CONTRACT

LAW

Contents

Preface

Any monograph on Australian contract law written at the dawn of the twenty-first century must of necessity take into account modern means of communication. Technology permeates all spheres of business dealings, increasing the opportunities to contract in a global context. Nevertheless, the principles upon which contract law is based still strongly reflect historical influences. For example, all Australian jurisdictions still require certain contracts to be made or evidenced in writing, based on the 1677 English *Statute of Frauds*.

Anglo-Australian parliaments have never sought to codify contract law. However, from the end of the nineteenth century, statutory interventions such as the *Sale of Goods Acts* were considered necessary to give parliamentary sanction to contractual rules developed to that time. While the English Commercial Court of the early twentieth century gave full vent to the concept of freedom of contract, by the end of the century, some of these freedoms have been whittled away by other statutes that dictated norms of contractual behaviour. These statutes gave recognition to the greater social and political interest in consumer protection now reflected in Australia in, for example, Federal trade practices legislation, and state fair trading and contract review legislation.

This work recognises and identifies these trends in its analysis of contract law. In doing so, it also concedes that the development of the law in this area has been far from consistent. Seven state jurisdictions, augmented in the mid-1970s by an Australian federal jurisdiction, have fed numerous cases into the equation. Aggrieved parties to contracts now often concurrently enjoy a statutory remedy as well as one at common law. In some areas, this has given rise to differing judicial approaches, with judgments resting upon inferences drawn from complex facts rather than from any consistently applied principles, which were previously the building blocks of contract law. This work provides a scholarly analysis and critique of the modern principles and theories of contract law as applicable in Australia in a form accessible to lawyers, academics and other professionals.

In addition, any modern treatise on contract law can no longer ignore the effect of an international perspective on the development of law in Australia. Australian courts are increasingly having regard to legal developments in other countries. This has created a greater need to become acquainted with areas of divergence in the law of other jurisdictions, and the persuasive impact of those laws on Australian contract law. Each chapter of this work includes perspectives from three of Australia's major trading partners—New Zealand, the United States of America, and Japan. Further, international contracts are considered in Chapter 26.

We have many people to thank in the production of this book. First, three other academics contributed chapters in their areas of expertise. We would like to thank Simon Fisher, Reader, University of Queensland for his contribution to Chapter 1 and for Chapters 2, 26 and 27 in the areas of negotiation, international contracts and theories of contract law. Likewise, we would like to thank Peter MacFarlane, Associate Professor, Queensland University of Technology, for Chapter 10 on capacity to contract, and Ms Veronica Taylor, Director, Asian Law Centre, University of Washington, for the Japanese perspectives. Their contribution to this work has enriched it considerably, and we are most grateful for the time and effort that they expended in researching, writing and presenting their contributions for publication as part of this book.

Grateful thanks must also go to Ms Michelle Bradfield and Ms Nikki Low, who undertook a great part of the underlying research for the book, and Ms Anne Overell, who also undertook research as well as editing the tables of cases and statutes. The authors also appreciate the assistance of Ms Anne Matthew for her help in the final stages. Des and Sharon would like to gratefully thank Mrs Margaret Barlow, their Personal Assistant, who undertook the bulk of the typing and formatting. The authors also thank Ms Caroline Miall for her efficient efforts in helping to finalise the project.

The authors would like to acknowledge the support of their academic colleagues, in particular Professor Bill Duncan and Professor Stephen Corones, who provided helpful input throughout the course of this project. Funds were provided by the Faculty of Law, which assisted with research, and for which the authors are grateful.

Finally, thanks must also go to our publishers, Oxford University Press, particularly Ms Jill Henry, who has supported and guided this work through to its successful completion, and Ms Trish Baker, our editor, who worked tirelessly under difficult time constraints.

Readers should note that as part of the publishing requirements, two scholars in the field of contract law refereed this text and a number of the referees' suggestions were incorporated into the final manuscript. We have endeavoured to state the law as at 1 April 2001.

Lindy Willmott
Sharon Christensen
Des Butler
May 2001

Table of cases

References are to paragraphs

References are to paragraphs

Table of statutes

References are to paragraphs

Part I

Overview

This Part addresses two preliminary issues before examining the substantive law that occupies the bulk of the book.

It is important to provide an introduction to the matters covered in this book, and set them in context. Chapter 1 establishes the framework of the book, and addresses questions about the essence of contract law, common terminology, and the role of courts in contract law. It also includes a short examination of the historical development of contract law in Australia, and explains why each chapter includes perspectives from three select overseas countries: New Zealand, the United States, and Japan.

The second chapter in this Part addresses an element that underlies all contracts to a greater or lesser extent: the negotiation process. Negotiation may play a role at a variety of stages of a contract including the initial formation, any variation in performance, and resolution of disputes. This chapter examines negotiation both from the perspective of the underpinning theory and from the more practical perspective of the way negotiation can be effectively conducted.

Chapter 1

Introduction

'Law is a form of conflict resolution created in the process of politicization and pacification of society. Contract law is a form of law that emerged with trade and the division of labour. It presupposes freedom, equality and security of people that attracted private fortunes in the marketplace in order to maximize their return expressed in money values. Law has forms and is a form as well. It is the ruling and enforced communication on normative behaviour in modern societies.'[1]

1.1 The essence of Australian contract law

[1.05] The aim of this book is to provide readers with a concise examination of Australian contract law. This introductory chapter outlines the essence of contract law. A first working definition of contract law is this: contract law is the body of law that provides for the creation, performance and termination of duties voluntarily assumed by legal actors in relation to other legal actors.

[1.10] The following case gives a snapshot of the role of contract law from a court's point of view. In *Commonwealth v Verwayen*,[2] McHugh J remarked that 'the enforcement

---

1   U Riefner, 'The Vikings and the Romans: Contract Law and Social Economy' in T Wilhelmsson (ed), *Perspectives on Critical Contract Law*, Dartmouth Publishing, Aldershot, 1993, pp 169–209, 180.

2   (1990) 170 CLR 394.

of promises is the province of contract',[3] which does illustrate that contract law is concerned with the act of promising—but does it also capture the essence of contract law? Arguably, it does, for the following reasons.

First, there must be a *subject matter* of contract law. The law attributes significance to certain kinds of acts—in this context, people making some kind of solemn promise or undertaking to do or not to do something. Not every undertaking falls within the ambit of contract law, so contract law must call upon some kind of 'bright line' rule to decide which kinds of promises are enforceable, and which are not. Australian contract law also uses various rules of recognition to decide which types of promises can be enforced by the legal system. These bright-line rules are dealt with at various points in this book.

Secondly, there is a class of *persons* who make promises. This is the class of legal actors known as persons. Legal personality has been extended beyond natural persons to encompass artificial entities such as corporations.[4]

The third observation that flows from McHugh J's dictum in *Commonwealth v Verwayen*[5] is implied by the nature of promising itself: it is a voluntary rather than an involuntary act. As Tipping J remarked in *Sinclair Horder O'Malley and Co v National Insurance Company of New Zealand Ltd*,[6] the law of obligations is divided into voluntary and involuntary obligations.[7] Contract law is the branch of law where obligations are voluntarily assumed. Building on this, promises are voluntary acts. If some promises are enforceable, it follows that voluntarily made promises can also create obligations for the promise maker (called the promisor) that are enforceable by the person to whom the promise is made (the promisee). These promises become legal acts, and are subject to the apparatus of the legal system (such as courts).

[1.15] McHugh J's dictum in *Commonwealth v Verwayen*[8] encapsulates the essence of contract, but there are some circumstances outside the area of contract law in which a person will be prevented ('estopped') from going back on what they have said. In these cases, where there is a deficiency in promise making and enforcement under the law of contract, the courts can call upon principles in other areas of law designed to ensure the attainment of justice.[9]

[1.20] Examining the essence of contract law from a broader perspective, contract scholars generally agree that contract law has three legitimate functions. The first function is to specify which agreements are legally binding and which are not. The second function is to define the rights and duties (in other words, obligations) created by enforceable but otherwise ambiguous agreements. The third function is to indicate the consequences of an unexcused breach of contract.[10]

---

3   Ibid at 501.
4   See S Fisher, L Wiseman & C Anderson, *Corporations Law*, 2nd edn, Butterworths, Sydney, 2001 for a survey of Australian corporations law.
5   (1990) 170 CLR 394 at 501.
6   [1992] 2 NZLR 706 at 719.
7   An obligation is a relationship between two people, one of whom owes a duty (the debtor), with the other person being a person to whom the duty is owed (the creditor). The creditor enjoys a right against the debtor. Thus an obligation is a double-ended bond or tie between two legal persons: see R Zimmermann, *The Law of Obligations: Roman Foundations of the Civilian Tradition*, Juta & Co Ltd, Cape Town, 1990, p 1.
8   (1990) 170 CLR 394 at 501.
9   This concept is explored further in Chapter 7.
10 A Kronman, 'Contract Law and Distributive Justice' 89 *Yale Law Journal* 472, 472 (1980).

Beyond the purely doctrinal or internal view of contract law, it is possible, by taking a broader perspective of contract law, to see other threads to the rich tapestry of contract. Collins wrote, on this theme:

> The practising lawyer identifies the key function of contracts as the planning of an economic relation. The legal scholar views the rules of contract law as a particular source of private law obligations. The socio-legal scholar perhaps considers contract law as a tool for the regulation of economic and social trans-actions. Finally, the judge treats contracts as creating binding rules of law between the parties, breach of which provides a justification for the imposition of state sanctions.[11]

Collins argues that contract expresses a central form of human association in modern society, and that contract as an organising principle of human association defines the meaning of social life.[12]

1.2 The architecture of contract law

[1.25] The architecture of contract law consists of those basic elements that make up the contract law superstructure under the Australian legal system. Various theoretical and practical frameworks can be employed to sketch the main contours of this archi-tecture, but here it is sufficient to explain the key terms of contract law and identify the main legal actors involved.

At its most basic level, contract law involves persons and voluntarily assumed obli-gations.[13] The contracting persons are described in various ways. The generic term is 'parties'. It is common in many contracts for the parties to assume more specific labels such as 'seller' and 'buyer' in sale of goods contracts (with the terms 'vendor' and 'pur-chaser' being common in older legal literature and primary legal sources).[14]

[1.30] Next, the *contents* of contracts are expressed in what are generically called *terms*. Much of contract law is concerned with determining the contents of a partic-ular contract.[15] Conventionally, there are three main classes of terms in a contract: conditions, warranties and intermediate (or innominate) terms. Contractual terms are often categorised as either express terms or implied terms. This distinction is drawn because of the way these types of terms become part of any particular contract. Because contracts express voluntarily assumed obligations, the law also provides machinery for the *duration* of contract. Just to confuse the novice in contract law, this is also known as the 'term' of the contract. The duration of any contract can be either fixed or open-ended. Contracts have a fixed term when it is possible to deter-mine how long the contract is to last. Where the length of a contract cannot be determined, the contract is open-ended—the law then implies machinery for termi-nation, usually by performance by both or all contracting parties, or by allowing one

---

11   H Collins, *Regulating Contracts*, OUP, Oxford, 1999, p 12.
12   Ibid.
13   See [1.10] above.
14   On sale of goods contracts, see A Tyree, *Sale of Goods*, Butterworths, Sydney, 1998; KCT Sutton, *Sales and Consumer Law*, 4th edn, LBC Information Services, 1995; and S Fisher, *Commercial and Personal Property Law*, Butterworths, Sydney, 1997, Chapter 12.
15   See Chapter 9 for a discussion of 'Contents'.

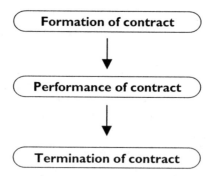

Figure 1.1 The formation–performance–termination paradigm of contract law

of the contracting parties to terminate the contract by giving reasonable notice of termination.

[1.35] A tool that can be used to explain the operation of contract law is the 'formation–performance–termination' paradigm (see Figure 1.1). This tool is not so much a conceptual framework for contract law as a working blueprint that can be used to break contract down into its three distinct phases. Still, it fits neatly into the architecture of contract law, and in fact it is an important part of the contract law superstructure, since it helps to order contract law.

[1.40] The structure of this book may be viewed in terms of this paradigm. The notion of 'Formation' includes a number of issues. First there is the mechanical operation involved in negotiating a contract: this is dealt with in Chapter 2. Next there are the essential elements of a binding contract, with the associated issue of equitable estoppel. These are discussed in Part 2 (chapters 3–7). Once it is determined that a valid contract has been formed, two related issues arise: what terms form part of the contract, and the interpretation or significance of each of those terms. These two issues are discussed in Part 3 (chapters 8–9). In some cases, the necessary elements are present but there is nevertheless some limitation on the parties who may rely on the contract. These circumstances include the contractual capacity of the contracting parties, requirements of writing, and privity of contract. They are dealt with in Part 4 (chapters 10–12). A fourth bundle of issues concerns factors which, if they occur as the contract is being made, have the effect of invalidating ('vitiating') the contract. These factors are examined in Part 5 (chapters 13–18).

'Performance' represents the fulfilment or carrying out of the promises in the contract. It also reflects 'termination', since most contracts are brought to an end by being terminated. Performance involves issues such as the time for performance, the type of performance required, and the degree of performance actually rendered. These issues are examined in Chapter 19, in Part 6.

The balance of Part 6 (chapters 20–22) examines the other means of termination. Besides performance, a contract may be discharged, or brought to an end in one of three ways: termination by agreement, termination for breach of a term, and termination by frustration. Associated with termination for breach is the area of remedies. Part 7 (chapters 23–25) looks at the remedies that are relevant in a contractual setting: damages, equitable remedies such as specific performance, and injunction and restitutionary remedies.

Each of these chapters includes international comparisons. They are complemented by Chapter 26, which addresses the special issues arising in international contracts, including international conventions such as the United Nations Convention on Contracts for the International Sale of Goods (the Vienna Sales Convention).

The book concludes with Chapter 27—an examination of different theories, themes and ideologies of contract law.

1.3   Courts and contract law

[1.45] The intersection of the courts and contract law may be examined at two levels: the institutional and the operational.

[1.50] At the institutional level, the organ used by civil societies to resolve disputes is the judicial system.[16] In western liberal democratic thought and practice, generally there are three branches of government: legislative, executive, and judicial. It is the role of the judicial branch of government to order and resolve disputes between people, whether on a public-to-public basis or on a public-to-private basis. When it comes to contracts, the courts have an integral role in resolving contract law disputes. The classical model of contract law[17] presupposes that the judicial process is intended to serve one or both of two important social goals. The first goal is that legal actors should comply with socially desired standards of behaviour. This is reinforced by the threat of penalties or sanctions, or the promise of reward. The second social goal is that society (through the judicial system) should provide machinery for the settlement of disputes by peaceful and fair means.[18] Both of these goals present a passive role for the courts right through the process of contracting: they see the courts' role in the contract process as arising only if the parties are unable to resolve their own difficulties, or one party seeks to bring the behaviour of another contracting party to account in some appropriate and neutral forum.

[1.55] At the operational level, two distinct processes work to bring about judicial intervention in contract disputes. The first is the interpretation of contracts; the second is their construction. In one American case, *Fashion Fabrics of Iowa v Retail Investors Corp*,[19] the court said that interpretation 'involves ascertaining the meaning of contractual words; construction refers to deciding their legal effect'.[20] In the area of adjustment of contracts, the courts have a very limited role, and they will intervene only in very specific instances. Conventional contract theory holds that the courts will not

---

16   Besides the court system, there is also the phenomenon of Alternative Dispute Resolution (also called dispute management). For details, see G Clarke, 'Dispute Resolution', Chapter 6 in S Fisher (ed), *The Law of Commercial and Professional Relationships*, FT Law and Tax, Melbourne, 1996; H Astor & C Chinkin, *Dispute Resolution in Australia*, Butterworths, Sydney, 1992; L Boulle, *Mediation: Principles, Process, Practice*, Butterworths, Sydney, 1996; Australian Law Reform Commission, *Review of the Adversarial System of Litigation: ADR, its Role in Federal Dispute Resolution*, Sydney, 1998.

17   According to Atiyah, the classical model of contract law is derived from its nineteenth-century liberal antecedents, under which the law enforces bilateral executory agreements because it seeks to give effect to the acts of will or intentions of the parties to a particular contract: PS Atiyah 'Contracts, Promises and the Law of Obligations' (1978) 94 *Law Quarterly Review* 193, 193–194 and PS Atiyah, *Essays on Contract*, Clarendon Press, Oxford, 1986, pp 11–13.

18   See PS Atiyah, 'Contracts, Promises and the Law of Obligations' (1978) 94 *Law Quarterly Review* 193, 197. (Also reproduced in PS Atiyah, *Essays on Contract*, Clarendon Press, Oxford, 1986, Chapter 2).

19   266 NW 2d 22 at 25 (1978).

20   For a detailed study of the interpretation of contracts, see K Lewison, *The Interpretation of Contracts*, 2nd edn, Sweet & Maxwell, London, 1997.

adjust a contract between willing contracting parties on the basis that, in hindsight, the bargain appears to be unevenly weighted as regards the interests of the parties, or even grossly disadvantageous to one of them: see *Biotechnology Australia Pty Ltd v Pace*[21] and *Kofi-Sunkersette Obu v A Strauss & Co.*[22] This rule provides a limited role for courts in contract law disputes and shows how the courts practise judicial restraint instead of judicial activism. Since this is a common law rule, it can be abrogated by statute.

[1.60] There are some well-known examples of statutory adjustment of contract by courts in the Australian legal system. The first example that should be mentioned is the power of the Federal Court of Australia to make orders under s. 87(2) of the *Trade Practices Act* 1974 (Cth) varying contracts or arrangements that are associated with contraventions of provisions of Parts IV, IVA, IVB and V of the *Trade Practices Act*. A second example of a judicial charter to adjust contracts concerns the powers conferred upon the courts of New South Wales under the *Contracts Review Act* 1980 (NSW).[23] Another example arises under the *Consumer Credit Code* (which applies uniformly throughout Australia as State and Territorial law): courts adjudicating consumer credit disputes can make changes to consumer credit contracts on the ground of hardship (s. 66) as well as having the power to reopen unjust consumer credit transactions under s. 70 of the *Consumer Credit Code*.[24] It would be a mistake of legal method to assume from these specific instances of judicial adjustment of contracts that Australian courts have general jurisdiction to adjust contracts between contracting parties. But this cursory review of Australian law does show specific instances where courts are empowered to adjust certain types of contracts on the basis of criteria that are articulated in statutes.

1.4 The development of Australian contract law

[1.65] It is impossible to analyse the origins of Australian contract law without acknowledging its English heritage—for it is from this English legal inheritance that Australian contract law arises.[25] While Australian lawyers acknowledge the importance of the English legal heritage of the Australian common law, it does not follow that we

---

21 (1988) 15 NSWLR 103 at 135 per Kirby P.

22 [1951] AC 243 at 250. If people wish to classify the degree or extent of intervention of courts, then the attitude of the courts as expressed in these rules is closer to the judicial restraint end of the spectrum than the activist end.

23 See S Fisher, 'Judicial Review of Contracts Between Financiers and Security Providers' [1991] 11 JIBFL 556–561 & 12 JIBFL 608–616 and JR Peden, *The Law of Unjust Contracts: including the Contracts Review Act 1980 (NSW) with Detailed Annotations and Pleadings*, Butterworths, Sydney, 1982.

24 See D McGill & L Willmott, *Annotated Consumer Credit Code*, LBC Information Services, Sydney, 1999, pp 434–533.

25 For an historical survey of contract law, see OW Holmes Jr, *The Common Law*, Little, Brown and Co, Boston, 1881, pp 247–288; SJ Stoljar, *The History of Contract at Common Law*, Australian National University Press, Canberra, 1975; AWB Simpson, *A History of the Common Law of Contract: the Rise of the Action of Assumpsit*, Clarendon Press, Oxford, 1975; J Gordley, *The Philosophical Origins of Modern Contract Doctrine*, Clarendon Press, Oxford, 1991. For a more general study on the development of contract law from an English perspective, see PS Atiyah, *The Law of Contract*, 4th edn, Clarendon Press, Oxford, 1989, Chapter 1 as well as PS Atiyah, *The Rise and Fall of Freedom of Contract*, Clarendon Press, Oxford, 1979.

should adopt a kind of cultural cringe and slavishly follow modern English law in any field of public or private law.[26] Cases such as *Cook v Cook*[27] and *Nguyen v Nguyen*[28] have loosened the grip of the English common law and English precedents on Australian common law. Nothing since these landmark cases has changed the view that Australian law and English law will continue to diverge, and the indications are that this gap will widen as Australian law pursues its own path and engages more intensively with other legal systems and cultures.[29] Although Australian lawyers and Australian legal institutions will still consider the merits of English common law doctrines and principles, the fact remains that Australian law in general (and contract law in particular) will carve its own distinctive niche in the common law legal family as the body of Australian law develops.

Legal anthropology throws some light on the development of contract as a legal institution.[30] A famous observation made by Maine says that contractual obligations are characteristic of modern societies, and that as societies develop, they entail a movement from *status to contract*.[31] The sociologist Durkheim[32] and others further refined Maine's theory until it was challenged by legal anthropologists—beginning with Redfield in 1950—on the basis of new ethnographic data.[33] Thus, contrary to Maine's theory of legal evolution and development, some societies have developed in such a way that contract can precede status, rather than the issue of status preceding contract. Legal anthropology points out that contract law takes the elements of social structures and assesses how they interact with the notion of contractual obligations in societies.

[1.70] Translating these concerns to the Australian legal environment, in particular the pre-white settlement dating from 1788, Ellinghaus then argues that the Aboriginal people did in fact have a conception of contract in 1788. They traded many articles across the Australian continent, and they established great trading routes across the Australian landmass. The evidence cited by Ellinghaus goes further, and demonstrates that not only goods, but also services and rights were traded between Aboriginal groups.[34] Ellinghaus goes on to argue that modern Australian contract law needs to

---

26   For a review and analysis of the cultural cringe in contract law, see MP Ellinghaus, 'Towards an Australian Contract Law', in MP Ellinghaus, AJ Bradbrook & AJ Duggan (eds) *The Emergence of Australian Law*, Butterworths, Sydney, 1988, 44–69, especially at 46–53.

27   (1986) 162 CLR 376.

28   (1990) 169 CLR 245.

29   A related development is the passage of the Australia Acts 1986 legislative package by the United Kingdom, the Commonwealth and State Parliaments. This has 'repatriated' legislative competence over Australia's legislative affairs to Australia and her States. For a detailed study, see B O'Brien, 'The Australia Acts', in MP Ellinghaus, AJ Bradbrook & AJ Duggan (eds) *The Emergence of Australian Law*, Butterworths, Sydney, 1988, pp 337–354.

30   Legal anthropology is the discipline devoted to the study of the discourse, practices, values and beliefs which all societies consider essential to their operation and reproduction: see N Rouland, *Legal Anthropology*, trans PG Planel, The Athlone Press, London, 1994, § 1.

31   See H Maine, *Ancient Law: its Connection with the Early History of Society and its Relations to Modern Society*, John Murray, London, 1861, reprinted Dorset Press, 1986, p 141.

32   See S Lukes & A Scull (eds), *Durkheim and the Law*, Martin Robertson, Oxford, 1983; and A Hunt, *The Sociological Movement in Law*, Macmillan, London, 1978, pp 85–88 (as cited in S Wheeler & J Shaw, *Contract Law: Cases, Materials and Commentary*, Clarendon Press, Oxford, 1994, pp 46–49).

33   See N Rouland, *Legal Anthropology*, trans PG Planel, The Athlone Press, London, 1994, §§ 131 and 132.

34   MP Ellinghaus, 'Towards an Australian Contract Law', in MP Ellinghaus, AJ Bradbrook & AJ Duggan (eds) *The Emergence of Australian Law*, Butterworths, Sydney, 1988, 44–69, especially at 54–63.

integrate its Aboriginal antecedents because our civilisation cannot come to maturity without the complete integration of its indigenous components.[35]

[1.75] A convenient starting point for tracing the development of contract law in Australia[36] is the writ system employed by the common law in mediaeval England. The system was based on a limited number of causes of action recognised by the common law. Each cause of action was represented by a form of writ for pleading the relevant case. If the wording of a particular writ could accommodate the circumstances that arose in a particular case, the plaintiff was entitled to a remedy.

This system originally did not include a writ for a cause of action similar to a modern allegation of breach of contract. There was a writ of covenant (for breach of an obligation contained in a document under seal), but it did not suit many cases of breach of promise. There was also a writ of debt, but this had a number of limitations, including a requirement that work had been fully performed, or that, where money had been lent, the sum in dispute was an agreed amount. These limitations also made this writ unsuitable for cases involving an informal exchange of promises.

[1.80] Another writ recognised by the common law was that of trespass. Under this writ, a plaintiff could plead that the defendant had wrongly done something (described as *misfeasance*), such as wrongly (in the sense of poorly) mending a hole in the road. With the application of a little ingenuity, this writ came to be used to plead that the defendant had wrongly *failed* to do something (called *non-feasance*), such as wrongly failing to mend a hole in the road. Specifically, it was adapted to plead that the defendant had wrongly failed to perform his promise. This new form of writ became known as a writ of *assumpsit*—based on the defendant's assumption of an obligation.[37]

[1.85] An element of the pleading of assumpsit was the 'consideration'—the motive behind the defendant's promise.[38] Consideration was little more than a matter of evidence, and it was so easily demonstrated that disreputable plaintiffs often fraudulently claimed against hapless, usually illiterate defendants with whom they may have had little if any prior dealing—a practice that ultimately led to the passing of the *Statute of Frauds* in 1677.[39]

By the late sixteenth century it was recognised that either advantage to the promisor or disadvantage to the promisee could amount to good consideration. But viewing consideration only in terms of the reason for the promise meant that moral obligations or 'ties of conscience' were sufficient for the purpose.[40] This remained so, until the notion was finally rejected in the early nineteenth century.[41]

In time, consideration was viewed as more than just an essential aspect of pleading the plaintiff's claim; it began to be seen as an essential element of a binding contract. To be enforceable, a promise had to be either made under seal or supported by con-

---

35   Ibid, especially at 65–69.

36   More detailed accounts of the historical development of contract law in Australia may be found in DW Greig & JLR Davis, *Law of Contract*, Law Book Co, Sydney, 1987, Chapter 1; N Seddon & MP Ellinghaus, *Cheshire and Fifoot's Law of Contract*, 7th edn, Butterworths, Sydney, 1997, Chapter 26.

37   See *Slade's case* (1602) 4 Co Rep 91; 76 ER 1072.

38   AWB Simpson, *A History of the Common Law of Contract*, Clarendon Press, Oxford, 1975, p 321.

39   See [11.05].

40   See, eg, *Hawkes v Saunders* (1782) 1 Cowp 289; 98 ER 1091.

41   *Eastwood v Kenyon* (1840) 11 A&E 438; 113 ER 482.

sideration that was regarded as having value in the eyes of the law.[42] At approximately the same time, the emphasis changed: instead of focusing on a promise, it began to focus on an *agreement*—in the sense of an exchange of promises. Also, improvements in communications and the growing tendency to conduct business dealings by correspondence that occurred around the beginning of the nineteenth century led the courts to recognise that contracts could be formed by means of an offer that was later accepted.[43] With the Industrial Revolution and the emergence of free enterprise in the nineteenth century, contract law came to be regarded as a law of bargains: something for something.

[1.90] The next major development in Australian contract law did not occur until the High Court's decision in *Waltons Stores (Interstate) Ltd v Maher* in 1988.[44] Until this time, the body of law known as equity had ameliorated some harsh consequences of the need to show consideration at common law by applying a doctrine of fairness known as promissory estoppel. This doctrine applied where a party to a contract had promised the other party that certain rights under the contract would not be enforced, and that other party had relied on the promise, changing his or her position because of it.[45] In such a case, equity prevented the promisor from reneging on the promise, even though no consideration had been provided for it. But the doctrine was subject to an important limitation—it could only be used as a defence when a promisor attempted to exercise the right in question. No action lay against the promisor for breach of his or her promise. In other words, promissory estoppel was regarded as a 'shield' but not a 'sword'.[46] This was due to fears that to do so would be tantamount to enforcing a promise not supported by consideration.[47]

In 1988, the High Court reappraised the doctrine. It held that the doctrine was based on equitable notions of unconscionability. Looked at that way, there was no real distinction between unconscionability associated with a broken promise not to insist upon a right and unconscionability associated with a broken promise to create a right.[48] The doctrine—now called 'equitable estoppel'—could therefore be relied upon as a cause of action, and not merely as a defence—a sword as well as a shield. But the case did not uproot the rules of consideration, because the remedy of equitable estoppel had to be proportionate to the unconscionability to be avoided. In most cases, this is more likely to be compensation for wasted expenditure rather than making good the promise. In some cases, however, it will be necessary to enforce the promise.[49]

[1.95] Equitable estoppel is only one example of the way equitable notions of unconscionability have encroached on contract law. Unconscionability reflects equity's concern to avoid unfairness or injustice in the circumstances surrounding the formation of a contract. It can also be seen in the law's treatment of contracts entered into where a

---

42   *Rann v Hughes* (1778) 7 Term Reps 350n; 101 ER 1014n.
43   *Huddleston v Briscoe* (1805) 11 Ves Jr 583; 32 ER 1215; *Adams v Lindsell* (1818) 1 B&Ald 681; 106 ER 250.
44   (1988) 164 CLR 387. See Chapter 7.
45   *Central London Property Trust Ltd v High Trees House Ltd* [1947] KB 130.
46   See [7.25].
47   *Combe v Combe* [1951] 2 KB 215 at 220.
48   *Waltons Stores (Interstate) Ltd v Maher* (1988) 164 CLR 387 at 425–6. See further [7.25].
49   See [7.225].

party is incapacitated by intoxication or mental impairment,[50] unilateral mistake,[51] or material disadvantage exploited by a stronger party.[52] In New South Wales, unconscionability of this kind is also the subject of statutory prohibition.[53] Legislatures outside New South Wales have as yet done little to prohibit unconscionability (in the sense of striking down terms of contract that operate unfairly or oppressively).[54]

The main exception has been statutory intervention in areas such as consumer contracts and credit transactions. Legislation such as the *Trade Practices Act* 1974 and the equivalent State and Territory *Fair Trading Acts* and the uniform *Consumer Credit Code* represent statutory intervention into the kinds of contracts that routinely involve a substantial imbalance in bargaining power. These statutes operate by, for example, providing remedies for misleading or deceptive conduct, implying enforceable rights or obligations in consumer contracts, or prescribing contract formalities that benefit consumers.

1.5   Comparative aspects of contract law

[1.100] The primary focus for discussion in this book is contract law in Australia—and in appropriate cases, its parent law in England. However, modern means of transport and communication, the influence of international finance and multinational corporations, and the ability to choose the law that governs the contract are among the factors that make it increasingly important for the modern lawyer to become at least acquainted with areas of divergence in the law of other jurisdictions.

[1.105] Accordingly, this book includes at the end of each chapter perspectives from three of Australia's major trading partners: New Zealand, the United States of America, and Japan. It is not the intention of this book to provide an exhaustive examination of the law of contract in each of these jurisdictions. Instead, it is intended to identify the major issues that arise in those jurisdictions and to briefly point out areas where the law differs from that in Australia. Readers can pursue further readings in specialist texts if the need arises.

[1.110] New Zealand is Australia's closest trading partner, and trade between the two countries has been encouraged through agreements such as the *Australia New Zealand Closer Economic Relations Trade Agreement* (Canberra, 28 March 1983; Aust TS 1983 No 2) (called the 'Closer Economic Relations Agreement' for brevity). Like Australia, New Zealand is a common law country that traces the origins of its contract law to the law in England. However, in a number of important respects, the law in New Zealand differs from that in Australia, usually because of statutory enactment (two examples are the *Contractual Mistakes Act 1977* (NZ) and the *Contracts (Privity) Act 1982* (NZ)).

[1.115] The United States is one of Australia's largest trading partners. Like Australia, its contract law is common-law based. Unlike the High Court of Australia, however, the United States Supreme Court does not serve as the highest court in the hierarchy in matters not involving federal jurisdiction. Instead, State Supreme Courts serve this

---

50   See [10.160].
51   See [14.290].
52   See [17.05].
53   See, eg, *Trade Practices Act* 1974, ss 51AA, 51AB, 51AC. See [17.85–17.115].
54   See, eg, *Contracts Review Act* 1980 (NSW).

role. In other words, there is a single common law in Australia,[55] but in the United States there are effectively 50 distinct bodies of law. This does not necessarily mean that the law will differ from state to state, but such a possibility exists. Often states will be influenced by the law in other states with which they are geographically linked, or with which they share characteristics (such as being industrial or farm states).

[1.120] Assistance in the synthesis of the laws of various states has been provided by an encyclopaedic publication called *The Restatement*. This publication is sponsored by the American Law Institute, comprising senior academics, judges and attorneys, and it seeks to identify common themes across different states in selected areas of law. The principles set out in the Restatement are supported by comments and illustrations. It does not have the standing of law, although it is not uncommon for a court to base its decision on the relevant *Restatement* section on the ground that it reflects a consensus in the law. Contract law is one of the areas of law that have been subjected to this treatment. The latest edition of the contract section, commonly referred to as the *Restatement (Second) of Contracts*, was published in 1981.

[1.125] A further source of contract law in the United States is the Uniform Commercial Code (UCC). The Code was designed to replace the Uniform Sale of Goods Act, modelled on the English *Sale of Goods Act* 1893 and other statutes dealing with commercial dealings. The Code has been enacted with slight variations in all states except Louisiana, which has enacted the Code with major variations of the sections dealing with sales. The Code has 11 articles, with two having particular relevance for the general law of contract: Article 1—General Provisions and Article 2—Sales.[56] In general, Article 2 is limited to contracts for the sale of goods.[57] It does not apply to, for example, a contract for services or for the sale of land.

[1.130] It is not traditional in a book like this to make references to the law of a country like Japan. However, there are good reasons for including such references, even if only in short form. First, Japan is one of Australia's most important trading partners. Secondly, Japan is a civil law country. The contrast between Australian laws and Japanese laws is therefore a contrast between the common law and civil law. It may therefore be useful to identify concepts that are unfamiliar to a common lawyer but may be significant in a contract governed by Japanese law.

---

55   *Lange v Australian Broadcasting Corporation* (1997) 189 CLR 520.
56   Other articles deal with topics including leases (Art 2A), negotiable instruments (Art 3), bank deposits (Art 4), letters of credit (Art 5), bills of lading (Art 7) and investment securities (Art 8).
57   UCC 2-102.

Chapter 2

Negotiation

2.1 Introduction to negotiation

2.1.1 *Negotiation as a social process*

[2.05] Negotiation is a social process.[1] This is so despite its role as a legal phenomenon, and as an element of (or rather a process of) the law of contract. And if negotiation is a social process, then its defining characteristics, its elements and its internal processes come from outside the legal system. This chapter introduces negotiation as a social process, and offers some thoughts about its points of contact with the law of contract. First, negotiation is approached by mapping its contours. Secondly, the elements of negotiation are spelt out. The third stage examines the two main bargaining strategies

---

1   See R Kramer & D Messick (eds), *Negotiation As a Social Process*, SAGE Publications, Thousand Oaks, California, 1995.

in the process of negotiation. The fourth stage stresses the importance of preparation for negotiation, and then concludes with the negotiation process itself.[2] [2.10] The following definition captures the essence of negotiation, together with some of its alternatives:

> Negotiation is a response to conflict. Conflict arises at a decision point when (a) one has interests perceived to be incompatible with the interests of others, and (b) these particular others are capable of affecting achievement of one's interests. Negotiation is one of three alternatives for pursuing one's interests in the conflict. The other two are by using power (the ability to impose a solution) and conflict resolution (which involves reconceptualising the dispute in less divisive terms). Negotiation differs from the use of power in that negotiating parties voluntarily commit themselves to the course of action they agree upon, whereas power users overcome resistance in the way that results in compliance rather than commitment. Negotiation differs from conflict resolution in that the latter, as the term is used here, involves a cognitive restructuring that actually diminishes the perceived incompatibility of interests between the parties. Negotiation, therefore, involves acceptance of an outcome that, except in the case of perfect integrative solutions of the bridging variety, only partially serves negotiator's interests. From this perspective, negotiation can be construed as interactive decision making in that each party decides whether or not to accept a particular settlement as a result of the interaction; power-induced outcomes are unilateral rather than interactive decisions (citations omitted).[3]

People usually associate conflict with divisiveness and irreconcilable positions. But the sense in which conflict has been used in the passage above is that it is associated with the pursuit of opposing interests by two or more parties, where those interests clash (or conflict).

[2.15] Another dimension to conflict is that it stems from competition.[4] The promotion of competing interests by two or more interest-holders can produce conflict. The process of advancing (and where possible reconciling) the pursuit of these competing interests is the domain of negotiation as a social process. In the sense in which negotiation has been talked about so far, it can be seen as a branch of the social sciences.

[2.20] Rather than just reflecting a pursuit of competing interests, negotiation can also sit within the framework of Alternative Dispute Resolution (ADR).[5] ADR embraces a number of processes that have as their broad aim the resolution of conflict—including

---

2   This chapter is indebted to the valuable work performed by N Spegel, B Rogers & R Buckley, *Negotiation: Theory and Techniques*, Butterworths, Sydney, 1998.

3   See L Greenhalgh & D Chapman, 'Joint Decision Making: The Inseparability of Relationships and Negotiation', Chapter 8 in R Kramer & D Messick (eds), *Negotiation As a Social Process*, SAGE Publications, Thousand Oaks, California, 1995, p 167.

4   See G Tillett, *Resolving Conflict: A Practical Approach*, Sydney University Press, Sydney, 1991, p 7 (cited by by N Spegel, B Rogers & R Buckley, *Negotiation: Theory and Techniques*, p 99).

5   See G Clarke, 'Dispute Resolution', Chapter 6 in S Fisher (ed), *The Law of Commercial and Professional Relationships*, FT Law & Tax, Melbourne, 1996, pp 147–161. See also L Boulle, *Mediation: Principles, Process, Practice* (Butterworths, Sydney 1996); G Goodpaster, *A Guide to Negotiation and Mediation*, Irvington-on-Hudson, N.Y, Transnational Publishers, 1997); L Riskin & J Westbrook, *Dispute Resolution and Lawyers*, West Publishing Co, St. Paul, Minn, 1987, Supplement 1993.

mediation, conciliation, arbitration, mini–trials, expert appraisal, expert determination, and expert recommendation.[6] ADR provides alternative pathways for the resolution of disputes to the time-honoured method of litigation (dispute resolution through the courts, or curial dispute resolution). Curial dispute resolution can be used in conjunction with ADR, and frequently is, in the context of court-annexed mediation and arbitration.[7] ADR is facilitative, advisory or determinative.[8] Negotiation is an element of ADR rather than a distinct type of ADR.

[2.25] Negotiation does not take place in a vacuum. It is closely tied to social relationships, which include legal relationships.[9] Some commentators consider that no clear science of relationships has emerged, but it is possible to define relationships in both conceptual and operational senses. Greenhalgh and Chapman offer a conceptual definition of relationship as the meaning assigned by two or more individuals to their connectedness or co-existence. To place this within the context of negotiation, relationship involves the thinking that causes a negotiator to adopt a particular attitude towards the other party.[10] By adopting this view of negotiation, one can place it within a conceptual framework of sorts. That is, negotiation is both a *social relationship* as well a *social process* that describes the way people advance their own interests in competition with others, where those interests bring them into some form of relationship. In turn, this advancement of interests takes place in the context of the way societies at large allow people of all types and descriptions to undertake the activities that result in their wants and needs being satisfied. Contract law provides one particular framework for negotiation as it has been described in this chapter.

2.1.2   The contours of negotiation

[2.30] The 'contours of negotiation' are those broad features of the negotiation landscape that can be mapped to guide people through it. In other words, the contours signify the big picture of negotiation, rather than its minute detail. The contours of negotiation contain the following features.

[2.35] Above all, negotiation is a *process*. Yet at the same time, negotiation is not a process that is divorced from outcomes. People participate in the process of negotiation to achieve outcomes—that is to say, negotiation has a purpose. Applying some of

---

6   See the short definitions of each of these processes at Australian Commercial Disputes Centre (under Dispute Resolution Methods): <http://www.austlii.edu.au/au/other/acdc/Methods/Me1_Disp.html> [accessed 2 January 2001]; George Raitt's website: <http://www.vicnet.net.au/users/georaitt/> [accessed 2 January 2001]; and at the National Alternative Dispute Resolution Advisory Council (NADRAC): <http://law.gov.au/aghome/advisory/nadrac/adrdefinitions.htm> [accessed 2 January 2001]. Some useful URL links are collected at the University of Queensland Law Library <http://www.library.uq.edu.au/law/weblawadr.html> [accessed 2 January 2001].

7   See the *Federal Magistrates Act* 1999 (Cth), ss 21–32.

8   See The National Alternative Dispute Resolution Advisory Council (NADRAC) *Alternative Dispute Resolution Definitions*, Canberra, March 1997 <http://law.gov.au/aghome/advisory/nadrac/adrdefinitions.htm> (accessed 2 January 2001).

9   For a study of some key legal relationships, see S Fisher (ed), *The Law of Commercial and Professional Relationships*, FT Law & Tax, Melbourne, 1996.

10   See Greenhalgh & Chapman, 'Joint Decision Making: The Inseparability of Relationships and Negotiation', p 179.

this thinking to the concerns of this book, negotiation intersects with contract law at three key points.

The first point is in the formation of contract, where negotiation describes the preliminary steps or exchanges between two or more parties, which results in the formation of a contract between them. Negotiations between two or more contracting parties concerning the formation of a contract are designed to advance the wants and needs of each of those contracting parties and provide an external framework (the Australian legal system) within which rights under that contract can be enjoyed and duties performed. Within the body of contract law, the specific processes that are included in negotiation include offer and acceptance.[11]

The second point of contact between negotiation and contract law concerns the termination of contract, and in particular attempts by one contracting party to reach a settlement of a contractual dispute with the other contracting party or parties.[12] In a relational sense, the second point of contact between negotiation and contract law takes as its focus the *closure* of the relationship rather than its formation.

The third connection between negotiation and contract law as a process concerns the adjustment of contractual rights and duties—in other words, variation of contract.[13] If the parties to a contract want to vary its terms, they need to negotiate the variation, or the other party may make a claim for non-performance of the contract.

2.2   The elements of negotiation

[2.40] An 'element' is an irreducible component of any system. In turn, elements combine to form processes and processes combine to form systems. The elements of negotiation are the style of the negotiator; the status of the negotiator as a member of a community or profession; negotiation as a transaction-based exchange; the relational aims of negotiation when viewed as a process; the objects of any particular negotiation; the values negotiators bring to the negotiation; and the skill base of negotiators.

[2.45] Commentators point out that the personal style of negotiators has an important bearing and impact on the process of negotiation.[14] Personal style is often explained by the discipline of psychology (a behavioural science), with less scientifically rigorous accounts of psychology known as 'pop psychology'. Observable human behaviour can be categorised as more or less extroverted or introverted, and more or less people-oriented or task-oriented. These dimensions refer to observable behaviour in people and not their internal mental processes.[15] In perhaps more familiar language, these dimensions correspond to the *style* a person has in his or her personal communications and relations. These attributes can be grouped together under the label of 'people skills'.[16] Another model that is used to help people identify their predominant behavioural

---

11   See Chapter 3.
12   Contractual disputes arise out of claims that one party to a contract has not performed his or her duties under the contract for the benefit of the other contracting party (or sometimes a third party). On performance of contract, see chapters 3 and 19.
13   See Chapter 11, where variation of contract is considered.
14   See N Spegel, B Rogers & R Buckley, *Negotiation: Theory and Techniques*, Chapter 7.
15   See N Spegel, B Rogers & R Buckley, *Negotiation: Theory and Techniques*, 7.8.
16   See generally, R Bolton, *People Skills*, Simon & Schuster Australia, Brookvale, NSW, repr 2000.

characteristics is DISC (Directing, Influencing, Stabilising, and Conscientious), with sub-classification of each quadrant into behaviours, needs, and fears.[17]

[2.50] Negotiation can be viewed as a transaction-based exchange between two people. As negotiation is a social process, the subject matter of the 'transaction' is an exchange of something of value (not necessarily an exchange of things of equal value) between those social actors. Transactions, used in the sense of the negotiation process, involve the interplay of needs and wants, and trading or bargaining between the negotiators to satisfy those needs and wants. The contribution of social exchange theory to negotiation lies in its axiom that all social relations have an instrumental foundation. People will only form and remain in relationships, of whatever kind, so long as they receive individual rewards better than those available elsewhere.[18] In other words, there has to be some point to the particular negotiation between any two or more people.

If a bridge is made between this view of transaction and contract law, then transacting involves contracting—that is, the exchange of mutual promises between two or more contracting parties. Contract law provides the internal and external conditions under which it is prepared to recognise any given contract and to provide, if necessary, the coercive machinery of the state to intervene in the performance or adjustment of a contractual relationship.

[2.55] The total transaction in negotiation can be divided into the phases of preparation, negotiation, and agreement, which generally occur in that sequence.[19] In the preparation phase, each negotiating or contracting party identifies their own needs and wants that they think can be satisfied by some transaction-based exchange with another person. This will involve some preliminary research (whether intuitive or sophisticated or somewhere in between) and making contact with the other contracting party.[20] The negotiation phase requires each side to identify their own positions and interests, to generate options to meet those interests, to bargain or trade with the other person to satisfy or meet their own interests as well as those of the other side, and to express some commitment to any agreement that is reached.[21] The agreement phase includes implementation of the commitment that has been reached, and a post-implementation phase.[22]

[2.60] Another issue that is relevant to the negotiation process is whether the negotiation is designed to secure a single outcome, or some outcome that is to be continued or repeated. If it is a one-off transaction, the relationship between the negotiators is likely to be transitory, confined only to the particular transaction that has been negotiated. It does not follow that if agreement has been reached, the parties will not need to re-enter a negotiation; they may in fact need to do so—particularly if difficulties

---

17 See N Spegel, B Rogers & R Buckley, *Negotiation: Theory and Techniques*, 7.17.
18 See E Lawler & J Yoon, 'Structural Power and Emotional Processes in Negotiation: a Social Exchange Approach', Chapter 7 in R Kramer & D Messick (eds), *Negotiation As a Social Process*, SAGE Publications, Thousand Oaks, Calif, 1995, p 147.
19 See N Spegel, B Rogers & R Buckley, *Negotiation: Theory and Techniques*, 1.19.
20 See N Spegel, B Rogers & R Buckley, *Negotiation: Theory and Techniques*, 1.19–1.22, Chapter 3 and [2.5] below.
21 See N Spegel, B Rogers & R Buckley, *Negotiation: Theory and Techniques*, 1.19, 1.23 and 1.24.
22 See N Spegel, B Rogers & R Buckley, *Negotiation: Theory and Techniques*, 1.19, 1.25 and 1.26.

emerge in the implementation or post-implementation phases.[23] If the transaction is one of a repeated series of identical or similar transactions, or if the transactions are dissimilar, but between the same people, then there must be an added factor if the ongoing relationship is to be sustained: the trust that is developed and built up through the cycle of repeat transactions.

[2.65] The status of the negotiator is an important factor in negotiation as a process. Status as a phenomenon is connected with social stratification and social mobility.[24] There is a considerable volume of literature on the socialisation of the legal profession stemming from sociological research into the legal profession that does not need to be covered in this book.[25] Nevertheless, the reason for mentioning the status of negotiators is that when lawyers participate in negotiation, there is a perception that all lawyers are skilled and confident negotiators because of their legal training and because lawyers negotiate in one form or another every working day. While lawyers may participate in negotiations often, it does not follow that they are skilled negotiators—and indeed, most law schools provide very little in the way of training in negotiation. So being a lawyer does not equate to being a skilled and competent negotiator.

[2.70] The relational aims of negotiation when viewed as a process combine several strands of thought and levels of personal commitment. Some commentators have captured the relational aims of negotiation in these terms:

- the parties want to feel that they have been treated fairly;
- the parties want the opportunity to give their side of the story;
- the parties want to feel they have retained some control over the negotiating process;
- the parties are willing to negotiate with each other again;
- the parties will have achieved an outcome with which they can live.[26]

These relational aims of negotiation are important, because they invest the process with some utility, as well as reflecting some important human values in the way that social relationships (including legal relationships, as a subset) are formed and performed.

[2.75] The objects of any particular negotiation signify what each negotiating party wants to achieve by participating in the negotiation in the first place. One dimension of the objects of negotiation is the important relational aim, referred to above, that the parties want to achieve an outcome with which they can live. Another dimension is that the parties should select negotiation as a process, rather than one of the competing alternatives such as power-centred solutions and conflict resolution.

[2.80] The values people bring to negotiation affect the strength or weakness of their commitment to this important social process. In addition, values set internal standards and principles that negotiators will adhere to (more or less) in the negotiation process. Negotiators will have greater satisfaction with the process of negotiation if something

---

23   See N Spegel, B Rogers & R Buckley, *Negotiation: Theory and Techniques*, 1.26.
24   See A Bullock & S Trombley (eds), *The New Fontana Dictionary of Modern Thought* (3rd edn, HarperCollins Publishers, London, 1999: entries on 'social mobility', p 803; and 'social stratification', p 805.
25   See C Parker, 'The Logic of Professionalism: Stages of Domination in Legal Service Delivery to The Disadvantaged' (1994) 22 *International Journal of the Sociology of Law* 145.
26   See N Spegel, B Rogers & R Buckley, *Negotiation: Theory and Techniques*, 1.8.

of their values has been incorporated into the negotiation process. Negotiators will be prepared to live with negotiated outcomes if those outcomes are consistent with—or, at the worst, not too far removed from—their values.

[2.85] The skill base of negotiators is an important element in the successful outcome of negotiation as a process. Commentators have identified a bank of essential skills in negotiation, including research skills, communication skills, lateral thinking skills, analytical skills, and drafting skills.[27]

Having seen that the elements of negotiation are multi-faceted and multi-dimensional, the next aspect to consider is bargaining strategies.

2.3 Bargaining strategies

[2.90] Bargaining strategies can be divided into two groups: interest-based bargaining and adversarial bargaining. Each of these topics has its place in negotiation as a social process. They also have their place as tools in the practice of the law of contract. Each of these bargaining strategies is examined here.

2.3.1 Interest-based bargaining

[2.95] Interest-based bargaining is an approach to negotiation that concentrates on satisfying interests rather than arguing over or defending positions. Interest-based bargaining is also called principled bargaining.[28] Leading negotiation theorists and practitioners, Fisher and Ury, developed a widely followed four-part matrix to achieve successful negotiations, as follows:

1 *People*: separate people from the problem.

2 *Interests*: focus on the interests, not positions.

3 *Options*: generate a variety of options before deciding what to do.

4 *Criteria*: insist that the result of negotiation be based on some objective standard.[29]

This matrix is examined more closely below.

(a) People

[2.100] The axiom that people should be separated from their problems in the process of negotiation is designed to ensure that negotiators concentrate on substantive issues rather than getting sidelined on people issues. This axiom also recognises that people are more important than their problems. The prime task early in the negotiation process is to provide some mechanism to deal with people issues first. This might mean, for example, providing an opportunity for people to release their disappointment or express their anger about the conflict that has resulted in the need to negotiate.[30]

The application of the axiom that people should be separated from their problems takes place continuously during the negotiation. The following steps represent practi-

---

27   See N Spegel, B Rogers & R Buckley, *Negotiation: Theory and Techniques*, 2.4 and R Bolton, *People Skills*, Simon & Schuster Australia, reprinted 2000.

28   See N Spegel, B Rogers & R Buckley, *Negotiation: Theory and Techniques*, 2.7.

29   See R Fisher, W Ury & B Patton, *Getting To Yes: Negotiating Agreement without Giving In*, 2nd edn, Penguin, New York, 1991, pp 11, 17–98.

30   See N Spegel, B Rogers & R Buckley, *Negotiation: Theory and Techniques*, 2.8.

cal measures to achieve separation of people from their problems. Commentators advocate 'active listening', which embraces listening to an opponent's argument without interrupting or justifying one's own case.[31] The next step is to acknowledge the points made by one's opponent—this involves acknowledging the feelings of an opponent, and when necessary offering an apology (without capitulating), while at the same time continuing to project confidence.[32] Other measures adopted in the negotiation process are for negotiators to agree wherever they can, and to do so without conceding (this is called 'accumulating yesses') and to use non-verbal cues to communicate with an opponent.[33] Another strategy in separating people from their problems is to acknowledge the other person, and his or her authority and competence, and make some attempt to build a working relationship.[34]

(b) Interests

[2.105] The concept of 'interests' in negotiation is one of the poles of two extremes: interests and positions. A position is what somebody wants, and the interests are why he or she wants it.[35] In other words, interests explain the positional posture of a negotiator. The commentator Moore has identified three types of interests: substantive interests, procedural interests, and relationship or psychological interests. Substantive interests refer to a desired outcome. Procedural interests sit alongside substantive interests, referring to needs associated with the negotiation process itself, such as the need to be heard and the need to be treated fairly. Relationship or psychological interests are more intangible than substantive interests, but influence the negotiation process nevertheless. These include the desire to maintain one's reputation, or the need for security.[36]

(c) Options

[2.110] An option is a method for meeting an interest. Negotiation commentators advocate the practice of generating options for mutual gain as a step along the path to securing desired outcomes.[37] Some of the particular strategies or measures that are used to generate options include:

- Separate the act of creating options from the evaluation of options. At the same time, do not ignore the process of the evaluation of options that have been generated.

---

31   See W Ury, *Getting Past No: Negotiating with Difficult People*, Century Business, London, 1992, pp 37–40; N Spegel, B Rogers & R Buckley, *Negotiation: Theory and Techniques*, 2.9. The process of reflective listening is also helpful in negotiations (and indeed in all forms of communication): see R Bolton, *People Skills*, pp 27–113.

32   W Ury, *Getting Past No: Negotiating with Difficult People*, pp 40–44.

33   W Ury, *Getting Past No: Negotiating with Difficult People*, pp 44–47.

34   W Ury, *Getting Past No: Negotiating with Difficult People*, pp 47–50.

35   See N Spegel, B Rogers & R Buckley, *Negotiation: Theory and Techniques*, 2.10.

36   See N Spegel, B Rogers & R Buckley, *Negotiation: Theory and Techniques*, 2.13, citing C Moore, *The Mediation Process: Practical for Strategies Resolving Conflict*, 2nd edn, Jossey-Bass Publishers, San Francisco, 1996.

37   See N Spegel, B Rogers & R Buckley, *Negotiation: Theory and Techniques*, 2.15–2.17 and R Fisher, W Ury & B Patton, *Getting To Yes: Negotiating Agreement without Giving In*, pp 58–83.

- Identify one's own options, as well as the options available to the other negotiator.
- Generate a range of options, including those that might not be particularly obvious. Options include 'probables' as well as 'possibles'.
- Options should be beneficial to both parties, not just to the proponent of a particular option.
- Where possible, more than one person should be involved in generating options.
- Options should strive for optimality.[38]

[2.115] The process of inventing options for mutual gain involves option diagnosis and the prescription of options.[39]

(d) Criteria

[2.120] Conventional wisdom holds that if negotiators can agree upon objective and neutral criteria as the framework within which a negotiation takes place, it is more likely than not that the parties will reach agreement, as well as being capable of fulfilling or performing that agreement.[40] The attractiveness of objective criteria is that they apply even-handedly to both parties,[41] and also calibrate the standard of performance expected of a party to the negotiations. Objective criteria shift attention away from the imposition of will or the exercise of power within a negotiation. The objective criteria necessary for any negotiation can be drawn from a wide variety of disciplines or fields of human endeavour, including the law itself, social norms, industry standards and practice, or independent expert determination.[42]

[2.125] Negotiators should employ objective criteria in negotiation by (1) framing each issue as a joint search for objective criteria; (2) reasoning and being open to reason as to which standards are the most appropriate and how they should be applied; and (3) never yielding to pressure, only to principle.[43]

2.3.2 Adversarial bargaining

[2.130] Adversarial bargaining is at the heart of our system of law. It is what lawyers are renowned for—and in some cases, it is what they are good at. By contrast with interests-based bargaining, adversarial bargaining focuses on positions, not interests (adversarial bargaining is also called positional bargaining).[44] A negotiation centred upon adversarial bargaining is concerned with promoting and protecting one's own position, not with forging some kind of community of interests. Adversarial bargaining can involve the exertion of pressure and the use of hard-nosed tactics to achieve an outcome desired by a negotiator.

---

38 Adapted from N Spegel, B Rogers & R Buckley, *Negotiation: Theory and Techniques*, 2.15.
39 R Fisher, W Ury & B Patton, *Getting To Yes: Negotiating Agreement without Giving In*, pp 62–83.
40 See N Spegel, B Rogers & R Buckley, *Negotiation: Theory and Techniques*, 2.18.
41 N Spegel, B Rogers & R Buckley, *Negotiation: Theory and Techniques*, 2.18.
42 N Spegel, B Rogers & R Buckley, *Negotiation: Theory and Techniques*, 2.18.
43 R Fisher, W Ury & B Patton, *Getting To Yes: Negotiating Agreement without Giving In*, pp 91–96.
44 N Spegel, B Rogers & R Buckley, *Negotiation: Theory and Techniques*, 2.22; R Fisher, W Ury & B Patton, *Getting To Yes: Negotiating Agreement without Giving In*, pp 7–14.

2.4   Preparation for negotiation

[2.135] Preparation in any activity consists of those prior measures undertaken to equip the participants for the activity. It goes without saying that preparation is integral to many activities in modern life, and to negotiation no less. When preparation is factored into negotiating, its goals are:

- To create an environment for constructive negotiation;
- To increase the ability of negotiators to make measured and considered responses when under pressure;
- To increase each negotiator's understanding of the other side and the way they operate;
- To be able to make informed decisions during the completion of the negotiation.[45]

[2.140] When viewed as a process, preparation for negotiation entails the following steps:

1   Defining objectives. (What do the negotiators want to achieve, and is this feasible?)

2   Considering the range of process options available (negotiation, assisted negotiation, mediation, expert appraisal, arbitration, and litigation).

3   Considering the negotiator's own interests (or those of his or her client) and prioritising them, and repeat this exercise in connection with any opponents' interests.

4   Mapping the negotiation (mapping is done to define goals, assemble interests, develop options, consider consequences, and develop better understandings).

5   Generating options.

6   Developing the parameters of the negotiation (divided into the 'walk away zone' and the 'aspiration level').

7   Preparing the logistics for the negotiation (this includes considering the data to be used, who will negotiate (in the case of groups that are being represented in the negotiation), and the venue for the negotiation and the mode of the negotiation).

8   Preparing for the other side (this involves each negotiator putting himself or herself into the shoes or place of the other negotiator or party, as well as researching the backgrounds and positions on the other participants to the negotiation).[46]

2.5   The processes of negotiation

[2.145] This final section considers the processes employed in a negotiation (each negotiation is different, and thus atypical, but the processes applied to them can be divided into patterns).

[2.150] All negotiators should be alive to the possibility that the other side may engage in tactics to unsettle them and gain the ascendant position in the negotiation. The conventional response is for the negotiator to expose these, and seek their cessation or

---

45   See N Spegel, B Rogers & R Buckley, *Negotiation: Theory and Techniques*, 3.13–3.17.
46   See N Spegel, B Rogers & R Buckley, *Negotiation: Theory and Techniques*, 3.18–3.33.

reversal.[47] If there are no tactics, or the tactics that have been employed have been defused, the next stage is to consider the three types of opening to the negotiation.

[2.155] The 'maximalist' opening is known as the 'soft high'. A soft high opening is one where the negotiator makes a demand that is is very favourable to his or her own interests or client, but accompanies it with a signal that indicates that the opening is flexible.[48]

The next type of opening is the 'firm reasonable' (or equitable opening). The firm reasonable opening is one that is used where one negotiator has (or sees) only a small degree of movement between the positions of the parties to the negotiation.[49]

The third type of opening in negotiation is the 'problem-solving' opening. It involves interest-based bargaining and the formation of a relationship that takes as its centrepiece a constructive approach to the negotiation.[50]

[2.160] The stage beyond the opening stage is the exploration stage. This is the stage where the negotiators gather intelligence from each other using the framework of concerns, interests and agendas (CIA for short). Each negotiator listens to the concerns of the other side, identifies the interests that motivate them, and then establishes an agenda to address those interests.[51]

[2.165] If there has been success in the information-gathering process, it is more probable than not that the parties will reach agreement. Commentators say it is important to focus on the basics (including never conceding an issue: instead, trade it for something else; and knowing the value of what the negotiator is offering and the value of what that person is getting in return).[52]

[2.170] When it comes to actually locking in an agreement, it is necessary to select between one of two approaches. The first is the layered agreement, where each issue is bedded down before the parties move on to resolve the next issue in turn. The second measure occurs where the issues are interrelated; then it is necessary to strive for conditional, linked bargaining. This seeks a once-and-for-all final resolution on all issues before even provisionally accepted commitments become firm.[53] Then, with a view to the ultimate implementation of whatever agreement has been reached, it is necessary for the negotiators to reality-test all of the important elements of their agreement.[54]

[2.175] The key final phase of the process of negotiation is closure by recording and documenting the 'negotiation agreement'[55] (assuming agreement has been reached; the phrase 'negotiation agreement' is used to signify the agreement reached as a result of the negotiation, and not to mean an agreement to negotiate). This is where skills training in drafting comes to the fore.[56] Some signposts to consider when drafting the clo-

---

47 See N Spegel, B Rogers & R Buckley, *Negotiation: Theory and Techniques*, 4.3.
48 See N Spegel, B Rogers & R Buckley, *Negotiation: Theory and Techniques*, 4.6.
49 See N Spegel, B Rogers & R Buckley, *Negotiation: Theory and Techniques*, 4.7.
50 See N Spegel, B Rogers & R Buckley, *Negotiation: Theory and Techniques*, 4.8.
51 See N Spegel, B Rogers & R Buckley, *Negotiation: Theory and Techniques*, 4.9–4.13.
52 See N Spegel, B Rogers & R Buckley, *Negotiation: Theory and Techniques*, 4.14.
53 See N Spegel, B Rogers & R Buckley, *Negotiation: Theory and Techniques*, 4.15 and 4.16.
54 See N Spegel, B Rogers & R Buckley, *Negotiation: Theory and Techniques*, 4.15–4.17.
55 See N Spegel, B Rogers & R Buckley, *Negotiation: Theory and Techniques*, 4.24–4.26.
56 See R Macdonald & D McGill, *Butterworths Skills Series: Drafting* Butterworths, Sydney, 1997.

sure of the negotiation via a document intended to be legally binding are set out below:

- First establish whether or not it is possible to draft the agreement including the negotiating at the negotiation itself. This will normally only be possible in the case of simple or single-issue negotiations. It is possible to fashion a *Masters v Cameron* agreement that provides for an immediately enforceable agreement that is intended to be replaced in the future with a fuller and more precise version.[57]
- Clearly draft the obligations (that is, the complex of rights-and-duties) of the parties. A poorly drafted document will exacerbate, not resolve or enhance, the relationship between the parties.
- Separate substantive matters from procedural matters, and be alert to the possibility that agreements regarding process matters may not be enforceable if they are 'agreements to agree'.[58]
- The document should be comprehensive, and deal with all of the substantive and procedural issues on which agreement has been reached between the parties.
- Provide clear time limits for the parties' specific duties and responsibilities, covering matters such as the time of payment and the time of performance of non-financial duties.
- Reality-test the performance of the promises each party makes to the other before the document is signed off.
- Consider whether conditions precedent need to be built into the performance of key responsibilities by any of the negotiating parties, including matters such as finance from external sources, approvals by management or company boards, or approvals from external agencies.
- Once the negotiation agreement has been signed by all parties, put in place practical procedures for monitoring the performance of that agreement, including performance by the negotiator and by the other side.[59]

[2.180] To sum up: negotiation is a social process that has a deep resonance within the law. It draws on cognate disciplines, including some branches of the social sciences (such as psychology) and conflict resolution and management. The processes of negotiation described in this chapter provide an embryonic framework within which those approaching contract law can participate in negotiations with some confidence.

---

57   See [4.310]–[[4.340].
58   See chapters 3 and 4.
59   See N Spegel, B Rogers & R Buckley, *Negotiation: Theory and Techniques*, 4.27–4.33 for other matters that should be taken into account in the drafting of a negotiation agreement.

Part II

Formation

This Part considers the elements necessary for formation of a valid contract. In most transactions made between individuals, the parties do not give specific attention to each of these discrete elements. Someone agrees to buy and someone agrees to sell; the price is fixed and the bargain completed. However, when a dispute arises, the courts look to see if the agreement satisfies the established elements of agreement (offer and acceptance), certainty, intention to create legal relations and consideration. These are the issues considered in this Part.

The traditional approach used to establish agreement between the parties—sometimes referred to as *consensus ad idem*, or 'a meeting of the minds'—involves the making of an offer followed by the acceptance of that offer. However, this approach is simplistic: it fails to recognise the complexities associated with, for example, counter offers, previous dealings, and protracted negotiations. In *Empirnall Holdings Pty Ltd v Machon Paul Partners Pty Ltd* (1988) 14 NSWLR 523 Kirby P (as he then was) approached the question of agreement by considering all the indicia for and against assent by the parties, without the need to find a specific offer followed by a specific acceptance. The traditional approach had earlier been criticised by Professor Atiyah in the third edition of *An Introduction to the Law of Contract*:

> It may be very difficult, if not impossible, to find a real offer and acceptance or to decide who is the offeror and who the offeree. Such cases show that to insist on the presence of a genuine offer and acceptance in every case is likely to land one in sheer fiction ...

It should also be noted that, in reality, there is a merging of the elements of agreement, certainty and intention to create legal relations. Thus, the lack of certainty may be indicative of the fact that there was no final offer or acceptance. But how certain must the agreement be? Many contracts include terms that are not actually agreed between the parties, or ambiguities in the language, or things are left unsaid. A contract may be concluded by a general understanding and a handshake, or with words such as: 'I'll get it to you as soon as I can' or, 'I'll take whatever you think is a fair price.' This poses a dilemma for the law; on one hand, it wishes to give effect to agreements made between the parties, but on the other hand, it must be able to determine what exactly the parties meant.

In the same way that certainty can impact on whether there has been agreement between the parties, the notion of an intention to be legally bound is also a relevant factor. The law makes the presumption that certain agreements are not intended by the parties to be legally binding, and thus binding in good faith only. A mother's offer to her adult son to pay him $5 per week if he mows the lawn each Saturday may be accepted by the son—and yet it is unlikely that the agreement will be legally binding. This Part considers the circumstances that give rise to the presumption, and the rationale for the rule.

Consideration is fundamental to contract formation and involves the notion of payment or benefit for the promise of another. It is generally the price paid, or the promise to pay, for the goods or services given or delivered. However, as a matter of policy, why should the courts not give effect to agreements made between parties where there is a clear offer and acceptance, certainty as to terms, and an intention to be bound by that agreement? Why should the promise to make a gift, or vary an existing agreement, not be enforced simply because of a lack of consideration? The matter has troubled the courts—and law reform committees—for some time.

One of the principles applied by the courts to give effect to promises that are relied upon by the parties but where consideration is lacking, is the principle of equitable estoppel. This involves preventing or estopping one of the parties from reneging on a promise made, even if that promise was not paid for, or supported by consideration. Equitable estoppel is grounded in equity and fairness, where the notion of unconscionability is important.

Chapter 3

Agreement

3.1 Introduction

[3.05] The fundamental requirement for any contract is that the parties have reached agreement. This is sometimes described as a 'concluded bargain'.[1] Under traditional contractual theory, an agreement is reached where an offer is made, and the offeree accepts that offer. Most contemporary transactions can comfortably be analysed in this fashion, whether the contract is entered into by the parties face to face, or electronically. A simple contract for the sale and purchase of a computer illustrates the point.

Example

A makes an offer to buy a computer for $3000. B accepts the offer by agreeing to sell the computer to A for this amount. A concluded bargain has been reached.

[3.10] Many transactions, however, are more complex than the simple contract for sale just described. Sometimes negotiations between parties extend over a long period, and comprise many items of communication. In addition, there may be other kinds of conduct by a party which, although not expressing acceptance to the contractual arrangement in any direct way, signify an understanding of the existence of a contractual relationship. While it may be impossible or difficult in the circumstances of a particular case to isolate an 'offer' and an 'acceptance' of that offer, it may be that the parties themselves consider a concluded bargain to have been reached.

[3.15] The modern judicial approach both in Australia and New Zealand appears to be to recognise and accommodate this commercial reality. A court will examine the whole course of dealings between the parties—including communication between them—together with their other conduct.[2] If, based upon such facts, an objective bystander would consider a concluded bargain to have been reached, the contractual

---

1   See, for example, *May and Butcher Ltd v The King* [1934] 2 KB 17 at 21 per Lord Dunedin.

2   *Empirnall Holdings Pty Ltd v Machon Paull Partners Pty Ltd* (1988) 14 NSWLR 523 at 531; *Integrated Computer Services Pty Ltd v Digital Equipment Corp (Aust) Pty Ltd* (1988) 5 *Butterworths Property Reports* [97 326] at 11 117; *Vroon BV v Foster's Brewing Group Ltd* [1994] 2 VR 32 at 81; *Toyota Motor Corporation Australia Ltd v Ken Morgan Motors Pty* Ltd [1994] 2 VR 108; *Marist Brothers Community Inc v Shire of Harvey* (1995) 14 WAR 69 at 73–75; *Meats v Attorney-General* [1983] NZLR 308 at 377. There has also been recognition for some time in England that the whole course of dealings including the conduct of the parties is relevant in determining contract formation: *Brogden v Metropolitan Railway Co* (1877) 2 App Cas 666 at 682 and *Gibson v Manchester City Council* [1978] 1 WLR 520 at 523–524.

requirement of agreement will be satisfied. This is sometimes referred to as the 'global' approach to contractual analysis.[3]

[3.20] The potentially complex nature of contract negotiation and formation also illustrates the overlapping issues relevant to contract formation. As will be seen in later chapters, to be a legally recognised contract, the agreement must be complete, and the parties must have agreed on the terms with sufficient certainty. Further, before legal consequences will attach, the parties must have intended to become legally bound. In cases where parties are involved in protracted negotiations, these elements may be inextricably linked. If the parties are still in the process of negotiating details of the proposed agreement, no concluded agreement would have been reached. This may be apparent from the fact that the agreement is incomplete, or its terms vague and uncertain. It is also likely that, at this stage of the process, the parties could not have intended to be legally bound. The interrelationship of traditional contractual concepts has been judicially recognised on a number of occasions.[4]

3.2   Understanding the concept of offer

[3.25] An offer may be defined as the expression to another of a willingness to be legally bound by the stated terms.[5]

[3.30] A contract for the sale of a computer was referred to at [3.05]. The offer in this case is made by A: A offers to buy B's computer for $3000. By examining this offer, three features that must be present for the offer to be legally effective can be identified.

1   *Statement by offeror (A) containing stated terms.* The offer may be contained in a formal document. However, an offer could be made through other means such as a verbal statement, e-mail, advertisement in various media including the television, radio or the Internet, or any combination of these forms. The statement (or other vehicle for making the offer) must contain all of the essentials of the proposed agreement. Further, the terms must be sufficiently certain.[6]

2   *Statement made to another person.* A statement made by a person in the privacy of his or her own room to no other person will not constitute a valid offer. The offer must be made to another legal entity. Here, A makes the offer to B. It should be noted, however, that an offer need not be limited to a single person or other legal

---

3   For a useful examination of the alternative concepts of contract formation, see D Khoury, 'Identifying agreement: questioning the traditional approach' (1997) *Law Institute Journal* 51.

4   See, for example, *Carlill v Carbolic Smoke Ball Company* [1893] 1 QB 256 at 263; *G Scammell & Nephew Ltd v HC & JG Ouston* [1941] AC 251 at 268; *Australian Woollen Mills Pty Ltd v The Commonwealth* (1953) 92 CLR 424 at 457; *Masters v Cameron* (1954) 91 CLR 353 at 360; *Marist Brothers Community Inc v Shire of Harvey* (1995) 14 WAR 69 at 74.

5   There are very few judicial attempts to define the concept of offer. See, however, the consideration of offer in *Australian Woollen Mills Pty Ltd v Commonwealth* (1954) 92 CLR 424 at 456–457 [the decision being affirmed in *Australian Woollen Mills Pty Ltd v Commonwealth* (1955) 93 CLR 546]. There have been attempts by academic writers to define the term. See, for example, the description of an offer in JW Carter & DJ Harland, *Contract Law in Australia*, 3rd edn, Butterworths, North Ryde, 1996, p 25: '... as the indication by one person to another of his or her willingness to enter into a contract with that person on certain terms.' Offer has also been defined in Halsbury's Laws of Australia as '... the expression of willingness to contract on terms stated: what is alleged to an offer must have been intended to give rise, on its acceptance, to legal relations.'

6   See Chapter 4 for issues of completeness and certainty.

entity. A valid offer can be made to more than one person or, as will be examined later, even to the world at large.

3   *Offeror indicates a preparedness to be bound.* The final requirement is that the offeror must be prepared to be bound if the offer is accepted by the offeree. Ordinarily, it will be implied from both the language used and the conduct of the party that the person is making the offer in order to reach a binding agreement.

[3.35] Although the above three elements must be present in all legally recognised offers, the nature of the offer can vary according to whether the contract being negotiated is bilateral or unilateral. Special features of an offer arise where it is made to the public at large or, as is increasingly the case today, through the Internet.

3.2.1   Offers in bilateral contracts

[3.40] Most contracts entered into are bilateral contracts. A useful definition of such a contract was provided by Lord Diplock in *United Dominions Trust (Commercial) Ltd v Eagle Aircraft Services Ltd:*[7]

> Under contracts of the former kind [bilateral contracts] each party undertakes to the other party to do or to refrain from doing something, and in the event of his failure to perform his undertaking, the law provides the other party with a remedy.

An 'offer' in the context of a bilateral contract then is one which, if accepted, is effective to bind *both* parties to perform his or her undertaking. The offer made by A above in the hypothetical example of the sale of a computer is of such a nature. If the offer is accepted by B, a bilateral contract is formed. A promises to pay $3000 to B, while B promises to pass title in the computer to A. A party failing to perform the respective promise will be in breach of contract.

3.2.2   Offers in unilateral contracts

[3.45] Unilateral contracts arise less frequently. Lord Diplock in *United Dominions Trust (Commercial) Ltd v Eagle Aircraft Services Ltd*[8] also provided a definition of a unilateral contract:

> Under contracts which are only unilateral—which I have elsewhere described as 'if' contracts—one party, whom I will call 'the promisor,' undertakes to do or to refrain from doing something on his part if another party, 'the promisee,' does or refrains from doing something, but the promisee does not himself undertake to do or to refrain from doing that thing.

When examining the concept of unilateral contracts in *Australian Woollen Mills Pty Ltd v The Commonwealth,*[9] the High Court considered the term 'unilateral contract' to be 'unscientific and misleading', as there must always be two parties to a contractual obligation. The Court continued:

---

7   [1968] 1 WLR 74 at 82.
8   [1968] 1 WLR 74 at 83.
9   (1953) 92 CLR 424.

The position in such cases is simply that the consideration on the part of the offeree is completely executed by the doing of the very thing which constitutes acceptance of the offer.[10]

[3.50] Examples of unilateral contracts best demonstrate their unique nature:

- *Offers of reward*: a government may offer a reward of an amount of money in exchange for information leading to the conviction of a murderer;[11] or an owner may offer a reward for the finding and returning of lost property.[12]
- *Offers for prizes*: a manufacturer of a product may advertise that if a person purchases a certain quantity of the product, he or she will receive a prize.[13]

[3.55] In these cases, the offerors are the government, the owner of lost property, and the manufacturer respectively. The offerees are anyone who provides information so as to satisfy the terms of the reward offer, or any purchaser of the product who complies with the stated stipulations required to receive the prize. A unilateral contract differs from a bilateral contract in that it does not immediately impose an obligation on either party to perform. The obligation on the offeror to perform only arises if the offeree performs the required task (in the examples above, providing the relevant information, or buying the requisite quantity of a product).[14] The offeree, on the other hand, will never be under an enforceable obligation to perform.

3.2.3 Offers to public at large

[3.60] In the example of the sale of the computer, the offer by A was made to one other person, B. It will often be the case that a contracting party will comprise more than one person. A contract for the sale of land, for example, will often involve two sellers and two buyers. The more complex issue that has received some judicial consideration is whether a legally recognised offer can be made to the world at large. The landmark case on this point is *Carlill v Carbolic Smoke Ball Company*.[15]

Example: Carlill v Carbolic Smoke Ball Company

The defendant (the Company) was the manufacturer of a product called the Carbolic Smoke Ball, which was designed to prevent the user of the smoke ball from contracting the flu. To promote its product, the Company advertised in a newspaper to pay £100 to any person who contracted the flu after using one of their smoke balls in the specified manner for a specified period. The plaintiff relied on the advertisement, purchased one of the smoke balls, and used it in the prescribed manner and for the prescribed period. The plaintiff contracted the flu and sued the Company to recover the £100.

---

10   Ibid at 456.
11   See, for example, *The Crown v Clarke* (1927) 40 CLR 227.
12   *Australian Woollen Mills Pty Ltd v The Commonwealth* (1953) 92 CLR 425 at 456.
13   See, for example, *Esso Petroleum Ltd v Commissioners of Customs and Excise* [1976] 1 All ER 117, *Chappell and Co v Nestlé and Co Ltd* [1960] AC 87 and *Carlill v Carbolic Smoke Ball Company* [1893] 1 QB 256.
14   Note, however, that the offeror may be under an obligation not to withdraw the offer once the offeree has commenced acceptance. See [3.295]–[3.300].
15   [1893] 1 QB 256.

The English Court of Appeal held that the plaintiff was entitled to recover the £100 from the Company. The court rejected the Company's argument that the promise was not binding because it was not made with anyone in particular. As stated by Lindley LJ, 'in point of law this advertisement is an offer to pay £100 to anybody who will perform these conditions, and the performance of the conditions is the acceptance of the offer'.[16]

[3.65 In *Carlill's case*,[17] the offer made to the world at large formed the basis of a unilateral contract. This will not always be the case. Depending on the terms of the advertisement to the general public, the advertisement may constitute an offer which, if accepted, forms a bilateral contract.[18]

3.2.4   *Offers made through the Internet*

[3.70] In recent times, there has been an enormous increase in the extent to which commerce is transacted through the Internet. The expansion of electronic commerce has also highlighted a number of difficulties, particularly in relation to issues of contract formation. Given the extent to which such trade is transacted across jurisdictions, difficult legal problems can arise—such as establishing the place and time of formation of the contract, and the appropriate legal regime to govern the transaction. These issues are examined elsewhere in this chapter,[19] and later in this book.[20] However, where goods and services are advertised for sale over the Internet (and provided Australian law governs the transaction), some of the traditional contractual concepts will continue to be relevant. The principles relating to offers made to the public at large provide an example. Offers made on the Internet may be offers made to the public at large in the same way as the advertisement in *Carlill's case*.[21] The fact that offers made electronically can potentially reach a wider audience does not, in itself, affect these legal principles.[22]

3.3   What is not an offer

[3.75] Where statements are made in a commercial or business context, it is sometimes difficult to determine the precise legal effect of a particular statement or exchange. Depending on the circumstances of the case, a statement, while having some features akin to an offer, may be in fact something less. The other party will therefore be unable to 'accept' to form a binding agreement. The commentary that follows explains the way these statements differ from offers.

---

16   Ibid at 262.
17   [1893] 1 QB 256.
18   See [3.115]–[3.130].
19   See [3.660]–3.670].
20   See [26.380]–[26.400].
21   [1893] 1 QB 256.
22   It may, however, be the case that the wide nature of the audience receiving the offer may influence a court's determination on whether the particular communication constitutes an offer or an invitation to treat.

3.3.1 Mere puff

[3.80] A common feature of advertising, particularly in years gone by, is to make exaggerated or perhaps unsustainable claims about products. [23] The following examples illustrate the point:

Example A

We make the most powerful and effective cockroach baits on the market. If you use our product, you will never see another cockroach again.

Example B

The special formula in our new toothpaste incorporates the latest developments in medical research. We are so confident with our product that if you use it according to the directions, and you suffer any decay while using our product, we will pay your dentist's bill.

Example C

Use our shampoo and you, too, can have Bette Davis hair. It will change your life.

[3.85] Sometimes such statements can be regarded only as 'mere puffery'—the claims are made only for advertising purposes and 'mean nothing'.[24] Example C above is likely to fall into this category. A purchaser using the product whose hair does not become like the hair of Bette Davis and whose life is not transformed will not be able to sue the manufacturer of the product for breach of contract. The manufacturer was clearly not making a promise that was intended to be taken seriously.

[3.90] Not all statements made in advertising, however, can be dismissed so lightly. The case of *Carlill v Carbolic Smoke Ball Company*[25] provides such an example. In that case,[26] it was held that the statement was more than mere puffery. The deposit of £1000 in the bank was an indication of the manufacturer's intention that the offer was genuine.[27] It may be that Example B above falls within this category.

[3.95] Some advertising statements may fall between these two extremes. Example A may be such a case. In determining whether the advertisement is a mere puff or an offer capable of being accepted and forming a contract, the court must consider how a reasonable person in the position of the offeree would interpret the advertisement.[28]

---

23 See further [8.210] and [13.40].
24 *Carlill v Carbolic Smoke Ball Company* [1893] 1 QB 256 at 261.
25 [1893] 1 QB 256.
26 For the facts and decision see [3.60] above.
27 See also *Byers v Dorotea Pty Ltd* (1987) 69 ALR 715 where units being constructed and sold were described as being 'bigger and better' than those in a nearby building. The Federal Court considered (at 720) that in the circumstances of the case, such a statement could not be regarded as merely a puff. Contrast, however, the American case involving an advertisement by a soft drink manufacturer suggesting that a person collecting sufficient 'Pepsi Points' may have a chance to win a Harrier Jump Jet (valued at US$23 million). This advertisement was held not to constitute an offer as it was not sufficiently 'clear, definite and explicit'. See S Graw, 'Puff, Pepsi and "That Plane"—The John Leonard Saga' (2000) 15 *Journal of Contract Law* 281.
28 *Manufacturers' Material Insurance Ltd v John H Boardman Insurance Brokers Pty Ltd* (1992) 27 NSWLR 630 at 638; *Lark v Outhwaite* [1991] 2 Lloyd's Rep 132 at 139.

Factors such as the vagueness of the statement, and the other details of the advertisement itself would be relevant considerations.

3.3.2 Supply of information

[3.95] In the course of contractual negotiations, enquiries are frequently made of the other party, and information is exchanged. It is sometimes difficult to decide whether a statement by one party constitutes an offer or is merely a response to a request for information. The case of *Harvey v Facey*[29] provides a good illustration of this point.

Example: Harvey v Facey

One party was anxious to purchase property of another, the property being known as 'Bumper Hall Pen'. The prospective purchasers sent a telegram to the owners in the following terms: 'Will you sell us Bumper Hall Pen? Telegraph lowest cash price.' The owners responded: 'Lowest price for Bumper Hall Pen £900'. The final communication was by the purchasers to say: 'We agree to buy Bumper Hall Pen for £900 asked by you ...' The purchasers later brought an action for specific performance when the owners refused to complete the purchase.

The Privy Council did not grant the relief sought because a contract had not been formed. The plaintiff made two enquiries of the owners: whether they were willing to sell; and what the lowest price of the sale would be. The owners responded only to the second question by supplying the information. It could not be implied that they responded to the first question by agreeing to sell.

In coming to its decision, the Privy Council gave a very literal interpretation to the exchange of telegrams. It follows that a clearer indication of a preparedness to enter into a contract is required then merely providing terms or information upon which a party may be prepared to enter into such a contract.

3.3.3 Invitation to treat

[3.100] An invitation to treat is a technique used by a person who wants another person or persons to make an offer. It is an indicator of that person's willingness to negotiate entry into a contract. In a legal sense, the invitation falls short of a valid legal offer. The party making the invitation does not indicate a willingness to be bound on the terms contained in the invitation, and the invitation cannot be accepted by the other party to conclude an agreement. In *Carlill's case*,[30] Bowen L J described an invitation to treat in the following terms:

> cases in which you offer to negotiate, or you issue advertisements that you have got a stock of books to sell, or houses to let, in which case there is no offer to be bound by any contract. Such advertisements are offers to negotiate—offers to receive offers—offers to chaffer, as, I think, some learned judge in one of the cases has said.

---

29   [1893] AC 552.
30   [1893] 1 QB 256 at 268.

As Bowen L J pointed out, advertisements for sale, such as those appearing in catalogues or even the display of goods on shelves in a supermarket will generally be regarded as invitations to treat.[31] They are not offers by themselves, but 'offers to receive offers'. They are designed to generate offers by others. Therefore, an invitation to treat cannot be accepted by the other person and bind the person who advertised the product.

[3.105] Some kinds of transactions have had their legal character defined by an established body of case law. Advertisements and displays of goods are examples; these are considered in more detail below. Categorisation can be more difficult in other cases. It can be a fine line between a statement constituting an invitation to treat and an offer. Ultimately, the test is how the statement would be regarded by a reasonable person in the position of the offeree. This can only be determined by considering all the circumstances of the case.

3.4   Categorising transactions

[3.110] The foregoing discussion provides some general principles relevant to determining whether an offer has been made. Transactions that at first glance resemble offers, but in fact were something different, were also considered. In this part of the chapter, a variety of common business practices are identified and analysed by isolating the elements of offer and acceptance. For a number of these standard practices, case law has developed to suggest the transaction will generally be categorised in a certain way. But care must be taken not to generalise. While it might be true to say, for example, that courts usually treat advertisements in a newspaper as invitations to treat, in the end, each case must be decided on its merits. It is a question of construction in each case.

3.4.1   Advertisements

[3.115] Manufacturers and retailers use a variety of means to promote their products: advertisements over the radio, on television, in a newspaper, or on an Internet home page; circulars delivered to letterboxes door to door, or forwarded through the mail; catalogues or magazines given or sold to the public; or displays of goods in shop windows and on the shop floor itself. As a general proposition, most advertising techniques are regarded as invitations to treat by the party placing the advertisement. However, whether the advertiser has gone one step further—so the advertisement can be regarded as an offer—will depend on the language used, as well as any other relevant circumstances.

(a)   Advertisement in a catalogue or through a circular

[3.120] To promote sales of merchandise, retailers often produce catalogues designed for wide public circulation. Another common advertising strategy is the printing and delivery of circulars to individual householders. Such advertising material is likely to

---

31   See [3.120] and [3.135] for a more detailed examination of the legal implications of these kinds of advertisements and displays.

describe the items for sale by words or photograph, together with price. The question is whether the advertisement in the catalogue or circular represents an invitation to treat or an offer. Categorisation of the advertisement may be significant for a number of reasons.

1   *Where the 'offer' for sale of particular items is regulated by statute.* Legislation may restrict or regulate the extent to which certain kinds of goods (or possibly fauna and flora) may be offered for sale.[32] A retailer will only have to comply with statutory requirements if the advertisement is an offer, but not if it is an invitation to treat.

2   *Where the retailer has exhausted the stock of advertised items.* A retailer who has sold all stock of the advertised item may be in breach of contract if the advertisement is regarded as an offer. In such a case, a person seeing the advertisement and placing an order with the retailer would be accepting the offer, and a contract would be formed. A retailer who was unable to provide the item would be in breach of the contract. The outcome will be different if the advertisement is regarded as an invitation to treat.

The legal status of circulars and catalogues that provide information about items for sale and their prices is reasonably settled. Such material is only an invitation to treat. Placing an order will be an offer, which can be accepted or rejected by the retailer.[33]

This approach makes sense. The retailer placing the advertisement could not have intended that any order placed would constitute a binding contract for the amount of the order. If this were the case, a successful catalogue or circular that generated a large number of orders that could not be filled would result in the retailer being in breach of multiple contracts. The retailer must have intended to be able to accept or reject orders placed in response to the advertisement.

(b) Advertisement in newspapers and magazines

[3.125] Another common way to promote sales of a product or to gain a commercial benefit in some other way is to place advertisements in newspapers and magazines. Advertisements of this kind raise similar legal issues to those discussed above in relation to catalogues and circulars. An advertisement that gives information about goods for sale, and their price, will generally be an invitation to treat rather than an offer.[34]

Notwithstanding this general proposition, however, it is possible for an advertisement to be couched in terms that indicate the retailer's willingness to be bound if the specified terms are accepted.[35]

---

32   See, for example, the legislation at issue in *Partridge v Crittenden* [1968] 1 WLR 1204.
33   *Grainger & Son v Gough* [1896] AC 325 at 333.
34   *Partridge v Crittenden* [1968] 1 WLR 1204.
35   See, for example, *Re Mount Tomah Blue Metals Ltd (in liq)* [1963] ALR 346 which involved an advertisement in a newspaper and a circular distributed to shareholders of a company requesting shareholders to send in money to assist the company's financial situation. In exchange, the shareholders were to receive debenture stock. The Supreme Court of the Australian Capital Territory held that the advertisement and circular constituted an offer that could be accepted by the shareholders forwarding a cheque to the company.

Example

Savealot Supermarket will sell all 15 washing machines on its shop floor to the first 15 customers who enter the store on Monday and can pay $200.00 cash. Limit of 1 machine per customer.

This advertisement is an offer capable of acceptance. To use the definition of offer provided earlier, it is an expression to another [here the public at large] of a willingness to be bound by the stated terms.[36] This advertisement is in a different class to most advertisements. As in *Carlill's case*,[37] 'there is the promise, as plain as words can make it'.[38] It is not an invitation for customers to make an offer. It is a promise to sell 15 fridges on the shop floor to the first 15 customers on Monday who have $200.00 cash.

(c)   Advertisements appearing on the Internet

[3.130] Many manufacturers and retailers now advertise their products on the Internet. Potential customers access the manufacturers' home pages and see the material on the site. As always, the question of whether such advertisements are invitations to treat or offers capable of acceptance is one of construction. The legal status of such advertisements is likely to be determined by applying the traditional principles explained above. An advertisement to the general public may well be construed in the same way as an advertisement in a catalogue—that is, as an invitation to treat. This is particularly likely to be so where, for example, information appears on the site advising potential customers that the price will only be debited to the specified credit card when the retailer has established that the particular product is in stock. In such a transaction, the customer's order is probably an offer to purchase. On the other hand, it is possible to design an advertisement that constitutes an offer, even though it is made to the world at large—as occurred in *Carlill's case*.[39] This may be the case if the particular site makes it clear that when the customer takes the prescribed steps that result in confirmation of the customer's order, the product (whether or not currently in stock) will be supplied.

(d)   Display of goods

[3.135] The display of goods in a retail outlet is another form of advertising, whether the display occurs in a shop window or by storing goods on a shelf in a self-service store. From time to time, a question has arisen about the legal effect of the display. Can the display of those goods be regarded as an offer to sell the goods for the stated price—that offer being accepted when their customer selects the item by taking it from the shelf and placing it in his or her basket or trolley? Alternatively, is it merely an invitation for the customer to make an offer to purchase the item?

Members of the public asked to consider this question are likely to say the store is making an offer to sell that particular item. However, this is clearly not the legal position. The display of an article together with its price constitute an invitation to

---

36   See [3.25] above.
37   [1893] 1 QB 256.
38   Ibid at 262.
39   [1893] 1 QB 256.

treat.[40] A customer who selects the item and takes it to the counter for payment makes the offer. It is then open to the retailer (or agent) to accept the offer to form an agreement, or reject it.

3.4.2   Auctions

[3.140] Auctions are a common method of sale where the subject matter is unique. It is for this reason that sales of land frequently occur by auction. But auctions are not limited to subject matter of this kind, and the same legal principles apply regardless of the item being sold.

(a)   Advertisements for auction

[3.145] To attract the maximum number of potential bidders, auction sales are generally advertised. While advertisements will vary in format depending on the nature of the auction, they will always describe the property to be auctioned and give the location of the auction. At common law, the advertisement does not bind the auctioneer to carry out the auction. The auctioneer may withdraw various lots at the auction itself, or cancel the auction altogether without incurring any liability from potential bidders.[41]

(b)   Auctions with a reserve

[3.150] For most property sold by auction, the owner will set a reserve price. This means that the auctioneer cannot sell the property unless he or she receives a bid at or greater than the reserve price. If the bids do not reach the reserve, the property is said to be 'passed in', and the property is not sold.

For auctions where there is a reserve price, the call for bids by the auctioneer is akin to an invitation to treat. Each bid made at the auction represents an offer that may be accepted or rejected by the auctioneer. Acceptance of the offer occurs, and the agreement is formed, when the auctioneer knocks the property down to the successful bidder. Because the agreement is not formed until a bid is knocked down, a bidder can withdraw a bid (offer) before this time.[42]

(c)   Auctions without a reserve

[3.155] It is less common for auctions to occur without a reserve price being set. The legal status of an auction of property where it is advertised that the property will be sold to the highest bidder (that is, an auction without a reserve) is not entirely settled.[43] There is early English authority to suggest that where an auction is advertised to be without reserve, a contract is made between the auctioneer and the highest bona fide bidder. An auctioneer who refuses to knock down the property to

---

40   *Fisher v Bell* [1961] 1 QB 394; *Pharmaceutical Society of Great Britain v Boots Cash Chemists (Southern) LD* [1953] 1 QB 401.

41   *Harris v Nickerson* (1873) LR 8 QB 286. Liability may flow, however, if the auctioneer advertises an auction and, at the time the auction was advertised, he or she did not intend to hold the auction. See [13.420]. Compare the situation where the auction advertisement is one without a reserve. See Warlow v Harrison (1859) 120 ER 295 discussed at [3.155].

42   *Payne v Cave* (1789) 100 ER 502; *AGC (Advances) Ltd v McWhirter* (1977) 1 *Butterworths Property Reports* [97045].

43   For the position in New Zealand, see [3.680]–[3.685].

that bidder will be in breach of contract.[44] The suggestion in *Warlow v Harrison*[45] was that an auctioneer in such a case 'pledges himself that the sale shall be without reserve' and that he in fact 'contracts that it shall be so; and that this contract is made with the highest bidder'.[46] To this extent, an auction without a reserve is on a different legal footing from an auction with a reserve. Where the auction does have a reserve, an auctioneer will not incur contractual liability by failing to knock the property down to the highest bidder.

[3.160] While it may be the case that an auctioneer who advertises an auction as being 'without reserve' incurs contractual liability by not knocking the property down to the highest bidder, it is quite a separate issue whether bids made at such an auction have a different legal status from bids at an auction *with* a reserve. Where there is a reserve, bidders make the offer, which is accepted if and when the auctioneer knocks down the property. If an auctioneer undertakes to conduct an auction without a reserve (and may incur contractual liability if he or she reneges on that promise), the question arises as to whether this constitutes an offer to the highest bidder, with each bidder making a conditional acceptance. Under this view, acceptance (and therefore contract formation) is conditional upon the bidder being the highest bidder.

[3.165] The legal nature of an auction without a reserve was considered by the Supreme Court of New South Wales in *AGC (Advances) Ltd v McWhirter*.[47] There, the auction was originally advertised as being with a reserve, but ultimately proceeded without one. The legal status of bids made at the auction arose because the auctioneer knocked the property down to the second-highest, not the highest, bidder. The highest bidders lodged a caveat over the property on the basis that they were the purchasers of the property—the contract having been formed when they made the highest bid. The sellers then brought an action against the highest bidders for removal of the caveat. The Court held that the caveat should be removed, as the sellers had not entered into a contract with them. According to the Court, even in an auction without a reserve, each bid represents an offer that could be accepted or rejected by the auctioneer. As the bid was not accepted, a contract had not been formed. The Court did not differentiate between the legal character of bids at an auction on the basis of whether or not there was a reserve price set.[48]

---

44   *Warlow v Harrison* (1859) 120 ER 925. This case was applied in an early decision of the Victorian Supreme Court in *Ulbrick v Laidlaw* [1924] VLR 247, and the facts and decision reached were cited without adverse comment by the same Court in *Hordern House Pty Ltd v Arnold* [1989] VR 402 and by the Queensland Supreme Court in *Wright v Madden* [1992] 1 QdR 343. It was followed recently by the English Court of Appeal in *Barry v Davies (trading as Heathcote Ball & Co)* [2000] 1 WLR 1962. Although the auction was advertised as being without a reserve, two engine analysers (each valued at £14 000) were withdrawn from sale as the highest bid was £200 for each. The unsuccessful bidder recovered £27 600 (the difference between the bid and the market price) as damages for breach of a collateral contract to sell to the highest bidder.

45   (1859) 120 ER 925.

46   Ibid at 928.

47   (1977) 1 *Butterworths Property Reports* [97045].

48   The Court also referred to *Warlow v Harrison* (1859) 120 ER 925 but noted that the decision related to liability of an auctioneer where the auction was stated to be without reserve, not the issue of contract formation. Nevertheless, the New South Wales Supreme Court queried whether the English decision could be consistent with the long-standing authorities on the legal nature of auctions: (1977) 1 *Butterworths Property Reports* [97047] at 9458.

3.4.3   Tendering

[3.170] Tendering is a process used in both the private and government sectors. It can be used, for example, where a landowner or developer wants a complex built. Owners who want to ensure they receive a range of competitive quotes may invite builders to tender for the project. Builders then submit tenders that contain a price for which the project can be provided, based on the specifications stipulated by the owner. The owner then has the option of accepting the most attractive bid. Tenders can also be used to obtain competitive selling prices. If a seller has a quantity of stock that is no longer needed, but is still of some commercial value, the seller may invite the public, or a section of the public to whom such stock may be valuable, to tender for it. Again, once the tenders are submitted, the seller may chose to sell to the person submitting the most attractive (presumably in such a case the highest) bid.

(a)   Advertisements for tender

[3.175] A request for tenders will usually be advertised. From a legal perspective, an advertisement requesting tenders is similar to an advertisement promoting an auction. Most advertisements are designed to maximise tenders (or bids, as the case may be). The legal status of an advertisement inviting tenders will generally be the same as an advertisement of an auction with a reserve.[49] The advertisement is an indication of a person's readiness to receive offers (akin to an invitation to treat).[50] Liability will there-fore generally not arise if the person chooses not to accept any of the tenders, or does not even consider all tenders in a bona fide way.

[3.180] While an advertisement will generally be regarded in this light, each case must be considered on its own facts.[51] There are at least two situations in which a person inviting tenders may incur liability as a result of the tendering process. The first arises where the advertisement inviting tenders indicates that the highest (or lowest, as the case may be) bid will be accepted. An advertisement inviting tenders worded in this way has been interpreted as an offer to the highest bidder. Acceptance occurs when a person submits the tender that turns out to be the highest tender.[52]

[3.185] The second exception to the general proposition that a person inviting tenders incurs no liability to individual tenderers was suggested by the English Court of Appeal in *Blackpool & Fylde Aero Club Ltd v Blackpool Burrow Council*.[53] While the Court did not doubt the correctness of the general proposition, a person could—depending on the circumstances—incur contractual liability for failing to comply with the agreed tendering process. This could occur if they failed to consider a conforming tender. On the facts of that case, the Court held that the invitation to tender indicated all tenders submitted in the correct form by the due date would be considered. This was sufficient to create a contract between the party seeking tenders and the tenderer.

49   There is a suggestion that the position may be different if the advertisement is of an auction without reserve: [3.145] and [3.155].
50   *Spencer v Harding* (1870) LR 5 CP 651 at 564.
51   *Hughes Aircraft Systems International v Airservices Australia* (1997) 146 ALR 1 at 25–26.
52   *Harvela Investments Ltd v Royal Trust Company of Canada (CI) Ltd* [1986] 1 AC 207. This proposition is also supported by dicta in *Spencer v Harding* (1870) LR 5 CP 561 at 564.
53   [1991] WLR 1195.

Failure to consider the tender put the party in breach of contract. *Hughes Aircraft Systems International v Airservices Australia*[54] is an Australian case in which liability attached for failure to comply with the tendering process. A letter setting out details of the tendering process, including evaluation criteria and their priorities, and evaluation methodology, was prepared by the body calling for tenders and signed by the two prospective tenderers. On signing, this letter was held to constitute a contract binding on the party calling for tenders—a contract requiring that body to comply with the agreed tendering process. Consideration for this promise was the tenderers' participation in the tendering process.[55]

(b) Individual tenders

[3.190] In the usual case, at advertisement inviting tenders will make it clear that the party is under no obligation to accept any tender made. In such a case, each tender will be regarded as an offer that can be accepted or rejected. On the other hand, if a party indicates that the highest (or lowest) bidder will be accepted, as mentioned earlier, there is authority to suggest that the advertisement will constitute an offer that is accepted by the person submitting the highest performing tender.[56]

3.4.4   *Standing offers*

[3.195] A standing offer is an indication by one party of his or her willingness to provide goods or services over a specified period.[57] For example, A may be successful in a tender to supply a government department with stationery for 12 months. The parties may agree that A will provide various items of stationery that the department may order from time to time during that period, at specified prices.

Because the offer of A may, unless it is withdrawn, be effective for 12 months, it is referred to as a 'standing offer'. The standing offer is accepted every time an order for stationery is placed by the government department. After placing the order, the contract is formed and the parties are bound in relation to that particular order. If the goods are not delivered, the offeror (here A) will be in breach of contract,[58] as will be the case if the offeree (the government department) wrongly refuses to take delivery of the goods. Because of the nature of a standing offer, it is likely to be accepted by the offeree a number of times during the relevant period.

[3.200] Unlike an option,[59] the offeror is entitled to withdraw the offer at any time before acceptance of the offer by placing an order. Further, unless the parties expressly agree to the contrary, there is no obligation by the offeree (the government department) to order stationery only from the offeror.[60] The offeree will not be in breach of

---

54   (1997) 146 ALR 1. For an impact of this decision on the law on tender, see A Phang 'Tenders, Implied Terms and Fairness in the Law of Contract' (1998) 13 *Journal of Contract Law* 126.
55   For the New Zealand position, see [3.680]–[3.685].
56   See [3.180] above.
57   Such offers often arise at a result of a call for tenders by a party requiring such goods or services. The legal implications of a tender were examined at [3.170]–[3.190].
58   *The Great Northern Railway Co v Witham* (1873) LR 9 CP 16.
59   See further below.
60   *Colonial Ammunition Co v Reid* (1900) 21 LR (NSW) 338.

contract by not placing an order. In other words, the offeree may choose not to accept the standing offer.

3.4.5   Options

[3.205] Ordinarily, an offeror may revoke an offer at any time before it is accepted. This is the case even if the offeror promises to keep the offer open for a time.[61] The position is different, however, if the offeree provides consideration—for example, by paying money—for the offeror to keep the offer open. This arrangement then becomes one under which the offeree is granted an option. An option may be useful in the following context.

Example

A purchaser of land may only wish to purchase a particular block (block A) if he or she can also purchase the adjoining block (block B). In exchange for payment of a sum of money, the seller of block A gives the purchaser an option, for a specified period, to buy that block.

As the purchaser provides consideration to the seller to keep the offer open for some period, the offer cannot be withdrawn during that period. There has been considerable academic and judicial argument about the true nature of an option. On one theory, the option itself is a separate agreement: the offeree provides consideration to the offeror to keep the offer open for a specified period. The offer is therefore irrevocable.[62] The alternative theory is that by entering the option, the parties enter a conditional contract. In the above example, the seller and purchaser enter a conditional sale. The sale becomes unconditional if and when the buyer exercises the option and does what is required of him or her to complete the transaction.[63]

[3.210] In most cases, it has little practical significance whether the true nature of an option is described by the first or the second theory. In the example above, if the seller fails to keep the offer open for the agreed period and sells to another party, he or she will be in breach of a contractual obligation and, depending on the circumstances, liable to damages, regardless of the theory used to categorise the transaction.

3.4.6   Purchase of tickets for transport

[3.215] Contracts for transport can take a variety of forms. The contract may be for carriage on public transport such as bus, train, tram, or ferry; or private transport such as plane, taxi, boat or ship. The method of contract formation can also vary considerably. What these contracts will generally have in common, however, is that the passenger will receive a ticket of some kind. Issues of contract formation—and precisely when that takes place—are important because tickets for transport commonly contain

---

61   *Routledge v Grant* (1828) 130 ER 920.

62   *Gilbert J McCaul (Aust) Pty Ltd v Pitt Club Ltd* (1959) 59 SR (NSW) 122; *Bowman v Durham Holdings Pty Ltd* (1973) 131 CLR 8 at 10 and 17–18; *United Dominions Trust (Commercial) Ltd v Eagle Aircraft Services* [1968] 1 WLR 74 at 81; *Goldsbrough, Mort & Co Ltd v Quinn* (1910) 10 CLR 674 at 691–692.

63   *Traywinds Pty Ltd v Cooper* [1989] 1 QdR 222; *Laybutt v Amaco Australia Pty Ltd* (1974) 132 CLR 57 at 71–76; *Goldsbrough, Mort & Co Ltd v Quinn* (1910) 10 CLR 674 at 678–679.

exemption or exclusion clauses. Such clauses will, of course, only assist a carrier if they are introduced *before* the contract has been formed. The different circumstances in which tickets can be purchased and contracts formed are considered below.

(a) Tickets from automatic vending machines

[3.220] It is now commonplace for public transport tickets to be purchased through automatic vending machines. An intending passenger puts money into a slot and receives a ticket. The precise point at which the contract is formed in such a case is considered at [3.255]. The presence of the machine ready to accept the money constitutes an offer, and the passenger accepts the offer by inserting the coins. After this point, it is too late for terms to be introduced to govern the transaction. Any terms appearing on the ticket issued by the machine that were not drawn to the passenger's attention beforehand could not be regarded as forming part of the contract.

(b) Purchase of tickets prior to carriage

[3.225] It is also common to buy tickets before the trip. For example, a person may purchase a bus, train, ferry, or train pass that allows carriage over a certain period or for a specified number of journeys. Sometimes notices are displayed at the place where the tickets are purchased. Depending on the prominence of the display, such terms may be incorporated into the contract.[64] Sometimes, however, the ticket that is issued upon payment by the passenger will contain additional terms. It is a difficult legal point to determine precisely when the contract of carriage is formed. This exchange can be analysed in different ways.

Option 1

Passenger makes an offer to pay for transport, the offer being accepted by the carrier when the money is handed over and the ticket is issued. It is then too late for any terms on the ticket to be incorporated into the contract.

Option 2

Passenger makes an offer to pay for transport. A counter-offer is then made by the carrier, who issues a ticket containing new terms. This counter-offer is accepted by the passenger if he or she does not return the ticket after having a reasonable time to read the terms and consider their suitability. If a passenger does not return the ticket within that time, a contract including the terms on the ticket will have been formed.

Whether a particular set of facts falls into option 1 or 2 is likely to depend on the circumstances of the case. A crucial factor is the extent of time a passenger has to read the terms before actual carriage.[65]

[3.230] The following examples illustrate different ways that contracts of carriage can be formed.

---

64   See [8.125]–[8.145].
65   *Thornton v Shoe Lane Parking Ltd* [1971] 2 QB 163 at 169; *MacRobertson Miller Airline Services v Commissioner of State Taxation (Western Australia)* (1975) 133 CLR 125 at 136–139.

Example A

A person wants to catch a ferry to the city. When the ferry docks, an agent of the carrier stands at the entry to the ferry. As each passenger boards, the agent takes the fare and gives the passenger a ticket.

Example B

An intending passenger approaches an airline counter at an airport. The airline issues a ticket in exchange for payment of money by the passenger. The ticket facilitates carriage of a passenger to a particular destination.

It is likely that a court faced with Example A would categorise it as falling within option 1 above. The passenger does not have a chance to read the terms on the ticket and decide whether he or she is prepared to accept them. The situation is the same when the person boards a bus, pays the fare, receives a ticket, and then takes a seat. The contract is formed at the time the fare is handed over and the ticket received.[66] There is no opportunity for the passenger to read the terms on the ticket and consider whether they are prepared to be bound by them.

[3.235] The position may be different if the ticket for carriage is prepaid. In this case, the passenger purchases the ticket before the trip and has an opportunity to read the terms and consider whether he or she is prepared to accept the counter-offer on this basis. The issue of contract formation in the context of purchasing an airline ticket—as in Example B above—has been examined by the High Court.

Example: MacRobertson Miller Airline Services v Commissioner of State Taxation (Western Australia) [67]

To secure a flight with the airline company, a passenger would approach the company and, if there was an available seat on the plane, the passenger would pay the fare and be issued with a ticket. The stage of that transaction that is regarded as contract formation was pivotal to the issue before the High Court.

In the course of his judgment, Justice Stephen provided a useful examination of contract formation in ticket cases. In relation to airline tickets, His Honour considered the ticket to be the offer. The passenger accepted the offer on the terms in the ticket either by conduct (boarding the plane) or by not returning the ticket after having a reasonable opportunity to read the terms.

[3.240] Although *MacRobertson's case*[68] involved the purchase of a ticket over the counter, many (if not most) plane tickets are not bought in this way. Flights are generally prebooked and prepaid, with the passenger being sent the ticket in the mail or picking it up prior to the flight. In these circumstances, it is possible to argue that the contract for carriage was formed over the phone when the flight was booked and payment made. If this is the case, it may be argued that the terms on the ticket would not form

---

66   *Wilkie v London Passenger Transport Board* [1947] 1 All ER 258 at 259.
67   (1975) 133 CLR 125.
68   Ibid.

part of the contract.[69] Clearly this would not be the outcome desired or expected by the carrier. But because both parties would expect the contract to take place subject to certain terms, a court might find that the contract was entered into subject to any implied terms that ordinarily govern such contracts.[70] Alternatively, a court might adopt an approach similar to that in *MacRobertson's case*.[71] If intending passengers are advised that a ticket will be sent to them by mail, or can be picked up at the airport, a court may find that a contract is formed when the passenger has reviewed the ticket containing the terms of carriage and fails to object to those terms within a reasonable time of receiving them.

[3.245] The position is further complicated where a passenger rings an airline to book and pay for a ticket, and on arrival at the airport, collects a boarding pass, not a ticket, upon showing identification. The passenger is not advised that the contract is subject to any terms, either at the time of booking the flight or when collecting the boarding pass; nor does the boarding pass contain any terms. In this case, it is likely that the contract is formed at the time of the phonecall, when the passenger books the ticket, and the airline agrees to the carriage. In the absence of express terms being incorporated into the contract, a court may hold that the contract is subject to the usual terms that govern contracts of carriage by plane.

(c) Purchase of ticket during course of carriage

[3.250] It is also possible to purchase a ticket in the course of the carriage. In such cases, the contract is formed before the purchase of the ticket. Precisely what constitute the offer and the acceptance is an interesting academic point, but likely to have little practical significance. It may be that the offer is made by the carrier in allowing the passenger on board, and the offer is accepted by the passenger's boarding of the transport. Once again, it is likely that the parties would contract on terms that usually govern such contracts.[72]

3.4.7   Automatic vending machines

[3.255] Automatic vending machines are in widespread use, and serve a variety of functions. They are commonly used for the automatic issue of snack food, tickets for public transport, and entry into public car parks. Owners of vending machines may sometimes attempt to impose terms on the other contracting party (generally to exclude or limit liability), so it may be important to determine precisely when the contract is formed. After the offer is accepted, it is too late to impose additional terms.[73]

---

69   See, for example, *Oceanic Line Special Shipping Co Inc v Fay* (1988) 62 ALJR 389 which involved the issue of a ticket for carriage on a cruise vessel. At the time of purchase, the passenger received an 'exchange order' which was exchanged for a ticket on the particular cruise vessel upon boarding. The High Court held that the contract was formed when the earlier 'exchange order' was received by the passenger, so the terms on the ticket issued on boarding did not form part of the contract.

70   *Hollingworth v Southern Ferries Ltd (The Eagle)* [1977] 2 *Lloyd's Rep* 70 at 75, where Ogden J suggested there would be an implied term in a contract of carriage that a shipowner could impose reasonable rules on passengers for their safety and for the proper running of the vessel.

71   (1975) 133 CLR 125.

72   *Hollingworth v Southern Ferries Ltd (The Eagle)* [1977] 2 *Lloyd's Rep* 70 at 75.

73   Terms displayed on the vending machine itself may form part of the contract: see [8.130]–[8.145].

The timing of contract formation in such transactions was considered by the English Court of Appeal in *Thornton v Shoe Lane Parking Ltd*[74]—a case involving an automatic ticket vending machine that allowed access to a car park. Once the car approached the machine, a ticket was issued to the customer automatically. The question was whether the terms referred to on the ticket issued automatically by the machine as the car approached formed part of the contract. In finding that they did not, the Court of Appeal considered that generally for vending machines, 'the offer is made when the proprietor of the machine holds it out as being ready to receive money'.[75] The proposition is slightly different in the car park context. If a notice is displayed—giving prices and stating that cars are parked at owner's own risk—the offer is contained in the notice. Acceptance occurs when the car proceeds to the machine and the ticket is taken by the driver.

3.5   Communication of an offer

[3.260] Acceptance must take place in reliance upon the offer.[76] If the offeree performs a particular act that corresponds to the terms of the offer without knowledge of the offer, there is no agreement, and no contract comes into existence. A different issue arises where the offeree hears of the terms of the offer, not from the offeror himself or herself, but from a third party.

Example
Anna knows that Carrie wishes to buy her old car and tells Barry that she is going to sell it to Carrie for $5000. Barry advises Carrie of Anna's plans.

The general position is that for an offer to be valid, it must be communicated to the offeree.[77] The communication must be by the offeror or someone authorised by the offeror.[78] In the example above, unless Barry was authorised by Anna to convey her offer to Carrie, a valid offer was not made to Carrie.

There are sound reasons for requiring an offer to be communicated by the offeror or the offeror's agent. It may be that the offeror intends to make an offer to the offeree. However, until the time that offer is communicated, it is open for the offeror to change his or her mind. Allowing an unauthorised person to communicate the offer would alter this position. If the communication by Barry in the above example was effective, Carrie could accept the offer and bind Anna to perform the contract. If Anna changed her mind after speaking to Barry, and sold the car to another person, Anna would then be in breach of contract with Anna. This would not be a desirable outcome.

[3.265] The requirement that the offeror must communicate the offer to the offeree is likely to operate differently where an offer is made to the public at large, as in *Carlill's*

---

74   [1971] 2 QB 163.
75   Ibid at 169.
76   See [3.365]–[3.370].
77   *Cole v Cottingham* (1937) 173 ER 406; *Banks v Williams* (1912) 12 SR (NSW) 382 at 390–391.
78   Ibid.

case.[79] It could happen in such a case that a person does not read the advertisement or hear the announcement for himself or herself, but is advised of the terms of the offer by someone else. It may be clear from the advertisement containing the offer that the offeror intends to be bound immediately, and the offer could be accepted by anyone fulfilling the requirements of the offer. In such a case, the way a person is advised of the terms of the offer is largely irrelevant. Communication may be by reading the advertisement or by the details being passed onto the offeree by another party.

[3.270] When considering the requirement of communicating the offer, the method of communication is largely irrelevant. The same principles apply whether the offer is sent by post, facsimile, or e-mail, or is displayed on the Internet. In the usual course, until the offer is communicated by the offeror to the offeree, it will not constitute an offer capable of acceptance.

3.6   Termination of an offer

[3.275] As long as an offer remains valid, it is capable of being accepted so as to form an agreement. Once it is terminated, it is no longer capable of acceptance by an offeree. An offer will cease to be effective in various circumstances.

3.6.1   Withdrawal by offeror

[3.280] As a general rule, an offer can be withdrawn by an offeror at any time before acceptance.[80] This is so even if the offeror has promised to keep the offer open for a period.[81] To be a valid withdrawal of offer, there needs to be actual communication of the withdrawal to the offeree.[82] There is no equivalent to the postal acceptance rule that operates in this context.[83]

[3.285] Although actual communication of the withdrawal is required, the communication may be effective even if made by someone other than the offeror or someone authorised by the offeror.

Example: Dickinson v Dodds[84]

The owner offered to sell his property and advised the offeree that he would keep the offer open until 5 January. Before this date, the owner sold to a third party. The original offeree was advised of the sale by another party who was not authorised by the offeror. The offeree subsequently purported to accept the original offer.

---

79   [1893] 1 QB 256.
80   *Goldsbrough Mort & Co Ltd v Quinn* (1910) 10 CLR 674 at 678; *Veivers v Cordingley* [1989] 2 QdR 278 at 297.
81   If the offeree has provided consideration to the offeror to keep the offer open, however, the position is different. An option is created and the offeror is required to keep the offer open for the requisite period. See [3.205]–[3.210] above.
82   *Byrne & Co v Leon Van Tien Hoven & Co* (1880) 5 CPD 344 at 347; *Sommerville v Rice* (1912) 31 NZLR 370.
83   If the postal acceptance rule operates, an acceptance of an offer occurs when the letter of acceptance is posted. See [3.495].
84   [1876] 2 ChD 463. See also *King v Homer* (1913) NZLR 222.

The Chancery Division held that the offer to sell to the offeree had been validly withdrawn. There is no requirement for there to be an express or actual withdrawal of the offer.

[3.6.1.3] The focus of the courts in determining the validity of an agreement is whether the 'two minds were at one, at the same moment of time'.[85] On the facts of *Dickinson v Dodds*,[86] this was not the case. That the offeree was advised that the offer was withdrawn by a third party did not alter this fact. The only requirement is that the offeree be informed about the withdrawal from a reliable source. What constitutes a reliable source is a question of fact that must be established in each case.

[3.290] Special rules about withdrawal of offers operate where the contract is a unilateral contract; where the offer has been made to the world at large; or the parties have entered into an option agreement.[87]

(a) Withdrawal in unilateral contracts

[3.295] The nature of unilateral contracts was examined earlier, at [3.45]. Special problems arise because of the nature of such contracts where the offeror wishes to withdraw the offer. Because of the way acceptance occurs in a unilateral offer, injustice could occur if an offeror were permitted to withdraw the offer before acceptance of the offer was completed. In *Carlill's case*,[88] for example, a person might have acted in response to the advertisement by buying and using the smoke balls as directed. That person would be disadvantaged if the Smoke Ball Company could withdraw the offer at that stage, just before the person contracted the flu and thereby became eligible to claim the £100.

To avoid such injustice, there is long-standing authority to suggest that an offeror cannot effectively withdraw an offer after that offeree has commenced acceptance of it.[89] In *Veivers v Cordingly*,[90] McPherson J framed the position where the offer is made in exchange for the doing of an act or acts in the following way:

(1) acceptance takes place when the offeree 'elects' to do the relevant act or acts; and

(2) the offer becomes irrevocable once the act or acts, which will constitute consideration for the offer, have been partly performed.[91]

His Honour left open whether a simple election is sufficient to accept the offer or communication of the acceptance is required. Perhaps this is a matter that turns on an interpretation of the particular offer in question.

---

85   Ibid at 472.
86   [1876] 2 ChD 463.
87   The withdrawal of an offer in the context of options was considered earlier at [3.205]–[3.210].
88   [1893] 1 QB 256.
89   *Abbott v Lance* (1860) 2 Legge 1283.
90   [1989] 2 QdR 278.
91   Ibid at 298.

[3.300] The most recent development on this issue is the judgment of the Full Court of the Federal Court in *Mobil Oil Australia Ltd v Lyndel Nominees Pty Ltd*.[92] After reviewing the relevant authorities, the Federal Court did not agree that there was a general proposition that an offeror could not revoke an offer after acceptance had commenced.[93] Further, even if in a particular fact situation there is an implied promise not to revoke the offer after acceptance has commenced, any purported revocation by the offeror would be effective. The relief open to an offeree in such circumstances would be an action in damages for breach of the implied promise.

It may be that the approach taken by the Full Court of the Federal Court will not lead to a different result. As suggested by the Federal Court, in these cases the offeror may be regarded as having entered into an implied ancillary contract not to revoke, or the offeror may be estopped from falsifying an assumption that the offeree will not be deprived of the chance of completing the act of acceptance.[94] Once again, the precise analysis of a particular case will turn on the specific facts.

(b) Withdrawal where offer is to world at large

[3.305] Different issues arise where the offeror wishes to withdraw an offer made to the world at large. It would be impossible for the offeror to ensure that all offerees receive actual communication of withdrawal of the offer. For this reason, it is likely that something less than actual communication will be sufficient to effectively withdraw the offer. As a matter of prudence, the offeror should, to the extent possible, use the same medium to advise of withdrawal as was used to advise of the offer. If the offeror takes these steps, he or she may be able to maintain that the offer is validly withdrawn even if one or more offerees were not made aware of the withdrawal.[95]

3.6.2 Rejection by offeree

[3.310] If the offeree rejects the offer, the offer is terminated.[96] It will not then be open for the offeree to change his or her mind and accept the offer. To be an effective rejection, it must be communicated to the offeror. The formulation by the offeree of a decision to reject the offer will not without more operate to revoke the offer.[97]

[3.315] As discussed below,[98] if the offeree responds to the offer by changing its terms, this amounts to a counter-offer by the offeree and operates as a rejection of the initial

---

92   (1998) 81 FCR 475.
93   Ibid at 506.
94   Ibid.
95   While there is no authority on this point in Australia, there is American authority (*Shuey v United States* 92 US 73 (1875)) which supports this view). See [3.720].
96   *Stevenson Jaques & Co v McLean* (1880) 5 QBD 346; *Baker v Taylor* (1906) 6 SR (NSW) 500.
97   An interesting point on which there appears to be no reported authority is the effect of a rejection of an offer posted by the offeree, followed by the posting of a letter of acceptance. The offeror should, in the ordinary course of post, receive the revocation prior to the acceptance. However, if the postal acceptance rule were applicable (see [3.495] below), the contract would be formed when the letter of acceptance was posted. Were this matter to be litigated, it is submitted that a court would be reluctant to hold that a contract existed notwithstanding the operation of the postal acceptance rule. It would be an absurd outcome for the offeror to be potentially in breach of a contract with the offeree if he or she acted on the revocation received first and entered into a contract with a third party.
98   See [3.375]–[3.405].

offer.[99] However, a counter-offer must be distinguished from a request for information or a request to clarify certain terms by the offeree. While the distinction between the two concepts is sometimes subtle, such requests will not operate as a rejection of the original offer.[100]

3.6.3   Lapse of time

[3.320] It is open to an offeror to specify a date or a time upon which the offer will lapse. Once this date or time has passed, the offer lapses and the offeree is unable to accept it to form an agreement. Where the offeror does not specify such a time or date, the offer will lapse within a 'reasonable' time after the offer has been made.[101] What is reasonable will vary from case to case, and will depend on the particular circumstances.

[3.325] In *Manchester Diocesan Council for Education v Commercial & General Investments Ltd*,[102] Buckley J considered two possible bases for the rule that an offer would lapse within a reasonable time:

(1) It is implied into the offer that if it is not accepted within a reasonable time, it is withdrawn; or

(2) If the offeree does not accept the offer within a reasonable time, the offeree must be regarded as having refused it.[103]

While the legal basis for this rule would generally not alter an assessment of what constitutes a 'reasonable' time, Buckley J considered that in some instances, this could influence the outcome. Under the first approach, what is reasonable must be determined at the date of the offer, based on the circumstances existing at that time and circumstances reasonably likely to arise during the continuance of the offer. If the second approach is adopted, it would be appropriate to consider the actual conduct of the offeree after the offer is made. Buckley J favoured the second approach, allowing him to take into consideration the conduct of the offeree subsequent to the making of the offer.

3.6.4   Failure of a condition in a conditional offer

[3.330] Offers can be made which are expressly or impliedly subject to conditions.[104] If the condition is not complied with by the offeree, the offer will cease. The following example illustrates a conditional offer.

---

99   *Hyde v Wrench* (1840) 49 ER 132.

100   *Stevenson Jaques & Co v McLean* (1880) 5 QBD 346.

101   *Ramsgate Victoria Hotel Co Ltd v Montefiore* (1866) LR 1 Ex 109 at 111; *Ballas v Theophilos* (1958) 98 CLR 193; *Kean v Dunfoy* [1952] NZLR 611.

102   [1970] 1 WLR 241.

103   Ibid at 247.

104   This is particularly common where parties are in a lease and certain conditions must be complied with for the lessee to exercise an option to renew the lease, as in *Gilbert J McCaul (Aust) Pty Ltd v Pitt Club Ltd* [1959] SR (NSW) 122.

Example

A offers to buy a quantity of B's stock which A has previously inspected. A's offer to buy at a specified price is expressed to be subject to the goods being in the same condition as when earlier inspected by A.

If the stock has deteriorated, the condition has not been satisfied and the offer cannot be accepted.[105]

3.6.5 Death of the offeror or offeree

[3.335] The effect of death of one of the parties before acceptance of the offer is not entirely settled. The outcome may depend on whether it is the offeror or offeree who has died, the intention of the parties, the subject matter of the contract, or whether the offeree was granted an option.

(a) Death of the offeror

[3.340] It is difficult to state in any definitive way the effect of an offeror's death. Perhaps a helpful starting point is the following dicta of Mellish L J in *Dickinson v Dodds*:[106]

> It is admitted law that, if a man who makes an offer dies, the offer cannot be accepted after he is dead ... for it makes the performance of the offer impossible.[107]

Notwithstanding the categorical terms in which the law was stated, in the context of that case, it is likely that the Lord Justice is referring to the situation where the offeree purports to accept when he or she has knowledge of the offeror's death. Where the offeree has no such knowledge, whether the offeror's death terminates the offer may depend upon the intention of the offeror as derived from a construction of the offer itself. For example, if the contract relates to personal services such as a commission for the offeror to perform some painting or writing, it would be the intention of the offeror that such an offer would lapse on the offeror's death. The offeror may not be regarded as having the same intention if the contract were for the sale of property and the transaction could be completed by the deceased's estate.

(b) Death of offeree

[3.345] The effect of an offeree's death on an offer was examined by Lord Sterndale MR in *Reynolds v Atherton*.[108] After reviewing the commentary in various texts, the Master of the Rolls concluded:

---

105 For a case involving comparable facts, see *Financings Ltd v Stimson* [1962] 3 All ER 386. The English Court of Appeal held that a contract did not come into existence because an implied condition of the offer was not fulfilled.
106 [1876] 2 ChD 463.
107 Ibid at 475. This dicta was applied in *Fong v Cilli* (1968) 11 FLR 495.
108 (1921) 125 LT 690.

the offer having been made to a living person who ceases to be a living person before the offer is accepted, there is no longer an offer at all. The offer is not intended to be made to a dead person or to his executors, and the offer ceases to be an offer capable of acceptance.[109]

While the first sentence seems absolute in its terms, there is an indication from the remainder of the quote that, once again, the test may be that of intention. If the contract is one for the offeree's personal services, it would have been intended that the offer would cease on the offeree's death. A contract for the sale of property may not, however, be considered in the same light.

(c) Options

[3.350] An option raises different considerations. As discussed earlier, under an option agreement, the offeror has agreed to keep the offer open for a specified period. This may mean that the parties *intended* the offer to be one that could be accepted notwithstanding the death of the offeror or offeree. Viewed in this way, an option creates rights that are not personal to the offeror and offeree, and could be exercised by their respective estates. But this general proposition cannot be advanced without a warning. If the contract is one that involves personal services, and that person dies, the parties could not have intended the option to be exercisable following the death.

There has also been some suggestion that the effect of death on an option may depend on the legal nature of options.[110] The different views on this point were raised earlier.[111] If an option is regarded as a conditional contract, the option may confer on the offeree a right to specific performance of the contract. Such a right could be enforced by or against the estate of a deceased person. On the other hand, if an option is regarded as creating an irrevocable offer only, the offer may not be considered to be capable of acceptance following death.[112]

3.7 Requirements for acceptance

[3.355] Under traditional contractual theory, an agreement is formed once an offer is accepted. The fact of acceptance is significant because after this time, neither the offer nor the acceptance can be withdrawn without exposing the withdrawing party to potential contractual liability. There are generally two requirements to be satisfied for a valid acceptance to occur:

1   The offeree must intend to accept the terms of the offer; and
2   That intention must be communicated to the offeror.

In [3.05] and [3.30] above, an agreement for the sale of a computer was referred to. If A made the offer in writing and B responded to A in writing, accepting the terms of the offer, both of these requirements for valid acceptance would be satisfied.

---

109   Ibid at 695.
110   *Laybutt v Amoco Australia Pty Ltd* (1974) 132 CLR 57 at 72.
111   See [3.205] above.
112   Compare, however, the views of Isaacs J in *Carter v Hyde* (1923) 33 CLR 115 at 123–125 where he regarded an option as an irrevocable offer, yet considered the right of the offeree to exercise the option to pass to the executors on the offeree's death.

The offeree (B) agreed to the terms set out in the offer. No new terms were added nor counter-offer made. Further, the offeree (B) communicated the fact of acceptance to the offeror by writing to A.

The two requirements (and the extent to which they are displaced or modified in particular circumstances) are considered in more detail next.

3.8 Acceptance must correspond to offer

[3.360] The first requirement for a valid acceptance is that the offeree must assent to the terms of the offer. The acceptance must be unqualified, and there must not be an attempt to introduce new terms. It is implicit in the notion of acceptance that the offeree must have knowledge of and be responding to that offer.

3.8.1 Offeree must have knowledge of, and act in reliance on, offer

[3.365] Central to traditional contract theory is the notion of *consensus ad idem*. For the parties to be regarded as having entered an agreement, the offeror must have been making the offer and the offeree must have been agreeing to the terms of the offer at the one moment in time. For this to occur, the offeree must have knowledge of the terms of the offer at the time of purported acceptance. An acceptance therefore cannot be considered to have occurred in the following circumstances.

Example

Anna is aware that Bernadette wants to sell her car. Anna leaves Bernadette a note in her letterbox offering to buy the car for $3000. By coincidence, at the same time Bernadette rings Anna and leaves a message on Anna's answering machine that she would be happy to sell her car to Anna for $3000.

While both Anna and Bernadette agree on terms for the sale of Bernadette's car, no agreement has been formed. There have been two offers made, but neither has been accepted. The actions could not be construed as an offer and acceptance because neither party had knowledge of the offer of the other.[113]

[3.370] Further, where an act is to represent acceptance of an offer, the act must be performed for the purpose of accepting the offer. While this is unlikely to occur frequently, a person may perform the act of acceptance without knowledge of the offer. In other words, in performing the act, he or she is motivated by something other than the offer. But this can occur, as is illustrated by the case of the *Crown v Clarke*.[114] In that case, the issue before the High Court was whether Mr Clarke could collect reward money of £1000.00 for providing information that led to the arrest and conviction of the murderer of two police officers. Mr Clarke provided such information, but he gave the information not to receive the reward, but to ensure he was not charged with the murders. For this reason, the High Court held Mr Clarke unable to

---

113 *Tinn v Hoffman & Co* (1873) 29 LT 271.
114 (1927) 40 CLR 227.

collect the reward despite the fact that he knew of the offer when he provided the information.

3.8.2 A counter-offer is not acceptance

[3.375] To constitute a valid acceptance, the offeree must agree to all of the terms of the offer. If the offeree indicates acceptance of the offer, but on the basis of different terms suggested by the offeree, this will not constitute acceptance. The offeree has made a counter-offer, which can then be accepted or rejected by the original offeror. The following case illustrates that a suggested alteration to the offeror's terms cannot be acceptance of the original offer, and amounts to a counter-offer.

Example: Hyde v Wrench[115]

A seller offered to sell his farm for £1000. The buyer replied that he would buy it for £950. The seller refused. The buyer later purported to accept the seller's original offer to buy the farm for £1000.

In an action for specific performance by the buyer, the Master of the Rolls held that no contract existed between the parties. By making the counter-offer for £950, the buyer rejected the seller's original offer. The original offer cannot later be revived by the buyer's purported acceptance of it.

[3.380] The fact that a counter-offer had been made in *Hyde v Wrench*[116] was obvious, and not disputed by the parties. The position is not so clear in the context of some modern contractual negotiations. This is particularly evident where parties contract on the basis of standard forms that have been drafted to suit the requirements and to protect the business interests of the party proposing a particular form. Even in simple contracts for the sale and purchase of commodities, parties may transact business on the basis of their respective standard forms. While the parties may agree on the basics of sale (such as the subject matter, amount and price), the other terms in the respective forms may, and are likely to, differ. The difficulty this creates is sometimes referred to as the 'battle of the forms'. *Butler Machine Tool Co Ltd v Ex-cell-o Corporation (England) Ltd*[117] illustrates the problem that can arise.

Example: Butler Machine Tool Co Ltd v Ex-cell-o Corporation (England) Ltd

The seller of machinery quoted a price on a standard form. The form contained a clause entitling the seller to vary that price. The buyer placed an order for the same machinery on its own order form. The order form contained different standard conditions. The seller acknowledged the order by returning the acknowledgment form (which formed part of the buyer's order form) to the buyer.

The English Court of Appeal held that the seller was not entitled to rely on the price variation clause as it did not form part of the contract. The buyer's order

---

115 (1840) 49 ER 132. See also *Reparoa Stores Ltd v Treloar* [1958] NZLR 177 and *Cross v Davidson* (1898) 17 NZLR 861.
116 Ibid.
117 [1979] 1 WLR 401.

constituted a counter-offer because it contained terms different to the seller's original offer. That counter-offer was accepted when the seller returned the acknowledgment.

[3.385] In *Hyde v Wrench*,[118] no contract was formed because there had been a rejection by the offeree of a fundamental term of the contract—the price. However, the current Australian position is that even if there is agreement on the fundamental terms of the transaction, if the offeree adds an additional term, a counter-offer is made.[119] A contract will not be formed until that counter-offer is accepted. Therefore, in *Turner Kempson & Co Pty Ltd v Camm*,[120] where the offeree purported to accept an offer to sell a quantity of raspberry pulp at a stated price, a contract was held not to exist because the offeree purported to add a term requiring delivery in three separate lots, with approximately 10 days between each delivery.

[3.390] As demonstrated by the preceding commentary, the Australian and English authorities operate in a rather inflexible way in determining whether the parties can be regarded as having reached agreement. The purported introduction of a new term by the offeree will constitute a rejection of the original offer. However, in limited circumstances something less than apparently unqualified acceptance of the terms of the offer may be regarded as acceptance. These circumstances will now be considered.

(a) Acceptance couched in different language

[3.395] Where an offer is accepted by tearing off an acknowledgment on an offeror's standard form and returning it, or by indicating a simple assent to the terms proposed by the offeror, there is clearly an acceptance in the same terms as the offer. Sometimes, however, parties enter into a course of correspondence during contractual negotiations. The purported acceptance by an offeree may use language different from that used by the offeror. By using different language, it may be arguable that the offeree did not accept on the same terms offered by the offeror. In such a case, a determination of whether an agreement has been formed will be based on a construction of the terms of the offer and acceptance. If the court is satisfied that the parties have reached agreement on the terms, it is likely to find that a contract has come into existence despite differences in the language of offer and acceptance.[121]

(b) Request by offeree for modification of performance

[3.400] An offeree may choose to accept the terms of an offer even if not entirely satisfied with those terms. Expressions of dissatisfaction by the offeree will not prevent contract formation if the offeree also indicates acceptance of those terms.[122] Further, agreement is not prevented if the offeree, at the time of acceptance, seeks a concession

---

118 (1840) 49 ER 132.

119 The position is more flexible in the United States: see [3.725]–[3.730] below, and possibly in New Zealand where there is a recent trend towards adopting a global approach to contract formation: see JF Burrows, J Finn & SMD Todd, *The Law of Contract in New Zealand*, 8th edn, Butterworths, Wellington, 1997, pp 56–57.

120 [1922] VLR 498.

121 *Carter v Hyde* (1923) 33 CLR 115; *Cavallari v Premier Refrigeration* (1952) 85 CLR 20; *Quadling v Robinson* (1976) 137 CLR 192 at 197.

122 *Joyce v Swann* (1864) 144 ER 34 at 41 and 42.

from the offeror in terms of contractual performance.[123] Once again, provided acceptance of the terms is unqualified, a request by the offeree that the offeror allow a different method of performance will not prevent contract formation.

(c) Divergence from terms of offer for benefit of offeror

[3.405] It is possible for acceptance to occur by conduct without the need for acceptance
of the terms to be communicated to the offeror.[124] If the conduct does not correspond to
the terms of the offer, there will generally be no agreement. However, on the rare occasion that the offeree's conduct represents terms more favourable to the offeror than those
in the offeror's offer, a court is likely to find that agreement exists.[125]

3.8.3   Acceptance must be unqualified

[3.410] To be a valid acceptance, it is not enough for the offeree to agree on all of the
terms proposed by the offeror. Acceptance must also be unqualified. As examined
later,[126] a party may accept all of the terms proposed by the offeror, yet make the
agreement 'subject to contract'. Whether or not there has been acceptance in such a
case, and an agreement formed, will depend on the intention of the parties. If their
intention is not to make a concluded bargain until execution of a formal contract, the
offeree cannot be regarded as having given an unqualified acceptance of the offer. In
such a case, there will be no binding contract. If, on the other hand, there is agreement on all terms and the parties intend to be bound immediately, but they still want a
formal agreement to be drawn up, there will be a binding contract. There is an
unqualified acceptance by the offeree of the terms of the offer.

3.8.4   Mere inquiry does not constitute acceptance

[3.415] After receiving an offer, an offeree may want further clarification of one or
more terms. For example, if a person offers stock for sale at a particular price, the
offeree may be interested to know whether the seller would be prepared to accept
credit. If an offeree's response is regarded as a mere inquiry into the terms of the offer,
it does not operate as a rejection of the offer.[127] Unlike a counter-offer, where the
offeree alters or adds to the terms of the original offer, the offeree is simply seeking
clarification of the terms contained in the original offer. On the other hand, the
inquiry will not be regarded as an acceptance of the offer. In the example above, the
offeree is not indicating a willingness to accept the terms in the offer. While the
inquiry may constitute intimation that the offeree may be interested in accepting the
offer if satisfied with the outcome of the inquiry, the inquiry itself falls short of acceptance. At that stage, although the offer is not rejected, it also cannot be regarded as
having been accepted.

---

123   *Clive v Beaumont* (1848) 63 ER 1121.
124   See [3.440]–[3.465].
125   *Ex parte Fealey* (1897) 18 LR (NSW) 282.
126   See [4.310]–[4.340].
127   *Stevenson Jaques & Co v McLean* (1880) 5 QBD 346. See also comments of Cooke J in *Powierza v Daley*
      [1985] 1 NZLR 588 at 561 that 'the line between rejecting an offer and merely inquiring as to a possi-
      ble variation is a fine one, but the basic test is the effect on a reasonable person in the shoes of the
      offeror'.

3.9 Notification to offeror of fact of acceptance

[3.9.1] For agreement to occur, it is not enough for an offeree to decide to accept the offer. There must be some outward manifestation of that decision. For this reason, the general rule is that an offeree must communicate acceptance of the offer to the offeror, and agreement is not complete until such communication is effected.[128] In some cases, however, communication of acceptance is not a prerequisite to contract formation. Principles relevant to contract formation in a variety of circumstances are considered next.

3.9.1 Method of acceptance

[3.425] Contracts may be formed in a variety of ways. In some cases, the offeror prescribes the way an offeree should advise the offeror of acceptance. In other cases, the parties do not discuss this issue at all. What is an appropriate method of acceptance leading to contract formation in any given situation will depend on the particular facts. A determination of this issue is important. Whether acceptance has occurred depends on whether the offeree has complied with the requirements of the method of acceptance for the particular transaction.

If the offeror has not specified the way in which the offeree should advise the offeror of acceptance, the appropriate method of acceptance will depend on the intention of the parties as derived from the particular facts. In most cases, it will probably be open for the offeree to accept in a variety of ways. For example, if an offer is made in a face-to-face meeting between the parties, in the absence of a stipulation to the contrary, a valid acceptance could occur through another meeting, or by telephone, facsimile, post, or electronic communication. Provided the acceptance is communicated to the offeror, acceptance will be effective to conclude the agreement.[129] The precise moment of contract formation will depend on the particular method of acceptance used, and any stipulations made by the offeror. The principles that govern contract formation in these different circumstances are considered later in this commentary.[130]

(a) Method of acceptance stipulated by offeror

[3.430] An offeror may stipulate how acceptance should take place—for example, by indicating that an offeree could accept by performing according to the terms of the offer. The need for communication of acceptance would be impliedly waived in such a case.[131] The offeror may indicate that the offeree's acceptance should be made by 'return post'—thus indicating a quick response is required by the offeree. Failure to respond in the manner specified may be a bar to contract formation. Whether this is because the offer is regarded as having lapsed, or because the acceptance does not

---

128 *Powell v Lee* (1908) 99 LT 284; *Soares v Simpson* [1931] NZLR 1079.
129 Note, however, that acceptance must be communicated by the offeree or a duly authorised agent of the offeree: *Powell v Lee* (1908) 99 LT 284.
130 See [3.470]–[3.610].
131 See further 'Acceptance by conduct' below. As to the limitations on the ability of the offeror to stipulate methods of acceptance, see 'Acceptance by silence' below.

comply with the terms of the offer, is probably only of academic significance. No agreement would have been formed.

[3.435] Although an offeree puts himself or herself at risk by accepting in a manner other than that stipulated by the offeror, in some cases that will not be fatal to contract formation. First, if the offeree accepts in a manner that is more advantageous to the offeror, acceptance will be valid. Therefore, if an offeror sends an offer by mail and requires a response by 'return post', acceptance by telephone or facsimile is likely to constitute a valid acceptance.[132] Second, if the method of acceptance was inserted for the convenience of the offeree, the offeree may waive the benefit of the clause and accept in a different way.[133] Thirdly, even if a manner of acceptance is prescribed in the offer, on a true construction of the terms of the offer, this may not be the *only* method of acceptance that will be effective.[134]

(b) Acceptance by silence

[3.440] Generally, an offeror may dictate the manner of acceptance. Unless acceptance occurs in this way, there is no agreement. There is one important restriction, however, on the extent to which the offeror can dictate the method of contract formation. It is not open to an offeror to make an offer and advise the offeree that an agreement will have been formed unless the offeree communicates rejection of the offer.[135] To put it another way, the offeror cannot stipulate that silence constitutes consent.

[3.445] Consent to an offer by silence has more commonly arisen in the context of aggressive marketing techniques used by hopeful sellers delivering unrequested products to the homes of potential buyers. Using this technique, sellers deliver goods together with a notice that unless the goods are returned within a specified period (or rejection of the offer is communicated in another way), the buyer will be taken to have agreed to buy the product on the stated terms. Such practices are now prohibited by statute, and contract formation cannot occur in this way.[136]

(c) Acceptance by conduct

[3.450] An offeror may stipulate the manner of acceptance by advising the offeree that if he or she wishes to accept the offer, the offeree should perform stipulated acts. In such a case, the offeror waives the need for the offeree to communicate acceptance. The sufficiency of acceptance by conduct rather than communication to the offeror

---

132 *Tinn v Hoffman & Co* (1873) 29 LT 271 at 274.

133 *Manchester Diocesan Council for Education v Commercial & General Investments Ltd* [1970] 1 WLR 241.

134 Ibid.

135 *Felthouse v Bindley* (1862) 142 ER 1037; *Empirnall Holdings Pty Ltd v Machon Paull Partners Pty Ltd* (1988) 14 NSWLR 523 at 527; *Braund v Mutual Life and Citizens' Assurance Co Ltd* [1926] NZLR 529. In limited circumstances, however, the offeree may be regarded as having a duty to communicate rejection of the offer if he or she does not wish to accept it—a duty arising out of the general course of dealings between the parties: *Empirnall Holdings Pty Ltd v Machon Paull Partners Pty Ltd* (1988) 14 NSWLR 523 at 534.

136 *Trade Practices Act* 1974 (Cth), ss 64 and 65. See also the Fair Trading equivalents: *Fair Trading Act* 1989 (Qld), ss 52 and 53; *Fair Trading Act* 1987 (NSW), ss 58 and 59; *Fair Trading Act* 1999 (Vic), ss 24, 25 and 26; *Fair Trading Act* 1987 (SA), ss 72 and 73; *Consumer Affairs and Fair Trading Act* 1990 (NT), ss 58 and 59; *Fair Trading Act* 1992 (ACT), ss 29 and 30.

may be express or implied. The following illustrates a case of an express stipulation that conduct is sufficient acceptance.

Example

A buyer wishes to buy a specified quantity of certain goods from a supplier at a stated price. The buyer places the order and advises the seller to forward the goods to the buyer if the supplier agrees to the terms.

[3.455] In some unilateral contracts, communication of acceptance is impliedly waived. *Carlill's case*[137] is an example. Performance of the conditions was held to constitute acceptance. It was implicit from the facts of the case that the Smoke Ball Company did not require those intending to accept the offer to communicate the acceptance.

[3.460] In some cases, courts may infer acceptance of an offer from the conduct of the parties, even if it was originally contemplated that acceptance would occur in a more formal way, such as by signing a written agreement. Lord Hatherley recognised this to be the case in *Brogden v The Directors of the Metropolitan Railway Company*,[138] where he stated:

> although there has been no formal recognition of the agreement in terms by the one side, yet the course of dealing and conduct of the party to whom the agreement was propounded has been such as legitimately to lead to the inference that those with whom they were dealing were made aware by that course of dealing, that the contract which they had propounded had been in fact accepted by the persons who so dealt with them.

[3.465] The following Australian case illustrates how conduct can constitute acceptance in such circumstances.

Example: Empirnall Holdings Pty Ltd v Mark Machon Paull Partners[139]

A property developer engaged an architect to undertake a property development. The architect forwarded a printed contract to the property developer. The property developer preferred not to sign contracts, and the architect was told this. Nevertheless, building work proceeded and a number of progress claims were paid by the property developer to the architect. In a claim for payment of outstanding fees, the property developer denied the existence of a contract.

It was held by the New South Wales Court of Appeal that a contract existed between the parties. Although the offeror (the architect) indicated that acceptance should be effected by signing and returning the formal document, the conduct of the offeree (property developer) indicated acceptance of the terms of the offer.

---

137 [1893] 1 QB 256. For facts of the case, see [3.60].
138 (1877) 2 App Cas 666 at 682.
139 (1988) 14 NSW LR 523.

3.9.2 Instantaneous communication: acceptance must be communicated

(a) General rule

[3.470] Where the mode of acceptance is by 'instantaneous communication', the general rule of law is that the contract will be formed when acceptance of the offer is communicated to the offeror. The contract is formed when and where the offeror receives that communication.[140] The rule regarding contract formation in the context of instantaneous communication has been described by Lord Wilberforce as a 'general' rather than a 'universal' rule. As the following extract demonstrates, the real test of contract formation must be determined by, among other things, the intention of the parties.

> Since 1955 the use of telex communication has been greatly expanded, and there are many variants on it. The senders and recipients may not be the principals to the contemplated contract. They may be servants or agents with limited authority. The message may not reach, or be intended to reach, the designated recipient immediately: messages may be sent out of office hours, or at night, with the intention, or upon the assumption, that they will be read at a later time. There may be some error or default at the recipient's end which prevents receipt at the time contemplated and believed in by the sender. The message may have been sent and/or received through machines operated by third persons. And many other variations may occur. No universal rule can cover all such cases: they must be resolved by reference to the intentions of the parties, by sound business practice and in some cases by a judgment where the risks should lie …[141]

(b) Meaning of 'instantaneous communication'

[3.475] Some methods of communication clearly fall within the 'instantaneous' category. Negotiations can take place between parties in each other's presence, and acceptance of an offer by a statement made directly to the offeror is clearly instantaneous communication. Negotiation by telephone is regarded in the same way.[142] Although telex messages involve greater delays than the telephone, it appears that these methods will generally also be regarded as instantaneous communication for the purpose of contract formation.[143] As stated by Parker LJ in *Entores L D v Miles Far East Corporation:*[144]

---

140 *Entores L D v Miles Far East Corporation* [1955] to QB 327 at 335; *Hamstead Meats Pty Ltd v Emerson & Yates Pty Ltd* [1967] SASR 109, *Mendelson-Zeller Co Inc. v T & C Providores Pty Ltd* [1981] 1 NSWLR 366 at 369; *Brinkibon Ltd v Stahag Stahl und Stahlwarenhandels-Gesellschaft mbH* [1983] 2 AC 34; *Reese Bros Plastics v Hammon-Sobelco Australia Pty Ltd* (1988) 5 *Butterworths Property Reports* [97325] at 11 108 per Gleeson CJ.

141 *Brinkibon Ltd v Stahag Stahl und Stahlwarenhandels-Gesellschaft mbH* [1983] 2 AC 34 at 42.

142 *Entores LD v Miles Far Easts Corporation* [1955] 2 QB 327 at 332; *Hamstead Meats Pty Ltd v Emerson & Yates Pty Ltd* [1967] SASR 109; *Union Steamship Co v Ewart* (1895) 13 NZLR 9.

143 *Entores L D v Miles Far East Corporation* [1955] 2 QB 327; *Brinkibon Ltd v Stahag Stahl und Stahlwarenhandels-Gesellschaft mbH* [1983] 2 AC 34; *Reese Bros Plastics Ltd v Hammon-Sobelco Australia Pty Ltd* (1988) 5 *Butterworths Property Reports* [97325]; *Egis Consulting Australia Pty Ltd v First Dynasty Mines Ltd* [2001] WASC 22 (2 February 2001). Contrast the position where a public telex is used: *Leach Nominees Pty Ltd v Walter Wright Pty Ltd* [1986] WAR 244.

144 [1955] 2 QB 327 at 337.

So far as Telex messages are concerned, although the dispatch and receipt of a message is not completely instantaneous, the parties are to all intents and purposes in each other's presence just as if they were in telephonic communication, and I can see no reason for departing from the general rule that there is no binding contract until notice of the acceptance is received by the offeror.

Transmissions by facsimile are regarded in the same way.[145]

[3.480] As would be expected, acceptance by post is treated differently. In the usual course of events, there is at least one day's delay (generally greater) between posting of the letter and its receipt by the offeror. This kind of communication cannot therefore be regarded as instantaneous, and different rules will apply.[146]

[3.485] Whether courts regard electronic communication as instantaneous has not yet been tested. The implications of this kind of communication are considered separately below.[147]

3.9.3 Postal acceptance rule

[3.490] The general rule is that a contract will be formed only where the offeree's acceptance is communicated to the offeror. An exception to this general rule may arise where the post is used in contract formation, as in the following scenario.

Example

A seller writes to a prospective buyer offering to sell a specified quantity of wool. On receipt of the letter, the buyer responds by accepting the offer. Before the letter of acceptance is received by the seller (but after it is posted), the seller sells the wool to a third party.

(a) Statement of the rule

[3.495] The classic pronouncement of the postal acceptance rule that has been adopted in both England and Australia for more than a century is that of Lord Herschell in *Henthorn v Fraser*:[148]

Where the circumstances are such that it must have been within the contemplation of the parties that, according to the ordinary usages of mankind, the post might be used as a means of communicating the acceptance of an offer, the acceptance is complete as soon as it is posted.

Applying this rule to the example above, a contract will be formed when the buyer posts the letter, not when the offeror actually receives it.[149]

[3.500] The postal acceptance rule operates only where the post 'must have been within the contemplation of the parties' as a possible way of communicating accept-

---

145 *Reese Bros Plastics Ltd v Hammon-Sobelco Australia Pty Ltd* (1988) 5 *Butterworths Property Reports* [97325]; *Entores L D v Miles Far East Corporation* [1955] 2 QB 327.

146 See [3.490]–[3.545].

147 See [3.550]–[3.600].

148 [1892] 2 Ch 27 at 33.

149 The facts of this example represent the facts of *Adams v Lindsell* (1818) 106 ER 250, the court finding that the contract was formed when the letter of acceptance was posted.

ance of the offer. This is likely to be the case where the offer was made by post.[150] It may also be the case if the offer is made in person, but the parties live a considerable distance apart.[151] Acceptance by post may also be contemplated where an offer capable of acceptance by more than one person is made to the world at large through a medium such as a newspaper. In making a determination about whether acceptance by post is contemplated, each case will be judged on its facts, with a court looking at all of the circumstances.[152]

[3.505] If the postal acceptance rule operates, acceptance is effective, and a contract is formed once the letter is posted. It does not affect the validity of the contract if the letter takes longer than usual to reach the offeror, or is completely lost in the post. The offeror bears this risk.[153]

(b) Policy behind the rule

[3.510] The first application of the postal acceptance rule was in 1818 in *Adams v Lindsell*,[154] where the court delivered a very brief judgment. The court's justification for the ruling was that any other view would mean that a contract could never be formed by post. The court's approach was that if the offeror should not be bound until actual receipt of acceptance, then the offeree should not be bound until actual receipt of advice that the offeror received the acceptance. And so it would go on. A later (and probably more persuasive) justification for the rule was given by Parker LJ in *Entores L D v Miles Far East Corporation*.[155] The general rule that acceptance is effective only when communicated to the offeror is to protect the offeror. If the offeror indicates that acceptance by post is acceptable, the offeror has impliedly waived the requirement that actual communication of the acceptance is necessary. The contract is therefore complete when the acceptance is posted.

[3.515] While the rule has been criticised from time to time, the enduring attractiveness of the postal acceptance rule is its promotion of contractual certainty.[156] Provided the post is contemplated by the parties, once acceptance is posted, the offeree can proceed on the basis that a contract has been formed. Further, as will be examined below, an offeror has the option of displacing the operation of the rule by stipulating that he or she will not be bound until actual receipt of the offeree's acceptance.

(c) To what communication does the rule extend?

[3.520] It is axiomatic to state that the postal rule can only apply to communication by post. There are, however, some forms of communication that share some but not all features of communication by post. Courts have had to make determinations about the applicability of the postal acceptance rule to such communications. While telex, fac-

---

150   *Adams v Lindsell* (1918) 106 ER 250; *The Household Fire and Carriage Accident Insurance Company (Ltd) v Grant* (1879) 4 Ex D 216.
151   *Henthorn v Fraser* [1892] 2 Ch 27.
152   See further below as to other circumstances in which the postal acceptance rule will be displaced.
153   *Household Fire and Carriage Insurance Co (Ltd) v Grant* (1879) LR 4 Ex D 216.
154   (1818) 106 ER 250.
155   [1955] 2 QB 327.
156   Compare RA Samek, 'A re-assessment of the present rule relating to postal acceptance' (1961) 35 ALJ 38.

simile, and telephone have been regarded as instantaneous communication and therefore outside the operation of the rule,[157] communications by telegram are regarded by the courts as being more akin to ordinary mail.[158] Therefore, acceptance occurs when the information is given to the post office to be sent to the offeror.

[3.525] The document exchange service ('DX' system) is another method of communication that can be used by parties if they are members of the system. The DX operates by giving members an exchange point they can visit regularly to pick up documents left for them there and place outgoing documents in the boxes of other members for them to pick up. Because this system operates differently from the postal system, it has been suggested (though not decided) that the postal acceptance rule would not operate when the DX system is used.[159]

(d) When is the rule displaced?

[3.530] From the formulation of the rule given earlier, it can be seen that it will only apply where it was contemplated by the parties that the post might be used as a method of acceptance. A court is likely to reach such a conclusion where, among other circumstances, an offer was made by post, or the parties live a considerable distance away from each other. As a corollary, the rule is displaced if a court does not consider that post was within the contemplation of the parties as a means of communicating the acceptance, or if the offeror indicates that he or she will not be bound until actual receipt of the acceptance.

Example: Bressan v Squires[160]

A buyer was given an option to buy land. The option was to be exercised 'by notice in writing addressed to me at any time on or before 20 December, 1972.' Notice was posted by the offeree on 18 December but not received until 21 December. The offeree argued that the postal acceptance rule applied and acceptance occurred on 18 December, within the time stipulated by the offeror.

The New South Wales Supreme Court held that the postal acceptance rule did not apply in the circumstances of the case. The wording of the option implied that the seller required *actual notice* by the specified date. This requirement was not fulfilled by simply posting a letter of acceptance.

---

157 See [3.470]–[3.485].

158 *Cowan v O'Connor* (1888) 20 QBD 640; *Bruner v Moore* [1904] 1 Ch 305. See also *Leach Nominees Pty Ltd v Walter Wright Pty Ltd* [1986] WAR 244 where the offer was made by telex, but the offeree accepted through a public telex system, it having no telex system of its own. Master Seaman QC concluded that acceptance was complete as soon as the message was committed to the public telex operator. The Master considered that the justification for the postal rule applied equally in this case. Response by public telex was contemplated by the parties, and once the offeree committed the message to the public telex operator, the offeree would not necessarily know if it was communicated to the offeror. It was arguable that the contract was complete at that time.

159 *Coot Pty Ltd v Admin Management Pty Ltd,* Unreported decision of New South Wales Supreme Court, No 13254/97, 3 November, 1998.

160 [1974] 2 NSWLR 460.

[3.535] It appears then, that whether the postal acceptance rule is displaced turns on the intention of the offeror. This intention may be distilled from construing the terms of the offer. If the offeror says or implies that actual notification is required before an agreement is formed, as in *Bressan v Squires*,[161] the postal acceptance rule will be displaced.[162] Secondly, it is suggested that the circumstances of the case itself might indicate a displacement of the rule. In *Talleman & Company Pty Ltd v Nathan's Merchandise (Victoria) Pty Ltd*,[163] Dixon CJ and Fullagar J stated in dicta that:

> the general rule is that a contract is not completed until acceptance of an offer is actually communicated to the offeror, and a finding that a contract is completed by the posting of a letter of acceptance cannot be justified unless it is to be inferred that the offeror contemplated and intended that his offer might be accepted by the doing of that act. ... In ... [*Henthorn v Fraser*] it was easy to draw such an inference, but, in such a case as the present, where solicitors are conducting a highly contentious correspondence, one would have thought that actual communication would be regarded as essential to the conclusion of agreement on anything.[164]

Support for this approach can also be found in a fairly recent decision of the Victorian Supreme Court of *Nunin Holdings Pty Ltd v Tullamarine Estates Pty Ltd*.[165] This case involved a contract for the sale of land, the contract to be effected by an exchange of contracts. Hedigan J did not apply the postal acceptance rule in this case because, although the parties may have contemplated use of the post to exchange the contracts, the correspondence from the offeror's solicitor indicated that the contract would be formed upon receipt by the offeror's solicitor of a contract signed by the offeree. The intention of the offeror as reflected in the letter was that the contract would not be formed by merely posting the signed contract to the offeror. This construction left no scope for the operation of the postal acceptance rule.

(e) Revocation of acceptance prior to receipt

[3.540] Strict adherence to the technical operation of the postal acceptance rule can lead to a perhaps surprising result where an offeree wishes to withdraw a mailed acceptance and does so prior to its being received by the offeror. This could occur, for example, if the acceptance was mailed and the offeree subsequently advised the offeror that he or she did not accept the offer (or that the acceptance was withdrawn) by telephone. Applying the postal acceptance rule, the contract is formed when the letter of acceptance is posted. A subsequent purported withdrawal of that acceptance will be ineffective. A lay person would probably regard this outcome as illogical. A contract is formed even though the offeror is notified of the rejection of the offer before receiving a letter of acceptance. In such a case, the offeror would not be disadvantaged by a

---

161 Ibid.
162 See also *Holwell Securites Ltd v Hughes* [1974] 1 WLR 155.
163 (1956) 98 CLR 93 at 111–112.
164 Ibid at 111–112.
165 [1994] 1 VR 74.

conclusion that a contract had not been formed. He or she has not acted in reliance upon the existence of a contract.

[3.545] There is still no definitive Australian authority on whether acceptance by mail can be effectively withdrawn by a more speedy means of communication. There are some early New Zealand dicta to suggest that an acceptance cannot be withdrawn in this way,[166] and even earlier Scottish authority to suggest that it can.[167] In a more recent decision of the Victorian Supreme Court, however, it was assumed that if the postal acceptance rule applied, the contract would be formed when the acceptance was posted, and a subsequent telephone call withdrawing the acceptance would be ineffective.[168] While this opinion was expressed in *obiter dicta*, the Supreme Court finding that the postal acceptance rule did not operate on the facts, it provides at least some indication that courts may favour the strict adherence to the postal acceptance rule in such a case.

3.9.4 Electronic communication

[3.550] The time of contract formation where the contract is formed by electronic communication is still open to some speculation. The common law provides that a contract is formed at the time an acceptance is communicated to the offeror.[169] As examined below, however, there may be different views as to precisely when communication occurs in the context. In the commentary below, the relevance of the traditional 'instantaneous' categorisation is considered, as well as the impact of the electronic transactions legislation which has been drafted in all Australian jurisdictions.

(a) Traditional classification: 'instantaneous' or 'non-instantaneous'

[3.555] When the postal acceptance rule was originally formulated and refined, alternative communication in the form of electronic communication such as e-mail was not in existence—or, for that matter, even contemplated. As modern technology evolved and methods of communication such as telexes and facsimile transmissions began to be used, the courts had to adjudicate upon whether the postal acceptance rule applied to them. In making these determinations, distinctions were drawn between 'instantaneous' and 'non-instantaneous' methods of communication. The postal acceptance rule was considered inappropriate for instantaneous communications. The policy underpinning the postal acceptance rule was not considered relevant, so telex, facsimile and telephone, being regarded as instantaneous communications, are therefore outside the operation of the rule.

[3.560] The applicability of the postal acceptance rule to electronic communication through e-mail is still to be judicially determined by Australian courts.[170] It may be

---

166 *Weinkheim v Arndt* (1873) NZ Jurist 73.

167 *Dunmore (Countess) v Alexander* (1839) Sh (Ct of Sess) 190.

168 *Nunin Holdings Pty Ltd v Tullamarine Estates Pty Ltd* [1994] 1 VR 74.

169 *Powell v Lee* (1908) 99 LT 284; *Soares v Simpson* [1931] NZLR 1079.

170 For a useful summary of the postal acceptance rule, the policy underlying it and the extent to which it should be extended to e-mail, see K O'Shea & K Skehan, 'Acceptance of offers by e-mail—how far should the postal acceptance rule extend?' (1997) 13 *QUTLJ* 247.

that an assessment of whether the rule will operate depends on whether electronic communication can be regarded as instantaneous. Given the different ways in which information can be transmitted electronically and the varying degrees of delay that can operate in individual transactions, this may turn out to be a difficult assessment to make. After a person (the offeree) transmits an e-mail to another (the offeror), the e-mail generally goes through the offeree's server, the Internet, the offeror's server and ultimately to the offeror's computer. Depending on the location of the offeree and offeror, and the computer systems involved in the particular transmission, there can be some delays. The computer systems of third parties are often involved in the transmission. Less frequently, in circumstances where the offeror and offeree conduct considerable business, direct links can be set up between the computer system. Transmission of e-mail in such circumstances should involve less delay.

[3.565] While delays can and do occur in e-mail transmissions, in a sense, they can be regarded as instantaneous. Once sent, transmission is via telephone lines. In the absence of computer system breakdowns or delays due to congestion, unlike the postal service, there is no inherent delay involved in such communication.

[3.570] Further, the fact that a communication is something less than 'instantaneous' has not prevented courts from holding that the postal acceptance rule is not applicable. In *Entores Ld v Miles Far East Corporation*,[171] it was recognised that telex messages were not 'completely instantaneous'. Nevertheless, this form of communication was regarded in the same way as communication by telephone. While there is considerable scope and justification for a court to come to a contrary finding, it may be open for a court to consider electronic communication as virtually instantaneous communication.[172] If so, the postal acceptance rule would not be relevant to this kind of communication.

(b) Alternative classification

[3.575] Despite the traditional approach of the court to categorise a particular form of communication as 'instantaneous' or 'non-instantaneous' to determine whether the postal acceptance rule applies, the time is now ripe for a fresh examination of principles that should govern contract formation in an electronic age. The varying degrees of delay that can be involved in electronic communication demonstrate the difficulty of categorising such communication as either 'instantaneous' or 'non-instantaneous'. And other issues complicate a determination of the precise time of contract formation. An e-mail may be received centrally by the offeror's organisation but not forwarded to the offeror for some time. For offerors who have computers on their desks, an e-mail may be accidentally (or perhaps purposely) trashed without being opened, so that actual communication of the content of the e-mail never occurs. Such matters make it difficult to determine when the acceptance is actually communicated.

---

171 [1955] 2 QB 327.

172 It has been suggested by writers in New Zealand that electronic communication may be regarded as instantaneous communication and therefore be governed by the same rules: JF Burrows, J Finn & SMD Todd, *Law of Contract in New Zealand*, 8th edn, Butterworths, Wellington, 1997, p 64.

Problems of contract formation where electronic communication is used can be avoided if parties reach agreement on these matters in advance. Of course, in the usual case this will not occur. Contractual principles must be adopted and developed to address these issues. But it does seem that the postal acceptance rule is not appropriate in the electronic age. There are also some difficulties involved in regarding such communications as instantaneous. It may be that the words of Lord Wilberforce cited earlier—that contract formation must be resolved by reference to 'the intentions of the parties, by sound business practice and in some cases by a judgment of where the risks should lie'[173]—will assume greater significance. Given the variety of factors that can operate and the range of technologies used, a universal rule may be neither appropriate nor desirable. The end result may be that a contract is formed only when communication of acceptance is received. If the acceptance is sent by e-mail, in the absence of evidence indicating a contrary intention by the offeror, this may be considered to be communicated once the e-mail is received by the offeror's server.

(c) Legislative intervention

[3.580] It is always open for the legislature to resolve uncertainties with the common law by enacting legislation. Over recent years, there has been consultation between the Commonwealth, States and Territories with a view to developing a model law to deal with electronic commerce. The proposal of the Commonwealth was to develop a national uniform legislative scheme under which 'all governments enact legislation within their jurisdiction to facilitate the removal of existing legal impediments to electronic commerce'.[174] Legislation has been drafted in all Australian jurisdictions to implement this policy.[175]

[3.585] The object of the legislation is to provide a regulatory framework that:

1 recognises the importance of the information economy to the future economy and social prosperity of Australia;

2 facilitates the use of electronic transactions;

3 promotes business and community confidence in the use of electronic transactions; and

4 enables business and the community to use electronic communications in their dealings with government.[176]

An important function of the legislation is to facilitate compliance with statutory obligations through electronic communication. For example, if a statute requires information to be lodged, or a document produced, the legislation allows this to be done electronically.

---

173 *Brinkibon Ltd v Stahag Stahl und Stahlwarenhandels-Gesellschaft mbH* [1983] 2 AC 34 at 42.

174 Explanatory Memorandum to the *Electronic Transactions Bill* 1999 (Cth).

175 *Electronic Transactions Act* 1999 (Cth); *Electronic Transactions Act* 2000 (NSW); *Electronic Transactions (Victoria) Act* 2000; *Electronic Transactions (Queensland) Bill* 2001; *Electronic Transactions Bill* 2000 (WA); *Electronic Transactions Act* 2000 (SA); *Electronic Transactions Act* 2000 (Tas); *Electronic Transanctions (Northern Territory) Bill* 2000; *Electronic Transactions Act 2001* (ACT). Although a number of the above Acts have been passed, at the time of writing, only the Commonwealth and Victorian legislation is in operation.

176 *Electronic Transactions Act* 1999 (Cth), s 3; *Electronic Transactions (Victoria) Act* 2000, s 4.

[3.590] The legislation also contains provisions for the time and place of receipt and dispatch of an electronic communication,[177] which may assist in determining the time and place of contract formation at common law. The common law provides that a contract is formed at the time and place an acceptance is communicated to the offeror.[178] As stated earlier, the main difficulty in an electronic environment is determining when an acceptance is communicated or received by the offeror. The possible times communication could occur are when the electronic communication leaves the offeree's computer, when the communication is received by the offeror's Internet service provider, when the communication enters the offeror's computer or when the offeror reads the communication. Section 14 (3) and (4) of the *Electronic Transactions Act* 1999 (Cth) and the state equivalents establish some basic rules for the time of receipt of an electronic communication.[179] It is arguable that these sections clarify the issue by providing that an electronic communication is received at the time the communication comes to the attention of the addressee. This would most likely be at the time the addressee reads the communication or at the earliest at the time the addressee notices that the communication has been received into their computer. As the state legislation is expressed to apply to 'the law of the jurisdiction',[180] it is arguable that the relevant sections should be read as providing a time of receipt for the purposes of the common law relating to the formation of contract.

---

177 *Time of dispatch*: If an electronic communication enters a single information system outside the control of the originator, unless otherwise agreed between the parties, the dispatch of the electronic communication is taken to occur when it enters that information system: *Electronic Transactions Act* 1999 (Cth), s 14(1); *Electronic Transactions (Victoria) Act* 2000, s 13(1). There is also a deeming provision for the time of dispatch where an electronic communication enters successively two or more information systems outside the control of the originator: *Electronic Transactions Act* 1999 (Cth), s 14(2); *Electronic Transactions (Victoria) Act* 2000, s 13(2).

    Time of receipt: If the addressee of an electronic communication (the offeror for the purposes of contract formation) has designated an information system for the purpose of receiving electronic communications, unless otherwise agreed between the parties, the time of receipt of the electronic communication is the time when the communication enters that information system: *Electronic Transactions Act* 1999 (Cth), s 14(3); *Electronic Transactions (Victoria) Act* 2000, s 13(3). If the addressee has not designated an information system for the purpose of receiving such communication, the time of receipt is when the communication comes to the attention of the addressee: *Electronic Transactions Act* 1999 (Cth), s 14(4); *Electronic Transactions (Victoria) Act* 2000, s 13(4).

178 *Powell v Lee* (1908) 99 LT 284; *Soares v Simpson* [1931] NZLR 1079.

179 See note 177.

180 See *Electronic Transactions (Victoria) Act* 2000 where 'law of this jurisdiction' is defined in s 3(1) to mean 'any law in force in this jurisdiction, whether written or unwritten, but does not include a law of the Commonwealth.' Equivalent provisions appear in legislation in the other jurisdictions. Compare the Commonwealth legislation, which is expressed to apply to the 'laws of the Commonwealth'. On the few occasions that it has been judicially considered, the prevailing view is that there does not exist an identifiable common law of the Commonwealth: *R v Kidman* (1915) 20 CLR 425 at 445 per Isaacs J and *Jackson v Gamble* [1983] 1 VR 552 at 559 per Young CJ. There is also authority to suggest that the phrase 'law of the Commonwealth' is limited to the legislation passed by the Commonwealth Parliament: Lane PH, The Australian Federal System, Law Book Company 1979 2nd edn, p 867; *The Commonwealth and The Central Wool Committee v Combing, Spinning and Weaving Company Ltd* (1922) 31 CLR 421 at 431 per Knox CJ and Duffy J; *Spratt v Hermes* (1965) 114 CLR 226 at 247 per Barwick CJ; *Butterworths Australian Legal Dictionary* 1997, definition of 'Commonwealth law', *Laws of Australia*, Law Book Company, para 19.5 [14]. It may be the case, therefore, that the Commonwealth legislation does not affect contract formation in the same way that the state legislation does.

The consequence of this interpretation is that in the case of acceptance by e-mail, the general rule that an acceptance is effective at the time of communication could be used with the legislation clarifying the time of receipt.

[3.595] An alternative interpretation is that the legislation does not impact on any determination of contract formation. Previously courts have determined the point at which a contract is formed by differentiating between instantaneous and other forms of communication. The Electronic Transactions legislation[181] does not assist this debate, as there is no provision for acceptance to be effective for an electronic communication at the time of receipt. The legislation merely provides for the time an electronic communication is deemed to be received. It follows that until a court determines that a contract made by electronic means is formed at the time acceptance is communicated, the legislation is unable to provide assistance.

[3.600] As the intention of the legislation is to remove any existing legal impediments that may prevent a person from using electronic communications to satisfy legal obligations, a court is likely to prefer the view that the legislation extends to contractual issues.

3.9.5   Acceptance combining technologies

[3.605] It is possible for an offeree to accept an offer by using more than one technology. While perhaps a rare occurrence, there has been a Queensland case in which acceptance was effected by using both instantaneous and non-instantaneous methods of communication. In *Express Airways v Port Augusta Air Services*,[182] the acceptance was by telegram to the Post Office; the Post Office communicated this by telex to the telex machine of the offeror. Applying the rules set out earlier, if acceptance was sent by telegram, the postal acceptance rule may have operated. On the other hand, response by telex is regarded as instantaneous communication and outside the operation of the rule. Without any detailed consideration of the basis for so deciding, Douglas J held that the rule set out in *Entores Ltd v Miles Far East Corporation*[183] should apply, so that acceptance occurred only when communication was received by the offeror. Despite the fact that acceptance also involved the use of telegrams, acceptance was regarded as complete, and contract formation occurred when, and at the place that, the telex was received.

[3.610] A contrary approach was taken by Master Seaman QC in *Leach Nominees Pty Ltd v Walter Wright Pty Ltd*,[184] a case also involving both instantaneous and non-instantaneous methods. The offeree accepted by telephoning the message to a public telex operator, who sent it to the offeror's telex machine. The Master considered the rationale for the postal rule applied equally to this case. The parties contemplated that acceptance would be by public telex, and when the message was committed to the public telex operator, the offeree had no way of knowing whether it was effectively communicated to the offeror. Therefore, it was arguable that the contract was formed at that time.

The Western Australian decision was helpful in that the Master provided a useful examination of the justification for the postal rule, and why it was appropriate to apply the rule, on the facts of the case. Given the increased variety of methods of communication, and the fact that acceptance using a combination of methods is possible, it

---

181   *Electronic Transactions Act* 1999 (Cth), s 14; *Electronic Transactions (Victoria) Act* 2000, s 13.
182   [1980] QdR 543.
183   [1955] 2 QB 327.
184   [1986] WAR 244.

would have been helpful for Douglas J to provide a more detailed explanation of why the postal rule was not applicable. In both cases, it may be that there was considerable reliance on the intention of the parties.[185] In the Queensland decision, for example, contractual negotiations took place person-to-person and by phone. While it was not overtly considered in his judgment, this may have been relevant to the decision that the parties only intended to be bound upon actual communication of the acceptance. In the Western Australian decision, on the other hand, the parties intended the acceptance to be by public telex. This, according to Master Seaman QC, may have been enough to indicate the offeror's willingness to waive communication of acceptance before being contractually bound.

3.10 Acceptance in unilateral contracts

[3.615] Acceptance in the context of unilateral contracts raises issues that do not arise in bilateral contracts.

3.10.1 *Acceptance commonly by conduct*

[3.620] The nature of unilateral contracts was examined earlier.[186] Common examples of unilateral contracts are agreements to pay a reward for information or the finding of a lost item, or agreements to provide a prize for performance of specified acts. In these situations, the requirement for acceptance to be communicated is often impliedly waived.[187] Acceptance is effected by the offeree performing the requirements specified by the offeror.

3.10.2 *Withdrawal of offer after acceptance commenced*

[3.625] The rules governing the ability of an offeror to withdraw an offer were discussed earlier.[188] These rules operate differently in the context of a unilateral contract. While the result may depend on the circumstances of the particular case, once an offeree has begun to accept the offer by performing the acts stipulated, it is likely to be too late for the offeror to withdraw the offer and claim there has been no contract formation.[189]

3.11 Who may accept offer?

[3.630] An offer can only be accepted by the person to whom it is made.[190] If A makes an offer to sell A's car to B, the offer cannot be accepted by C. Whether a person falls within the class of persons entitled to accept the offer is a matter of construction of the terms of the offer.

[3.635] It is, of course, possible for offers to be made to more than one person. This occurs where the offer is made to the public at large through, for example, a newspaper

---

185 As suggested to be appropriate by Lord Wilberforce in *Brinkibon Ltd v Stahag Stahl und Stahlwarenhandels-Gesellschaft mbH* [1983] 2 AC 34 at 42.
186 See [3.45]–[3.55].
187 *Carlill v Carbolic Smoke Ball Company* [1893] 1 QB 256.
188 See [3.455].
189 See [3.280]–[3.305].
190 *Reynolds v Atherton* (1921) 125 LT 690; *McMahon v Gilberd & Co Ltd* [1995] NZLR 1206.

advertisement, or where the offeror makes individual contact with a number of offerees. It is a question of construction in each case whether the offer is one capable of acceptance by more than one party, thereby creating a number of contracts. *Carlill's case*[191] is a classic example. The offer made to the public at large was capable of acceptance by anyone performing the acts specified in the advertisement. On the other hand, advertisements for a reward for information leading to an arrest and conviction is likely to be interpreted differently. As in *Carlill's case*,[192] it is possible for more than one person to be in a position to accept. More than one person may have information that would qualify them for a reward. Nevertheless, courts have interpreted an advertisement for a reward as an offer that is accepted by the first person to come forward with the relevant information.[193] Only one contract is capable of being formed in such a case.

[3.640] An offeror will be in a difficult situation where the subject matter is such that only one contract can be performed, but there has been more than one purported acceptance. Such a situation could arise where an offeror makes an offer to sell his or her real property to two people. If the offer is accepted by one person and, before the offeror withdraws the offer to the other, that other also accepts, two valid contracts will have been formed.[194] In such circumstances only one contract is capable of being performed. The offeror will then be in breach of contract with the other offeree and potentially liable for damages.

3.12 Contract formation: time and place

[3.645] There are a variety of reasons why it may be important to establish precisely when and where a contract is formed. Time of formation may be relevant if the offeror has changed his or her mind and wishes to withdraw the offer. Once the contract is formed, it is too late to withdraw the offer. Further, if an offer can be accepted only up until a particular date, determining the date of contract formation may be critical. Place of contract formation is significant if a dispute arises between the contracting parties. It may be a relevant consideration in determining the appropriate jurisdiction in which to bring an action for breach of the contract. The time and place that the contract is formed depends on the method of contract formation. The different methods of contract formation and the rules applicable to them were examined earlier.[195]

3.12.1 *Instantaneous communication*

[3.650] It will be recalled that negotiations made face to face, by telephone, telex, and facsimile are all instantaneous methods of communication. In such cases, the contract is formed when and where the offeror receives the acceptance communicated.[196] There-

---

191 [1893] 1 QB 256. For facts of this case, see [3.60].
192 Ibid.
193 *Robinson v M'Ewan* (1865) 2 WW & a'B (L) 65 at 67.
194 *Patterson v Dolman* [1908] VLR 354.
195 See [3.420]–[3.610].
196 *Entores L D v Miles Far East Corporation* [1955] to QB 327 at 335; *Hamstead Meats Pty Ltd v Emerson & Yates Pty Ltd* [1967] SASR 109, *Mendelson-Zeller Co Inc v T & C Providores Pty Ltd* [1981] 1 NSWLR 366 at 369; *Brinkibon Ltd v Stahag Stahl und Stahlwarenhandels-Gesellschaft mbH* [1983] 2 AC 34; *Reese Bros Plastics v Hammon-Sobelco Australia Pty Ltd* (1988) 5 *Butterworths Property Reports* [97325] at 11 108 per Gleeson CJ.

fore, if negotiations took place, for example, by facsimile and, unbeknown to the offeree, the offeree's facsimile machine malfunctioned when sending the acceptance so it was never received, no contract would come into existence. The position would be the same where negotiations took place by telephone and, due to a fault with the lines, the offeror was unable to hear the offeree's acceptance.

3.12.2 Post

[3.655] If the postal acceptance rule applies, the contract is formed when, and at the place that, the letter of acceptance is posted. This is the case even if, due to a fault in the postal service, the letter is never delivered. In this way, unlike the situation where communication is instantaneous, any risk in failure of the communication medium is borne by the offeror.

3.12.3 Electronic communication

[3.660] As noted earlier, the Australian courts have not yet made a determination in relation to issues surrounding contract formation where parties correspond by electronic communication.[197] To overcome this legal vacuum and to ensure certainty of business arrangements, traders who regularly transact business in this way may agree on issues surrounding contract formation. Parties may, for example, agree that formation does not occur until acceptance is received at the offeror's computer. Agreement may also be reached about the effect of computer failure. The majority of electronic commerce transactions, however, will occur in the absence of such agreement. As examined earlier, the legal position on contract formation in the electronic environment has not yet been tested in the courts.

[3.665] The legal uncertainty on issues of contract formation in the electronic environment is exacerbated when contracts occur with people in other countries. Given that commerce through the Internet is becoming increasingly popular, and parties to the contract will often come from countries with different legal systems, conflict of laws problems will inevitably arise. The difficulties that can arise are exemplified by the following real incident involving the purchase and sale of a CD.[198] While the transaction was a simple one, the legal issues arising out of it were anything but simple.

Example

An English website advertised a CD for sale for £9. Loundy, a Chicago lawyer, ordered the CD through the website and received an e-mail acknowledgment of the order. Later Loundy received a note from the mail-order representative that the advertised price was an error and asked if he were still interested in buying the CD for £13. Loundy responded that he wished to buy the CD for the price initially advertised.

[3.670] These facts raise complex legal issues. What law should govern the situation? As this transaction may constitute a valid contract in one jurisdiction but not another

---

197 See [3.550]–[3.575].

198 C Kaplan, 'On the web, it's buyer beware. But where?', March 26, 1999, *Cyber Law Journal* http://www.nytimes.com/library/tech/99/03/cyber/cyberlaw/26law.html (accessed 27 April 2001).

(which was alleged to be the position in this case), a determination of this issue may be crucial. What happens if United States law dictates that it only has jurisdiction because the contract was formed there, while different rules apply in the United Kingdom indicating it was the appropriate jurisdiction?[199] These legal issues are further exacerbated because many jurisdictions have not developed or refined their own rules of contract formation involving electronic communication. The CD case also highlights practical problems that arise. If contract formation had occurred in England, it would not be feasible for Loundy, a citizen of the United States, to commence an action in a foreign jurisdiction. The cost and inconvenience involved would generally be prohibitive.

3.13 International perspective

3.13.1 New Zealand

[3.675] The New Zealand law on contract formation largely reflects the Australian position as outlined in this chapter. As is the trend in Australia and England, some recent New Zealand decisions have recognised that a global approach to issues of contract formation may in some circumstances be more appropriate than the traditional approach of requiring identification of offer and acceptance.[200]

[3.680] Special mention, should be made, however, of auctions without reserves, and similar transactions. The auction process and the legal effect of an advertisement of an auction, an auctioneer's call for bids, the bids made and the final knockdown by the auctioneer were examined earlier.[201] Whether an auction without a reserve should be treated in a different way was also addressed. It was noted that the English case of *Warlow v Harrison*[202] suggests that where an auction takes place without a reserve, an auctioneer may be exposed to contractual liability if the property is not subsequently knocked down to the highest bidder. It was also noted that there is Australian authority suggesting an auctioneer will not be liable in such situations.[203]

The more recent New Zealand authorities suggest that where, as in *Warlow v Harrison*,[204] a party indicates that he or she agrees to be bound by a particular bid or tender, that party may be contractually bound. This is sometimes referred to as the 'two contract approach'.[205] The first contract is the primary one, whether for the sale of goods, the construction of a building or some other enterprise. The secondary contract relates to the way the parties have agreed that formation of the primary contract should occur. If, for example, a party agrees to sell property to the highest tenderer, a person submitting a tender accepts the offer and the secondary contract is formed. The following case provides an example.

---

199 See [26.380]–[26.400].
200 *Boulder Consolidated Ltd v Tangaere* [1980] 1 NZLR 560; *Meats v Attorney-General* [1983] NZLR 308.
201 See [3.4.2].
202 (1859) 120 ER 925.
203 *AGC (Advances) Ltd v McWhirter* (1977) 1 *Butterworths Property Reports* [97045]. Compare *Ulbrick v Laidlaw* [1924] VLR 247.
204 (1859) 120 ER 925.
205 JF Burrows, J Finn & SMD Todd, *Law of Contract in New Zealand*, 8th edn, Butterworths, Wellington, 1997, p 44.

Example: Markholme Construction Ltd v Wellington City Council[206]

A seller advertised in a paper for the sale of a number of pieces of land for a specified price. The advertisement further stated that if there was more than one bid for the one piece of land, a ballot would be held of the bidders. Although the seller received more than one bid, it refused to hold a ballot. One of the bidders brought an action for breach of contract.

The New Zealand High Court held that the seller was liable for breach of contract to hold a ballot. The seller in this case was in breach of the secondary contract. The bidder had lost the chance to participate in the ballot.

[3.685] The two contract approach may also be relevant if an advertisement calling for tenders indicates the lowest (or highest, as the case may be) conforming tender will be accepted. The English Court of Appeal decision of *Blackpool & Fylde Aeroclub Ltd v Blackpool Burrow Council*[207] was mentioned earlier in the chapter.[208] As the Council inviting tenders failed to consider a conforming tender, the Council was held to be in breach of contract. Using the two contract approach, the Council was in breach of the secondary contract. In the New Zealand case of *Pratt Contractors Ltd v Palmerston North City Council*,[209] an advertisement by the defendant advised that the lowest conforming tender was to be accepted. Although the plaintiff submitted such a tender, it was not accepted. The plaintiff took legal action and was awarded damages against the defendant. Although the defendant was in breach of the secondary contract only, the damages award was the amount necessary to put the plaintiff in the same position that it would have been in had its tender been accepted.

If the two contract approach were adapted to auctions conducted without a reserve price, an auctioneer may be liable under the secondary contract for failure to knock the item down to the highest bidder.

3.13.2   United States

[3.690] The requirement of agreement as fundamental to contract formation is equally applicable in America. Traditionally, existence or non-existence of agreement is examined by deciding whether there is an offer and corresponding acceptance, and ensuring the requisite degree of mutuality exists. As in other common law jurisdictions, the objective theory prevails when considering aspects of agreement such as, for example, whether the words used by the alleged offeror can properly be regarded as constituting an offer. The increased complexity of the precontractual negotiation phase and the fact that many drafts of contracts may be prepared and negotiated by the parties themselves or through their legal representatives have led to judicial recognition that it is not always possible to analyse contractual arrangements in terms of offer and acceptance. Instead, a global approach to contract formation is recognised more accurately as reflecting commercial reality.[210]

---

206   [1985] 2 NZLR 520.
207   [1991] WLR 1195.
208   See [3.185].
209   [1995] 1 NZLR 469.
210   The global approach to contract formation is reflected in §22 of the Restatement (Second).

[3.695] The Restatement (Second) largely reflects the common law principles on matters relating to agreement, with §3 providing as follows:

> An agreement is a manifestation of mutual assent on the part of two or more persons. A bargain is an agreement to exchange promises or to exchange a promise for a performance or to exchange performances.[211]

However, the Restatement (Second) does not simply adopt all of the traditional terminology. To give one example, the terms 'bilateral contract' and 'unilateral contract' are not used, as the distinction between these terms was perceived to serve little or no purpose.

[3.700] In a text of this kind, it would serve little purpose to focus on the minute detail of differences between America and Australia on the law of agreement. However, it may be helpful to focus on specific aspects of American law where there has been a divergence of judicial opinion within Australia, or where there has been little consideration of the particular point of law by the Australian courts.

(a) Auctions

[3.705] The precise moment of contract formation in cases of auctions with reserve and without reserve was examined earlier.[212] While diverse views have been expressed about whether an auctioneer's call for bids in an auction without a reserve being set constitutes an invitation to treat or an offer, the prevailing Australian view appears to be that the auction should be treated in the same way as an auction with a reserve. The call for bids is an invitation to treat, and any subsequent bid constitutes an offer that may be rejected or accepted by the auctioneer. A contract is concluded only on a fall of the hammer.

The American common law generally appears to reflect the Australian position in that an auctioneer's call for bids is regarded as inviting offers, with each bid constituting an offer. This is also the position under the Restatement (Second) and the Uniform Commercial Code where the auction is one with reserve.[213] The position is different under both the Restatement (Second) and the Code where the auction is without reserve. Inviting bids in such a case is regarded as an irrevocable commitment by the auctioneer to sell to the highest bidder. The auctioneer makes an offer to sell at any price, and the goods cannot be withdrawn unless no bid is made within a reasonable time.[214] It should logically follow from this that upon the highest bid being made, the contract of sale is formed. Interestingly, though, although the auctioneer is not entitled to withdraw his or her offer, under both the Restatement and the Code, a bidder can retract his or her bid before the auctioneer declares that the bid is accepted and a sale completed.[215]

---

211   See also Restatement (Second), §§17, 18, 22, 23 and 26.
212   See [3.150]–[3.165] above.
213   Restatement (Second) §28(1)(a) and Uniform Commercial Code 2-328(2).
214   Restatement (Second) §28(1)(b) and Uniform Commercial Code 2-328(3).
215   Restatement (Second) §28(1)(c) and Uniform Commercial Code 2-328(3).

(b) Option contracts

[3.710] The operation of option contracts was explored earlier in the text.[216] The American common law is the same as the Australian position: for an offer to be irrevocable, it must be given under seal, or consideration must be provided by the offeree. The concept of an 'option contract' is recognised by the Restatement (Second),[217] but limitations are imposed on the extent to which the offer can remain irrevocable. Pursuant to §87(1)(a), an offer is binding as an option contract if it:

'is in writing and signed by the offeror, recites a purported consideration for the making of the offer, and proposes an exchange on fair terms within a reasonable time …'

The Uniform Commercial Code refers to irrevocable offers as 'firm offers'.[218] Such an offer will be binding under the Code provided it is in writing and signed by the offeror. The offer will remain open for the time specified, a reasonable time if none is specified and, in any event, for no more than for three months.

(c) Withdrawal of offer in unilateral contracts

General principle

[3.715] It was observed earlier, in the Australian context, that there is a divergence of views on whether an offeror can revoke a unilateral offer after the offeree has commenced acceptance.[219] There has been a similar debate in America. On a traditional analysis, an offeror can withdraw an offer until acceptance has taken place. In a unilateral contract, acceptance is complete only after performance has been completed. The potential risk to which an offeree commencing acceptance may be exposed in such a case has been resolved by the Restatement (Second) by turning the offer into an option contract once the offeree begins to render performance.

(1) Where an offer invites an offeree to accept by rendering a performance and does not invite a promissory acceptance, an option contract is created when the offeree tenders or begins the invited performance or tenders a beginning of it.

(2) The offeror's duty of performance under any option contract so created is conditional on completion or tender of the invited performance in accordance with the terms of the offer.[220]

Where offer to public at large

[3.720] In general, an offer will terminate under American law in the same circumstances as operate in Australia. One such way is by the offeror withdrawing the offer. In both jurisdictions, withdrawal of an offer is usually only effective when it has been communicated to the offeree. This, of course, poses difficulties where the offer has been made to

---

216 See [3.205]–[3.210].
217 Restatement (Second) §25.
218 Uniform Commercial Code 2-205.
219 See [3.295]–[3.300].
220 Restatement (Second) § 45.

the public at large. It is impossible to ensure that all people who were potentially able to accept the offer could be notified of its withdrawal in such circumstances. Notwithstanding this problem, it has been held in America that provided the withdrawal of the offer receives the same publicity as the initial offer, that is sufficient to revoke the offer.[221] If that requirement is met, a prospective offeree is unable to accept the offer even if he or she is not in fact aware of the offer having been withdrawn.

(d) Battle of the forms

[3.725] The difficulties relating to contract formation that arise where the offeror and offeree each negotiate by using their standard forms was canvassed earlier.[222] In contrast to the relatively inflexible Australian and English approach, the American courts have attempted to develop techniques to mitigate the extent to which the rules work against contract formation. To illustrate, one technique is to find contract formation upon the offeree responding on his or her own form. This acceptance can be regarded as being on the terms proposed by the offeror, coupled with a suggested modification of the terms of the contract so formed in the manner suggested by the offeree's form.[223] A different approach that has also been employed is to regard the original offer as being modified in the manner indicated by the offeree's form and a contract in this modified form having been concluded.[224]

[3.730] The Uniform Commercial Code was drafted to overcome the problems associated with the battle of forms. Article 2-207 provides as follows:

(1) A definite and seasonable expression of acceptance or a written confirmation which is sent within a reasonable time operates as an acceptance even though it states terms additional to or different from those offered or agreed upon, unless acceptance is expressly made conditional on assent to the additional or different terms.

(2) The additional terms are to be construed as proposals for addition to the contract. Between merchants such terms become part of the contract unless:

(a) the offer expressly limits acceptance to the terms of the offer;

(b) they materially alter it; or

(c) notification of objection to them has already been given or is given within a reasonable time after notice of them is received.

(3) Conduct by both parties which recognises the existence of a contract is sufficient to establish a contract for sale although the writings of the parties do not otherwise establish a contract. In such case the terms of the particular contract consist of those terms on which the writings of the parties agree, together with any supplementary terms incorporated under any other provision of this Act.

---

221 *Shuey v United States* 92 US 73 (1875). This position is now reflected in the Restatement (Second) §46.
222 See [3.375]–[3.405] above.
223 *Valashinas v Koniuto* 124 NE 2d 300 (NY 1954).
224 *Poel v Brunswick-Balke-Collender Company* 110 NE 619 (NY 1915).

While intended to provide some certainty to contracting parties and to ensure agreements entered into and acted upon are regarded as valid, the ensuing litigation on the Code provisions is testimony to a fresh set of problems arising from the drafting. For example, while it is clear that paragraph (1) suggests contract formation occurring on the terms suggested by the offeror, difficulties arise in determining the extent to which there can be 'an expression of acceptance' where the purported acceptance contains additional or different terms. Many other problems of construction have arisen from this and paras (2) and (3).

It is beyond the scope of this text to examine the difficulties encountered by the American courts in interpreting the Code provisions. It is clear from the American experience, however, that there is greater recognition of the practical realities of commercial transactions. Wherever possible, whether applying common law principles or interpreting the Uniform Commercial Code, the courts try to find that agreement has been reached, particularly where the parties have clearly conducted their affairs on that basis.

(e) Postal acceptance or 'mailbox' rule

[3.735] The postal rule or 'mailbox' rule as it is called in America, also operates in the United States. Consistent with the Australian and English approaches, the rule does not apply to instant communication. According to one leading American author, instantaneous communication covers electronic mail as well as the more widely recognised forms of telephone, telex, and facsimile transmissions.[225]

[3.740] The question whether a rejection by an offeree that overtakes an earlier acceptance made by post is effective is also the subject of debate in this jurisdiction. Given the emphasis on mutuality of obligations, one leading academic suggests that where an offeree posts an acceptance of the offer, that acceptance should be binding on the offeree as well as on the offeror.[226] The offeree should not be entitled to take the benefit of any change in market conditions by changing his or her mind and rejecting the offer (or withdrawing the acceptance) in a speedier manner of communication. If the offeror is bound at the time of posting the acceptance, so, too, should the offeree.

3.13.3 Japan

[3.745] The Japanese rules on formation are slightly different from their common law counterparts, although they produce similar results. There are three recognised ways in which a contract can be formed through the parties' mutual intent: (1) offer and acceptance; (2) cross offers and (3) acceptance by performance.

[3.750] In most cases, the parties' intention will be declared through offer and acceptance. Acceptance of a firm offer (whether oral or in writing) is all that is required to form a contract. Where the communication of offer and acceptance is not instantaneous, Article 526(1) of the Civil Code provides that a contract is formed when the acceptance is dispatched. The effect of the 'dispatch rule' is that contracts are formed comparatively

---

225   EA Farnsworth, *Contracts*, 3rd edn, Aspen Law and Business, New York, 1999, p 177.
226   EA Farnsworth, *Contracts*, 3rd edn, Aspen Law and Business, New York, 1999, pp 178–179.

early.[227] The person receiving the offer has no obligation to reply to it. If there is no reply to the offer, the usual position is that a contract has not been formed. The exception to this principle, however, is found in the Commercial Code, which governs transactions between' 'merchants' (defined in Article 4, Commercial Code). Article 509 of the Commercial Code deems an offer to have been accepted by a party where he or she and the offeror have regular business relations, unless the party receiving the offer expressly dispatches notice of rejection. A fairly abstract interpretation debate has developed about the 'dispatch rule' (*hasshin shugi*) and the 'delivery rule' (*tôtatsu shugi*) centring on conformity with articles 521, 526 and 527 of the Civil Code. It concerns the question of who should bear the risk of possible revocation of the offer or acceptance and the risk of non-delivery of the expression of intent.[228]

As with the common law, the terms of the offer and acceptance must match. There are rules on firm offers, so that an offer specifying a period for acceptance may not be revoked (Civil Code Article 521) and failure to accept within the specified time frame causes an offer to lapse. The Civil Code is silent about offers that do not prescribe a time frame for acceptance. Where no time frame is given, the offer may be revoked within a reasonable time, or will lapse if it is not accepted within a reasonable time. By contrast, the Commercial Code makes it clear that in commercial transactions the offer lapses if not accepted within a reasonable time (Commercial Code Article 508). Delayed acceptance constitutes a new offer.

By contrast, the Civil Code contains no explicit rules about offer and acceptance in situations where the parties are engaged in conversation or negotiation. Whether a contract was formed or not requires the application of common sense after the fact. However, in commercial dealings, Article 507 of the Commercial Code provides that as between parties in conversation, where an offer is made and is not immediately accepted, the offer loses its efficacy. This can be applied analogously to non-commercial transactions, where, if agreement is not reached before the end of the conversation, the offer can be said to have lapsed.

[3.755] The distinction between an offer and an invitation to submit an offer is treated in a similar way in Japanese law as it is treated elsewhere: the question turns on the facts including the parties' identities, the degree of detail, and the transaction type.

[3.760] It is possible to form a contract through cross-offers. Although not expressly recognised by the Civil Code, case law recognises that, in some cases, a contract may emerge from the exchange of expressions of intention or exchange of documents, particularly between parties who have a continuing business relationship.[229]

---

227   Shoji Kawakami, 'Formation of Contract: Some Thoughts on Modern Contract Theory' (Part 1) (S Steele and V Taylor trans, unpublished) Japanese original: (1988) *Hanrei Taimuzu* (No. 655) (15 March 1988); See also Shoji Kawakami 'Precontractual Liability: Japan' in (E. Hondius ed. 1991) Precontractual Liability: Reports to the XIIIth Congress International Academy of Comparative Law Montreal Canada 18–24 August 1990, 205–221.

228   Shoji Kawakami, 'Formation of Contract: Some Thoughts on Modern Contract Theory' (Part 1) (S Steele and V Taylor trans, unpublished) Japanese original: (1988) *Hanrei Taimuzu* (No. 655) (15 March 1988); See also Shoji Kawakami 'Precontractual Liability: Japan' in (E. Hondius ed. 1991) Precontractual Liability: Reports to the XIIIth Congress International Academy of Comparative Law Montreal Canada 18–24 August 1990, 205–221.

229   Uchida Takashi, *Minpô II* [Civil Law II] 1997, Tokyo Daigaku Shuppankai Tokyo p 40.

[3.765] Acceptance by performance is recognised in Civil Code Article 526(2), and is supported by business custom in many situations such as the dispatch of goods.

[3.770] Although, in theory, the rules of offer and acceptance under the Civil Code appear clear, determining whether a contract has in fact been formed is not always clear-cut; courts in many cases take a substantive approach, evaluating all of the surrounding circumstances.

[3.775] At present, Japan has no specific legislation relating to formation of contracts in electronic commerce. This is scheduled for drafting and submission to the Diet (Parliament) in 2001.

Chapter 4

Certainty and completeness

4.1 Introduction

[4.05] Before parties will be regarded as having entered into a binding legal contract, there must be an agreement. An offer must have been communicated by one party to the other party, and the offeree must have accepted the terms of that offer. As discussed in the next chapter, before a contract will be enforced by a court, the parties must have intended to enter into legal relations with each other. A separate, yet related, requirement for contract formation is that of certainty and completeness. A court will only enforce a contract if the terms of the agreement are formulated with sufficient certainty and agreement has been reached on all of the terms necessary to carry out the contract.[1]

[4.10] That there is overlap between the formation requirements of offer and acceptance, intention to create legal relations and certainty is demonstrated by the well-known case of *Carlill v Carbolic Smoke Ball Company*.[2] The argument posed by the Carbolic Smoke Ball Company, in its denial of any obligation to pay £100, was summarised by Lindley LJ in the following terms:

> First of all it is said that this advertisement is so vague that you cannot really construe it as a promise—that the vagueness of the language shews that a legal promise was never intended or contemplated.[3]

Although this argument was not accepted by the English Court of Appeal on the facts of the case, it demonstrates that concepts of uncertainty or vagueness are relevant to a determination of whether there has been an offer made which is capable of acceptance, and whether the parties could have had the requisite intention to enter into legal relations. If an offer is so vague that the respective obligations of the parties on acceptance are unclear, it is unlikely to be a valid offer in legal terms. Similarly, if the terms of the offer are vague and uncertain, it may indicate that the parties have not yet reached the stage of negotiations at which each intends to be legally bound to the

---

1   See [4.25]–[4.50].
2   [1893] 1 QB 256. See facts set out at [3.60].
3   [1893] 1 QB 256 at 263.

other party. The direct correlation between intention and certainty was also pointed out by Lord Wright in *G Scammell and Nephew Ltd v HC & JG Ouston*:[4]

> There are in my opinion two grounds on which the court ought to hold that there was never a contract. The first is that the language used was so obscure and so incapable of any definite or precise meaning that the court is unable to attribute to the parties any particular contractual intention.

[4.15] The volume of case law that considers issues of uncertainty illustrates the difficult task faced by the court in determining whether the particular contract is so vague and uncertain as to be unenforceable. Where one party claims that the contract is invalid on the basis of uncertainty, or for failure of the parties to reach agreement on all terms, and that claim is denied by the other party, the court must balance two policy objectives. The first is that the court wants to give effect to an agreement made by the parties if it appears that they intended to be bound by that agreement.[5] The second is that the court does not wish to hold parties to obligations where the agreement is cast in such vague terms that there is no indication they intended to be bound by it. While each case must be judged on its facts, it seems that 'the modern tendency is to give content and effect to contractual terms despite a superficial vagueness'.[6]

[4.20] The rule governing certainty of contract is set out at [4.25]. While stating the rule is easy, its application to individual cases has caused the judiciary considerable difficulty. Views can legitimately differ as to whether it is possible to give meaning to a particular clause. Herron CJ of the New South Wales Supreme Court commented that this area of law is one 'as to which there is much room for a difference of opinion, for it raises one of the most contentious aspects of the law of contract'.[7] It is for this reason that decisions on whether a provision is enforceable frequently contain dissenting judgments.[8]

4.2 Statement of the rule

[4.25] The classic statement of the rule regarding certainty of contractual obligations was made by Viscount Maugham in *G Scammell and Nephew Ltd v HC and JG Ouston*:

> In order to constitute a valid contract the parties must so express themselves that their meaning can be determined with a reasonable degree of certainty. It

---

4   [1941] AC 251 at 268.

5   *Hillas and Co Ltd v Arcos Ltd* (1932) 147 LT 503 at 512; *G Scammell and Nephew Ltd v HC & JG Ouston* [1941] AC 251 at 268; *Meehan v Jones* (1981) 149 CLR 571 at 589; *Upper Hunter County District v Australian Chilling & Freezing Co Ltd* (1968) 118 CLR 429 at 436–437; *Rowella Pty Ltd v Hoult* [1987] 1 QdR 386 at 393; *Hawthorn Football Club Ltd v Harding* [1988] VR 49; *Biotechnology Australia Pty Ltd v Pace* (1988) 15 NSWLR 130 at 132–133.

6   *Upper Hunter County District v Australian Chilling & Freezing Co Ltd* (1968) 118 CLR 429 at 436–437; *Hawthorn Football Club Ltd v Harding* [1988] VR 49 at 56–57; *Rowella Pty Ltd v Hoult* [1987] 1 QdR 386 at 393.

7   *Stocks and Holdings (Constructors) Pty Ltd v Arrowsmith* (1964) 64 SR (NSW) 211 at 217.

8   See, for example, *Whitlock v Brew* (1969) 118 CLR 445; *Hall v Busst* (1960) 104 CLR 206; *Placer Development Ltd v The Commonwealth* (1969) 121 CLR 353; *Biotechnology Australia Pty Ltd v Pace* (1988) 15 NSWLR 130.

is plain that unless this can be done it would be impossible to hold that the contracting parties had the same intentions; in other words the consensus ad idem would be a matter of mere conjecture.[9]

[4.30] There are a number of facets to this statement of principle.

- A contract containing language that is 'so obscure and so incapable of any definite or precise meaning that the court is unable to attribute to the parties any particular contractual intention' will be unenforceable.[10] The uncertainty may relate to one or more pivotal terms of the agreement,[11] or may go to the very heart of the agreement—such as where parties agree to negotiate in the future.[12]
- Even where uncertain or ambiguous language is not used, if the parties have not agreed on all of the essential terms of the agreement, the contract will be unenforceable.[13]
- A contract will be unenforceable if it reserves a discretion for one party not to carry out his or her obligations.[14]

[4.35] There is a considerable body of case law on issues of certainty, and some lack of consistency in the terminology. Distinctions have been drawn both in the case law and academic writings between contracts that are illusory and those that are uncertain or ambiguous. In their joint judgment in the High Court case of *Placer Development Ltd v The Commonwealth*,[15] Taylor and Owen JJ said:

> a promise to pay an unspecified amount of money is not enforceable where it expressly appears that the amount to be paid is to rest in the discretion of the promisor and the deficiency is not remedied by a subsequent provision that the promisor will, in his discretion, fix the amount of the payment. Promises of this character are treated by Pollock (Principles of Contract, 12th ed (1946) pp 38, 39) not as vague and uncertain promises—for their meaning is only too clear—but as illusory promises …[16]

[4.40] If the three facets of the statement of principle listed above are viewed in this light, only the first two limbs can be regarded as raising issues of certainty; the third would be regarded as a contract containing an illusory promise. As observed by Taylor and Owen JJ, while an illusory promise is not enforceable, its meaning will be clear. Because the nature of the obligations undertaken by each party can be stated definitively, it falls outside the kind of contractual deficiency described by Viscount Maugham in *G Scammell and Nephew Ltd v HC & JG Ouston*.[17] Notwithstanding these technical distinctions, the case law illustrates the blurring of the boundaries between

---

9   [1941] AC 251 at 255.
10   *G Scammell and Nephew Ltd v HC and JG Ouston* [1941] AC 251 at 268.
11   See [4.60]–[4.70].
12   See [4.75]–[4.95].
13   See [4.195].
14   *Thorby v Goldberg* (1965) 112 CLR 597 at 605; *Meehan v Jones* (1981) 149 CLR 571 at 587.
15   (1969) 121 CLR 353.
16   Ibid at 359–360.
17   [1941] AC 251.

illusory and uncertain promises.[18] In the end, the classification is not pivotal. Neither promise is enforceable.

[4.45] While the contracting parties may, and are likely to, take opposing views on the certainty of a particular clause, the court must make an objective assessment about its enforceability.[19]

[4.50] Finally, it should be remembered that where a party seeks to bring an action based on a clause in a contract, the onus will be on the plaintiff to demonstrate the validity of the clause.[20]

4.3 Ambiguity and uncertainty

[4.55] Issues of ambiguity and uncertainty can arise in a variety of contexts. The following scenarios demonstrate this point.

Scenario 1

One party wishes to sue another for damages for breach of contract, the other claiming that the particular clause is void for uncertainty.[21]

Scenario 2

One party brings an action for specific performance of a contract, the other defending the action claiming that the contract contains an uncertain term, which makes the contract void.[22]

Scenario 3

Parties enter an agreement entitled 'Heads of Agreement' under which they agree on certain principles, and outline their intentions in relation to other matters that are not yet finalised. One party seeks to enforce the agreement, but the other claims that it is unenforceable as it is too uncertain.

The action contemplated in scenario 1 is a common law action, the plaintiff seeking damages for breach of a contractual term. The plaintiff in scenario 2, on the other hand, seeks equitable relief in the form of specific performance. Both contracts could be of the same kind—for example, a contract for the sale of land. In each case, if the contract is uncertain or ambiguous, the plaintiff's action will fail.[23] However, it has been suggested that a court, in exercising its equitable jurisdiction, may be more lenient in its deliberations as to whether a clause can be regarded as certain. Therefore, in *Hall v Busst*,[24] where a contract of sale conferred on a seller of land an option to repur-

---

18   See for example, *Biotechnology Australia Pty Ltd v Pace* (1988) 15 NSWLR 130 at 137.
19   *Biotechnology Australia Pty Ltd v Pace* (1988) 15 NSWLR 130 at 135.
20   *Falck v Williams* [1900] AC 176.
21   *Hall v Busst* (1960) 104 CLR 206.
22   *Fitzgerald v Masters* (1956) 95 CLR 420; *Lend Lease Financial Planning Ltd v Southcap Pty Ltd* Butterworths unreported judgments BC 9802393, Queensland Court of Appeal, 2 June 1998.
23   This is assuming that issues such as severance and waiver discussed in [4.135]–[4.140] and [4.150]–[4.155] respectively are not relevant.
24   (1960) 104 CLR 206.

chase for a price that required the calculation of the 'value' of various assets and liabilities, the seller could not sue the purchaser for breach of that term. It was suggested that the position may have been different if an action seeking specific performance of a contract for sale at a *fair* value had been brought.[25]

4.3.1 Individual terms

[4.60] A number of different terms have been used to describe clauses that are struck down for want of certainty. Whether the clause is said to be 'vague', 'ambiguous', or 'uncertain' is unlikely to make any difference. The clause will be void. Sometimes the court will label a term 'meaningless' or 'illusory'. These terms have a slightly different connotation from the others. A meaningless clause is, of course, one to which a meaning cannot be attributed. Although instances of such clauses are relatively rare, the case of *Fitzgerald v Masters*[26] provides a good example of such a clause and is examined later in this paragraph. A meaningless clause will be treated in the same way as an uncertain clause. An 'illusory' clause raises slightly different considerations, referred to earlier.[27]

[4.65] Given that each determination turns on the facts of the individual case, it may be instructive to provide case examples of the kinds of clauses that have been either struck down or upheld for reasons relating to certainty.

Example: Whitlock v Brew[28]

The parties entered into a contract for the sale of land. On part of the land, a petrol service station business was being conducted. The contract required the purchaser to grant a lease of a portion of the land sold 'to the Shell Co of Australia Ltd upon terms that the said land leased as aforesaid be used by Shell or their sub-tenant or licensee for the sale of [Shell] products and upon such reasonable terms as commonly govern such a lease.' The contract went on to provide for an arbitrator to resolve any disputes that arose in relation to the interpretation of the agreement. The majority of the High Court (Kitto, Taylor, Menzies and Owen JJ, McTiernan J dissenting) held that the clause was uncertain, as it did not prescribe the term of the lease or the rent.

Example: Hall v Busst[29]

The parties entered into a contract for the sale of land. The seller was given an option to repurchase the property at a sum of '£3157 4s 0d to which shall be added the value of all additions and improvements to the said property since the date of purchase by the [purchaser] (such values to be taken as at the date of exercise of this option) and from shall be subtracted the value of all deficiencies of chattel property and a reasonable sum to cover depreciation of all buildings and other property on the land'. A majority of the High Court (Dixon CJ, Fullagar, and Menzies JJ, Kitto and Windeyer JJ dissenting) held that the option to purchase was void because the price was not stated with sufficient certainty.

---

25 Ibid at 223 per Fullagar J.
26 (1956) 95 CLR 420.
27 See [4.35]–[4.40].
28 (1967) 118 CLR 445.
29 (1960) 104 CLR 206.

Example: G Scammell and Nephew Ltd v HC & JG Ouston[30]

The parties agreed on the sale of a van, 'on the understanding that the balance of purchase price can be had on hire-purchase terms over a period of two years'. The House of Lords held that the agreement was too uncertain to be enforceable. As there were no common hire purchase terms, the agreement required further agreement of the parties.

Example: Fitzgerald v Masters[31]

The parties agreed to the sale of an interest in a farm. The final clause in the contract purported to embody a set of conditions of sale 'so far as they are inconsistent (sic)' with the terms of their agreement. In fact, no such set of conditions existed. The High Court held that this clause was meaningless and therefore void.[32]

Example: Biotechnology Australia Pty Ltd v Pace[33]

As part of an employment contract, a senior research scientist was given 'the option to participate in the Company's senior staff equity sharing scheme'. At the time the contract was entered into and at the time of termination, no such scheme had been established. The New South Wales Court of Appeal (Kirby P and McHugh JA, Hope JA dissenting) held that the reference to the scheme did not give rise to an enforceable contractual obligation.

Example: Lend Lease Financial Planning Ltd v Southcap Pty Ltd[34]

The parties entered into an agreement for lease. In relation to 'outgoings', the tenant agreed to 'pay a proportion based on the area of the tenancy to include airconditioning electricity costs'. The Queensland Court of Appeal held that this clause was sufficiently certain and ordered specific performance of the lease agreement.

[4.70] It will be interesting to monitor the evolving case law in this area. The modern approach, as demonstrated by the various judgments in the recent decision of the Queensland Court of Appeal in *Lend Lease Financial Planning Ltd v Southcap Pty Ltd*,[35] increasingly appears to emphasise the court's willingness to uphold an agreement entered into by the parties, particularly where the circumstances indicate that the parties intended to be bound by the agreement.

4.3.2   Agreements to negotiate

[4.75] Parties who are interested in pursuing some kind of joint venture, but are not yet at the stage of being able to commit to final, specific terms, may choose to enter an agreement to negotiate at a later stage. Sometimes these agreements are labelled 'heads

---

30   [1941] AC 251.
31   (1956) 95 CLR 420.
32   Note, however, that the court was prepared to sever the clause in the circumstances of the case. See further [4.135]–[4.140].
33   (1988) 15 NSWLR 130.
34   [1998] QCA 117; Butterworths unreported judgments, Queensland Court of Appeal, BC 9802393, 2 June 1998.
35   Ibid.

of agreement'. Enforceability issues arise where one party no longer wishes to continue negotiations, or where one party considers the other not to be negotiating in good faith, or otherwise breaching the terms of the agreement to negotiate.

[4.80] The legal status of an agreement to agree in the future is discussed in more detail below.[36] The basic proposition is that if parties do not reach final agreement on essential terms, instead agreeing to finalise such matters at a later time, that contract is an agreement to agree. As such, it is incomplete and will not be enforced.[37] If an agreement to negotiate is regarded as an agreement to agree, it too will be unenforceable and no action can be brought if one party withdraws from negotiations or does not negotiate in good faith.[38]

[4.85] Australia, England, and the United States have divergent approaches to the enforceability of agreements to negotiate. The House of Lords in England has adopted a conservative approach to the enforcement of such agreements. In *Walford v Miles*,[39] the House of Lords held a prospective seller of a photographic processing business not to be in breach of an agreement to negotiate by withdrawing from negotiations. In the opinion of Lord Ackner, the concept of a contractual obligation to negotiate was 'inherently repugnant to the adversarial position of the parties when involved in negotiations'.[40]

[4.90] While the American courts have not taken a consistent approach on this issue, the case law reveals a greater preparedness to enforce agreements to negotiate.[41]

[4.95] The current Australian position seems to fall somewhere between the traditional English and the more flexible American approaches. The leading decision on this point is that of the New South Wales Court of Appeal in *Coal Cliff Collieries Pty Ltd v Sijehama Pty Ltd*.[42] The parties were involved in negotiations for a complex joint venture agreement for a coal mine. They executed a 'Heads of Agreement' document in which they agreed to 'proceed in good faith to consult together upon the formulation of a more comprehensive and detailed Joint Venture Agreement'. Although, on the facts of the case, the Heads of Agreement document was held to be unenforceable, it was contemplated by Kirby P (with whom Waddell A-JA was in general agreement) that in appropriate circumstances, an agreement to negotiate could be enforceable. In the course of his detailed judgment, Kirby P reviewed the legal position governing agreements to negotiate in England, the United States and Australia. He concluded that if the parties provided good consideration and the terms of the agreement to

---

36   See [4.160].

37   *Booker Industries Pty Ltd v Wilson Parking (Qld) Pty Ltd* (1982) 149 CLR 600 at 604.

38   Professor McLauchlan in 'Rethinking Agreements to Agree' (1998) 18 *New Zealand Universities Law Review* 77 criticises this approach. If the parties intend to be bound by their agreement to agree on certain matters in the future, Professor McLauchlan believes such an agreement should be upheld. He argues that, for this reason, the time has come to rethink the established line of authorities relying on principles set out in *May & Butcher v The King* [1934] 2 KB 17. Compare also the legal status of a contractual obligation to mediate or conciliate which has been distinguished from a duty to negotiate in good faith: *Hooper Bailie Associated Ltd v Natcon Group Pty Ltd* (1992) 28 NSWLR 194 at 209.

39   [1992] 2 WLR 174.

40   Ibid at 181. See also *Courtney & Fairbairn Ltd v Tolaini Brothers (Hotels) Ltd* [1975] 1 WLR 297 at 301 per Lord Denning MR.

41   See further at [4.395]–[4.405].

42   (1991) 24 NSWLR 1.

negotiate were sufficiently certain, such agreements might be enforceable. One mechanism to make an agreement to negotiate more certain, it was suggested, would be to include a provision referring matters in dispute to a third party.

The direction taken by the judiciary in this area will be awaited with interest.[43] The increasing volume of literature from both Australia and the United States attests to the practical implications of whether such agreements can be enforceable.[44] There has been resistance to the view—as expressed by Kirby J—that an appropriately drafted agreement to negotiate may be enforceable. In *Coal Cliff Colieries Pty Ltd v Sijehama Pty Ltd*[45] itself, Handley JA adopted an orthodox approach by holding that a promise to negotiate is illusory. Many see a contractual obligation to negotiate as being repugnant to the very nature of the process of negotiation. On the other hand, an increasing number of academics and practitioners consider it time to free contracting parties from the shackles of contractual orthodoxy.[46] If parties indicate a desire to be contractually bound to negotiate in the future, and the language of the agreement is such that the courts can attribute a meaning to it, the agreement should be enforceable.[47] To do otherwise would be to frustrate the commercial expectations of the parties. Given the increasing extent to which the Australian courts have been influenced by the United States experience, it may be that the trend will be to assess each agreement on its merits rather than to adopt an approach of blanket refusal to enforce such agreements. Where the parties have built in strategies to ensure that meaning can be given to the agreement—whether by referral of matters in dispute to a third party or by reference to some other external standard—it may no longer be appropriate to label a contract to negotiate or head of agreement as an agreement to agree and, therefore, unenforceable.

43 In a recent decision of the Federal Court, Lindgren J cites Kirby P's comments in *Coal Cliff Collieries Pty Ltd v Sijehama Pty Ltd* (1991) 24 NSWLR 1 at 26, and notes that there is still uncertainty surrounding the question whether an agreement to negotiate in good faith is enforceable: *Vivian Fraser & Associates Pty Ltd v Shipton*, [1999] FCA 60, Federal Court of Australia New South Wales Registry, BC 9900162 (5 February 1999). In the case before the Federal Court, as the parties had not entered an explicit agreement to negotiate, a determination as to the enforceability of such an agreement did not need to be made. See also the comments of the New South Wales Court of Appeal in *Australis Media Holdings Pty Ltd v Telstra Corporation Ltd* (1998) 43 NSWLR 104 at 126–127 (cited by McMurdo P and Davies JA in the Queensland Court of Appeal in *Seymour CBD Pty Ltd v Maroochydore Convenience Centre Pty Ltd* [2000] QCA 327 at 7), that although Australian courts will not enforce an agreement to agree, 'the status of contracts to negotiate is more uncertain'.

44 EA Farnsworth, 'Pre-contractual Liability and Preliminary Agreements: Fair Dealing and Failed Negotiations' (1987) 87 *Columbia Law Report* 217 at 264; H Beale, 'Commentary on 'Good Faith and Fairness in Failed Contract Negotiations' ' (1995) 8 *Journal of Contract Law* 120 at 123; J Beaton, 'Commentary on "Good Faith and Fairness in Negotiated Contracts"' (1995) 8 *Journal of Contract Law* 138 at 139; RP Buckley, '*Walford v Miles*: False Certainty about Uncertainty —An Australian Perspective' (1993) 6 *Journal of Contract Law* 58; GK Flint, ' 'Enforce Them All': A Battle Cry for the Beleaguered Agreement to Negotiate' (1995) 13 *Australian Bar Review 262*; IB Stewart, 'Good Faith in Contractual Performance and in Negotiation' (1998) 72 ALJ 370.

45 (1991) 24 NSWLR 1.

46 IB Stewart, 'Good Faith in Contractual Performance and in Negotiation' (1998) 72 ALJ 370; AF Mason, 'Contract, Good Faith and Equitable Standards in Fair Dealing' (2000) 116 *Law Quarterly Review* 66.

47 After a comprehensive examination of the law in this area, Einstein J of the New South Wales Supreme Court in *Aiton v Transfield* [1999] NSWSC 996 (1 October 1999) indicated that, in appropriate circumstances, an agreement to negotiate would be enforceable if couched in sufficiently certain terms.

4.4   Saving ambiguous, uncertain or meaningless contracts

[4.100] The desire of courts to uphold rather than frustrate agreements is illustrated by the various techniques that have been used to hold parties to their promises notwithstanding the uncertainty or meaninglessness of one or more of the terms.

4.4.1   Link to external standard

[4.105] A clause in a contract which, on its face, appears uncertain may be enforceable if a meaning can be given to it by reference to an external standard. The parties may provide for 'a standard, machinery or formula designed by the parties to take the place of their own agreement'. [48] The reference may be made in a direct way by, for example, incorporating standard hire purchase terms used by the particular hiring company. If such a set of standard hire purchase terms exists, the clause will be valid. [49] Recourse may also be made to external standards, even where the contract itself does not expressly provide such a link. For example, in *Hillas and Co Ltd v Arcos Ltd*, [50] the contract for sale of Russian softwood timber also gave the purchaser an option to buy more timber for delivery in the next year. The option was held to be valid even though it did not state the kind, size or quality of the timber to be supplied, or the dates or ports of shipment. In coming to its decision, the House of Lords relied in part on the specifications agreed in the original contract for sale. To this extent, specifications in the contract could be regarded as an external standard.

[4.110] In contrast, the inability of the court to establish an external standard denied a senior research scientist relief when he sued to obtain the benefits under his employment package in *Biotechnology Australia Pty Ltd v Pace*. [51] Under the contract of employment, in addition to salary entitlements, the employee was given 'the option to participate in the Company's senior staff equity sharing scheme'. At the time of the contract and at the time of termination of employment, such a scheme had not been established. [52]

[4.115] Sometimes, the contract may provide for one or more terms to be inserted by a third party. In a fashion, this is also a link to an external standard. The extent to which such a mechanism will save an otherwise uncertain or incomplete agreement is considered later. [53]

4.4.2   Link to reasonableness standard

[4.120] Illustrative of the court's desire to be the upholders of contracts is their willingness to adopt principles of reasonableness to make certain something that, on its

---

48   *Hawthorn Football Club v Harding* [1988] VR 49 at 55.
49   Compare G *Scammell and Nephew Ltd v HC & JG Ouston* [1941] AC 251 where a similar reference was held to be invalid because of the numerous forms of hire purchase transactions and the varying terms which were incorporated in them.
50   (1932) 147 LT 503.
51   (1988) 15 NSWLR 130.
52   Failure to establish an external standard was also relevant to the decisions in *Whitlock v Brew* (1967) 118 CLR 445 and *Hall v Busst* (1960) 104 CLR 206.
53   See [4.175]–[4.180] below.

face, is uncertain. Lord Wright in *Hillas and Co Ltd v Arcos Ltd*[54] stated the proposition in the following way:

> ... there are appropriate implications of law, as for instance, the implication of what is just and reasonable to be ascertained by the court as matter of machinery where the contractual intention is clear but the contract is silent on some detail.[55]

Given that the parties in that case had clearly intended to be bound by the contract, the House of Lords was prepared to give meaning to clause 9 of the contract of sale which gave the purchasers an option to buy '100 000 standards for delivery during 1931'. The conclusion that this was a reference to a hundred thousand standards 'of softwood goods of fair specification' was reached by the House of Lords, both by reference to an earlier clause in the contract and by its preparedness to imply standards of reasonableness to otherwise uncertain clauses.

[4.125] Contracts for the sale of land that are subject to the purchaser obtaining satisfactory finance have also been challenged on uncertainty grounds. As will be examined later,[56] standards of reasonableness may also be relevant when considering the obligations of a purchaser in these circumstances, and whether such clauses will be void for uncertainty.

(a) Implying reasonable price

[4.130] Although a court is prepared to rely on standards of reasonableness to give meaning to an otherwise uncertain clause, the complete failure of a contract of sale to provide for the price of the property raises different issues. These are explored later.[57]

4.4.3 Severance

[4.135] A contract may comprise many terms, only one of which is void for uncertainty. The invalidity of one term will not necessarily mean that the whole contract will be struck down. In some circumstances, the invalid term can be severed and the remainder of the contract will be enforceable. The test for when a term may be severed from a contract was examined by the High Court in *Fitzgerald v Masters*.[58] It will be recalled[59] that this case involved a contract for the sale of an interest in land, clause 8 of the contract incorporating a set of conditions that did not in fact exist. On whether the contract could be saved by simply severing the meaningless clause 8, McTiernan, Webb and Taylor JJ had this to say:

> In the circumstances of the case it [clause 8] must be regarded simply as a compendious provision inserted by way of more abundant caution to cover such incidental matters as did not obtrude themselves for the consideration of the parties. But their intention that they should be bound by the declared terms is

---

54   (1932) 147 LT 503.
55   Ibid at 514.
56   See [4.285]–[4.305].
57   See [4.240]–[4.275].
58   (1956) 95 CLR 420.
59   See [4.65].

clear. And it is equally clear that they intended their agreement to subsist even if the provisions of clause 8 should fail to incorporate some term or terms from an identifiable form containing 'usual conditions'.[60]

As the parties would have intended to be bound in the absence of clause 8, the High Court upheld the contract of sale.

[4.140] A contrary decision will be reached where the offending clause forms a pivotal part of the contract, so that the parties would not have intended to be bound in its absence. The case of *Whitlock v Brew*[61] falls into this category. The granting of the lease to Shell was considered to be 'definitive of the ultimate rights which it is contemplated the purchaser is to get under his contract'.[62] Therefore, severance was not possible and the contract was held to be void for uncertainty.

4.4.4 Divisible obligations

[4.145] Most contracts cover one subject. It is unlikely for the same contract to provide for a sale of land from A to B as well as making provision for A to engage B's services as an architect. Nevertheless, parties are generally free to contract on whatever terms they wish and on whatever subject matter they desire. Where parties enter into a contract containing different kinds of obligations, and issues of uncertainty arise in relation to one aspect of their arrangement, severance of the latter part may be possible. The following case illustrates this point.

Example: The Life Insurance Company of Australia Ltd v Phillips[63]

A life insurance company entered into a policy of life insurance with Mr Phillips. The policy provided for payment of a specified sum on the death of Mr Phillips (the insured). In addition, the policy provided for the insured to borrow certain moneys from the insurance company in the circumstances set out. The insured claimed, among other things, that the policy of life insurance was void on the basis that the terms of the loan arrangement were ambiguous.

In finding in favour of the insurance company, the High Court held that even if the clauses relating to the loan arrangement were void for uncertainty, this part of the agreement could be severed and the remainder of the policy remained valid. In coming to its decision, the focus of the various Justices was on the independent nature of the obligations arising under the insurance policy. The first related to an obligation to pay an amount of money on the insured's death. The second related to the insurance company's obligation to advance money to the insured. Even if that obligation was ambiguous or uncertain, it was an independent, divisible obligation that could be severed from the agreement.[64] Knox CJ stated the test for severance in the same terms as discussed at [4.135]–[4.140]: that the question of whether the whole contract will be void depends on the intention of the parties to be gathered from the instrument as a whole. His Honour then went on to note that if the con-

---

60 (1956) 95 CLR 420 at 438.
61 (1967) 118 CLR 445. For facts of this case, see [4.65].
62 (1967) 118 CLR 445 at 461–462.
63 (1925) 36 CLR 60.
64 Ibid at 72 per Knox CJ, at 81–82 per Isaacs J and at 86 per Starke J.

tract is divisible, the part that is void may be separated from the rest without affecting its validity.[65]

Despite the reference to the intention of the parties, surprisingly the Justices did not examine whether both parties would have entered into the policy of life insurance if the promise to advance money did not form part of the contract. Perhaps this means that the test for severance, when used in the context of a contract containing independent or divisible obligations, may be applied differently from the way it is applied in the usual case where a contract relates to just one theme or subject matter.

4.4.5   *Waiver or removal of uncertainty*

[4.150] If a clause is inserted in a contract for the benefit of a party, that party may waive the benefit of the clause and the contract can continue to be performed.[66] As will be seen, this principle can be relevant where not all of the terms of a contract are in writing, as required by statute.[67] If the term that is not in writing is designed solely for the benefit of one party, that party can waive the benefit of the clause, and the remainder of the contract will be specifically enforceable. The same principles are equally relevant where one clause is void for uncertainty. If the clause is inserted for the benefit of one party only, but is drafted in such vague terms as to make it void, that party can choose to waive the benefit of the clause and have the remainder of the contract specifically enforced.[68]

[4.155] Applying the same principles, if the uncertainty in a contract is removed before a party tries to have the contract specifically enforced, the court will be able to grant specific enforcement even though the contract would not have been enforceable when it was first entered into. The following case provides an example.

Example: MacAulay v Greater Paramount Theatres Ltd[69]

The parties entered a contract for the sale of a 30-year leasehold interest in land. The purchaser was required to obtain the written approval of the head lessors to 'plans and specifications of the new building' prior to completion of the contract. Although the contract did not set out what the plans and specifications were to be, by the time the matter came before the court, the purchasers had obtained plans and specifications which, according to an expert witness, were sufficient for an architect to work on.

As the uncertainty was removed before the action commenced, the New South Wales Supreme Court granted specific performance of the contract.[70]

---

65   Ibid at 72.
66   See also [9.225].
67   See [11.80] and [11.125].
68   *Whitlock v Brew* (1967) 118 CLR 445 at 461.
69   (1922) 22 StRNSW 66.
70   See also *Bradford v Zahra* [1977] QdR 24 where the Queensland Supreme Court granted specific performance of a contract for sale on the same grounds.

4.5 Incomplete agreement

[4.160] Parties must reach final agreement on the essential aspects of the contract before they will be regarded as having entered a contract. It is not enough for them to leave a matter to be agreed upon at a later stage. That would be an agreement to agree which, as evidenced by the following extract from the judgment of Gibbs CJ, Murphy J, and Wilson J, is unenforceable:

> It is established by authority, both ancient and modern, that the courts will not lend their aid to the enforcement of an incomplete agreement, being no more than an agreement of the parties to agree at some time in the future.[71]

[4.165] The only word of caution to add to this statement is that while the principle that an agreement to agree cannot constitute an enforceable contract has not been the basis of widespread challenge,[72] argument has arisen about whether particular arrangements can properly be regarded as such agreements. Agreements to negotiate including 'Heads of Agreement' are an example.[73] Secondly, even if the parties do not finalise all the terms of the agreement themselves, but provide a mechanism for doing so, the agreement may no longer be regarded as an agreement to agree, and will be enforceable. The extent to which such reference can save an otherwise incomplete agreement is considered next.

4.5.1 Agreement contains mechanism to complete

[4.170] It may suit the needs of contracting parties not to finalise various aspects of their agreement, but rather to insert in it a mechanism for determining one or more terms at a later date. As we have seen, the parties may wish to link an aspect of their agreement to an external standard.[74] Another common technique is to leave matters to be determined by a third party.

(a) Reference to a third party

[4.175] It is well established that parties to a contract may leave terms of the contract to be decided by a third party. This principle extends even to essential terms.[75] For example, in a lease agreement containing an option for a further term, the parties could agree for rental during the option period to be determined by a third party.

[4.180] Sometimes, instead of a contract providing for a matter to be agreed by a third party, it may provide for the matter to be agreed by the parties themselves and, if they are unable to reach agreement, to be resolved by a third party, often an arbitrator. Despite the fact that the contract initially provides for future agreement by the parties themselves, such agreements are enforced by the courts. As the contract contains a

---

71 *Booker Industries Pty Ltd v Wilson Parking (Qld) Pty Ltd* (1982) 149 CLR 600 at 604. For a recent example of the refusal of the New Zealand Court of Appeal to enforce an agreement in which an essential term was left for later agreement by the parties, see *Barrett v IBC International Ltd* [1995] 3 NZLR 170.
72 Compare, however, views of Professor McLauchlan referred to in note 38 above.
73 See [4.75]–[4.95]
74 See [4.105]–[4.115].
75 *Godecke v Kirwan* (1973) 129 CLR 629 at 645.

mechanism to resolve any impasse, the parties are not *required* to agree in the future. The agreement will not offend the fundamental principle of completeness. Therefore, a contract for a football player to play for a named football club which provided 'the terms upon which the player shall represent [the Club] ... shall be such as shall be agreed between the parties ... as being fair and reasonable to both parties and in the event that any dispute or difference may arise for settling of such terms and conditions then such dispute or difference shall be referred to the determination of two arbitrators' was held by the Supreme Court of Victoria to be valid.[76] The machinery put in place by the parties meant that no further agreement was necessary for the contract to be carried out. Similarly, a lease that contained an option of a new term, the rent to be 'as may be mutually agreed between the lessor and the lessee and failing agreement then such rental as may be fixed by an arbitrator' was held by the High Court to be valid.[77] As the lease provided a mechanism for determining the rental, no further agreement between the parties was necessary.[78]

(b) Discretion retained by a contracting party

[4.185] A contract may purport to leave some matters to the discretion of one of the contracting parties. It may provide for one of the contracting parties, at a later stage, to finalise one or more terms of the agreement, or may leave to one of the parties a discretion as to the method of carrying out a particular obligation. Both of these techniques can raise difficult issues of enforceability, either because it is incomplete or uncertain, or because the promises contained in the agreement are illusory.

[4.190] There can be no doubt that a contract that leaves essential matters for later determination by one of the contracting parties will be unenforceable.[79] However, there is authority to suggest that a contract may be binding even if it leaves some matter to be determined by one of the contracting parties.

Example: Godecke v Kirwan[80]

The parties entered into an agreement relating to the sale of land. Clause 6 of the agreement provided that: 'if required by the vendor, the [purchaser] shall execute a further agreement to be prepared ... by [the vendor's] appointed solicitors containing the foregoing and such other covenants and conditions as they may reasonably require.' The vendor refused to complete the sale and claimed, on a number of grounds, that the contract was unenforceable.

The High Court held that the contract was binding. In relation to clause 6, Walsh J expressed the view that there was 'no reason in principle for holding that there

---

76   *Hawthorn Football Club Ltd v Harding* [1988] VR 49.

77   *Booker Industries Pty Ltd v Wilson Parking (Qld) Pty Ltd* (1982) 149 CLR 600.

78   Compare the strict approach adopted by the Court of Appeal in *May and Butcher v The King* [1934] 2 KB 17. A contract for the sale of goods provided for the price to be as agreed between the parties, and contained a separate clause referring disputes arising from the agreement to arbitration. The contract was held to be unenforceable. Viscount Dunedin commented (at 22) that failing to agree could not be regarded as a dispute, so could not be referred to arbitration. Therefore, it was held that there was no mechanism for determining the price.

79   *May and Butcher Ltd v The King* [1934] 2 KB 17 at 20.

80   (1973) 129 CLR 629.

cannot be any binding contract if some matter is left to be determined by one of the contracting parties'.[81] It was relevant to His Honour's determination that the clause only allowed a term to be inserted in the contract if it was not inconsistent with the terms of the offer, and if the term was reasonable. Gibbs J did not decide whether an agreement could leave further terms to be settled by one of the parties.[82] His Honour suggested that the position may be different if an agreement had been reached on all essential terms, and a subsidiary matter was left to the determination of one of the parties.[83] On the facts before the Court, however, a determination of this matter was not required because insertion of further terms was left to a third party (the vendor's solicitor), not to the vendor himself.[84]

It is unfortunate that different views were expressed by the Justices of the High Court on this important point. Given the limited extent to which Walsh J (with whom Mason J agreed) suggested that power to insert further terms could be validly conferred on a contracting party, and the failure of Gibbs J to support such a proposition, serious doubts must be cast over a contract that leaves a matter to be decided later by a party to the contract. This is particularly the case where the matter is other than a subsidiary one.

[4.195] Different considerations arise where a party is given discretion in relation to performance of stated contractual obligations. It is possible for a contract to confer on a party such a wide discretion that the party cannot be regarded as making any promise at all.[85] In such a case, that party's promise is illusory and cannot be regarded as amounting to an enforceable contract. On the other hand, if the discretion merely relates to the way the party carries out the contractual obligation, it will be enforceable.[86] It is sometimes difficult to distinguish between a promise that leaves some matter for the final determination of the contracting party, a promise which gives the promisor such a discretion as to render it illusory, and a promise that confers on the promisor a legitimate discretion governing the way in which he or she may perform a contractual obligation.

Example: Yaroomba Beach Development Company Pty Ltd v Coeur De Lion Investments Pty Ltd[87]

As part of an arrangement to sell property, a share agreement was entered into between the seller and purchaser. Under the agreement, the seller was to receive six life member class shares in a country club to be incorporated by the buyer. While

---

81   Ibid at 642.

82   Ibid at 646.

83   Ibid at 647.

84   Gibbs J did not explain the basis upon which a party's solicitor, retained to act on behalf of that party, could be regarded as a third party for these purposes.

85   See, for example, *Loftus v Roberts* (1902) 18 TLR 532 which involved an arrangement for the plaintiff to perform in a play that the defendant may have staged in a West-End theatre. As the defendant had a discretion whether to stage the play, and the plaintiff whether to act, there was held to be no contract which could be sued upon.

86   *Thorby v Goldberg* (1965) 112 CLR 597; *Yaroomba Beach Development Company Pty Ltd v Coeur De Lion Investments Pty Ltd* (1989) 18 NSWLR 398.

87   (1989) 18 NSWLR 398.

certain rights were to attach to such shares, details of those rights could not be final-ised until the club was incorporated. It was contended by the seller that the agree-ment was void because it was left to the purchaser to determine what rights would attach to the shares.

The New South Wales Supreme Court held that the share agreement was valid. Because the parties agreed on basic matters in relation to the shares, the fact that the purchaser had a 'latitude of choice' as to the way certain stipulations were to be car-ried into effect did not make the agreement void.

Again, the validity of such clauses is a matter of construction, and will turn on the individual facts of each case.[88]

4.5.2   Breakdown of mechanism to complete

[4.200] While parties may leave essential terms to be determined through some speci-fied mechanism, such as a decision of a third party, difficult legal issues can arise where the mechanism breaks down. The traditional view of contract formation is that the court will not rewrite the agreement for parties where the parties themselves have failed to agree on all terms. Following such an approach, if the parties have established a mechanism for determining a term and that mechanism fails, the court will not sub-stitute its own view and complete the agreement.[89] To do so would also be to com-plete the agreement for the parties.

[4.205] However, the High Court case of *Booker Industries Pty Ltd v Wilson Parking (Qld) Pty Ltd*[90] may signal a more relaxed application of these long-established principles.

Example: Booker Industries Pty Ltd v Wilson Parking (Qld) Pty Ltd[91]

The parties entered into a lease agreement under which the lessee was given an option to take a further term. The rental for that further term was 'to be agreed with the lessor or failing agreement to be determined by an arbitrator'.

The High Court held that the option constituted a valid agreement. In his judg-ment, Brennan J drew a distinction between a clause for determining price or rent where the manner of calculation as set out in the clause was essential to the parties, and a clause where the mechanism was simply one by which the parties could ascer-tain a reasonable price or rent. While in the former case, completion of the contract would be conditional upon determination of the price or rent in the manner specified, the same could not be said of the latter case. If the parties simply wish to establish a reasonable price or rent and the mechanism stated failed, Brennan J suggested that a court would be more inclined to substitute its own objective determination of a rea-sonable price or rent and uphold the agreement.

---

88   *Re Theodorou* [1993] 1 QdR 588 at 592–593.
89   *Milnes v Gery* (1807) 33 ER 574
90   (1982) 149 CLR 600.
91   Ibid.

[4.210] A similar approach was taken by the House of Lords in *Sudbrook Trading Estate Ltd v Eggleton*.[92] This case involved a contract under which the lessees were granted an option to purchase the property at a price 'as may be agreed upon by two valuers one to be nominated by the lessor and the other by the lessee and in default of such agreement by an umpire appointed by the ... valuers'. The House of Lords considered that the mechanism to establish a price was designed to obtain a fair and reasonable amount. In these circumstances, if the machinery broken down, the court indicated its preparedness to substitute its own machinery to determine a fair and reasonable price.

[4.215] While the High Court may not have departed from established principles to the same extent as the House of Lords, given the increased preparedness of courts to uphold agreements, particularly in a commercial context where the parties have indicated an intention to be bound, the courts may be more willing to treat clauses of the kind referred to above as merely devices designed to establish a reasonable price, rather than reflecting the parties' desire to obtain a 'price idiosyncratically fixed by a third party'.[93] Therefore, if the stated mechanism breaks down, a court may be prepared to determine a fair and reasonable price, and not to regard that determination as completing the agreement for the parties.

[4.220] Different principles apply where the contract is for the sale of goods and the price is to be fixed by the valuation of a third party. Here, the matter is governed by the sale of goods legislation in the various Australian jurisdictions.[94] Where the third party cannot or does not make such valuation, the agreement is void.[95] However, if the third party is prevented from so doing by the fault of one party, the other may maintain an action in damages against the former.[96] Further, notwithstanding the above, if any of the goods have been delivered to and appropriated by the buyer, he or she must pay a reasonable price for them.[97]

4.6 Saving incomplete agreements

[4.225] As discussed in relation to ambiguous, uncertain, and meaningless contracts, the desire of the courts to uphold agreements is also evident in the strategies used to enforce agreements that, on their face, appear to be incomplete.

---

92 [1983] AC 444.

93 *Booker Industries Pty Ltd v Wilson Parking (Qld) Pty Ltd* (1982) 149 CLR 600 at 614.

94 *Sale of Goods Act* 1896 (Qld), s 12; *Sale of Goods Act* 1923 (NSW), s 14; *Goods Act* 1958 (Vic), s 14; *Sale of Goods Act* 1895 (WA), s 9; *Sale of Goods Act* 1895 (SA), s 9; *Sale of Goods Act* 1896 (Tas), s 14; *Sale of Goods Act* 1972 (NT), s 14; *Sale of Goods Act* 1954 (ACT), s 14.

95 *Sale of Goods Act* 1896 (Qld), s 12(1); *Sale of Goods Act* 1923 (NSW), s 14(1); *Goods Act* 1958 (Vic), s 14(1); *Sale of Goods Act* 1895 (WA), s 91(1); *Sale of Goods Act* 1895 (SA), s 9(1); *Sale of Goods Act* 1896 (Tas), s 14(1); *Sale of Goods Act* 1972 (NT), s 14(1); *Sale of Goods Act* 1954 (ACT), s 14(1).

96 *Sale of Goods Act* 1896 (Qld), s 12(2); *Sale of Goods Act* 1923 (NSW), s 14(2); *Goods Act* 1958 (Vic), s 14(2); *Sale of Goods Act* 1895 (WA), s 9(2); *Sale of Goods Act* 1895 (SA), s 9(2); *Sale of Goods Act* 1896 (Tas), s 14(2); *Sale of Goods Act* 1972 (NT), s 14(2); *Sale of Goods Act* 1954 (ACT), s 14(2).

97 *Sale of Goods Act* 1896 (Qld), s 12(1A); *Sale of Gods Act* 1923 (NSW), s 14(1); *Goods Act* 1958 (Vic), s 14(1); *Sale of Goods Act* 1895 (WA), s 9(1); *Sale of Goods Act* 1895 (SA), s 9(1); *Sale of Goods Act* 1896 (Tas), s 14(1); *Sale of Goods Act* 1972 (NT), s 14(2); *Sale of Goods Act* 1954 (ACT), s 14(1).

4.6.1 Implication of terms

[4.230] The willingness of the courts to imply terms into agreements was illustrated by the decision of the House of Lords in *Hillas and Co Ltd v Arcos Ltd*,[98] a case involving the enforceability of an option to sell Russian softwood timber. The contract did not specify the quality or price of the timber nor the dates for delivery. Discussing the English legal maxim '*verba ita sunt intelligenda ut res magis valeat quam pereat*',[99] Lord Thankerton had this to say:

> That maxim, however, does not mean that the court is to make a contract for the parties, or to go outside the words they had used, except insofar as there are appropriate implications of law, as for instance, the implication of what is just and reasonable to be ascertained by the court as matter of machinery where the contractual intention is clear but the contract is silent on some details. Thus in contracts for future performance over a period, the parties may neither be able nor desire to specify many matters of detail, but leave them to be adjusted in the working out of the contract. Save for the legal implication I have mentioned, such contracts might well be incomplete or uncertain; with that implication in reserve they are neither incomplete nor uncertain. As obvious illustrations I may refer to such matters as prices or times of delivery in contracts for the sale of goods, or times for loading or discharging in a contract of sea carriage. Furthermore, even if the construction of the words used may be difficult, that is not a reason for holding them to ambiguous or uncertain to be enforced if the fair meaning of the parties can be extracted.[100]

[4.235] Naturally, there are limits on the extent to which a court will imply a term or terms. If the parties have not reached agreement on the essential terms, the contract is unlikely to be saved in this way. Further, the greater the number of terms not finally agreed upon by the parties, the less inclined a court will be to exercise its discretion to imply a term. Of course, each case will be decided on its own facts. In *Hall v Busst*,[101] concerning a contract for the sale of land, Fullagar J opined that the contract could only be regarded as concluded if the parties agreed on the three essential elements: the parties, the subject matter, and the price. His Honour continued that if these elements had been agreed upon with sufficient certainty, 'the law will supply the rest'.[102]

It is difficult to predict with any certainty whether a court will be prepared to imply terms in a particular case. The inconsistency in the case law is especially pronounced where the contract relates to the sale of goods or land and the parties have not reached final determination as to price.[103] Having said that, however, it appears

---

98 (1932) 147 LT 503.
99 Translated, this Latin maxim means that words are to be so construed that the thing may avail rather than perish: P Butt & PE Nygh (editors), *Butterworths Concise Australian Legal Dictionary*, 2nd edn, North Ryde, 1998.
100 (1932) 147 LT 503 at 514. Courts, both in England and Australia, have continued to apply such principles: see, for example, *G Scammell and Nephew Ltd v HC & JG Ouston* [1941] AC 251 at 255 and *Hawthorn Football Club Ltd v Harding* [1988] VR 49 at 56.
101 (1960) 104 CLR 206.
102 Ibid at 222.
103 For this reason, this topic is dealt with separately at [4.240]–[4.275].

that two other factors may be relevant in the courts determination. First, if it is clear that the parties have gone beyond the stage of negotiation and intend to be contractually bound, the court will be more minded to imply a term and enforce the agreement.[104] Secondly, and related to the first consideration, if the contract has been partly executed—for example in a contract for the sale of goods, property has been delivered and title has passed—the court will seek to imply a term necessary for the validity the agreement.[105]

4.6.2 Failure to specify price

[4.240] Issues of incompleteness frequently arise where parties fail to expressly fix a price in contracts for the sale of goods or land, or for rental in an option to renew a lease for a further period. While failure to specify price is merely one example of incompleteness, given its prevalence in the case law and practical importance, this aspect will be considered separately. Whether the agreement will be upheld can turn on precisely how the agreement makes provision [or fails to make provision] for the price. The outcome may also depend on the subject matter of the agreement. Before proceeding, it is worth observing the comments of Menzies J in *Hall v Busst*[106] in relation to contracts for sale generally:

> The starting point in considering this must be that there can be no binding contract of sale without agreement as to price.[107]

(a) Contract is silent on price

[4.245] The general principle is that a contract will only be regarded as validly constituted if the parties have agreed on its essential terms. Applying this principle, failure of the parties to agree on price would mean that the contract is not complete, and would not be upheld by the court. However, the common law on this point is not so straightforward. First, it appears that contracts for the sale of land are treated differently from contracts for the sale of goods. In the latter case, the courts are sometimes prepared to imply a term that the purchaser will pay a reasonable price for the goods.[108] A court will more readily make such an implication where both parties clearly intend to be bound by the agreement. This intention is demonstrated, for example, where the contract is partly executed and property in the goods has passed.[109] A contract for the sale of land is treated differently. A court will not imply a term for payment at a reasonable price into a contract for the sale of land.[110]

---

104 *Hillas and Co Ltd v Arcos Ltd* (1932) 147 LT 503 at 514; *O'Sullivan v The National Trustees Executors and Agency Company of Australasia Ltd* [1913] VLR 173; *Palmer v Bank of NSW* [1973] 2 NSWLR 244.
105 *Hall v Busst* (1960) 104 CLR 206 at 233.
106 (1960) 104 CLR 206.
107 Ibid at 232.
108 *Hall v Busst* (1960) 104 CLR 206 at 240–243 per Windeyer J.
109 *Hall v Busst* (1960) 104 CLR 206 at 242 per Windeyer J; *F&G Sykes (Wessex) Ltd v Fine Fare Ltd* [1967] 1 Lloyd's Rep 53 at 57–58 per Lord Denning MR.
110 *Hall v Busst* (1960) 104 CLR 206 at 240 per Windeyer J; *Stocks & Holdings (Constructors) Pty Ltd v Arrowsmith* (1964) 112 CLR 646 at 650 per Barwick CJ.

[4.250] With the enactment of the sale of goods legislation throughout Australia, the position is now clear for contracts for the sale of goods. If the contract is silent as to price, the buyer is required to pay a reasonable price.[111]

(b) Contract provides for parties to agree in future

[4.255] An agreement to agree in the future also offends against the general principle of completeness. Although the parties in such a case have turned their minds to the issue of price, this will not necessarily mean that the contract will be upheld. Unfortunately, the case authorities are not entirely consistent. However, it can at least be said that the outcome is likely to differ depending on the nature of the contract. If the contract is for a sale of goods, there is authority to suggest that a court may imply a term that the goods will be sold at a reasonable price, and the contract will be upheld.[112] On the other hand, an agreement by the parties to agree later on a price in a contract to sell land, or on rental in an option to renew a lease, is unlikely to be upheld.[113] it is submitted that contracts dealing with land where parties agree to agree in the future about price or rental are likely to be treated in the same way as contracts that are silent on those matters.

(c) Contract makes provision for mechanism to complete

[4.260] A contract that contains a mechanism for setting a term at a later time is likely to be valid. It is not uncommon for such a mechanism to be used in relation to setting a price. The legal position is not so settled where the mechanism provided for by the contract breaks down. Both of these issues were addressed earlier.[114]

(d) Contract provides for payment of a reasonable price

[4.265] The law is also not entirely settled where the parties agree to sell for a 'reasonable price' or a 'fair value', but do not otherwise provide a mechanism for establishing what that price might be. Once again, whether the agreement is upheld as being sufficiently certain may turn on the nature of the subject matter in dispute. A

---

111 *Sale of Goods Act* 1896 (Qld), s 11(2); *Goods Act* 1958 (Vic), s 13(2); *Sale of Goods Act* 1923 (NSW), s 13(2); *Sale of Goods Act* 1895 (WA), s 8(2); *Sale of Goods Act* 1895 (SA), s 8(2); *Sale of Goods Act* 1896 (Tas), s 13(2); *Sale of Goods Act* 1954 (ACT), s 13(2); *Sale of Goods Act* 1972 (NT), s 13(2). Note, however, that these provisions will only be of assistance where the parties have reached agreement on all other essential terms of the agreement: *Australia and New Zealand Banking Group Ltd v Frost Holdings Pty Ltd* [1989] VR 695 at 703.

112 *Foley v Classique Coaches Ltd* [1934] 2 KB 1. Contrast *May and Butcher v The King* [1934] 2 KB 17. It may also be that the *Sale of Goods* legislation in the various jurisdictions will be relevant here. Where the parties agree to agree on price in the future, they may not be regarded as having fixed the price in accordance with the relevant provision: *Sale of Goods Act* 1896 (Qld), s 11(1); *Sale of Goods Act* 1923 (NSW), s 13(1); *Goods Act* 1958 (Vic), s 13(1); *Sale of Goods Act* 1895 (SA), s 8(1); *Sale of Goods Act* 1895 (WA), s 8(1); *Sale of Goods Act* 1896 (Tas), s 13(1); *Sale of Goods Act* 1972 (NT), s 13(1); *Sale of Goods Act* 1954 (ACT), s 13(1). Therefore, the buyer may be required to pay a reasonable price for the goods: *Sale of Goods Act* 1896 (Qld), s 11(2); *Sale of Goods Act* 1923 (NSW), s 13(2); *Goods Act* 1958 (Vic), s 13(2); *Sale of Goods Act* 1895 (SA), s 8(2); *Sale of Goods Act* 1895 (WA), s 8(2); *Sale of Goods Act* 1896 (Tas), s 13(2); *Sale of Goods Act* 1972 (NT), s 13(2); *Sale of Goods Act* 1954 (ACT), s 13(2).

113 *Stocks & Holdings (Constructors) Pty Ltd v Arrowsmith* (1964) 112 CLR 646 at 650 per Barwick CJ; *Randazzo v Goulding* [1968] QdR 433 at 441.

114 See [4.170]–[4.195] and [4.200]–[4.220].

contract for the sale of goods at a reasonable price is likely to be valid.[115] 'Reasonable price' is an objective standard that can be determined without further agreement between the parties. If one party breaches the agreement, the court can assess the price to be attributed to the goods, and damages can be awarded accordingly.[116]

[4.270] It has been suggested that the position may be different if the contract is for the sale of land—or perhaps even for a sale of goods, if they are unique or of a very special character, such as an original painting by a master. In *Hall v Busst*,[117] for example, the contract was for the sale of land, the purchase price being calculated by reference to 'the value of all additions and improvements to the said property since the date of purchase' and to 'the value of deficiencies of chattel property and a reasonable sum to cover depreciation of all buildings and other property on the land'. In a split decision by the High Court, an action for damages for breach of the contract failed. The clause to determine the sale price was held to be void for uncertainty. On the facts of that case, Dixon CJ and Menzies J found that the clause was not sufficiently certain as there was not an established market for the particular property in question. Two strong dissenting judgments were delivered by Kitto and Windeyer JJ. In upholding the validity of the contract, they concluded that it was possible to attach a value to the subject matter.

[4.275] Given the more liberal approach taken by the High Court in *Booker Industries Pty Ltd v Wilson Parking (Qld) Pty Ltd*[118] in relation to the court's preparedness to substitute its own mechanism for arriving at a reasonable rental where the mechanism established by the parties breaks down, it will be interesting to observe the approach of the Australian courts on this issue in the future.

4.7 'Subject to' agreements

[4.280] Sometimes parties may be ready to sign a contract but not able or not prepared to commit to one or more aspects of the agreement. In these circumstances, parties may decide to enter into agreements 'subject to' the happening of a particular event. 'Subject to finance' agreements and agreements that are 'subject to contract' are common illustrations of such agreements. Both kinds of agreement raise aspects of uncertainty and incompleteness.

4.7.1 'Subject to finance' agreements

[4.285] Most purchasers of land have insufficient personal funds to complete the purchase themselves, and need to borrow from a lending institution. A purchaser who has found a house to buy but has not yet had finance approved may not wish to enter an

---

115 This is particularly the case as the *Sale of Goods* legislation in the various jurisdictions provide for payment by the buyer of a reasonable price in the circumstances set out: *Sale of Goods Act* 1896 (Qld), s 11(2); *Sale of Goods Act* 1923 (NSW), s 13(2); *Goods Act* 1958 (Vic), s 13(2); *Sale of Goods Act* 1895 (SA), s 8(2); *Sale of Goods Act* 1895 (WA), s 8(2); *Sale of Goods Act* 1896 (Tas), s 13(2); *Sale of Goods Act* 1972 (NT), s 13(2); *Sale of Goods Act* 1954 (ACT), s 13(2).

116 *British Bank of Foreign Trade Ltd v Novinex Ltd* [1949] 1 KB 623. Contrast the views expressed in *Hall v Busst* (1960) 104 CLR 206 at 234–235 per Menzies J.

117 (1960) 104 CLR 206.

118 (1982) 149 CLR 600, as discussed in [4.205].

unconditional contract.[119] If an unconditional contract is entered into and the purchaser cannot obtain the necessary finance to pay the vendor the purchase price, the purchaser will be in breach of contract and potentially liable to pay the vendor damages. To accommodate purchasers in such cases, contracts for sale may contain a clause stating that the contract is subject to 'the purchaser receiving approval for finance on satisfactory terms and conditions'. This is referred to as a 'subject to finance' clause. The contract is binding immediately on the parties, but will come to an end if the purchaser is unable to obtain finance and terminates the contract pursuant to its terms. It is an example of a condition subsequent, considered further later.[120]

'Subject to finance' clauses have been challenged on the bases that they are too uncertain, and that because they give such a wide discretion to a purchaser concerning the rejection of finance, the purchaser's promise to buy is illusory. More particularly, two practical issues can arise from the subject to finance clause. First, the uncertainty surrounding the 'satisfactory' nature of the finance. Secondly, the uncertainty surrounding the steps that must be taken by the purchaser to obtain such finance in order to satisfy the obligations imposed by the contract. Both of these matters were addressed by the High Court in *Meehan v Jones*.[121]

(a) 'Satisfactory finance'

[4.290] It was argued in *Meehan v Jones* [122] that a clause which provided for finance to be obtained on 'satisfactory terms' was either too uncertain to be valid, or gave the purchaser such a wide discretion that it was illusory. This view was not accepted by the High Court. As the clause was inserted for the benefit of the purchaser, the determination of whether the finance was satisfactory was left to the purchaser. Interpreted in this way, none of the Justices considered the clause too uncertain. Gibbs CJ, Mason, and Wilson JJ were of the view that in making this determination, the purchaser was required, at the very least, to act honestly.[123] On this interpretation, the clause would not be too uncertain, as the court is able to make a determination about whether the purchaser acted honestly. Further, as the purchaser was under an obligation to act honestly, it could not be said that the purchaser's promise was illusory.

(b) Steps to be taken to obtain finance

[4.295] The finance clauses in most standard land contracts impose an obligation on the purchaser to take all steps reasonably necessary to obtain finance approval. The nature of the purchaser's obligation where the finance clause is silent on this point is not entirely settled. This issue was considered by three Justices in *Meehan v Jones*.[124]

---

119   In this context, 'unconditional contract' means a contract which does not contain a term stating that the contract is subject to the purchaser being able to arrange finance.

120   See [9.225].

121   (1981) 149 CLR 571.

122   Ibid.

123   The Justices considered that there may be an additional requirement for the purchaser to act reasonably in determining whether the finance was satisfactory. However, the clause would also be valid if this were the test. Murphy J did not consider that an obligation to act honestly added anything to a purchaser's obligation. While His Honour also considered that there was no justification for implying that the purchaser act reasonably, he nevertheless considered the clause to be valid.

124   (1981) 149 CLR 571.

Unfortunately, the issue was dealt with only briefly, and the approaches taken were not entirely consistent. Gibbs CJ was not prepared to imply into the contract an obligation on the part of the purchaser to make reasonable efforts to obtain finance.[125] His Honour noted that although the parties may have expected that to be the case, they did not contract to that effect. Mason and Wilson JJ, on the other hand, were of the view that the purchaser was required to do all that was reasonable to obtain the finance.[126] The approach taken by Mason and Wilson JJ seems to reflect more accurately the intention of the parties. As the contract was made subject to the purchaser obtaining satisfactory finance, the parties must have contemplated that the purchaser would seek to obtain finance.

[4.300] The views expressed by Mason and Wilson JJ are even more persuasive if purchasers undertake to use their 'best endeavours' to obtain finance.[127] Such a clause was considered by the Supreme Court of Western Australia in *Jetcity Pty Ltd v Yenald Nominees Pty Ltd*.[128] While Owen J noted that the obligation to use best endeavours has an established meaning,[129] the phrase had to be considered in the context of the way it was used in the case before him, namely in a subject to finance clause. Owen J considered the comments of the High Court in *Meehan v Jones* [130] and a recent decision of the Full Court of the Supreme Court of Western Australia[131] that the subject to finance clause conferred on a purchaser a duty to act honestly, and perhaps honestly and reasonably. His Honour concluded that on the facts of the case before him, at the very least there was a requirement to act honestly in using best endeavours to obtain the loan.

[4.305] Where a purchaser undertakes to use best endeavours to obtain finance, the contract can be distinguished from that considered by the High Court in *Meehan v Jones*.[132] Notwithstanding the approach taken by Owen J outlined above, there appear to be two distinct issues in such a case. The first relates to steps that must be taken by the purchaser to obtain finance. While the court was divided on this point in *Meehan v Jones*,[133] the contract under consideration did not contain a best endeavours clause. If the contract contains a best endeavours clause, it is submitted that an objective test should be used to ascertain whether a purchaser has used best endeavours to obtain finance. The purchaser will be required to act reasonably in obtaining finance. The second and distinct issue is whether, after using such steps to obtain finance, the finance is satisfactory. The comments made by the High Court remain relevant here. In determining whether finance is satisfactory, at the very least the purchaser has an obligation to act honestly, or perhaps honestly and reasonably.

---

125 Ibid at 581.
126 (1981) 149 CLR 571 per Mason J at 591 and per Wilson J at 598.
127 See further [9.360].
128 Butterworths unreported judgment, Supreme Court of Western Australia (9 April 1999), BC9901721.
129 *Paltara Pty Ltd v Dempster* (1991) 6 WAR 85 at 89; *Transfield Pty Ltd v Arlo International Ltd* (1980) 144 FCLR 83 at 101; *Sheffield District Railway Co v Great Central Railway Co* (1911) 27 TLR 451.
130 (1981) 149 CLR 571.
131 *Erley Pty Ltd v Gunzberg Nominees Pty Ltd*, unreported decision, library number 980153, 3 April 1998.
132 (1981) 149 CLR 571.
133 Ibid.

4.7.2 'Subject to contract'

[4.310] In the course of negotiations, parties may come to agreement on all relevant terms, yet make their agreement 'subject to contract'. It is not always an easy task to determine whether, before the formal contract is entered into, the parties are contractually bound. The High Court directly addressed this issue in *Masters v Cameron*[134] and concluded that, in such circumstances, the case could fall into one of three categories:[135]

- The parties have reached finality in arranging all terms and intend to be immediately bound to perform those terms, but at the same time propose to have the terms restated in a form which will be fuller or more precise but not different in effect—binding contract formed.

- The parties have completely agreed upon all terms and intend no departure from or addition to those terms, but have made performance of one or more of the terms conditional upon the execution of a formal document—binding contract formed.

- The intention of the parties is not to make a concluded bargain at all, unless and until they execute a formal contract—no binding contract formed.

[4.315] The category a particular case falls into turns on the intention of the parties. If the parties intend the agreement to be binding on them even before entry into the final contract, the contract will fall into one of the first two categories above.

[4.320] In the course of its judgment, the High Court comments, in relation to terms such as 'subject to contract' and 'subject to the preparation of a formal contract' that:

> It has been recognised throughout the cases on the topic that such words prima facie create an overriding condition, so that what has been agreed upon must be regarded as the intended basis for a future contract and not as constituting a contract.[136]

At face value, these words suggest that the use of terms such as 'subject to contract' might raise a presumption of some kind against there being a binding contract. However, this approach has not been adopted in the Australian courts.[137] The real question is that of the intention of the parties and, in gleaning that intention, the language used in the first agreement will be a relevant factor. It will not, however, be the only factor. Also relevant is the conduct of the parties.[138]

[4.325] The case law provides illustrations of the three categories described by the High Court in *Masters v Cameron*.[139]

---

134 (1954) 91 CLR 353.

135 Ibid at 360.

136 (1954) 91 CLR 353 at 363.

137 See, for example, *Sheehan v Zaszlos* [1995] 2 QdR 210 at 213. Contrast the more restrictive approach of the New Zealand courts, as set out in [4.375].

138 *Sheehan v Zaszlos* [1995] 2 QdR 210 at 213. See, for example, *Marek v Australasian Conference Association Pty Ltd* [1994] 2 QdR 521 where it was suggested that engaging solicitors to assist in the preparation of a contract for the sale of land indicates a likelihood that the parties do not wish to be finally committed before that contract is executed.

139 (1954) 91 CLR 353.

(a) First category

[4.330] There are a number of examples of cases falling within the first category described in *Masters v Cameron*.[140]

Example: Branca v Corbarro [141]

The parties agreed to the sale of a mushroom farm, the buyer paying a deposit to the seller. The agreement contained a clause stating that the agreement was 'a provisional agreement until a fully legalised agreement, drawn up by a solicitor and embodying all the conditions herewith stated, is signed'.

The English Court of Appeal held that the parties intended to be bound immediately. Relevant to this determination was the use of the words 'provisional' and 'until'. Also relevant was payment by the purchaser to be made by a date before the formal agreement was to be executed.

(b) Second category

[4.335] Agreements where parties use the term 'subject to contract' are most likely to fall within the first or third categories. Cases falling within the second are rare, but one such example is set out below.

Example: Niesmann v Collingridge[142]

The parties agreed on the sale of land, the seller signing a written document which provided for a certain portion of the price to be payable 'on the signing of contract'. The document also contained a statement that 'value received for option sixpence' and that amount was paid by the purchaser to the seller.

The New South Wales Supreme Court held that the parties had entered into a binding agreement. The offer was not expressed to be 'subject to' or 'conditional upon' the execution of a formal contract. The execution of the contract was simply relevant for the fixing of a date for payment of the purchase money. All of the essential terms had been agreed upon.

(c) Third category

[4.340] The High Court decision of *Masters v Cameron* [143] itself provides an example of a case falling within the third category.

Example: Masters v Cameron [144]

The parties agreed to the sale of a farm. The agreement was stated to be 'subject to the preparation of a formal contract of sale which shall be acceptable to [the vendor's] solicitors on the above terms and conditions'. The purchaser agreed to the purchase in these terms, paid a deposit to the vendor's agent and, among other things,

---

140 Ibid.
141 [1947] 1 KB 854. See also *Southcoast Oils (Qld and NSW) Pty Ltd v Look Enterprises Pty Ltd* [1988] 1 QdR 680.
142 (1921) 29 CLR 177.
143 (1954) 91 CLR 353.
144 Ibid.

made some minor structural alterations to the property. The purchaser subsequently claimed that a binding contract had not been entered into.

The High Court agreed, and held that a binding agreement had not been entered into. The parties had not intended to be bound until they entered into a formal document. The payment of deposit to the seller was made on the basis that if a formal contract should be executed, that amount should be treated as a deposit and, if such an agreement were not entered into, should be returned to the purchaser.

4.8 International perspective

4.8.1 New Zealand

[4.345] The New Zealand law on the requirements of certainty and completeness is largely the same as the Australian law. The leading New Zealand authority is the Court of Appeal decision of *Attorney-General v Barker Bros Ltd*,[145] a case concerning the enforceability of an option to renew in a lease that stated: 'the terms and conditions of any such lease shall be as agreed upon by the parties at the time, but the rent shall not be less than the amount paid hereunder'. The lease also contained an arbitration clause. The Court of Appeal held that the option was enforceable and, after a review of the relevant authorities, considered that the cases supported the following three propositions:[146]

1 If it appears that the true intention of the parties was not to enter into a binding arrangement until and unless certain unsettled terms of their bargain were settled by agreement between them, then no contract can come into existence in the absence of such further agreement;

2 If the court is satisfied that the real intention of the parties was to enter into an immediate and binding agreement then the court will do its best to give effect to that intention; and

3 Apparent lack of certainty will be cured if some means or standard can be found whereby that which has been left uncertain can be rendered certain.

[4.350] These principles are consistent with those operating in Australia. However, there has been some divergence between the jurisdictions in the way these broad principles have manifested themselves in decisions.

(a) Agreements to negotiate

[4.355] The divergent approaches taken in England, Australia and the United States were discussed earlier.[147] The conservative English approach is that an agreement to negotiate can only be regarded as an agreement for the parties to agree in the future and, as such, is unenforceable. Traditionally, the cases have demonstrated a reluctance by the New Zealand judiciary to depart from these established principles.[148] Having

---

145   [1976] 2 NZLR 495.
146   Ibid at 498–499.
147   See [4.85]–[4.95].
148   JF Burrows, J Finn & SMD Todd, *Law of Contract in New Zealand*, 8th edn, Butterworths, Wellington, 1997, pp 79–80.

said this, however, in a recent decision of the New Zealand Court of Appeal,[149] no doubts were raised about the validity of such a clause. The parties in that case had entered into a contract for the provision of residential care beds for the elderly. The contract was for a specified period, and contained a clause that on the expiration of the existing term, the parties would negotiate in good faith on the terms of a new agreement. On these facts, the Court held that the parties intended to be legally bound by the agreement to negotiate the terms of a future agreement. This approach appears to reflect that taken by Kirby P in *Coal Cliff Collieries Pty Ltd v Sijehama Pty Ltd*,[150] where his Honour suggested that such an agreement should be enforceable if the parties indicated a desire to be contractually bound, and the agreement was such that the courts could attribute a meaning to it.[151]

(b) Mechanisms to determine terms in agreements to agree

[4.360] As in Australia, a contract may be regarded as sufficiently certain, even if not all of the essential terms have been settled by the parties, if the parties have agreed upon a mechanism by which these matters could later be determined. However, in one important respect, the New Zealand law seems to be more liberal than the Australian law. The New Zealand case law indicates an increased preparedness to uphold an agreement despite the failure of a mechanism to determine an essential term or, further, the failure of parties to overtly insert such a mechanism. *Money v Ven-Lu-Ree Ltd*[152] is a case involving the sale of shares. The parties agreed that the sellers would seek a valuation of them from each shareholder's accountant as at a particular date. The agreement did not provide any guidance as to the basis upon which the valuation would occur, or how the parties would resolve any dispute about such a valuation. Despite the deficiencies in the mechanism for determining the share price, the New Zealand Court of Appeal (and in turn the Privy Council) upheld the agreement. The New Zealand Court of Appeal was prepared to imply a term that the matter should proceed to arbitration if the parties failed to agree on a price. This was so despite the failure of the agreement itself to provide such a mechanism. The more radical basis for upholding the agreement suggested by the Court of Appeal (and accepted by the Privy Council), however, was the significance attached to the fact that the parties intended the price to be determined objectively. According to the Court, this alone meant that the contract was sufficiently certain. In other words, an indication that a particular term is to be determined according to objective criteria may in itself constitute the machinery to make the contract sufficiently certain. To that extent, the New Zealand judiciary has taken a more liberal approach than appears to be the case in both Australia and England.

---

149 *Residential Care (New Zealand) Incorporated v New Zealand Hospitals Association Incorporated* [2000] NZCA 128 (17 July 2000).
150 (1991) 24 NSWLR 1.
151 It is also consistent with the views of Professor McLauchlan as referred to in footnote 38 above.
152 [1988] 2 NZLR 414 (Court of Appeal decision) and [1989] 3 NZLR 129 (Privy Council decision).

(c) 'Subject to' agreements

[4.365] In general terms, similar considerations to those in Australia are relevant in New Zealand in determining whether a 'subject to' agreement is enforceable. However, two areas of difference are worthy of note.

Agreements that are 'subject to finance'

[4.370] The New Zealand approach to subject to finance clauses is slightly different from the Australian position as expressed in *Meehan v Jones*.[153] It will be recalled that there are two issues where the validity of a contract containing a subject to finance clause is called into question. The first is the steps that must be taken by the purchaser to obtain finance. In the absence of a clause requiring a purchaser to take reasonable steps to obtain such finance, the High Court refrained from implying a term to that effect in a contract.[154] However, New Zealand courts are more likely to imply a term that a purchaser must take reasonable steps in seeking finance.[155] The second issue is how to determine whether the available finance is 'satisfactory'. While the position in Australia appears to be that the purchaser must at least act honestly in this regard, the question as to whether the purchaser should also be required to act reasonably has not been definitively determined. The position is different in New Zealand. The Court is likely to imply a term that the purchaser must act reasonably in determining whether the terms of the finance should be accepted.[156]

Agreements that are 'subject to contract'

[4.375] As is the case in Australia, where agreement is expressed to be 'subject to contract' or parties have stated in the course of negotiations that they intend to enter a formal agreement, whether they are legally bound depends on their intention. While the test of intention is the same, it appears that a New Zealand court may be more likely to draw an inference that the parties do not intend to be bound until a formal document is drawn up and executed. The leading New Zealand authority on the point is *Carruthers v Whitaker*,[157] a case involving the sale of land. Here, the parties reached preliminary agreement, but then put the matter in the hands of their solicitors. In determining that the parties lacked legal intention, the ordinary and customary manner of becoming bound was considered relevant. For contracts for the sale of land, parties and solicitors contemplate that a person will only be bound once a formal agreement is signed. In this way, both parties are protected and certainty is given to the agreement. The inference to be drawn from these factors is a lack of intention to be legally bound until a formal document is signed.

Subsequently, this inference has been applied by the Court of Appeal to cover more general cases of commercial contracts where there is no formality requirement.[158] More recently, the Court of Appeal has described it as a 'principle of some

---

153 (1981) 149 CLR 571.
154 See [4.295]–[4.305].
155 *Connor v Pukerau Store Ltd* [1981] NZLR 384 at 388.
156 JF Burrows, J Finn and SMD Todd, *Law of Contract in New Zealand*, 9th edn, Butterworths, Wellington, 1997, p 229.
157 [1975] 2 NZLR 667.
158 *Concorde Enterprises Ltd v Anthony Motors (Hutt) Ltd* [1981] 2 NZLR 385.

importance, for it provides a prima facie rule of some certainty'—at least in the commercial area and in contracts dealing with purchasers and vendors.[159]

4.8.2 United States

[4.380] An equivalent requirement applies in the United States: a contract must be sufficiently certain and complete to be valid. If the agreement reached by the parties on a material term is too indefinite, or no agreement has been reached at all, the prima facie proposition is that the contract is void.[160] However, in two noteworthy areas, the American law operates differently.

(a) Saving indefinite agreements

[4.385] American courts are more willing to uphold agreements by resorting to 'gap-fillers'—at least where the contract is silent on a material term. As the label suggests, a gap-filler operates like an implied term. There is considerable debate about the rationale upon which a court will supply a gap-filler to complete a contract. However, it appears that most gap-fillers are based on the intention of the parties. As in Australia, where price is omitted from a contract, an obligation to pay a reasonable price is likely to be implied. Unlike Australia, this implication is likely to extend to contracts for the sale of land.

[4.390] The Restatement (Second) and the Uniform Commercial Code also seek to ensure incomplete or uncertain agreements are upheld wherever possible. Provided the parties have indicated an intention to be contractually bound (and there is a reasonably certain basis for giving an appropriate remedy), the contract will not fail for indefiniteness.[161] If the contract is one with 'open terms'—in the sense that the parties have not stated a price for the goods being sold—the missing term will be supplied by the court.[162] The result is the same if the contract provides that the price is to be settled by agreement between the parties, yet they fail to agree.[163] The contract is enforceable, the price that is implied being the same as if the contract were silent as to price. A reasonable price at the time of delivery will be implied. Relief in these circumstances might not have been available under the American common law.

(b) Agreement to negotiate

[4.395] The American position departs from that in Australia in a more dramatic way where agreements to negotiate are concerned. The traditional view, even in the United States, was that agreements to agree were unenforceable because they were indefinite. Although it is generally accepted that parties to a contract must perform the obligations imposed by the contract in good faith, this duty does not arise before contract formation. There is no common law duty to negotiate in good faith. As in Australia, parties are entitled to act in their own interests, which may result in negotiations being broken off to pursue more attractive proposals.

---

159 *Shell Oil New Zealand Ltd v Wordcom Investments Ltd* [1992] 1 NZLR 129 at 132.
160 The common law position is reflected in both the Restatement (Second) § 33(1) and implicitly in the Uniform Commercial Code 2-204.
161 Restatement (Second) § 33 and Uniform Commercial Code 2-204 (3).
162 Restatement (Second) § 33 commentary e and Uniform Commercial Code 2-305.
163 Ibid.

[4.400] A different question arises, however, where the parties agree by contract to enter into further negotiations with a view to reaching a concluded contract. Not all American courts take the same approach to this issue. Nevertheless, the weight of judicial authority suggests that an agreement to negotiate in good faith is enforceable. Provided there is a clear indication by the parties that they intend to be bound by the agreement, it is likely that the contract will be held to be enforceable. One of the cases frequently cited to support this proposition is *Itek Corporation v Chicago Aerial Industries*.[164] The contract for sale required the parties 'to make every reasonable effort to agree upon and have prepared as quickly as possible a contract'. The parties had already agreed on a number of terms, which were set out in the contract. The Supreme Court of Delaware held that by entering into the agreement, the parties obligated themselves to attempt in good faith to reach final agreement. The seller breached this duty by calling off negotiations to pursue a more favourable offer elsewhere.

[4.405] In recent decades, the courts have been inclined to uphold agreements to agree even if not coupled with a 'reasonable efforts' or 'best efforts' clause. Such contracts have been held to be valid because the courts imply into the agreement a duty to negotiate in good faith. In one case, for example, the parties entered a contract under which the buyer was given an option to buy real property for $23 500 'on payments and terms to be negotiated provided the same is exercised by June 1'. The buyer sought to exercise the option prior to June 1. As the seller no longer wanted to sell the land, he refused to negotiate. In finding for the buyer, the court expressed the view that the contract entitled the buyer to suggest a method of payment, following which the parties were obliged to negotiate in good faith. As the seller no longer wanted to sell, he was in breach of this duty.[165]

The Restatement (Second)[166] and the Uniform Commercial Code[167] reflect the increased preparedness of the courts to enforce contracts where a term has been left for later agreement by the parties.

4.8.3 Japan

[4.410] The Japanese Civil Code makes it clear that the 13 'type' contracts covered by specific Code provisions require elements such as offer and acceptance for their formation. Sales contracts, for example, must include the 'exchange of property rights' and 'payment of the purchase price' (Article 555); leases must stipulate the 'right to use certain items' and the 'payment of rent' (Article 601). The question of how certain these terms must be is not strictly defined within the Civil Code.

[4.420] Traditionally, Japanese jurisprudence requires that contracts comply with four overarching conditions to be valid: certainty; ability to be performed; legality; and social acceptability. The certainty requirement is similar to its counterpart in the common law; that is, the important aspects of a contract must be certain, or must be able to be made certain through interpretation. It is not necessary that every provi-

---

164 248 A 2ed 625 (Del 1968). This case was cited by Kirby P in *Coal Cliff Collieries Pty Ltd v Sijehama Pty Ltd* (1991) 24 NSWLR 1 at 25.

165 *Kier v Condrack* 25 Utah 2d 139, 478 P 2d 327 (1970).

166 Restatement (Second) § 33 ill 8.

167 Uniform Commercial Code 2-204 (3) and 2-305 (1)(b).

sion of the contract be certain for it to be valid.[168] Case law suggests that the scope of the object of the contract can be ascertained by interpretation,[169] and the contract may be said to have been formed even where the object of the contract was not completely certain.[170]

[4.425] Japanese law and practice tolerate a high degree of uncertainty about price. It is not at all uncommon for sales contracts or service contracts to be concluded with no discussion of, nor reference to, price. A contract in writing may similarly be silent about price—or it may stipulate that the 'equivalent price be paid'. It is also legally acceptable for the price to be determined subsequently as the current market price, either by the parties (for example, *atogime* contract, where a wholesale contract price is determined after performance, according to the retail price actually paid), or by the court. This approach is consistent with the pattern of repeated long-term dealings within Japanese industries, and a degree of uniformity in market pricing, which meant that even implicit understandings could yield a high degree of certainty as to the content of the agreement.[171]

[4.430] In interpreting contracts to render them certain, Japanese courts and scholarly writing today, in theory, give more weight to ascertaining the parties' subjective intent than they do to following the external indications of the parties' intent, but in practice the two approaches tend to converge.[172] As occurs under the common law, courts tend to favour interpretations that will render the contract valid.

168 Takashi Uchida, *Minpô 1* [Civil Code Vol 1] (2000, 2nd edn) Tokyo: Tokyo Daigaku Shuppankai, 260.
169 9 (11) *Minshu* 1521 (Supreme Court 4 October 1955).
170 Shoji Kawakami, 'Formation of Contract: Some Thoughts on Modern Contract Theory' (Part 1) (S Steele and V Taylor trans, unpublished) Japanese original: (1988) *Hanrei Taimuzu* (No. 655) (15 March 1988); See also Shoji Kawakami 'Precontractual Liability: Japan) in (E. Hondius ed. 1991) Precontractual Liability: Reports to the XIIIth Congress International Acadamy of Comparative Law, Montreal Canada 18–24 August 1990, 205–221.
171 Shoji Kawakami, 'Formation of Contract: Some Thoughts on Modern Contract Theory' (Part 1) (S Steele and V Taylor trans, unpublished) Japanese original: (1988) *Hanrei Taimuzu* (No. 655) (15 March 1988); See also Shoji Kawakami 'Precontractual Liability: Japan) in (E. Hondius ed. 1991) Precontractual Liabilit?: Reports to the XIIIth Congress International Acadamy of Comparative Law, Montreal Canada 18–24 August 1990, 205–221.
172 Takashi Uchida, *Minpô 1* [Civil Code Vol 1] (2000, 2nd edn) Tokyo: Tokyo Daigaku Shuppankai, 262.

Chapter 5

Intention to create legal relations

5.1   Introduction

[5.05] In previous chapters, various aspects of contract formation have been examined. Before a valid contract can come into existence, an offer must be made, acceptance of the offer must occur, and consideration must be provided. The contract must be complete, and the terms agreed with sufficient certainty. However, this alone is not enough. For example, people living together in a domestic arrangement may agree for one person to perform chores inside the house while the other maintains the outside areas. It is unlikely that parties would intend the bargain to be enforceable at law if one side does not perform his or her promise. For that reason, a requirement for entry into a valid contract is that the parties possess the requisite intention to create a contract. This is commonly referred to as having an intention to create legal relations.

In an attempt to ascertain the intention of parties who appear to have entered into contracts, the courts have developed certain rebuttable presumptions. These presumptions, the circumstances in which they arise and can be rebutted, and other factors that influence a court's determination on contractual intent, are considered in this chapter.

Before proceeding, however, it should be noted that a determination of whether the requisite intention exists cannot be made in isolation. Where intention or lack of it arises as an issue, there may be associated questions about whether the parties have in fact reached agreement with sufficient certainty. The overlap of these concepts was canvassed earlier.[1]

5.2   Statement of the rule

[5.10] Before a contract can be created, the parties must have intended to enter into legal relations. The rule was succinctly stated by Atkin LJ in *Rose and Frank Co v JR Crompton & Bros Ltd*[2] in the following way:

> To create a contract there must be a common intention of the parties to enter into legal obligations, mutually communicated expressly or impliedly.[3]

It can be seen from this quote that it is open for the parties to use express language to indicate an intent (or lack of intent) to impose legal obligations on each other. Alternatively, this intention can be implied from the circumstances. One of the circumstances particularly relevant here is the context in which the agreement was reached. Different presumptions arise depending on the circumstances surrounding the formation. If the parties enter an agreement in the context of a domestic or social relationship, a presumption arises that they did not intend their agreement to have legal consequences. Conversely, if parties contract in a commercial context, it is presumed that they did negotiate with the necessary legal intent. There are also other indicators of contractual intent, such as the language used in the agreement and subsequent conduct of the parties. These matters are considered later.

---

1   See [3.20] and [4.10] below.
2   [1923] 2 KB 261.
3   Ibid at 293.

[5.15] The courts use an objective test in making a determination about the intention of the parties. As stated by Lord Denning MR in *Merritt v Merritt*:[4]

> In all these cases the court does not try to discover the intention by looking into the minds of the parties. It looks at the situation in which they were placed and asks itself: would reasonable people regard the agreement as intended to be binding?[5]

In other words, in making an objective determination of the parties' intention, the court looks at all of the surrounding circumstances.[6]

5.3 Domestic and social relationships

[5.20] Where a party seeks to enforce an agreement made with a family member or an agreement formed in a social context, he or she may have difficulty proving that the parties possessed the requisite intention at the time the agreement was formed.

5.3.1 Presumption

[5.25] The intention of the parties can be gleaned from the surrounding circumstances. One such circumstance is the nature of the relationship of the parties who enter the agreement. For example, where the agreement is between a husband and wife, courts are reluctant to find that the parties intended such agreement to have legal consequences. The nature of the relationship of husband and wife is regarded as being such a strong indicator of intention (or, more accurately, lack of intention) that a presumption is said to arise in such circumstances.

> When a husband and wife are living together in amity it is natural enough to presume that their discussions about money matters are not intended to create legally binding contracts.[7]

[5.30] This presumption is not limited to cases of married couples. In *Jones v Padavatton*,[8] Danckwerts LJ observed that the principles applied in *Balfour v Balfour*[9] to a married couple 'apply to dealings between other relations, such as a father and son and daughter and mother'.[10]

[5.35] This presumption can be extended beyond interfamilial agreements. If negotiations and agreement take place between friends, for example, the circumstances might give rise to a presumption that the parties did not intend to enter legal relations.[11]

---

4   [1970] 1 WLR 1211.
5   Ibid at 1213. See also *Fleming v Beevers* [1994] 1 NZLR 385 at 390.
6   *Bowerman v Association of British Travel Agents Ltd* [1996] CLC 45. For the difficulties in applying the objective test where there are a number of different people involved in the negotiations, all having different degrees of background knowledge, and possibly different actual intentions, see comments of Megan J in *Edwards v Skyways Ltd* [1964] 1 WLR 349 at 355–356.
7   *Merritt v Merritt* [1970] 1 WLR 1211 at 1213.
8   [1969] 1 WLR 328.
9   [1919] 2 KB 571 at 578–580.
10 1969] 1 WLR 328 at 332.
11 *Heslop v Burns* [1974] 1 WLR 1241. See [5.90].

5.3.2   Rebutting the presumption

[5.40] While the presumption of lack of legal intent may be a helpful starting point for the courts, the cases demonstrate that the presumption can be easily rebutted. For example, if parties who are in a familial relationship are contracting in a business context, or if a husband and wife enter into an agreement in circumstances in which they are no longer living in harmony, or the agreement is between other family members where there is hostility in the relationship, the court may well find the necessary legal intent present. Similarly, despite the contractual negotiations occurring between people in a close domestic or social relationship, if the words used in the contract indicate a legal intention, the presumption that may otherwise have arisen would be rebutted.

5.3.3   Case examples

[5.45] The case law provides useful illustrations of the extent to which the court is likely to rely on the presumption of lack of intent in the domestic or social context, and the circumstances in which the courts will find that the presumption is rebutted on the facts.

(a) Husband and wife

[5.50] The presumption of lack of intent was applied by the English Court of Appeal in the following case to prevent an agreement made between the parties being sued upon by the wife.

Example: Balfour v Balfour[12]

After the parties were married in England in 1900, they moved to and lived in Ceylon where the husband had a government posting. They returned to England in 1915 for a holiday. Although the husband went back to Ceylon in 1916, his wife remained in England for health reasons. Before the husband left for Ceylon, they entered an agreement that if the wife supported herself and did not call on the husband for any further maintenance, the husband would pay the wife £30 per month.

When the wife later sued on the agreement, an issue before the court was whether the parties intended the agreement to have legal consequences. All of the Lord Justices considered the agreement to be unenforceable on the basis that the parties were in a domestic relationship and did not intend legal consequences to flow from their arrangement. As Atkin LJ put it, 'one of the most usual forms of agreement which does not constitute a contract appears to me to be the arrangements which are made between husband and wife.'[13]

[5.55] Given that many couples now choose to cohabit without marrying, the same presumption should apply where an agreement is entered into between a couple living in a de facto relationship. While there is no reported case law directly on point, the presumption would, as a matter of logic, extend to both heterosexual and same-sex couples.

---

12   [1919] 2 KB 571.
13   Ibid at 578.

(b) Separated husband and wife

[5.60] The policy behind the presumption that arises in domestic relationships was discussed by Atkin LJ in *Balfour and Balfour*.[14] Such agreements do not form valid contracts 'because the parties in the inception of the arrangement, never intended that they should be sued upon'.[15] In explaining why this is the case, he continued:

'The common law does not regulate the form of agreements between spouses. Their promises are not sealed with seals and sealing wax. The consideration that really obtains for them is that natural love and affection which counts for so little in these cold Courts.'[16]

[5.65] Where the parties are divorced, separated, or in the process of separating, the negotiations do not take place in the context of 'natural love and affection' as described by Atkin LJ. Therefore, the same presumption is less likely to arise, and a court will generally find that the requisite contractual intent existed.

Example: Merritt v Merritt[17]

After the parties to the marriage separated (but before their divorce) they agreed that the wife would continue to pay off the mortgage over the former matrimonial home (in which she still lived), and when that had been fully paid, the husband would transfer his interest in the house to her. The husband also signed a document to that effect. The wife paid off the mortgage, but the husband refused to transfer his interest to the wife.

In finding for the wife, the English Court of Appeal held that the parties possessed the requisite legal intention when agreeing on the arrangements for the house. In the words of Widgery LJ, 'once that natural love and affection has gone, as it normally has when the marriage has broken up, there is no room at all for the application of such a presumption'.[18]

(c) Other familial relationships

[5.70] A presumption that parties in other familial relationships do not intend to create legal relations arises for the same reason as for married (or de facto) couples. Agreements made in this context are based on natural love and affection and are not intended by the parties to have legal consequences. Perhaps, as would be expected, the bond of natural love and affection is likely to weaken according to the remoteness of the tie.[19] The bond between a husband and a wife would generally be stronger than that between a woman and her sister-in-law, for example. It follows that the presumption of lack of legal intention is more likely to be rebutted for other familial relationships than for husbands and wives.

---

14 [1919] 2 KB 571.
15 Ibid at 579.
16 Ibid.
17 [1970] 1 WLR 1211.
18 Ibid at 1214.
19 The comments of McPherson J (as he then was) at first instance in *Riches v Hogben* [1985] 2 QdR 292 at 297 tend to support this view.

[5.75] In fact, this position is reflected in the case law. In those cases where the court finds that the presumption has been rebutted, one or more of the following factors are often relevant:

- The seriousness of the conduct involved (such as moving countries or giving up paid employment);
- The expense involved, especially if the relevant party is not wealthy;
- Whether there is or has been a degree of hostility in the relationship;
- The closeness of the family ties (for example whether it is a mother–daughter relationship or great-aunt–great-niece relationship);
- Whether the subject matter of the agreement is business or commercial in nature.

Example: Jones v Padavatton[20]

A mother, resident in England, invited her daughter, who lived and worked in the United States, to move to England to study for the Bar. The mother promised to provide her with maintenance of $200 (US) a month to do so. The daughter agreed. Subsequently, the mother and daughter altered their arrangements so that, instead of being paid, the daughter was able to live in her mother's house. A dispute arose, and the mother brought an action to evict the daughter from the house.

The English Court of Appeal found for the mother on the basis that there was no legally binding agreement between the parties regarding the provision of maintenance (and later the offer to live in the mother's house). Relying on the presumption that family members do not intend to enter legal relations, it was held that there was merely 'one of those family arrangements which depend on the good faith of the promises which are made and are not intended to be rigid, binding agreements'.[21] This was the case notwithstanding the seriousness of the actions of the daughter taken in reliance on the mother's promise and the obvious expense involved in moving from the United States.[22]

[5.80] It appears that Australian courts may be more willing to find that the presumption has been rebutted in such circumstances.

Example: Wakeling v Ripley[23]

The defendant was an elderly man of considerable wealth who lived in Australia. He invited his sister and her husband (the plaintiffs) to come to Australia to live with and care for him until his death. In consideration of this, the defendant promised to provide them with an income for life, and to leave them his property on his death. The plaintiffs agreed, the husband giving up secure employment in England. A dispute arose and the plaintiffs sued the defendant for breach of contract.

The New South Wales Court of Appeal found in favour of the plaintiffs. It was held that, in the circumstances of the case, the agreement was 'something very much

---

20   [1969] 1 WLR 328.

21   Ibid at 332 per Danckwerts LJ.

22   Although Fenton Atkinson LJ concurred that there was no legal intention, Salmon LJ concluded that the presumption had been rebutted on these facts.

23   (1951) 51 SR (NSW) 183.

more than a mere family or social agreement'.[24] Relevant to this finding was the serious consequences of the arrangement for the plaintiffs, namely the husband giving up his salaried position and pension, and both of them moving permanently to Australia.[25]

[5.85] Finally, where the agreement is primarily a business arrangement for the advantage of each contracting party, a court is likely to find that the necessary legal intent existed, despite the parties being related to each other.

Example: Roufos v Brewster[26]

Mr and Mrs Brewster owned a motel at Coober Pedy, while their son in law, Mr Roufos, ran a small store. Mr Roufos drove the Brewster's truck to Adelaide for repairs. It was agreed between them that if Mr Roufos could arrange for someone to drive the truck back the Coober Pedy, Mr Roufos could transport goods for his business back on the truck. The truck was involved in an accident on the way back, and the Brewsters sued Mr Roufos for the cost of repairing the truck.

Although the Brewsters were unsuccessful in their action, the court held that the parties had entered a binding contract. As the setting of the agreement was commercial, and not domestic or social, a legal relationship had been created between the parties.

(d) Social relationships

[5.90] The presumption of lack of legal intent can extend beyond familial relationships to agreements entered into in a social context, or agreements made between friends. An example is provided by *Heslop v Burns*.[27] The deceased allowed his friends to stay in a house owned by him free of charge. In an action for possession by the deceased's executors against the friends, the friends argued they were in possession as tenants at will. The friends were unsuccessful, the court finding that, in the circumstances in which possession was given, the parties had not entered legal relations.

[5.95] A court will not always find that the parties lacked legal intention, even when the arrangement is clearly made between friends or relatives in a social setting. For example, there is authority to the effect that parties who pool funds to enter a competition in one person's name may intend that arrangement to have legal consequences.[28] Therefore, if the person wins, action can be brought to force that person to share the

---

24 Ibid at 186.
25 A similar result occurred in *Todd v Nicol* [1957] SASR 72 where an elderly woman living in South Australia invited her sister in law and niece to move from Scotland to live with her. In consideration for their move, they were permitted to live with her until her death, or until the niece married. On these facts, the South Australian Supreme Court found that the parties had the requisite legal intention when they entered the contract. Compare, however, a recent decision of the Western Australian Supreme Court in *Gors v Henderson; Henderson v Perpetual Trustee WA Ltd* (1999) Aust Contract Reports 90-099. The defendants gave up accommodation and employment to live with and look after the deceased (stepgrandmother of the defendants), in exchange for receiving real property on her death. The defendants' action for damages and compensation on a *quantum meruit* basis for services rendered was unsuccessful. One of the reasons for the decision was lack of requisite legal intention.
26 [1971] 2 SASR 218.
27 [1974] 1 WLR 1241.
28 *Simpkins v Pays* [1955] 1 WLR 975; *Welch v Jess* [1976] NZ Rec Law 185.

winnings with other members of the group. While this result is undoubtedly fair and would reflect the intention of the parties who participated in the syndicate, it is perhaps more doubtful whether any of the parties would have contemplated the arrangement to have legal consequences. It may be that in cases that involve people winning considerable amounts of money in these circumstances, the court may be more easily persuaded about matters of intention.

5.4 Commercial agreement

[5.100] As most people would expect, where parties enter an agreement in a commercial context, or make an agreement that relates to a business matter, it is likely that a court would find they had the necessary legal intent to create a valid contract.

5.4.1 Presumption

[5.105] Where parties negotiate and agree in a business setting, it is presumed that the parties intended the agreement to have legal consequences.

> Now it is quite possible for parties to come to an agreement by accepting a proposal with the result that the agreement does not give rise to legal relations. The reason for this is that the parties do not intend that their agreement shall give rise to legal relations. This intention may be implied from the subject matter of the agreement, but it may also be expressed by the parties. In social and family relations such an intention is readily implied, while in business matters the opposite result would ordinarily follow.[29]

[5.110] Therefore, the party alleging that an agreement relating to business matters is of no legal effect has the onus of demonstrating that to be the case. It has been judicially stated that, in those circumstances, that onus is heavy.[30] For the presumption to arise, the agreement must relate to a business matter. Ordinarily, it is easy to determine whether an agreement relates to a business matter. However, the issue of whether a transaction could truly be regarded as having taken place in a business setting was in dispute in *Esso Petroleum Ltd v Commissioners of Customs and Excise*.[31]

Example: Esso Petroleum Ltd v Commissioners of Customs and Excise[32]

For promotional purposes, Esso Petroleum distributed millions of coins to petrol stations that sold Esso petrol. The coins were of little intrinsic value, but each featured one of the members of the English Soccer team. There were 30 coins in the series. It was advertised to the public that for every 4 gallons of Esso petrol they bought, they would receive one of these coins. The advertisements indicated that these coins were

---

29 *Rose and Frank Co v JR Crompton and Bros Ltd* [1923] 2 KB 261 at 288 per Scrutton LJ. This case went on appeal to the House of Lords ([1925] AC 445). On this point, however, the determination of the Court of Appeal was unanimously upheld.
30 *Edwards v Skyways Ltd* [1964] 1 WLR 349 at 355.
31 [1976] 1 All ER 117.
32 Ibid.

a 'gift' and were being given 'free'. The matter before the Court was whether the coins were being 'sold' (and therefore liable to be assessed for purchase tax). One of the issues crucial to the Court's determination was whether the parties had the necessary intention to form a contract of sale.

The House of Lords was split 3:2 on this point. Three of the Lords[33] held that the parties possessed the requisite legal intent in relation to the provision of the coins upon a customer buying 4 gallons of petrol. Lord Simon provided a number of grounds for this conclusion.[34] First, the promotion took place in a business setting. It was intended that sales would be promoted as a result of the coins. Secondly, this scheme had a potentially large commercial benefit to Esso. Thirdly, this view was supported by authority.[35]

The contrary view was reached by Viscount Dilhorne.[36] Central to his Lordship's argument was that 'the offer of a gift of a free coin' could not properly be regarded a business matter that attracted the presumption of legal intention.[37]

It is submitted that the view held by the three Lords in this case is far more persuasive. Despite the comments of Viscount Dilhorne, it is difficult to regard this transaction as not falling within a commercial or business setting. The purpose of the scheme was to promote sales of Esso petrol. It was a business decision to offer the coins in exchange for the sale of petrol. It follows that it was a business transaction, despite the small intrinsic value of the coins. It is further submitted that in any future case of this kind, the broader approach to what constitutes a commercial or business setting will be adopted.

5.4.2 Rebutting the presumption

[5.115] Even if the agreement is made in a commercial or business setting, it is possible for the parties to intend the agreement not to have legal consequences. If a person can prove this lack of intent, the presumption will be rebutted and the court will find that no contract came into existence. The intention not to create legal relations may be evident in a number of different ways. For example, the agreement may contain an express clause that no legal consequences flow from the document, or the overall tenor of the particular document may indicate that the parties had no intention to enter legal relations. These and other indicators of intent are examined at [5.155]–[5.215].

5.5 Government activities

[5.120] When examining the extent to which the law of contract is relevant in the context of contracts made with governments and government instrumentalities, two different types of activities should be identified. The first is where the government, or

---

33 Lords Wilberforce, Simon and Fraser.
34 [1976] 1 All ER 117 at 121–122.
35 In this regard, Lord Simon cited *Rose and Frank Co v JR Crompton and Bros Ltd* [1923] 2 KB 261 at 288 and 293 and *Edwards v Skyways Ltd* [1964] 1 All ER 494 at 500.
36 In a separate judgment, Lord Russell also held that the requisite legal intention did not exist.
37 [1967] 1 All ER 117 at 121.

any of its instrumentalities, enters into commercial negotiations and agreements with another party. The second is where acts are carried out or statements made by government officials in the course of administering government policy.

5.5.1 Commercial agreements

[5.125] As part of ordinary governmental activity, the government must necessarily enter into commercial agreements. Contracts to purchase stationery, contracts to construct buildings, and contracts to purchase government vehicles are illustrations. In such cases, the usual contractual principles apply to determine whether a contract has been formed. As for all other contracts, before such contracts can be sued upon, it must be demonstrated that all parties formed the requisite intention to create legal relations. In most commercial agreements, existence of legal intention will not be an issue.[38] However, in *Coogee Esplanade Surf Motel Pty Ltd v Commonwealth of Australia*,[39] it was contended by Coogee Esplanade Surf Motel Pty Ltd ('the motel') that it had entered a contract to sell the motel to the Commonwealth. No contract had been executed, but there had been negotiations followed by a contract being forwarded to the relevant Commonwealth Department 'for approval and if satisfactory, for execution'. The Permanent Head of the Department advised the Director of the motel that approval had been given and funds authorised, and that the 'transaction' would be settled in July. A 'letter of intent' was then sent by the Permanent Head to the Director of the motel. In an action by the Director of the motel for specific performance of the contract, the court held that the parties had not formed the requisite legal intent to contract. Interestingly, the President of the New South Wales Court of Appeal indicated that the phrase 'settlement of the transaction' might have a different effect if used in the context of a personal seller and a personal buyer.[40] If that is correct, it may be the case that where one of the contracting parties is a government, increased formality may be required to demonstrate the necessary legal intent.

5.5.2 Policy initiatives

[5.130] Where the government activity relates to a policy initiative—for example, to provide assistance to a particular section of the community or to promote a specific activity or industry—a court may be less likely to find that the parties intended to enter contractual relations. For example, in *The Administration of the Territory of Papua New Guinea v Leahy*,[41] the Department of Agriculture of the Territory, at the request of Mr Leahy, provided assistance to help Mr Leahy eliminate an infestation of cattle tick on his property. Such action was consistent with the government policy of tick eradication. After the exercise, the Department was sued by Mr Leahy, who claimed damages for breach of contract on the basis that the departmental officers did not perform their activities skilfully. In finding for the Department, the High Court held that

---

38   *Rothmans of Pall Mall (NZ) Ltd v Attorney-General* [1991] 2 NZLR 323; *Attorney-General v Barker Bros* [1976] 2 NZLR 495.
39   (1976) 50 ALR 363.
40   Ibid at 370 per Moffitt P.
41   (1960) 105 CLR 6.

the arrangement between the parties was not contractual in nature. It was not the common intention of the parties to enter into legal obligations.

> The conduct of the parties constituted an administrative arrangement by which the Administration in pursuance of its agricultural policy gave assistance to an owner to prevent that stock contracting a disease which was prevalent in the Territory. The work done by the Administration was analogous to a social service which generally does not have as its basis a legal relationship of a contractual nature and for which no right of action would arise in favour of the citizen who is receiving the services if the Government acts inefficiently in performing them.[42]

For similar reasons, in *Australian Woollen Mills Pty Ltd v The Commonwealth*,[43] a company was unsuccessful in its action against the Commonwealth for breaching the subsidy arrangement announced some years previously. According to the High Court, the announcement of the subsidy arrangement was merely an announcement of policy. It could not be construed as anything that could, if accepted, lead to contractually binding obligations.

5.6 Voluntary associations

[5.135] Voluntary associations and clubs are formed for a variety of reasons, and are common throughout Australia. They facilitate gatherings of people for a common purpose. Such associations vary in size and formality and cover a range of different activities. Voluntary associations may be formed because people share the same hobbies or, in the case of political parties, as the cases reveal, this structure is used to further political ends. Sporting bodies also commonly rely on this structure.

[5.140] The conduct of members of voluntary associations and clubs and the way transactions to which they are a party can take place are governed by a set of rules or a constitution developed for that purpose. The question that arises from time to time is the extent to which courts can interfere with or adjudicate upon an alleged breach of the rules or constitution. The crux of the matter is whether the rules or constitution constitute a binding legal contract between parties. Relevant to a determination of this matter is whether the parties intended to create legal relations by joining the association or club.

This matter was first considered by the High Court in *Cameron v Hogan*[44] in the context of an alleged breach of the rules of association of the Australian Labour Party. A former member of the party brought an action against the executive for improperly excluding him from the Party in breach of Party rules. The High Court denied the member declaratory or injunctive relief because the rules of the association did not

---

42   Ibid at 11. Compare *Rothmans of Pall Mall (NZ) Ltd v Attorney-General* [1991] 2 NZLR 323 where an agreement that involved issues of governmental policy was held not to be valid, not because of lack of contractual intention, but because of lack of consideration.

43   (1954) 92 CLR 44.

44   (1934) 51 CLR 358.

create enforceable contractual rights between the parties. The Court noted that associations of this kind are established on a consensual basis only,

> unless there were some clear positive indication that the members contemplated the creation of legal relations *inter se*, the rules adopted for their governance would not be treated as amounting to an enforceable contract.[45]

The High Court indicated that the result might have been different if the member had a proprietary interest in the assets of the association.

[5.145] Whether the same result would occur today if the matter were to go to the High Court is perhaps open to debate. In a more recent decision of the Queensland Supreme Court, *Baldwin v Everingham*,[46] a member of the Liberal Party (Queensland branch), brought an action against various members of the executive claiming breaches of the constitution in relation to endorsement procedures. The Queensland Supreme Court was prepared to grant declaratory relief; it noted that the expectations of people involved in political parties has altered since the 1930s, when *Cameron v Hogan*[47] was decided. Dowsett J was able to distinguish *Cameron v Hogan* on the basis of the increased statutory recognition conferred on voluntary associations since the High Court decision was reached. Given that such associations in the 1990s have, for example, greater power to deal with property, Dowsett J considered that political parties had been taken 'beyond the ambit of mere voluntary associations'.[48]

[5.150] The importance of proprietary interests and rights conferred on a member in establishing whether a breach of rules is a justiciable matter is further illustrated by *Finlayson v Carr*.[49] This case arose out of an attempt by the Australian Jockey Club ('AJC') to alter its rules to specifically exclude women from its membership, and to establish a separate class of membership—'AJC Associates'—available to women. A member of the club claimed that the rules did not empower such amendments to be made, and brought an action challenging them. On the preliminary point of whether the member could bring such an action, the New South Wales Supreme Court noted that membership of the AJC carried with it important proprietary rights. On this basis, the rules must be considered to create legal relations between the parties. Accordingly, the member was entitled to bring the action.

5.7 Circumstances indicating absence of intention

[5.155] Where a party to an agreement defends a claim made on the basis that he or she did not intend to enter legal relations, the court must make a determination on the issue of intention. As state earlier,[50] intention can be gleaned through the parties' express language, or on the basis of the circumstances in which agreement was

---

45   Ibid at 371.
46   [1993] 1 QdR 10.
47   (1934) 51 CLR 358.
48   [1993] 1 QdR 10 at 20.
49   [1978] 1 NSWLR 657.
50   See [5.10].

reached. Some of these circumstances have already been examined. There are other phrases that are commonly used with the intention that their use will prevent legal consequences from attaching. Some of the more common ones are now considered.

5.7.1 Honour clauses

[5.160] The presumption that arises in a commercial context is quite clear. The court will presume that the parties intended to create legal relations by entering the agreement. Of course, it is open for the parties to form a contrary intention. They can indicate by express words in their agreement that they did not intend the agreement to have legal consequences. Such clauses are sometimes referred to as 'honour clauses'. The following clause is illustrative.

> This arrangement is not entered into, nor is this memorandum written, as a formal or legal agreement, and shall not be subject to legal jurisdiction in the Law Courts either of the United States or England, but it is only a definite expression and record of the purpose and intention of the three parties concerned, to which they each honourably pledge themselves, with the fullest confidence—based on past business with each other—that it will be carried through by each of the three parties with mutual loyalty and friendly co-operation. This is hereinafter referred to as the 'honourable pledge' clause.[51]

This clause was used in the context of an agency agreement between an English company (supplier) and an American company (sole agents). Although this was clearly a commercial arrangement, the existence of the honour clause prevented the American company from bringing an action against the English supplier when it terminated the agreement without notice.

[5.165] A clause inserted on the back of a football coupon by a company running pools on football matches was held in *Jones v Vernon's Pools Ltd*[52] to have the same effect. The clause provided that:

> Everybody who comes into these pools must understand that there are no legal obligations either way in connection with these pools. We are going to do our best. Every care will be taken, and we employ accountants, but this money must be sent in on the clearest understanding that this is a gentlemen's agreement, an agreement which carries with it no legal obligations on either side, and confers no legal rights.

This clause prevented the plaintiff from recovering against the defendant company, even if it could be established that the plaintiff filled in and sent a winning coupon to the defendant.

5.7.2 Promotional puff and 'free gifts'

[5.170] In the world of commerce, various techniques may be used to promote the sales of products. It can sometimes be difficult to determine whether such advertisements can give rise to legally enforceable contracts. Once again, the issue of the inten-

---

51 *Rose and Frank Co v JR Crompton and Bros Ltd* [1925] AC 445.
52 [1938] 2 All ER 626.

tion of the parties becomes relevant. Where language such as the offer of a 'free gift' is used, or an apparently extravagant claim is set out in an advertisement, there may be a tendency to think that a person who acts in response to the advertisement may not intend legal consequences to flow. A person who promises to give another a gift would generally not expect there to be legal consequences if the promisor reneges.

[5.175] The courts, however, do not adopt such an approach. To determine whether the requisite intention exists, they look not only at the words used, but at the entire context in which the advertising takes place. For example, if such language is used in a business setting, or to promote a commercial end, a court may be persuaded that the necessary intention existed. It is for this reason that three members of the House of Lords in *Esso Petroleum Ltd v Commissioners of Customs and Excise*[53] regarded the offer of a free coin upon the purchase of 4 gallons of Esso petrol as capable of creating legal relations.[54]

[5.180] The intention of the parties was also an issue in *Carlill v Carbolic Smoke Ball Company*.[55] This case was examined in detail earlier.[56] It will be recalled that the Carbolic Smoke Ball Company advertised that it would pay £100 to anyone who contracted influenza after using its product in the specified manner. The Court of Appeal held that this advertisement was more than a promotional puff. The intention of the parties, as evidenced by the company depositing £1000 in a bank for the purpose of payment, was relevant in finding that an offer had been made which, if accepted, would give rise to enforceable obligations.

5.7.3   Ex gratia payments and 'without prejudice' offers

[5.185] Where parties are negotiating to resolve a particular matter, one party may offer to make an *ex gratia* payment to the other.[57] Alternatively, one party (often a solicitor) may write a 'without prejudice' letter to the other in which an offer is made to conclude the matter between the parties. The question may arise concerning the legal consequences which flow if such an *ex gratia* payment is made, or a without prejudice offer is accepted.

Both of these situations were referred to by Megaw J of the Queens Bench Division in *Edwards v Skyways Ltd*[58]—a case involving a redundancy package for crew members negotiated between an airline company and the British Air Line Pilots Association. Agreement was reached to pay redundant air crew members an 'ex gratia amount approximating to the company's contributions for each member of the pension and superannuation fund'. The company later refused to pay this amount and was sued by one of the pilots made redundant. Despite the use of the words '*ex gratia* payment', Megaw J held that the parties intended to create legal relations when negotiating the redundancy package. Of the term '*ex gratia*', his Honour made the following comments:

---

53   [1976] 1 All ER 117.
54   For more detail of this decision, see [5.110].
55   [1893] 1 QB 256.
56   See [3.60].
57   Butterworths' *Encyclopaedic Australian Legal Dictionary* defines an *ex gratia* payment as 'from favour. Payment of money made or given as a concession, without legal compulsion.'
58   [1964] 1 WLR 349.

the words 'ex gratia,' in my judgment, do not carry a necessary, or even a probable, implication that the agreement is to be without legal effect. It is, I think, common experience amongst practitioners of the law that litigation or threatened litigation is frequently compromised on the terms that one party shall make to the other a payment described in express terms as 'ex gratia' or 'without admission of liability'. The two phrases are, I think, synonymous. No one would imagine that a settlement, so made, is unenforceable at law. The words 'ex gratia' or 'without admission of liability' are used simply to indicate … that the party agreeing to pay does not admit any pre-existing liability on his part; but he is certainly not seeking to preclude the legal enforceability of the settlement itself by describing the contemplated payment as 'ex gratia'.[59]

5.7.4 Letters of comfort

[5.190] What is meant by a letter of comfort and the circumstances in which it is given are examined at [11.50]–[11.55]. Where an advance is made—for example, to a subsidiary company—the lender may request the holding company to guarantee performance of the borrower's obligations. If the holding company is not prepared to give a guarantee, the lender may instead request that a letter of comfort be provided. A letter of comfort gives an assurance, or at least suggestion, that the subsidiary company will be able to meet its obligations when they fall due.

[5.195] Whether a letter of comfort can be sued upon by the lender if the borrower defaults depends on whether a contract has been created between the writer of the letter and the lender. Central to this determination is whether the parties intended to create legal obligations by the giving and receiving of the letter. To determine this, the courts look at the construction of the document and the circumstances surrounding its sending, in particular whether it has been given in a commercial context. In *Banque Brussels Lambert SA v Australian National Industries Ltd*,[60] a principal shareholder of the borrower gave various assurances concerning the line of credit provided by the bank. The shareholder promised not to reduce its shareholding in the borrowing company without first giving 90 days' notice to the lender. It also confirmed its practice to ensure that the borrowing company would continue to be in a financial position to meet its obligations when they accrued. On the borrower's default, the lender sued upon this letter. The following points were considered in the determination of the New South Wales Supreme Court that the parties had intended the letter to have legal consequences:

- On a construction of the letter, the terms were sufficiently promissory in nature.[61]
- The letter was part of a commercial transaction in which there is a presumption that legal relations were intended.

---

59 Ibid at 356. That acceptance of a 'without prejudice' offer will be legally binding on the parties is also apparent from the comments of Dixon FJ and Fllagar J in *Tallerman & Co Pty Ltd v Nathan's Merchandise (Victoria) Pty Ltd* (1956) 98 CLR 93 at 110.
60 (1989) 21 NSWLR 502.
61 Compare *Australian European Finance Corporation Ltd v Sheahan* (1993) 60 SASR 187; *Kleinwort Benson v Malaysia Mining Corp BHD* [1989] 1 All ER 785; *Commonwealth Bank of Australia v TLI Management Pty Ltd* [1990] VR 510.

- Intention is deduced from 'the document as a whole seen against the background of the practices of the particular trade or industry'.[62]

5.7.5 'Subject to contract' clauses

[5.200] For some contracts, the negotiation phase can be protracted. The parties may reach agreement on a number of matters, but state that such agreement is 'subject to contract' or 'subject to the preparation of a formal contract'. Whether the parties have entered into an enforceable contract at that stage was considered by the High Court in *Masters v Cameron*.[63] This case was considered at [4.340]. Where parties conclude negotiations with the understanding that the subject matter will subsequently be dealt with by a formal contract, whether a concluded agreement has been reached depends on their intention. As stated in the joint judgment of Dixon CJ, McTiernan and Kitto JJ:

> 'The question depends upon the intention disclosed by the language the parties have employed, and no special form of words is essential to be used in order that there shall be no contract binding upon the parties before the execution of their agreement in its ultimate shape ...'[64]

5.7.6 'Letters of intent' and 'understandings'

[5.205] Parties sometimes conduct their affairs on the basis of an 'understanding' between them. Such an understanding may arise orally, or be put in writing. Questions about its contractual standing may arise where one party no longer wishes to be bound by it. A related issue arises in the area of letters or documents of intent. While the court will consider all the circumstances of the case to ascertain the parties' intention, the use of terms such as 'letter of intent' or 'understanding' may indicate something short of an intention to enter a concluded agreement.

[5.210] The facts and decision of *Coogee Esplanade Surf Motel Pty Ltd v Commonwealth of Australia*[65] were discussed earlier.[66] Following negotiations for the sale of a motel but before entry into a formal contract, the Permanent Head of the relevant Department sent a letter of intent to the seller. The letter advised that approval had been given for the purchase and that the Permanent Head was requested to complete the transaction in the near future. In the opinion of Moffitt P, a 'letter of intention' indicated only the intention of one party—there the Commonwealth—to enter into a contract to buy. Further, it was inconsistent with there already being a contract to buy. Glass JA agreed with the President's conclusion that a binding contract had not been entered into. In a dissenting judgment, Hutley JA expressed the view that a letter of intent represented a 'common but revocable intention on the major issues'.[67] It resulted from bilateral discussions. Because the Departmental officer described the letter as 'conclusive', Hutley

---

62   Citing from DW Greig & JLR Davis, *The Law of Contract*, The Law Book Company Limited, North Ryde, 1987, pp 229–230.
63   (1954) 91 CLR 353.
64   Ibid at 362.
65   (1976) 50 ALR 363.
66   See [5.125].
67   *Coogee Esplanade Surf Motel Pty Ltd v Commonwealth of Australia* (1976) 50 ALR 363 at 381.

JA considered the letter irrevocable on the part of the writer of the letter. In short, the parties had the requisite legal intent to form a binding contract.

While the letter of intent was relevant in the Court's determination that neither party possessed the requisite legal intention, a court could well come to a different conclusion in different circumstances. The nature of the language used, whether one or both parties signed the letter, and possibly whether one of the parties is a Government Department may be relevant factors.[68]

[5.215] The reaching of an 'understanding' between parties has been likened to an expression of present intention, resulting in something less than a binding contract. Therefore, if a solicitor writes to a prospective client to 'place on record the understanding that all the legal work of and incidental to the completion' of a particular project be performed by that solicitor, and that understanding is accepted, it is unlikely that the parties would have entered a binding legal contract for retainer of the solicitor's services.[69] In this context, an 'understanding' is a vague term and unlikely to be interpreted as imposing legally binding obligations on the parties.

5.8   International perspective

5.8.1   New Zealand

[5.220] The legal position in New Zealand on intention to create legal relations is substantially the same as that in Australia, and requires no separate examination.[70]

5.8.2   United States

[5.225] The United States position on intention is largely the same as the law in Australia. As a general proposition, the parties will not be bound by the contract if the circumstances surrounding entry into the agreement indicate they do not intend legal consequences to flow.[71] There are perhaps two features of the American law worth highlighting. First, despite a clear indication that the parties do not intend the agreement to have legal consequences, it may be enforced if the parties have acted on the agreement and it would be unfair not to enforce it.[72] In similar circumstances, relief may be available in Australia on principles of promissory estoppel.[73] However, in Australia, even if the plaintiff satisfies the required elements, the remedy has to be propor-

---

68 See comments of Moffitt P *in Coogee Esplanade Surf Motels Pty Ltd v Commonwealth of Australia* (1976) 50 ALR 363 at 370.

69 *JH Milner & Son v Percy Bilton Ltd* [1966] 2 All ER 894.

70 Compare, however, comments of J Francis in 'Letters of Comfort: possible avenues of interpretation' (1993) NZLJ 185 that the New Zealand position concerning the enforceability of letters of comfort is not entirely settled. On balance, however, it is likely that legal principles enunciated by the English Court of Appeal in *Kleinwort Benson Ltd v Malaysia Mining Corp BHD* [1989] 1 All ER 785 also represents the New Zealand law: *Bank of New Zealand v Ginivan* [1991] 1 NZLR 178.

71 This position is reflected in the Restatement (Second) § 21.

72 Examples of cases falling within this category involve pension plans entered into by employers and employees, such plans expressed to be non-contractual in nature. Because of the reliance on these plans by the employees, the agreements were enforceable although they were expressed not to be contractual in nature.

73 See Chapter 7 for more detail on this form of relief.

tionate to the detriment suffered. Such restrictions will not bar enforcement of the contract in America.

[5.230] Secondly, some agreements made in the domestic or social context may not be enforced even if the parties have indicated an intention to be legally bound. One example is an agreement by one partner to pay the other a specified amount every month. Reluctance to enforce such agreements is grounded in public policy considerations. Given the potential number of these kinds of agreements—which may be entered into by couples and others in a domestic or social context—there is a perceived danger that courts would be inundated with claims. Other factors influencing courts have been concerns about family disharmony should these agreements be the subject of litigation. The position is different in Australia. Provided the parties intend the agreement to have legal consequences, it will be enforceable in the same way as a commercial agreement.

5.8.3 Japan

[5.235] The key element in formation of contracts under Japanese law is mutual intention to contract, and the declaration of that intention [*ishihyôji*]. The Civil Code recognises both subjective intention and the objective manifestation of that intention,[74] and courts will determine the parties' intentions with regard to both factors.

Unlike the common law, Japanese contract law has not developed presumptions about contractual intent based on the status of the parties. So, for example, there is no presumption against contractual intent as between spouses, relatives or friends. Whether a contract was actually intended is a question of fact, based on the circumstances. In commercial transactions, as we have seen in previous chapters, the effect of the rules of offer and acceptance can be that contracts are formed relatively early. In more complex situations, the issue tends not to be whether there was an intention to contract, but at what point in the negotiation the contract should be treated as having come into being. This is a question of interpreting the facts in the particular case. One response to this problem has been the use of remedies for negotiations that are broken off before a contract was formed, but after some harm has accrued to the other party. This issue is examined in Chapter 7.

[5.240] Japanese law also recognises a major exception to the intent to contract: the mental reservation. Civil Code Article 93 provides that:

> A declaration of intention shall not be invalidated by the fact that it differs from the declarant's real intention; but such declaration of intention shall be null and void, if the other party was aware, or should have been aware, of the real intention of the declarant.

Where a party wishes to avoid being bound by a contract and relies on this defence, he or she has the burden of proving that the other party knew or should have known of his or her mental reservation. Where one party lacks real intent and the other party seeks to avoid the contract on this basis, the party seeking to avoid the contract will be allowed to do so under Article 93 of the Civil Code. Article 93 is a

---

74   Takashi Uchida, *Minpô 1* [Minpo Volume 1] (2000, 2nd edn) Tokyo Daigaku Shuppankai 47.

protective provision for such 'innocent' parties. The rationale is that, as between the party who acts as if they were prepared to contract (but reserved his or her real intention) and the party who relied on those signals of intention, the latter is more likely to have suffered loss and is more deserving of remedial assistance.[75] Again, this is a question of fact.

[5.245] Japanese law also recognises intermediate situations in which undertakings, though not fraudulent, may fall short of a complete intention to be bound contractually. One such category is the 'gentlemen's' agreement', recognised in Japanese case law as not contractually binding. Another possibility is the 'natural obligation' [*shizen saimu*], which emerges originally from Roman law. In a contractual setting, this may create an obligation if the promising party begins to act on the promise (somewhat analogous to promissory estoppel). However, it falls short of being a contractually binding obligation compellable by the other party simply on the basis of, for example, an oral undertaking.[76] The *Marutama Café Waitress Case* cited by Uchida is a famous example.[77] Here, a café patron became close to a waitress, and hoping to gain her approval, promised to give her enough money to allow her to set up her own establishment. When she sought performance of the promise, the patron reneged. The Daishin'in (the precursor to Japan's Supreme Court) found that the patron's undertaking would have been enforceable as an obligation (*saimu*) had he moved to peform it of his own volition. As a simple promise, however, it was not enforceable by the waitress. The point here is that although the promise lacked the bindingness of contract, it had the potential to be transformed into a binding obligation.

---

75   Takashi Uchida, *Minpô 1* [Minpo Volume 1] (2000, 2nd edn) Tokyo Daigaku Shuppankai 47.
76   Takashi Uchida, *Minpô 1* [Minpo Volume 1] (2000, 2nd edn) Tokyo Daigaku Shuppankai 49.
77   Decision of the Daishin'in 25 April 1935 *Shimbun* 3835-5 (*Kafe marutama jyokyû jiken*) discussed in Takashi Uchida, *Minpô 1* [Minpo Volume 1] (2000, 2nd edn) Tokyo Daigaku Shuppankai 49.

Chapter 6

Consideration

6.1 Introduction

[6.05] The concept of agreement is fundamental to contract formation. Where an offer has been made and accepted, promises are involved. Whether or not a promise that is part of an agreement can be enforced depends on, among other things, whether the promisee has given 'consideration' for the promise. The example given in the introduction to chapter 3 is illustrative.

Example

A makes an offer to buy a computer for $3000. B accepts this offer by agreeing to sell the computer to A for this amount. A concluded bargain had been reached.

Upon agreement, B promises to pass title in the computer to A. If B subsequently refuses to pass title as agreed, the question arises whether A can enforce the promise. The answer depends on whether A has 'paid for' B's promise. In the example given, A has paid for B's promise by agreeing to pay B $3000. In legal terms, the price paid for the promise is referred to as consideration. A valid contract is formed (and therefore an action for breach of a promise can be brought) only if the promisee provides legally recognised consideration for the promise.

[6.10] The requirement for the existence of consideration in contract formation reflects an important matter of policy. The common law will only enforce a promise for which a price is paid.[1] If, in the above example, B promised to transfer title in a computer to A because B had two computers and A had none, and B subsequently reneged, A would have no recourse. A has not provided consideration for B's promise. In a similar way, if an adult child promises to take care of a frail parent, this promise alone will not be enforceable. The fact that the promisor may be regarded as having a moral obligation to honour that commitment is not sufficient to enforce the promise. If the promisee agrees to transfer property to the adult child on the basis of the promise, the situation may be different. The promisee has 'paid for' the promise and it may be enforceable.

[6.15] In practical terms, only in rare cases is doubt likely to arise about whether a promise is supported by consideration. However, the notion of consideration and the requirement that it be present before a promise can be enforced is open to criticism.

---

1   While this clearly represents the modern position, it should be noted that the existence of consideration has not always been a requirement for a promise to be enforced. In earlier times, issues of reliance rather than consideration were relevant to courts in determining whether a promise should be enforced.

The following example demonstrates what some may regard as a shortcoming in the doctrine.

Example

An owner of a shopping complex enters into a three-year lease with tenant X. During the term of the lease, X struggles to make the rental payments and the parties alter their existing rental agreement to reduce the rent for the balance of the period.

Entry into the lease does not raise any difficulties in relation to consideration. In consideration for allowing X to occupy the premises for a fixed period, X will pay a set rental. However, difficulties may arise where the parties vary their rental agreement. From a commercial perspective, this arrangement may benefit both parties. X is able to remain in business, and the owner retains a tenant. In an economic environment in which it is difficult to attract tenants, this alteration to the lease agreement may be of commercial benefit to the owner. However, it is doubtful whether X can be regarded as having provided consideration for the owner's promise to decrease the rental. If this is correct, the owner can later sue X for the shortfall of rent. Although this might be the legal position, it is unlikely to reflect what reasonable people would regard as a fair, sensible, or commercially realistic outcome.

[6.20] As the above example demonstrates, a strict application of rules of consideration may lead to harsh results. But recognition of the shortfalls of the doctrine, coupled with a desire for the law to more closely reflect people's expectations, can lead to application of principles in a more flexible way.[2] The English case of *Williams v Roffey Brothers and Nicholls (Contractors) Ltd*[3] is a classic example. While the case may be open to criticism for pushing the boundaries of the rules on consideration, the decision itself reflects the commercial reality of operating in the construction industry. Occasional judicial pronouncements also suggest, at least in limited circumstances, that the absence of consideration may not prevent enforcement of a promise. For example, Toohey J in *Trident General Insurance Co Ltd v McNiece Bros Pty Ltd*[4] thought that a contractor could sue an insurer although consideration had not moved from the contractor. Further, the development of the doctrine of promissory estoppel under which a promise that has been relied on to another's detriment may be enforced by that other despite the lack of consideration provides another example of the law evolving to accommodate expectations of reasonable people.[5] Such developments certainly demonstrate the fact that common law is not static, and its evolution may continue to witness further developments in the rules governing consideration.[6]

---

2   J Steyn, 'Contract law: fulfilling the reasonable expectations of honest men' (1997) 113 *The Law Quarterly Review* 433 at 437.

3   [1992] WLR 1153.

4   (1987) 165 CLR 107 at 172.

5   It is suggested by P Prindable in 'Is offer and acceptance no longer a consideration? An examination of the implications of the *Waltons v Maher* concept of promissory estoppel' (1996) 16 *Queensland Lawyer* 169 at 178 that the role of the doctrine of consideration has in fact been enhanced by this High Court decision.

6   See, for example, comments of Santow J in *Musumeci v Winadell Pty Ltd* (1994) 34 NSWLR 723 at 740 about the 'continuing trend to side-step the artificial results of a strict doctrine of consideration'.

Nevertheless, today the requirement of consideration for contract formation is undisputed. This is reflected in all texts and judicial pronouncements on the issue.

6.2   Nature of consideration

[6.25] Consideration is a difficult concept to understand. When describing one of the important cases on consideration, Lord Dunedin commented that 'this case is to my mind apt to nip any budding affection which one might have had for the doctrine of consideration'.[7] In this part of the chapter, some of the definitions of the term are considered, as well as the way the concept differs in the context of bilateral and unilateral contracts. The terms 'executed' and 'executory' consideration are also explained.

6.2.1   Definitions and examples of consideration

[6.30] One of the classic descriptions of the concept of consideration was the formulation by Sir Frederick Pollock that was adopted by Lord Dunedin in *Dunlop Pnuematic Tyre Company Ltd v Selfridge & Company Ltd:*[8]

> An act or forbearance of one party, or the promise thereof, is the price for which the promise of the other is bought, and the promise thus given for value is enforceable.

The tables below set out a number of simple contracts to distil what can be regarded as the 'act or forbearance by one party [the promisee], or the promise thereof' which constitutes the consideration for the promise of the other [the promisor].

No	Example	A's promise	B's consideration
I	Agreement for sale of land by A to B for $200 000	A to pass title to B	B's promise to pay $200 000
II	Agreement for A to paint B's house for $5000 payment to be made on completion	A to paint B's house	B's promise to pay $5000
III	Agreement for A to provide tennis coaching to C and D if B (C and D's mother) provides remedial mathematics lesson to E (A's son)	A to provide tennis coaching to C and D	B's promise to give remedial mathematics lesson to E

[6.35] Another definition in common parlance is that of Lush J in *Currie v Misa:*[9]

> A valuable consideration, in the sense of the law, may consist either in some right, interest, profit, or benefit accruing to the one party, or some forbearance, detriment, loss or responsibility, given, suffered or undertaken by the other ...

Examples I–III could be regarded as 'some right, interest, profit, or benefit accruing to the one party', namely the promisor (A), while examples IV–VII below are

---

7   *Dunlop Pneumatic Tyre Company Ltd v Selfridge & Company Ltd* [1915] AC 847 at 855.
8   [1915] AC 847 at 855. This formulation is sometimes shortened by referring to consideration 'as the price paid for the promise'.
9   (1875) LR 10 Ex 153 at 162.

examples of 'some forbearance, detriment, loss or responsibility given, suffered or undertaken by the other', the promisee (B).

No	Example	A's promise	B's consideration
IV	A and B are neighbours and are in dispute over the fence line, B claiming it is built on her property. They agree that if A pays B $3000, B will not litigate the matter	A to pay B $3000	B's promise not to litigate
V	A needs transport for a week but does not own a car. A and B agree that if B lends her car to A for this time, A will pay for the car to be serviced	A to service the car	B promises to give A her car for a week
VI	Agreement between A (an employer) and B (an employee) that if B assumes higher duties, she will be paid an increased salary	A to pay an increased salary	B to assume higher duties
VII	A company that manufactures smoke balls (A) promises B that if B uses the smoke balls in the manner directed and still contracts the flu, A will pay B $100	A to pay B $100 if B contracts the flu after using the smoke balls as prescribed	B buying and using the smoke balls in the manner directed (if B chooses to do so)

[6.40] In all of the above examples, agreement has been reached between A and B. If A reneges on a promise, B will be entitled to bring action in relation to that breach as B has provided consideration for the promise. What is important to recognise, however, is that in all of these cases, promises have been exchanged by A and B. In each case B has made a promise to A. Importantly, A has also paid for B's promise (as listed in the second column). Therefore, if B reneges, A is also entitled to bring action for that breach.

6.2.2 Consideration in bilateral contracts

[6.45] The nature of a bilateral contract and principles of offer and acceptance that arise in that context were examined in chapter 3 on agreement.[10] The description of a bilateral contract given by Diplock LJ in *United Dominions Trust (Commercial) Ltd v Eagle Aircraft Services Ltd*[11] is informative not only in relation to principles of agreement, but also to the notion of consideration. Where parties enter bilateral contracts, 'each party undertakes to the other party to do or to refrain from doing something …'.[12] In other words, a bilateral contract is formed where the parties exchange promises. At the time agreement is reached, each party makes a promise. The price paid for that promise—the consideration—is the other party's promise. Each party promises to do an act or refrain from doing an act. Examples I–VI above are all illustrations of bilateral contracts. All involve an exchange of promises. This is the case whether the contract is for a single transaction, such as a sale of land (in example I), or involves ongoing obligations, as in an alteration to an employment contract (in example VI).

---

10   See [3.40].
11   [1968] 1 WLR 74.
12   Ibid at 82.

6.2.3   Consideration in unilateral contracts

[6.50] Because a unilateral contract is different in nature from a bilateral contract, consideration operates differently. As emphasised by Lord Diplock, in a unilateral contract, the promisee does not himself or herself undertake to do or to refrain from doing a particular act.[13] Unlike a bilateral contract, there is not an exchange of promises. The only promise is the one made by the promisor to do or refrain from doing an act *if* the promisee does or refrains from doing a specified act. Example VII above, based on the facts of *Carlill v Carbolic Smoke Ball Company*,[14] is such an example. A is the promisor and has promised to pay B \$100 if B contracts the flu after using the smoke balls as prescribed. B does not make a promise to use the smoke balls and is, therefore, under no obligation to do so. However, if B does, it is the act of buying and using the smoke balls in the manner directed (and subsequently contracting the flu) that is the consideration for A's initial promise. In unilateral contracts, the act or forbearance itself—rather than a promise—constitutes the consideration. It is the absence of an obligation undertaken by the promisee that distinguishes a unilateral contract from a bilateral contract.

6.2.4   Executed and executory consideration

[6.55] The distinction between a bilateral and a unilateral contract underlies the concepts of 'executory' and 'executed' consideration. The terms 'executed' and 'executory' have technical meanings when used in the context of consideration. A bilateral contract is formed when the parties exchange promises. In example I above, A promises to transfer land to B. B's consideration for A's promise is a promise to pay A \$200 000. Consideration in this case is regarded as executory. This means that the obligation to perform has not yet fallen due. As indicated above, however, the position is different for a unilateral contract.[15] The parties do not exchange promises. In example VII, it is only A who has made the promise. A's obligation to pay B arises only if B carries out the specified acts. Consideration for A's promise is not executory because B has not promised to perform. If B chooses to and does perform the specified acts, consideration is said to be executed.[16]

6.3   Rules governing consideration

[6.60] The preceding discussion provided some definitions of the concept of consideration and explained how consideration differs depending on whether used in the context of bilateral or unilateral contracts. To fully understand how the doctrine operates, however, it is necessary to be aware of the various rules that have developed throughout the evolution of this doctrine.

---

13   *United Dominions Trust (Commercial) Ltd v Eagle Aircraft Services Ltd* [1968] 1 WLR 74 at 83.
14   [1893] 1 QB 256. For a further example, see *Holloway v Attorney-General* [1994] 2 ERNZ 528.
15   See [6.50].
16   For an explanation of the distinction between 'executed' and 'past' consideration, see [6.160].

6.3.1   Consideration must move from the promisee

[6.65] It is implicit from the preceding discussion that for there to be a contract between the promisor and promisee, consideration must move from the promisee.[17] This occurred in the examples listed above. B promised to pay the money or perform the particular act specified as consideration for a promise. Failure of a litigant to provide consideration to the promisor was one of the reasons that the plaintiff was unsuccessful in the following important but complex case.

Example: Dunlop Pnuematic Tyre Company Ltd v Selfridge & Company Ltd[18]

Dunlop Pnuematic Tyre Company Ltd ('Dunlop') sold some products to a third party at a discount price. In consideration for the discount price, the third party agreed that if it onsold for a discount price, it would require an undertaking by that purchaser not to sell at less than the list price. The third party sold to Selfridge & Company Ltd ('Selfridge') and obtained the required undertaking. Selfridge did not honour this undertaking and was sued by Dunlop for breach of contract.

The House of Lords found in favour of Selfridge. Even if it could be considered that an agreement was entered into between Dunlop (the third party acting as agent for Dunlop, an undisclosed principal) and Selfridge, Dunlop could not be regarded as having provided consideration for Selfridge's promise not to sell at less than the list price. Consideration for this promise moved only from the third party.

(a)   Benefit need not move to promisor

[6.70] It will generally be the case that consideration moves from the promisee to the promisor, whether the promisee promises to pay money, or do or forbear from doing an act. This occurred in most of the above examples. However, this need not necessarily be the case. It is sufficient if consideration moves from the promisee to a third party at the direction of the promisor. Example III illustrates this point. In consideration for A's promise, B promises to give remedial mathematics lessons to A's son, E.

(b)   Joint promisees

[6.75] The agreement in all of the above examples is between A and B. It is possible, however, for agreements to take place between more than two parties.

Example

B and C agree with A that A may quarry and remove stone from land owned by B in exchange for A paying royalties to B and C.

---

17   *Dunlop Pnuematic Tyre Company Ltd v Selfridge & Company Ltd* [1915] AC 847; *Tweddle v Atkinson* (1861) 121 ER 762. A promise was once considered to be enforceable if consideration was provided by someone close to the promisee. However, this notion was finally overruled in *Tweddle v Atkinson* (1861) 121 ER 762.

18   [1915] AC 847.

These facts disclose a valid agreement. In consideration of A's promise to pay B and C royalties for the quarried stone, B allows A access to the land and rights to quarry and remove stone. In this case, B and C are joint promisees. Consideration need only flow from one of the promisees.[19] This contract is therefore enforceable by C, even although C has not provided consideration for A's promise.[20]

(c) Overlap with doctrine of privity

[6.80] The doctrine of privity is examined in Chapter 12. In simple terms, it provides that only a person who is a party to a contract can sue on it. We have just seen that a promisee is only able to sue on a promise if the promisee has given consideration for that promise. As demonstrated by the following example, there exists considerable overlap between these doctrines.

Example

A and B agree that if B does specified work for A, A will pay C $500. B does the work but A refuses to pay the $500.

Applying common law principles, C will not be successful in an action against A to enforce A's promise. There are two possible bases for this. First, C is not a party to the contract, so is unable to sue upon it. This is because of the doctrine of privity. Alternatively, it could be argued that C has not provided consideration for A's promise, and therefore cannot sue upon it. On this occasion, rules of consideration come into play. Unfortunately, the case law does not provide clear and consistent guidance as to the real reason for C's inability to sue. The following early English decision, and later comment on the basis of the decision, provide a good illustration of the dilemma.

Example: Tweddle v Atkinson[21]

A man (the plaintiff) and a woman were engaged to be married. The plaintiff's father and the deceased (the woman's father) agreed for each to pay specified amounts to the plaintiff upon the marriage. The deceased died without paying the agreed sum. The plaintiff sued the deceased's estate to recover the amount.

It was held that the plaintiff could not succeed. The reason provided was that an action could not be brought upon a promise where the plaintiff is a 'stranger to the consideration'.

The brief judgments were couched in language of consideration. However, in *Trident General Insurance Company Ltd v McNiece Bros Pty Ltd*[22] (the *Trident* case), Toohey J noted the difficulty in determining the true ratio of the English case. His Honour's

---

19   *Coulls v Bagot's Executor and Trustee Company Ltd* (1966) 119 CLR 460.
20   Compare *Coulls v Bagot's Executor and Trustee Company Ltd* (1966) 119 CLR 460. On similar facts, it was held by the High Court that the agreement was not enforceable by C, as C was not a party to the contract. It was accepted by the majority of Justices, however, that if B and C were joint promisees, it was enough for consideration to be provided by one of them only.
21   (1861) 121 ER 762.
22   (1987) 165 CLR 107.

tentative conclusion was that the plaintiff failed on both grounds: because he was not a party to the contract, and because he had not provided any consideration.[23]

[6.85] Because of the overlap between the operation of these doctrines, debate has arisen as to whether two doctrines exist, or whether they are both, in fact, different formulations of the one doctrine. The interrelationship between the doctrines of consideration and privity has been considered, albeit relatively briefly, by the High Court on two occasions. In *Coulls v Bagot's Executor and Trustee Company Ltd*,[24] Barwick CJ expressed the view that there are two separate doctrines, and was critical of the fact that they were sometimes not kept distinct. His Honour continued:

> Indeed, on some occasions when lack of privity is the real reason for not allowing a plaintiff to succeed on a promise not made with him, an unnecessary and irrelevant reason is given that the plaintiff was a stranger to the consideration; that is to say, that he was not merely not a party to the agreement but was not a party to the bargain.[25]

More recently in the *Trident* case, it was the tentative conclusion of the three Justices who considered the issue that consideration and privity were two separate, though interrelated, principles.[26]

[6.90] Until further consideration of the issue, therefore, it appears that the doctrine of consideration will be regarded as being different from the doctrine of privity. The following example was given at the outset.

Example

A and B agree that if B does specified work for A, A will pay C $500. B does the work but A refuses to pay the $500.

Assuming that the doctrines of privity and consideration are distinct, it is the view of the authors that the legal implications of this agreement are most correctly described in the following way. B, the promisee, has provided valid consideration for A, the promisor's, promise. A valid contract therefore exists between A and B. If A fails to pay C, B can sue A for breach of contract. C, however, is unable to sue A because C is not a party to that contract. As stated by Barwick CJ and quoted earlier 'an unnecessary and irrelevant reason is given that the plaintiff [here, C] was a stranger to the consideration.'[27] Where C is not a party to the contract, the doctrine of privity prevents C from bringing an action on the contract. It is unnecessary to consider issues of consideration.

[6.95] Different legal issues arise if C is a party to the contract, as in the following case.

---

23   Ibid at 163.
24   (1966) 119 CLR 460.
25   Ibid at 478.
26   (1987) 165 CLR 107 at 115 per Mason C J and Wilson J and at 164 per Toohey J.
27   *Coulls v Bagot's Executor and Trustee Company Ltd* (1966) 119 CLR 460 at 478.

Example

A, B and C sign a contract under which A agrees to pay C $500 if B does specified work. B does the work but A refuses to pay the $500.

Here, as C is a party to the contract, the doctrine of privity will not bar an action by C against A for A's breach. However, the doctrine of consideration is likely to be relevant. C will be unable to sue A for breach because C has not provided consideration for A's promise.[28] In this case, therefore, it is the doctrine of consideration, not privity, which prevents a successful action being brought by C.

6.3.2 Consideration must be bargained for

[6.100] An act or forbearance (or promise to forbear) can only constitute valid consideration if it is bargained for. The notion of 'bargain' involves both the promisor and the promisee. The action or forbearance from action of the promisee must be in reliance on the promisor's promise. In addition, the act or forbearance must be done at the request of the promisor. As stated by the High Court, there must exist the requisite 'quid pro quo' between the promisor's promise and the act or forbearance of the promisee.[29] In another case, Lord Justice Denning, as he then was, spoke of the nexus between the promise and consideration in the following terms.

> Unilateral promises of this kind have long been enforced, so long as the act or forbearance is done on the faith of the promise and at the request of the promisor, express or implied.[30]

[6.105] For most contracts, there will be no dispute about whether consideration has been bargained for. Where a bilateral contract is entered into under which an owner of land promises to pay a specified sum to a builder who agrees to build a house, there is no room for debate about whether the builder's actions in building the house are done in reliance on the owner's promise to pay money, or whether those actions are done at the request of the owner. The nature of unilateral contracts, however, is different. As illustrated by the following case, it may be more difficult to demonstrate the link between the promise and consideration in such contracts.

Example: Coombe v Coombe[31]

After a married couple separated, the husband promised to pay the wife £100 per year. Because of this promise, the wife did not apply to the Divorce Court for maintenance. The husband failed to pay the money as promised, and the wife brought action to recover the payments.

The English Court of Appeal found in favour of the husband. The parties had not entered a contract for the payment of £100 per year as the wife had not provided consideration for the husband's promise. The wife's forbearance from bringing an

---

28   If B and C can be regarded as joint promisees, however, the contract will be enforceable by C if consideration is provided by either B or C: see [6.75] above.
29   *Australian Woollen Mills Pty Ltd v The Commonwealth* (1954) 92 CLR 424 at 456–457.
30   *Combe v Coombe* [1951] 2 KB 215 at 221.
31   [1951] 2 KB 215.

action for maintenance did not constitute consideration because it was not done at the express or implied request of the husband.

[6.110] The required nexus between the promise and consideration has also been examined by the High Court.

Example: Australian Woollen Mills Pty Ltd v The Commonwealth[32]

The Commonwealth implemented a subsidy scheme to lower the purchase price of wool for local manufacturers. Upon discontinuance of the scheme, a local manufacturer sued the Commonwealth for breach of contract to recover the outstanding subsidy. The manufacturer claimed that a contract was in existence between it and the Commonwealth, the manufacturer buying quantities of wool in consideration for the Commonwealth's promise to provide a subsidy.

In finding in favour of the Commonwealth, the High Court was not persuaded that a contract had come into existence. There was no indication that the Commonwealth's promise was made to induce the manufacturer to purchase wool, nor that the manufacturer purchased the wool because of the Commonwealth's promise.

6.3.3 Consideration must be sufficient

(a) General principle

[6.115] To be valid consideration, the price paid by the promisee for the promisor's promise must be 'sufficient'. Consideration must be 'something which is of some value in the eye of the law'.[33] The decisions, in turn, provide guidance concerning the kinds of acts, forbearance or promises that can be regarded as something of value for this purpose.

[6.120] In the usual case—particularly where contracts are formed in a commercial context—there will be no dispute over the sufficiency of the consideration. Each party is attempting to obtain some benefit from the agreement. In a contract under which an owner of real estate promises to sell that real estate to a buyer for $200 000, the buyer's consideration (the promise to pay the agreed price) will be sufficient. However, the agreements that can be entered into are many and varied. Consideration may be valid although it cannot be given a monetary equivalent.

Example: Chappell & Co Ltd v Nestlé Co Ltd[34]

Nestlé Co Ltd ('Nestlé') manufactured chocolate. To promote chocolate sales, Nestlé promised to give a record to any member of the public who sent in 1s 6d plus three chocolate wrappers. The issue before the Court was whether the three chocolate wrappers (as well as the 1s 6d) could properly be regarded as part of the 'sale price' of the record.[35]

---

32   (1954) 92 CLR 424.
33   *Thomas v Thomas* (1842) 2 QB 851 at 859 per Patteson J. It is not therefore surprising that a promise to do something illegal, or even to refrain from doing something illegal cannot be regarded as 'something of value in the eyes of the law': *Jamieson v Renwick* (1891) 17 VLR 124. Compare also the concept of an illusory promise as discussed at [4.35]–[4.40]
34   [1960] AC 87.
35   If it were so regarded, Nestlé would be in breach of the *Copyright Act* 1956 (Eng).

The House of Lords held that the chocolate wrappers did form part of the sale price. Consideration for the record was both the money paid and the three chocolate wrappers. The sending in of the wrappers was of value to Nestlé. Given the large number of records sold, there would be a large number of wrappers sent in. This was of commercial benefit to Nestlé. The fact that the chocolate wrappers could not be converted into money was irrelevant.

This House of Lords decision demonstrates that even if an item lacks intrinsic value, requiring it to be provided can constitute good consideration. It is interesting to contrast this notion with principles governing 'moral consideration'. As explored later, such consideration is not sufficient.[36] As noted below, consideration will be valid even if it is not 'adequate' in an objective way when compared with the promise, or if it is nominal only. The extent to which the rules on consideration can be justified on any kind of logical basis is considered later in this paragraph.[37]

(b) Consideration need not be adequate

[6.125] A lay person asked to articulate the distinction between 'adequate' and 'sufficient' would be unlikely to provide any sensible response. However, this distinction is critical in the context of consideration. Consideration, it is said, must be sufficient but need not be adequate.[38] When used in relation to consideration, adequacy is a reference to the commercial value of the consideration. By saying that consideration need not be adequate, it means that a court is not interested in ensuring that a promisee provides value for the promisor's promise. If parties agree to the sale of real estate valued at $200 000 for a purchase price of $180 000, it is not open for a court to find there was no consideration because the promisee's promise to pay less than the market value was inadequate to support the promisor's promise to pass title.[39]

(c) Consideration can be nominal

[6.130] Not only is the court not concerned to establish that consideration for the promise is adequate, consideration will be regarded as valid even if it is 'nominal' only.[40] Provided agreement arises from a bargain, a promisor can confer a benefit of considerable value upon a promisee in exchange for the promisee's promise to pay $10.[41]

(d) Sustainability of sufficiency principles

[6.135] The requirement that consideration be 'valid', 'good' or 'sufficient' for an agreement to be formed is, in itself, sound, and consistent with the bargain theory of

---

36   See [6.175]–[6.210].

37   See [6.135]–6.145].

38   For the reason why the judiciary does not embark upon an examination of the adequacy of consideration, see the judgment of Kirby P in *Woolworths Ltd v Kelly* (1991) 22 NSWLR 189 at 193–194.

39   For an example of a contract for the transfer of land being enforced despite the commercial inadequacy of the consideration, see *Re Murphy* [1933] NZLR 583.

40   *Thomas v Thomas* [1842] 2 QB 851; *Niesmann v Collingridge* (1921) 29 CLR 177; *Barnett v Ira L & AC Berk Pty Ltd* (1952) 52 SR (NSW) 268; *Carallari v Premier Refrigeration Co Pty Ltd* (1952) 85 CLR 20.

41   See, for example, *Lennox v Cameron* (1997) 8 Butterworths Property Reports [97696], a case involving an option to purchase land being given in exchange for consideration of $1.

contract formation. Over the decades, rules have developed to establish whether a particular act or forbearance (or promise to forbear) can be regarded as sufficient consideration in particular circumstances. Whether these principles fit comfortably together can perhaps be queried. The following examples illustrate the problem. In all cases, the father wishes to transfer his real estate valued at $200 000 to his daughter.

Examples

I   A father promises to transfer real estate to his daughter in consideration of the daughter paying him $100 000.

II   A father promises to transfer real estate to his daughter in consideration of the daughter paying him $1.

III   A father promises to transfer real estate to his daughter in consideration of the daughter's love and affection for her father.

IV   A father promises to transfer real estate to his daughter in consideration of his daughter agreeing to 'conduct herself with sobriety, and in a respectable, orderly and virtuous manner'.[42]

V   A father promises to transfer real estate to his daughter in consideration of the daughter agreeing to complete the sale of an original Dobell painting to her father, the contract of sale having been entered into one month earlier.

Comment on examples

I   The father's promise is enforceable because the daughter's consideration is sufficient. Consideration need not be adequate. The fact that consideration is less than the value of the real estate does not mean that the consideration is not sufficient.

II   The father's promise is enforceable because the daughter's consideration is sufficient. Consideration is sufficient even though it is nominal only.

III   The father's promise is not enforceable because the daughter's consideration is not of value in the eyes of the law.[43]

IV   There is authority to suggest that the father's promise is enforceable because the daughter's consideration is or may be of value in the eyes of the law.[44]

V   The father's promise is unenforceable because the daughter's consideration is not of value in the eyes of the law. It is insufficient consideration for the promisee to promise to perform a pre-existing legal duty owed to the promisor.[45]

[6.140] The legal status of the consideration in most of the above examples is reasonably well settled.[46] When the enforceability of the promises in the scenarios are compared, it must be queried whether the different outcomes are sustainable from the perspective of the reasonable expectations of ordinary people. In examples I and II, the father clearly wants to provide his daughter with a benefit by transferring the real

---

42   This was the consideration provided by a divorced wife in *Dunton v Dunton* [1892] VLR 114. See [6.190].

43   See [6.185].

44   *Dunton v Dunton* [1892] VLR 114. See [6.190].

45   See [6.220].

46   Note, however, that there can be a fine line between consideration that is regarded as sufficient in the eyes of the law and the consideration that is not in cases such as III and IV above.

estate to her at half the market value (I), or for nominal consideration only (II). In both cases, it is likely that the father is motivated by the love and affection he and his daughter have for each other. However, if such love and affection is expressed to be the consideration, it is not good consideration. In all cases, the daughter receives a benefit because that is the father's desire. Where consideration is, in a legal sense, contrived by the giving of a token payment (as in example II), the promise is enforceable. However, statement of the *motivation* for the transfer (as in example III) does not constitute good consideration.

[6.145] The enforceability of promises that involve some feature of moral consideration—as in examples III and IV—raise further difficulties. As elaborated below, it can be a fine line between consideration that is regarded as sufficient and consideration that is not. Example V is also not without difficulty. The difficulties surrounding the performance of existing legal duties as consideration is explored later in this chapter.[47]

6.3.4   Consideration must not be past

(a)   General principle

[6.150] Consideration moving from the promisee will not be valid to support a promisor's promise if that consideration is past. Consideration will be regarded as being past if it has already flowed from the promisee to the promisor.[48] There are very few reported cases that examine this issue. However, the following early English decision demonstrates the operation of the principle.

Example: Roscorla v Thomas[49]

A buyer bought a horse from a seller. After the sale, the seller promised that the horse was 'free from vice'. The horse was vicious, and the buyer sued the seller for breach of his promise that the horse was free from vice.

Chief Justice Lord Denman dismissed the buyer's action as he did not provide any consideration for the seller's promise. Agreement to buy the horse could not be regarded as consideration because the sale had already taken place.

[6.155] There is no room for doubt that past consideration cannot support a promisor's promise. However, in limited circumstances, where a promise relates to previous work done or assurances given by a promisee on the understanding that the work or assurance would subsequently be rewarded, a promisor's promise may be enforced. The circumstances in which such a promise is enforceable, and how its enforcement is consistent with the principle that past consideration is not good consideration, are explored later.[50]

---

47   See [6.255].

48   There are exceptions to this rule: consideration regarded as valuable under the *Bills of Exchange Act* 1999 (Cth), s 32(1)(b); an acknowledgment of a debt being regarded as an implied promise to pay although not supported by consideration; ratification of a voidable contract by a minor upon reaching majority will bind the minor in the absence of consideration by the other party. See further JW Carter & DJ Harland, *Contract Law in Australia*, 3rd edn, Butterworths, North Ryde, 1996, pp 110–111.

49   (1842) 3 QB 234. For further examples, see *Re McArdle* [1951] Ch 669 and *Tranzequity Holdings Ltd v Malley* (1990) 5 NZCLC 66343.

50   See [6.420]–[6.435].

(b) Past consideration distinguished from executed consideration

[6.160] Consideration is said to be 'executed' once it has been performed.[51] When considered in the abstract, 'executed' consideration can look like past consideration. However, as the following examples illustrate, this is not the case.

Examples

I   A promises to pay B $10 000 to paint the exterior of A's house, payment to be made within thirty days of B completing the work.

II As for example I above. After B completes the painting, B advises A that the particular kind of paint used was specially treated to keep away cobwebs and wasp nests for five years.

Comment on examples

I   A and B have entered a valid contract for the painting of the house. Once B has finished the painting, B's consideration for A's promise to pay $10 000 is said to be executed. B is entitled to payment after thirty days from the date of completion.

II As for I, a valid agreement exists for the painting of the house. Therefore B is entitled to payment of $10 000 thirty days after completion. However, A is not able to sue B if the paint does not keep away cobwebs and wasp nests as promised. A has provided no consideration for this promise. A's agreement to enter the original contract cannot be regarded as consideration because that had already taken place. It was past consideration and therefore not good consideration.

In summary, to determine whether consideration is regarded as executed or past, the legal position must be examined at the time the relevant promise is made. If, at that time, the act, forbearance, or promise that is claimed to be consideration has already occurred or been given, the consideration is past, not executed. It will not be good consideration to support the promise.

6.4   Consideration and formal agreements

[6.165] For hundreds of years, it has been recognised that all contracts fall into one of two categories: formal agreements and simple agreements.[52] Formal agreements are signed under seal, and are more commonly referred to as deeds.[53] Because of the solemnity or seriousness of the manner of execution of such documents, the common law has recognised these agreements as valid even if consideration has not been provided by the parties to them.[54] Simple agreements are agreements other than formal

---

51 For an examination of 'executed' and 'executory' consideration, see [6.55] above.

52 *Rann v Hughes* (1778) 101 ER 1014 refers to these categories as 'specialty' and 'parol' agreements. In this context, parol means all agreements that are not specialty agreements, so it includes written agreements other than deeds and also oral agreements.

53 In this context, a seal is defined as 'a mark or symbol attached to a document to indicate authenticity or as a formal requirement': *Butterworths Business and Law Dictionary*, Butterworths, 1997.

54 A possible exception to this rule is where the parties execute a deed, but do not intend it to operate as a deed: *Rose & Burgess v Commissioner of Stamps (SA)* (1979) 22 SASR 84 at 89.

agreements, and can be either oral or written. For such agreements to be valid contracts, consideration must be present.

6.5   Consideration: specific examples

[6.170] Notwithstanding the existence of well-established rules governing consideration, applying those rules to particular fact situations can create challenges. In this part of the chapter, the extent to which particular kinds of acts or promises can constitute valid consideration is examined, together with the difficulties that the courts have encountered in making such determinations.

6.5.1   Moral consideration

[6.175] As examined earlier,[55] to constitute good consideration, the act, forbearance, or promise must be of value in the eyes of the law.[56] This does not mean that the consideration must be a commercial equivalent to the thing promised. Further, the consideration need not have any intrinsic value at all.[57] How then is a determination made of whether something is of value? This question is particularly vexed where the purported consideration contains some component of behaviour not related to any kind of commercial outcome, or is linked in some way to the motivation for the promisor's promise.

[6.180] As a starting point, it appears that a promise made because of a sense of moral obligation to the promisee will not be sufficient consideration to support that promise.

Example: Eastwood v Kenyon[58]

Upon the death of a girl's father, the father's executor (the plaintiff) looked after the girl's interests and investments, and spent his own money in the process. When the girl attained majority, she undertook to repay the plaintiff. This promise was adopted by the girl's husband (the defendant) when she married. The plaintiff brought action against the defendant to recover the amount promised.

The plaintiff was unsuccessful, the English court finding that the plaintiff had not provided any consideration for the husband's promise. Any moral obligation that the defendant may have felt on the basis of the care taken of his wife and money expended by the plaintiff on her over the years did not constitute valid consideration.[59]

[6.185] Secondly, a promise made because of the love and affection that the promisor and promisee have for each other, or that the promisor has for the promisee, is not legally recognised.[60] While such emotions may well be the motivation behind an

---

55   See [6.115].
56   *Thomas v Thomas* (1842) 2 QB 851 at 859.
57   See [6.120].
58   (1840) 113 ER 482.
59   The court also noted that the services provided by the plaintiff to the wife over the years could not be regarded as good consideration for the promise because they were past acts.
60   *White v Bluett* (1853) 23 LJ (Exch) 36; *Bret v J S* (1600) 78 ER 987.

agreement, they cannot constitute valid consideration. That motivation cannot be good consideration is evident from the following case.

Example: Thomas v Thomas[61]

On his deathbed, a testator indicated that he wanted his wife to receive his house. The house was conveyed to the wife 'in consideration of such desire'. In the same agreement, the wife was required to pay the executors £1.1.0 yearly towards the rent payable in respect of the house, and to keep the house in repair. The executors refused to transfer the property.

The English court held that the executors were required to transfer the house to the wife. The wife's promise to pay £1.1.0 and to keep the premises in repair was consideration for the promise to transfer the property. However, the court held that fulfilling the testator's desire could not form part of the legal consideration for the agreement.

[6.190] Beyond these principles, it is difficult to predict whether a court will regard consideration that encompasses notions of good, moral or proper behaviour as valid, even where that behaviour or conduct is bargained for. The way promises such as these have been regarded by the courts in the past may provide some guidance.

Example: Dunton v Dunton[62]

Upon separation of a married couple, the husband promised to pay the wife specified maintenance if she, among other things, promised to 'conduct herself with sobriety, and in a respectable, orderly and virtuous manner'. The majority of the Supreme Court of Victoria held this to constitute valuable consideration.[63]

Example: Hamer v Sidway[64]

A person's promise to give up tobacco and liquor until he turned 21 was held by the New York Court of Appeals to constitute good consideration for the payment of $5000.

Example: Jamieson v Renwick[65]

A promisee promised, among other things, not to live in a particular area, or visit or annoy the promisor, in exchange for payment of an annual sum of £25. The Victorian Supreme Court held that this constituted good consideration for the promise.

Example: White v Bluett[66]

A son was disappointed about the way his father had distributed some property, and made repeated complaints about this distribution to his father. The son and father agreed that if the son ceased complaining about the distribution, and also because of

---

61   (1842) 2 QB 851.
62   (1892) 18 VLR 114.
63   Hood J dissented on the basis that the stated consideration was too uncertain to be valid.
64   (1891) 27 NE 256.
65   (1891) 17 VLR 124.
66   (1853) 23 LJ (Exch) 36.

the natural love and affection the father had for his son, the son would not have to pay money owing to his father. An English court held that the son had not provided good consideration for the father's promise. Pollock CB noted that the son had no right to complain because his father had a right to distribute property in any way he saw fit. The son promising not to do what he had no right to do could not constitute consideration.

[6.195] The question then is whether any conclusions can be drawn from the decisions about what attributes of the bargained-for conduct must be present for it to constitute valid consideration. It may be possible to reconcile these decisions if regard is given to the comments of Pollock CB in *White v Bluett*[67] that the son had no right to complain about the father's distribution of property. Promising to abstain from such complaints could not, therefore, constitute consideration. In the other three cases, the parties had every right to act or behave in the way they promised they would not. The promises therefore were regarded as constituting consideration.

[6.200] However, this distinction is not an appropriate one to draw and should not be the yardstick against which sufficiency of consideration should be measured. Notwithstanding the observations of Pollock CB, there was nothing unlawful about the son complaining to the father. The fact that the son had no legal right to upset the property distribution is irrelevant. Undertaking to give up this right to complain constituted a forbearance to do something he was entitled to do, just as much as a promise to refrain from smoking cigarettes.

[6.205] From a common-sense prospective, the decision of the court in *White v Bluett*[68] is certainly justifiable. If a promise to stop complaining is regarded as valid consideration, it is easy to envisage many instances of consideration being contrived to support a promise. As mentioned earlier, however, given the ability of nominal consideration to support a promise, it must be queried whether consideration of the kind contemplated in *White v Bluett* is any less supportable in principle.

[6.210] In summary, a bargained-for promise to behave in a particular way can constitute consideration, even if that behaviour is of no commercial value, and of only personal value (from the promisor's perspective). The fact that it would be difficult (if not impossible) to assess the amount of damages that would flow as a result of the breach should be irrelevant in determining the validity of the consideration. In fact, where the consideration relates to some aspect of behaviour and is not in a commercial context, it would be unlikely for the damages to be easily quantifiable. The difficulty faced by the courts is in drawing the line between the kinds of promises that are of value in the eyes of the law, and the kinds that are not. As the nature of such promises can vary widely, it is difficult to offer concrete guidelines. In practical terms, it may be that this is no longer a significant problem. Few of the reported cases on this topic are recent.

---

67   Ibid.
68   Ibid.

Perhaps, in deciding whether the contract is valid in such situations, the court may take a more global approach to contract formation. Relevant factors in determining contract validity may be whether the promisee's promise is too vague or uncertain to form the basis of a contract. Allied to this may be questions about whether the parties could have possessed the requisite contractual intent. Upon consideration of such factors, the court may be satisfied that a valid contract has not been formed. The reason given by the court may, depending on the facts of the case, be couched in terms of the consideration not being of value in the eyes of the law.

6.5.2   *Performance of existing duties*

[6.215] A person may be under an obligation to act in a particular way, the obligation arising either out of a contract previously entered into or because of a public duty imposed on that person. If another person (the promisor) promises to do an act in consideration of that person's (the promisee's) promise to perform the promisee's existing duty, the question arises whether that consideration is sufficient to support the promise. The resolution of this issue depends on whether the existing obligation arises under a contract or is in the nature of a public duty, and on who the parties to the subsequent agreement are. These issues are dealt with separately below.

(a) Performance of existing contractual duties

[6.220] It is now a long-standing legal principle that a promise by one party (the promisee) to perform an existing contractual duty owed to another party (the promisor) does not constitute good consideration for the promisor's promise.[69]

[6.225] The promise to perform existing contractual duties may be in the context of an agreement that involves subject matter different from the first agreement, as in the following case.

Example

A and B enter into a contract for B to build a house for A for $200 000 (first agreement). A and B later agree that, in consideration of B building the house, A will do some landscaping work for B (second agreement).

The second agreement is not enforceable by B because B has provided no consideration for A's promise to landscape. B was already contractually bound to A to build A a house. It is more common, however, for this issue to arise in the context of a second agreement relating to the first agreement.

Example

A and B enter into a contract for B to build a house for A for $200 000 (first agreement). B realises that she has underquoted for the work and will make a loss. A and B subsequently agree that, in consideration of B finishing the construction work, A will pay B an additional $30 000 (second agreement).

---

69   *Wigan v Edwards* (1973) 47 ALJR 586 at 594. This rule also applies in New Zealand: *Cook Island Shipping Co Ltd v Colson Builders Ltd* [1975] 1 NZLR 422.

This example, in essence, involves the variation of an existing contract. The rules governing such variation are examined later.[70] As will be seen, for a variation of existing contractual arrangements to be effective, consideration must be provided for each party's promise.[71] In the above example, A has promised to pay B an additional $30 000. However, B has not promised to do anything more than perform the existing contractual duties. On a traditional analysis, B's promise is not supported by consideration, and therefore not enforceable by B.

[6.230] A trilogy of English cases must be examined in order to understand the extent to which performance of pre-existing contractual obligations can constitute consideration. These cases are informative about the traditional operation of the rule,[72] the circumstances in which exceptions to the rule operate,[73] and the modern attempt to redefine or reformulate the rule (or perhaps to depart from it) to accommodate commercial realities.[74]

Example: Stilk v Myrick[75]

The plaintiff was a seaman who was employed as a crew member to work a ship from London to the Baltic and back. In the course of the voyage, two of the seamen deserted. Because the captain was unable to replace these men, he entered an agreement with the rest of the crew to distribute the wages of the two deserters equally among them if they continued to work the ship back to London. They proceeded to do so, but the captain refused to distribute the wages of the deserters. The plaintiff brought an action to claim his portion of the wages.

The plaintiff was unsuccessful, the English court finding the agreement to share the wages void for want of consideration. As part of the original agreement, the crew had undertaken to do all that they could under all the emergencies of the voyage. The desertion of part of the crew was such an emergency. As the crew members were merely performing what they were originally bound to do under the existing contract, they did not provide consideration for the captain's promise.

[6.235] The *Stilk v Myrick* principle will not prevent enforcement of a subsequent agreement, however, where the promisee promises to do something more than he or she originally contracted to do, as illustrated by the following case.

Example: Hartley v Ponsonby[76]

The plaintiff was a seaman who was part of a crew of 19 employed to work a ship from Australia to Bombay. While the ship was in harbour, some of the seamen deserted. To induce the remaining crew to complete the voyage, the master promised

---

70   See [21.50] below.
71   *NZ Needle Manufacturers Ltd v Taylor* [1975] 2 NZLR 33.
72   *Stilk v Myrick* (1809) 170 ER 1168.
73   *Hartley v Ponsonby* (1857) 119 ER 1471.
74   *Williams v Roffey Bros & Nicholls (Contractors) Ltd* [1991] All ER 512.
75   (1809) 170 ER 1168.
76   (1857) 119 ER 1471. For an equivalent New Zealand case where there was held to be consideration provided to justify an increase in the price of goods being sold, see *Moyes and Groves Ltd v Radiation (NZ) Ltd* [1982] 1 NZLR 368.

to pay them a sum of money in addition to their wages. The plaintiff later brought an action against the captain to recover the additional money promised.

An English court found in favour of the plaintiff. After the desertions, it was dangerous to life for the ship to go to sea. This operated to release the original crew from their contracts. Therefore, the plaintiff agreeing to remain on the ship for the rest of the voyage was consideration for the captain's promise to pay additional money.

[6.240] The rule in *Stilk v Myrick*[77] can be justified. It prevents a party to the contract from later attempting to obtain a further benefit from the other party by suggesting that he or she will be unable (or unprepared) to continue performance of the contract unless an additional benefit is conferred. On the other hand, the rule has been criticised for ignoring commercial realities. There are some circumstances in which a promisor may be prepared to confer an additional benefit on the promisee to ensure he or she completes performance of the existing contractual duties in the manner originally agreed. A promisor may wish to confer the benefit to avoid a penalty he or she may suffer if the contract is not finished on time, or because the promisor and promisee contract with each other on a regular basis and such a concession may maintain or promote good business relations between them. It may also be the case that promising an additional benefit to ensure completion makes better business sense than having the promisee breach the contract and the promisor taking action for damages for the breach. It is difficult to accommodate these commercial realities while applying the strict rule in *Stilk v Myrick*.

[6.245] Depending on the circumstances of the case, to accommodate the reasonable expectations of contracting parties, the court may attempt to use other techniques to enforce a subsequent promise made by a contracting party. For example, a court may be prepared to find that the parties have agreed to abandon the original contract and enter into a new one.[78] Alternatively, principles of promissory estoppel may prevent the promisor from reneging on the subsequent promise made to the promisee. Another, more controversial, way the courts have enforced a subsequent promise is illustrated by the third important case in the trilogy.

Example: Williams v Roffey Bros & Nichols (Contractors) Ltd[79]

The defendant building contractors contracted to refurbish a block of 27 flats. The carpentry work was subcontracted to the plaintiff for £20 000. After the plaintiff had performed less than half of the work and received interim payments amounting to £16 200, the plaintiff realised that he was in financial difficulties because he had underquoted for the work. The defendant was anxious for the plaintiff to complete the work within the time originally agreed, because the defendant would incur penalties under its head contract if the work was not completed on time. At the defendant's instigation, the parties entered into a subsequent agreement under which the plaintiff undertook to complete the work on time in consideration for the defendant paying an

---

77   (1809) 170 ER 1168.
78   This was in fact the basis for the decision in *Hartley v Ponsonby* (1857) 119 ER 1471.
79   [1991] All ER 512.

additional £10 300. The plaintiff subsequently sued the defendant to recover the additional money.

The English Court of Appeal found in favour of the plaintiff. The Court held that the benefit received by the defendant—avoiding a penalty under the main contract or having to engage another subcontractor—was sufficient consideration for the defendant's promise to pay the additional £10 300. The agreement was enforceable even though the plaintiff promised to do no more than what he had originally contracted to do. In coming to its decision, the Court of Appeal carefully examined the issue of consideration. After reviewing the relevant authorities, Glidewell LJ summarised what he considered to be the existing state of the law through a number of propositions:

(i)   if A has entered into a contract with B to do work for, or to supply goods or services to, B in return for payment by B; and

(ii)   at some stage before A has completely performed his obligations under the contract, B has reason to doubt whether A will, or will be able to, complete his side of the bargain; and

(iii) B thereupon promises A an additional payment in return for A's promise to perform his contractual obligations on time; and

(iv)   as a result of giving his promise B obtains in practice a benefit, or obviates a disbenefit; and

(v)   B's promise is not given as a result of economic duress or fraud on the part of A, then;

(vi)   the benefit to B is capable of being consideration for B's promise, so the promise will be legally binding.[80]

[6.250] Following this Court of Appeal decision, there was speculation in Australia on whether this new approach to consideration would be adopted. It was not long before the matter was considered by Santow J of the Supreme Court of New South Wales.

Example: Musumeci v Winadell Pty Ltd[81]

The plaintiffs (the lessees) and the defendant (the lessor) had entered into a lease of premises in a shopping centre. Because the lessor had given a lease to a competitor of the plaintiff lessees, the lessees' trade was affected and they were unable to remain viable while continuing to paying the full rent. The parties therefore entered into an agreement under which the lessees were permitted to pay only two-thirds of the rent originally specified. The plaintiff lessees sought a declaration to that effect.

The Supreme Court found in favour of the plaintiff lessees on the basis that the original lease had been altered. Santow J held that there had been consideration for the lessor's promise to decrease the rental: the practical benefit of continuing with the lessees as viable tenants rather than having to find other tenants and suing the lessees for the rental shortfall. This was particularly the case as the lessees may have been entitled to plead a number of defences and cross-claims in any action brought by the lessor.

---

80   Ibid at 521–522.
81   (1994) 34 NSWLR 723.

After a detailed consideration of the relevant policy implications, Santow J was of the view that *Williams v Roffey Bros & Nicholls (Contractors) Ltd*[82] should be followed in Australia.[83] He reached this view notwithstanding widespread criticism of the way the Court of Appeal purported to apply *Stilk v Myrick*[84] in that case. His Honour identified three arguments for not enforcing a contract to perform pre-existing obligations, and suggested why each was not sustainable.[85] First, failing to enforce such an agreement may protect a promisor from extortion that could result from a promisee threatening to abandon the contract unless granted a concession. Santow J countered that the value of this argument had been lessened by the development of principles of economic duress as a vitiating factor. Duress is a more appropriate avenue through which to regulate illegitimate pressure of this kind than principles of consideration. Secondly, Santow J noted the argument that the promise should not be enforced because the promisee suffers no legal detriment by performing what he or she was already obliged to do, and the promisor does not receive any legal benefit by receiving what was already due. This proposition was answered by recognising that in a practical sense, a benefit is received by the promisor. If that were not the case, the concession would not have been agreed to. It would be of greater benefit to the promisor to have the contract performed according to its terms rather than taking legal action to have it enforced. Finally, it was argued that the effect of the extension in *Williams v Roffey Bros & Nicholls (Contractors) Ltd* is that it leaves no room for the operation of the rule in *Stilk v Myrick*. This, too, was refuted by Santow J. His Honour was of the view that the rule in *Stilk v Myrick* continued to operate where the promisor's promise was 'wholly gratuitous'. In other words, for *Williams v Roffey Bros & Nicholls (Contractors) Ltd* to apply and for the promise to be enforced, the promisee must be able to demonstrate that the promise to perform an existing contractual obligation was of sufficient practical benefit to the promisor. In *Williams v Roffey Bros & Nicholls (Contractors) Ltd*, for example, the performance by the subcontractor was worth more to the contractor than damages that could be obtained by the contractor for breach.

[6.255] What then can be regarded as the Australian position on whether a promise to perform pre-existing contractual duties can be valid consideration? Is the decision in *Williams v Roffey Bros & Nicholls (Contractors) Ltd* (adopted in *Musumeci v Winadell Pty Ltd*) a departure from the traditional principles set out in *Stilk v Myrick* and reiterated by Mason J in *Wigan v Edwards?*[86] The English Court of Appeal in *Williams v Roffey Bros & Nicholls (Contractors) Ltd* purported to approve the early decision in *Stilk v Myrick*, and expressly denied that the proposition expressed in its decision contravened those principles. The crux of the issue is whether benefits secured by an agreement can be consideration for the promisor's promise. Whether the Court of Appeal has merely redefined and reformulated the principle enunciated in *Stilk v Myrick*, or has effectively departed from the ratio of the case, has been the subject of considerable academic

---

82   [1990] 1 A11 ER 512

83   It also appears that this shift has occurred in New Zealand: *United Food and Chemical Workers Union of NZ v Talley* [1993] 2 ERNZ 360 at 376 and *Newmans Tours Ltd v Ranier Investments Ltd* [1992] 2 NZLR 68 at 80.

84   (1809) 170 ER 1168.

85   (1994) 34 NSWLR 723 at 741–746.

86   (1973) 47 ALR 586 at 594.

comment.[87] This divergence of view is recognised and explored in the judgment of Santow J in *Musumeci v Winadell Pty Ltd*.

While as a matter of policy it may now be appropriate to depart from the strict rule of consideration espoused *Stilk v Myrick*, the basis upon which this movement away from the rule occurred is difficult to justify on an application of established rules of consideration. In circumstances where a subsequent agreement is entered into because a party to a contract suggests that he or she may be unable or unwilling to complete the contractual obligations without receiving a further concession, the promisor must necessarily foresee a benefit from completion. If not, the promisor's promise would not have been made. If this is correct, it is hard to envisage room for the continued operation of the rule in *Stilk v Myrick*. Promises made in consideration of performing existing contractual obligations would be enforceable. Given the commercial realities mentioned earlier, this may be a desirable outcome. However, it may have been preferable, in terms of a rational evolution of the common law, to recognise the inappropriateness of the rule and expressly abandon it, rather than arrive at the desired outcome by purporting to apply traditional rules.

(b) Performance of public duty

[6.260] Just as there is a rule that performance of pre-existing contractual duties cannot be consideration for a promise, there is an equivalent rule that relates to performance of a public duty. In the context of whether a promise to compensate an attorney for his time when subpoenaed to give evidence could be enforced, Lord Tenterden CJ had this to say.

> If it be a duty imposed by law upon a party regularly subpoenaed, to attend from time to time to give his evidence, then a promise to give him any remuneration for loss of time incurred in such attendance is a promise without consideration.[88]

[6.265] The rationale for the rule is that if a person is obliged by law to do a particular act, then in undertaking to perform that act in exchange for a promise, he or she is providing no consideration. That act would have been performed in any event. Applying this reasoning, if the promisee promises to do something over and above what the public duty requires, there would be consideration for the promise. This was the basis upon which Viscount Finlay held that the Glamorgan County Council could recover the promised fees in *Glasbook Brothers Ltd v Glamorgan County Council*.[89]

Example: Glasbook Brothers Ltd v Glamorgan County Council

During a national coal strike, a colliery manager sought protection of the colliery by the police. The manager thought that adequate protection could only be provided by billeting police on the premises. The police superintendent, however, was of the view that sufficient protection could be provided by a mobile force. An agreement was subsequently entered into between the owners of the mine and the Council for a police force

---

87   See, for example, R Meyer-Rocho, 'The Requirement of Consideration' (1997) 71 ALJ 532 and J Adams and R Brownsword, 'Contract, Consideration and the Critical Path' (1990) NLR 536.

88   *Collins v Godefroy* (1831) 109 ER 1040 at 1042.

89   [1925] AC 270. For a further example, see *Black White and Grey Cabs Ltd v Reid* [1980] 1 NZLR 40.

to be billeted on the premises in exchange for an undertaking by the coal mine to pay for those services. The Council later took action to obtain the promised payment.

The House of Lords held (by a majority of 3:2) that the agreement was enforceable. Viscount Finlay thought there was no duty on the police to give the special protection asked for. In his view, 'there was abundant consideration' for the promise to pay for the services. The other members of the majority agreed that the promise to pay was enforceable, but based their decision on principles of public policy rather that consideration.

[6.270] Cases dealing with performance of public duties cover a range of subject matter. The notion of public duty embraces the provision of police services, health services (at least in the public sector), fire-fighting services, and garbage removal services, to name just a few. Some obligations of a more personal nature are also properly regarded as legal duties. The most common duty of this kind is the legal obligation imposed on parents to maintain their children. On separation, if one party promises to care for a child as consideration for a promise by the other to pay a certain sum, can it be said that consideration is given for the promise to pay? The promisee was always under a legal duty to maintain the child.

[6.275] The cases have not taken an entirely consistent approach in determining enforceability of contracts involving the discharge of public duties. In cases involving the discharge of public duties by government authorities, regard is often given to matters of public policy. In *Glasbook Brothers Ltd v Glamorgan County Council*,[90] for example, two of the majority of three Lords cast their judgment in terms of public policy considerations. The agreement was enforceable because it was not illegal or contrary to public policy, there being no determination of whether consideration had been given for the promise to pay the cost of the operation. A different approach appears to have been taken in relation to the legal duty to care for children. In the mid-nineteenth century, only the mother had a duty to care for an illegitimate child. A number of cases considered whether a father's promise to pay a sum of money if the mother continued to care for the child was enforceable, given that the mother had a legal duty to do so in any event.[91] In all these cases, the courts enforced the promises to pay. The judgments indicate a preparedness to find the existence of sufficient consideration. This latitude in finding the existence of consideration has been demonstrated by the courts even in more recent times.[92]

[6.280] In the preceding commentary on performance of pre-existing contractual duties as consideration, the unsatisfactory state of the law was noted. Difficulties also arise where the purported consideration for a promise is the performance of public duties. Perhaps the time is ripe for a reassessment of the rules of consideration in this context. There is some judicial support for a move to recognise the performance of public duties as constituting consideration.[93] This is particularly persuasive in modern

---

90   [1925] AC 270.
91   *Jennings v Brown* (1842) 152 ER 210; *Linnegar v Hodd* (1848) 136 ER 948; *Hicks v Gregory* (1849) 137 ER 556; *Crowhurst v Laverack* (1852) 155 ER 1322.
92   *Ward v Byham* [1956] 1 WLR 496; *Popiw v Popiw* [1959] VR 197.
93   *Ward v Byham* [1956] 1 WLR 496 at 498 per Denning LJ; *Williams v Williams* [1957] 1 WLR 148 at 151 per Denning LJ; *Popiw v Popiw* [1959] VR 197 at 199 per Hudson J.

times, as an increasing number of government services must be paid for by consumers of those services. Assuming validity of consideration, it would then remain open for a court to determine whether, on public policy grounds, it would be appropriate for the contract to be enforced.

(c)   Where promise is made to a third party

[6.285] In the preceding discussion on whether the promise to perform pre-existing contractual obligations (or actual performance) can constitute consideration, the following example was given.

Example

A and B enter into a contract for B to build a house for A for $200 000. A and B enter into a subsequent agreement that, in consideration of B building a house, A will do some landscaping work for B.

It was observed that the subsequent agreement between A and B was not valid because B did not provide A with consideration for A's promise to do the landscaping. The legal position is different, however, if the subsequent agreement is made between B and C. If B and C agree that, in consideration of B building a house for A, C will do some landscaping work for B, C's promise is enforceable by B. A promise to perform an existing contractual duty owed to another party (or the actual performance of the duty) can be good consideration for a promise. There are a number of possible rationales for this. Firstly, it may be of benefit for the promisor (C) to ensure that the original agreement is carried out. If the promisee (B) has indicated that he or she may choose not to carry out the original agreement, the promisor may wish to ensure this occurs by entering a subsequent contract. Secondly, although the promisee (B) may be contractually bound to perform the original agreement, by entering into the subsequent agreement, he or she incurs further liability to the promisor (C) if the first agreement is not performed. In this sense, the promisee has changed the existing position by entering into a second agreement.

[6.290] One of the early decisions in which this principle was applied is the case of *Scotson v Pegg*.[94]

Example: Scotson v Pegg

The plaintiff had contracted to sell goods to a third party, the goods to be delivered to the third party or the third party's nominee. The third party nominated the defendant. Subsequently, the plaintiff and defendant agreed that in consideration of the defendant unloading the same goods from the plaintiff's ship at a specified rate, the plaintiff would deliver the goods to the defendant.

The English Court held that the agreement between the plaintiff and the defendant was valid even though the plaintiff promised to do no more than to carry out the existing contractual duty owed to the third party.

---

94   (1861) 158 ER 121.

[6.295] The principle set out in *Scotson v Pegg*[95] was more recently endorsed by the Privy Council in *New Zealand Shipping Co Ltd v A M Satterthwaite & Co Ltd*.[96] The facts of this case will be explored in more detail later.[97] Applying the principles set out in *Scotson v Pegg*, the Privy Council held that a valid contract existed between the shipper and the stevedore to unload the vessel, even though the stevedore was bound by its contract with the carrier to do the same. Performance of its contractual obligation constituted acceptance of the shipper's offer. In relation to the sufficiency of this conduct as consideration, the Privy Council noted the following:

> An agreement to do an act which the promisor is under an existing obligation to a third party to do, may quite well amount to valid consideration and does so in the present case: the promisee obtains a benefit of a direct obligation which he can enforce.[98]

[6.300] Shortly after that decision, the Privy Council again endorsed the principle in *Pao On v Lau Yiu Long*.[99] The Privy Council held that the contract of indemnity could be enforced. The plaintiff (the owners of shares in a private company) had, in a prior agreement with the public company, undertaken not to sell 60 per cent of the shares for at least one year. However, this promise could also constitute consideration in a later agreement with a different party (the defendant—the majority shareholder in the public company), under which that party provided the plaintiff with an indemnity against loss.

[6.305] While there is not an abundance of case law on point in Australia, the High Court has accepted that a promise to carry out pre-existing contractual duties owed to a third party can provide good consideration.[100]

6.5.3   *Part payment of debt*

(a)   Rule in *Pinnel's case*

[6.310] If an amount of money is owing by a debtor to a creditor, and those parties enter into a subsequent agreement that the creditor will accept a lesser amount in full satisfaction of the amount owing, the later agreement will generally not be binding. It is not binding because the debtor has not provided consideration for the creditor's promise to forgo the balance due. Therefore, even if the debtor acts on this agreement by paying the lesser sum agreed—and this sum is accepted by the creditor—the creditor will generally be able to sue the debtor for the balance due. The principle that the promise to pay part of a debt cannot constitute consideration for a creditor's promise to forgo the balance is commonly referred to as the 'rule in *Pinnel's case*'.[101] The decision of *Foakes v Beer*[102] is one of the best-known applications of this rule.

---

95   (1861) 158 ER 121.
96   [1975] AC 154.
97   See [12.230].
98   Ibid at 168.
99   [1980] AC 614. See [6.430] for a more detailed examination of the facts of this case.
100   *Port Jackson Stevedoring Pty Ltd v Salmond & Spraggon (Aust) Pty Ltd* (1978) 139 CLR 231 at 243–244.
101   Although the principle was applied in earlier decisions, *Pinnel's case* (1602) 77 ER 237 is the decision usually cited as authority for this principle.
102   (1884) 9 App Cas 605.

Example: Foakes v Beer

A creditor (Mrs Beer) obtained judgment against the debtor (Dr Foakes) for £2090.19s. As the debtor was unable to pay this amount, the parties entered an agreement under which the debtor paid the amount off over a period of time. If payment was made in accordance with the agreement, the creditor undertook not to 'take any proceedings whatever on the said judgment'. A judgment creditor is entitled to be paid interest on a judgment debt until payment of the debt is received in full. If the agreement was enforceable, the creditor would not be entitled to bring an action for the interest.

The House of Lords held that the creditor was entitled to receive the interest claimed. As the debtor had not provided consideration for the creditor's promise to forgo the interest, the agreement not to bring further proceedings on the judgment was not enforceable.

(b) Circumstances in which the rule will not operate

[6.315] There are a number of circumstances in which the rule in *Pinnel's case* will not operate, so that a creditor is unable at a later time to claim the balance owing to him or her.

Parties enter into a deed

[6.320] As explained, the rule in *Pinnel's case* is based on principles of consideration. A creditor's promise to forgo part of a debt owing is not enforceable, because the debtor does not provide consideration for the promise. Consideration is not required, however, for specialty agreements.[103] If the parties enter into a deed under which the creditor forgoes part of the amount owing, that arrangement will be enforceable despite the absence of consideration.

Accommodation to benefit the creditor

[6.325] The rule in *Pinnel's case* is based on the absence of consideration. If the debtor provides consideration for the creditor's promise, the rule will not apply. For example, if the circumstances surrounding payment altered to accommodate the wishes of the creditor so that the creditor received some benefit from the new arrangement, consideration may have been provided for the creditor's promise. Examples of how the arrangement could be altered to assist the creditor are:

- payment on an earlier than scheduled date;
- payment at a location more convenient to the creditor;
- payment in a currency more desirable to the creditor.[104]

[6.330] It follows that where the time and place of payment of the debt is altered for the convenience of the *debtor*, this will not provide consideration for the creditor's promise to forgo the balance of the debt.[105]

---

103 See [6.165].
104 The Court of Common Pleas in *Pinnel's case* (1602) 77 ER 237 described this concession by a debtor in the following terms:'… it appears to the Judges that by no possibility, a lesser sum can be satisfaction to the plaintiff for a greater sum: but the gift of a horse, hawk, or robe, etc, in satisfaction is good. For it shall be intended that a horse, hawk or robe, etc, might be more beneficial to the plaintiff than the money …'.
105 *Vanbergen v St Edmunds Properties Ltd* [1933] 2 KB 223.

Amount owing is disputed

[6.335] The rule in *Pinnel's case* operates only where there is no dispute between the debtor and creditor about the existence and quantum of the debt. If the parties cannot agree on the amount owing, they may wish to enter a compromise agreement. For example, debtors may agree to pay an amount more than they think is owing, while creditors may agree to accept less as full payment. The rule in *Pinnel's case* will not apply to such an agreement. In the case of a compromise, although the creditor promises to accept an amount less than what the creditor contends is the amount of the debt in full settlement of the debt, the debtor has provided consideration for the creditor's promise. The debtor has agreed to pay an amount more than the debtor believes to be due. This is good consideration even if the creditor is, in fact, correct and the amount claimed by the creditor is actually due. If such an agreement were not enforceable, it would be difficult for parties to validly settle a disputed claim.[106] For the rule in *Pinnel's case* to be avoided in this way, there must be a genuine dispute about the amount owing. It is not enough that the debtor is unhappy about paying the amount.

Example: H B F Dalgety Ltd v Moreton[107]

A real estate agent was appointed by sellers to find a seller for their farm. It was agreed that the real estate agent should be paid in accordance with the professional scale of charges adopted by the Real Estate Institute of New Zealand. After the sale, the sellers were invoiced for $9786.98 in accordance with the scale. The sellers forwarded to the real estate agent a cheque for $2450.00, being the sellers' 'estimate of costs on a 'work done' basis'. The cheque was banked by the real estate agent. The agent subsequently sued for the balance of the commission due.

The High Court in New Zealand found in favour of the real estate agent. The fact that the sellers were reluctant to pay the amount owing to the real estate agent did not mean that there was a genuine dispute about the amount owing to him. Therefore, payment of the lesser amount could not be consideration for forgoing the balance due.

Payment by a third party

[6.340] If a debtor is in financial difficulty and unable to pay debts as they become due, a friend or relative may wish to provide some assistance to the debtor. To placate a creditor and bring the matter to an end, such a third party may offer to pay the creditor a sum less than the full amount owing in full satisfaction of the debt. As the third party is not indebted to the creditor, his or her promise to pay an amount should be good consideration for the creditor's promise to forgo the balance of the debt.[108] The fact that payment is by a third party and not the debtor takes the case outside the operation of the rule in *Pinnel's case*. The contract between the third party and creditor is therefore regarded as valid.

[6.345] The more difficult legal point is determining the effect of this agreement on a contractual relationship between the debtor and creditor. Is there any legal defence

---

106   Applying the same principles, forbearance to sue by one party can operate as valid consideration for another party's promise: see [6.400]–[6.415].

107   [1987] 1 NZLR 411.

108   *Hirachand Punamchand v Temple* [1911] 2 KB 330 at 337 and 340.

available to a debtor who is later sued by the creditor for the balance of the debt? In the relatively few reported cases in which creditors have brought such action, they have been unsuccessful.[109] While this outcome is clearly just, the courts have grappled with the legal basis for this outcome. In the most recent reported case, *Hirachand Punamchand v Temple*,[110] the Court of Appeal unanimously found in favour of the debtor, but alternative bases for the decision were canvassed. There seemed to be a general consensus that the agreement between the creditor and third party operated to extinguish the debt. Subsequent action therefore could not be brought by the creditor on the balance due. There was less certainty about the basis upon which a defence is pleaded by the debtor in a later action. One possibility expressed was that an action could not be brought by the creditor because it would be an abuse of the process of the court to do so. To allow the action to proceed would be to allow a fraud on the third party. The alternative basis for a defence was the simple recognition that the debt had been extinguished.

Notwithstanding any doubts surrounding the legal basis for these decisions, there is little doubt that the objective of such arrangements involving third parties—namely the release of a debtor from liability—will not be frustrated by any technical argument involving consideration.

Composition with creditors

[6.350] If a debtor is in financial difficulties with creditors and is unable to meet outstanding obligations as they fall due, the debtor may seek to enter a 'composition with creditors'.[111] Under such an arrangement, the creditors all agree to accept payment of something less than the full amount owing by the debtor, in exchange for giving the debtor a full release. Creditors may agree to such an arrangement if it appears that this is the most likely avenue to recover any amount from the debtor. Such arrangements may take a variety of forms. A composition may be entered into just between the creditors themselves, between the creditors and debtor, or the debtor may enter into individual arrangements (or releases) with each creditor.

[6.355] The legal validity of such an arrangement may be called into question if a creditor later seeks to recover an amount from the debtor over and above the amount agreed in the composition. As between the creditors, it is clear that consideration has been provided, each promises to forgo a portion of the debt due in exchange for the other creditors agreeing to do the same. As between an individual creditor and debtor, however, the position is different. It may be argued that on a strict application of the rule in *Pinnel's case,* the creditor has not received consideration for his or her promise to accept part payment in full satisfaction of all of the debt owing, so the composition is not a valid agreement. The creditor is therefore free to sue the debtor for the balance.

---

109 *Welby v Drake* (1825) 171 ER 1315; *Cook v Lister* (1863) 143 ER 215; *Hirashand Punanshand v Temple* [1911] 2 KB 330.
110 [1911] 2 KB 330.
111 These kinds of arrangements are expressly contemplated by Part X of the *Bankruptcy Act* 1966 (Cth): see the s 187(1) definition of 'composition'.

[6.360] The difficulty in establishing consideration in such an arrangement was noted by Bollen J of the South Australian Supreme Court in the case of *In the Estate of Whitehead*.[112] His Honour spent some time reviewing the literature on this issue and noted the apparent acceptance of the validity of such compositions notwithstanding the uncertainties surrounding the existence of consideration.[113]

[6.365] A number of different grounds can be suggested for upholding the composition. The first relies on the principles enunciated in *Coulls v Bagot's Executor and Trustee Company Ltd*.[114] If the agreement is between all of the parties (creditors and the debtor), it may be possible to construe the agreement as involving joint promisees. For each individual creditor, the agreement is as between that creditor on the one hand, and the other creditors and the debtor on the other. The other creditors have provided consideration for the individual creditor's promise not to sue for the balance because they agreed to do the same. As the other creditors have provided consideration, there is no requirement for the other joint promisee, (the debtor) to do so. At best, however, this theory requires a court to be imaginative in its construction of the agreement. Further, it is difficult to see how the theory would operate at all if the debtor enters separate agreements with each individual creditor.[115]

[6.370] The second possible ground for upholding the agreement is on the same principles as were relevant in *Hirachand Punamchand v Temple*.[116] As between the creditors themselves, the composition is valid. The agreement between the creditors is equivalent to the agreement between the creditor and third party in *Hirachand Punamchand v Temple*.[117] The court should not allow a creditor to successfully sue a debtor for the balance for the same reason that the creditor could not succeed in *Hirachand Punamchand v Temple*.[118] To do so would represent a fraud on the other creditors. The analogy to the situation involving a composition with a body of creditors was made by Farwell LJ in *Hiranchand Punamchand v Temple*.[119]

[6.375] Bollen J in *In the Estate of Whitehead*[120] was prepared to uphold the validity of a composition notwithstanding 'the absence of consideration or despite the inability to perceive consideration moving from the debtor'.[121] As with the case of payment of a lesser sum by a third party to a creditor, the validity of a composition by debtors with creditors will continue to be upheld even though there may be lingering doubt as to the legal justification for doing so.

---

112   (1986) 44 SASR 402.
113   Ibid at 403–404.
114   (1966) 119 CLR 460.
115   It was for this reason that Bollen J held that this principle could not apply in the case of *In the Estate of Whitehead* (1986) 44 SASR 402.
116   [1911] 2 KB 330.
117   Ibid.
118   Ibid.
119   [1911] 2 KB 330 at 341. Compare comments of Bollen J in *In the Estate of Whitehead* (1986) 44 SASR 402 at 406.
120   (1986) 44 SASR 402.
121   Ibid at 406.

Judicature Act 1908 (NZ)

[6.380] There is a further exception in New Zealand arising from the *Judicature Act* 1908. Pursuant to s 92, an acknowledgment in writing by a creditor (or agent of the creditor) of the receipt of part of the debt in full satisfaction of the entire debt operates to discharge the balance owing to the creditor.

(c) Criticisms of the rule in *Pinnel's case*

[6.385] The rule in *Pinnel's case* has been with us for centuries. As is often the case with common law principles of long standing, it has become so entrenched that it is apparently now difficult to depart from. However, the rule has been the subject of judicial and academic criticism for some time.[122] The thrust of the problem is that the rule does not reflect the expectations of reasonable people, or modern commercial realities. The rule does not allow business people to enter agreements that may provide each with a commercial benefit. In circumstances where a debtor has indicated an inability to pay the full amount at the required time, it may be preferable from the creditor's perspective to accept a smaller sum at the specified date, rather than pursue legal action with the possibility (or likelihood) of the debtor being unable to make good any judgment against him or her in any event.

[6.390] It is to accommodate commercial realities that some exceptions to this rule have evolved. The rule will not apply where payment is made by a third party, or a composition has been entered into between creditors and the debtor. As alluded to above, however, the legal basis for departing from the rule is perhaps questionable. In developing such exceptions, the courts have been attempting to avoid the inappropriateness of the rule in these specified cases.

[6.395] It was also a recognition of commercial realities that prevented the landlord from recovering against the tenant in *Musumeci v Winadell Pty Ltd*.[123] An agreement by the parties to a decrease in the rental payable was held to be enforceable.[124] While not directly on point with *Pinnel's case,* an agreement that *in future* the tenant had to pay the landlord only two-thirds of the previously agreed rental arguably raises the same principle as a creditor forgiving part of a *past* debt. It is difficult to justify the former arrangement as being enforceable, but the latter not.[125] The rule in *Pinnel's case* is, of course, consistent with the notion that a promise to perform pre-existing contractual duties does not constitute good consideration. There is increasing support for the view that both of these rules of consideration fail to reflect the expectations of reasonable people and need to be reconsidered.

---

122 See, for example, the comments of Lord Blackburn in *Foakes v Beer* (1884) 9 App Cas 605 at 622: 'What principally weighs with me in thinking that Lord Coke [in *Pinnel's case*] made a mistake of fact is my conviction that all men of business, whether merchants or tradesmen, do everyday recognise an act on the ground that prompt payment of a part of their demand may be more beneficial to them than it would be to insist on their rights and enforce payment of the whole'. This concern was also noted by Santow J in *Musumeci v Winadell Pty Ltd* (1994) 34 NSWLR 723 at 739.

123 (1994) 34 NSWLR 723.

124 See [6.250].

125 See *Musumeci v Winadell Pty Ltd* (1994) 34 NSWLR 723 at 739 where Santow J notes the tension between his decision and the rule in *Pinnel's case.*

6.5.4 Forbearance to sue

[6.400] Disputes can arise between parties in the course of a contractual relationship. Each party may take a different view of his or her respective rights and obligations arising under the contract. In an attempt to avoid litigation, parties may attempt to resolve such disputes between themselves. The following examples illustrate the context in which such agreements may take place.

Examples

I   A engaged B to do some building work. When it came time to settle the account, B maintained that $10 000 was owed to her, while A had calculated the outstanding sum to be only $5000. To avoid litigation, the parties agreed that A should pay B $7500 in final settlement of the account.

II   A entered into a contract to sell her business to B for a set sum. In the course of negotiations, B alleged A had made some fraudulent misrepresentations. As B needed an extension of time to obtain the necessary funds to purchase the business, the parties agreed that if A extended the settlement date, B would not bring action against A for the fraudulent misrepresentation.

[6.405] In both cases, the question of enforceability of the agreements arises. What would be the position if, in example (I), A later sued to recover the $2500 paid or, in example (II), A refused to give B the extended time in which to settle? Has B provided consideration for A's promise in each case? Would it make a difference if, on a proper legal analysis, A in example (I) in fact only owed $5000 and, in example (II), there has been no fraudulent misrepresentation by A?

In both cases, it is likely that the agreements will be upheld. As a matter of policy, settlement of legal action is encouraged. To promote settlement of potential (or actual) legal claims, the court is prepared to recognise the validity of agreements to compromise claims or agreements to forbear from suing even if the claim by the party is one that may not have succeeded. In other words, a promise not to sue may be good consideration for the other party's promise even if *in fact* that claim would have been unsuccessful. Although in strict legal terms it is difficult to see how forfeiting a claim that could not succeed can be regarded as consideration, it not being of actual value, it can be so regarded in the eyes of the law. If this were not the case, it would be impossible for parties to be able to settle actions with any confidence. If facts were later discovered to indicate the action would not have been successful, this would impact on the validity of the consideration.

[6.410] Not all compromises of an action or promises not to sue will provide good consideration for the other party's promise. The party promising not to sue or foregoing part of the claim must be acting in good faith. He or she must have an honest belief that the claim may be successful.[126] In other words, the parties must be in a genuine dispute.

---

126   *Wigan v Edwards* (1973) 47 ALJR 586.

Example: Hercules Motors Pty Ltd v Schubert[127]

Following negotiations between Hercules Motors Pty Ltd ('Hercules') and Schubert, a lender bought a car from Hercules and sold it to Schubert on hire purchase terms. There were certain faults when the vehicle was delivered to Schubert. A dispute arose between Hercules and Schubert concerning whether Schubert was to be provided with a new car. They subsequently agreed for Hercules to re-duco the car. Schubert contended that the work was not done to specification and brought an action against Hercules. In defence, Hercules claimed that it was not in breach of the agreement because Schubert had not given consideration for its promise to repair the surface of the car.

The Full Court of the New South Wales Supreme Court held that Schubert was entitled to damages for breach of contract. As there was a genuine dispute between the parties over their rights and obligations under the original contract, the compromise provided consideration for the promise of Hercules to repair the surface of the car.

Provided that the claim is made in good faith, it does not matter that the belief was not well founded, or that the claim was in fact bad in law.

[6.415] It has also been suggested that the claim must not be vexatious or frivolous.[128] It is unlikely that a claim will be vexatious or frivolous if the claimant is acting in good faith. Nevertheless, in theory this could occur. When considering the issue of compromise claims in *Wigan v Edwards*,[129] however, the High Court did not make a determination on whether this additional limitation applied.

6.5.5 *Bargained-for conduct already performed*

[6.420] The rules governing past consideration were examined earlier.[130] Consideration will generally be ineffective to support a promise if, at the time the promise is given, the consideration has already been performed. As illustrated by the following case, however, there is an important exception to this rule.

Example: Lampleigh v Braithwaite[131]

The defendant (Mr Braithwaite) had been convicted of murder and asked the plaintiff (Mr Lampleigh) to do what he could to obtain a pardon from the King. The plaintiff acted upon this request, incurring personal expense in the process. After the plaintiff carried out these services, the defendant promised to pay him £100. The plaintiff sued to recover this amount.

---

127 (1953) SR (NSW) 301.
128 *Miles v New Zealand Alford Estate Co* (1886) 32 Ch D 266 at 291–292 per Bowen L J. In the leading New Zealand authority, *Couch v Branch Investments Ltd* [1980] 2 NZLR 314 at 320, it was suggested that if the claim were sufficiently 'unmeritorious or unconscionable' forbearance from pursuing it may not constitute consideration.
129 (1973) 47 ALJR 586.
130 See [6.150]–[6.160].
131 (1615) 80 ER 255. For a further example, see *Casey v Commissioner of Inland Revenue* [1959] NZLR 1052.

The English Court found in favour of the plaintiff. Although the promise to pay the £100 was made after the plaintiff performed the services, it was presumed by the parties at the time the defendant requested the services that they would be paid for. The plaintiff performed the services on that basis, and the later promise to pay was regarded as part of the same transaction.

On a strict approach to consideration, the subsequent promise by Mr Braithwaite to pay £100 was not supported by consideration from Mr Lampleigh. The only possible consideration for the promise to pay was the performance of services, and this was past. However, the court took a more realistic approach to the problem by recognising that the services would only have been provided on the basis of payment.

[6.425] The approach adopted by the English Court in 1615 reflects the commercial realities of today. Services are frequently provided without discussion of payment, but it is presumed by all parties that there will be payment for those services. Obtaining the professional services of a medical specialist for a particular complaint, or an accountant for the preparation of a taxation return, or a hairdresser for a style cut are but three examples of where this could occur.

[6.430] The circumstances in which past services or promises can operate as good consideration for a subsequent promise have been refined since the early decision of *Lampleigh v Braithwaite*.[132] The Privy Council in *Pau On v Lau Yiu Long*[133] provides useful guidance on this issue.

Example: Pau On v Lau Yiu Long[134]

The plaintiffs owned the capital of a private company. The private company owned a building that a public company wished to acquire. To effect this transaction, the plaintiffs sold their shares in the private company to the public company. In exchange, the plaintiffs received shares in the public company. The defendant, the majority shareholders in the public company, requested that the plaintiffs give the public company an undertaking not to sell 60 per cent of those shares for one year. This was to ensure that the market was not flooded with the shares in the public company, which could adversely affect the share price. To ensure that the plaintiffs would not be disadvantaged if the shares decreased in value, the defendant agreed to buy 60 per cent of the shares after the period had expired, at $2.50 a share.

Subsequently, the plaintiffs realised that, should the second agreement be carried out, the plaintiffs would not benefit from any increase in the share price. Accordingly, the plaintiffs and defendant entered into an agreement to replace the previous agreement to purchase the shares at $2.50 each, under which the defendant agreed to indemnify the plaintiffs for any loss in respect of 60 per cent of their holding, which would occur if the market closed at the end of the period at less than $2.50 a share.

The share prices dropped and the plaintiffs sought to rely on the contract of indemnity. The defendant refused to indemnify them on the basis that the plaintiffs did not give consideration for the promise to indemnify.

---

132 Ibid.
133 [1980] AC 614.
134 Ibid.

The Privy Council found in favour of the plaintiffs. In the circumstances of the case, the plaintiffs could be regarded as having provided consideration for the defendant's indemnity. Consideration was the plaintiffs' agreement with the public company under the first agreement not to sell the shares for a year. This promise was given at the defendant's request. The parties understood at that time that the plaintiffs needed to be compensated for any drop in price that should take place during that period.[135]

[6.435] Although this case involved a promise to give an indemnity rather than to make a payment, the same principles apply. A benefit is conferred upon the promisee. In all cases where a promisee seeks to enforce a promise made after the provision of the services (or other conduct relied upon), the promisee must be able to demonstrate the following:

1   the act must have been done at the promisor's request;
2   the parties must have understood that the act was to be remunerated either by a payment or the conferment of some other benefit;
3   payment, or the conferment of a benefit, must have been legally enforceable had it been promised in advance.[136]

6.6   International perspectives

[6.440] A recurring theme throughout this chapter has been a questioning of whether the common law concept of consideration and the rules that have developed as part of the concept reflect the expectations of reasonable people. The challenge to consideration as a necessary and appropriate requirement for contract formation is widespread. An example can be seen in the development of UNIDROIT Principles of International Commercial Contracts and the Vienna Sales Convention.[137] Under the UNIDROIT Principles, commercial contracts operate without requiring consideration to be present,[138] and a sale governed by the Vienna Sales Convention may be modified or terminated by the mere agreement of parties, without the requirement of consideration.[139]

6.6.1   New Zealand

[6.445] The legal position on consideration in New Zealand is substantially the same as that in Australia, and requires no separate examination.

6.6.2   United States

[6.450] The legal position on consideration in the United States is also largely the same as that in Australia. This is certainly true in relation to the starting proposition that a promise will only be enforced if the promisee has given consideration for it.[140] The

---

135   The fact that the plaintiffs were already contractually bound to the public company (a third party) not to sell 60 per cent of their holding did not adversely affect the plaintiffs' claim. A promise to perform an obligation owed to a third party can constitute good consideration. See [6.285]–[6.305].
136   *Pau On v Lau Yiu Long* [1980] AC 614 at 629.
137   Both of these are examined in Chapter 26.
138   UNIDROIT Principles of International Commercial Contracts Article 3.2 (1994).
139   Vienna Sales Convention, Article 29(1).
140   The Restatement (Second) reflects the common law in this regard, Chapter 4 of that work being devoted to various aspects of consideration.

notion that consideration must involve legal detriment and be bargained for also represents the American position.[141] Similar distinctions between specialty (or formal) and parol (or informal) contracts and the requirement of consideration in the latter kind only also exist.[142]

[6.455] The problems associated with the doctrine of consideration highlighted in this chapter have formed the basis of extensive debate in the United States. The perceived inappropriateness of the doctrine has led to a greater erosion of the orthodoxy of the concept than has occurred in Australia. First, many jurisdictions have enacted legislation that makes certain types of promises enforceable if they are in writing, even in the absence of consideration. The reasoning behind such legislation is that if the agreement is reduced to writing, there must have been a degree of deliberation by the parties. In such a case, it is appropriate to enforce the promise despite the lack of consideration.[143] The Uniform Commercial Code also reflects this legislative trend in relation to certain types of agreements.[144]

[6.460] Secondly, the American judiciary has demonstrated a greater preparedness to depart from the orthodoxy of principles of consideration on what appear to be an *ad hoc* basis. One example relates to the rule that the promise to perform a pre-existing duty cannot constitute valid consideration. In some jurisdictions where this rule has not been abolished by statute, it has been modified by the courts. The courts have enforced the agreement notwithstanding a lack of consideration on the basis that one of the parties has encountered difficulties in performing the contract, and those difficulties were not originally contemplated by the parties. There are other examples of promises being enforced by the courts where the promisor has some kind of moral obligation, even though the obligation falls short of the technical requirements of consideration.[145]

[6.465] Thirdly, consideration is not required to enforce a 'stipulation' made by a party. A stipulation is 'a promise or agreement with reference to a pending judicial proceeding, made by a party to the proceeding or an attorney for a party'.[146] If the stipulation is made in the manner prescribed, it will be enforced despite a lack of consideration. No doubt there are public policy imperatives to recognise stipulations, not least of which is to relieve the matters so stipulated from determination by the judiciary.

[6.470] Promises are enforced in the above cases, despite the lack of consideration, because other matters of principle are perceived to take precedence. For example,

---

141   Restatement (Second) § 71.
142   In many American jurisdictions, the principle that a document executed under seal is a formal document, therefore not requiring consideration has been abolished by statute. However, there are other ways in which contracts are deemed to be formal and, if in such form, enforceable notwithstanding the absence of consideration.
143   As an example, legislation has been enacted in some jurisdictions to make written agreements to modify contractual obligations enforceable even in the absence of consideration. Another example is the enactment of legislation to enforce a promise if it is in writing even although the consideration expressed for the promise is past or executed.
144   See, for example, Uniform Commercial Code 2-209(1).
145   Examples include promises by guarantors to pay upon the default of the debtor after the guarantor has been released from the guarantee on technical grounds, or the promise of a father of a child conceived out of wedlock to pay a specified amount even though he may not be under a legal obligation to pay such sum.
146   JD Calamari & JM Perillo, *The Law of Contracts*, 4th edn, West Group, St Paul, Minnesota, 1998, pp 245–246. See also Restatement (Second) § 94.

some jurisdictions have enacted legislation to ensure that written modifications of contractual obligations are enforceable despite a lack of consideration. The overriding
public policy consideration may be to accommodate the reasonable expectations of
people engaged in commerce. Again for reasons of public policy, an argument has
been advanced for the complete abandonment of the doctrine of consideration. In the
United States, there is widespread recognition that parties must act in good faith in
performing and enforcing contractual obligations. The overriding obligation of the
promisor to act in good faith becomes the 'glue that binds the parties to a contract'[147]
rather than consideration provided by the promisee. While it may still be some time
before such a proposition is adopted by the judiciary, it is consistent with the erosion
of consideration as an essential contractual requirement across American and other
jurisdictions.

6.6.3   Japan

[6.475] Consideration is a peculiar invention of the common law. In most of the
world's legal systems—that is, the civil law world—contracts are formed simply on the
basis of the parties' mutual intent, as discussed in Chapter 5.

Of course, in civil law contracts—as in common law contracts—intent needs to be
evidenced in some way. This can be done through oral declarations, conduct, preparing contract documents or pointing to supporting documents, or through payment of
money. However, in a civil law jurisdiction such as Japan's, 'consideration' in the
common law sense is not required.

[6.480] As a practical matter, many types of contract in Japan actually call for payment
of a deposit. In a sales contract this is 'earnest money' [tesuke]. To a common law
observer, the deposit or earnest money may seem to perform the function of consideration, and to the extent that we see consideration as evidence of serious contractual
intent, the functions are very similar. However, the significance of the earnest money
in Japanese law depends on the contract between the parties. As well as evidencing the
agreement, it may also represent the prepayment of a penalty in case of breach, or it
may be viewed as establishing a right to rescission (that is, abandonment or return of
the earnest money, depending on which party rescinds.)

---

147   JD Calamari & JM Perillo, *The Law of Contracts*, 4th edn, West Group, St Paul, Minnesota, 1998, p 166.

Chapter 7
Equitable estoppel

7.1 Introduction

[7.05] The doctrine of equitable estoppel was developed in response to the injustice that could follow from a person reneging on a promise that he or she has made. It has been seen that under contract law a gratuitous promise—that is, a promise not supported by sufficient consideration moving from the promisee—is not enforceable. Accordingly, under contract law there is nothing stopping a person from resiling from a gratuitous promise, no matter how unjust or unfair it may be for the promisee in the circumstances. Where equitable estoppel applies, however, a person will be prevented or 'estopped' from going back on his or her word. In some circumstances, equitable estoppel may involve the enforcement of a gratuitous promise. Consequently, the operation of equitable estoppel has implications for the law of contract.

Nevertheless, it is important to emphasise the need for unconscionability before equitable estoppel will apply: it is not available as a back-up submission in every case where the parties have failed to establish a binding contract.[1]

7.2 Common law estoppel

[7.10] Equitable estoppel may be contrasted with common law estoppel, in particular common law estoppel by conduct (also known as common law estoppel in pais).[2] Essentially, common law estoppel by conduct prevents a person from unjustly departing from an assumption or representation *of past or existing fact* that the other party has adopted or relied upon and which, unless the assumption or representation is adhered to, will cause that other party to suffer detriment.[3] Common law estoppel is traditionally classified as a rule of evidence that prevents a person denying what he or she has represented and instead trying to prove the true facts. Common law estoppel is referred to as a rule of evidence because it may help form the factual foundation for an action—but it is not a cause of action in itself. Accordingly, if the estoppel relates to the existence of a contract between the parties, the legal relationship between the parties is ascertained by reference to the terms of the contract that has been assumed to exist. If, in the assumed state of affairs, the contract confers a cause of action on the party raising the estoppel, the cause of action may be enforced. The source of legal obligation in that event is the assumed contract: the estoppel is not a source of legal obligation except in the sense that the estoppel compels the party bound to adhere to the assumption that the contract exists.[4] For example, where a company led a supplier

---

1   *Milchaus Investments Pty Ltd v Larkin* (1989) ATPR 50,431 at 50,438 per Young J.

2   'Estoppel in pais' means estoppel without documents, that is an estoppel arising otherwise than on the basis of a document: A Leopold, 'The elements of estoppel' (1991) *Building and Construction Law* 248 at 265–266. An additional type of common law estoppel is 'estoppel by convention' which arises from the parties' mutual assumption of a particular state of affairs as the basis of their relationship: see, for example, *Con-Stan Industries of Australia Pty Ltd v Norwich Winterthur Insurance (Aust) Ltd* (1986) 160 CLR 226; *Stuart Miller & Co Pty Ltd v Custom Credit Holdings Ltd* (1985) 4 ACLC 105. In such a case both parties are estopped from denying the common assumption.

3   *Thompson v Palmer* (1933) 49 CLR 507 at 547 per Dixon J; *Grundt v Great Boulder Pty Ltd Gold Mines Ltd* (1937) 59 CLR 641 at 674 per Dixon J.

4   *Waltons Stores (Interstate) Ltd v Maher* (1988) 164 CLR 387 at 415 per Brennan J.

of goods to assume that it was the purchaser of goods in fact received by an associated company of similar name, the first company was held bound by the contract between itself and the supplier that its conduct had led the supplier to assume to exist.[5]

[7.15] By operating only in relation to representations of past or existing fact, common law estoppel does not compel adherence to representations of intention or promises. Equity follows the common law, so in this respect the same limitation applies both at common law and in equity.[6]

7.3 Development of the doctrine of equitable estoppel

7.3.1 *High Trees and promissory estoppel*

[7.20] The origins of modern equitable estoppel, so far as is relevant to contract law, lie in the 1947 decision of Denning J in *Central London Property Trust Ltd v High Trees House Ltd*,[7] which in turn drew upon dicta in two nineteenth-century cases. In the first, *Hughes v Metropolitan Railway Co*,[8] a landlord had given six months' notice to a tenant to carry out repairs on the premises being leased. Thereafter, the landlord and tenant entered into negotiations concerning the possibility of the landlord purchasing the tenant's interest. When the negotiations finally broke down, the landlord attempted to rely on the failure to repair within the stipulated six months as entitling it to terminate the lease. In the House of Lords, Lord Cairns stated that: 'it is a rule of equity that if parties enter into contract and then negotiate, which has the effect of leading one party to suppose that strict rights under the contract will not be enforced, or will be suspended, a person seeking to enforce those rights will not be allowed to where it would be inequitable to enforce them.'[9] *Hughes* was subsequently applied in the second case, *Birmingham & District Land Co v London and North Western Railway Co*.[10] In this case, parties to a building contract had tacitly agreed that periods stipulated under the contract would not run while building work was suspended. Bowen LJ interpreted the *Hughes* principle as meaning that 'where a party to a contract A induces by his conduct the other party B to believe rights under the contract will not be enforced or will be suspended for a time, equity will not let A enforce those rights until the time passes without the parties being in the same position as before.'[11]

[7.25] Independent of any general principle, therefore, these cases held that in equity—either because of negotiations or the conduct of one of the parties—a party to a contract could not insist on certain rights under the contract. This notion formed the basis of the development of the doctrine of promissory estoppel by Denning J[12] in the *High Trees* case. In that case, the defendant leased a block of flats from the plaintiff at a

---

5   *Laws Holdings Pty Ltd v Short* (1972) 46 ALJR 563.
6   *Jorden v Money* (1854) 5 HLC 185 at 214–215; 10 ER 868 at 882.
7   [1947] KB 130.
8   (1877) 2 App Cas 439.
9   Ibid, at 448.
10   (1888) 40 Ch D 268.
11   Ibid at 286.
12   As he then was; later Denning LJ.

certain ground rent. When the Second World War broke out, there was a downturn in business and the flats were not fully occupied. When it became clear that the defendant could not pay the ground rent out of profits from subletting the flats to others, it was agreed that the rent should be reduced by half indefinitely. At the end of the war, the business recovered and the flats were once again fully let. The receiver of the landlord company commenced an action claiming that it was entitled to the full rent for the entire period.[13] Denning J (in *obiter dicta*) relied upon the *dicta* in *Hughes* and *Birmingham* as supporting a principle that where a promise is made which, to the knowledge of the person making the promise, is going to be acted upon by the person to whom it is made, the promisor will not be allowed to renege or act inconsistently with the promise.[14] Subsequently, in *Combe v Combe*,[15] Denning LJ took the opportunity to more fully state the principle:

> The principle … is that, where one party has, by his words or conduct, made to the other a promise or assurance which was intended to affect the legal relations between them and to be acted upon accordingly, then, once the other party has taken him at his word and acted on it, the one who gave the promise or assurance cannot afterwards be allowed to revert to the previous legal relations as if no such promise or assurance had been made by him, but he must accept their legal relations subject to the qualification which he himself has so introduced, even though it is not supported in point of law by any consideration but only by his word.[16]

Denning LJ was careful to restrict this 'promissory estoppel' to the limited sense of not allowing the promisor to act inconsistently with the promise. He made it clear that the case was not authority for the creation of a new cause of action in damages for breach of the promise. Promissory estoppel was merely the foundation of a defensive equity: promissory estoppel was a 'shield but not a sword.'[17] As Denning LJ stressed: 'Seeing that the principle never stands alone is giving a course of action in itself, it can never do away with the necessity of consideration when that is an essential part of the cause of action. The doctrine of consideration is too firmly fixed to be overthrown by a side-wind.'[18]

The doctrine was subsequently approved and applied by the House of Lords[19] and the Privy Council.[20] After being applied in a number of State court decisions,[21]

---

13 Although the receiver argued that it was entitled to the full rent for the entire period, in fact it sought to recover only the rent for the last two quarters of 1945 in the action. Denning J held that the true construction of the agreement was that the arrangement was to last only while there was difficulty in finding tenants, so that full rent had been payable from the beginning of 1945: [1947] KB 130 at 135.

14 Ibid at 134.

15 [1951] 2 KB 215.

16 Ibid, at 220.

17 The recognition of promissory estoppel was not precluded by the rule in *Jorden v Money* that in equity estoppel in pais did not apply to statements of intention or promises, since promissory estoppel did not seek to enforce such a promise and instead only concerned the non-enforcement of certain contractual rights.

18 [1951] 2 KB 215 at 220.

19 *Tool Metal Manufacturing Co Ltd v Tungsten Electric Co Ltd* [1955] 1 WLR 761.

20 *Ajayi v RJ Briscoe (Nigeria) Ltd* [1964] 1 WLR 1326.

21 See, for example, *Je Maintiendrai Pty Ltd v Quaglia* (1981) 26 SASR 101; *Gollin & Co Ltd v Consolidated Fertilizers Sales Pty Ltd* [1982] Qd R 435.

promissory estoppel was finally adopted as part of the law in Australia by the High Court in *Legione v Hateley*[22]—'at least between parties in a pre-existing contractual relationship.'[23]

7.3.2 Recognition of equitable estoppel

[7.30] Promissory estoppel was not the only type of estoppel recognised in equity. For some time equity had also recognised estoppel by acquiescence,[24] estoppel by encouragement,[25] and proprietary estoppel (where equity bound the owner of property who induced another to expect that an interest in the property would be conferred on that other).[26] The relationship between these hitherto separate and distinct lines of authority was considered in the watershed case *Waltons Stores (Interstate) Ltd v Maher*.[27] In that case, the owner of land entered into negotiations with Waltons: the owner would demolish a building on the land and construct a new one to Waltons' specifications, which Waltons would then lease. Waltons made it clear to the owner that it was working to a tight timetable. The necessary documents were prepared, and Waltons' solicitors wrote to the owner's solicitors stating that they thought that Waltons' approval would 'be forthcoming' and that they would let them know the next day if there were any amendments. Several days later, the owner's solicitors had heard nothing further and submitted a document signed by the owner 'by way of exchange'. The owner then proceeded to demolish the building. About a week later, Waltons underwent a restructuring that included a reconsideration of whether it wished to proceed with the transaction. It therefore instructed its solicitor to 'go slow', although it became aware that the demolition was proceeding. Two months later, it informed the owner that it did not wish to proceed. By that time, the building was about 40 per cent completed. At no time had there been an exchange of contracts necessary for the conclusion of a binding contract.

[7.35] A majority of the court (Mason CJ and Wilson in a joint judgment, and Brennan J) interpreted the facts as indicating that the owner had been led to believe, and had acted on the belief, that an exchange of contracts *would* take place. In seeking relief, therefore, the owner was confronted by two closely connected difficulties:

- to seek relief on the basis of an estoppel would be to rely upon it as a source of rights rather than a mere defensive tool as had been previously stressed by Denning LJ in *Combe v Combe*; and

- in the absence of an agreed consideration, to grant a remedy would be tantamount to enforcing a gratuitous promise.

[7.40] In finding for the owner, their Honours recognised that promissory estoppel was but one instance where an equity was created by estoppel. A common thread

---

22   (1983) 152 CLR 406 (purchasers of land led to believe by a secretary in the office of the vendors' solicitors that a requested extension to a settlement date had been granted).

23   Ibid at 434. Since the parties in that case were in such a pre-existing contractual relationship, it was unnecessary for the court to decide whether the doctrine of promissory estoppel should be accepted as a general doctrine applicable regardless of the existence of that relationship: ibid at 435.

24   See, for example, *Laws Holdings Pty Ltd v Short* (1972) 46 ALJR 563.

25   *Legione v Hateley* (1983) 152 CLR 406 at 430.

26   See, for example, *Ramsden v Dyson* (1866) LR 1 HL 129; *Plimmer v Wellington Corporation* (1884) 9 App Cas 699.

27   (1988) 164 CLR 387.

linked the various types of estoppel recognised in equity—namely 'the principle that equity will come to the relief of a plaintiff who has acted to his detriment on the basis of a basic assumption in relation to which the other party to the transaction has "played such a part in the assumption that it would be unfair or unjust if he were left free to ignore it".'[28] Equity comes to the relief of such a plaintiff on the footing that it would be unconscionable conduct on the part of the other party to ignore the assumption.[29] Brennan J was of a similar view: although the equity created by estoppel had been differently expressed from time to time, its foundation, in all its instances, was the recognition of unconscionable conduct by the party bound by the equity.[30]

Accordingly, the various estoppels recognised by equity, including promissory estoppel, have been subsumed into a single doctrine of equitable estoppel. The familiar categories now do no more than serve to identify the characteristics of the circumstances that have been held to give rise to an equity in the party who is raising the estoppel.[31]

[7.45] Once it is acknowledged that the basis for equitable estoppel is the prevention of unconscionable conduct, a logical difficulty arises in attempting to limit the principle so it applies only to promises to suspend or extinguish existing rights and not to the creation of new rights. Unconscionable conduct may arise equally in either case. Consequently, there was no basis for restricting the operation of equitable estoppel to a defensive role and to not recognise it as being a source of new rights in appropriate circumstances. Equitable estoppel is therefore both a shield and a sword.[32]

This approach did not, however, necessarily raise the spectre of enforcement of non-contractual promises that had been identified by Denning LJ. The basis of equitable estoppel was unconscionable conduct rather than the enforcement of promises. In some cases, the avoidance of unconscionable conduct requires the enforcement of a promise.[33] In such cases, the equitable estoppel almost wears the appearance of contract—but they nevertheless remain distinct. As Brennan J pointed out, the differences include:

- a contractual obligation is created by the agreement of the parties whereas an equity created by estoppel may be imposed irrespective of any agreement by the party bound;

- a contractual obligation must be supported by consideration whereas an equity created by estoppel need not be supported by what is, strictly speaking, consideration; and

- the measure of a contractual obligation depends on the terms of the contract and the circumstances in which it is applied whereas the measure of an equity created by estoppel varies according to what is necessary to prevent detriment resulting from the unconscionable conduct.[34]

---

28   Ibid at 404, citing Dixon J in *Grundt v Great Boulder Pty Ltd Gold Mines Ltd* (1937) 59 CLR 641 at 675 and *Thompson v Palmer* (1933) 49 CLR 507 at 547.
29   (1988) 164 CLR 387 at 404.
30   Ibid at 419; see also *Olsson v Dyson* (1969) 120 CLR 365 per Kitto J.
31   See *Waltons Stores (Interstate) Ltd v Maher* (1988) 164 CLR 387 at 420 per Brennan J.
32   Ibid at 426.
33   Ibid at 405 per Mason CJ and Wilson J.
34   Ibid at 425.

[7.50] Here, Waltons' conduct in standing by, when it knew that the owner was attempting to comply with the strict timetable that Waltons had specified in the course of negotiations and that the owner had executed the counterpart deed and forwarded it to Waltons' solicitor, amounted to clear encouragement or inducement to the owners to act on the basis of the assumption that completion of the exchange was a formality. It was unconscionable for Waltons to do so, knowing that the owner was exposing himself to detriment by acting on the basis of the false assumption. Accordingly, Waltons was estopped from retreating from its implied promise to complete the contract.[35]

7.3.3 A unified estoppel?

[7.55] It is clear from the judgments in *Waltons v Maher* that a number of elements are common to both equitable estoppel and common law estoppel in pais. Given this commonality, it is natural to ask whether the law has developed to a stage at which a single unified estoppel applies both at common law and in equity. Such a development was advocated by two of the judges in *Commonwealth v Verwayen*.[36]

[7.60] In *Commonwealth v Verwayen*, Mason CJ argued in favour of a 'single overarching doctrine' of estoppel that provided that a court may do what is required to prevent a person resiling from an assumption as to a present, past or future state of affairs which that party had induced another to detrimentally rely upon. A central element of such a doctrine would be proportionality between the remedy and the detriment to be avoided: it would be wholly inequitable and unjust to insist upon a disproportionate 'making good' of the relevant assumption.[37]

[7.65] By contrast, Deane J was in favour of a 'general doctrine of estoppel by conduct' that precluded departure from an assumed state of affairs. Under this formulation, relief is framed on the basis of the assumed state of affairs, unless in the circumstances that would be inequitably harsh. In such circumstances, some lesser form of relief would be awarded.[38]

[7.70] However, the notion of a unified doctrine of estoppel was not accepted by other members of the court.[39] As McHugh J pointed out:

> One important difference between the common law doctrine of estoppel in pais and the equitable doctrines of promissory and proprietary estoppel is that the common law doctrine is concerned with the rules of evidence, notwithstanding that a common law claim of estoppel must be pleaded, while the equitable doctrines are concerned with the creation of new rights between the parties.[40]

---

35 Ibid at 407 per Mason CJ and Wilson J, 428 per Brennan J.
36 (1990) 170 CLR 394.
37 Ibid at 413; see also Mason CJ in *Foran v Wight* (1989) 168 CLR 385 at 411–413; Gaudron J in *Commonwealth v Verwayen* (1990) 170 CLR 394 at 487.
38 Ibid at 443; see also Deane J in *Waltons Stores (Interstate) Ltd v Maher* (1988) 164 CLR 387 at 451; *Foran v Wight* (1989) 168 CLR 385 at 435. See generally A Robertson, 'Towards a Unifying Purpose for Estoppel' (1996) 22 *MULR* 1.
39 See *Commonwealth v Verwayen* (1990) 170 CLR 394 at 422 per Brennan J, 454 per Dawson J, 499–501 per McHugh J.
40 Ibid at 500.

Further, representations or assumptions concerning the future can only be dealt with by equitable estoppel and not by common law estoppel in pais.[41] So it seems a number of issues remain to be resolved before it can be said that the law has developed to the stage of a unified estoppel applicable both at common law and in equity.[42]

7.4 Elements of equitable estoppel

7.4.1 General

[7.75] While it was unnecessary in *Legione v Hateley* to enquire whether the doctrine of promissory estoppel could apply where there was no pre-existing contractual relationship,[43] it is clear from *Waltons Stores (Interstate) Ltd v Maher*[44] that equitable estoppel may apply in the absence of pre-existing relationship of any kind.[45]

Consequently, an equitable estoppel may arise from pre-contractual negotiations.[46] However, a different result may apply where the parties subsequently execute a formal contract that is expressed to constitute the whole of the contract between the parties, but where one party asserts that the other is estopped from relying on rights created by the written contract due to an assumption formed during negotiations.[47] If it were otherwise, a new element of uncertainty would be introduced and the solemnity of formal contracts would be seriously undermined.[48]

[7.80] Unconscionable conduct is the touchstone for the operation of equitable estoppel and requires more than a mere failure to fulfil a promise or a mere reliance on a promise to do something resulting in a promisee changing his or her position or suffering detriment. Instead, unconscionable conduct denotes a creation or encouragement by the defendant in the other party of an assumption that a contract will come into existence or a promise will be performed and for the other party to have relied upon

---

41 Ibid at 499–500.

42 In the most recent case concerning estoppel to have been considered by the High Court, *Giumelli v Giumelli* (1999) 73 ALJR 547 at 549 the joint judgment of Gleeson CJ, McHugh, Gummow, and Callinan JJ declined to consider whether the various doctrines and remedies in the field of estoppel were to be brought under a unified doctrine. It has been suggested, however, that resolution of the appropriate remedy—specifically whether the remedy ought to be based on protection against detrimental reliance, prevention of unconscionable conduct or fulfilment of expectations—would be a major step in the facilitation of a transition to a unified estoppel: see, for example, A Robertson (1996) 22 *MULR* 1 at 27.

43 See (1993) 152 CLR 406 at 435 per Mason and Deane JJ.

44 (1988) 164 CLR 387.

45 See, for example, ibid at 400. See also, for example, *Birstar Pty Ltd v The Proprietors 'Ocean Breeze' Building Units Plan No 4745* [1997] 1 Qd R 117 at 127 per Macrossan CJ (with whom Thomas J agreed on this point).

46 See, for example, *Waltons Stores (Interstate) Ltd v Maher* (1988) 164 CLR 387; *State Rail Authority (NSW) v Heath Outdoor Pty Ltd* (1986) 7 NSWLR 170 (CA); *Silovi Pty Ltd v Barbaro* (1988) 13 NSWLR 466 (CA); *Austotel Pty Ltd v Franklins Selfserve Pty Ltd* (1989) 16 NSWLR 582 (CA).

47 *Skywest Aviation Pty Ltd v Commonwealth* (1995) 126 FLR 61 at 105.

48 See *State Rail Authority (NSW) v Health Outdoor Pty Ltd* (1986) 7 NSWLR 170 at 177 per Kirby P; *Johnson Mathey Ltd v AC Rochester Overseas Corporation* (1990) 23 NSWLR 190 at 195–196; *Cafdawn Pty Ltd v Waltons Stores (Interstate) Ltd* (unreported, Fed Ct, Beaumont J, 28 March 1991); *Skywest Aviation Pty Ltd v Commonwealth* (1995) 126 FLR 61 at 103–105. In the latter case it was suggested (at 105) that such a result was consistent with the principle that a collateral contract cannot be inconsistent with the terms of the main agreement: see [8.340].

that assumption to his or her detriment to the knowledge of the first party.[49] As Brennan J stated in *Waltons Stores (Interstate) Ltd v Maher*:

> To establish an equitable estoppel, it is necessary for a plaintiff to prove that (1) the plaintiff assumed that a particular legal relationship then existed between the plaintiff and the defendant or expected that a particular legal relationship would exist between them and (in the latter case) that the defendant would not be free to withdraw from the expected legal relationship; (2) the defendant has induced the plaintiff to adopt that assumption or expectation; (3) the plaintiff acts or abstains from acting in reliance on the assumption or expectation; (4) the defendant knew or intended him to do so; (5) the plaintiff's action or inaction will occasion detriment if the assumption or expectation is not fulfilled; and (6) the defendant has failed to act to avoid that detriment whether by fulfilling the assumption or expectation or otherwise.[50]

In this formulation, the second, fourth, and sixth elements reflect the necessary unconscionable conduct.[51] The Brennan elements have since been cited with approval on numerous occasions.[52]

[7.85] The elements of estoppel must be positively proved and will rarely if ever be inferred. This is clearly evident in relation to the detriment suffered[53] but applies equally to the other elements.[54]

[7.90] Judges often adopt the terms 'plaintiff' and 'defendant' as convenient descriptions of the parties involved. This is accurate where the equitable estoppel is relied upon as a cause of action. However, it should be borne in mind that equitable estoppel may still be used as a defensive shield,[55] in which case the party alleging estoppel will be the defendant and the party estopped will be the plaintiff.[56] Nevertheless, for

---

49   *Waltons Stores (Interstate) Ltd v Maher* (1988) 164 CLR 387 at 406 per Mason CJ and Wilson J.

50   Ibid at 428–429.

51   Cf a formulation of equitable estoppel suggested by the New South Wales Court of Appeal, which essentially comprised the first three elements suggested by Brennan J 'in circumstances where departure from the assumption by the defendant would be unconscionable': see *Silovi Pty Ltd v Barbaro* (1988) 13 NSWLR 466 at 472 (CA); see also *Austotel Pty Ltd v Franklins Selfserve Pty Ltd* (1989) 16 NSWLR 582 at 585, 610 (CA); *Mobil Oil Australia Ltd v Lyndel Nominees Pty Ltd* (1998) 153 ALR 198 at 234 (Fed Ct FC).

52   See, for example, *Trippe Investments Pty Ltd v Henderson Investments Pty Ltd* (1992) 106 FLR 214 at 229 (NT CA); *Re Ferninando* (1993) 42 FCR 243; *S & E Promotions Pty Ltd v Tobin Brothers Pty Ltd* (1994) 122 ALR 637 (Fed Ct FC); *Birstar Pty Ltd v The Proprietors 'Ocean Breeze' Building Units Plan No 4745* [1997] 1 Qd R 117 at 127–8 per Macrossan CJ (with whom Thomas J agreed on this point); *Mobil Oil Australia Ltd v Lyndel Nominees Pty Ltd* (1998) 153 ALR 198 at 234 (Fed Ct FC); *Woodson (Sales) Pty Ltd v Woodson (Australia) Pty Ltd* (1996) 7 BPR 14,685; *Forbes and Bundock v Australian Yachting Federation Inc* (unreported, NSW SC, Santow J, 4 April 1996); *Wright v Hamilton Island Enterprises Ltd* (unreported, Qld SC, Thomas J, 17 March 1998); *Homesun Pty Limited v Crawley* (unreported, ACT SC, Higgins J, 3 December 1996).

53   See, for example, *Commonwealth v Verwayen* (1990) 170 CLR 394 at 416 per Mason CJ and McHugh J; *Potter Partners Ltd v Balanda* (unreported, Qld FC, 30 June 1989).

54   *Chellaram & Co v China Ocean Shipping Co* [1991] 1 Lloyd's Rep 493 at 502, 513.

55   *Taylor Farms (Aust) Pty Ltd v A Calkos Pty Ltd* (unreported, NSW SC, Kirby J, 12 March 1999) [1999] NSWSC 186 at [82]; cf

56   As in, for example, *Central London Property Trust Ltd v High Trees House Ltd* [1947] KB 130.

convenience this chapter will use 'plaintiff' and 'defendant' to denote the party seeking to rely on estoppel and the party against whom estoppel is asserted, respectively.

7.4.2 Assumption or expectation

(a) Future state of affairs

[7.95] The relevant assumption or expectation has been described in a variety of ways. In *Waltons v Maher*, Mason CJ and Wilson J identified the relevant assumption or expectation as being 'that a contract will come into existence or a promise will be fulfilled.' In *Silovi Pty Ltd v Barbaro*, Priestley JA (with the concurrence of the other members of the New South Wales Court of Appeal) used the same formulation, explaining that equitable estoppel operated upon representations or promises as to future conduct, including promises about legal relations.[57] Such descriptions are understandable when describing the operation of equitable estoppel when it occurs in the form of promissory estoppel.

[7.100] The relevant assumption or expectation was cast in wider terms by Brennan J in *Waltons v Maher* as being that a particular legal relationship then existed or would exist between the plaintiff and the defendant.[58] Similarly, in *Austotel Pty Ltd v Franklins Self Serve Pty Ltd*,[59] the New South Wales Court of Appeal found the description of the relevant assumption or expectation by Mason CJ and Wilson J in *Waltons v Maher* and in *Silovi v Barbaro* as being unduly restrictive when confronted by circumstances in which equitable estoppel arose in the form of proprietary estoppel. In *Austotel v Franklins*, store premises were constructed and adapted to suit the purposes of a supermarket proprietor. The supermarket proprietor acquired special equipment and fittings and moved to terminate the lease on its existing premises. However, negotiations failed to produce agreement as to the rent payable for the new premises. Priestley JA acknowledged that the proposition set out in *Silovi v Barbaro*, while appropriate for the circumstances arising in that case, did not fully cover the field of equitable estoppel. *Silovi v Barbaro*, like *Waltons v Maher*, dealt with the situation where there was no dispute about any of the terms of the agreement. But it had been established that equitable relief of a proprietary kind could be granted even where the plaintiff was unable to point to precise terms describing what they expected from the defendant.[60] Accordingly, his Honour thought the relevant assumption or expectation suggested in *Silovi v Barbaro* should be expanded, and would more properly be described as an assumption or expectation 'that a contract will come into existence or a promise be performed or an interest granted to the plaintiff by the defendant'.[61] Kirby P indicated that he was content with the expansion suggested by Priestley JA of the *Silovi v Barbaro* description of the relevant assumption or expectation, although the description that he ultimately preferred was that the assumption or expectation be 'that a contract will come into existence, or a

---

57   (1998) 13 NSWLR 466 at 472.
58   (1998) 164 CLR 387 at 428.
59   (1989) 16 NSWLR 582.
60   *Austotel Pty Ltd v Franklins Self Serve Pty Ltd* (1989) 16 NSWLR 582 at 604, referring to, for example, *Plimmer v Mayor of Wellington* (1884) LR 9 App Cas 699.
61   (1989) 16 NSWLR 582 at 610.

promise be performed, or a transaction [be] carried out between the plaintiff and the defendant.'[62] Priestley JA's expanded interpretation has since attracted support.[63]

These expanded formulations indicate the essentially prospective nature of equitable estoppel.[64]

(b) Clear and unambiguous

[7.105] A concept shared by both common law estoppel at pais and equitable estoppel is that the assumption or expectation acted upon by the plaintiff must have been clear and unambiguous.[65]

[7.110] Estoppel requires a greater degree of certainty than that required for a contractual undertaking. This requirement was explained by Lord Denning MR as follows:

> The representation is put forward as a *variation* [of contract], and is fairly capable of one or other of two meanings, the judge will decide between those two meanings and say which is right. But, if it is put forward as an *estoppel*, the judge will not decide between the two meanings. He will reject it as an estoppel because it is not precise and unambiguous. There is good sense in this difference. When a contract is *varied* by correspondence, it is an *agreed* variation. It is the duty of the court to give effect to the agreement if it possibly can: and it does so by resolving ambiguities, no matter how difficult it may be. But, when a man is *estopped*, he has not agreed to anything. Quite the reverse. He is stopped from telling the truth. He should not be stopped on an ambiguity. To work in estoppel, the representation must be clear and unequivocal.[66]

[7.115] A representation cannot be said to be clear and unequivocal if important information is omitted.[67] Further, it is insufficient for conduct to merely be consistent with a particular assumption or expectation if it does not *unequivocally* support that assumption or expectation. Thus, in *Lorimer v State Bank of New South Wales*[68] one reason given by Handley JA for rejecting the argument that an estoppel was established in the circumstances was that the only conduct on the part of a Bank that could have supported an assumption made by one of its customers occurred within the framework of the existing relationship of banker and customer, such as the honouring of cheques and permitting the customer's overdraft to increase. That conduct was merely consistent with the bank conveying the representation that it would back certain plans rather than unequivocally conveying that representation.

---

62   Ibid at 585.
63   See, for example, *Woodson (Sales) Pty Ltd v Woodson (Australia) Pty Ltd* (1996) BPR 14,685; *Forbes and Bundock v Australian Yachting Federation Inc* (unreported, NSW SC, Santow J, 4 April 1996).
64   The inclusion by Brennan J in *Waltons v Maher* of an assumption that a legal relationship 'then existed' between the parties (see (1988) 164 CLR 387 at 428), may be thought to indicate an overlap with common law estoppel. It would seem that the rules of equity would prevail in such a case: see Kirby P in *Lorimer v State Bank of New South Wales* (unreported, NSWCA, 5 July 1991).
65   *Legione v Hateley* (1983) 152 CLR 406 at 436 per Mason and Deane JJ; see also *Chellaran & Co v China Ocean Shipping Co* [1991] 1 Lloyd's Rep 493 at 501, 509.
66   *Woodhouse AC Israel Cocoa Ltd SA v Nigerian Produce Marketing Co Ltd* [1971] 2 QB 23 at 64.
67   *Mobil Oil Australia Ltd v Lyndel Nominees Pty Ltd* (1998) 153 ALR 198 at 237.
68   Unreported, NSWCA, 5 July 1991.

[7.120] In *Legione v Hateley*, Mason and Deane JJ pointed out that it is not necessary for a representation to be clear in its entirety, provided that so much of the representation as is necessary to found the propounded estoppel satisfies the requirement. So a representation that a particular right would not be asserted for at least X days will not be unclear or unequivocal merely because the words used are equivocal as to whether the relevant period is X days, X + 1 day or X + 2 days. If what is said or done amounts to a clear and unequivocal representation that the particular right will not be exercised for a period of at least X days, a representation to that effect can be relied upon to establish an estoppel.[69]

(c) Assumptions may be of fact or law

[7.125] It seems that equitable estoppel will apply to assumptions or expectations of law as well as those as to future fact. Indeed, on some occasions the two assumptions may be difficult if not impossible to separate. For example, in *Lorimer v State Bank of New South Wales*,[70] a cotton farmer acted on the assumption that his bank would finance the hire-purchase of certain machinery in the development of part of his land. Handley JA of the New South Wales Court of Appeal held that the farmer may have honestly but mistakenly believed that his assumption was as to the true facts (a mistake of fact), or that what were the true facts amounted to a contract that obliged the bank to finance his plans (a mistake of law). Similarly, in *Waltons v Maher* the owner might have been viewed as having assumed that an exchange of contracts would take place in due course (an assumption of fact), or that he would have a future legal relationship with Waltons (an expectation of law).[71] Certainly the distinction between mistakes of fact and mistakes of law has been removed in other respects besides estoppel.[72]

7.4.3   *Encouraged or induced*

(a) Words or conduct

[7.130] An essential aspect of unconscionable conduct is that the defendant played a part in the other party adopting the assumption or expectation. Perhaps the clearest way an assumption or expectation may be encouraged or induced is as a result of a promise or representation made by the defendant.

[7.135] However, this does not mean that the representation must necessarily be express. A clear and unambiguous representation may be implied from words used, or be adduced from a failure to speak, where there was a duty to speak, or from conduct.[73] As to whether silence was capable of inducing the adoption or an assumption or expectation, Brennan J in *Waltons v Maher* thought the observations of Dixon J in *Thompson v Palmer* in reference to common law estoppel in pais applied equally to equitable estoppel:

---

69   (1983) 152 CLR 406 at 439.
70   Unreported, NSWCA, 5 July 1991.
71   See also *Commonwealth v Verwayen* (1990) 170 CLR 394 at 413 per Mason CJ; at 445 per Deane J.
72   See, for example, *David Securities Pty Ltd v Commonwealth Bank of Australia* (1992) 175 CLR 353.
73   *Legione v Hateley* (1983) 152 CLR 406 at 438–439 per Mason and Deane JJ.

Whether a departure by a party from the assumption should be considered unjust and inadmissible depends on the part taken by him in occasioning its adoption by the other party. He may be required to abide by the assumption because it formed the convention or basis upon which the parties entered into contractual or other mutual relations, such as bailment; or because he has exercised against the other party rights which would exist only if the assumption were correct ... or because knowing the mistake the other laboured under, he refrained from correcting him when it was his duty to do so; or because his imprudence, where care was required of him, was a proximate cause of the other party's adopting and acting upon the faith of the assumption; or because he directly made representations upon which the other party founded the assumption.[74]

Thus, an assumption or expectation may be adopted not only as the result of an express promise by the defendant, but also in certain circumstances as the result of encouragement by the defendant for the plaintiff to adhere to an assumption or expectation he or she has already formed, or as the result of being 'lulled into a false sense of security' by a failure by the defendant to object to an assumption or expectation on which the plaintiff is known to be conducting his or her affairs.[75] Silence will be unconscionable only where there is an attempt to afterwards assert a legal relationship different from the one which, to the knowledge of the silent party, the other party assumed or expected. A person who knows or intends that the other should conduct his or her affairs on the basis of the assumption or expectation has two options open to him or her:

- either to warn the other that he or she denies the correctness or assumption of the expectation when he or she knows that the other may suffer detriment by acting on the basis of the assumption or expectation; or
- to act so as to avoid any detriment that the other may suffer in reliance on the assumption or expectation.

It will be unconscionable to refrain from making a denial and then to leave the other party to suffer whatever detriment is occasioned by the non-fulfilment of the assumption or expectation.[76]

[7.140] It is essential that the defendant knows or ought to know of the mistake being made by the plaintiff.[77] In this respect, the defendant cannot escape where he or she has wilfully shut his or her eyes to what should have been obvious.[78]

---

74   (1933) 49 CLR 507 at 547.
75   *Waltons Stores (Interstate) Ltd v Maher* (1988) 164 CLR 387 at 427 per Brennan J; *S & E Promotions Pty Ltd v Tobin Brothers Pty Ltd* (1994) 122 ALR 637 at 656 (Fed Ct FC); *Skywest Aviation Pty Ltd v Commonwealth* (1995) 126 FLR 61 at 112.
76   *Waltons Stores (Interstate) Ltd v Maher* (1988) 164 CLR 387 at 428 per Brennan J.
77   *Ampol Ltd v Matthews* (1991) 4 ACSR 592.
78   *S & E Promotions Pty Ltd v Tobin Brothers Pty Ltd* (1994) 122 ALR 637 at 656 (Fed Ct FC) applying *The Zamora (No 2)* [1921] 1 AC 801 at 803, 812.

Example: Ampol Ltd v Matthews[79]

The construction business of a corporate customer of Ampol was taken over by a new company bearing a similar name. The change was reflected in the repainting of the company vehicles and the printing of new letterhead. However, the bank accounts, or at least the numbers of the accounts, remained the same and cheques were drawn on the accounts sometimes in the old name but more often in the new. Nothing was done to close the account with Ampol in the name of the old company or to open a new account in the name of the new company. Further, no steps were taken to revoke a guarantee of the old company's obligations given to Ampol by the principals of the old company. The business continued to be run in the same way as it was before and Ampol continued to supply the new company in the same way as it had previously supplied the old company.

The Full Court of the Supreme Court of South Australia held that the failure by the old company to bring to the notice of Ampol that the company had ceased to trade and that thereafter Ampol should look to the new company for payment of the account amounted to unconscionable conduct and gave rise to an estoppel. In relation to whether the old company knew of the mistake that Ampol was making, 'wilful blindness' on the part of the old company could be equated with knowledge: it was enough that those associated with it had closed their eyes and gone ahead without bothering to do anything one way or another.

By contrast, in *Lorimer v State Bank of New South Wales*[80] a bank was unaware that one of its customers, a cotton farmer, was acting under the assumption that the bank would finance his development plans. The customer was unable to rely on an estoppel against the bank based on its routine lending of money to him pending its decision upon his request for finance, since two bank officers had made it quite clear before he committed himself that they could give no assurance that the bank would provide the funding.

[7.145] Moreover, it will be insufficient if the plaintiff orchestrates matters so that it appears that the defendant's conduct allowed the plaintiff to adopt the assumption where the reality is otherwise.[81]

Example: Skywest Aviation Pty Ltd v Commonwealth[82]

Skywest provided surveillance services off the North Australian coast directed principally at illegal fishing and unauthorised landings on Australian territory. After this contract was not renewed, a contract was awarded to Amman Aviation, but this contract was promptly terminated by the Commonwealth.[83] When the Australian Customs Service again invited tenders for the Coastwatch contract, Skywest submitted a tender based on three Westwind aircraft appropriately modified for surveillance operations. It was found by the trial judge that when Skywest submitted its tender, it was aware that the cost of modification of aircraft available to it for purchase would exceed the amount it had stated in its tender. In the course of pre-contractual negoti-

---

79   (1991) 4 ACSR 592.
80   Unreported, NSWCA, 5 July 1991.
81   *Skywest Aviation Pty Ltd v Commonwealth* (1995) 126 FLR 61 at 113.
82   (1995) 126 FLR 61.
83   See [20.465].

ations with various Customs Service officers, the chief executive of Skywest and project manager at Skywest both adopted a strategy of introducing into conversations the concept of 'equalisation' (intended to denote that the Commonwealth would be responsible for these extra costs) in such a way that the Customs Service officers did not know what it meant. It was held that the purpose of the strategy was to put the Commonwealth in a position where its officers could not deny the conversations in which the so-called assumption about equivalence was expressed. Skywest was awarded the tender. Skywest subsequently claimed that the Commonwealth was estopped from denying responsibility for the costs of modification of the aircraft it purchased.

Miles CJ of the ACT Supreme Court held that far from the Commonwealth fostering any relevant assumption on the part of Skywest, all the fostering was on the part of Skywest. There was nothing in the conduct of the Customs Service officers to induce a belief in Skywest that the Commonwealth would pay for or contribute any cost of modification outside of the tender and contract. Indeed, the Customs Service officers had no or little appreciation of the concept of 'equalisation'. Skywest knew this, and was concerned to keep it that way. The Commonwealth therefore had not induced or caused Skywest to adopt the claimed assumption.

A similar result will follow if the representation by the defendant upon which an estoppel is said to be based was induced by the plaintiff's misrepresentation.[84]

(b) Mere hope

[7.150] The defendant must have 'played such a part in the adoption of the assumption that it would be unfair or unjust if he were left free to ignore it'.[85] If a party plays *no* part in the adoption of the assumption or expectation, there will be no unconscionable conduct by that party.[86] The assumption in such a case is likely to be no more than a mere hope rather than being the consequence of words or conduct by the party claimed to be estopped.

[7.155] Departure from an assumption or expectation formed in the face of an express statement intended to dissuade such a belief will not be unconscionable. Accordingly, in *Lorimer v State Bank of New South Wales*,[87] despite express statements by two bank officers that the bank was not yet committed to the development plans, the plaintiff farmer may be seen as having taken a gamble and relied upon his own hope that the bank would ultimately provide finance, rather than any belief encouraged or induced by the bank. Similarly, in *Valbirn Pty Ltd v Powprop Pty Ltd*,[88] despite a clear indication by a restaurant proprietor that it would not lease particular premises, the owner of the premises risked the expense of making design and layout changes to its building in the hope that it might successfully secure the restaurant proprietor as a tenant. When negotiations between the parties were unsuccessful, the

---

84 *Official Trustee in Bankruptcy v Tooheys Ltd* (1993) 29 NSWLR 641 (CA) (fraudulent misrepresentation); *Trippe Investments Pty Ltd v Henderson Investments Pty Ltd* (1992) 106 FLR 214 (NT CA) (innocent misrepresentation).

85 *Waltons Stores (Interstate) Ltd v Maher* (1988) 164 CLR 387 at 675.

86 *Canberra Bushrangers Baseball Team Pty Limited v Byrne* (unreported, ACT SC, Higgins J, 21 December 1997); *Homesun Pty Limited v Crawley* (unreported, ACT SC, Higgins J, 3 December 1996).

87 Unreported, NSWCA, 5 July 1991 per Priestley and Handley JJA.

88 [1991] 1 Qd R 295.

restaurant proprietor was held to not be estopped from denying that there was an agreement to lease.

[7.160] Mere hope can be seen in operation where a particular interpretation is placed on an ambiguous representation by the party claiming estoppel. This may be illustrated by New South Wales Court of Appeal decision in *Chellaram & Co v China Ocean Shipping Co*.[89] In that case, solicitors for the defendant wrote to the solicitors for the plaintiff in the following terms: 'we trust ... it will not be necessary for your client to commence proceedings until settlement has been fully explored.' When the time limitation on the action for breach of the contract of carriage expired, the plaintiff alleged that the solicitors' letter estopped the carrier from relying on the time bar. But it was held that nothing in the statement by the solicitors for the defendant suggested or justified the conclusion that nothing further needed to be said or done about the limitation period.[90] Any assumption that the time bar would not be invoked by the defendant might be explained more from the mere hope on the part of the plaintiff that the time bar would not be invoked—and of this, the defendant had no knowledge either actual or constructive.[91]

(c) Unauthorised representations

[7.165] No estoppel will arise if a representation is made by an agent who has no authority to bind his or her principal, and this fact is known or ought to be known to the party claiming estoppel.[92] However, the mere fact that a representation is unauthorised will not necessarily prevent an estoppel being established. When an unauthorised statement is made to the knowledge of the principal in circumstances where the principal knows or ought to know that the statement is being relied upon, a failure to deny the statement may amount to an encouragement by the principal for others to believe that the statement is in fact authorised and may reasonably be relied upon by the other party. In other words, an estoppel may arise not on the basis of the initial unauthorised statement by the agent, but rather upon the later encouragement by the principal (in the form of his or her failure to denounce the statement when he or she had the opportunity to do so). The unconscionability lies in the principal's failure to disabuse the party acting in reliance of the statement, when combined with knowledge of that reliance and a failure to avoid the consequential detriment.

Example: Corpers (No. 664) Pty Ltd v NZI Securities Australia Ltd[93]

The defendant, an Australian subsidiary of a New Zealand finance company, was the mortgagee of a building in the Sydney central business district. The owner of the building was continually in default and went into receivership, and the defendant attempted unsuccessfully to sell the building by mortgagee's auction. After the auc-

---

89 [1991] 1 Lloyd's Rep 493.

90 Ibid at 501 per Gleeson CJ (with whom Samuels JA agreed), at 513 per Kirby P.

91 Cf *S & E Promotions Pty Ltd v Tobin Brothers Pty Ltd* (1994) 122 ALR 637 at 651–652 (Fed Ct FC) where it was held that the plaintiff's failure to exercise an option on a lease in the permitted time was due to protracted negotiations between the parties for a new long term lease which included the defendant asking for an amendment to the new lease without imposing a limit for the amendment to be accepted or chasing up the matter.

92 *State Rail Authority (NSW) v Heath Outdoor Pty Ltd* (1986) 7 NSWLR 170 (CA).

93 (1989) ASC 58,402.

tion, representatives of the plaintiff approached a senior officer of the defendant with a proposal involving the defendant lending the plaintiff $65 million to buy the building. Three days later, the defendant's officer advised the plaintiff's representatives that he had 'referred it to New Zealand and they have approved it'. The following day he supplied a letter setting out the terms on which the defendant would provide the $65 million financing, and on the same day, the plaintiff entered into an agreement to purchase the building. Meanwhile, the defendant and its New Zealand parent company were undergoing changes in its management and the executives were issued with written instructions limiting their lending authority. Following a review of the deal by executives in New Zealand, the defendant indicated that there was no way it would proceed with the deal.

Young J of the New South Wales Supreme Court held that although the officer had no actual or ostensible authority to write the letter that the plaintiff had relied upon, a common law estoppel—and alternatively an equitable estoppel—had been made out. The defendant's conduct in knowingly and silently watching the plaintiff enter into the contract to purchase the building when it must have known that it was only doing so because of the letter, gave rise to an estoppel. Accordingly, the defendant was held bound by a contract to lend the plaintiff $65 million in the same way as it would have been bound had its officer had the appropriate authority.

7.4.4 Reliance

[7.170] The plaintiff's reliance upon an assumption or expectation induced by the defendant must have been reasonable. Departure from an assumption or expectation that is unreasonably formed or unreasonably relied upon will not normally constitute unconscionable conduct by the defendant.[94] It has been suggested that when determining whether the plaintiff reasonably adopted and relied on an assumption or expectation, only the plaintiff's actual knowledge is relevant—not any constructive notice (including constructive notice that the assumption or expectation was untrue).[95]

[7.175] The requirement of reasonableness may be a significant impediment to a party seeking to establish an equitable estoppel on the basis of a non-contractual promise. This is because a promisee may reasonably be expected to appreciate that because a voluntary promise does not form part of a binding contract, he or she cannot safely rely upon it.[96] A similar difficulty confronts a party seeking to establish an estoppel preventing parties from refusing to proceed with a transaction expressed to be 'subject to contract'.[97]

[7.180] In assessing the reasonableness of any reliance, the characteristics of the plaintiff—including whether he or she was being advised by solicitors at the time—are relevant.[98] For example, in *Capital Market Brokers Pty Ltd v Hamelyn UPC Ltd*[99] no estoppel was held to arise where the parties were stockbrokers and merchant bankers

---

94   *Australian Securities Commission v Marlborough Goldmines Ltd* (1993) 177 CLR 485 at 506; *Standard Chartered Bank Aust Ltd v Bank of China* (1991) 23 NSWLR 164 at 180–81.
95   *Standard Chartered Bank Aust Ltd v Bank of China* (1991) 23 NSWLR 164 at 181.
96   *Waltons Stores (Interstate) Ltd v Maher* (1988) 164 CLR 387 at 406 per Mason CJ and Wilson J, citing *Amalgamated Property Co v Texas Bank* [1982] 1 QB 84 at 107. See also *Kirton v Nethery* (unreported, NSW SC, McClelland CJ in Eq, 15 July 1996).
97   Ibid, citing *Attorney-General (Hong Kong) v Humphreys Estate Ltd* [1987] 1 AC 114.
98   A fortiori where the plaintiff is a practising solicitor or barrister himself or herself: see, for example, *Kirton v Nethery* (unreported, NSW SC, McClelland CJ in Eq, 15 July 1996).
99   Unreported, NSW Supreme Court, Young J, 2 May 1989.

experienced in commerce who intended to have their solicitors prepare formal documentation. Similarly, in relation to large commercial entities represented by solicitors, Kirby P observed in *Austotel Pty Ltd v Franklins Self Serve Pty Ltd*:

> We are not dealing here with ordinary individuals invoking the protection of equity from the unconscionable operation of a rigid rule of the common law. Nor are we here dealing with parties which were unequal in bargaining power. Nor were the parties lacking in advice either of a legal character or of technical expertise. The Court has before it two groupings of substantial enterprises, well resourced and advised, dealing in a commercial transaction having a great value. … they did not reach the point of formulating their agreement in terms which would be enforced by the law of contract. This is not, of itself, a reason for denying them the beneficial application of the principles developed by equity. But it is a reason for scrutinising carefully the circumstances which are said to give rise to the conclusion that an insistence by the appellants on their legal rights would be so unconscionable that the Court will provide relief from it.[100]

However, the mere fact that the parties may have had the benefit of legal advice or were contracting according to customary practice will not, by itself, necessarily prevent an estoppel from arising. It is possible, as illustrated by *Waltons v Maher* itself, that a party's solicitor may be encouraged or induced to make the same mistake as his or her client.

[7.185] Notwithstanding the necessity for any reliance to be reasonable, there may be circumstances in which a prima facie unreasonable reliance still forms the basis of an equitable estoppel. It has already been seen that in some cases, even a departure from an unauthorised representation may be unconscionable. This may be the case where a principal is aware of the unauthorised representation but takes no steps to disavow that representation and effectively adopts it as his or her own. The important features of such a case are the principal's knowledge that the other party is relying on unauthorised representation and the failure by the principal to either warn the other party of his or her mistake or to act otherwise to prevent the other party incurring detriment.

A similar position can be seen where an assumption or expectation is being unreasonably relied upon. The failure by the defendant to dissuade the plaintiff from relying on that assumption or expectation can amount to an encouragement of that assumption or expectation. In such circumstances, the equitable estoppel would be based not on the unreasonable reliance upon the original assumption or expectation, but upon a reasonable reliance upon an assumption or expectation that if the original assumption or expectation was wrong, the defendant would have dissuaded the plaintiff from relying on it.[101]

7.4.5 Knowledge or intention

[7.190] The party who induces the adoption of an assumption or expectation must know or intend the other party to act or abstain from acting in reliance on the assumption or expectation.[102] Brennan J elaborated on this point in the following terms:

---

100 (1989) 16 NSWLR 582 at 585; see also Rogers AJA at 621.
101 See A Leopold, 'The Elements of Estoppel' (1991) BCL 248 at 259–260.
102 *Waltons Stores (Interstate) Ltd v Maher* (1988) 164 CLR 387 at 406 per Mason CJ and Wilson J, 423 per Brennan J; see also *Crabb v Arun District Council* [1976] Ch 179 at 188. Cf *Berry v Hodsdon* [1989] 1 Qd R 361 at 363.

When the adoption of an assumption or an expectation is induced by the making of a promise, the knowledge or intention that the assumption or expectation will be acted upon may be easily inferred. But if a party encourages another to adhere to an assumption or expectation already formed or acquiesces in the making of an assumption or the entertainment or an expectation when he ought to object to the assumption or expectation—steps which are tantamount to inducing the other to adopt the assumption or expectation—the inference of knowledge or intention that the assumption or expectation will be acted on may be more difficult to draw.[103]

An example where the inference may be drawn in the second situation contemplated by Brennan J may be where, in the course of negotiations, the defendant stipulates or communicates special requirements or specifications and subsequently becomes aware that the plaintiff is acting with the obvious intent of fulfilling those requirements or specifications, but nevertheless chooses to remain silent. For example, in both *Waltons v Maher*[104] and *Marvan Pty Ltd v Yulara Development Co Ltd*,[105] the plaintiff was 'lulled into a false sense of security' when it renovated or constructed premises to meet the defendant's requirements in anticipation of the execution of a lease, to the defendant's knowledge but without objection or caution from the defendant.[106]

7.4.6 *Detriment*

[7.195] The relevant detriment is that of the plaintiff, not the defendant.[107] Further, there must be a link between the assumption or expectation created or encouraged and the detriment suffered.[108]

[7.200] It is insufficient for the plaintiff merely to change his or her position in reliance upon the assumption or expectation. Instead, for both common law estoppel in pais and equitable estoppel, it is necessary that the party claiming estoppel suffer detriment in the sense that 'as a result of adopting [the assumption] as the basis of action or inaction, [the plaintiff] will have placed himself [or herself] in a position of material disadvantage if departure from the assumption be permitted'.[109] Accordingly, there must be disadvantage in the sense of the party being in some way worse off. It may involve the plaintiff pursuing a particular course of action—such as failing to take the necessary steps to become ready and willing to perform the contract, where that is required.[110]

---

103 Ibid at 423.
104 (1988) 164 CLR 387. In this case there was the additional element of urgency which pervaded the negotiation of the terms of the proposed lease: ibid at 407 per Mason CJ and Wilson J.
105 (1989) 98 FLR 348.
106 *S&E Promotions Pty Ltd v Tobin Brothers Pty Ltd* (1994) 122 ALR 637 at 649 (Fed Ct FC).
107 *Gobblers Inc Pty Ltd v Stevens* (1993) 6 BPR 97488 at 13,597.
108 Ibid; *Re Ferdinando* (1993) 42 FCR 243 at 248; *Australia and New Zealand Banking Group v PA Wright and Sons Pty Ltd* [1999] NSWSC 628 (25 June 1999).
109 *Thompson v Palmer* (1933) 49 CLR 507 at 547 per Dixon J; *Newbon v City Mutual Life Assurance Society Ltd* (1935) 52 CLR 723 at 734 per Rich, Dixon and Evatt JJ; *Legione v Hateley* (1983) 152 CLR 406 at 437; *Lorimer v State Bank of New South Wales* (Unreported, NSWCA, 5 July 1991); *Hawker Pacific Pty Ltd v Helicopter Charter Pty Ltd* (1991) 22 NSWLR 298 at 307 (CA); *Austral Standard Cables Pty Ltd v Walker Nominees Pty Ltd* (1992) 26 NSWLR 524 at 538 (CA).
110 *Foran v Wight* (1989) 168 CLR 385; *Austral Standard Cables Pty Ltd v Walker Nominees Pty Ltd* (1992) 26 NSWLR 524 (CA).

By contrast, it will be insufficient if, for example, the plaintiff merely spent money that he or she was always planning to spend, but at an earlier time and with no resulting altered mode of living or other disadvantage.[111] The detriment is determined as at the date the defendant seeks to resile from the assumption or expectation he or she has encouraged or induced, and upon which the other party has acted.[112]

[7.205] Although a single peppercorn may constitute valuable consideration, such a small loss would not amount to 'material' or 'significant' disadvantage as required for the purposes of the law of estoppel. This is because consideration is decided by agreement between the parties, while the relevant detriment is not something that the defendant has agreed as the price binding him or her to the expectation he or she created or encouraged.[113]

However, the disadvantage need not be substantial. For example, relevant detriment has been found where the plaintiff has been required to pay arrears of rental in a bulk amount rather than on a periodic basis;[114] been required to negotiate an agreement for the removal of a caveat;[115] and been forced to return to court and to fight a case on its merits after the defendant had reneged on a settlement agreement reached by counsel involved in the case.[116]

[7.210] There will be no estoppel if the plaintiff suffers detriment *after* learning that the assumption or expectation on which he or she relied was without basis.[117] Further, any detriment must be suffered by the plaintiff himself or herself, and not by an associated party such as a related company.[118]

7.4.7 Failure to avoid detriment

[7.215] The purpose of equitable estoppel is to prevent detriment being suffered. As Brennan J explained in *Waltons v Maher*, 'the object of the equity is not to compel the party bound to fulfil the assumption or expectation; it is to avoid the detriment which, if the assumption or expectation goes unfulfilled, will be suffered by the party who has been induced to act or abstain from acting on it'.[119] Depending on the circumstances, the defendant may be required to do no more than warn the plaintiff that the assumption or expectation is mistaken before the plaintiff incurs irreversible detriment.[120]

[7.220] It may be possible to show the relevant detriment where the defendant has made an attempt to avoid detriment being suffered by the plaintiff but the attempt proves to be inadequate. In other words, equitable estoppel may be relied upon even

---

111 See, for example, *Potter Partners Ltd v Balanda* (unreported, Qld FC, 30 June 1989).
112 *Lorimer v State Bank of New South Wales* (Unreported, NSWCA, 5 July 1991); *Ashton Mining Ltd v Commissioner of Taxation* (2000) 44 ATR 249.
113 *Hawker Pacific Pty Ltd v Helicopter Charter Pty Ltd* (1991) 22 NSWLR 298 at 308.
114 *Je Maintiendrai v Quaglia* (1980) 26 SASR 101.
115 *Stevens v Standard Chartered Bank* (1988) 53 SASR 323 at 346.
116 *Collin v Holden* [1989] VR 510.
117 *Milchas Investments Pty Ltd v Larkin* (1989) 11 ATPR 50,431 at 50,439.
118 Ibid.
119 *Waltons Stores (Interstate) Ltd v Maher* (1988) 164 CLR 387 at 423.
120 *Lorimer v State Bank of New South Wales* (Unreported, NSWCA, 5 July 1991) per Kirby P; *Waltons Stores (Interstate) Ltd v Maher* (1988) 164 CLR 387 at 428. See also *Forbes and Bundock v Australian Yachting Federation Inc* (unreported, NSW SC, Santow J, 4 April 1996).

where the defendant has taken steps to avoid the detriment but those steps do not go far enough. This may be the case where, for example, a contractual provision intended to preserve rights enjoyed by the plaintiff is inserted in a dealing with a third party, and the provision proves to be insufficient to properly secure those rights.[121]

7.5 Relevant remedy

[7.225] The appropriate remedy is within the court's discretion.[122] In moulding its decree, the court, as a court of conscience, goes no further than necessary to prevent unconscionable conduct.[123] In other words, there should be proportionality between the remedy and the relevant detriment.[124] This has been described as the court determining what is the 'minimum equity to do justice for the plaintiff.'[125] The remedy therefore varies according to the circumstances of the case; it will depend in each case on a close examination of the detriment occasioned to the party claiming estoppel.[126] The object of equitable estoppel is not to enforce promises but rather to avoid detriment.[127] In some circumstances, however, the enforcement of a promise may be the only means of avoiding the detriment.[128] That was the case in *Waltons v Maher* itself.

[7.230] In *Commonwealth v Verwayen*, Mason CJ pointed out a difference between detriment that brings estoppel into play and detriment for which estoppel grants a remedy. His Honour stated:

> When a person relies upon the correctness of an assumption which is subsequently denied by the party who has induced the making of the assumption, two distinct types of detriment may be caused. In a broad sense, there is detriment which would result from the denial that the correctness of the assumption upon which the person has relied. In a narrower sense, there is the detriment which the person has suffered as a result of his reliance upon the correctness of the assumption ... While detriment in the broader sense is required in order to found an estoppel (and it would be strange to grant relief if such detriment were absent), the law provides a remedy which will often be closer in scope to the detriment suffered in the narrower sense.[129]

---

121   See *Silovi Pty Ltd v Barbaro* (1988) 13 NSWLR 466.
122   *Austotel Pty Ltd v Franklin's Self Serve Pty Ltd* (1989) 16 NSWLR 582 at 616.
123   *Waltons Stores (Interstate) Ltd v Maher* (1988) 164 CLR 387 at 419 per Brennan J.
124   See also, for example, *Birstar Pty Ltd v The Proprietors 'Ocean Breeze' Building Units Plan No 4745* [1997] 1 Qd R 117 at 128 per Macrossan CJ (with whom Thomas J agreed on this point); *Forbes and Bundock v Australian Yachting Federation Inc* (unreported, NSW SC, Santow J, 4 April 1996).
125   *Crabb v Arun District Council* [1976] Ch 179 at 198; *Waltons Stores (Interstate) Ltd v Maher* (1988) 164 CLR 387 at 404 per Mason CJ and Wilson J.
126   *Waltons Stores (Interstate) Ltd v Maher* (1988) 164 CLR 387 at 419 per Brennan J; *Lorimer v State Bank of New South Wales* (Unreported, NSWCA, 5 July 1991).
127   *Mobil Oil Australia Ltd v Lyndel Nominees Pty Ltd* (1998) 153 ALR 198 at 238.
128   *Waltons Stores (Interstate) Ltd v Maher* (1988) 164 CLR 387 at 427 per Brennan J; *Commonwealth v Verwayen* (1990) 170 CLR 394 at 411–412 per Mason CJ, 429 per Brennan J, 501 per McHugh J. See also *S & E Promotions Pty Ltd v Tobin Brothers Pty Ltd* (1994) 122 ALR 637 at 651 (Fed Ct FC) (relief analogous to specific performance held to be appropriate in the circumstances).
129   (1990) 170 CLR 394 at 396; see also ibid at 429–430 per Brennan J, 504 per McHugh J.

In other words, the court may order compensation based on the plaintiff's reliance loss rather than on his or her expectation loss.

Example: Commonwealth v Verwayen[130]

In 1964, the aircraft carrier HMAS *Melbourne* collided with the destroyer HMAS *Voyager*. Due to legal opinion at the time, which was based on certain *obiter dicta* in a High Court decision to the effect that it was public policy that a member of the armed forces could not recover damages for the negligence of another member of the armed forces in the course of duty, no action for compensation was commenced by the plaintiff, a survivor of the collision. That *obiter* was subsequently disapproved by the High Court in 1982 in a decision that broadened the ambit of the law of negligence in the context of the armed forces. Subsequently, a number of survivors, including the plaintiff in this case, took action against the Commonwealth. Over a prolonged period, the Commonwealth made public declarations that it would neither seek to rely on the statute of limitations nor plead that it owed no duty of care to members of the armed forces. Similar statements were made in correspondence between the solicitors acting for the parties. Nevertheless, in late 1985, the Commonwealth reconsidered its policy in relation to claims arising from the collision and began to plead that the claim was time-barred and that no duty was owed to the survivors. Verwayen argued that the Commonwealth was either estopped from relying on the defences or had waived those defences.

A majority of the High Court held that the Commonwealth was not entitled to rely on the defences. Of the four judges in the majority, two (Deane and Dawson JJ) decided the case on the basis of equitable estoppel, while two (Toohey and Gaudron JJ) based their decision on waiver. Deane J applied his concept of a general doctrine of estoppel by conduct extending to representations about future facts and held that there was a prima facie entitlement to relief based on the assumed state of affairs (in this case, that the two defences would not be relied upon). Dawson J identified the real detriment in the circumstances as being the strain of litigation and false raising of hopes, which could only be satisfied by holding the Commonwealth to fulfil its assumption by not relying on the defences. This was in contrast to the view taken by Mason CJ and Brennan and McHugh JJ, who also dealt with the case on the basis of estoppel but who held that the minimum equity to do justice in the circumstances was to compensate the plaintiff for his reliance loss—that is, to compensate the plaintiff for the legal costs from the time the Commonwealth had stated that it would not contest liability or plead the statute of limitations up until the time of the change of policy. In adopting this approach, Mason CJ said he regarded the allegation that the Commonwealth's conduct in changing its policy had caused a deterioration in the plaintiff's emotional condition as 'sheer speculation'. Similarly, McHugh J noted that while it was possible that the plaintiff had suffered more worry and stress as a result of the assurance of the Commonwealth than he would have otherwise have suffered if the Commonwealth had not given the assurance, the plaintiff had led no evidence to

---

130   (1990) 170 CLR 394.

that effect, and he did not think it could be inferred. By contrast, Brennan J dismissed a plaintiff's emotional state as a possible relevant detriment.[131]

This case is commonly cited as authority for the view that a court should only grant a remedy that is the minimum necessary to do justice between the parties, and that this ought to be in the nature of reliance loss. However, this has not prevented a number of courts from granting a remedy focused on the nature of the plaintiff's expectation.[132]

[7.235] In relation to the circumstances in which the maximum remedy of making good an assumption or expectation relied upon by the plaintiff, Mason CJ suggested, *obiter*, that each case was one of degree, and that it would be appropriate for the expectation to be fulfilled where there had been reliance for an extended period—or where there had been substantial and irreversible detriment suffered in reliance upon the assumption, or from detriment that could not satisfactorily be compensated or remedied.[133] It would appear from the judgments in *Commonwealth v Verwayen* that ill health, worry, and stress might suffice if they can be affirmatively proved.[134]

[7.240] A broader approach to the relevant remedy can be seen in the concept of a general doctrine of estoppel by conduct favoured by Deane J. Such a concept favours a prima facie entitlement to relief based on the assumed state of affairs the defendant is estopped from denying. It is only qualified where the relief would exceed what could be justified by the requirements of conscientious conduct, and would be unjust to the defendant.[135] By contrast, Gaudron J has expressed the view that 'where the nature or likely extent of the detriment cannot be accurately or adequately predicted it may be necessary in the interests of justice that the assumption be made good to avoid the possibility of detriment even though the detriment cannot be said to be inevitable or more probable than not'.[136]

In the High Court's most recent consideration of equitable estoppel, *Giumelli v Giumelli*,[137] the joint judgment of Gleeson CJ, McHugh, Gummow, and Callinan JJ referred to the different approaches adopted by the various judges in *Commonwealth v Verwayen* and held that there was nothing in those judgments to preclude the court below granting relief in accordance with a prima facie entitlement. Although this indicates support for Deane J's approach, their Honours did not discuss the merits of the competing approaches.[138]

[7.245] There are different views as to whether a court should grant relief that may have an adverse effect on the rights of third parties. In *Silovi Pty Ltd v Barbaro*, the

---

131 See (1990) 170 CLR 394 at 416 per Mason CJ, 429 per Brennan J and 504 per McHugh J.

132 See, for example, *Edwater Grazing Pty Ltd v Pincevic Nominees Pty Ltd* [2001] NSWSC 157 (15 March 2001) (making good representation that fence would be removed held to be minimum remedy to do justice).

133 (1990) 170 CLR 394 at 416.

134 Such an approach was adopted in another case involving a claim by a survivor of the *Voyager* disaster, *Commonwealth v Clark* [1994] 2 VR 333 at 343 per Marks J, 380 per Ormiston J.

135 *Commonwealth v Verwayen* (1990) 170 CLR 394 at 442.

136 Ibid at 487.

137 (1999) 73 ALJR 547.

138 See ibid at 556.

remedy awarded was the grant of a personal licence to the plaintiffs coupled with an interest in the nature of a profit à prendre, which, taken together, were sufficient to prevent the later equitable interest of the purchaser (which had been acquired under a contract for sale) from prevailing over the earlier equitable rights.[139] In other cases, the potential adverse effect on a third party may influence the court in framing the appropriate relief. In *Giumelli v Giumelli*,[140] the High Court held that in making its orders and fashioning the equitable relief that should be granted to the plaintiff, the court was obliged to consider, among other circumstances, the matters that stood in the way of a simple order to convey the land to the plaintiff in accordance with the assumption he had been encouraged to make. Such an order would have resulted in an injustice to others and could have exceeded what was required for conscientious conduct by the defendant. Accordingly, the High Court substituted an order for payment of money to the value of the land for the lower court's order that the land be transferred to him. Similarly, in *Forbes and Bundock v Australian Yachting Federation Inc*[141] it was held that where a two-man yachting crew had suffered detriment in reliance upon Olympic selection criteria published by the defendant Federation, the appropriate remedy was compensation for the wasted expenditure they had incurred—buying and air-freighting boating equipment at their own expense—to mitigate the competitive disadvantage they would otherwise have suffered in the circumstances. In ordering the Federation to pay that compensation, Santow J of the Supreme Court of New South Wales was satisfied that no injury would be caused to innocent third parties—as would have occurred if, for example, the court had ordered the cancellation or denial of the Olympic nomination of the crew selected ahead of the plaintiffs.

7.6   International perspectives

7.6.1   New Zealand

[7.250] New Zealand has not yet taken the final step of supporting an equitable estoppel in the same terms as *Waltons Stores (Interstate) Ltd v Maher*,[142] however, there are strong signs that New Zealand law is heading in that direction.[143] First, it has been held that promissory estoppel does not depend upon there being a pre-existing contractual relationship.[144] Secondly, the New Zealand Court of Appeal has said that 'any suggestion that estoppel is available only as a shield has disappeared'.[145] Accordingly, there is some recognition that estoppel may found a cause of action.[146] Thirdly, it has been recognised that unconscionable conduct is the underlying basis of the doctrine.[147] As a consequence, it has been acknowledged that the court has a discretion to find the

---

139   (1988) 13 NSWLR 466 at 475, citing *Reid v Moreland Timber Co Pty Ltd* (1946) 73 CLR 1.
140   (1999) 73 ALJR 547.
141   Unreported, NSW SC, Santow J, 4 April 1996.
142   (1988) 164 CLR 387.
143   See JF Burrows, J Finn & S Todd, *Law of Contract in New Zealand*, Butterworths, Wellington, 1997, p 140–2.
144   *Burbery Finance v Hinds Bank Holdings Ltd* [1989] 1 NZLR 356; *Harris v Harris* (1989) 1 NZ Conv. C190, 406; *McDonald v Attorney-General* (unreported, High Court, 20 June 1991).
145   *Old Star Insurance Co Ltd v Gaunt* (1991) 3 NZBLC 102,294 at 102,299.
146   See also *McDonald v Attorney-General* (unreported, High Court, 20 June 1991).
147   *Mortensen v NZ Harness Racing Conference* (unreported, High Court, 7 December 1990).

appropriate means of addressing the detriment that has been suffered.[148] Lastly, it has been recognised in the New Zealand Court of Appeal that there is a common link between proprietary and promissory estoppel.[149] These statements are similar to statements in *Waltons Stores (Interstate) Ltd v Maher* regarding aspects of equitable estoppel in Australia.

[7.255] Accordingly, there is good reason to believe that it will only be a matter of time until a *Waltons v Maher* style of doctrine of equitable estoppel is recognised by the New Zealand Court of Appeal.

7.6.2   United States

[7.260] In the United States, the direct enforcement of promises made without consideration by means of promissory estoppel is well established.[150] The Restatement Second §90(1) states:

> A promise which the promisor should reasonably expect to induce action or forbearance on the part of the promisee or a third person and which does induce such action or forbearance is binding if injustice can be avoided only by enforcement of the promise. The remedy granted for breach may be limited as justice requires.

The Restatement Second §90 has been described as the 'most significant departure from its stated policy of following precedents' and has been described as the 'fountainhead of recovery based on reliance on a broad range of situations'.[151]

[7.265] The section may be seen as having four requirements:

- There must have been a promise. Such a promise must be clear and unambiguous.[152] Accordingly, a mere expression of opinion or prediction will be insufficient.[153]
- The promisor must have had reason to expect reliance on the promise. Accordingly, no estoppel will arise where the promisor has no reason to expect any reliance at all or had reason to expect reliance but not of the sort that actually occurs.[154]
- The promise must have induced the reliance. While there must have been an actual reliance, there is no requirement in §90 that the reliance be detrimental. Nevertheless, many cases have assumed that it must result in detriment.[155]

---

148 *Harris v Harris* (1999) 1 NZ Conv. C190, 406; *McDonald v Attorney-General* (unreported, High Court, 20 June 1991); *National Westminster Finance NZ Ltd v National Bank of NZ (1993)* [1996] 1 NZLR 548 at 549 (CA) per Tipping J.

149 *Gillies v Keogh* [1999] 2 NZLR 327 at 331 per Cooke P, 346 per Richardson J; *Gold Star Insurance Co Ltd v Gaunt* (1991) 3 NZBLC 102,294 at 102,299 per Holland J; *National Westminster Finance NZ Ltd v National Bank of NZ (1993)* [1996] 1 NZLR 548.

150 See also *Waltons Stores (Interstate) Ltd v Maher* (1988) 164 CLR 387 at 401–402 per Mason CJ and Wilson J.

151 EA Farnsworth, *Contracts*, 3rd edn, Aspen Law and Business, New York, 1999, §2.19.

152 *Cyberchron Corp v Calldata Systems Development* 47 F 3d 39 (2nd Cir, 1995).

153 *Major Mat Co v Monsanto Co* 969 F 2d 579 (7th Cir, 1992).

154 *D & G Stout v Bacardi Imports* 805 F Supp 1434 (ND Ind 1992).

155 See, for example, *Chesser v Babcock & Wilcox* 753 F 2d 1570 (11th Cir, 1985); *Fregara v Jet Aviation Business Jets* 764 F Supp 940 (DNJ 1991); cf *Vastoler v American Can Co* 700 F 2d 916 (3rd Cir 1983).

The circumstances must have been such that an injustice can be avoided only by enforcement of the promise. This aspect of the section has only been discussed in a small number of cases and only ever rarely invoked to deny recovery.[156]

Where the four elements are established, the section states that recovery is 'limited as justice requires.' This has been interpreted to mean that recovery is generally limited to damages based on reliance loss.[157] There may, however, be circumstances where the promisee is entitled to recover expectation loss, such as a lack of good faith on the part of the promisor,[158] or where there is a difficulty in calculating recovery on a reliance loss basis.[159]

[7.270] The section reflects an attitude adopted by American courts—treating promissory estoppel as the equivalent of consideration in particular circumstances.[160] This is because in the United States, consideration is subject to a number of limitations that do not operate in Australia. In other words, there will be circumstances in which an Australian court would be prepared to find sufficient consideration, but an American court would, not due to the constraints affecting consideration in that country. In the United States, therefore, promissory estoppel tends to occupy ground left vacant due to these constraints on consideration.[161]

[7.275] Promissory estoppel in the United States is therefore more closely connected with general contract law than in Australia, where equitable estoppel is based on the equitable notion of unconscionable conduct. The American doctrine also emphasises the promisor's reasonable expectation that the promise will induce action or forbearance, as opposed to encouraging or inducing an expectation in the promisee in Australia. There are, nevertheless, similarities—in the sense that there needs to be an expectation on the part of the promisor that the promisee will act in reliance on the promise and the impossibility of avoiding injustice by other means.[162]

7.6.3 Japan

[7.280] Japanese law recognises procedural estoppel (*kin'hangen*: literally the prohibition on repudiating one's own statements), which operates in an analogous way to its common law counterpart. Equitable estoppel, including promissory estoppel, and the situations that give rise to these claims are deal with under the rubric of good faith in Japan. This is discussed more broadly in Chapter 17.

[7.285] Here the focus is on the application of good faith that arises in pre-contractual situations—the obligation to compensate the other party when contractual negotiations are wrongfully destroyed. Lower-level Japanese courts had long held that the

---

156 See, for example, *Kiley v First National Bank* 649 A 2d 1145 (Md App 1994) (where depositors had benefit of bank cheque account for 5 years, court held that justice did not compel application of promissory estoppel).

157 See, for example, *D & G Stout v Bacardi Imports* 805 F Supp 1434 (ND Ind 1992).

158 Restatement Second §90 illustrations 8 and 9; see also duty of good faith discussed in [8.945]–[8.950].

159 *Goldstick v ICM Realty* 788 F 2d 456 (7th Cir 1986).

160 See, for example, *Allegheny College v National Chautauqua County Bank* 246 NY 369 at 374 (1927) per Cardozo CJ (dealing with the case of charitable subscriptions).

161 See the analysis of Mason CJ and Wilson J in *Waltons Stores (Interstate) Ltd v Maher* (1988) 164 CLR 387 at 402.

162 Ibid.

obligation to act in good faith extends to the pre-contractual stage. This has now been confirmed by the Supreme Court.[163] It follows that, where the other party's legitimate expectation that a contract had (or would be) formed is wrongfully betrayed, the party terminating or destroying the negotiations will be liable to pay compensation to the innocent party. The scope of compensation is limited to actual loss, such as reliance expenditure. Asserting contributory negligence may also reduce it.

[7.290] This extension of liability to the pre-contractual stage in Japan has, as elsewhere, given rise to a vast amount of legal debate and scholarly writing. One argument is that the problems to which it is the implicit solution could quite readily be compensated using Japanese tort law. Article 709 of the Civil Code states that 'a person who violates intentionally or negligently the right of another is bound to make compensation for damage arising therefrom' and has traditionally been interpreted in a flexible way. Article 709 forms the basis of a claim in tort, using rules on actually loss, causation and proximity that are virtually identical to those in the common law.

However, Japanese lawyers generally characterised pre-contractual problems as requiring contractual solutions. One explanation for this is that the German concept of *culpa in contrahendo* (fault in contract formation or, in Japanese, *keiyakuteiketsujô no kashitsu*) was adopted relatively early in Japanese scholarly writing and court reasoning. This concept is now employed broadly to cover a range of pre-contractual situations, including improper destruction of contract negotiation but extending through other duties of care at the pre-contractual stage. The multiplicity of pre-contractual problems resolved by Japanese courts under this heading has weakened its predictive value. A key issue for Japanese contract law now is how to separate the different legal principles bundled under this conceptual label.[164]

[7.295] A second application of the doctrine of good faith at the pre-contractual stage is the duty to provide information (the duty of disclosure). Three classical situations arise in Japan. The first is the duty to inform in real estate transactions. The Residential Building and Land Transactions Industry Law requires that brokers of residential buildings and land must give explanations to prospective buyers about issues listed under the law.[165] The same duty to investigate and inform also applies as a matter of general civil law.[166] The second situation is where a prospective franchisee with little business experience is relying on the knowledge of a franchisor. In this situation, Japanese courts have held that the franchisor has a duty to provide objective, accurate information.[167] A third and expanding category concerns financial investment products such as warrant transactions and insurance policies that generate income, where parties who are apparently making their own investment decisions are in fact relying on the statements made by financial institutions and securities firms. The income-generating insurance (so-called *hengaku hoken*) cases are interesting because although the financial product

---

163 Saihan 18 September 1984 *Hanji* 1137–51.

164 Uchida Takashi, *Minpô II* (Civil Code 2) (1997) Tokyo Daigaku Shuppankai, p 28.

165 Civil Code Article 35.

166 Tokyo District Court 31 March 1977 *Hanji* 858–69) holding that the seller or an apartment has the duty to disclose proposed plans to erect a building next door which would damage the view from the property in question where he or she knew of this matter or could have easily obtained such information: Uchida Takashi, *Minpô II* (Civil Code 2) (1997) Tokyo Daigaku Shuppankai, p 28.

167 See, for example, Kyoto District Court 12 December 1991 *Hanji* 1413-102.

was designed to be an investment subject to ordinary market risk, in practice the explanation and the fact that the product was being offered by insurance companies gave it the appearance of a kind of savings scheme with implicitly guaranteed rates of return. When Japan's economic collapse made the expected rates of return impossible, numerous suits were commenced, and there are numerous lower court decisions on these problems. In 1996 the Supreme Court held that, in the case of a contract of this kind entered into at the invitation of the insurance company, the company bears a duty to explain the risks and failure to do so results in tortious liability.[168] The duty of good faith is a general civil law obligation: of course, so in fashioning a remedy the court can treat its breach as either a question of tort or of contract. Whether the duty to explain extends to a duty to advise is still a matter of debate in Japan.

---

168 Saihan 28 October 1996 *Kinyûhômujôhô* [Finance Law Reports] 1469-49; Uchida Takashi, *Minpô II* (Civil Code 2) (1997) Tokyo Daigaku Shuppankai, p 28.

Part III

Content

This Part examines the content of the contractual arrangement entered into by the parties. Determining the extent and legal nature of the obligations that the parties have undertaken is a two-step process. First, the contractual terms that govern the transaction must be established. Secondly, the meaning and significance of those terms must be determined. This Part examines both steps in the process.

A contract can consist of two kinds of terms: those expressly agreed upon by the parties, and those implied in the contract either to reflect the presumed intention of the parties, or for public policy reasons. The rules that govern whether oral or written statements can be regarded as express terms, and therefore form part of the contract, are reasonably well settled. Despite the diverse and ever-changing contexts in which contract formation can occur—the most recent example of which is electronic commerce—the established rules continue to apply. Movement has been noticeable over the past decade, however, in relation to the preparedness of the courts to imply terms that impact on contractual performance. The evolving obligation for contracting parties to perform contractual duties in good faith is the most obvious example of this development. All of these issues relate to establishing the contractual terms, and are considered in Chapter 8.

Chapter 9 focuses on construction of those terms. The courts have developed general rules of construction to assist in determining the meaning of the contract. While this process involves an attempt to establish the intention of the parties, there is an important rule of evidence that can, in some circumstances, restrict the extent to which such intention can be given in evidence. This rule (and the exceptions to it) can impact on the construction ultimately attributed to the terms.

Another important aspect of contract construction is the legal effect of particular types of terms. Some terms are promissory in nature, and legal consequences flow from their breach. Those consequences differ according to how the term is categorised. Different rules apply if a term provides for a contingency, or if the term seeks to exclude or limit liability should particular loss, injury or damage occur. Other kinds of terms are also identified and their significance are briefly examined in Chapter 9.

Chapter 8

Terms I: Establishing contractual terms

8.1   Introduction

[8.05] Contracts can take a variety of forms. Parties who seek formality in their dealings may require the contract to be in writing and signed by each party. In such a case, their contract generally will consist of, at the very least, the terms contained in that document. But there may be other terms governing the contractual relationship. In the course of negotiating entry into the contract, various oral statements are likely to have been made. Difficult questions can arise about the legal status of such oral statements. Sometimes the parties intend these statements to form part of the contract—but even if they do, rules of evidence may prevent reliance on them should a dispute later arise. Further, there may be additional terms, not even discussed by the parties or included in the written document, that form part of the contract. In some circumstances, certain terms are implied in the contract to reflect the presumed, if not actual, intention of the parties.

In contrast, many contracts are made orally—not reduced to writing by the parties. Again, it is not always easy to determine which oral statements are intended to be contractual in nature, and which are not. The law has developed various means of determining these issues. Even in the context of oral contracts, in some circumstances terms may be implied to reflect the presumed intention of the parties.

Some contracts are primarily oral agreements, but issues arise as to whether a written statement forms part of the contract. Oral agreements in which one of the contracting parties receives a ticket, or where a notice containing a contractual term is displayed at the place where the parties form their agreement are examples of how this could arise.

Issues concerning the establishment of contractual terms can conveniently be considered under two heads:

- express terms;
- implied terms.

Under the first head, different ways parties can incorporate terms into the contract will be considered. This requires consideration of both written terms (whether in a document signed by the parties, a notice, or an unsigned document such a ticket) and oral terms. Relevant to the issue of incorporating oral terms is an examination of the 'parol evidence rule'.

The second head involves consideration of both the common law and statute. Some well established common law principles provide the basis on which terms are implied into a contract. This area of the law is, however, very fluid. Of increasing emphasis in recent times is the extent to which a duty to act in good faith will be imposed on parties. Statutes can also impact in a significant way on contractual obligations. There has been recent movement in this area as well.

8.2   Incorporating written terms

[8.10] Most contracts entered into in modern times—particularly in the commercial context—will involve some element of writing. Contracts involving considerable sums of money such as construction contracts, franchise agreements, and other mercantile contracts are likely to be in writing and signed by the contracting parties. In other situations, the arrangement may involve a written document that is not signed by the parties. Common examples of this are tickets issued as part of a contact of carriage. Terms can also be contained in written notices displayed in prominent places. Agreements can be formed where such notices are displayed—for example, by appearing on a board at the entrance to a car park. Alternatively, businesses may display terms on their websites. Sometimes, parties may purport to contract on the basis of terms not expressly set out in the document or discussed orally, but set out in another document referred to by the parties.

While each of these scenarios raises different considerations about whether the written term forms part of the contractual relationship between the parties, a common thread runs through all such cases. The court examines the circumstances of the case to determine whether the parties can be regarded as having assented to the written terms.[1]

8.2.1 Incorporation by signature

(a) General rule

[8.15] Parties sometimes wish their contractual arrangement to be formalised by reducing the agreement to writing, the written document being signed by the contracting parties. If this occurs, both parties will generally be bound by all of the terms contained in the agreement, regardless of whether the document was read or the parties were aware of the existence of the terms contained in the agreement. The reason for the rule is that a person who signs a document indicates agreement to the terms contained in it. It is that person's responsibility to ensure he or she is satisfied that those terms reflect the agreement made. A party who chooses not to read the terms of the document before signing assumes the risk. To allow parties to escape contractual liability because they have not read the document would erode commercial certainty to an unacceptable extent. The following case is generally cited as authority for the proposition that a person is bound by the terms contained in an agreement signed by that person.

> **Example: L'Estrange v F Graucob Ltd[2]**
>
> The buyer bought an automatic slot machine. She signed the seller's order form, which contained a number of terms. Some of these were in ordinary print, while the exemption clause was typed in small print. The machine did not work satisfactorily upon delivery, and the buyer claimed damages for breach of an implied warranty that the machine was fit for the purpose for which it was sold. The seller defended the action on the basis of the exclusion cause.
>
> The English Court held that the exclusion clause formed part of the contract and was effective to deny the buyer damages for breach of the implied warranty. When a document containing contractual terms is signed, in the absence of fraud or misrepresentation, the party signing the document is bound by its terms. It is immaterial whether the signing party has read the document or not.

(b) When the rule is displaced

[8.20] The reason for the rule that parties should be bound by the terms in a contract they have signed is persuasive.

In limited circumstances, however, courts have held a person not to be bound by the terms of a document that he or she has signed. The rule in *L'Estrange v F Graucob*

---

1   See, for example, *Olly v Marlborough Court Ltd* [1949] 1 KB 532 at 549.
2   [1934] 2 KB 394. This decision was applied in *Jones v Aircrafts Pty Ltd* [1949] StRQd 196.

Ltd[3] has been displaced in circumstances where the signature does not signify assent to the terms. Where this has occurred, there has been some competing interest—such as the need to protect the signing party—that outweighs the desire for contractual certainty achieved by holding a person to the terms in a signed document.

Misrepresentation of the effect of the clause

[8.25] In *L'Estrange v F Graucob Ltd*[4] itself, the court indicated that the general rule that a party is bound by all of the terms of a document signed by him or her will not apply where the person is induced to sign by fraud or misrepresentation. Misrepresentation of the effect of a clause prevented a dry cleaning company from relying on an exclusion clause in the following case.

Example: Curtis v Chemical Cleaning & Dyeing Co[5]

Mrs Curtis took a white satin wedding dress to the dry cleaners. She was handed a paper headed 'Receipt' by a shop assistant and was asked to sign it. Before she did so, she asked why she was required to do this. The assistant said the dry cleaning company was not prepared to accept liability for specified risks such as the risk of damage to beads and sequins, with which the dress was trimmed. In fact, the receipt contained a wider exclusion clause excluding the company from 'any damage howsoever arising'. The wedding dress was stained in the dry cleaning process and Mrs Curtis brought action against the dry cleaners for damage. The dry cleaning company relied on the exclusion clause.

The English Court of Appeal found in favour of Mrs Curtis. The dry cleaning company was unable to rely on the exclusion clause in the receipt. Notwithstanding that a person is generally bound by the terms in a document he or she has signed, this rule will not apply where a false impression has been created about the existence or extent of a clause—here the exemption clause. Because the shop assistant indicated that the exemption clause related only to damage to beads and sequins, the dry cleaning company was unable to rely on the clause. It did not matter that the misrepresentation was innocent.

Document signed is not contractual in nature

[8.30] If a party signs a document believing it is something other than a contractual document, he or she may not be bound by its terms. The reason is that signing a document in these circumstances does not signify assent to the terms. Lord Justice Denning (as he then was) referred to this possible scenario in *Curtis v Chemical Cleaning & Dyeing Co*[6] when considering whether the exclusion clause had been incorporated into the dry cleaning contract. The Lord Justice suggested that, in the circumstances of that case, if a document were given to the customer on the handing over of the garment for cleaning, and no discussion about the content of the document had taken place, it might reasonably be regarded as 'only a voucher for the customer to produce when

---

3   [1934] 2 KB 394.
4   Ibid.
5   [1951] 1 KB 805.
6   Ibid.

collecting the goods, and not understood to contain conditions exempting the cleaners from their common law liability for negligence'.[7] In other words, if such a document is not regarded as contractual in nature, the terms will not be incorporated into the contract, even if signed by the party.[8]

[8.35] Difficult issues arise where parties have finalised their agreement, and some time later sign a written document—but the writing contains terms not previously agreed to. Although the document may look like a contractual document, if it is signed after verbal agreement is reached, the cases indicate that it is likely not to be so regarded. The signer therefore may not be bound by the terms. In examining this issue, it may be helpful to distinguish two different factual scenarios: where performance occurs before signing, and where oral agreement is reached (but performance has not occurred) before signing. Each is considered in turn.

[8.40] Parties may reach a verbal agreement and carry out (at least in part) the contractual obligations, and then sign a document containing contractual terms. Whether the written terms form part of the contract in such a situation was considered in the following case.

Example: DJ Hill & Co Pty Ltd v Walter H Wright Pty Ltd[9]

A carrying company (the defendant) verbally contracted with the plaintiff to carry machinery for the plaintiff. Once the machinery was delivered, an employee of the defendant handed two documents to the plaintiff's employee for signature. One of these documents related to the carriage of the machinery and contained a clause excluding liability for loss or damage that occurred to the machinery in transit. Over a seven-month period, the defendant transported goods for the plaintiff on about ten separate occasions. On one such occasion, machinery was damaged in transit, and the plaintiff brought action against the defendant for damages for negligent performance of the contract of carriage. The issue for determination by the court was whether the exclusion clause in the document formed part of the contract between the parties.

The Supreme Court of Victoria held that the exclusion clause did not form part of the contract, and the plaintiff was entitled to damages. The Full Court made the following comment in relation to whether the exclusion clause could form part of the contract:

> On the occasion of the first dealing between the [defendant] and the [plaintiff]…it is clear that the contract was oral, that the contract was made before the form was presented, and moreover, that performance of the contract by the [defendant] was complete by that time. On that occasion the form, in our opinion, was plainly not a contractual document between the parties.[10]

---

7   Ibid at 809.
8   See also *Mihaljevic v Eiffel Tower Motors Pty Ltd and General Credits Ltd* [1973] VR 545 where a person considering purchasing a semi trailer on hire purchase terms signed an offer to a credit provider, the document negating any warranties that had been given to the person seeking credit by employees of the motor dealer. The Supreme Court of Victoria considered this document to have no legal effect as a contract as there was no consideration for the offeror's promise to negate the warranties. As such, the offeror was not bound by the terms in this document. The position is the same in New Zealand: *Holmes v Burgess* [1975] 2 NZLR 311.
9   [1971] VR 749.
10   Ibid at 753.

In this case, the court also had to consider whether the exclusion clause was incorporated by a previous course of dealings.[11] Where there has not been a previous consistent course of dealings between the parties, it seems appropriate that a person should not be bound by a clause in a document signed by him or her after the agreement is concluded and the bargained for service provided. In these circumstances, it is unlikely to be regarded as a contractual document. Because the document was signed on delivery, the parties regarded it as no more than a delivery docket.

[8.45] The second, and more difficult issue to resolve, is where the parties verbally agree on all terms of their transaction, and the signing of the document relating to that transaction takes place contemporaneously with, not following, contract performance. Unlike the previous scenario, signing the document may precede or be contemporaneous with performance—so the argument that the principle in *L'Estrange v F Graucob Ltd*[12] should apply is stronger. On the other hand, if it is established that the parties have reached agreement verbally—so the contract is concluded at that stage—it may be argued that a subsequent signing of a written document will only incorporate additional or different terms if the parties, by signing that document, intend to vary the original agreement. That reasoning was adopted by the Supreme Court of South Australia in the following case.

Example: Warming's Used Cars Ltd v Tucker[13]

Both the plaintiff and defendant traded in used cars. As part of a transaction involving the sale and purchase of a number of vehicles, the defendant bought a vehicle from a third party. The plaintiff was aware of the circumstances surrounding this purchase. The defendant, in turn, agreed to sell this vehicle to the plaintiff. The terms of sale of this vehicle were settled verbally. To finalise the transactions, the next day the defendant's agent signed in the plaintiff's 'Purchases Book'. A signature from the seller (here, the defendant) was required by statute. The document signed certified that the car was the property of the seller and free from encumbrances. In fact, the third party had not owned the vehicle before sale to the defendant. The plaintiff subsequently sued the defendant for breach of the warranty that the vehicle was the defendant's property and free from encumbrances.

The Supreme Court of South Australia held that the written term in the Purchases Book did not form part of the contract. The basis of the court's reasoning was that the contract between the parties was entered into the day before the book was signed. Napier CJ was of the view that the oral contract alone, therefore, governed the contractual obligations of the parties unless there was evidence of a new agreement varying the oral contract. His Honour did not consider the signing of the Purchases Book revealed any intention to alter the earlier agreement.

Cases such as these are likely to be rare. Generally, where parties sign a written agreement, the document is intended to form the basis of the contractual arrangement between the parties.[14] Moreover, as indicated by Napier CJ, the signing of

---

11   See [8.580]–[8.635].
12   [1934] 2 KB 394.
13   [1956] SASR 249.
14   In such cases, the parol evidence rule may operate so as to exclude evidence of prior verbal discussions: see [8.370]–[8.410].

the Purchases Book was to 'implement' the transaction, not to form the basis of the agreement or vary the earlier oral contract. Legislation required the seller to sign a document regarding the sale. This decision can be justified on the basis that the document signed by the seller cannot be regarded as contractual in nature. The seller's agent did not sign to give assent to the written terms. It is therefore consistent with authority in such a case for the person signing not to be bound by the written terms.

If the elements of this defence are established, the signer could not be regarded as having assented to the terms.

Defence of *non est factum*

[8.50] *Non est factum* is a defence available only to a limited class of people who have signed a contractual document, and wish to escape the legal consequences of that contract. The thrust of the defence is that the person who signed the document did not know what he or she was signing. The person relying on the defence must show that the document signed was radically different from the document the person thought he or she signed. As stated by the High Court, a person can only rely on this defence if they are:

> unable to read owing to blindness or illiteracy and … must rely on others for advice as to what they are signing; it is also available to those who through no fault of their own are unable to have any understanding of the purport of a particular document.[15]

If the elements of this defence are established, the signer could not be regarded as having assented to the terms.

8.2.2   Incorporation by notice: unsigned document

[8.55] In many contractual arrangements, some kind of written document changes hands although no document is signed by the contracting parties. The following are just some examples:

- tickets issued upon payment of specified fare to gain access to transport on bus, train, plane, or ferry;
- ticket issued upon parking a car in a car park;
- ticket issued upon payment to allow entry to a performance, amusement park, or similar venue;
- ticket issued upon payment to enable a person to ride on an attraction such as those in amusement parks;
- brochure given to prospective bidders at an auction describing the lots to be auctioned.

A number of contractual arrangements also involve a written document signed by one party only, the party seeking to rely on the written terms. An example of this may be a quotation given by a tradesperson.

---

15   *Petelin v Cullen* (1975) 132 CLR 355 at 359–360. This defence, and the other requirements that must be satisfied before it will be successful, are considered in detail later in this text. See [14.255]–[14.280].

[8.60] In all these cases, the written document may contain a number of terms. It is particularly common for these terms to include a clause that excludes one party from liability should harm, injury or loss occur in the course of the contractual arrangement. To determine the rights and obligations of the parties, it must be established whether the written terms in the document form part of their contract. As both parties have not signed the written document, the rule in *L'Estrange v F Graucob Ltd*[16] will not apply. The general proposition that the parties will be bound by the terms will not operate. It does not follow from this that such terms will never form part of the agreement. But if they are to form part of the agreement, there must be other evidence that the parties have assented to the terms.[17]

[8.65] A review of the case law indicates that a person is likely to be bound by the terms in a written document (not signed by him or her) if reasonable notice of the existence of the terms has been given, and this notice was given before or upon contract formation. If both of these limbs are satisfied, that party can be considered to have assented to the terms. For ease of reference in the following commentary, the person seeking to rely on the written terms will be referred to as the defendant, and the party unaware of the terms, the plaintiff.

(a) Reasonable steps taken by defendant

[8.70] Whether the defendant took reasonable steps to draw the written terms to the attention of the plaintiff is a question of fact.[18] If, prior to buying a train ticket, for example, the prospective purchaser is advised that the ticket contains a number of terms, and the purchaser reads the terms and then buys a ticket, the purchaser will be bound by the terms. By being advised of the terms, and reading them, then buying the ticket, the purchaser has assented to those terms in the same way as if he or she signed the document. The terms will therefore form part of the contract. In reality, however, intending contracting parties are rarely advised of terms in such an explicit way. Consequently, many contracts are entered into without one party being aware of the existence of any terms at all. In these cases, a number of factors are relevant to determining whether the written terms should be regarded as forming part of the contract.

[8.75] If, at the time of contact formation, the plaintiff is given a document by the defendant that a reasonable person would regard as being a contractual document, the plaintiff will generally be bound by the terms in the document. By taking the document without objecting to or discussing the terms, the plaintiff can be regarded as having assented to them, and will be regarded as having been bound by them.[19] On the other hand, if the document is not one that a reasonable person would regard as contractual in nature, and no extra steps have been taken by the defendant to advise the plaintiff that the document contains contractual terms, the plaintiff would not ordinarily be bound by the written terms. For these reasons, it is crucial to determine whether, in the given circumstances, the document is one that would usually be regarded as contractual in nature.

---

16   [1934] 2 KB 394.
17   *Parker v The South Eastern Railway Company* (1877) 2 CPD 416 at 421.
18   *Parker v The South Eastern Railway Company* (1877) 2 CPD 416 at 423; *Hood v Anchor Line (Henderson Bros) Ltd* [1918] AC 837 at 844.
19   *Mendelsshon v Normand Ltd* [1970] 1 QB 177 at 182.

[8.80] The cases provide illustrations of documents that can be so regarded. In a contract under which parties arrange for goods to be carried by sea, a bill of lading will be presented to the shipper. In this kind of a contract, all parties would expect the document to contain contractual terms.[20] There are also case examples of courts finding that certain documents cannot be regarded as contractual in nature. For example, it has been held that documents received by a customer upon handing over garments at a dry cleaning store would fall within this category. The document might reasonably be regarded as a voucher for the customer to produce when collecting the goods, rather than a contractual document containing terms.[21] The courts have made a similar assessment of a ticket issued to a person by a railway company when he deposited luggage in a cloakroom.[22] Such a ticket could reasonably be regarded as a voucher for the receipt of luggage, which was also necessary to identify when the passenger sought to reclaim it. The case of *DJ Hill & Co Pty Ltd v Walter H Wright Pty Ltd*[23] provides a further illustration. That case involved a contract for transport of machinery. As the document was handed over (and, in that case, signed by the plaintiff) upon delivery, it was unlikely to be regarded as a contractual document. In the circumstances, the document would be akin to a delivery docket. The same result would follow if the document were not signed.

[8.85] Some of the ticket cases referred to in the preceding paragraph occurred many decades ago. At the time of the decisions, the public perception about whether a document is likely to contain contractual terms was probably different from the public perception today. If such cases were litigated today, courts might make a different assessment about whether a particular document would be regarded by a reasonable person as contractual in nature. A receipt issued by a dry cleaning outlet may be such a case.

[8.90] As a final point, it should be noted that where the defendant wants to show that the plaintiff is bound by the terms, the onus is on the defendant to demonstrate that the document was not delivered to the plaintiff merely as a voucher or receipt, but as a contractual document.[24]

[8.95] Even where the kind of document given to the plaintiff is ordinarily regarded as contractual, there may be some circumstances in which the plaintiff will not be bound by its terms. The first is where the circumstances indicate that the particular document, although usually of a contractual kind, does not contain contractual terms. Examples of this may occur in the following situations:

- the notice on the ticket directing the passenger to 'further conditions at back' is illegible when the ticket is issued;[25]
- the document is folded so as to indicate it does not contain written terms;[26]
- the ticket sets out only the place of departure and destination on the front, the terms being printed on the other side.[27]

20   *Parker v The South Eastern Railway Company* (1877) 2 CPD 416 at 422.
21   *Causer v Browne* [1952] VLR 1. See also the *dicta* of Lord Justice Denning in *Curtis v Chemical Cleaning & Dyeing Co* [1951] 1 KB 805 at 809.
22   *Parker v The South Eastern Railway Company* (1877) 2 CPD 416.
23   [1971] VR 749.
24   *Causer v Browne* [1952] VLR 1 at 5.
25   *Sugar v London Midland & Scottish Railway Company* [1941] 1 All ER 172.
26   *Richardson Steamship Co Ltd v Rowntree* [1894] AC 217.
27   *Henderson v Stevenson* (1875) LR 2 HLSc 470.

[8.100] Secondly, if the document contains a term that is unusual for that kind of contract, or is particularly harsh, the mere handing over of the ticket, although accepted as being a contractual document, may not be sufficient to bring notice of that particular term to the plaintiff's attention. In such circumstances, what are reasonable steps to take to draw the term to the plaintiff's attention may be different from the steps required if the term is of a kind that would ordinarily be found in the document. Support for this proposition is provided by the *dicta* of Bramwell LJ in *Parker v The South Eastern Railway Company*[28] where he commented as follows:

> What if there was some unreasonable condition, as for instance to forfeit £1000 if the goods were not removed in forty-eight hours? Would the depositor be bound? I might content myself by asking; would he be, if he were told 'our conditions are on this ticket,' and he did not read them? In my judgment he would not be bound in either case. I think there is an implied understanding that there is no unreasonable condition to the knowledge of the party tendering the document and not insisting on its being read.[29]

It follows from this dictum that more would be required for an unreasonable term to be regarded as forming part of the contract between the parties.

[8.105] The preceding commentary concerned contractual documents. It is also possible for a person to be bound by terms in a document that is not a contractual document. This will be the case if the defendant takes reasonable steps to draw the terms to the plaintiff's attention.[30] The plaintiff will be bound by the written terms because he or she will be regarded as having assented to them.

Effect of person not being able to read or understand terms

[8.110] In determining whether reasonable steps have been taken to bring the term to the attention of the plaintiff, the defendant must do what is 'sufficient to inform people in general that the ticket contains conditions'.[31] If this is done, a person cannot argue that he or she is not bound by the terms on account of his or her 'exceptional ignorance or stupidity or carelessness'.[32] In other words, a plaintiff who is particularly unworldly, and does not know that a particular kind of document will contain contractual terms, will still be bound by those terms, provided the defendant took reasonable steps to bring that fact to the notice of people in general. In this context, the rule is harsh in its operation. The outcome is also unfortunate if the plaintiff is unable to read or understand the terms because of illiteracy or lack of familiarity with the English language.[33] Such people will also be bound by the written terms.

[8.115] If the particular disability preventing a person from reading or understanding the term is expressly brought to the defendant's attention, however, it is possible that the outcome will be different. The basis upon which a person is regarded as being

---

28 (1877) 2 CPD 416.
29 Ibid at 428. This *dictum* was cited with approval in *Thompson v London Midland & Scottish Railway Company* [1930] 1 KB 41 at 49, 53–54. See also *J Spurling Ltd v Bradshaw* [1956] 1 WLR 461 at 466.
30 *Parker v The South Eastern Railway Company* (1877) 2 CPD 416 at 423.
31 Ibid.
32 Ibid.
33 See, for example, *Thompson v London Midland & Scottish Railway Company* [1930] 1 KB 41 at 46 where Lord Henworth MR commented that 'the plaintiff in this case cannot read; but, having regard to the authorities, and the condition of education in this country, I do not think that avails her in any degree'.

bound by the terms in a written document is that he or she has assented to them. If the plaintiff has indicated to the defendant that he or she is unable to read (or this fact is patently obvious in the particular circumstances), the plaintiff could not be regarded as having assented to the terms. In such a case, it is at least arguable that the terms will not be incorporated into the agreement.

(b)   Reasonable steps taken before or upon contract formation

[8.120] Once the contract has been formed, it is too late for fresh terms to be introduced. Therefore, for the terms in a document to form part of the contract, the reasonable steps to bring them to the attention of the plaintiff must occur before or at the time of contract formation. If an agreement is formed, and a ticket is later handed to the plaintiff, the terms on the ticket may not be regarded as forming part of the contract. Reasonable steps to bring the terms to the attention of the plaintiff were not taken before or at the time of contract formation. It was for this reason that the terms on the ticket in *Thornton v Shoe Lane Parking Ltd*[34] were held not to form part of the contract between the parties.[35]

8.2.3   *Incorporation by notice: signs*

[8.125] Some contractual arrangements are entered into without any exchange of documentation, but notices or signs may be displayed, containing terms later relied upon by one of the parties. This can occur in the following kinds of cases:

- sign displayed at the entrance to a skating rink, informing patrons that they enter at their own risk;
- sign displayed at a luggage counter at railway station, informing travellers that the railway company will not be liable for loss relating to goods deposited to an amount more than a specified sum;
- sign at a motel counter, informing guests that the motel is not responsible for goods stolen during the visitor's stay at the motel.

Possible examples are endless. In some cases, a contracting party may use both signs and tickets to convey the content of the terms. As with the earlier cases, these contracts often come before the courts for a determination of whether the term formed part of the contract. Again, the crux of the matter is whether, in the circumstances of the case, the party (referred to in this commentary as the plaintiff) can be regarded as having assented to the terms. If the plaintiff was aware of the term, it will form part of the contract regardless of the nature of the sign. The same result would follow if the other party (the defendant) drew his or her attention to the term, and this advice was ignored. Difficulties arise where the plaintiff denies observing the sign at the time of contract formation.

In such a case, the position is the same as for incorporating terms in unsigned documents: did the defendant take reasonable steps to bring the term to the attention of the plaintiff? If so, did this occur before or at the time of contract formation?

---

34   [1971] 2 QB 163.
35   For more information on the time of contract formation in the context of a ticket issued by an automatic vending machine, see further [3.255].

(a) Reasonable steps taken by defendant

[8.130] The test for incorporation of terms contained in a sign is equivalent to that used in the context of unsigned documents. The crucial factor is the reasonableness of notice given to the plaintiff. Griffith CJ, in the *Balmain New Ferry Company v Robertson*,[36] considered whether a notice placed over the entrance to a private wharf was sufficient to incorporate the term into the contract of carriage. Where the passenger had not used the ferry before—so no issue of incorporation of the term by previous consistent course of dealings arose—his Honour treats the test of incorporation by notice in a sign in the following way:

> If he had been a stranger who had never before been on the premises, it would have been sufficient for the defendants to prove that they had done what was reasonably sufficient to give the plaintiff notice of the conditions of admittance.[37]

[8.135] At times, the test has been couched in language that puts a greater onus on the defendant by suggesting that the steps taken could only be regarded as sufficient if the plaintiff actually became aware of the term. In *Mendelssohn v Normand Ltd*,[38] Lord Denning couched the test in the following language:

> Such a notice is not imported into the contract unless it is brought home to the party so prominently that he must be taken to have known of it and agreed to it ... That was not so here. The garage company did not prove that Mr Mendelssohn knew of the terms of this notice or that he agreed to it. They cannot, therefore, rely upon it.[39]

In that case, the English Court of Appeal had to determine whether a notice placed at the reception desk formed part of the contract between the garage proprietors (the defendants) and the plaintiff who parked his motor vehicle at the defendants' garage. The notice contained the words 'Customers' Property. Important Notice' in large letters, with an exclusion clause appearing in smaller letters below. The Court of Appeal held that this notice did not form part of the contract between the parties (for the reasons given by Lord Denning in the quote above).

[8.140] Lord Denning's test should not be taken literally. It could not be the case that reasonable steps will only be regarded as having been taken if the plaintiff was in fact made aware of the term. It may have been implicit in the judgment of Lord Denning that he was referring to a plaintiff who was acting *reasonably* in the circumstances. If the notice was not brought to his or her attention, the term would not be incorporated.

[8.145] On balance, therefore, it is likely that the terms in a sign or notice will be incorporated if the defendant has taken reasonable steps to bring the information in the

---

36 (1906) 4 CLR 379.
37 Ibid at 386. On the facts of the case, however, it was held that the passenger had actual knowledge of the term as a result of previous consistent course of dealings. On this basis, the term formed part of the contract and the court did not have to decide whether the sign was sufficient to incorporate the term.
38 [1970] 1 QB 177.
39 Ibid at 182.

sign or notice to the plaintiff's attention. If that has been done, it does not matter whether or not the particular plaintiff read the terms on the notice or sign—or even, as indicated below, whether the plaintiff was able to read or understand the writing on the sign or notice.

Effect of person not being able to read or understand terms

[8.150] It generally does not matter that the particular plaintiff under consideration is unable to read or understand the terms, or for some other reason peculiar to that plaintiff, does not read the terms. Provided reasonable steps were taken to bring the terms to the attention of an ordinary person in the position of the plaintiff, that is sufficient.[40]

(b)   Reasonable steps taken before or upon contract formation

[8.155] As was discussed earlier in relation to incorporating unsigned documents, the reasonable steps taken by a defendant to incorporate the terms in a sign or notice must be taken before, or upon, contract formation. This requirement was not satisfied in *Olley v Marlborough Court Ltd*,[41] a case involving a hotel guest who lost certain property during the stay with the hotel. The notice in the bedroom that purported to excuse the motel from liability in such circumstances was held not to form part of the contract between the parties, as the contract had already been formed. It was too late for such a term to be incorporated in the contract.

8.2.4   *Incorporation by notice: website*

[8.160] Computers are being used increasingly in commercial transactions. Issues of time and place of contract formation where orders for goods and services are made through the Internet was considered earlier in this work.[42] This method of contract formation also raises questions about the terms that form part of the contractual relationship. Frequently, but not always, the website of a business contains terms that are intended by the provider of the goods or services to form the basis of the contractual relationship. Assuming that Australian law is applied,[43] it is likely that the traditional principles considered above will continue to be relevant. The person placing the order (the customer) will be bound by the terms appearing on the website only if he or she can be regarded as having assented to them. This will be the case if the provider has taken reasonable steps to bring the terms to the attention of the customer, and that this occurred before, or upon, contract formation.

[8.165] Whether reasonable steps were taken before or upon contract formation will depend on precisely what the customer was required to do to place an order, and when this was done. Some websites display the terms that govern any transaction entered into, and require the consumer to indicate agreement to the terms in the manner prescribed (for example, clicking on the relevant icon). If the consumer does so, and then places an order, there would be a strong argument that the provider has taken reasonable steps to bring the terms to the attention of the consumer. By indicat-

---

40   See [8.110]–[8.115].
41   [1949] 1 KB 532.
42   See [3.660]–[3.670].
43   The relevant conflict of laws issues are considered at [26.380]–[26.400].

ing agreement to the terms, the consumer is regarded as having assented to them. As this occurred before the order was placed, the consumer will be bound by the terms.

[8.170] It is also possible for the provider to display terms on its website, but not require the consumer to consent to them expressly. If a contract is made in person and one party advises the other that terms govern the transaction, and provides the other with a document setting out the terms, this will be regarded as reasonable notice, and the person will be bound.[44] Where the contract is formed electronically and the configuration of the website allows the consumer to order the goods or services without acknowledging that the terms form part of the agreement, the courts may be less inclined to find that they form part of the contract. Because computer users often scroll through options until they reach the one relevant to them (in this case, the placing of the order), it is unlikely that any of the terms that appeared on the site earlier will have been read. If the consumer was not required to indicate agreement to the terms, he or she may not even have noticed that terms had been displayed on the screen at all. In these circumstances, and because many businesses transacting through a website require consumers to consent expressly to the terms, the courts may not regard the mere display of the terms as reasonable notice. If an order is placed, the consumer may not be regarded as having assented to the terms on the website.

[8.175] The position is different again if no terms appear on the website. It is unlikely that terms will govern a contract formed electronically in this case, even if the consumer is aware that terms would be imposed by the provider if the contract were formed through another medium.

8.2.5 Incorporation by reference

[8.180] Sometimes a party may wish to incorporate a number of terms into a contract and, instead of listing them in the contract, incorporate them by reference. This is common practice where lending institutions advance money and take a mortgage over land to secure that advance. There are many standard terms a lender may wish to incorporate into all such mortgage transactions. Instead of each mortgage transaction listing these terms in full, the mortgage document can incorporate the terms by reference to another document that sets them out in full. In most jurisdictions, legislation facilitates standard terms becoming part of the mortgage by incorporation in this way.[45]

[8.185] While the above example relies on statute, the common law also recognises that terms can be incorporated into a contract by reference. In *Smith v South Wales Switchgear Co Ltd*,[46] for example, parties agreed for the plaintiff to overhaul the defendant's electrical equipment. The written purchase order that was later accepted by the

---

44 See [8.70].

45 See, for example, *Land Title Act* 1994 (Qld), s 170; *Real Property Act* 1990 (NSW), s 42; *Transfer of Land Act* 1958 (Vic), s 42; *Real Property Act* 1886 (SA), s 69; *Transfer of Land Act* 1893 (WA), s 68; *Land Titles Act* 1980 (Tas), s 40; *Land Title Act* 2000 (NT) s 169; *Land Titles Act* 1925 (ACT), s 58.

46 [1978] 1 WLR 165. For a more recent example of incorporation by reference, see the decision of the Federal Court of Australia in *Rivenwood International Australia Pty Ltd v McCormick* [2000] FCA 889, BC200003663 (4 July 2000). Various entitlements in the employer's 'Company Policy and Practices' was held (by 2:1 majority) to be incorporated into the employment contract, thereby entitling the employee to an additional redundancy payout.

plaintiff stated that the supply of services was subject to the defendant's 'general conditions of contract ... obtainable on request'. Although the plaintiff did not request such general conditions, a copy was forwarded to the plaintiff, at some later point, with an amended purchase order. The plaintiff began work shortly afterwards. The English House of Lords held that the general conditions had been incorporated into the contract. Lord Fraser seemed to imply that this would have been the result even if the general conditions had not been forwarded to the plaintiff.[47]

[8.190] As demonstrated by *Smith v South Wales Switchgear Co Ltd*,[48] there is no doubt that terms can be incorporated into an agreement by reference, thus avoiding the need to set out the individual terms in full. However, whether the terms have effectively been incorporated by reference in any given case will depend on the surrounding circumstances, and the principles examined earlier remain relevant. If the parties discussed the terms in the other document and both are content with those terms, each party is considered to have assented to them. If the parties sign the document, this, too, may be regarded as assent to the terms—even if the party later claiming not to be bound by the terms (the plaintiff) has not been given, or has not read, the standard terms. Whether a clause incorporating other terms included in an unsigned document (such as a ticket) or on a sign is sufficient will turn on whether the party seeking to rely on the term (the defendant) has done all that is reasonable in the circumstances. What constitutes reasonable steps may vary according to the nature of the terms the defendant seeks to incorporate. In the following case, reference in a ticket to the existence of other terms was held to be sufficient to incorporate those other terms into the contract of carriage.

Example: Thompson v London, Midland & Scottish Railway Company[49]

An excursion ticket for carriage by rail was purchased for the plaintiff. On the ticket were printed the words: 'Excursion. For conditions see back.' On the back, the ticket contained a notice that it was issued subject to the conditions in the railway company's timetables and excursion bills. The timetables contained an exclusion clause. The plaintiff incurred injury while on the railway journey and sued the railway company. The railway company sought to rely on the exclusion clause in the timetable.

The English Court of Appeal found in favour of the railway company on the basis that the exclusion clause formed part of the contract. The Court considered that, on the facts of the case, any terms that formed part of the ticket formed part of the contract. The ticket stated plainly on its face that it was issued upon a number of conditions. Lord Hanworth continued:

> and that one of the conditions is that the person shall find them at a certain place and accept them, and that is I think quite a plain indication that the carrier has made that offer upon those terms and conditions only, and that any

---

47   Ibid at 171.
48   [1978] 1 WLR 165.
49   [1930] 1 KB 41.

answer that he had not brought the conditions sufficiently to the notice of the person accepting the offer must be set aside as perverse.[50]

[8.195] In summary, the case law suggests that terms can be incorporated into a contract by reference, regardless of whether the document incorporating the terms is signed by the parties, or is a ticket or a sign. The test, as before, appears to be whether the plaintiff can be regarded as having assented to the terms incorporated by reference. For signed documents, this will generally be satisfied. For other documents, the test of whether reasonable steps were taken will be relevant. If the plaintiff can be regarded as having assented to the terms, it should make no difference that the plaintiff has chosen not to procure and read a copy of those terms.

8.3 Incorporating oral terms

[8.200] Before entering into an agreement, parties usually engage in some kind of verbal exchange. In a contract for the sale of a car, for example, clarification may be sought about the car's capabilities, age, or any problems the previous owner may have experienced with it. Such negotiation or discussion is likely to occur regardless of whether or not an agreement subsequently reached is reduced to writing. Issues relating to whether oral terms form part of an agreement, therefore, apply equally to contracts in writing.

[8.205] Disputes can arise where pre-contractual statements are later discovered to be false. For example, a buyer may seek relief if a car turns out to be an earlier model than that indicated in conversation with the seller prior to the sale. The nature of any relief for the party being given incorrect information (the 'innocent party') depends on the way the statement is classified. Legal implications do not flow from all oral statements made. An off-the-cuff comment made by a salesperson that was clearly not intended to be taken seriously is unlikely to have any legal consequences. Other statements may influence entry into the contract, but may not have been intended by the parties to form part of the contract. These distinctions can be difficult to make. Further, if the statement was intended by the parties to have contractual effect, it may be necessary to determine whether that term forms part of the main contract, or is more appropriately regarded as forming the basis of a collateral contract.

8.3.1 Mere puff

[8.210] It has been a common advertising technique—particularly in the days before consumer protection legislation—to exaggerate the qualities of a particular product, or to make other claims that obviously could not be substantiated. Examples include:

- 'This skin cream will remove all of your freckles, wrinkles and other blemishes overnight and make you the most desirable person in town.'
- 'Buying this car at this price is the best deal you will find anywhere in the world.'

Such statements are likely to be regarded as 'mere puffery' because they are not intended to be taken seriously, and could not be regarded as truly representing the

---

50   Ibid at 51.

position.[51] No consequences arise at common law from such sales talk. If a person buys the skin cream and that person's wrinkles do not disappear, he or she could not successfully sue the seller for the falsity of the advertisement.

[8.215] However, people making excessive or exaggerated claims are now in danger of being in breach of statute. The *Trade Practices Act* 1974 (Cth) (and its fair trading equivalents in the various jurisdictions) regulate such behaviour by prohibiting misleading or deceptive conduct.[52] A person who makes false statements beyond the reach of the common law may therefore incur liability under these statutes.

8.3.2 *Representation or term*

[8.220] It is easy to determine whether a statement falls within the realm of puffery. It is generally more difficult to determine whether the statement possesses the qualities needed to be a contractual term, or falls short of this mark, and can only be regarded as a representation. The remedy available to an innocent party turns on this classification.

Example

Parties entered into a contract for the sale of a car. The seller thought the particular car was a 1998 model and advised the prospective buyer accordingly. In fact, it was a 1995 model and its market value was $5000 less than the market value of a 1998 model (the price paid by the buyer).

If the statement of the car's vintage is a contractual term, the buyer will be entitled to sue the seller for its breach, with damages likely to be assessed at $5000. On the other hand, if the statement is regarded as a representation only—having no contractual force—the seller will not be liable to pay damages for breach of contract. At common law, the buyer will be entitled to the more limited relief available for innocent misrepresentation.[53]

[8.225] A statement will be a term of a contract if it is intended to be promissory in nature. A statement will be promissory in nature if the statement-maker 'warrants' its truth.[54] Lord Denning LJ (as he then was) provided a helpful description of what is meant by the term 'warrants' when used in this context:

> In saying that he must prove a warranty, I use the word 'warranty' in its ordinary English meaning to denote a binding promise. Everyone knows what a man means when he says 'I guarantee it' or 'I warrant it' or 'I give you my

---

51 See, for example, *Byers v Dorotea Pty Ltd* (1986) 69 ALR 715 where the statement-maker suggested that units being built were 'bigger and better' than the prospective purchaser's existing unit. (The Federal Court held this statement to be misleading and deceptive within s 52 of the *Trade Practices Act* 1974 (Cth)). See also *Dimmock v Hallett* (1866) LR 2 Ch App 21 at 27 where a statement by an auctioneer that land was 'fertile and improvable' although it had been abandoned as useless, was regarded by the court as being 'a mere flourishing description by an auctioneer'.

52 See [13.40] and [13.425]

53 Note, however, that damages may be available to the buyer in these circumstances in actions arising under the *Trade Practices Act* 1974 (Cth) and the State *Fair Trading Acts* in the various jurisdictions. See [13.430].

54 Note that the term 'warrants' used in this context is different from the term which is used in the context of classifying contractual terms. See [9.165]–[9.170].

word on it.' He means that he binds himself to it. That is the meaning it has borne in English law for 300 years ...[55]

If the statement-maker cannot be regarded as warranting (or guaranteeing) the truth of the statement, it will not be a term of the contract, and will not have contractual force. The statement will be a representation only.

[8.230] The test of whether the parties intended the statement to be promissory in nature is determined objectively. The court should not 'look into the minds of the parties to see what they themselves intended'.[56] Instead, regard should be had to how an intelligent bystander would understand the situation. This is assessed by observing the conduct of the parties—their words and behaviour—rather than by making inquiries about their thoughts.[57] In making this determination, the intelligent bystander must be placed in the situation of the parties.[58]

[8.235] The test for determining whether a statement is a term or representation is easy to state. It is, however, much more difficult to apply. This is demonstrated by the different conclusions on this point reached by the Justices of the High Court in the following case.

Example: Hospital Products Ltd v United States Surgical Corporation[59]

The United States Surgical Corporation ('USSC') manufactured surgical stapling devices and disposal loading units. It entered a distributorship agreement with Blackman, under which Blackman was to be the sole Australian distributor of USSC products. The nature of the arrangement was discussed by representatives of USSC and Blackman in a restaurant about one month prior to agreement being reached. In that discussion, Blackman agreed, among other things, to promote USSC products in Australia and not to deal in or promote any products that would be in competition with the USSC products he was promoting. In later correspondence confirming the agreement, a number of terms were set out. The statements made by Blackman at the restaurant were not, however, incorporated into that correspondence. Hospital Products International Pty Ltd ('HPI') (an entity with links to Blackman) was later substituted for Blackman as the Australian distributor. Later, contrary to the oral statements made by Blackman, HPI began supplying existing customers of USSC with products in direct competition with those of USSC. In an action by USSC against HPI, Blackman and related companies, one of the issues before the High Court was whether the oral statements made at the restaurant formed express terms of the distributorship agreement.

The High Court (by a majority of 4:1) held that those statements formed part of the express terms of the distributorship agreement, and were breached by the

55   *Oscar Chess Ltd v Williams* [1957] 1 WLR 370 at 374.
56   *Oscar Chess Ltd v Williams* [1957] 1 WLR 370 at 375.
57   Ibid.
58   See *Reardon Smithline v Hansen-Tangen* [1976] 1 WLR 989 at 996 per Lord Wilberforce where he stated: '… what must be ascertained is what is to be taken as the intention which reasonable people would have had if placed in the situation of the parties.'
59   (1984) 156 CLR 41.

conduct of HPI and Blackman. Although Gibbs CJ dissented, his Honour applied the test of the intention of the parties to determine whether the statement was promissory in nature, or merely representational. After a review of the evidence, Gibbs CJ concluded that the statements were not promissory in nature. The other Justices, however, after a less detailed consideration of the law on the point, agreed with the findings of the New South Wales Court of Appeal that these statements were promissory and formed express terms of the contract between the parties.

[8.240] A court may have regard to a number of indicators to assist it in determining whether the requisite intention for the statement to form part of the contract did exist. These indicators are not determinative of the issue, but, depending on the circumstances of the case, one or more of them may provide helpful guidance about the intention of the parties. These indicators are now considered in turn.

(a)   Words and conduct of the parties

[8.245] The test of intention of the parties is objective. The court must have regard to all of the evidence. The words used by the parties are relevant in this regard. If the words of the statement-maker indicate that he or she warrants the truth of the statement, this is strong evidence that the statement was intended to be contractual in nature. The relevance of the words used is highlighted by Denning LJ (as he then was) in the following extract:

> Turning now to the present case, much depends on the precise words that were used. If the seller says 'I believe it is a 1948 Morris. Here is the registration book to prove it,' there is clearly no warranty. It is a statement of belief, not a contractual promise. But if the seller says 'I guarantee that it is a 1948 Morris. This is borne out by the registration book, but you need not rely solely on that. I give you my own guarantee that it is,' there is clearly a warrantee. The seller is making himself contractually responsible, even though the registration book is wrong.[60]

[8.250] Other conduct of the parties may be indicative of contractual intent. The facts of the following case demonstrate how important conduct of the parties can be.

Example: Harling v Eddy[61]

A heifer was put up for auction and, as no bids had been made, the seller advised the audience that the animal was sound and the seller could guarantee it in all respects. The buyer subsequently bid for, and bought, the heifer, but the statement was incorrect; the heifer died of advanced tuberculosis within months of the sale. The buyer sued for breach of contract.

In finding for the buyer, the main issue considered by the English Court of Appeal was whether this oral statement could be enforced, given that a written term of the printed conditions acknowledged that no warranty was given in relation to the animal

---

60   *Oscar Chess Ltd v Williams* [1957] 1 WLR 370 at 375.
61   [1951] 2 KB 739.

sold. It was the view of the Court that the express oral statement was a condition of the contract, and the seller was liable for breach notwithstanding the exclusion clause. While not examining the reasons why the statement was regarded as a term rather than a representation, it is likely that the importance of the term (as evidenced by the conduct of the parties) was relevant.

[8.255] Having said this, however, importance of the statement alone is not determinative of whether the statement can be regarded as promissory in nature. In *JJ Savage & Sons Pty Ltd v Blakney*,[62] for example, a statement by the seller about the estimated speed of a motor cruiser being purchased was clearly important to the buyer. Nevertheless, the High Court held that the statement did not constitute a contractual term. In the course of the joint judgment, it was observed that the fact that the statement related to a matter of importance and was relied upon by the buyer does not necessarily warrant the conclusion that the statement was promissory.[63]

(b) Knowledge or expertise of the statement-maker

[8.260] The test of whether a statement is a term of the contract is whether it was intended to be promissory in nature. The extent to which the statement-maker can be regarded as promising or guaranteeing its truth will depend on the knowledge of the statement-maker.[64] As is illustrated by the following two cases, where the statement-maker professes to have personal knowledge of the relevant information, it is more likely that he or she can be regarded as guaranteeing its truth. If, on the other hand, the statement-maker is merely passing on information of which he or she has become aware, but does not profess to have any personal knowledge in relation to the information, it would be more difficult to regard that statement as promissory.

Example: Oscar Chess Ltd v Williams[65]

As part of a hire purchase deal, the defendant traded in his Morris to the plaintiff car dealers. The car had been acquired by the defendant's mother in 1954. In the course of negotiations, the defendant described the Morris as a 1948 model, and produced the registration book. The registration book indicated that it was first registered in 1948, and had subsequently changed owners five times. In fact, the Morris was a 1939 model, worth £115 less. The plaintiff sued to recover this amount as damages, claiming that the defendant's oral statement was a term of the contract.

The English Court of Appeal found in favour of the defendant. The defendant's oral statement was not intended to be a term of the contract. The defendant was merely stating his belief, not making a contractual promise.[66]

---

62   (1970) 119 CLR 435.
63   Ibid at 443.
64   *Mihaljevic v Eiffel Tower Motors Pty Ltd* [1973] VR 545 at 556.
65   [1957] 1 WLR 370.
66   Ibid at 375 (see earlier in this paragraph for the extract referred to). See also *Routledge v McKay* [1954] 1 WLR 615 at 636 where the seller 'stated that it was a 1942 model and pointed to the corroboration found in the book.' In these circumstances, the Court held the statement to be a mere representation having no contractual effect.

[8.265] Even if a statement-maker does not claim to have personal knowledge of the accuracy of the statement, if the person is in a better position to ascertain its accuracy than the innocent party, the court will more readily infer that it was intended to be promissory.

Example: Dick Bentley Productions Ltd v Harold Smith (Motors) Ltd[67]

In a conversation prior to the sale of a car, the seller, a motor dealer, said the vehicle had been fitted with a replacement engine and gear box and, since that time, had travelled 20 000 miles. In fact, the vehicle had travelled almost 100 000 miles since the work was done. The buyer sued the seller for breach of the contractual term.

The English Court of Appeal found in favour of the buyer as the statement was a term of the contract. Relevant to its determination was the fact that the seller was a motor dealer, and therefore in a better position to ascertain the history of the vehicle than if it had been a private seller.

(c) Statement maker has control in relation to information

[8.270] An indicator that follows on from the previous indicator is where the pre-contractual statement relates to subject matter that is, or should be, in the control of the statement-maker. The case of *Hospital Products Ltd v United States Surgical Corporation*,[68] discussed above, is a good illustration of this point.[69] Because the undertakings given by Blackman at the restaurant related to his conduct in the course of the distributorship agreement, he had control over the subject matter. He was therefore in a position to guarantee the truth of the statements. While not expressly stated to be a factor, this may have influenced the majority of the High Court Justices in finding that the statements were terms of the contract.

(d) Oral statement not reduced to writing

[8.275] Where, following pre-contractual negotiations, the agreement is reduced to writing and the oral statement upon which the innocent party seeks to rely is omitted from the document, this may indicate that the parties did not intend the statement to be contractual in nature.

Example: Routledge v McKay[70]

The parties entered into a contract for the sale of a motorcycle. Seven days before the sale, the seller told the buyer it was a 1941 model. When the agreement was subsequently reduced to writing, this statement was omitted. In fact, the motor cycle was a 1930 model. The buyer sued the seller for damages for breach of contract.

---

67   [1965] 1 WLR 623. See also *Couchman v Hill* [1947] KB 554 in which case a farmer stated prior to sale that the heifer was unserved. This statement was held to be promissory in nature, it being relevant that the information was within, or should have been within, the farmer's own knowledge and information about which the buyer was ignorant.
68   (1984) 156 CLR 41.
69   See [8.235].
70   [1954] 1 WLR 615. See also *Oscar Chess Ltd v Williams* [1957] 1 WLR 370 at 376.

The English Court of Appeal found in favour of the seller. Relevant to its determination was the failure of the parties to record this statement in the written contract.

[8.280] As all of these factors are indicators of intention only, failure to reduce an oral statement to writing is not determinative of the matter.[71] Once again, *Hospital Products Ltd v United States Surgical Corporation*[72] is illustrative. The oral statements made by Blackman at the restaurant were regarded by the majority of the High Court to be express terms even though they were not included in subsequent correspondence between the parties that set out other contractual terms.

[8.285] The corollary to this indicator is also of assistance. If an oral statement later becomes part of the written agreement, it is likely that it was intended to form part of the contract.[73]

[8.290] Of course, this indicator is of no assistance where the later agreement is only verbal.

(e) Interval of time

[8.295] There is authority to suggest that the interval of time between when the statement is made and when the contract is formed may also indicate whether the parties intended the statement to be promissory—and therefore to form part of the contract.[74] The greater the interval, the less likely it will be regarded as promissory. In *Routledge v McKay*,[75] for example, the seven-day delay between making the statement and entering the contract was a factor considered by the court in finding that the statement did not form part of the contract. On the other hand, in *Hospital Products Ltd v United States Surgical Corporation*,[76] the fact that there was a one-month delay between the oral statements made by Blackburn in the restaurant and entry into the distributorship agreement did not prevent the oral statements forming part of the contract.

On balance, it is submitted that a consideration of the lapse of time is likely to be of subsidiary importance in a court's determination of this issue.

8.3.3   Collateral contracts

(a)   Nature of a collateral contract

[8.300] An oral statement that is established as being promissory in nature will generally form part of the contract being considered. In *Hospital Products Ltd v United States Surgical Corporation*,[77] for example, as the oral statements were regarded as promissory, they were held to form part of the distributorship agreement (the main contract). In some cases, however, the oral statement may not be regarded as forming part of the

---

71   *Oscar Chess Ltd v Williams* [1957] 1 WLR 370 at 376.
72   (1984) 156 CLR 41.
73   *Oscar Chess Ltd v Williams* [1957] 1 WLR 370 at 376.
74   *Routledge v McKay* [1954] 1 WLR 615. While this point was not expressly considered in *Harling v Eddy* [1951] 2 KB 739, the statement made by the seller at auction immediately prior to the buyer's bid was regarded as a term of the contract.
75   [1954] 1 WLR 615.
76   (1984) 156 CLR 41.
77   Ibid.

main agreement, but instead form the basis of a collateral contract. The following case illustrates how a collateral contract operates.

Example: De Lassalle v Guildford[78]

In the course of negotiating entry into a lease, the prospective tenant refused to hand over his copy of the lease to the landlord unless he received an assurance that the drains were in order. The landlord gave this assurance. The lease was silent as to the condition of the drains. The drains were not in good order, and the tenant brought action to recover damages for breach.

The English Court of Appeal held that the verbal statement about the condition of the drains was a warranty made by the lessor that was contractual in nature. The warranty, however, did not form part of the lease agreement. It was collateral to the lease.

[8.305] It can be seen from this case that a collateral contract is one in which the consideration for the promisor's promise is the promisee's entry into the main contract.[79] The following separate agreements were held to exist in *De Lassalle v Guildford*.[80]

- *Collateral contract:* the landlord (the promisor) assured the prospective tenant (the promisee) that the drains were in good working order. The promisee's consideration for this promise was entry into the lease agreement (the main contract).

- *Main contract:* lease agreement between the landlord (promisor under the collateral contract) and tenant (promisee under the collateral contract).

[8.310] As with all contracts, for consideration to be valid, it must not be past. The promisee's consideration for the promisor's promise under a collateral contract is entry into the main agreement. If the promisee has already entered into the main agreement at the time the collateral contract is formed—that is, when the promisor's statement is made—the promisee's consideration will be *past*, and a valid collateral contract will not exist.[81]

[8.315] In *JJ Savage & Sons Pty Ltd v Blakney*,[82] the High Court had to determine whether a collateral contract had been entered into. From the joint judgment of the Court, it appears that the following must be satisfied before a statement will give rise to a collateral contract:

- a statement is made to induce entry into the contract;
- the statement is relied upon; and
- the statement relied upon was promissory in nature.

---

78 [1901] 2 KB 215.
79 *Heilbut Symons & Co v Buckleton* [1913] AC 30 at 47 per Lord Moulton: 'It is evident both on principle and on authority that there may be a contract the consideration for which is the making of some other contract'.
80 [1901] 2KB 215.
81 See, for example, *Hercules Motors v Schubert* (1953) 53 SR (NSW) 301 where the promisor's statement about the condition of the car being purchased was made after the main contract was entered into. Therefore, no collateral contract was formed, the consideration for the promisor's statement being past.
82 (1970) 119 CLR 435.

The third element was discussed earlier. If the statement-maker intends to guarantee the truth of the statement, it will be regarded as a contractual term. The same considerations referred to earlier are also relevant to a determination in this context.[83] The other elements relating to inducement and reliance are also relevant to the vitiating factor of misrepresentation; they are examined in detail later in this text.[84]

[8.320] Applying these principles, the High Court held that the plaintiff had not proved the existence of a collateral contract, and so was not entitled to damages for its breach.

Example: JJ Savage & Sons Pty Ltd v Blakney[85]

Prior to entering into a contract for the purchase of a motor boat, the seller sent a letter to the buyer making comments and recommendations about various engines he regarded as suitable for that boat. The buyer bought the motor boat with the recommended engine. When the engine did not run the boat as well as the seller had suggested, the buyer sued the seller for damages. The buyer claimed, among other things, that the promise made in the letter formed the basis of a collateral contract.

The High Court held that a collateral contract did not exist. In relation to the information concerning the capacity of the engine, the High Court considered that the buyer could have done one of three things:
- required the attainment of a specified speed to be a condition of the contract;
- made the seller promise that the boat could attain a specified speed; or
- made his own judgment based on the seller's opinion.

A collateral contract would have been formed if the second option had been adopted. In fact, the seller did not guarantee the truth of the statement, and the buyer relied on his own judgment, based on the seller's opinion expressed in the letter. Accordingly, a collateral contract had not been formed.

[8.325] If a collateral contract is established and the statement that forms the basis of the contract is false, the statement-maker (promisor) will be in breach of the collateral contract. As in all cases of breach, the promisor will be liable in damages for loss resulting from that breach. Because the statement is not a term of the main contract, however, no remedy arises in relation to that contract. The falsity of the statement does not entitle the promisee to terminate the main contract.

(b) Bipartite and tripartite collateral contracts

[8.330] Collateral contracts may be either bipartite or tripartite. As the name suggests, a collateral contract is bipartite where the parties to it are the same as those who enter

---

83   For a further example of a pre-contractual statement being made which was regarded as non promissory in nature, see *Robertson v Kern Land Pty Ltd* (1989) 96 FLR 217. Prior to entering into a contract for the sale of land, a statement concerning possible road access to that land was made by an employee of the seller. The Queensland Supreme Court rejected the contention that a collateral contract existed because the statement was not promissory in nature.

84   See [13.75]–[13.100].

85   (1970) 119 CLR 435.

the main agreement. In the following case, the High Court found a collateral contract between the buyer of land and the Council.

Example: Shepperd v The Council of the Municipality of Ryde[86]

This case involved the sale of land by the Council of the Municipality of Ryde to Shepperd. Before entering into the contract, the Council advised Shepperd that the land opposite the house would become a park. This information was also set out in a promotional brochure issued by the Council. The importance of this land becoming a park was made clear to the Council. A year after the sale, the Council decided to subdivide the land. The buyer sought an injunction to restrain this action on the basis of the promise made prior to entering into the contract of sale.

The High Court found in favour of the buyer and granted the interlocutory injunction sought. The Court held that there was sufficient evidence of a collateral warranty by the Council that the land would be used as a park and not be subdivided.

[8.335] Tripartite collateral contracts arise less frequently. In these cases, the parties to the collateral contract are different from the parties to the main contract. Notwithstanding that the parties to the main contract are different from those in the collateral contract, the receiver of the information under a collateral contract is still entitled to sue for breach if that information turns out to be false.

Example: Wells (Mersthan) Ltd v Buckland Sand & Silica Ltd[87]

The defendant was a sand merchant who assured the plaintiff, a commercial flower grower, that certain sand sold by it had a particular composition suitable for the plaintiff's needs. Because of this advice, the plaintiff purchased the sand from a third party, the third party having purchased it from the defendant. The sand did not conform to the assurances made by the defendant. The plaintiff suffered a loss, and sued the defendant for breach of its promise.

The English Court found in favour of the plaintiff. The Court accepted that there was a contractual liability in respect of the statement. As such, a collateral contract had been entered into on the basis of the promise made by the defendant. It did not matter that the contract for the purchase of the sand was made with a third party.

(c)   Consistency with the main contract

[8.340] There is an important limitation on the effectiveness of the collateral contract in providing relief where a false pre-contractual statement induces entry into the main contract. In Australia and New Zealand at least, the courts will only recognise a collateral contract if it is not inconsistent with the terms of the main contract. Such inconsistency operated to deprive the sub-lessee of a remedy in the following case.

---

86   (1951) 85 CLR 1.
87   [1965] 2 QB 170.

Example: Hoyt's Pty Ltd v Spencer[88]

A landlord leased a building to Spencer ('the lessee'). Under this head lease, the landlord could terminate the lease by giving four weeks notice in writing to the lessee. The lessee then granted a sub-lease to Hoyt's ('the sub-lessee'). A clause in the sub-lease allowed the lessee to terminate the sub-lease at any time by giving four weeks' notice in writing. However, in pre-contractual negotiations, the lessee advised the sub-lessee that it would only rely on the clause if the lessee was given a notice of termination by the head lessor. Notwithstanding this undertaking, the lessee later relied on the clause to terminate the sub-lease even though such notice had not been given by the head lessor. The sub-lessee claimed the lessee was unable to do this because it was contrary to the collateral contract entered into.

The High Court found in favour of the lessee. A collateral contract could not be held to exist because it would be inconsistent with the main agreement. Under the main agreement (the sub-lease), the lessee could terminate at any time, provided four weeks' notice were given. The oral statement made before entering into the lease limited this right.

[8.345] The justification for not allowing a collateral contract to have force if it is inconsistent with the terms of the main contract was explained by Knox CJ in the following terms:

> The reason for this conclusion is that the alleged consideration for the collateral contract is the assumption by the purchaser of the obligations specified in the main contract, which obligations are immediately varied or abrogated by the collateral contract.[89]

[8.350] Whether this rationale can be supported is perhaps questionable. The requirement for consistency has been criticised since this decision (although it has never been overruled). The main basis for the criticism is that the rule does not give effect to the actual intention of the parties. There may be a number of reasons why parties would not alter or delete a term in the main agreement (such as the sub-lease in *Hoyt's Pty Ltd v Spencer*)[90] even if it is inconsistent with the promise made as part of the collateral contract. One commentator has suggested that there may be psychological reasons why a promisee may not wish to insist on the main contract being altered

> such as that it would show a lack of trust in the [promisor's] word, or that the parties might be reluctant to alter in handwriting an engrossed document. Or, there may be, in other circumstances, practical reasons, such as that the

---

88 (1927) 27 CLR 133. The requirement for consistency has prevented the finding of a collateral contracts in a number of later decisions. See, for example, *Maybury v Atlantic Union Oil Co Ltd* (1953) 89 CLR 507 at 518 and *State Rail Authority of New South Wales v Heath Outdoor Pty Ltd* (1986) 7 NSWLR 170 at 192. See also *Donovan v Northlea Farms Ltd* [1976] 1 NZLR 180. There appears to be a trend in New Zealand, however, for the courts to take a relatively liberal approach to interpreting oral and written statements, so that they will be less inclined to find an inconsistency: JF Burrows, J Finn & SMD Todd, *Law of Contract in New Zealand*, 8th edn, Butterworths, Wellington, 1997, p 169.

89 Ibid at 139–140.

90 (1927) 27 CLR 133.

document, being a standard form contract, does *not* represent the parties' bargain, and is thus not regarded by the beneficiary of the collateral promise as of vital importance.[91]

Clearly the objective intention of the parties is to be bound by the statement made in the collateral contract rather than an inconsistent one in the main contract. In *Hoyt's Pty Ltd v Spencer*,[92] for example, a bystander witnessing the pre-contractual negotiations would regard the agreement to be that the lessee would not terminate the sub-lease unless the head lessor gave him notice to terminate the head lease. Denying the existence of the collateral contract fails to give effect to this intention. Further still, it could operate to promote sharp practice. The promisor can say a clause will not be enforced, even though he or she may intend later to rely on it. Fraud in such a case would be difficult for a promisee to prove.[93]

[8.355] As illustrated by the following decision, the requirement for consistency does not apply in England.

Example: City and Westminster Properties (1934) Ltd v Mudd[94]

The parties had negotiated the renewal of a lease of a ground-floor shop and basement. The new lease contained a clause that required the premises to be used only for the purposes of trade. In previous years, the tenant had slept in a small apartment that formed part of the premises. When negotiating the new lease, the tenant advised the landlord that he would not execute a new lease unless he were allowed to continue sleeping on the premises. The landlord agreed. The landlord subsequently brought action for forfeiture of the lease on the basis that the tenant was in breach of this covenant by sleeping in the premises. The tenant relied on the oral covenant to defend the claim.

The English Court found in favour of the tenant. Because the tenant signed the lease in reliance on the landlord's promise, the tenant was entitled to rely on the promise.

(d)   Circumstances in which collateral contracts likely to be pleaded

[8.360] To some extent, the notion of parties entering into a collateral contract is contrived. It is a legal device that can operate to bind a statement-maker to promises made, even where the parties may not have intended to enter a separate contract in relation to the statement. The existence of a collateral contract will be particularly important where the parties have entered into a written agreement and intend that contract to contain all of the terms of the contract. In such a case, the parol evidence rule operates to prevent oral evidence being led to add to the written document.[95] This means an innocent party is unable to sue for damages for breach of that contract

---

91   N Seddon, 'A plea for the reform of the rule in *Hoyt's Pty Ltd v Spencer*' (1978) 52 ALJ 372 at 379.
92   (1927) 27 CLR 133.
93   Contrast the position where a pre-contractual oral statement can be given effect to if the court finds that the parties intended it to form a clause of the *main* contract, notwithstanding it may be inconsistent with a term in the main contract: *Couchman v Hill* [1947] KB 554.
94   [1959] 1 Ch 129.
95   See [8.370]–[8.390].

in relation to a false oral statement made before entry into the main agreement. If, however, the innocent party can show the oral statement formed the basis of a collateral contract, he or she may be entitled to damages for breach of the collateral contract. This can be the outcome even if the parties had not consciously intended to enter into a separate collateral contract.

[8.365] The collateral contract concept may also be relevant in the context of contracts required to be in writing to be enforceable.[96] The case of *Shepperd v The Council of the Municipality of Ryde*[97] is illustrative. The contract there was for the sale of land, and such contracts are enforceable only if they are in writing. The statement about the proposed use of nearby land did not form part of the contract for sale of land, so an action for breach could not be brought. However, as the statement was held to form the basis of a collateral contract, the buyer was entitled to damages for its breach. The strict effect of legislation requiring contracts for the sale of land to be in writing before they can be enforced was circumvented.

8.4   Parol evidence rule

8.4.1   *Statement of the rule*

[8.370] The foregoing commentary examined the circumstances in which an oral statement made prior to contract formation is likely to form part of that contract.[98] The test is whether, from an objective perspective, the parties intended the statement to be promissory. There is, however, a rule of long standing that may prevent evidence of the oral term being led in some instances where the contract is later reduced to writing. This rule is a rule of evidence; it is commonly referred to as the 'parol evidence rule'. One of the early formulations of the rule is that of Lord Denman in *Goss v Nugent*:[99]

> By the general rules of the common law, if there be a contract which has been reduced into writing, verbal evidence is not allowed to be given of what passed between the parties either before the written agreement was made, or during the time that it was in a state of preparation, so as to add to or subtract from or in any manner vary or qualify the written contract.

[8.375] The parol evidence rule, as described by Lord Denman, has been adopted and still operates in Australia.[100] However, a number of comments need to be made about this formulation of the rule, and how it has subsequently developed. First, Lord Denman referred to the exclusion of 'verbal evidence' of what transpired between the parties during pre-contractual negotiations and at the time of contract preparation. While it is certainly correct that the rule applies to verbal evidence, the rule is also

---

96   See Chapter 11.
97   (1951) 85 CLR 1.
98   See [8.220]–[8.295].
99   (1833) 110 ER 713 at 716.
100   See, for example, *Mercantile Bank of Sydney v Taylor* (1891) 12 LR (NSW) 252 at 262, *Codelfa Construction Pty Ltd v State Rail Authority of New South Wales* (1982) 149 CLR 337 at 347, *Robertson v Kern Land Pty Ltd* (1989) 96 FLR 217 at 231.

effective to exclude other kinds of extrinsic evidence such as other documents relating to the contract or previous drafts of the written contract ultimately entered into.[101]

[8.380] Secondly, the formulation by Lord Denman excluded the introduction of parol evidence 'so as to add to or subtract from or in any manner vary or qualify the written contract'. As noted by Mason J in the High Court decision of *Codelfa Construction Pty Ltd v State Rail Authority of New South Wales*,[102] the original formulation of the rule did not prevent extrinsic evidence being introduced to assist in the *interpretation* of the written agreement. Nevertheless, the case law demonstrates an evolution of the parol evidence rule to exclude extrinsic evidence for this purpose as well. As a result, it is often said that there are two aspects to the rule:

1   To exclude extrinsic evidence so as to add to or subtract from or in any manner vary or qualify the written contract; and

2   To exclude extrinsic evidence to assist in the interpretation of the written contract.

[8.385] Thirdly, Lord Denman suggested that the rule applies 'if there be a contract which has been reduced into writing'. While the rule will only apply if there is a written contract, it will not apply in all such cases. The situations in which the rule will apply are explored in more detail later.[103]

[8.390] In this text, both aspects of the rule will be dealt with separately. The first is relevant to establishing the actual content of the agreement between the parties (or at least, the evidence of the agreement that may be led in court). This part of the rule will therefore be examined in this chapter. As the second aspect relates to matters of interpretation, it will be considered in chapter 9: Construction of terms.

8.4.2   Rationale of the rule

[8.395] The parol evidence rule as originally formulated was designed to promote certainty of contractual dealings. If parties reduce their agreement to writing, one party dissatisfied with that written agreement should not be able to introduce other evidence to affect the contractual arrangements. The rationale of the rule was put concisely by Latham CJ in *Hope v RCA Photo Phone of Australia Pty Ltd*:[104]

> When parties express their agreement in writing they do so for the purpose of securing certainty and preventing disputes. They may choose to leave their arrangements to the risks and chances of verbal evidence but if they have recourse to writing for the purpose of recording their agreement, they cannot afterwards change their attitude and, by seeking to give parol evidence, introduce the very element of uncertainty which the adoption of writing was intended by both parties to exclude.

An appreciation of the rationale of the rule assists in understanding why the exceptions to the rule have evolved.[105]

---

101   *Codelfa Construction Pty Ltd v State Rail Authority of New South Wales* (1982) 149 CLR 337 at 347; *Nemeth v Bayswater Road Pty Ltd* [1988] 2 QdR 406 at 414.
102   (1982) 149 CLR 337 at 347.
103   See [8.400]–[8.410]
104   (1937) 59 CLR 348 at 357. See also *Gordon v MacGregor* (1909) 8 CLR 316 at 323–324.
105   See [8.415]–[8.455].

8.4.3 When the rule applies

[8.400] The parol evidence rule will not apply to all contracts that are evidenced by writing. The rules only applies where the terms of the agreement are wholly in writing.[106] If the parties intend the contract to consist of both oral and written terms, the rule will not apply. It was for this reason, in *Hospital Products Ltd v United States Surgical Corporation*,[107] that the parol evidence rule did not exclude evidence being led of the oral statements made at the restaurant. The High Court (by majority) held that the parties intended the contract to be constituted by both the statements made at the restaurant, and by the terms of the subsequent letter. The parol evidence rule therefore did not apply.[108]

[8.405] Where the written agreement between the parties is formal, and appears to represent the entirety of the contract, the party seeking to introduce the oral term may have difficulty demonstrating that the parties intended the contract to consist both of this document and to oral terms. In *Gordon v MacGregor*,[109] for example, the parties entered a written agreement to buy and sell timber of certain specifications. The seller did not perform, and sought to introduce oral evidence relating to the girth of the required timber and the time of delivery of the timber to excuse his non-performance. Isaacs J had this to say about whether the contract also consisted of these oral statements:

> Now that document, when it is looked at, uses words that are appropriate only to a definite absolute contract: 'I undertake to purchase' on the one hand with all the particulars, and 'I undertake to supply and agree under the above conditions' on the other … It is an almost irresistible presumption that the parties agreed that that should be the record of their bargain and I can find no scrap of evidence to displace that presumption, and, therefore, I say it matters under the circumstances of this case not at all whether there was evidence as to the girth and as to the time. The rule in many cases has been affirmed over and over again.[110]

Having referred to the 'irresistible presumption' that the written agreement constituted the entire contract, however, Isaacs J noted that it was 'always open to the parties to show whether or not the written document is the binding record of the contract'.[111] This means that a party is entitled to lead oral evidence to demonstrate that the parties intended oral (or other) terms to form part of the contract.[112] The parol evidence rule

---

106 *Gordon v MacGregor* (1909) 8 CLR 316 at 323; *Hospital Products Ltd v United States Surgical Corporation* (1984) 156 CLR 41 at 60–61; *State Rail Authority of New South Wales v Heath Outdoor Pty Ltd* (1986) 7 NSWLR 170 at 191; *Robertson v Kern Land Pty Ltd* (1989) 96 FLR 217 at 231; *Tak and Co Inc v AEL Corporation* (1995) 5 NZ BLC 103887 at 103892.

107 (1984) 156 CLR 41.

108 See also *Couchman v Hill* [1947] 1 KB 554, referred to in note 67. Without expressly referring to the parol evidence rule, the English Court of Appeal allowed the introduction of oral evidence about the condition of the heifer. It seems implicit in the decision that the parties intended the contract to be made up of the prior oral statement as well as the terms and conditions of auction, leaving no operation for the parol evidence rule. For a New Zealand example, see *AM Bisley & Co Ltd v Thompson* [1982] 2 NZLR 696. Compare *Robertson v Kern Land Pty Ltd* (1989) 96 FLR 217.

109 (1909) 8 CLR 316.

110 Ibid at 322.

111 (1909) 8 CLR 316 at 323, citing Baron Bramwell in *Wake v Harrop* 6 H & N 768 at 774.

112 *State Rail Authority of New South Wales v Heath Outdoor Pty Ltd* (1986) 7 NSWLR 170 at 191–193.

only operates to exclude extrinsic evidence once it is established that the parties intended the written document to represent the entire agreement.

[8.410] One further point that must be considered in determining whether the parties intended their agreement to be wholly in writing is the effect of a clause being inserted in the agreement, to the effect that the document represents the entire agreement between the parties and there is no other agreement between the parties in relation to the subject matter of the contract. Clauses of this kind are referred to variously as 'entire agreement', 'entire contract' or 'merger' clauses; they are considered in more detail in the next chapter.[113] In brief, there is authority to suggest that such clauses may be effective in demonstrating the parties' intention for the writing to represent the entire agreement.[114] It follows that the parol evidence rule would apply, and the oral statements could not be regarded as forming part of the agreement.

8.4.4   Exceptions to the rule

[8.415] Even where the parties intend the writing to represent the entire agreement, at times a court will admit oral or other extrinsic evidence that may impact on the contractual obligations of the parties as set out in the writing. The circumstances in which evidence is admitted despite the parol evidence rule are examined below. For ease of reference, these have been listed under the heading of 'Exceptions' to the parol evidence rule. However, for most of these cases, it is probably more correct to regard them as situations where the rule does not come into play, rather than examples of exceptions to the rule.

(a)   Evidence of collateral contract

[8.420] The nature and operation of a collateral contract was examined earlier.[115] Where a collateral contract exists, the promisee's consideration for the promisor's promise is entry into the main contract. If the main contract is reduced to writing and the parties intend the writing to constitute the entire agreement, the parol evidence rule excludes extrinsic evidence to add to, subtract from or vary that agreement. The collateral contract, however, is a separate contract. The parol evidence rule preventing extrinsic evidence being led to affect the main contract does not apply to the collateral contract. Therefore, oral evidence relating to that contract can be led.[116]

[8.425] The case of *De Lassalle v Guildford*,[117] discussed above,[118] provides an example. The English Court of Appeal admitted evidence of a collateral agreement concerning the condition of the drains, notwithstanding that the parties had subsequently entered a later written tenancy agreement. The Court was satisfied that the parties had entered

---

113   See Chapter 9.
114   *Hope v RCA Photophone of Australia Pty Ltd* (1937) 59 CLR 349.
115   See [8.300]–[8.365].
116   For this reason, leading evidence of a collateral contract is not really an exception to the parol evidence rule. That rule continues to operate in relation to the main agreement.
117   [1901] 2 KB 215.
118   See [8.300].

into two separate agreements. The parol evidence rule related to the tenancy agreement, but did not prevent evidence of the earlier collateral contract being led.[119]

(b) Evidence that written contract is not yet in force

[8.430] The parol evidence rule operates to exclude extrinsic evidence to add to, subtract from or vary the agreement only if the contract is in force, and the written document reflects the contractual arrangement. It follows that oral evidence that the contract has not yet commenced operation is admissible, even although the parties have signed a written agreement.

Example: Pym v Campbell[120]

Parties were negotiating a contract to sell an invention. They verbally agreed the contract would proceed only if approval to the invention was obtained from an engineer. Because of the practical difficulties involved in the relevant parties being able to meet at the one time to sign the agreement, the parties agreed to sign the written contract for sale of the invention on the basis that the sale would only be effective if the engineer approved the invention. This approval was not given. The seller subsequently brought an action on the written agreement.

The English Court found in favour of the buyer. Despite the fact that the agreement for sale was reduced to writing, the court was prepared to hear oral evidence that the agreement had not yet come into effect.

Cases such as *Pym v Campbell*[121] do not truly represent an exception to the parol evidence rule. If parties have not reached an agreement, the parol evidence rule does not come into operation.

(c) Evidence that the written contract was *later* varied or discharged

[8.435] Parties who have reduced their contract to writing may later wish to vary or completely discharge that agreement. Unless the contract is one required to be in writing to be enforceable, neither the variation nor discharge need be in writing.[122] Therefore, oral or other evidence can be led that the written agreement (which at the time may have represented the entire agreement of the parties) has been subsequently varied or discharged.[123] The parol evidence rule prevents introduction of extrinsic evidence that the parties added to, subtracted from or varied the agreement *before* it was reduced to writing, not evidence that the parties *later* agreed to its variation or discharge.

---

119   Compare *Clough v Rowe* (1888) 14 VLR 70, a case involving the sale of sheep. Before entering into the contract, the seller advised the buyer that the sheep would not lamb before the second week in April. The parties later entered a written agreement for sale that did not include the earlier statement by the seller. The court considered that the seller's oral statement related to the main agreement, so did not find that a collateral contract had been formed. As such, the parol evidence rule prevented the admission of the seller's earlier statement.

120   (1815) 119 ER 903.

121   Ibid.

122   See [11.415]–[11.440].

123   *Narich Pty Ltd v Commissioner of Pay-roll Tax* [1983] 2 NSWLR 597 at 601.

(d) Evidence to imply a term

[8.440] In some circumstances, the common law recognises that a term forms part of the contractual relationship between the parties even though it is not expressed in the written document. The term is said to be one that is 'implied' by the common law.[124] Depending on the basis upon which a term is sought to be implied, the court may need to hear evidence. The nature of the evidence will depend upon the basis upon which a contracting party seeks to imply the term. Relevant evidence may, for example, relate to the custom or usage in a particular industry or evidence of previous course of dealings between the parties. The extent to which a court is prepared to accept extrinsic evidence seems to vary according to the basis of implication. The effect of the parol evidence rule on the implication of terms is examined separately later in this chapter. As will be seen, in some cases the court is prepared to accept extrinsic evidence to determine whether to imply a term even if the parties intended the document to represent their entire agreement.

(e) Evidence necessary for rectification

[8.445] From time to time, parties may verbally agree on all contractual terms, but make an error when reducing their agreement to writing. A simple example is an agreement to sell property for a specified sum, but when the agreement is reduced to writing, a different sum is recorded as the price. Although the parol evidence rule will generally prevent the introduction of evidence to add to, subtract from or vary the agreement, the rule will not exclude such evidence if it is necessary to rectify the written document so as to correct such error.[125]

[8.450] A more difficult issue arises where there has not been a mistake in reducing the agreement to writing, but the written agreement cannot be regarded as reflecting the common intention of the parties, as evidenced by the pre-contractual negotiations. Where the parties are operating on the basis of a common assumption of fact, which they adopted as the basis of their relationship, the issue of estoppel by convention arises. Ordinarily, the contracting parties would be estopped from later alleging that the common assumption was not correct.[126] Where the written document purports to represent the entire agreement between the parties and is silent about the common assumption, the question is whether the parol evidence rule prevents evidence being led of pre-contractual negotiations to demonstrate the common assumption under which the parties were operating. The following case illustrates the tension between the parol evidence rule and the operation of the doctrine of estoppel by convention.

Example: Whittet v State Bank of New South Wales[127]

A husband and wife were negotiating entry into a mortgage of their home to secure advances needed for the husband's business. The wife was prepared to give the mortgage only if it was limited to $100 000. Her solicitor negotiated this requirement with

---

124 The circumstances in which a term will be implied at common law is considered in more detail later in this chapter: see [8.460]–[8.790].

125 *NSW Medical Defence Union Ltd v Transport Industries Insurance Co Ltd* (1986) 6 NSWLR 740. This is the case even if the contract contains an 'entire agreement' clause: *Macdonald v Shinko Australia Pty Ltd* [1999] 2 QdR 152.

126 Estoppel by convention is a species of common law estoppel. See [7.10].

127 (1991) 24 NSWLR 146.

officers of the bank, and agreement was reached. However, the mortgage did not reflect this agreement: it was expressed to be unlimited in its operation. One of the issues before the Court was whether the parol evidence rule prevented evidence being led of the pre-contractual negotiations under which it was agreed that the mortgage be limited to $100 000.

The New South Wales Court of Appeal held that such evidence could be led so that the mortgage secured advances to a limit of $100 000. Rolfe J summarised the position in the following words:

> The application of principles of rectification, a parol collateral contract to a written principal contract, and of estoppel by convention are all capable of outflanking the parol evidence rule.[128]

[8.455] The case authorities have not been entirely consistent on whether the parol evidence rule is effective to exclude the operation of estoppel by convention in such cases. While the New South Wales Court of Appeal in *Whittet's case* considered that the parol evidence rule was giving way to the 'widening ambit of the doctrine of estoppel by convention',[129] Bryson J of the same Court more recently, in *dicta*, expressed concern about introducing verbal evidence of pre-contractual exchanges to support arguments of estoppel where the parties had subsequently entered into a written document that represented a final and considered impression of their contractual intention.[130]

8.5　Implied terms

[8.460] The focus of this chapter so far has been on the legal character of matters discussed by the parties or set out in writing before or at the time of contract formation. If the discussions resulted in the statement forming part of the contract, it would be an express term. But a contract between parties can include terms in addition to terms expressly agreed upon by the parties. Such terms are referred to as 'implied' terms. There are a number of different grounds upon which terms can be implied into a contract; the most common are examined in the rest of this chapter. The eight grounds for implying terms (considered below) can be divided into two broad categories.

[8.465] The first category is that of terms implied to reflect the presumed intention of the parties. These can be:
- a term implied to provide the contractual arrangement with business efficacy;
- a term implied from previous consistent course of dealings between the parties;
- a term implied from custom or usage;
- a term implied to complete the contract.

Because these are implied rather than express terms, generally either one or both of the parties will not have specifically turned their minds to the particular term.

128　Ibid at 151. This decision was followed by the same Court in *State Bank of SA v Macintosh* (unreported, 31 May 1995).

129　*Whittet v State Bank of New South Wales* (1991) 24 NSWLR 146 at 154 per Rolfe J citing from McLelland J in *Bentham v ANZ Banking Group Ltd* (26 June 1991, unreported).

130　*Australian Co-operative Foods Ltd v Norco Co-operative Ltd* (1999) 46 NSWLR 267 at 279 following the views expressed by McLelland J in *Johnson Matthey Ltd v AC Rochester Overseas Corporation* (1990) 23 NSWLR 190, and declining to follow the views of Rolfe J in *Whittet v State Bank of New South Wales* (1991) 24 NSWLR 146.

Nevertheless, the common law regards the term as forming part of the contract because, in the circumstances of the case, it is presumed to reflect their intention had they done so.[131] Because implication occurs to reflect the presumed intention of the parties, a term will not be implied under any of these heads if there is an express term to the contrary in the agreement.

[8.470] The second category is that of terms implied regardless of intention. These can be:

- a term implied as a legal incident of a particular class of contract;
- a term implied imposing on the parties a general duty to cooperate;
- a term implying duties of good faith, fair dealing and reasonableness;
- a term implied by statute.

The terms in the second category are implied regardless of the intention of the parties. To some extent, these categories are driven by public policy considerations. Terms are implied under the first three points in the second category to reflect how the judiciary considers contracting parties should act in the course of performing a contract, or performing certain kinds of contracts. In a similar way, the legislative imposition of terms reflects standards which the legislature considers appropriate in particular circumstances. Notwithstanding the relevance of public policy considerations, in most of these cases, parties are free to contract out of the implied term. The extent to which this is possible is considered later.

[8.475] While it may be helpful to categorise implied terms in the two categories (eight sub-categories) identified above, it should be borne in mind that there can be considerable overlap between the categories.[132] A term that may be implied by one court to give business efficacy to the arrangement may be implied by another court as part of the duty of the parties to cooperate in the performance of the contract. Even on the facts of a single case, a court may be prepared to imply the same term on more than one ground.[133] Furthermore, the list of grounds for implying terms given above is neither definitive nor static. Implied terms can also be categorised in other ways—and, as demonstrated later, the common law is still evolving. For example, while people in commerce in the early twenty-first century may reasonably be expected to perform their contractual obligations in good faith, it is unlikely that an equivalent obligation would have existed fifty years ago.[134]

[8.480] Finally, it should be noted that terms can be implied in a contract regardless of whether that contract is oral or written. If the contract is one in which the parties have reduced their entire agreement to writing, difficulties may arise in relation to the operation of the parol evidence rule and the extent to which extrinsic evidence can be

---

131   For a recent examination of the relevance of parties' intentions when courts seek to imply terms in fact, see JM Paterson, 'Terms Implied in Fact: The Basis for Implication' (1998) 13 *Journal of Contract Law* 103.

132   This overlap has been recognised judicially on a number of occasions. See, for example, *Renard Constructions (ME) Pty Ltd v Minister for Public Works* (1992) 26 NSWLR 234 at 255 and 260 per Priestley JA, and *Hughes Aircraft Systems International v Airservices Australia* (1997) 146 ALR 1 at 38.

133   See, for example, *Renard Construction (ME) Pty Ltd v Minister for Public Works* (1992) 26 NSWLR 234 per Priestley JA and *Hughes Aircraft Systems International v Airservices Australia* (1997) 146 ALR 1.

134   See [8.750]–[8.790].

admitted. The extent to which the parol evidence rule may impact on the implication of terms is examined throughout the remainder of this chapter.

8.5.1   Term implied on the basis of business efficacy

(a)   Rationale of implication

[8.485] Parties entering into contractual arrangements will generally attempt to make provision for incidents that may occur during the life of the contract. However, there may be one or more matters about which the parties have not negotiated or expressly agreed. This may be because the parties thought the position was so obvious there was no need to expressly agree on it, or because the parties had not (consciously at least) turned their minds to that particular aspect of the agreement. If, as the contract unravels, the existence or non-existence of such a term becomes relevant to the contractual obligation or liability of the parties, the courts may be called upon to consider whether the term needs to be implied into the particular contract so that it can be effectively carried out. Terms that are implied in contracts in these circumstances are commonly said to be implied on the basis of business efficacy. It is sometimes said that the term is implied 'in fact'. This is because the focus of the court is on the facts of the particular case before it. The issue is whether, on the facts surrounding that particular contract (not for contracts of that class in general), implication is necessary.[135] As can be seen from the criteria that must be satisfied before a term will be implied, terms implied on this ground are intended to reflect the presumed intention of the parties.

[8.490] The following are case illustrations of terms being implied a term on this ground.

Example 1: The Moorcock[136]

The parties entered a contract for the plaintiff ship owner to leave his vessel at the defendant's jetty. It was known by the parties that at low tide, the vessel would rest on the bottom of the River Thames. When this occurred, the vessel sustained damage as a result of the uneven condition of the bed of the river. The Court implied a term that the defendant would take reasonable care to ensure that the bed of the river was in a condition not to cause damage to the vessel.

Example 2: Commonwealth v Ling[137]

This case involved a contract between Chinese students and an educational institution under which the students paid fees in exchange for a course of study. It was implied in the agreement that if the students were unable to obtain a visa that permitted them to study in Australia, their fees would be reimbursed.

Example 3: RDJ International Pty Ltd v Preformed Line Products (Australia) Pty Ltd[138]

This contract involved the sale of a manufacturing business under which the purchaser agreed to pay the seller 5 per cent of the sales revenue for three years. It was an

---

135   Compare a term implied as a matter of law in all contracts of a particular category. See [8.690]–[8.725].
136   (1889) 14 PD 64.
137   (1993) 118 ALR 309.
138   (1996) 39 NSWLR 417.

implied term of the agreement that the purchaser would not voluntarily do anything that would make it more difficult for the seller to continue to receive the royalty for the three-year period.

[8.495] Courts have been prepared to imply a term for reasons of business efficacy for more than a century. In *The Moorcock*,[139] Bowen LJ of the English Court of Appeal explained the basis for the implication in the following way.

> I believe if one were to take all the cases … it will be found that in all of them the law is raising an implication from the presumed intention of the parties with the object of giving to the transaction such efficacy as both parties must have intended that at all events it should have. In business transactions such as this, what the law desires to effect by the implication is to give such business efficacy to the transaction as must have been intended at all events by both parties who are business men …[140]

Since this time, the test for implication has received considerable judicial attention and, in the process, been significantly refined. Nevertheless, the thrust of the test remains the same: whether implication of the term is necessary to provide business efficacy to the transaction.

(b) Five-tier test

[8.500] In 1978, the case of *BP Refinery (Westernport) Pty Ltd v Shire of Hastings*[141] went on appeal from Victorian Supreme Court to the Privy Council. While the above passage from *The Moorcock*[142] was cited with approval, the Privy Council provided additional guidance by setting out five conditions that had to be satisfied before it would regard a term as being implied on the basis of business efficacy:[143]

- the term must be reasonable and equitable;
- the term must be necessary to give business efficacy to the contract, so that no term will be implied if that contract is effective without it;
- the term must be so obvious that 'it goes without saying';
- the term must be capable of clear expression;
- the term must not contradict any express term of the contract.

As is apparent from the following commentary, there is considerable overlap between these five elements.[144]

---

139 (1889) 14 PD 64.
140 Ibid at 68.
141 (1977) 180 CLR 266.
142 (1889) 14 PD 64.
143 This test has subsequently been adopted by the High Court and applied by Australian Courts on many occasions. See for example, *Codelfa Construction Pty Ltd v State Rail Authority of New South Wales* (1982) 149 CLR 337. The test has also been cited with approval by the New Zealand Court of Appeal: *Devonport Borough Council v Robbins* [1979] 1 NZLR 1 at 23.
144 The possibility of overlap was recognised by the Privy Council itself in *BP Refinery (Westernport) Pty Ltd v Shire of Hastings* (1977) 180 CLR 266 at 283.

Implication must be reasonable and equitable

[8.505] Because a term implied for reasons of business efficacy is intended to reflect the presumed intention of the parties, the term must be both reasonable and equitable. If the term were unreasonable or inequitable, a person could not be regarded as intending the term to form part of the contract. This limb was relevant to the determinations made by the Privy Council in the following case.

Example: BP Refinery (Westernport) Pty Ltd v Shire of Hastings[145]

To encourage BP Refinery (Westernport) Pty Ltd to establish an oil refinery in Victoria, the Shire of Hastings entered into a rating agreement under which the company received discounted rates for a forty year period. A separate agreement was entered into between the State of Victoria and the company facilitating the establishment of a refinery ('the refinery agreement'). As a result of the restructure of the parent organisation, the company gave up occupation of the refinery site but, some time later, resumed occupation. The Shire claimed that there was an implied term of the rating agreement that the concessions would only apply while the company was in occupation and had terminated when the company ceased occupation. The Full Court of the Victorian Supreme Court held that an implied term of this kind formed part of the rating agreement.

When the matter came before the Privy Council, it held that a term such as that suggested by the Victorian Supreme Court could not be implied in the agreement. To imply such a term would be wholly unreasonable and inequitable. It was clearly within the contemplation of the company that the organisation could be restructured at any time. Such restructure was expressly contemplated in the refinery agreement, that agreement being referred to in the recitals of the rating agreement. This was particularly likely given that the rating agreement was to subsist for a forty year period. In the circumstances, it would be both unreasonable and inequitable to suggest that the benefits of the rating agreement would only subsist for the time that the company was in occupation. The Privy Council instead implied a term that any assignee of the company would receive the benefit under the rating agreement.

Implication must be necessary to give business efficacy to the contract so that no term will be implied if the contract is effective without it

[8.510] The fact that the term sought to be implied is reasonable and equitable as between the parties is not, of itself, enough. The second requirement is that it must be *necessary* to imply the term to give business efficacy to the contract. Latham CJ in *Scanlan's New Neon Ltd v Tooheys Ltd*[146] couched the test of necessity in the following terms.

> And the test of whether it is clearly necessary is whether the express terms of the contract are such that both parties, treating them as reasonable men — and they cannot be heard to say that they are not — must clearly have intended the

---

145   (1977) 180 CLR 266.
146   (1943) 67 CLR 169.

term, or, if they have not adverted to it, would certainly have included it, if the contingency involving the term had suggested itself to their minds.[147]

This test of necessity had been described as 'stringent'.[148] If it is applied stringently, it imposes a difficult onus of proof for a person seeking to imply a term to meet. The courts have not been entirely consistent in terms of the rigour with which this test is applied. However, the weight of authority suggests that it is a reasonably difficult hurdle to overcome.

[8.515] Different judicial standards regarding what is 'necessary' in the circumstances to provide business efficacy to the contract can result in cases that are difficult to reconcile. In *Con-Stan Industries of Australia Pty Ltd v Norwich Winterthur Insurance (Australia) Ltd*,[149] for example, the Court was not prepared to imply a term either that the broker alone was liable to the underwriter for payment of the premium, or that payment by the insured to the broker discharged the obligation to pay the underwriter.[150] The High Court recognised the difficulty in demonstrating that imposition of a term is 'necessary' for the operation of the contract:

> [T]here is real difficulty in the proposition that either term is necessary to make the contract work. The contract is capable of sensible operation in the absence of the implied terms, and the [Insured's] submission amounts to little more that an assertion that the terms are necessary to make the contract work in a manner that will avoid additional liability of the [Insured].[151]

This can be contrasted with the decision of the Federal Court in *Commonwealth v Ling*.[152] As mentioned earlier,[153] it was held to be an implied term of the contract for the provision of educational services that if the student did not obtain the necessary visas, the educational fees would be refunded. However, on a strict application of this test, it must be queried whether it has been satisfied. If the student had been able to obtain the visa, the educational services would have been provided. The term was not necessary to carry out that contract. If the student had been unable to obtain the visa, the contract certainly could not have been carried out. However, it was the inability to obtain the visas rather than the failure to refund the money paid that made it impossible to carry out the contract.

[8.520] It is submitted that, on balance, the courts interpret this limb relatively strictly. Where this occurs, the requirement is a difficult one to satisfy.[154]

---

147 Ibid at 195.
148 *Shell UK Ltd v Lostock Garage Ltd* [1977] 1 All ER 481 at 491.
149 (1985) 160 CLR 226.
150 For more detail regarding the facts and decision, [8.650].
151 Ibid at 241.
152 (1993) 118 ALR 309.
153 See earlier in this paragraph.
154 See, for example, *Shell UK Ltd v Lostock Garage Ltd* [1977] 1 All ER 481, *Scanlan's New Neon Ltd v Two-hey's Ltd* (1943) 67 CLR 169, *Hospital Products Ltd v United States Surgical Corporation* (1984) 156 CLR 41 and *Byrne v Australian Airlines Ltd* (1995) 185 CLR 410.

Term must be so obvious that 'it goes without saying'

[8.525] The third requirement, which overlaps to some degree with the second, is that the term must be so obvious that it goes without saying. In determining whether this criterion has been met, the perception of an officious bystander apprised of all of the relevant circumstances is relevant. In the judgment of the majority of the Privy Council in *BP Refinery (Westernport) Pty Ltd v Shire of Hastings*,[155] the question was whether the term:

> was something so obvious that it went without saying, and if an officious bystander had asked whether that was the common intention of the parties the answer would have been 'Of course'.[156]

In that case, a term that 'the Company' as used in the rating agreement was a reference to any assignees of the company was held to satisfy this test.

[8.530] If the term is necessary for the purpose of giving business efficacy to the transaction, it will generally be a term that is so obvious that it goes without saying. However, this will not always be the case. In *Codelfa Construction Pty Ltd v State Rail Authority of New South Wales*,[157] for example, while Mason J conceded that the term sought to be implied may have been necessary for the purpose of business efficacy, in the circumstances of the case it was not a term that was so obvious that it went without saying.

Example: Codelfa Construction Pty Ltd v State Rail Authority of New South Wales[158]

A construction company entered into a contract with the New South Wales State Rail Authority to carry out some excavation work to construct an underground railway. To complete the work within the time specified in the contract, the company intended to operate three eight hour shifts per day, six days per week. Because of the disturbance created, the company was restrained from working between 10 pm and 6 am. The company claimed there was an implied term in the contract that if it was restrained from carrying out the work in the manner contemplated, the Rail Authority would indemnify it against the additional costs incurred.[159]

The High Court was not prepared to imply the term urged by the company. At the time of negotiation, both contracting parties were operating under the assumption that an injunction could not be granted to restrain the work proceeding in the manner contemplated. It was therefore impossible to suggest that a term allowing for additional payment to the company in such an event was one that went without saying. As Mason J said:

> This is not a case in which an obvious provision was overlooked by the parties and omitted from the contract. Rather it was a case in which the

---

155   (1977) 180 CLR 266.
156   Ibid at 28.
157   (1982) 149 CLR 337.
158   Ibid.
159   There was an alternative claim that the contract was frustrated by the grant of the injunction. See [22.80].

parties made a common assumption which masked the need to explore what provisions should be made to cover the event which occurred. In ordinary circumstances negotiation about that matter might have yielded any one of a number of alternative provisions, each being regarded as a reasonable solution.[160]

[8.535] This limb also presented an obstacle in *Hospital Products Ltd v United States Surgical Corporation*[161] to the implication of a term in a distributorship agreement that the distributor would not '... do anything inimical to the market in Australia for USSC's Surgical Stapling Products'. If asked before entering into the contract whether such a term was part of the agreement, the parties, according to the High Court, would not have responded 'Of course; that is so clear that we did not bother to say it.'[162] Gibbs CJ predicted that a more likely response may have been that such a term was too far-reaching in its operation, as it could have prevented the distributor from taking such action as was reasonable in the course of carrying out its distributorship arrangement.

Term must be capable of clear expression

[8.540] Generally, if a term is so obvious that it goes without saying, it will be capable of clear expression. Nevertheless, it is a separate requirement that must be met before a court will imply a term on these grounds. An inability to formulate a term with sufficient specificity proved an obstacle to the implication of a term in the following decision of the English Court of Appeal.

Example: Shell UK Ltd v Lostock Garage Ltd[163]

Shell and Lostock (the operator of a garage) entered into a solus agreement under which Shell required Lostock to sell only petrol supplied by Shell. A petrol price war occurred in the neighbourhood of Lostock's garage. To assist some of the garages tied to Shell, Shell introduced a support scheme under which it subsidised garages supplying its products. It did not provide such a subsidy to Lostock. One of the issues that arose in litigation between Shell and Lostock was whether there could be implied into the solus agreement a term that Shell would not abnormally discriminate against Lostock in favour of competing garages.

One of the grounds upon which the Court of Appeal refused to imply the term suggested was the difficulty in phrasing the implied term. Relevant in this regard was the vagueness and ambiguity inherent in the words 'discriminate' and 'abnormality'.

Term must not contradict any express term of the contract

[8.545] A term implied on the basis of business efficacy is designed to reflect the presumed intention of the parties. If they have agreed upon and inserted into the contract

---

160   (1982) 145 CLR 337 at 355–356. The view that no one term could be regarded as going without saying is further supported by the fact that different terms were implied by the Arbitrator, Ash J at first instance and the New South Wales Court of Appeal.
161   (1984) 156 CLR 41.
162   Ibid at 66–67.
163   [1977] 1 All ER 481.

an express term that is inconsistent with the implied term, the implied term cannot be regarded as reflecting their intention. For this reason, the Privy Council inserted a fifth requirement—that the term must not contradict an express term of the contract.[164]

[8.550] Inconsistency with an express term was one of the grounds upon which Brennan J in *Codelfa Construction Pty Ltd v State Rail Authority of New South Wales*[165] refused to imply the term concerning payment of additional money and increasing the extension date should the construction company be restrained from working to the originally contemplated schedule. His Honour considered such a term to be inconsistent with the provisions in the contract governing time for completion and payment for the work performed.[166]

(c) Impact of parol evidence rule

[8.555] The extent to which the parol evidence rule operates to exclude evidence that may be relevant to the implication of a term on the basis of business efficacy is a difficult issue. As we have seen, a term implied to give business efficacy to the transaction will reflect the presumed intention of the parties. If this is the case on a set of facts, the parties must not have intended the written document to represent all of the terms of the contract. On this logic, it could be argued that the parol evidence rule would not apply and extrinsic evidence relevant to the implication of the term would be admissible.[167]

[8.560] This was not the approach adopted by the High Court, however, in *Codelfa Construction Pty Ltd v State Rail Authority of New South Wales*.[168] One of the issues considered by the Court was whether the parol evidence rule prevented evidence being admitted to support the implication of a term. Mason J considered in some detail how the parol evidence rule originated and subsequently developed. His Honour noted that evidence of surrounding circumstances is admissible to assist in the interpretation of a contract if it contains provisions with ambiguous meanings.[169] This is done in an attempt to ascertain the presumed intention of the parties. Mason J continued, saying that the implication of a term is also a matter of construction of a contract. The same evidence should therefore be admitted in deciding whether a term should be implied on grounds of business efficacy. On this basis, Mason J considered it appropriate to admit evidence of the parties' common understanding of the way the work was to be carried out in the course of determining whether to imply a term.[170] In other words, the objective background to the contract is admissible in determining whether it is

---

164 It appears, however, that the fact that one or more terms touches on subject matter similar or related to the terms sought to be implied will not necessarily prevent its implication: See, for example, *Shepherd v Felt & Textiles of Australia Ltd* (1931) 45 CLR 359.

165 (1982) 149 CLR 337.

166 Ibid at 406.

167 Compare the extent to which extrinsic evidence is admissible where a term is sought to be implied on the basis of previous consistent course of dealings or custom or usage: see [8.635] and [8.675].

168 (1982) 149 CLR 337.

169 Ibid at 352. See further [9.35]–[9.40].

170 Compare Brennan J at pp 400–404 who appeared to take a more restrictive view of the circumstances in which terms can be implied. Nevertheless, his Honour indicated that it was appropriate to determine the issue of implication of terms 'in the matrix of the facts' in which it arose.

appropriate in the circumstances of the case to imply a term necessary to give business efficacy to the transaction.[171]

(d) Relevance of formality of contract

[8.565] As a general proposition, the more formal and detailed the written document is, the more reluctant a court will be to imply a term on the basis of business efficacy. If the parties have gone to some lengths to reduce their agreement to writing and to ensure it reflects their intentions, it is difficult to suggest they have omitted a term that is *necessary* to give their agreement business efficacy, and to suggest that the term omitted is so obvious that it goes without saying.[172]

[8.570] Similar reasoning applies to standard form contracts. Where one party has reduced its contractual arrangements to terms on a standard form, it is likely that the party contracts only on the basis of those terms. It is difficult to argue that there may exist, in addition to these terms, a term that is *necessary* to give business efficacy to the transaction. The fact that a standard contract was used in *Codelfa Construction Pty Ltd v State Rail Authority of New South Wales*[173] was a relevant consideration for Mason J in declining to imply a term.

> My reluctance to imply a term is the stronger because the contract in this case was not a negotiated contract. The terms were determined by the Authority in advance and there is some force in the argument that the Authority looked to Codelfa to shoulder the responsibility for all risks not expressly provided for in the contract. It is a factor which in my view makes it very difficult to conclude that either of the terms sought to be implied is so obvious that it goes without saying.[174]

[8.575] For verbal agreements or other agreements where the parties have not attempted to reduce the entire agreement to writing, parties may not have negotiated the terms with the same rigour or precision. There may therefore be further scope for the implication of a term on the basis of business efficacy. In fact, there is a suggestion in two High Court decisions that the test for implication may be different (or at least applied in a less rigorous fashion) if the contract lacks the formality that existed in *BP Refinery (Westernport) Pty Ltd v Shire of Hastings*.[175] Deane J in *Hospital Products Ltd v United States Surgical Corporation*[176] warned against 'an over-rigid application of the cumulative criteria', particularly in relation to the requirement that the term be necessary to give business efficacy to the transaction. About a decade later, McHugh and Gummow JJ in *Byrne v Australian Airlines Ltd*[177] considered that in such cases, 'the question is whether the implication of that particular term is necessary for the reasona-

---

171 This approach was adopted by the Federal Court in *Adelaide Petroleum NL v Poseidon Ltd* (1990) 98 ALR 431 at 534.
172 This was one of the reasons advanced by the High Court in refusing to imply a term in *Ansett Transport Industries v Commonwealth* (1977) 139 CLR 54.
173 (1982) 149 CLR 337.
174 Ibid at 356. See also similar remarks by Aickin J at 374.
175 (1977) 180 CLR 266.
176 (1984) 156 CLR 41 at 121.
177 (1995) 185 CLR 410.

ble or effective operation of the contract in the circumstances of the case'.[178] Whether an application of this test is easier to satisfy than the Privy Council's five-tier test remains to be seen.[179] Regardless of the particular test used, clearly the more comprehensive the contractual arrangement between the parties is, the less scope there is for implication of a term. The corollary to this statement applies in relation to verbal or otherwise less formal agreements.

8.5.2   Terms implied from previous consistent course of dealings

(a)   General principle

[8.580] Where parties contract on a regular basis, it is not uncommon for them to incorporate the same terms each time they contract. If, on one occasion, the contract is formed without expressly incorporating such terms, the question arises whether the terms that formed part of the previous contracts can be regarded as forming part of the later contract.

Example

A car owner, C, always has his car repaired at B's garage. Whenever C drops his car off, he signs a form containing various terms. On the last occasion, C's car broke down and C telephoned B advising her to repair the car. Agreement is reached without express mention of the usual terms. C's car is towed to B's garage. Are the terms that are usually in a document signed by C part of the contract to repair the car that was made by the parties over the telephone?

[8.585] The weight of authority suggests that the test of whether a term can be incorporated into the contract on the basis of a course of dealing is one based on reasonableness.[180] In the circumstances of the case, is it reasonable to hold that the parties entered into the contract on the basis, and with the knowledge, that their agreement would be on the terms set out in previous contracts entered into?[181] Lord Reid explained the circumstances in which a term will be incorporated on these grounds in the following way:.

> If two parties have made a series of similar contracts each containing certain conditions, and then they make another without expressly referring to those conditions it may be that those conditions ought to be implied. If the officious

---

178   Ibid at 442, citing with approval *Hawkins v Clayton* (1988) 164 CLR 539 at 573.

179   For an examination of whether the more relaxed criteria suggested by McHugh and Gummow JJ is likely to result in different outcomes, see GJ Tolhurst and JW Carter, 'The New Law on Implied Terms' (1996) 11 *Journal of Contract Law* 76.

180   As examined later in [8.620]–[8.630], the case law governing the incorporation of a term on the basis of previous consistent course of dealings between the parties is not entirely consistent. Nevertheless, the courts generally accept reasonableness as the basis for implication.

181   *Henry Kendall & Sons v William Lillico & Sons Ltd* [1969] 2 AC at 91. Compare comments of Lord Denning in *British Crane Hire Corporation Ltd v Ipswich Plant Hire Ltd* [1975] 1 QB 303 at 311, where he suggested that a term could be implied not on the basis of a course of dealing, but on the common understanding which is derived from the conduct of the parties. As the parties were aware of the terms which were 'habitually imposed by the supplier' of the machines under consideration, those terms formed part of the contract between the parties.

bystander had asked them whether they had intended to leave out the conditions this time, both must, as honest men, have said 'of course not'.[182]

If this can be demonstrated, a term will be implied to reflect the presumed intention of the parties. Naturally, if the parties have expressly agreed to incorporate different or inconsistent terms, there is no room for implying a term on this basis.

(b) Criteria relevant to establish previous consistent course of dealings

[8.590] It then remains to determine the circumstances in which parties will be regarded as having an expectation that the contract is entered into on terms incorporated in previous contracts. The relevant term or terms obviously must have formed part of earlier agreements between the parties. And there must be evidence of an earlier consistent course of dealings between the parties. Relevant in this assessment are:
- the number of dealings between the parties; and
- the consistency of dealings between the parties.

However, there are no rules dictating how many dealings are required, or over what period they must have taken place. The following cases may provide useful indicators concerning what will be regarded as sufficient to establish a consistent course of dealings.

Example 1: Horrier v Rambler Motors (AMC) Ltd[183]

This case involved a contract for the repair of a car. Contracts to repair on three or four occasions over the previous five years were not regarded as sufficient to constitute a course of dealings.

Example 2: Henry Kendall & Sons v William Lillico & Sons Ltd[184]

In this case (discussed below), three to four contracts per month over the previous three years were regarded as sufficient to constitute a course of dealing.

Example 3: Chattis Nominees Pty Ltd v Norman Ross Homeworks Pty Ltd[185]

This case involved deliveries of furniture from the plaintiff to the defendant. While the case report does not indicate the number of prior contracts of sale entered into between the parties, there are references to 'a series of sales' taking place throughout 1991 and 'frequent and regular dealings' between the parties.[186] This was held to be sufficient to constitute a course of dealing.

[8.595] As would be expected, the greater the number of prior dealings, the greater the likelihood of incorporating the term. Consistency of contractual dealings is also important. The argument for incorporating a term on the basis of prior dealings is less

---

182 *McCutcheon v David MacBrayne Ltd* [1964] 1 WLR 125 at 128.
183 [1972] 2 QB 71.
184 [1969] 2 AC 31.
185 (1992) 28 NSWLR 338.
186 Ibid at 343.

compelling if the terms are incorporated into earlier contracts on some occasions, but not on others.[187]

(c)   Term incorporated after earlier contract formed

[8.600] In the example given in [8.590], the terms in the earlier contracts to repair the car were agreed upon at the time of contract formation. As such, the terms clearly formed part of the earlier contract. More difficult issues arise where the term is purportedly introduced into the earlier contract after its formation (or possibly even performance). Whether such a term can be incorporated as a result of previous dealings was considered by the English House of Lords in the following case.

Example: Henry Kendall & Sons v William Lillico & Sons Ltd[188]

The parties had entered into contracts for the sale of meal for feeding to pheasants and partridges. It was the practice to conclude the contract orally; the seller then forwarded a sale note to the buyer later that day or the next day. The sale note contained a clause under which the buyer undertook responsibility for any latent defect in the product. The parties contracted in this way three or four times a month over three years. One of the issues for determination by the House of Lords was whether those terms had been incorporated into the contract on the basis of the previous dealings.

The House of Lords held that the terms had become part of the contracts of sale. In the circumstances of the case, it was reasonable to hold that when the buyer placed an order, it did so on the basis, and with the knowledge that, an acceptance of the order would be on the terms and conditions set out in the sale note.

[8.605] The decision of the House of Lords seems sensible. Even though the terms in the sale note could not have formed part of the first contract because they were introduced after contract formation, the same result should not follow for all subsequent contracts entered into. The basis for the parties not being bound by the terms in the first contract is that they could not be regarded as having assented to them. This reasoning may also have applied to the second or third contracts entered into. However, it defies logic to suggest that because they were always given at the end of the particular contract, they could never be regarded as forming part of the contract. The test should be whether the parties could be regarded as having assented to the terms. Where the parties have been contracting over a long period, with such a note always being sent after contract formation, it would be reasonable to assume that, at some stage, the parties have contracted on the basis of these terms. When that stage is reached (as it had been in this case), the terms will be implied on the basis of the previous course of dealings.

[8.610] Notwithstanding the persuasiveness of the decision, a different approach to this issue was taken by the Full Court of the Victorian Supreme Court in *DJ Hill & Co Pty*

---

187   See, for example, *McCutcheon v David MacBrayne Ltd* [1964] 1 WLR 125 where receipts were sometimes issued and sometimes not issued on the shipping of goods. On the facts of the case, the House of Lords was not prepared to imply a term on the basis of previous dealings.

188   [1969] 2 AC 31.

Ltd v Walter H Wright Pty Ltd,[189] discussed above.[190] The defendant admitted it was aware there were terms on the delivery docket. However, the Court accepted that the defendant had never read the terms, and was unaware of their content. As in *Henry Kendall & Sons v William Lillico & Sons Ltd*,[191] the first contract between the parties would not incorporate the terms in a docket as it was signed after both contract formation and performance. However, the Court did not consider that these terms could be incorporated by subsequent dealings of the parties.

[8.615] It is perhaps possible to distinguish this case from *Henry Kendall & Sons v William Lillico & Sons Ltd*[192] on the basis that the defendant in *DJ Hill & Co Pty Ltd v Walter H Wright Pty Ltd*[193] at no time regarded the document that was signed upon delivery of the machinery as anything more than an acknowledgment of delivery of the goods. By contrast, the sale notes in the English case were recognised by the parties as contractual documents. Further, in *DJ Hill & Co Pty Ltd v Walter H Wright Pty Ltd*,[194] there had been only ten or so previous dealings between the parties, by comparison with more than a hundred dealings in *Henry Kendall & Sons v William Lillico Ltd*.[195] It would be interesting to speculate on the outcome of the Victorian case if the parties had contracted in the same way several times a month over several years. In such circumstances, it would be more difficult to sustain the position that such a document, which was always signed after delivery was completed, and which, to the knowledge of the defendant, contained terms, was not a contractual document.

(d) Requirement of actual knowledge

[8.620] In some cases, it has been suggested that incorporation by a prior course of dealings is possible only if the party has actual knowledge of the terms. The following extract from the judgment of Lord Devlin in *McCuthcheon v David MacBrayne Ltd*[196] is representative of this school of thought.

> The previous dealings are relevant only if they prove knowledge of the terms, actual and not constructive, and assent to them. If a term is not expressed in a contract, there is only one other way in which it can come into it and that is by implication. No implication can be made against a party of a term which was unknown to him. If previous dealings show that a man knew of and agreed to a term on ninety nine occasions there is a basis for saying that it can be imported into the hundredth contract without an express statement. It may or may not be sufficient to justify the importation — that depends on the circumstances; but at least by proving knowledge the essential beginning is made. Without knowledge there is nothing.[197]

---

189   [1971] VR 749.
190   See [8.40].
191   [1969] 2 AC 31.
192   Ibid.
193   [1971] VR 749.
194   Ibid.
195   [1969] 2 AC 31.
196   [1964] 1 WLR 125.
197   Ibid at 134.

[8.625] While there has been some support for such a view in Australia,[198] it is contrary to the views expressed by the English Court of Appeal in *Horrier v Rambler Motors (AMC) Ltd*[199] and by the House of Lords in *Henry Kendall & Sons v William Lillico & Sons Ltd.*[200] As emphasised by Lord Guest in *Kendall*, the rest of the members of the House of Lords in *McCutcheon v David MacBrayne Ltd*[201] did not concur in these comments of Lord Devlin. Further, Lord Guest regarded those comments as *obiter dictum* only.

[8.630] It would severely restrict the operation of the doctrine if incorporation were only permitted if a party had actual knowledge of the term. For a start, proof that the person had such knowledge would be difficult to establish. Secondly, there does not appear to be any logical basis upon which this view can be sustained. It is also inconsistent with the approach taken by the courts generally in relation to incorporating terms into the contract. As observed in various contexts earlier in this chapter, actual knowledge of the content of a term is not determinative. The issue is whether, in the circumstances of the case, the parties can be regarded as having assented to the term.[202] If parties have contracted using the same terms over a long period without either party objecting to the terms, it is reasonable to regard the parties as having assented to them. It should not matter that one of the parties has chosen not to familiarise himself or herself with their content.

(e) Impact of parol evidence rule

[8.635] It is apparent from the cases on this topic that a party often seeks to rely on a previous course of dealing to incorporate a term into the contract where the later contract is verbal and the earlier contracts are in writing.[203] Because the later contract is not in writing, the parol evidence rule will not operate. Therefore, extrinsic evidence of previous dealings can be admitted. This would also be the position in cases such as *Henry Kendall & Sons v William Lillico & Sons Ltd,*[204] where the agreement is always made orally and followed by the issue of a document containing contractual terms. In the rare case where the parties have entered into a written agreement, but there is an attempt to imply a term on the basis of previous dealings, it could be argued that the parol evidence rule will not apply. A term is implied on the basis of a course of dealing to reflect the presumed intention of the parties. If the test for implication of a term is satisfied, the parties must have intended to contract on the basis of the terms in the written document as well as the implied term. Therefore, the parol evidence rule will not apply.[205]

---

198   *Eggleston v Marley Engineers Pty Ltd* (1979) 21 SASR 51 at 62–66; *DJ Hill & Co Pty Ltd v Walter H Wright Pty Ltd* [1971] VR 749 at 752.
199   [1972] 2 QB 71.
200   [1969] 2 AC 31.
201   [1964] 1 WLR 125.
202   See [8.10]. There is also suggestion in the High Court decisions of *Sydney City Council v West* (1965) 114 CLR 481 and *Thomas National Transport (Melbourne) Pty Ltd v May & Baker (Australia) Pty Ltd* (1966) 115 CLR 353 that a term can form part of a contract regardless of actual notice.
203   See, for example, *Hollier v Rambler Motors* (ANC) Ltd [1972] 2 QB 71.
204   [1969] 2 AC 31.
205   Compare [8.555]–[8.560] regarding the operation of the parol evidence rule where parties seek to imply a term on the basis of it being necessary for business efficacy.

8.5.3   Terms implied from custom or usage

[8.640] Within a particular trade or profession, contracting parties may regard themselves as being bound by certain terms even if those terms are not expressly agreed upon. Terms can form part of the contract because parties in the particular trade or profession always contract on the basis of those terms. Where terms are incorporated into a contract in this way, they are said to be implied on the basis of custom or usage. The term is implied to give effect to the presumed intention of the parties. For example, in an early English decision, an employer of a weaver was held to be entitled to deduct an amount from the weaver's wages for cloth that was not properly woven.[206] Although there was no an express term to that effect in the employment contract, because the custom was followed in 85 per cent of the mills in the region, it was implied in the contract on the basis of custom or usage.

[8.645] In recent times, terms are less likely to be implied on this basis than on many of the other grounds discussed in this commentary. This may be because parties are less likely to leave matters like this to chance. If a term is generally accepted within a particular trade or profession, it is likely to be incorporated into the contract, or expressly negatived.

[8.650] In a more recent Australian decision, the High Court had to consider whether a particular custom existed in the insurance industry.

Example: Con-Stan Industries of Australia Pty Ltd v Norwich Winterthur Insurance (Australia) Ltd[207]

The insured paid a premium to a broker who should have passed the payment on to the underwriter. The broker did not, and the insured was sued by the underwriter for payment of the premium. The High Court was called upon to consider whether there was a custom in the insurance industry that the underwriter can look only to the broker for payment of the premium or, alternatively, that payment by the insured to the broker was a sufficient discharge of the insured's obligation to pay the underwriter.

The High Court held that there was insufficient evidence of either of the customs alleged. The underwriter was therefore entitled to recover the premium from the insured.

In the course of its joint judgment, the High Court extracted from the relevant case law four propositions that are relevant to establish whether a term will be regarded as implied on the basis of custom or usage.[208]

1   [8.655] The existence of a custom or usage that will justify the implication of a term into a contract is a question of fact.

   In making a determination on this issue, the focus must be on the custom or usage in the particular trade or profession under consideration. Of relevance in *Con-Stan Industries of Australia Pty Ltd v Norwich Winterthur Insurance (Australia)*

---

206   *Sagar v Ridehalge* [1931] 1 Ch 310.
207   (1985) 160 CLR 226.
208   Compare the leading New Zealand case of *Woods v NJ Ellingham & Co Ltd* [1977] 1 NZLR 218 in which Henry J summarised the five principles which he regarded as relevant for implying a term on the basis of custom.

Ltd,[209] therefore, is the practice within the insurance industry. As emphasised by the High Court, 'there is little to be gained by referring … to the practices of the London marine market in the last century'.[210]

2   [8.660] There must be evidence that the custom relied on is so well known and acquiesced in that everyone making a contract in that situation can reasonably be presumed to have imported that term into the contract.

There are really two aspects to this requirement. Firstly, there must be sufficient evidence that a custom of the kind alleged in fact exists. The custom must be sufficiently widespread and consistent that it can be articulated with some certainty. Secondly, and related to the first limb, the custom must be so widespread that it is well known to the people within the trade or profession. In other words, the custom must achieve a sufficient degree of notoriety that it must be regarded as reflecting the presumed intention of the parties.[211]

Provided these limbs are satisfied, a term can be implied even if it is not universally accepted or adopted within the trade or profession. The fact that one person does not contract on the basis of such a term will not be regarded as enough to negative the existence of such a custom.

3   [8.665] A term will not be implied into a contract on the basis of custom where it is contrary to the express terms of the agreement.

A term is implied on the basis of custom and usage to reflect the presumed intention of the parties. If the parties expressly exclude such a term, or insert a term inconsistent with it, the term cannot be regarded as reflecting their intention so will not be implied. It was for this reason that the seller of marble was unsuccessful in *Summers v Commonwealth*.[212] The contract was for the sale of marble of sizes specified in a schedule. The seller delivered blocks of marble of a larger size, out of which the specified sizes could be cut. The High Court rejected the seller's submission that it was the custom to provide marble of a size from which smaller sizes could be cut because it contradicted the express terms of the contract between the parties.

4   [8.670] A person may be bound by a custom notwithstanding the fact that he or she had no knowledge of it.

Unless the parties have agreed to the contrary, a term is implied provided the elements of the second limb above are established. One of the requirements is that the term has sufficient notoriety. If this is satisfied, parties to the contract are presumed to have contracted on the basis of the term forming part of the contract. It follows that a party to the contract will be bound even if he or she does not have actual knowledge of the custom. Provided the custom is sufficiently

---

209 Ibid.

210 Ibid at 236.

211 Similar sentiments were expressed by McHugh and Gummow JJ of the High Court in *Byrne v Australian Airlines Ltd* (1995) 185 CLR 410 at 440 where they commented: 'The question is always whether the general notoriety of the custom makes it reasonable to assume that the parties contracted with reference to the custom so that it is therefore reasonable to import such a term into the contract. Where there is such an established usage, the Courts are spelling out what both parties know and would, if asked, unhesitatingly agree to be part of the bargain'.

212 (1918) 25 CLR 144.

widespread and well known, the contracting party is regarded as having constructive knowledge of the term. If this were not the case, a person could avoid being bound by the term merely by denying knowledge of the custom.

Impact of parol evidence rule

[8.675] Evidence of custom or usage within a particular trade or profession can be admitted even if the parties have entered into a written agreement. The parol evidence rule will not operate to exclude evidence of the custom or usage. The reason is the same as articulated above in relation to business efficacy. As a term is implied to reflect the presumed intention of the parties, the parties must not have intended the writing to form the entire agreement. They intended to contract on the basis of the implied term also. As such, the parties must not have intended the writing to form the entire agreement.[213]

8.5.4　*Term implied to complete agreement*

[8.680] In Chapter 4, the requirement for parties to reach agreement on all essential aspects of the contract was examined. Without such agreement, the contract will be incomplete and unenforceable. It was further noted, however, that the judiciary attempts to uphold agreements if at all possible—particularly where it is clear from the conduct of the parties that they regard themselves as being bound by the contract. As a means of upholding agreements where not all of the terms have been finalised, in an appropriate case the courts may be prepared to imply a term. In *Hillas & Co Ltd v Arcos Ltd*,[214] for example, the contract contained an option to sell Russian softwood timber but did not specify the quality or price of the timber nor the dates for delivery. The House of Lords was prepared to imply terms in relation to both matters, and in so doing, concluded that the option was neither uncertain nor incomplete. Relevant to its decision was the fact that elsewhere in the contract was reference made to the sale of such timber. Lord Thankerton noted that courts do not make contracts for parties except where it is appropriate to make implications of law, for example, 'the implication of what is just and reasonable to be ascertained by the court as matter of machinery where the contractual intention is clear but the contract is silent on some detail'.[215]

Impact of parol evidence rule

[8.685] The cases in which terms will be implied on this basis are comparatively rare. There is little guidance therefore on the extent to which the parol evidence rule will prevent admissibility of evidence to enable the court to imply a term necessary to complete an agreement. It is submitted that the rules governing admissibility of evidence to imply a term on these grounds will be the same as for implication for the purpose of business efficacy.[216]

213　*Hutton v Warren* (1836) 150 ER 517 at 521; *Royal Insurance Australia Ltd v Government Insurance Office of New South Wales* [1994] 1 VR 123 at 133.
214　(1932) 147 LT 503.
215　Ibid at 514. See [4.230]–[4.235].
216　See [8.555]–[8.560]. Therefore, the courts can be appraised of the factual matrix surrounding contract formation as well as the express terms of the contract agreed upon by the parties.

8.5.5   Term implied as a legal incident of a particular class of contract

[8.690] In particular classes of contracts the courts have imposed obligations on one or both parties even though such obligations were not expressly agreed upon by the parties. Here, the terms are implied by the court not to reflect the presumed intention of the parties, but because the courts have taken the view, on policy grounds, that such terms *should* be implied.[217] The following illustrates one such category of contract in which a term is implied on this basis.

Example: Liverpool City Council v Irwin[218]

The Liverpool City Council rented out a 15-storey tower block for residential purposes. The tenants withheld rent to protest the condition of the building. The Council brought action for possession and the tenants counter-claimed on the basis that the Council was in breach of its duty to maintain the common parts of the building including lifts, staircases, rubbish chutes and passages.

The House of Lords held that the Council was in breach of such a duty. In all contracts for tenancy, the landlord is under an obligation to ensure that the tenants were able to use these areas or facilities.

[8.695] In cases of this kind, the implication is not made because, on the facts of the case, the particular contract (here, a tenancy agreement) needed such a term to be implied. To this extent, it is different from a term being implied to give business efficacy to the transaction. The implication here is based on general considerations that apply to all contracts of that kind. A term implied on these grounds is commonly referred to as one implied 'as a matter of law' for contracts of that kind.

[8.700] Although terms implied to give business efficacy to transactions are implied on different grounds from terms implied as a matter of law in a particular class of contract, there can be some overlap between these categories. The Federal Court decision of *Hughes Aircraft Systems International v Airservices Australia*[219] demonstrates this overlap.[220] The facts of this case were referred to in an earlier chapter.[221] The case involved a request for tenders to provide services for a Commonwealth Authority. One of the issues before the Court was whether there should be a term implied into a contract between the Authority and a prospective tenderer that the Authority would act fairly in the process of requesting and evaluating tenders. Finn J, after a detailed review of

---

217   *Australis Media Holdings Pty Ltd v Telstra Corporation Ltd* (1998) 43 NSWLR 104 at 123; *Renard Constructions (ME) Pty Ltd v Minister for Public Works* (1992) 26 NSWLR 234 at 261–262; *Codelfa Construction Pty Ltd v State Rail Authority of New South Wales* (1982) 149 CLR 337 at 345–346; *Liverpool City Council v Irwin* [1977] AC 239 at 254–255; *Shell UK Ltd v Lostock Garage Ltd* [1977] 1 All ER 481 at 487; *Con-Stan Industries of Australia Pty Ltd v Norwich Winterthur Insurance (Australia) Ltd* (1985) 160 CLR 226 at 237.
218   [1977] AC 239.
219   (1996) 146 ALR 1.
220   See also *Renard Constructions (ME) Pty Ltd v Minister for Public Works* (1992) 26 NSWLR 234 at 260.
221   See [3.185].

the law, was prepared to imply such a term on the basis of business efficacy as well as a legal incident of this kind of contract.[222]

[8.705] The example of terms being implied into tenancy agreements has already been given. Further illustrations of categories of contract where terms are implied as a legal incident of the contract are:

1 *Contracts for the provision of goods and services:* the common law provides a term that goods be reasonably fit for the purpose for which they were supplied and services fit for the purpose for which they were rendered.[223]

2 *Contracts for the provision of professional services*: the common law will imply a term that reasonable care be taken by the professional in providing such services.[224]

3 *Contracts of employment:* the common law recognises a number of implied terms that are incidents of the contract of employment. One example is the employer's duty to provide a safe place of work.[225] Another is the implied duty to advise employees of their rights where such rights are exercisable only within a particular period.[226]

4 *Building contracts:* in a contract to build a house, the common law implies a term that the completed house will be reasonably fit for habitation, and that work carried out will be done in a proper and workmanlike fashion.[227]

5 *Franchise agreements:* it has been suggested recently by the Supreme Court of Victoria that a term of good faith and fair dealing is a legal incident of a franchising agreement.[228] According to the Court, this term 'obliges each party to exercise the powers conferred upon it by the agreement in good faith and reasonably, and not capriciously or for some extraneous purpose'.

[8.710] The categories of contract to which legal incidents will be attached in this way are not closed. Even if a court has not implied a term in a particular kind of contract before, it is open for the court to consider whether such implication should be made.[229] While there has been some controversy about the test to be used for the implication of a term as a matter of law, the accepted test appears to be that of neces-

---

222 His Honour also considered that the term could be implied in law on the basis of a duty of good faith and fair dealing. See [8.750]–[8.790].

223 *Samuels v Davis* [1943] 1KB 526; *Derbyshire Building Co Pty Ltd v Becker* (1961) 107 CLR 633.

224 *Greaves & Co (Contractors) Ltd v Baynham* [1975] 1 WLR 1095 at 1100; *Clark v Kirby-Smith* [1964] 2 All ER 835.

225 *McLean v Tedman* (1984) 155 CLR 306 at 312; *Hamilton v Nuroof (WA) Pty Ltd* (1956) 96 CLR 18.

226 *Scally v Southern Health and Social Services Board* [1992] 1 AC 294.

227 *Perry v Sharon Developments Co Ltd* [1937] 4 All ER 390; *Miller Construction Ltd v Olsen* [1973] 1 NZLR 265.

228 *Far Horizons v McDonald's Australia Ltd* [2000] VSC 310 (18 August 2000). For a recent comment on the developments in the common law concerning implication of terms and the unconscionability provisions of the *Trade Practices Act* 1974 (Cth) insofar as they apply to franchising agreements, see S Corones, 'Implied good faith and unconscionability in franchises: moving towards relational contract theory' (2000) 28 *Australian Business Law Review* 462.

229 See, for example, *Esso Australia Resources Ltd v Plowman (Minister for Energy and Minerals)* (1995) 128 ALR 391 where the High Court considered whether a duty of confidentiality should be implied as a matter of law into agreements to arbitrate. See also the recent recognition by the Supreme Court of Victoria in *Far Horizons Pty Ltd v McDonald's Australia Ltd* [2000] VSC 310 (18 August 2000) of the duty of good faith and fair dealing to be implied as a legal incident of a franchise agreement.

sity.[230] There is less certainty about how a court determines whether it is necessary to imply a term in a particular class of contract. On a narrow interpretation, it is necessary to imply a term only if the contract would be rendered nugatory, worthless or be seriously undermined without it being implied.[231] The more liberal approach is to take into account general policy considerations in determining whether such a term can be or should be regarded as a necessary incident of contracts of that kind. The requirement for implication—that the absence of the term would render the contract nugatory or worthless or would seriously undermine the contract—may be difficult to demonstrate. Further, such a strict interpretation seems contrary to the notion that terms of this kind be implied into particular classes of contract to reflect general policy considerations.[232]

[8.715] These conflicting approaches were referred to by Finn J in *Hughes Aircraft Systems International v Airservices Australia*.[233] His Honour suggested that a narrow construction of the necessity test may not adequately explain all situations where terms are imposed on this basis. In some cases, the implication of a term has been based on considerations of public policy rather than on the narrow construction of the necessity test.[234] The more liberal test for implying terms on this ground was also adopted by Priestley JA in *Renard Constructions (ME) Pty Ltd v Minister for Public Works*.[235] His Honour expressed the view that the term 'necessary incidents' of the type of contract did not mean that the term was required for the effective carrying out of the contract.[236] Rather, the test should be whether, in light of contemporary thinking, it would be appropriate or reasonable to imply a term of the kind. On this basis, his Honour considered that a term should be implied into construction contracts generally that, in exercising a discretion to take action under the contract, the discretion should be exercised reasonably.

[8.720] Although terms of this kind are implied on grounds of necessity—however that may be defined—the parties may expressly agree to the contrary.[237] For example, if someone hires a chattel such as an electric saw to another, the owner may expressly exclude any warranty that the chattel is reasonably fit for the purpose.[238]

---

230 *Lister v Romford Ice and Cold Storage Co Ltd* [1957] AC 555; *Liverpool City Council v Irwin* [1977] AC 239; *Scally v Southern Health and Social Services Board* [1992] 1 AC 294; *Byrne v Australian Airlines Ltd* (1995) 185 CLR 410; *Hughes Aircraft Systems International v Airservices Australia* (1997) 146 ALR 1.

231 See, for example, comments of McHugh and Gummow JJ in *Byrne v Australia Airlines Ltd* (1995) 185 CLR 410 at 450.

232 See note 218.

233 (1997) 146 ALR 1.

234 Ibid at 39, citing *Simonous Vischer & Co v Holt & Thompson* [1979] 2 NSWLR 322 at 348; *Tournier v National Provincial and Union Bank of England* [1924] 1 KB 461 at 473; *Perry-Jones v Law Society* [1969] 1 Ch 1 at 7–8; *Lister v Romford Ice and Cold Storage Ltd* [1957] AC 555 at 576.

235 (1992) 26 NSWLR 234.

236 Ibid at 261.

237 *Byrne v Australian Airlines Ltd* (1995) 185 CLR 410 at 449; *Gemmell Power Farming Co Ltd v Nies* (1935) 35 SR (NSW) 469.

238 *Derbyshire Building Co Pty Ltd v Becker* (1961) 107 CLR 633 at 645.

Impact of parol evidence rule

[8.725] As a final point, it should be mentioned that the parol evidence rule is not relevant to the implication of terms under this head. Implication is based on principles of necessity, not on the presumed intention of the parties, which may only be discernible by considering discussions between the parties or other circumstances surrounding entry into the contract.

8.5.6 *General duty of co-operation*

[8.730] It is an implied term of all contracts that each party agrees to do all things necessary to enable the other party to have the benefit of the contract.[239] This term is generally referred to as the duty of co-operation. It is a term implied as a matter of law in the sense that it is implied into contracts generally, and not because the facts of a particular case warrant the implication. Notwithstanding that courts have implied such a term for reasons of policy, it is open for the parties to agree that they are not under a duty to co-operate.[240]

[8.735] The operation of the 'general rule' as it was originally referred to in *Butt v McDonald*[241] is illustrated by the decision itself. The parties contracted to sell real property but the seller was not the owner of that property. The buyer was successful in an action against the seller for breach of an implied warranty that the buyer was to receive title to the property. The Queensland Supreme Court held that the warranty was implied by applying the general rule that each party to a contract agrees to do all such things as are necessary to enable the other party to have the benefit of the contract.[242]

[8.740] The notion that a duty of co-operation can be implied into contracts generally has been applied and endorsed on many occasions in Australia.[243] It is difficult to argue against a general proposition that contracting parties should co-operate so that both may enjoy the benefit of the contract. However, it is sometimes difficult to determine the extent of the obligation imposed by this duty. At some point, the duty to ensure that the other party obtains the benefit from the contract may conflict with action that will maximise the benefits of the first party. Mason J explored this issue in the High Court case of *Secured Income Real Estate (Australia) Ltd v St Martins Investments Pty Ltd*.[244] His Honour drew a distinction between doing acts that are necessary to perform obligations fundamental to the contract, and doing acts that will entitle the other party to a benefit under the contract, but are not essential to the performance of that

---

239   *Butt v McDonald* (1896) 7 QLJ 68 at 70–71.

240   *Butt v McDonald* (1896) 7 QLJ 68 at 71; *Secured Income Real Estate (Australia) Ltd v St Martins Investments Pty Ltd* (1979) 144 CLR 596 at 607–608.

241   (1896) 7 QLJ 68.

242   For another example of a duty of co-operation being implied into a contract, see *Adelaide Petroleum NL v Poseidon Ltd* (1990) 98 ALR 431, a case involving the take over of a company. A statement by a director that it would not assist in an underwriting arrangement contemplated by the Heads of Agreement entered into between the companies was held to be a breach of the implied duty to co-operate.

243   *Secured Income Real Estate (Australia) Ltd v St Martins Investments Pty Ltd* (1979) 144 CLR 596 at 607; *Hospital Products Ltd v United States Surgical Corporation* (1984) 156 CLR 41 at 137–138; *Adelaide Petroleum NL v Poseidon Ltd* (1990) 98 ALR 431 at 535; *Himbleton Pty Ltd v Kumagai (NSW) Pty Ltd* (1991) 29 NSWLR 44 at 59–60; *RDJ International Pty Ltd v Preformed Line Products (Australia) Pty Ltd* (1996) 39 NSWLR 417 at 420–421.

244   (1979) 144 CLR 596.

party's obligations under the contract, or fundamental to the contract itself.[245] This case provides an example of an obligation falling into the second category, thereby falling outside the scope of the duty to co-operate.

Example: Secured Income Real Estate (Australia) Ltd v St Martins Investments Pty Ltd[246]

The sellers sold a large office building to the buyers. The balance purchase price of $170 000 was due to be paid by the buyer approximately five months after settlement date. The contract provided for this amount to be reduced by a formula if the rental from the premises had not reached a specified figure. It looked as if the rental would not reach the specified figure. The seller therefore offered to rent as much of the building as was necessary to increase rental to the figure so that the balance purchase price had to be paid by the buyer. The buyer did not agree to lease the premises to the seller. One of the issues before the Court was whether there was an implied obligation arising out of the contract of sale to lease the premises to the seller.

The High Court held that the buyer was not in breach of its duty to co-operate by not granting the lease requested by the sellers. The Court was prepared to imply an obligation on the buyer to do all things reasonably necessary to enable leases to be granted. It was the common intention of the parties that the buyer was not entitled to capriciously or arbitrarily refuse to grant a lease to the seller. On the facts of that case, however, the Court held that the buyer was justified in not granting the lease sought, because it had reasonable doubts concerning the ability of the seller to pay the rent promptly.[247]

[8.745] The duty to co-operate and the point at which that duty does not require specific conduct by contracting parties was considered more recently by Young J of the New South Wales Supreme Court in *RDJ International Pty Ltd v Preformed Line Products (Australia) Pty Ltd*.[248] His Honour noted that the duty as developed in Australia does not go so far as to require a party 'to interrupt his or her own activities merely to help the other if he or she sees the other getting into difficulties'.[249] By the same token, Young J recognised that the law requires certain action in some circumstances to bring about 'the substantial requirement of the contract'.[250] In determining what the substantial requirement of the contract is, the court must seek to establish the common intention of the parties. This is achieved by reference to the terms of the contract itself and the substance of the contract. Once the intention of the parties in entering the contract is established, the extent to which the duty of co-operation will require action by the parties can be assessed. The case before the Court involved the sale of a business. The purchase price was $300 000 together with payment to the seller of roy-

245 Ibid at 607.
246 (1979) 144 CLR 596.
247 See also *Himbleton Pty Ltd v Kumagai (NSW) Pty Ltd* (1991) 29 NSWLR 44 where the New South Wales Supreme Court held that the duty to co-operate did not extend to the prospective buyer doing what was requested of the seller to ensure that the buyer exercised the option to buy property.
248 (1996) 39 NSWLR 417.
249 Ibid at 421.
250 Ibid.

alties equivalent to five per cent of the amount of revenue received from sales of the manufactured product for three years. Due to the poor performance of the business, the purchaser stopped manufacturing the product after eighteen months. The Supreme Court held that by ceasing manufacture, the buyer was in breach of an implied duty not to do anything voluntarily that would make it materially more difficult for the seller to receive the royalty stream.[251] Relevant to determining whether such a duty formed part of the buyer's duty to co-operate was the intention of the parties in entering the contract.

8.5.7   Implication of duties of good faith, fair dealing and reasonableness

[8.750] Notions of good faith, fair dealing, and reasonableness are becoming increasingly relevant in a variety of different legal contexts, not all of them relating to issues of contract law.[252] In the arena of contract law, the trend appears to be to an increasing recognition of such concepts in many aspects of the contracting process. The following are just a few examples:

- the requirement of 'reasonableness' in implying a term based on business efficacy;[253]
- the preparedness of courts to imply a reasonable price where the contract is silent;[254]
- statutory implication of a reasonable price in a contract for the sale of goods;[255]
- implication of a term that is 'just and reasonable' in limited circumstances to complete an agreement;[256]
- suggestion that there may be a duty on a prospective buyer to act 'reasonably' as well as honestly in determining whether finance is satisfactory in a contract to purchase;[257]
- relevance of 'reasonableness' where terms are implied as a legal incident of a contract for the provision of goods and services or a contract for the provision of professional services.[258]

[8.755] The concepts of reasonableness and the like have also been relevant in relation to required standards of contractual performance in a more general way. There have been cases where courts have implied a duty to perform contractual obligations reasonably in order to provide business efficacy to the transaction,[259] or because the duty to perform in that way is a legal incident of that category of contract.[260] However, it is quite a different proposition to suggest that for all contracts

---

251   Compare comments of Barwick CJ in *Ansett Transport Industries (Operations) Pty Ltd v The Commonwealth of Australia* (1977) 139 CLR 54 at 61 that a term should be implied 'to maintain and not to destroy or relevantly alter the basis upon which the parties have contracted'.
252   In *Gibson v Parkes District Hospital* (1991) 26 NSWLR 9, for example, the duty to act in good faith was held by the New South Wales Supreme Court to apply to the obligation of a workers' compensation insurer and employer in processing a worker's compensation claim.
253   See [8.505].
254   See [4.245].
255   See [4.250].
256   See [8.680].
257   See [4.295]–[4.305].
258   See [8.705].
259   *Renard Constructions (ME) Pty Ltd v Minister for Public Works* (1992) 26 NSWLR 234.
260   *Hughes Aircraft Systems International v Airservices Australia* (1997) 146 ALR 1.

entered into there will be implied a duty of fair dealing by the parties, or that they will perform their contractual obligations in good faith or reasonably.[261] Whether the common law has evolved to a stage where parties are required to act in this way to satisfy an implied duty is an issue not entirely settled in Australia. It certainly is a topic that has attracted much speculation (both in Australia and elsewhere) over the past decade.[262]

[8.760] The proposition that notions of good faith, fair dealing and reasonableness may be relevant to contractual performance as a general proposition was first suggested by Priestly JA in *Renard Constructions (ME) Pty Ltd v Minister for Public Works*.[263] The parties had entered into a construction contract under which the principal was given certain powers upon the contractor's default. On default, the principal could call upon the contractor to show cause why the principal should not exercise its powers under the contract (for example, to exclude the contractor from the site and take over the work to be completed). One of the issues before the New South Wales Court of Appeal was whether there was a duty implied on the principal in exercising its powers under the construction contract. In a detailed and considered judgment, Priestley JA turned his mind to possible grounds upon which a term could be implied into the construction contract that would impact on the way in which the principal exercised its discretion. First, his Honour considered that it was appropriate, to give business efficacy to the transaction, to imply a term that the principal act reasonably in exercising a discretion under the contract. Secondly, he noted that construction contracts of this kind were standard contracts and, as such, there was no reason why such a term would not be implied as a matter of law in all contracts of that type. A requirement to exercise the relevant discretions reasonably therefore was implied as a legal incident of all such construction contracts. Thirdly, his Honour suggested that even if it were not possible to categorise construction contracts as a class of contracts, an obligation of reasonableness may be implied as a matter of law into the contract before the court. This implication was not based on any of the recognised grounds. His Honour, relying on an extract from an earlier High Court judgment, indicated that the basis of the implication was a combination of the particular facts of the case as well as an implication of

---

261 While distinctions have been drawn between the terms 'good faith', 'fair dealing' and 'reasonableness' (see, for example, Priestley JA in *Renard Constructions (ME) Pty Ltd v Minister for Public Works* (1992) 26 NSWLR 234), on many occasions they are used in such a way as to indicate the same kind of standard. The use of the terminology in the case law reflects a great deal of overlap with these terms: see, for example, *Hughes Aircraft Systems International v Airservices Australia* (1997) 146 ALR 1, *Service Station Association Ltd v Berg Bennett & Associates Pty Ltd* (1993) 117 ALR 393 and *GSA Group Pty Ltd v Siebe Plc* (1993) 30 NSWLR 573.

262 HK Lucke, 'Good Faith and Contractual Performance' in PD Finn (ed), *Essays on Contract*, Law Book Co, Sydney, 1987; E Moloney, 'Contracts and the Concept of Good Faith' (1993) 23 ACLN 32; TRH Cole, 'The Concept of Reasonableness in Construction Contracts' (1994) 10 BCL 7; TRH Cole, 'Law: All in Good Faith' (1994) 10 BCL 18; Lord Justice Staughton, 'Good Faith and Fairness in Commercial Contract Law' (1994) 7 *Journal of Contract Law* 193; IB Stewart, 'Good Faith in Contractual Performance and in Negotiation' (1998) 72 ALJ 370; A Phang, 'Tenders Implied Terms and Fairness in the Law of Contract' (1998) 13 *Journal of Contract Law* 126; JM Paterson, 'Duty of Good Faith: Does it have a place in contract law?' (2000) 48 *Law Institute Journal* 48; JF O'Connor, *Good Faith in English Law*, Dartmouth, 1990, Chapter 8; A Mason, 'Contract, Good Faith and Equitable Standards in Fair Dealing' (2000) 116 *Law Quarterly Review* 66; EA Farnsworth, 'Good Faith and Contract Performance' in J Beatson and D Friedman (eds), *Good Faith and Fault in Contract Law*, Clarendon Press, Oxford, 1995.

263 (1992) 26 NSWLR 234.

law.[264] As Priestley JA held that the duty to perform reasonably had been implied on more established grounds, however, it was unnecessary to elaborate further.

The other Justices of the Court of Appeal took different approaches. Handley JA agreed that the principal had to act reasonably in exercising the discretion conferred by the contract, but not for the reasons suggested by Priestley JA. Instead, such a duty arose as a matter of construction of the contract. Meagher JA, on the other hand, did not accept that there was any basis upon which an obligation to act reasonably could be imposed on the contractor.

[8.765] The notion that an obligation to exercise a discretion reasonably can be implied, as a matter of law, as a legal incident of contracts of that kind (or as a result of a combination of an ad hoc implication and an implication as a matter of law) does, of itself, represent a development in the law of implied terms. However, as noted earlier in this chapter,[265] the classes of contracts in which a term can be implied as a legal incident of the contract are not closed. It is always open for the judiciary to add to these categories, as did Priestley JA in relation to standard form construction contracts, so that in future cases a term will be implied into contracts of that kind. However, Priestley JA pushed the boundaries even further. As a separate and distinct issue unrelated to construction contracts, his Honour considered whether a duty that parties act in good faith in carrying out contractual obligations should be implied into contracts generally. The suggestion was that the time may be ripe for the imposition 'in all contracts of a duty upon the parties of good faith and fair dealing in its performance'.[266] His Honour considered that the recognition of such a duty is in line with existing community standards. While the duty to act in good faith was not the basis of his decision, he did deal with the concept in considerable detail, referring to the development of the doctrine particularly in the United States and Canada.

[8.770] There has been a huge body of academic writing both in Australia and elsewhere on the infusion of good faith obligations into the law governing the performance of contracts,[267] and an ever-increasing number of cases which, to a greater or lesser extent, have considered such principles. In *Presmist Pty Ltd v Turner Corporation Pty Ltd*[268] and *Hughes Bros Pty Ltd v Trustees of the Roman Catholic Church for the Archdiocese of Sydney*,[269] the New South Wales Supreme Court followed *Renard's case* in finding that a principal's discretion conferred by a construction contract had to be exercised reasonably. More recently, in *Alcatel Australia Ltd v Scarcella*,[270] the New South Wales Court of Appeal considered whether parties to a contract of lease were under an obligation to act in good faith in performing obligations and exercising rights under the lease. After a thorough review of the Australian and American decisions and writings in the area, the Court concluded that there was no reason why a duty to act in good faith should not be implied as part of the lease. Again, in *Australian Co-operative Foods Ltd v Norco Co-operative*

---

264 Ibid at 262–263 citing extracts of the judgment of Dixon J in *Gullett v Gardner*, a case partly reported in (1948) 22 ALJ 151.
265 See [8.710].
266 Ibid at 268.
267 See note [262].
268 (1992) 30 NSWLR 478.
269 (1993) 31 NSWLR 91.
270 (1998) 44 NSWLR 349.

Ltd[271] Bryson J recognised the 'openness' of the New South Wales Court of Appeal to the 'implication of a duty of good faith both in performing obligations and in exercising rights'.[272] Finally, Byrne J and the Victorian Supreme Court recently noted the 'considerable body of authority in this country' that has followed *Renard's case* and as such did not consider himself at liberty to depart from it.[273]

[8.775] It has been interesting to observe the response of the Federal Court to the suggestion that, as a general proposition, it may be appropriate to impose a duty to act in good faith in performing contractual obligations. When the matter came before the Federal Court in *Service Station Association Ltd v Berg Bennett & Associates Pty Ltd*,[274] shortly after *Renard's case*, Gummow J was not prepared to imply a new term, as a matter of law, that affected the quality of contractual performance.[275] In a later decision of the same Court, *Hughes Aircraft Systems International v Airservices Australia*,[276] Finn J also considered whether to imply a term based on the duty to act in good faith and fair dealing. While indicating that his own view accorded more closely with that expressed by Priestley JA in *Renard's case* than with that of Gummow J in the earlier Federal Court decision, his Honour was not required to make a final determination on the issue. Interestingly, in a more recent decision of the same Court, there appeared to be an assumption based on *Hughes Aircraft Systems International v Airservices Australia*[277] (and other decisions) that the imposition of a general duty of good faith and fair dealing now formed part of the contractual landscape and should be implied into the dealership agreement before the court.[278]

[8.780] The increasing trend towards the implication of a duty of good faith or fair dealing or to act reasonably in performing contractual obligations cannot be denied. Despite the earlier reluctance in some quarters of the New South Wales judiciary, the case law indicates a general acceptance of an implied duty to act in good faith in contractual performance in that jurisdiction. Even in the Federal Court, Finkelstein J ventured that 'in appropriate contracts, perhaps even in all commercial contracts, such a term will ordinarily be implied ... as a legal incident of the relationship'.[279] This trend is also evidenced by the extent to which the topic continues to be explored both in the case law and in academic writings, and the increased reliance of the Australian

---

271 (1999) 46 NSWLR 267.
272 Ibid at 282. His Honour did express the view (at 282), however, that 'it cannot be said that a general obligation of good faith in the execution of contracts has been established'.
273 *Far Horizons Pty Ltd v McDonald's Australia Ltd* [2000] VSC 310 (18 August 2000). See also the decision of the New Zealand Court of Appeal in *Bigola Enterprises Ltd v Lambton Quay Books Ltd* [2000] NZCA 113 (6 July 2000) which, when applying New South Wales law, appeared to accept that a duty of good faith in performing express contractual obligations could be implied in a franchise agreement. (However, this duty was not sufficient to impose an obligation of confidentiality that prevented the franchisee from disclosing information about financial details of the franchisee's business to another party.)
274 (1993) 117 ALR 393.
275 Ibid at 406. In a later case of *Dorrough v Bank of Melbourne* (unreported, 27 September 1995), Cooper J considered that in the Federal Court jurisdiction there was no general principle by which a duty of good faith is implied in every contract.
276 (1997) 146 ALR 1. For a consideration of this decision, see A Phang, 'Tenders, Implied Terms and Fairness in the Law of Contract' (1998) 13 *Journal of Contract Law* 126.
277 (1997) 146 ALR 1.
278 *Garry Rogers Motors (Aust) Pty Ltd v Subaru (Aust) Pty Ltd* (1999) ATPR 41-703.
279 (1999) ATPR 41-703 at 43,014. In the recent decision of the Victorian Supreme Court of *Far Horizons Pty Ltd v McDonald's Australia Ltd* [2000] VSC 310 (18 August 2000), Byrne J regarded a term of good faith and fair dealing as a legal incident of a franchising contract.

judiciary upon the American experience.[280] As this duty becomes increasingly accepted as forming part of the common law of contracts in Australia, further attention will inevitably be directed to what behaviour can properly be encompassed within the concepts.[281] Of course, defining the parameters of the obligation of good faith could impact directly on the outcome of the case. In a recent decision of the Victorian Supreme Court, for example, it was conceded that a term of good faith and fair dealing is implied in all franchise agreements.[282] This required each party to exercise the powers conferred by such contract in good faith and reasonably, and not capriciously or for some extraneous purpose. Notwithstanding the imposition of such duty, however, McDonald's was held not to be in breach of that duty by establishing a store in the vicinity of another franchisee even although such conduct would have an adverse financial impact on the other franchisee. Further, the duty did not prevent McDonald's from using confidential financial information provided by the franchisee to assist in making a determination to establish a store in direct competition with the franchisee. Perhaps a more vigorous interpretation of what might be encompassed by a duty to act in good faith may have resulted in a different outcome.

[8.785] In the seminal decision of *Renard Construction (ME) Pty Ltd v Minister for Public Works*[283] it was suggested that imposing on parties to a contract a duty of good faith and fair dealing would be reflective of community expectations of contractual behaviour. To this extent, the duty is imposed in the interests of justice and regardless of the intention of the parties. Given the basis for implying this duty, it would perhaps be surprising if parties were permitted to contract out of the duty. To allow them to do so would seem to defeat the reason for implying the term in the first place—to reflect community expectations. Nevertheless, there are some indications that the parties may be able to contract out of such a duty. The first draws an analogy with another ground for implying a term for reasons of public policy. As we have seen, terms that are implied as a legal incident of a particular category of contract can be expressly negatived notwithstanding that the term would otherwise be implied largely on policy grounds. If terms of this kind can be contracted out of, it could be argued that the same should apply to a duty to act in good faith. Secondly, there is a suggestion by the New South Wales Supreme Court that the conduct of the parties may indicate an intention not to carry out contractual performance in

---

280 See, for example, the review in *Renard Construction (ME) Pty Ltd v Minister for Public Works* (1992) 26 NSWLR 234, *GSA Group Pty Ltd v Siebe Plc* (1993) 30 NSWLR 573, *Service Station Association Ltd v Berg Bennett & Associations Pty Ltd* (1993) 117 ALR 393 and *Hughes Aircraft Systems International v Airservices Australia* (1997) 146 ALR 1.

281 Although Priestley JA made a number of observations about the nature of the obligation to act in good faith, in a particular case, it may be difficult to delineate obligations which flow from the duty to act in good faith and how they differ, if at all, from obligations arising out of a duty to act reasonably. There has already been considerable academic writing on the topic. See, for example, ER Good, 'The Concept of "Good Faith" in English Law', paper delivered at the *Centro Di Studi E Ricerche Di Diritto Comparata E Straniero*, Rome, page 3; SJ Burton, 'Good Faith Performance of a Contract within Article 2 of the Uniform Commercial Code' (1981) 67 *Iowa Law Review* 1; TRH Cole, 'Law — All in Good Faith' (1994) 10 BCL 18; LJ Priestley, 'Contract: The Burgeoning Maelstrom' (1987) 6 *Journal of Contract Law* 15. More recently, Einstein J of the New South Wales Supreme Court in *Aiton v Transfield* [1997] NSWSC 996 (1 October 1999) undertook a comprehensive review of the meaning of the term.

282 *Far Horizons Pty Ltd v McDonald's Australia Ltd* [2000] VSC 310 (18 August 2000).

283 (1992) 26 NSWLR 234 at 268.

good faith.[284] If it is possible to negate such a duty by conduct, it follows that it could be negated by an express term to that effect, or by an express term that is inconsistent with such an implied duty.[285]

The doctrine of good faith in performance of contractual obligations is still evolving in Australia. No definitive statements can be made about those contracts in which a duty of good faith will be implied and further direction is needed to delineate the ambit of the duty with more precision. Further guidance is also needed on the ability of parties to contract out of the implied duty.

Impact of parol evidence rule

[8.790] As for duties implied as a legal incident to a particular class of contract and the general duty of co-operation, duties of good faith, fair dealing and reasonableness are imposed to reflect community standards. Their implication is unaffected by the operation of the parol evidence rule.

8.5.8 *Term implied by statute*

[8.795] It has been seen that there is scope within the common law for terms to be implied in contracts to reflect the changing expectations of society. The obligation imposed on a principal to act reasonably (and possibly also in good faith) in exercising discretion under a construction contract is an example.[286] Enactment of legislation is another way that obligations or standards of conduct can be imposed upon contracting parties. Legislation regulates conduct or standards in many different kinds of contracts: contracts providing consumer credit,[287] contracts for the sale of goods and services,[288] contracts of hire purchase,[289] and contracts of insurance,[290] to name just a few. Some statues allow parties to contract out of the statutory provisions and others do not. To illustrate the way legislation[291] can impact on contractual obligations, a simple contract for the sale of goods and services is considered below. In addition, reference is made to provisions of the *Trade Practices Act* 1974 (Cth), which impact on contractual performance not only by implying terms into the contract, but by prohibiting certain kinds of conduct.

(a) Contracts for the sale of goods and services

[8.800] Sale of goods legislation exists in all Australian jurisdictions. The statutes regulate aspects of a sale transaction including contract formation (covering such issues as capacity, subject matter, price, and conditions and warranties to be included in the

---

284 *GSA Group Pty Ltd v Sieve PLC* (1993) 30 NSWLR 573 at 580. Similarly, in *Far Horizons Pty Ltd v McDonald's Australia Ltd* [2000] VSC 310 (18 August 2000), the question was raised whether an entire agreement clause was sufficient to exclude an implied duty to act in good faith. On the facts of that case, however, a determination did not have to be made, and the question was left open.

285 *Hurley v McDonald's Australia Ltd* (1999) ASAL 55-037.

286 See [8.760]–[8.765].

287 *Consumer Credit Code* 1994.

288 See [8.800]–[8.810].

289 *Hire Purchase Act* 1959 (Qld); *Hire Purchase Act* 1959 (Vic); *Hire Purchase Act* 1959 (WA); *Hire Purchase Act* 1959 (Tas).

290 *Insurance Contracts Act* 1984 (Cth).

291 Sale of goods legislation in all Australian jurisdictions as well as the *Trade Practices Act* 1974 (Cth).

contract), performance of the contract (including duties of the parties as to delivery and payment), and remedies of the buyer and seller upon breach. Of relevance in the context of this chapter is the implication in the contract of sale of various conditions and warranties, the most important ones being listed below.[292]

- Implied condition that the seller has title to the goods being sold, or will have title at the time property in the goods is to pass.[293]
- Implied warranty that the buyer will have quiet possession of the goods.[294]
- Implied warranty that the goods are free from any charge or encumbrance.[295]
- In a contract for the sale of goods by description, an implied condition that the goods correspond with the description (and if the sale is by sample as well as by description, it is not sufficient that the bulk of the goods corresponds with the sample if the goods do not also correspond with the description).[296]
- Where the buyer (expressly or by implication) makes known to the seller the particular purpose for which the goods are required, so as to show that the buyer relies on the seller's skill or judgment, and the goods are of a description that it is in the course of the seller's business to supply, an implied condition that the goods are reasonably fit for that purpose.[297]
- When goods are bought by description from a seller who deals in goods of that description, an implied condition that the goods are of merchantable quality.[298]
- In a contract for sale by sample, implied conditions that the bulk corresponds with the sample in quality, that the buyer will have a reasonable opportunity of comparing the bulk with the sample, and that the goods are free from any defect, rendering them unmerchantable, which would not be apparent on reasonable examination of the sample.[299]

---

292 For a more detailed examination of the terms implied by *Sale of Goods legislation*, reference should be made to specialist texts in this area.

293 *Sale of Goods Act* 1896 (Qld), s 15(a); *Sale of Goods Act* 1923 (NSW), s 17(1); *Goods Act* 1958 (Vic), s 17(a); *Sale of Goods Act* 1895 (WA), s 12(i); *Sale of Goods Act* 1895 (SA), s 12I; *Sale of Goods Act* 1896 (Tas), s 17(a); *Sale of Goods Act* 1972 (NT), s 17(a); *Sale of Goods Act* 1954 (ACT), s 17(a).

294 *Sale of Goods Act* 1896 (Qld), s 15(b); *Sale of Goods Act* 1923 (NSW), s 17(2); *Goods Act* 1958 (Vic), s 17(b); *Sale of Goods Act* 1895 (WA), s 12(ii); *Sale of Goods Act* 1895 (SA), s 12II; *Sale of Goods Act* 1896 (Tas), s 17(b); *Sale of Goods Act* 1972 (NT), s 17(b); *Sale of Goods Act* 1954 (ACT), s 17(b).

295 *Sale of Goods Act* 1896 (Qld), s 15(c); *Sale of Goods Act* 1923 (NSW), s 17(3); *Goods Act* 1958 (Vic), s 17(c); *Sale of Goods Act* 1895 (WA), s 12(iii); *Sale of Goods Act* 1895 (SA), s 12III; *Sale of Goods Act* 1896 (Tas), s 17(c); *Sale of Goods Act* 1972 (NT), s 17(c); *Sale of Goods Act* 1954 (ACT), s 17(c).

296 *Sale of Goods Act* 1896 (Qld), s 16; *Sale of Goods Act* 1923 (NSW), s 18; *Goods Act* 1958 (Vic), ss 18 and 87; *Sale of Goods Act* 1895 (WA), s 13; *Sale of Goods Act* 1895 (SA), s 13; *Sale of Goods Act* 1896 (Tas), s 18; *Sale of Goods Act* 1972 (NT), s 18; *Sale of Goods Act* 1954 (ACT), s 18.

297 *Sale of Goods Act* 1896 (Qld), s 17(a); *Sale of Goods Act* 1923 (NSW), s 19(1); *Goods Act* 1958 (Vic), s 19(a); *Sale of Goods Act* 1895 (SA), s 14I; *Sale of Goods Act* 1896 (Tas), s 19(a); *Sale of Goods Act* 1972 (NT), s 19(a); *Consumer Affairs and Fair Trading Act* 1990 (NT), s 64(2); *Sale of Goods Act* 1954 (ACT), s 19(2).

298 *Sale of Goods Act* 1896 (Qld), s 17(c); *Sale of Goods Act* 1923 (NSW), s 19(2); *Goods Act* 1958 (Vic), s 19(b); *Sale of Goods Act* 1895 (WA), s 14(ii); *Fair Trading Act* 1987 (WA), s 38(1); *Sale of Goods Act* 1895 (SA), s 14II; *Consumer Transactions Act* 1972 (SA), s 8(4); *Sale of Goods Act* 1896 (Tas), s 19(b); *Sale of Goods Act* 1972 (NT), s 19(b); *Consumer Affairs and Fair Trading Act* 1990 (NT), s 64(1); *Sale of Goods Act* 1954 (ACT), s 19(4).

299 *Sale of Goods Act* 1896 (Qld), s 18; *Sale of Goods Act* 1923 (NSW), s 20; *Goods Act* 1958 (Vic), s 20; *Sale of Goods Act* 1895 (WA), s 15; *Sale of Goods Act* 1895 (SA), s 15; *Sale of Goods Act* 1896 (Tas), s 20; *Sale of Goods Act* 1972 (NT), s 20; *Sale of Goods Act* 1954 (ACT), s 20.

[8.805] In some cases, the parties may contract out of the statutory conditions and warranties that are implied in the contract of sale.[300]

[8.810] The *Trade Practices Act* 1974 (Cth) also regulates aspects of consumer transactions. Part IV Division 2 implies conditions and warranties into consumer transactions that largely equate with those implied by the sale of goods legislation.[301]

However, the following important differences are worthy of note.

First, the sale of goods legislation will apply to all transactions for the sale of goods (provided there is the necessary link with the particular jurisdiction). By contrast, the terms implied by the *Trade Practices Act* 1974 (Cth) will only operate where the supplier is a corporation and the acquirer is a consumer within the statutory definitions;[302] or if the transaction falls within one of the categories of extended application of the legislation (for example, if the transaction occurred as part of the supplier engaging in trade or commerce internationally, interstate or between a state and a territory).[303] Depending on the circumstances of the case, therefore, a transaction for the sale of goods may fall within the ambit of both the sale of goods legislation and the *Trade Practices Act* 1974 (Cth).

Secondly, terms implied by the *Trade Practices Act* 1974 (Cth) are not limited to contracts for the 'sale of goods' but extend to their 'supply'. Supply is defined to include sale, exchange, lease, hire or hire-purchase.[304] Thirdly, the *Trade Practices Act* 1974 (Cth) also implies terms in contracts for the provision of services. Section 74 implies in a contract for supply of services, a warranty that the services will be rendered with due care and skill and that any materials supplied will be reasonably fit for the purpose for which they are supplied. In some cases, a further warranty will be implied that the services and materials supplied in connection with them will be reasonably fit for the purpose for which the services are required—or of such a nature and quality that they might reasonably be expected to achieve the result.[305]

---

300 *Sale of Goods Act* 1896 (Qld), s 56; *Sale of Goods Act* 1923 (NSW), s 57; *Goods Act* 1958 (Vic), s 61; *Sale of Goods Act* 1895 (WA), s 54; *Sale of Goods Act* 1895 (SA), s 54; *Sale of Goods Act* 1896 (Tas), s 59; *Sale of Goods Act* 1972 (NT), s 57; *Sale of Goods Act* 1954 (ACT), s 58. In some jurisdictions, however, legislation prohibits parties to a 'consumer' transaction from excluding these terms: *Sale of Goods Act* 1923 (NSW), s 64; *Goods Act* 1958 (Vic), s 95; *Fair Trading Act* 1987 (WA),Part III; *Consumer Transactions Act* 1972 (SA), s 8; *Consumer Afffairs and and Fair Trading Act* 1990 (NT), Part V Division 2.

301 Section 69 implies undertakings as to title, encumbrances and quiet possession; section 70 implies conditions where there is a supply of goods by description; section 71 implies undertakings as to quality and fitness; section 72 implies conditions where there is a supply by sample. As is the case in many of the other jurisdictions, there are limitations on the extent to which parties can contract out of terms implied. The general proposition is that any term of a contract that purports to exclude, restrict or modify the implied terms is void (s 68). However, where the supply does not relate to goods or services ordinarily acquired for personal, domestic or household use, the supplier may be entitled to limit the extent of a liability for a breach of an implied condition or warranty (s 68A).

302 *Trade Practices Act* 1974 (Cth), ss 4 and 4B respectively.

303 *Trade Practices Act* 1974 (Cth), s 6(2)(c).

304 *Trade Practices Act* 1974 (Cth), s 4.

305 *Trade Practices Act* 1974 (Cth), s 74(2). The provision further sets out those services not falling within the ambit of the provision: s 74(3).

(b) Statutory prohibition of unconscionable conduct

[8.815] The way the common law implies terms into contracts can impact on contractual performance. The duty imposed to act reasonably (and perhaps in good faith) on the principal in exercising a discretion under a construction contract is an example.[306] Statutes can also impact on contractual performance. While the common law and statutes do this by implying terms into a contract, statutes can also affect contractual performance by prohibiting or requiring certain behaviour.[307] A good illustration of this is Part IVA of the *Trade Practices Act* 1974 (Cth), which prohibits 'unconscionable' conduct.[308] Part IVA contains three substantive provisions:

- A corporation is prohibited from engaging in unconscionable conduct in the course of trade or commerce.[309] For the purpose of this provision, unconscionable conduct has the meaning attributed to it by the 'unwritten law, from time to time, of the States and Territories'.

- A corporation is prohibited from engaging in unconscionable conduct in the course of trade or commerce where goods or services are supplied for personal, domestic or household use or consumption.[310] For the purpose of determining whether a corporation has acted in an unconscionable way for this section, the court may have regard to five matters listed in the legislation itself. For the purpose of this provision, therefore, the term 'unconscionable' is unlikely to reflect the common law meaning.

- The third provision targets unconscionable conduct in the course of small business transactions.[311] Unconscionable conduct is prohibited in relation to both the supply and acquisition of goods and services where the amount involved is $1 000 000 or less.[312] In determining the meaning of unconscionable conduct in this context, the court may have regard to the eleven matters listed. These matters are wide in scope; the final provision refers to the 'extent to which the supplier and business consumer acted in good faith'.[313]

[8.820] It has been suggested that the precise scope of these provisions is unclear.[314] The meaning to be attributed to the term 'good faith', and the extent to which that may deny self-interest have been flagged in particular as a potential problem. Never-

---

306 *Renard Constructions (ME) Pty Ltd v Minister for Public Works* (1992) 26 NSWLR 234.
307 For a recent consideration of the way in which both common law (in particular the implied duty to act in good faith) and statute (the unconscionability provisions of the *Trade Practices Act* 1974 (Cth)) can affect responsibilities arising from a franchising agreement, see S Corones, 'Implied good faith and unconscionability in franchises: moving towards relational contract theory' (2000) 28 *Australian Business Law Review* 462.
308 Another example of considerable practical significance is the prohibition of misleading or deceptive conduct: *Trade Practices Act* 1974 (Cth), s 52 and the equivalent provisions in the Fair Trading legislation. These are considered in Chapter 13.
309 *Trade Practices Act* 1974 (Cth), s 51AA. This provision is stated not to apply to conduct that is prohibited by ss 51AB or 51AC.
310 *Trade Practices Act* 1974 (Cth), s 51AB.
311 *Trade Practices Act* 1974 (Cth), s 51AC.
312 *Trade Practices Act* 1974 (Cth), s 51AC(9) and (10).
313 *Trade Practices Act* 1974 (Cth), s 51AC(3)(k).
314 S Corones, 'Does 'Good Faith' in s 51AC of the Trade Practices Act Deny Self-interest?' (1999) 27 *Australian Business Law Review* 414.

theless, the duties imposed by the *Trade Practices Act* 1974 (Cth) illustrate an important phenomenon in contract law, namely the increasing extent to which statute impacts on the ability of parties to agree upon terms and have their contractual performance regulated by those terms and those terms alone.

8.6   International perspective

8.6.1   New Zealand

[8.825] The New Zealand law on the topics examined in this chapter largely reflects the Australia position and, for the most part, requires no further comment. However, the following comparisons are worthy of note.

(a)   Incorporating oral terms

[8.830] Historically, the New Zealand law drew the same distinction between oral statements that merely induced entry into the contract (often referred to as 'mere representations'), and oral statements that constituted a term of the contract. Categorisation was crucial because different remedies flowed from each. The test to determine the nature of the oral statement is the same as that applied in Australia: whether the parties intended the statement to be promissory in nature.[315] Further, the same subsidiary tests are relevant in New Zealand to assist in ascertaining that intention.

[8.835] Since the enactment of the *Contractual Remedies Act* 1979 (NZ), however, the practical consequences that flow from categorisation as a mere representation or contractual term have largely disappeared. Pursuant to section 6, a party will be entitled to damages for a false representation 'in the same manner and to the same extent as if the representation were a term of the contract that has been broken'.[316] Although the practical need for distinguishing between a representation and term has largely been abolished because of this enactment, the New Zealand common law on the nature of a representation and a term, and the test to determine when a statement will be regarded as such remains unaltered.

(b)   Implied terms

[8.840] The common law bases for the implication of a contractual term are substantially the same as exist in Australia. One area in which the jurisdictions differ, however, is the extent to which the implication of an obligation of good faith and fair dealing can be regarded as forming part of the New Zealand common law. In 1992, the High Court in *Livingstone v Roskilly*[317] was not prepared to reject the notion that 'parties to a contract must act in good faith in making and carrying out the contract'.[318] Since that time, however, there has not been an equivalent degree of judi-

---

315   See [8.225].
316   For more detail on the operation of this legislation, see [14.325]–[14.340].
317   [1992] 3 NZLR 230.
318   Ibid at 237 per Thomas J. See also the comments of Master Kennedy-Grant in *Allen v Southland Building Society* (1995) 6 TCLR 638 that it was at least arguable that a term of this kind could be implied.

cial consideration and adoption of the concept as has occurred among the Australian judiciary.[319]

[8.845] Secondly, as in Australia, various statutes imply terms into particular contracts.[320] In relation to contracts for the sale of goods, of particular importance are ss 14–17 of the *Sale of Goods Act* 1908 (NZ), which imply terms concerning title and quality of the goods.

8.6.2 United States

(a) Incorporating oral and written terms
Pre-contractual oral statements

[8.850] In America, whether an oral statement made before entry into the contract forms part of the terms of that contract seems less problematic than is the case in Australia. There are fewer decisions on point, and virtually no coverage of the topic in the major texts. This is because of the significance attached to the final agreement reached between the parties. A substantive rule of law exists where it is found that the parties have formed a contractual intent: an earlier tentative agreement will be rejected in favour of a later expression that is final.[321] This also means that the final agreement supersedes earlier statements made in the course of negotiating that agreement.[322] Because of this substantive rule of law, pre-contractual oral statements made in the course of negotiations are less likely to form part of the final agreement between the parties, and the courts therefore have not been required to formulate tests to ascertain whether the parties intended such statements to have contractual force.

Incorporating written terms

[8.855] As in Australia, the traditional test for determining whether written terms have been incorporated into a contract is that of assent. If the parties can be regarded as having assented to its terms, they will be bound by them. Relevant to this determination is whether the contracting party seeking to escape liability under the written terms has discharged his or her 'duty to read' the document. The traditional approach is to regard a contracting party as having an obligation to read a document that he or she signs, or is handed to him or her (such as a policy document, bank book containing terms, tickets and the like), as well as notices containing terms that are prominently displayed at the time the parties contract. It follows from this obligation to read that a person entering into the contract must be regarded as having assented to the contractual terms. That party is prevented from later claiming that he or she had not read the document or for some other reason was unaware of the content of the terms.

---

319   The existence of a general duty to act in good faith in the course of a franchise agreement was considered by the New Zealand Court of Appeal in *Bigola Enterprises Ltd v Lambton Quay Books Ltd* [2000] NZCA 113 (6 July 2000). However, as the parties had agreed that the law of New South Wales was to govern the contractual obligations, the decision did not directly develop the New Zealand common law in this area.

320   See, for example, *Hire Purchase Act* 1971, *Motor Vehicle Dealers Act* 1975 and *Carriage of Goods Act* 1979. See also the *Fair Trading Act* 1986 (particularly ss 9–15) which relate to conduct that is misleading or deceptive, or likely to mislead or deceive.

321   JD Calamari & JM Perillo, *The Law of Contracts*, 4th edn, West Group, St Paul, Minnesota, p 121.

322   Ibid.

[8.860] Once again, the American law reflects the Australian position by recognising that in some situations, a party cannot be taken to have assented to the terms despite having signed or having been given an opportunity to read the document. A party is unlikely to be bound by written contractual terms in these circumstances:

- the document is not legible;[323]
- terms are not sufficiently drawn to the party's attention;
- there are vitiating factors.

[8.865] In deciding whether terms have been sufficiently drawn to the party's attention, the notion of reasonableness is relevant. Consideration is given to the same kind of factors that are relevant to Australian courts in determining whether the terms on a ticket or notice form part of the contract. Also relevant under this exception is whether the particular document could be regarded as being contractual in nature. If not, the term could not be regarded as having been sufficiently drawn to the other party's attention.

[8.870] Vitiating factors can arise in several ways—there are a number of reasons why a person may not understand the content of a contract. Some stem from the conduct (such as fraud or misrepresentation) of the other party, while some may arise from the party himself or herself not taking sufficient safeguards when entering into the contract (for example, the person being blind and not taking sufficient steps to familiarise himself or herself with the content of the document). In some of these cases, a party may escape liability under the contract.[324]

The above overview of the traditional American approach to incorporation of written terms reveals many similarities to the Australian law. The same cannot be said for the more modern approach taken by many American courts over recent decades, particularly in relation to standard-form contracts. In such cases, the courts have expressed concern that the unequal bargaining positions of the parties result in contracts being entered into where the weaker party has no real opportunity to negotiate the contractual terms. The dominant party presents the weaker party with a standard form contract on a 'take it or leave it basis', the contract often containing unfair and unreasonable terms. When issues of enforceability of such contracts arise, the modern approach of the American courts tends to be to focus less on the outward manifestation of assent (central to the objective approach to contract formation), and more on whether there has been true assent to the contractual terms. Where a standard-form contract is used, the onus shifts to the dominant party to show that the particular terms have been drawn to the attention of the other party and that he or she has consciously agreed to be bound by them. However, even if it can be shown that there has been true assent, the court may choose to strike down the particular term (or the whole contract if that term cannot be severed) if the term is so unfair that it can be regarded as contrary to public policy or unconscionable.

[8.875] Notwithstanding this trend, it cannot be said that the American courts take a consistent approach on this issue. A number of decisions illustrate the courts' preparedness to

---

323 *Baker v Seattle* 79 Wn 2d 198, 484 P2d 405 (1971).
324 For more detail on the extent to which vitiating factors will enable a person to avoid liability under a contract, see Part V.

look at whether there has been true assent to contractual terms and whether, in any event, one or more terms should be struck down for reasons relating to public policy.[325] At this stage, it appears that the liberal approach is generally limited to cases in which the parties use a standard contract containing detailed and onerous provisions.

[8.880] The liberal common law approach is reflected in the Restatement (Second), § 211, which provides as follows:

(1) Except as stated in subsection (3), where a party to an agreement signs or otherwise manifests assent to a writing and has reason to believe that like writings are regularly used to embody terms of agreements of the same type, he adopts the writing as an integrated agreement with respect to the terms included in the writing.

(2) Such a writing is interpreted wherever reasonable as treating alike all those similarly situated, without regard to their knowledge or understanding of the standard terms of the writing.

(3) Where the other party has reason to believe that the party manifesting such assent would not do so if he knew that the writing contained a particular term, the term is not part of the agreement.

[8.885] The Restatement (Second) recognises that parties may choose to contract on the basis of a standard form, and that they will generally be bound by the terms in such a contract (paras (1) and (2)). However, the Restatement contains an important safe-guard not unlike that being developed under the common law. A party is not likely to be regarded as having assented to a term in a standard form contract if the dominant party has reason to believe that the party would not have entered into the contract had he or she been aware of the existence of the term (para (3)). In making a determina-tion on this issue, it is relevant whether a clause of that kind would ordinarily be con-tained in such a contract, whether the terms of the clause are harsh and oppressive, and whether such a term detracts from the operation of terms expressly agreed upon by the parties (and possibly the overall purpose of the contract).

(b) Parol evidence rule

[8.890] In Australia, the parol evidence rule excludes the use of extrinsic evidence to add to, subtract from, or in any manner vary or qualify the language of a written instrument.[326] The United States position is substantially the same, although there are some variations as to its application.[327] In that jurisdiction, the final written agreement is said to be 'integrated'[328]—that is, intended as a final written expression of one or

---

325 See, for example, *Weaver v American Oil Company* 257 Ind 458, 276 NE 2d 144 (1971), *Henningsen v Bloomfield Motors* 32 NJ 358, 161 A 2d 69 (1960) and *Williams v Walker-Thomas Furniture Company* 350 F 2d 445 (DC Cir 1965).

326 See [8.370]–[8.380] above. The interpretation aspect of the rule so far as the United States position is concerned is discussed in [9.435]–[9.440].

327 Restatement Second §§ 214 and 215.

328 The agreement is referred to as being integrated on the basis that it integrates or brings together terms that have been previously agreed or negotiated. The integrated terms may have been agreed upon in writing, for example by way of letters or memoranda.

more terms of the agreement.[329] If the agreement is integrated, the second question is whether the integration is total or partial.

[8.895] A writing that is final and complete of all that the parties intended, is called a total integration. A writing that is final but does not completely express the party's contract is a partial integration.[330] The focus here is on the intention of the parties and thus the length and detail of the agreement and whether the agreement includes a merger clause[331] are factors to take into account.

[8.900] Where the writing represents a total integration, then it cannot be contradicted or supplemented by other terms even if they are consistent with the writing.[332] Having said this, the Restatement (Second) indicates that an agreement is not totally integrated if the consistent additional terms are (a) made for an additional consideration, or (b) if the offered terms might naturally be omitted from the writing.[333] Where the integration is partial, extrinsic material cannot be used to contradict the written agreement, but may be used to supplement it, provided the additional terms are not inconsistent with the written agreement.[334]

[8.905] Under the Restatement (Second), the legal effect of a determination that the agreement is integrated is that evidence of prior or contemporaneous agreements or negotiations is not admissible to contradict a term of the writing. The provisions of the Uniform Commercial Code[335] are similar:

> Terms with respect to which the confirmatory memoranda of the parties agree or which are otherwise set forth in a writing intended by the parties as a final expression of their agreement with respect to such terms as are included therein may not be contradicted by evidence of any prior agreement or of a contemporaneous oral agreement, but may be explained or supplemented.

Under the same provision, the writing may be explained or supplemented: (a) by course of dealing or usage of trade or by course of performance; and (b) by evidence of consistent additional terms *unless the court finds the writing to have been intended also as a complete and exclusive statement of the terms of the agreement.*[336]

[8.910] Finally, it should be noted that the exceptions to the rule (or more correctly the situations where the rule does not come into play) include the exceptions that apply in Australia, such as the later variation of the contract, evidence that the written rectification contract is not yet in force, evidence of a collateral contract, evidence necessary to demonstrate a mistake in the writing.[337]

---

329 Restatement Second § 209.
330 Restatement Second § 210.
331 A merger clause is of the kind that 'this writing represents the full, complete and entire agreement of the parties and is conclusive of every matter and term that forms part of this contract.'
332 *Farmers Co-Op Assn v Garrison*, 248 Ark 948, 454 SW 2 644 (1970); Restatement Second § 216.
333 Restatement Second § 216.
334 JD Calamari & JM Perillo, *The Law of Contracts*, 4th edn, West Group, St Paul, Minnesota, p 122.
335 Article 2-202 of the Uniform Commercial Code.
336 Emphasis added. That is, if there has been a total integration, the provisions of (a) and (b) would not apply.
337 See generally EA Farnsworth, *Contracts*, 3rd edn, Aspen Law & Business, New York, 1999, p 442.

(c) Implied terms

[8.915] As noted earlier in this chapter, some contracts comprise terms that have not been expressly agreed upon by the parties.[338] These omissions are resolved by the courts by implying a term:

> The parties have failed to reach the illusory goal of the 'perfectly contingent contract' ... They have written what is sometimes called an 'incomplete contract'. Courts must resolve such disputes arising from the omission by some process other than that of interpretation.[339]

[8.920] In the United States, cases alleging that a contract contains terms apart from those that have been expressed in written or oral form are referred to as 'omitted cases'. The rules used by the courts to determine the construction of these terms are known as 'default rules' and the terms supplied by the court are known as 'implied terms' or 'constructive terms'. In this area of implied terms, the United States position is similar to the Australian common law. However, there are some differences in approach. First, the increased focus by United States courts on giving effect to the intention of the parties. In addition, there is a more developed application of principles such as good faith than currently exists in Australian contract law.[340]

The basis for implying a term

[8.925] The reason for implying a term is to rectify a void in the agreement between the parties.[341] The general rule therefore, is that where the agreement is clear on the point, a term will not be implied.[342] This is one reason why the rules for implication of terms are called 'default rules'.

[8.930] In deciding whether a term should be implied, the United States courts look first to the actual expectations of the parties, applying a subjective test. This test requires consideration of what the parties themselves would have understood to be the case, rather than an objective test based on reasonableness. However, it is recognised that the parties may be found to have different expectations—in which case the courts apply an objective standard based on whether one party should reasonably have known of the other's expectation.[343] The courts rely on common practice, previous dealings, and habits, as well as the express terms of the agreement,[344] in order to give effect to the parties' actual or presumed intentions. Thus, the more detailed the agreement, the

---

338 See [8.460]–[8.820].

339 EA Farnsworth, *Contracts*, 3rd edn, Aspen Law & Business, New York, 1999, p 494.

340 See [8.750]–[8.790].

341 Sometimes the implication of terms by the court is referred to in the United States as gap-filling. This is where the courts supply a term either because the court thinks the parties would have agreed on the term if it had been brought to their attention or because it is a term which accords with the requirements of justice.

342 In *City of Yonkers v Otis Elevator Co* 844 Of 2nd 42 (2nd Cir 1988) it was noted that the 'court will generally not imply a term in the face of the parties' expressed intent to the contrary.'

343 In *Parev Prods Co v I Rokeach & Sons* 124 Of 2nd 147, 149 (2nd Cir 1941) the court noted: 'What we should seek is therefore that which will most nearly preserve the status created and developed by the parties.'

344 Thus where an express term applies to a particular situation, the courts may consider this when dealing with an analogous situation.

less likely it is that the court will conclude that the case before it is an 'omitted case'. In the language of one court:

> Terms are implied not because they are just or reasonable, but rather for the reason that the parties must have intended them.[345]

If there is no reliable indication of expectations and no objective basis for determining what those expectations may have been, then a court may imply a term on the basis of what justice demands. A court may, for example, justify the term it supplies on the ground that the term prevents one party from being in a position of 'economic servility' and 'completely at the mercy' of the other.[346]

[8.935] The implication of a term is not restricted to unforeseen events. It can also arise where the parties foresee an event but there is no consensus or agreement on how to deal with it. In these cases the courts still apply the default rules.[347]

Examples of implied terms

[8.940] Three examples of implied terms that are common in the United States and which relate to general contractual provisions, are: terms imposing a duty of good faith; terms imposing a duty of best efforts; and terms providing for termination of the agreement. As is the case with implied terms in general, the nature of these terms is to give effect to the subjective intentions of the parties. Except perhaps for 'good faith', they can therefore be expressly negated by agreement.

Duty of good faith

[8.945] The Restatement (Second) § 205 notes:

> Every Contract imposes upon each party a duty of good faith and fair dealing in its performance and its enforcement.[348]

As far as *good faith* is concerned, one writer has noted:

> Courts have often supplied a term requiring both parties to a contract to exercise what is called 'good faith' or sometimes 'good faith and fair dealing'.[349]

Under the provisions of the Uniform Commercial Code, the requirement to act in good faith 'may not be disclaimed by agreement' although the parties may, by agreement, determine the standards by which the performance of that obligation is to be

---

345   *Barco Urban Renewal Corp v Housing Auth* 674 F 2nd 1001, 1007 (3rd Cir 1982). The UNIDROIT Principles of International Commercial contracts, Art 4.8 notes that in filling a gap or implying a term the court should take into account (a) the intention of the parties; (b) the nature and purpose of the contract; (c) good faith and fair dealing; and (d) reasonableness.

346   EA Farnsworth, *Contracts*, 3rd edn, Aspen Law & Business, New York, 1999, p 501.

347   See comment to the Restatement Second § 261: 'Factors such as the practical difficulty of reaching agreement on the myriad of conceivable terms of a complete agreement may excuse a failure to deal with improbable contingencies'. Farnsworth at 499 notes on this point: 'When this is so, the court should recognise that it is faced with an omitted case even though the dispute was foreseeable.'

348   Article 1-203 of the Uniform Commercial Code is in similar terms.

349   EA Farnsworth, *Contracts*, 3rd edn, Aspen Law & Business, New York, 1999, p 504. JD Calamari & JM Perillo, *The Law of Contracts*, 4th edn, West Group, St Paul, Minnesota, 1998, p 408: 'Omitted terms are often supplied by looking through the lens of the covenant of good faith and fair dealing'.

measured—so long as the standards are not manifestly unreasonable. A similar restriction has been imposed on contracts that do not come within the provisions of the Code.[350] In view of the fact that the United States courts put so much emphasis on giving effect to the intention of the parties, it is not surprising that conflict has arisen in reconciling the mandatory character of the duty of good faith with the principle, often repeated by courts, that there is no such duty if it would conflict with an express provision of the contract.[351]

[8.950] The second matter to note in respect of good faith is whether it applies to the terms of an agreement or is all-pervasive (in that it creates rights independent of the language of the agreement). Although there is authority that the Code's provision on good faith does not create 'independent' rights, separate from those created by the provisions of the contract, not all courts have felt so constrained.[352]

Duty of best efforts

[8.955] In relation to the duty of *best efforts* it has been noted that:

> [This term] requires a party to make such efforts as are reasonable in the light of that party's ability and the means at its disposal and of the other party's justifiable expectations. Although the scope of this duty is no better defined than is the scope of the duty of good faith, it is clear that the duty of best efforts is more onerous than that of good faith.[353]

The obligation to use best efforts has been said to create a standard of conduct 'above and beyond the implied obligation of good faith'.[354]

Termination of contract

[8.960] Concerning *termination*, this will arise where, for example, one party seeks to terminate an agreement where the contract is silent on the point; or where a party claims—giving effect to the subjective test for determining terms—that since the contract says nothing about termination, the agreement can be terminated at will. In these cases, the courts have dealt with the matter by implying a term appropriate to the omitted case.[355]

---

350 EA Farnsworth, *Contracts*, 3rd edn, Aspen Law & Business, New York, 1999, p 504.

351 *Riggs National Bank of Washington v Linch* 36 F 3rd 370 (4th Cir 1994) where it was noted that the implied duty of good faith 'cannot be used to override or modify explicit contractual terms.' This can be compared with what the court said in *Carmichael v Adirondack Bottled Gas Corp* 635 A 2nd 1211 (Vt 1993) that the duty of good faith 'is imposed by law and is not a contractual term that the parties are free to bargain in or out as they see fit.'

352 EA Farnsworth, *Contracts*, 3rd edn, Aspen Law & Business, New York, 1999, pp 505–506. See also JD Calamari & JM Perillo, *The Law of Contracts*, 4th edn, West Group, St Paul, Minnesota, 1998, pp 457–460. See also comments to Art 1-203 of the Uniform Commercial Code: 'This section does not support an independent course of action for failure to perform or enforce in good faith'.

353 EA Farnsworth, *Contracts*, 3rd edn, Aspen Law & Business, New York, 1999, Id at p 509.

354 *TSI Holdings v Jenkins* 924 P 2nd 1239 (Kan 1996).

355 EA Farnsworth, *Contracts*, 3rd edn, Aspen Law & Business, New York, 1999, p 511.

Conclusion

[8.965] Australian law has a more rigid categorisation of implied terms, and the courts tend to classify them according to the reasonably well established categories examined in this chapter. In the United States these same issues arise, but in the context of putting a greater focus on the intention of the parties. There is also a much more developed approach in respect of the requirement to act in good faith than currently exists in Australian contract law. It is likely that our jurisdiction will pay increasing regard to the development of the United States principles in this regard.

8.6.3 Japan

[8.970] The principle of freedom of contract in Japan—including freedom of form—means that the parties are free to stipulate the terms of their contracts orally, in writing, or in a combination of oral statements, written contract and other documentation. The absence of a *Statute of Frauds* equivalent in Japan means that written terms are not necessarily privileged over oral terms. The ultimate test of what forms the terms of a contract is the parties' mutual intent.

[8.975] A practical application of this idea is the Japanese courts' treatment of pre-printed contracts. A wide range of these are sold at stationer's shops. They are usually simple agreements designed for use in situations such as employment, house or land leases, or distribution agreements. Even where the pre-printed agreement is detailed and has been sealed (the equivalent of signature), if a dispute arises, parts of the contract may be set aside if one of the parties can show that the form does not evidence the parties' original intent. Where courts look behind printed contracts in this way they treat the terms as *reibun* (or 'model clauses') rather than as evidence of the parties' agreement.[356]

[8.980] Freedom of contract also means that the parties are free to adopt or to reject contract rules set out in the Civil or Commercial Codes. Most of the Codes' contract provisions are optional provisions (*nin'i kitei*), which apply to contracts only to the extent that the parties do not evidence a different intent (Article 91 Civil Code).

[8.985] As discussed in Chapter 4, it is also not uncommon for parties to have tacit (unarticulated) agreement on some terms or for the parties or the court to refer to industry practices in order to identify contract terms after the fact.

[8.990] Other terms may apply to the contract, regardless of the parties' intent. The most important category is the mandatory provisions of the Civil Code (*kyôkô kitei*), for example, those requiring juristic acts (including contracts) to be exercised in accordance with good faith (Article 1(2))[357] and in conformity with public order (Article 90). If terms agreed by the parties breach either of these requirements, the contract may require a curative interpretation (for example, holding the infringing part of the contract invalid, while upholding the non-infringing provision).[358]

By way of illustration, a contract between a manufacturer (either within or outside Japan) and a distributor in Japan may provide that, in the case of breach—as defined in

---

356 For applications of this idea see: V Taylor 'Continuing Transactions and Persistent Myths: Contracts in Contemporary Japan' (1993) 19 *Melbourne University Law Review* 352.

357 On the implied principles of good faith and fair dealing, see [17.180]–[17.200].

358 See eg Takashi Uchida, *Minpô 1* [Civil Code 1] (2000 2nd edn) Tokyo Daigaku Shuppankai, 265.

the contract—the distribution contract may be terminated by the manufacturer after 14 days' notice. On its face, this would appear to be a valid contract clause. If, however, the parties had been contracting continuously for a number of years and if the distributor's business was largely or wholly dependant on the manufacturer's business, a Japanese court would be likely to view a strict attempt to enforce the clause as written as a breach of good faith. The Japanese court would require the manufacturer to perform—and terminate—the contract in good faith, which would require sufficient notice (some months, depending on the length of the original contract) as well as an opportunity to cure the defect or breach.[359]

[8.995] In interpreting the parties' contract, Japanese courts make reference to (a) custom; (b) the optional provision of the Code; (c) *jôri* (or jurisprudential insight) and (d) the doctrine of good faith.[360] Custom is recognised explicitly as a source of potential party agreement by Article 92 of the Civil Code and by Article 2 of the *Law on the Application of Laws (Hôrei)*. For legal acts covered by the Commercial Code (including commercial contracts), Article 1 of that Code provides that 'Where no provision exists in this Code as to a commercial matter, the commercial customary law shall apply, and where there is no such law, the Civil Code shall apply'.

Traditionally, Article 2 of the *Hôrei* was interpreted as covering customary law *(kanshûhô) and* Article 92 of the Civil Code simply custom (or trade usage). Customary law applies to a fairly narrow range of universally binding unwritten rules, now largely confined to areas such as banking and finance. Consequently, in more recent years, both customary law and custom are treated as equally applicable, or of equal status, for the purposes of contract interpretation.[361]

---

359   See: V Taylor 'Continuing Transactions and Persistent Myths: Contracts in Contemporary Japan' (1993) 19 *Melbourne University Law Review* 352.
360   See eg Takashi Uchida, *Minpô 1* [Civil Code 1] (2000 2nd edn) Tokyo Daigaku Shuppankai, 265.
361   Takashi Uchida, *Minpô 1* [Civil Code 1] (2000 2nd edn) Tokyo Daigaku Shuppankai 266.

Chapter 9
Terms II: Construction of terms

9.1　Introduction

[9.05] Having determined what terms form part of the contract,[1] the next question is the proper construction of the contract. This question may conveniently be looked upon in two respects:

- the *meaning* of the terms of the contract; and
- the *significance* of those terms.

The first of these issues involves the approach taken when interpreting the contract, including the information that may be taken into account. This involves, amongst other things, a further reference to the 'parol evidence' rule as well as other guidance on the approach adopted by courts when interpreting a contract.

The second question involves issues including the classification of terms and the consequences of such classification. It also involves an appraisal of particular types of clauses that frequently appear in contracts and may raise particular sub-issues of their own.

9.2　Interpreting the meaning of terms

9.2.1　General approach

[9.10] 'Construction' of contracts may be seen as involving two activities: first, ascertaining the meaning of the words used, and secondly, determining the legal effect of those words.[2] The meaning of a contract is a matter of fact in the sense that it is a question depending on the words of the particular contract under consideration. By contrast, the legal effect of a contract is a question of law, which may involve reference to previous cases.

[9.15] A document is construed as a whole, rather than extracting provisions and attempting to construe them in isolation.[3] The objective is to construe the document so as to produce a consonant whole, if possible.[4]

[9.20] When a court construes a contract, it attempts, as far as possible, to give effect to the bargain: the law is not the 'destroyer of bargains.'[5] In other words, the process

---

1　See Chapter 8.

2　*Life Insurance Co of Australia Ltd v Phillips* (1925) 36 CLR 60 at 78.

3　See, for example, *George v Cluning* (1979) 28 ALR 57 (HC); *Amalgamated Television Services Pty Limited v Television Corporation Limited* (1969) 123 CLR 648.

4　*Hume v Rundell* (1824) 2 Sim & St 174 at 177; 57 ER 311 at 312; *Lloyd v Lloyd* (1837) 2 My & Cr 192 at 202; 40 ER 613 at 617.

5　*Hillas & Co Ltd v Arcos Ltd* (1932) 147 LT 503 at 512.

of construing a contract involves the court giving effect to the intentions of the parties wherever possible, especially where the contract has been entered into by lay persons.[6] In determining the parties' intention, the court must not be too astute or subtle[7]—nor narrow or pedantic[8]—in seeking defects sufficient to exclude a valid contract. Similarly, when construing a contract made between commercial parties, courts will try to avoid a placing a construction on the language that makes commercial nonsense or is commercially inconvenient, since it will be inferred that commercial parties would not themselves normally agree in such a way.[9] Indeed, at a general level, courts prefer to avoid constructions that lead to consequences that appear to be capricious, unreasonable, inconvenient or unjust.[10]

Although the court's purpose is to ascertain the intention of the parties, it adopts an objective approach that seeks to give effect to the meaning obtained from a reasonable third party's viewpoint rather than the subjective or actual intentions of the parties.[11]

9.2.2   Admissible evidence

(a)   The parol evidence rule

[9.25] An issue that arises when a court is attempting to ascertain the intention of the parties to a contract is the evidence that may properly be taken into account. It has been held by the High Court that where the contract has been wholly reduced into writing, the intention of the parties is to be gathered from the 'four corners of the instrument.'[12] This approach is a manifestation of the parol evidence rule, which provides that where the written document is intended to be a complete record of the contract, extrinsic evidence is not admissible to add to, vary or contradict the language of the document.[13] The objective of the rule is to preserve the sanctity of the written document and to avoid the process of construction being muddled by 'uncertain testimony of slippery memory.'[14]

[9.30] The parol evidence rule is not an area of law without its difficulties. Different formulations of the rule have been expressed in the courts and by commentators and a number of exceptions to its operation have been recognised. It is clear, though, that where the document is not intended to be a complete or final record of the contract,

---

6   *York Airconditioning & Refrigeration (Australasia) Pty Ltd v Commonwealth* (1949) 80 CLR 11 at 26; *Gangemi Holdings Pty Ltd v Salter* [1999] NSWSC 1004 (Studdert J 1 October 1999).

7   *Hillas & Co Ltd v Arcos Ltd* (1932) 147 LT 503 at 514 per Lord Wright.

8   *Upper Hunter County District Council v Australian Chilling & Freezing Co Ltd* (1968) 118 CLR 429 at 437 per Barwick CJ.

9   *Hide & Skin Trading Pty Limited v Oceanic Meat Traders Limited* (1990) 20 NSWLR 310 at 313–314 per Kirby P.

10   *Australian Broadcasting Commission v Australasian Performing Rights Association Ltd* (1973) 129 CLR 99 at 109–110.

11   *Hospital Products Ltd v United States Surgical Corporation* (1984) 156 CLR 41 at 62; *Taylor v Johnson* (1983) 151 CLR 422 at 429.

12   *Allen v Carbone* (1975) 132 CLR 528 at 531.

13   *Goss v Lloyd Nugent* (1833) 5 B&D 58 at 65; 110 ER 713 at 716; *Gordon v McGregor* (1909) 8 CLR 316 at 323. The title 'parol' (that is 'oral') is something of a misnomer since the rule excludes all evidence which is extrinsic to the document rather than merely evidence of oral statements. Another manifestation of the rule is in relation to determining the terms that form part of the contract; see [8.370].

14   *Bacchus Marsh Concentrated Milk Co Ltd v Joseph Nathan & Company Limited* (1919) 26 CLR 401 at 451–452.

or the contract is made partly orally and partly in writing, the parol evidence rule will not apply, and extrinsic evidence will be admissible to assist in interpretation.

(b) Factual matrix

[9.35] When a court embarks upon a process of construing a document, it must 'place itself in thought in the same factual matrix as that in which the parties were.'[15] Accordingly, when determining the parties' intentions, the court may validly take into account not only the words recorded in the document but also evidence of the surrounding circumstances.[16] The evidence of surrounding circumstances must be known to both parties, although if facts are notorious, the court may presume knowledge of them.[17]

Exactly what constitutes the 'surrounding circumstances' may be difficult to define.[18] It has been suggested that in a commercial contract it is appropriate for the court to have reference to the commercial purpose of the contract, which in turn presupposes knowledge of the way the transaction started, its background, and the context and market in which the parties are operating.[19]

[9.40] There are different views as to when it is appropriate to take account of evidence of surrounding circumstances. In the face of statements that such evidence helps to establish the context of the contract in all cases,[20] it has been suggested that the 'true rule' is that evidence of surrounding circumstances is only admissible to assist in the interpretation of a contract if the language is ambiguous or susceptible to more than one meaning, and is not admissible to contradict the language of the contract when it has a plain meaning.[21]

(c) Exceptions to the parol evidence rule

[9.45] The impact of the parol evidence rule has been tempered by the recognition of a number of exceptions that enable the court to have reference to its extrinsic evidence. The chief exceptions are as follows.

Ambiguity

[9.50] It has long been established that extrinsic evidence may be admitted to resolve an ambiguity in the contract. Indeed, many of the following specific exceptions are

---

15   *Reardon Smith Line v Yengvar Hansen-Tangen* [1976] 1 WLR 989 at 997; *Prenn v Simmonds* [1971] WLR 1381 at 1383–1384.

16   *Allen v Carbone* (1975) 132 CLR 528 at 531; *DTR Nominees Pty Ltd v Mona Homes Pty Ltd* (1978) 138 CLR 423 at 429; *Lakatoi Universal Pty Ltd v Walker* [2000] NSWSC 113 (10 March 2000).

17   *Codelfa Construction Pty Ltd v State Rail Authority of New South Wales* (1982) 149 CLR 337 at 352 per Mason J; *DTR Nominees Pty Ltd v Mona Homes Pty Ltd* (1978) 138 CLR 423 at 429; *B&B Constructions (Aust) Pty Ltd v Brian A Cheeseman & Associates Pty Ltd* (1994) 35 NSWLR 227 at 237, 246–247.

18   *Reardon Smith Line Ltd v Yengvar Hansen-Tangen* [1976] 1 WLR 989 at 995.

19   Ibid at 996, cited with approval in *Codelfa Construction Pty Ltd v State Rail Authority of New South Wales* (1982) 149 CLR 337 at 350.

20   See, for example, *DTR Nominees Pty Ltd v Mona Homes Pty Ltd* (1978) 138 CLR 423 at 429; *Prenn v Simmonds* [1971] 1 WLR 1381 at 1383–1384.

21   *Codelfa Construction Pty Ltd v State Rail Authority of New South Wales* (1982) 149 CLR 337 at 352 per Mason J. Strictly speaking, therefore, Mason J may be seen as suggesting that evidence surrounding circumstances may be admitted as an exception to the parol evidence rule: see [9.50].

merely specific examples of ambiguity in the contract. 'Ambiguity' has a wide embrace. As many, if not most, documents are reasonably capable of more than one meaning,[22] this exception has serious ramifications for the efficacy of the general rule.[23]

'Ambiguity' extends not only to patent ambiguity—language that on its face is capable of more than one possible meaning, or is otherwise made unclear by the other language in the document[24]—but also latent ambiguity, which arises where an apparently clear meaning is shown to be ambiguous when extrinsic facts are taken into account.[25] Recognition of the possibility of latent ambiguity demonstrates that it may not always be safe to assume that the words of a document will simply carry their plain or ordinary meaning.[26]

Identification of subject matter

[9.55] Extrinsic evidence is admissible to resolve ambiguity about the subject matter of the contract.[27] This is usually as a result of latent ambiguity. Thus the doubt created by extrinsic knowledge is resolved by extrinsic evidence.[28]

Example: White v Australian & New Zealand Theatres Ltd[29]

By contract with the defendant, the plaintiffs agreed to render their 'exclusive professional services to act, perform, sing, dance or otherwise exercise their talents ... as directed' by the defendant. The basis of the contract was a theatre revue. After the opening of the revue, the defendant told the plaintiffs that it was too demanding to expect them to both produce and perform in the review; it consequently brought in another person to produce the show. The plaintiffs thereupon sought damages for breach of contract and refused to appear in the show.

The High Court held that the phrase 'professional services' was not precisely stated in the contract. In order to ascertain exactly what professional services the artists had contracted to render under the agreement, it was necessary to ascertain the particular professional services the artists were personally qualified to render and what parts had been assigned to them in the particular production. In light of this

---

22 *Life Insurance Co of Australia Ltd v Phillips* (1925) 36 CLR 60 at 70.

23 The suggestion that virtually every case will involve words capable of more than one meaning, and so may require reference to extrinsic evidence for interpretation, may mean it is better to say simply that all contracts have to be construed in their factual context: see *Trawl Industries of Australia Ltd v Effem Foods Pty Ltd trading as 'Uncle Ben's of Australia'* (1992) 27 NSWLR 326 at 358–359; *B&B Constructions (Aust) Pty Ltd v Brian A Cheeseman & Associates Pty Ltd* (1994) 35 NSWLR 227 at 235–236, 245.

24 *White v Australian and New Zealand Theatres Ltd* (1943) 67 CLR 266; see, for example, *Matthews v Smallwood* [1910] 1 Ch 77.

25 *Hope v RCA Photophone of Australia Pty Ltd* (1937) 59 CLR 348 at 356 per Latham CJ; *DTR Nominees Pty Ltd v Mona Homes Pty Ltd* (1978) 138 CLR 423 at 429; *B&B Constructions (Aust) Pty Ltd v Brian A Cheeseman & Associates Pty Ltd* (1994) 35 NSWLR 227 at 236 per Kirby P.

26 *Codelfa Construction Pty Ltd v State Rail Authority of New South Wales* (1982) 149 CLR 337 at 248; see also *B&B Constructions (Aust) Pty Ltd v Brian A Cheeseman & Associates Pty Ltd* (1994) 35 NSWLR 227 at 234 per Kirby P: 'There is now a growing appreciation of the ambiguity of all languages but of the English language in particular.' Cf *Folks Leader v Duffy* (1888) 8 HL(I) 294 at 301 per Lord Halsbury LC; *Allgood v Blake* (1873) LR 8 Ex 160 at 163 per Blackburn J.

27 *Cameron & Co v Slutzkin Pty Ltd* (1923) 32 CLR 81 at 86.

28 *Great Western Railway & Midland Railway v Bristol Corporation* (1918) 87 LJ Ch 414 at 429 per Lord Wrenbury.

29 (1943) 67 CLR 266.

extrinsic evidence, the proper meaning of 'professional services' included producing the show. Accordingly, the defendant was in breach.

[9.60] There may be a different result where the ambiguity relates to the character of the subject matter rather than the identification of a particular subject matter.

Example: Hope v RCA Photophone of Australia Pty Ltd[30]

The plaintiff entered into a written contract to lease 'electrical sound-reproduction' equipment from the defendant for a specified period. The equipment supplied by the defendant matched the description in the schedule to the contract but was second-hand rather than new. The plaintiff sought to adduce extrinsic evidence that the agreement was intended to refer to new equipment.

The High Court held that the evidence of character that the plaintiff wanted to admit was not in the strict sense evidence of identification. Existence of ambiguity is not established by the fact that a general description applies to all persons or things falling within a certain class. It cannot be said that ambiguity is being removed or that language is being interpreted when what is being sought is the qualification of the description of a class by the addition of an attribute. In fact, when an attempt is made to adduce extrinsic evidence for the purpose of showing that the equipment referred to in the agreement was not new equipment, an attempt was being made not to explain the contract, but rather to vary it by adding a new term.

Identification of the parties

[9.65] Extrinsic evidence is admissible where there is ambiguity concerning the identity of the parties to the agreement, or concerning their relationship or the capacity in which they have entered into the contract.

Example: Edwards v Edwards[31]

A deed provided that a property was transferred to 'John Edwards' in consideration of the payment of a small sum by the said John Edwards. The deed was executed by a 'John Edwards Junior'. The evidence showed that the grantor's father was called John Edwards. The party to the deed was the grantor's brother, John Edwards (which explained the addition of the suffix 'Junior' to his signature). The deed, however, referred in its recitals to the 'natural love and affection' that the grantor had for 'her nephew the said John Edwards.' The grantor's brother John Edwards had a nine-year-old son, who was also called John Edwards. Accordingly, the deed was capable of referring to three different people all with the same name: the grantor's father, the grantor's brother, and the grantor's nephew.

It was held that the insertion of the reference to the nephew John Edwards resulted in an ambiguity as to which John Edwards was the true grantee. Conflict in the names caused an ambiguity that permitted the admission of extrinsic evidence; that evidence showed

---

30   (1937) 59 CLR 348.
31   (1918) 24 CLR 312.

that the insertion of the word 'nephew' in the recitals had been by error. The grantor had intended to transfer the property to her brother and no other.

In another case, extrinsic evidence was adduced to disclose the identity of 'our client'.[32]

[9.70] Extrinsic evidence may also be used to resolve ambiguity concerning the capacity or relationship between parties, such as showing the existence or nature of an agency relationship.[33] Accordingly, evidence was admitted in one case to show that the defendant was the correct principal, despite his or her agent having purported to enter into the contract on behalf of another person.[34]

Identification of real consideration

[9.75] Extrinsic evidence is admissible to prove the real consideration under a contract where:

* no consideration or nominal consideration is expressed in the instrument;
* the expressed consideration is in general terms or ambiguously stated; or
* a substantial consideration is stated but an additional consideration exists, provided the additional consideration proved is not inconsistent with the instrument.[35]

Example: Yaroomba Beach Development Co v Coeur De Lion Investments Pty Ltd[36]

A package of three agreements was negotiated in connection with the sale of land for a golf course adjacent to a tourist resort and beachfront land. Under the agreements (a land purchase agreement, a licence agreement, and a share agreement), in exchange for the land and access to the beachfront land under the share agreement, the vendor was to receive a large sum of money and the rights of six life memberships in the country club that was to be formed. For stamp duty purposes, the share agreement did not refer to the land purchase agreement or the licence agreement. The purchaser claimed that it was not obliged to pay the money or issue memberships because there was no consideration for either promise.

It was held that there was no consideration on the face of the share agreement. Accordingly, the real consideration could be proved by evidence extrinsic to the instrument. On that evidence, the real consideration for the purchasers' promises was the sale of the land and the licence to access the beachfront because the transaction was one package with three components.

Where the additional consideration is of a different kind, it will not be inconsistent unless perhaps the written instrument says that the stated consideration is the only consideration. Where a substantial consideration is stated, and the additional consideration

---

32   *GR Securities Pty Ltd v Baulkham Hills Private Hospital* (1986) BPR 9,315 (NSW CA).
33   *Giliberto v Kenny* (1983) 48 ALR 620 at 623.
34   *Minter v Jamieson* (1924) 25 SR (NSW) 589.
35   *Pau On v Lau Yiu Long* [1980] AC 614 at 631.
36   (1989) 18 NSWLR 398.

is the same kind, for example the stated consideration is $100 000.00 and the true consideration is claimed to be $150 000.00, the argument for inconsistency is stronger.[37]

Custom or usage

[9.80] Where the language used in the instrument has a particular meaning—for example, by custom or usage in a particular trade, industry or region, evidence of that meaning is admissible, even if there is no patent ambiguity.[38] This would include providing evidence of the English meaning of words in a foreign language.[39]

Rectification

[9.85] It has long been recognised that extrinsic evidence may be admitted to show that the parties' intention was not accurately recorded in the written instrument. In appropriate circumstances the document may be rectified so that it accords with the parties' actual agreement.[40]

9.2.3   Inadmissible evidence

[9.90] While evidence of 'surrounding circumstances' may be admissible—either on one view to establish the context of the contract, or on a narrower view, where there is some kind of ambiguity in the contract that needs to be resolved—it seems that evidence of certain matters is treated as being inadmissible.

(a)   Subjective intention

[9.95] Evidence of the actual, subjective intentions of the parties is not admissible. As noted at [9.20], when a court seeks to ascertain the intention of the parties by construction of the contract, it is doing so from the objective rather than subjective point of view. A court cannot receive evidence from a party regarding his or her intentions and construe the contract by reference to those intentions.[41]

(b)   Prior negotiations

[9.100] Evidence of negotiations that precede the written document is generally not admitted. This is not for a technical reason or even for reasons of convenience—although such evidence may have the effect of prolonging the case and adding to its expense—but simply because such evidence is unhelpful.[42] The nature of negotiations is that even if the parties' intentions are convergent, they are still not the same. It is only the final document that properly reflects a consensus between the parties.[43]

---

37   *Yaroomba Beach Development Co v Coeur De Lion Investments Pty Ltd* (1989) 18 NSW LR 398.
38   *Thornley v Tilley* (1925) 36 CLR 1. See, for example, *Tummon v Crick* [1963] QWN 33 (architect agreeing to do work for builder 'on usual terms'); *Max Cooper & Sons Pty Ltd v Sydney City Council* (1980) 54 ALJR 234 ('payloadings' in the building industry); *Appleby v Purcell* (1973) 2 NSWLR 879 at 889 ('push and stack' given rural land usage rather than given dictionary meaning).
39   *Di Sora v Phillipps* (1863) 10 HLC 624; 11 ER 1168.
40   *Bacchus Marsh Concentrated Milk Co Ltd v Joseph Nathan & Co Ltd* (1919) 26 CLR 410 at 427. In relation to rectification see [14.135].
41   *Life Insurance Co of Australia Ltd v Phillips* (1925) 36 CLR 60 at 71; *DTR Nominees Pty Ltd v Mona Homes Pty Ltd* (1978) 138 CLR 423 at 429.
42   *Prenn v Simonds* [1971] 1 WLR 1381 at 1384 per Lord Wilberforce.
43   Ibid at 1384.

[9.105] Difficulty arises, however, where evidence of prior negotiations is adduced in order to establish objective background facts, which are known to both parties, and the subject matter of the contract. Such evidence is admissible to the extent to which they have this tendency. However, so far as the evidence consists of statements and conduct of the parties that reflect their actual intentions and expectations, they are inadmissible.[44] Such expressions of intention are presumed to be superseded by, and merged in, the contract itself.[45] This distinction between leading evidence of prior negotiations as evidence of intention as opposed to establishing the surrounding circumstances may be easier to state in theory than to apply in practice.

(c) Subsequent conduct

[9.110] There are different views about the extent to which the parties' subsequent conduct may be permitted as evidence to aid interpretation of the written instrument. The House of Lords has concluded that evidence of subsequent conduct cannot be referred to for the purpose of interpreting the contract.[46] In the words of Lord Reid, it is 'now well settled that it is not legitimate to use as an aid in the construction of the contract anything which the parties said or did after it was made.'[47]

[9.115] The Privy Council has treated such statements as reflecting the position in Australia as well.[48] However, the true position in Australia may not be so clear. Ample authority has supported the use of evidence of subsequent conduct as an aid to construction.[49] More recent authorities, however, tend to support[50] the English approach.[51] In *Hide & Skin Trading Pty Ltd v Oceanic Meat Traders Ltd*,[52] Kirby P explained that the 'dangers and disadvantages' of allowing reference to subsequent conduct included that the parties may tailor their post-contract behaviour according to the case they believe they later have to present in court; they may seek to advance their understanding of the agreement simply to persuade the other party to accept their construction; the expansion in the field of inquiry would add to the burden of fact finding and consequently the length and cost of litigation; and subsequent conduct may be based on an erroneous understanding of the parties' rights. Opposed to this is

---

44   *Codelfa Construction Pty Ltd v State Rail Authority of New South Wales* (1982) 149 CLR 337 at 352 per Mason J. See, for example, *Skywest Aviation Pty Ltd v Commonwealth* (1995) 126 FLR 61.

45   Ibid.

46   *James Miller & Partners Ltd v Whitworth Street Estates (Manchester) Ltd* [1970] AC 583; *L Schuler AG v Wickman Machine Tool Sales Ltd* [1974] AC 235.

47   *James Miller & Partners Ltd v Whitworth Street Estates (Manchester) Ltd* [1970] AC 583 at 603.

48   *Australian Mutual Providence Society v Chaplin* (1978) 18 ALR 385 at 392; *Narich Pty Ltd v Commissioner of Pay-Roll Tax* (1983) 50 ALR 417 at 420–421.

49   See, for example, *Hart v McDonald* (1910) 10 CLR 417; *Farmer v Honam* (1919) 26 CLR 183 at 197; *Thornley v Tilley* (1925) 36 CLR 1 at 11; *Sinclair Scott & Co v Naughton* (1929) 43 CLR 310 at 327; *White v Australian & New Zealand Theatres Ltd* (1943) 67 CLR 266 at 271 per Latham CJ, 275 per Starke J and 281 per Williams J.

50   See, for example, *Administration of Papua & New Guinea v Daera Guba* (1973) 130 CLR 353 at 446; *Codelfa Construction Pty Ltd v State Rail Authority of New South Wales* (1982) 149 CLR 337 at 348; *FAI Traders Insurance Co Ltd v Savoy Plaza Pty Ltd* [1993] 2 VR 343; cf *Spunwill Pty Ltd v BAB Pty Ltd* (1994) 36 NSWLR 290.

51   See generally S Charles, 'Interpretation of ambiguous contracts by reference to subsequent conduct' (1991) 4 JCL 16.

52   (1990) 20 NSWLR 310.

the possibility that by clear and mutual conduct, the parties may evidence what they originally intended.[53]

[9.120] If the English approach is to prevail in Australia, and evidence of subsequent conduct is to be regarded as inadmissible, it may be possible to ameliorate the effect of this exclusion in an appropriate case where the conduct forms the basis of an estoppel[54] or variation.[55]

9.3   Legal effect of words: types of terms

[9.125] Contracts may contain a wide variety of terms. The legal effect of the words used depends upon the type of term. Contrary to the belief of many lay persons, not all terms in a contract are of a type which, if breached, give rise to a remedy for the innocent party. This is certainly the case in relation to 'promissory' terms. However, other terms may be, for example, more mechanical or procedural in nature and not capable of breach in the same sense.

9.3.1   *Promissory terms*

[9.130] A promissory term is one pursuant to which a party promises or undertakes to do or refrain from doing something, or that a state of affairs will or will not exist. Where the party fails to do or refrain from doing something, or the state of affairs does or does not occur, in accordance with his or her promise or undertaking, that party will have breached the term. The effect of such a breach depends upon whether the term is classified as a condition, a warranty, or an intermediate term. Determination of the appropriate classification is an objective test of the parties' intention, taking into account their words and conduct.[56]

(a)   Conditions

[9.135] The word 'condition' can have a wide range of meanings. In ordinary usage, it frequently refers to the terms of a contract in a generic sense, as in 'see conditions on back of ticket'.[57] However, in contract law the word has a much more specific meaning. A 'promissory condition'—referred to as a 'condition' for short—is a term that lies at the root of the contract and is so important that any breach of it entitles the innocent party to terminate further performance of the contract and to claim damages for the breach.[58] The right to terminate in such a case arises by virtue of the nature of the term and is available regardless of whether or not the effect of the breach has serious consequences for the innocent party. Conditions are also known as 'essential terms'.[59]

---

53   Ibid, at 316.
54   See, for example, *Grundt v Great Boulder Gold Mines Ltd* (1938) 59 CLR 641; *Stevens v Standard Chartered Bank Australia Ltd* (1988) 53 SASR 323.
55   See, for example, *Australian Mutual Providence Society v Chaplin* (1978) 18 ALR 305 at 392–293; *Australian Energy Ltd v Lennard Oil NL* [1996] 2 Qd R 216 at 237.
56   *Bowes v Chaleyer* (1923) 32 CLR 159; *Associated Newspapers Ltd v Banks* (1951) 83 CLR 322.
57   *L Schuler AG v Wickman Machine Tool Sales Ltd* [1974] AC 235 at 250 per Lord Reid.
58   Ibid, at 251.
59   *Luna Park (NSW) Ltd v Tramways Advertising Pty Ltd* (1938) 61 CLR 286.

[9.140] The High Court in *Associated Newspapers Ltd v Banks*[60] approved the test for conditions suggested by Jordan CJ in *Tramways Advertising Pty Ltd v Luna Park (NSW) Ltd*:

> The test of essentiality is whether it appears from the general nature of the contract considered as a whole, or from some particular term or terms, that the promise is of such importance to the promisee that he would not have entered into the contract unless he had been assured of a strict or a substantial performance of the promise, as the case may be, and this ought to have been apparent to the promisor.[61]

The quality of essentiality has been described as depending upon a determination of the general nature of the contract and the particular provision, taking into account the importance attached to the provision by the parties as evidenced by the contract itself in the surrounding circumstances.[62]

[9.145] The High Court has suggested that courts do not readily construe a term as a condition; where considerations are finely balanced they prefer to hold that a term is not of that kind, due to the automatic right to terminate and the court's preference for construing a contract in such a way as to encourage performance rather than avoidance of obligations.[63] Description of a term by the parties as being a 'condition' is persuasive but not conclusive.[64] One factor that may persuade a court to construe a term as a condition is if damages are an inadequate remedy for breach of the term, or if damages for breach would be difficult to prove.[65] The court may also be influenced if a particular construction leads to an unreasonable result.[66] This consideration may either favour construction of the term as a condition[67] or lead to a contrary result.[68]

Example: Associated Newspapers Ltd v Bancks[69]

A cartoonist was contracted by a newspaper to provide a weekly strip entitled *Us Fellers* featuring the character Ginger Meggs. The newspaper undertook that the strip would appear on the front page of the comic section of the Sunday edition. On three occasions the strip appeared on the third page of the section. The cartoonist purported to terminate the contract for breach of condition.

The High Court held that the promise to publish the strip on the front page of the comic section was an essential term, applying the test formulated by Jordan CJ in

---

60   (1951) 83 CLR 322; see also the High Court's subsequent endorsement in, for example, *DTR Nominees Pty Ltd v Mona Homes Pty Ltd* (1978) 138 CLR 423 at 430–431; *Shevill v Builders Licensing Board* (1982) 149 CLR 620 at 627; *Ankar Pty Ltd v National Westminster Finance (Australia) Ltd* (1987) 162 CLR 549 at 556.
61   (1938) 38 SR (NSW) 632 at 641–642.
62   *DTR Nominees Pty Ltd v Mona Homes Pty Ltd* (1978) 138 CLR 423 at 431.
63   *Ankar Pty Ltd v National Westminster Finance (Australia) Ltd* (1987) 162 CLR 549 at 556–557.
64   *L Schuler AG v Wickman Machine Tool Sales Ltd* [1974] AC 235 at 251.
65   *Ankar Pty Ltd v National Westminster Finance (Australia) Ltd* (1987) 162 CLR 549 at 556–557; *McDougall v Aeromarine of Emsworth Ltd* (1958) 1 WLR 1126 at 1133; *Bunge Corp New York v Tradax Export SA Panama* [1981] 1 WLR 711 at 720.
66   *L Schuler AG v Wickman Machine Tool Sales Ltd* [1974] AC 235 at 251, 265.
67   As in, for example, *Associated Newspapers Ltd v Bancks* (1951) 83 CLR 322; *Ankar Pty Ltd v National Westminster Finance (Aust) Ltd* (1987) 162 CLR 549.
68   As in, for example, *L Schuler AG v Wickman Machine Tool Sales Ltd* (1974) AC 235.
69   (1951) 83 CLR 322.

Tramways Advertising v Luna Park. In the circumstances, the cartoonist would not have agreed to provide the weekly strip unless he had been assured that his work would have been published in the agreed manner. It was of prime importance to Bancks that there should be a continuity of publication so that his work should be kept continuously before the public; be published as a whole, not mutilated; and be published on the most conspicuous page of the comic section.

In support of the treatment of the term as a condition it might be suggested that in light of the fact that the most important thing for the cartoonist was to have continuous conspicuous publication, the only effective remedy for a breach of that promise was to terminate the relationship, rather than to allow only an award of damages.

[9.150] The court must determine the real intention of the parties from the language they have used and the surrounding circumstances. The court may take into account the probable effect of non-performance, weighed as the parties would have weighed it when making the contract. A term will be regarded as a condition where the stipulation is so important that a breach would make further performance the performance of a substantially different contract or would destroy the main object of the contract.[70]

[9.155] It is possible for the parties, by the use of appropriate language, to elevate any term to the status of a condition—even a term that might otherwise be regarded as of little significance.[71] For example, a lease may provide that any breach of its terms by the lessee entitles the lessor to terminate the lease and retake possession.

[9.160] In the case of a sale of goods only, although strictly speaking the term 'condition' is not defined in the sale of goods legislation,[72] it is clear that the legislation contemplates that a condition is a term the breach of which gives rise to a right to 'repudiate' (terminate) the contract.[73] However, in some jurisdictions, where the contract is for specific goods and the contract has been executed, any breach of condition must be treated as a breach of warranty *ex post facto*.[74] The effect of these provisions is that where a contract for specific goods has been executed, there will only be a right to claim damages. Any claim to terminate for a breach of condition will have been lost.

(b) Warranties

[9.165] The word 'warranty' can also be given a range of interpretation. In common parlance, it may refer to the promise by a manufacturer to repair goods that are faulty when sold. In contract law, by contrast, the word is capable of at least three meanings. It may refer to a promise that constitutes a collateral contract (sometimes referred to as a 'collateral warranty'),[75] or a term in an insurance contract that is treated as being essential. The third meaning of the word—and the relevant sense in the context of the

---

70   *Bowes v Chaleyer* (1923) 32 CLR 159 at 181 per Isaacs and Rich JJ (dissenting); see also *Betini v Gye* (1876) 1 QBD 183 at 188.

71   *Shevill v Builders Licensing Board* (1982) 149 CLR 620 at 627; *Hongkong Fir Shipping Co Ltd v Kawaski Kissen Kaisha Ltd* [1962] 2 QD 26 at 63 per Upjohn LJ.

72   Cf the express definition of 'warranty': see [9.170].

73   *Sale of Goods Act* 1954 (ACT) s 16 (2); *Sale of Goods Act* 1923 (NSW), s 16(2); *Sale of Goods Act* 1972 (NT), s 16(2); *Sale of Goods Act* 1896 (Qld), s 14(2); *Sale of Goods* (1895) (SA), s 11(2); *Sale of Goods* 1896 (Tas), s 16(2); *Goods Act* 1958 (Vic), s 16(2); *Sale of Goods Act* 1895 (WA), s 11(2).

74   *Sale of Goods Act* 1972 (NT), s 16(4); *Sale of Goods Act* 1896 (Qld), s 14(3); *Sale of Goods* 1896 (Tas), s 16(3); *Sale of Goods Act* 1895 (WA), s 11(3). In Victoria the provision only applies to sales to 'consumers': see *Goods Act* 1958 (Vic), ss 16(3), 85, 99(1). No equivalent provision appears in the legislation in the ACT, New South Wales or South Australia.

75   See [8.30].

tripartite classification of promissory terms—is that denoting a term subsidiary to the main purpose of the contract, breach of which gives rise to only a right to claim damages. There is no right to terminate for breach of warranty.[76]

Example: Ellul v Oakes[77]

The vendor of a house completed a form setting out particulars of the house for use by a real estate agent. In answer to the question whether the house was sewered or served by a septic tank, the vendor crossed out the word 'septic' and wrote 'yes' beside the word 'sewer'. Although the area was sewered, in fact the house was only served by a septic tank.

The Full Court of the Supreme Court of South Australia held that objectively, the vendor intended to guarantee the accuracy of the statement regarding sewerage. The statement was therefore promissory and not merely a representation. Nor, in the circumstances, was it sensible to talk in terms of the statement preceding a principal contract. The promise was therefore not a collateral contract but a term of the sale contract. While the purchasers later claimed that they would not have entered the contract had they known that sewerage was not connected, the court preferred the evidence of the estate agent that the purchasers were in fact quite happy with their bargain and the low price they had paid. The term was held to be a warranty, and the purchasers were entitled to an award of damages equal to the cost of connecting sewerage to the house.

In *Shevill v Builders Licensing Board*,[78] the High Court held that a promise in a lease to pay rent in advance would not, without more, be an essential term that had the effect that any failure, however slight, to make the payment at the specified times would entitle the lessor to terminate the lease.[79] In other words, such a promise is only a warranty. Naturally, it is possible for the parties to stipulate that the term is to be regarded as fundamental, so that any breach may result in termination.[80] Alternatively, it is possible for repeated breach of a warranty to amount to a repudiation that will entitle the innocent party to terminate.[81]

[9.170] This definition is echoed with respect to contracts for the sale of goods in the State and Territory sale of goods legislation. This legislation defines a warranty as meaning:

> An agreement with reference to goods which are the subject of a contract of sale, but collateral to the main purpose of such contract, the breach of which gives rise to a claim for damages, but not to a right to reject the goods and treat the contract as repudiated.[82]

---

76   *Bettini v Gye* (1876) 1 QBD 183 at 188.
77   (1972) 3 SASR 377.
78   (1982) 149 CLR 620.
79   Ibid, at 627 per Gibbs CJ, with whom Murphy and Brennan JJ agreed.
80   See [9.155].
81   See [20.115]–[20.120].
82   *Sale of Goods Act* 1954 (ACT), s 5(1); *Sale of Goods Act* 1923 (NSW), s 5(1); *Sale of Goods Act* 1972 (NT), s 5(1); *Sale of Goods Act* 1896 (Qld), s 3(1); *Sale of Goods Act* 1895 (SA), s 60(1); *Sale of Goods Act* 1896 (Tas), s 3(1); *Goods Act* 1958 (Vic), s 3(1); *Sale of Goods Act* 1895 (WA), s 60(1). See, for example, *O'Dempsey v Hansen* [1939] QWN 22 (promise that ewes were in lamb to Corriedale rams, when some were not in lamb and others were in lamb to Merino rams, held to be a warranty).

This definition is so well established that it has been suggested that the formulation of the common law definition derives from it, and that the definition provided in the sale of goods legislation should be able to be cited, at least by analogy, in the case of contracts not concerning a sale of goods.[83]

(c) Intermediate or innominate terms

[9.175] In *Hongkong Fir Shipping Co Ltd v Kawasaki Kissen Kaisha Ltd*[84] the English Court of Appeal recognised for the first time that a third class of term stood somewhere between a condition and a warranty, and could not be satisfactorily classified as either. The remedy for breach of such a 'intermediate' or 'innominate' term varies according to the gravity of the breach. If the breach is serious—in the sense that it deprives the innocent party of substantially the whole of the benefit of the contract—then the innocent party will be entitled to terminate the contract and/or claim damages. Where, on the other hand, the effect of the breach is not sufficiently serious, the innocent party will only be entitled to claim damages for the breach.[85] The existence of this third category of promissory term has since been accepted by both the House of Lords[86] and High Court.[87]

[9.180] In the *Hongkong Fir* case, the focus of the court was directed to the consequences of breach of a term—in that case a promise of seaworthiness of a vessel—which could not be properly classified as either a condition or a warranty. The court was not called upon to develop a definition for the third category of term.[88] Subsequently, an intermediate term was defined as one that may be foreseen in advance as being capable of a variety of breaches, some trivial, some serious.[89] For example, a promise of a vessel being 'in every way' seaworthy is capable of being breached in only a minor way, such as a nail being out of place, or of being breached in a serious way, such as defects leading to its total loss.[90]

[9.185] Nothing in the recognition of a third category of promissory term in *Hongkong Fir* suggested any departure from the basic and long-standing rule for determining the appropriate category of a particular term. In other words, the court is still required in the first instance to determine the intention of the parties by looking at the contract in light of the surrounding circumstances.[91]

---

83   *Associated Newspapers Ltd v Bancks* (1951) 83 CLR 322 at 339.
84   [1962] 2 QB 26.
85   See, in particular, ibid at 69–70 per Diplock LJ.
86   See, for example, *Reardon Smith Line v Yengvar Hansen-Tangen* [1976] 1 WLR 989; *Bunge Corp New York v Tradax Export SA Panama* [1991] 1 WLR 711.
87   See, for example, *Shevill v Builders Licensing Board* (1982) 149 CLR 620 at 626, 637; *Ankar Pty Ltd v National Westminster Finance (Australia) Ltd* (1987) 162 CLR 549 at 562. DW Greig & JLR Davis, *Law of Contract*, Law Book Co, Sydney, 1987, pp 1212–1213 suggest that the High Court's acceptance of the third category was in fact foreshadowed in language used by the High Court in *Associated Newspapers Ltd v Bancks* (1951) 83 CLR 322 at 339.
88   *Bunge Corp New York v Tradax Export SA Panama* [1981] 1 WLR 711 at 726 per Lord Roskill.
89   Ibid, at 715.
90   *Hongkong Fir Shipping Co Ltd v Kawaski Kissen Kaisha Ltd* [1962] 2 QB 26.
91   *Bunge Corp New York v Tradax Export SA Panama* [1981] 1 WLR 711 at 715–716 per Lord Wilberforce, 719 per Lord Lowry, 725 per Lord Roskill.

Example: Bunge Corp New York v Tradax Export SA Panama[92]

The parties entered into a contract for the purchase of a number of shipments of soya bean meal. Under the contract, the purchasers undertook, in respect of the June shipment, to give at least 15 consecutive days' notice of the probable readiness of the carrying vessel and of the approximate quantity required to be loaded. This notice was in fact provided on the 17 June (two days late). The seller purported to terminate the contract for breach of condition. The purchasers argued, however, that the decision in the *Hongkong Fir* case meant that the proper approach was to first enquire into the effect of the breach. Since in the circumstances the two-day delay in providing notice had not caused the seller to suffer any significant loss, the purchasers claimed that the term should be treated as only giving a remedy in damages.

The House of Lords held that the purchasers' argument was based on a misconception of the *Hongkong Fir* decision. That judgment did not support the proposition that the court's first enquiry should be in relation to the effect of the breach committed. That enquiry was relevant only in the event of the court deciding that the relevant term was an intermediate term. This was not the case in relation to a time clause in a mercantile or commercial contract such as was in issue. Such a clause is only capable of one kind of breach: to be late. The supplier under a mercantile or commercial contract must have the certainty of knowing whether he or she is still obliged to provide the goods. A supplier should not be expected to wait after a breach of one, two, three, or any other number of days before he or she knows whether there is a right to terminate the contract. The time stipulation was therefore a condition entitling the seller to terminate the contract, regardless of the seriousness of the consequences of the breach in fact. The point that in the actual circumstances the seller had suffered little as a result of the two-day delay in giving notice was entirely irrelevant.

[9.190] Consequently, the court must first ascertain the intention of the parties with respect to the correct classification of a promissory term—that is, whether it is a condition, warranty, or intermediate term. It is only in the event that the court decides it is an intermediate term that it then proceeds to a second query: determining whether in the circumstances of the case the breach has deprived the innocent party of substantially the whole of the benefit of the contract. In deciding the second question, a number of matters may be taken into account, including:

- the degree of performance up to the time of the breach compared with the performance required under the contract;
- whether damages would adequately compensate the lost expectations of the innocent party;
- whether the expectations of the party in breach would be unfairly prejudiced by terminating the contract;
- the attitude and conduct of the party in breach, including the likelihood of the breach persisting.[93]

---

92   [1981] 1 WLR 711.
93   This list was extracted in DW Greig & JLR Davis, *Law of Contract*, Law Book Co, Sydney, 1987, p 1214.

Example: Hongkong Fir Shipping Co Ltd v Kawaski Kissen Kaisha Ltd[94]

The vessel Hongkong Fir was chartered for a period of 24 months. The charter contained a promise that the vessel was 'in every way fitted for ordinary cargo service'—in other words, that the shipowner promised that vessel was seaworthy. The charterers took delivery of the vessel in Liverpool and sailed it in ballast to Virginia, where it picked up a cargo of coal bound for Osaka, Japan. On delivery in Liverpool, the vessel's machinery was in reasonably good condition; but due to its age it needed to be maintained by an experienced, competent, careful, and adequate engineering staff. However, when the vessel sailed, the chief engineer was inefficient and drunk, and the engine room complement was insufficient. As a consequence, the machinery broke down on several occasions, and by the time the vessel reached Osaka it had been at sea for eight and a half weeks, but had spent five weeks being repaired. On arrival in Osaka, it was found that a further 15 weeks were required for the vessel to be repaired to a state of seaworthiness. The charterers claimed that the vessel's unseaworthiness in terms of both the crew (which is regarded as an aspect of seaworthiness) and machinery entitled it to terminate the charterparty.

The English Court of Appeal held that while the vessel was unseaworthy on delivery to the charterers by reason of the incompetent and insufficient engineering staff, the charterers were not entitled to terminate the charterparty for a number of reasons. First, as soon as the troubles came to the shipowners' attention, they had taken all steps to attempt to remedy them. No money was spared on repairs during the voyage, and the vessel undertook a very thorough overhaul when it was in Osaka. The chief engineer was dismissed and replaced by a most competent, experienced and reliable chief engineer and a competent and sufficient engineering staff was engaged. Secondly, after being repaired in Osaka, the vessel was still available for about 17 of the 24 months under the charterparty; the comparative amount of time lost by virtue of the breach was thus not large. Thirdly, there was an inference that the financial loss flowing from the owners' breach was not serious, since the charterers' counterclaim for damages had been abandoned at trial. Finally, it would be unfair to the shipowners if termination were permitted after several months when the charterers may have been able to terminate the charter before performance had commenced. In the circumstances, therefore, the charterers had not been deprived of substantially the whole of the benefit under the contract, and were therefore limited to their remedy in damages. They were not entitled to terminate the charterparty.

[9.195] Although the sale of goods legislation only refers to conditions and warranties, it has been held—in England, at least—that the concept of an intermediate term may also apply to a contract for the sale of goods. This is because the legislation expressly preserves the operation of the 'rules of the common law'.[95]

---

94   [1962] 2 QB 26.
95   *Cehave MV v Bremer Handelsgesellschaft GmbH (The Hansa Nord)* [1976] QB 44 (CA); *Reardon Smith Line Ltd v Yengvar Hansen-Tangen* [1976] 1 WLR 989. In New South Wales the *Sale of Good Act* (1923), s 4(5) was amended to introduce a tripartite classification of terms in contracts for the sale of goods.

[9.200] It has been suggested by some textbook writers that while the *Hongkong Fir* case contemplated a tripartite classification of terms, there is good reason for arguing that there should in fact only be two categories of obligations: conditions and intermediate terms. The basis for this suggestion may be grounded both upon a historical analysis of the late nineteenth-century authorities and upon the practical difficulty of holding a term to be a warranty once the concept of an intermediate term is admitted.[96] The suggestion is not without merit, particularly in terms of flexibility of remedy permitted by re-classifying all warranties as intermediate terms, while still retaining the notion that the parties are able to agree that a term is so important to their transaction that any breach of it should entitle the innocent party to have the right to terminate the dealing.

9.3.2   Contingencies

[9.205] The parties may wish to make the existence or the continued operation of the contract, or of an obligation in the contract, conditional upon the occurrence or non-occurrence of an event. The provision for such an event is known as a contingency.

[9.210] Contingencies may be either *conditions precedent* or *conditions subsequent*. Once again, the use of the word 'condition' may lead to confusion. The word is not used to denote any relationship with a 'condition' as in the sense of a promissory condition. In the case of a contingency, as opposed to a promissory condition, neither party undertakes or guarantees that the event will occur or will not occur. Non-fulfilment of a contingency does not result in a disappointed party being entitled to a remedy in the same way that breach of a promissory term does. Contingencies are merely external events that may have an effect upon the existence or operation of the whole or part of a contract.

Further confusion may result from the use by some judges, particularly in older cases, of 'condition precedent' to mean a promissory condition.[97]

[9.215] A 'condition precedent' in a sense of a contingency is an event that must occur before a contract comes into existence or an obligation under the contract arises. If the event fails to occur, there will either be no contract or the obligation will not arise. For example, in one case, a contract for the purchase of a share in an invention was made subject to the condition precedent of an engineer approving the invention—failure of which led to the court holding that no agreement had come into existence.[98] Where there is doubt about whether the contingency is a condition precedent to the existence of the contract, or merely of an obligation under the contract, it seems the court will favour the latter interpretation, since it gives greater scope in determining and adjusting the rights of the parties. The condition will not normally be construed as

---

96   See, for example, DW Greig & JLR Davis, *Law of Contract*, Law Book Co, Sydney, 1987, pp 1209–1222; JW Carter & DJ Harland, *Contract Law in Australia*, 3rd edn, Butterworths, Sydney, 1996, p 245. In N Seddon & MP Ellinghaus, *Cheshire and Fifoot's Law of Contract*, 7th edn, Butterworths, Sydney, 1997, p 745 the authors argue that the concept of an intermediate term is unnecessary, while suggesting that a contract may be terminated for either breach of condition or a so-called 'fundamental breach,' that is a breach which takes into account the effect of the breach and whether the innocent party has been deprived of the substantial benefit of the contract.

97   See, for example, *Bettini v Gye* (1876) 1 QB 183 at 187.

98   *Pym v Campbell* (1856) 6 E&B 370; 119 ER 903.

a condition precedent to the formation of a contract unless the contract read as a whole plainly compels that conclusion.[99]

[9.220] By contrast, a 'condition subsequent' is an event whose occurrence may give rise to a right to terminate further performance of the contract. For example, contracts for the purchase of land frequently provide that the purchase is subject to the purchaser obtaining finance for the purchase.[100] Similarly, where a horse was sold on the condition that it had and could hunt with Bicester hounds, and that the purchaser could return the horse if it did not have this ability, the proviso was construed as a condition subsequent that enabled the purchaser to terminate the contract if it should be unfulfilled, but without giving rise to a right to damages [101]

[9.225] Generally, the party for whose benefit the condition subsequent was inserted will be the party who has the right to terminate on non-occurrence. In the case of a contract made 'subject to finance' clause, this will usually be the purchaser, not the vendor.[102] Further, the purchaser is entitled in such a case to waive the benefit of the clause.

If the clause is for the benefit of both parties, either may be able to terminate. For example, a clause making a sale 'subject to subdivisional approval' may be seen as being for the benefit of both purchaser and vendor when the vendor retains adjoining land.[103] Such a clause may only be waived with the consent of both parties.

Where, on the other hand, the clause provides that the contract is to be rendered void on non-occurrence of an event, and the event is beyond the control of both parties, the contract may be automatically ended if the event occurs. For example, a clause that provides that the contract will be void if it rains for a particular day will automatically void the contract if it in fact rains.[104]

[9.230] The High Court has cautioned against placing undue emphasis on deciding whether a particular contingency is properly described as a condition precent or a condition subsequent. The difference may be no more than a 'matter of words'[105] or merely 'an artificial and theoretical question'.[106] Since the one contingency may, depending on the perspective of the respective parties, be at once a condition precedent and a condition subsequent,[107] the essential question is the effect of the contingency.[108]

[9.235] The courts tend to prefer an interpretation of contingencies as requiring an election to terminate on the part of one or both of the parties (rather than the occurrence or non-occurrence of the event having the effect of automatically terminating the contract).[109] It seems that where the contingency is for the benefit of one of the

---

99 *Perri v Coolangatta Investments Pty Ltd* (1982) 149 CLR 537 at 552 per Mason J.
100 See, for example, *Meehan v Jones* (1982) 149 CLR 571.
101 *Head v Tattersall* (1871) LR 7 Ex 7.
102 See, for example, *Meehan v Jones* (1982) 149 CLR 571.
103 See, for example, *Raysun v Taylor* [1971] Qd R 172; cf *Associated Developments (Australia) Pty Ltd v Allied & General Pty Ltd* (1994) Q Conv R 54-458 (for benefit of purchaser only where vendor not retaining adjoining land).
104 See, for example, *Carpentaria Investments Pty Ltd v Airs* [1972] Qd R 436.
105 *Meehan v Jones* (1982) 149 CLR 571 at 582 per Gibbs C J; see also *Perri v Coolangatta Investments Pty Ltd* (1982) 149 CLR 537 at 541.
106 Ibid at 592 per Mason J.
107 *Maynard v Goode* (1926) 37 CLR 529 at 540 per Isaacs J; see also *Perri v Coolangatta Investments Pty Ltd* (1982) 149 CLR 537 at 564–565 (completion of sale of Cronulla property made subject to completion of sale of Lilli Pilli property).
108 *Perri v Coolangatta Investments Pty Ltd* (1982) 149 CLR 537 at 541.

parties, it may be waived by that party, with the effect that the other party is unable to rely on the non-occurrence of the event as terminating the contract.[110] In an appropriate case, a party may estopped from relying upon the contingency.

9.3.3   Exemption clauses

[9.240] It is not uncommon for a party to insert an 'exemption' clause—also known as an 'exclusion', 'exception' or 'limitation' clause. Such a clause may be one of three main kinds:

- It may purport to exclude a party's liability—for example, 'no responsibility will be accepted by the carrier for any loss of, or damage to … goods … either in transit or in storage for any reason whatsoever.'[111]
- It may limit the extent of liability to a particular maximum amount—for example, 'Any liability on [X's] part or on the part of its servants or agents for damages … arising out of … the relationship established by this agreement … shall not in any event … exceed $100.00.'[112]
- It may make liability subject to certain pre-conditions, such as the commencement of any suit or the giving of notice of a default within a certain time—for example, 'The carrier [is] discharged from all liability whatsoever in respect of the goods unless suit is brought within one year of their delivery or of a date when they should have been delivered.'[113]

The High Court has expressly held, however, that irrespective of the kind of exclusion, the court is to apply the same rules of interpretation.[114]

[9.245] Exemption clauses may involve the determination of two separate issues:

- whether the clause forms part of the contract; and
- whether, on the true construction of the clause, it covers the liability that has arisen.[115]

The former issue has been dealt with elsewhere.[116] The issues concerning the true construction of the clause follow.

(a)   General approach

[9.250] The High Court has explained the general approach to exemption clauses in the following terms:

---

109   See, for example, *Gange v Sullivan* (1966) 116 CLR 418 at 441; *Perri v Coolangatta Investments Pty Ltd* (1982) 149 CLR 537 at 544–545, 567.

110   *Perri v Coolangatta Investments Pty Ltd* (1982) 149 CLR 537 (contingency that contract was 'subject to sale of buyers' present property' regarded as being able to be waived by the buyers).

111   See, for example, *Thomas National Transport (Melbourne) Pty Ltd v May & Baker (Australia) Pty Ltd* (1966) 115 CLR 353.

112   See, for example, *Darlington Futures Ltd v Delco Australia Pty Ltd* (1986) 161 CLR 500.

113   See, for example, *New Zealand Shipping Co Ltd v A N Satterthwith & Co Ltd (The Eurymedon)* [1975] AC 154; *Port Jackson Stevedoring Pty Ltd v Salmond & Spraggon (Australia) Pty Ltd (The New York Star)* (1980) 144 CLR 300.

114   *Darlington Futures Ltd v Delco Australia Pty Ltd* (1986) 161 CLR 500 at 510; cf the suggestion that a distinction should be drawn between *exclusion* and *limitation* clauses in *Ailsa Craig Fishing Co Ltd v Melbourne Fishing Co Ltd* [1983] 1 All ER 101.

115   In some, but not all, cases there may also be an issue whether a third party purportedly covered by the exemption clause is able to claim its benefit: see [12.220].

116   See [8.10]–[8.195].

Interpretation of an exclusion cause is to be determined by construing the clause according to its natural and ordinary meaning, read in the light of the contract as a whole, thereby giving due weight to the context in which the clause appears including the nature and object of the contract, and, where appropriate, construing the clause contra proferentem in the case of ambiguity.[117]

Accordingly, the court will take into account, for example, related terms that have been cross-referenced,[118] and any relevant headings.[119]

[9.255] It follows that an appropriately worded clause may exempt liability for what some English courts in particular have described as a 'fundamental breach'—a breach considered so serious that it strikes the root of the contract, such as the carrier of goods deviating from the usual and reasonable route for carriage of goods.[120]

[9.260] While exemption clauses are read according to their ordinary and natural meaning and in context, Windeyer J[121] pointed out that there are nevertheless 'certain established rules of law that must govern their interpretation,' namely:

- the *contra proferentum* rule;
- special rules that govern attempts to exempt negligence; and
- the 'four corners' rule.

(b) *Contra proferentum* rule

[9.265] The *contra proferentum* rule provides that, in Windeyer J's words, an exemption clause will be ordinarily construed strictly against the *proferens*—the party for whose benefit it is inserted.[122]

Example: Eimco Corporation v Tutt Bryant Ltd[123]

The vendor was a tractor dealer; it sold certain tractors to the buyer. At the time of the contract, the vendor provided a written statement, called a 'warranty', which provided that the goods would be free from defects in workmanship and material for one year; that the vendor's obligations under the warranty were limited to replacement of defective parts; and that the warranty was expressly in lieu of 'all other warranties express or implied'. The tractors proved to be defective.

The New South Wales Court of Appeal held that the condition of merchantability implied in the contract by the *Sale of Goods Act* had been breached. This condition continued in force because, read strictly and *contra proferentum*, the written statement only

---

117 *Darlington Futures Ltd v Delco Australia Pty Ltd* (1986) 161 CLR 500 at 510; see also *Port Jackson Stevedoring Pty Ltd v Salmond & Spraggon (Aust) Pty Ltd* (1978) 138 CLR 231 at 238; *Thomas National Transport (Melbourne) Pty Ltd v May & Baker (Australia) Pty Ltd* (1966) 115 CLR 353 at 376 per Windeyer J.

118 See, for example, *Amalgamated Television Services Pty Ltd v Television Corporation Ltd* (1969) 123 CLR 648; *George v Cluning* (1979) 28 ALR 57.

119 See, for example, *Ansett Transport Industries Pty Ltd v Commonwealth* (1977) 139 CLR 54; *George v Cluning* (1979) 28 ALR 57.

120 See, for example, *Thomas National Transport (Melbourne) Pty Ltd v May & Baker (Australia) Pty Ltd* (1966) 115 CLR 353; *The Antares (Nos 1 & 2)* [1987] 1 Lloyd's Rep 424 at 429–430.

121 *Thomas National Transport (Melbourne) Pty Ltd v May & Baker (Australia) Pty Ltd* (1966) 115 CLR 353 at 376–377.

122 Ibid, at 276 per Windeyer J.

123 [1970] 2 NSWR 249; see also *Wallis Son & Wells v Pratt & Haynes* [1911] AC 394; *Elders Smith Goldsbrough Mort Ltd v McBride* [1976] 2 NSWLR 631 at 642–643.

replaced 'all other *warranties* express or implied'. Further, although the buyer had accepted delivery and thus was required to treat the condition as a warranty *ex post facto*,[124] this meant only that the buyer could not terminate for breach. It did not reclassify the condition as a warranty for the purposes of the written statement. Accordingly, the buyer was entitled to damages and was not limited to replacement parts.

(c) Attempts to exempt negligence

[9.270] Windeyer J explained that an exemption clause will relieve a party of liability for his or her negligence, or that of his or her servants or agents, if it expressly or impliedly covers such liability. A clause will impliedly cover such liability if there can be no ground of liability other than negligence to which it could refer.[125] The rules regarding attempts to exempt negligence were stated in the Privy Council in *Canada Steamship Lines Ltd v The King*[126] as follows:

(1) an express exemption of liability for negligence must be given effect and is sufficient to exclude liability;

(2) where there is no express reference to negligence, the court must decide whether the ordinary meaning of the words used in the clause are wide enough to exclude negligence. Any doubt in this regard is resolved *contra proferentum*; and

(3) if the words used in the clause are wide enough to cover negligence, but there is some other ground of liability other than negligence, the clause will be read as applying only to that other ground of liability and will not operate to exclude the claim for negligence.[127]

[9.275] The three rules in effect provide for two eventualities: where the parties express an intention in unequivocal language that liability for negligence is to be exempted (rule 1) and where no such express intention is shown (rules 2 and 3). It would seem that for rule 1 to apply the word 'negligence' or a close synonym must be used.[128] To allow the exemption in such a case is to simply give effect to the clear intention of the parties.

---

124 See [9.160].

125 *Thomas National Transport (Melbourne) Pty Ltd v May & Baker Australia Pty Ltd* (1966) 115 CLR 353 at 376.

126 [1952] AC 192 at 208.

127 Different views have been expressed regarding whether the rules in *Canada Steamship Rules* survived the High Court's judgment in *Darlington Futures Ltd v Delco Australia Pty Ltd* (1986) 161 CLR 500: see *Schenker & Co (Aust) Pty Ltd v Maplas Equipment & Services Pty Ltd* [1990] VR 834 at 846 (rules inconsistent); *Glebe Island Terminals Pty Ltd v Continental Seagram Pty Ltd* [1994] 1 Lloyd's Rep 213 at 248 (rules inconsistent); *Graham v Royal National Agricultural and Industrial Association of Queensland* [1989] 1 Qd R 624 at 630–1 (rules consistent). Certainly Windeyer J in *Thomas National Transport (Melbourne) Pty Ltd v May & Baker Australia Pty Ltd* (1966) 115 CLR 353 had no difficulty applying a statement resembling that expressed in *Darlington v Delco* in conjunction with a statement resembling the rules in *Canada SS v The King* and it may be that the rules are simply an application in a particular case of the ordinary rules that an intention to exempt particular liability should be clearly expressed and that exemption clauses are interpreted strictly, *contra proferentum*: see also JW Carter & DJ Harland, *Contract Law in Australia*, 3rd edn, Butterworths, Sydney, 1996, p 264; DW Greig & JLR Davis, *Law of Contract*, Law Book Co, Sydney, 1987, p 629–630.

128 *Smith v South Wales Switchgear Ltd* [1978] 1 WLR 165.

[9.280] Unless the *proferens* is in such a strong bargaining position that he or she is able to name his or her terms, it may be more likely that the parties will be reluctant to use such explicit language as 'negligence' or 'neglect'. In such a situation, rules 2 and 3 are called into play to determine whether liability in negligence is excluded. These two rules together involve a two-stage enquiry:

- first, are the words used wide enough to cover negligence; and
- secondly, if so, is there some ground of liability other than negligence?

[9.285] Some authorities suggest that while the use of words such as 'all liability' or 'any loss' are insufficient, the addition of the words 'whatever its cause' or 'howsoever caused' will mean that the clause is wide enough to cover liability in negligence.[129] However, many cases have treated the words used as being capable of embracing liability in negligence according to their ordinary meaning.[130] It may be, therefore, that a court today will be reluctant to dismiss an exemption clause on the basis that on its ordinary construction it does not apply to liability for negligence.[131]

[9.290] Assuming that upon their ordinary meaning the words for the clause are capable of extending to liability and negligence, the next enquiry is a ground for liability other than negligence. In many types of contracts, the *proferens* will be under a duty to take reasonable care by virtue of both tort and the contract.

Example: Alderslade v Hendon Laundry Ltd[132]

The plaintiff took 10 linen handkerchiefs to the defendant launderers for washing. The defendants failed to return the handkerchiefs. There was evidence of negligence by the defendants, but they purported to rely upon a clause in the contract which provided that 'the maximum amount allowed for lost or damaged articles is 20 times the charge made for laundering'.

The English Court of Appeal held that in the case of a bailment of goods, such as had occurred in the present circumstances, the bailee is under a contractual obligation to take reasonable care for the protection of the goods. Accordingly, the only way the defendants could be made liable for the loss of the goods—whether in contract or in tort—was if it could be shown that they had been guilty of negligence in performing their duty to take care of the goods. Thus the only ground for liability was one in negligence—and the plaintiff could not avoid the application of the exemption clause by suing in tort rather than contract.

Similarly, under a contract of carriage, the carrier normally undertakes to use reasonable care in the carriage of the plaintiff or his or her goods. In the event of injury to the plaintiff or loss or damage to the goods, the plaintiff will have to show a failure to take

---

129 See, for example, *Rutter v Palmer* [1922] 2 KV 87 at 94; *Commissioner for Railways (NSW) v Quinn* (1946) 72 CLR 345 at 372. See generally JW Carter & DJ Harland, *Contract Law in Australia*, 3rd edn, Butterworths, Sydney, 1996, p 262.

130 See, for example, *Davis v Pearce Parking Station Pty Ltd* (1954) 91 CLR 642 ('not be responsible for loss or damage of any description' treated as capable of referring to liability for negligence); *Darlington Futures v Delco Australia Pty Ltd* (1986) 161 CLR 500 ('any loss arising in any way' regarded as capable of referring to liability for negligence).

131 See DW Greig & JLR Davis, *Law of Contract*, Law Book Co, Sydney, 1987, p 630.

132 [1945] KB 189.

reasonable care in order to show breach of contract, or alternatively a breach of the duty to exercise reasonable care in tort. Consequently, the only ground of liability in such cases is one based on negligence, and the exemption clause will operate to exclude liability. The same applies in the case of a contract for the provision of services, which will normally include a contractual undertaking by the contractor to take reasonable care in carrying out the services requested.

[9.295] A different result will follow, however, where there is an alternative cause of action not based on a failure to take reasonable care. This will be the case where, for example, a plaintiff may claim damages for—alternatively—breach of a strict obligation, or negligence in tort.

Example: White v John Warwick & Co Ltd[133]

The plaintiff hired a tricycle from the defendants for use in the delivery of newspapers. The contract contained a clause that purported to exempt the defendants from liability 'for any personal injuries to the riders of the machines hired'. While riding a tricycle provided by the defendants while his own was being repaired, the seat slipped forward and propelled the plaintiff over the handlebars, resulting in injury.

The English Court of Appeal held that in the circumstances there were two possible heads of liability: one for negligence and the other for breach of contract. The action for breach of contract was based on breach of the implied promise to provide a machine that was reasonably fit for the purpose for which it was hired. This promise was 'strict' in the sense that its breach did not require the plaintiff to prove that the defendants had failed to use reasonable care. Accordingly, the exemption clause was read as covering the strict liability in contract, but not the liability in tort for negligence.

[9.300] Possible alternative heads of damage may be identified with a little imagination, but they must not be so fanciful or remote that the *proferens* cannot be supposed to have desired protection against them.[134]

Example: Graham v Royal National Agricultural and Industrial Association of Queensland[135]

The plaintiff entered his palomino quarterhorse colt 'Bob's Chex' as an exhibit in the annual Royal National Show, commonly known as the Exhibition or 'Ekka'. The contract between the plaintiff and the RNA included an exclusion of liability in the following terms: 'The association will not under any circumstances hold itself responsible for any loss, damage to or any misdelivery of any exhibits.' One morning while it was being exercised—and due to the negligence of an RNA employee—the colt took fright and ran into a nearby road, where it became entangled with a car. As a consequence, the colt was seriously injured and ultimately had to be put down.

---

133 [1953] 2 All ER 1021.

134 *Canada Steamship Lines Ltd v The King* [1952] AC 192 at 208; *LSB Gillespie Bros & Co Ltd v Roy Bowles Transport Ltd* [1973] 1 QB 408 at 414.

135 [1989] 1 Qd R 624.

Connolly J of the Supreme Court of Queensland held that the meaning of the clause was that the parties agreed that liability was excluded. His Honour considered the rules in the *Canada SS* case were firmly established principles that the High Court had not intended to reverse in *Darlington Futures v Delco*. There was no express exclusion of negligence in this case. Applying the second and third rules from the *Canada SS* case, the wording of the clause was wide enough to cover negligence but the RNA's potential liability to exhibitors went beyond liability for negligence. It was not difficult to envisage causes of action for loss, damage or misdelivery of exhibits that were not founded on negligence when regard was had to the wide variety of activities conducted on the RNA's premises during the Ekka, including the great concentrations of people, livestock, agricultural and industrial exhibits, and the need for reserves of combustible fuels, electrical and water supplies, as well as the rides and machinery in the sideshow alley. The RNA was the sole supplier of electricity, and in the event of an interruption of supply without negligence on its part, could be liable for damage to exhibits caused by a failure of light or refrigeration. The RNA provided accommodation for animals for reward; it could conceivably be liable for breach of contract for damage caused by the unsuitability of that accommodation. The RNA undertook to feed poultry; it might be liable for breach of an implied term that the feed would be fit for consumption independent of any negligence on its part. Accordingly, the exemption clause did not extend to cover the RNA's negligence, and it was held liable to the plaintiff.

[9.305] It should be noted, however, that some State courts have preferred *Darlington Futures v Delco* to the *Canada SS* rules and have resolved questions involving attempts to exempt negligence by simply determining the natural and ordinary meaning of the clause in the context of the contract as a whole.[136]

(d) Four corners rule

[9.310] An exemption clause will only operate to exclude liability arising within the 'four corners' of the contract. A *proferens* can only rely on conditions that were intended to protect him or her if he or she carried out the contract in the way he or she had contracted to do it. It will not be effective where the *proferens* acts in a way Windeyer J described as 'quite alien to [the] contract.[137]

Example: Davis v Pierce Parking Station Pty Ltd[138]

The plaintiff parked her car in the defendant's parking station. The terms of the contract were contained in a receipt she was given. These included a term that the vehicle was 'garaged at owner's risk' and that the defendant would 'not be responsible for loss or damage of any description'. The defendant was held to be negligent in having left the car near a public street without removing the ignition key and in not taking

---

136 See, for example, *Glenmont Investments Pty Ltd v O'Loughlin* [2000] SASC 429 (FC) (20 December 2000); *GL Nederlands (Asia) Pty Ltd v Expertise Events Pty Ltd* [1999] NSWCA 62; *Schenker & Co (Aust) Pty Ltd v Maplas Equipment and Services Pty Ltd* [1990] VR 834.

137 *Thomas National Transport (Melbourne) Pty Ltd v May & Baker (Australia) Pty Ltd* (1966) 115 CLR 353 at 377; see also *Gibaud v Great Eastern Railway Co* [1921] 2 KB 426 at 435 per Scrutton LJ.

138 (1954) 91 CLR 642.

immediate steps to notify the police when it became apparent the car had been stolen. The car was later recovered, badly damaged.

The High Court held that bailees in the position of the defendant have a contractual duty to exercise reasonable care in and about the custody of the goods placed in their hands. In particular, they should exercise reasonable care to safeguard the property against theft. Moreover, if the property is stolen, they are bound, as soon as they become aware of that fact, to notify the bailor or the police so that immediate steps may be taken towards its recovery. Be that as it may, the duty to take steps for recovery was but one aspect of the bailee's general duty to take reasonable care in and about the garaging of the car, and the risk of loss or damage consequential on theft was a risk attached to the garaging of the car. In other words, the risk of loss or damage consequential on theft was a risk contemplated by the contract. The clause therefore operated to exempt the bailee's liability.

[9.315] By contrast, an exemption clause will not apply where the loss or damage results from conduct that is neither authorised nor permitted by the contract.[139]

Example: Sydney City Council v West[140]

The plaintiff parked his car at a parking station owned and operated by the defendant council. The plaintiff was given a ticket containing a number of clauses. One of the clauses read: 'The Council does not accept any responsibility for the loss or damage to any vehicle or for loss of or damage to any article or thing in or upon any vehicle or for any injury to any person however such loss, damage or injury may arise or be caused.' A second clause read: 'This ticket must be presented for time stamping and payment before taking delivery of the vehicle.' In spite of this, the council delivered the vehicle to a thief who claimed to have lost his ticket and who tricked the council into issuing a substitute ticket. When the plaintiff sued for damages—claiming breach of an implied promise of safekeeping or alternatively a course of action in detinue—the council tried to rely on the exemption clause.

A 3:2 majority of the High Court held that the council was unable to rely on the protection of the exemption clause. Under the terms of the contract, possession of any car was to be retained by the council until presentation and surrender of a ticket by the driver of the car. Accordingly, the act of the parking station attendant in allowing the thief to hand over a substitute ticket he had obtained by deception constituted an act done with respect to a bailor's goods that was neither authorised nor permitted by the contract.

Similarly, it would normally be outside the contemplation of either party for one of them to deliberately breach the contract, including deliberately or maliciously damaging goods held under a bailment or being carried under a contract of carriage.[141]

---

139 *The Council of the City of Sydney v West* (1965) 114 CLR 481 at 488–489.
140 (1965) 114 CLR 481.
141 See, for example, *Davies v Pearce Parking Station Pty Ltd* (1954) 91 CLR 642 at 652; *Sydney City Council v West* (1965) 114 CLR 481 at 488, 493; *TNT (Melbourne) Pty Ltd v May & Baker (Aust) Pty Ltd* (1966) 115 CLR 353 at 385 per Windeyer J.

(e) Statute

[9.320] The extent of protection offered by an exemption clause may reflect the degree of inequality of bargaining power between the parties. At common law, the court has no absolving power and cannot refuse to enforce a valid exemption clause even where it operates unreasonably.[142] This position has been altered by two statutes in particular that warrant mention.

[9.325] In New South Wales, the *Contracts Review Act* 1980 (NSW) allows a court to intervene in the case of contractual terms deemed to be 'unjust'. In such a case, the court is entitled to enforce the term only so far as it deems fit.[143] These provisions are of general application and would include within their ambit any exemption clause deemed to operate unreasonably.

[9.330] Statutory provisions that apply more particularly to exemption clauses may be found in the *Trade Practices Act* 1974 (Cth). Section 68 renders void any term that purports to exclude, restrict, or modify the application of terms implied under that statute, including terms regarding the quality or fitness of goods or services. The Act generally applies to the supply of goods or services by corporations or by natural persons in other areas of Commonwealth jurisdiction. However, an exception is provided by section 68A in the case of goods or services other than those acquired for personal, domestic, or household use, but which are sold at a price less than $40 000.[144] Section 68A provides that in such a case, a term of a contract for the supply of goods and services will not be void under section 68 by reason only that it limits the liability of the corporation in the following ways.

In the case of goods, any one of the following:
- the replacement of the goods or the supply of equivalent goods;
- repair of the goods;
- the payment of the cost of replacing the goods or acquiring equivalent goods; or
- the payment of the cost of having the goods repaired.

In the case of services:
- the supplying of the services; or
- the payment of a cost of having services supplied.

However, these permitted exclusions will not be allowed where the person to whom the goods or services were supplied establishes that it is not fair or reasonable for the corporation to rely on that term of the contract. In determining whether reliance on the term is fair or reasonable, the court must have regard to all the circumstances of the case, and in particular the following:
- the relative strength of bargaining positions, taking into account among other things the availability of equivalent goods or services and suitable alternative sources of supply;
- whether the buyer received an inducement to agree to the term or had the opportunity of acquiring the goods and services from any source of supply under a contract that did not include the term;

---

142   *Faramus v Film Artistes' Association* (1963) 1 All ER 636.
143   See [17.120].
144   See *Trade Practices Act* 1974 (Cth), s 4B.

- whether the buyer knew or ought reasonably to have known of the existence and extent of the term (having regard, among other things, to the custom of the trade and any previous course of dealing between the parties);
- in the case of the supply of goods, whether the goods were manufactured, processed, or adapted to the special order of the buyer.

9.3.4 Other common clauses

[9.335] A wide array of other types of terms may be found in contracts. Those discussed below are not exhaustive.

(a) Definition clauses

[9.340] Definition clauses are used to assign particular meanings to particular words used in the contract. These definitions may provide, for example, technical meanings or more extensive and specific meanings to particular words. For example, a clause may provide that: "Property' in this agreement means the property situated at 2 George Street, Brisbane.'

Such clauses are not promissory in nature and are not capable of being breached.

(b) Duty to act in good faith

[9.345] It has already been seen that Australian courts are prepared to imply a duty of good faith into contracts.[145] However, such an obligation may also be found in an express term of the contract. For example, a clause may provide: 'The purchaser and supplier shall make diligent and good faith efforts to resolve all disputes in accordance with the provisions of this [clause].'[146]

[9.350] Such a term may be appropriate in the case of a contract requiring concurrent performance or co-operation between the parties. What is enforced is not the cooperation itself but performance in a process.[147] This may be contrasted with a promises to 'negotiate in good faith' the terms of an agreement; such promises have been regarded as illusory on the ground that they are nothing more than an agreement to agree.[148]

[9.355] The effect of a breach of a duty of good faith will depend upon the clause and the circumstances. For example, a breach may prevent one party from relying on a term of the contract or from exercising a particular right under the contract, or may give rise to a liability in damages.

(c) Best endeavours clause

[9.360] A clause may provide that '[the agent] will use its best endeavours to promote and extend the sale of the product in the territory'.[149] Or it may require 'reasonable

---

145 See [8.750]–[8.785].

146 Cf cl 28.1 of the construction contract considered in *Aiton v Transfield* [1999] NSWSC 996 (Einstein J 1 October 1999).

147 *Hooper Bailie Associated Ltd v Natcon Group Pty Ltd* (1992) 28 NSWLR 194 at 206.

148 *Coal Cliff Collieries Pty Ltd v Sijehama Pty Ltd* (1991) 24 NSWLR 1 (although a majority was prepared to accept such an agreement in appropriate circumstances); *Tobias v QDL Ltd* (unreported, NSW SC, Simos J, 12 September 1997).

149 Cf cl 7(a) in the distributorship agreement considered in *L Schuler AG v Wickman Machine Tool Sales Ltd* [1974] AC 235.

endeavours' or 'all reasonable endeavours'. Such a clause is often found in distributor-ship agreements and license agreements,[150] although it is not restricted to those types of contract.[151] These clauses are designed to provide a measure of protection to the promisee by imposing an obligation on the promisor.[152]

What a promisor is required to do under a 'best endeavours' clause is determined by what is reasonable in the circumstances, taking account of the nature, capacity, qualifications, and responsibilities of the party to the contract viewed in light of the particular contract.[153] A best endeavours clause places a party under an obligation not to hinder or prevent the fulfilment of its purpose.[154] However, the obligation does not require the party to venture beyond the bounds of reason. He or she is required to do all that reasonably can be done in the circumstances to achieve the contractual object, but no more.[155]

(d) Entire contract (merger) clause

[9.365] The parol evidence rule may be reinforced by a provision known as an 'entire contract' or 'merger' clause that expressly states that the written contract is conclusive of the parties' bargain. For example, a clause may provide: 'The agreement as herein set forth contains the entire understanding of the respective parties with reference to the subject matter hereof and there is no other understanding, agreement, warranty or representation express or implied in any way binding, extending, defining or otherwise relating to … any of the matters [herein].'[156]

[9.370] Such a clause is effective to exclude extraneous terms or interpretations, as well as any representations at common law[157]—at least those that are not fraudulent.[158] Its effect on misleading or deceptive conduct may be questionable, unless in the particular circumstances it serves to break the chain of causation between the conduct and any subsequent contract. In other words, the question would be whether, in light of the clause, the contract was formed irrespective of the conduct.[159]

[9.375] The clause will not, however, preclude the receipt of evidence showing that the contract did not record the common intention of the parties for the purpose of the equitable remedy of rectification. This is because rectification operates outside a contract and independent of the parol evidence rule.[160]

---

150 *Hospital Products Ltd v United States Surgical Corporation* (1984) 156 CLR 41 at 91 per Mason J. See also *Transfield Pty Ltd v Arlo International Ltd* (1980) 144 CLR 83.

151 See, for example, *Ankar Pty Ltd v National Westminster Finance (Australia) Ltd* (1987) 162 CLR 549 (surety agreement).

152 *Hospital Products Ltd v United States Surgical Corporation* (1984) 156 CLR 41 at 91 per Mason J.

153 *Transfield Pty Ltd v Arlo International Ltd* (1980) 144 CLR 83 at 97 per Mason J.

154 *Shepard v Felt & Textiles of Aust. Ltd* (1931) 45 CLR 359 at 378; *Hospital Products Ltd v United States Surgical Corporation* (1984) 156 CLR 41 at 65 per Gibbs CJ.

155 *Sheffield District Railway Co v Great Central Railway Co* (1911) 27 TLR 451; *Paltara Pty Ltd v Dempster* (1991) 6 WAR 85 at 89 (FC); *Hospital Products Ltd v United States Surgical Corporation* (1984) 156 CLR 41 at 92 per Mason J.

156 Cf cl 27 of the hire contract considered in *Hope v RCA Photophone of Australia Pty Ltd* (1937) 59 CLR 348.

157 *Life Insurance Co of Australia v Phillips* (1925) 36 CLR 60 at 82–83 per Isaacs J.

158 This is because 'fraud opens all doors': *Macdonald v Shinko Australia Pty Ltd* [1999] 2 Qd R 152 at 154.

159 See [13.605].

160 *Macdonald v Shinko Australia Pty Ltd* [1999] 2 Qd R 152 at 155, 156.

(e) Agreed damages clause

[9.380] An agreed damages clause is a clause that provides for the payment of an amount that is a genuine pre-estimate of the loss resulting from any breach. For example, a clause may provide that: 'If during the hiring [the borrower] defaults in any payment or commits any breach of this agreement [the lender] may retake possession of the goods and recover from [the borrower] as liquidated damages the recoverable amount being the total rent less all moneys paid by [the borrower] to [the lender] by way of deposit and rentals for the goods, the value of the goods and a rebate of charges calculated in accordance with this clause.'[161]

The purpose of such a clause is to remove the need to prove the actual extent of loss. This may mean a shorter trial or no need to proceed to trial at all. Agreed damages clauses are common in, for example, shipping and construction contracts, where certain types of breach may be not uncommon.[162] They also are common in hire purchase agreements, where they are known as 'acceleration clauses'.

The validity of an agreed damages clause is governed by the law related to penalties.[163]

(f) Termination clause

[9.385] A termination clause confers a contractual right to terminate the contract for breach. Such a right may be general—in which case it will arise on a breach of any term—or specific, in which case it will arise only where there has been a breach of a specific term. For example, a clause may provide: 'In the event that [party A] fails to carry out the contract or comply with a condition of the contract to the satisfaction of [party B], [party B] may require [party A] to show cause why the contract should not be cancelled.'[164]

An issue that may arise in relation to termination clauses is whether the contract may only be terminated in the way specified by the clause, or whether the clause merely provides additional ways of terminating the contract apart from those available at common law.[165]

(g) *Force majeure* clause

[9.390] A *force majeure* clause provides for the disposition of a contract in the event of its being affected by circumstances beyond the control of the parties—such as an act of God. For example, a clause may provide that: 'the above sale is subject to strikes, floods, war, accidents, fire, failure of manufacturers to deliver, non-receipt, non-delivery or mistakes in cables, and/or other contingencies causing delay or non-shipment'.[166]

---

161 Cf cll 5 and 6 in the hire purchase contract considered in *Esanda Finance Corporation Ltd v Plessnig* (1989) 166 CLR 131.

162 For example, where a ship takes longer to load or unload than promised (a not infrequent occurrence) damages at an amount per hour or per day (called 'demurrage') become payable for detaining the ship in port in breach of contract.

163 See [20.50].

164 Cf cl 2.24 of the contract for services considered in *Commonwealth v Amann Aviation Pty Ltd* (1991) 174 CLR 64.

165 See [23.425]–[23.470].

166 Cf the clause in the sale contract considered in *Ringstad v Gollin & Co Pty Ltd* (1924) 35 CLR 303 at 313.

A *force majeure* clause may operate in relation to events that are not ordinarily regarded as of the kind that would render the contemplated performance of a contract impossible at common law. Further, a *force majeure* clause may provide that if one of the catalogued events occurs, the contract will be terminated, suspended, renegotiated, or otherwise dealt with in accordance with its express terms.[167]

(h) Restraint of trade

[9.395] A restraint of trade clause is a promise by one party to give up a freedom with respect to his or her trade for the benefit of the other party. For example, a contract might contain a promise by a television presenter that he or she will not 'engage in any other presentation activity during the term of this agreement ... without the prior written consent of [the employer]'.[168]

At common law, all restraints are prima facie void, but may be justified if they are shown to be reasonable. Breach or threatened breach of a valid restraint may give rise to a remedy—particularly an injunction restraining breach. Restraints of trade are considered in more detail below.[169]

(i) Dispute resolution clause

[9.400] A dispute resolution clause provides that any dispute between the parties arising under the contract should first be referred to an alternative means of resolution. For example, a clause may provide: 'All disputes arising out of the Contract during the progress of the works or after completion or as to any breach or alleged breach shall be decided by arbitration.'[170] Alternatively, the clause may require disputes to be referred to mediation.

[9.405] Such clauses provide a procedure to be followed for a resolution of disputes. They are common in the construction and shipping industries. Dispute resolution clauses have been held to be not contrary to the public policy that prevents attempts to oust the court's jurisdiction.[171] Failure to observe a dispute resolution clause may constitute a breach of contract that gives rise to a remedy, including an injunction staying any court proceedings commenced contrary to its terms,[172] and/or damages for breach.[173]

(j) Law of contract

[9.410] A contract has the capacity to span jurisdictions. The law that governs the rights and liabilities of the parties is referred to as the 'proper law' of the contract.[174] In determining the proper law of a contract, a court will be guided by the express or

---

167 The relationship between force majeure clauses and the common law concerning frustration is considered at [22.170].

168 Cf cl 2(iii) in the employment contract considered in *Curro v Beyond Productions Pty Ltd* (1993) 30 NSWLR 337.

169 See [18.35].

170 Cf cl G56(1) of the construction contract considered in *Codelfa Construction Pty Ltd v State Rail Authority of New South Wales* (1982) 149 CLR 337. Such a clause may more specifically be described as an 'arbitration clause.'

171 Such a clause is often referred to as a '*Scott v Avery* clause': see further [18.105].

172 *CSR Ltd v Cigna Insurance Ltd* (1997) 189 CLR 345.

173 *The Jay Bola* [1997] 2 Lloyd's Rep 279 at 285.

174 *Merwin Pastoral Co Pty Ltd v Moolpa Pastoral Co Pty Ltd* (1933) 48 CLR 565 at 573.

presumed intention of the parties.[175] An example of an express statement of intention is: 'This contract shall be governed by the laws of Queensland.'

[9.415] Generally speaking, the parties have an unfettered right to choose the proper law of their contract.[176] Indeed, parties to a contract made in Queensland and to be performed in Queensland could declare that the contract was to be governed by the law of another country, such as New Zealand, with which the contract had no connection at all—provided such a measure is bona fide and not contrary to public policy.[177] In the absence of an express statement, the proper law of the contract is that of the jurisdiction with which the contract has most real connection.[178]

9.4　International perspective

9.4.1　New Zealand

[9.420] There are some minor differences between the law in Australia and in New Zealand with respect to the various matters examined in this contract. A line of authority in New Zealand supports the view that, like Australia and England, subsequent conduct may not be used to aid the interpretation of a contract.[179] However, a recent majority of the Court of Appeal purported—apparently without considering any House of Lords or High Court decisions—to state the current law in terms of its being possible for meaning to be illuminated by subsequent conduct.[180]

[9.425] In relation to the significance attached to particular promissory terms, the *Contracts Remedies Act* 1979 s 7(4) provides that the remedy for a breach of term depends upon the seriousness of its consequences. A party may terminate where the effect of the breach is to substantially reduce the benefit to the innocent party, to substantially increase the burden of the innocent party, or to make the benefit or burden substantially different from that contracted for by the innocent party. In other words, New Zealand law now regards all promissory terms as being intermediate terms.[181]

[9.430] In relation to exemptions clauses, while New Zealand has not taken steps to regulate exemption clauses such as those taken in England,[182] in particular instances, validity of an exemption clause may be questioned; these include hire purchase contracts, door-to-door sales, insurance contracts, minor's contract, small disputes, pre-contractual negotiations, transactions caught by the *Fair Trading Act* 1986, and transactions caught by the *Consumer Guarantees Act* 1993.[183]

175　*Moonlighting International Pty Ltd v International Lighting Pty Ltd* [2000] FCA 41 (Finckelstein J, 31 January 2000).
176　*Kay's Leasing Corp Pty Ltd v Fletcher* (1964) 64 SR (NSW) 195 at 205.
177　*Vita Food Products Inc v Unus Shipping Co* [1939] AC 277 at 290.
178　*Bonython v The Commonwealth* (1948) 75 CLR 589 at 601.
179　See, for example, *McLaren v Waikato Regional Council* [1993] 1 NZLR 710 at 731; *New Zealand Post Ltd v ASB Bank Ltd* [1995] 2 NZLR 508 at 511; *Supercool Refrigeration & Airconditioning v Hoverd Industries Ltd* [1994] 3 NZLR 300 at 317. These decisions were all at High Court level.
180　*Valentines Properties Pty Ltd v Hunico Corp Ltd* [2000] 3 NZLR 16 at 27 per Keith and Gallen JJ, Paterson J dissenting.
181　See [20.545]–[20.560]. This section does not affect an innocent party's right to terminate for repudiation: see s 7(2).
182　See *Unfair Contract Terms Act* 1977 (UK).
183　See JF Burrows, J Finn & S Todd, *Law of Contract in New Zealand*, Butterworths, Wellington, 1997, pp 210–218.

9.4.2 United States

[9.435] American courts regard the process of interpretation as an exercise in attempting to determine the meaning that the parties themselves attach to their language. This will not necessarily reflect the objective meaning that may be ascribed to the words used.[184] Even where a common meaning is not shared by both parties—so that there has been what may be described as a 'misunderstanding'—American courts will still enquire whether there is still some reason for preferring the meaning of one party over that of the other. This will usually occur where one party actually knows or has reason to know that the other party has attached another meaning, and also knows what that meaning is. In such a case, the meaning attached by the first party is preferred.[185] It is only where there is no true meeting of the minds—when the parties attach materially different meanings with their manifestations and neither party knows or has reason to know the meaning attached by the other—that there is no contract for lack of assent.[186] Such a result also follows in the even rarer case where there is a stand-off because each party knows (or each party has reason to know) the meaning attached by the other.[187]

[9.440] In seeking to achieve this interpretative end, an American court is entitled to look to all the relevant circumstances surrounding the transaction when interpreting the contract. This includes 'all writings, oral statements, and other conduct which the parties manifested their assent, together with any prior negotiations between them and any applicable course of dealing, course of performance, or usage.'[188] Since the objective is to ascertain the meaning to be given to the language, there is no requirement that the language be ambiguous, vague or otherwise uncertain before recourse is had to the surrounding circumstances.[189] In other respects, the interpretative process involves familiar concepts including that the agreement is to be read as a whole,[190] and that in cases of ambiguity, the contract is read contra proferentem.

[9.445] The American approach to the classification of terms is substantially different from the Australian approach. In the United States, it is recognised that a party who has not received an expected performance may pursue a claim for damages. However, in some limited cases, the innocent party may in addition exercise a right to suspend its own performance—which may ultimately lead to a refusal to perform if the other party fails to perform. This additional remedy depends upon the American concept of 'condition'.[191]

[9.450] The Restatement Second §224 defines a condition as 'an event not certain to occur, which must occur, unless occurrence is excused, before performance under a contract becomes due.' This means that the term 'condition' embraces:

---

184   EA Farnsworth, *Contracts*, 3rd edn, Aspen Law and Business, New York, 1999, §7.7, 7.9; cf *Eustis Mining Co v Beer, Sondheimer & Co* 239 F 976 at 984–985 (SDNY 1917) per Learned Hand J.

185   See also Restatement Second §201.

186   Restatement Second §20.

187   Ibid.

188   EA Farnsworth, *Contracts*, 3rd edn, Aspen Law and Business, New York, 1999, §7.10.

189   Ibid.

190   *Brinderson-Newberg Joint Venture v Pacific Erectors* 971 F 2d 272 (9th Cir 1992).

191   EA Farnsworth, *Contracts*, 3rd edn, Aspen Law and Business, New York, 1999, §8.1.

- an event within the control of the promisor (often referred to as the 'obligor' in America), such as a promisor's duty to pay for painting on his or her 'honour satisfaction with the job';
- an event largely within the control of the promisee (often referred to as the 'obligee' in America), such as an insurer's duty to pay for loss due to fire when the insured provides proof of loss;
- an event largely within the control of a third person, such as the promise by a purchaser to complete settlement on condition that the bank approve finance; or
- an event largely beyond the control of anyone such as the promise by an insurer to pay under an insurance policy on condition that damage result from fire.[192]

The promisor need not render performance until the condition occurs.[193] A condition need not be material or significant[194]—reflecting the Australian notion that any term may be elevated to the status of a promissory condition.

[9.455] While generally speaking any event may be made a 'condition,' the Restatement Second definition excludes three kinds of events:

- events that must occur before a contract comes into existence;
- events that are certain to occur; and
- events that extinguish a duty after its performance has become due.

Accordingly, the Restatement Second excludes as a 'condition' events that Australian courts might describe as conditions precedent to formation or conditions subsequent.

[9.450] The non-occurrence of a condition of a promisor's duty may have two effects:

- the promisor is entitled to suspend performance on the ground that the performance is not due as long as the condition has not occurred; or
- if it becomes too late for the condition to occur, the promisor is entitled to treat the duty as discharged and the contract as terminated.[195]

A suspension of performance cannot last indefinitely, so it naturally follows that at some point the promisor must be allowed to treat the duty as discharged. The time between suspension and final discharge may be expressly stipulated in the agreement, or implied to be a reasonable time.

[9.465] In relation to exemption clauses, it has been held that a party cannot exempt itself from liability in tort for harm that it causes intentionally or recklessly.[196] However, a party is able to exempt itself from liability—or limit liability in tort for harm caused by negligence—provided the clause is not unconscionable.[197] However, as has been noted elsewhere,[198] that there have been cases in which an exemption clause has been unenforceable because it affects the public interest and the other party is a member of a protected class. The two main examples involve an employer attempting to exempt itself from liability to its employee for negligence, and a common carrier or

---

192 Ibid at §8.2.
193 Ibid.
194 *Jungmann & Co v Atterbury Bros* 163 NE 123 (NY 1928).
195 Restatement Second §225.
196 *Martin Marietta Corp v International Telecommunication Satellite Organisation* 991 F 2d 94 (4th Cir 1993).
197 *O'Callaghan v Waller & Beckwith Realty Co* 155 NE 2d 545 (Ill 1958).
198 See [18.530].

utility attempting to exempt itself from liability to its passenger or customer for negligence (although a limit of liability may be allowed where it is in exchange for a cheaper rate). There has also been support for striking down exemption clauses contained in residential leases,[199] although there has been disagreement about whether a seller of a product may exempt itself from strict liability imposed for physical harm caused by the product's unreasonable dangerous condition.[200] It seems that such an exemption may be permitted in the case of a contract negotiated between two businesses of equal bargaining power for the sale of an experimental product.[201]

9.4.3 Japan

[9.470] In common law countries such as Australia, the division of contract terms into conditions, warranties, and intermediate terms is an exercise in determining the relevant consequences of breach. In Japanese contract law, the key question is rather whether contract termination (*kaijo*) is possible, and in what circumstances. Most commentators translate *kaijo* in English as rescission because the obligation set out in article 545 is to restore the innocent party to their original position, without prejudicing the rights of bona fide third parties. This is procedural rescission, rather than the equitable concept of the same name. A claim for rescission under Japanese law does not preclude a claim for damages for real loss such as the loss of expected contract profits.[202]

[9.475] Contracts in Japan may be terminated as of right or by operation of law. A typical example of termination by right is the frequently used contract clause that lists the circumstances in which the contract will be automatically terminated. In a commercial contract, these usually include events such as change of company president, the commencement of corporate reorganisation or bankruptcy-related procedures, and a criminal investigation of office-holders of either party or the like. The parties are free to indicate other terms of the contract where breach will result in termination, but the courts may reinterpret those choices.

[9.480] In contracts other than continuing contracts, termination of the contract by law will be permitted where there is:

- a breach of the contract;
- the breach can be attributed to the fault of the other party; and
- the procedures set out in Civil Code article 541 have been followed.

Article 541 provides that 'if one of the parties does not perform his obligation the other party may fix a reasonable period and demand its performance, and may rescind the contract, if no performance is effected within such a period.' The kinds of breaches that traditionally ground the right to terminate are delay in performance,[203] impossibility of performance[204] and incomplete performance.

The requirement that, in cases other than that of impossibility, the other party be offered a chance to cure faulty performance before terminating the contract is typical of civil law systems.

---

199   *Henrioulle v Marin Ventures* 573 P 2d 465 (Cal 1978).
200   *Sterner Aero v Page Airmotive* 499 F 2d 709 (10th Cir 1974).
201   *Keystone Aeronautics Corp v RJ Enstrom Corp* 499 F 2d 146 (3rd Cir 1974).
202   Civil Code Article 545(3).
203   Civil Code Articles 541 and 542.
204   Civil Code Article 543.

[9.485] Termination by operation of law depends on whether the contract is a single transaction or a continuing contract. This distinction is important, because the legal rules about continuing contracts may operate to override the parties' agreement. Continuing contracts—including leases, contracts of employment, entrustment (sub-contracting) contracts and the like—are subject to some specific provisions under the Civil Code. For example, article 620 provides that leases may only be rescinded with prospective effect. Contracts of mandate (such as agency agreements) and sub-contracts are also subject to the limitation that the right of rescission may only be exercised if the other party is compensated adequately.

[9.490] The consequences of terminating as of right or at law are spelt out in the case law for particular contract types. A typical example of this is the long-term distribution contract, where renewal is tacitly expected and is essential to the livelihood of one of the parties. In one leading case, the court held that where the renewal of the contract was of this kind, despite the parties being free to terminate the contract at will, such a decision would have to be supported by a compelling reason. In the absence of a compelling reason, the terminating party may be liable for substantial damages.[205] Similarly, other distribution cases have held that, where a contract period is for a year but the contract itself has been repeatedly renewed and there is an expectation of renewal, then a contract provision allowing 30 days' notice for termination by either party will be ineffective. The notice period actually required will be closer to six months or a year, in the absence of the terminating party being able to show some kind of compelling reason (such as a breach going to the fundamental nature of the contract) in order to support the termination clause.

[9.495] The absolute liability for performing a contract at common law—which in Australia often results in the inclusion of an exemption clause—is not a feature of Japanese contract law. As a result, exemption clauses were seldom a feature of traditional Japanese contract theory or practice. They are more evident in standard-form contracts (for example, in sales of consumer goods). This can be partly explained as a kind of pre-emptive reaction to the 1996 *Product Liability Law*, which imposes strict liability for loss arising from flaws in the manufacture, design or sale of consumer goods.

---

205   Sapporo High Court 30 September 1987 *Hanji* 1258–76.

Part IV

Limits on Enforcement of Contracts

In some circumstances, the three essential elements of a binding contract—agreement, intention to create legal relations and consideration—may be present and yet the contract is unable to be enforced. This Part examines three factors that limit the persons who may enforce a contract or the circumstances in which a contract may be enforced.

This Part commences with an examination of the concept of capacity to contract. The capacity of a contracting party is often not in issue. However, a party who is a minor (a person who has not yet turned 18), is mentally impaired by illness or intoxication by alcohol or drugs, or has become insolvent, may be able to rescind the contract. This will mean the other party will be unable to enforce the contract against the one lacking capacity—or may only be able to enforce it in limited circumstances. On the other hand, a person who lacks capacity may still be able to enforce the contract against the other party. The capacity of corporations, associations and the government are also discussed.

The next major topic discussed in this Part is the requirement of writing. Although, generally speaking, a contract does not have to be in writing to be enforceable, in a small number of situations, the contract must be either made in writing (in a formal document) or sufficiently evidenced in writing to be enforceable. The law in this area originated with the English *Statute of Frauds* 1677, which has been re-enacted to a greater or lesser extent in the different Australian States.

The third chapter in this Part examines the concept of privity of contract. Privity has two main aspects. First, only the parties to a contract are able to enforce it. Thus, even if the parties intend a person who is not a party to the contract (referred to as a 'third party') to receive a benefit under the contract, the third party is not able to enforce it. A variety of legislation has been enacted to overcome this limitation. Further, the third party might effectively overcome the limitation by relying on one of the so-called 'exceptions to privity'—in fact other principles of law that give the third party rights in the circumstances. Secondly, only the parties to a contract may be subject to liabilities (or 'burdens') under it. Thus parties to a contract are not able to impose a burden on a third party. Once again, in some cases a third party might be made subject to a burden as a result of the application of other principles in the circumstances.

Chapter 10
Capacity

10.1 Introduction

[10.05] The law assumes that those who enter into contracts have the legal capacity to do so. However, contract law is no different from other areas of law where by virtue of a person's age, state of mind, or status, the person is given protection by the law.[1] In the area of tort law, for instance, a person who has insufficient maturity and lacks understanding about the nature of proposed medical treatment cannot give a valid consent to that treatment[2]—and in the area of negligence, the age of the defendant is a factor that goes to the question of breach of duty.[3] In the area of criminal law, a child under the age of 14 is protected from certain criminal liability.[4] Children under the age of 18 are generally prohibited from marrying.[5]

These are but some examples of the way the law, recognising there is a need to protect the vulnerable and the young, provides exceptions to the assumption of capacity.

[10.10] In contract law, however, when we refer to a 'lack of capacity' we are not referring to a lack of understanding. Indeed, there would be many competent adults who, when entering into an agreement, do not fully understand the nature or extent of their promises; yet the courts do not routinely declare these contracts void or voidable. Likewise, there would be many agreements made by minors where the terms are fully understood by both parties and yet the contract is not binding on the minor. And the old common law concerning the incapacity of married women to enter into a binding contract was not based on some notion as to their 'lack of understanding', but rather the legal fiction that they had no legal personality separate from that of their husbands.[6] The practical effect of legislation is that married women now have full contractual capacity.[7]

When we are referring to a lack of capacity in contract law we are really referring to persons in a particular circumstance or with a characteristic that invokes the protection of the law—or, for reasons of policy, restricts the rights of one of the parties to

---

1   'Person' here refers not just to individuals but also to organisations, corporations and governments.
2   In *Secretary, Department of Health and Community Services v JWB and SNB* (1992) 175 CLR 218 the High Court noted the House of Lords decision in *Gillick v West Norfolk AHA* [1985] 3 All ER 402 and concluded: 'A minor is, according to this principle, capable of giving informed consent when he or she achieves a sufficient understanding and intelligence to enable him or her to understand fully what is proposed. This approach, though lacking the certainty of a fixed age rule, accords with experience and with psychology. It should be followed in this country as part of the common law.' In some Australian jurisdictions legislation has changed the common law concerning consent to medical treatment by minors. See for example the *Consent to Medical Treatment and Palliative Care Act* 1995 (SA) and the *Minors (Property and Contracts) Act* 1970 (NSW). In the case of an adult suffering an intellectual disability the test of capacity to consent to treatment is also in terms of understanding. In most Australian jurisdictions there is now legislation in place that sets up a statutory scheme for approving treatment to adults who lack understanding.
3   In *McHale v Watson* (1964) 111 CLR 384, for example, the fact that the defendant was a child was a significant factor in deciding that there had been no negligence.
4   At common law a person under seven cannot incur criminal liability, a person between seven and 14 can be convicted of a criminal offence only if the Crown can also prove that the defendant at the time of the offence had the mental capacity to understand that he or she was doing something that was wrong: *M* (1977) 16 SASR 589. The common law rule is adhered to in Tasmania. In Victoria and the ACT, the minimum age of criminal responsibility has been raised to eight and in NSW, SA, Qld, WA and the NT to ten.
5   This may however in certain cases be lowered to 16 years: *Marriage Act* (1961) (Cth), s 12.

hold the other to their promise. Thus, many contracts concerning minors and the mentally disabled are in fact binding. In this sense, it is misleading to speak of certain classes of persons lacking capacity to contract.

In their book *The Law of Contract*, Greig and Davis note:

> It is however, a misnomer to talk in this context of a lack of capacity. A minor, for instance is fully capable of entering into a variety of contracts, and with regard to other contracts the minority of one party bestows upon him the privilege of being able to repudiate, or of not being bound by a contract, but does not prevent the contract from being enforced by him. With regard to the mentally ill or someone who is drunk, the fact that they may not be subject to the obligations of a contract stems from the power of the courts, in their equitable jurisdiction to set aside a contract on the grounds of unconscionability, rather than any lack of capacity on the part of the person affected. In the case of married women, any restriction on their liability under a contract is an incident of their rights to property and not of their contractual capacity.[8]

[10.15] Concerning minors, the arbitrary notion that individuals below the age of 18 require protection from certain bargains seems out of step with modern psychology and the economic realities of life.[9] Perhaps a more modern approach would be to look at the level of maturity and understanding of the parties. This would be consistent with the way other areas of law deal with young people. Much of our law is still grounded in common law principles that historically put minors in the same category as lunatics and married women, and as such in need of protection. Society has moved a long way since those categorisations could (if they ever could) be described as appropriate.

[10.20] Finally, by way of introduction, the development of international trade agreements and Internet transactions has required a reassessment of much of the law of contract. The issue of capacity has not escaped these developments. The market-place

---

6   At common law, the property of a married woman vested in her husband and any contracts she made were void because she had no legal personality separate from her husband. A means of avoiding this conclusion was where property was conveyed to her for her sole and separate use, in which case equity required her husband or trustee to hold his legal interest as trustee for her. This is what the case law means when referring to the liability of married women being proprietary and not personal. It was also possible for property to be vested in a married women in such a way that it could not be disposed of by her under the influence of her husband. This was referred to as 'Restraints upon anticipation'. This common law position has also been subject to statutory reform and either abolished or amended so as to allow courts to release a married woman's property from a restraint upon anticipation where this is for her benefit and with her consent.

7   See for example *Law of Property Act* 1936 (SA); *Married Women's Property Act* 1935 (Tas); *Marriage Act* 1958 (Vic); *Married Persons' Property Act* 1986 (ACT); *Married Persons (Equality of Status) Act* 1989 (NT); *Law Reform Act* 1995 s 18 (Qld); *Married Persons (Equality of Status) Act* 1989 (NSW); *Married Women's Property Act* 1892 (WA).

8   DW Greig & JLR Davis, *The Law of Contract,* The Law Book Company Limited, North Ryde, 1987, p 757.

9   In terms of the psychology, this is a reflection of the fact that evidence suggests that the capacity to make an intelligent choice, involving the ability to consider different options and their consequences, generally appears in a child somewhere between the ages of 11 and 14. See *Secretary, Department of Health and Community Services v JWB and SNB* (1992) 175 CLR 218 at 238. The economic reality is that young people do have disposable income and are increasingly entering into commercial agreements.

is no longer the corner store but the world wide web. Important statutory provisions (especially in New South Wales) have also amended or abrogated the common law in this area. Both these matters are considered later in this chapter.

10.2 Minors

[10.25] In Australia, a minor is a person under the age of 18.[10] The general position in respect of contracts entered into by minors is that they are voidable.[11] However, at common law, contracts in a particular group are binding on the minor. These are contracts for necessaries, or contracts relating to employment or apprenticeship. Other contracts are binding on the minor unless *repudiated*, or not binding on the minor unless they are *ratified* upon attaining adulthood. This division is an attempt by the law to balance competing policy considerations: protecting young people as well as giving effect to contractual promises.[12]

10.2.1 *Contracts that are binding*

(a) Contracts for necessary goods and services

[10.30] Contracts for necessaries (be they goods or services) will be binding on both parties; the normal remedies for a breach of contract will apply where the minor fails to carry out her or his promise. The rationale is that if the contract is one for necessary goods or services, then there can be no detriment or disadvantage by enforcing the agreement. However, in this context, benefit alone is not enough—the goods or services must also fall within the definition of necessaries or, as we shall see, the contract must be one of employment or apprenticeship.[13] Moreover, a minor is not bound by a trading contract, no matter how beneficial the contract may have been.[14] In *Cowern v Nield*[15] Phillimore J noted:

> It is no doubt correct to say, in a general sense that contracts of a certain character are enforceable against an infant if they are for his benefit, but an infant is

---

10 *Age of Majority Act* 1974 (ACT) s 5; 1974 (NT) s 4; 1973 (Tas) s 3; 1977 (Vic) s 3; 1972 (WA) s 5; *Minors (Property and Contracts) Act* 1970 (NSW) s 8 and s 17 *Law Reform Act* 1995 (NSW); *Age of Majority (Reduction) Act* 1971 (SA), s 3; *Law Reform Act* 1995 (Qld), s 17. In New Zealand, by the *Age of Majority Act* 1970 an infant or minor is a person who has not attained 20 years of age.

11 A necessary qualification to this statement is that in some jurisdictions (especially New South Wales) legislation has changed the position. The relevant legislative provisions are included at the end of this section. In New Zealand the position is determined by the provisions of the *Minors' Contracts Act* 1969.

12 In New Zealand the position is covered by the *Minors' Contracts Act* 1969 discussed at [10.260]–[10.280].

13 In the case of *Bojczuk v Gregorcewicz* [1961] SASR 128 the Supreme Court held that a minor was not bound by a promise to pay for a ticket to enable her to emigrate from Poland to Australia although the contract was for her benefit. 'The mere fact that the contract was for the benefit of the defendant is not in itself reason for holding that it is a contract binding on her ... The contract was plainly not in itself a contract for employment or instruction or education, and in my opinion it was not closely connected with any such contract or incidental or ancillary to any such contract, or similar in character to the classes of agreements which have been held to be binding upon infants if for their benefit' (per Ross J at 132 and 134).

14 *Cowern v Nield* [1912] 2 KB 419 where a minor who had established himself in business was not bound by a contract whereby he agreed to sell goods in the course of his business; *Merchantile Union Guarantee Corp Ltd v Ball* [1937] 2 KB 498 where a minor was not liable on a contract involving the hire-purchase of goods acquired by him for use in his business.

15 [1912] 2 KB 419 at 422.

not necessarily liable on a contract merely because it is for his benefit. I am satisfied from the authorities which have been cited to us that the only contracts which, if for the infant's benefit, are enforceable against him are contracts relating to the infant's person, such as contracts for necessaries, food, clothing, and lodging, contracts of marriage, and contacts of apprenticeship and service. In my opinion a trading contract does not come within that category.

In *Nash v Inman*,[16] an action was brought by a tailor for clothes supplied to the defendant while he was an undergraduate at Cambridge University. Fletcher Moulton LJ noted:

> An infant, like a lunatic, is incapable of making a contract of purchase in the strict sense of the words; but if a man satisfies the needs of the infant or lunatic by supplying to him necessaries, the law will imply an obligation to repay him for the services so rendered, and will enforce that obligation against the estate of the infant or lunatic.[17]

[10.35] Of course, the most litigated issue in this area is what constitutes 'necessaries'. The common law has developed a two-tiered test. The first part asks whether the goods or services are capable of being a necessary and the second part asks whether the goods actually are a necessary in the circumstances.[18] In all jurisdictions (except New South Wales) legislation provides that where necessaries are sold and *delivered* to a minor, the minor must pay a reasonable price.[19] The statutory definition of necessaries accords with the common law: they are goods suitable to the condition in life of such minor, and necessary to his or her actual requirements at the time of sale and delivery.[20]

[10.40] Whether the goods concerned are capable of being regarded as necessaries is a question of law for the judge to decide. The onus of establishing this matter rests with the plaintiff. It is a question of fact for the jury (if there is one) to determine whether the goods actually are necessaries in terms of the actual requirements of the minor.[21]

---

16 [1908] 2 KB 1.

17 Ibid at 8. In this case the appeal by the tailor was dismissed because 'there was no evidence on which the jury might properly find that that these goods were necessary to the actual requirements of the infant at the time of sale and delivery.' Per Fletcher Moulton LJ at 11.

18 *Nash v Inman* [1908] 2 KB at 9. In *Sultman v Bond* [1956] StRQd 180, Stanley J noted at 189: 'The test whether anything is a 'necessary' is whether it was of a nature suitable to the infant's condition in life and actually required by him at the time, and that he was not at the time otherwise sufficiently provided with things of that sort.'

19 If the goods have not been delivered, any dispute arising under the contract would be determined according to the common law.

20 See *Sale of Goods Act* 1954 (ACT), s 7; *Sale of Goods Act* 1992 (NT), s 7; *Sale of Goods Act* 1896 (Qld), s 5; *Sale of Goods Act* 1895 (SA), s 2; *Sale of Goods Act* 1896 (Tas), s 7; *Sale of Goods Act* 1895 (WA), s 2; *Goods Act* 1958 (Vic), s 7. In New South Wales, the provision concerning necessaries is found in s 7 of the *Sale of Goods Act* 1923, however, that section only applies to those who are suffering from mental incapacity or drunkenness. In respect of contracts made with minors, the position in NSW is regulated by the *Minors (Property and Contracts) Act* 1970 details of which are given at [10.115] of this chapter.

21 *Bojczuk v Greforcewicz* [1961] SASR 128 at 134: 'Although it was found as a fact that the transaction was beneficial to the defendant, it was held as a matter of law that it did not constitute a contract for necessaries.' *McLaughlin v Darcy* (1918) 18 SR (NSW) 585 where Pring J held that the contract was capable of being regarded as one for necessaries and directed the jury to decide whether it was so in fact.

Example: Ryder v Wombwell[22]

In this case, the plaintiff sued the defendant, a minor, for the price of a pair of jewelled solitaires and an antique goblet. The defendant was the son of a baronet.

The court held there was no evidence of either article being a necessary and found against the plaintiff. In a joint judgment the court noted:

> The general rule of law is clearly established, and is that an infant is generally incapable of binding himself by a contract. To this rule there is an exception introduced, not for the benefit of the tradesman who may trust the infant, but for that of the infant himself. [Referring to the statement by Parke, B. in Peters v Fleming] 'From the earliest time down to the present the word necessaries is not confined in its strict sense to such articles as were necessary to the support of life, but extended to articles fit to maintain the particular person in the state, station and degree in life in which he is' ... It is enough for the decision of this case if we hold that such articles as are here described are not prima facie necessary for maintaining a young man in any station of life, and that the burden lay on the plaintiff to give evidence of something peculiar making them necessaries in this special case, and that he has given no evidence at all to that effect.[23]

[10.45] Thus, it can be seen that the question of necessaries varies according to social and economic circumstances; for example, clothes are necessary, but expensive labels may not be. To a young person who is a student, a computer may be a necessity, but to another young person it may not. Apart from the goods themselves, the needs of the actual young person at the time have to be considered.[24]

[10.50] A contract with a minor might involve the supply of goods or services, or both—such as materials and labour for the construction of a house. As noted earlier, the concept of necessaries, while applying generally to goods, has been extended to include necessary services that benefit the minor. In these cases the question as to whether such services are necessary will be one of balance—balancing the benefit derived from the service with the detriment or burden. It will be appreciated that this exercise may involve a determination as to whether the minor has in fact made a good bargain—something the courts do not generally consider.[25]

---

22   (1868) LR 4 Ex 32.
23   Ibid at 38.
24   This is a subjective issue and the question has been raised as to the capacity of a judge to make any accurate assessment of what might be a necessary for a particular young person. In *Ryder v Wombwell* (1868) LR 4 Ex 32 at 40 the court noted: 'The Lord Chief Baron, in his judgment, questions whether under any circumstances it is competent for the judge to determine as a matter of law, whether particular articles are or are not to be deemed necessaries suitable to the estate and condition of an infant ... But the judges do know, as much as juries, what is the usual and normal state of things, and consequently whether any particular article is of such a description as that it may be a necessary under such usual state of things. If a state of things exists (as it well may) so new or so exceptional that the judges do not know of it, that may be proved as a fact, and then it will be for the jury under a proper direction to decide the case.'
25   [The] present law is based upon the proposition that the courts will not look into the adequacy of consideration; that is to say, they will not assess whether the promisor has received adequate value for his promise: DW Greig & JLR Davis, *The Law of Contract,* The Law Book Company Limited, North Ryde, 1987, p 88.

Example: Sultman v Bond[26]

The plaintiff claimed an amount owing for labour and materials supplied for the construction of the defendant's matrimonial home. The defendant minor refused to pay.

The court found in favour of the defendant. In the course of his judgment, Stanley J noted:

> The defendant's liability depends upon the contract being for necessaries provided for him, which contract as a whole was for his benefit. It is doubtful if anything can be more beneficial for young married man than to begin his married life in his own home. But it is a different matter if he is so overloaded with debt that his repayments are out of proportion to his income ... I am not at all satisfied that this contract was really for his benefit as a whole. But assuming that it was, was the provision of this home a necessary? ... Had the defendant not been engaged to be married it could not have been argued that a house was a necessary for a single youth in his position ... Marriage during infancy might have been advantageous to the defendant but in my opinion the expenditure and liability incurred for that purpose are not shown to be necessaries within the meaning of the doctrine being considered ... I decline to hold that the contracts were for necessaries or that the common law enables the plaintiff to recover as for necessaries supplied to an infant in the circumstances of this case.[27]

Example: McLaughlin v Darcy[28]

Darcy, a minor, was a professional boxer; he employed a solicitor to assist him in obtaining a passport so that he might travel to the United States to box.[29] Darcy agreed to pay the solicitor for his services whether successful or not in obtaining a passport. The solicitor spoke to the authorities, who promised to consider Darcy's request favourably at an early date. But Darcy did not wait; he absconded to America without a passport, and he later died there. The plaintiff solicitor sued Darcy's executors to recover his remuneration.

The minor was held liable to the solicitor. Cullen CJ noted:

> The case set up by the plaintiff on the uncontradicted evidence was that the services he was engaged to render were for the purpose of enabling the minor to obtain employment at the calling on which his living depended, and not merely employment, but certain practical training and experience which were necessary to enable him to carry out that employment effectively. That being so, I think his Honour was right in forming the opinion that the contract set up was one capable according to the circumstances of being regarded as a contract for necessaries within the meaning of that expression as used in the authorities.[30]

---

26   [1956] StRQd 180.
27   Ibid at 189 and 193.
28   (1918) 18 SR (NSW) 583.
29   This case is also cited as an example of a contract that is regarded as being analogous or incidental to an employment agreement and thus enforceable against the minor.
30   (1918) 18 SR (NSW) 583 at 589.

In *Chapple v Cooper*,[31] the provision of necessary services extended to services contracted for by a minor in respect of the funeral of the minor's spouse.[32] Minors who are married are liable not only for necessary goods and services purchased for their personal use, but also for those purchased for their spouse and children.[33]

[10.55] In terms of legal effect, where the contract is for necessaries, title will pass (if goods are involved) and the contract will be enforceable against the minor, who can be required to pay a reasonable price. But minors are only liable on contracts for necessaries *as such*; they are not liable to repay a loan given for necessaries—the rationale being that they might dissipate the money. However, at common law, a person purchasing necessaries for a minor at the minor's request may recover their reasonable cost from the minor—and in equity, one who lends money to a minor for the purchase of necessaries is subrogated to the seller's rights against the minor in respect of so much of the money as was actually spent on necessaries.[34]

(b) Contracts of employment and apprenticeship

[10.60] A minor under 18 years of age is bound by contracts of employment or apprenticeship during his or her minority, provided the contract is for the minor's benefit.[35] Once the agreement is found to be one of employment, the only issue is whether, viewed in its totality, it is of advantage or benefit in the sense that it is not unfair or oppressive. The contract, in these circumstances, is presumed to be necessary. These agreements are sometimes referred to as beneficial contracts of service. The reason for holding such contracts to be binding on the minor is that they do not place her or him under any disadvantage or burden such that the minor requires the protection of the law.[36] However, unlike contracts for necessaries—which will always bind a minor—a contract of employment or a beneficial contract of service may be repudiated by the minor upon attaining his or her majority, even though such a contract was and continues to be for his or her benefit.

---

31 (1884) 153 ER 105.
32 Alderson B concluded at 108 that 'Now there are many authorities which lay it down that a decent Christian burial is a part of a man's own rights; and we think it is no great extension of the rule to say that it may be classed as a personal advantage and reasonably necessary to him … It may be observed that as the ground of our decision arises out of the infant's previous contract of marriage, it will not follow from it that an infant child, or more distant relation, would be responsible upon a contract for the burial of his parent or relative.'
33 *Chapple v Cooper* (1844) 153 ER 105 at 106: 'The cases referred to on the other side, of the supply of necessaries for a man's wife, or children, or servant are not disputed.' See also *Sultman v Bond* [1956] StRQd 180.
34 JW Carter & DJ Harland, *Contract Law in Australia*, 3rd edn, Butterworths, North Ryde, 1996, pp 281 and 282.
35 Per Isaacs J in *Hamilton v Lethbridge* (1912) 14 CLR 236 at 261 and 262, supporting the view of earlier cases that during his minority a minor can no more dissolve such a contract which the court sees is beneficial to him than he can make one which the court sees is to his prejudice. Barton J in the same case noted that such contracts 'hold good unless expressly repudiated at majority'. Also per Stanley J in *Sultman v Bond* [1956] StRQd 180 at 191. For the purpose of determining the question the whole of the contract must be looked into and not a particular portion only.
36 As Isaacs J remarked in *Hamilton v Lethbridge* (1912) 14 CLR 236 at 261, the reason for such a contract of employment being binding on the minor 'is that it is the means of maintaining himself, and he is during his minority protected to this extent that he is not allowed to destroy it'.

Example: De Francesco v Barnum and Ors[37]

The plaintiff, George Giuseppe de Francesco, brought an action against two infant defendants alleging that they were bound as apprentices and that they had been enticed away from the plaintiff's service by the defendants. The claim was for money earned by the defendants while in the service of Barnum, and an injunction to restrain the infants from further performances with Barnum, and for damages.

The court found in favour of the defendants on the grounds that the infants' agreement with the plaintiff was not binding. Fry LJ noted:

Now, from a very early date it has been held that one exception as to the incapacity of an infant to bind himself relates to a contract for his good teaching or instruction whereby he may profit himself afterwards ...There is another exception, which is based on the desirableness of infants employing themselves in labour; therefore, where you get a contract for labour and you pay a remuneration of wages, that contract, I think, must be taken to be, prima facie, binding upon an infant ... The court must look to the whole contract, having regard to the circumstances of the case, and determine, subject to any principles of law which may be ascertained by the cases, whether the contract is or is not beneficial. [After discussing the terms of the apprenticeship Fry LJ continued] Those are stipulations of an extraordinary and an unusual character, which throw, or appear to throw, an inordinate power into the hands of the master without any correlative obligation on the part of the master. I cannot, therefore, say that on the face of this instrument it appears to be one, which the Court ought to hold to be for the benefit of the infant.'[38]

In *Hamilton v Lethbridge*,[39] the High Court was asked to determine the status of Articles of Clerkship, entered into by a minor, which included a restraint of trade clause. The Court held that since the contract was ratified upon the minor reaching his majority, it continued to be binding. Griffith CJ noted:

When an infant comes of age he is free to affirm or disaffirm the contract as to anything remaining to be done under it. If he affirms it the question of it being for his benefit no longer arises. If he disaffirms it there is an end of the matter. He must do one thing or the other.[40]

[10.65] Other cases have found that contracts concerning employment or apprenticeship and the like bind the minor—at least until they are repudiated at adulthood. In *Roberts v Gray*,[41] the Court of Appeal held that a contract involving a minor in a billiard-playing tour was held to be a contract of employment for the benefit of the minor, and was therefore binding on him. In *Doyle v White City Stadium Ltd*,[42] a professional boxer who

---

37   (1890) 45 Ch D 430.
38   Ibid at 439.
39   (1912) 14 CLR 236.
40   Ibid at 241. His Honour also found that the restraint of trade clause was not invalid.
41   [1913] 1 KB 520.
42   [1935] 1 KB 110.

was a minor was said to be bound by a licence agreement that restricted his right to a share of the income 'if he should commit a foul'; and in *Chaplin v Leslie Frewin (Publishers) Ltd*,[43] a minor entered into a publishing contract that was held to be for his general benefit as an author, and therefore binding. The minor was therefore unable to prevent publication of the book as agreed in the terms of the contract.[44]

[10.70] One of the few cases where the 'employment' contract was found not to be for the general benefit of the minor was the Canadian case of *Toronto Marlboro Major Junior 'A' Hockey Club v Tonelli*[45] involving a 16-year-old ice hockey player who had entered into a contract to play exclusively for the plaintiff club for four years. In return, he was to receive payment of $25 per week plus other benefits such as board and school fees. The contract also contained a term requiring the minor to pay the club 20 per cent of gross remuneration if at any time within three years after termination of the contract he joined a professional ice hockey club. The Court concluded that this contract was not binding on the defendant, as it was not, when viewed overall, for his benefit.

10.2.2 Contacts that are voidable by the minor

(a) Contracts that are binding unless repudiated[46]

[10.75] At common law, the scope of the category of contracts that are binding unless repudiated concerns contracts under which a minor acquires property of a permanent nature, or to which continuing obligations are attached. Examples include a contract for an interest in land;[47] a contract for the purchase of shares;[48] contracts concerning marriage settlements;[49] and contracts for the purchase of the goodwill of a business,[50] or concerning the joining of a partnership.[51]

---

43 [1966] Ch 71.

44 Lord Denning at 88 dissented on the issue of whether the contract was for the plaintiff's benefit because the publication involved scandalous information that would bring shame and disgrace on others and expose the minor author to claims for libel: 'It is not for his good that he should exploit his discreditable conduct for money, no matter how much he is paid for it.'

45 (1979) 96 DLR (3rd) 135.

46 The language is unfortunate. It is something of a nonsense to talk about a contract being binding when one party can repudiate it at any time.

47 *Whittingham v Murdy* (1889) 60 LT 956; *Davies v Beynon-Harris* (1937) TLR 424. See also *In Re Willmott* (1948) StRQd 256 at 258 where Philp J noted: 'At common law an infant was capable of making a contract for the sale of land and of making a grant thereof, but he had and has the privilege of avoiding his contract or his grant.' In the same case the court disagreed with an earlier Queensland case of *In Re McGill (infant)* [1944] QWN 31. In connection with contracts involving the transfer of land it should also be noted that the Torrens title land registration system deems the register to be a conclusive record of ownership and this may, where for example there is no knowledge of the fact of infancy, abrogate the common law principles in this area: *Percy v Youngman* [1941] VLR 275. The matter was recently considered in *Horvath v Commonwealth Bank of Australia* [1998] Vic SC CA (30th September 1998) which approved *Percy v Youngman* and supported the view that a registered mortgage is effective as against an infant despite s 49 of the *Supreme Court Act* 1986 (Vic) which states that a contract entered into by a minor for the repayment of money lent or to be lent is void.

48 *Vickery's Motors Pty Ltd v Tarrant* [1924] VLR 195; *Steinberg v Scala (Leeds) Limited* [1923] 2 Ch 452; *Norman Baker Pty Ltd (in liq) v Catherine Baker* (1978) 3 ACLR 856 at 859.

49 *Edwards v Carter* [1893] AC 360.

50 *Aroney v Christianus* (1915) 15 SR (NSW) 118.

51 *Lovell v Beauchamp* [1894] AC 607 at 611; *Goode and Bennion v Harrison* 5 B & Ald 147 at 151: 'Here, the infant, by holding himself out as a partner, contracted a continual obligation; and that obligation remains till he thinks proper to put an end to it.'

So far as these contracts are concerned, they are voidable in the sense that while initially binding on both parties, the minor may repudiate her or his obligations during minority, or within a reasonable time of attaining majority.

A minor is not liable for any future obligations under a repudiated contract. However, liabilities that were accrued and became due prior to repudiation are enforceable against the minor.[52]

[10.80] What amounts to a reasonable time will of course depend on the circumstances of the case.[53] If the minor choses to be inactive, this might be taken as affirmation of the contract, and the opportunity to repudiate will be lost.[54] No formalities are required; but in practice, repudiation will usually occur when steps are taken to enforce the contract against the minor. This general principle is, however, subject to certain statutory modifications (discussed later in this chapter).

[10.85] In a claim by the minor for money paid under the contract prior to repudiation, recovery is available only if there has been a total failure of consideration.

Example: Steinberg v Scala (Leeds) Limited[55]

The plaintiff had entered into a contract for the purchase of certain company shares and had her name duly entered on the register. She did not attend any meeting of the defendant company and did not receive any dividend on the shares. Some two years after entering into the contract, the plaintiff wrote to the defendant company repudiating the contract and claiming the return of her money. The company refused to remove her name from the register and refused to repay her money.

In the Court of Appeal there was no argument over the fact that the plaintiff had the right to rescind the contract and have her name removed from the register. However in relation to the claim for return of the money Lord Sterndale MR noted:

> Now the plaintiff has had the shares; I do not mean to say that she had the certificates; she could have had them at any time if she had applied for them; she has had the shares allotted to her and there is evidence that they were of some value ... In those circumstances is it possible to say that there was a total failure of consideration? ... If she has obtained something which has money's worth then she has received some consideration, that is, she has received the thing for which she paid her money ... I cannot see any

---

52 *Norman Baker Pty Ltd (in liq) v Catherine Baker* (1978) 3 ACLR SA(WA) 856 at 859, where the Western Australian Full Court noted: 'upon the infant repudiating she is simply freeing herself from further obligation. She is not rescinding the agreement as from the beginning; she is bringing it to an end so as to escape from any future liability.'

53 In *Edwards v Carter* [1893] AC 360 at 366, Lord Herschell LC concluded in relation to a settlement in contemplation of marriage: 'Has a reasonable time been exceeded? The learned judges in the court below expressed their opinion that the period which elapsed, a period of between four and five years, was more than a reasonable time ... It is enough to say that in my opinion it is impossible to hold that the learned judges in the court below have in any way erred in saying that more than a reasonable time had elapsed.' See also *Rain v Fullerton* (1900) 17 WN (NSW) 161 at 162.

54 In *Hamilton v Lethbridge* (1912) 14 CLR 236 at 257, Griffith CJ noted at p 243: 'In this case after the defendant came of age he continued to serve under the articles for more than two years after the assignment. That of itself amounts to ratification and adoption by the infant.' See also the comments by Barton J at page 257 approving *Edwards v Carter* [1893] AC 360 : 'If he does nothing within a reasonable time after he attains twenty-one, the presumption is that he has affirmed the contract.'

55 [1923] 2 Ch 452.

difference when you come to consider whether there has been consideration or not, between the position of a person of full age and an infant.[56]

Similarly, minors who have transferred goods under a contract may, upon repudiation, recover those goods only if they received no part of the consideration promised
for them and restitution is possible.[57] On this point, the Queensland Law Reform
Commission Report *Minors: Civil Law Capacity* noted:

> These rules clearly offend elementary considerations of justice and fairness. A
> minor who inadvisably parts with property and receives only a small portion of
> the promised consideration cannot recover the property, whereas a rogue who
> takes advantage of his or her minority to obtain the benefit of a contract with-
> out honouring his or her own obligations under the contract can escape liabil-
> ity under the contract.[58]

(b) Contracts that are not binding unless ratified by the minor

[10.90] At common law, contracts that do not fall into the category of necessaries, or
beneficial contracts of service or binding contracts that have not been repudiated, will
not be enforceable against a minor unless and until she or he chooses to ratify them
within a reasonable time of attaining majority. Unless the minor takes some positive
step to confirm the contract, she or he is not bound by it; however, the minor can
enforce the contract against an adult party to the agreement. Furthermore, the contract, while voidable by the minor, is effective to transfer property—although once
property has been transferred, it cannot be recovered unless there has been a total failure of consideration and restitution is possible.[59]

[10.95] The common law rule requiring the minor to take positive steps to ratify the
contract was said to leave the minor open to potential undesirable pressure from creditors. As a result, Western Australia, the Australian Capital Territory, the Northern
Territory, and South Australia have legislation to the effect that such ratification must
be in writing and signed by the minor. In Victoria, no ratification is effective, whether
in writing or not.[60]

---

56   Ibid at 459.
57   *Pearce v Brain* [1929] 2 KB 310. Note that in South Australia the *Minors Contacts (Miscellaneous Provisions)
      Act* 1979, s 7 gives the courts a discretion to permit recovery of property by a minor who has avoided a
      contract, despite there not having been a total failure of consideration. See also *Minors (Property and
      Contracts) Act* 1970 (NSW), s 37.
58   Queensland Law Reform Commission, Report number 50 of 1996 at 19.
59   See footnote 57 where the same legislation allows for such a transfer.
60   *Mercantile Law Act* 1962 (ACT), s 15; *Statute of Frauds Amendment Act* 1828 (Imp) (NT); *Statute of Frauds
      Amendment Act* 1828 (Imp) (WA); *Supreme Court Act* 1986 (Vic), s 50. The Victorian provision also
      applies whether or not there was any new consideration for the promise or ratification. Section 51 of
      the same Act provides that any agreement, whether in writing or not, made after majority to repay a
      loan contracted during minority is void except in special circumstances. *Minors Contacts (Miscellaneous
      Provisions) Act* 1979 (SA), s 4 requires that the written ratification be on or after the day on which the
      minor attains majority.

10.2.3 The impact of legislation

[10.100] New South Wales has enacted legislation that establishes a Code for the operation of contracts concerning minors. Other jurisdictions have also legislated in respect of the operation of contracts concerning minors, but have also retained the common law. There seems to be a clear case for uniform legislation in this area. The rights of parties to a contract made in Australia should not be dependent upon the State or Territory in which the contract was made. The area has been the subject of a number of Law Reform Commission Reports.[61]

(a) Victoria

[10.105] The common law rules outlined above have been modified in Victoria by the *Supreme Court Act* 1986. Division 4 of that Act relates to 'Contracts of Minors'. The Act makes void the following contracts entered into by a minor: (a) contracts for the repayment of money lent or to be lent; (b) contracts for payment of goods supplied or to be supplied, other than necessaries; and (c) accounts stated.[62]

Further, under the Act, no action can be brought against a minor in respect of a promise made after attaining majority to pay a debt contracted during his or her minority; or in respect of any ratification made after majority of a promise or contract made during minority. This is said to apply whether or not there was any new consideration for the promise or ratification.[63] Thus a fresh promise to perform a contract other than a debt will be enforceable, though a mere ratification will not.

If a minor contracts for a loan, that contract is void under (a) above, and any agreement upon majority to repay all or part of the loan is also void. However, where a person in good faith (and for value, and without notice) is the holder or assignee of the instrument, that person may recover from the minor the amount secured by the instrument. If that person does recover from the minor, the minor may in turn recover that amount from the person to whom the minor gave the instrument.[64]

---

61 The NSW Law Reform Commission report on *Infancy in Relation to Contracts and Property* (LRC 6, 1969) noted at p 20 that the authorities on the law of infancy in relation to contracts and dispositions of property are in a disorderly condition and the law cannot be stated both coherently and accurately. The fact that Law Reform Commissions in other jurisdictions have also considered the area to be in need of reform supports the view that a common legislative framework is desirable. See for example South Australia Law Reform Commission Report No 41 *Contractual Capacity of Infants* (1977); Queensland Law Reform Commission Report No 50 *Minors' Civil Law Capacity* (1996); Tasmanian Law Reform Commission Report No 48 *Contracts and the disposition of property by minors* (1987); Western Australia Law Reform Commission Report No 25 *Minors' Contracts* (1988); Victorian Chief Justice's Law Reform Committee Report *Infancy in Relation to Contracts and Property* (1970). For the position in New Zealand see the discussion at [10.260]–[10.280].

62 *Supreme Court Act* 1986 (Vic), s 49. An account stated refers to an admission of a debt and is evidence of an amount owing. Such amount may be rebutted by contrary evidence 'and therefore, in the contracts declared by the Act to be void, the inclusion of accounts stated is almost superfluous': JG Starke, NC Seddon & MP Ellinghams, *Cheshire and Fifoot's Law of Contract,* 7th edn, Butterworths, North Ryde, 1997, p 652. Note that not all contracts are excluded. In particular section 49 does not apply to contracts for the supply of services to a minor or to contracts of employment. Nor does it apply to those contracts that are binding on a minor unless and until repudiated.

63 *Supreme Court Act* 1986 (Vic), s 150.

64 *Supreme Court Act* 1986 (Vic), s 51. At common law, a minor cannot be liable on a negotiable instrument. The significance of *Supreme Court Act* 1986 (Vic), s 51(2) is that bona fide holders or assignees for value without notice of negotiable instruments executed by a minor are protected.

(b) South Australia

[10.110] In South Australia, the relevant legislation is the *Minors Contracts (Miscellaneous Provisions) Act* 1979. The object of the Act is to make provision in relation to contracts entered into by minors, and for related purposes. Where a minor has entered into a contract that is, by reason of her or his minority, unenforceable against her or him, the contract remains unenforceable unless it is ratified by the minor, in writing, on or after the day on which the minor attains majority.[65] Under the Act, a contract with a minor will be valid and enforceable if the contract was entered into with the approval of a court. Such approval may be given upon application by the minor or by her or his parent or guardian, or by any other party to the proposed contract.[66] Where a minor has avoided a contract on the ground of her or his minority, and before the minor did so, property passed to some other contracting party, then a court may, on an application by or on behalf of the minor, order restitution of that property on such terms and conditions as it considers just.[67] Finally, the Act specifies that a court may, on the application of a minor, parent, or guardian, appoint a person to transact any specified business or execute any documents on behalf of the minor; where this is done, any liabilities incurred are enforceable against the minor.[68]

(c) New South Wales

[10.115] The relevant legislation in New South Wales is the *Minors (Property and Contracts) Act* 1970. Under this Act, where a minor participates in a civil act (defined to include a contract), that civil act is *not* binding on the minor except as provided by the Act.[69] Further, a minor will not be bound where he or she lacks the understanding necessary for participation in such civil act.[70]

Contracts that are binding on a minor

[10.120] The Act provides that the following contracts will be presumptively binding on a minor:[71]

- where a minor enters a contract that is for her or his benefit at the time. Under s 43 of the Act, a court may seek guidance on this question from a parent, guardian or referee;
- where a minor enters into a contract for the purchase or sale of real or personal property, so long as the contract is not manifestly unfair. Thus cash sales by a minor would be binding, as long as they are not unfair, even if they were not for the minor's benefit;

---

65   *Supreme Court Act* 1986 (Vic), s 4.
66   *Supreme Court Act* 1986 (Vic), s 6.
67   *Supreme Court Act* 1986 (Vic), s 7.
68   *Supreme Court Act* 1986 (Vic), s 8.
69   *Minors (Property and Contracts) Act* 1970 (NSW), 17. This matter was considered in the case of *Homestake Gold of Australia v Peninsula Gold* (1996) *Aust Contracts Reports* 90-066 at 90,395 where the Supreme Court of NSW held that the minors concerned had not participated in the execution of deeds transferring shares in their name. The Court continued at 90,397: 'Accordingly, although the minors' names are on the Register, those names are at present liable to be removed from the Register and the minors do not have a legal or equitable interest in these shares previously held by Peninsula.'
70   *Minors (Property and Contracts) Act* 1970 (NSW), s 18.
71   *Minors (Property and Contracts) Act* 1970 (NSW), ss 19–25.

- where a minor makes a disposition of property wholly or partly as a gift, which is reasonable at the time;
- where a minor participates in a civil act pursuant to a contractual or other duty binding on the minor;
- where a minor makes an investment in government securities or stocks;
- where an innocent third party acquires property consequent to the contract with the minor or alters their position on the basis of the civil act by the minor;[72]
- contracts concerning rents or other income on the part of a married minor.

Apart from the above cases, a minor may make application to the court for a grant of capacity to participate in any civil act or to rescind or vary any order.[73] Further, where a certificate is given to the effect that the minor understood the true purpose and effect of the disposition of property and agreed freely, and the consideration was not manifestly inadequate, then that contract will be presumptively binding on the minor.[74]

Affirmation

[10.125] Any contract that is not presumptively binding may be affirmed by the minor upon reaching 18 years of age, or affirmed by his or her personal representative after the minor's death. Alternatively, the Act provides for affirmation of the contract by an order of a court while a person is a minor.[75] Where a contract is affirmed under this provision, it is presumptively binding on the minor. Such affirmation may be by words, written or spoken, or by conduct and need not be communicated to any person.

Repudiation

[10.130] A minor may repudiate a contact that is not presumptively binding—either during her or his minority, or before attaining the age of nineteen. If the minor does not repudiate the contract before turning 19, it becomes presumptively binding on the minor.[76] The repudiation does not have effect if it appears that at the time of the repudiation, the contract is for the benefit of the minor. To be effective, the repudiation must be in writing, and served on the other party.[77]

Apart from repudiation by the minor, a court can repudiate a contract on behalf of a minor at any time during her or his minority, where that contract is held not to be for the benefit of the minor.[78] The effect of repudiation is to discharge the minor from his or her obligations under the contract. However, it does not have this effect against any other person or association of which the minor may be a member.[79]

---

72 This section was discussed in the case of *Homestake Gold of Australia v Peninsula Gold* (1996) *Aust Contracts Reports* 90-066 at 90,396.
73 *Minors (Property and Contracts) Act* 1970 (NSW), ss 26 and 27.
74 *Minors (Property and Contracts) Act* 1970 (NSW), ss 28 and 29. Such certificate is to be given by a solicitor instructed and employed independently of any other party to the transaction or by the Public Trustee.
75 *Minors (Property and Contracts) Act* 1970 (NSW), s 30.
76 *Minors (Property and Contracts) Act* 1970 (NSW), ss 31 and 38.
77 *Minors (Property and Contracts) Act* 1970 (NSW), s 33.
78 *Minors (Property and Contracts) Act* 1970 (NSW), s 34.
79 *Minors (Property and Contracts) Act* 1970 (NSW), s 35.

[10.135] In cases where a contract is *not* presumptively binding on the minor, a court may, upon application by a person interested in the contract (for example an adult party), *affirm* or repudiate the contract on behalf of the minor.[80] Where a contract is repudiated by a minor, the court can give directions about the adjustment of rights arising under the contract.[81]

10.2.4 Contracts concerning guarantees

[10.140] Where an adult guarantees the credit of a minor and the minor's contract is voidable at the minor's option, the guarantor will not be liable if the minor repudiates the principal contract. However, the guarantor will be liable if the contract is construed as one of indemnity rather than one of guarantee.

Statutory provisions have changed the common law in some jurisdictions. In New South Wales, s 47 of the *Minors (Property and Contracts) Act* 1970 provides that a guarantor of an obligation of a minor is bound by the guarantee to the extent to which he or she would be bound if the minor were not a minor. In South Australia and Tasmania, similar provisions apply.[82] Section 55(3) of the *Consumer Credit Code* deals with guarantees given in respect of persons under 18 years of age.[83] It has been suggested that this section could be interpreted as making a guarantor of a minor's liability liable under the guarantee provided that the required prominent statement referred to in s 55 appears. However, the more likely interpretation is that it simply superimposes a further statutory requirement that must be met for the guarantee to be enforceable.[84]

10.2.5 Liability in tort

[10.145] Although minors are generally liable for their torts, they cannot (except in New South Wales) be liable in tort where to do so indirectly gives effect to a contract to which they are not bound.[85] The case of *R Leslie Ltd v Sheill*[86] is an example of the common law position.

---

80 *Minors (Property and Contracts) Act* 1970 (NSW), s 36.
81 *Minors (Property and Contracts) Act* 1970 (NSW), s 37.
82 In South Australia, section 5 of the *Minors Contracts (Miscellaneous Provisions) Act* 1979 provides that 'Where a person (other than a minor) guarantees the performance by a minor of his obligations under a contract, the guarantee shall be enforceable against the guarantor to the same extent as if the minor had, before entering into the contract to which the guarantee relates, attained his majority. This section does not operate to render a guarantee enforceable if it would, apart from this section, be unenforceable otherwise than by reason of the minority of the person whose obligations are guaranteed.' The same provision is found in *Minors Contracts Act* 1988 (Tas), s 4.
83 *Consumer Credit Code*, s 55(3) reads: 'A guarantee which guarantees the liability of a debtor who was under 18 years of age when the liability was incurred cannot be enforced against the guarantor unless it contains a prominent statement to the effect that the guarantor may not be entitled to an indemnity against the debtor'.
84 D McGill & L Willmott, *Annotated Consumer Credit Code,* LBC Information Services, North Ryde, 1999, p 375.
85 In New South Wales, section 48 of the *Minors (Property and Contracts) Act* 1970 provides: 'Where a person under the age of twenty-one is guilty of a tort, the person is answerable for that tort whether or not (a) the tort is connected with a contract; or (b) the cause of action for the tort is in substance a cause of action in contract.' In New Zealand, the *Minors' Contracts Act* 1969 expressly preserves a minor's immunity at common law from liability in tort for procuring a contract by means of fraudulent representations as to his or her age but the court is to take such matters into account when deciding any matter involving a contract made with a minor.
86 [1914] 3 KB 607.

Example: R Leslie v Sheill[87]

The plaintiffs were a firm of money-lenders and they sued the defendant to recover money lent, on the ground that the defendant had obtained the funds by fraudulently representing that he was of full age when in fact he was still a minor.

The English Court of Appeal found in favour of the defendant, Lord Sumner noting:

> [B]ecause of his [the defendant's] fraud the plaintiffs have been induced to make and act upon an unenforceable contract. So long ago as *Johnson v Pye* (1665) 1 Sid 258, it was decided that, although an infant may be liable in tort generally, he is not answerable for a tort directly connected with a contract which, as an infant, he would be entitled to avoid … It is perhaps a pity that no exception was made where, as here, the infant's wickedness was at least equal to that of the person who innocently contracted with him, but so it is. It was thought necessary to safeguard the weakness of infants at large, even though here and there a juvenile knave slipped through.[88]

10.2.6 Restitutionary claims

[10.2.6.1] Although the common law will not make a minor liable if to do so would give effect to a contract to which she or he is not bound, nevertheless, the deceit by the minor in these circumstances does not leave the other party without any remedy. True, they cannot rely on contract or tort law for a remedy; however, the equitable doctrine of restitution may be invoked. If a minor obtains non-necessary goods for example by fraudulently misrepresenting her or his age, equity will compel the minor to restore the goods, as long as they are still in her or his possession. If the goods are no longer in the minor's possession, it seems the minor will not be compelled to restore their value, or any proceeds of sale. For this reason, equity will not compel minors to repay money obtained by fraudulently misrepresenting their age unless they have the actual coins or notes in their possession.

This matter was also raised in *R Leslie Limited v Sheill*,[89] where Lord Sumner concluded:

> I think that the whole current of decisions down to 1913, apart from *dicta* which are inconclusive, went to show that, when an infant obtained an advantage by falsely stating himself to be of full age, equity required him to restore his ill-gotten gains, or to release the party deceived from obligations or acts in law induced by the fraud, but scrupulously stopped short of enforcing against him a contractual obligation entered into while he was an infant, even by means of fraud … In the present case … the money was paid over in order to be used as the defendant's own and he has so used it and, I suppose spent it. There is no question of tracing it, no possibility of restoring the very thing got by the fraud.[90]

---

87   Ibid.
88   Ibid at 611.
89   [1914] 3 KB 607.
90   Ibid at 618–619.

In the later case of *Mercantile Credit Limited v Spinks*,[91] a minor, by fraudulently misrepresenting his age, induced a finance company to advance him money for the purchase of a motor vehicle. The court held that the contract was for necessaries (the minor being a salesman) but went on to apply another equitable principle based on the right of the lender to be subrogated to the rights of a person who sells necessaries to a minor.

[10.155] The common law has been modified in some jurisdictions by statutory provisions, which declare that certain contracts entered into by a minor are void. These provisions were outlined earlier.[92] If these contracts are declared to be void, then money or property can be recovered as long as the minor has not suffered a total failure of consideration.[93]

10.3 Mentally disabled and intoxicated persons[94]

[10.160] Under the common law, a contract made by or with a mentally disabled person (as opposed to a person who is certified as insane)[95] is valid unless, when it was made, she or he was incapable of understanding the nature of the transaction and the other party knew or ought to have known of this. The purpose of the rule is protective.

[10.165] For a time, such contracts were said to be void on the grounds that there could be no *consensus ad idem* (the 'meeting of minds' required for there to be agreement); however, this was later qualified by a rule that a person could not plead her or his own unsoundness of mind in order to avoid a contract she or he had made. This in turn gave way to a further rule that such a plea was permissible if it could be shown that the other contracting party knew of the insanity.[96]

[10.170] Once a contracting party has recovered from the mental disability, any words or conduct consistent with ratification of the agreement will make it binding. If rescission does not take place promptly, the silence may be deemed an affirmation of the agreement.[97]

---

91   [1968] QdR 67.
92   See para 10.2.3 above
93   *Pearce v Brain* [1929] 2 KB 310. See also the discussion in JW Carter & DJ Harland, *Contract Law in Australia*, 3rd edn, Butterworths, North Ryde, 1996, pp 291 and 292.
94   These cases need to be distinguished from cases of *non est factum* where a person is mistaken as to the nature or character of a document, for example that they are signing a contract of sale rather than a lease. See comment by Fullagar J in *Blomley v Ryan* (1956) 99 CLR 362 at 401.
95   Persons found to be incapable of managing their property or affairs are subject to Mental Health legislation and the power of the Supreme Court to appoint a committee or official for these purposes. In *Gibbons v Wright* (1953) 91 CLR 423 at 439 the court noted in reference to lunatics who were insane: 'Such a person is held incompetent to dispose of his property, not because of any lack of understanding (indeed he remains incompetent even in a lucid interval) but because the contract custody and power of disposition of his property has passed to the Crown to the exclusion of himself. Accordingly his disposition is completely void.'
96   *Hart v O'Connor* [1985] 1 AC 1000 at 1018 and 1019.
97   JW Carter & DJ Harland, *Contract Law in Australia*, 3rd edn, Butterworths, North Ryde, 1996, p 304.

Example: Gibbons v Wright[98]

In this case, the High Court considered an appeal by Bessie Gibbons (the plaintiff) against a decision of the Full Court of the Supreme Court of Tasmania in favour of Reginald Wright, who was the executor of the wills of two sisters—Olinda Gibbons and Ethel Gibbons. After the deaths of Olinda and Ethel Gibbons, a dispute arose over the entitlement of Bessie Gibbons to certain property. The plaintiff argued that the two sisters lacked the mental capacity to understand a deed they had executed prior to their death concerning the property. The effect of the deed was that instead of the last survivor of the three joint tenants becoming entitled to the whole of the property, each of them would be entitled to a one-third share, which would pass to her estate if she still owned it at her death.

The Court dismissed the appeal on the grounds that the contract was not in fact avoided by the two sisters, and was therefore valid. In a joint judgment the Court noted:

> The law does not prescribe any fixed standard of sanity as requisite for the validity of all transactions. It requires, in relation to each particular matter or piece of business transacted, that each party shall have such soundness of mind as to be capable of understanding the general nature of what he is doing by his participation ... [having found that the sisters lacked the capacity for the validity of the instruments the court continued at 449] ... Upon the authorities as they now stand, it appears to us that we ought to regard it as settled law that an instrument of conveyance executed by a person incapable of understanding its effect, in the sense of its general purport, is not on that account void, though in the circumstances it may be voidable by the conveyor or his representatives.[99]

[10.175] The question of any mental incapacity must be pleaded and proved by the one who seeks to set the contract aside. In addition, it would need to be established that the other party had knowledge of the fact of the incapacity.

[10.180] Once a contracting party has recovered her or his mental capacity, his or her words or conduct consistent with the contract's continuance will render it binding. Likewise, where necessaries are sold and delivered to a mentally disabled person, there is a statutory requirement that the person pay a reasonable price for them. The definition of necessaries is the same as for minors—goods suitable to the condition in life of such person, and to her or his actual requirements at the time of the sale and delivery.[100]

---

98   (1954) 91 CLR 423.
99   Ibid at 437.
100   Section 7 of the *Sale of Goods Act* 1954 (ACT) is an example of the relevant provision: 'Where necessaries are sold to an infant or to a person who, by reason of mental incapacity or drunkenness, is incompetent to contract, he must pay a reasonable price for the goods.' See equivalent provisions in the other jurisdictions: *Sale of Goods Act* 1896 (Qld), s 5; *Sale of Goods Act* 1923 (NSW), s 7; *Goods Act* 1958 (Vic), s 7; *Sale of Goods Act* 1895 (WA), s 2; *Sale of Goods Act* 1895 (SA), s 2; *Sale of Goods Act* 1896 (Tas), s 7; *Sale of Goods Act* 1992 (NT), s 7; *Sale of Goods Act* 1908 (NZ), s 4(1).

A more recent case in this area is *Hart v O'Connor*,[101] which went on appeal to the Privy Council from the New Zealand Court of Appeal.

Example: Hart v O'Connor[102]

The vendor of land, O'Connor, farmed it in partnership with two of his brothers. He entered into an agreement to sell the land to the defendant (Thomas Hart). The vendor was 83, and unknown to the defendant, was of unsound mind. The plaintiffs (one of the O'Connor brothers and his two sons) instituted proceedings against the defendant, claiming a declaration that the land contract should be rescinded for (among other things) want of mental capacity by the vendor.

The New Zealand Court of Appeal found for the plaintiffs and granted the declaration. The Privy Council reversed this decision. In their reasons for decision their Lordships noted:

> The traditional view in English law was that it must be proved that the other contracting party knew of or ought to have appreciated such incapacity. Otherwise the contract stood ... But in Archer v Cutler [1980] 1 NZLR 386 it had been decided that a contract made by a person of insufficient mental capacity was voidable at his option not only if the other party knew of or ought to have appreciated his unsoundness of mind, but also if the contract 'was unfair to the person of unsound mind' ... In the opinion of their Lordships, to accept the proposition enunciated in Archer v Cutler ... is illogical and would distinguish the law of New Zealand from the law of Australia.[103]

[10.185] A person under the extreme influence of drugs or alcohol is said to be in the same position, in relation to contracts, as a person who is mentally disabled. Such a person lacks contractual capacity if he or she was so incapable as not to understand the effect of what he or she was doing, and the other party had knowledge of that fact. The contract then is voidable; on regaining sobriety, the affected person may withdraw from the contract. In practice, it would be difficult to show that the other party was *not* aware of the disability.

[10.190] Intoxication that does not prevent understanding of the transaction[104] is generally not a ground for avoidance of contractual liability. This is another area where contract and equity cross paths: while a person may not be able to have such a contract set aside for lack of contractual capacity, nevertheless the contract may be unfair in the sense of being unconscionable, and may be set aside in equity for that reason.

This matter was considered by the High Court *in Blomley v Ryan*.[105]

---

101   [1985] 1 AC 1000.

102   Ibid.

103   Ibid at 1014 and 1027. See also *Scott v Wise* [1986] 2 NZLR 484.

104   The test of the nature and extent of influence has been variously described as 'so lunatic, or drunk, as not to know what he was about when he made a promise or sealed an instrument'; 'not capable of understanding the nature of the contract'. See JW Carter & DJ Harland, *Contract Law in Australia*, 3rd edn, Butterworths, North Ryde, 1996, p 301.

105   (1956) 99 CLR 362. See also *Peeters v Schimanski* [1975] 2 NZLR 328.

Example: Blomley v Ryan[106]

The plaintiff, Graham Blomley, was seeking an order for specific performance on a contract for the sale and purchase of a property near Boggabilla in New South Wales. The defendant (Ryan, the vendor) was an old man who alleged that for some days prior to, and upon, the day he signed this agreement, his condition was such, as a result of over-indulgence in alcoholic liquor (mainly rum) that he did not possess the requisite contractual capacity. The facts indicated that he had drunk himself practically, if not entirely, into a state of insensibility.

Taylor J of the High Court (who heard the matter at first instance) noted:

> About 7 am he was lying sprawled across the bed and about 8 am or 9 am he had more to drink. Apparently he had not undressed during the night, and it is more than probable that at least on several of the nights succeeding 18th April he went to bed in the suit of clothes which he was wearing when the shearers commenced to arrive ... [The plaintiff] gave evidence to the effect that the defendant did not appear to be other than his normal self ... I find it impossible to accept this evidence.[107]

In the Full High Court Fullagar J endorsed the view that:

> A Court of Equity ought not to give its assistance to a person, who has obtained an agreement, or deed from another in a state of intoxication; and on the other hand ought not to assist a person to get rid of any agreement or deed, merely upon the ground of his having been intoxicated at the time ... As to that extreme state of intoxication, that deprives a man of his reason, I apprehend, that even at law it would invalidate a deed, obtained from him while in that condition. So we find it again and again that mere drunkenness affords no ground for resisting a suit to enforce a contract. Where however, there is real ground for thinking that the judgment of one party was, to the knowledge of the other, seriously affected by drink, equity will generally refuse specific performance at the suit of that other, leaving him to pursue a remedy at law if he so desires.[108]

By majority (Kitto J dissenting), the Court ordered that the contract be set aside upon the ground that it was an unconscionable bargain.[109]

---

106 Ibid.
107 Ibid at 369.
108 Ibid at 404 and 405.
109 The dissent by Kitto J was on the grounds that 'I find myself unable to avoid the conclusion that the defendant all along acted deliberately, even if not as hard-headedly as he might have; that he was quite capable of judging of his interests and of dealing with Blomley and Stemm on equal terms ...The defendant was not the 'poor and ignorant man' who figures in the cases as a ready victim for the unscrupulous ... His decision to accept a price so much below that which he had been demanding does not need any more probable explanation than that being, as he said, in a bad mood, tired of managing the property, feeling his age and the depressing effects of indifferent health ... he came to the conclusion that the best thing to do was to take Blomley's offer and be done with it': (1956) 99 CLR 362 at 429 and 430.

10.4 Bankrupts[110]

[10.195] In their book *Contract Law in Australia*, Carter and Harland note:

> Bankruptcy does not affect contractual capacity, that is, the capacity of a person to become contractually bound, but affects the operation of contracts made by a person who is at the time, or subsequently becomes, bankrupt. Upon bankruptcy, contracts previously entered into do not come to an end; the bankrupt's contractual rights vest under s 58(1) of the *Bankruptcy Act* 1966 (Cth) in the trustee in bankruptcy for the benefit of the bankrupt's creditors.[111]

The purpose of the rule concerning bankruptcy is to protect the assets of the bankrupt for the benefit of creditors; thus a trustee is able to avoid any contract, made by the bankrupt prior to bankruptcy, which is unprofitable—and any other contract, with the consent of the court.[112] Where a trustee declines or neglects to act on an application by the other party to make such election, the trustee will lose the right to disclaim and is deemed to have adopted the contract. A person who has accrued a right under a contract (for example a right to damages or a right to sue for breach of contract) in circumstances where the other contracting party subsequently becomes bankrupt, becomes a creditor in the bankruptcy.

[10.200] So far as post-bankruptcy contracts are concerned, the trustee or estate will be bound where a person deals with a bankrupt in good faith and for valuable consideration in respect of property acquired by the bankrupt on or after the day she or he became a bankrupt, if the contract is completed before any intervention by the trustee.[113] In view of the fact that entering into a contract with a bankrupt may expose the other party to the risk of non-compliance, it is an offence for an undischarged bankrupt to enter into certain types of contracts without disclosing their status.[114] Where a bankrupt contracts in breach of this prohibition, the contract is unenforceable by the bankrupt and the other party is entitled to rescind the contract.[115]

[10.205] The court has wide powers to set aside a contract and make an order on terms it considers just and equitable.[116]

---

110 This section represents a brief overview of the law in this area. The *Bankruptcy Act* 1966 (Cth) is a detailed piece of legislation that regulates most of the law in this area. Only certain sections have been highlighted in order to demonstrate the consequences of bankruptcy on contracts.

111 JW Carter & DJ Harland, *Contract Law in Australia*, 3rd edn, Butterworths, North Ryde, 1996, p 318.

112 *Bankruptcy Act* 1966 (Cth), s 133 (1AA,1AB,5A,5B). A trustee is not entitled to disclaim a lease without leave of the court and without giving certain notice: s 133(4). So far as the right to disclaim onerous contracts is concerned the trustee has an election. JW Carter & DJ Harland, *Contract Law in Australia*, 3rd edn, Butterworths, North Ryde, 1996, p 318. The powers exercisable at the discretion of a trustee are set out in s 134 of the Act.

113 *Bankruptcy Act* 1966 (Cth), s 126(1).

114 See, for example, section 269 of the *Bankruptcy Act* 1966 (Cth) in relation to obtaining credit, entering into a hire-purchase agreement, or a contract for leasing or hiring of goods or obtaining certain goods or services, or carrying on a business.

115 See generally *Halsbury's Laws of Australia* Reed International [110-2920].

116 The *Bankruptcy Act* 1966 (Cth) confers jurisdiction on State and Territory Supreme Courts and the Family Court; however the Federal Court deals with most bankruptcy matters.

10.5 Corporations and unincorporated associations

10.5.1 Corporations

[10.210] A corporation is an individual or group of individuals invested with legal personality (the capacity to have legal rights and duties) other than the legal personality that is consequent to each individual upon birth. A corporation may be granted corporate status or personality in a number of ways. For example, it may be created by virtue of some Act of Parliament or by Royal Charter. The most common method of incorporation of companies is pursuant to the *Corporations Law*.[117]

[10.215] Prior to legislative reform, corporations were required to state the objects of the company in the Memorandum of Association and were incapable of entering into any contract that was not within the stated objects or powers.[118] The validity of contracts could thus depend on the skill of the drafter as to the Memorandum of Association of the company, and it was not uncommon for very wide powers and discretions to be included. This notion of limiting the power of a company by virtue of its objects invoked the doctrine of *ultra vires* (where the company acts beyond power). This has now changed, and where a contract is outside the powers of a company's objects, noncompliance with those powers or objects is no longer a barrier to enforcement of the contract.[119] A company has the legal capacity of a natural person as well as specified powers appropriate to companies.[120]

[10.220] The question of agency is relevant here. Corporations cannot act on their own account; they need human beings as their hands and minds. Where a corporation authorises another person to be its agent then the acts of the agent, acting in the course of his or her authority as agent, bind the company. This authority might be express (written or oral) or implied by virtue of the position the person has in the company—for example, the purchasing manager. Where the authority of the agent has been exceeded, the company will only be liable if it can be shown that it had previously represented the agent as having sufficient authority to make such contracts (sometimes referred to as 'apparent' or 'ostensible' authority). Secondly, the company will be bound if the company ratifies the contract.[121] Apart from agency, a company can be liable for the acts or intentions of its directors or officers when these are sufficiently connected to the company.[122]

---

117 In New Zealand most trading corporations are created by complying with the provisions of the *Companies Act* 1993.

118 *Ashbury Railway Carriage and Iron Co v Riche* (1875) LR 7.

119 *Corporations Law*, ss 124 and 125; *Companies Act* 1993 (NZ) s 16.

120 *Corporations Law*, s 124.

121 Regarding pre-incorporation contracts the *Corporations Law* empowers a company within a reasonable time after incorporation to ratify such contracts entered into a reasonable time before incorporation. This was to avoid the old common law that a contract made on behalf of a non-existent company did not bind the company once it was incorporated; nor could the company ratify it.

122 In this case, the acts or intentions can be attributed to the company itself. See for example *HL Bolton (Engineering) Co Ltd v TJ Graham & Sons Ltd* (1957) 1 QB 159; *Tesco Supermarkets Ltd v Nattrass* [1972] AC 153 per Lord Reid at 170.

10.5.2 Unincorporated associations

[10.225] The position of companies can be contrasted with an unincorporated association such as a social club that has no legal personality distinct from that of its members. However, this does not mean that the management committee of an unincorporated association is immune from liability.[123] In *Bradley Egg Farm Ltd v Clifford*,[124] the English Court of Appeal held that the executive council of the Lancashire Utility Poultry Society were the principals of a servant who negligently carried out a test that resulted in a number of birds dying. The executive council was liable personally to the plaintiffs, members of the Poultry Society. It seems that where the members of a council or management committee change after the contract is entered into then the old members do not remain liable indefinitely.[125] However, the new committee may be bound by contracts entered into by an old committee if it is clear that the intention is to bind both parties to the future performance of the agreement.[126]

[10.230] Unincorporated clubs and associations can be given an independent legal status if they incorporate under the relevant State or Territory legislation.[127] This protects individual members of the association and the management committee from being personally liable in contract or tort.[128]

10.6 Governments and the Crown[129]

[10.235] The idea that a government or a government body may lack power to enter into a contract seems, at first sight, to be strange. Historically, the government was equated with the Crown which, in turn, related back to the person of the sovereign. There was no doubt that the sovereign could enter into contracts with the same capacity as any other person. In modern times it is not satisfactory to equate the government with the person of the sovereign. It is more appropriate to regard the government as akin to a corporation with defined powers. This is certainly true of the Common-

---

123 For example in *Ward v Eltherington* [1982] QdR 561 the court held that all persons who were, at the relevant time, members of the committee were bound by a contract between an unincorporated association (the Indooroopilly Services Club) and the plaintiff for work done prior to the proposed construction of a clubhouse.

124 [1943] 2 All ER 378.

125 In *Carlton Cricket and Football Social Club v Joseph* [1970] VR 487 the court noted that 'the members of the [original] committee could not be regarded in the circumstances of this case as authorising the undertaking of obligations of the kind dealt with in the document in such a way as to make themselves personally liable for the performance of those obligations over the years.' The contract in question involved a 21-year licence agreement. The result was that no one was bound by the contract.

126 Thus in *Peckham v Moore* [1975] 1 NSWLR 353 a professional footballer promised his continued services to the club and to the successive managers and they promised that as a club they would continue to employ him.

127 *Associations Incorporation Act* 1981 (Qld); *Associations Incorporation Act* 1984 (NSW); *Associations Incorporation Act* 1981 (Vic); *Associations Incorporation Act* 1985 (SA); *Associations Incorporation Act* 1987 (WA); *Associations Incorporation Act* 1964 (Tas); *Associations Incorporation Act* 1963 (NT); *Associations Incorporation Act* 1991 (ACT).

128 See, for example, *Liddle v Aboriginal Legal Aid Service* (1999) 150 FLR 142, which involved an application for a declaration by a former employee of the Service, which was a voluntary association registered under the *Associations Incorporation Act* 1963 (NT).

129 For a comprehensive discussion of these issues see NC Sedden, *Government Contracts: Federal, State and Local*, 2nd edn, Federation Press, Sydney, 1999.

wealth government, whose powers are limited by the Constitution. The States and Territories, on the other hand, probably have unlimited capacity to enter into contracts, as long as they do not trespass into areas of Commonwealth power.[130]

The Crown (at State or Commonwealth level) has the power to enter into contracts and is liable in most instances as a party to an action for breach of contract, although there may be specific statutory bars to the bringing of proceedings against the Crown in certain specific cases.[131]

[10.240] A contract with the Crown should not be confused with a contract made with a government body that has independent corporate status under a separate statute or under the *Corporations Law*.[132]

An example of the Crown being found liable on a contract is the case of *New South Wales v Bardolph*.[133]

Example: New South Wales v Bardolph[134]

An officer of the NSW Premiers Department entered into an advertising contract with a resident of South Australia for the weekly insertion in a newspaper of advertisements for the NSW Tourist Bureau. The contract was not expressly authorised by the legislature or by the executive, although moneys had been appropriated by the government for government advertising. Shortly after making the contract, the government changed, and the new administration refused to use or pay for any further advertising space. Notwithstanding this, the plaintiff continued to insert the advertisements, and at the end of the period named in the contract, brought an action for recovery of the total unpaid amount.

The High Court held that the contract made with the Crown was binding on the Crown. Dixon J (with whom the others agreed) noted:

> In considering whether the Crown was affected with responsibility for the agreement made on its behalf by the Superintendent of Advertising, that is, whether, independently of parliamentary provision of funds, it became the contract of the Crown, it is a matter of primary importance that the subject matter of the contract notwithstanding its commercial character, concerned

---

130 NC Seddon, *Government Contracts: Federal State and Local*, 2nd edn, Federation Press, Sydney, 1999, p 39. Note also that sections 106, 107 and 108 of the Constitution preserve the law-making powers of the States. On the other hand Territories have a more limited power and are subject to s 122 of the Constitution.

131 *Judiciary Act* 1903 (Cth); *Crown Proceedings Act* 1992 (ACT); *Crown Proceedings Act* 1988 (NSW); *Crown Proceedings Act* 1993 (NT); *Crown Proceedings Act* 1980 (Qld); *Crown Proceedings Act* 1992 (SA); *Crown Proceedings Act* 1993 (Tas); *Crown Proceedings Act* 1958 (Vic); *Crown Suits Act* 1947 (WA). See also PW Hogg, *Liability of the Crown*, 2nd edn, LBC Information Services, North Ryde, 1989, p 163. In terms of certain Crown protections the *Trade Practices Act* 1974 (Cth) exempts the Crown from any prosecutions under the Act. The comments made in *Commonwealth v Evans Deakin Industries Ltd* (1986) 161 CLR 254 at 265 support the capacity of the Crown to enter into binding contracts.

132 See generally the *Laws of Australia*, LBC, Legal Entities Part D where the following example is given: 'The Australian Heritage Commission is a body corporate whereas the Alligator Rivers Region Research Institute is not an incorporated body so that a contract with that institute would be with the Crown in right of the Commonwealth.'

133 (1934) 52 CLR 455.

134 Ibid.

a recognized and regular activity of Government in New South Wales ... No statutory power to make a contract in the ordinary course of administering a recognized part of the government of the State appears to me to be necessary in order that, if made by the appropriate servant of the Crown, it should become the contract of the Crown, and subject to the provision of funds to answer it, binding upon the Crown.[135]

[10.245] An interesting point that flows from this is that a subsequent government that decides not to proceed with a contract may be liable in damages. This aspect of the law does not sit easily with the view that governments are sovereign and that one government cannot bind a future government. In *L'Huillier v Victoria*,[136] Callaway JA drew a distinction between cases where a government cannot bind future government action—thus any such contract would be void—with those cases where a government breaks a contract because of (for example) a change in policy. In the case of *L'Huillier*, the majority found that the agreement was not void, because it did not contain an impermissible fetter on the exercise of a public law discretion.[137] The case came about because the Government of Victoria had agreed to the re-appointment of the plaintiff for a five-year term as Chairman and Chief Executive Officer of a statutory body. Subsequently, the Government reappointed him by a series of short-term appointments, ending after two years. He sued the State for breach of contract.

The middle course suggested by the majority was that in cases involving some change of policy or the exercise of a discretion, there is a valid contract, but it is subject to an implied term that the government may have to withhold performance if performance would be inconsistent with the exercise of that discretion. In this case, the Government did not avail itself of that term by making a positive decision not to reappoint the plaintiff and was therefore bound by the agreement.[138]

[10.250] Finally, there may be constitutional reasons why a government lacks the capacity to enter into binding contracts—for example, the Commonwealth may lack the power under the Constitution, or a State or Territory government may lack contractual capacity because the area comes within Commonwealth responsibility. The effect on a contract if power is lacking, or it is exceeded, is that the contract is void.[139]

---

135   Ibid at 507.

136   [1996] 2 VR 465.

137   Callaway JA (with whom Charles JA agreed) commented at [1996] 2 VR 465 at 484: 'A contractual provision to the effect that the repository of a public law discretion will, at a future time, exercise the discretion in a particular way is void if, and only if, on its true construction it means that the repository will exercise the discretion in that way in any event ... even if in breach of the duty to exercise the discretion according to law.' Callaway JA also noted at 480 the importance of being able to conclude binding agreements with the Crown: 'If governments had no such capacity, it would often be impossible to secure the services of those best qualified. They would choose a binding and lucrative engagement in private enterprise in preference to an unenforceable promise by the Crown.'

138   For a discussion of these matters see NC Seddon, *Government Contracts: Federal State and Local*, 2nd edn, Federation Press, Sydney, 1999, Chapter 5.

139   NC Seddon, *Government Contracts: Federal State and Local*, 2nd edn, Federation Press, Sydney, 1999, pp 66 and 67.

10.7 International perspective

[10.255] It is becoming increasingly common for individuals, companies, and governments to enter into contracts with persons or governments who are overseas. The explosion of the Internet and global shopping raises particular questions concerning the capacity to enter into binding agreements.[140] Many disputes in this area concern the law that is to be applied to a contract under dispute. The general rule is that the law of the place where the contract is formed will govern the dispute—but there are a number of exceptions based on the express wishes of the parties and certain international treaty obligations and protocols.[141]

As far as 'global shopping' is concerned, it will be exceedingly difficult to detect the age or mental capacity of a person purchasing goods over the Internet. At least in face-to-face dealings some proof of identity and the general demeanour of the person can alert the adult party in the transaction of the need for caution.

10.7.1 New Zealand

[10.260] The law concerning capacity to contract in other common law jurisdictions is a mixture of common law and legislation—a common law base with a legislative overlay. The age of majority in New Zealand is 20. The law relating to contracts with minors is governed by the *Minors' Contracts Act* 1969 (NZ). Under the Act, there are three levels of enforceablility:

1 contracts that have the same effect as if the minor were of full age and capacity;

2 contracts that are presumptively enforceable, but in respect of which the court has certain powers to intervene to cancel or vary the contact; and

3 contracts that are presumptively unenforceable against the minor but in respect of which the court has power to intervene to enforce the contract in whole or in part.[142]

[10.265] In the first place, minors who are or have been married have full contractual capacity. Secondly, contracts made by minors over 18 and beneficial contracts of service are given full force and effect as though made by an adult; however, the court still has power to declare them unenforceable where the consideration is inadequate or where the contract is harsh or oppressive to the minor.[143] In the third category are contracts made by minors under the age of 18; these are unenforceable against the minor, but if the court finds that a contract was fair and reasonable when it was entered into, it may enforce the contract and declare it binding in whole or in part.[144]

---

140 See, for example, the Review by R Chalmers, 'Going Digital' (2000) 25 *Alternative Law Journal* 46, concerning a Report by Fitzgerald (ed) et al entitled *Going Digital: Legal Issues for electronic commerce, multimedia and the Internet*, Prospect Media Pty Ltd 1998, in which the authors recognise the difficulties of the law regulating the rapidly changing and borderless environment of the Internet.

141 This is outside the scope of this chapter but see generally the United Nations Convention on Contracts for the International Sale of Goods 1980 which was enacted as part of our domestic law in 1989 via the *Sale of Goods (Vienna Convention) Act* in the various Sates and Territories. See also Chapter 26.

142 See generally JF Burrows, J Finn & SMD Todd, *Law of Contract in New Zealand*, 8th edn, Butterworths, Wellington, 1997.

143 *Minors' Contracts Act* 1969 (NZ), ss 5(2) and 7.

144 *Minors' Contracts Act* 1969 (NZ), s 6.

[10.270] In relation to the tortious liability of minors, the Act expressly preserves a minors' immunity at common law from liability in tort for procuring a contract by means of fraudulent representations but goes on to provide that the court will take such representations into account when making any orders.

[10.275] Concerning corporations, most trading corporations in New Zealand are created by conditions laid down in the *Companies Act* 1993 (NZ). Changes made to the Act remove the difficulty of enforcing contracts made with a company when the company has acted beyond its powers. The broad effect is to allow innocent third parties to make contracts with companies without the risk of having them set aside as being beyond power.

[10.280] In relation to persons who are mentally disordered or drunk, New Zealand, for the most part, applies the common law.[145]

10.7.2 United States

[10.285] The law regulating capacity to contract in the United States is based largely on common law principles, many of which are reflected in the Restatement (Second).[146] As in Australia, capacity is generally assumed. The two main areas where capacity arises as an issue in the United States concerns contracts made with minors and contracts with those who are mentally incompetent.

[10.290] In the United States, for the purposes of contract law, a person is a minor if he or she is under the age of 18.[147] The reason for maintaining special rules for minors and the competing policy issues was noted long ago by the New York Court of Appeal:

> [A] protracted struggle has been maintained in the courts, on the one hand to protect infants or minors from their own improvidence and folly, and to save them from the depredations and frauds practiced upon them by the designing and unprincipled, and on the other to protect the rights of those dealing with them in good faith and on the assumption that they could lawfully make contracts.[148]

[10.295] The effect of minority is that the contract is generally voidable at the option of the minor.[149] An infant cannot generally avoid transactions where the law compels performance, or contracts for necessaries for the minor's children.[150] This right to avoid the contract is referred to as 'disaffirmance' and may be express, or implied by words or conduct.[151] The failure by the minor to disaffirm the contract may amount to

---

145 In respect of necessaries s 4(1) of the *Sale of Goods Act* 1908 (NZ) is in similar terms to provisions that exist in Australian jurisdictions and referred to at footnote 19.

146 Restatement (Second) § 12.

147 The age of 21 was amended by statute. In addition, a few states have enacted statutes making exceptions to the 18-year-old majority rule so far as capacity is concerned for minors engaged in a business. Thus the Restatement (Second) notes at § 14: 'Unless a statute provides otherwise, a natural person has the capacity to incur only voidable contractual duties until the beginning of the day before the person's eighteenth birthday'.

148 *Henry v Root* 33 N.Y. 526, 536 (1895) New York Court of Appeal. The same considerations support the Australian law in this area.

149 EA Farnsworth, *Contracts*, 3rd edn, Aspen Law and Business, New York, 1999, p 226.

150 JD Calamari & JM Perillo, *The Law of Contracts,* 4th edn, West Group, St Paul, Minnesota, 1998, p 282.

151 The entire contract must be disaffirmed, not merely the portions that are burdensome to the minor.

ratification. Ratification can only take place after majority. Ratification can be demonstrated by (a) failure to make a timely disaffirmance; (b) express ratification; or (c) conduct manifesting ratification. In relation to the requirement for a minor to repudiate a voidable contract within a reasonable time of attaining majority it has been noted:

> By holding the right of election open [indefinitely], the minor would be enabled, after majority, to speculate upon fluctuations in value, to affirm or disaffirm, as his subsequent interest might dictate; whereas the other party would be helpless until the minor might see fit to act. The protection which the rule affords is against the deleterious effects of contracts made during minority. Beyond that date ... he should be required to act within a reasonable time in all cases where not to require it would be inequitable or unjust to the other party.[152]

[10.300] Upon a minor's avoidance of a contract, the United States law requires the minor to restore the goods, or the consideration, if they are in his or her possession:

> At the very least, the minor is expected to return what remains of anything that was received from the other party. The minor is also expected to return what remains of anything acquired from third persons in exchange for what the minor received from the other party.[153]

Where services have been used, or the property is unable to be returned, there is no obligation to make restitution by way of payment. However, this general rule has not been followed in all cases. In *Bartlett v Bailey*,[154] the New Hampshire Supreme Court held that a minor who was a milk dealer was liable for the reasonable value of milk supplied to him in the course of his business. On this view, if the infant has received a benefit, then the infant is liable to make restitution to the value of the benefit. Although a few courts have followed the New Hampshire view, in most States the other party's right to restitution depends on whether that party can bring the case within one of the several exceptions mentioned below.

[10.305] In the United States the minor who contracts for necessaries may disaffirm the contract, but can be required to make restitution.[155] This is unlike the position in Australia, where such contracts are deemed to be binding and the requirement to pay a 'reasonable price' arises from the contract itself. In the United States, a contract of loan for the purpose of paying for necessaries is treated as a contract for necessaries on the reasoning that the lender succeeds by subrogation to the rights of the person who furnished the necessaries.[156] Where the minor, as plaintiff, seeks recovery of money paid for goods, as opposed to cases where the minor, as defendant, merely sets up minority as a defence to non-payment, then, upon return of the money, the one who furnished

---

152   *Walker v Stokes Bros & Co* 226 S.W. 158, 160 (Tex. Civ. App. 1924).
153   *Whitman v Allen* 121 A 160 (Me 1923).
154   59 NH 408 (1879).
155   EA Farnsworth, *Contracts,* 3rd edn, Aspen Law & Business, New York, 1999, p 233. JD Calamari & JM Perillo, *The Law of Contracts,* 4th edn, West Group, St Paul, Minnesota, 1998, p 292 suggest that a minor may disaffirm a contract for necessaries but is liable in quasi-contract for the reasonable value of the necessaries furnished.
156   *Price v Sanders* 60 Ind 310 (1878).

the goods to the minor is entitled to their return. In some cases, courts have offset the return of the minor's money by an amount based on the use made of the goods or their depreciation. Where the goods or services are supplied on credit, there is an assumption of the legal and practical risk of non-payment, and the supplier is not entitled to their return, or restitution.[157]

[10.310] If the minor has made a misrepresentation as to his or her age, the view in the majority of states is that the one who has been deceived can recover in tort for the misrepresentation. In other states, it is not possible to sue the minor in tort if the tort represents, in essence, a breach of the contract.

[10.315] As far as those who are mentally incompetent[158] are concerned, the traditional test used in the United States to establish such incapacity is 'whether the party lacks the capacity to understand the nature and consequences of the transaction in question.'[159] This is known as the cognitive test.[160] To this traditional test, the Restatement (Second) adds a reference to cases where the person understands the nature and consequences of the transaction in question, but nevertheless lacks effective control, and where the other party has reason to know of the incapacity.[161] The burden of proving incompetence in relation to capacity rests with the person who seeks relief on the grounds of mental incompetence.

[10.320] So far as intoxication is concerned, § 16 of the Restatement Second states that the inability to understand, by reason of intoxication, makes a contract voidable only if the other party has reason to know of the inability to understand the transaction or the inability to act in a reasonable manner in relation to the transaction. This is in line with the common law in Australia.

[10.325] Under § 15 of the Restatement (Second), the effect of mental incompetence is that the contract is voidable at the instance of the mentally incompetent party. In a few states, statutory provisions make such contracts null and void rather than voidable. As is the case with minors, the right of the mentally incompetent to avoid the contract may be lost by ratification or delay.[162]

[10.330] The remedies available to a party where a contract has been disaffirmed lie in restitution. In relation to contracts made with a person who is mentally incompetent, the other party is under a greater disadvantage than if the contract had been made with a minor. This is because the test of mental incompetence gives rise to more uncertainty than does the test of immaturity, which is based on age. However, the other party's rights to restitution are greater as against a mental incompetent than as against a

---

157 JD Calamari & JM Perillo, *The Law of Contracts,* 4th edn, West Group, St Paul, Minnesota, 1998, p 289.

158 As opposed to persons whose property is under guardianship by reason of an adjudication of mental illness or defect. Such a person lacks capacity to contract. Restatement (Second) § 13.

159 *Lloyd v Jordan* 544 So 2nd 957 (Ala 1989).

160 Apart from the capacity to understand, the Australian position also requires knowledge of the incapacity by the other party. See para 10.3.

161 This is known as the volitional test. 'If by reason of mental illness or defect ... he is *unable to act* in a reasonable manner in relation to the transaction and the other party has *reason to know* of his condition.' (The Restatement (Second), para. 15 emphasis added). The qualification that the other party has reason to know was reaffirmed in *Ortelere v Teachers Retirement Board* 250 NE 2nd 460, 465 (NY 1969).

162 Apart from this, where the contract is made on fair terms and the other party is without knowledge of the mental illness or defect the power to avoid the contract may be lost (The Restatement (Second) para 15 (2)).

minor. The minor is ordinarily accountable only for the benefits that remain in the minor's hands,[163] but the mental incompetent is generally required, as a condition of relief, to make restitution in full to the extent of any benefit received.

> Even if the incompetent has dissipated or squandered it during incompetence, so that it cannot be returned in kind, the incompetent must restore the status quo by making compensation in money.[164]

10.7.3 Japan

[10.335] In Japanese law, mutual intention is required to form a contract, and persons who lack the ability to form mutual intention are regarded as lacking capacity to contract.[165] There is no Civil Code provision that states this explicitly; it is simply accepted in Japanese jurisprudence as a proposition necessary to the accurate interpretation of the Civil Code.[166] An example of such mental incapacity [ishimunôryoku] would be the inability to form the necessary intention to contract because the person concerned was heavily under the influence of alcohol.

[10.340] Originally, the effect of contractual incapacity was that it voided the contract automatically. In more recent times, however, it has been regarded as a principle employed for the protection of the person lacking capacity. The trend in Japanese law is to allow that person to assert that the contract is void (something close to treating the contract as voidable at the option of that party).

[10.345] In Japan, issues of contractual capacity are generally classified as cases of mental incapacity (such as the example given above) and cases of legal incapacity. New legislation substantially reforming the Civil Code position on legal incapacity in Japan was enacted in December 1999 and came into effect on 1 April 2000.

[10.350] Prior to these amendments, Japanese law after the Second World War defined three categories of people lacking legal capacity: minors, incompetents, and quasi-incompetents. The new revisions abolish these categories and introduce a scheme of protection in which the terms 'lacking capacity' and 'incapacitated' are no longer used. Instead, new classifications provide for three categories of 'persons of limited capacity'. The amendments are the most dramatic changes made to the Civil Code since its enactment, apart from the immediate post-war revisions to family and gender equality.[167] A new *Law on Voluntary Guardianship* also establishes a new system under which contracts between people requiring protection and the guardian charged with ordering their affairs and acting in their place (for example, to make arrangements for their care) are drawn under the supervision of the Family Court and are registered with the Court.[168]

---

163 Except in relation to necessaries, which also applies to those who are mentally incompetent.
164 *Sparrowhawk v Erwin* 246 P 541 (Ariz 1926). However the United States courts have not required full restitution where the other party acted unfairly and with knowledge of the incompetence.
165 Decision of the Daishin'in [forerunner to the Japanese Supreme Court] 11 May 1905 *Nichiminroku* 11-706.
166 Takashi Uchida, *Minpô I* [Civil Code Vol 1] (2000) 2nd edn, Tokyo Daigaku Shuppankai, Tokyo, 101.
167 Takashi Uchida, *Minpô I* [Civil Code Vol 1] (2000) 2nd edn, Tokyo Daigaku Shuppankai, Tokyo, 102.
168 For a complete description, see: Takashi Uchida, *Minpô I* [Civil Code Vol 1] (2000) 2nd ed Tokyo: Tokyo Daigaku Shuppankai, 149–154.

[10.355] The first new category of persons with limited capacity is that of persons requiring the appointment of a guardian or assistant. These must be declared by the Family Court. The procedure can be instituted by a spouse, a close relative, one of a number of kinds of guardian or assistants, or the police (Civil Code Article 7 as revised). Contracts concluded by people requiring guardianship are voidable, with the exception of contracts for necessities.[169] These contracts can also be affirmed by the legal guardian.

[10.360] The second kind of limited capacity (previously quasi-incompetency) is defined as a situation in which a person has mental capacity, but has obviously less than average ability to manage his or her assets.[170] That person, a spouse, or other defined persons may apply to the Family Court for a declaration to this effect, and the Court appoints of someone to assist the person in their legal affairs.

[10.365] The third new category of limited capacity enables a person suffering from mild mental or emotional incapacity to apply to the Family Court (or to have an application made on his or her behalf) for a hearing, and the appointment of someone to assist in their legal affairs. This category covers people who are capable of making decisions, but who, for mental or emotional reasons, are likely to be swayed in their decision-making by other people in a way that prevents their decisions from being their own. This level of limited capacity is less stringent than the traditional definition of quasi-incompetence in Japanese law.[171] The effect of both the second and third categories of limited capacity is that a person declared to have limited capacity may make contracts, but these contracts will be voidable either at his or her option or at the option of the guardian or assistant, unless the latter has given consent. If the guardian or assistant improperly withholds consent, the person of limited capacity may apply directly to the Family Court for permission to form the contract.[172]

[10.370] Different issues arise in relation to minors. The age of majority in Japan is 20 (Civil Code Article 3). Accordingly, legal acts performed by a minor require the consent of his or her legal representative to be valid (Article 4(1)). Where a minor is without parents, the legal representative will be the minor's legal guardian. Where a minor forms a contract without the consent of his or her legal representative (or guardian), that contract is voidable at the minor's option. A legal representative or guardian may also cancel such a contract (Civil Code Article 120).[173] It is also possible for either the minor or the legal representative or guardian to affirm such contracts (Civil Code Article 122).

[10.375] Article 5 of the Civil Code allows minors to dispose of property (including money) freely to the extent permitted by their legal guardians. This underpins the validity of ordinary sales contracts concluded by minors. Article 6 of the Civil Code also permits minors to carry on a business and to be deemed to have the same capacity as an adult in this respect, for example, in the case of someone earning his or her living through music or the performance of traditional arts.[174]

---

169 Takashi Uchida, *Minpô I* [Civil Code Vol 1] (2000) 2nd edn, Tokyo Daigaku Shuppankai, Tokyo, 109.
170 Until 1979 this included people with hearing, sight and speech disabilities, but they are now treated as having full capacity unless declared otherwise.
171 Takashi Uchida, *Minpô I* [Civil Code Vol 1] (2000) 2nd edn, Tokyo Daigaku Shuppankai, Tokyo, 114.
172 Takashi Uchida, *Minpô I* [Civil Code Vol 1] (2000) 2nd edn, Tokyo Daigaku Shuppankai, Tokyo, 115.
173 Takashi Uchida, *Minpô I* [Civil Code Vol 1] (2000) 2nd edn, Tokyo Daigaku Shuppankai, Tokyo, 105.

[10.380] As a matter of practice, when someone under 20 contracts for high-value consumer goods such as a mobile phone, the provider will typically require a counter-signature by a parent or guarantor. The 'Dial Q' cases are an interesting response by Japanese courts to the problem of underage consumers of expensive goods and serv-ices. In these cases, minors had dialled up telephone services (for example telephone sex providers) from home telephones. The telephone company then argued that the parents were liable for the telephone charges, either because the services-by-phone contracted for were ancillary to the main contract for the telephone line, or because the parents had impliedly guaranteed payment of the services-by-phone contract because the calls were placed from home. In most cases, the courts have found in favour of the parents—that is, the contracts for services-by-phone were voidable.

---

174 The *Labour Standards Law* contains other protective provisions on the employment of minors.

Chapter 11

Formalities

11.1 Introduction

[11.05] It is a common misconception of many non-lawyers that a contract must be in writing to be enforceable. In fact, this is rarely the case. Provided a contract is validly formed and there are no vitiating factors, action can usually be brought to enforce a verbal contract. Notwithstanding this general proposition, however, a limited number of contracts must be evidenced by writing to be enforceable. This chapter examines this requirement of formality.

Legislation exists in all Australian jurisdictions requiring some degree of formality before certain kinds of contracts can be enforced. This legal position originated in the United Kingdom with the enactment of the *Statute of Frauds* in 1677. The reason for passing the Imperial legislation was to overcome difficulties arising out of an early rule of evidence. It used to be the case that people could not give evidence to support their own case in actions brought against them. In the absence of evidence of some other kind, therefore, it was difficult to resist spurious claims brought against a person. To prevent such bogus actions, legislation was enacted to prevent certain kinds of contracts from being enforced unless they were in writing and signed by the party to be charged—namely the defendant. Contracts considered to be of particular significance were subject to this requirement; not least of these were contracts concerning land.

Failure to comply with the *Statute of Frauds* (Imp) led to the peculiar result of the contract being valid but unenforceable.

As can be imagined, strict compliance with the statutory requirement of writing could lead to injustice. For example, if the plaintiff had substantially carried out his or her side of the bargain but the defendant had not, and refused to complete, the performing party (the plaintiff) could be disadvantaged. To alleviate the harshness of the statutory requirement, the courts of equity intervened to require performance by the defendant in some circumstances. This doctrine of part-performance is also examined here.

The relevant provisions of the *Statute of Frauds* (Imp) have been re-enacted in most Australian jurisdictions. The requirement of formality is retained for a number of different kinds of contracts. The two most important, for practical purposes, are contracts of guarantee and some contracts concerning land.[1] This chapter deals with contracts of these types.

11.2 Guarantees

[11.10] In most Australian jurisdictions, there is a statutory requirement that the contract of guarantee must be in writing and signed by the party to be charged in order to be enforceable. Section 56(1) of the *Property Law Act* 1974 (Qld) is illustrative of these provisions. It provides as follows:

> No action may be brought upon any promise to guarantee any liability of another unless the promise upon which such action is brought, or some memorandum or note of the promise, is in writing, and signed by the party to be charged, or by some other person by the party lawfully authorised.[2]

11.2.1 Nature of a guarantee

[11.15] A contract of guarantee has been defined as 'a contract to answer for the debt, default or miscarriage of another who is to be primarily liable to the promisee'.[3] The

---

1   A number of other kinds of contracts are required to be in writing to be enforceable. These include contracts made in consideration of marriage: *Statute of Frauds* (Imp) 1677, s 4 (NT) and *Mercantile Law Act* 1935 (Tas), s 6; contracts where executor assumes personal liability: *Statute of Frauds* (Imp) 1677, s 4 (NT) and *Mercantile Law Act* 1935 (Tas), s 6; contracts that are not to be performed within one year of their formation: *Statute of Frauds* (Imp) 1677, s 4 (NT) and *Mercantile Law Act* 1935 (Tas), s 6; contracts for the sale of goods valued at $20 or more: *Sale of Goods Act* 1972 (NT), s 9; *Sale of Goods Act* 1896 (Tas), s 9; *Sale of Goods Act* 1895 (WA), s 4; hire purchase contracts: *Hire-Purchase Act* 1961 (NT), ss 6–7; *Hire Purchase Act* 1959 (Tas), ss 5–6; certain building contracts: *Home Building Act* 1989 (NSW), s 7; credit contracts governed by *the Consumer Credit Code*: *Consumer Credit Code*, s 12; bills of exchange: *Bills of Exchange Act* 1909 (Cth), s 8(1); contracts for marine insurance: *Marine Insurance Act* 1909 (Cth), s 27.

2   Equivalent requirements exist in Victoria (*Instruments Act* 1958, s 126), Western Australia (*Law Reform (Statute of Frauds) Act* 1962, s 2), Tasmania (*Mercantile Law Act* 1935, s 6), the Australian Capital Territory before 1986 (for guarantees entered after that time, the requirement having been removed: *Imperial Acts (Substituted Provisions) Act* 1986, s 3(1)) and the Northern Territory (*Law of Property Act* 2000 (NT), s 58). Contrast the position in New South Wales (*Imperial Acts Application Act* 1969, s 8(1)) and South Australia (*Statutes Amendment (Enforcement of Contracts) Act* 1982, s 3). See also the obligation imposed by s 50 *Consumer Credit Code* that a guarantee governed by the Code be in writing and be signed by the guarantor. 'Guarantee' is defined widely in Schedule 1 to include an indemnity.

3   *Yeoman Credit Ltd v Latter* [1961] 1 WLR 828 at 831.

person who provides the guarantee is referred to interchangeably as the 'guarantor' or 'surety'. In contemporary Australian society, contracts of guarantee are relatively commonplace. They may, for example, be given in the following situations:

- loan to a person to buy a house for personal use, with a guarantee given by that person's parents;
- loan to a person to help establish that person in business with a guarantee from that person's spouse;
- loan to a company for business purposes, with a guarantee being obtained from the directors of the business.

[11.20] In situations where a guarantee is given, there will be two separate transactions. The first is referred to as the principal transaction. Where a guarantee is given of a person's obligations under a contract of loan (as is commonly the case) the principal transaction will be the loan contract entered into between the lender and the debtor. The debtor is primarily liable under that contract of loan. The contract of guarantee, entered into between the lender and the guarantor, is referred to as the secondary transaction. The guarantor is secondarily liable to the lender. Liability of the guarantor arises only if the principal transaction between the lender and the debtor is valid, and there has been default under the principal transaction. If, for some reason, the principal transaction is not valid and therefore cannot be enforced against the debtor, it will generally also be the case that the guarantor will not be liable under the guarantee.

11.2.2 Transactions which are not guarantees

[11.25] A number of transactions resemble contracts of guarantee, yet technically are not so regarded. Those transactions need not comply with the statutory requirement of formality.[4]

(a) Contracts of indemnity

[11.30] In the preceding discussion, it was explained that a contract of guarantee confers secondary liability on a guarantor. In the example above of a guarantee of repayment of a loan, the primary liability lay with the debtor to repay the lender, while the guarantor had secondary liability only. In many ways, a contract of indemnity has the same effect as a contract of guarantee. The distinction between a guarantee and an indemnity, however, is that under the latter the surety undertakes *primary* liability. This means the surety may be liable notwithstanding that the principal transaction is unenforceable. The following case illustrates the distinction between a guarantee and indemnity.

Example: Yeoman Credit Ltd v Latter[5]

Yeoman Credit Ltd, a finance company, let a car on hire-purchase terms to Mr Latter, who was a minor at the time of contract. Because the hirer was a minor, an adult was

---

4 Note, however, that a guarantee is defined in Schedule 1 of the *Consumer Credit Code* to include an indemnity. If the indemnity is one regulated by the Code, therefore, it must be in writing to satisfy s 50 of the Code, even though it may not be a guarantee within the common law understanding of that term: see [11.30].

5 [1961] 1 WLR 828.

asked to sign a document headed 'Hire-purchase indemnity and undertaking'. Pursuant to clause I of the document, the adult agreed with the finance company to 'indemnify you against any loss arising from or arising out of the agreement and to pay to you the amount of such loss or demand and whether or not at the time of demand you shall have exercised all or any of your remedies in respect of the hirer or the chattels but so that upon payment in full by me of my liabilities hereunder I shall obtain such of your rights as you may at your discretion assign to me'. Under English law, the principal transaction between Yeoman Credit Ltd and Mr Latter was void because Mr Latter was a minor at the time he entered the contract. As a result, on the default of Mr Latter, Yeoman Credit Ltd brought action against the surety.

The issue for determination by the court was whether the document was a guarantee or an indemnity. If the former, Yeoman Credit Ltd could not recover from the surety because liability under a guarantee is secondary, and dependant upon a valid principal contract. On the other hand, if the document signed was an indemnity, the surety would be undertaking primary liability—which would subsist notwithstanding the unenforceability of the principal transaction.

On a proper construction of the document, having regard to the nature of the obligations undertaken by the surety, the court held that the document was an indemnity. The surety had undertaken primary liability for the obligations of the minor under the hire-purchase agreement, so was liable to Yeoman Credit Ltd.

(b)   Promise of guarantee made to the debtor

[11.35] Under a contract of guarantee, the guarantor makes a promise to the person (commonly a lender) with whom the principal obligor (commonly a debtor) contracts. In other words, the guarantor promises the lender that if the debtor defaults, he or she will pay amounts due to the lender. It is also possible for a person to promise the principal obligor (the debtor) that he or she will pay the debt of the debtor. As this promise is not made to the person with whom the principal obligor contracts (the lender), the contract is not one of guarantee.[6]

(c)   Person agrees to take over the debt of another

[11.40] Where a debtor and creditor have entered into a contract of loan, it could occur that a third party agrees with the creditor to take over the debt of the debtor. Such an arrangement is not a contract of guarantee and therefore need not comply with the statutory requirement of formality. Such a transaction was examined in the following case.

Example: Gray v Pearson[7]

The debtor, Mr Cocks, was unable to meet debts due to a number of his creditors. He called a meeting of creditors, at which it was decided that the creditors would accept payment from the defendant of a percentage of the money due to them, in exchange for the defendant being entitled to the assets of Mr Cocks' estate. Although

---

6   *Eastwood v Kenyon* (1840) 113 ER 482.
7   (1877) 3 VLR 81.

this arrangement was not in writing, it was held to be enforceable against the defendant as it was not a contract of guarantee.

(d)   The agreement imposes no personal liability on the person

[11.45] Where a guarantor undertakes secondary liability under a contract of guarantee, that guarantor will be personally liable if the principal transaction is valid and the principal obligor defaults. The situation is different, however, if a person does not undertake personal liability, but instead proffers his or her property as security to the promisee under the principal transaction. A transaction of this kind was examined by the High Court in the following case.

Example: Harvey v Edwards, Dunlop & Co Ltd[8]

Edwards, Dunlop & Co Ltd ('Edwards') was owed money by a third party. In consideration of Edwards not suing the third party, Mr Harvey agreed to pay the money by allowing the sale of his property in Scotland. To effect the sale, he forwarded to a solicitor in Scotland a power of attorney. Mr Harvey later refused to pay Edwards the money owed by the third party and was sued on his promise. Part of Mr Harvey's defence was that the agreement to pay was not in writing. One of the issues for determination by the High Court was whether the arrangement between Edwards and Mr Harvey was that of guarantee.

The only Justice to make a determination on this issue was Higgins J. In his view, the arrangement was not one of guarantee, and therefore did not have to comply with the statutory requirements of formality. Liability was imposed only on the proceeds of sale of the property in Scotland. Mr Harvey had not 'promised to answer for the debt of the company'.[9] If the proceeds of sale were insufficient to cover the debt, there was no obligation on Mr Harvey to pay out of his other assets. If this had been a guarantee, he would have been required to pay from his own assets.

(e)   Letters of comfort

[11.50] Guarantees are generally obtained when the creditor is concerned that the debtor may be unable to meet his or her contractual liability under the principal transaction. But sometimes third parties are not prepared to provide the lender with a guarantee. As a compromise, however, the third party may be prepared to give the lender some assurance about the likelihood of the debtor meeting obligations under the principal contract. Such assurances are commonly referred to as letters of comfort. Letters of comfort are sometimes given by a director or shareholder where an advance is made to a company, or by a holding company where an advance is made to a subsidiary company. As indicated by the case law, letters of comfort often contain the following kind of information:

- the third party is aware of the facility the lender is providing to the debtor;
- the terms of the facility are accepted with the consent and knowledge of the third party;

---

8   (1927) 39 CLR 302.
9   Ibid at 312.

- it is the policy of the third party (if it is a holding company and the advance is to a subsidiary company) to ensure that the debtor is at all times in a position to meet its liabilities when they fall due.

[11.55] Whether a letter of comfort is binding as a contractual document—so that the third party may be called upon to pay pursuant to that letter—depends on the construction of the document. Frequently, the issue is whether there was an intention by the parties, namely the third party and the lender, to create legal relations.[10] In determining the intention of the parties, the presumption that the parties intend to create legal relations if they enter into a commercial transaction may be relevant. In these circumstances, the onus then shifts to the third party to show that, despite giving a letter of comfort, the parties did not intend to establish legal relations.[11]

11.2.3   Requirement of writing: content

[11.60] For a contract of guarantee to be enforceable, the relevant statutory provision requires either the promise to be in writing, or some 'memorandum or note' of the promise to be in writing.[12] The provision does not, however, elaborate on precisely the information that must be contained in the writing to satisfy the statutory requirement. Guidance must therefore be obtained from the case law. The High Court case of *Harvey v Edwards, Dunlop & Co Ltd*[13] provides a starting point. In the joint judgment of Knox CJ, Gavan Duffy and Starke JJ, it is said that the document must contain 'all the essential terms of the agreement'.[14]

(a)   Information particular to the guarantee

[11.65] First, the guarantee must contain the names of the relevant parties: the lender, the debtor, and the guarantor. It may happen that the guarantee makes reference to a party without expressly identifying who that party is. The authorities suggest that even if a party is not expressly identified, a description of the party will be sufficient if 'the description used can be explained by extrinsic evidence without having to resort to evidence to prove the intention of the author'.[15] In *Rosser v Austral Wine & Spirit Co Pty Ltd*,[16] the guarantee was in favour of 'each and every number of the Wholesale Spirit Merchants Association of Victoria Wine and Brandy Producers' Association of Victoria'. The Supreme Court of Victoria held this to be a sufficient description, and parol evidence was admissible to identify who such members were.

[11.70] Secondly, the relevant terms of the guarantee must be stated. This would generally require the amount of debt being guaranteed to be specified.[17] If the guarantee is given of the amount advanced by the lender together with interest on that amount,

---

10   *Banque Brussels Lambert SA v Australian National Industries Ltd* (1989) 21 NSWLR 502.
11   Ibid at 521.
12   For the extent to which an electronic document can satisfy this requirement, see [11.240]–[11.265].
13   (1927) 39 CLR 302.
14   Ibid at 307.
15   *Rosser v Austral Wine & Spirit Co Pty Ltd* [1980] VR 313.
16   [1980] VR 313.
17   Note, however, the comments made by the Supreme Court of New South Wales in *Vetro Glass Pty Ltd v Fitzpatrick* (1963) 63 SR (NSW) 697 at 701 that a guarantee complied with the formality requirement by guaranteeing 'advances' made.

the interest payable by the debtor should also be specified in the guarantee. In addition to these obvious content requirements, the guarantee should also contain any other material terms of the guarantee. For example, if the guarantee is supported by a mortgage, details of that mortgage should be included in the guarantee. If the guarantee is for a specified term or the guarantor is entitled to be advised of certain information concerning the principal transaction, that information should be set out as well.

[11.75] There are two important caveats to the general proposition that a guarantee must contain all of the essential terms. The first relates to disclosure of consideration for the guarantee. Although the lender must provide valuable consideration to the guarantor for a valid contract of guarantee to be formed, the nature of that consideration is not required to be contained in the guarantee.[18]

[11.80] Secondly, where a material term has been omitted from the guarantee, there may be limited circumstances in which the guarantee will still be enforceable against the guarantor. This could occur if the material term that has not been reduced to writing is a term for the benefit of the lender. In such a case, the lender will be entitled to waive the benefit of the oral term and enforce the guarantee as modified.[19] For example, parties may orally agree for the guarantor to guarantee an advance by the lender to the debtor together with payment of interest—yet when the agreement is reduced to writing, the parties may fail to insert the reference to the interest rate. On the debtor's default, the lender may choose to waive the benefit of the oral term concerning recovery of the interest. The court may be prepared to enforce the guarantee with the guarantor's liability restricted to the amount advanced without the interest.

(b)   Acknowledgment of agreement

[11.85] In addition to containing information about the content of the particular guarantee, it is likely that the guarantee must indicate that the guarantor has undertaken the obligation to guarantee.[20] The issue of acknowledgment of agreement is more contentious in relation to the equivalent statutory provision for contracts concerning land. This will be dealt with later.[21] It is less likely to be an issue in the context of guarantees because, by the very nature of the agreement, if the parties have reduced the agreement to writing, it will probably include the guarantor's undertaking to repay on the debtor's default.

11.2.4   Requirement of writing: signed by party to be charged or agent

[11.90] To satisfy the statutory provision, the promise or note or memorandum of the promise must be 'signed by the party to be charged, or by some other person by the

18   *Property Law Act* 1974 (Qld) s 56(2); *Instruments Act* 1958 (Vic) s 129; *Mercantile Law Amendment Act* 1856 (UK), s 3 adopted in Western Australia by *Imperial Acts Adopting Ordinance* 1867; *Mercantile Law Act* 1935 (Tas) s 12; *Mercantile Law Act* 1962 (ACT) s 12; *Law of Property Act* 2000 (NT), s 58(2). In New South Wales and South Australia, there is no formality requirement for guarantees. For the position in the Australian Capital Territory, see also note 2 above.

19   *Hawkins v Price* [1947] Ch 645.

20   J O'Donovan & J Phillips, *The Modern Contract of Guarantee*, 3rd edn, LBC Information Services, North Ryde, 1996, pp 85–86, the authors citing as authority decisions concerning contracts of land.

21   See [[11.30]–[11.155].

party lawfully authorised'.[22] Upon the debtor's default, the lender will seek to enforce the guarantee against the guarantor. Therefore, it is the guarantor who is the 'party to be charged' within the meaning of the provision. To satisfy the formalities requirement, therefore, the guarantee must be signed by the guarantor. Generally this will not be a problem. A guarantor's signature will usually appear at the end of the guarantee. Over recent years, intending guarantors often obtain independent legal advice before executing a guarantee. If solicitors are involved in the execution of guarantees, it is even less likely that there will be any difficulties concerning execution. However, this is not always the case. In some cases, the courts have been called on to decide whether something less than the full signature of the guarantor (or his or her agent) is sufficient to satisfy the statutory requirement.

Example: Durrell v Evans[23]

A sale of hops from the plaintiff to the defendant was negotiated by the plaintiff's agent. At the time of entry into the contract, the agent filled in a sales note in duplicate, with the intention of one copy being given to the defendant and one being retained by the plaintiff. When the agreement was concluded, the agent printed the defendant buyer's name at the top of one copy of the sale note, and gave it to the defendant. The plaintiff seller's name was printed on the top of the other copy. No document was ever signed by the defendant.

The defendant failed to proceed with the transaction, and the issue before the court was whether the English equivalent of the formalities provision applicable to a contract of this kind had been satisfied. In particular, the court had to determine whether the printing of the defendant's name at the top of the sales note by the agent was sufficient to satisfy the statutory requirement. The court held that it was. Citing from an earlier English decision,[24] the court stated that 'when it is ascertained that he meant to be bound by it as a complete contract, the statute is satisfied, there being the note in writing shewing the terms of the contract, and recognised by him'.[25] As the court was satisfied that, for the purpose of signing the document, the agent was also acting as agent for the defendant, the statute had been satisfied.

[11.95] This concept is sometimes referred to as the 'authenticated signature fiction'. Reference was made to this so-called fiction by the High Court in *Pirie v Saunders*,[26] noting the meaning attributed to it by the Full Court of the New South Wales Supreme Court (in the judgment being appealed from) 'that if the name of the party to be charged (not being a signature in the ordinary sense of the word) is placed on the document said to constitute the written memorandum of the contract, it is to be treated as a signature for the purposes of the statute if such party expressly or impliedly indicates that he recognises the writing as being an authenticated expression of the contract'.[27]

---

22   For the extent to which an electronic signature can satisfy this requirement, see [11.270]–[11.285].
23   (1862) 158 ER 848.
24   *Johnson v Dodgson* (1837) 150 ER 918 at 921.
25   (1862) 158 ER 848 at 853.
26   (1960) 104 CLR 149.
27   Ibid at 154.

To apply this principle in the context of a guarantee: if the guarantor's name appears on the guarantee, and it is the guarantor's intention that the name authenticates the document, it will be sufficient to satisfy the statutory requirement. As is clear from *Durrell v Evans*,[28] provided this is satisfied, it does not matter whether the name appears at the beginning, middle or end of the document or whether initials or some kind of mark is used to authenticate the document.

[11.100] The statutory provision makes it clear that the signature can be by the guarantor or the agent acting on the guarantor's behalf. Appointment of the agent is not required to be in writing.[29]

11.3   Contracts relating to land

[11.105] All Australian jurisdictions have a statutory requirement of formality where the contract concerns land.[30] Although the wording is not identical in all jurisdictions, the thrust of the provisions is largely the same. The relevant provision in Queensland is s 59 of the *Property Law Act* 1974, which provides as follows:

> No action may be brought upon any contract for the sale or other disposition of land or any interest in land unless the contract upon which such action is brought, or some memorandum or note of the contract, is in writing, and signed by the party to be charged, or by some person by the party lawfully authorised.

To satisfy the statutory provision, one of two things must exist. Either the contract must be in writing, or some memorandum or note of the contract must be in writing.

11.3.1   *Nature of contract needing writing*

[11.110] The requirement of formalities applies to a contract for the sale of land or any interest in land as well as a contract for the 'other disposition' of land or any interest in land. 'Disposition' is a wide term; it will include such transactions as the mortgage of land, lease of land, and the declaration of a trust in relation to the land. As reflected in the case law, difficulties concerning the enforcement of a contract in relation to land generally relate to contracts for the sale of land.

11.3.2   *Requirement of writing: content*

[11.115] As was the case for guarantees, the statutory provision does not give guidance as to the required content of the contract or note or memorandum of the contract to satisfy the statutory requirement. Once again, recourse must be had to relevant case authorities. Although it concerned the statutory requirement for guarantees, presumably the comments in the majority judgment in *Harvey v Edwards, Dunlop & Co*

---

28   (1862) 158 ER 848.
29   *Pain v Flynn* (1884) 10 VLR 131.
30   *Property Law Act* 1974 (Qld) s 59; *Conveyancing Act* 1919 (NSW) s 54A; *Instruments Act* 1958 (Vic) s 126; *Law Reform (Statute of Frauds) Act* 1962, s 2 (WA); *Law of Property Act* 1936 (SA) s 26; *Conveyancing and Law of Property Act* 1884 (Tas) s 36: *Imperial Acts (Substituted Provisions) Act* 1986 Sch 2 Pt 11 clause 4 (ACT); *Law of Property Act* 2000 (NT), s 5(c).

Ltd[31] that the document must contain 'all the essential terms of the agreement' is also relevant here.[32]

(a) Information particular to the contract

[11.120] It was suggested by the New South Wales Supreme Court in relation to a contract involving land that there were four matters that must be recorded to satisfy the statutory requirement.[33] First, the document must contain the parties to the contract.[34] As was mentioned in the context of guarantees, as long as the intention of the parties was clear, extrinsic evidence may be introduced to establish the identity of the parties.[35] Secondly, the property must be adequately described.[36] If the property the subject of the sale is part only of a particular lot, care must be taken to specifically identify the portion being sold.[37] By way of contrast, if freehold property is sold subject to an existing leasehold and the leasehold interest is known to the purchaser, there is authority to suggest that the property is sufficiently described even if there is no reference to the lease.[38] Thirdly, the consideration for the promise, namely the price, must be recorded.[39] Finally, the principal terms of the contract must be disclosed. For example, if the parties require time to be of the essence, that condition should be included in the contract.

[11.125] As mentioned for guarantees, failure to include in the document all essential terms might not necessarily be fatal to a plaintiff. If the term omitted is for the benefit of the plaintiff, the plaintiff may be entitled to waive the benefit of that clause and seek enforcement of the contract without that clause.

Example: Petrie v Jensen[40]

The parties entered into a contract for the sale of land that included a requirement for the seller to obtain an undertaking from tenants of the property to quit the premises within 60 days of the date of the contract. The seller was not able to obtain the undertaking, and treated the contract as at an end.

In the buyer's action for specific performance, the Queensland Supreme Court found in the buyer's favour. As the clause regarding the tenant's undertaking to quit was inserted solely for the buyer's benefit, he was entitled to waive the benefit of the term and insist on performance of the contract.

While this case was not concerned with formalities, it illustrates the significance of categorising a clause as being for the exclusive benefit of the plaintiff. This is also rele-

---

31   (1927) 39 CLR 302.
32   For the extent to which an electronic document can satisfy this requirement, see [11.240]–[11.265].
33   *Twynam Pastoral Co Pty Ltd v Anburn Pty Ltd* (1989) NSW Conv R 55-498 at 58,633.
34   *Williams v Byrnes* (1863) 15 ER 660; *Riley v Melrose Advertisers* (1915) 17 WALR 127; *Sims v Robertson* (1921) 21 SR (NSW) 246.
35   *Rosser v Austral Wine & Spirit Co Pty Ltd* [1980] VR 313.
36   *South Coast Oils (Qld & NSW) Pty Ltd v Look Enterprises Pty Ltd* [1988] 1 QdR 680.
37   *Pirie v Saunders* (1961) 104 CLR 149.
38   *Timmins v Moreland Street Property Co Ltd* [1958] 1 Ch 110.
39   *Wain v Warlters* (1804) 102 ER 972.
40   [1954] StR Qd 138.

vant in the context of formalities. If the written contract for sale had not contained the term about the tenant's undertaking, the buyer would have been entitled to waive the benefit of the term and enforce the contract without that term.

To be successful, the plaintiff must satisfy the court that the term was solely for his or her benefit. If the term is for the benefit of both parties, the term cannot be waived and the contract will not be enforceable.[41]

(b)   Acknowledgment of agreement

[11.130] In the course of negotiation, parties may exchange letters or otherwise record in writing details of their transaction. An issue that has arisen on a number of occasions is whether it is sufficient to satisfy the legislation for the writing to contain terms of the transaction, or whether the writing should also contain an acknowledgment that the parties have reached a concluded agreement. The policy reason for for requiring the writing to contain such an acknowledgment is clear. It is to protect a party where the terms of the proposed transaction have been documented in the negotiation stage, but agreement was never finally reached.

[11.135] For a time in England, there were two lines of authority: one requiring the writing to contain both the terms and a recognition that agreement between the parties had been reached, and the other requiring only that it contain the terms.[42] The issue was ultimately resolved by the English Court of Appeal in *Tiverton Estates Ltd v Wearwell Ltd*,[43] with all Justices indicating that the writing needed to contain an acknowledgment of agreement to satisfy the statutory requirement.[44]

[11.140] This approach has also been adopted in Australia.[45] The writing must contain an acknowledgment of agreement as well as the terms of the agreement. Such acknowledgment may be expressed or implied in the writing. In fact, in a number of Australian decisions where this requirement was held to have been satisfied, it is difficult to discern what was regarded by the courts as the acknowledgment of agreement.[46]

Because agreements have been regarded as satisfying this limb without an overt acknowledgment of the existence of an agreement, some have taken the view that it is more accurate to say that the writing is sufficient provided there is no express denial of the contract.[47] While the facts in some cases may support such a view, it does not accord with the express pronouncements of the courts on the matter. There is still a requirement that the writing contain an acknowledgment of agreement—whether that acknowledgment is express or implied. The case law, does demonstrate, however, that the judiciary is lenient in interpreting what constitutes acknowledgment of agreement for such purposes.

---

41   *Hawkins v Price* [1947] 1 Ch 645.

42   *Tiverton Estates Ltd v Wearwell Ltd* [1975] 1 Ch 146 at 156–157.

43   [1975] 1 Ch 146.

44   Ibid at 157 per Lord Denning MR, at 168 per Stamp LJ and at 172 per Scarman LJ.

45   *Pirie v Saunders* (1961) 104 CLR 149; *Woden Squash Courts Pty Ltd v Zero Builders Pty Ltd* [1976] 2 NSWLR 212; *Coogee Esplanade Surf Motel Pty Ltd v Commonwealth of Australia* (1976) 50 ALR 363.

46   See, for example, *Duncan Properties Pty Ltd v Hunter* [1991] 1 QdR 101.

47   N Seddon and M Ellinghous, *Cheshire and Fifoot's Law of Contract*, Butterworths, Sydney, 1997, 7th edn, p 600.

11.3.3 Requirement of writing: signed by party to be charged or agent

[11.15] Finally, to satisfy the statutory requirement, the document must be signed by the party to be charged.[48] If there is a purported contract for the sale of the land and the seller claims not to be bound by the agreement, the seller will be the party to be charged for the purposes of any action brought. In the same way, if a buyer alleges not to be bound by an agreement, the buyer will be the party to be charged for the purpose of satisfying the statutory requirement.

[11.150] As to what is meant by the term 'signed' or 'signature' for the purpose of this provision, the earlier discussion in the context of guarantees[49] is equally applicable here. To recapitulate: a person may be taken to have signed a document although he or she has not put a signature to it. If the name of the party is placed on the document, and that party expressly or impliedly indicates that he or she recognises the writing as being an authenticated expression of the contract, that is likely to be sufficient to satisfy the statutory requirement.[50]

[11.155] Once again, it is sufficient if the document is signed by a person who is duly authorised by the party to be charged. As for guarantees, the agent must be expressly authorised to sign the document on behalf of the party. Even if a person engages a solicitor to negotiate a contract of sale of land, that is not sufficient to authorise the solicitor to execute the contract on the client's behalf.[51] While the authorisation of the agent must be express, only in the Victorian provision is there a requirement for the authorisation to be in writing.[52]

11.4   Joinder of documents

[11.160] It is possible to satisfy the statutory requirement of writing even if all of the relevant information is not contained in the one document. In certain circumstances, more than one document may be joined together and, if the documents so joined contain all the material terms, the contract will be enforceable.

[11.165] The test to determine whether documents can be joined has evolved over many years. At first, a plaintiff had to satisfy a very strict test before joinder would be allowed. While it is likely that a wider formulation of the joinder rule operates in Australia today, given the strict approach taken in an early High Court decision,[53] the matter is not free from doubt.

[11.170] The position in England can be stated with certainty. Jenkins LJ in *Timmins v Moreland Street Property Co Ltd*[54] described the circumstances in which a document can be joined to another which is signed by the party to be charged (the defendant).

---

48   For the extent to which an electronic signature can satisfy this requirement, see [11.270]–[11.285].
49   See [11.90]–[11.100].
50   *Pirie v Saunders* (1960) 104 CLR 149 at 154. For examples of cases where a loose interpretation of the word 'signature' has been applied by the courts, see *Leeman v Stocks* [1951] 1 Ch 941, *Short v Graeme Marsh Ltd* [1974] 1 NZLR 722. Compare *Van der Veeken v Watsons' Farm (Pukepoto) Ltd* [1974] 2 NZLR 146.
51   *Nowrani Pty Ltd v Brown* [1989] 2 QdR 582. See also *Lynn Borough v Auckland Bus Co Ltd* [1964] NZLR 511 (and on appeal at [1965] NZLR 542).
52   *Instruments Act* 1958 (Vic), s 126.
53   *Thomson v McInnes* (1911) 12 CLR 562.
54   [1958] 1 Ch 110.

in order to justify the reading of documents together for this purpose … there should be a document signed by the party to be charged, which, while not containing in itself all the necessary ingredients of the required memorandum, does contain some reference, express or implied, to some other document or transaction. Where any such reference can be spelt out of a document so signed, then parol evidence may be given to identify the other document referred to, or, as the case may be, to explain the other transaction, and to identify any document relating to it. If by this process a document is brought to light which contains in writing all the terms of the bargain so far as not contained in the document signed by the party to be charged, then the two documents can be read together so as to constitute a sufficient memorandum …[55]

[11.175] When the issue of joinder was first considered by the High Court in *Thomson v McInnes*,[56] Griffith CJ took a much narrower approach. As can be seen from the following extract, joinder was considered to be possible only if the relevant document referred to another document. It was not sufficient to refer to a transaction.

It is sufficient if the note signed by the party to be charged refers to some other document in such a manner as to incorporate it with the document signed, so they can be read together … but the whole contract must be shown by the writing. The reference, therefore, in the document signed must be to some other document as such, and not merely to some transaction or event in the course of which another document may or may not have been written.[57]

[11.180] The matter came before the High Court again in *Harvey v Edwards, Dunlop and Co Ltd*.[58] Without reference to the earlier discussion of the High Court and relying instead on later English authority, Knox CJ, Gavan Duffy, and Starke JJ (in a joint judgment) considered it possible to join documents either by reference to another document or to some other transaction.

It is well settled that any document signed by the party to be charged or by some person authorised by him which contains all the essential terms of the agreement is a sufficient memorandum. It is also well settled that the memorandum 'need not be contained in one document; it may be made out from several documents if they can be connected together.' They may be connected by reference one to the other; but further, 'if you can spell out of the document a reference in it to some other transaction, you are at liberty to give evidence as to what that other transaction is, and, if that other transaction contains all the terms in writing, then you get a sufficient memorandum within the statute by reading the two together' (*Stokes v Whicher*).[59, 60]

---

55   Ibid at 130.
56   (1911) 12 CLR 562.
57   Ibid at 569.
58   (1927) 39 CLR 302.
59   [1920] 1 Ch 411 at 418.
60   (1927) 39 CLR 302 at 307.

[11.185] For the sake of certainty, it would have been helpful for the High Court, in its later decision, to expressly reject the earlier restrictive approach taken by Griffith CJ. The continuing doubt as to the correct position is reflected by a query raised by the Federal Court in *ANZ Banking Group v Widin*[61] as to 'whether the more restrictive approach taken in *Thomson v McInnes* is still good law having regard to *Harvey v Edwards, Dunlop and Co Ltd*'.[62] On balance, it is submitted that the later adoption by the High Court of the expansive English approach must represent the current Australian position.[63] Therefore, a document may be able to be joined if there is a reference, express or implied, to another document or to a transaction.

11.4.1   Reference to a document

[11.190] Despite the different approaches taken by the courts on whether joinder is permissible where reference is to a 'transaction', the position is clear where the document signed by the defendant makes reference to another 'document'. Joinder of that document is permitted. The following example illustrates the operation of the rule.

Example: Tonitto v Bassal[64]

The buyers and sellers negotiated entry into an option to purchase the sellers' land. The buyers signed the option agreement and sent it, with a deposit, to the sellers' solicitor. Later, the sellers no longer wished to proceed with the sale and their solicitor wrote a letter to the buyers advising them that the sellers did not consider themselves bound by the option, and returning the deposit. The letter contained a reference to 'the option to purchase' and 'the option agreement'. It was not in issue that the solicitors were authorised to sign the letter on the sellers' behalf. The question before the court was whether the option agreement could be 'joined' to the solicitor's letter.

The New South Wales Court of Appeal held that the documents could be joined. The terms 'option to purchase' and 'option agreement' in the letter were sufficient to incorporate the terms of the written option agreement.

[11.195] As the document joined in this way is referred to in the document signed by the defendant, it follows that the joined document will be in existence at the time the document is signed by the defendant. There are, however, two caveats to this general proposition.

(a)   Documents that are physically connected

[11.200] There is authority that a document physically connected to the document signed by the defendant may be joined.[65] An application of this principle is the ability

---

61   (1990) 102 ALR 289.
62   Ibid at 300 per Hill J. On the facts of the case, it was not necessary for the Court to make a determination on that issue.
63   Support for this position can be found in *Woden Squash Courts Pty Ltd v Zero Builders Pty Ltd* [1976] 2 NSWLR 212 at 218 per Holland J.
64   (1992) 28 NSWLR 564.
65   *M'Ewan v Dynon* (1877) 3 VLR 271.

to join an envelope to a letter. Where a letter is signed by the defendant and sent to the plaintiff, but the letter does not, on its own, contain the necessary information, the court will allow the envelope to be joined to the letter. In this way, there will be a note or memorandum of the information on the envelope, namely the name of the plaintiff.[66]

(b) Documents that are executed at the same time

[11.205] In a contract for the sale of land, it is not uncommon for a buyer to write a cheque for a deposit, send it to the seller, and later receive a receipt from the seller. If the seller is the party to be charged, it is likely that the cheque could be joined to the receipt (the document signed by the party to be charged).[67] The position is probably different if the buyer is the party to be charged. The seller is unlikely to be able to join the receipt to the cheque, because it is executed later than the cheque. As such, it is difficult to suggest that the cheque contained any express or implied reference to the later document.[68]

[11.210] The position may, however, be different if the writing and exchange of cheque and receipt occurs at the one time and place.

Example: Timmins v Moreland Street Property Co Ltd[69]

The parties entered an oral agreement for the defendant to buy the plaintiff's property. The defendant buyer later refused to proceed with the transaction. The issue before the court was whether there was a sufficient note or memorandum of the agreement. The documents relied on by the plaintiff were the cheque signed by the defendant and the receipt signed by the plaintiff. One of the defences raised by the defendant was the inability to join the receipt to the cheque because the receipt was signed after the cheque. Therefore, the document (cheque) signed by the party to be charged (the buyer) could not be considered to refer expressly or impliedly to the receipt signed by the plaintiff.

This proposition was not accepted by the English Court of Appeal. Jenkins LJ was of the view that 'where two documents relied on as a memorandum are signed and exchanged at one and the same meeting as part of the same transaction, so that they may fairly be said to have been to all intents and purposes contemporaneously signed, the document signed by the party to be charged should not be treated as incapable of referring to the other document merely because the latter, on a minute investigation of the order of events at the meeting, is found to have come second in the order of preparation and signing.'[70]

This view was shared by the other Lord Justices.[71]

---

66 *Pearce v Gardner* [1897] 1 QB 688.
67 See, for example, *Saunderson v Purchase* [1958] NZLR 588.
68 See further in this regard the discussion at [11.230]–[11.235].
69 [1958] 1 Ch 110.
70 Ibid at 123.
71 Despite being successful on this ground, the plaintiff was unable to enforce the oral agreement. See [11.230].

11.4.2   Reference to a transaction

[11.215] In most of the reported cases, the courts are asked to decide whether joinder of a document should be allowed on the basis of a reference to a 'transaction' rather than another 'document'. Joinder was allowed on this basis in the following case to facilitate enforcement of an oral agreement.

Example: Fauzi Elias v George Sahely and Co (Barbados) Ltd[72]

The parties orally agreed for the plaintiff to buy the defendant's property. The plaintiff's solicitor wrote to the defendant's solicitor confirming the details of the purchase and enclosing a cheque for the deposit. The defendant's solicitor sent back a receipt in which he wrote that he had received the money as a deposit on the property 'agreed to be sold' by the defendant to the plaintiff. The defendant did not wish to proceed with the transaction. The plaintiff brought an action for specific performance of the oral agreement and relied on a combination of the receipt and the letter to satisfy the statutory requirement of writing.

  The court accepted the plaintiff's submission and allowed the receipt and letter to be read together. Because the receipt made reference to the property 'agreed to be sold', this was a reference to a 'transaction'—namely the contract to sell the defendant's property to the plaintiff. As stated in their judgment, where there is a reference to a transaction, 'parol evidence can ... be given to explain the transaction, and to identify any document relating to it. Such evidence was led in the present case; it brought to light a document, namely (the solicitor's) letter ... which does contain in writing all the terms of the bargain'.[73]

[11.220] Other examples of references to 'transactions' have been considered sufficient to justify hearing oral evidence about whether other documents exist in relation to that transaction. They include:

- reference in a letter to the fact that the buyer was pleased to 'mutually agree terms for the purchase of ... [the] Holiday Camp' facilitated joinder of a written sale contract;[74]
- reference in a receipt to a sum received 'as a deposit on the purchase' of certain land facilitated joinder of a contract containing details of the sale;[75]
- receipt signed by seller facilitating joinder of cheque signed by buyer.[76]

[11.225] These examples can be contrasted with the restrictive approach taken by the High Court in *Thomson v McInnes*,[77] where reference to 'purchase money' was held to be insufficient to allow reference to be made to other documents. It will be recalled, however, that the plaintiff had to show a reference to another 'document' rather than

---

72   [1983] 1 AC 646.
73   Ibid at 655.
74   *Burgess v Cox* [1951] 1 Ch 383.
75   *Long v Millar* (1879) LR 4 CPD 450.
76   *Stokes v Whicher* [1920] 1 Ch 411. Note, however, this was only one of the matters referred to by the court to facilitate joinder.
77   (1911) 12 CLR 562

to a 'transaction' to satisfy the test for joinder. A reference to 'purchase money' may, therefore, be treated differently today.

[11.230] A difficult issue that has not been definitively resolved by the case law is the extent to which a cheque, as a document signed by the party to be charged, can be regarded as an implied reference to a transaction (or other document). This matter was alluded to in *Timmins v Moreland Street Property Co Ltd*,[78] where there was an exchange of a cheque and receipt at the same time. The plaintiff seller sought to rely on the information contained in both the cheque and receipt to satisfy the requirement of writing. The cheque was signed by the party to be charged, the buyer in this case. The seller was confronted with an additional hurdle, however, in that the payee of the cheque was the seller's solicitor, not the seller himself, yet the receipt was given by the seller. Given that the cheque was made payable to a firm of solicitors and not the seller himself, the court was not prepared to join the receipt to the cheque.

[11.235] This leaves unanswered the issue of whether the receipt could be joined to the cheque (the buyer being the party to be charged) if the payee of the cheque were the same as the person who signed the receipt. Roma LJ in *Timmins v Moreland Street Property Co Ltd*[79] recognised the possibility of joinder in such a case, but did not have to decide the point. It appears that Jenkins LJ took a different approach. He did not accept that it was possible to 'spell out of this cheque any reference, express or implied, to any other document or to any transaction other than the order to pay a sum of money constituted by the cheque itself.'[80] He continued that 'the cheque ... gives no indication whatever of the purpose for which the payment was to be made, and I think it is clear that the mere fact that the payment must have been made for some purpose or for some consideration cannot reasonably be held to amount to a reference to some other document or transaction ...'.[81]

The reasoning of Lord Justice Jenkins is persuasive. While it may be possible for a receipt to expressly or impliedly refer to a cheque, the reverse does not follow. Therefore, even if the payee under a cheque is the same as the person signing the receipt, it is submitted that in the ordinary course of events, joinder of the documents, where the buyer is the party to be charged, will not be possible.

11.5 Adequacy of electronic 'writing' and 'signature'

[11.240] With the increased use of electronic communication in contract negotiation, an issue that will need resolution is how the statutory requirements of formality will be satisfied where the 'writing' and 'signing' occur electronically. Of relevance to a land transaction or a contract of guarantee is whether an electronic communication sent by a party to the contract can fulfil the statutory requirements for a 'contract' or 'some memorandum or note of the contract' to be 'in writing' and 'signed by the party to be

---

78   [1958] 1 Ch 110.
79   Ibid at 134.
80   [1958] 1 Ch 110 at 130–131.
81   Ibid.

charged'. This issue may be of greater academic than practical interest in most cases. In practice, a party to a contract who is sent an electronic communication containing relevant details of the contract is likely to print it out. Once this occurs, 'writing' in the traditional sense of the word exists, and the only issue is whether the sender can be regarded as having signed the document. In this determination, the established common law rules on whether the name appears to authenticate the content of the document will continue to apply. Where a computer-generated facsimile of the person's signature is used, it is likely that this test will be satisfied, unless it is proved the person did not cause the signature to appear on the document.

[11.245] However, if the electronic communication is not reduced to printed form, will the electronic version be sufficient to satisfy the statutory requirements? In 1999, the Commonwealth enacted the *Electronic Transactions Act,* which addresses a number of issues concerning electronic communications.[82] Sections 9 and 10 of that Act are relevant where 'under a law of the Commonwealth, a person is required to give information in writing' and where 'under a law of the Commonwealth, the signature of a person is required' respectively. In these circumstances, the requirement can be satisfied if the person gives the information by means of an electronic communication. As discussed earlier, it is unlikely that the State and Territory legislation, which deal with issues of formality, will be regarded as 'a law of the Commonwealth'.[83] Despite the suggestion in the Explanatory Memorandum that 'law of the Commonwealth' is 'intended to be read in its broadest sense', it is suggested that it cannot be regarded as extending to State and Territory legislation. On this view, sections 9 and 10 of the Commonwealth Act will not be relevant in resolving whether electronic documents and signatures are sufficient to satisfy references to writing and signing in State or Territory legislation.

[11.250] However, all States and Territories intend to enact legislation equivalent to the Commonwealth Act so a uniform approach to electronic communication exists.[84] Legislation has been drafted in all Australian jurisdictions to implement this policy.[85]

[11.255] Sections 8 and 9 of the Victorian legislation are equivalent to sections 9 and 10 of the Commonwealth Act, but refer to 'a law of this jurisdiction' that requires the giving of information to be in writing or requires the signature of a person to be given. As already examined in this chapter, legislation exists in most jurisdictions requiring contracts of guarantee and contracts concerning the creation or disposal of interests in land to be in writing and signed by the party to be charged in order to be enforceable.[86] The issue then is whether sections 8 and 9 (or their equivalents in the other States and Territories) apply to the formality provisions for such contracts where parties to a transaction use an electronic communication for the 'writing' and 'signing' of the contract. The issues of writing and signature are considered separately.

---

82   For more information concerning the objects of the legislation, see [3.9.4].
83   The meaning of this term was considered earlier in this text. See [3.9.4].
84   Explanatory Memorandum to the *Electronic Transactions Bill* 1999 (Cth), p 2.
85   *Electronic Transactions Act* 1999 (Cth); *Electronic Transactions Act* 2000 (NSW); *Electronic Transactions (Victoria) Act* 2000; *Electronic Transactions (Queensland) Bill* 2001; *Electronic Transactions Bill* 2000 (WA); *Electronic Transactions Act* 2000 (SA); *Electronic Transactions Act* 2000 (Tas); *Electronic Transactions (Northern Territory) Bill* 2000; *Electronic Transactions Act* 2001 (ACT). Although a number of the above Acts have been passed, at the time of writing, only the Commonwealth and Victorian legislation were in operation.
86   See notes 2 and 30 above.

[11.260] Relevantly, s 8 of the Victorian legislation provides that where a person is required to give information in writing, the requirement is met if the person gives the information by an electronic communication.[87] The first requirement for the operation of the section is that 'a person is required to give information in writing'. The term 'give information' is defined broadly in s 8(5) of the Act,[88] but none of the examples given would suggest that 'give information' includes the creation of a 'contract or memorandum' as known under the relevant statues. In other words, it is not possible to paraphrase s 8 as 'If under a law of the jurisdiction a person is required to [enter/form a contract] in writing'. In addition, it may be difficult to conclude that the relevant formality legislation actually 'requires' a contract or memorandum to be in writing. The legislation usually only provides that a contract will not be enforceable unless it is in writing. While the drafting of both the Commonwealth and State legislation appears to facilitate the electronic submission of information, particularly to Government departments, it does not integrate satisfactorily with the formalities legislation. It is therefore doubtful that s 8, in its current form—referring to a law requiring a person to 'give information in writing'—could extend to the formality requirements for contracts of guarantee or contracts concerning the creation or disposal of interests in land.

[11.265] Even if the difficulties of language are overcome, the section will not apply to a transaction unless the other two requirements (namely, the information being readily accessible so as to be useable for subsequent reference, and the consent of the person to whom the information is required to be given) are met. In relation to the requirement for consent, it is suggested that both parties need to consent to the contract being formed using an electronic communication. Consent is defined to include 'consent that can reasonably be inferred from the conduct of the person concerned'.[89] It is clear that consent may be given where the person expressly consents either orally or in writing. Possible situations where consent may be inferred could include:

- in a previous course of dealings electronic communication was used;
- a person commenced correspondence or made an offer via electronic communication; or
- a person handed to another a business card with an e-mail address indicating the card included contact details.

Situations that are less clear are where an e-mail address appears in a contract, which forms the basis of an offer or on a company's letterhead used in correspondence. In each case the person's conduct would be considered in light of their express statements. For example, a person may send a letter by e-mail indicating that any negotiations for a contract should take place in paper form, and not electronically. The mere act of sending an e-mail would not in that case be considered 'consent'.

---

87   The section contains two provisos relating to the form of the communication and the consent of the recipient.
88   Pursuant to section 8(5), 'giving information' includes, but is not limited to, the following matters: making an application; making or lodging a claim; giving, sending or serving a notification; lodging a return; making a request; making a declaration; lodging or issuing a certificate; making, varying or cancelling an election; lodging an objection; giving a statement of reasons.
89   *Electronic Transactions (Victoria) Act* 2000, s 3(1).

[11.270] The final relevance of the electronic transactions legislation to the formalities legislation is in relation to the requirement for a contract to be signed by the party to be charged. Section 9 of the *Electronics Transactions (Victoria) Act* 2000 provides that where a signature is required under a law of the jurisdiction, this will be met for an electronic communication if a method is used to identify the person and to indicate the person's approval of the information communicated.[90] In accordance with the objective of being technologically neutral,[91] the legislation does not prescribe any particular method for ensuring the approval of communications over the Internet.

[11.275] Digital signatures are emerging as one method of ensuring that the communication is sent by a particular person and has not been changed in transit. It is suggested that where the integrity of a document is important (as in the case of a land transaction or guarantee) the parties will need to use a method that not only provides approval of the document but also maintains the integrity of the document. Importantly, a digital signature is not a digitised image of a handwritten signature. This would not comply with the legislation and could be easily copied. Digital signatures operate by using asymmetric cryptography in the form of a public key and a private key. Essentially, messages are encrypted using a computer program and password (private key), which is unique to the sender of the message. The key will appear as a jumble of random numbers and letters at the bottom of the document. This will be unique to the particular document. The jumbled string would be different if the signer (or someone else) altered the document even by a single letter and re-signed it. A digital signature can therefore prove who signed the document and that it has not been altered since it was signed. If the document is changed after signing, the document and signature will no longer correspond and this will be evident to the person opening the message. The recipient of the message will then decrypt the message using a program that recognises that person's digital signature. This is referred to as a public key.[92]

[11.280] A digital signature can therefore, be used to indicate the identity and approval of an electronic document by a person in accordance with the legislation. It also has the advantage of being able to verify the integrity of a document from the time of signing, to the time of receipt. However, the fact that a digital signature does not look like a signature in the traditional sense and the relative inexperience of individuals with the technology may impact upon the willingness of parties to consent to the formation of land transactions and guarantees by electronic methods. Unless the parties consent under s 8 and s 9 of the Victorian Act to the use of an electronic communication and the method of signing, the legislation will not apply.[93]

---

90 Section 9(1) contains a further two provisos relating to the reliability of the communication and the consent of the recipient. Consent for the purpose of s 9 is the same as discussed above for s 8.

91 Technology neutral means that different forms of technology will be treated equally by the law. The Commonwealth government decided that this would be the most effective method of ensuring the legislation would have lasting application in the face of changes to technology.

92 A person's public key can be obtained from a Certification Authority. The Authority will check and certify the public key. A Certification Authority will be a body that holds records of public and private keys as well as certifying their validity. The Commonwealth Government has established the National Electronic Authentication Council, which will be involved in developing appropriate policies for private certification authorities to follow.

93 This will also apply to the equivalent legislation in other jurisdictions.

[11.285] Ultimately the common usage of electronic communications for the formation of land transactions and guarantees will depend on the interpretation given to the various sections by the courts. As indicated above, a narrow interpretation of phrases such as 'required to give information' may mean that the legislation is not effective in protecting electronic land transactions or guarantees due to the difference in drafting between the electronic transactions legislation and formalities legislation. If this is correct, it may be necessary for State and Territory legislatures, given the importance of the electronic agenda at federal and international levels, to consider amendment of formalities legislation to provide protection to parties contracting electronically.

11.6 Effect of statutory non-compliance: common law

[11.290] The effect of failing to comply with the relevant statutory provision concerning formality is that 'no action may be brought' on the particular contract. The common law and equitable consequences which flow from statutory non-compliance differ, so will be dealt with separately. In this part, consideration is given to the common law effect of non-compliance.

11.6.1 Contract is unenforceable

[11.295] As 'no action can be brought' on a contract failing to comply with the requirements of formality, that contract is 'unenforceable'. Under common law principles, where one of the parties refuses to complete, action cannot be taken by the other to enforce the contract. Action cannot be brought for specific performance[94] or for damages for breach.[95] For the same reason, a defendant is unable to rely on an unenforceable contract to resist a claim by a plaintiff. To do so would, in effect, be to permit the enforcement of the contract.

Example: Gray v Ellis[96]

The plaintiff, the owner of a racehorse, entered an oral agreement to lease the horse to the defendant for two years, the defendant to give the plaintiff a portion of the winnings during this period. The contract was required by statute to be in writing. The defendant took possession of the horse. In the plaintiff's action to recover possession of the racehorse, the defendant pleaded the oral agreement. This defence was rejected by the court. If the court allowed the defence to succeed, the effect would be to enforce an unenforceable contract.

11.6.2 Contract valid to pass title

[11.300] Although a contact failing to comply with statutory requirements will be unenforceable, it will be a valid contract. This means that, if the contract is performed

---

94   *Tiverton Estates Ltd v Wearwell Ltd* [1975] 1 Ch 147.
95   *Timmins v Moreland Street Property Co Ltd* [1958] 1 Ch 110; *Freedom v AHR Constructions Pty Ltd* [1987] 1 QdR 59.
96   [1925] StR Qd 209.

by the parties, it will be effective to pass good title. As stated by Webb J in *Watson v Royal Permanent Building Society*:[97]

> There may be a valid contract for the sale of land, although by reason of its not being in writing no action can be brought upon it, nor probably could any action be brought in which the establishment of the contract would be necessary to the plaintiff's case.[98]

In that case, there were two contracts of sale of the one piece of land. In determining who had priority, the lack of writing for one of those contracts was not considered relevant.

11.6.3 Recovery of money paid under unenforceable contract

[11.305] Where parties enter into an oral contract for the sale of land, a buyer may, pursuant to that contract, pay the seller a deposit or other amount of money. If one of the parties refuses to complete the purchase (relying on failure to comply with the statutory requirements), the question arises whether the buyer can recover money so paid.

(a) Recovery of deposit

[11.310] A deposit paid by a buyer is considered to be an 'earnest to bind the bargain'.[99] If the sale is not completed due to the buyer's default, the deposit is liable to forfeiture to the vendor.[100] This is the position if the contract is one which complies with the statutory requirement of formality. From the decision of the Queensland Supreme Court in *Freedom v AHR Constructions Pty Ltd*,[101] it can be seen that this will also be the case where the buyer defaults under an oral contract of sale.

Example: Freedom v AHR Constructions Pty Ltd

The parties entered an oral agreement for the plaintiff to buy a unit from the defendant for $140 000. A total of $47 000 was paid by the plaintiff before the plaintiff advised the defendant that she was unable to complete the purchase. The plaintiff sued to recover the $47 000 paid.

The court considered the nature of the $47 000 paid by the plaintiff and concluded that, given that it represented more than one-third of the purchase price, it could not properly be regarded as a deposit. On the basis that a deposit generally represents 10 per cent of the purchase price, McPherson J concluded that the deposit here was $14 000. This amount was forfeited on the buyer's default. The defendant was entitled to retain this amount, notwithstanding failure to comply with the formal requirements because 'the defendant has no need to bring an action' within the meaning of the section to hold the deposit.

---

97   (1888) 14 VLR 283.
98   Ibid at 291.
99   *Howe v Smith* (1884) 27 ChD 89 at 101; *McDonald v Dennys Lascelles Ltd* (1933) 48 CLR 457 at 470.
100   *Freedom v AHR Constructions Pty Ltd* [1987] 1 QdR 59 at 65.
101   [1987] 1 QdR 59.

[11.315] Where an enforceable contract for the sale of land is not completed because of the seller's default, the position is different. The deposit is recoverable by the buyer. The deposit is recoverable as money had and received upon a total failure of consideration, where the consideration for which it was paid is the conveyance or transfer that has not taken place.[102] In other words, the action is one brought in restitution, not on the contract.

(b)   Recovery of amount more than deposit

[11.320] As illustrated by the facts of *Freedom v AHR Constructions Pty Ltd*,[103] the buyer under an unenforceable contract may pay more than the deposit before the contract is terminated. The buyer is likely, in such circumstances, to seek recovery of the payment so made. Where the buyer is in default, as was the case in *Freedom v AHR Constructions Pty Ltd*,[104] the court will attempt to establish what portion of the payment constituted a deposit. For the reasons given earlier, that amount can be retained by the seller. In *Freedom v AHR Constructions Pty Ltd*,[105] the balance of $33 000 was recoverable by the plaintiff because the plaintiff could recover without seeking directly to enforce the contract. In such circumstances, the plaintiff is entitled to recover money paid 'unless it was intended to be a deposit liable to forfeiture in event of the contract going off by her default'.[106] The money is recoverable by proceedings for restitution—as money had and received—not by proceedings on the contract.

11.6.4   Other restitutionary claim may still be available

[11.325] Where money paid under an unenforceable contract is recoverable, the action is based on restitutionary, not contractual principles. Restitutionary principles may also be relevant in those limited circumstances in which services are provided under an unenforceable contract. Section 45 of the *Builders Licensing Act* 1971 (NSW)[107] provided such an example.

Example: Pavey & Matthews Pty Ltd v Paul[108]

Pursuant to an oral building contract, the plaintiff builder undertook to carry out certain building work for the defendant. On completion of the building work, the defendant refused to pay claiming the contract was unenforceable because it failed to comply with the formalities requirement of s 45 of the *Builders Licensing Act*.

The High Court held that although the plaintiff was unable to recover the contract price due to failure to comply with the statutory requirement, he could successfully claim on a *quantum meruit* basis for the value of the work done and materials supplied under an oral contract. Recovery was permissible because it was brought on restitutionary, not contractual grounds.

---

102   *Fullbrook v* Lawes (1876) 1 QBD 284 at 289.
103   [1987] 1 QdR 59.
104   Ibid.
105   Ibid.
106   Ibid at 69.
107   See now ss 7 and 10 of the *Home Building Act* 1989 (NSW).
108   (1986) 162 CLR 221.

11.7 Effect of statutory non-compliance—equity

[11.330] Various equitable doctrines can alleviate the harsh common law consequences of non-compliance with the statutory requirement of writing. These doctrines will more commonly arise in the context of contracts concerning land.[109]

11.7.1 Doctrine of part-performance

[11.335] If parties enter into an oral contract for the sale of land and, relying on that contract, one party does certain acts, the courts may be prepared to grant that person specific performance of the contract. To obtain such equitable relief, four conditions must be satisfied.

(a)   Acts are unequivocally referable to some such contract as that alleged

[11.340] To satisfy the first limb, the plaintiff must be able to demonstrate a nexus between his or her actions and the contract which the plaintiff is seeking to enforce. The extent to which the plaintiff's acts must be 'referable' to the contract has presented some difficulty. The original formulation of the referability requirement was strict. The Earl of Selborne LC stated in *Maddison v Alderson*[110] that 'the acts relied upon as part performance must be unequivocally, and in their own nature, referable to some such agreement as that alleged'.[111] Therefore, in that case, the plaintiff was unable to enforce an oral agreement with the deceased that if she performed duties as housekeeper for him until his death for no wages, he would give her an interest in his house. Her acts of housekeeping were held not to be evidence of a contract, let alone a contract concerning the deceased's land.

[11.345] In England, this test was relaxed to a degree in *Steadman v Steadman*.[112] Lord Reid phrased the rule in the following way:

> In my view, unless the law is to be divorced from reason and principle, the rule must be that you take the whole circumstances, leaving aside evidence about the oral contract, to see whether it is proved that the acts relied on were done in reliance on a contract: that will be proved if it is shown to be more probable than not.[113]

There was no additional requirement that the contract had to be one concerning land.

---

109   There is no reason in principle, however, why the doctrine of part-performance and the doctrine of estoppel could not apply to a contract of guarantee. However, in relation to the doctrine of part-performance, there may be practical difficulties in showing that the acts of part-performance (particularly where the guarantee is of repayments under a contract of loan) were unequivocally referable to some such contract as that alleged and done in reliance on the contract of guarantee. See further (a) and (b) below and the discussion in J O'Donovan & J Phillips, *The Modern Contract of Guarantee*, 3rd edn, LBC Information Services, North Ryde, 1996, pp 117–118.
110   (1883) 8 App Cas 467.
111   Ibid at 479.
112   [1976] AC 536.
113   Ibid at 541–542.

[11.350] In Australia, when the High Court first addressed the issue, the earlier strict English approach was adopted.[114] The High Court had a further opportunity to develop the doctrine in 1976.

Example: Regent v Millett[115]

The parties entered into an oral contract for the plaintiff buyer to purchase the defendant seller's property. Under the terms of the agreement, the buyer was to enter possession and take over the seller's mortgage repayments. The seller agreed to transfer the property to the buyer once the mortgage was paid off. Upon taking possession, the buyer effected substantial repairs to the premises. The seller refused to complete the transfer and the buyer sought specific performance of the contract.

In determining whether there were sufficient acts of part performance, the High Court adopted the strict test used in *Maddison v Alderson*[116] that the acts must be unequivocally, and in their own nature, referable to some such agreement as that alleged. The court continued that the giving and taking of possession by itself was a sufficient act of part performance. While conceding that it may be proved that the taking of possession is referable to some authority other than the contract alleged, that was not the case here. The circumstances surrounding possession indicated the existence of a contract, and 'possession was unequivocally referable to some such contract as that alleged'. Unfortunately the judgment did not elaborate on what circumstances of the case indicated that possession was so referable. Perhaps relevant in this regard was the taking over of the seller's mortgage repayments and making improvements to the premises.

It is interesting to observe that although the more liberal approach of the House of Lords in *Steadman v Steadman*[117] was available to the High Court at the date of judgment (and was indeed referred to in the judgment), the court was not inclined to adopt it.

[11.355] There are more recent case examples in which the doctrine of part-performance has been relied upon in actions for specific performance. In *Australia and New Zealand Banking Group Ltd v Widin*,[118] the ANZ Bank successfully enforced a mortgage agreement that was not sufficiently evidenced by writing. The following acts of part-performance were held by the Full Court of the Federal Court to be sufficient:

- provision of financial accommodation to the debtor;
- obtaining an indemnity agreement;
- taking a mortgage in blank and an authority to complete it.

Hill J undertook a thorough review of the different formulations of the referability test. The conclusion his Honour reached was that until the matter is reconsidered by the High Court, the more liberal approach adopted by the House of Lords in *Steadman*

---

114   *McBride v Sandland* (1918) 25 CLR 69 at 78; *Cooney v Burns* (1922) 30 CLR 216 at 222.
115   (1976) 133 CLR 679.
116   (1988) 8 App Cas 467.
117   [1976] AC 536.
118   (1990) 102 ALR 289.

v Steadman[119] does not represent the law in Australia. It seemed implicit in his judgment that he favoured the adoption of a more liberal approach in Australia.

[11.360] The other case worthy of mention is *Darter Pty Ltd v Malloy*,[120] which involved an oral contract for the sale of a building unit. The unusual feature of this case was that the application for specific performance was brought by the seller, not the buyer. Before entering into the contract of sale, the defendant buyer's parents were renting the unit. It was agreed that, until settlement, the parents would continue to occupy the premises at a reduced rental. The Queensland Supreme Court relied on the following acts of part-performance by the seller to order specific performance of the contract:

- allowing the defendant into possession (by his parents continuing to occupy the premises);
- accepting a decreased rental from the parents pending settlement of the contract.

Applying the strict test set out in *Maddison v Alderson*,[121] the court considered that retention of existing possession, if coupled with a reduction in the weekly rent, was referable to a new contract between the buyer and seller. There was no discussion of how continued possession by the *defendant's parents* could be referable to a contract between the plaintiff and defendant. Further, it must be presumed that if there were no decrease in the rent, the acts could not be referable to the contract as alleged. This point was not expressly considered in the judgment.

[11.7.1.8] While the strict test continues to apply in Australia, the cases demonstrate a more relaxed application of that test. For that reason, it is difficult to be categorical about what acts of part-performance will be sufficient to persuade a court to order specific performance of a contract. Nevertheless, the following review may provide some guidance.

Entry into possession

[11.370] Given the decision of *Regent v Millet*,[122] it is clear that allowing and taking possession of premises, if coupled with payment and improvement of the property, will be enough for a buyer to enforce the contract. Whether possession alone will be enough has not been categorically decided. While there is an indication to that effect in the case,[123] the High Court also indicated that entry into possession may, in some circumstances, be on the basis of an authority other than the contract. If that were the case, presumably entry into possession would not be a sufficient act of part-performance. It is difficult to discern the circumstances particular to that case that indicated entry into possession being on the authority of the contract. It may have been the payment of the seller's mortgage instalments, or carrying out improvements to the property. On the other hand, the Queensland Court of Appeal in *Darter Pty Ltd v Malloy*[124] indicated that *Regent v Millet*[125] was authority for the more general proposition that 'in the case of an

---

119   [1976] AC 536.
120   [1993] 2 QdR 615.
121   (1883) 8 App Cas 467.
122   (1976) 133 CLR 679.
123   Ibid at 683.
124   [1993] 2 QdR 615.
125   (1976) 133 CLR 679.

agreement to purchase, giving and taking of possession is a sufficient act of part perform-ance'.[126] Further judicial comment on this point is awaited with interest.

Payment of money

[11.375] The question can also arise whether payment of money alone can be regarded as a sufficient act of part-performance. Applying the strict test of referability, the ques-tion can only be answered in the negative.[127] The payment of money, on its own, could not be regarded as being referable to a contract concerning land. In *Australia and New Zealand Banking Group Ltd v Widin*,[128] there were held to be sufficient acts of part-performance to enforce a contract of mortgage. Provision of financial accommo-dation was only one act relied upon, and the Full Court of the Federal Court indicated that, on application of the strict test, this alone may not have been sufficient. In the absence of other acts, it would be impossible to argue that payment was referable to the contract as alleged. As clear from the cases, payment may be made pursuant to a mortgage agreement or a contract for the sale of land.

Preparation of documents

[11.380] Where an oral contract is concluded, a party may instruct a solicitor to pre-pare the relevant documentation. Giving instructions and the ensuing preparation of documents are unlikely to be considered sufficient acts of part-performance.[129]

(b) Acts done in reliance on the agreement and with knowledge of other party

[11.385] To obtain equitable relief, the plaintiff must show that the acts were done in reliance on the agreement and with the knowledge of the other parties.[130] Although it has been suggested that to qualify, such acts must be *required* by the contract, this was rejected by the High Court in *Regent v Millet*.[131] If this were required, the usefulness of the doctrine would be severely limited.

(c) Acts done by party seeking to enforce contract

[11.390] Specific performance is an equitable remedy. Although a court may be prepared to order specific performance on the grounds of part-performance, those acts of part-per-formance must be by the person seeking to enforce the contract—namely the plaintiff. It is not sufficient for this purpose to look at the actions of the defendant.[132]

(d) Oral contract must be otherwise enforceable

[11.395] To obtain the equitable remedy of specific performance, the plaintiff must also be able to show that the contract would have been enforceable had it satisfied the

---

126 [1993] 2 QdR 615 at 622.
127 This view is also consistent with the early judicial pronouncements: *Maddison v Alderson* (1883) 8 App Cas 467 at 478–479; *Cooney v Burns* (1922) 30 CLR 216 at 222–223. Contrast the broader stance adopted by Lord Reid in *Steadman v Steadman* [1976] AC 536 at 541.
128 (1990) 102 ALR 289.
129 *Steadman v Steadman* [1976] AC 536 at 554; *Cooney v Burns* (1922) 30 CLR 216 at 222.
130 *McBride v Sandland* (1918) 25 CLR 69 at 79.
131 (1976) 133 CLR 679 at 683–684.
132 *King v Grimwood* (1891) 17 VLR 253 at 258.

statutory requirement of writing. The agreement must be concluded,[133] and satisfy the usual contractual requirements for enforceability.[134]

11.7.2   Estoppel

[11.400] The equitable doctrine of estoppel is reviewed in Chapter 7. As illustrated by the landmark case of *Waltons Stores (Interstate) Ltd v Maher*,[135] the doctrine of estoppel may facilitate the enforcement of an oral contract concerning land. The High Court decision was examined in some detail there.[136]

11.7.3   Constructive trust

[11.405] As a result of the evolution of various equitable doctrines and remedies, in some circumstances, an interest in land can be created in favour of a person in the absence of writing. This will occur where equity recognises the creation of a resulting or constructive trust. It is beyond the scope of this text to examine the evolution and refinement of these doctrines. However, the increased prevalence of the constructive trust based on unconscionability justifies a brief explanation of the circumstances in which it will arise. Constructive trusts of this kind commonly arise in the context of the breakdown of a de facto relationship, where a person who owns property seeks to deny his or her former partner an interest in the property.

Example: Baumgartner v Baumgartner[137]

The parties lived in a de facto relationship for just over four years. There was a child of the relationship. Towards the beginning of the cohabitation, the parties purchased a property; it was registered in the de facto husband's name. This property was the principal place of residence of the couple. Both parties worked for the duration of the relationship (except for a brief period during which the de facto wife stayed at home following the birth of their child), and they pooled their funds for the purpose of their joint relationship. On determination of the relationship, the de facto husband brought an action claiming full beneficial ownership of the property.

The High Court held that, in the circumstances of the case, particularly the pooling of funds and the purchase of the house for the benefit of the relationship, it would be unconscionable for the de facto husband to deny the de facto wife an interest in the property. Accordingly, the High Court held that a constructive trust had been created and that the husband held the property beneficially for both the de facto husband and wife.

[11.410] The effect of creation of a constructive trust is that an action can be brought in relation to an interest in land, even though the creation of the interest is not evidenced in writing. Given the circumstances (as in the case above) in which a court will

---

133 *McBride v Sandland* (1918) 25 CLR 69 at 79.
134 Compare *McBride v Sandland* (1918) 25 CLR 69 where the High Court was not satisfied that the parties had entered into an agreement.
135 (1988) 164 CLR 387.
136 See [7.30]–[7.50].
137 (1987) 164 CLR 137.

recognise the creation of a constructive trust, however, it is unlikely to be of assistance to a plaintiff who is seeking to enforce an oral contract for the sale of land in circumstances where the defendant wishes no longer to proceed.

11.8 Variation and termination of contract

[11.415] The statutory provisions that require certain contracts to be in writing are silent about the way such contracts can be effectively terminated or varied. There is no direction concerning whether the agreement to terminate or vary the contract must be in writing. Recourse therefore must be had to the case law.

[11.420] First, it is clear that a contract required to be in writing to be enforceable can be terminated by oral agreement between the parties.[138] However, this is not the position if the parties wish to vary the contract. For any variation agreed upon by the parties to be effective, it must be evidenced in writing.[139] This must occur in order to satisfy the statutory provision: an action on the promise (here an agreement to vary the contract) can only be brought if evidenced in writing. If the original agreement is in writing and the variation is only oral, the original contract unaffected by the variation will be enforceable, even though this will not reflect the intention of the parties.

[11.425] Given that a contract that is required to be in writing can be orally terminated, but only varied if the variation is done in writing, it may be crucial to decide whether the later arrangement entered into between the parties is properly categorised as a termination or variation. Generally, this will be easy to ascertain. However, it may be the case that the proposed alteration to the contract is so far-reaching that it in fact operates to discharge the oral contract and put in place a new one. The test used by the courts to determine whether the contract has been terminated or varied is that of the intention of the parties.[140]

Example: Electronic Industries Ltd v David Jones Ltd[141]

The parties entered into an agreement under which Electronic Industries Ltd were to install and demonstrate television equipment in a David Jones store over a specified two-week period. Because of industrial action that affected retail trade, David Jones asked for the demonstration period to be postponed. Electronic Industries Ltd agreed to this request. Subsequent attempts to reschedule a demonstration time failed, and David Jones advised Electronic Industries Ltd that it no longer wished to proceed with the demonstration.

In an action by Electronic Industries Ltd for breach of contract, the High Court had to decide the effect of negotiations that took place after contract formation. In finding for Electronic Industries Ltd, the Court held that the parties at no stage intended to terminate the original contract. It was merely the intention of the parties to vary the original contract by altering the date for the demonstration.

---

138   *Tallerman and Co Pty Ltd v Nathan's Merchandise (Victoria) Pty Ltd* (1957) 98 CLR 93 at 113.
139   Ibid; *Phillips v Ellinson Bros Pty Ltd* (1941) 65 CLR 221 at 243.
140   *British and Benningtons Ltd v North Western Cachart Tea Co Ltd* [1923] AC 48 at 69.
141   (1954) 91 CLR 288.

[11.430] Turning to contract concerning land, if the intention is to discharge the contract and substitute a new one, but the new contract is not in writing, no contract would exist between the parties. If it is considered to be a variation that is not evidenced in writing, then the parties would continue to be bound by the original agreement. Ironically, neither outcome would reflect the actual intention of the parties.

[11.435] However, if the subsequent arrangement could be categorised as a 'waiver' rather than a variation, then it may be possible to give effect to it despite the absence of writing. Where the oral arrangement relates to an alteration in the mode or manner of performance, rather than to an alteration of the principal obligations themselves, it may be enforceable despite the lack of writing.[142] In the context of a contract for the sale of land, one party, at the request of another, may agree to settle at a different date from that specified in the contract. Whether the obligation to settle is effectively altered in this way depends on the way that later agreement is categorised.

[11.440] Finally, circumstances may arise where a party is prevented from enforcing the original contract that is evidenced in writing, even though the variation agreed to by the parties is oral only. This could occur where the principles of equitable estoppel as espoused by the High Court in *Waltons Stores (Interstate) Ltd v Maher*[143] apply.[144]

11.9 International perspective

[11.445] In the introduction to this chapter, it was noted that the origins of the various Australian statutes on formalities were based upon the United Kingdom legislation, the *Statute of Frauds* 1677. The legislation in New Zealand and the United States is also largely modelled on this enactment.

11.9.1 New Zealand

[11.450] The New Zealand situation on the statutory requirement of formalities for certain contracts largely reflects the Australian position. The relevant statute in New Zealand is the *Contracts Enforcement Act* 1956, s 2 of that Act providing as follows:

2. Proof of contracts relating to land and to guarantees —

(1) This section applies to —

    (a) Every contract for the sale of land;

    (b) Every contract to enter into any disposition of land, being a disposition that is required by any enactment to be made by deed or instrument or in writing or to be proved by writing;

    (c) Every contract to enter into any mortgage or charge on land;

    (d) Every contract by any person to answer to another person for the debt, default, or liability of a third person.

(2) No contract to which this section applies shall be enforceable by action unless the contract or some memorandum or note thereof is in writing and

---

142 *Phillips v Ellinson Bros Pty Ltd* (1941) 65 CLR 221 at 243.
143 (1988) 164 CLR 387.
144 See Chapter 7 for a detailed examination of these principles.

is signed by the party to be charged therewith or by some other person lawfully authorised by him.

(3) Nothing in this section shall —

    (a) Apply to any sale of land by order of the Supreme Court or through the Registrar of that Court;

    (b) Apply to any alienation of Maori land by a Maori, being an alienation that is required by the Maori Affairs Act 1953 to be confirmed by the Maori Land Court, or to any sale of Maori land by order of that Court;

    (c) Affect the operation of the law relating to part performance.

(4) For the purposes of this section —

'Disposition' includes any conveyance, transfer, grant, partition, exchange, lease, assignment, surrender, disclaimer, appointment, settlement, or other assurance; and any declaration or creation of a trust; and any devise, bequest, or appointment by a will;

'Land' means any estate or interest, whether freehold or chattel, in real property.

(5) The foregoing provisions of this section apply only to contracts made after the passing of this Act.

(6) This section is in substitution for section four of the Statute of Frauds 1677 of the Parliament of England, and that section shall cease to be in force in New Zealand, except in respect of contracts made before the passing of this Act.

(a)   Similarities to Australian equivalent

[11.455] Section 2(2) of the *Contracts Enforcement Act* 1956 imposes the same requirement of formality as the equivalent Australian provisions. Even much of the drafting is the same. The following similarities exist.

- A contract failing to comply with the requirement of formality will not be enforceable by action.
- The contact or some memorandum or note thereof must be in writing and signed by the party to be charged.
- To satisfy the provision, the contract may also be signed by someone lawfully authorised by the person to be charged.

As the drafting of the provision is the same to this extent, the Australian and New Zealand case law respectively on these points will be persuasive in the other jurisdiction.

[11.460] In relation to contracts for guarantee, the New Zealand legislation[145] also reflects the Australian equivalent that the statutory requirement of formality may be satisfied even if the consideration given for the guarantee is not contained in the document.

[11.465] Finally, the New Zealand legislation is similar to its Australian counterpart because of the express statement in s 2(3)(c) of the *Contracts Enforcement Act* 1956 that

---

145 *Contracts Enforcement Act* 1956, s 3.

the formality requirement does not affect the operation of the law relating to part-per-formance. Equivalent provisions exist in most Australian jurisdictions.[146]

(b) Differences from Australian equivalent

[11.470] Despite the obvious similarities to its Australian counterpart, there are some differences worthy of note.

Contracts concerning land

[11.475] Paragraphs (a)–(c) of s 2(1) of the *Contracts Enforcement Act* 1956 set out the contracts concerning land that must satisfy the formality requirement. While the drafting differs from the Australian equivalent, the effect is largely the same. Paragraphs (a) and (c) relate to contracts for the sale of land, and mortgages and charges over land, respectively. All of these fall within the ambit of the equivalent Australian provisions.

Paragraph (b), however, represents a departure from the Australian position. For other dispositions of land (not caught by paras (a) and (c)), the parties must comply with the formality requirement only if *another* enactment requires the disposition to be in writing. Therefore, unless a statute expressly requires a disposition of land (other than those referred to in paras (a) and (c)) to be in writing, the *Contracts Enforcement Act* 1956 will not apply to it. The operation of the formality requirement therefore is narrower in scope than the Australian equivalent.

Contracts of guarantee

[11.480] Section 2(1)(d) of the *Contracts Enforcement Act* 1956 does not refer to a contract of 'guarantee' but a contract 'to answer to another person for the debt, default, or liability of a third party'. By contrast, the *Statute of Frauds* (Imp) applied to promises concerning the 'debt, default or miscarriage' of another. There was some doubt about whether 'miscarriage' as used in the Imperial legislation extended only to liability under contract, or was broad enough to extend to tortious liability. To remove such doubt, the New Zealand provision substituted 'liability' for 'miscarriage'. 'Liability' is wide enough to encompass contractual and tortious liability.

The language used is different from that used in the Australian jurisdictions. In Victoria, Western Australia, Tasmania, and the Northern Territory, the language in the Imperial legislation is used.[147] The provisions operate if a person promises to 'answer for the debt default or miscarriages of another person'. As set out earlier, in Queensland the requirement of formality extends to 'any promise to guarantee any liability of another'.[148] Although there is no express reference in the Queensland section to 'debt' or 'default' as in the New Zealand provision, it is submitted that 'liability' is

---

146 *Property Law Act* 1974 (Qld), s 6(d); *Conveyancing Act* 1919 (NSW), s 54A(2); *Property Law Act* 1958 (Vic), s 55(d); *Property Law Act* 1969 (WA), s 36(d); *Law of Property Act* 1936 (SA), s 26(2); *Conveyancing and Law of Property Act* 1884 (Tas), s 36(2); *Imperial Acts (Substituted Provisions) Act* 1986 Sch 2 Pt 11, clause 4(2) (ACT); *Law of Property Act* 2000 (NT), s 5(d).

147 *Instruments Act* 1958 (Vic), s 126; *Law Reform (Statute of Frauds) Act* 1962 (WA), s 2; *Mercantile Law Act* 1935 (Tas), s 6; *Law of Property Act* 2000 (NT), s 5(c).

148 *Property Law Act* 1974 (Qld), s 56.

wide enough to encompass such terms. Therefore, there appears to be no practical difference between the Australian and New Zealand positions.

(c)   Proposed reform in New Zealand

[11.485] In December 1997, the New Zealand Law Commission published a Discussion Paper, 'Repeal of the Contracts Enforcement Act 1956'.[149] As the title suggests, the Commission formed the tentative view that the time might be right for the abolition of a formality requirement for contracts concerning land and contracts of guarantee. In relation to guarantees, the Commission noted a current anomaly: guarantees must be in writing, yet indemnities need not be. Instead of recommending that the requirement be altered to extend to indemnities, the Commission favoured the abolition of the requirement for guarantees. The Commission further considered, in relation to contracts concerning land, that the historical reason for requiring formality may no longer be as relevant. For this reason, the Commission considered that it might now be appropriate to abolish the *Contracts Enforcement Act* 1956. At the time of writing, the legislation has not been repealed.

11.9.2   United States

[11.490] Most American States have legislation requiring certain kinds of contracts to be in writing to be enforceable. The United Kingdom statute upon which the American legislation is based has undergone considerable amendment, so some categories of contracts previously required to be in writing to be enforceable no longer fall within the statute. By contrast, most of the American legislation has not been similarly altered. The result is that more contracts fall within the ambit of the American statutes and must be in writing to be enforced than is the position in the United Kingdom.

(a)   Contracts governed by statute

[11.495] In most American states, six categories of contract fall within the ambit of the legislation.

A contract of an executor or administrator to answer for a duty of his decedent[150]

[11.500] This head covers promises made by a deceased person's executor to be held personally responsible for debts of the deceased estate, for example, for medical expenses before death or funeral expenses of the deceased. The requirement for writing is intended to protect executors from fraudulent allegations made by creditors in connection with debts that may be owing by the estate.

A contract to answer for the duty of another[151]

[11.505] The policy behind this class of contract and its ambit of operation largely reflects the Australian position on contracts of guarantee and will be given no further coverage here.

---

149   New Zealand Law Commission Discussion Paper 13.
150   Restatement (Second) § 110.
151   Restatement (Second) § 110.

A contract made upon consideration of marriage[152]

[11.510] In modern times, the fact that this kind of contract has to be in writing to be enforceable is of little practical significance. It is interesting to observe that an early American decision held that a contract formed by the exchange of promises to marry fell outside the ambit of this provision.[153]

A contract for the sale of an interest in land[154]

[11.515] The terminology used in the legislation has given rise to considerable litigation in an attempt to determine its precise ambit. There has been uncertainty arising from the phrase 'contract for sale', and what is meant by the words 'interest' and 'land'.[155] Suffice it to say that in general the courts have given the legislation a broad scope. Notwithstanding that the legislation refers to contracts 'for sale' of an interest in land, contracts of mortgage and lease, for example, fall within the operation of the legislation, as is the case in Australia.

A contract that is not to be performed within one year from the making thereof[156]

[11.520] A contract will fall within this provision, regardless of its subject matter, if the completion of the contract does not occur within one year from entering into it. The requirement for formality in such cases has been the subject of much criticism on the basis that it is difficult to rationalise. Notwithstanding such criticism, it continues to operate in most American States.

A contract for the sale of goods for a price of $500 or more

[11.525] The requirement of formality for contracts of this kind was incorporated into separate legislation from the categories of contracts already described,[157] and now a modified version of the requirement is contained in article 2-201 of the Uniform Commercial Code. Article 2-201 differs from the previous legislation in terms of what the memorandum must contain and the circumstances in which the contract will be enforced despite failure to comply with the requirements of the article.

(b)   Requirements of the statute

[11.530] Most American statutes adopt the same wording as the United Kingdom legislation requiring the agreement or some memorandum or note thereof to be in writing and to be signed. Further, the terms that must be in writing to satisfy the legislation are largely the same.[158] While the position is not entirely settled in Australia, the Restatement (Second) expressly provides that the writing must be 'sufficient to indicate that a contract ... has been made between the parties or offered by the signer to

---

152   Restatement (Second) § 110.
153   *Withers v Richardson* 21 Ky (5 TB Mon) 94 (1827).
154   Restatement (Second) § 110.
155   EA Farnsworth, *Contracts*, 3rd edn, Aspen Law & Business, New York, 1999, p 388.
156   Restatement (Second) § 110.
157   The formality requirement was contained in the *Uniform Sales Act*, legislation adopted in most States.
158   Restatement (Second) § 131.

the other party'.[159] As in Australia, there is also some flexibility surrounding the signature requirement. It is generally sufficient if the person's intention is to authenticate the writing as his or her own.[160] Principles of joinder are also relevant in America.[161]

(c)   Effect of failing to comply with statutory requirements

[11.535] Once again, the American position where the statute is not complied with is largely the same as applies in Australia: the contract is unenforceable, yet there are some circumstances in which a party wishing to enforce the agreement may be entitled to relief. First, the doctrine of part-performance operates for most contracts required to be in writing. In the United States, in a contract for the sale of land, the same strict test of the performance being unequivocally referable to the agreement is used as in Australia. However, the doctrine is not applicable to contracts of suretyship. Secondly, as in Australia, in some circumstances where one party has acted in reliance on the existence of the contract, the other party may be estopped from relying on the legislation as a defence. The operation of estoppel in America is examined elsewhere in this text.[162] In practical terms, the extent to which relief has been granted on the basis of estoppel arguments has led to a significant erosion of the statutory requirements.[163] Thirdly, where one party has acted in reliance on the unenforceable agreement and, in so doing, has conferred a benefit on the other party, he or she may be entitled to a restitutionary remedy. The party may be entitled to recover money paid under the contract or recover the reasonable value of services provided to the other party. While principles of unjust enrichment as a basis for providing restitutionary relief have been applied in Australia, they are of relatively recent origin and are still evolving.[164] The use of the remedy in Australia with respect to unenforceable contracts for the sale or disposition of land is generally limited to moneys paid under the contract. By contrast, under American law, the restitutionary remedies of an injured party are likely to be similar whether or not the contract is enforceable.[165]

11.9.3   Japan

[11.540] In Japan, as in other civil law systems, party autonomy is a core concept within contract law. This means: (a) freedom to conclude a contract—or not to conclude it; (b) freedom to decide the contents of the contract; and (c) freedom of contract form. Freedom with regard to content and form means that, although the Japanese Civil Code refers to 13 classical contract 'types' (or 'named' contracts) and provides general rules for these, parties can, in principle, create any type of contract they wish. Distributorships, franchises, new forms of insurance, and many financial services contracts are all examples of contracts created outside the Code framework, but to which Civil Code provisions are applied by analogy.

---

159   Ibid.
160   Restatement (Second) § 134.
161   Restatement (Second) § 132.
162   See [7.260]–[7.275].
163   EA Farnsworth, *Contracts* 3rd edn, Aspen Law & Business, New York, 1999, p 417.
164   See [24.25]–[24.75].
165   EA Farnsworth, *Contracts* 3rd edn, Aspen Law & Business, New York, 1999, p 414.

Freedom of contract form also means that the Civil Code does not prescribe formalities that the parties must follow to make a contract valid: a contract is formed merely through their agreement (or 'mutual intention'). Historically Japan, like China, used written contracts extensively for important transactions, but between parties with repeat dealings oral contracts were often the norm. Code law followed this commercial practice by adopting the civil law approach and recognising that the parties' agreement need not be in writing. In contemporary Japanese law, there is no *Statute of Frauds* equivalent. Even where writing is prescribed by special legislation overriding the Civil Code, the failure to comply does not necessarily render the contract unenforceable.

[11.545] Some exceptions to the general rule can be found. One is contracts for the sale of land, where courts are reluctant to find an agreement legally binding until the documentation has been formalised.[166] The *Real Estate Business Regulation Act* 1952 requires real estate agents to supply written proof of major conditions of the transaction to the other party (Article 37). Another example is the Civil Code provision governing gifts (Article 550), which allows a contract for a gift, when not made in writing, to be revoked by either party. A third example is life insurance contracts. In theory, these are consensual and informal contracts (that is, no writing required). In practice, however, they are invariably formal contracts because insurers require applicants to use a standard application form. In other cases, for example, where the life insurance is payable on the death of the insured but the policy holder is a third person, Commercial Code, Article 674 requires, as a matter of public policy, that the consent of the insured be given in order for the contract to be valid. This consent is invariably given in writing.

[11.550] The Civil Code rules then appear to make writing completely optional in all but a very few situations in Japan. This is the principle that the Tokyo District Court upheld in *Marubeni Iida v Ajinomoto*,[167] where processed food manufacturer Ajinomoto sought to rescind a purchase agreement for soy beans worth $5 million because the market price had plummeted. Ajinomoto argued that its oral agreement with the seller should be set aside because there was no contract in writing. The court disagreed. It held that there was insufficient evidence that contracts in writing were part of commercial custom in these circumstances, and found no reason to overturn the consensual contract principle.

[11.555] In practice, however, contract informality in Japan is much less prevalent today than in the past. This differs from industry to industry. Oral agreements can be common in some primary or traditional industries, or where there is a continuing relationship. In many cases, special laws for that industry require contracts to be in writing, or provide for the creation of industry-wide rules approved by the relevant regulator, which may be treated as binding on parties subsequently unless expressly excluded.[168] In other cases—for example, leases, franchises, and guarantees—preparation of a contract in writing is customary. Much of this documentation is sealed by the

---

166 Eg S Michida (V Taylor trans), 'Contract Societies: Japan and the United States Compared' (1992) 1 *Pacific Rim Law and Policy Journal* 199.
167 8 *Kakyu Minshu* 1366 at 1415–1416 (Tokyo District Court, 31 July 1957).
168 V Taylor, (1997) 'Consumer Contract Governance in a Deregulating Japan' 27 *Victoria University of Wellington Law Review* 99.

parties—that is, they stamp the document with a personal, inked chop. Sealing is a formal act, like signing, and in transactions is usually taken as prima facie evidence of serious intent or consent. The end result is that in Japan today writing may form all or part of the contract and standard form agreements are widely used in both commercial and consumer transactions. In the case of a dispute, however, the question of whether or not a binding contract was formed is a question for the court, based on the totality of the evidence. This may include the presence (or absence) of writing; what is customary practice in transactions of this kind; the degree of detail in the document; and the nature of the transaction.

One consequence of the relatively flexible rules on contract formation in Japan is that the point at which a contract has been reached during negotiations is not always clear. An increasingly important area of the law is precontractual liability, discussed in Chapter 7.

Chapter 12

Privity

12.1 Introduction

[12.05] The doctrine of privity of contract states that only the parties to a contract are legally entitled to enforce it, or be bound by it. In other words, while performance of a contract may in the circumstances result in a benefit[1] or burden as a matter of *fact* upon a third party to the contract, as a matter of law, a third party cannot enforce the contract nor be subject to limitations imposed by the contract.

[12.10] The doctrine does not have a long history. It seems to have emerged in the early-to-mid nineteenth century with the development of the bargain theory of contract, whereby only the parties to a bargain could enforce obligations undertaken by the bargain.[2] However, it appears that the doctrine was also promulgated as the result of a complex combination of historical, legal, social and economic factors, some of which are no longer relevant today. These include such matters as the concept of a contract as representing a private relationship between its parties; the different needs of a primarily agrarian economy built around small villages that lack the relatively complex commercial situations of today; fears that third parties could bring champertous actions in which they were not naturally concerned; and the unenforceability of simple oral promises in medieval times.[3] The privity doctrine is closely associated with the rules of consideration, inasmuch as it is sometimes suggested that an alternative explanation for why a person cannot enforce the benefit of a contract to which he or she is not a party is that the he or she cannot enforce a promise for which he or she has provided no consideration. This notion is reflected by the requirement that consideration

---

1   See, for example, *Dunlop Pneumatic Tyre Co Ltd v Selfridge & Co Ltd* [1915] AC 847 at 853 where this rule was stated by Viscount Haldane LC as: 'only a person who was a party to a contract can sue on it. Our law knows nothing of a jus quaesatum tertio arising by way of contract.' See also *Coulls v Bagot's Executor and Trustee Co Ltd* (1967) 119 CLR 460 at 478 per Barwick CJ, 494 per Windeyer J.

2   See, for example, *Price v Easton* (1833) 4 B&Ad 433; 110 ER 518; *Tweddle v Atkinson* (1861) 1 B&S 393; 121 ER 762.

3   I Stewart, 'Why place trust in a promise? Privity of contract and enforcement of contracts by third party beneficiaries' (1999) 73 ALJ 354 at 355 citing Palmer, *The Paths to Privity: the History of Third Party Beneficiary Contracts at English Law*, Austin & Winfield, 1992.

must move from the promisee.[4] Nevertheless, the better view seems to be that they are distinct rules.[5]

[12.15] The privity doctrine, particularly in so far as it prevents a third party from enforcing the benefit of the contract, has been the subject of extensive judicial criticism. The injustice that may result from the rule arises not only from its failure to give effect to the express intention of the parties to the contract, but also because those who are aware of the promise may reorder their affairs in accordance with it. For this reason, in some jurisdictions the privity doctrine has been abrogated to give a third party to the contract the right to enforce the promise made for his or her benefit. Other jurisdictions have legislated to abrogate the effect of the doctrine in relation to specific types of contract. Even where the privity doctrine has been regarded as binding, courts have developed methods of evading its effects by applying other principles of law in the circumstances. In some cases, these detours are not restricted to attempts to enforce the benefit but also extend to the imposition of burdens; they may also only apply to the imposition of burdens on third parties. This chapter will examine each of these areas in turn.

12.2 General rule

[12.20] The general rule dictates that where promisor A enters into an agreement with promisor B which provides that promisor A will confer a benefit on C, a third party to the contract, C is unable to claim the benefit of the promise despite that being the clear intention of parties A and B. Perhaps less troublesome is the other aspect of the doctrine, which holds that where parties A and B enter into a contract, they cannot by their bargain impose a liability of third party C. It is easy to conceive of the travesties that could be perpetrated were the law to permit parties A and B to agree between themselves that each should be paid a sum of money of their choosing by a stranger C.[6]

[12.25] In a sense, denial of a right to enforce the contract on the part of third party C does not necessarily lead to an unsatisfactory result. For example, whatever the position relating to third party C, nothing changes the fact that a contract has been entered into between A and B. Accordingly, should promisor A fail to perform his or her promise to benefit third party C, B has available the normal remedies for breach of contract. In particular, the remedy of specific performance may be a valuable remedy since it has the effect of forcing the promisor to perform the promise.[7] It is available as a remedy since damages would not be an adequate remedy[8] for the promisee B: where

---

4   *Tweddle v Atkinson* (1861) 1 B&S 393 at 397; 121 ER 762 at 763–4.
5   It would therefore be possible for a person to be a party to the contract but nevertheless unable to enforce a promise due to his or her failure to provide consideration for it: see, for example, *Coulls v Bagot's Executor and Trustee Co Ltd* (1967) 119 CLR 460; *Trident General Insurance Co Ltd v McNiece Bros Pty Ltd* (1988) 165 CLR 107 at 115–116. See further [6.80]–[6.95].
6   See, for example, *Atlas International Travel Pty Ltd v Bennet* [1999] NSWSC 877 (2 September 1999).
7   *Coulls v Bagot's Executor and Trustee Co Ltd* (1967) 119 CLR 460 at 478 per Barwick CJ and 503 per Windeyer J; *Beswick v Beswick* [1968] AC 58 at 81 per Lord Hodson, 88–92 per Lord Pearce, 97–102 per Lord Upjohn; *Trident General Insurance Co Ltd v McNiece Bros Pty Ltd* (1988) 165 CLR 107 at 120.
8   See [25.05]–[25.45].

A has promised to confer a benefit on C the only person who suffers substantial loss by a failure to perform that promise is C. B therefore would only be entitled to nominal damages, unless there were some other circumstance in which a failure to confer the benefit on C will, according to the usual course of things or to the knowledge of promisor A, result in substantial loss to promisee B.[9]

The disadvantage of specific performance as a remedy suited for all cases where a promisor has breached a promise to confer a benefit on a third party is that it requires the willingness of promisee B to commence action with a view to ensuring third party C receives the promised benefit.[10] It may be that party B and third party C are closely associated, so B will be motivated to commence an action. But if promisee B and third party C have no association, B may have no interest in commencing proceedings for the benefit of a stranger.[11]

[12.30] Another unsatisfactory aspect of the privity doctrine is that as a third party to the contract, C has no influence over any variation or revocation of the promise agreed to by A and B. This becomes particularly important where third party C has relied upon the existence of the promise in its original, unaltered state and has thereby incurred detriment or may suffer detriment should the promise be varied or revoked.

[12.35] The injustice that may result from the doctrine of privity has led to its criticism on numerous occasions.[12] One judge has described it as a 'blot on our law and thoroughly unjust'[13] while another referred to it as an 'anachronistic shortcoming that has for many years been regarded as a reproach to English private law.'[14] The English Law Revisions Committee in 1937 recommended the abolition of the rule in its *Sixth Interim Report* (CMD 5449).[15] The UK Parliament finally acted on this recommendation in 1999,[16] enabling third parties to enforce terms that purport to confer benefits on them[17] where the parties have so intended.[18]

[12.40] In Australia, such judicial reform came very close to reality in the recent case of *Trident General Insurance Co Ltd v McNiece Bros Pty Ltd*.[19] In that case, a construction company called Blue Circle entered into a contract of insurance with Trident General Insurance with regard to a construction site. The policy defined the assured as Blue Circle, its subsidiaries and 'all contractors and subcontractors'. McNiece was Blue Circle's principal contractor. It was held liable when sued by a crane driver for negligence for injuries he sustained on site. McNiece subsequently made a claim under the insurance policy between Trident and Blue Circle. By a 4:3 majority, the High Court held that McNiece was entitled to coverage. Three of the four majority judges (Mason CJ

---

9   In *Trident General Insurance Co Ltd v McNiece Bros Pty Ltd* (1988) 165 CLR 107 at 158 Dawson J suggested the example of where the promise is to pay a sum which will reduce the promisee's indebtedness to the third party.

10   *Trident General Insurance Co Ltd v McNiece Bros Pty Ltd* (1988) 165 CLR 107 at 120.

11   As occurred in *Trident General Insurance Co Ltd v McNiece Bros Pty Ltd* (1988) 165 CLR 107.

12   See also Stewart (1999) 73 ALJ 354 at 359.

13   *Forster v Silvermere Golf and Equestrian Centre Ltd* [1983] AC 598 at 611.

14   *Swain v Law Society* [1983] 1 AC 598 at 611.

15   See paragraph 48.

16   *Contracts (Rights of Third Parties) Act* 1999.

17   Section 81.

18   Ibid.

19   (1988) 165 CLR 107.

and Wilson J in joint judgment, and Toohey J) were in favour of abolishing privity, at least in an insurance context. Mason CJ and Wilson J stated that it was the duty of the High Court to reconsider rules that operated unjustly or unsatisfactorily. Toohey J also thought the rule lacked a sound foundation in jurisprudence and logic and, since it was only 120 years old, was not so deeply entrenched that it could not be changed. An important reason for allowing the third party to sue was the expected reliance by a third party in the sense of ordering his or her affairs by reference to the promise. While, in the final analysis, all three judges decided to limit their decision to claims of a beneficiary under an insurance policy, Mason CJ and Wilson J expressed their views in very general terms; and Toohey J expressly stated that it would be unreal to think that their decision in that case would not have implications for privity elsewhere.

12.3   Statutory abrogation of privity

[12.45] The doctrine of privity of contract has been abrogated by statue in Western Australia and Queensland. The Commonwealth Government has abrogated privity in relation to the special areas of insurance and maritime contracts of carriage. Other legislation has modified or abrogated privity in relation to particular types of contract.

12.3.1   Western Australia

[12.50] The recommendation of the 1937 English Law Revision Committee was adopted in Western Australia. The *Property Law Act* 1969, s 11(2) provides that where a contract expressly in its terms purports to confer a benefit directly on a person who was not named as a party to the contract, the contract is enforceable by that person in his or her own name. This provision is subject to a proviso in subsection (3) that, unless the contract otherwise provides, the contract may be cancelled or modified by the mutual consent of the persons named as parties at any time before the beneficiary has adopted it, either expressly or by conduct.

Example: Westralian Farmers' Co-operative Ltd v Southern Meat Packers Ltd[20]

The plaintiff livestock agent negotiated the sale of some cattle to the defendant on behalf of a farmer. The contract of sale entered into between the farmer and the defendant contained a statement to the effect that to enable the agents to protect their claim to commission, the full purchase price was to be payable by the buyer to and be recoverable by the agents alone. The plaintiff credited the farmer with the purchase price less its commission. Despite the provision in the contract, the defendant paid the full purchase price directly to the farmer. The plaintiff then sued the defendant for the full purchase price.

The Full Court of the Western Australian Supreme Court held that the agent was entitled to recover this amount pursuant to the *Property Law Act* 1969 (WA), s 11(2). Since the contract contained a provision for payment to the agent 'alone,' it could be

---

20   [1981] WAR 241.

said that the agreement expressly conferred a benefit on the agent within the terms of the section. The court rejected an argument by the defendant that the payment of the price to the farmer was a modification of the contract within the terms of s 11(3), since even if it were properly construed as a modification, it had occurred after the plaintiff had adopted the contract by crediting the farmer with the price in its books.

[12.55] Under the section, each person named as a party to the contract must be joined as a party to the action or proceeding by the beneficiary.

[12.60] It is essential, if the legislation is to apply, that the third party be named as a third party beneficiary. In other words, the legislation may not be invoked by an incidental beneficiary who stands to be indirectly benefited from the contract.[21]

Example: Visic v State Government Insurance Co Ltd[22]

A worker recovered a damages judgment against his employer for injuries at work. The employer was insured by an insurance policy, but it was an indemnity policy that did not provide for coverage of workers against the consequences of accidents. The policy only covered the employer in respect of possible liability. The worker attempted to directly enforce the insurance policy but the insurance company refused indemnity.

It was held that the policy neither named the worker as a party nor specifically named him as a beneficiary, even though as a matter of practice injured workers often negotiated directly with the employer's insurer. Accordingly, the worker was neither within the ambit of the *Insurance Contracts Act* 1994 (Cth)[23] nor the *Property Law Act* 1969 (WA), s 11.

[12.65] The section provides that any defence that would be available to the defendant had the beneficiary been a party to the contract will be available in an action by the beneficiary.[24] Further, it is possible for a third party to be made subject to an obligation, but only in a case where at the same time the contract purports to confer a benefit on him or her.

12.3.2   Queensland

[12.70] The *Property Law Act* 1974 (Qld), s 55(1) provides that a promisor who, for a valuable consideration moving from the promisee, promises to do or refrain from doing an act or acts for the benefit of a beneficiary shall, upon acceptance by the beneficiary, be subject to a duty enforceable by the beneficiary to perform that promise. This section was also prompted by the English Law Revision Committee Report of 1937. Unlike the Western Australian section, there is a considerable—and growing—body of cases that have considered the operation of s 55, although in many cases the section has been called upon by way of alternative argument rather than being the

---

21   *Visic v State Government Insurance Co Ltd* (1990) 3 WAR 122.
22   (1990) 3 WAR 122.
23   See [12.155].
24   See s 11(2)(a).

main focus of the action. There have, however, been a few cases in which the only issue has been the claim of a third party beneficiary, and the case has been resolved in favour of the beneficiary by an unremarkable application of the section.[25]

(a)   Promisor

[12.75] It seems that the relevant 'promisor' under the statute is the party who actually makes the promise for the benefit of the beneficiary. In the absence of an assignment, the promise is not binding upon a new party who merely stands in the shoes of the promisor who makes the promise. Thus, where the promise is made by a trustee of a trust who is subsequently replaced by a new trustee, the promise will not be binding on the new trustee.[26]

(b)   Beneficiary

[12.80] A party may clearly be a 'beneficiary' for the purposes of s 55 if he or she is expressly named in a contract as receiving the benefit of performance of work under a contract.[27] A live issue regarding 'beneficiary' is whether a person who is not named in the promise—but is incidentally benefited by the promise—can enforce the promise under s 55. There is authority supporting both competing views; the better view seems to be that an 'incidental beneficiary' cannot rely on the section.[28]

Example: Re Burns Philp Trustees[29]

A mortgagor owned land at the Gold Coast on which a unit development was planned. A mortgage was granted in favour of Burns Philp. There were two subsequent securities: a bill of encumbrance in favour of Mexican Village and a mortgage in favour of the Commonwealth Bank. There were also several unsecured creditors. The mortgagor struck financial problems and the first mortgagor, Burns Philp, sold the land and paid out its debt. The surplus from the sale was insufficient to pay out the remaining debts. Indeed, if the surplus had been used towards either of the Mexican Village or the Commonwealth Bank debts, there would have been no funds to pay any of the other claimants. In September 1993 there was a meeting between Mexican Village and the unsecured creditors. The view was expressed that if there was a forbearance by the various claimants so that the project proceeded through to completion, the various creditors could hope to be paid in full. To ensure that the unsecured creditors would be paid, or perhaps merely to induce them to exercise the necessary forbearance, Mexican Village agreed with each of them that it would relinquish its

---

25   See, for example, *Batchelor v Ocean Downs Pty Ltd* (unreported, Qld SC, Ambrose J, 16 September 1985) (promising contract of a sale of real estate agency to continue the employment of the manager of the agency); *Orpin v AGC (Advances) Ltd* (unreported, Qld SC, de Jersey J, 8 October 1987) (payment of sum by promisee to satisfy a debt owed by the beneficiary to the promisor in return for the promisor releasing the beneficiary from a registered mortgage).

26   *Re Davies* [1989] 1 Qd R 48.

27   See, for example, *Re Eagle Star Trustees Ltd* (unreported, Qld SC, Ambrose J, 25 March 1994).

28   *Re Burns Philp Trustees* (unreported, Qld SC, Macrossan J, 17 December 1986); *Robt Jones (363 Adelaide Street) Pty Ltd v First Abbott Corporation Pty Ltd* (unreported, Qld SC, White J, 28 October 1997).

29   Unreported, 17 December 1986.

prior entitlement to payment. At the meeting and in the deed recording the terms of agreement, attention was not given to the Commonwealth Bank's debt, and the significance of its position and the size of its debt were overlooked. The Commonwealth Bank subsequently claimed the benefit of the promise by Mexican Village to relinquish its prior entitlement, contained in the agreement between it and the other creditors. The Commonwealth Bank claimed that since Mexican Village had relinquished its priority, the Bank as the next registered creditor was entitled to the whole of the surplus in payment of its debt.

Macrossan J of the Queensland Supreme Court rejected the Commonwealth Bank's argument. The clear intention of the agreement was to adjust entitlements only as between the parties to the agreement. There was no promise to do or refrain from doing anything for the benefit of the Commonwealth Bank, which was mentioned nowhere. The Bank could therefore not rely on s 55.

[12.85] The issue of an 'incidental beneficiary' was considered by some of the judges in the High Court in *Northern Sandblasting Pty Limited v Harris*[30] in the context of a landlord of residential premises who undertook to have a defective electrical appliance repaired before tenants entered into possession. A licensed electrician performed the repairs negligently, with the result that those in possession of the premises were placed at risk of death or injury. The plaintiff (the daughter of the tenants) received a severe electrical shock and suffered permanent and disabling injuries. The section was argued as an alternative basis for compensation. Of the two judges who directly considered the issue, the dissenting judge, Kirby J, considered that although the promise was in the contract between the landlord and the tenants, the plaintiff as the daughter of the tenants—who also was known by the landlord to be living in the house—was an incidental beneficiary to the promise and could enforce it under s 55.[31]

By contrast, Brennan CJ, who was a member of the majority, strongly rejected the suggestion that an incidental beneficiary could rely on s 55. He stated that from the context of s 55, it appeared that the identity of the beneficiary must be ascertainable from the terms of the promise made. The beneficiary is not any person who, in the event, would have been benefited had the promise been fulfilled. If that had been the intention of the legislature, the duty that s 55 imposes would have been owed to the world at large—or, at least, to any person who may foreseeably have been benefited by the discharge of that duty.[32] Allowing s 55 to apply in a case like the present, he thought, would make it impossible to predict on any logical basis the categories of beneficiaries who might be entitled to make a claim under s 55.[33]

---

30   (1997) 188 CLR 313.

31   Ibid, at 413.

32   Ibid, at 329.

33   Ibid. As a matter of strict doctrine of precedent, weight cannot be given to Kirby J's comments because they are the words of a dissenting judge, whereas greater weight may be assigned to Brennan CJ's rejection of incidental beneficiaries since he was a member of the majority. However, the issue is complicated because Gaudron J agreed with Kirby J's comments but was nevertheless a member of the majority.

(c)   Promise

[12.90] 'Promise' is defined in s 55(6) as being a promise:

- which is or appears to be intended to be legally binding, and
- which creates or is intended to create a duty enforceable by a beneficiary.

A contractual term that merely regulates the relationship between promisor and promisee will not be enforceable by a third party if it does not amount to a promise to benefit the third party and create an enforceable duty.[34]

[12.95] It would seem that the definition in s 55(6) is in terms that are not apt to include an obligation inserted in a contract by operation of statute—such as a duty imposed on a landlord to maintain premises under the *Residential Tenancies Act* 1975 (Qld). Instead, 'promise' is treated by s 55 in terms of intention. It is one thing to acknowledge that statutes impose contractual obligations on a landlord in relation to the state of the premises, for example, but another to then make the leap to allowing such an obligation to be enforced by a third party as a promise under s 55.[35] A promise to benefit a beneficiary may be made subject to the fulfilment of specific preconditions. Failure to satisfy the preconditions will prevent s 55 arising as an issue.[36]

[12.100] It would also appear to be an open question whether an exemption clause that purports to extend coverage to a third party amounts to a promise to confer a benefit on the third party. While a broad interpretation of 'benefit' may include an exemption from liability,[37] a different result might follow if the term is given a meaning similar to the meaning that is well established in restitution.[38]

(d)   Acceptance

[12.105] Section 55(6) defines 'acceptance' as an assent by words or conduct communicated by or on behalf of the beneficiary to the promisor—or to a person authorised on his or her behalf—in the manner (if any) specified in the promise and within the time specified in the promise (or, if no time is specified, within a reasonable time of the promise coming to the notice of the beneficiary). In a number of respects, therefore, the subsection expressly refers to agents: the acceptance may be communicated by *or on behalf of* the beneficiary, to the promisor *or to some person authorised on his or her behalf*. However, by the terms of the subsection the 'reasonable time' for acceptance does not start until the promise comes to the notice of *the beneficiary*. Nevertheless, it may still be sufficient if the promise comes to the notice of the beneficiary's agent, such as the beneficiary's solicitor.[39]

---

34   See, for example, *Davis v Archer Park Newsagency Rockhampton* (unreported, Qld SC, Demack J, 17 July 1984) (Gold Lotto entrant, not paid for having winning numbers due to destruction by fire of original coupon, unable to recover from newsagent on basis of term in agency contract between Gold Lotto organisers and newsagent requiring safe keeping of original coupons by newsagent).

35   *Northern Sandblasting Pty Ltd v Harris* (1997) 188 CLR 313 at 329 per Brennan CJ, 382 per Gummow J (with whom Dawson and Toohey JJ agreed in this respect); cf 413 per Kirby J (with whom Gaudron J concurred). Once again, difficulties are posed by virtue of s 55 being an alternative issue. Only Brennan CJ and Toohey J were in the majority of the decision, like Gaudron J who agreed with Kirby J in finding in favour of the plaintiff on the point.

36   *Remar v Graham-Hall-Downer Pty Ltd* (unreported, Qld SC (FC), 17 November 1988).

37   Cf the express definition of benefit to include exemption clauses in the New Zealand *Contracts (Privity) Act* 1982. See also the express reference to exclusion clauses in the *Contracts (Rights of Third Parties) Act* 1999 (UK), s 1(6).

38   See [12.365].

39   *Re Davies* [1999] 1 Qd R 48 at 49, 51.

[12.110] It seems that any assent by the beneficiary must on its face purport to 'accept' the promise. It may be insufficient for there to be words or conduct that are merely *consistent* with an acceptance for the purposes of the section.[40] However, provided the beneficiary's assent purports to accept the promise, it is immaterial if in fact the purported acceptance precedes the promise to benefit the beneficiary.[41]

Example: Hyatt Australia v LTCB Australia Ltd[42]

Discovery Bay owned a hotel that was managed by Hyatt. Under the management agreement, Discovery Bay promised that the land on which the hotel stood would be kept free of mortgage or encumbrances. In 1988, Discovery Bay obtained finance secured by mortgages over its land, including the land on which the hotel stood. In deference to the Management Agreement, it was agreed that a clause would be inserted in the bill of mortgage over the land on which the hotel stood; by that clause, the mortgagee agreed that while the Management Agreement remained in force, the mortgagee would not interfere with the operation of the hotel by Hyatt. In November 1988, Hyatt forwarded an 'acknowledgement of security' that included a statement that Hyatt had consented to the grant of the mortgage and 'acknowledges and confirms' that the mortgage did not 'materially and adversely affect the operation of the hotel' by Hyatt. The mortgage was finally signed on 21 July 1992. Subsequently, Discovery Bay went into receivership and a dispute arose between the mortgagee and Hyatt concerning disposal of proceeds from the operation of the hotel.

The Queensland Court of Appeal noted that the purported acceptance in November 1988 preceded by some $3\frac{1}{2}$ years the relevant promise (the mortgage executed on 21 July 1992). However, the court had no difficulty in recognising the concept of an 'anticipatory acceptance' that was in advance of the promise to benefit the third party. The court drew an analogy with the notion of a conditional acceptance that takes effect as a counter-offer, itself capable of acceptance by further promise. The simplest way of frustrating such an anticipatory acceptance—if that was what the promisor and promisee wished to achieve—was simply to refrain from going on to make the primary promise. If the primary promise was never made, there would be nothing for the anticipatory acceptance to fasten onto. In any event, the issue of the writ commencing proceedings by Hyatt was sufficient conduct manifesting an intention to accept the promise. In deciding that this had been within a reasonable time, it was considered a relevant factor that the decision-makers for the various parties were located in far-apart places such as Japan, Hong Kong, and the United States.

It might be queried whether geographic location is necessarily of any, or any great, relevance in a technological age. Further, a question not addressed in this *obiter* comment is how it sits with the view that 'reasonable time' commences when the promise comes to the attention of the beneficiary's agent, who may well be situated locally.

---

40   *Re Davies* (unreported, Qld SC Ryan J, 22 December 1986) not considered on appeal [1989] 1 Qd R 48; *Robt Jones (363 Adelaide Street) Pty Ltd v First Abbott Corporation Pty Ltd* (unreported, Qld SC, White J, 28 October 1997); cf *Northern Sandblasting Pty Ltd v Harris* (1997) 188 CLR 313 at 413 per Kirby J (with whom Gaudron J agreed).

41   *Hyatt Australia Ltd v LTCB Australia Ltd* [1996] 1 Qd R 260 at 264.

42   [1996] 1 Qd R 260.

(e) Defences

[12.115] Section 55(4) provides that any matter that would otherwise be relied on as rendering a promise void, voidable, or unenforceable will be available by way of defence in proceedings for the enforcement of a duty under s 55. The Law Reform Commission's explanatory note described the intended object of this subsection as being 'to ensure that defences such as mistake, fraud, misrepresentation, Statute of Frauds and Statute of Limitations, payment, etc, which may be available to the promisor against the promisee are also available to the former against the beneficiary.'[43] In other words, the subsection is:

> Concerned for the obvious reasons of justice to ensure that the beneficiary coming in from outside, as it were, to enforce the promise for his own benefit, will not be unduly advantaged by being placed in a stronger position than the original promisee had that person himself sought to enforce the promises.[44]

However, the subsection should not be interpreted as an exclusive statement of the matters that could modify or abate the amount recoverable when the third party beneficiary sues the promisor. Where, for example, a statutory enactment imposes a limit on liability, it may operate to directly limit the extent of liability a third party beneficiary may enforce under s 55, just as much as it would limit the amount a directly contracting promisee could recover.[45]

(f) Variation or rescission of promise

[12.120] Under s 55(2), *before* acceptance, the parties to the contract may vary or rescind the promise. However, s 55(3)(d) provides that *after* acceptance, the terms of the promise and the duty of the promisor or beneficiary may be varied or discharged only with the consent of the promisor and the beneficiary.

(g) Imposition of burdens

[12.125] Like the Western Australian legislation, s 55 may incidentally allow an obligation to be imposed upon the beneficiary. Section s 55(3)(b) states that the beneficiary will be bound by any promise or duty that is imposed as part of the promise that benefits him or her. In other words, an obligation may be imposed upon the beneficiary— but only as part of a promise that confers a benefit upon him or her.

(h) Common law still applicable

[12.130] Section 55(7) provides that the section does not affect any right or remedy that exists or is available apart from the section. This subsection has the effect of saving the common law so that where the statute cannot be applied—perhaps because the requirement of acceptance has not been complied with—the common law applies. Consequently, a beneficiary who is unable to make out a case under the statute would

---

43   Queensland Law Reform Commission, Report No 16, at 40–41.
44   *Wallis v Downard-Pickford(North Queensland) Pty Ltd* (1992) ATPR 41-197 at 40,651.
45   Ibid; see also *Remar v Graham-Hall-Downer Pty Ltd* (unreported, Qld SC (FC) 17 November, 1988) where it was suggested that the matter such as waiver and prevention of performance might be relied upon in an appropriate case.

be left to rely on an exception to the privity doctrine, if one were available in the circumstances.

12.3.3 Insurance

[12.135] In *Vandepitte v Preferred Accident Insurance Corporation of New York*,[46] the Privy Council applied the privity rule to an insurance policy that was expressed to be for the benefit of persons who were not parties to the contract. As a consequence, persons who were named as beneficiaries under the insurance policy, but who were not actually parties to the policy, were unable to claim coverage under the policy.

[12.140] Today in Australia, insurance cases are the subject of legislation enacted to overcome the privity rule.

(a)   Marine insurance

[12.145] The *Marine Insurance Act* 1909 (Cth), s 20(2) provides that a mortgagee, consignee or other person having an interest in the subject matter of a marine insurance contract may insure not only on his or her own behalf but also on behalf of, and for the benefit of, other persons who may be interested.

(b)   Compulsory third party motor vehicle insurance

[12.150] Motivated by the obvious policy need to ensure an effective scheme of compensation for victims of road accidents, all Australian jurisdictions have enacted legislation that compels the owner of a motor vehicle, on registration of the vehicle, to insure against death or personal injuries, and provides that the insurer must indemnify not only the owner of the vehicle but also any person using it—with or without the owner's permission—even though that person is not a party to the contract of insurance entered into between the insurance company and the owner.[47]

(c)   Insurance in general

[12.155] The 1982 Australian Law Reform Commission report *Insurance Contracts* noted the displacement of the *Vandepitte* decision in respect of compulsory third party motor vehicle insurance in all Australian jurisdictions. Nevertheless, *Vandepitte* was still available in order to deny insurance coverage in other circumstances, and it had been used to do so as recently as 1979.[48] The Commission concluded that this problem could not be resolved by the application of principles such as trust and agency, and therefore recommended that persons falling within the class of persons expressed by an insurance policy as being entitled to indemnity should be able to sue on the policy.[49] The Commission suggested that such an alteration in the law should be uncontroversial, because as a matter of practice most insurers already acted as though they were under such a liability to such third parties.[50] This recommendation was ultimately

---

46   [1933] AC 70.

47   See *Motor Traffic Act* 1936 (ACT), s 54(1); *Motor Vehicles (Third Party Insurance) Act* 1942 (NSW), s 10(7);
      Motor Accidents (Compensation) Act 1979 (NT), s 6(1); *Motor Vehicles Insurance Act* 1936 (Qld), s 3(2); *Motor
      Vehicles Act* 1959 (SA), s 104; *Motor Accidents (Liabilities and Compensation) Act* 1973 (Tas), s 14(1); *Motor
      Car Act* 1958 (Vic), s 46(1); *Motor Vehicle (Third Party Insurance) Act* 1943 (WA), s 3(1).

48   See *Janovovic v Broers* (1979) 25 ACTR 39.

49   Australian Law Reform Commission, *Insurance Contracts,* Report No 20 (1982), at para [122].

50   Ibid, at para [124].

given effect by the enactment of the *Insurance Contracts Act* 1984 (Cth), s 48. That provision applies to all contracts of insurance entered into after the Act came into force on 1 January 1986.[51]

12.3.4 Maritime contracts of carriage

[12.160] Legislation has abolished the privity rule in at least some respects in relation to maritime contracts of carriage—specifically servants and agents of sea carriers, and consignees and indorsees of sea carriage documents.

(a) Servants or agents of sea carriers

[12.165] If the privity rule were to be applied, then the usual exemptions from liability that appear in contracts of carriage exempting the carrier from liability to the owner of goods for loss or damage to the goods could be simply evaded by, for example, suing instead the servants or agents of the carrier (including the master and crew of the vessel) who actually caused the loss or damage.

[12.170] In the past, this risk has been avoided by the inclusion in the bill of lading evidencing the contract of carriage a provision known as a '*Himalaya* Clause', which has the effect of making the carrier the agent for its servants, agents or independent contractors in relation to an exemption of liability for loss or damage to the goods.[52] Such a clause has been held effective to exempt from liability third parties to the contract of carriage such as the master, crew, or stevedores who are entrusted with loading and unloading the goods. Recently, however, the Commonwealth enacted the *Carriage of Goods by Sea Act* 1991, which gives effect to the International Carriage Convention known as the 'Hague Rules,' as amended by the 'Visby' and 'SDR' Protocols and as modified in accordance with Australian shipping circumstances. The 'modified amended Hague' Rules (as they are sometimes known) provide that the servants and agents of the carrier are entitled to the same exemptions from liability as the carrier. Accordingly, now by force of law rather than as a provision in a contract, parties such as the master and crew—but not independent contractors such as stevedores—may now rely on the exemptions contained in the contract entered into between the carrier and the owner of goods shipped by sea.

(b) Consignees and indorsees

[12.175] The other important aspect of sea carriage in which privity has been abrogated concerns the routine action of the owner of goods selling a part or the whole of the cargo to a third party before, or while, the goods are in transit. In such a case, the contract of carriage is entered into between the original owner and the carrier of the goods. A longstanding issue has been whether the buyer, as a consignee or indorsee,[53]

---

51 This provision was enacted after the accident which gave rise to the proceedings in *Trident General Insurance Co Ltd v McNiece Bros Pty Ltd* (1988) 165 CLR 107, but before the case was decided. If the same circumstances arose today they would be caught within the ambit of the section.

52 See [12.220].

53 A 'consignee' is a third party to whom the original owner dispatches or consigns goods. An 'indorsee' is a third party who purchases goods which are being shipped by the original owner to itself, while the goods are in transit. Where such a sale takes place, the relevant shipping documents such as the bill of lading are 'indorsed' to the 'indorsee.'

is entitled to make a claim against the carrier if the carrier breaches any of the provisions of the contract of carriage including breaches resulting in loss or damage to the goods. Privity of contract has long been a substantial obstacle for such buyers, who were thus placed at a distinct disadvantage; they may have paid a substantial sum for goods that arrived damaged (or not at all) but had no recourse against the party who was likely to have been responsible. Similarly, the situation was not satisfactory from the carrier's position. The carrier often could find itself delivering goods to a third party such as a consignee or indorsee and being unable to enforce outstanding liabilities under the contract owed by original owner, such as freight charges, because it would amount to imposing a burden on a third party to the contract.

[12.180] This unsatisfactory situation has now been remedied by the enactment of a statute in identical terms in all Australian jurisdictions. The effect of the *Sea Carriage Documents Acts*[54] is twofold. First, all rights in the original contract of carriage are transferred to a third party buyer as from the time of consignment or indorsement. Effectively, therefore, a consignee or indorsee may now enforce rights under a contract to which he or she was a third party. Secondly, all outstanding liabilities under the original contract of carriage are transferred to a third party buyer when he or she demands or takes delivery of the goods. Thus, it is possible to impose a burden on a consignee or indorsee despite the fact that he or she was a third party to the original contract of carriage.

12.3.5   Other legislation

[12.185] Other sporadic legislation abolishes or modifies the privity rule. Under Commonwealth legislation, certain negotiable instruments—including cheques, bills of exchange and promissory notes—which contain promises may be passed on to subsequent holders, who are able to enforce those promises.[55] For example, it is possible for a person named as the payee of a cheque to endorse the cheque to another person, who is then legally able to enforce the cheque.

[12.190] In some jurisdictions, legislation enables subsequent owners of residential properties to sue a builder of substandard construction work.[56] Clearly, such subsequent owners would not be privy to the original contract between the builder and the first owner.

[12.195] More problematic is the effect of legislation based on the English *Law of Property Act* 1925, s 56(1)—re-enacted in each Australian jurisdiction—and its impact on property. The section states that:

> A person may take an immediate or other interest in land or other property, or
> the benefit of any condition, right of entry, covenant or agreement over or

---

54   The template legislation is: *Sea-Carriage Documents Bill* 1996 (ACT), cll 8, 10; *Sea-Carriage Documents Act* 1997 (NSW), ss 8, 10; *Sea-Carriage Documents Act* 1998 (NT), ss 8, 10; *Sea-Carriage Documents Act* 1996 (Qld), ss 6, 8; *Sea-Carriage Documents Act* 1998 (SA) ss 7, 9; *Sea-Carriage Documents Act* 1997 (Tas), ss 7, 9; *Sea-Carriage Documents Act* 1998 (Vic), ss 8, 10; *Sea-Carriage Documents Act* 1997 (WA), ss 8, 10.

55   See, *Bills of Exchange Act* 1909 (Cth), ss 36–43; *Cheques Act* 1986 (Cth), s 73.

56   See, for example, *Queensland Building Services Act* 1991 (Qld), s 71; *Defective Houses Act* 1976 (SA), s 4(3); *Building Work Contractors Act* 1995 (SA), s 32; *Housing Indemnity Act* 1992 (Tas), s 7; *House Contracts Guarantee Act* 1987 (Vic), s 8.

respecting land or other property, although he may not be named as a party to the conveyance or other instrument.[57]

The word 'property' is defined in legislation as including any form of property, real or personal, including a chose in action.[58] It has been argued that the section may be interpreted as abrogating privity of contract because the right to enforce a term of a contract is regarded as constituting a chose in action.[59] However, that argument was rejected by the House of Lords in *Beswick v Beswick*, on the basis that the English enactment was only a consolidating statute, and that this gave rise to a strong presumption that it was not intended to effect such a radical change in the existing law.[60]

It has been pointed out that the same observation does not hold true for the Australian legislation.[61] However, the Western Australian provision concerning privity of contract is often pointed to as showing that the Australian provisions were not intended to effect a wholesale abolition of privity. The English section was adopted in Western Australian in s 11(1) of the *Property Law Act* 1969, which then proceeded in ss (2) and (3) to largely abrogate the privity rule in that State. Had the English provision been intended to have the effect of abrogating privity of contract, these two subsections would not have been necessary.[62]

Indeed, it may be argued that the purpose of the English section was limited to doing away with an old common law rule that in an indenture *inter partes*, the covenantee had to be named as a party to the indenture before he or she could take the benefit of an immediate grant of the benefit of a covenant. The provision therefore enabled beneficiaries who were not named in such an indenture, but who were in existence and identifiable at the time the deed was entered into, to take that benefit.[63] In other words, while prima facie the words of the statute appear to abolish the rule that a third party is unable to enforce a promise that purports to confer a benefit on him or her, on closer analysis, the section only addresses a limited circumstance of little modern-day relevance.

---

57   *Conveyancing Act* 1919 (NSW), s 36C(1); *Law of Property Act* 1936 (SA), s 34(1); *Conveyancing and Law of Property Act* 1884 (Tas), s 61(1); *Property Law Act* 1958 (Vic), s 56(1); *Property Law Act* 1969 (WA), s 11(1); cf *Property Law Act* 1974 (Qld), s 13(1); *Real Property Act* 1852 (SA), s 4 (which is applicable in the NT).

58   A 'chose in action' is something recoverable by action or court proceeding.

59   *Drive Yourself Hire Co (London) Ltd v Strutt* [1954] 1 QB 250 at 274 per Lord Denning MR. It is for this reason that the difficulty does not arise in either Queensland nor the Northern Territory where the relevant legislation only refers to 'interest in land' and omits the phrase 'or other property': see *Property Law Act* 1974 (Qld), s 13(1); *Real Property Act* 1852 (SA), s 4 (which is applicable in the NT). No corresponding legislation was enacted in the ACT at all.

60   [1968] AC 58 at 77 per Lord Reid, 81 per Lord Hodson, 87 per Lord Guest, 93 per Lord Pearce, 105 per Lord Upjohn.

61   DW Greig & JLR Davis, *Law of Contract*, Law Book Co, Sydney, 1987, p 1045; N Seddon & MP Ellinghaus, *Cheshire and Fifoot's Law of Contract*, 7th edn, Butterworths, Sydney, 1997, p 248.

62   Ibid.

63   See *Beswick v Beswick* [1968] AC 58 at 106 per Lord Upjohn. See also DW Greig & JLR Davis, *Law of Contract*, Law Book Co, Sydney, 1987, pp 1046–1047.

12.4 So-called 'exceptions' at common law

[12.200] Where there is no statute abrogating or modifying the privity rule, or where there is a statutory provision, but its preconditions have not been met,[64] a beneficiary seeking to enforce a promise for his or her benefit will need to rely upon one of the so-called 'exceptions' to privity. Although the term 'exceptions' is commonly used, there is no true exception to the doctrine of privity. Instead, the apparent exceptions are, in fact, applications of other legal principles to the contractual relationship of promisor, promisee, and third party beneficiary.[65] Similarly, there are 'exceptions' that enable a third party to be subject to a liability originally contained in the contract between two other parties.

[12.205] Some principles operate as 'exceptions' in respect of both benefits and burdens; some only for benefits; and some only for burdens. As to attempts to confer a benefit on a third party, Brennan and Deane JJ in *Trident General Insurance Co Ltd v McNiece Bros Pty Ltd*[66] recently pointed out that the main principles that may provide a remedy for a disappointed beneficiary are agency, trust, and estoppel. To this list Brennan J added recovery of damages,[67] while Deane and Gaudron JJ added unjust enrichment. Some of the exceptions may be better termed 'evasions' in the sense that, despite first appearances that party C is a third party, they in fact represent normal contractual relations between party A and party C.

12.4.1 Agency

(a) Generally

[12.210] Where A has entered into a contract with B, who is acting as agent on behalf of C, then in fact the contract is between A and C, and the privity rule never becomes an issue. The principal, C, will be able to sue and be sued on the contract. The principal (C) will be able to enforce the benefit when his or her agent (B) was acting with actual authority—or where principal C later ratifies the unauthorised act of B. Principal C will be liable on the contract where agent B was acting with actual or ostensible authority.

[12.215] Normally it is immaterial that A is unaware that B is contracting as agent for C. In the case of such an undisclosed principal, A will still be taken to have contracted with C if A has indicated he or she is willing—or has led the agent B to believe that he or she is willing—to treat as a party to the contract anyone on whose behalf B may have been authorised to contract. Such a willingness may be assumed by B in the case of an ordinary contract unless either A has manifested his or her unwillingness, or there are some other circumstances that should lead B to realise that A was unwilling.[68]

---

64 As may occur, for example, in Queensland where there has not been 'acceptance' within a reasonable time as required by the *Property Law Act* 1974 (Qld), ss 55(1) and (6).

65 See, for example, *Trident General Insurance Co Ltd v McNiece Bros Pty Ltd* (1988) 165 CLR 107 at 135 per Brennan J, 143 per Deane J.

66 (1988) 165 CLR 107 at 139–40 per Brennan J, 145–147 per Deane J.

67 This addition has already been addressed above: see [12.25].

68 *Teheran Europe Co Ltd v ST Belton (Tractors) Ltd* [1968] 2 QB 545 at 555 per Lord Diplock.

In the case of an undisclosed principal, either the agent B or undisclosed principal C—but not both—may sue or be sued on the contract.[69]

(b)   Exemption clauses and third parties

[12.220] A particular issue that has frequently arisen is whether a person who is not party to a contract may nevertheless rely upon an exemption from liability contained in that contract. The issue has arisen, in particular, in relation to the carriage of goods—whether by sea, land or air. It has already been mentioned[70] that it is customary for the carrier of goods to insert into the relevant contract of carriage an exemption of liability for loss or damage to those goods. Such an exemption may purport to extend to cover third parties such as the carrier's servants, agents and independent contractors. This measure may be necessary to avoid the owner of goods bypassing the carrier's exemption and instead seeking to make third parties liable. Of course, where the third parties are servants or agents, any liability might ultimately be sheeted home to the carrier on the grounds of vicarious liability. In the case of independent contractors, the carrier may wish to protect an ongoing relationship that may be threatened if the independent contractor is held liable for damage or loss. Prima facie, persons such as the carrier's servants, agents or independent contractors are not protected by such exemptions, despite the exemption purporting to extend protection to them, because they are not parties to the contract of carriage entered into between the carrier and the person shipping the goods.[71]

[12.225] Lord Reid, in *Scruttons Ltd v Midland Silicones Ltd*,[72] suggested that an exclusion clause in a document like a bill of lading may be drafted so as to effectively protect third parties such as stevedores if four conditions were met:

1   the relevant bill of lading must make it clear that the stevedore is intended to be protected;

2   the bill of lading must also make it clear that the carrier is contracting not only on its own behalf but also as agent for the stevedores in relation to the exemption;

3   the carrier was so authorised by the stevedores, although later ratification by the stevedores will do; and

4   any difficulties concerning consideration moving from the stevedores are overcome.[73]

If these four conditions are satisfied, the carrier–promisee effectively contracts as agent for the stevedore–beneficiary with respect to the promise by the cargo owner–promisor not to hold the stevedore liable for any loss or damage to the goods. So long as the stevedore provides consideration, a contract is concluded between the cargo owner and the stevedore that effectively contains the solitary promise by the cargo owner not to hold the stevedore liable.

[12.230] It has since been customary for bills of lading that evidence the contract of carriage to include a '*Himalaya* clause' that complies with Lord Reid's test, and thus effec-

69   *Bain Securities Ltd v Curmi* [1990] 1 ACSR 794.
70   See [12.170].
71   *Wilson v Darling Island Stevedoring and Lighterage Co Ltd* (1956) 95 CLR 43.
72   [1962] AC 446.
73   Ibid at 474.

tively extends the protection of immunities and exemptions contained in the contract to third parties such as the carrier's servants, agents, and independent contractors.[74]

Example: The Eurymedon[75]

A drilling machine was shipped under a bill of lading from England to New Zealand. On arrival in Wellington, the machine was damaged—allegedly as a result of the negligence of the stevedore. The consignee under the bill commenced an action against the stevedore for the loss. The stevedore sought to rely on a clause in the bill that stated: 'No servant or agent of the carrier (including every independent contractor ...) shall in any circumstances whatsoever be under any liability whatsoever to the shipper, consignee or owner of the goods ... for any loss or damage ... arising or resulting directly or indirectly from any act, neglect or default on his part ... and the purpose of all the foregoing provisions of this clause the carrier is or shall deemed to be acting as agent or trustee on behalf of and for the benefit of all persons who are or might be his servants or agents from time to time (including independent contractors).'

A majority of the Privy Council held that the stevedore was able to successfully rely upon the exemption. Applying Lord Reid's test, the first condition was satisfied because the bill made it clear that the independent contractor was to be covered. The second condition was satisfied because it was also made clear in the clause that the carrier was deemed to be acting as agent on behalf of the stevedore. The third condition was satisfied in this case because the stevedore that carried out all stevedoring work in Wellington for the carrier's ships was the wholly owned subsidiary of the stevedore, and the stevedore generally acted as the carrier's agent in New Zealand. If there was not actual authority, then later ratification was sure to follow. Finally, the fourth condition was satisfied because the stevedore was performing an existing contractual duty to a third party—namely the carrier—and this constituted sufficient consideration.[76]

[12.235] Lord Reid's test has since been applied to road carriage cases.[77] It may also be possible to apply the test in the case of a contract not involving carriage of goods but which contains an exemption clause that purports to extend protection to third parties to the contract.

---

74 See, for example, *New Zealand Shipping Co Ltd v AM Satterthwaite & Co Ltd* (the *Eurymedon*) [1975] AC 154; *Port Jackson Stevedoring Pty Ltd v Salmond & Spraggon (Aust) Pty Ltd* (the *New York Star*) (1978) 139 CLR 231 (HC); (1980) 144 CLR 300 (PC). The clause is commonly known as a '*Himalaya* clause' after the name of a vessel in an earlier case *Adler v Dickson* [1955] 1 QB 158, which held that a passenger was entitled to sue the master and crew of the vessel despite a clause in the contract of carriage purporting to exclude them from liability.

75 *New Zealand Shipping Co v AM Satterthwaite & Co Ltd* [1975] AC 154.

76 See [6.220]. The carrier is described as 'the third party' in this sense because it was a third party to the contract being constructed between the cargo owner and the stevedore for which consideration was required to move from the promisee stevedore to support the cargo owner's promise not to hold the stevedore liable. It should not be confused with the prima facie appearance that the stevedore was a third party to the contract of carriage between the cargo owner and the carrier.

77 See, for example, *Celthene Pty Ltd v WKJ Hauliers Pty Ltd* [1981] 1 NSWLR 606; *Life Savers (Australasia) Pty Ltd v Frigmobile Pty Ltd* [1983] 1 NSWLR 431.

12.4.2 *Trust*

[12.240] The privity rule may be evaded where a trust is recognised as having been created. Where a trust is created, a trustee holds property (which may include a promise as a chose in action) on behalf of a beneficiary (also referred to as 'cestui que trust'). It has long been recognised that trust may be a means of averting any hardship that follows from the privity rule where in particular circumstances the promisee B may be regarded as holding the benefit of the promise as trustee for and on behalf of the third party C.[78] Where the promisee is a trustee, the third party does not become a party to the contract but instead acquires an equitable interest in the promise.[79] The contract binds only the promisor and the promisee; the third party beneficiary is unable to enforce the promise as if he or she were privy to the contract. The third party can enforce the promise indirectly by an action in which the promisee is joined as a defendant.[80]

[12.245] For a trust to be recognised, there need only be the requisite intention to create a trust. However, the greatest obstacle to the trust device being utilised as a sufficient response to the injustice that may follow an application of the privity rule has been the inconsistent approaches taken by the courts on the question of whether the requisite intention has been shown.[81] While an express statement of intention should pose no problem, greater difficulty has been encountered when attempting to infer the requisite intention. Indeed, the cases are full of contradictory decisions on seemingly identical facts.[82] Some cases cautioned against inferring the necessary intention from general words,[83] while others readily inferred the existence of a trust—sometimes merely from the circumstance that the contract was made for the benefit of a third party.[84]

[12.250] In *Trident General Insurance Co Ltd v McNiece Bros Pty Ltd* Mason CJ and Wilson J suggested a way forward:

> [The] apparent uncertainty should be resolved by stating that the courts will recognize the existence of a trust when it appears from the language of the parties, construed in its context, including the matrix of circumstances, that the parties so intended. We are speaking of express trusts, the existence of which depends on intention. In divining intention from the language which the parties have employed the courts may look to the nature of the transaction and

---

78   *Lloyd's v Harper* (1880) 16 Ch D 290; *Les Affréteurs Réunis Société Anonyme v Leopold Walford (London) Ltd* [1919] AC 801; *Wilson v Darling Island Stevedoring & Lighterage Co Ltd* (1956) 95 CLR 43 at 67.

79   *Construction Engineering (Aust) Pty Ltd v Hexyl Pty Ltd* (1985) 155 CLR 541.

80   *Birmingham v Renfrew* (1937) 57 CLR 666 at 686; *Trident General Insurance Co Ltd v McNiece Bros Pty Ltd* (1988) 165 CLR 107 at 135 per Brennan J.

81   *Trident General Insurance Co Ltd v McNiece Bros Pty Ltd* (1988) 165 CLR 107 at 120–1 per Mason CJ and Wilson J.

82   N Seddon & MP Ellinghaus, *Cheshire and Fifoot's Law of Contract*, 7th edn, Butterworths, Sydney, 1997, p 272 usefully provides a list of different types of contracts together with, in each case, cases which have and which have not recognised the requisite intention.

83   *Vandepitte v Preferred Accident Insurance Co Corp of New York* [1933] AC 70 at 79–80; *Re Schebsman* [1944] Ch 83 at 104.

84   *Robertson v Wait* (1853) 8 Ex 299; 155 ER 1360; *Lloyd's v Harper* (1880) 16 Ch D 290; *Les Affréteurs Réunis Société Anonyme v Leopold Walford (London) Ltd* [1919] AC 801; *Williams v Baltic Insurance Association of London Ltd* [1924] 2 KB 282.

the circumstances, including commercial necessity, in order to infer or impute intention.[85]

Similarly, Deane J stated:

> The requisite intention should be inferred if it clearly appears that it was the intention of the promisee that the third party should himself be entitled to insist upon performance of the promise and receipt of the benefit and if trust is, in the circumstances, the appropriate legal mechanism for giving effect to that intention. A fortiori, equity's requirement of an intention to create a trust will be at least prima facie satisfied if the terms of the contract expressly or impliedly manifest that intention as the joint intention of both promisor and promisee.[86]

Despite these clearer directions, there still appears to be a reluctance to recognise the existence of a trust in some circumstances.[87]

[12.255] It has been suggested that one means by which the difficult question of establishing the requisite intention might be avoided would be if, instead of seeking to establish an express or implied trust, the court were prepared to impose a *constructive* trust on one or other of the parties to a contract where it would be unconscionable to allow the promisor to renege.[88] However, like the equitable estoppel exemption,[89] such an approach would not provide a complete answer, because not all cases of attempts to confer benefits on third parties involve unconscionable conduct by the promisor.

12.4.3   Equitable estoppel

[12.260] In *Trident General Insurance Co Ltd v McNiece Bros Pty Ltd*, Brennan J and Deane J raised the possibility of a third party being able to enforce the benefit of a promise by means of an equitable estoppel. Estoppel may be an available recourse where the promisor A's promise has induced third party C to act or refrain from acting in reliance such that he or she will suffer detriment if A is allowed to resile from the promise.[90] Naturally, the difficulty in relying on estoppel as a solution to the hardships created by the privity rule is that it requires unconscionable conduct on the part of promisor A, which will not be present in all cases of third parties seeking to obtain the benefit of the promise. Further, any remedy that is yielded by the estoppel will be proportionate to the detrimental reliance,[91] which only in some cases will involve enforcing A's promise.

---

85   (1988) 165 CLR 107 at 121.

86   Ibid, at 147.

87   See, for example, *Burleigh Forest Estate Management Pty Ltd v Cigna Insurance Australia Ltd* [1992] 2 Qd R 54 (FC).

88   N Seddon & MP Ellinghaus, *Cheshire and Fifoot's Law of Contract*, 7th edn, Butterworths, Sydney, 1997, p 275.

89   See [12.4.3].

90   *Waltons Stores (Interstate) Ltd v Maher* (1988) 164 CLR 387.

91   See [7.225].

12.4.4 Unjust enrichment

[12.265] In *Trident General Insurance Co Ltd v McNiece Bros Pty Ltd*, Deane J suggested that where a promisor (such as an insurer under an insurance policy) had received consideration (such as the moneys payable for a promised indemnity) but then refused to observe that promise—by, for example, refusing to indemnify the third party on the ground that the third party was not a party to the contract of insurance—then conceivably the circumstances could give rise to a cause of action founded upon principles of unjust enrichment.[92] His Honour acknowledged, however, that 'the path by which relief would be granted in such a case might well involve some reassessment of the extent of curial powers, both statutory and inherent, to mould the relief appropriate to do justice in the circumstances of a particular case.'[93] However, he did not think it necessary in the *Trident* case to embark upon that exercise.

[12.270] In the same case, however, Gaudron J did venture a formulation of unjust enrichment that would provide the third party with a remedy. Her Honour was of the view that where the consideration is wholly executed in favour of a promisor under a contract made for the benefit of a third party, a rule that the third party may not bring an action to secure the benefit of the contract permits the possibility that the promisor may be unjustly enriched to the extent that the promise is not fulfilled.[94] She suggested that a promisor who has accepted agreed consideration for a promise to benefit a third party is unjustly enriched at the expense of the third party to the extent that the promise is unfulfilled and the non-fulfilment does not attract proportional legal consequences. This possibility may be prevented, in her Honour's view, by recognition that a promisor who has accepted agreed consideration for a promise to benefit a third party owes an obligation to the third party to fulfil that promise and that the third party has a corresponding right to bring action to secure the benefit of the promise.[95] The circumstances that warranted the imposition of an obligation—the acceptance of agreed consideration for a promise to benefit a third party—also necessarily required that the content and duration of that obligation should ordinarily correspond with the content and duration of the contractual obligation owed by the promisee. Thus, if the obligation as between promisor and promisee is varied, modified or extinguished, then correspondingly the obligation of the promisor to the third party will be varied, modified, or extinguished.[96]

12.4.5 Torts

[12.275] In some cases an action in torts may offer a detour around the privity rule. For example, in appropriate case a third party might effectively obtain the benefit of a

---

92 (1998) 165 CLR 107 at 145–146, referring to *Pavey & Matthews Pty Ltd v Paul* (1987) 162 CLR 221 at 227, 256–257; *Australia and New Zealand Banking Group Ltd v Westpac Banking Corporation* (1988) 164 CLR 662 at 673–674.
93 (1988) 165 CLR 107 at 146.
94 Ibid at 175–176.
95 Ibid at 176.
96 Ibid at 177. This approach has been subject to criticism: see KB Sho, 'Privity of contract and restitution' (1989) 105 LQR 4; DA Butler, 'Privity of contract in Queensland' (1990) 10 *Queensland Lawyer* 147.

contract by bringing an action for economic loss arising out of negligent performance of the contract.

[12.280] The potential for such claims has been enhanced by recent decisions by the High Court.[97] In *Bryan v Maloney*,[98] a builder was held to owe a duty of care to a subsequent purchaser of a house. A builder and a subsequent purchaser were considered to be in a proximate relationship for a number of reasons, including the fact that for many a home is the most expensive investment they will make in their lives. The end result is that although a subsequent purchaser is not privy to the contract between the builder and the original owner—and is therefore unable to enforce the promises made in that contract by the builder, including those relating to the quality of the work performed—the subsequent purchaser will nevertheless have an action for the economic loss that he or she suffers due to negligent construction resulting from the breach of the builder's tortious duty of care.

Further support for a tortious detour around privity is provided by *Hill v Van Erp*.[99] In that case, a solicitor breached her contract of retainer by failing to ensure that a will was validly executed by a testator—with the result that the intended beneficiary was disappointed. Although the intended beneficiary was not privy to the contract between the testatrix and the solicitor, the High Court held that the disappointed beneficiary nevertheless had an action in negligence for the solicitor's breach of a duty of care. Once again, the constraints of the privity rule were avoided, and a third party to a contract was able to recover with respect to her economic loss.

Significant considerations that support the recognition of a duty of care in such cases include the known vulnerability of the third party and the finite class to which the third party belongs, so there is little risk of the imposition of a duty amounting to 'an indeterminate amount for an indeterminate time to an indeterminate class.'[100] Naturally, however, this option does not offer a panacea for all cases of third parties seeking a remedy.

12.4.6   Trade Practices Act

[12.285] In a similar fashion to the recognition of a claim for the third party in tort, a third party to a contract may obtain relief pursuant to the *Trade Practices Act* 1974 (Cth), s 52 in the case of a promisor who has engaged in misleading or deceptive conduct.[101]

Example: Accounting Systems 2000 (Developments) Pty Ltd v CCH Australia Ltd[102]

The promisor acquired the right to use, but not the copyright in, a computer program. The promisor then purported to assign the copyright in the software to the promisee, warranting that it was entitled to do so. This was a false statement by the

---

97   See, for example, *Bryan v Maloney* (1995) 182 CLR 609; *Hill v Van Erp* (1997) 188 CLR 159.
98   (1995) 182 CLR 609.
99   (1997) 188 CLR 159.
100   *Bryan v Maloney* (1995) 182 CLR 609 at 618 citing *Ultramares Corporation v Touche* 174 NE 441 at 444 (1931).
101   See Stewart (1999) 73 ALJ 353 at 365.
102   (1993) 42 FCR 470.

promisor, although it did represent its honest belief. The promisee was controlled by CCH, although CCH was a third party to the agreement between the promisor and the promisee. CCH was under the belief that copyright had been assigned to the promisee, and therefore took a licence from the promisee and thereafter made certain expenditures.

The Full Court of the Federal Court held that CCH could successfully claim damages under s 52 for the promisor's false statement that it held the copyright in the software and was entitled to grant licences for its use. Where misleading conduct was found in the making of the actual promise by the promisor, the absence of privity between the complainant and the corporation that engaged in the misleading and deceptive conduct is irrelevant. Accordingly, while CCH was a third party to the contract between the promisor and the promisee and therefore unable to enforce warranties contained in that contract, it was nevertheless able to obtain a remedy by virtue of s 52.

[12.290] It was also held in relation to the correct measure of damages under s 82 in such a case that where the misleading conduct complained of is of a promissory nature, the court should not feel itself limited to applying the usual tort measure of loss. Instead, the court should focus on the causative consequences of the conduct that is the basis of the complaint.[103]

12.4.7   Assignment and novation

[12.295] Promisee B may effectively assign the benefit of his or her rights to the third party C. Assignment effects an 'exception to the privity rule since a person who is not party to the original contract is nevertheless able to enforce rights arising under it.

[12.300] Each Australian jurisdiction has enacted legislation[104] in similar form, prescribing three requirements for an effective assignment:

- the assignment must be absolute, inasmuch as the entire interest of the assignor (the promisee) must be transferred to the assignee (the third party);
- the assignment must be in writing, signed by the assignor (the promisee);
- notice must be given to the debtor.

If these three requirements are satisfied, the promisor A may be sued by the assignee/third party C alone, in his or her own name.

[12.305] Where, however, the assignment fails to comply with all three requirements, it may still be effective as an equitable assignment, in which case the assignee/third party C must join the assignor/promisee B either as a co-plaintiff or a co-defendant in the action.[105] No particular form is required for the assignment to be effective in equity. It need not be in writing, nor is it necessary to give notice to the debtor/

---

103   (1993) 42 FCR 470 at 510.

104   *Conveyancing Act* 1919 (NSW), s 12 (also applies in ACT: *Law of Property (Miscellaneous Provisions) Ordinance* 1958 (ACT)); *Property Law Act* 1974 (Qld), s 199; *Law of Property Act* 1936 (SA) s 15 (also applies in NT); *Conveyancing and Law of Property Act* 1884 (Tas), s 86; *Property Law Act* 1958 (Vic), s 134; *Property Law Act* 1969 (WA), s 20.

105   *Williams v Atlantic Assurance Co* [1933] 1 KB 81.

promisor A—although the debtor/promisor will not be bound by the assignment until he or she receives notice.[106]

[12.310] An assignment of contractual rights will not be possible where the contract excludes such an assignment,[107] or where the contract involves a degree of personal relations (as, for example, in an employment agreement).[108]

[12.315] In some instances, the assignment of contractual rights to a stranger to the original contract is effected by operation of law. Examples are the passing of rights on death to the personal representative of the deceased party under a contract not involving personal characteristics[109] and the vesting of rights under a contract in a trustee in bankruptcy upon a person becoming insolvent.[110]

[12.320] While the benefit under the contract may be assigned, it is not possible to assign a burden or liability under the contract unless the burden is assigned as a condition of enjoying the rights.[111] However, both benefits and burdens may be transferred to a third party under an arrangement known as a 'novation'. A novation occurs where an original contract between A and B is discharged and replaced by a fresh contract between A and B, or between A and C.[112] In the latter case, the effect is that rights and liabilities that were enjoyed or owed by B may be subsequently enjoyed or owed by C, a third party to the original contract. Unlike assignment, a novation involves the creation of new rights and liabilities rather than the transfer of existing rights or liabilities. Consequently, novation requires that all three persons involved— A, B, and C—must agree to the transaction, in contrast to an assignment, which is a transaction between the creditor B and the assignee C, to which the assent of the debtor A is not needed.[113]

12.4.8 Use of property

[12.325] Principles of land law provide exceptions to the privity rule in relation to the transfer of a lease and in respect of the use of land. This is because a lease, for example, not only creates contractual rights but also an interest in the land.

[12.330] Accordingly, where a lessee transfers a lease to a new lessee, the new lessee will be able to enforce the benefit and be bound by those covenants in the lease that 'touch and concern' the land—such as covenants concerning the repair and maintenance of the property and the uses to which the property may be put. A similar position applies where the landlord transfers his or her interest in the reversion.

[12.335] Where the owner of land sells part of it, he or she may wish to restrict the use the purchaser may make of the property. The privity rule would ordinarily prevent a third party who is a subsequent purchaser from being bound by such a covenant.

---

106 *Stocks v Dobson* (1854) 4 De GM&G 11; 43 ER 411.
107 *Helstan Securities Ltd v Hertfordshire County Council* [1978] 3 All ER 262.
108 *Nokes v Doncaster Amalgamated Colleries Ltd* [1940] AC 1014.
109 *Stubbs v Holywell Railway Co* (1867) LR 2 Ex 311.
110 *Bankruptcy Act* 1966 (Cth), s 58.
111 *Aspden v Seddon (No 2)* (1876) 1 Ex D 496 (right to mine certain land assigned on condition that the assignee pay compensation for any disturbance to buildings on the surface of the property).
112 *Scarf v Jardine* (1882) 7 App Cas 345 at 351 per Lord Selborne.
113 *Olsson v Dyson* (1969) 120 CLR 365 at 388 per Windeyer J.

Nevertheless, equity may grant an injunction preventing breach of the covenant where the subsequent purchaser acquires the land with notice of the covenant.[114]

Example: Tulk v Moxhay[115]

The plaintiff owned vacant land and houses in Leicester Square. He subsequently sold the land in the centre of the square to Elms, who covenanted to keep and maintain the land as a square garden and a leisure ground. Subsequently, the land was resold a number of times until it was purchased by the defendant. The defendant knew of the covenant, but nevertheless intended to build on the land.

It was held that the plaintiff was entitled to an injunction restraining the defendant from building on the land. If such a purchaser had notice of the covenant but was not bound by the covenant, land retained by the vendor nearby might lose value, which equity as a court of conscience would not allow.

Consequently, there are three elements that a plaintiff seeking to enforce a covenant against a subsequent purchaser of the land must show:

- the covenant must be negative in character;[116]
- the covenant must touch and concern the land which is benefited;[117] and
- the plaintiff must retain land that is in the close vicinity of the land subject to the covenant.[118]

[12.340] Although it was made clear in *Tulk v Moxhay* that an essential element was that the vendor must retain property in the neighbourhood of that burdened by the covenant, the rule was nevertheless applied with respect to the mortgage or purchase of a ship by a purchaser with notice that it was subject to an existing charterparty.[119]

Example: Lord Strathcona Steamship Co Ltd v Dominion Coal Co

The owner of the steamship *Lord Strathcona* chartered her for five years for use on the St Lawrence River in Canada each summer. Subsequently, the steamer was twice resold, the ultimate buyer knowing of the charterparty but refusing to allow the charterer to use the steamer.

The Privy Council held that since the ultimate buyer bought the ship with notice that it was subject to a restrictive covenant in favour of the charterer, it was bound by that covenant.

The decision of the Privy Council to grant the injunction in favour of the charterer was made despite the fact that, unlike the plaintiff in *Tulk v Moxhay*, the charterer had no proprietary interest in other property in the vicinity of the property being bur-

---

114 *Tulk v Moxhay* (1848) 2 Ph 774; 41 ER 1143.

115 (1848) 2 Ph 774; 41 ER 1143.

116 *Haywood v Brunswick Permanent Benefit Building Society* (1881) 8 QBD 403.

117 *Rogers v Hosegood* [1900] 2 Ch 388.

118 *Clem Smith Nominees Pty Ltd v Farrelly* (1978) 20 SASR 227. It may be open to doubt the extent to which the rule in *Tulk v Moxhay* may still be called upon in jurisdictions which have enacted a Torrens system of land based on indefeasibility of registered title.

119 *De Mattos v Gibson* (1858) 4 De G&J 276 at 282; 45 ER 108 at 110 per Knight-Bruce LJ; *Lord Strathcona Steamship Co Ltd v Dominion Coal Co* [1926] AC 108.

dened. An important component in the defendant's unconscionable conduct was missing. Notwithstanding this difficulty, the *Lord Strathcona* case has in the past been accepted as binding on Australian courts, although it has been confined to its narrowest terms in the form of a ship acquired with notice that it is subject to a charterparty, and only so far as can be protected by injunction, on the basis that a ship is a chattel of peculiar value to the person in whom the right to use it is vested.[120]

12.4.9 Collateral contract

[12.345] There may be a case where, despite appearances that C is a third party to a contract between A and B, the correct analysis is that the consideration for a promise by C was A's entry into the contract with B, a tripartite collateral contract.[121] For example, a manufacturer of goods may make a promise about their quality, in return for which the consumer enters into a contract with a retailer for the purchase of the goods.[122]

[12.350] In such a case—as in agency—there would be a normal contractual relationship between A and C, and the privity issue does not arise. Under that contract, party C agrees to be subject to a liability that party A may enforce.

12.4.10 Restraint of trade

[12.355] It is discussed elsewhere[123] that prima facie, all restraints on trade are void. However, a restraint may be valid if it can be justified as being reasonable both in the interests of the parties to the contract and in the public interest. It has been held that although restraint of trade is generally a matter between the parties to the contract, it may incidentally have significance for third parties. For example, it has been recognised that the governing body of a sporting competition and the public have an interest in teams taking part in the competition having a spread of talent, so the competition is not dominated by one team or a few teams. For this reason, a reasonable player draft or salary cap system might be agreed between the governing body of a competition and individual clubs, which effectively burden individual players who are third parties to that agreement.[124]

12.5 International perspectives

12.5.1 New Zealand

[12.360] In relation to a third party beneficiary seeking to enforce the benefit of a promise made for his or her benefit, as in Queensland and Western Australia, the privity rule has been abrogated by statute in the form of the *Contracts (Privity) Act* 1982.

---

120 *Shell Oil of Australia Ltd v McIlraith McEacharn Ltd* (1944) 45 SR (NSW) 144 at 150.
121 See, for example, *Wells (Merstham) Ltd v Buckland Sand & Silica Co Ltd* [1965] 2 QB 170.
122 See also *Trade Practices Act* 1974 (Cth), Part V, Div 2A (consumer may in certain circumstances bring an action against a manufacturer where goods are not fit for the purpose for which they were purchased (s 74B); do not correspond with a description by which they were sold (s 74C); are not of merchantable quality (s 74D); or where sold by sample do not correspond in quality with the sample (s 74E)).
123 See [18.35].
124 See, for example, *Adamson v NSW Rugby League Ltd* (1991) 31 FCR 242; *Wickham v Canberra District Rugby League Football Club Ltd* (1998) ATPR 41-664.

Section 4 of the Act provides that where a promise contained in a deed or contract confers or purports to confer a benefit on a person (designated by name, description or reference to a class) who is not a party to the deed or contract (whether or not the person is in existence at the time when the deed or contract is made) the promisor is under an obligation, enforceable at the suit of that person, to perform that promise.

[12.365] Unlike the Queensland and Western Australian statutes, the New Zealand statute defines 'benefit' in s 2 as including any advantage, any immunity, any limitation or other qualification of an obligation to which a person is or maybe subject or a right to which a person is or maybe entitled and any extension or other improvement of a right or rights to which a person is or maybe entitled. The definition contemplates, therefore, that the benefit may be by way of exclusion of liability as well as by way of a positive grant. Although s 4 refers to the right of a third party beneficiary to 'enforce' the promise—which is not strictly the same thing as a beneficiary seeking to rely on a benefit by way of a defence—it has been held that a third party may be treated as enforcing a promise that confers an immunity by pleading it in his or her defence to a claim by the promisor.[125]

[12.370] It is clear that the need to designate the beneficiary in specific terms precludes the claim of an 'incidental beneficiary' who is not named but nevertheless receives or should receive a benefit as an incidence of its performance.[126] The section is also subject to a proviso that means either of the contracting parties may seek to show that it was not intended that the promise should create an obligation enforceable at the suit of the beneficiary. It may include an express agreement that there was no such intention, or even evidence that a benefit has been conferred on a designated third party by mistake.[127]

[12.375] Pursuant to s 5, the parties to the contract may vary or cancel the promise until:

- the position of the beneficiary has been materially altered by his or her own or another's reliance on the promise;
- the beneficiary has obtained judgment upon the promise; or
- the beneficiary has obtained the award of an arbitrator or upon a submission relating to the promise.

This section is subject to two exceptions. Section 6 allows the contracting parties to vary or discharge the contract:

- by agreement between the parties and the beneficiary; or
- pursuant to an express provision in the contract known to the beneficiary, where the beneficiary has not materially altered his or her position in reliance on the promise before the provision became known to him or her.

Section 7 allows either contracting party to apply to a court to authorise a variation or discharge. In such a case, the court may order the payment of compensation to the beneficiary as it thinks just. Like the Australian provisions, s 9 provides that the promi-

---

125   *Steel & Tube Ltd v Works & Development Services Ltd* (unreported, High Court, 12 June 1992).
126   See, for example, *Cassidy v Woolworths (NZ) Ltd* [1993] DCR 638 (principal shareholder of contracting company not designated as beneficiary).
127   See, *McKenzie v Smith* (unreported, High Court, 12 July 1990).

sor may assert any contractual defences he or she may have in answer to a claim by the beneficiary.

[12.380] The *Contracts (Privity) Act* 1982 does not effect the common law.[128] Accordingly, where the terms of the statute are not satisfied, the common law and its exceptions will still be relevant.

[12.385] The statute does not have any effect on the privity rule in relation to attempts to impose burdens on third parties. In this connection, the same issues concerning the recent recognition of duties of care in respect of, for example, defective buildings as recently identified in *Bryan v Maloney* arise equally in New Zealand.[129]

12.5.2 United States

[12.390] United States courts also observe a general rule that while performance of a contract may benefit persons other than the parties who made it, they cannot enforce it.[130] However, two exceptional cases were developed in which a third party could enforce the benefit of a contract: the case of a 'creditor beneficiary' whereby the creditor of a promisee was entitled to enforce the promise by a promisor to pay the promisee's debt,[131] and the case of a 'donee beneficiary', whereby a promisee obtained the promise from the promisor with the intention of making a gift to the beneficiary, who was in some way related to the promisee, or conferring upon him or her a right against the promisor.[132]

[12.395] The Restatement (Second) has had a major influence on courts in many jurisdictions with respect to privity.[133] The Restatement (Second) is cast in terms of 'intended beneficiary' (a term used to denote a beneficiary who acquires rights under a contract)[134] and 'incidental beneficiary' (a term used to denote a beneficiary who does not acquire rights under a contract).[135] Under the Restatement (Second) §302(1), an intended beneficiary is one who satisfies two requirements:

1   recognition of a right to performance in the beneficiary is appropriate to effectuate the intention of the party; and

2   either:

   (a)   the performance of the promise will satisfy an obligation of the promisee to pay money to the beneficiary; or

   (b)   the circumstances indicate that the promisee intends to give the beneficiary the benefit of the promised performance.

This definition resolves previous disagreement about who must have the necessary intention to benefit the third person, in favour of it being the promisee's intention. It

---

128   See s 14.

129   *Invercargill CC v Hamlin* [1996] 1 NZLR 513.

130   *Mississippi High School Activities Association v Farris* 501 So 2d 393 (Miss 1987); *Burke & Thomas v International Organisation of Masters, Mates and Pilots* 600 P 2d 1982 (Wash 1979).

131   *Lawrence v Fox* 20 NY 268 (1859).

132   *Seaver v Ransom* 120 NE 639 (NY 1918) (promisee agreeing with promisor that the promisor would provide for the promisee's favourite niece in his will).

133   See, for example, *Choate, Hall & Stewart v SCA Service* 392 NE 2d 1045 (Mass 1979); *Guy v Liederbach* 459A 2b 744 (Pa 1983).

134   See §302.

135   See §315.

is therefore not necessary for both parties to so intend.[136] It is not necessary for the beneficiary to be identified at the time the promise is made, provided the beneficiary may be identified at the time the promise is to be performed.[137] However, failure by the contract to identify the beneficiary may in some cases be interpreted as meaning that the beneficiary is only incidental.[138]

[12.400] One means used by some courts to determine whether there was an intention to benefit the beneficiary is to ask whether the promisor is required to render the promised performance directly to the beneficiary, rather than to the promisee. If the performance is rendered directly to the promisee, there may be a stronger basis to argue that the third party is merely an incidental beneficiary and therefore unable to recover.[139] The court will also give effect to an express provision that the third party has the right to enforce the contract[140] or that the third party does not have that right.[141]

[12.405] An intended beneficiary has a right against the promisor and need not join the promisee in any action.[142] In addition, the beneficiary retains any right he or she may have had against the promisee prior to the contract between the promisor and the promisee. Naturally, in addition to the beneficiary's rights, the promisee retains his or her rights against the promisor. The promisee is able to bring an action for damages or specific performance in the usual manner—although where the rights of the beneficiary arise from a 'gift' promise,[143] the promisee will suffer no substantial loss, and therefore may only recover nominal damages. In such a case, specific performance may present the only effective remedy.[144] By contrast, where the performance of the promise will satisfy the duty of the promisee to pay money to the beneficiary, the promisee will usually have no difficulty in showing substantial damages.[145]

[12.410] American courts have agreed that there is a time at which the beneficiary's right becomes 'vested', such that it is no longer at risk of being discharged or modified by the agreement of the promisor and promisee. The Restatement (Second) §311(3) states that the promisor and promisee have the power to discharge or modify the duty until, before receiving notification of any discharge or modification, the beneficiary materially changes his or her position in justifiable reliance on the promise or brings suit on it or manifests assent to it at the request of the promisor or promisee. The time of assent by the beneficiary is therefore the earliest time at which the beneficiary's right

---

136 Cf *Spires v Hanover Fire Insurance Co* 70 A 2d 828 (Pa 1950).
137 *Commercial Insurance Co v Pacific-Peru Construction Corp* 558 F 2d 948 (9th Cir 1977).
138 Restatement (Second) §308 comment (a).
139 *Buchman Plumbing Co v Regents of University* 215 NW 2d 479 (Minn 1974); *Lonsdale v Chesterfield* 662 P 2d 385 (Wash 1983).
140 See, for example, *Cobert v Home Owners' Warranty Corp* 391 SE 2d 263 (Va 1990).
141 *Mississippi High School Activities Association v Farris* 501 So 2d 393 (Miss 1987).
142 *Bourer v Devenes* 121 A 566 (Conn 1923).
143 That is, where the promisee intended to confer the benefit on the third party as a gift, rather than its being in fulfilment of a prior obligation such as a debt owed by the promisee to the third party.
144 *Drewen v Bank of Manhatten Co* 155 A 2d 529 (NJ 1959) (specific performance if the remedy at law is inadequate).
145 *Heins v Byers* 219 NW 287 (Minn 1928).

can become vested.[146] It is, however, possible for the contract to stipulate a different time for vesting of the beneficiary's right.[147]

[12.415] Generally, the beneficiary's right is subject to any defences in claims that the promisor may have against the promisee under the contract.[148] These defences include misrepresentation, mistake, duress, and illegality.[149] Once again, this is subject to the contract expressly providing that the beneficiary's right is not subject to the defences available to the promisor against the promisee.[150] Similarly, the promisor may conduct itself in such a way as to estop itself from relying on defences that might otherwise have been available.[151]

12.5.3   Japan

[12.420] As noted in previous chapters, the rules on offer and acceptance in Japanese law function relatively similarly to those in common law jurisdictions. In most cases, the identity of the parties contracting will be clear, and issues of privity or standing to assert a claim in contract do not arise. In some circumstances, however a court may find contractual privity to achieve a desired result. A case cited by Ramsayer and Nakazato[152] is a good example. In *Okazaki v Nankai kotsu*, the plaintiff routinely made bookings with a particular taxi driver who worked for the Nankai kotsu taxi company. The driver would frequently fail to charge her a fare. On one occasion, instead of taking her home, the taxi driver took the plaintiff to a secluded place and raped her. The plaintiff sued the taxi company, Nankai, for breach of the promise to transport her safely. The issue was whether there was a contract between the plaintiff and Nankai, given that she probably had no intention of paying. The court found that there was, and that Nankai was liable in contract. What the case also illustrates is the tendency identified by some Japanese law scholars for courts to characterise situations as contractual rather than tortious.

[12.425] Japanese courts will also enforce contracts made for the benefit of third parties. If a contract is made for the benefit of a third party, then the third party acquires an independent right to enforce the contract.[153] If follows, however, that either party to the contract can also assert its defences in relation to the contract against the third party.[154]

---

146   See, for example, *Olson v Etheridge* 686 NE 2d 563 (Ill 1997).
147   Restatement (Second) §311(1). For example, the contract may stipulate that the right vests as soon as the contract is made.
148   Restatement (Second) §309.
149   See, for example, *Rouse v United States* 215 F 2d 872 (DC Cir 1954).
150   *Goldstein v National Liberty Insurance Co* 175 NE 359 (NY 1931).
151   *Levy v Empire Insurance Co* 379 F 2d 860 (5th Cir 1967).
152   *Okazaki v Nankai kotsu KK* 179 *Hanrei taimuzu* 128 (Osaka District Ct 30 June 1965) cited in *Japanese Law* (U Chicago, 1999) 48.
153   Civil Code Article 537.
154   Civil Code Article 539.

Part V
Vitiating Factors

Although the elements of a valid contract may appear to be present, in certain situations, either one of the parties to a contract may be entitled to rescind the contract due to the conduct of the other party; or the contract may be void due to the lack of one of the essential elements of the contract.

The right to rescind a contract may arise where one party has made a misrepresentation to another, and it induced the contract, or where one party has unduly influenced the decision of the other, unlawfully compelled the other's decision, or engaged in unconscionable conduct or sharp practice to induce the agreement. A right to rescind the contract may also be given by statute where one party has engaged in prohibited conduct—such as misleading or deceptive conduct under the *Trade Practices Act* 1974 (Cth)—or one party has engaged in illegal conduct, such as the commission of a crime. The second type of situation referred to above is where the contract is actually void *ab initio*. This means that the contract was void from the beginning and never actually existed. A contract will be void *ab initio* where there has been a common mistake, mutual mistake, or unilateral mistake as to identity, or where a statutory provision provides for a contract to be void for illegality. In each case, one or more of the essential elements of a contract will be missing. For example, in the case of mutual mistake, the parties will be at cross purposes, and therefore lack consensus in their agreement.

Although the two general situations described above are related, in that they ultimately result in a contract's being void, a contract may only be rescinded through the act of one of the parties—whereas no act is required for a contract that is void *ab initio*. An important consequence of this distinction is that although a contract may be voidable and therefore susceptible to rescission, it will still come into existence, and rights and obligations may ensue. By contrast, a contract void *ab initio* never existed; therefore, no rights or obligations are created.

This Part considers the effects of misrepresentation, mistake, duress, undue influence, unconscionability, and illegality of a contract.

Chapter 13

Misrepresentation and misleading or deceptive conduct

13.1 Introduction

[13.05] During the course of most contractual negotiations, the parties will frequently make oral statements concerning the proposed arrangement. These pre-contractual statements may eventually form part of the contract as a term, or may remain mere representations that were intended to induce a party to enter the contract.[1] Where a pre-contractual oral statement is untrue, the misinformed party may seek redress from the maker of the statement by arguing one or all of the following:

- the statement formed part of the contract (that is, it was a term) and as the statement is now untrue, there has been a breach of the contract that may entitle the misinformed party to terminate the contract and seek damages; or
- the statement was a representation, and as the statement is now untrue there has been a misrepresentation that may entitle the misinformed party to rescind the contract and, in some cases, seek damages.
- The statement constituted misleading or deceptive conduct that may entitle the misled party to rescind the contract and seek damages pursuant to either the *Trade Practices Act* 1974 or the relevant State *Fair Trading Act*.

The misinformed party may pursue any of these claims but will ultimately be required to elect at judgment.[2]

[13.10] Before considering the rights of a party at common law for a misrepresentation, the effect of statutory regulation in the area of misrepresentation is briefly examined. The *Trade Practices Act* 1974 (Cth) and the equivalent State *Fair Trading Acts*[3] have, in certain circumstances, usurped the common law concept of misrepresentation. Section 52 of the *Trade Practices Act* 1974 (Cth) prohibits a corporation from engaging in misleading or deceptive conduct in the course of trade and commerce.[4] Since its commencement in 1974, this section has become increasingly significant as a tool for regulating the conduct of commercial entities and providing redress for misled parties in situations where the common law may not have recognised a valid right. The courts have interpreted s 52 as having wide application limited only by the wording of the section itself. In a significant number of cases, although the courts are in no way bound by the common law, the judges have drawn upon, and sought guidance from,

---

1   The effect of an oral statement becoming a term of the contract was considered at [8.220]–[8.295].
2   *Bissett v Wilkinson* [1926] All ER 343.
3   NSW: *Fair Trading Act* 1987, s 42; Qld: *Fair Trading Act* 1989, s 38; Vic: *Fair Trading Act* 1985, s 11; SA: *Fair Trading Act* 1987, s 56; WA: *Fair Trading Act* 1987, s 10.
4   NSW: *Fair Trading Act* 1987, s 42; Qld: *Fair Trading Act* 1989, s 38; Vic: *Fair Trading Act* 1985, s 11; SA: *Fair Trading Act* 1987, s 56; WA: *Fair Trading Act* 1987, s 10.

the common law principle of misrepresentation[5] in reaching a decision concerning s 52—especially in regard to the interpretation of misleading conduct and the appropriate remedies. Therefore, it is appropriate to consider the principles underlying the common law first, and then to examine the operation of the statutory overlay provided by the *Trade Practices Act* 1974 (Cth).

13.2 Common law: elements of misrepresentation

[13.15] Misrepresentation can be defined as a false statement of past or existing fact made by the representor to the representee, at or before the contract was entered into, which induced, and was intended to induce, the contract.[6] Each of these elements is considered in turn.

13.3 False statement of past or present fact

[13.20] A misrepresentation is founded upon the existence of a false statement of past or present fact. The statement made by the representor must actually be false in fact. No claim will lie for a representation that is true. Whether a statement of past or present fact has been made is a question of fact. It may be possible for conduct such as 'a nod or a wink, or a shake of the head or a smile intended to induce'[7] to form a representation of fact, particularly where it occurs in response to a question. A statement of past or present fact must be distinguished from other types of statements such as opinions, law, intention, promises, and puffs. The general proposition is that those types of statements are not actionable as misrepresentations, unless the person making the statement has misrepresented the state of his or her mind.[8]

13.3.1 Statement of future intent, promise or assurance

[13.25] It is often simply stated that a representation about a person's intention or a future state of affairs will not amount to a misrepresentation. This will be true where the statement amounts to a promise or assurance not to do a certain act in the future.[9] Does this mean that where a statement is couched in the future tense it cannot form the basis of a representation? Whether a statement, although couched in the future tense, is actually a statement of present fact is more than a question of grammar. For example, if a person states that a supermarket is selling all goods at 10 per cent off for the week, that is a statement of present fact. If the person instead states that 'If you go to that supermarket, they will sell you any item at 10 per cent less' that is a statement in the future tense, but it is in essence a statement of present

---

5   *Gates v City Mutual Life Assurance Society* (1986) 160 CLR 1; *Marks v GIO Australia Holdings Pty Ltd* (1998) 158 ALR 333.
6   Note negligent misrepresentation is not limited to statements of fact. Refer to [13.130].
7   *Walters v Morgan* (1861) 3 De GF & J 718; 45 ER 1056 at 1059.
8   *Edgington v Fitzmaurice* [1881–85] All ER 856; *Munchies Management Pty Ltd v Belperio* (1988) 84 ALR 700.
9   *Civil Service Co-operative Society of Victoria Ltd v Blyth* (1914) 17 CLR 601.

fact. It means the same as the first statement. This was the case in *Balfour & Clark v Hollandia Ravensthorpe NL*,[10] where a sales agent represented that 'in two years' time [the purchasers] would be able to borrow from the Hindmarsh Building Society a sum equal to 90 per cent of the value of the property secured by first mortgage only, provided that they promptly opened an account with the society and that they had saved 10 per cent of the purchase price'. This amounted to a representation that the existing policy of the building society was to lend the amount stated subject to two conditions only. This was not true.[11]

Can a statement that relates to the intention of a person amount to a statement of fact and therefore, a misrepresentation? That question should be answered in the affirmative. It has been very clearly stated by Bowen LJ[12] that 'the state of a man's mind is as much a fact as the state of his digestion'. This suggests that a person may just as easily defraud another about the state of her or his mind as about an objective fact. For example, a person who represents that 'in six months' time I will repay the debt' is making a statement about her or his intention—and also impliedly stating a present intention to repay the debt in the future. If the person does not presently hold that intention, the statement will be a fraudulent misrepresentation.

Example: Edgington v Fitzmaurice[13]

The plaintiff, after receiving a prospectus from the directors of the Army and Navy Provisions (Market) Ltd, took up debenture bonds in the company. The prospectus provided that the object of issuing the debentures was first, to complete certain alterations to existing buildings owned by the company, and secondly, to purchase horses and vans to save transport costs. After taking up the debenture bonds, the plaintiff discovered that the moneys were not used for the purposes stated in the prospectus, but were instead used to pay various debts of the company. The plaintiff commenced an action for misrepresentation, and succeeded. The defendant argued that the statements in the prospectus were mere statements of future intention and not statements of presently existing fact. Therefore, the statements could not amount to misrepresentations. In response to this argument, Cotton LJ said:

> It was argued that this was only the statement of an intention, and that the mere fact that an intention was not carried into effect could not make the Defendant liable to the Plaintiff. I agree that it was a statement of intention, but it is nevertheless a statement of fact, and if it could not be fairly said that the objects of the issue of the debentures were those which were stated in the prospectus the Defendants were stating a fact which was not true; and if they knew that it was not true, or made it recklessly not caring whether it was true or not, they would be liable.[14]

---

10   (1978) 18 SASR 240.
11   Refer also to *Aaron's Reefs Ltd v Twiss* [1896] AC 273.
12   *Edgington v Fitzmaurice* [1881–85] All ER 856.
13   [1881–85] All ER 856.
14   Ibid at (at 479–480).

13.3.2 Statement of opinion

[13.30] A statement of opinion or expression of belief may be considered in the same way as a statement of future intention, and should be distinguished from a statement of fact.[15] While the statement of opinion is not itself a statement of present fact, it may convey an inherent representation that the person making the statement holds that opinion, or is aware of facts that justify that opinion.[16] In *Smith v Land and House Property Corporation*,[17] the seller of a property described the tenant as 'a most desirable tenant'. While this was considered a statement of opinion, it was evidently not true, as the tenant was consistently late in paying the rent. Bowen LJ stated:

> [I]t is often fallaciously assumed that a statement of opinion cannot involve the statement of a fact. In a case where the facts are equally well known to both parties, what one of them says to the other is frequently nothing but an expression of opinion. The statement of such opinion is in a sense a statement of a fact, about the condition of the man's own mind, but only of an irrelevant fact, for it is of no consequence what the opinion is. But if the facts are not equally known to both sides, then a statement of opinion by the one who knows the facts best involves very often a statement of a material fact, for he impliedly states that he knows facts which justify his opinion.[18]

From this statement, it appears that the following matters will be relevant to a determination of whether a statement of opinion is a misrepresentation:

- the relative knowledge and position of each of the parties;
- the actual words used and meaning conveyed;
- whether fraud is established. Did the person giving the opinion have a genuine belief in his or her opinion no matter how erroneous?[19]

Where the maker of the statement is in exclusive possession of facts relevant to the opinion stated, the person is really stating that there are facts within his or her knowledge that make the opinion reasonable.[20] If, based upon the facts known, a reasonable person in that position would not hold that opinion,[21] or if the opinion is actually not held, a fraudulent misrepresentation will exist.

Example: Bisset v Wilkinson[22]

Prior to entering into a contract for the sale of a farming property to the defendant, the plaintiff represented that in his opinion, if the property was worked with a good six-horse team, it should carry 2000 head of sheep. It was common knowledge between the parties that the vendor had not at any time operated a sheep farm, and that the purchasers were not experienced in the operation of a sheep farm. After the

---

15   *Fitzpatrick v Michael* (1928) 28 SR (NSW) 285.
16   Ibid at 289.
17   (1885) 28 Ch D 7.
18   At 15. Refer also to *Ritter v North Side Enterprises Pty Ltd* (1975) 132 CLR 301.
19   See further [13.115].
20   *Smith v Land and House Property Corporation* (1885) 28 Ch D 7; *Brown v Raphael* [1958] Ch 636.
21   *Bisset v Wilkinson* (1926) All ER 343.
22   (1926) All ER 343.

purchasers went into occupation and commenced their farming operations, they found themselves in difficulties. The purchasers refused to pay the balance of the purchase moneys to the vendor, who commenced an action for recovery of the moneys. In defence of the vendor's claim, the purchasers alleged that the pre-contractual statement made by the vendor was a misrepresentation.

The court found that the pre-contractual statement made by the vendor was an opinion. The court then considered the circumstances in which an opinion could amount to a fraudulent misrepresentation. The statement by Bowen LJ in *Smith v Land & House Property Corporation*[23] was approved and applied. The court considered that the material facts of the transaction, the knowledge of the parties and their relative positions, and the words of the representation used, were all relevant in deciding whether a misrepresentation of the vendor's opinion had occurred. The court considered it to be material that both parties were aware that the vendor had not—and so far as appears, no other person had—at any time carried on sheep farming upon the unit of land in question. The court concluded that the statement did not amount to a misrepresentation.

13.3.3 Statement of law

[13.35] The general proposition is that a statement of law is not a misrepresentation. This arises from the conclusion that a statement of law is merely a statement of opinion until adjudicated on by a court. Some difficulties have arisen in distinguishing between statements of fact and law.[24] However, this difficulty will not prevent the representor from being liable for misrepresentation where:

- the statement of law is made fraudulently (without belief in the truth of the statement);[25]
- the statement of law is given in a situation where the representor owes the representee a duty of care to ensure that any advice or information given is accurate, and it is reasonable for the representee to rely on it (for example, where the representor is a legal practitioner advising her or his client);[26] or
- it would be unconscionable in all the circumstances to allow the representor to escape liability, such as where an estoppel is created.[27]

13.3.4 Puffs

[13.40] Sales talk or flourishing descriptions by sales people are generally not considered significant enough to constitute statements of fact and therefore, not to be misrepresentations at common law. A description by an agent that land is 'fertile and improvable' was considered unimportant to a sale.[28] However, sales talk or puffery

---

23 (1884) 28 Ph D 7.
24 Refer to *Eaglesfield v Marquis of Londonderry* (1876) 4 Ch D 693.
25 *Public Trustee v Taylor* [1978] VR 289 at 297; *British Workman's & General Insurance Co Ltd v Cunliffe* (1902) 18 TLR 502; *Oudaille v Lawson* [1922] NZLR 259.
26 See *L Shaddock & Associates v The Council of the City of Parramatta* (1981) 150 CLR 225 at 250, where a local government was found to owe a duty of care when providing information.
27 Refer to [7.125].
28 *Dimmock v Hallet* (1866) LR 2 Ch App 21 at 27.

may constitute misleading or deceptive conduct under the *Trade Practices Act* 1974 (Cth)[29] if a reasonable person would be misled by the comments.

13.3.5 Silence

[13.45] At common law misrepresentation requires an actual statement to be made by one party to another. Where a person creates a false impression in the mind of another person due to a failure to make a statement, the common law will not recognise that conduct as a misrepresentation except in certain circumstances. Mere silence will not give rise to a misrepresentation at common law unless a special relationship between the parties imposes an obligation to disclose. A positive act or representation is required before a misrepresentation will be found. At common law, the law will provide a remedy for misrepresentation by silence in three broad categories of circumstance.

(a)　Half truths

[13.50] A half truth may be defined as a statement which, although it is literally true, creates a false impression in the mind of the representee because other information is not disclosed. Despite the fact that every word of the statement may be true, if something is left out that would have qualified it, a false statement will have been made.[30] For example, if a real estate agent when selling a property represents that the property is fully let, but fails to inform the buyer that the tenant has served notice to quit, a misrepresentation has been made.[31] The initial statement is made untrue by the failure to disclose all relevant information. Where the information is deliberately withheld, or the representor has been reckless, the statement will be a fraudulent misrepresentation.[32] If the representor owes a duty of care to the representee and has been careless in not ascertaining the additional information, there will be a negligent misrepresentation. However, a misrepresentation will not generally arise if no duty of care is owed and the representor is not aware of the additional facts that make the statement false.[33]

(b)　Statement that becomes false prior to contract

[13.55] A statement that was originally correct but later becomes false may found a claim for misrepresentation. The representor owes a duty to the representee to correct any untrue statements prior to a contract being executed.[34] Likewise, where the statement was untrue from the beginning, and the representor discovers prior to contract that the statement is untrue, a duty arises to disclose this fact to the other party.[35] It is clear that once a statement is made for the purpose of inducing the formation of a contract, the representor takes on a continuing duty to ensure the representee is fully

---

29　Refer to *Byers v Doretea Pty Ltd* (1986) 69 ALR 715, where the statement that a unit was the 'biggest unit on the Coast' was held to be misleading.

30　*Arkwright v Newbold* (1881) 17 Ch D 301.

31　*Dimmock v Hallett* (1866) LR 2 Ch App 21.

32　*Jennings v Zihali-Kiss* (1972) 2 SASR 493.

33　However, where the representor is in a fiduciary relationship or it is a contract *uberrimae fidei*, a failure to disclose even if innocent, will be a breach of duty for which damages may be recoverable.

34　*With v O'Flanagan* [1936] 1 Ch D 575; *Jones v Dumbrell* [1881] VR 199.

35　*Davies v London Marine Insurance Company* (1878) 8 Ch D 469 at 475.

informed of any changes to the accuracy of the statement that occur prior to execution of the contract.

Example: Davies v London Marine Insurance Company[36]

The secretary of a company who believed monies had been wrongfully retained by the company's agent ordered the arrest of the agent for a felony. Friends of the agent approached the company and offered to deposit a sum of money into an account by way of security for any deficiency. On the same day, the company was advised that the conduct of the agent did not amount to a felony, and the arrest warrant was withdrawn. Later that day, the friends of the agent had a further meeting with the company and agree to deposit a sum of £2000 with the company. No mention was made of the withdrawal of the arrest warrant. The company subsequently tried to claim the monies deposited to repay the debt. The plaintiffs claimed rescission of the contract on the basis of misrepresentation, and succeeded. Fry J identified the relevant principle as:

> [I]f one of the negotiating parties has made a statement which is false in fact, but which he believes to be true and which is material to the contract and during the course of the negotiation he discovers the falsity of that statement. He is under an obligation to correct his erroneous statement; although if he had said nothing he very likely might have been entitled to hold his tongue throughout. So again if a statement has been made which is true at the time, but which during the course of the negotiations become untrue, then the person who knows that it has become untrue is under an obligation to disclose to the other the change of circumstance.[37]

(c)   Duty of disclosure

[13.60] Parties who are contracting with one another are entitled to remain silent in respect of salient facts where no duty of disclosure is imposed by law. This will apply even though the undisclosed facts may affect the bargaining position and ultimate decision of the other party. A duty of disclosure arises at common law in a limited number of circumstances. The first is where there is a fiduciary relationship between the parties—as in the case of a principal and agent,[38] solicitor and client, parent and child, or trustee and beneficiary. Parties in these types of relationship may only enter a contract together, if at all, after ample disclosure by the agent, solicitor, parent, or trustee. The second circumstance is where there is a contract *uberrimae fidei*—a contract of the 'utmost good faith'. In such contracts, the parties are required to make full disclosure of all material facts. A failure to disclose will amount to a misrepresentation. A contract of the utmost good faith can be found between insurer and insured,[39] and within a

---

36   (1878) 8 Ch D 469.
37   Ibid at 475.
38   *McKenzie v McDonald* [1927] VLR 134.
39   *Khoury v Government Insurance Office of New South Wales* (1984) 165 CLR 622; *Mayne Nickless Ltd v Pegler* [1974] 1 NSWLR 228; *Dixon v Royal Insurance Australia* (1997) ANZ Ins Cas 61-346; *Toikan International Insurance Broking v Plastell Windows Australia* (1989) 94 FLR 362; *Elston v Phoenix Prudential Aust* [1987] 2 Qd R 354; *Barclay Holdings (Aust) v British National Insurance* (1987) 8 NSWLR 514.

partnership. The requirement for full disclosure in an insurance contract has been given statutory effect by s 21 of the *Insurance Contracts Act* 1984 (Cth).

Each of these relationships represents an exception to the general principle that mere silence will not amount to a misrepresentation at common law. The representee will be able to rely on the fact that no statement was made, and therefore, no material facts exist that would affect the contractual relationship. This should be contrasted with the situation of a half-truth, or where an untrue statement is discovered prior to contract. In both of these cases, the misrepresentation is founded upon the combined effect of a positive statement and an omission—and therefore is not a case of mere silence amounting to a misrepresentation.[40]

13.4 Addressed to the representee by the other party

[13.65] The representation that induces the contract should be made by the other party to the contract or that party's authorised agent.[41] A representation that induces the representee to enter a contract with a third party will not allow the representee to rescind the contract with the third party. However, the representor may be liable to compensate the representee if reliance on the statement can be proved.[42]

13.5 At or before the time when the contract was made

[13.70] Only representations made prior to the time of the contract, and intended to induce the contract, can be misrepresentations. This generally limits the scope of misrepresentations to pre-contractual negotiations. False statements made after a contract is executed will not entitle the representee to rescind the existing contract. However, the misrepresentation may have caused the representee to suffer other loss in reliance on the statement, and that loss may be recoverable.

13.6 Which was intended to and did induce the representee to make the contract

[13.75] There are two aspects to this final requirement. First, the representor must have intended that the statement induce the contract. Secondly, the representee must, in fact, have been induced to enter the contract because of the statement by the repre-

---

40   The *Trade Practices Act* 1974 (Cth) has modified the general law in relation to liability for misleading conduct arising from silence. Refer to [13.395]–[3.410].

41   In relation to the liability of a principal for the conduct of their agent refer to *McCormick v Nowland* (1988) ATPR 40-852.

42   Damages will only be recoverable if the statement is negligent or fraudulent. Refer for example to *Shaddock v The Council of the City of Parramatta* (1981) 10 CLR 225 where the local government was liable in damages for a negligent misrepresentation but the buyer of the property was not entitled to rescind the contract with the seller.

sentor. Usually the crucial issue for decision by the court will be 'Did the representee rely on the statement?'.

13.6.1   Intention to induce

[13.80] The intention of the representor to induce the contract will not usually be in issue. It is generally readily apparent that if the statement is made in the course of pre-contractual negotiations, the representor intends to induce the contract by the statement. Nevertheless, if a statement is made innocently and with no intention to induce the contract in circumstances where it would be unreasonable for the representee to rely upon the statement, inducement may not be established.

Difficulties may also occur where the statement is not made during negotiations for the contract. For example, in *Peek v Gurney*,[43] the plaintiff bought shares from some existing shareholders in reliance upon the statements in the original prospectus. The House of Lords held that as the statements in the prospectus had been addressed to original allottees of the shares (as a class) and not to the plaintiff, the company had no intention to induce the contract between the plaintiff and the allottees, as the prospectus was no longer current.[44]

13.6.2   Reliance by the representee

[13.85] The representee must rely upon the statement made by the representor. The onus of proving the representee relied upon the statement rests with the representee.[45] What is the degree of reliance required? In *Edgington v Fitzmaurice*,[46] the English Court of Appeal considered that it was not necessary for the plaintiff to show that the misrepresentation was the sole inducing factor, but it was necessary for the misrepresentation to be material to the decision to enter the contract. It did not matter that the plaintiff had entered into the contract as a result of the misrepresentation as well as the plaintiff's own mistake or motives. The fact was that the plaintiff was influenced by the misrepresentation to enter the contract. The High Court gave detailed consideration to the issue of reliance in *Gould v Vaggelas*,[47] where Wilson J laid down four principles relevant to reliance, which subsequent courts have adopted:[48]

1   Notwithstanding that a representation is both false and fraudulent, if the representee does not rely upon it, he or she has no case.

2   If a material representation is made which is calculated to induce the representee to enter into a contract and that person in fact enters into a contract there arises a fair inference of fact that he or she was induced to do so by the representation.

---

43   (1873) LR 6 HL 377.
44   cf. *Fraser v NRMA Holdings Ltd* (1995) 127 ALR 543; a different result may be reached under the *Trade Practices Act* 1974 (Cth).
45   *Gould v Vaggelas* (1985) 157 CLR 215.
46   [1881–85] All ER 856.
47   (1985) 157 CLR 215 at 236.
48   *Collins Marrickville v Henjo Investments* (1987) 72 ALR 601; *Netaf v Bikane* (1990) 92 ALR 490; *Kizbeau Pty Ltd v WG&B Pty Ltd* (1995) 131 ALR 363.

3   The inference may be rebutted, for example, by showing that the representee, before he or she entered into the contract, either was possessed of actual knowledge or the true facts and knew them to be true or alternatively made it plain that whether, he or she knew the true facts or not, he or she did not rely on the representation.

4   The representation need not be the sole inducement. It is sufficient so long as it plays some part, even if only a minor part, in contributing to the formation of the contract.

Some of the common situations involving the issue of reliance in which the courts have adjudicated include the following.

(a)   The statement is ignored by the representee

[13.90] Despite the fact a statement may be made to the representee prior to contract, the representee may choose to ignore the statement, or may instead rely upon her or his own knowledge or judgement in entering the contract.[49]

(b)   The representee has knowledge of the true state of affairs at the time of contract

[13.95] If the representee has knowledge of the fact that the statement made by the representor is untrue at the time of contract, no claim for misrepresentation will lie. The representor is required to establish that the representee had actual knowledge of the falsity of the statement, and proceeded in any event.[50] The knowledge possessed by the representee must be such as to destroy the effect of the statement as an inducement to enter the contract. Consequently, knowledge that the statement is partly untrue may not be enough to constitute a bar to recovery by the representee.[51]

Example: Holmes v Jones[52]

The owners of a pastoral property wrote to the respondents (Jones) offering to sell the pastoral property. The offer misrepresented the amount of stock the property currently carried. The respondents instructed a third person to carry out an inspection of the property and then report back to them. Following this inspection, the respondents became aware that the statements made in the letter of offer were inaccurate. The respondents made a fresh offer to purchase the property, which was accepted. Following execution of the contract, the respondents tried to have the contract set aside due to the misrepresentation contained in the first letter.

The High Court refused the respondents' claim, concluding they had not relied upon the statements made in the first letter. Griffith CJ stated:

> The first observation to be made is that it is clear that, in order that the action may be maintained, the representation must have been continuing down to the time when the contract was entered into and must have been

---

49   *Holmes v Jones* (1907) 4 CLR; *Wilcher v Stain* [1962] NSWR 1136.
50   Refer to *Holmes v Jones* (1907) 4 CLR 1692.
51   Refer to *Gipps v Gipps* [1978] 1 NSWLR 454
52   (1907) 4 CLR 1692.

believed by the plaintiffs at that time, so as to be at that time an inducement to enter into the contract.

It appears to me to be common sense as well as law that, when a purchaser chooses to rely on his own judgement or upon that of his agent, he cannot afterwards say that he relied upon a previous representation made by the vendor.[53]

(c) The representee has the means of discovering the falsity of the statements

[13.100] A person may still be held to have relied upon the statements of another person despite the fact that they may have been able, with reasonable diligence, to discover the falsity of the statement. Carelessness of the representee in protecting his or her own interests will not be a bar to recovery if it is proved that the representee relied upon the statement.[54]

13.7 Need to distinguish categories of misrepresentation

[13.105] Three types of misrepresentation have been recognised by the general law:
- innocent misrepresentation;
- fraudulent misrepresentation; and
- negligent misrepresentation.

It is necessary to distinguish between the different types of misrepresentation as the available remedies differ. The primary remedy available for each type of misrepresentation is rescission of the contract at the election of the representee. Damages are also available for fraudulent and negligent misrepresentation, either in addition to rescission, or alone. The different types of misrepresentation and the available remedies are examined below.

13.8 Innocent misrepresentation

[13.110] An innocent misrepresentation occurs where the representor has been neither fraudulent nor negligent. There must be no evidence of fraud, as outlined in *Derry v Peek*,[55] and the maker of the statement must not be under a duty of care to the other person.[56] The onus will lie on the representee to allege and prove either fraud or negligence.[57] The four elements of misrepresentation as outlined from [13.15] to [13.100] must be proved to establish an innocent misrepresentation.

If an innocent misrepresentation is proved, the representee may, at her or his election, choose to rescind the contract. The election to rescind should be made within a reasonable time, and in the case of a sale of land or shares, must be

---

53 Ibid at 1697, 1702.
54 *Redgrave v Herd* (1881) 20 Ch D 1 at 13–14.
55 (1889) 14 App Cases 337.
56 Refer to [13.125].
57 *Dorotea v Christos Doufas Nominees Pty Ltd* [1991] 2 Qd R 91.

exercised prior to completion of the contract.[58] Damages are not available for an innocent misrepresentation.[59]

13.9   Fraudulent misrepresentation

[13.115] A fraudulent misrepresentation will occur where all of the elements detailed at [13.15]–[13.100] are present, and the representor has acted fraudulently. As stated in *Derry v Peek*,[60] a statement will be fraudulent where a false representation has been made:

- knowingly; or
- without belief in its truth; or
- recklessly, careless whether it be true or false

with the intention that it should be acted upon by another party who is thereby induced to act upon it.

As indicated by the definition, the courts employ a subjective test in determining whether a person has been fraudulent. This requires the presentation of evidence regarding the state of mind of the particular person.[61]

The most readily detectable type of fraudulent misrepresentation will occur where the statement-maker is aware of the dishonesty of his or her statement.[62] However, fraud will also be proved where there is an absence of a genuine belief in the truth of the statement. Accordingly, it is immaterial whether the representor knows it to be untrue, or is merely ignorant or doubtful of the truth. An absence of genuine belief in the truth of the statement will also occur where the representor is recklessly careless about whether it is true or not. The reference in this context to recklessness and carelessness has at times caused some confusion, and the authors of Salmond and Williams[63] provide useful guidance on the distinction between fraud and negligence:

> But such a reference to recklessness and carelessness in this connection is a fertile source of confusion of thought. It suggests that negligence may be equivalent to fraud. This is not so, for these two states of mind are mutually exclusive. No one can make a statement fraudulently who makes it carelessly or negligently. Nor does the law recognise in this connection any form of constructive fraud which is in reality merely negligence. When, therefore, it is said that a statement is fraudulent if made recklessly, not caring whether it is true or false, what is really meant is that a statement is fraudulent if made without any genuine belief in its truth.

As is the case for innocent misrepresentation, if fraudulent misrepresentation is proved, the representee will be entitled to elect for rescission of the contract. This right of election must be exercised within a reasonable time and is not, unlike inno-

---

58   The limits on rescission of the contract are discussed at [13.195]–[13.255].
59   *Redgrave v Hurd* (1881) 20 Ch D 1.
60   (1889) 14 AC 337.
61   *Derry v Peek* (1889) 14 AC 337.
62   For example, *Alati v Kruger* (1955) 94 CLR 216; *Gould v Vaggelas* (1985) 157 CLR 215.
63   JW Salmond and J Williams, *Principles of the Law of Contracts* Sweet & Maxwell, 1945, London, p 244.

cent misrepresentation, barred by the completion of the contract.[64] The representee will also be entitled to claim damages for any losses suffered as a result of the misrepresentation. The measure of damages will be the same as those for the tort of deceit.[65]

13.10 Negligent misrepresentation

[13.120] The law of negligent misrepresentation emerged in the 1960s with the recognition by the House of Lords, in *Hedley Byrne & Co Ltd v Heller & Partners Ltd*,[66] that a person to whom a negligent statement had been made could recover damages in tort if a special relationship existed. Until this time, a person who made a statement carelessly and without fraud was treated as having made an innocent misrepresentation.[67] Consequently, a person could only recover damages for a statement made by another person if fraud was involved, or there was an existing fiduciary relationship. Compared with the earlier development of the law of negligence,[68] the principle of negligent misrepresentation was slow to develop, due in part to the reluctance of the courts to expose parties to liability for pure economic loss.[69] Some of these initial doubts about the expansive operation of the principle of negligent misrepresentation were to some extent overcome by limiting recovery to parties in a 'special relationship'.

13.10.1 Requirements

[13.125] As with fraudulent and innocent misrepresentation, negligent misrepresentation requires proof of the elements (except for the requirement that the statement be one of fact) discussed at [13.15]–[13.100], in addition to the following:
- that the representor owed the representee a duty to take reasonable care that the statement made by the representor was true and reliable;
- that the representor breached such duty; and
- the false representation led to the representee's suffering loss or damage.

[13.130] The existence of a duty to take reasonable care is what distinguishes this type of misrepresentation from innocent and fraudulent misrepresentation. In addition, another point of distinction is that if a special relationship is present, a negligent misrepresentation may occur where the representor is providing an opinion. It is not necessary for the statement to be one of fact—only that the representor is providing advice or information. The breach of a duty of care through the provision of false information will be enough to allow the representee to recover damages in negligence for any loss suffered. However, to obtain rescission of a contract, the representee must prove that the statement was made prior to entry into the contract, and that the representee relied on the statement when entering the contract.

---

64 See for example *Alati v Kruger* (1955) 94 CLR 216 where the court allowed rescission for fraudulent misrepresentation despite the closure of the business.
65 Refer to *Gould v Vaggelas* (1985) 157 CLR 215 and the discussion at [13.260].
66 (1964) AC 465.
67 For example, *Derry v Peek* (1889) 14 App Cas 337.
68 In 1932 with the decision of *Donoghue v Stevenson* (1932) AC 562.
69 *Ultramares Corp v Touche Niven & Co 255 NY 170* (1931) per Cardozo CJ.

13.10.2 What is a special relationship?

[13.135] Since the landmark decision of the House of Lords in *Hedley Byrne v Heller & Partners*,[70] the High Court has broadened and refined the concept of negligent misrepresentation and the meaning of 'special relationship'. It is clear that more than reasonable foreseeability of loss or damage to a person is required to found a claim in negligent misrepresentation. There must be a relationship of proximity between the parties—usually shown by the existence of reasonable reliance on the statement.[71]

[13.140] In *MLC Assurance v Evatt*,[72] Barwick CJ stated that a special relationship arises:

> whenever a person gives information or advice to another ... upon a serious matter, [in] circumstances [where] the speaker realises ... or ought to realise, that he is being trusted ... to give the best of his information or advice as a basis for action on the part of the other party and it is reasonable in the circumstances for the other party to act on that information [or] advice.

[13.145] On appeal, the Privy Council[73] restricted the special relationship to circumstances where the person owing the duty was carrying on or professing to carry on a profession, business, or occupation involving the possession of skill and competence. However, the restricted view of the Privy Council was rejected by the High Court in *L Shaddock & Associates v The Council of the City of Parramatta*:[74]

> I find it difficult to see why in principle the duty should be limited to persons whose business or profession includes giving the sort of advice or information sought and to persons claiming to have the same skill and competence as those carrying on such a business or profession, and why it should not extend to persons who, on a serious occasion, give considered advice or information concerning a business or professional transaction.[75]

[13.150] The court confirmed the statement by Barwick CJ in *MLC Assurance v Evatt*[76] about when a special relationship will arise. Arising out of the statement formulated by Barwick CJ, there are several points of note. First, liability for negligent misrepresentation is not confined to those carrying on or professing to carry on a profession, business, or occupation involving the possession of skill and competence. Policy reasons for adopting a wider approach to liability for negligent misrepresentation and rejecting the restricted view of the Privy Council in *Mutual Life & Citizens' Assurance Co Ltd v Evatt*[77] were outlined by Mason J in *L Shaddock & Associates v The Council of the City of Parramatta*.[78]

---

70   [1964] AC 465.
71   *Hawkins v Clayton* (1988) 164 CLR 539; *Norris v Sibberas* [1990] VR 161; *Davis v Radcliffe* [1990] 1 WLR 821.
72   (1968) 122 CLR 556 at 572–573.
73   (1970) 122 CLR 628
74   (1981) 150 CLR 225.
75   Ibid, 234–235, per Gibbs CJ.
76   (1968) 122 CLR 556 at 572–573.
77   [1971] AC 793.
78   (1981) 150 CLR 225 at 250–251.

[13.155] Secondly, a person will not be under a duty to take reasonable care unless he or she knows or ought to know that the other person is relying on him or her to take reasonable care, and it is reasonable for that other person to rely on the first person for the information. It may not be reasonable to rely on information given casually on some social or informal occasion unless the advice or information concerned a business or professional transaction and the representee makes clear the gravity of the inquiry and the importance and influence attached to the answer.

[13.160] However, a request for advice or information is not required before a duty of care will arise. Information voluntarily given with the intention of inducing a contract or other action may also give rise to liability. In such a case, the requirement to prove reasonableness may not be necessary for success.[79]

[13.165] Examples of negligent misrepresentation in a contractual context arise commonly in the course of negotiations for the sale of property involving real estate agents.[80]

[13.170] It is accepted that a real estate agent owes a duty of care to the buyer of a property to ensure that information provided to the buyer is accurate where the agent knows, or ought to know, that the buyer is relying on the agent for the accuracy of the information.[81] An agent who fails in this duty and provides false information to the buyer due to a lack of care will be liable for negligent misrepresentation. Where the statements made are within the actual or implied authority of the agent[82] and the statements are effective in inducing the contract, the buyer may also seek rescission and damages against the seller. The seller will be vicariously liable for the statements of the agent made within the agent's actual or implied authority.

Example: McCormick v Nowland[83]

A real estate agent advertised the vendor's property for sale. In the advertisement and auction brochure, the agent represented that the house on the property was made of brick, and that a pool at the rear of the property adjoined a parkland. The plaintiffs entered into a contract for the purchase of the property relying upon the statements in the advertisement and the brochure. Between contract and completion, the plaintiffs discovered that the area to the rear of the pool was not parkland, and the house was built of concrete blocks, not brick. After receiving legal advice, the plaintiffs claimed rescission of contract for negligent misrepresentation. The plaintiffs alleged that the vendor was vicariously liable for the statements made by the agent in the advertisement and the auction brochure.

The plaintiffs succeeded in claiming damages from both the real estate agent and the vendor. The court also granted rescission of the contract with the vendor, on the basis that the vendor was vicariously liable for the agent's statement. The court held

---

79   *San Sebastian Pty Ltd v Minister Administering the Environment Planning and Assessment Act 1979* (1986) 162 CLR 340 at 344–345, 371.

80   For example *Rawlinson & Brown Pty Ltd v Witham* (1995) Aust Torts Reports 81-341; *Esso Petroleum v Mardon* (1976) QB 801; *Ellul v Oakes* (1972) 3 SASR 377.

81   *Roots v Oentory* [1983] 2 Qd R 745; *McCormick v Nowland* (1988) ATPR 40-852; *Rawlinson & Brown Pty Ltd v Witham* (1995) Aust Torts Reports 81-341.

82   Refer to *Mullens v Miller* (1882) 22 Ch D 194 at 199 in relation to the authority of a real estate agent.

83   (1988) ATPR 40-852.

that the vendor would be liable for all statements made within the actual or implied authority of the real estate agent. In relying upon the authority of *Mullins v Miller*,[84] the court concluded that the statements made by the agent in describing the property were within the agent's actual or implied authority.

13.11 Remedies

[13.175] Two primary remedies are available for misrepresentation. A misrepresentation of any type will allow the representee to elect to rescind the contract.[85] The right to rescind, however, may be subject to certain limits.[86] The second type of remedy a representee may seek is damages. Damages are only available if a negligent or fraudulent misrepresentation is proved. Damages are not available for innocent misrepresentation.[87]

13.12 Rescission

[13.180] Prior to the *Judicature Acts*, rescission of a contract could be ordered either at common law or in equity. There are several differences between rescission in the two jurisdictions. At common law, rescission of a contract could only be ordered where there was evidence of fraud. In equity, evidence of fraud was not necessary.[88] Following the merging of the courts of equity and common law by the *Judicature Acts*, the principles concerning rescission in equity have been consistently applied by the courts in the case of misrepresentation.[89]

[13.185] Accordingly, if any type of misrepresentation has occurred, the representee may elect to rescind the contract. This means that the representee has a choice whether to rescind or affirm the contract following the misrepresentation. To ensure a valid rescission occurs, the representee should take steps within a reasonable time to bring the contract to an end and communicate this decision in clear and unequivocal terms to the representor.[90] Rescission may be effected either orally or in writing, but writing is preferred from an evidentiary point of view.

13.12.1 *Effect on the contract*

[13.190] Following an effective rescission of the contract, the parties will be returned substantially to their pre-contractual positions and the contract will be void. Neither party will be entitled to enforce obligations that previously existed under the contract, but damages may be recoverable for conduct, such as misrepresentation, that gives rise to a liability in tort for negligence or fraud.

---

84   (1882) 22 ChD 194.
85   Rescission is the act of making the contract void. That is, the parties are returned to their pre-contractual position as though the contract never existed. This has a consequence for enforcement of accrued rights. Refer to [20.25].
86   The applicable limits are discussed below.
87   *Redgrave v Hurd* (1881) 20 Ch D 1.
88   Ibid at 12.
89   *Redgrave v Herd* (1881) 20 Ch D 1 at 12; *Alati v Kruger* (1955) 94 CLR 216 at 223.
90   *Ivanof v Phillip Levy* [1971] VR 167; cf. *Car Finance Ltd v Caldwell* [1965] 1 QB 525.

3.12.2   Limits on right to rescind

[13.195] The right of the representee to rescind the contract will not be unfettered in all circumstances. The courts have recognised various limits on the representee's right to rescind a contract.

(a)   Affirmation of the contract

[13.200] Once a misrepresentation is discovered, a representee may elect either to affirm or to rescind the contract. If the representee elects to affirm, the right to rescind for that particular misrepresentation will be lost. Once an election is made it cannot be retracted.[91] Any election to affirm must be made in clear and unequivocal terms to be effective. Whether affirmation of the contract has occurred may be ascertained from the words or conduct of the representee. However, there is doubt concerning the exact degree of knowledge required by the representee before his or her conduct or words will amount to an affirmation of the contract. Does the representee require knowledge of both the falsity of the statement and the right to rescind, or is mere knowledge of the false statement enough? If the election is between contractually conferred rights, it is clear that an election can be made even where the elector does not have knowledge of the legal effect of his or her election.[92] In other cases—such as the general law right to affirm or rescind for misrepresentation or mistake—the matter does not appear to be settled. Several authorities favour the proposition that the elector does need to have knowledge of the legal effect of his or her election before his or her conduct is binding as an election,[93] but others are equivocal, and some authority rejects the proposition.

[13.205] The High Court decision of *Sargent v ASL Developments Ltd*[94] provides a detailed examination of the principles of election. The purchasers of a property were attempting to avoid the contract pursuant to a special condition within the agreement. The court considered in detail the requirements of a valid election. Stephen J noted that the doctrine of election requires an element of knowledge on the part of the elector, and words or conduct sufficient to amount to the making of an election. However, the nature of the knowledge is not clear from the authorities. In each case, the authorities suggest that the elector must at least have knowledge of the facts that give rise to the legal right to rescind, terminate, or affirm. The question is whether there must also be knowledge of the right of election between the two available rights. In *Elder's Trustee Case*,[95] the court concluded that knowledge of the facts giving rise to the legal right was all that was necessary where the conduct of the elector was unequivocal. However, if the conduct was not quite unequivocal and therefore viewed as no more than evidence of election, the knowledge of the right of election may be relevant, and point to a natural inference that an election has in fact been made. Stephen J noted the decision in *Coastal Estates v Melevende*,[96] where the Victorian Full

---

91   *Sargent v ASL Developments Ltd* (1974) 131 CLR 634 at 656 per Mason J.
92   Ibid; see also *O'Connor v SP Bray Ltd* (1936) 36 SR (NSW) 248.
93   Refer in particular to *Coastal Estates v Melevende* [1965] VR 433.
94   (1974) 131 CLR 634.
95   (1941) 65 CLR 603.
96   [1965] VR 433.

Court concluded that in a case of fraudulent misrepresentation, an election could only be made where the person had knowledge of the facts and the right of election. Herring CJ considered there was authority for a divergence of views in relation to rights given under the contract and rights available at common law. The first view is that knowledge of the facts is sufficient. The second view is that knowledge of the right to rescind is also necessary. Whether an election has occurred is a question of fact. It is possible that where the elector has no knowledge of the right to rescind, it may be inferred that the conduct is not of such an unequivocal character that the elector should be refused the right to rescind. Stephen J appeared to prefer the second view that as the right to rescind was not given by the contract—the party required to elect needed to have knowledge of his or her legal rights, before his or her conduct could be viewed as an election.

[13.210] Mason J, in the same case, was not in favour of applying different rules to the cases of termination and rescission for misrepresentation, and although he did not express a view, preferred the principles of election to be the same across all areas of the law.[97]

[13.215] The difference in judicial opinion is yet to be satisfactorily resolved. It is suggested that in all cases the issues of election and consequently, of whether a contract has been affirmed, will be a question of fact considered in the light of all the surrounding circumstances.

(b) Lapse of time

[13.220] The right to rescind must be exercised within a reasonable time of discovering the falsity of the statement, or the representee will risk affirming the contract by his or her conduct. It would also appear to be the case that an election to rescind for an innocent misrepresentation should be exercised within a reasonable time of the representee's having the opportunity to prove or disprove the statement.[98] As a matter of policy, commercial transactions require some degree of certainty which would not be achieved if contracts remained open to rescission indefinitely. In any event, this would not apply in the case of fraud where rescission will be available provided the right is exercised within a reasonable time of discovering the fraud.

(c) Impossibility of *restitutio in integrum*

[13.225] The very essence of rescission is that the parties should be returned to their original positions. This is referred to as *restitutio in integrum*. At common law, if precise *restitutio in integrum* was not possible, the court was unable to grant rescission to the representee. However, a more flexible approach has been adopted in equity, where rescission will be granted provided the parties can be *substantially* restored to their pre-contractual positions. Particularly in the case of fraudulent misrepresentation, a court of equity may be willing to grant compensation or indemnification[99] where this would more substantially restore the parties to their original positions, and may make what-

---

97 (1941) 65 CLR 603 at 658.
98 *Leaf v International Galleries* [1950] 2 KB 86 at 92.
99 *Brown v Smit* (1924) 34 CLR 160.

ever financial adjustment is appropriate to restore the parties to those positions. Examples may include compensation for deterioration in property;[100] compensation for improvements made to the property; or compensation for repairs to the property. Collateral losses involved in carrying on a business would not be recoverable in equity, but damages may be available.[101] The flexible approach adopted by the courts is exemplified by the decision of *Alati v Kruger*.[102]

Example: Alati v Kruger[103]

Kruger purchased a fruit business together with the goodwill, stock in trade and certain assets from Alati. After completion of the contract, Kruger discovered that Alati had made certain fraudulent misrepresentations about the average takings of the business. Kruger immediately began an action in the Supreme Court against Alati claiming rescission of the contract, return of the purchase money, and damages. During this time, Kruger continued to carry on the business, which declined and started to make a loss. Before judgment was given the business had closed down, and the landlords had re-entered the premises. Alati argued that rescission of the contract was no longer possible due to the closure of the business.

The High Court rejected Alati's argument, concluding that rescission of the contract was possible:

> equity had always regarded as valid the disaffirmance of a contract induced by fraud even though precise restitutio in integrum is not possible, if the situation is such that, by the exercise of its powers, including the power to take accounts of profits and to direct inquiries as to allowances proper to be made for deterioration, it can do what is practically just between the parties, and by so doing restore them substantially to the status quo.[104]

[13.230] In *Alati v Kruger*,[105] the court went on to note that the function of a court in proceedings for rescission in equity was to adjudicate upon the validity of a purported disaffirmance of the transaction by the applicant, and to give effect to it. The approach taken by equity allowed the court to provide for any adjustments necessary where the simple handing-back of property or repayment of money would not put them in as good a position as before they entered into their transaction. This allows equity to concede the right of a defrauded party to rescind in a much wider variety of cases than the common law could recognise. The right of rescission in equity, however, is subject to the usual equitable discretions. The court considered whether Kruger should be entitled to rescission, having discontinued the business and left the premises before judgment. However, the test applied by the court was whether Kruger had acted unconscientiously during the pendency of the action causing the loss of a valuable leasehold and goodwill by abandoning the premises without giving Alati a reasonable

---

100   *Balfour v Hollandia Ravensthorp NL* (1978) 18 SASR 240.
101   *Brown v Smit* (1924) 34 CLR 160; *Gould v Vaggelas* (1984) 157 CLR 215 at 221–222.
102   (1955) 94 CLR 216.
103   Ibid.
104   Ibid at 223.
105   Ibid.

opportunity to take it back. As this had not occurred, the fact that the business no longer existed was not a bar to the rescission of the agreement.

(d) Where third party rights have intervened

[13.235] Where a third party acquires an interest in property, the subject of the contract, a court will not be able to grant rescission—the primary reason being that the parties can no longer be placed in their original positions. The court will generally be unable to divest the interest of the third party and return the property to the original owner. As the contract will remain valid and enforceable until rescission, a third party may acquire valid and enforceable rights in the property as against other parties.[106]

(e) Contract is completely performed

[13.240] This final limit on the right to rescind is referred to as 'the rule in *Seddon's case*' and applies only to innocent misrepresentation. The cases of *Seddon v North Eastern Salt Company Ltd*[107] and *Wilde v Gibson*[108] suggest that once a contract is executed (fully performed by the parties) the representee is unable to rescind the contract for innocent misrepresentation. *Seddon v North Eastern Salt Company Ltd*[109] involved the purchase by Seddon of shares in the London Salt Company. During the course of negotiations, the trading losses of the company were misrepresented to Seddon. In reliance on the representations, Seddon purchased the shares but discovered shortly after completion that the trading losses were grossly understated. The court refused rescission of the contract, relying on the decision of *Wilde v Gibson*.[110] Lord Campbell in the later case stated that 'where the conveyance has been executed ... a Court of Equity will set aside the conveyance only on the ground of actual fraud.'[111]

[13.245] The rule in *Seddon's case* has been criticised by commentators and the judiciary. The application of the rule to transactions for the sale of goods is uncertain, and it is suggested that the rule should be limited to contracts for the sale of land. In *Leason Pty Ltd v Prince Farm Pty Ltd*,[112] the plaintiff purchased a thoroughbred race horse in reliance upon a representation by the defendant that the horse was of a particular blood line. Once it was discovered that the statement was false, the plaintiff sought to return the horse, but the defendant refused. It was argued that as the contract had been executed, the horse had been accepted and could not be returned. Helsham CJ examined in detail the emergence of the rule in *Seddon's case* and whether it should be applicable to a contract for the sale of goods. His Honour validly points out that the rule in *Seddon's case* relies primarily on the decision in *Wilde v Gibson*,[113] which in essence concerned misrepresentation as to title, not a sale of goods. The rights of a buyer following execution of a land transaction are further complicated by the doctrine of merger,[114] which operates to prohibit the reconvey-

---

106 *Phillips v Brooks Limited* [1919] 2 KB 243.
107 [1905] 1 Ch 326.
108 (1848) 9 ER 897.
109 [1905] 1 Ch 326.
110 (1848) 9 ER 897.
111 Ibid at 909.
112 [1983] 2 NSWLR 381.
113 (1848) 9 ER 897.
114 This doctrine is highlighted in the case of *Svanosio v McNamara* (1956) 96 CLR 186.

ance of land following completion except in the case of fraud or total failure of consideration. The unclear relationship between this doctrine and the equitable principle of rescission for misrepresentation may have contributed to the decision in *Wilde v Gibson*.[115] In conclusion, Helsham CJ stated that 'the remedy of rescission for innocent misrepresentation is available in the case of an executed contract for the sale of goods'[116] subject of course to the other limits, such as affirmation, on the exercise of the court's equitable jurisdiction.

[13.250] The decision in *Leason Pty Ltd v Prince Farm Pty Ltd*[117] has, however, been met with criticism from Wood J of the New South Wales Court of Appeal in *Vimig v Contract Tooling*.[118] That case involved the sale of a business where misrepresentations were made in relation to the profits of the business. Wood J was not persuaded by the judgment of Helsham CJ in *Leason Pty Ltd v Prince Farm Pty Ltd*,[119] and departed from the rule in *Seddon's case*.

[13.255] In cases involving a sale of goods, the preferable approach is that the rule in *Seddon's case* does not apply. The primary criterion for determining whether rescission is available should be whether *restitutio in integrum* is possible despite execution of the contract. Several states of Australia have adopted this position through legislation.[120] However, in the case of a sale of land, rescission of the contract for innocent misrepresentation is not available following execution of the contract and the passing of title, because of the operation of the doctrine of merger.[121]

13.13 Damages

13.13.1 Measure of damage

[13.260] Damages may be sought for negligent or fraudulent misrepresentation in addition to, or instead of, rescission. Damages for misrepresentation are calculated in accordance with the principles for recovery of damages in tort for negligence or deceit. The loss recoverable in tort should be contrasted with the measure of damages in contract.[122] The object of damages in tort is to place representees in the position they would have been in had the tort not occurred.[123] In contrast, the object of damages in contract is to place plaintiffs in the position they would have been in had the contract been performed.[124] This means that in tort the plaintiff/representee will be compensated for the loss suffered as a result of relying on the misrepresentation. Therefore, where a misrepresentation has induced a person to purchase property the measure of damage will be the difference between the real value of the property at the

---

115 (1848) 9 ER 897.
116 *Leason Pty Ltd v Prince Farm Pty Ltd* [1983] 2 NSWLR 381 at 387.
117 [1983] 2 NSWLR 381.
118 (1986) 9 NSWLR 731.
119 [1983] 2 NSWLR 381.
120 ACT: s 3(b) *Law Reform (Misrepresentation) Act* 1977; SA: s 6(1)(b) *Misrepresentation Act* 1971; NSW: s 4(2A) *Sale of Goods Act* 1923; Vic: s 100(1) *Goods Act* 1958.
121 Refer to *Montgomery v Continental Bags (NZ) Ltd* [1972] NZLR 884 in relation to the operation of the merger principle in Torrens title.
122 Refer to *Holmes v Jones* (1907) 4 CLR 1692 at 1709.
123 *Gould v Vaggelas* (1985) 157 CLR 215.
124 *Robinson v Harman* (1848) 1 Ex 850 at 855; *Wenham v Ella* (1972) 127 CLR 454 at 471; *Commonwealth v Amann Aviation Pty Ltd* (1991) 174 CLR 68 at 80, 98.

time of purchase and what the person actually paid for the property. The court will, in effect, draw a comparison between the plaintiff's financial position prior to entering into the contract and the position after the contract is entered into. This will also allow the court to award damages for consequential losses resulting from the operation of a business[125]—but representees will generally not be able to recover their lost expectation or anticipated profit.[126] Lost expectation is recoverable in tort only if the representee can prove that but for the misrepresentation, the representee would have entered into another available arrangement that would have resulted in his or her expectations being met.[127]

[13.265] In contrast, a plaintiff will be compensated after breach of contract for the loss of what he or she expected to receive through performance of the contract. The usual measure of damage will be the difference between the market value of the property at the date of breach and the contract price. In essence, the court will look to a comparison of the position of the plaintiff at the date of breach and the position he or she expected to be in after performance of the contract. This allows the plaintiff to claim any loss of profits not received due to the breach.

[13.270] Where a misrepresentation has also become a term of the contract, the choice between claiming damages for breach of contract or damages for misrepresentation may be significant, as highlighted in the case of *Ellul v Oakes*.[128] The plaintiff purchased a property in reliance upon a representation by the vendor's agent that the property was fully sewered. The same statement was included in the contract. Several months after the sale, the purchaser discovered that the property was not sewered and sued the vendor, in the alternative, for breach of warranty and negligent misrepresentation. In relation to the claim for negligent misrepresentation, Bray CJ said:

> the ... claim must fail because it is based on tort and damages is the gist of the action and no damage was shown. The measure of damages ... is the difference between the value of what the plaintiff parted with and the value of what he got in consequence of relying on the representation. It is not the contractual standard of the difference between the value of what he got and the value of what he would have got if the representation had been true.[129]

[13.275] The plaintiff failed in his claim for negligent misrepresentation because there was no evidence that the property with a septic system was worth any less than a sewered property. However, the plaintiff succeeded in the claim for breach of warranty because he did not receive what he bargained for when entering the contract.

13.13.2 Requirements of causation and remoteness

[13.280] As in contract, damages in tort are only recoverable if the plaintiff can prove that the loss was caused by the misrepresentation, and that the loss was not too remote. A detailed discussion of the rule of causation and remoteness in tort are beyond the

---

125 *Kizbeau Pty Ltd v WG & B Pty Ltd* (1995) 184 CLR 281.
126 Refer to *Marks v GIO Australia Holdings Ltd* (1998) 158 ALR 333.
127 *Marks v GIO Australia Holdings Ltd* (1998) 158 ALR 333.
128 [1972] 3 SASR 377.
129 Ibid at 379.

scope of this book and will only be examined briefly.[130] The traditional test for establishing causation in contract and in tort is the 'but for' test. That is, the loss would not have occurred but for the breach or wrong of the defendant. However, where there are multiple causes of the loss, there has been a judicial shift towards considering the question of causation based on policy or 'common sense' considerations. This is occurring both in contract and in tort.[131]

[13.285] In contract, remoteness is governed by the two limbs of the rule in *Hadley v Baxendale*,[132] and centres around the question of whether the loss is 'sufficiently likely to result' from the breach of contract. In tort, remoteness is generally governed by the reasonable foreseeability test.[133] In the case of negligent misrepresentation, the court will be concerned with whether the loss caused by the statement was reasonably foreseeable in the circumstances. However, in the case of fraudulent misrepresentation, it seems all losses that flow directly from the misrepresentation will be recoverable. Whether it must also be reasonably foreseeable is not clear as pointed out in *Gould v Vaggelas*:[134]

> There is no reason in principle why the defrauded purchaser should not recover damages for all the loss that flowed directly from the fraudulent inducement (unless, possibly, the loss was not foreseeable). If the purchaser, besides paying more for the business than it was worth, has suffered additional losses that resulted directly from the fraud he ought to be compensated for them. Of course the court must be satisfied that the loss did result directly from the fraud and not from some supervening cause such as the folly, error or misfortune of the purchaser himself.

13.13.3   Measure of damage if contract affirmed

[13.290] The measure of damages for misrepresentation where the contract is affirmed will generally be the difference between the real value of the property at the time of purchase and what the person actually paid for the property. This measure of damage allows the representee to recover the prejudice or disadvantage suffered by reason of reliance on the representor's statement. Take, for example, a situation where the seller of a property misrepresents the value of the property to be $250 000. As a result of the representation, a buyer purchases the property for $200 000. In that example, the buyer would be able to recover any difference between the contract price and the real value of the property. If the real value of the property is less than $200 000, the buyer will recover the difference. The buyer will not be able to recover the loss of expecta-

---

130 Reference should be made to RP Balkin & JLR Davis, *Law of Torts*, 2nd edn, Butterworths, Sydney, 1996; JG Fleming, *The Law of Torts*, 9th edn, LBC Information Services, North Ryde, 1998.

131 Refer to *March v E & M Stramare Pty Ltd* (1991) 171 CLR 506 and in relation to causation in contract to [23.35]–[23.95].

132 (1854) 9 Ex 341; 156 ER 145.

133 Refer to *Overseas Tankship (UK) Ltd v Morts Dock and Engineering Co Ltd (Wagon Mound) (No 1)* [1961] AC 388; *Overseas Tankship (UK) Ltd v the Miller Steamship Co (Wagon Mound) (No 2)*[1967] 1 AC 617; *Hughes v Lord Advocate* [1963] AC 837 and *Nader v Urban Transit Authority of NSW* (1985) 2 NSWLR 501.

134 (1984) 157 CLR 215 at 221–222 per Gibbs CJ.

tion as a result of the property's not being worth $250 000. To recover such loss, the buyer would need to prove a breach of contract.[135]

13.13.4 Measure of damage after rescission of contract

[13.295] A representee who elects to rescind a contract for misrepresentation will be entitled to a refund of the purchase price, provided the property is returned to the representor. In the above example,[136] this would entitle the purchaser to return the property and receive a refund of the contract price. The value of the property is irrelevant. No additional damages would be recoverable unless the representee can prove that consequential damages were suffered.[137]

13.14 Statutory reform of the common law of misrepresentation

13.14.1 Introduction

[13.300] The most significant statutory reform of the common law of misrepresentation occurred with the enactment of the *Trade Practices Act* 1974 (Cth) and the State *Fair Trading Acts*. Section 52 of the *Trade Practices Act* 1974 (Cth) provides that:

> A corporation shall not in trade or commerce, engage in conduct that is misleading or deceptive or is likely to mislead or deceive.

[13.305] A mirror provision appears in all of the State Fair Trading legislation—except that the State legislation prohibits misleading conduct by 'persons' and not just corporations.[138] However, both the Commonwealth and State legislation are limited in their operation to conduct in 'trade or commerce'. Each State's *Fair Trading Act* contains an identical provision except for the Queensland Act, which limits the recovery of damages to consumers as defined in s 6 of the *Fair Trading Act* 1989 (Qld).[139]

[13.310] Since the commencement of s 52 of the *Trade Practices Act* 1974 (Cth), it has become an important part of the arsenal of commercial lawyers—even being referred to as an Exocet missile for commercial litigators. The section, while simple on its face, has generated a significant amount of litigation and case law since its inception. The discussion within this text focuses on the effect of s 52 of the *Trade Practices Act* 1974 (Cth) on the common law of misrepresentation and highlight the areas in which the rights of a representee have been expanded by the legislation.

---

135 See for example, *Ellul v Oakes* [1972] 3 SASR 377 and the commentary at [13.270].

136 Refer to [13.3.3].

137 Consequential loss may be things such as legal expenses, stamp duty or agent's commission.

138 NSW: *Fair Trading Act* 1987, s 42; Qld: *Fair Trading Act* 1989, s 38; Vic: *Fair Trading Act* 1985, s 11; SA: *Fair Trading Act* 1987, s 56; WA: *Fair Trading Act* 1987, s 10.

139 'Consumer' is defined in s 6 to include: (1) a person who purchases goods, services or an interest in land otherwise than in the course of, or for the purposes of, a business carried on by that person. In this case there is no limit on the value of the goods or services or interest in land. (2) A person who buys goods, services or an interest in land where the price does not exceed $40 000. In this case the person may purchase the goods or services or interest in land for the purposes of the business. (3) A corporation who purchases goods, services or an interest in land for a value not exceeding $40 000.

13.15 Overview of s 52 *Trade Practices Act* 1974 (Cth)

[13.315] The primary purpose of s 52 is to impose a norm or standard of conduct upon parties to commercial transactions with the aim of limiting the so-called 'smart practices' often employed in business dealings.[140] The section has been so effective in the prohibition of misleading or deceptive conduct by corporations in trade or commerce, that it has superseded the common law of misrepresentation in this area. However, there is still scope for the operation of the common law of misrepresentation in private dealings between individuals, and it is usually pleaded in the alternative to misleading conduct in actions against corporations. The *Trade Practices Act* 1974 (Cth) gives several significant advantages to a person claiming damages or rescission for misleading conduct. First, the section catches unintentional conduct. There is no requirement for an intention to mislead under s 52. Consequently, a person who makes a false statement honestly, may still be guilty of misleading conduct. Secondly, s 52 is wider than the common law in its application to conduct. Misleading conduct may occur through words, actions or silence. The potential application of s 52 to silence or non-disclosure is far greater than the limited instances already discussed under the common law.[141] Thirdly, although s 52 is found in Part V 'Consumer Protection' in the Act, the section is not limited to consumer transactions.[142]

13.16 Elements of s 52

13.16.1 Application to corporations and persons

[13.320] Section 52 of the *Trade Practices Act* 1974 (Cth) applies principally to corporations. A corporation is defined in s 4(1) to mean a body corporate that is:

(a) a foreign corporation;[143]

(b) a trading or financial corporation formed within the limits of Australia;[144]

(c) incorporated in a territory;

(d) a holding corporation of one of the corporations mentioned above.

[13.325] The operation of the *Trade Practices Act* 1974 has also been extended to natural persons in certain circumstances. These circumstances are limited by s 6 of the

---

140 *Commonwealth Bank of Australia v Mehta* (1991) 23 NSWLR 84; *Fraser v NRMA Holdings Limited* (1995) 127 ALR 543; Hon Mr Justice RS French, 'The Action for Misleading or Deceptive Conduct: Future Directions' in C Lockhart (ed) *Misleading or Deceptive Conduct: Issues and Trends,* Federation Press, Sydney, 1996, p 283.

141 Refer to [13.45]–[13.60].

142 *Bevanere Pty Ltd v Lubidineuse* (1985) 59 ALR 334; *Concrete Constructions (NSW) Pty Ltd v Nelson* (1990) 169 CLR 594.

143 For further discussion on the meaning of foreign corporations see *Trade Practices Act* 1974 s 4 and *Nauru Local Government Council v Australian Shipping Offices Association* (1978) 27 ALR 435.

144 For further discussion on the meaning of trading or financial corporations see *Trade Practices Act* 1974, s 4; the Constitution s 51(xx); *Hughes v Western Australian Cricket Association Inc* (1986) 69 ALR 660 at 671–672; *Re Federal Court of Australia; Ex parte Western Australian National Football League* (1979) 143 CLR 190; *E v Australian Red Cross Society* (1991) 99 ALR 601.

Trade Practices Act 1974, and extend the operation of s 52 to persons who engage in misleading and deceptive conduct while in the course of or in relation to:

(a) interstate or overseas trade or commerce;

(b) trade between the states or territories;

(c) supplying goods to the commonwealth;

(d) the use of postal telegraphic or telephonic services or a radio or television broadcast;[145] or

(e) professional persons engaged in promotional activities.

[13.330] Section 82(1) also extends the liability for breach of a provision of the *Trade Practices Act* 1974 to natural persons 'involved in the contravention'. This phrase is defined in the *Trade Practices Act* 1974, s 75B and is sufficiently wide to include the relevant officers and directors of the corporation involved in the contravention of s 52 with a corporate entity.[146]

13.16.2 Liability of a corporation for conduct of agents

[13.335] A corporation, although a separate legal entity, cannot act except through its directors, servants and agents. To overcome any difficulties of attributing conduct to a corporation, s 84(2) of the *Trade Practices Act* 1974 deals with conduct engaged in by directors, servants or agents on behalf of bodies corporate. The section acts to deem the conduct of a relevant person, acting within his or her actual or apparent authority, to be conduct of the corporation.[147] This means that if a director of a corporation engages in misleading conduct towards another person, and that director is acting within the course of his or her actual or ostensible authority, the corporation will also have engaged in that same misleading conduct, therefore proving one of the elements of s 52.[148]

Whether a director, servant or agent is acting within the course of his or her actual or ostensible authority should be determined according to the ordinary rules of principal and agent having regard to any statutory alterations.[149] It is important to note that the words 'on behalf of' in the section are wider than the usual test of whether an employee was acting in the course of employment.[150] Therefore, it is possible that

---

145 See *Snyman v Cooper* (1990) 91 ALR 209 where the conduct complained of was constituted by a misleading advertisement appearing in the Yellow Pages. The court held that telephonic services as that phrase was used in s 6(3) was to be interpreted widely enough to include official directories published pursuant to the *Telecommunications Act* 1975 (Cth). In *Green v Ford* (1985) ATPR 40-603 the court found that an individual was in breach of the *Trade Practices Act* in relation to magazines sent through the post. The conduct must also occur in trade and commerce: *Dataflow Computer Services Pty Ltd v Goodman* (1999) ATPR 41-730.

146 Refer to [13.350].

147 *Wright v Wheeler Grace and Pierucci Pty Ltd* (1988) ATPR 40-865; *Keen Mar Corporation Pty Ltd v Labrador Park Shopping Centre Pty Ltd* (1985) 61ALR 504.

148 Section 84(2) only deems the corporation to have engaged in misleading conduct. It does not deem the corporation to have been acting in trade and commerce. Therefore the corporation will only be liable under s 52 if the other elements of trade or commerce are proven by the plaintiff.

149 Refer in particular to ss 125–129 of the *Corporations Law.*

150 *TPC v TNT Management Pty Ltd* (1985) 58 ALR 423; *Wallis v Walplan Pty Ltd* (185) 59 ALR 771.

conduct of an employee or director acting within his or her apparent authority, but in some way that was forbidden, would still be within s 84(2).[151]

13.16.3   Application to government entities

[13.340] Section 2A of the *Trade Practices Act* 1974 states that the Commonwealth government and its instrumentalities[152] are bound when carrying on a business[153] by the provisions of s 52. The exact meaning of 'carries on a business' is, however, unclear in the context of government purchasing and some other contracting activities.[154]

[13.345] The Crown in right of the State is not bound by s 52 of the *Trade Practices Act* 1974.[155] The Crown in right of the State will include any State statutory authority entitled to Crown immunity. To determine if the statutory authority is entitled to Crown immunity, the legislation by which the authority is established and the activities engaged in pursuant to that legislation must be analysed.[156] A statutory body that does not have Crown immunity may be caught by the provisions of the *Trade Practices Act* 1974 if it is considered to be a corporation acting in trade and commerce.[157]

13.16.4   Liability of a party involved in a contravention of s 52

[13.350] Sections 82 and 87 provide that remedies may be claimed against a corporation or person that contravened s 52 and any person who is 'involved in the contravention'. This will allow the injured party to claim a remedy, not only from a corporation that contravenes s 52, but also from any director or agent of the corporation who actively engages in the same conduct. Section 75B defines a person involved in a contravention to include a person who has aided, abetted or procured the contravention; or a person who is in any way directly or indirectly knowingly concerned in or party to the contravention. It is clear that for a person to be knowingly concerned in the contravention of s 52 by another person or corporation they must have knowledge of the relevant facts constituting the contravention, and have participated in the

---

151 *Serrata Investments Pty Ltd v Rajane Pty Ltd* (1991) 6 WAR 419.

152 'Authority of the Commonwealth' is defined in s 4(1) of the *Trade Practices Act* 1974. The Act applies to those bodies corporate either established under a law of the Commonwealth or in which the Commonwealth has a controlling interest. For example Telstra is a Commonwealth statutory corporation to which the Act applies; *Tytel Pty Ltd v Australian Telecommunications Commission* (1986) 67 ALR 433.

153 Business includes a non-profit business: see s 4(1) of the *Trade Practices Act* 1974.

154 Refer to N Seddon, *Government Contracts: Federal, State and Local*, 2nd edn, Federation Press, Sydney 1999, pp 201–208.

155 However, the Crown in right of the States and Territories is bound by Part IV of the Act relating to competition policy. Refer to ss 2B–2C of the *Trade Practices Act* 1974. These provisions commenced on the 20 July 1996.

156 Refer to *Bropho v Western Australia* (1990) 171 CLR 1; *Wardley Australia v Western Australia* (1992) 175 CLR 514.

157 For example in *E v Australian Red Cross Society* (1991) 27 FCR 310 the Royal Prince Alfred Hospital, a State statutory corporation was held to be a trading corporation for the purposes of the *Trade Practices Act* and not an emanation of the Crown. In *State Superannuation Board v Trade Practices Commission* (1982) 60 FLR 165, the Federal Court found that the State Superannuation Board, a Victorian statutory corporation, had been established with such independence from government control that it was not entitled to immunity. However, note the contrasting decisions in *State Government Insurance Corporation v Government Insurance Office of New South Wales* (1991) 28 FCR 511; *Burgundy Royale Investments Pty Ltd v Westpac Banking Corporation* (1988) 18 FCR 212; *Bradken Consolidated Ltd v BHP* (1979) 145 CLR 107.

contravention in some way.[158] Therefore, unlike a person who directly contravenes s 52, a person involved in the contravention must have a certain degree of knowledge of the facts or elements constituting a contravention of the section.[159] The exact extent of the knowledge required is not entirely clear. It is not necessary to prove intent to contravene the section, but a reckless statement has been held to infringe s 75B,[160] and constructive knowledge of a contravention is insufficient.[161]

[13.355] As outlined above,[162] a corporation may be deemed to have engaged in misleading conduct through its servant, agent or director. Can that servant, agent or director also be a party involved in the contravention of the Act by the corporation? Initially, in the case of *York v Lucas*,[163] the court suggested that a director whose conduct created liability for a corporation pursuant to s 84(2) of the *Trade Practices Act 1974* would not be regarded as a person who was involved in the contravention of the Act by the corporation. However, in *Wheeler Grace & Pierucci v Wright*[164] the Full Federal Court reconsidered the issue and concluded that both the corporation and the individual who contributed to the breach by the corporation would be liable.[165] This would allow a plaintiff to sue both the director and the corporation, even though a successful claim against the director involved in the contravention does not depend upon the corporation's being a party to the action.[166]

13.16.5 Meaning of 'in trade or commerce'

[13.360] 'Trade or commerce' is defined in the *Trade Practices Act 1974* s 4 to mean trade or commerce within Australia or between Australia and places outside Australia. In *Re Ku-ring-gai Corporation Building Society (No 12) Ltd*, Bowen CJ said 'the terms trade and commerce are ordinary terms which describe all material communities, the negotiations verbal and by correspondence, the bargain, the transport and the delivery which comprised commercial arrangements'.[167]

[13.365] Normally, conduct of any corporation will be conduct in the course of trade or commerce. As the majority of corporations (charitable institutions being one exception) are incorporated for the purpose of trading in some manner,[168] most conduct of the corporation should be regarded as conduct in trade and commerce.[169] Generally, therefore, trade and commerce has been given a wide meaning in most of the authorities. However, in *Concrete Constructions (NSW) Pty Ltd v Nelson*,[170] the majority of the

---

158 *Yorke v Lucas* (1985) 158 CLR 661. Refer also to S Corones and S Christensen, 'Vicarious and Ancillary Liability for Misleading Conduct under the *Trade Practices Act 1974* (Cth)' (1996) 4 *Current Commercial Law* 99.

159 *Wheeler Grace and Pierucci v Wright* (1989) ATPR 40-940; *Sutton v AJ Thompson Pty Ltd* (1987) 73 ALR 233; *Henjo Investments Pty Ltd v Collins Marrickville Pty Ltd* (1988) 78 ALR 83.

160 *Gokora Pty Ltd v Montgomery Jordon & Stevenson Pty Ltd* (1986) ATPR 40-722 at 47,916–17.

161 *Crocodile Marketing v Griffith Vintners* (1992) 28 NSWLR 539; *Richardson & Wrench (Holdings) Pty Ltd v Ligon No 174 Pty Ltd* (1994) 123 ALR 681.

162 Refer to [13.335].

163 (1985) 158 CLR 661.

164 (1989) ATPR 40-940.

165 This followed the High Court decision of *Hamilton v Whitehead* (1988) 166 CLR 121.

166 *Richardson & Wrench (Holdings) Pty Ltd v Ligon No 174 Pty Ltd* (1994) 123 ALR 681.

167 (1978) 36 FLR 134 at 139.

168 Or for financial purposes: see definition of corporation in s 4 *Trade Practices Act 1974*.

169 *Bevanere Pty Ltd v Lubidineuse* (1985) 7 FCR 325; 59 ALR 334.

170 (1990) 169 CLR 594 at 604.

High Court restricted the operation of trade or commerce by finding that a corporation was acting in trade or commerce when its conduct was 'towards persons …with whom it has or may have dealings in the course of those activities or transactions which of their nature bear a trading or commercial character'. Conduct such as misleading statements to employees or negligent driving by an employee while delivering materials were not considered to be 'in' trade or commerce but were incidental to trade or commerce.[171] Likewise, misleading statements in an email about the conduct of a corporation have been held to be 'in relation to' trade and commerce but not 'in' trade and commerce.[172]

[13.370] Trade or commerce has also been interpreted to include the conduct of professional persons when acting for remuneration. In *Bond Corporation Pty Ltd v Thiess Contractors Pty Ltd*,[173] French J held that professional advice given by an engineer was conduct in trade and commerce. In his Honour's opinion where the conduct of a professional involves the provision of services for reward then there is 'no conceivable attribute of that aspect of professional activity which will take it outside the class of conduct' falling within trade or commerce.[174] It appears, therefore, that the advice given by professionals, such as doctors or lawyers, to clients will be given in trade or commerce.[175] This will only be the case where the professional is incorporated, otherwise liability is limited to promotional activity under the *Trade Practices Act* 1974, s 6(4). Politicians and priests on the other hand are clearly not engaged in trade or commerce.[176]

[13.375] Purely domestic transactions such as the sale of private dwellings are not in the course of trade or commerce.[177] However, a real estate agent selling private or domestic dwelling will be acting in trade or commerce and may be liable for misleading statements made to purchasers of the property.[178]

---

171 Ibid at 602–603; see also, *Firewatch Australia Pty Ltd v Country Fire Authority* (1999) ATPR (Digest) 46-198. Compare: *Barto v GPR Management Services Pty Ltd* (1991) 33 FCR 389, where the Federal Court ruled that misleading statements made during negotiations with present or prospective employees regarding that person's employment contract might be regarded as occurring in trade or commerce; *NRMA Limited v Yates* (1999) ATPR 41-721, where a director as part of a re-election campaign made misleading TV and radio advertisements alleging mismanagement by the Board; the statements were held to be in trade and commerce due to the director's intention to influence future trade and commerce of NRMA.

172 *Dataflow Computer Services Pty Ltd v Goodman* (1999) ATPR 41-730.

173 (1987) 14 FCR 215; 71 ALR 615.

174 Ibid at 220.

175 Solicitor: *Argy v Blunt & Lane Cove Real Estate Pty Ltd* (1990) 94 ALR 719; accountants: *Mackman v Stengold* (1991) ATPR 41-105; architects: *Multiplex Constructions Pty Ltd v Amdel Pty Ltd* (1991) ATPR 41-154; *Latella v LJ Hooker Ltd* (1985) ANZ Conv R 141. Compare *Tobacco Institute of Australia v Woodward* (1993) 32 NSWLR 559, where statements concerning judicial proceedings made by a professional consultant speaking for Action on Smoking and Health Ltd were held not to have been made in trade and commerce.

176 *Durant v Greiner* (1990) 21 NSWLR 119. Likewise, policy statements by a Commonwealth minister which related to the international wool trade were found not to have been in trade and commerce: *Unilan Holdings Pty Ltd v Kerin* (1992) 35 FCR 272.

177 *Bevanere Pty Ltd v Lubidineuse* (1985) 7 FCR 325; 59 ALR 334; *O'Brien v Smolonogov* (1983) 53 ALR 107; *Franich v Swannell* (1993) 10 WAR 459 where a corporation was held to be engaged in trade and commerce when selling a fruit business. It was necessary for the company to be engaged in the business of selling commercial premises.

178 *Aliotta v Broadmeadows Bus Service Pty Ltd* (1988) ATPR 40-873 and *Argy v Blunt & Lane Cove Real Estate Pty Ltd* (1990) 94 ALR 719; *MacCormick v Nowland* (1988) ATPR 40-852.

13.16.6   Engaging in conduct

[13.380] Section 52 is directed at prohibiting any misleading or deceptive conduct. Initially, the authorities attempted to confine the operation of s 52 to conduct that contained or conveyed a misrepresentation.[179] However later authorities have held that the clear words of the section should not be restricted—and this allows the section to apply to cases of silence.[180] This would appear to be the preferred view, and is in accordance with the wide definition of conduct in s 4(2)(b) of the *Trade Practices Act 1974*, which includes doing or refusing to do any act (otherwise then inadvertently) or making it known that the act will not be done.[181]

13.16.7   When is conduct misleading or deceptive?

[13.385] The central focus of s 52 is upon the establishment of misleading or deceptive conduct. Whether the conduct is misleading or deceptive should be viewed from the perspective of the type of persons or class of persons exposed to the conduct. There is no requirement for the person engaging in the misleading or deceptive conduct to do so intentionally—therefore, except in some circumstances, the perspective or view of the party engaging in the conduct will be irrelevant.[182] It is only necessary for an applicant to prove that the conduct engaged in either misled or deceived them. There has been some judicial debate about whether the words 'misleading' and 'deceptive' are synonymous, but in reality most applicants need only prove a minimum requirement of misleading conduct.[183] Proof that a person has been misled requires evidence that they have been led astray by action or conduct, or led into error, or caused to err.[184] However, proof that a person has been deceived would require evidence that the party has been induced to believe a thing that is false and which the person practising the deceit knows or believes to be false.[185]

[13.390] The test of whether conduct is misleading or deceptive is objective; it is based upon a consideration of the conduct of the defendant in light of the type of person who is likely to be exposed to that conduct. When applying this yardstick, it should be borne in mind that the hypothetical member of the determined class of people at whom the conduct is aimed 'may not be particularly intelligent or well informed, but perhaps somewhat less than average intelligence and background knowledge, but not a

---

179   *Taco Co of Australia Inc v Taco Bell Pty Ltd* (1982) 42 ALR 177 at 201; *Global Sportsmen Pty Ltd v Mirror Newspapers Pty Ltd* (1984) 2 FCR 82 at 88.

180   *Rhone-Poulenc Agrochimie SA v UIM Chemical Services Pty Ltd* (1986) 12 FCR 477; *Henjo Investments Pty Ltd v Collins Marrickville Pty Ltd* (1988) 79 ALR 83; *Demagogue Pty Ltd v Remensky* (1992) 39 FCR 31; 110 ALR 608.

181   See s 4(2)(c) *Trade Practices Act 1974* (Cth).

182   The knowledge of a person engaging in the conduct will be relevant to a conclusion of whether he or she is a party involved in the contravention as defined in s 75B of the *Trade Practices Act 1974*. Whether the person engaging in the conduct acted recklessly or dishonestly will also be relevant where the conduct engaged in is characterised as an opinion, intention, or relates to some other future matter.

183   In *Henjo Investments Pty Ltd v Collins Marrickville Pty Ltd* (1988) 79 ALR 83, Lockhart J stated that they were not necessarily synonymous whereas in *Parkdale Custom Furniture Pty Ltd v Puxu Pty Ltd* (1982) 149 CLR 191 at 198 Gibbs CJ proffered the view that 'the two words in quotation marks are in my view tautologous'.

184   *Henjo Investments Pty Ltd v Collins Marrickville Pty Ltd* (1988) 79 ALR 83.

185   *Re London & Globe Financial Corporation Ltd* [1903] 1 Ch 728 at 732.

person who is quite unusually stupid'.[186] Evidence of the fact that a person has actually been misled or deceived is not necessary, but may be persuasive.[187] Evidence of actual deception may be difficult to acquire particularly in the case of misleading advertising, but it is sufficient for the applicant to prove that the conduct was likely to mislead or deceive.[188] In contrast, where the misleading conduct consists of oral pre-contractual statements, it will be necessary for the representee to prove that they were actually misled or deceived (in other words they relied upon the conduct) if the remedies of damages or rescission are being claimed.[189]

13.16.8   Silence as conduct

[13.395] It is clear from the wide definition of conduct in s 4(2) of the *Trade Practices Act* 1974 that silence or refraining from engaging in conduct that is, in all the circumstances, misleading will be caught by s 52. Unlike the restrictive principles of the common law regarding silence, the courts have adopted a general test for whether silence or failure to disclosure is misleading or deceptive. The court will usually view all of the surrounding circumstances to ascertain whether there is a reasonable expectation on the part of the plaintiff that if some relevant fact existed it would have been disclosed.[190] In determining what conduct will amount to misleading or deceptive conduct, the courts have drawn upon the principles underlying the common law of misrepresentation, but have refused to restrict the operation of s 52 to the same circumstances as the common law. The recognition at common law of silence as an actionable misrepresentation relies heavily upon the existence of particular types of relationships, such as fiduciary relationships or contracts of good faith. For silence to be actionable under s 52, no such relationship need exist. An abundance of academic comment has arisen concerning whether s 52 implies a duty upon a party in pre-contractual negotiations to disclose all relevant information to the other party.[191] However, the authorities have preferred the view that the section imposes a minimum level of commercial probity upon parties to commercial transactions rather than a duty of disclosure.[192] The cases illustrate that although there was no requirement for a blanket

186   *McWilliams Wines Pty Ltd v McDonalds System of Australia Pty Ltd* (1980) 33 ALR 394.

187   *Taco Bell Pty Ltd v Taco Co of Australia* (1981) 40 ALR 153; *Parkdale Custombuilt Furniture Pty Ltd v Puxu Pty Ltd* (1982) 149 CLR 191; *McWilliams Wines Pty Ltd v McDonalds Systems of Australia Pty Ltd* (1980) 33 ALR 394.

188   See *Global Sportsmen Pty Ltd v Mirror Newspapers Ltd* (1984) 2 FCR 82 at 87. 'Likely to mislead' has been judicially interpreted to mean a real chance or possibility: *State of Western Australia v Wardley Australia Ltd* (1991) 30 FCR 245 at 261.

189   *Brown v Jam Factory Pty Ltd* (1980) 35 ALR 79; *Jones v Acompareold Investments Pty Ltd* (1985) 6 FCR 512; *Pappas v Soulac Pty Ltd* (183) 50 ALR 231.

190   *Kimberley NZI Finance Ltd v Torero Pty Ltd* (1989) ATPR (Digest) 46-054 at 53,195; *Demagogue Pty Ltd v Ramensky* (1992) 110 ALR 608; *Fraser v NRMA Holdings Ltd* (1995) 127 ALR 543; *Arbest Pty Ltd v State Bank of New South Wales Ltd* (1996) ATPR 41-481.

191   D Skapinker, 'The Imposition of a positive duty of disclosure under section 52 of the *Trade Practices Act* 1974 (Cth)' (1991) 2 JCL 75; A Robertson, 'The Circumstances in which Silence can Constitute Misleading and Deceptive Conduct' (1991) QLSJ 21; D Skapinker, 'Silence is Golden: or is it?' (1995) 69 ALJ 1654; E Webb, 'Representations of Shop-Centre Leases, What is the tenant "entitled to expect"' (1994) 8(8) *Australian Property Law Bulletin* 115.

192   See *Commonwealth Bank of Australia v Mehta* (1991) 23 NSW LR 84; *Fraser v NRMA Holdings Ltd* (1995) 127 ALR 543, (Black CJ, von Doussa and Cooper JJ); *Demagogue Pty Ltd v Ramensky* (1992) 39 FCR 31 at 40 (Gummow J); *Park v Allied Mortgage Corp Ltd* (1993) ATPR (Digest) 46-105 at 53,471.

disclosure of all information that may influence the mind of a party during negotiations, if the conduct of one party is such as to create an impression that a certain matter does exist, or that there is nothing unusual in the transaction, then disclosure may be necessary to ensure the conduct is not misleading.[193]

[13.400] The treatment given to this area by the courts is somewhat *ad hoc*, but it is clear that the existence of a corresponding common law duty of disclosure is not essential to a finding of misleading conduct by silence. The obligation imposed by s 52 has not been restricted by the courts to coincide with the common law duties, and is considered by some judges to have created new rights and remedies where previously none have existed.[194] Due to the *ad hoc* nature of the courts' consideration of silence and its relationship with s 52, it is difficult to find common principles that a court may take into account when assessing the factual matrix. It appears, however, that the court will take into account factors such as the information that would usually be disclosed to a person in that particular type of commercial activity,[195] the knowledge of the silent party, the experience and consequent expectation of the plaintiff,[196] the nature of the information not disclosed, the object of remaining silent—and, finally, the reliance by the plaintiff on the silence. Of particular note is the fact that, according to s 4(2) of the *Trade Practices Act* 1974, silence is only conduct if the person has refrained from doing an act otherwise than inadvertently. This means that 'while a failure to disclose may in fact mislead, it will not be actionable as misleading conduct unless this failure was intentional'.[197] Therefore, a person who fails to disclose information must have actual knowledge of the undisclosed fact. It is also necessary for the person with the knowledge to be aware that the other person has a reasonable expectation that the information will be disclosed. This awareness may arise from the nature of the information or the surrounding circumstances.

[13.405] It appears that both criteria must be present. In *General Newspapers v Telstra Corporation*,[198] the respondent was aware of the relevant undisclosed information, but the court concluded there was no evidence the plaintiff had a reasonable expectation of disclosure. The relevant circumstances may have arisen if the plaintiff had asked a relevant question or made known to Telstra that they thought that a certain state of affairs existed. An expectation of disclosure may not arise where parties to a commercial transaction have equal bargaining power. It has been stated that commercial people expect a certain degree of 'evasion or of obfuscation by [others] seeking to resist disclosing information which is confidential'.[199] It is also expected that not all the cards will be laid on the table—as in *Lam v Ausintel Investments Australia Pty Ltd*,[200] where

---

193 Refer to *Demagogue Pty Ltd v Ramensky* (1992) 110 ALR 608.
194 *Demagogue Pty Ltd v Ramensky* (1992) 39 FCR 31.
195 Refer to *Henjo Pty Ltd v Collins Marrickville Pty Ltd* (1988) 79 ALR 83, *Great Australian Bite Pty Ltd v Menmel Pty Ltd* (1996) ATPR 41-506.
196 Refer to *Lam v Ausintel Investments Australia Pty Ltd* (1989) 97 FLR 458, *Commonwealth Bank of Australia v Mehta* (1991) 23 NSW LR 84; *Fraser v NRMA Holdings Ltd* (1995) 127 ALR 543.
197 *Edgar v Farrow Mortgage Pty Ltd (in liq)* (1992) ATPR (Digest) 46-096, *Zaknic Pty Ltd v Svelte Corporation Pty Ltd* (1996) ATPR (Digest) 46-159.
198 (1993) 117 ALR 629.
199 *General Newspapers Pty Ltd v Telstra* (1993) 117 ALR 629 at 642.
200 (1989) 97 FLR 458.

the respondents were entitled to assume that the applicant, as an intelligent and experi-enced banker and businessman, would not expect information that would better his bargaining position to be disclosed. The position will be different if the conduct of the respondent creates a false impression of the situation in the mind of the applicant. This will usually be the case where the person contravening the section has actually pur-ported to provide some type of explanation or information but failed to provide the full story, thereby leading the other person into error. This situation will commonly give rise to a half-truth, which will also be recognised as a misrepresentation by the common law.

Example: Finucane v New South Wales Egg Corporation[201]

Mr Finucane had purchased an egg run from the Egg Corporation. The Egg Corpora-tion had conducted interviews with potential applicants, and during those interviews discussed extensively the operation concerned. While the Egg Corporation disclosed that it was investigating a reorganisation of the distribution system, it refrained from disclosing that if a reorganisation occurred, the principle of 'last in first out' would operate, and that compensation would not be paid. The court held that the conduct of the Egg Corporation was misleading or deceptive within the meaning of s 52. In coming to the conclusion, the court considered in this case the whole of the circum-stances including the content of the negotiation and the knowledge and experience of the other party. It is also important to note that although the silence was not intended to induce the contract, the mere fact the Egg Corporation refrained from disclosing the information in circumstances where it should have been obvious that the information was relevant, was sufficient to evoke the operation of s 52.

[13.410] While s 52 does not impose a duty on contracting parties to put all their cards on the table, it does impose an obligation on a party when advice or any information is provided to ensure that the full picture is given. If the context in which the infor-mation or advice is given creates a misleading impression in the mind of the other party, then a failure to speak up at that point will be regarded as misleading or decep-tive.[202] Ultimately, whether conduct (including silence) amounts to misleading or deceptive conduct is a question of fact for the court, based upon evidence of all the surrounding circumstances. One of those surrounding circumstances must be whether a reasonable expectation of disclosure has been created.[203] The authorities clearly indi-cate that while there is some coincidence between the operation of s 52 and the

---

201 (1988) 80 ALR 486. See also *General Newspapers Pty Ltd v Telstra Corporation* (1993) 117 ALR 629 at 643 and *Karmot Autospares Ltd v Dominelli Ford (Hurstille Pty Ltd)* (1992) 35 FCR 560.

202 Refer for example to *Demagogue Pty Ltd v Ramensky* (1992) 39 FCR 31 where a real estate agent was found to have engaged in misleading conduct by failing to disclose the existence of a road licence to the purchaser, following a direct inquiry by the purchaser. Although there was no duty on the real estate agent to disclose the existence of this licence, once questioned and having volunteered information the agent should have ensured that the full picture was made clear to the purchaser.

203 Some difficulties have arisen in the operation of s 52 with a party's duty of confidentiality. Refer to *Kabwand Pty Ltd v National Australia Bank Ltd* (1989) ATPR 40-950; *Winterton Constructions Pty Ltd v Hambros Australia Ltd* (1992) 111 ALR 649; *Warner v Elders Rural Finance Ltd* (1992) 113 ALR 517; *Le Gleeson Pty Ltd v Sterling Estates Pty Ltd* (1991) 23 NSW LR 571.

common law of misrepresentation, the courts are not bound to follow the principles at common law, and may, if appropriate, create new rights and remedies where none may previously have existed.

13.16.9 Fact, law, and opinion: can they be misleading?

[13.415] Conduct as defined by s 4(2) of the *Trade Practices Act* 1974 is not limited to representations of fact. This means that statements of fact and law that provide inaccurate information are capable of being misleading. The position of statements of opinion, however, are not as clear. As with the common law, a statement of opinion that turns out to be wrong will not of itself amount to misleading or deceptive conduct.[204] The general approach taken by the authorities in relation to opinions has been influenced to a large extent by the common law. Therefore, where an opinion is based upon a question of fact, it may be found to be misleading where the person knows that the facts do not support the opinion or the opinion does not represent the state of mind of the person.[205] For example, an accountant's opinion about trading figures was held to be misleading where it was based on erroneous facts.[206] In the context of the broad test applied by the courts under s 52, an opinion will be misleading or deceptive if it is such as to lead the person to whom it is given into error.[207]

13.16.10 Statements concerning future matters

[13.420] Statements concerning future matters may include statements of intention, promises and predictions. Predictions would normally only be misleading or deceptive if the person making the prediction either knew it to be false or made it with reckless disregard for whether it was true or false.[208] The position is the same in relation to statements of intent[209] or where the statement is one of present intention or ability rather than about a future event.[210] It is accepted that s 52 is no wider than the common law in this regard. However, the position under the *Trade Practices Act* 1974 is affected by s 51A, which provides that a representation as to a future matter will be taken to be misleading unless the maker of the misrepresentation can prove that he or she had reasonable grounds for making the representation. The purpose of s 51A is to facilitate the evidentiary procedures in representation cases involving statements as to future matters, by reversing the onus of proof. This requires the representor to prove that he or she had reasonable grounds for making the statement. Despite the intended objective of s 51A, the issue of whether representations concerning future matters are misleading and the approach of the courts still appears unclear. For example, in

---

204 *Elders Trustee & Executor Co Ltd v EG Reeves Pty Ltd* (1987) 78 ALR 193.
205 *Global Sportsmen Pty Ltd v Mirror Newspapers Pty Ltd* (1984) 2 FCR 82.
206 *Mackan v Stengold* (1991) ATPR 41-105; *Sweetman v Bradfield Management Services Pty Ltd* (1994) ATPR 41-290.
207 *Cohen v Centrepoint Freeholds Pty Ltd* [1982] ATPR 40-289; *National Australia Bank Ltd v Nobile* (1988) 100 ALR 227; *Batman v Slatyer* (1987) 71 ALR 553.
208 *Thompson v Mastertouch TV Service Pty Ltd (No 1)* (1977) 29 FLR 270; *TN Lucas Pty Ltd v Centrepoint Freeholds Pty Ltd* (1984) 1 FCR 110.
209 *Cohen v Centrepoint Freeholds Pty Ltd* (1982) 66 FLR 57.
210 *Stack v Coast Securities No 9 Pty Ltd* (1983) 46 ALR 451; *Bill Acceptance Corp Ltd v GWA Ltd* (1983) 50 ALR 242 at 247–50; *Futuretronics International Pty Ltd v Gadzhis* [1992] VR 209 at 233–234.

Futuretronics International Pty Ltd v Gadzhis,[211] the defendant was a successful bidder at an auction for the sale of land. He refused to sign the written contract and the contract was not signed by the auctioneer on his behalf. This created an unenforceable contract, as there was no note or memorandum in writing executed by the defendant.[212] The vendor sued the defendant, arguing that he had engaged in misleading conduct by bidding at the auction and then refusing to sign. Ormiston J discussed at length the relationship between promises and misleading conduct. His approach indicates that the mere fact a promise or statement of intent is not fulfilled will not give rise to misleading conduct. His Honour relied upon previous authority that indicated that a promise or statement of intention will be misleading only if it is made fraudulently or recklessly. This is consistent with the approach at common law.

13.16.11 Puffery

[13.425] At common law, puffery or sales talk usually engaged in by sales persons will not be a misrepresentation. However, s 52 is likely to cover this kind of conduct in circumstances where the sales talk or puffery leads the recipient into error. For example, in *Byers v Dorotea Pty Ltd*,[213] a statement by the agent that units on the Gold Coast were bigger and better than any others near by was held to be misleading. As a general principle, whether puffery or sales talk amounts to misleading or deceptive conduct will be a question of fact turning primarily on the question of whether it was reasonable for the other party to rely upon the statement in the circumstances.

13.17 No requirement for intention

[13.430] Intent is not an element of s 52. A corporation may have engaged in misleading or deceptive conduct even though it did not intend to do so. Whether conduct is misleading or deceptive will be ascertained objectively by the court. In other words, the court will look to see whether in fact the applicant has been misled or whether it is likely that the applicant or the particular class of persons could be misled by the conduct. The court will not inquire as to whether the person engaging in the conduct actually intended to mislead or deceive the applicant.[214] This would suggest that any requirement for deceptive conduct is redundant. However, in some circumstances, proof of deception may encourage the court to exercise its discretion more favourably than if the conduct was merely misleading, particularly in a case of rescission.[215] Generally, the focus in a claim pursuant to s 52 of the *Trade Practices Act* 1974 is on how the other party perceived the conduct, rather than on the intention or knowledge of the person engaging in the conduct. This should be contrasted with the position at common law in the case of fraudulent misrepresentation.

---

211 [1992] VR 209.
212 Refer to Chapter 11 Formalities.
213 (1986) 69 ALR 715; and see *MacFarlane v John Martin* (1977) 1 ATPR 40-034; *Given v Pryor* (1979) 39 FLR 437.
214 *Parkdale Custombuilt Furniture Pty Ltd v Puxu Pty Ltd* (1982) 149 CLR 191 at 197.
215 For example, in a case such as *Alati v Kruger* (1955) 95 CLR 216, the court was more disposed to the granting of rescission, despite the business being closed due to the existence of fraud.

[13.435] There are certain exceptions to the general proposition that intention is not a requirement for misleading or deceptive conduct:

1   Where the conduct is characterised as a statement of opinion or intention, or concerns some future matter, then the statement will not be misleading unless it is proved that the statement-maker made the statement dishonestly, recklessly, or without belief in its truth.[216]

2   A person who is alleged to be involved in a contravention of the *Trade Practices Act* 1974 as defined by s 75B will not be liable unless it is proved that he or she was knowingly concerned in the contravention of the legislation. This will require proof that the person had knowledge of the essential facts constituting the contravention.

3   Where the conduct complained of is characterised as silence, the definition of conduct in s 4(2) of the *Trade Practices Act* 1974 would require that the person had refused or refrained from disclosing the information deliberately.[217]

13.18 Time limits

[13.440] An aggrieved party may obtain a remedy for misleading or deceptive conduct pursuant to s 82 or s 87. Each section imposes a time limit for commencing a claim. Proceedings for compensation pursuant to s 82(2) must be commenced within 3 years of the date on which the cause of action accrued. An action for rescission or some other remedy under s 87 must also be commenced within the same period.[218] Whether a time limit has been exceeded is an issue that should be raised by the defendant as a defence. Once pleaded, it may act as a bar to recovery.[219] There is no provision within the *Trade Practices Act* 1974 (Cth) for extension of the time periods, and a party is unable to rely upon the State *Limitation of Action Acts*[220] or equitable discretions[221] to extend the time for commencement of a claim.

[13.445] Despite the similarity of expression in ss 82 and 87, the time limit for commencing a claim may actually start to run from different times under each of the sections. The gist of a claim pursuant to s 82 is that either loss or damage has occurred at the time the cause of action has commenced. Therefore, a cause of action will not accrue for the purposes of s 82 until the aggrieved party has suffered loss or damage.[222] The time period will not start to run under s 82 where there is merely where a prospective loss—it must have actually occurred.[223] Where the misleading or deceptive

---

216 Refer to [13.415].

217 Refer to [13.400].

218 Section 87(1CA)(b) *Trade Practices Act* 1974 (Cth). However, a claim for rescission arising out of unconscionable conduct alleged under Part IVB of the Act must be commenced within 2 years of the date the cause of action accrued.

219 *James v ANZ Banking Group Ltd* (1986) 64 ALR 347 at 396–397; *AMP Society v Specialist Funding Consultants Pty Ltd* (1991) 24 NSWLR 326 at 331.

220 *Vink v Schering Pty Ltd* (1991) ATPR 41-064; *Keen Mar Corporation Pty Ltd v Labrador Park Shopping Centre Pty Ltd* (1988) ATPR 40-853; *New South Wales v McCloy Hutcherson Pty Ltd* (1993) 116 ALR 363 at 377–80; *Jekos Holdings Pty Ltd v Australian Horticultural Finance Pty Ltd* (1994) 2 Qd R 515.

221 *Wardley Australia Ltd v Western Australia* (1992) 175 CLR 514.

222 *Coleman v Gordon M Jenkins & Associates Pty Ltd* (1989) ATPR 40-960.

223 *Wardley Australia Ltd v Western Australia* (1992) 175 CLR 514.

conduct induces a person to enter into a contract, generally the cause of action will accrue at the time the person enters into the relevant contract.[224] Exceptions may occur where the effects of the misleading conduct are delayed—as where the person gives a guarantee or indemnity. In *Wardley Australia Ltd v Western Australia*,[225] an indemnity was granted as a result of misleading or deceptive conduct. The question for the court was: When did the applicant suffer loss or damage for the purposes of the time limitation in s 82 of the *Trade Practices Act* 1974?

[13.450] The High Court was strongly of the view that a cause of action for damages under s 82 would not start to run until such time as the actual loss or damage was suffered. Usually, loss or damage will be suffered at the time the contract is entered into—or, at the latest, on the date the contract is completed.

[13.455] In *Wardley*, the High Court considered that the time did not start to run until the indemnity had been called up. Although there may be detriment in entering into a disadvantageous contract, this did not necessarily equate to the suffering of loss or damage at that time. The fact that potential loss or damage may be suffered is not enough. A further factor that impacted on the High Court's decision was the existence of an obvious injustice in compelling the institution of an action prior to the loss being ascertained or ascertainable.[226]

[13.460] In contrast, relief may be obtained pursuant to s 87 of the *Trade Practices Act* 1974 (Cth) where loss or damage is *likely* to be suffered. Proof of actual loss is not necessary. Consequently, a cause of action under s 87 may arise at the time a contravention occurs or in the case of a contingent loss at the time the contract is entered into. Despite the fact the loss may never actually occur, it may still be a situation where the person is *likely* to suffer loss or damage.

13.19 Effect of a contravention of s 52

13.19.1 Overview

[13.465] A party who is aggrieved by a contravention of s 52 of the *Trade Practices Act* 1974 may claim a range of remedies. Where the misleading conduct takes the form of a misrepresentation that induced a contract, the aggrieved party would usually seek damages (s 82) or rescission (s 87).[227] Damages pursuant to s 82 may be sought as the principal remedy by the aggrieved party. Rescission may be sought as ancillary relief under s 87 or as principal relief independently of any claim for compensation.[228]

---

224 *Keen Mar Corporation Pty Ltd v Labrador Park Shopping Centre Pty Ltd* (1988) ATPR 40-853; *Elna v International Computers (Australia) Pty Ltd* (1987) 75 ALR 271 at 279–281; *Emanuele v Chamber of Commerce and Industry (SA) Inc* (1994) ATPR 53,565.

225 (1992) 175 CLR 514.

226 Refer also to *Hawkins v Clayton* (1988) 164 CLR 539 at 602; *SWF Hoists and Industrial Equipment Pty Ltd v State Government Insurance Commission* (1990) ATPR 41-045.

227 A contravention of s 52 will allow a claim for an injunction pursuant to s 80, however in a situation involving misrepresentation inducing a contract a claim for an injunction is unlikely. Other remedies such as variation of the contract or repayment of monies may also be sought under s 87.

228 Refer to s 87(1), which applies to a claim for rescission that is made ancillary to a principal claim for compensation, and s 87(1A) which applies to a principal claim for rescission independent of a claim for compensation under s 82. See also *Fielding v Vagrand Pty Ltd* (1992) 111 ALR 368 at 374.

[13.470] A claim for compensation pursuant to s 82 of the *Trade Practices Act* 1974 will not succeed unless the applicant proves that actual loss or damage has occurred as a result of a contravention of s 52. This should be contrasted with a claim for rescission pursuant to s 87, which may succeed where no actual loss or damage has occurred, but loss is likely to occur in the future.

13.19.2   Is a contravention an offence?

[13.475] Unlike the other provisions of Part V of the *Trade Practices Act* 1974 a contravention of s 52 is not a criminal offence.[229] This means a court cannot impose a penalty for a contravention of s 52 unless the conduct also constitutes a contravention of another provision of Part V. For example, a misleading representation made by a real estate agent to a purchaser concerning the potential use of a property would be a contravention of both s 52 and s 53A.[230] A penalty could be imposed by the court for the contravention of s 53A in accordance with s 79.

13.19.3   Measure of damage: s 82

[13.480] Recovery of compensation for loss or damage pursuant to s 82 of the *Trade Practices Act* 1974 is subject to proof of:

•   a contravention of Part IV or Part V; and

•   loss or damage suffered as a result of the contravention.[231]

Compensation is recoverable from the person whose conduct gave rise to the loss or damage and from any person involved in the contravention.[232]

[13.485] The section itself does not provide any guidance on the measure of loss to be applied. Caution should be exercised in drawing too close an analogy between s 82 and the common law. Although, in claims for misleading conduct arising from misrepresentation, the courts have continually preferred the tortious measure of damage over the contractual measure, they have warned against reaching definitive analogies between the common law of tort and s 82.[233] Section 82 provides a vehicle for recovering loss for multifarious forms of contravention of Parts IV and V. Claims for a contravention of s 52 constitute only one aspect of those Parts. Nevertheless, one rationale given for adopting the tortious measure is the similarity to a claim for misrepresentation and the indication in section 82 itself that only the loss suffered as a result of the conduct is recoverable.[234]

[13.490] A clear indication of the method to be adopted by the courts was set by the High Court in *Gates v City Mutual Life Assurance Society Ltd*.[235] This case involved the

---

229   See s 79 of the *Trade Practices Act* 1974.

230   *Benlist Pty Ltd v Olivetti Australia Pty Ltd* (1990) ATPR 41-043; *Latella v LJ Hooker Ltd* (1985) 5 FCR 146.

231   It is important in all instances that the applicant provide evidence of the loss which has been suffered: *Voss Real Estate v Schreiner* (1998) ATPR 41-627.

232   Section 75B defines 'a person involved in the contravention', refer to [13.350].

233   Refer to *Gates v City Mutual Life Assurance Society* (1986) 160 CLR 1; *Akron Securities Ltd v Iliffe* (1997) 4 NSWLR 353 at 364; *Marks v GIO Australia Holdings Ltd* (1998) 158 ALR 333 per McHugh, Hayne, Callinan JJ at 344–345, Gummow J at 360, Kirby J at 366.

234   *Gates v City Mutual Life Assurance* (1986) 160 CLR 1 at 11–14.

235   (1986) 160 CLR 1.

misrepresentation by an insurer to a proposer that the total disability clause in a life insurance policy would entitle him to benefits if he were totally disabled from following his occupation as a builder. The proposer suffered an injury that prevented him from being a builder but not from engaging in other types of work. The clause did not operate in that event.

[13.495] An important question for the High Court was whether the insured party was entitled to recover compensation on the basis of his lost expectations, that is the insurance proceeds. The majority of the court clearly concluded that a claimant for compensation pursuant to s 82 of the *Trade Practices Act* 1974 for misleading or deceptive conduct should only be entitled to recover the loss suffered as a result of the conduct:

> there is much to be said for the view that the measure of damage in tort is appropriate in most, if not all, Pt V cases, especially those involving misleading or deceptive conduct and the making of false statements. Such conduct is similar in character and effect to tortious conduct ...[236]

[13.500] Generally this will mean that the applicant is entitled to recover the monies spent in reliance on the representation. Recovery of compensation that puts the applicant in the position as if the representation had been true is only recoverable if the applicant can prove that, but for reliance on the misleading conduct, the applicant would have obtained the expected benefit by entering into another contract.[237] Although the High Court appeared to prefer the tortious method of calculating loss, the majority clearly stated that 'the courts are not bound to make a definitive choice between the two measures [contract and tort] of damages so that one applies to all contraventions to the exclusion of the other'.[238]

[13.505] If the measure of damage applied in *Gates v City Mutual Life Assurance Society Ltd*[239] is used, an aggrieved party will be compensated for the prejudice or disadvantage suffered as a result of relying on the misleading conduct. A party will only be compensated for unrealised expectations if the conduct prevented entry into a similar contract with another party, or if the representation amounted to a warranty or collateral contract.[240] Later decisions have continued to apply this approach,[241] and it is possible to draw from the authorities principles for common types of transactions.

[13.510] Where misleading conduct induces a person to purchase property the measure of damage will generally be the difference between the real value of the property at the time of purchase and what the person actually paid for the property.[242] The

---

236 Ibid at 14, Mason CJ, Wilson, Dawson JJ.

237 Ibid at 14–15. See also *Marks v GIO Australia Holdings Limited* (1998) 158 ALR 333, followed in *Zipside Pty Ltd v Anscor Pty Ltd* [2000] QCA 395.

238 (1986) 160 CLR 1 at 14.

239 (1986) 160 CLR 1.

240 In the case of a warranty or collateral contract, the plaintiff will need to elect between damages under the *Trade Practices Act* 1974, or damages in contract. Both will not be available.

241 *Brown v Jam Factory Pty Ltd* (1981) 53 FLR 340; *Yorke v Ross Lucas Pty Ltd* (1982) 69 FLR 116; *Kenny & Good Pty Limited v MGICA (1992) Limited* (1997) ATPR 41-576; *Marks v GIO Australia Holdings Limited* (1998) 158 ALR 333.

242 *Kenny &Good Pty Ltd v MGICA (1992) Limited* (1997) ATPR 41-576.

court will, in effect, draw a comparison between the plaintiff's financial position prior to entering into the contract and that after the contract is entered into. It is emphasised in the cases that the usual measure may not apply in all cases and the ultimate question is how much worse off the applicant is as a result of the conduct. Particular difficulties arise where the value of the property declines sharply after the purchase. The usual measure of loss will not allow the applicant to recover any loss suffered as a result of the decline in value. Where it is clear that the applicant would not have entered into the contract but for the misleading conduct, the loss suffered due to the decline in value may be recoverable.[243] If the applicant would have entered into the relevant transaction even if the misrepresentation had not been made, any losses flowing from the transaction as such cannot be said to flow directly from the inducement. In such a case, the applicant would have been exposed in any event to the precise risk that ultimately eventuated, and the loss in value is not recoverable. The mere fact that the applicant entered into a contract that confers different rights and obligations does not establish that loss or damage has been suffered.[244]

[13.515] The application of this general principle will also allow the court to award consequential losses resulting from the operation of a business,[245] but representees will generally not be able to recover their lost expectation or anticipated profit.[246] Lost expectations, such as profits, are only recoverable under s 82 if the applicant can prove that, but for the misrepresentation, the applicant would have entered into a another available arrangement that would have resulted in the expectations being met.[247]

[13.520] Other types of loss that may be recoverable include damages for loss of an opportunity,[248] damages for mental distress,[249] and interest.[250]

13.19.4   Recovery of loss or damage: s 87

[13.525] Pursuant to s 87 of the *Trade Practices Act* 1974, the court may at its discretion make an order for the payment of compensation in the amount of any loss or damage suffered.[251] The power of the court to grant relief pursuant to s 87 of the *Trade Practices Act* 1974 is predicated upon:

* the applicant's suffering (or likelihood of suffering) loss or damage by the conduct of another party; and
* the conduct's being a contravention of Parts IVA or V.

[13.530] The purpose of s 87 is to provide the court with power to make such orders as the court considers appropriate with the object of compensating an aggrieved party for loss or reducing or preventing potential loss. This appears to provide an aggrieved

---

243   *Kenny &Good Pty Ltd v MGICA (1992) Limited* (1997) ATPR 41-576; *Gentry Bros Pty Ltd v Wilson Brown and Associates Pty Ltd* (1996) Q Conv R 54-471.
244   Refer to *Jobbins v Capel Court Corp Ltd* (1989) 25 FCR 226; *Marks v GIO Australia Holdings Limited* (1998) 158 ALR 333.
245   *Kizbeau Pty Ltd v WG & B Pty Ltd* (1995) 131 ALR 363.
246   Refer to *Marks v GIO Australia Holdings Limited* (1998) 158 ALR 333.
247   Ibid.
248   *Sellars v Adelaide Petroleum NL* (1994) 179 CLR 332.
249   *Steiner v Magic Carpet Tours Pty Ltd* (1984) ATPR 40-490.
250   Interest may be awarded pursuant to s 51A of the *Federal Court of Australia Act* 1976 (Cth). The *Trade Practice Act* 1974 does not empower the court to award interest.
251   Section 87(2)(d) *Trade Practices Act* 1974.

party with a second alternative for the recovery of loss or damage arising from a contravention of s 52. An important issue for an aggrieved party will be whether s 87 of the *Trade Practices Act* 1974 provides any advantage over s 82 of the *Trade Practices Act* 1974.

[13.535] Several features of s 87 may act to distinguish it from s 82. The first feature is that relief may be obtained where loss or damage is likely to be suffered. It is not necessary for an aggrieved party to prove that actual loss or damage has been suffered by conduct of another person. However, an order pursuant to s 87(2)(d) of the *Trade Practices Act* 1974 would require a person engaged in conduct to pay the aggrieved party the loss or damage suffered as a result of the conduct. This should be contrasted with the other orders set out in s 87(2) of the *Trade Practices Act* 1974, which include the words 'is likely to suffer' loss or damage.[252] This means that in the context of a claim for compensation, both s 82 and s 87 require proof of loss or damage. Where loss or damage is likely to be suffered, it may be appropriate for the court to grant a type of relief different from compensation.

[13.540] The second feature of s 87 is that the court is empowered to make such order or orders as the court thinks appropriate. It has been suggested that the existence of such a discretion would allow the court to grant compensation of a different kind from that available pursuant to s 82.

[13.545] The issue of the type of damage recoverable under s 87 did not receive detailed consideration by the High Court until the case of *Marks v GIO Australia Holdings Limited*.[253] The High Court considered claims by the holders of a loan facility from GIO, which increased its interest rate contrary to representations made at the time of contract. The trial judge awarded the applicants damages to compensate for the increased rate—in essence the equivalent of the lost expectation on the bargain. The Full Federal Court allowed an appeal by GIO, and the applicants appealed to the High Court.

[13.550] The High Court followed the decision in *Gates v City Mutual Life Assurance Society*,[254] holding that the customers were only entitled to damages for the detriment suffered as a result of entry into the contract. This equated to the prejudice or disadvantage of altering their position to enter into the contract. As the loan cost the applicants less than any other loan on the market, the majority of the court considered that no loss or damage had been sustained. The applicants were not entitled to claim the lost expectation or profit. They had argued that the type of loss or damage recoverable under s 87(1A) was different from the loss or damage recoverable under s 82. After considering the purpose of both s 82 and s 87, the High Court concluded that:[255]

> The loss or damage spoken of in ss 82 and 87 is not confined to economic loss.
> ... But central to them all, when it is said that the loss was, or will probably be,
> caused by misleading or deceptive conduct, is that the plaintiff has sustained (or

---

252 See s 87(2)(a), (e), (f), (g) *Trade Practices Act* 1974.
253 (1998) 158 ALR 333.
254 (1986) 160 CLR 1.
255 (1998) 158 ALR 33 at 347

is likely to sustain) a prejudice or disadvantage as a result of altering his or her position under the inducement of the misleading conduct.

[13.555] Even though the measure of compensation given under ss 82 and 87 will be subject to the same principles, s 87 is not confined to cases where loss or damage has been sustained. Relief may be obtained where it is shown that a person is *likely* to suffer loss or damage in the future and relief is available to prevent or reduce that loss. The inquiry remains one about whether it is likely that as a result of the contravention the party concerned will suffer some prejudice or disadvantage. Something more than the entry into a contract that is different from the type represented will need to be shown before it is likely that loss or damage will have been suffered.[256] In practical terms, the type of relief granted where actual loss is sustained will differ from the type where loss is only foreseeable.

13.19.5 Are causation and remoteness necessary?

[13.560] In order to recover loss pursuant to both ss 82 and 87 the party must suffer the loss 'by' conduct in breach of the Act. This requirement was examined by Mason CJ in *Wardley Australia Ltd v Western Australia:*[257]

> 'By' is a curious word to use. One might have expected 'by means of', 'by reason of', 'in consequences of' or 'as a result of'. But the word clearly expresses the notion of causation without taking up the common law practical or common-sense concept of causation recently discussed by this court in *March v Stramare (E & MH) Pty Ltd*,[258] except in so far as that concept is modified or supplemented expressly or impliedly by the provisions of the Act. Had Parliament intended to say something else, it would have been natural and easy to have said so.[259]

[13.565] The authorities indicate that causation is proved if there is a relevant nexus between the conduct complained of and the loss or damage suffered.[260] The person induced to enter the contract must show not only that the transaction was induced by the misleading conduct, but also that the losses suffered flow directly from the contravention.[261] Where a representation forms the basis of the misleading conduct the applicant must first satisfy the court of the fact they relied upon the conduct when entering the contract.[262] The common law principles concerning reliance are applied under the *Trade Practices Act* 1974.[263] In particular, the misleading conduct need not be the sole inducement so long as it plays a material part in contributing to entry into the transaction.[264] The second requirement is that the losses suffered actually flow from the

---

256 Cf. *Demagogue Pty Ltd v Ramensky* (1992) 110 ALR 608
257 (1992) ATPR 41-189 at 40,571.
258 (1991) 171 CLR 506.
259 See also *Munchies Management Pty Ltd v Belperio* (1988) 58 FCR 274 at 286–287.
260 *Janssen-Cilag Pty Ltd v Pfizer Pty Ltd* (1992) 37 FCR 526.
261 *Gates v City Mutual Life Assurance Society* (1986) 160 CLR 1; *Kenny & Good Pty Ltd v MGICA (1992) Limited* (1997) ATPR 41-576.
262 Where misleading conduct is constituted by a passing off, it may not be necessary to prove reliance. See *Janssen-Cilag Pty Ltd v Pfizer Pty Ltd* (1992) 37 FCR 526.
263 Refer to [13.470].

inducement. Common law principles of causation will be relevant. In particular, the commonsense approach to causation in *March v Stramare* appears to be favoured.[265] If the applicant would have entered into the transaction even if the representation had not been made, then the losses suffered cannot be said to flow directly from the inducement.[266] Likewise, where the loss is contingent on events occurring after the date of contract, action of the representor that provides an option for avoiding the loss may break the chain.[267]

[13.570] Examples of situations where the applicant failed to prove a causal connection between the misleading conduct and the loss suffered are:

- A financier who agreed to lend funds on the basis of a misleading valuation failed to show the money would not have been lent even if the valuation were true. The financier would have been exposed to the actual risk that eventuated irrespective of the misleading conduct. As a result, the decline in the value of the property through a market correction could not be said to flow directly from the contravention of s 52.[268]

- A person who entered an agreement to defer debts owing by a corporation to him failed to proved that he relied on advice by the bank about the transaction. The person, as an intelligent and experienced businessman, was found to have relied upon his own commercial judgement.[269]

[13.575] The existence of any contributory negligence on the part of the applicant will generally be irrelevant to the question of reliance. However, there may be circumstances where the applicant is so negligent in the protection of his or her own affairs that the misleading conduct may, on the facts, not have been a real inducement to enter the contract.[270]

13.19.6   Can damages be apportioned between the contravening parties?

[13.580] There is no express provision in the *Trade Practices Act* 1974 for the apportionment of loss between co-defendants.[271] However, judicial consideration has been given to an apportionment of loss between an applicant and a respondent pursuant to s 87 of the *Trade Practices Act* 1974. In *I & L Securities Pty Ltd v HTW Valuers (Bne) Pty Ltd*,[272] the Queensland Court of Appeal held that s 87 provided a broad discretionary power to take account of a wide range of factors, including the fault of each party. The Court concluded that a financial institution was only entitled to

---

264   *Gentry Bros Pty Ltd v Wilson Brown and Associates Pty Ltd* (1996) Q Conv R 54-471; *Kabwand Pty Ltd v National Australia Bank Ltd* (1989) ATPR 40-950 at 50,378.

265   *Gentry Bros Pty Ltd v Wilson Brown and Associates Pty Ltd* (1996) Q Conv R 54-471; *Wardley Australia Ltd v Western Australia* (1992) ATPR 41-189 at 40,571.

266   *Kenny & Good Pty Ltd v MGICA (1992) Limited* (1997) ATPR 41-576.

267   Refer to *Marks v GIO Australia Holdings Ltd* (1998) 158 ALR 333 per Gummow J at 362.

268   *Kenny & Good Pty Ltd v MGICA (1992) Limited* (1997) ATPR 41-576.

269   *Lam v Austinel Investments Australia Pty Ltd* (1990) 97 FLR 458.

270   *Argy v Blunts and Land Cove Real Estate Pty Ltd* (1990) 26 FCR 112.

271   However, there may be a claim at law or in equity for contribution where there are concurrent claims. See *Gentry Bros Pty Ltd v Wilson Brown and Associates Pty Ltd* (1996) Q Conv R 54-471.

272   [2000] QCA 383

recover part of its loss from a defaulting valuer where the institution's conduct partially contributed to its loss.

13.19.7 Ancillary orders

[13.585] In addition to the substantive remedy of damages, an applicant aggrieved by a contravention of s 52 may also obtain a range of other remedies pursuant to s 87 of the *Trade Practices Act* 1974. Section 87 provides the court with a discretion to make orders that compensate a person for loss or damage suffered or that is likely to be suffered as a result of a contravention of Parts IV, IVA or V. As discussed above, s 87 differs from s 82 in that it is not necessary to prove that loss or damage has actually been suffered. It is sufficient if loss or damage is likely to be suffered in the future.[273] The types of orders a court may make include inter alia:

- an order for rescission of the contract (s87(2)(a));
- an order varying a contract (s 87(2)(b));[274]
- an order directing a person to refund money or return property (s 87(2)(c)); or
- an order directing a person to pay loss or damage (s 87(2)(d)).[275]

[13.590] The type of relief granted by the court will depend upon the circumstances. The relief considered most appropriate to either compensate the applicant or prevent or reduce loss or damage to the applicant will be given. One or more of the orders listed in s 87(2) of the *Trade Practices Act* 1974 may be given.[276]

[13.595] In the context of misleading conduct, one of the most common remedies sought is rescission. The circumstances in which a court may order the rescission of a contract were considered in *Henjo Investments Pty Ltd v Collins Marrickville Pty Ltd*.[277] The Full Court of the Federal Court rejected a claim for rescission of a contract for the sale of a business. The principles of equity concerning rescission were considered as useful guidelines,[278] although the Court did not consider itself constrained by the limitations of the general law relating to restoration of the status quo. Particular weight was given by the court to the conduct of the applicant after he discovered the misleading conduct.[279] Rescission of the contract was possible even if the status quo could not be exactly restored[280]—but in the circumstances, the conduct of the applicant in running the business and the delays in progressing the claim made rescission of the contract inappropriate. The court considered that damages were sufficient to compensate the applicant for its loss. Therefore, while issues such as affirmation, *restitutio in integrum*, delay, adequacy of damages, and third party rights are relevant to the matrix of facts considered by the court, they will not be determinative of the position. The

273 *Demagogue Pty Ltd v Ramensky* (1992) 110 ALR 608; *Marks v GIO Australia Holdings Limited* (1998) 158 ALR 333.
274 See for example *Kizbeau Pty Ltd v WG& B Pty Ltd* (1995) 131 ALR 363; *Mister Figgins Pty Ltd v Centrepoint Freeholds Pty Ltd* (1981) 36 ALR 23.
275 Refer to [13.525]–[13.555].
276 *Munchies Management Pty Ltd v Belperio* (1988) 84 ALR 700
277 (1988) 79 ALR 83.
278 See also *Munchies Management Pty Ltd v Belperio* (1988) 84 ALR 700; *Demogogue Pty Ltd v Ramensky* (1992) 110 ALR 608; *Byers v Dorotea* (1986) 69 ALR 715.
279 See also *Mister Figgins Pty Ltd v Centrepoint Freeholds Pty Ltd* (1981) 36 ALR 23 at 60.
280 *Alati v Kruger* (1955) 94 CLR 216.

overriding question for the court will be whether an order for rescission is appropriate to compensate the applicant for loss sustained or likely to be sustained.

[13.600] Another important distinction between the general law right to rescind and rescission under the *Trade Practices Act* 1974 is that the former is the act of one of the parties and the latter is the act of the court. In equity, a party has a right to elect to rescind the contract for misrepresentation. Under the *Trade Practices Act* 1974, a party must seek an order for rescission from the court. This is another reason why principles such as affirmation of the contract, while relevant to the exercise of the court's discretion, may not be determinative of the issue under the *Trade Practices Act* 1974.[281]

13.20 Exclusion of liability for misleading conduct

[13.605] The effectiveness of an exclusion clause to nullify the effect of s 52 of the *Trade Practices Act* 1974 or its state equivalents[282] has been viewed with scepticism by the courts. While contracting out of the *Trade Practices Act* 1974[283] is not specifically prohibited, it is clear that any attempt to do so will be met with resistance from the court. The only circumstance in which an exclusion clause has been effective is where the clause has the effect of breaking the chain of causation between the misleading conduct and the entry into the agreement.[284] The success of this type of exclusion clause has not been universal, as courts are very reluctant to allow a party to avoid the operation of the *Trade Practices Act* 1974. This has led to the development of some inventive clauses and arguments to try to persuade the court to give effect to the clause.

[13.610] The current authorities are consistent with the following principles, even though different decisions may be reached on the evidence presented to the court. Exclusion clauses are usually ineffective for several reasons.

* It is not possible to evade the operation of the *Trade Practices Act* 1974 or its State equivalents by inserting an exclusion clause.[285] In addition, the conduct will usually occur prior to entry into a contract—therefore, the insertion of an exclusion clause in the contract will not affect the party's reliance on the conduct.[286]

* An exclusion clause is only one of the factors the court will take into account in determining whether a purchaser has actually been misled by the vendor's conduct.[287]

---

281 *Myers v Transpacific Pastoral Co Pty Ltd* (1986) 8 ATPR 40-673; *Byers v Dorotea Pty Ltd* (1986) 69 ALR 715

282 Section 42 *Fair Trading Act* 1987 (NSW); s 38 *Fair Trading Act* 1989 (Qld); s 56 *Fair Trading Act* 1987 (SA); s 14 *Fair Trading Act* 1990 (Tas); s 11 *Fair Trading Act* 1985 (Vic); s 10 *Fair Trading Act* 1987 (WA); s 42 *Consumer Affairs and Fair Trading Act* 1990 (NT); s 12 *Fair Trading Act* 1992 (ACT).

283 Note that a prohibition on contracting out exists in the *Fair Trading Act* 1987 (SA), s 96; *Fair Trading Act* 1989 (Qld), s 107; *Fair Trading Act* 1990 (Tas), s 50.

284 *Keen Mar Corp Pty Ltd v Labrador Park Shopping Centre Pty Ltd* (1989) ATPR (Digest) 46-048.

285 *Henjo Investments Pty Ltd v Collins Marrickville Pty Ltd* (1988) 79 ALR 83; *Clarke Equipment Australia Ltd v Covcat Pty Ltd* (1987) 71 ALR 367; *Byers v Dorotea Pty Ltd* (1987) ATPR 40-760.

286 *Petera Pty Ltd v EAJ Pty Ltd* (1985) ATPR 40-605; *Karmot Auto Spares Pty Ltd v Dominelli Ford (Hurstville) Pty Ltd* (1992) ATPR 41-175.

287 *Netaf Pty Ltd v Bikane Pty Ltd* (1990) ATPR 41-011.

- An 'entire agreement' clause may only be effective if it breaks the chain of causation between the conduct and the entry into the contract, such that the party could not have relied on the conduct when entering the contract.[288] This will be a matter of evidence and not law.
- There is a suggestion that to allow any clause to exclude liability under the *Trade Practices Act* 1974 would be against the policy of the legislation.[289]

[13.615] In order for an exclusion clause to have any effect, the clause must act to break the chain of causation between the misleading conduct and the entry into the arrangement. An example of such a clause can be found in *Keen Mar Corporation Pty Ltd v Labrador Park Shopping Centre Pty Ltd*.[290] In that case, the plaintiff leased certain premises from the defendant in a shopping centre. Prior to entering into the lease, the plaintiff received certain brochures, and representations were made by a real estate agent employed by the defendant. The plaintiff was required to specify in a deed any representations that had been made to them concerning the leased premises. The deeds were signed after consultation with its solicitors. Morling and Wilcox JJ accepted that it was not possible to contract out of s 52 of the *Trade Practices Act* 1974.[291] However, their Honours' judgment confirms that a properly drafted exclusion clause drawn to the attention of the contracting party, and on which the contracting party receives legal advice, may be of considerable assistance in resisting a claim that the party has been induced to enter the contract as a result of misleading conduct. The deed contained a statement by the plaintiff of the representations made and relied upon when entering the lease, and these were confirmed by the plaintiff's solicitor. The representation complained of by the plaintiff was not included in the document, and the plaintiff did not, prior to commencing the action, make a complaint about the matter the subject of the alleged representation, even though other matters were complained of. But the decision in this case should not be viewed as providing the magic formula in terms of drafting an effective entire agreement clause. In all situations, it will depend very much on the evidence presented to the court. As was stated in *Netaf Pty Ltd v Bikane Pty Ltd*:[292]

> [an entire agreement clause] may provide some evidence upon the issue of the making of the representation. However, that statement is only one element in the complex of relevant facts; its importance will vary from case to case.

[13.620] It is suggested that this is a preferable view of the operation of entire agreement clauses. Such a clause will not automatically operate to negate liability under the *Trade Practices Act* 1974. Placing such a clause in a contract will have no contractual effect in relation to the *Trade Practices Act* 1974, but the existence of the clause should

---

288   *Kewside Pty Ltd v Warman International Ltd* (1990) ATPR (Digest) 46-059; *Waltip Pty Ltd v Capalaba Park Shopping Centre Pty Ltd* (1989) ATPR 40-975.

289   *Henjo Investments Pty Ltd v Collins Marrickville Pty Ltd* (1988) 79 ALR 83.

290   (1989) ATPR (Digest) 46-048.

291   Refer also to *Clark Equipment Australia Ltd v Covcat Pty Ltd* (1987) ATPR 40-768; (1987) 71 ALR 367; *Collins Marrickville Pty Ltd v Henjo Investments Pty Ltd* (1987) ATPR 40-782; (1987) 72 ALR 601 and on appeal (1988) 79 ALR 83.

292   (1990) ATPR 41-011 at 51,230.

be a factor the court takes into account, together with the surrounding circumstances, in deciding if the plaintiff has actually been misled.[293]

[13.625] As s 52 and its state equivalents are not concerned with intention or motive, all representations should be treated in the same way under the Act. Therefore, in terms of whether an exclusion clause will be effective, it is irrelevant that the conduct is innocent, negligent or fraudulent. The question should simply be whether the conduct is misleading or deceptive. The effect of the exclusion clause should then be examined in light of this conclusion.

13.21 International perspectives

13.21.1 New Zealand

[13.630] There is no substantive difference between the common law in Australia and New Zealand in relation to when a representation will be a misrepresentation.

However, the possible remedies for a misrepresentation in New Zealand are regulated by the *Contractual Remedies Act* 1979 (NZ). Sections 6 and 7 of the Act provide for the remedies of damages and cancellation of a contract following a misrepresentation but are subject to any contrary provisions in the contract itself. Section 6 provides that a party is entitled to damages if he or she is induced to enter into a contract by a misrepresentation of any kind made by the other party. In contrast to the measure of damages recoverable in Australia, s 6 provides for a party to receive the contractual measure of damages for breach of a term instead of damages in tort for either deceit or negligence. This means that the aggrieved party will be placed in the position he or she would have been in, had the representation been true, and removes any distinction between representations and terms.[294] Section 6 does not provide its own measure of damage, but defers to the common law principles governing an award of damages in contract.[295] Compensation is also available pursuant to s 9 of the Act, which was originally inserted to empower a court to relieve against the consequences of cancelling a contract. Some of the authorities, however, have given s 9 a wide application—suggesting that it empowers a court with a broad remedial discretion extending to an award of the statutory equivalent of damages on an expectation basis.[296] Conflicting academic comment suggests that a wide interpretation of s 9 is not justified.[297]

---

293 The intention of the party inserting the clause is irrelevant. A different view is expressed in A. Terry, 'Disclaimers and Deceptive Conduct' (1986) 14 *ABLR* 478 in the context of disclaimers. The view that conduct under s 52 should be categorised in accordance with common law principles is not in accordance with the current interpretation of s 52 expressed in *Demagogue Pty Ltd v Ramensky* (1992) 110 ALR 608 and followed in subsequent decisions.

294 Contrast the position in Australia where damages are awarded according to the tortious measure: [13.260].

295 Section 6 is intended to apply to all types of contracts including a sale of goods. *Contractual Remedies Act* 1979, s 6(2) provides for the Act to apply despite contrary provisions in the *Sale of Goods Act* 1908.

296 *Gallagher v Young* [1981] 1 NZLR 734 at 740; *Newmans Tours Ltd v Ranier Investments Ltd* [1992] 2 NZLR 68 at 89–90; *Thomson v Rankin* (1992) 2 NZ Conv C 191,400 at 191,404.

297 F Dawson and D McLauchlan, '*Gallagher v Young*: the *Contractual Remedies Act* 1979' (1982) 10 *New Zealand University Law Review* 47 at 55; CT Walker, 'Section 9 of the *Contractual Remedies Act* 1979: Opening Pandora's Box' (1995) *Auckland University Law Review* 527.

[13.635] Section 7 of the *Contractual Remedies Act* 1979 provides for the cancellation of a contract for either misrepresentation or breach. The Act has removed the distinction between the claims for rescission and termination empowering a court to cancel a contract and make such other orders it considers appropriate. These other orders include restoration of property and payment of money.[298] The effect of cancelling the contract is the same as termination for breach. The obligations of the parties are cancelled as to the future and each party retains property or money that has passed at that time. For the equivalent of rescission to occur, the court must order the return of property under s 9 of the *Contractual Remedies Act* 1979. Cancellation of the contract may occur where the parties have expressly or impliedly agreed that the truth of the representation is essential or the party is substantially deprived of the benefit of the contract or has received something substantially different from what was contracted for.[299] The discretion to order cancellation of a contract for an effective misrepresentation is expressly limited by affirmation.[300] In contrast, the discretion of the court to grant additional relief (such as restitution) under s 9 is limited expressly by the rights of bona fide third parties for value, and where such an order would give rise to inequity.[301] Cancellation of the contract does not prevent a party from also claiming damages.[302]

[13.640] The common law of misrepresentation has also been affected by the introduction of the *Fair Trading Act* 1986 (NZ), which prohibits persons from engaging in misleading conduct in trade and commerce.[303] As there is no substantive difference between a claim for misleading conduct in Australia and New Zealand, this does not require separate examination.[304]

13.21.2 United States

[13.645] The principles and policy considerations surrounding the law of misrepresentation in Australia are substantially reflected in the principles guiding relief from misrepresentation in the United States. The main distinction between the two systems lies in the clear dichotomy between the rights of an aggrieved party in contract and in tort. In Australia, a party would be able to avoid the contract and seek damages in tort for deceit or negligence. The American system, except in the case of a sale of goods,[305] requires a representee to make an election between avoiding the contract and claiming restitution in contract;[306] or affirming the contract and claiming damages in tort. A choice of remedy will depend not only on whether loss is suffered or restitution is still possible, but also on the type of misrepresentation. A claim for damages suffered due to a misrepresentation in tort requires proof of fraud

---

298   Refer to s 9 *Contractual Remedies Act* 1979.
299   Refer to s 7(4) *Contractual Remedies Act* 1979.
300   Refer to s 7(5) *Contractual Remedies Act* 1979.
301   Section 9(5) and (6) *Contractual Remedies Act* 1979.
302   Refer to s 10 *Contractual Remedies Act* 1979. Contrast the position in the United States [13.720].
303   Section 9 *Fair Trading Act* 1986.
304   Refer to [13.320]–[13.435] in relation to the Australian position.
305   Refer to Uniform Commercial Code § 2-721.
306   In some cases reliance damages may be recoverable: *Hammac v Skinner* 265 Ala.9, 89 So.2d 70 (1956); *Mock v Duke* 20 Mich.App 453, 174 NW 2d 161 (1969).

and materiality, while in contract a claim for rescission will succeed where the misrepresentation is either fraudulent or material.[307]

[13.650] A misrepresentation is simply defined as an assertion that is not in accord with the facts.[308] A misrepresentation may result in:

- a contract's being voidable at the election of the representee;
- the formation of a contract being prevented;[309]
- reformation of the contract by the court.[310]

[13.655] Damages are only available in tort. A detailed examination of the effect of misrepresentation in tort is outside the scope of this commentary.[311] Emphasis will be given to a comparative examination of the principles governing rescission of a contract for misrepresentation.

[13.660] Rescission of a contract for misrepresentation will be available if the following are proved:

- an assertion not in accordance with the facts;
- the assertion must be either fraudulent or material;
- the assertion must be relied on by the representee when making the contract; and
- the representee's reliance must have been justified.

(a) False assertion of fact

[13.665] As in Australia, the first element requires the false assertion to be one of past or existing fact, and commonly takes the form of either written or spoken words. The same issues about the effect of statements of intention, opinion, law and silence have arisen for consideration by the American courts. The general proposition in each case is that a statement of intention, opinion, law, or silence will not be an assertion of fact. Exceptions to this general proposition have been introduced, and in some cases have created doubt about the accuracy of the general rule. The exceptions are briefly summarised for comparative purposes.

Opinion

[13.670] The situations in which a statement of opinion may be interpreted as an assertion of fact are more tenuous than in Australia. There was a traditional reluctance by the American courts to relieve a person from the effect of a false opinion because it was merely sales talk or puffery, was immaterial to the contract, or there was 'no right to rely'[312] on the statement. A cohesive principle that details when an opinion will be considered an assertion of fact and may be relied on, is suggested by the Restatement (Second) Contract as:

---

307 No additional category of negligent misrepresentation arises. A misrepresentation is either fraudulent or non-fraudulent. Damages may be available separately for the tort of negligence.

308 Restatement (Second) § 159.

309 This circumstance is rare. A misrepresentation will only affect the formation of the contract if the elements of non est factum as laid down by the House of Lords in *Gallie v Lee* [1969] 1 All ER 1062 are proven. (Refer to[14.255]–[14.280] for discussion of non est factum.) This is followed in the Uniform Commercial Code § 3-305(a)(iii)(1990).

310 Reformation equates to rectification of a contract. Rectification is discussed at [14.135]–[14.170], [14.305]–[14.315].

311 Refer to Restatement (Second), Torts chs 22, 23.

312 Refer to [13.715].

Where the facts are not known to the recipient he or she may be justified in inferring that there are facts which justify the opinion or that there are no facts that are incompatible with the opinion.[313]

[13.675] If the statement of opinion is not considered to also be an assertion of fact, it may still be relied upon if:

- there is a relationship of trust and confidence between the parties;
- the representor is or claims to be an expert;
- the representee is for some special reason particularly vulnerable to misrepresentation of the type involved.[314]

Intention

[13.680] The law concerning statements of intention is substantially the same as Australian law. The case of *Edgington v Fitzmaurice*[315] is relied upon for the proposition that a statement of intention includes the assertion that the statement maker actually holds that intention at the time. Where the intention is not held, relief may be claimed only if reliance on the assertion is reasonable. Reliance may not be reasonable if the representee knows of facts that mean the representor cannot carry out his or her intention, or the statement of a false intention is not contrary to the ordinary standards of dealing in the particular transaction. For example, it may be consistent with reasonable standards of dealing for the buyer of real estate to misrepresent his or her intention concerning the use of the property to conceal a benefit the buyer will obtain from the purchase of the property.[316]

Law

[13.685] Statements of law may be either assertions of fact or opinion. A statement that a particular statute has been repealed will be an assertion of fact which, if false, will be a misrepresentation. However, statements concerning the possible outcome of a trial will be opinion—and actionable in the same circumstances as other opinions. The most important exception applicable to this type of opinion will be where the representor has some expertise or skill. This will be the case where a lawyer provides an opinion to a lay person. The lay person is entitled to rely upon the opinion as being founded on appropriate facts.[317]

Silence

[13.690] Similarly to the Australian position, the general proposition is that parties to a contract are not under any general obligation to disclose information to the other.[318] This general rule has been eroded by a large number of exceptions. In common with Australian law, silence will constitute a misrepresentation where:

313   This is similar to the position in Australian contract law. Refer to Restatement (Second) § 168.
314   Restatement (Second) § 169.
315   [1885] Ch D 459
316   *Lucas v Long* 125 Md 420, 94 A 12 (1915); *Finley v Dalton* 251 SC 586, 164 SE 2d 763 (1968). See also WP Keeton, 'Fraud: Statements of Intention' (1937) 15 *Tex L Rev* 185 at 188, 195.
317   Contrast Australian position at [13.35].
318   *Laidlaw v Organ* 15 US (2 Wheat) 178, 4 L Ed 214 (1817). Note the impact of the Uniform Commercial Code which imposes implied warranties concerning goods whether known to the seller or not: Uniform Commercial Code § 2-312–2-318.

- the representor knows that a previously true statement made by him or her is now false, and fails to inform the other party;
- the representor discovers that a previous statement was false, and fails to correct it;
- only a partial disclosure is made, creating a half truth;
- there is a relationship of trust and confidence (fiduciary relationship); or
- there is a contract of suretyship or insurance.

The additional exception to the rule not applicable in Australia is that a person should disclose facts known to him or her that would correct a mistake of the other party as to a basic assumption on which that party is making the contract, if non-disclosure of the fact amounts to a failure to act in good faith and in accordance with reasonable standards of fair dealing.[319] This final exception is similar in effect to s 52 of the *Trade Practices Act* 1974, but takes that section further by linking the expectation of disclosure to good faith and fair dealing. The exception would apply to require a builder to notify a contracting party of a mistake in a bid received from the contracting party. Like s 52 of the *Trade Practices Act* 1974, the exception does not require all cards to be laid on the table, but merely for prevailing standards in business ethics to be followed.[320]

(b) Assertion is fraudulent or material

[13.695] The second element requires the misrepresentation to be either fraudulent or material.[321] According to the Restatement (Second),[322] a misrepresentation is fraudulent if the maker intends his or her assertion to induce a party to manifest the party's assent and the maker:

(a) knows or believes that the assertion is not in accord with the facts; or
(b) does not have the confidence that he or she states or implies in the truth of the assertion; or
(c) knows that he or she does not have the basis that he or she states or implies for the assertion.

[13.700] The first two requirements replicate the definition of fraud in *Derry v Peek*,[323] while the third will operate even though the representor is convinced of the honesty of the assertion. There is no requirement that the assertion be both fraudulent and material.

[13.705] A misrepresentation does not have to be fraudulent to attract relief, but a non-fraudulent misrepresentation will not be actionable unless it is material.[324] Materiality exists where the misrepresentation would be likely to affect the conduct of a reasonable person, or 'if the maker of the representation knows that the recipient is likely to regard the fact as important' although a reasonable person would not.[325] For example, A makes a statement to B that a racehorse was bred at a particular stable. Unknown to A, this is incorrect; the horse was actually bred at a different stable. The specified stable was

---

319 Restatement (Second), § 161.
320 Refer to EA Farnsworth, *Contracts*, 3rd edn, Little Brown, Boston, 1999, at p 248–249; JD Calamari & JM Perrillo, *The Law of Contracts* 4th edn, West Group 1998 at §9.20.
321 Restatement (Second) §162.
322 § 162.
323 (1889) 14 App Cas 337.
324 This should be contrasted with the position in torts. A misrepresentation must be fraudulent to attract damages.
325 Restatement (Second) §162(2).

founded by B's grandmother. In the first instance, if B is induced by the statement to buy the horse but A is unaware of B's grandmother, the statement is not material, and therefore the contract is not voidable. If A knew of B's grandmother—and that B wanted to own a horse from the stable founded by her—the contract would be voidable. This would be either because the statement was material, or because the statement was fraudulent in accordance with the third part of the definition.

(c)   Reliance
[13.710] The third element requires the representee to have relied upon the misrepresentation when entering the contract.[326] Whether a representee was induced to enter a contract by a misrepresentation is a question of fact.[327]

(d)   Reliance is reasonable
[13.715] The fourth element is whether the representee acted reasonably in relying on the assertion. The fact the representee could have with reasonable diligence discovered the mistake prior to entering the contract does not bar relief.[328] The only exception to this is where the failure by the representee amounted to a breach of good faith or a failure to comply with reasonable standards of fair dealing.[329] A determination of whether this standard has been breached will include a consideration of the representee's peculiar qualities and characteristics and the circumstances of the particular cases including the fraudulent or innocent nature of the representation. Where discovery of the falsity could have been established by a cursory examination, reliance may not be justified.[330] It is expected that the representee would not rely blindly on the maker's assertion. However, mere failure to investigate would not deprive the representee of relief.

(e)   Remedies
[13.720] Proof of the four elements outlined above will ordinarily allow an aggrieved party to avoid the contract and seek restitution. In some cases, damages for consequential loss may be given as a method of returning the parties to their original positions.[331] Generally, though, a party must elect between rescission of the contract and damages. However, for a sale of goods under the Uniform Commercial Code, an election is not necessary, and an action for rescission and damages may be pursued provided there is no duplication of compensation.[332] For example, a person induced to purchase a horse by a representation that it is a stallion when in fact it is a gelding would be entitled to

---

326 *Eslamizar v American States Ins. Co* 134 Or App 138 P 2d 1195 (1995); Restatement (Second) §176.

327 The applicable principles are the same as in Australia.

328 Restatement (Second) §172. See also *Kendall v Wilson* 41 Vt 567, 571 (1869); *Spyder Enterprises v Ward* 872 F.Supp 8 (EDNY 1995) ('it is no excuse for a culpable misrepresentation that the means of proving it were at hand'). This also represents the position in Australia.

329 *Providence Jewelry Co v Crowe* 113 Minn. 209, 129 NW 224 (1911); *Volker v Connecticut Fire Ins Co* 22 NJ Super 314, 91 A 2d 883 (1952).

330 *Bailey v Bode Bros* 195 Wis. 264, 218 N.W. 174 (1928).

331 *Hammac v Skinner* 265 Ala 9, 89 So 2d 70 (1956); *Jennings v Lee* 105 Ariz 167, 461 P 2d 161 (1969).

332 Uniform Commercial Code § 2-721.

rescind the contract, return the horse, and claim damages for money expended on food, maintenance, and veterinary costs.[333]

[13.725] Rescission of a contract is possible either at common law or in equity. Originally, rescission of a contract was given only in equity; but the common law court also developed an ability to grant rescission through restitution. For some time the common law rule of requiring an offer to restore was favoured, but there is a discernible trend of granting rescission on the basis of equitable principles. This has been achieved either through legislation or by the creation of exceptions such as not requiring an offer to restore where it is useless or unfair to do so.[334] Since it is likely that the court would just order rescission conditional on restitution, there is no good reason to continue ignoring the equitable principles.[335]

[13.730] Other limits on the right to rescind include affirmation and delay.[336] Restitution of the property or money passed under the contract is a necessary corollary of rescission,[337] but a flexible approach of returning the property or compensation in money terms is adopted to ensure parties are returned as nearly as possible to their pre-contractual positions.[338] A general prohibition on the right to avoid after the contract is executed in the case of innocent misrepresentation has been rejected.[339]

13.21.3 Japan

[13.735] Traditionally, the problems that in common law are classified as misrepresentation and misleading and deceptive conduct were treated in Japan as pre-contractual issues. This kind of pre-contractual issue is resolved either through tort, or through the application of the doctrine of good faith, which has been interpreted by the courts to include an explicit duty to negotiate in good faith. Good faith also applies after formation, as an obligation to perform contracts in good faith. The doctrine of good faith is relied on relatively frequently in Japan, but has been criticised as being dependant on case law for its application and extension, particularly in consumer settings.

[13.740] The new *Consumer Contract Law* 2000 introduces for the first time explicit statutory provisions that approximate some of the measures used in common law countries and in the EU to combat misrepresentation and misleading or deceptive conduct. The new law provides, among other things, that a consumer may cancel a contract where the merchant (a) fails in his duty to provide important information necessary for the consumer to make a decision, or provides false information; or (b) engages in conduct that coerces or confuses the consumer, and without which the consumer could not have formed the intention to enter the contract. Contract

---

333 *Grandi v LeSage* 74 N.M 799, 399 P.2d 285 (1965).

334 Refer to JD Calamari & JM Perrillo, *The Law of Contracts* 4th edn, West Group, 1998 §9.23 at 344–345.

335 See EA Farnsworth *Contracts*, 3rd edn, Aspen Law & Business, New York, 1999, § 4.15.

336 Restatement (Second) § 380, 381.

337 *American Exch Bank v Smith* 23 P.2d 414 (Wash 1933).

338 *Bellefeuille v Medeiros* 139 N.E. 2d 413 (Mass 1957) (purchaser of business sold some property and lost some in flood; return of property and payment of money). *Miller v Sears* 636 P.2d 1183 (Alaska 1981) (representee required to account for use of property after notice of rescission given).

339 *Seneca Wire & Manufacturing Co v A.B. Leach & Co* 159 N.E. 700 (NY 1928); compare with the Australian position at [13.240]–[13.245].

provisions that the consumer could not have anticipated from the course of negotiations that are subsequently included in the contract will not form part of the contract.

[13.745] Although more explicit, this statutory language will also rely on court decisions and an analysis of the facts in each situation in order to build jurisprudence in this area. Amendments to the Code of Civil Procedure, effective in 1998, have also introduced a new small claims jurisdiction, which is expected to be one of the main arenas for litigating these kinds of claims. A new *Financial Services Law* is expected to provide analogous duties of disclosure in relation to the sale of financial services and products to consumers.

[13.750] It should also be noted that the operation of the 1947 *Antimonopoly Law* is basically limited to competition issues between corporations. Although important amendments in 2000 now allow individuals to bring claims under this law for the first time, the law itself has not been conceived of, or construed as, a consumer protection statute.

Chapter 14
Mistake

14.1 Introduction

[14.05] Mistakes by a party entering into a contract may take a wide variety of forms. A contracting party may be mistaken about, for example, the nature of the subject matter of the contract, the nature or content of a term or the obligations or benefits contained in the contract. A mistake may be said to be 'operative' when it is made by one or both of the parties prior to or at the time the contract is formed. Only operative mistakes can have the effect of vitiating the contract.

[14.10] The nature of an operative mistake will determine the effect upon the contract. For example, the type of mistake will dictate whether the appropriate remedy rests at common law or in equity. Such remedies may draw upon principles such as those governing *consensus ad idem*, certainty, construction of contracts, unconscionability, and the granting of equitable relief. For this reason it has been suggested that there is no true and distinct doctrine of mistake—but rather that 'mistake' merely represents an occasion for the confluence of a variety of legal and equitable principles.[1]

[14.15] It is possible for particular circumstances to call into play not only the principles governing mistake but also some other principles of contract law. For example, the mistake made by a party may have been induced by a misrepresentation by the other party. In such a case, the wider variety of remedies available for the misrepresentation—including remedies under statute—may mean that the primary focus in such a case is upon the misrepresentation rather than the mistake. However, there may be a case where the mistake provides a more desirable remedy—as where a mistake as to identity results in a contract being rendered void in circumstances where third party rights are involved.[2] In such a case, the plaintiff may wish to focus his or her claim for relief upon the mistake, rather than the misrepresentation.[3]

[14.20] Mistakes made by a party *after* the contract has been formed may be dealt with by other principles of contract law. For example, a mistake as to the interpretation of a contract may involve principles governing repudiation of contract.[4] Similarly, destruction of the subject matter of the contract without the knowledge of either party may result in a remedy for mistake,[5] whereas the same event occurring after the contract has been formed is instead the province of the doctrine of frustration.[6] Further, a mistake as existence of the subject matter—which may in some circumstances be dealt with as a case of mistake—may instead be dealt with as a breach of contract, if one party has made a positive guarantee of the existence of the item.[7]

---

1 (1951) 84 CLR 377 at 408. Cf N Seddon & MP Ellinghaus, *Cheshire and Fifoot's Law of Contract*, 7th edn, Butterworths, Sydney, 1997, p 470.
2 See [14.220]–[14.225].
3 Cf the plaintiff's claim in *Porter v Latec Finance (Qld) Pty Ltd* (1964) 111 CLR 177.
4 See, for example, *DTR Nominees Pty Ltd v Mona Homes Pty Ltd* (1978) 138 CLR 423.
5 See [14.80].
6 See [22.40]. Compare, for example, two cases arising from the postponement of the coronation activities for Edward VII: *Griffith v Brymer* (1903) 19 TLR 434 (a case of mistake) and *Krell v Henry* [1903] 2 KB 740 (a case of frustration).
7 See, for example, *McRae v Commonwealth Disposal Commission* (1951) 84 CLR 377. See [14.85].

[14.25] Traditionally, an operative mistake must be one of fact, not law.[8] However, as most mistakes of law involve some kind of mistake of fact, the distinction is unsatisfactory, and difficult to justify.[9] Moreover, the distinction has been abandoned in other contexts.[10] So it may be that if the High Court has the opportunity to consider the matter, it will abandon the distinction for operative mistakes as well.

14.2 Types of mistake

[14.30] Broadly speaking, there are three types of mistake: common mistake, mutual mistake, and unilateral mistake.

[14.35] A *common mistake* occurs where both parties make the same mistake. There is no difficulty concerning *consensus ad idem*, but each is mistaken about some underlying and material matter, such as the continued existence of the subject matter. For example, A may contract to sell his Lamborghini to B in circumstances where both parties are unaware that prior to the sale the car had been destroyed in an accident.

[14.40] A *mutual mistake* occurs where both parties are mistaken, but each makes a different mistake. In effect, the parties are at cross purposes. There is no true *consensus ad idem*, despite what may be the outward appearances. For example, A may contract to sell 'his car'—intending to sell his red Lamborghini—while B contracts to buy 'A's car'—intending to buy A's black Lamborghini.

Caution is warranted because on occasion, some judges have inappropriately treated the terms 'common mistake' and 'mutual mistake' as synonymous. For example, in *McRae v Commonwealth Disposals Commission* the High Court used the term 'mutual mistake' to describe a situation where both parties made the same mistake.[11]

[14.45] A *unilateral mistake* occurs where only one of the parties is mistaken and the other party knows, or ought to know, of the mistake. By contrast, where one party is mistaken and the other party neither knows nor ought know of the mistake, the mistake will be treated as mutual rather than unilateral. Whether the party who is not mistaken 'ought' to be aware of the other party's mistake will depend upon the surrounding circumstances. For example, if B agrees to purchase A's Holden under the mistaken belief that it is a collector's item, and A is in fact ignorant of that mistake, a court may nevertheless decide that it is a case of unilateral mistake because A *ought* to have been aware of the mistake due to the circumstances—for example, B's willingness to pay a price far in excess of the car's market value.

14.3 Effect of mistake

[14.50] An operative mistake may give rise to a remedy at common law or in equity.

---

8   *Con-Stan Industries of Australia Pty Ltd v Norwich Winterthur Insurance (Aus) Ltd* (1986) 160 CLR 226 at 245.

9   *Eslea Holdings Ltd v Butts* (1986) 6 NSWLR 175 at 186–189 per Samuels JA (Kirby P concurring).

10 See *David Securities Pty Ltd v Commonwealth Bank of Australia* (1992) 175 CLR 353 (action for money had and received); *Waltons Stores (Interstate) Ltd v Maher* (1998) 164 CLR 387 (equitable estoppel).

11 (1951) 84 CLR 377 at 408.

14.3.1 Common law

[14.55] At common law, a mistake may operate to negative or nullify contractual assent.[12] In such a case, the contract is said to be *void ab initio* (void as from the beginning). The parties are treated as if there had been no contract between them: any money or property transferred between them must be returned. Further, the contract will be insufficient to pass title. Consequently, the rights of a third party who has acquired an interest in the subject matter of the contract will be defeated.

[14.60] It has been suggested in Australia that in the case of a contract entered into by the parties under the common mistake that the subject matter is still in existence, it is more accurate to describe the situation as one in which the contract is unenforceable due to a total failure of consideration, than to describe it as a case of the contract being void.[13]

14.3.2 Equity

[14.65] In equity, a more flexible approach is taken to mistake. In equity mistake is to render the contract *voidable* and not *void*. Thus the contract may be rescinded by the mistaken party or the contract may be set aside by a court on such terms as it sees fit. However, this right is subject to similar limits to those applying to rescission for misrepresentation—including cases where *restitutio in integrum* is no longer possible, where an innocent third party has acquired an interest in the subject matter for value, affirmation, and perhaps lapse of time once the contract has been fully executed[14]—but not the execution of the contract.[15]

[14.70] Alternatively, the court may refuse a grant of specific performance at the request of a party seeking to take advantage of the mistake,[16] or may rectify the text of a contract where there has been a mistake in the recording of its terms.[17]

14.4 Common mistake

14.4.1 Common law

[14.75] A contract is void at common law for common mistake in only two circumstances: where there has been a common mistake as to the existence of the subject matter (*res extincta*) and common mistake as to title (*res sua*).[18]

(a) Res extincta

[14.80] Where—unknown to the parties—the subject matter of their contract no longer exists, the contract is clearly impossible to perform, and is accordingly void.[19]

---

12 *Bell v Lever Bros Ltd* [1932] AC 161 at 217 per Lord Atkin.
13 *McRae v Commonwealth Disposals Commission* (1951) 84 CLR 377 at 405–406; *Svanosio v McNamara* (1956) 96 CLR 186 at 209 (res sua).
14 *Solle v Butcher* [1950] 1 KB 671.
15 *Lukacs v Wood* (1978) 19 SASR 520.
16 See, for example, *Goldsbrough Mort & Co Ltd v Quinn* (1910) 10 CLR 674.
17 See, for example, *Maralinga Pty Ltd v Major Enterprises Pty Ltd* (1973) 128 CLR 336.
18 *Dell v Beasley* [1959] NZLR 89 at 96.
19 *Couturier v Hastie* (1856) 5 HLC 673; 10 ER 1065.

Example: Couturier v Hastie[20]

A consignment of corn was shipped from Salonica bound for England. In transit, the corn began to ferment, prompting the ship's master to sell the cargo at Tunis. Subsequently the consignor in England purported to sell the corn. When the buyer failed to pay, the consignor brought an action on the contract.

It was held by the House of Lords that the purchaser had agreed to purchase specific goods that had already perished. The purchaser has an obligation to pay on delivery of the shipping documents only if they represented, at the time of the making of the contract, goods in existence and capable of delivery. The bargain did not have the effect of a contract for goods 'lost or not lost'. Accordingly, the contract of sale could not be enforced against the buyer.

Sale of goods legislation now provides that where there is a contract for the sale of specific goods, and the goods, without the knowledge of the seller, have perished at the time the contract formed, the contract is deemed to be void.[21]

[14.85] *Res extincta* may be distinguished from two other situations: first, where the contract is for an 'adventure', it is a question of construction whether the purchaser has agreed to take a chance on whether or not the subject matter is in existence, or in the words of the court in *Couturier v Hastie*, a contract 'for goods lost or not lost'. In such a case, the true subject matter of the contract is not the goods themselves but the chance of their existence. Such contracts were more common in the days of goods being transported by sailing ship, when there was less certainty that vessels would arrive safely at their destinations. Secondly, where there is a warranty as to the existence of the subject matter: if it transpires in such a case that the goods either are no longer in existence or never existed in the first place, that party may be liable in damages for breach of contract.[22]

Example: McRae v Commonwealth Disposals Commission [23]

The Commonwealth placed newspaper advertisements calling for tenders for the purchase of an oil tanker, described as 'lying on Jourmaund Reef'. The plaintiff's tender was accepted. After the plaintiffs had incurred expense in fitting out a salvage expedition, it was discovered that no oil tanker had ever existed—and indeed there was no place known as Jourmaund Reef.

The High Court held that the plaintiffs were entitled to recover damages for breach of contract.[24] It was held that it was a question of the true construction of the contract. This was not a case in which the parties had proceeded on the basis of a erroneous assumption of fact so as to justify a conclusion that both parties were mistaken about the existence of the vessel. Certainly the officers of the Commission had

---

20 (1856) 5 HLC 673; 10 ER 1065.
21 *Sale of Goods Act* 1954 (ACT), s 11; *Sale of Goods Act* 1920 (NSW), s 11; *Sale of Goods Act* 1972 (NT), s 11; *Sale of Goods Act* 1896 (Qld), s 9; *Sale of Goods Act* 1895 (SA), s 6; *Sale of Goods Act* 1896 (Tas), s 11; *Goods Act* 1958 (Vic), s 11; *Sale of Goods Act* 1895 (WA), s 6.
22 *McRae v Commonwealth Disposals Commission* (1951) 84 CLR 377.
23 (1951) 84 CLR 377.
24 These damages were calculated on a reliance basis: see [23.395].

made an assumption, but the plaintiffs had not made an assumption in the same sense. They knew nothing except what the Commission had told them. The proper construction of the contract therefore was that the buyers had relied upon a promise by the Commission that there was a tanker in the position specified. Since this warranty had been breached, the Commission was liable in damages.

Alternatively, it was held that even if this were a case of mistake, where the mistake is caused by the fault of one party (here the Commission), that party is precluded from relying on the mistake as a basis for relief.[25]

(b) Res sua

[14.90] There are different views as to the effect of a mistake as to title. In *Bell v Lever Bros Ltd*, the House of Lords held that a contract is void where unknown to the parties, the buyer or lessee of property is already the owner of that property.[26] This involved a reconsideration of the previous decision in *Cooper v Phibbs* that where a fishery was leased to the party who actually owned it, the contract was merely voidable.[27] The *Bell v Lever Bros* conclusion appears to be logical, since the seller or lessor in fact has nothing to sell or lease—and, as in the case of *res extincta*, performance of the contract is impossible due to the absence of any subject matter. However, this interpretation was subsequently overlooked by the High Court, which regarded *Cooper v Phibbs* as an example of equitable relief for a total failure of consideration.[28]

[14.95] Once again, it may be a question of construction of the contract whether a common misapprehension has rendered the contract void, or alternatively, whether a vendor has undertaken to make title and thereby commited a breach of contract for which the purchaser is entitled to terminate and claim damages.[29]

14.4.2 Equity

[14.100] The equitable response to common mistake is much wider than the limited approach of the common law.

[14.105] First, equity generally follows the law, so that in the case of *res extincta* or *res sua*, equity will also treat the contract as having no effect, and may refuse specific performance or set aside the contract on such terms as it sees fit.[30] The equitable jurisdiction to provide relief for common mistake is part of the fundamental principle that a party having a legal right shall not be permitted to exercise it in a way that amounts to unconscionable conduct—in other words, 'fraud' in the wide equitable sense of the

---

25   Ibid, at 408–409.
26   *Bell v Lever Bros Ltd* [1932] AC 161 at 218 per Lord Atkin.
27   *Cooper v Phibbs* (1867) LR 2 HL 149.
28   *Svanosio v McNamara* (1956) 96 CLR 186 at 198, 208.
29   *Svanosio v McNamara* (1956) 96 CLR 186 at 196–197, 204–205 (sale of hotel which is discovered to be partly erected on adjoining land not owned by the vendor—held that the vendor could not make title and was in breach of contract); cf *McRae v Commonwealth Disposals Commission* (1951) 84 CLR 377.
30   See, for example, *Cochrane v Willis* (1865) LR 1 Ca App 58. As noted above, the original decision in *Cooper v Phibbs* (1867) LR 2 HL 149 was that the agreement was liable to be set aside on terms as the court saw fit. See [14.90].

term.[31] In order for the contract to be set aside for common mistake, three elements must be shown:

- a common misapprehension as to facts or as to the parties' rights;
- which is of a fundamental nature; and
- an absence of fault on the part of the party seeking to have the contract set aside.[32]

Example: Solle v Butcher[33]

The plaintiff leased a flat from the defendant. Both parties had acted on the incorrect assumption that the flat, which had been so substantially reconstructed that it was virtually a new flat, was no longer governed by the *Rent Restriction Acts* and that the plaintiff was no longer a protected tenant. The mistake was only discovered after two years. The plaintiff sought a declaration that the rent was capped under the Acts, and sought to recover the excess in rent that he had paid. The defendant counter-claimed for rescission of the lease on the ground of common mistake.

A majority of the English Court of Appeal held that the parties had been acting under a fundamental misapprehension about whether the premises were governed by the legislation. Further, the plaintiff was a surveyor employed by the landlord, who had advised the landlord on the appropriate rent. Accordingly, the landlord was not himself at fault. The majority held that it was inequitable for the plaintiff to claim a return of the overpayment of rent. Accordingly, the lease was set aside on terms that the landlord would comply with the necessary formalities to take the flat outside the ambit of the statute, and would then offer the plaintiff tenant a new lease for the unexpired portion of the old lease at the rental originally agreed by the parties.

[14.110] It would seem that a mistake may be described as 'fundamental' if it affects the nature or quality of the subject matter. This includes a mistake concerning the value of the subject matter.[34]

[14.115] The requisite equitable fraud—that is, unconscionability—may be satisfied merely by a party seeking to uphold the bargain when he or she is receiving an unexpected windfall under the contract due to the mistake.[35]

[14.120] The courts have displayed greater reluctance to set aside a conveyance of land on the basis of common mistake. It has been suggested that such a contract may only be set aside in equity in cases of fraud and where there is such a discrepancy between what has been sold and what has been conveyed that there is a total failure of consideration—or what amounts practically to a total failure of consideration.[36] One reason for such an attitude may be that in the case of a land conveyance, there is ordinarily ample opportunity to make the necessary enquiries and requisitions in relation to the vendor's title. Apart from anything else, if a common mistake persists despite such an opportunity, this

---

31   *Solle v Butcher* [1950] 1 KB 671 approved in *Svanosio v McNamara* (1956) 96 CLR 186; *Taylor v Johnson* (1983) 151 CLR 422 at 431.

32   Ibid, at 693 per Denning LJ.

33   [1950] 1 KB 671.

34   *Grist v Bailey* [1967] Ch 532.

35   *Lukacs v Wood* (1978) 19 SASR 520 at 531; see also *McGee v Pennine Insurance Co Ltd* [1969] 2 QB 507; *Solle v Butcher* [1950] 1 KB 671.

36   *Svanosio v McNamara* (1956) 96 CLR 186 at 198–199.

may constitute evidence of the party seeking to have the contract set aside being at fault, within the terms of the test propounded by *Solle v Butcher*.

[14.125] However, it may be that the formula 'what amounts practically to a total failure of consideration' should not be applied in an overly restrictive fashion.

Example: Lukacs v Wood[37]

The parties reached agreement on the sale of three vacant blocks of land. As a result of a mistake in relation to the volume and folio number inserted in both the contract and the transfer document, the purchaser actually acquired two vacant blocks of land and one block on which flats had been built. When the mistake was discovered, the purchaser refused to agree to a reconveyance of the block with the flats, and sought to keep his windfall.

The court held that there was in the circumstances 'what amounted practically to a total failure of consideration' since the contemplated vacant block was never bought and sold. Further, there was equitable jurisdiction because the purchaser sought to retain a windfall benefit by reason of common mistake of a highly advantageous bargain which he did not intend to make, and for which he had paid a wholly inadequate consideration. Accordingly, the court ordered a reconveyance of the wrong block and a conveyance of the correct vacant block of land.

[14.130] Rescission may also be refused where the plaintiff elects to affirm the contract after the mistake is discovered.[38]

(b)   Rectification

[14.135] At common law, a written record of a contract is conclusive of the parties' rights and obligations. Accordingly, if there has been an error in the recording of the parties' agreement, it is likely to result in advantage of some kind to one party and disadvantage to the other. There would be obvious injustice if the party who was advantaged by the error sought to maintain that advantage. This unconscionability provides a basis for the equitable remedy of rectification.

[14.140] In an order to rectify a common mistake in the recording of an agreement, two elements must be shown:

- a prior concluded contract—or at least a common intention that continued unaltered until the execution of the document; and
- 'convincing proof' that the written document does not embody the final agreement.[39]

[14.145] It was previously the position that in order for a common mistake in a document to be rectified, there must first have been a concluded contract between the parties.[40] Such a concluded contract needed to be binding, but did not need to be enforceable in the sense of any written formalities being satisfied.[41] It has now been

---

37   (1978) 19 SASR 520.
38   *Hudson v Jope* (1914) 14 SR (NSW) 351.
39   *Pukallus v Cameron* (1982) 180 CLR 447 at 452 per Wilson J.
40   *Australian Gypsum Ltd v Hume Steel Ltd* (1930) 45 CLR 54 at 63–64.
41   *United States v Motor Trucks Ltd* [1924] AC 196.

recognised that there need not even be a concluded contract if there is at least an intention common to both parties continuing down to execution of the contract.[42] Thus it is no longer necessary for the plaintiff even to show the formal requirements for a binding contract such as an offer and acceptance. Further, it seems that it is not necessary to have evidence of an outward expression of accord between the parties, and that the common intention can be proved by other means, including by inference from pre- and post-contractual facts.[43]

[14.150] There can be no rectification where there is a change in the common intention and the document in fact accurately reflects the final agreement between the parties.

Example: Maralinga Pty Ltd v Major Enterprises Pty Ltd[44]

At an auction sale of land, the auctioneer announced that the sale was subject to demolition of buildings on the land, but that the purchaser would have an option whether to demolish, or allow the buildings to remain. Further, the auctioneer stated that the vendor wanted settlement in cash but would take a mortgage back for the balance. The purchaser had seen a formal contract that had been prepared in advance. This form provided for demolition and payment of the balance in cash. After the property was knocked down but before the sale was settled, the purchaser sought to have the document amended to allow an option concerning demolition. The vendor refused. Believing that, although not clearly worded, the contract could be read as conferring an option concerning demolition, the purchaser signed the contract. After execution of the contract, the purchaser sought rectification to allow an option and a mortgage back for the balance.

A 2:1 majority of the High Court held that the purchaser was not entitled to rectification in either respect. Both parties had advance notice of the contract, and were aware that it differed from the antecedent bargain formed when the property was sold at auction. Despite this notice, they signed the contract. The written document was therefore not formed as a result of mistake as to its terms. The purchaser was mistaken as to its effect, but not its content. The purchaser failed to show that the executed document was intended to record the antecedent oral (and therefore unenforceable) agreement, or that the document, by common mistake, failed to conform to that agreement.

[14.155] The party seeking rectification bears a heavy onus of proof. There must be 'convincing proof' that the document differs from the parties' common intention. The omitted ingredient must be capable of such proof in clear and precise terms.[45] The court will not assume the task of making the contract for the parties.[46] Without such

---

42   *Slee v Warke* (1949) 86 CLR 271 at 280; *Maralinga Pty Ltd v Major Enterprises Pty Ltd* (1973) 128 CLR 336 at 350; *Pukallus v Cameron* (1982) 180 CLR 447 at 452, 456.
43   *NSW Medical Defence Union Ltd v Transport Industries Insurance Co Ltd* (1986) 6 NSWLR 740.
44   (1973) 128 CLR 336.
45   See, for example, *Warburton v National Westminster Finance Australia Ltd* (1988) 15 NSWLR 238 (rectification ordered where party left to fill in blanks in executed document made honest mistake and inserted incorrect material).
46   *Pukallus v Cameron* (1982) 180 CLR 447 at 452, approving *Joscelyne v Nissen* [1970] 2 QB 86 at 98.

proof, the certainty of contracts may be placed in jeopardy by a party seeking to assert prior negotiations as representing the true position.[47]

While it is not necessary to have evidence of an outward expression of the common intention, the absence of such proof may go towards whether the burden of proof may be discharged by the party seeking rectification.[48]

[14.160] Where a court orders a document to be rectified, it is treated as having been in its rectified form as from the date of execution.[49] Accordingly, a court will not order rectification where it would affect the rights of third parties.[50]

[14.165] Although authority suggests that a party who seeks to rely on the unrectified document is not treated to have 'affirmed' the contract and thereby prevented from seeking rectification,[51] it may be that asserting the document with knowledge of the mistake could form the basis of an estoppel preventing that party from seeking the remedy.[52]

[14.170] For the purposes of rectification, evidence of a common intention not recorded in the final document is treated as an exception to the parol evidence rule.[53]

(c)   Withhold specific performance

[14.175] Even where the circumstances do not involve a common mistake of fundamental nature, the court may, in its discretion, refuse a decree of specific performance where it would be a hardship on the promisor to specifically enforce the contract.[54]

14.5   Mutual mistake

14.5.1   Common law

[14.180] Where the parties are at cross-purposes, each making a different mistake, the position at common law depends upon whether any meaning may be objectively ascribed to the parties' apparent agreement. If it is not possible for a reasonable third party to prefer one meaning over another, the mutual mistake will render the contract void.[55]

Example: Raffles v Wichelhaus[56]

The parties contracted for the sale of goods 'ex-*Peerless* from Bombay'. In fact two ships called *Peerless* sailed from Bombay, one in October and the other in December.

---

47   *Anfrank Nominees Pty Ltd v Connell* (1989) 1 ACSR 365, applying *The Olympic Pride* [1980] 2 Lloyds Rep 67 at 73.

48   L Bromley, 'Rectification in Equity' (1971) 87 *Law Quarterly Review* 532 at 538: *Bishopsgate Insurance Australia Ltd v Commonwealth Engineering (NSW) Pty Ltd* [1981] 1 NSWLR 429 at 431; *Pukallas v Cameron* (1982) 180 CLR 447 at 452.

49   *Issa v Berisha* [1981] 1 NSWLR 261 at 265.

50   *Coolibah Pastoral Co v Commonwealth* (1967) 11 FLR 173 at 190.

51   *Market Terminal Pty Ltd v Dominion Insurance Co of Australia* [1982] 1 NSWR 105.

52   Cf *Standard Portland Cement Pty Ltd v Good* (1993) 47 ALR 107.

53   See [9.25].

54   *Dell v Beasley* [1959] NZLR 89.

55   *Raffles v Wichelhaus* (1864) 2 H&C 906; 159 ER 375; *Scriven Bros & Co v Hindley & Co* [1913] 3 KB 564.

56   (1864) 2 H&C 906; 159 ER 375.

The purchaser intended to refer to the October shipment while the vendor meant the December shipment.

It was held that the description of the goods matched both cargoes equally. There were no other circumstances that would favour one meaning over the other. Accordingly, the court could not assign any meaning to the agreement, and the purported contract was therefore void.

[14.185] Where, on the other hand, objectively the parties' agreement may bear a particular meaning, that will be the meaning imputed to it.[57]

Example: Goldsbrough Mort & Co Ltd v Quinn[58]

The defendant granted to the plaintiff an option to purchase certain lands that had been conditionally purchased under the *Crown Lands Act*. The purchase price was stated as being 'calculated on a freehold basis'. The defendant believed, when he granted the option, that he would receive the agreed price without deduction for converting the property into freehold. The plaintiff, on the other hand, asserted that the amount necessary to convert the Crown Lease lands to freehold should be deducted from the agreed purchase price.

The High Court held that the expression 'calculated on a freehold basis' was without ambiguity. Plainly it meant that there would be a deduction for conversion of the land into freehold. Accordingly, the defendant was bound by this interpretation, notwithstanding his intended meaning of the words.

14.5.2   *Equity*

[14.190] By definition, in the case of mutual mistake, neither party knows (nor ought know) of the other's mistake. Accordingly, there is no unconscionability to justify relief in equity.[59] At most, equity may withhold specific performance where particular hardship would result from holding a party to the contract.[60]

[14.195] Since equity generally follows the law, where the common law assigns a meaning, that meaning will also be assigned in equity.[61]

14.6   Unilateral mistake

14.6.1   *Common law*

[14.200] The effect of a unilateral mistake where only one party is mistaken and the other knows or ought to know of the mistake, was discussed by the High Court in *Taylor v Johnson*.[62] In that case, however, the court 'left to another day' two particular instances of unilateral mistake: mistake as to identity and mistake as to the nature of the contract '*non est factum*'. Both of these types of unilateral mistake have been the

---

57   *Houlahan v Australian and New Zealand Banking Group Ltd* (1992) 110 FLR 259.
58   (1910) 10 CLR 674.
59   *Riverlate Properties Ltd v Paul* [1975] Ch 133.
60   *Malins v Freeman* (1837) 2 Keen 25; 48 ER 537; *Tamplin v James* (1880) 15 Ch D 215 at 222, 223.
61   *Tamplin v James* (1880) 15 Ch D 215.
62   (1983) 151 CLR 422.

subject of specific analysis by the courts—and, in the absence of argument specifically on point, were therefore excluded from the more generally framed comments in *Taylor v Johnson*. Accordingly, these two exceptional types of unilateral mistake require separate treatment.

(a) Unilateral mistakes in general

[14.205] If a *subjective* approach were applied to the interpretation of contracts, a unilateral mistake would render the contract void. This is because according to a subjective approach—taking account of what the parties actually meant—there would be no consensus between the parties.[63]

Example: Ashley v Cook[64]

The plaintiff owned two properties. His homestead was on one; the other was a paddock. He intended to sell the paddock, but mistakenly advertised the homestead property. The defendant satisfied himself prior to the sale that the property advertised for sale was the homestead, and at the auction bid accordingly. The price he gave was cheap if he got the homestead but dear if he got the paddock.

It was held that the plaintiff did not intend to sell the homestead, but the defendant intended to purchase it. This unilateral mistake was taken as entitling the plaintiff to rescind the contract.

[14.210] It is now clear, however, that an *objective* theory is used in relation to contract construction.[65] Unlike the approach taken in cases like *Ashley v Cook,* a mistaken party now cannot rely on his or her own mistake as making the contract a nullity, even if it were a fundamental mistake and the other party knew about it, because to all outward appearances the parties will have reached an agreement, that is the version of the party who is not mistaken.[66]

Example: Taylor v Johnson[67]

Mrs Johnson granted an option to Taylor or his nominee to purchase two five-acre pieces of land for a total price of $15 000. Mrs Johnson subsequently refused to perform the contract on the basis that she believed the price had been $15 000 *per acre*.

A majority of the High Court held that Mrs Taylor's unilateral mistake did not render the contract void at common law because objectively the sale price was $15 000 in total. It was immaterial that subjectively one of the parties believed that the price was $15 000 per acre.

63 *Smith v Hughes* (1871) LR 6 QB 597 at 607–608 per Blackburn J, 610 per Hannen J, as explained in *Taylor v Johnson* (1983) 151 CLR 422 at 428.
64 (1880) 6 VLR 204. See also *Hartog v Colin & Shields* [1939] 3 All 566.
65 *Taylor v Johnson* (1983) 151 CLR 422 at 428–429. See also, *Bell v Lever Bros Ltd* [1932] AC 161; *Solle v Butcher* [1950] 1 KB 671.
66 (1983) 151 CLR 422 at 428.
67 (1983) 151 CLR 422.

Consequently, apart from the special cases of mistaken identity and *non est factum*, common law no longer renders a contract void for unilateral mistake.[68]

(b)   Mistake as to identity

[14.215] The cases have distinguished between various situations in which a person is mistaken as to the identity of a party with whom he or she is contracting depending upon whether the parties are dealing at a distance or dealing in each other's presence.

Generally

[14.220] Generally speaking, when a party is mistaken as to the identity of the other party to the contract, the issue is essentially one of the proper construction of the offer. A mistake as to the identity of the other party will void the contract where:

- at the time of the agreement between A and B, A regarded the identity of the other party to the contract as material;[69]
- A intended to contract not with B but with someone else (C);[70] and
- that intention was known, or ought to have been known, by B.[71]

Example: Cundy v Lindsay[72]

A rogue called Blenkarn sent a letter to the plaintiff Lindsay offering to buy certain goods. In the letter, the rogue called himself 'Blenkarn & Co of 37 Wood Street Cheapside' but signed the letter so that the name appeared to be 'Blenkiron & Co', which was a well-respected firm doing business at 123 Wood Street, Cheapside. The plaintiff knew of the high reputation of Blenkiron & Co, but not its exact address. Goods were forwarded to 37 Wood Street, Cheapside, where the rogue took delivery and subsequently resold them to the defendant.

The House of Lords held that the plaintiffs had intended to deal with Blenkiron alone, not Blenkarn, of whom they knew nothing. There could never be a consensus of mind between the plaintiff and the rogue, so the plaintiff's mistake voided the contract. Accordingly, no title passed to the rogue, and therefore could not in turn be passed to the defendant. The plaintiff succeeded in its action for the tort of conversion.

[14.225] There is authority to suggest that the effect of a unilateral mistake as to identity is that the contract is rendered voidable,[73] although the weight of authority in Australia is in favour of such a contract being rendered void.[74] It has been suggested that the flexibility that would be afforded by only treating such contracts as voidable

---

68   The High Court also left open whether this principle applies to an informal contract: (1983) 151 CLR 422 at 430.

69   *Boulton v Jones* (1857) 2 H&N 564; 157 ER 232.

70   *Cundy v Lindsay* (1878) 3 App Cas 459.

71   Cf the approach adopted by Kitto and Windeyer JJ in dissent in *Porter v Latec Finance (Qld) Pty Ltd* (1964) 111 CLR 177.

72   (1878) 3 App Cas 459.

73   *Lewis v Avery* [1972] 1 QB 198 at 207; *Westpac Banking Corp v Dawson* (1990) 19 NSWLR 614 at 629.

74   *Porter v Latec Finance (Qld) Pty Ltd* (1964) 111 CLR 177; *Roache v Australian Mercantile Land and Finance Co Ltd* [1965] NSWR 1015.

would be desirable, and in keeping with other developments concerning the treatment of mistake in Australia.[75] The issue is significant. If the correct approach is that the contract is void, then in no circumstances will a third party dealing with the rogue acquire good title in goods that the rogue has obtained under a contract formed by mistaken identity. By contrast, if the correct result is that the contract is merely rendered voidable, then the plaintiff's interest will be defeated by an innocent third party who acquires an interest for value in the subject matter of the contract prior to the plaintiff taking steps to rescind the contract.

[14.230] A contract may be void for mistaken identity where a plaintiff does *not* want to contract with someone but is deceived by a rogue into doing so.[76]

Face-to-face dealings

[14.235] Where, on the other hand, the contract is made by parties in each other's presence (*inter praesentes*), a rebuttable presumption arises that the contract is concluded with the person who is present.[77]

[14.240] The cases have not always been consistent about the steps necessary to rebut this presumption. In *Phillips v Brooks Ltd*,[78] a rogue presented himself to a jeweller as Sir George Bullough—someone known to the jeweller as a man of means—and was permitted to take away an emerald ring before his cheque cleared. The court held that the jeweller's step in looking up the name in a directory was insufficient to show that he intended to contract with Bullough and nobody else. Accordingly, the presumption that the jeweller had intended to sell the ring to the person physically present in the shop had not been rebutted, and the rogue had been able to pass title to a third party.[79] By contrast, in *Ingram v Little*,[80] a rogue represented to the sisters Ingram, who had advertised their car for sale, that he was a Mr PGM Hutchinson of Sandstead, Caterham. While the others chatted, one of the sisters slipped out and verified the name and address in a telephone directory at the local post office. Although the sisters had never heard of PGM Hutchinson, they allowed the rogue to take their car before his cheque for the sale price cleared.

The English Court of Appeal, by a 2:1 majority, held there was sufficient evidence to rebut the presumption that the contract had been made with the person who had been present—that is, the rogue. The majority was of the view that the initial contract with the person who was present was terminated when one of the sisters refused to take a cheque and called the deal off. The other sister's actions in checking the directory in the post office and the final agreement showed that the sisters intended to deal only with PGM Hutchinson. Accordingly, the contract was

---

75 See, for example, N Seddon & MP Ellinghaus, *Cheshire and Fifoot's Law of Contract*, 7th edn, Butterworths, Sydney, 1997, p 507.

76 *Said v Butt* [1920] 3 KB 497.

77 *Phillips v Brooks Ltd* [1919] 2 KB 243; *Lewis v Avery* [1972] 1 QB 198. Different considerations may apply where the rogue purports to contract as the agent for another person: *Roache v Australian Mercantile Land and Finance Co Ltd* [1965] NSWR 1015 at 1019.

78 [1919] 2 KB 243.

79 The jeweller may have been able to rescind for a fraudulent misrepresentation, but that right would have been lost due to the intervention of an innocent third party for value.

80 [1961] 1 QB 31.

held to be void, and title did not pass to the rogue—nor, thereafter, to the person who bought the car from the rogue.

[14.245] It may be difficult to reconcile these two cases. In *Phillips v Brooks Ltd* the jeweller at least knew of Sir George Bullough, whereas the sisters in *Ingram v Little* did not know of PGM Hutchinson. Subsequently, in *Lewis v Avery*,[81] the reasoning in *Phillips v Brooks Ltd* was preferred. In that case, a rogue represented himself to be 'Richard Greene', the star of the television series *Robin Hood*. He showed the plaintiff a special pass to the Pinewood Studios in the name 'Richard A Green', which bore an official-looking stamp. The plaintiff accepted a cheque filled out by the rogue signed 'RA Green', and allowed him to take his car before the cheque cleared. When the cheque was dishonoured, the plaintiff found that the rogue had resold the car to a bona fide purchaser. The English Court of Appeal held unanimously that nothing in the circumstances displaced the presumption of an intention to contract with the person who was physically present. Merely perusing identification tended by the rogue was insufficient. The contract was undoubtedly voidable for fraudulent misrepresentation, but the right to rescind had been lost due to the third party acquiring a right in the subject matter for value.[82]

[14.250] What is required to rebut the presumption will depend upon an assessment of the particular circumstances of the case. However, it seems that merely seeking to confirm an alleged identity by reference to a directory will be insufficient. Similarly, attempting to rely on identification proffered by the other person will not be sufficient to show either that the identity of the other person is material or that there was an intention to contract with another person.[83] It would also seem that any distinction between a person and that person's attributes (such as his or her wealth or social position) does not provide a valid basis for rebutting the presumption.[84]

(c)   Mistake as to the nature of the contract: *non est factum*

[14.255] The plea of *non est factum* ('it is not my deed') seeks to accommodate two competing policy considerations: the injustice of holding a person to a bargain to which he or she has not brought a consenting mind, and the necessity of holding a person who signs a document to that document—particularly in order to protect innocent persons who rely on that signature when there is no reason to doubt its validity.[85] In order to make out the plea, three elements must be shown:

*   the claimant belongs to the relevant class;
*   the claimant signed the document in the belief that it was radically different from what it was in fact; and
*   at least as against innocent persons, the claimant's failure to read and understand the document was not due to carelessness on his or her part.[86]

There is a heavy onus on a person seeking to rely upon the plea.[87]

---

81   [1972] 1 QB 198.
82   Ibid, at 207.
83   See [14.220].
84   See *Lewis v Avery* [1972] 1 QB 198 at 206.
85   *Petelin v Cullen* (1975) 132 CLR 355 at 359.
86   Ibid at 359–360.
87   Ibid at 360; *Saunders v Anglia Building Society* [1971] AC 1004 at 1019.

[14.260] The plea is often asserted in circumstances where a rogue misrepresents the nature of the document and thereby obtains a benefit that he or she may then try to transfer to a third party. Where the plea is established, the contract is void *ab initio*: no title may pass to the rogue, and accordingly any third party interest will be defeated. Where, on the other hand, the plea is not established, there may be rights with respect to, for example, fraudulent misrepresentation although the right to rescind must be exercised promptly—and before third party rights become involved—lest it be lost.

[14.265] The relevant class is restricted to those who:

- are unable to read, through blindness or illiteracy, and who must rely on others for advice as to what they are signing; or

- through no fault of their own are unable to have an understanding of the purport of the particular document.[88]

The class may include a foreign person who is unable to speak English very well.[89] The class may also include one who is suffering from a mental incapacity, provided the effect of the incapacity is that the claimant is not 'aware what were the motions his [or her] hand was performing' in the sense of being neither minded nor intending to sign a document of that character or class.[90] Where, on the other hand, the effect of the mental incapacity is that the person signing the document has no ability to understand or evaluate the document, the plea will fail, and the contract may instead be only voidable, not void.[91] In an exceptional case, it was held that the class included a person of full capacity who had been misled by a trusted friend to believe that he was merely witnessing the friend's signature on highly confidential documents that had material parts covered up.[92]

[14.270] It is a question of fact determined *subjectively* as to whether the document is radically or fundamentally different from what the signer of the document thought it to be.[93]

Example: Saunders v Anglia Building Society[94]

Mrs Gallie was a 78-year-old widow. She wanted to transfer her house to her nephew so he could raise money on it—but on condition that she remain in occupation until she died. The nephew and his friend, Lee, presented Mrs Gallie with a document to sign, which Lee represented to be a document that assigned the house by way of gift to the nephew. In fact, the document was a transfer of the house to Lee. Mrs Gallie had broken her glasses and was unable to read the document. On enquiring about the document, she was told by Lee that it was a deed of gift to her nephew. She thereupon executed the document. Subsequently, and without paying any money for the

---

88 *Petelin v Cullen* (1975) 132 CLR 355 at 359–360.
89 See, for example, *Lee v Ah Gee* [1920] VLR 278; *Nemtsas v Nemtsas* [1957] VR 191; *Petelin v Cullen* (1975) 132 CLR 355.
90 *Gibbons v Wright* (1954) 91 CLR 423 at 443.
91 Ibid at 443–444; *PT Ltd v Maradona Pty Ltd* (1991) 25 NSWLR 643; cf *Newman v Ivermee* (1989) NSW ConvR 55-493 (*non est factum* upheld where claimant was in such a distressed state of bereavement that on medical evidence she had no understanding of the nature of the document).
92 *Lewis v Clay* (1897) 67 LJQB 224.
93 *Petelin v Cullen* (1975) 132 CLR 355 at 361.
94 [1971] AC 1004.

house, Lee mortgaged the property to a building society. Mrs Gallie sought a declaration that the transfer to Lee was void on the basis of *non est factum*.

It was held in the House of Lords[95] that the plea of *non est factum* can only rarely be sustained by a person of full capacity. In this case, Mrs Gallie belonged to the relevant class despite the fact that her blindness was only temporary. However, it could not be shown that Mrs Gallie believed the document to be something radically different from what she thought she was signing. This was because whether the document was a gift to her nephew or a transfer to Lee, she had intended to divest herself of her interest in the house. Accordingly, there was not a radical or fundamental difference in the document that she actually signed. Accordingly, the plea failed.

Example: Petelin v Cullen[96]

Petelin spoke little English and could read none. He granted an option to purchase land to Cullen. After the option had expired, Cullen's agent wrote to Petelin requesting an extension and enclosing $50 in payment. Petelin signed the extension of the option in the belief that it was a receipt, having been told by the agent that he 'must sign' the document. Cullen later purported to exercise the option but Petelin refused to sell.

The High Court upheld Petelin's plea of *non est factum*. Petelin belonged to the relevant class because he had little appreciation of English and no capacity to understand the option agreement. Further, the document that he signed was radically different from what he thought he was signing: instead of being a mere receipt, it was in fact an option that enabled Cullen to purchase his land.

[14.275] In *Petelin v Cullen*, the High Court stressed that the third element of carelessness referred to a mere failure to take reasonable precautions in ascertaining the character of a document before signing it, rather than the tort of negligence with its constituent elements of duty, breach, and damage. The insistence that precautions be taken as a condition of making a defence was considered to be of fundamental importance when the defence was asserted against an innocent person, *whether a third party to the transaction or not*, who relied upon the document and the signature on it and who was unaware of the circumstances surrounding execution.[97] On the other hand, no such requirement applies where the plea is being asserted against a party who was aware of the circumstances attending execution and who knows, or has reason to suspect, that it was executed under some mistake concerning its character. In such a case, the plea will be successful because there will be no countervailing policy: no innocent person will have placed reliance on the signature without reason to doubt its validity.[98]

---

95   On appeal from the Court of Appeal sub nom *Gallie v Lee* [1969] 2 Ch 17. Mrs Gallie died following the decision of the Court of Appeal and her action was assumed by the executor of her estate.
96   (1975) 132 CLR 355.
97   *Petelin v Cullen* (1975) 132 CLR 355 at 360.
98   Ibid, at 360.

Example: Petelin v Cullen[99]

The High Court held that the third requirement had no relevance in the circumstances of this case. Petelin's mistaken belief that the document was a mere receipt was induced by a representation by the agent that the document only acknowledged the payment of the sum of $50. Petelin's difficulties in reading and understanding the document must have been clearly apparent to the agent, who was present when Petelin signed the document. In the face of Petelin's difficulties, the agent had only demanded that the document 'must be signed'—without offering any explanation of its character. Even if Cullen was not aware of the conduct of his agent, as his principal he was responsible for it. Cullen therefore was not an 'innocent person' in the circumstances.

In any event, the High Court did not believe Petelin had been careless. He had been faced with the choice of either relying on what the agent had said or incurring the expense and inconvenience of taking it to a solicitor for advice. Petelin had previously been advised by the agent to consult a solicitor when that was necessary, but on this occasion no such advice had been given, nor had he been given any indication that the document granted additional rights to those previously conferred.

[14.280] Where a document is signed with blank spaces left to be filled in at a later date by the other party, there may be an indication that the signer has been careless, thereby excluding the plea notwithstanding that the first two elements of belonging to the relevant class and believing the document to be something radically different may be demonstrated.[100]

14.6.2 Equity

[14.285] It has been noted that in the event of a unilateral mistake, equity may treat the contract as voidable, rectify the contract, or withhold the remedy of specific performance. The first two of these remedies warrant closer attention.

(a) Voidable contract

[14.290] At common law, a party cannot rely on his or her own mistake in order to void the contract. However, equity will set aside the contract in a case of unilateral mistake where the court is of the opinion that there has been 'sharp practice'—that is, it is unconscientious for parties to avail themselves of the legal advantage they have obtained by virtue of the contract.[101] Special circumstances are ordinarily required before it would be unconscientious for one party to a written contract to enforce it against another party who was under a mistake as to its terms or its subject matter.[102] In *Taylor v Johnson*[103] it was held that three elements must be shown:

99   (1975) 132 CLR 355.
100 Cf *Lewis v Clay* (1897) 67 LJQB 224; *United Dominion's Trust Ltd v Western* [1976] 1 QB 513.
101 *Torrance v Bolton* (1872) LR 8 Ch App 118 at 124 per James LJ with whom Mellish LJ agreed.
102 *Taylor v Johnson* (1983) 151 CLR 422 at 431; cf *Cielo v MG Kailis Gulf Fisheries Pty Ltd* (1991) 104 FLR 189 (no remedy where unilateral mistake but unconscionability by defendant).
103 (1983) 151 CLR 422.

- a party enters into a written contract under a serious mistake about its contents in relation to a fundamental term;
- the other party is aware or has reason to be aware that circumstances exist that indicate the first party is entering the contract under some serious mistake or misapprehension; and
- the other party deliberately sets out to ensure that the first party does not become aware of the existence of his or her mistake or misapprehension.[104]

In *Taylor v Johnson*, Mrs Johnson granted an option for a total price of $15 000, rather than $15 000 per acre. The value of the land, if a proposed rezoning became effective, was $195 000. By a 3:1 majority, the High Court held that, although Mrs Johnson had no remedy at common law, she was entitled to have the contract set aside in equity. The stipulation as to price was plainly a fundamental term of the contract. However, the majority was of the view that the proper inference to be drawn from the evidence was that Taylor was aware that Mrs Johnson was under some serious mistake or misapprehension about either the terms (the price) or the subject matter (its value) of the relevant transaction. Further, the avoidance of mention of the purchase price and the circumstances attending the execution of the option, including Taylor's incorrect statement that he did not have a copy of the option that he could make available to her, led to the inference that he deliberately set out to ensure that Mrs Johnson did not become aware that she was being induced to grant the option and to enter into the contract by a material mistake or misapprehension about the terms or subject matter of the contract.[105]

[14.295] What amounts to 'sharp practice' may depend upon the individual circumstances of the case. It may be that in a given case merely remaining silent with the knowledge or means of knowledge of the mistake may amount to unconscionable conduct and constitute 'deliberately setting out to ensure' that the mistaken party does not become aware of the existence of the mistake.[106]

[14.300] Once again, a contract will not be set aside for unilateral mistake where, for example, the contract has been affirmed, an innocent third party has acquired an interest in the subject matter of the contract for value,[107] or *restitutio in integrum* is no longer possible.[108]

(b)   Rectification

[14.305] Equity may rectify a written document where only one party mistakenly believes that the document accurately reflects the parties' agreement and the party who is not mistaken engages in unconscionable conduct or 'sharp practice'.[109] The necessary

---

104   (1983) 151 CLR 422 at 432; applied in *Deputy Commissioner of Taxation (NSW) v Chamberlain* (1990) 93 ALR 729 (attempt to conceal error in tax assessment); cf *Buseska v Sergio* (1990) 102 FLR 157.

105   Dawson J dissented on the ground that the court should have accepted the finding of the trial judge that Taylor did not know of the mistake and that as a consequence the case ought to have been treated as one of mutual mistake rather than unilateral mistake.

106   *Misiaria v Saydels Pty Ltd* (1989) NSW Conv R 55-474 at 58,448.

107   *McKenzie v McDonald* [1927] VLR 134.

108   *Spence v Crawford* [1939] 3 All ER 271.

109   *Riverlate Properties Ltd v Paul* [1975] Ch 133 at 140; *Commerce Consolidated Pty Ltd v Johnstone* [1976] VR 274.

elements for rectification after unilateral mistake were stated in *Thomas Bates & Son Ltd v Windham's (Lingerie) Ltd* as follows:

- the plaintiff wrongly believes that the written document contains a particular term or does not contain a particular term;
- the defendant is aware of the plaintiff's wrong belief;
- the defendant says nothing to correct the plaintiff's wrong belief; and
- the mistake either provides an advantage to the defendant or is a detriment to the plaintiff.[110]

[14.310] Although the elements are cast in terms of actual knowledge, it seems that it is sufficient if the defendant 'must have known' or 'strongly suspects' that the plaintiff is making a mistake.[111]

[14.315] There is ongoing debate about whether the court should be entitled to give the party not mistaken the option of having the contract rectified (which has the effect of preserving the contract) or set aside (which has the effect of destroying it).[112]

14.7 International perspectives

14.7.1 New Zealand

[14.320] The *Contractual Mistakes Act* (1977) provides a code governing relief for mistake. The statute purports to 'strike a balance between avoiding the unfairness of holding a party to an inappropriate transaction that was not fully assented to, and protecting other parties to the contract (and those claiming under them) who have a legitimate interest in seeing the contract performed'.[113]

[14.325] The statute represents a significant departure from mistake at the common law and in equity, the rules of which are displaced.[114] However, the Act makes it clear that certain areas are not affected, including the common law doctrine of *non est factum*, and the equitable remedy of rectification, or the law relating to frustration, illegality, payment of money under mistake of fact, undue influence, breach of fiduciary duty, fraud or misrepresentation.[115] The remedies for misrepresentation are more clearly stated in the *Contractual Remedies Act* (1979) and are less subject to judicial discretion, perhaps providing a better route for plaintiffs seeking relief under the *Contractual Mistakes Act* for mistakes induced by misrepresentation. The Act sets criteria by which it can be determined whether or not a mistake qualifies for potential relief.

---

110 [1981] 1 WLR 505; cf DW Greig & JLR Davis, *Law of Contract*, Law Book Co, Sydney, 1987, p 937 where it is argued that the fourth element ought only to be that the mistake was one calculated to benefit the unmistaken party since the basis of rectification is to prevent one party from unconscientiously taking advantage of the mistake in a document as written.

111 *Misiaria v Saydels Pty Ltd* (1989) NSW Conv R 55-474.

112 See, for example, *Garrard v Frankel* (1862) 30 Beav 445; 54 ER 961; *Paget v Marshall* (1884) 28 Ch D 255; *Coxon v Masters* [1930] QSR 337; DW Greig & JLR Davis, *Law of Contract*, Law Book Co, Sydney, 1987, pp 937–938; JW Carter & DJ Harland, *Contract Law in Australia*, 3rd edn, Butterworths, Sydney, 1996, pp 453–454; N Seddon & MP Ellinghaus, *Cheshire and Fifoot's Law of Contract*, 7th edn, Butterworths, Sydney, 1997, pp 505–506.

113 Contract and Commercial Law Reform Committee, *Report on the Effects of Mistakes on Contracts* (1976), para 5.

114 See s 5(1).

115 See s 5(2).

[14.330] In order to qualify for relief, an applicant must satisfy three elements:
- a mistake as defined by s 6(1)(a);
- an inequality of consideration consequent on the mistake; and
- that the applicant for relief was not obliged by the contract to bear the burden of any risk as to mistake.

There are three different kinds of mistake within s 6(1)(a): a mistake actually known to the other party;[116] a common mistake;[117] and mutual mistakes.[118]

[14.335] Unlike the requirement at common law that the mistake must be as to some 'fundamental' matter, the Act only requires that the party or parties be 'influenced' in the decision to enter the contract by the mistake. The second criterion requires an inequality of value or a benefit that is substantially disproportionate to the consideration. The third criterion only applies where the contract makes express or implied provision for a risk of mistake such as a standard-form contract for the sale of land placing on the purchaser the onus of establishing the boundaries of the property purchased.[119] Once it is shown that the mistake qualifies for relief, the court has a wide discretion to order relief as it thinks just, including but not limited to declaring the contract to be valid and subsisting in whole or in part or for any particular purpose; cancelling the contract; varying the contract; or granting relief by way of restitution or compensation.[120]

[14.340] The Act does not purport to extend to rectification or *non est factum*. In these two respects, therefore, there is no substantive difference between the law of Australia and of New Zealand.

14.7.2 United States

[14.345] A different nomenclature is observed in the United States:
- 'mutual mistake' is used to denote the case where one party's mistaken assumption is shared by the other party (in Australia and England this mistake would be described as a 'common mistake'); and
- a 'unilateral mistake', where one party's mistaken assumption is not shared by the other party (which would also be described as a 'unilateral mistake' in Australia).

The Australian concept of 'mutual mistake'—where the parties are at cross-purposes— is regarded by American courts as a question of interpretation. This is resolved by trying to discern the parties' intentions, rather than making a simple application of an objective test.[121]

[14.350] The Restatement (Second) §152 states that a contract can be avoided for 'mutual mistake' where the party adversely affected can show three elements:
- the mistake goes to a basic assumption on which the contract was made;
- the mistake has a material effect on the agreed exchange of performances; and
- the mistake is not one of which the party bears the risk.

---

116 See for example, *Weddel NZ Ltd v Taylor Preston Ltd* [1993] 2 NZLR 104 at 109.
117 See, for example, *Philips v Philips* [1993] 3 NZLR 159 (common mistake regarding enforceability of earlier oral agreement).
118 Referred to as 'different mistakes about the same matter of fact or law'.
119 See JF Burrows, J Finn & S Todd, *Law of Contract in New Zealand*, Butterworths, Wellington, 1997, p 286.
120 See s 7.
121 See [9.435].

These elements bear some resemblance to the elements suggested in *Solle v Butcher* for an equitable remedy for common mistake.

[14.355] It seems that a wide variety of assumptions may be regarded as 'basis' including those concerning the existence, identity, quantity, or quality of the subject matter.[122] The term 'basis' seems to be intended to exclude mistakes relating to collateral or peripheral matters.

[14.360] To show that a mistake has a material effect on the agreed exchange, a party must show more than a mere loss of advantage from the contract or that he or she would not have entered into the contract had there been no mistake. Instead, he or she must show that the resulting imbalance in the agreed exchange of promises is so severe that he or she cannot fairly be required to carry it out.[123] Courts have been more prepared to accept that there has been a material effect on the agreed exchange where the mistake has an impact on both parties rather than merely becoming less desirable for one party.[124]

[14.365] The third requirement has been posed as a means of reconciling a difficulty that has arisen where courts have denied relief even though the mistake has involved a basic assumption and had a material effect on the performance of the contract.[125] The Restatement (Second) lists three situations in which a party is deemed to have assumed the risk of the mistake: where the agreement expressly provides for such an assumption (such as by use of the words 'as is');[126] a party makes a contract with only limited knowledge of the facts and is aware of that limited knowledge;[127] and where the risk is allocated to a party by the court on the ground that it is reasonable in the circumstances to do so. The third instance is the most common.[128] This allocation is usually based on an exercise of common sense and an assessment of human behaviour. Suppose, for example, a builder agrees to construct a building but afterwards discovers that the land contains rock that will make the construction more expensive than either party had expected. It is unlikely the builder will be able to avoid the contract on the ground of a mistake in assuming, when they agreed upon a contract price, that the sewer conditions were normal. This will be because of the builder's generally greater expertise in judging subsoil conditions.[129]

It seems that a mistaken party is not precluded from obtaining relief merely because the mistake could have been avoided by that party exercising reasonable care.[130] The Restatement (Second) §157 suggests that relief for mistake is only pre-

---

122 *Dover Pool & Racquet Club v Brooking* 322 NE 2d 168 (Mass 1975).

123 Restatement (Second) § 152 comment c.

124 *Sherwood v Walker* 33 NW 919 (Mich 1887) (where sale of cow believed by the parties to be infertile when in fact was with calf the exchange became both less advantageous to the seller and more advantageous to the buyer).

125 See, for example, *Wood v Boynton* 95 NW 42 (Wis 1885) (sale of stone for $1 when it was in fact a rough diamond worth $700).

126 *Lenawee County Board of Health v Messerly* 331 NW 2d 203 (Mich 1982) (purchase of an apartment house 'as is' construed as assumption of risk of inadequate sewerage system).

127 See, for example, *Wood v Boynton* 95 NW 42 (Wis 1885) (seller having possession of stone for lengthy period without conducting investigation as to its intrinsic value assumed the risk that the stone was in fact a small diamond and therefore worth significantly more than contract price).

128 EA Farnsworth, *Contracts*, 3rd edn, Aspen Law and Business, New York, 1999, § 9.3.

129 See, for example, *Watkins & Son v Carrig* 21 A 2d 591 (NH 1941).

130 *Vermette v Anderson* 558 P 2d 258 (Wash App 1976).

cluded by fault where it amounts to 'a failure to act in good faith and in accordance with reasonable standards of fair dealing'. The remedy for mutual mistake is avoidance—in other words, the contact is voidable at the option of the disadvantaged party.[131] That remedy may be lost where that party fails to act within a reasonable length of time after he or she is or ought to be aware of the facts.[132]

[14.370] What Australian courts would describe as *res extincta* would seem in the United States to be able to be based on two alternative grounds: (American) mutual mistake or existing (as opposed to supervening), impracticability. In order to be excused on the ground of an existing impracticability, the four requirements imposed in the case of a supervening impracticability[133] must again be shown, namely:

- performance as agreed is impracticable;
- the event must have been a basic assumption on which the contract was made;
- the impracticability must have resulted without the fault of the party seeking to be excused; and
- the risk of the event must not have been assumed by a party.[134]

It has been acknowledged that an existing impracticability excuses the seller in a case of destruction of identified goods as at the time of contracting without the knowledge of either party.[135]

A number of distinctions between the alternative grounds may be recognised. A party relying on impracticability must show that it was impracticable for the party to perform—whereas a party relying only on mistake need only show that the mistake had a material effect on the agreed exchange of performances. However, to succeed on the ground of mistake, a party must show a mistake as to an existing fact and not merely an erroneous prediction as to the future. Further, it is more likely that a party will be regarded as having borne the risk in the case of mistake than in the case of impracticability or frustration.[136]

[14.375] A unilateral mistake occurs where only one party is mistaken. For a time, courts resisted granting relief where one party had an erroneous belief as to the facts that was not shared by the other party.[137] However, a limited right to avoid the contract for a unilateral mistake has now been recognised where:[138]

- the mistake went to a basis assumption on which the contract was made;
- the mistake had a material effect on the agreed exchange of performances;[139]
- avoidance is sought before any significant reliance by the other party;[140] and
- enforcement of the contract pursuant to the mistaken terms would be unconscionable.[141]

---

131   *Leavitt v Stanley* 571 A 2d 269 (NH 1990).
132   *Grymes v Sanders* 93 US 55 (1876)
133   See the discussion of frustration and supervening impracticability in [22.320].
134   See [22.320].
135   Uniform Commercial Code 2-613 Comment 2.
136   EA Farnsworth, *Contracts*, 3rd edn, Aspen Law and Business, New York, 1999, § 9.8.
137   See, for example, *Steinmeyer v Schroeppel* 80 NE 564 (Ill 1907).
138   Restatement (Second) § 153.
139   See, for example, *Elsinore Union Elementary School District v Kastorff* 353 P 2d 713 (Cal 1960); *Boise Junior College District v Mattefs Construction Co* 450 P 2d 604 (Id 1969).
140   *Boise Junior College District v Mattefs Construction Co* 450 P 2d 604 (Id 1969).
141   Ibid.

Unconscionability requires a degree of hardship if the contract were to be enforced, rather than mere materiality.[142] United States authorities[143] have held that unconscionability may be satisfied where there is mere knowledge or means of knowledge; or if some kind of 'sharp practice' is required, silence alone is sufficient. Corbin states:

> There is practically universal agreement that, if the material mistake of one party was caused by the other, either purposely or innocently, or was of such character and accompanied by such circumstances that he had reason to know of it, the mistaken party has a right to rescission.[144]

There may therefore be a divergence in this respect if the Australian approach of requiring knowledge or means of knowledge of the mistake, together with an active attempt to prevent the other party from discovering the mistake, is interpreted as requiring more than a mere silence with knowledge of the mistake.

[14.380] Further, even if these requirements are established, relief for unilateral mistake may still be withheld if the party seeking relief is judged to have borne the risk of the mistake—as where the mistake was one of judgment. Thus relief may be granted in the case of a clerical, arithmetical, or specification misreading error, but not where there is a mistake in judgment as to economic conditions for the continued existence of a price freeze.[145]

[14.385] Relief for unilateral mistake was first recognised in the case of general contractors making a unilateral mistake in the form of an error in the calculation of bids on construction contracts. Relief has also been granted where there has been a unilateral mistake about the identity of land or its boundaries;[146] where a seller of goods has made a unilateral mistake as to what goods he or she was offering;[147] and where the holder of a patent made a unilateral mistake as to whether its patent was capable of withstanding challenge.[148] The principles regarding unilateral mistake would now seem also to embrace cases of mistaken identity.[149] This is because the contract is voidable if the other party had reason to know of the mistake or caused it,[150] or if its enforcement would otherwise be unconscionable.

14.7.3   Japan

[14.390] Mistake in Japan (*sakugo*) is a subset of the concept of 'lack of real intention,' which renders a contract void. The other analogous components are mental reservation (*shinri ryûho*) and false declaration of intention (*kyogi hyôji*). In each case, there may be expressed intention, but no real meeting of minds—so the contract is treated as

---

142   Ibid at 606.
143   See, for example, *Coleman v Holecheck* 542 F(2d) 532 at 535–536 (1976); *De Paola v City of New York* 194 NYS (2d) 525 at 527–528 (1977); the majority also referred to Canadian cases, see *McMaster University v Wilchar Construction Ltd* (1971) 22 DLR (3d) 9 at 22; *Stepps Investments Ltd v Security Capital Corp Ltd* (1976) 73 DLR (3d) 351 at 362–364.
144   *Corbin on Contracts* (Vol 3, 1960) at 692 cited in *Taylor v Johnson* (1983) 151 CLR 422 at 432.
145   *Tony Down Food Co v United States* 530 F 2d 367 (Ct Cl 1976).
146   *Beatty v Depue* 103 NW 2d 187 (SD 1960).
147   *Colvin v Baskett* 407 SW 2d 19 (Tex Civ App 1966).
148   *Gamewell Manufacturing v HVAC Supply* 715 F 2d 112 (4th Cir 1983).
149   Restatement (Second) § 153 comment g.
150   *Patucek v Cordeleria Lourdes* 310 F 2d 527 (10th Cir 1962).

void, except where this would adversely affect the other party or an innocent third party.

[14.395] Mental reservation—for example, the joking offer—is dealt with in art 93 of the Civil Code, which provides that the declaration of intention, if accepted by the other party is valid 'unless the other party was aware or should have been aware of the true intention of the declarant'.

[14.400] Civil Code art 94 describes a false declaration of intention in the following terms:

1 A false declaration of intention made in collusion with another party is null and void.

2 The voidness of the declaration of intention referred to in the preceding section may not be set up against a third person who has acted in good faith.

[14.405] Mistake is the more usual vitiating factor. In the case of mistake, Civil Code art 95 provides that:

A declaration of intention shall be null and void if made under a mistake with regard to any essential element of the juristic act: however, if such mistake was caused by gross negligence on the part of the declarant, the declarant may not assert the contract's voidness.

Further, mistake may not be asserted against a third party who is acting in good faith.[151]

---

151 Civil Code 94(2) by analogy: the nullity of a declaration of intention as mentioned in the previous paragraph cannot be set up against a bona fide third person.

Chapter 15

Duress

15.1 Introduction

[15.05] The common law has long recognised that duress, in the form of a coercion of the plaintiff's will through illegitimate pressure or threats to the plaintiff's interests, renders a contract voidable.[1] Nevertheless, there is a dearth of modern cases consider-

---

1   See the historical analysis undertaken by Jacobs JA in the New South Wales Court of Appeal in *Barton v Armstrong* [1973] 2 NSWLR 598 at 606–610.

ing duress. One explanation for this phenomenon may be the 'stability of our society'.[2] A more likely reason is that circumstances that would traditionally constitute duress may also be seen as constituting actual undue influence. Duress may therefore, for all intents and purposes, have become subsumed by the equitable doctrine of undue influence.[3]

If duress is to be recognised as having a continued relevance, it may be due to its application in the relatively recent decision of the Privy Council in *Barton v Armstrong*.[4] Moreover, the early 1980s saw the emergence of a new doctrine of 'economic duress', which has since grown in significance. In the process, the emphasis appears to have shifted away from the notion of coercion of the will of the plaintiff to the lack of legitimacy in the pressure or compulsion.[5]

15.2 Types of duress

15.2.1 Threats to person

[15.10] The traditional common law concept of duress was limited to actual or threatened violence to the person of the plaintiff or his or her family.[6]

Example: Barton v Armstrong[7]

The plaintiff and defendant were two of four directors of a company. There had been antagonism between them for some time. The plaintiff and the other two directors reached the conclusion that the company would be better served if the defendant were excluded from its management. The defendant initially refused to resign when approached to do so by the plaintiff, but was voted out of various management positions he held. Finally, the parties agreed to a deed setting out the terms on which the plaintiff would buy the defendant out of the company and its interest in a large residential development. The trial judge found that the plaintiff was at least partly motivated to sign the deed by the defendant's threats to have the plaintiff murdered. Upon execution of the deed, the defendant and his nominees resigned from the company, but the cash payment required denuded the company of most of its liquid assets.

The Privy Council, on appeal from the New South Wales Court of Appeal, held that if a threat was made against a party's life and was one of the reasons for that party entering into a contract, relief should be granted for duress. It was immaterial that there may have been other reasons for entering the contract (including good business sense) if the threat contributed to the decision.

---

2   *Barton v Armstrong* [1973] 2 NSWLR 598 at 606 per Jacobs JA.

3   *Farmers' Cooperative Executors & Trustees Ltd v Perks* (1989) 52 SASR 399 at 405, agreeing with the suggestion by M Cope, *Duress, Undue Influence and Unconscientious Bargains* (1985), para 125. See also G Stevens, 'Over reaching: duress and undue influence' (1990) *Law Society Bulletin* 168 at 169.

4   [1973] 2 NSWLR 598.

5   *Crescendo Management Pty Ltd v Westpac Bank Corporation* (1988) 19 NSWLR 40 at 45–46 per McHugh JA; *Dimskal Shipping Co SA v International Transport Workers' Federation* [1992] 2 AC 152 at 166 per Lord Goff.

6   See also, for example, *Saxon v Saxon* [1976] 4 WWR 300 (threat to kill children).

7   [1973] 2 NSWLR 598.

[15.15] This notion extends to actual or threatened imprisonment or confinement.[8] By contrast, a contract resulting from a threat of a criminal prosecution for which there is sufficient ground will not amount to duress, provided that there is valuable consideration for the contract and no agreement to stifle the prosecution.[9]

Example: Scolio Pty Ltd v Cote[10]

Following an audit, it was discovered that the defendant manager had been misappropriating funds from the plaintiff company. On instructions from the plaintiff, the company auditor negotiated with the defendant the execution of a deed for repayment by the defendant of the amounts that he had misappropriated. When the plaintiff company sued for amounts overdue under the deed, the defendant claimed the deed was voidable, since he had signed it under duress. He claimed that on instructions from the plaintiff, the auditor had threatened him with police intervention if he did not sign the deed.

The Full Court of the Supreme Court of Western Australia held that the threat of prosecution was not enough to set aside a contract on the grounds of duress where the amount was in fact owing, and the person being threatened received consideration for entering into the contract. In this case, the consideration was in the form of the plaintiff allowing the defendant time to pay the outstanding debt. There was no evidence of impropriety. There was no agreement to stifle prosecution, since the defendant had not established that he signed the deed to prevent the plaintiff from informing the police in future, and had not established that the plaintiff believed the defendant had signed the deed for that purpose. Accordingly, there had not been duress in the circumstances.

15.2.2 Threats to personal property

[15.20] It has long been accepted that money paid in order to avoid wrongful seizure of goods or in order to obtain the release of goods wrongfully seized may be recovered in what is now known as restitution as 'money had and received'.[11] For some time, however, the law drew a distinction between an agreement to pay money for such a purpose and an agreement resulting from actual or threatened violence to person.[12]

[15.25] Today, where conduct amounting to duress to personal property is a reason for the plaintiff entering into a contract, that conduct will enable the plaintiff to avoid the contract.[13]

---

8   *Barton v Armstong* [1973] 2 NSWLR 598 at 609 per Jacobs JA, 616 per Mason JA. See, for example, *McLarnon v McLarnon* (1968) 112 Sol J 419 (threat to place plaintiff in a convent).
9   *Ward v Lloyd* (1843) 7 SNR 499; *Flower v Sadler* (1882) 10 QBD 572; *Scolio Pty Ltd v Cote* (1992) 6 WAR 475; cf *Mutual Finance Ltd v John Whetton & Sons* [1937] 2 KB 389.
10   (1992) 6 WAR 475.
11   *Astley v Reynolds* (1731) 2 Str 915, 93 ER 939; *Mackell v Horner* [1915] 3 KB 106; *Mason v New South Wales* (1959) 102 CLR 108 at 144 per Windeyer J.
12   See, for example, *Skeate v Beale* (1840) 11 Ad & El 983; 113 ER 688.
13   See, for example, *Hawker Pacific Pty Ltd v Helicopter Charter Pty Ltd* (1991) 22 NSWLR 298 at 302, 306; *Magnacrete Ltd v Douglas-Hill* (1988) 48 SASR 565 at 590.

Example: Hawker Pacific Pty Ltd v Helicopter Charter Pty Ltd[14]

A helicopter owned by the plaintiff charter company required repainting. This work was done by the defendant, but not to a satisfactory standard. Subsequently the helicopter was redelivered to the defendant for agreed rectification work. On completion of this work, representatives from the plaintiff sought to collect the helicopter, stressing that it was required urgently for certain charter work that day. Nevertheless, and although no express threat was made, the defendant made it clear that the helicopter would not be released unless an agreement was executed stipulating an amount due for the paint job and purporting to release the defendant company from any defective workmanship. The owner of the plaintiff company agreed to execute the agreement because he believed that it was the only practical way of getting possession of the helicopter that day.

The New South Wales Court of Appeal held that the agreement was voidable for duress. There was no distinction between recovery of money paid under compulsion in order to get possession of goods wrongfully detained and money paid under a contract made under duress to goods. Further, no express threat needs to be made if, as here, the victim forms a reasonable belief from the defendant's conduct.

It would seem, therefore, that the narrow ambit of duress has been expanded beyond duress to the person to, at least, duress to personal property. Such an expansion is also consistent with the recognition of the ground of economic duress.

15.2.3   Economic duress

[15.30] Australian courts have long held that money paid as a result of a threat to break an existing contract may be recovered in restitution as money had and received.[15] It was a small step from such authorities to the proposition that a contract entered into under pressure to a party's economic interests is voidable on the grounds of duress.[16] 'Economic duress' may therefore be defined as actual or threatened conduct deleterious to the plaintiff's economic interests.

[15.35] In *Crescendo Management Pty Ltd v Westpac Banking Corporation*[17] McHugh JA (with whom Samuels and Mahoney JJA concurred) held that the proper approach when determining whether there had been economic duress was to ask two questions:

- was any pressure applied to induce the victim to enter into the contract; and then
- did the pressure go beyond what the law was prepared to countenance as being legitimate?[18]

Pressure may be illegitimate if it consists of unlawful threats or amounts to unconscionable conduct. However, his Honour declared that the categories are not closed.

---

14   (1991) 22 NSWLR 298.

15   See, for example, *Nixon v Furphy* (1925) 25 SR (NSW) 151 at 160 (affirmed sub nom *Furphy v Nixon* (1925) 37 CLR 161); *White Rose Flour Milling Co Pty Ltd v Australian Wheat Board* (1944) 18 ALJ 324; *TA Sundell & Sons Pty Ltd v Emm Yannoulatos (overseas) Pty Ltd* (1955) 56 SR (NSW) 323.

16   See, for example, *Universe Tankships Inc v International Transport Workers' Federation* [1983] 1 AC 366.

17   (1988) 19 NSWLR 40 at 46.

18   Ibid at 46; see also *Universe Tankships Inc v International Transport Workers' Federation* [1983] 1 AC 366 at 400 per Lord Scarman.

Nevertheless, even overwhelming pressure not amounting to unconscionable or unlawful conduct will not necessarily constitute economic duress.[19]

The McHugh JA test has been subsequently applied.[20]

[15.40] It seems that use of the term 'unconscionable' in relation to economic duress is different from its usage in relation to the equitable doctrine of unconscionable conduct. In the equitable principle, the term 'unconscionable' refers to the nature of the advantage taken of a person in a position of special disadvantage. By contrast, 'unconscionable' for the purposes of economic duress refers to the nature of the duress or compulsion exercised—to its legitimacy or illegitimacy. However, present-day views of acceptable conduct play a part in both principles.[21]

[15.45] Economic duress may include a threat to break a contract unless it is renegotiated.

Example: North Ocean Shipping Co Ltd v Hyundai Construction Co Ltd (The Atlantic Baron)[22]

The plaintiffs engaged the defendant shipbuilders to build a tanker for a price fixed in US dollars. Payment was to be by way of instalments. After the first instalment was paid, the US dollar was devalued by 10 per cent. The shipbuilders then asked for the amount of all outstanding instalments to be increased by 10 per cent. Lengthy discussions followed in which it became clear that the shipbuilders would not agree to the original contract sum remaining as the price of the ship. Subsequently, the plaintiffs agreed to pay the increase but did so 'without prejudice' to their rights. This variation translated into a payment of about $3 million more than the contract price. The plaintiff subsequently sought to recover this amount (among other reasons) because it was an involuntary payment.

Mocatta J of the Queen's Bench Division held that a threat to break a contract may amount to 'economic duress' which, if leading to a contract, may render that contract voidable. Here the agreement to increase the price by 10 per cent was caused by what may be called 'economic duress'. The shipbuilders were adamant in insisting on the increased price without having any legal justification for doing so—and the plaintiffs realised that the shipbuilders would not accept anything other than an unqualified agreement to the increase. The plaintiffs might have claimed damages in arbitration against the shipbuilders, but that would have been with all the inherent unavoidable uncertainties of litigation. In the circumstances, it would have been unreasonable to decide that this is the course they should have taken. Prima facie, therefore, the agreement for the 10 per cent increase in the price had been reached under economic duress and gave the plaintiffs a right to rescind. However, in the circumstances, the plaintiffs had delayed in rescinding the contract and failing to register pro-

---

19   (1988) 19 NSWLR 40 at 46.

20   *Equiticorp Finance Ltd (in Liq) v Bank of New Zealand* (1993) 32 NSWLR 50; *News Limited v Australian Rugby Football League Ltd* (1996) 58 FCR 447; *McInerney v Blair* (unreported, Vic SC, Beach J, 13 Dec 1995); see also *Dimskal Shipping Co SA v International Transport Workers' Federation* [1992] 2 AC 152 at 165–166.

21   *Westpac Banking Corporation v Cockerill* (1997) 152 ALR 267 at 289 (Fed Ct FC); *Parras Holdings Pty Ltd v Commonwealth Bank of Australia* (unreported, Federal Court, Davies J).

22   [1979] 1 QB 705.

test in relation to some of the payments, and were therefore held to have affirmed the contract.

[15.50] Contract modification cases may be difficult to resolve in practice. It has been suggested that a threat to breach a contract unless it is modified may be distinguished from a warning, request or offer. A threat may be regarded as a proposal to bring about an unwelcome event unless the recipient of the proposal does something.[23] By contrast, a warning is a prediction that an unwelcome event will happen or that it will happen if certain circumstances arise—unlike a threat the speaker has no control over the unwelcome consequence. For example, subcontractors whose costs rise dramatically midway through the contract sometimes advise the head contractor that unless they are paid more, they will be forced to breach the contract. If as a result of higher costs such subcontractors really cannot complete the contract because they face bankruptcy if they continue, then they may only be giving a warning that they do not have the resources to finish the job. But subcontractors who make such statements when they are in fact able to complete the contract might be seen as making a threat.[24]

A request may occur where a party to a contract merely asks for new terms—perhaps combined with an explanation of the reason for the change. No unwelcome consequence is proposed, nor is an unwelcome consequence made conditional on non-performance of some action.[25] Finally, an offer occurs where a person making the proposal is attempting to alter the recipient's behaviour, but the difference is that in the case of an offer the proposal is not unwelcome.[26] Although the distinction between threats on the one hand and warnings, requests, and offers on the other might be clear in principle, it may be difficult to apply in practice—not least because the court must ascertain the substance of the proposal rather than merely relying on the words used.[27]

[15.55] Mere commercial pressure, even taken to the extreme, does not amount to illegitimate pressure.[28] Normally a threat to do something that is lawful is not illegitimate.[29] Thus a threat to commence legal proceedings will not usually amount to duress.[30] However, there may be circumstances in which such a threat is combined with an unlawful demand and therefore may be regarded as illegitimate.[31]

---

23   SA Smith, 'Contracting under pressure: a theory of duress' (1997) 56 *Cambridge Law Journal* 343 at 346, referring to G Lamond, 'Coercion, Threats and the Puzzle of Blackmail' in A Simester & ATH Smith (eds), *Harm and Culpability* Oxford University Press, Oxford, 1996.

24   For this reason Smith suggested that *Atlas Express Ltd v Kafco Ltd* [1989] QB 833 and *D & C Builders Ltd v Rees* [1966] 2 QB 617 involve threats whereas *Williams v Roffey Bros and Nicholls (Contractors) Ltd* [1991] 1 QB 1 only involved a warning: ibid at 346.

25   Ibid at 347.

26   Ibid at 347.

27   Ibid at 348–350.

28   *Smith v William Charlick Ltd* (1924) 34 CLR 38; *Pao On v Lau Yiu Long* [1980] AC 614; *Food Delivery Services Pty Ltd v ANZ Banking Group Ltd* (1996) 19 ACSR 345.

29   *Westpac Banking Corporation v Cockerill* (1997) 152 ALR 267 (Fed Ct FC).

30   See, for example, *Tejani v Gerrard* (unreported, NSW SC, Cohen J, 11 March 1998).

31   See, for example, *Kaufman v Gerson* [1904] 1 KB 591 (threat to prosecute victim's husband for a crime if the victim would not undertake to pay his debt held to be blackmail and therefore duress); *J&S Holdings Pty Ltd v NRMA Insurance Ltd* (1982) 41 ALR 539 (debtor threatened with legal proceedings to recover an amount in excess of debt owed, held to be subject to illegitimate pressure).

[15.60] It has been said that the presence or absence of protest is a relevant consideration when deciding whether the victim has acted voluntarily or the pressure was illegitimate.[32] By the same token, it has been recognised that there may well be a good reason in the circumstances for the victim having failed to object at a time when the pressure is at its maximum.[33]

[15.65] The McHugh JA test has been criticised by Kirby P[34] as resting on unsatisfactory criteria. What the law regards as 'legitimate' poses a question that can only be answered by characterising particular conduct as 'impermissible' economic duress or 'permissible,' even necessary, free market activity. The doctrine therefore rendered the law uncertain in an area where certainty was desirable. It invited judges and lawyers to substitute their opinions for those of commercial people, who will usually have a better appreciation of the economic forces at work.[35] For this reason, his Honour believed courts would be better able to provide relief for economic duress in a consistent and principled fashion under the doctrines of undue influence or unconscionability rather than 'by pretending to have economic expertise and judgement which they generally lack'.[36]

[15.70] In any event, Kirby P suggested that a court should be more circumspect about extending the remedy of economic duress to cases of the contracts between substantial businesses, particularly those availing themselves of high quality legal and managerial advice, than they may be in other cases of unequal bargaining power where different considerations may be relevant.[37]

15.3 Causal connection

[15.75] The alleged illegitimate pressure must be a material cause of the contract being formed. Provided the pressure is a material cause, it need not be the sole or even dominant inducement. It will be immaterial that there was a reason other than the threat, such as good business reasons.[38]

No matter how extreme, illegitimate pressure will have no effect on the contract if it had no material part to play in its formation.

Example: News Limited v Australian Rugby Football League Ltd[39]

News intended to form a new rugby league competition called 'SuperLeague', using teams and players contracted to the Australian Rugby League. The ARL forwarded Commitment Agreements to its contracted clubs, seeking their commitment to the ARL competition for a period of 5 years. SuperLeague subsequently arranged—sur-

---

32   *Mason v New South Wales* (1959) 102 CLR 108 at 142 per Windeyer J.
33   Ibid at 143; *Hawker Pacific Pty Ltd v Helicopter Charter Pty Ltd* (1991) 22 NSWLR 298 at 303 per Priestley JA with whom Handley JA agreed.
34   *Equiticorp Finance Ltd v Bank of New Zealand* (1993) 32 NSWLR 50 at 106.
35   Ibid, at 107.
36   Ibid; see also A Phang, 'Wither Economic Duress? Reflections on Two Recent Cases' (1990) 53 MLR 107 at 113.
37   Ibid, at 109.
38   *Barton v Armstrong* [1973] 2 NSWLR 598 at 613.
39   (1996) 58 FCR 447.

reptitiously, and by offers of large sums—for a considerable number of top players and coaches to be contracted to it. A number of clubs aligned with Super League claimed that the Commitment Agreements should be set aside on the ground that the clubs were subjected to economic duress by the ARL in the form of an alleged threat to exclude from its competition any club that did not sign.

Burchett J of the Federal Court held that the evidence showed many of the club Chief Executives felt that an assurance that they were to be in the competition for the next five years was extremely attractive, especially when they were clubs newly admitted to the ARL competition. Other club Chief Executives testified that the possibility of their clubs not being admitted to the competition was something they never seriously entertained. Accordingly, in the circumstances the clubs were not operating under any threat or fear of expulsion when they executed the Commitment Agreements.[40]

15.4   Remedies

15.4.1   Rescission

[15.80] As a contract entered into under duress is rendered voidable, not void, the principle remedy for duress is rescission of the contract.[41]

[15.85] Like misrepresentation, the right to rescind for duress may be lost in certain circumstances. Thus, the victim of duress may be taken to have affirmed the contract and be denied relief if, with full knowledge of the circumstances, he or she engages in conduct that unequivocally indicates adoption of the contract, or fails to promptly take steps to rescind the contract.[42] Similarly, the right to rescind will be lost where a third party has acquired an interest in the property that is the subject matter of the contract or where the parties are unable to be restored, or for any other reason *restitutio in integrum* is not longer possible—although it seems that at least substantial *restitutio in integrum* may be sufficient.[43]

15.4.2   Restitution

[15.90] Australian courts have treated some cases of duress as a development of the action to recover sums paid under coercion in restitution as money had and received.[44] No distinction has been drawn between an agreement entered into under duress and money paid due to coercion. Presumably, therefore, restitution may in an appropriate case offer an alternative remedy in the form of an action for recovery of money paid. The modern basis for such a restitutionary claim is unjust enrichment at the plaintiff's expense.[45]

---

40   The trial judge's finding on duress was not challenged on appeal to the Full Court: (1996) 139 ALR 193.
41   *North Ocean Shipping Co Ltd v Hyundai Construction Co Ltd* [1979] QB 705.
42   See, for example, *North Ocean Shipping Co Ltd v Hyundai Construction Co Ltd* [1979] QB 705 at 720; *Hawker Pacific Pty Ltd v Helicopter Charter Pty Ltd* (1991) 22 NSWLR 299 at 304, 305–306.
43   JW Carter & DJ Harland, *Contract Law in Australia*, 3rd edn, Butterworths, Sydney, 1996, p 476.
44   *Hawker Pacific Pty Ltd v Helicopter Charter Pty Ltd* (1991) 22 NSWLR 299 at 302.
45   See [25.40].

It is important to note, however, that the general rule is that restitution of moneys paid is not possible while the contract under which the payment was made remains on foot.[46] Accordingly, it is first necessary for the contract to have been either discharged or rescinded before a claim in restitution may be made.[47]

15.4.3 Damages

[15.95] There are conflicting views about whether damages may be recovered for duress. Some judges have suggested that duress is a tort if it causes damage or loss and thereby gives rise to a right to claim damages.[48] Others have been more equivocal, suggesting that while the particular form taken by economic duress in a given case may itself be a tort, conduct does not have to be tortious in order to constitute duress.[49]

15.5 Statute

15.5.1 Trade Practices Act and the Fair Trading Acts

[15.100] The *Trade Practices Act* 1974 (Cth) and state *Fair Trading Acts* prohibit certain forms of duress. For example, the statutes prohibit the use of physical force or undue harassment or coercion in connection with the supply or possible supply of goods or services to a consumer or the payment for goods or services by a consumer.[50] There is also a prohibition against physical force or undue harassment or coercion in connection with the sale or grant, or the possible sale or grant, of an interest in land or the payment for an interest in land.[51]

[15.105] In cases where the statutes have prohibited duress, they make available a wide range of remedies. These include injunctions[52] and ancillary orders including rescission, restitution, and variation of the contract.[53] Significantly, unlike the posi-

---

46 See [24.160].

47 See, for example, *The Evia Luck* [1992] 2 AC 152.

48 See, for example, *Universe Tankships of Monrovia v International Transport Workers' Federation (the Universe Sentinel)* [1983] 1 AC 366 at 400 per Lord Scarman; *Alec Lobb (Garages) Ltd v Total Oil (Great Britian) Ltd* [1985] 1 WLR 173 at 177.

49 *Universe Tankships of Monrovia v International Transport Workers' Federation (the Universe Sentinel)* [1983] 1 AC 366 at 385 per Lord Diplock.

50 *Trade Practices Act* 1974 (Cth), s 60; *Fair Trading Act* 1992 (ACT), s 26; *Fair Trading Act* 1987 (NSW), s 55; *Consumer Affairs and Fair Trading Act* 1990 (NT), s 55; *Fair Trading Act* 1989 (Qld), s 50; *Fair Trading Act* 1987 (SA), s 69; *Fair Trading Act* 1990 (Tas), s 26; *Fair Trading Act* 1985 (Vic), s 22; *Fair Trading Act* 1987 (WA), s 23.

51 *Trade Practices Act* 1974 (Cth), s 53A(2); *Fair Trading Act* 1992 (ACT), s 15(2); *Fair Trading Act* 1987 (NSW), s 45(2); *Consumer Affairs and Fair Trading Act* 1990 (NT), s 45; *Fair Trading Act* 1987 (SA), s 59(2); *Fair Trading Act* 1990 (Tas), s 17(2); *Fair Trading Act* 1985 (Vic), s 13(2); *Fair Trading Act* 1987 (WA), s 12(2).

52 *Trade Practices Act* 1974 (Cth), s 80; *Fair Trading Act* 1992 (ACT), s 44; *Fair Trading Act* 1987 (NSW), s 65; *Consumer Affairs and Fair Trading Act* 1990 (NT), s 89; *Fair Trading Act* 1989 (Qld), s 98; *Fair Trading Act* 1987 (SA), s 83; *Fair Trading Act* 1990 (Tas), s 34; *Fair Trading Act* 1985 (Vic), s 34; *Fair Trading Act* 1987 (WA), ss 74–76.

53 *Trade Practices Act* 1974 (Cth), s 87; *Fair Trading Act* 1992 (ACT), s 50; *Fair Trading Act* 1987 (NSW), s 72; *Consumer Affairs and Fair Trading Act* 1990 (NT), s 95; *Fair Trading Act* 1989 (Qld), s 100; *Fair Trading Act* 1987 (SA), s 85; *Fair Trading Act* 1990 (Tas), s 41; *Fair Trading Act* 1985 (Vic), s 41; *Fair Trading Act* 1987 (WA), s 77.

tion at common law, there is also no doubt that a court may in an appropriate case award damages.[54]

15.5.2 Contracts Review Act 1980 (NSW)

[15.110] In New South Wales,[55] duress may also be taken into account as a relevant factor by a court applying the *Contracts Review Act* 1980 (NSW). Section 9(2)(j) of that Act states that a court may have regard to whether 'any undue influence, undue pressure or unfair tactics' were exerted on or used against a party seeking relief under the Act when deciding whether the contract should be deemed unjust. Where a contract is so deemed, the court has a discretion regarding the degree to which the contract is enforced, should be set aside, or some other remedy such as restitution or compensation ordered.

15.6 International perspectives

15.6.1 New Zealand

[15.115] There is no substantive difference between the law relating to duress, including economic duress, in Australia and New Zealand.[56]

15.6.2 United States

[15.120] There appears to be no substantive difference between the law of duress in the United States and that in Australia.[57] The classic case of duress is regarded as one where the victim's intention or submission arises from a realisation that no practical choice is open. The Restatement (Second) provides in §175(1):

If a party's manifestation of assent is induced by an improper threat by the other party that leaves the victim no reasonable alternative, the contract is voidable by the victim.

The Restatement (Second) goes on in §176 to list the circumstances in which a threat shall be regarded as 'improper'. Clearly a threat will be improper if the threatened action infringes the victim's rights or is otherwise unlawful.[58] However, §176(2) provides more generally that:

A threat is improper if the resulting exchange is not on fair terms and:

(a) the threatened act would harm the recipient and would not significantly benefit the party making the threat;

---

54   *Trade Practices Act* 1974 (Cth), s 82; *Fair Trading Act* 1992 (ACT), s 46; *Fair Trading Act* 1987 (NSW), s 68; *Consumer Affairs and Fair Trading Act* 1990 (NT), s 91; *Fair Trading Act* 1989 (Qld), s 99; *Fair Trading Act* 1987 (SA), s 84; *Fair Trading Act* 1990 (Tas), s 37; *Fair Trading Act* 1985 (Vic), s 37; *Fair Trading Act* 1987 (WA), s 79.
55   See [17.120].
56   See JF Burrows, J Finn & S Todd, *Law of Contract in New Zealand*, Butterworths, Wellington, 1997, pp 343–348.
57   See, for example, *Rubenstein v Rubenstein* 120 A 2d 11 (NJ 1956) (threats including gangster violence and arsenic poisoning).
58   See also Restatement (Second) § 187(1).

(b) the effectiveness of the threat in inducing the manifestation or assent is significantly increased by prior unfair dealing by the party making the threat,
or

(c) what is threatened is a use of power for illegitimate ends.

Accordingly, in the United States it is sufficient but not essential for the threatened
action to be unlawful.

[15.125] Generally speaking, however, in America a threat by a party not to perform a
contractual duty is not regarded as amounting to duress. An agreement to modify the
original contract induced by such a threat may therefore still be valid. Nevertheless,
United States courts regard the parties to a contract as being bound by a duty of good
faith and fair dealing, and if such a threat amounts to a breach of that duty, it may be
regarded as being improper.[59]

15.6.3   *Japan*

[15.130] In contrast to the treatment of mistake in Japanese law, fraud and duress are
treated as vitiating factors that render the contract voidable rather than void.[60] The
rationale for the distinction is that scholarly interpretation characterises fraud and
duress as 'flawed declarations of intention', rather than situations in which there is a
'lack of real intention'.

[15.135] The innocent party may declare the contract void at his or her own option in
the case of either fraud or duress. However, timing is important. To rescind the contract, the innocent party must assert that the fraud or duress[61] occurred before formation.[62] If the vitiating factor occurred before formation, there are grounds for
rescission; however, if it was after, there can be no rescission.

Further, the innocent party may declare that the contract is void against an
innocent third party where the vitiating factor is duress, but not in the case of
fraud.[63]

[15.140] The effect of declaring a contract void in Japanese law is similar to that in the
common law—no claims based on the unperformed part of the contract will be effective. If contractual obligations have been performed, then unjust enrichment can be
avoided through applying Civil Code arts 703 and 704 to ground a claim for return of
whatever the other party received under the contract, or its fair market value. It is possible to claim compensatory damages in addition to the claim for return or property or
benefits, where the other party has acted in bad faith.[64]

---

59 Restatement (Second) § 205; Uniform Commercial Code 1-203; see also, for example, *Applied Genetics
International v First Affiliated Securities* 912 FD 1238 (10th Cir 1990). In relation to the American duty of
good faith.
60 Civil Code art 96.
61 The same principle applies to mistake: see [14.405].
62 With respect to tendering see: 14 (7) Minshu 115 (Sup Ct, 24 May 1960).
63 Civil Code art 93(3).
64 Civil Code arts 703, 704.

[15.145] Remedies in this area are subject to some limitation. Where the contract is void for reasons of public policy or good morals,[65] there will be no return of property, payments, or benefits unless it can be shown that the other party (the defendant) was solely at fault.[66] This is an extension of the principle that a party asserting bad faith or fault must themselves have acted in good faith or be able to show that they were not at fault.

---

65 Civil Code art 90.
66 Civil Code art 708.

Chapter 16

Undue influence

16.1   Introduction

[16.05] The limited application of the common law doctrine of duress to threats of violence against the person was avoided in equity by the application of the wider doctrine of undue influence. The basis of the equitable jurisdiction to set aside a contract on the ground of undue influence is the prevention of a unconscientious use of any special capacity or opportunity to affect the victim's will or freedom of judgment that may exist or arise.[1] The doctrine of undue influence has been described as having

---

1   *Johnson v Buttress* (1936) 56 CLR 113 at 134 per Dixon J.

'grown out of and been developed by the necessity of grappling with insidious forms of spiritual tyranny and with the infinite varieties of fraud'.[2]

[16.10] 'Undue influence' involves one person who occupies a position of ascendancy or influence over another improperly using that position for the benefit of himself or herself or someone else, so that the acts of the person influenced cannot be said to be his or her voluntary acts.[3] The party in the position of ascendancy falls under a duty that may be seen to contain fiduciary characteristics, since it is that person's duty to use the position of influence in the interests of no one but the person who is governed by the ascendant person's judgment, or who trusts the ascendant person.[4]

[16.15] Many of the cases that have considered the doctrine of undue influence have involved a gift being made by a donor in favour of a donee occupying a position of ascendancy or influence.[5] However, the doctrine is not restricted to gifts; it may apply, for example, to contracts of sale where it is shown or presumed that the transaction has been procured by the exercise of undue influence.[6] In that case, however, matters such as the adequacy of any consideration and 'the propriety of what wears the appearance of a business dealing' will be relevant.[7]

16.2 Classes of undue influence

[16.20] It was recognised by the English Court of Appeal in *Allcard v Skinner*[8] that there are two classes of undue influence. The first class is where the court is satisfied that the transaction is the result of actual undue influence exercised by a party in a position of ascendancy over another for the purpose of inducing the transaction. The second is where the relationship between the parties at the time of the transaction—or shortly before—is such as to raise a presumption that the party in a position of ascendancy exercised influence over the other. This approach has since been widely accepted in Australia[9] and England.[10]

---

2   *Allcard v Skinner* (1887) 36 Ch D 145 at 183 per Lindley LJ.
3   *Johnson v Buttress* (1936) 56 CLR 113 at 135; *Union Bank of Australia Ltd v Whitelaw* (1906) VLR 711.
4   *Johnson v Buttress* (1936) 56 CLR 113.
5   Where the transaction involves the party in ascendancy receiving a gift from the other party, the parties are sometimes referred to as 'donee' and 'donor' respectively.
6   *Poosathurdi v Kannappa Chettiar* (1919) LR 47 IA 1 (PC).
7   *Johnson v Buttress* (1936) 56 CLR 113 at 135–136 per Dixon J; cf *Berk v Permanent Trustee Company of NSW Ltd* (1947) 47 SR (NSW) 459 at 464;
8   (1887) 36 Ch D 145 at 171 per Cotton LJ; see also 181 per Lindley LJ.
9   See, for example, *Farmers' Co-operative Executors & Trustees Ltd v Perks* (1989) 52 SASR 399; *Johnson v Buttress* (1936) 56 CLR 113; *Union Fidelity Trustee Co of Australia v Gibson* [1971] VR 573.
10   *Poosathurdi v Kannappa Chettiar* (1919) LR 47 IA1; *National Westminster Bank Plc v Morgan* [1985] 1AC 686; *Bank of Credit and Commerce International SA v Aboody* [1989] 2 WLR 759. For a short time the English courts flirted with the notion that the relationship had to be of material disadvantage to the trusting party: see *National Westminster Bank Plc v Morgan* [1995] AC 686 at 704 per Lord Scarman followed by the Court of Appeal in *Midland Bank Plc v Shephard* [1988] 3 All ER 17 at 21. See also *Poosathurdi v Kannappa Chettiar* (1919) LR 47 IA 1 at 4 where it was held that while the relation of influence had been shown, the element which had not been proved was that the transaction constituted a disadvantage to the party seeking to avoid the contract. Australian law does not venture so far: *Baburin v Baburin* [1990] 2 Qd R 101 (confirmed on appeal [1991] 2 Qd R 240); cf *Farmers' Co-operative Executors & Trustees Ltd v Perks* (1989) 52 SASR 399 at 404.

16.3 Class 1: actual undue influence

[16.25] The first class concerns situations in which the transaction was entered into as a result of actual undue influence. The elements to be shown by a party seeking to rely on a plea of actual undue influence have been summarised as:

- one party to the transaction had the capacity to influence the other (the 'trusting party');
- that influence was exercised;
- its exercise was undue; and
- its exercise brought about the transaction.[11]

Example: Barton v Armstrong[12]

The defendant pressured the plaintiff to execute a deed between them by threatening to have the plaintiff murdered if he declined.

The Privy Council held that the plaintiff was entitled to relief, either because the threat amounted to duress[13] or alternatively actual undue influence.[14]

[16.30] Circumstances that constitute duress would also establish a case of actual undue influence. Indeed, it has been suggested that there is good reason for subsuming all duress cases under the first class of undue influence, the old common law kinds of duress constituting but an extreme example of actual undue influence.[15] For example, an agreement entered into under a threat that failure to do so would result in the party's son being prosecuted was held to constitute undue pressure and was the equivalent of actual undue influence.[16]

16.4 Class 2: presumed undue influence

16.4.1 Relevant relationships

[16.35] The second class involves the categories of relationship that are regarded as being of such a nature that they give rise to a presumption that undue influence induced any transaction between the parties. This class has itself been treated as being divided into two sub-classes: class 2A and class 2B.[17]

---

11   *Bank of Credit and Commerce International SA v Aboody* [1989] 2 WLR 758 at 782.
12   [1973] 2 NSWLR 598.
13   See [15.10].
14   See also the second ground for the decision in *Farmers' Co-operative Executors & Trustees v Perks* (1989) 52 SASR 399. In *Public Service Employees Credit Union Co-operative Ltd v Campion* (1984) 75 FLR 131 it was held that a threat to notify police in relation to misappropriation of money from an automatic teller machine by a father's son if the father did not execute a guarantee for repayment amounted to an application of actual undue influence.
15   See, *Farmers' Co-operative Executors & Trustees v Perks* (1989) 52 SASR 399 at 405, citing with approval M Cope, *Duress, Undue Influence and Unconscientious Bargains*, (1995) para 125.
16   *Public Service Employees' Credit Union Co-operative Ltd v Campion* (1984) 75 FLR 131 at 138-9 (ACT SC), following *Williams v Bayley* [1866] LR 1 HL 200.
17   *Barclays Bank Plc v O'Brien* [1994] 1 AC 180 at 189.

(a)   Class 2A: recognised relationships

[16.40] Class 2A contains certain well-defined categories accepted as naturally giving rise to a relationship of influence.[18] These include the relationships between trustee and beneficiary,[19] solicitor and client,[20] doctor and patient,[21] parent and child,[22] guardian and ward,[23] spiritual adviser and devotee[24] and, at least in the past, man and fiancée.[25] The characteristic common to all these relationships appears to be that the first-named person in such relationship is reasonably expected to advise and give guidance to the other, in and for the purpose of such relationship, solely in the interests and for the benefit of the other.[26]

[16.45] Cases of influence of a religious kind may be difficult, since such influence may be both powerful and hard to detect.[27] Indeed, the power of religious impressions under the ascendancy of a spiritual adviser may be seen as more powerful than anything inherent in the authority of a guardian—or even parental authority—with its ability to work upon passions, fears, hopes, and consciences.[28] Further, there is the ease and subtlety by which suggestions may be conveyed to, encouraged in, and absorbed by, those vulnerable to them as to what is the will of God in relation to their actions in particular matters.[29] Whether in any particular case a relationship in a religious context will be sufficient to found the presumption will depend upon whether the evidence establishes a reliance, dependence, or trust on the part of the claimant leading to a corresponding ascendancy on the party of the donee capable of influencing the making of the gift or transaction in question.[30]

[16.50] There is ample authority excluding from the recognised categories other relationships such as the relationship of husband and wife as such[31] and the relationship of banker, accountant, or financial adviser and client.[32]

---

18   See *Johnson v Buttress* (`1936) 56 CLR 113 at 134 per Dixon J; *Jenyns v Public Curator (Qld)* (1953) 90 CLR 113 at 133 per Dixon CJ, McTiernan and Kitto JJ; *Farmers' Co-operative Executors and Trustees Ltd v Perks* (1989) 52 SASR 399 at 403.

19   See, for example, *Dougan v MacPherson* [1902] AC 197; *Ellis v Barker* (1871) LR 7 Ch App 104; *Biningfield v Baxter* (1866) 12 App Cas 167

20   See, for example, *McPherson v Watt* (1877) 3 App Cas 254; *Gibson v Jeyes* (1801) 6 Bes Jun 266; 31 ER 1044; *Wright v Carter* [1903] 1 Ch D 27.

21   See, for example, *Mitchell v Homfray* (1881) 8 QBD 587.

22   See, for example, *Phillips v Hutchinson* [1946] VLR 270. No presumption arises where the child is emancipated from parental influence: *Lamotte v Lamotte* (1942) 42 SR (NSW) 99 (daughter aged 43 making gift of land to 75-year-old mother). The class 2A presumption does not arise where the child is the beneficiary: *Whereat v Duff* [1972] 2 NSWLR 147 at 167–168, *Spong v Spong* (1914) 18 CLR 544 unless circumstances warrant the presumption as a class 2B case.

23   See, for example, *Taylor v Johnston* (1882) 19 Ch D 603.

24   See, for example, *Norton v Relly* (1764) 2 Eden 286; 28 ER 908; *Allcard v Skinner* (1887) 36 Ch D 181; *Austin v McCaskill* (1922) 70 DLR 819; *Chennells v Bruce* (1939) 55 TLR 422; *Quek v Beggs* (1990) 5 BPR 11,761.

25   Cf *Zamet v Hyman* [1961] 1 WLR 1442.

26   *Union Fidelity Trustee Co of Australia Ltd v Gibson* [1971] VR 573; *Stivactas v Machaletos (No 2)* (1993) ACR 90-031 at 89,677 (NSWCA).

27   *Allcard v Skinner* (1997) 36 Ch D 181 at 183.

28   *Huguenin v Baseley* (1807) 14 Bes Jun 273 at 288; 33 ER 526 at 532.

29   *Quek v Beggs* (1990) 5 BPR 97405 at 11,766.

30   Ibid at 11,765.

31   See, for example, *Bank of Montreal v Stuart* [1911] AC 120; *Yerkey v Jones* (1940) 63 CLR 649.

32   *Cowen v Piggott* [1989] 1 Qd R 41.

(b) Class 2B: relationships attracting presumption

[16.55] However, the category of relationships in which undue influence is presumed is not closed. It rests upon principle, which applies whenever one party occupies or assumes towards another a position that naturally involves an ascendancy or influence over that other, or a dependence or a trust on his or her part. One occupying such a position falls under a duty in which fiduciary characteristics may be seen.[33] Thus, a relationship in a particular case may not be one of the well-established ones, but can nevertheless be recognised as giving rise to a presumption of undue influence.

Example: Johnson v Buttress [34]

A 67-year-old man who was wholly illiterate, and who was found by the trial judge to be of low intelligence and devoid of any capacity for, or experience in, business affairs, was habitually dependent on other persons for advice and assistance. After the death of his wife, the man transferred the land on which his house was built to the defendant, a blood relation of his wife, on the basis of his natural love and affection for her and the kindness she had shown his wife and himself from time to time. The transfer was signed in the office of the defendant's solicitor, the old man not having any independent advice.

The High Court held that the relationship between the old man and the defendant was one of an ignorant, labouring man habitually dependent on the guidance and support of others, who at the time of the transfer was dependent in many essential matters upon one whom he regarded as having all the advantages and position, and in whom he confided. The circumstances of the case, considered together with the character and capacity of the old man, led to the conclusion that a special relationship of influence existed between the old man and the defendant. As a result, a presumption of undue influence arose from the relationship. The onus therefore shifted to the defendant to rebut the presumption, which in the circumstances she was unable to do.

[16.60] Although the relationship between husband and wife is generally not regarded as a class 2A relationship that automatically gives rise to a presumption of influence, a *particular* husband–wife relationship may nevertheless be held to have that character.[35]

Example: Farmers' Co-operative Executors & Trustees Ltd v Perks[36]

A husband and wife lived alone on a remote farm. There was a long history of alcohol abuse by the husband and of domestic violence towards the wife. The wife executed a memorandum of transfer which transferred her share in the property to the husband.

It was held that while the relationship of husband and wife was not one in which influence was deemed to have existed, a special relationship of control and dominance may exist in particular circumstances of a case sufficient to give rise to a presumption

---

33 *Johnson v Buttress* (1936) 56 CLR 113 at 134.
34 (1936) 56 CLR 113.
35 *Farmers' Co-operative Executors & Trustees Ltd v Perks* (1989) 52 SASR 399.
36 (1989) 52 SASR 399.

of undue influence. Here the isolation and past abuse meant both that she was afraid of him, and that he had been able to exercise considerable influence over her. This was sufficient to give rise to a presumption of influence, which the husband had not rebutted on the evidence.

A similar observation may be made in relation to, for example, the relationship between banker and customer. While not ordinarily giving rise to a presumption of undue influence, the relationship of banker and customer may become one in which the banker acquires a dominating influence. If the banker does acquire a position of dominance and a manifestly disadvantageous transaction is proved, there would be room for a court to presume that it resulted from the exercise of undue influence.[37]

[16.65] It seems that when examining whether a relationship gives rise to a presumption of influence, the court will take into account matters such as the standard of intelligence and education, and the character, personality, age, state of health, blood relationship, and experience (or lack of it) in business affairs of the claimant. The length of friendship or acquaintanceship between the claimant and the other party in the intricacy of their business affairs may be factors to influence the claimant to depend upon the other party. Equally, the relative strength of character and personality of the other party, the period and closeness of the relationship, and the opportunity afforded to influence the claimant in business affairs are also important considerations.[38]

[16.70] It follows that where a person who is seeking to avoid a transaction on the basis of undue influence is not in one of the well established categories in which undue influence is presumed, he or she should first establish that in the circumstances undue influence ought to be presumed. Proof of that will shift the onus of proof to the other party to rebut the presumption. Where the party alleging undue influence is unsuccessful in showing that undue influence ought to be presumed, he or she will be left to actual proof of undue influence in the circumstances. This shifting of onus may become significant in a case where there is insufficient evidence in the circumstances to either prove or disprove undue influence. The existence of a presumption in such a case will be decisive.

16.4.2 Rebutting the presumption

[16.75] Where the parties stand in a relationship in which undue influence is presumed, the party in the position of influence cannot maintain a claim to the benefit of the transaction unless that party satisfies the court that he or she took no advantage of the claimant, and that the transaction was the independent and well-understood act of a person in a position to exercise a free judgment based on information as full as that of the recipient.[39] The facts that must be proved to satisfy the court that the dependent or trusting party was freed from influence are not always the same for the different

---

37   *National Westminster Bank v Morgan* [1985] 1 All ER 821 at 829; *James v Australia and New Zealand Banking Group* (1986) 64 ALR 347 at 389–390.

38   *Union Fidelity Trustee Co of Australia v Gibson* [1971] VR 573 at 577. See also *Nattrass v Nattrass* [1999] WASC 77 (25 June 1999) (presumption arose where dependent relationship between plaintiff and defendant and plaintiff was a senior citizen developing Alzheimer's disease).

39   *Johnson v Buttress* (1936) 56 CLR 113 at 134 per Dixon J.

relationships, since influence grows out of relationships in different ways and to different degrees.[40] However, relevant matters may include the trusting party's age, standard of intelligence, character, experience.[41]

[16.80] The party in ascendancy may rebut the presumption of undue influence, when it arises, by proving that the trusting party:

- knew and understood what he or she was doing; and
- was acting independently of any influence arising from the ascendancy.[42]

In relation to the second element, it is not necessarily sufficient to prove that the proposal to make the gift or transaction came from the trusting party[43] or that the party in ascendancy took no active steps to procure the gift or transaction.[44]

[16.85] Proof that the trusting party had independent advice may be relevant to rebutting the presumption of undue influence, but is not conclusive.[45] In an appropriate case, its absence may be a factor to be taken into consideration and may be a very potent fact.[46] Nevertheless, independent advice should be regarded as merely one way of showing the two elements required to rebut the presumption. Where advice is given, it must be both independent and effective for the purpose of enlivening the client's appreciation of the transaction, its legal effects and the alternatives (if any) that are open to the client.[47]

If the trusting party receives independent advice, and either misunderstands the advice or is given possibly erroneous advice resulting in his or her failure to appreciate or realise the financial implications and detriment to himself or herself inherent in the transaction, equity may still refuse to set aside the transaction if the trusting party otherwise understood the nature of the transaction and acted in relation to it in the full exercise of his or her will.[48] The nature of the presumed influence, the facts known to any solicitor advising the trusting party, and the nature of the advice given may, in particular circumstances, be insufficient to rebut the presumption.[49] Similarly, the question of whether the trusting party received independent advice might be disregarded if the court is satisfied that independent advice would have had no effect on the transaction.[50]

16.4.3 Undue influence and third parties

[16.90] The actual or presumed undue influence may result from the conduct of a third party. In such a case, beneficiaries who have notice of the circumstances of the relationship may have the onus cast upon them of proving that the transaction was a free, voluntary and well understood act of the trusting party.[51] Accordingly, for exam-

---

40 Ibid.

41 Ibid, at 119.

42 *Lancashire Loans Ltd v Black* [1934] 1 KB 380 at 409; *West v Public Trustee* [1942] SASR 109 at 119; *Inche Noriah v Shaik Allie Bin Omar* [1929] AC 127 at 135; *Quek v Beggs* (1990) 5 BPR 97-405 at 11,765.

43 *Spong v Spong* (1914) 18 CLR 544 at 549; *Whereat v Duff* [1972] 2 NSWLR 147 at 169.

44 *Allcard v Skinner* (1887) 36 ChD 181 at 183–184, 185–186; *Wright v Carter* [1903] 1 Ch 27 at 52–53.

45 *Inche Noriah v Shaik Allie Bin Omar* [1929] AC 127 at 135–136; *Bank of New South Wales v Rogers* (1921) 65 CLR 42; *Haskew v Equity Trustees, Executors and Agency Co Ltd* (1919) 27 CLR 231 at 234–235; *Whereat v Duff* [1972] 2 NSWLR 147; *Nattrass v Nattrass* [1999] WASC 77 (25 June 1999).

46 *Watkins v Combes* (1922) 30 CLR 180 at 196.

47 *Bester v Perpetual Trustee Co Ltd* [1970] 3 NSWR 30 at 36.

48 *Jenyns v Public Curator (Qld)* (1953) 90 CLR 113 at 132; *Union Fidelity Trustee Co of Australia v Gibson* [1971] VR 573 at 577.

49 *Quek v Beggs* (1990) 5 BPR 97-405 (NSW SC).

50 *Linderstam v Barnett* (1915) 19 CLR 528; *Barr v Union Trustee Co of Aust Ltd* [1923] VLR 236.

51 *Bank of New South Wales v Rogers* (1941) 65 CLR 42.

ple, creditors are not entitled to improve their position by inducing their debtors to obtain further security for their debts from their near relatives or other persons over whom they may have influence.[52]

Example: Bank of New South Wales v Rogers[53]

The plaintiff was a young woman who had lived with her uncle since the death of her parents. She sought his advice and followed it without question in all matters of business. She was of average intelligence and firmness, but had no business experience. She was induced by him to charge virtually all of her property in favour of his bank as security for his overdraft at a time when his affairs were looking bleak. The bank's manager knew that the plaintiff lived with her uncle, and while not actually aware of their relationship, had reason to believe that some special relationship existed between them—and could have discovered the nature of that relationship by reasonable inquiries. He had strong grounds for suspecting that the plaintiff had not had independent advice. In fact, it had not even been suggested to the plaintiff that she should obtain independent advice, and the full significance of the transaction was not explained to her nor was it understood by her.

The High Court held that a presumption of influence arose from the relationship between the uncle and plaintiff that operated at the time the plaintiff granted the charge. Further, the bank was so affected with notice of their relationship that the onus was cast upon it of rebutting the presumption and proving that the giving of the charge was the free, voluntary and well understood act of the plaintiff. The bank had failed to discharge that onus and accordingly the charge was set aside.

[16.95] While the relationship of husband and wife has not been seen as automatically giving rise to a presumption of undue influence, it has, in the words of Dixon J in *Yerkey v Jones* 'never been divested completed of what may be called equitable presumptions of an invalidating tendency.'[54] What has become known as the 'rule in *Yerkey v Jones*' states that a security given by a wife to her husband's creditor may be invalidated against the creditor where:

- the husband procures his wife's execution of a guarantee;
- the guarantee is for the immediate economic benefit not of the wife but of the husband;
- there are grounds to set aside the guarantee as against the husband (for example, a failure to explain the security adequately and accurately);
- the creditor relied upon the husband to obtain it from his wife; and
- the creditor had no independent grounds for reasonably believing that she fully comprehended the transaction and freely entered into it.[55]

---

52   *Sercombe v Sanders* (1865) 34 Beav 382 at 385; 55 ER 682 at 683; *Turnbull & Co v Duval* [1902] AC 429 at 435; *Bank of New South Wales v Rogers* (1941) 65 CLR 42 at 51.
53   (1941) 65 CLR 42.
54   (1940) 63 CLR 649 at 675.
55   See also *Garcia v National Australia Bank Ltd* (1998) 194 CLR 395 at 404–405; *Radin v Commonwealth Bank of Australia* (unreported, Fed Ct, Lindgren J, 3 Feb 1998); *Armstrong v Commonwealth Bank of Australia* [2000] ANZ ConvR 470 (NSWSC); *Westpac Banking Corp v Mitros* [2000] VSC 465 (3 November 2000).

Naturally, this rule may have great significance for banks or other lending institutions who, for example, obtain a guarantee from a wife for the debt of her husband. The validity of such a transaction may depend upon, for instance, the amount of detail of the information provided to her prior to her executing the document.

[16.100] It would appear that a husband can be said to have 'procured' his wife's execution of a document where the wife executes it otherwise than in the presence of the creditor. However, there are conflicting views about the case where a wife executes the document in the presence of the creditor.[56]

The rule does not apply where the wife obtains advantage from the transaction,[57] or if the guarantee benefits a relative of the husband.[58] By contrast, benefiting a company that is controlled by the husband—at least where the wife does not have a substantial interest in the company—will suffice.[59]

[16.105] The rule in *Yerkey v Jones* proceeds upon a particular assumption that married women occupy a disadvantaged position in society. It may be that in a contemporary society, when the position of a married woman is vastly different from that it was at the time of *Yerkey*, it may be more appropriate to allow the principle of unconscionability pronounced in *Amadio v Commercial Bank*, which clearly extend to a guarantee, to provide any protection required in particular circumstances. In other words, there may no longer be a case for retaining a separate doctrine drawn from from *Yerkey v Jones*.[60]

[16.110] Nevertheless, when the High Court had the opportunity to reconsider the rule in *Garcia v National Australia Bank Ltd*, a majority upheld it.[61] While acknowledging that Australian society, and particularly the role of women in that society, had changed in the six decades since the *Yerkey v Jones* decision, the joint judgment of Gaudron, McHugh, Gummow, and Hayne JJ insisted that the rationale of the rule was not to be found in notions based on the subservience or inferior economic position of women, nor any assumed vulnerability to exploitation due to their emotional involvement. Instead, the rule was based on the trust and confidence that is common between marriage partners. The marriage relationship was such that one of the parties, often the woman, may well leave business judgments to the other spouse. In such relationship, business decisions may be made with little consultation between the parties, or without the slightest hint of bad faith, the explanation of a particular transaction given by one to the other may be imperfect and incomplete, if not simply wrong.[62]

---

56   See, for example, *ANZ Banking Group Ltd v Lefkovic* (unreported, Vic SC, Tadgell J, 24 June 1992) (execution of guarantee by wife in presence of bank staff precluded reliance on rule) cf *Peters v Commonwealth of Australia* (1992) ASC 56-135 (execution of guarantee by wife in presence of bank staff did not preclude reliance on rule)

57   See, for example, *Commonwealth Bank of Australia v Cohen* (1988) ASC 55-681 at 58,160.

58   See, for example, *Geelong Building Society (in Liq) v Thomas* (1996) V Conv R 54-545.

59   See, for example, *Warburton v Whiteley* (1989) 5 BPR 97-398; *Broadlands International Finance Ltd v Sly* (1987) ANZ Conv R 328.

60   *Warburton v Whiteley* (1989) NSW Conv R 55-453 at 58,287 per Kirby P, 58,293 per Clarke JA with whom McHugh J agreed. For other calls for reform of the *Yerkey* rule See, for example, *European Asian of Australia Ltd v Kurland* (1985) 8 NSWLR 192 at 200; *Commonwealth Bank of Australia v Cohen* (1988) ASC 55-681 at 58,160; *Akins v National Australia Bank* (1994) 34 NSWLR 155 (CA); *Gregg v Tasmanian Trustees Ltd* (1997) 73 FCR 91 at 113–114.

61   (1998) 194 CLR 395.

62   Ibid, at 404.

Far from doing away from the rule, and leaving the field to be governed by the doctrine of unconscionable conduct, the majority thought, without finally deciding the point, that it may be that in modern society the rule should not be confined to wives executing transactions for the benefit of their husbands, but also apply to long-term relationships involving opposite or same-sex couples and perhaps might even find application where the husband acts as surety for the wife.[63]

16.5 Remedy

[16.115] Where actual undue influence is shown or where it is presumed and cannot be rebutted, the contract is rendered voidable. The right to rescind may, as in other cases, be lost where the trusting party has affirmed the contract or fails to act promptly,[64] *restitutio in integrum* is not at least substantially possible,[65] or an innocent third party has acquired for value an interest in the subject matter of the contract in question.[66]

Example: Quek v Beggs[67]

For the five years preceding her death, Mrs Quek regularly attended a church of which Mr Beggs was the pastor. A friendship developed between them. When Mrs Quek was diagnosed as suffering from cancer, Mr and Mrs Beggs provided significant practical, emotional, and spiritual support. Mrs Quek commenced making substantial payments of money to Mr Beggs as well as substantial gifts of real estate to Mr and Mrs Beggs to 'do the Lord's work'. After Mrs Quek's death, her daughter commenced proceedings to set aside the gifts of money and properties on the ground that they resulted from undue influence.

It was held that in the circumstances, the relationship between Mrs Quek and Mr Beggs, based in a religious context, established a reliance, dependence, or trust that led to a corresponding ascendancy on the part of Mr Beggs which was capable of influencing the making of the gifts. Further, the gifts were so substantial as to be not reasonably accounted for on the grounds of friendship, relationship, charity, or other ordinary motives on which ordinary persons act. Accordingly, a presumption of undue influence arose, which Mr Beggs had been unable to rebut. The gifts of the properties were therefore prima facie able to be rescinded. In this respect, the fact that Mrs Beggs was a joint recipient of the gifts of the properties was of no significance, since she was on notice of the relationship of presumed undue influence and gave nothing in return, and therefore could not be regarded as an innocent third party for value.

---

63 Ibid, at 404–405. Callinan J thought the rule too well established to change: ibid, at 441–442. Kirby P dissented on the basis that the rule was an anachronism, discriminatory and reinforced stereotypes, and favoured a more widely stated principle covering the obligations on credit providers where a surety is obtained from someone in a relationship of emotional dependence: ibid, at 421–432. In so doing, Kirby J agreed with the view of Lord Browne-Wilkinson in *Barclays Bank Plc v O'Brien* [1994] 1 AC 180 at 196; cf the criticism of this view in A Mason, 'The impact of equitable doctrine on the law of contract' (1998) 27 *Anglo-American Law Review* 1 at 6–7.

64 *Whereat v Duff* [1972] 2 NSWLR 147; cf *Kerr v West Australian Trustee Executor and Agency Co Ltd* (1937) 39 WALR 34.

65 *Quek v Beggs* (1990) 5 BPR 97405.

66 Ibid; *Bainbrigge v Browne* (1881) 18 Ch D 188.

67 (1990) 5 BPR 97405.

However, since the gifts of the money had been expended, in accordance with Mrs Quek's express desire, on improvements to a property owned by a person who was not a party to the proceedings, Mr Beggs could not be restored to the position he would have been in had the gifts never been made. Accordingly, Mr Beggs was not required to return the money to the estate.

Even where a right to rescind has been lost, a court may nevertheless be prepared to order equitable compensation,[68] or order an account of any profits made on any resale to a third party.[69]

16.6   International perspectives

16.6.1   New Zealand

[16.120] There is no substantive difference between the law of Australia and that of New Zealand in relation to undue influence.[70] There has been some support expressed for the view of the House of Lords in *National Westminster Bank v Morgan*[71] that in addition to a relationship of dominance or influence by one party over the other, it must be shown that the transaction was wrongful in that it constituted a manifest and unfair disadvantage to the person seeking to avoid it.[72] However, that view preceded the reconsideration of the matter in England and may itself therefore be open to reconsideration by the New Zealand Court of Appeal.[73]

[16.125] In relation to circumstances such as those arising in *Yerkey v Jones* of a relative guaranteeing a loan due to the undue influence of their son, there appears to be support in New Zealand for a plea of undue influence on one of two bases: that the person exerting the influence was acting as agent of the third person creditor, or alternatively, that the third person had actual or constructive notice of the undue influence.[74] The question may then be the appropriate circumstances in which to impute the lender notice of undue influence.

16.6.2   United States

[16.130] There do not appear to be substantive differences between the law in the United States and in Australia concerning undue influence. American law recognises that where there is a special relationship between the parties together with an improper persuasion of the weaker by the stronger, the weaker party is entitled to avoid any resulting contract. A special relationship is recognised as existing especially in the case of a relationship of trust of confidence in which the weaker party is justified in assuming that the stronger party will not act in a manner inconsistent with the

---

68   *Mahoney v Purnell* [1996] 3 All ER 61.
69   *Haywood v Roadknight* [1927] VLR 512.
70   See for example, *ASB Bank Ltd v Harlick* [1996] 1 NZLR 655; JF Burrows, J Finn & S Todd, *Law of Contract in New Zealand*, Butterworths, Wellington, 1997, pp 349-60.
71   [1985] AC 686.
72   *Contractors Binding Ltd v Snee* [1992] 2 NZLR 157 at 166.
73   JF Burrows, J Finn & S Todd, *Law of Contract in New Zealand*, Butterworths, Wellington, 1997, p 353.
74   *Contractors Binding Ltd v Snee* [1992] 2 NZLR 157. Citing with approval Slade LJ in *Bank of Credit & Commerce International SA v Aboody* [1989] 1 QB 923 at 972.

weaker party's welfare.[75] Such a relationship has been recognised in the case of familiar relationships such as parent and child,[76] physician and patient, and religious adviser and follower. Unlike Australia, in the United States it has also been recognised as including husband and wife[77] and, in some jurisdictions, engaged couples.[78]

[16.135] The requisite relationship has not been confined to the well-established instances. As with class 2B cases, courts have recognised that in certain circumstances a relationship may involve a relationship of trust in which a weaker party is entitled to assume the stronger party would not act against the weaker party's interests. For example, the requisite relationship has been held to exist in the case of an unmarried mother who was prevailed upon by her counsellor to surrender her child for adoption,[79] the case of a school teacher arrested on criminal charges of homosexual activity who, after 40 sleepless hours being questioned by police, was visited by the superintendent of the school district and the principal of his school with a view to obtaining his resignation,[80] and the case of a police officer influenced by his superiors to resign after a rape allegation against him.[81]

16.6.3 Japan

[16.140] The common law concept of undue influence has its functional equivalent in Japanese law in two areas. First, it can be treated as a subset of one of the vitiating factors looked at so far, in the sense that the influence exerted by another person results in a lack of real capacity to form the necessary contractual intent. Thus some cases of 'undue influence' in a common law setting may be seen as duress or misrepresentation in a Japanese context.

[16.145] Alternatively, Japanese contract law employs a broad duty to form and perform contracts in good faith, and the kind of conduct that would be classified as undue influence in the common law will almost certainly infringe the obligation of good faith in Japanese law. Good faith in Japanese law is discussed in Chapter 17.

---

75 Restatement (Second) § 177.
76 This relationship is reversible: See, for example, *Yount v Yount* 43 NE 136 (Ind 1896) (undue influence by adult son on elderly mother).
77 *Randolph v Randolph* 937 SW 2d 815 (Tn 1996).
78 See, for example, *Robert O v Ecmel A* 460A 2d 1231 (Del 1983).
79 *Methodist Mission Home v B* 451 SW 2d 539 (Tex 1970).
80 *Odorizzi v Bloomfield School District* 54 Cal Rptr 533 (Ct App 1966).
81 *Keithley v Civil Service Board* 89 Cal Rptr 809 (Ct App 1970).

Chapter 17

Unconscionable conduct

17.1 Introduction

[17.05] Equitable doctrines concerning unconscionable conduct have a strong influence upon modern Australian contract law.[1] That influence may be seen in equity's treatment of issues such as equitable estoppel, the contractual capacity of intoxicated and mentally disordered persons and unilateral mistake. Unconscionability was also manifested in the equitable doctrine of 'unconscionable conduct' in the watershed case *Commercial Bank of Australia Ltd v Amadio*.[2] In this case unconscionable conduct was defined as being a ground of relief 'whenever one party by reason of some condition or circumstance is placed at a special disadvantage vis-a-vis another and unfair or unconscious advantage is taken of the opportunity thereby created'.[3]

---

1   This influence has been more extensive than in England: see, for example, A Mason, 'The impact of equitable doctrine on the law of contract' (1998) 28 *Anglo-American Law Review* 1 at 2.
2   (1983) 151 CLR 447.
3   Ibid at 462.

[17.10] On occasions, there may be some overlap between undue influence and unconscionable conduct. However, the difference between the two equitable doctrines was explained in *Commercial Bank of Australia Ltd v Amadio* as follows:

> In [the doctrine of undue influence] the will of the innocent party is not independent and voluntary because it is overborne. In [the doctrine of unconscionable conduct] the will of the innocent party, even if independent and voluntary, is the result of the disadvantageous position in which he is placed and of the other party unconscientiously taking advantage of that position.[4]

Thus, the focus of undue influence is the plaintiff's overborne will, while the critical element is the defendant's conduct, which in the circumstances is not consistent with equity or good conscience.[5] There is no suggestion in the case of unconscionable conduct, therefore, that the party seeking to have the transaction set aside did not bring a free, voluntary and independent judgment to the making of the contract.[6] As such there is no reason for treating the two remedies are mutually exclusive in the sense that only one of them is available in a particular situation to the exclusion of the other.[7]

[17.15] As such, some judges, particularly in England, have perceived a possible threat to the certainty and security of commercial transactions.[8] On the other hand, Sir Anthony Mason has sought to allay concerns regarding the scope of unconscionable conduct:

> Commercial lawyers, among others, are uneasy with the notion that unconscionable conduct should play a part in influencing the shape of modern contract law. This unease arises from the suggested vagueness of the concept of unconscionable conduct and the potential for disrupting the certainty of commercial transactions which are inherent in the equitable doctrine of actual and constructive notice. Much of the unease should be dispelled if we think of unconscionable conduct, at least when it is a separate and independent ground of relief, as operating in a framework in which the parties are at two different levels. There is no scope for the operation of the doctrine in relation to a transaction between two commercial parties neither of whom stands in a position of special disability or disadvantage. Once that is appreciated, the criticism of unconscionable conduct is as ground of relief as between the parties to a transaction looses its force. It is seen as conduct which takes advantage of another's special disability or disadvantage, in a way that is harsh or oppressive.[9]

[17.20] This equitable jurisdiction has been taken up and enlarged by statute. The consequence is that, under statute, there may be a remedy in cases where there is an inequality of bargaining power and the terms of the contract are merely harsh or oppressive or otherwise unfair.

---

4   Ibid, at 462.
5   Ibid, at 474.
6   Mason (1998) 28 *Anglo-American Law Review* 1 at 9.
7   *Commercial Bank of Australia Ltd v Amadio* (1983) 151 CLR 447 at 462.
8   See, for example, *West Deutscher Bank v Islington London Borough Council* [1996] AC 669 at 704–705 per Lord Browne-Wilkinson.
9   Mason (1998) 28 *Anglo-American Law Review* 1 at 11–12; see also *Commonwealth v Verwayen* (1990) 170 CLR 394 at 441 per Deane J.

17.2 Unconscionable conduct in equity

17.2.1 Elements

[17.25] Equity may grant relief for unconscionable conduct where:

* one party is in a position of special disadvantage; and
* the other party knows or ought to know of that special disadvantage and takes unfair advantage of his or her position.[10]

Example: Commercial Bank of Australia Ltd v Amadio[11]

Mr and Mrs Amadio were quite elderly and had a limited knowledge of written English. Their son, Vincenzo, was the managing director of a building company that had an overdraft account with a bank. Vincenzo met regularly with the bank's manager, and it was clear to the manager from these meetings that the company was insolvent. Nevertheless, he agreed to assist Vincenzo in maintaining a facade of solvency by selectively dishonouring the company's cheques. Finally, the bank was no longer prepared to carry the company. Accordingly, Vincenzo convinced his parents to sign a mortgage over their property as a guarantee for the company's debt. The mortgage was executed at their home in the presence of the bank manager. Vincenzo had informed them that the guarantee would only be for six months, and have an upper limit of $50 000, when in fact there was no limit as to time or amount. The bank manager informed them that the guarantee was not limited to a six-month period, but otherwise they received no independent advice concerning the document. The company finally went into liquidation and the bank sought to recover an outstanding amount of $240 000 from Mr and Mrs Amadio.

The High Court held that the Mr and Mrs Amadio were able to avoid the guarantee. They were the weaker party in the transaction between themselves and the bank. The end result of the combination of their age, their limited grasp of written English, the circumstances in which the bank presented the document to them for their signature—and, most importantly, their lack of knowledge and understanding of the contents of the document—was that they lacked assistance and advice when assistance and advice were plainly necessary for there to be any reasonable degree of equality between themselves and the bank. That special disability was sufficiently evident to the bank to make it prima facie unfair for the bank to procure their execution of the guarantee. The bank acted through its manager in such a way that his actions were its actions, and his knowledge its knowledge. He was not unfamiliar with the personal circumstances of Mr and Mrs Amadio, was aware of the inability of the company to pay its debt and must also have been aware of the potential consequences to them of an unlimited guarantee. In the circumstances, it was prima facie unfair and unconscientious of the bank to proceed to procure the signatures of Mr and Mrs Amadio on the guarantee. The onus was therefore cast upon the bank to show that the transaction was just and reasonable. This it could not do.

---

10   *Commercial Bank of Australia Ltd v Amadio* (1983) 151 CLR 447 at 462 per Mason J; 474 per Deane J (with whom Wilson J agreed).

11   (1983) 151 CLR 447.

[17.30] 'Special disadvantage' has been defined as 'one which seriously affects the ability of the innocent party to make a judgment as to his own best interests, when the other party knows or ought to know of the existence of that condition or circumstance and of its effect on the innocent party.'[12] In *Blomley v Ryan*,[13] Fullagar J stated that relevant circumstances included poverty of any kind, sickness, age, sex, infirmity of body or mind, drunkenness, illiteracy or lack of education, and lack of assistance or explanation where assistance or explanation is necessary.[14]

This list should not, however, be regarded as being exhaustive of all the situations in which relief will be granted on the ground of unconscionable conduct.[15] For example, the High Court has recently decided that emotional dependence—or being subject to emotional influence—is a relevant disadvantage that might constitute a ground to set aside a transaction as unconscionable.[16] It has also been suggested that a special disadvantage might exist not only in the traditional 'constitutional disadvantage' such as age or infirmity, but also in 'situational disadvantage' such as disadvantage arising out of an intersection of the legal and commercial circumstances in which the plaintiff may find him or herself.[17]

[17.35] It is clear that actual knowledge of special disability is sufficient, but not necessary.[18] In *Commercial Bank of Australia Ltd v Amadio* Deane J said that the special disability must be 'sufficiently evident' to the defendant. In relation to the bank's knowledge in that case, he remarked:

> It would ... have been plain to any reasonable person, who was prepared to see and to learn that he was put on inquiry. The stage had been reached at which the bank, through [the manager] was bound to make a simple inquiry as to whether the transaction had been properly explained to Mr & Mrs Amadio. The bank cannot shelter behind its failure to make that inquiry.[19]

---

12   *Commercial Bank of Australia Ltd v Amadio* (1983) 151 CLR 447 at 462 per Mason J. The origins of the doctrine of unconscionable conduct may be traced back to the doctrine of 'catching bargains', which applied where young male heirs of family property sold or otherwise dealt with their interest for considerable undervalue and were allowed in equity to avoid the transaction on the basis of the inferred weakness from their situation and the advantage taken of it by the other party: see, for example, *Earl of Chesterfield v Janssen* (1750) 2 Ves Sen 125; 28 ER 82.

13   (1956) 99 CLR 362 at 405

14   Ibid at 405; see also Kitto J at 415: 'illness, ignorance, inexperience, impaired faculties, financial need or other circumstances [which] affect his ability to conserve his own interest.'

15   *Commercial Bank of Australia Ltd v Amadio* (1983) 151 CLR 447 at 462 per Mason J; *Blomley v Ryan* (1956) 99 CLR 362 at 405 per Fullagar J.

16   Louth v Diprose (1992) 175 CLR 621. See also *State of NSW v Sullivan* [1999] NSWSC 596 (14 July 1999) (lack of information and misinformation about transaction held to be special disability).

17   *Australian Competition and Consumer Commission v CG Berbatis Holdings Pty Ltd* [2000] FCA 1376 at [122] per French J (shopping centre tenant eager to sell business in order to care for ill daughter already placed under much stress after potential sale fell through); *Australian Competition and Consumer Commission v Samton Holdings Pty Ltd* [2000] FCA 1725 at [72] (plaintiffs 'over a barrel' through being mortgaged 'to the hilt' and at risk of losing their home and a large sum of money). These cases actually considered application of the *Trade Practices Act* 1974 (Cth), s 51AA: see [17.90].

18   Cf *Westwill Pty Ltd v Heath* (1989) 52 SASR 471 at 477.

19   (1983) 151 CLR 447 at 479.

A defendant cannot shelter behind a 'wilful ignorance' as a precluding knowledge of the special disability.[20] However relief will be refused where the stronger party neither knows nor ought know of the weaker party's special disadvantage.[21]

[17.40] It is not necessary for the stronger party to have created the special disadvantage under which the weaker party is labouring.

Example: Louth v Diprose[22]

The plaintiff, a practising solicitor, became infatuated with the defendant. The defendant, on the other hand, was largely indifferent to the plaintiff but tolerated his attentions because of the material advantages that resulted from their relationship. In addition to the plaintiff's emotional dependence on the defendant—which had a great influence on his actions and decisions—the defendant manufactured an atmosphere of crisis about her ability to continue living in her rented accommodation in order to influence him to provide money for the purchase of a house. She played upon his love for her by making suicide threats connected with her need for the house. Ultimately, despite his modest means, he gave her $58000 for the purchase of a house for occupation by herself and her children from a former marriage. Subsequently, the plaintiff sought to recover the money.

The High Court held that while the defendant was not responsible for the plaintiff's emotional dependence on her, it was sufficiently evident to her that it placed him under a special disability, which she sought to exploit. It was therefore prima facie unfair or unconscionable for her to procure, accept or retain any benefit from the impugned transaction.

[17.45] In most cases where relief is granted on the basis of unconscionable conduct, inadequate consideration will have been provided by the stronger party. However, this is not necessarily the case. Adequate consideration may move from the stronger party in cases where the transaction was nevertheless unreasonable and unjust from the perspective of the weaker party.[23]

[17.50] It is necessary for there to be a causal connection between the stronger party's unconscientious taking of advantage and the resultant contract.[24] No relief may be granted where the stronger party's exploitative conduct was not a material cause of the contract.

[17.55] To date, the doctrine of unconscionable conduct has been applied where a weaker party has entered into a disadvantageous contract. However, in *Commercial Bank of Australia Ltd v Amadio*, Mason J observed that:

Because times have changed, new situations have arisen in which it may be appropriate to invoke the underlying principle [of relief from unconscionable conduct]. Take, for example, entry into a standard form contract dictated by a

---

20   *Owen and Gutch v Homan* (1853) 4 HLC 997 at 1035; 10 ER 752 at 752 per Cranworth LC.
21   See for example, *Melverton v Commonwealth Development Bank of Australia* (1989) ASC 58,453.
22   (1992) 175 CLR 621.
23   (1983) 151 CLR 447 at 475 per Deane J.
24   *Louth v Diprose* (1992) 175 CLR 621 at 632.

party whose bargaining power is greatly superior, a relationship which discussed by Lord Reid and Lord Diplock in *Schroeder (A) Music Publishing Co v Macauley* ... In situations of this kind it is necessary for the plaintiff who seeks relief to establish unconscionable conduct, namely that unconscientious advantage has been taken of his disabling condition or circumstances.[25]

Standard-form contracts are typically used by parties who are in such a strong bargaining position with respect to the supply of goods or services that they are able to prescribe the terms on which they are prepared to contract—a 'take it or leave it' basis. It has been suggested that unconscionability may be capable of relating not only to formation of contracts (sometimes called 'procedural unconscionability') but also to the substantive terms contained in a contract (sometimes called 'substantive unconscionability'). If this proves to be the case, a court would be able to deem terms of a contract to be so unreasonable that they represented the stronger party taking advantage of a disability on the part of the weaker party—perhaps because of a pressing need for the goods or services.[26]

17.2.2 Justification

[17.60] Once the two elements are established by the weaker party, the onus shifts to the stronger party to justify the conduct by showing that the transaction was 'fair, just and reasonable'.[27] Proof that the weaker party had the benefit of independent advice may be one way of showing that the transaction was fair, just and reasonable, but it is not conclusive.[28]

17.2.3 Remedies

[17.65] The relief against unconscionable conduct will be designed to prevent the stronger party from acting against equity and good conscience by attempting to enforce, or retain the benefit of, a dealing induced by that conduct.[29] The main remedy will be rescission of the contract, although partial rescission (rescission to the extent of the unconscionability) may be possible in some cases.[30]

[17.70] As in other cases where rescission is an available remedy, this relief may be denied in certain circumstances. Thus, where the weaker party affirms or acquiesces in the contract in circumstances where he or she has knowledge of the right to disaffirm, rescission will not granted.[31] A practical difficulty in this connection, however, is that

---

25   (1983) 151 CLR 447 at 462–463.
26   See DW Greig & JLR Davis, *Law of Contract*, Law Book Co, Sydney, 1987, p 980. See, for example, *Familiar Pty Ltd v Samarkos* (1994) 115 FLR 443 ('administration fee' of $50 000 in respect of a loan of $50 000 set aside on the grounds that the payment was unconscionable).
27   *Commercial Bank of Australia Ltd v Amadio* (1983) 151 CLR 447 at 474; *Fry v Lane* (1888) 40 Ch D 312 at 321.
28   *Commercial Bank of Australia Ltd v Amadio* (1983) 151 CLR 447 at 479.
29   Ibid, at 480.
30   Ibid, at 480–481. At one stage Deane J (with whom Wilson J agreed) contemplated partial rescission to the extent that the Amadio's liability exceeded the $20 000 that they were prepared to incur, but he ultimately settled on full rescission in view of the lack of advice concerning the nature of the liability that they were guaranteeing. See also *Bridgewater v Leahy* (1998) 72 ALJR 1525 at 1544. The High Court was prepared to partially set aside a guarantee in *Vadasz v Pioneer Concrete (SA) Pty Ltd* (1995) 130 ALR 570.
31   See, for example, *Moffatt v Moffatt* [1984] 1 NZLR 600.

the weaker party normally does not understand the nature of the transaction in the first place, and so is unlikely to be aware of any right to have the contract set aside.[32]

Rescission may also be denied where an innocent third party without notice has acquired an interest for value in the subject matter of the contract, or where substantial *restitutio in integrum* is no longer possible.[33]

[17.75] In an appropriate case, ordering, for example, an account of profits may be an alternative remedy[34]—or perhaps equitable damages.[35]

[17.80] Naturally, being equitable relief, a remedy for unconscionable conduct may be refused on discretionary grounds, such as unclean hands[36] or laches (unreasonable delay).[37]

Example: Baburin v Baburin[38]

In 1966, the plaintiff—a 56-year-old widow whose native language was Russian but who had a reasonable grasp of English—held shares representing the controlling interest in a company. This company was managed by two of her sons and an accountant, upon whom the plaintiff placed great reliance and trust. In May 1966, the plaintiff was requested by one of her sons and the accountant to execute a transfer of the shares to her two sons for consideration of $21 000, and did so. In November 1985, the plaintiff sought to have the transfer set aside on a number of grounds including undue influence and unconscionable dealing.

It was held[39] that actual undue influence had not been established, and even if a presumption of undue influence arose, that presumption had been rebutted, since it could not be said that at the time of the transfer the plaintiff's will was not independent and voluntary. However, while the plaintiff had not been deprived of an independent and voluntary will, she had no real understanding of matters relating to the family company, and was accustomed to depend greatly upon the advice of one of her sons and an accountant. In these circumstances, the transfer was an unconscionable dealing, since unconscionable advantage had been taken of an innocent party who was unable to make a worthwhile judgment as to what was in her best interests. However, while mere delay did not constitute laches, during the delay of 19 years before the action was brought there had been a loss of relevant documents, death and impairment of recollection of witnesses, alteration in the nature of the rights attached to the shares, and the transfer of an interest in the shares to an innocent third party. There was no explanation for the delay. Accordingly, the delay was unreasonable, and the consequences were such that it would be unjust to grant the relief sought by the plaintiff.

32　See DW Greig & JLR Davis, *Law of Contract*, Law Book Co, Sydney, 1987, p 978.
33　Cf *Vadasz v Pioneer Concrete (SA) Pty Ltd* (1995) 130 ALR 570 (HC).
34　*McKenzie v McDonald* [1927] VLR 134; *Haywood v Roadknight* [1927] VLR 512
35　*Hill v Rose* [1990] VR 129.
36　*Adenan v Buise* [1984] WAR 61 at 70.
37　See, for example, *Adenan v Buise* [1984] WAR 61.
38　[1990] 2 Qd R 101.
39　The trial judge's decision was upheld on appeal: [1991] 2 Qd R 240.

17.3 Statute

[17.85] Unconscionable conduct is now also dealt with in a variety of ways under statute. Specific legislation deals with unconscionability in relation to, for example, consumer credit transactions and hire purchase agreements. Other legislation has addressed unconscionable conduct in a more general way. That legislation is considered in the following sections.

17.3.1 Expanded remedies under the Trade Practices Act 1974

[17.90] Section 51AA of the *Trade Practices Act* provides that a corporation must not, in trade or commerce, engage in conduct that is unconscionable within the meaning of the unwritten law of the States and Territories. In considering this provision, French J in *Australian Competition and Consumer Commission v CG Berbatis Holdings Pty Ltd*[40] observed:

> The concept of unconscionability is arguably to be found at two levels in the unwritten law. There is a generic level which informs the fundamental principle according to which equity acts. There is the specific level at which the usage of 'unconscionability' is limited to particular categories of case.

It is the second sense that is the focus of the section. It has been held that the primary objective of the provision is to make available the extensive and flexible remedies contained in the Act for conduct that otherwise constitutes unconscionable conduct in equity—that is, at least unconscionable according to the principles stated in *Commercial Bank of Australia Ltd v Amadio*.[41] In particular, the section enables the court to grant an injunction under s 80 or one of the flexible ancillary orders under s 87: such orders as the court thinks appropriate (such as an order varying the contract or an order refusing to enforce all or any of its provisions).[42] Although damages under s 82 are not available for unconscionable conduct under the *Trade Practices Act*, an order for compensation may be made under s 87.

An applicant who seeks these statutory remedies must bring an action within two years, rather than within the usual six-year limitation period applicable in contract cases.[43]

---

40   (2000) 169 ALR 324 at 334.
41   *Gregg v Tasmanian Trustees Ltd* (1997) 73 FCR 91 at 122–125; *HECEC Australia Pty Ltd v Hydro-Electric Corp* (1999) ATPR 46-196; *Swift v Westpac Banking Corporation* [1995] ATPR 40,426. However, it might be argued that 'unconscionability' extends beyond the *CBA v Amadio* doctrine to include matters such as equitable estoppel and relief from penalties and forfeitures for the harsh and oppressive exercise of rights: see, for example, *Australian Competition and Consumer Commission v CG Berbatis Holdings Pty Ltd* (2000) 169 ALR 324 at 334 per French J; P Finn, 'Unconscionable conduct' (1994) 8 JCL 37 at 39; A Mason, 'Contract, good faith and equitable standards in fair dealing' (2000) 116 LQR 66. In any event, s 51AA is not intended to apply to conduct already caught by s 51AB: see s 51AA(2).
42   N Seddon & MP Ellinghaus, *Cheshire and Fifoot's Law of Contract*, 7th edn, Butterworths, Sydney, 1997, p 563 also identify as benefits leading from s 51AA the provision of access to the Federal Court and enabling the Australian Competition and Consumer Commission to bring representative actions and to accept undertakings from corporations under s 87B.
43   *Trade Practices Act* 1974 (Cth), s 87(1CA).

17.3.2   Unconscionable conduct in the supply of goods or services

[17.95] Commonwealth and State legislation prohibits unconscionable conduct in trade or commerce in connection with the supply of goods or services to a consumer.[44] In other words, the goods or services supplied must be 'of a kind ordinarily acquired for personal, domestic or household use or consumption'. This might include a bank lending money to enable a person to buy a private residence.[45] However, it has been held that the sections do not apply, for example, to radio bookings supplied to taxi drivers,[46] a mortgage providing security for a business,[47] or the provision of finance or an overdraft to assist a corporation to carry on business activities.[48]

The Commonwealth prohibition is limited to conduct by corporations, while the state and territory provisions apply to 'persons' or 'suppliers'. It seems that neither embraces the State as supplier.[49]

[17.100] When determining whether the prohibition against unconscionable conduct has been contravened, the court may have regard to a number of factors as guidelines:

- the relative strengths of the bargaining positions of the parties;
- whether as a result of the conduct engaged in by the corporation, person, or supplier, the consumer was required to comply with conditions that were not reasonably necessary to protect the legitimate interests of the corporation, person, or supplier;
- whether the consumer was able to understand any documents relating to the supply or possible supply of the goods or services;
- whether any undue influence or pressure was exerted on, or any unfair tactics were used against, the consumer or a person acting on behalf of the consumer by the corporation, person, or supplier, or a person acting on its behalf in relation to the supply; and
- the amount for which and the circumstances under which the consumer could have acquired identical or equivalent goods or services from some other person.[50]

None of these guidelines are, however, conclusive of unconscionability.[51]

---

44   *Trade Practices Act* 1974 (Cth), s 51AB; *Fair Trading Act* 1992 (ACT), s 13; *Fair Trading Act* 1987 (NSW), s 43; *Consumer Affairs and Fair Trading Act* 1990 (NT), s 43; *Fair Trading Act* 1989 (Qld), s 39; *Fair Trading Act* 1987 (SA), s 57; *Fair Trading Act* 1990 (Tas), s 15; *Fair Trading Act* 1985 (Vic), s 11A; *Fair Trading Act* 1987 (WA), s 11. The limitation to consumer contracts may be explained on the basis of a perceived risk of introducing uncertainty into other business transactions: see, for example, JW Carter & DJ Harland, *Contract Law in Australia*, 3rd edn, Butterworths, Sydney, 1996, p 513. It has been held, for example, that the supply of banking services, involving finance of more than $10 million, to enable a group of companies to continue to carry on a diverse range of activities and to realise some or all of its assets did not constitute a 'supply of a service' with which *Trade Practices Act* 1974 (Cth), s 51AB is concerned.
45   *Begbie v State Bank of New South Wales Ltd* [1994] ATPR 41,881.
46   *Venning v Suburban Taxi Service Pty Ltd* [1996] ATPR 41,731.
47   *State Bank of New South Wales v Sullivan* [1999] NSWSC 596 (James J, 14 July 1999).
48   *Begbie v State Bank of New South Wales Ltd* [1994] ATPR 41,881; *Leitch v Natwest Australia Bank Limited* (unreported, Fed Ct, Cooper J, 12 October 1995). The latter case suggested that such a claim, if it is to be brought under the *Trade Practices Act*, is more suited to s 51AA: see [17.90].
49   *Bass v Permanent Trustee Co Ltd* (1999) 161 ALR 399.
50   See, for example, *Trade Practices Act* 1974 (Cth), s 51AB(2).
51   The guidelines are similar to those provided in the *Contracts Review Act* 1980 (NSW).

[17.105] The remedies for breach of s 51AB and its state equivalents are an injunction,[52] or ancillaries remedies as the court deems appropriate.[53]

[17.110] Section 51AB has been complemented by a further enactment, s 51AC, which is designed to provide protection for small business consumers or suppliers from unconscionable conduct in business transactions. The section has two main provisions:

- a corporation must not, in trade or commerce, engage in unconscionable conduct in connection with the supply of goods or services to, or acquisition of goods or services from, a person (other than a listed public company); and
- a person must not, in trade or commerce, engage in unconscionable conduct in connection with the supply of goods or services to, or acquisition of goods or services from, a corporation (other than a listed public company).

Once again, while no definition of 'unconscionable conduct' is offered, the section provides catalogues of factors relevant to determining whether the supply (or acquisition) should be deemed unconscionable. These catalogues mirror the factors set out in s 51AB[54] but include in addition matters such as:

- the requirements of any applicable industry code;
- any unreasonable failure to disclose that the supplier's (or acquirer's) conduct might affect the interests of the small business consumer (or supplier), or involve risk to the small business consumer (or supplier);
- the extent to which the supplier (or acquirer) was willing to negotiate the terms and conditions; and
- the extent to which the parties acted in good faith.

[17.115] There is a small but growing body of authority interpreting ss 51AB and 51AC. It has, however, been suggested that there is no reason to limit ss 51AB and 51AC to specific equitable principles. For one thing, the non-exhaustive catalogues of factors include undue influence and duress and other issues falling outside the equitable doctrines such as the *CBA v Amadio* doctrine.[55] In one case, 'unconscionability' for the purposes of s 51AC was held satisfied by conduct described as 'unfair'.[56]

It seems that both s 51AB and s 51AC prescribes a standard rather than a rule: the categories of conduct for each will never close, although the circumstances of the application of the standard in each of them is confined by the language of the section.[57] This may be contrasted with the rules governing the relevant application of the term 'unconscionable conduct' in s 51AA, which are judge-made rules that may change from time to time.[58]

---

52 See, for example, *Trade Practices Act* 1974 (Cth), s 80.
53 See, for example, *Trade Practices Act* 1974 (Cth), s 87. These orders include an order for compensation, although an order for damages is not available, because s 82 of the *Trade Practices Act* 1974 (Cth) and State equivalents do not apply to contraventions of the unconscionability provisions of the Acts. Compare *Fair Trading Act* 1990 (Tas), s 37.
54 See the list in [17.100] above.
55 *Australian Competition & Consumer Commission v CG Berbatis Holdings Pty Ltd* [2000] FCA 2 (14 January 2000) at [24] per French J; *Dai v Telstra Corp Ltd* [2000] FCA 379 (31 March 2000) at [29]; *Australian Competition & Consumer Commission v Simply No-Knead (Franchising) Pty Ltd* [2000] FCA 1365.
56 *Garry Rogers Motors (Aust) Pty Ltd v Subaru (Aust) Pty Ltd* (1999) ATPR 41-703.
57 *Australian Competition & Consumer Commission v C G Berbatis Holdings Pty Ltd* [2000] FCA 2 (14 January 2000) at [25] per French J.
58 Ibid, at [26].

It would seem that circumstances other than merely the terms of the contract are required to exist before ss 51AA, 51AB or 51AC can be applied.[59]

17.3.3 Review of contracts in New South Wales

[17.120] The *Contracts Review Act* 1980 (NSW) provides a wide power for courts exercising New South Wales jurisdiction to review contracts deemed to be unjust. It has been suggested that the Act does much to signal the end of classical contract theory in New South Wales.[60]

[17.125] The Act provides that the court may order a wide range of remedies if it deems a contract or a provision of a contract to have been unjust in the circumstances relating to the contract at the time it was made.[61] 'Unjust' is defined to include 'unconscionable, harsh or oppressive'.[62] The factors to be taken into account when determining whether the contract was unjust are set out in s 9(2), namely:

- whether or not there was a material inequality of bargaining power;
- whether or not there was negotiation of the terms;
- whether or not it was reasonably practicable for the party seek relief to have negotiated for the alteration of any terms;
- whether there were conditions that were unreasonably difficult to comply with or were not reasonably necessary for the protection of the legitimate interests of a party;
- whether any party was not reasonably able to protect his or her interests (or was represented by a party who could not do so), because of age, or physical or mental state;
- the relative economic circumstances, education, or background and literacy of the parties or their representatives;
- whether the contract was wholly or partly in writing: the 'physical form of the contract and the intelligibility of the language in which it is expressed';
- whether or not the party seeking relief had independent legal or other expert advice;
- the extent to which the provisions of the contract were explained to, and understood by, the party seeking relief;
- whether undue influence, pressure[63] or unfair tactics were used;
- the conduct of the parties in relation to similar contracts or courses of dealing; and
- the commercial or other setting, and the purpose and effect of the contract.

The court is also directed by s 9(1) to consider the public interest.

The list in s 9(2) is not intended to be exhaustive, although it is not unusual for a judge, when applying the section, to regard each factor in turn to see whether it is present in the circumstances of the case.[64] While the court is not to consider any injustice that was not reasonably foreseeable at the time the contract

---

59   *Hurley v McDonald's Australia Ltd* (2000) ATPR 41-741 (Fed Ct FC).
60   *West v AGC (Advances) Ltd* (1986) 5 NSWLR 610 at 611 per Kirby P, 621 per McHugh JA.
61   See s 7(1).
62   See s 4(1); *Amcor Ltd v Watson* [2000] NSWCA 21 (3 March 2000).
63   Cf *Davies v Camilleri* [2000] NSWSC 904 (12 September 2000), which held that the Act did not apply where a mortgagee was not aware of undue pressure exerted on the mortgagor by a mortgage broker.
64   See, for example, *Melverton v Commonwealth Development Bank* (1989) ASC 55-921 at 58,460; *Broadlands International Finance Ltd v Sly* (1997) ANZ Conv R 328.

was made,[65] the parties' behaviour with respect to performance may be taken into account when determining the appropriate relief.[66]

[17.130] Several of the factors in the s 9(2) list are personal to the party seeking relief, and it is not necessary for the particular circumstance to be known to either party,[67] although lack of knowledge might be relevant to the exercise by the court of its discretion when deciding the appropriate relief under s 7.[68] This may be contrasted with the narrower *CBA v Amadio* principle, which requires the defendant to have known of the plaintiff's special disadvantage.

[17.135] It seems that a contract may be 'unjust' because its terms, consequences or effects were unjust (substantive injustice) or because of the unfairness of the methods used to make it (procedural injustice). Many unjust contracts will be the product of both procedural and substantive injustice.[69]

[17.140] Once the court is satisfied that the contract is unjust, it has a wide range of remedies available to it under s 7 for the purpose of avoiding, so far as practicable, an unjust consequence or result.[70] The court may, for example, decide to refuse to enforce any or all of the provisions of the contract, declare it void in whole or part, or make an order varying any provision of the contract in whole or part. Where such an order is made, a court may also make orders for ancillary relief as set out in Schedule 1 to the Act.

[17.145] There is a general prohibition against attempts to exclude the provisions of the Act.[71] In addition to criminal penalties, any provision in the contract that has the effect of restricting or modifying the provisions of the statute, or which represents a waiver by a person of his or her rights under the Act, is void.[72]

[17.150] The operation of the Act is excluded from certain contracts—namely trade, business or professional contracts (apart from those in farming operations)[73]—and to award conditions in contracts of employment.[74] The Crown, a public or local authority, or a corporation cannot obtain relief under the Act.[75]

Despite these exclusions, courts have tended to take a wide approach to contracts that are subject to the provisions of the Act.[76] For example, in cases involving loans for business purposes, it seems that the involvement of family—as in the case of the mortgage being granted by the wife of the debtor—has been treated as a ground for applying the provisions of the Act.[77]

---

65 See s 9(4).
66 See *Baltic Shipping Co v Dillon* (1991) 22 NSWLR 1 at 20 per Kirby P.
67 *West v AGC (Advances) Ltd* (1986) 5 NSWLR 610 at 620; *Antonovic v Volker* (1986) 7 NSWLR 151.
68 *Collier v Morland Finance Corp (Vic) Pty Ltd* (1989) ASC 55-716 at 58,429–430 per Hope JA.
69 *West v AGC (Advances) Ltd* (1986) 5 NSWLR 610; *Baltic Shipping Co v Dillon* (1991) 22 NSWLR 1 at 20 per Kirby P.
70 *Amcor Ltd v Watson* [2000] NSWCA 21 (3 March 2000).
71 See s 18.
72 See s 17.
73 See s 6(2).
74 See s 21.
75 See s 6(1).
76 See, for example, *Beneficial Finance Corp Ltd v Karavas* (1991) 23 NSWLR 256 (loan to purchase an airline subject to the Act).
77 See, for example, *Peters v Commonwealth Bank of Australia* [1992] ASC 56-135; *Australian Guarantee Corp Ltd v McLelland* (1993) ATPR 41-254.

Example: West v AGC (Advances) Ltd[78]

Mrs West borrowed money from AGC for a dual purpose: to discharge an existing mortgage on the home (which she was having trouble in paying off) and to lend money to her husband's company. Mrs West was the only partner of a director who was prepared to risk her family home in this way. AGC could reasonably foresee that the company was at risk of being wound up but, unknown to AGC, the company was already insolvent, even with the loan from Mrs West. Mrs West received no independent legal advice and had no solicitor. She was advised against the transaction by her son and a barrister friend. Further, she knew that the wives of the other directors had refused to put their homes up as security. She was well aware that she was giving a mortgage, and that AGC could have recourse against the property in the event of default by the company. She also had some experience with business practice and concepts and was not (as McHugh JA commented) merely a suburban housewife or ordinary home owner. The company was subsequently wound up, and following her default on the loan, AGC sought to enforce the guarantee against her. Mrs West sought relief under the *Contracts Review Act* 1980 (NSW).

A majority of the New South Wales Court of Appeal held that the Act required the position and rights of both parties to be taken into account. Mrs West knew what she was letting herself in for when she executed the mortgage. She had independent advice from her son and a barrister friend and clearly understood the legal and practical effect of giving the mortgage. She knew and understood that the company was unable to pay its debts at the time she borrowed the money. So far as AGC was concerned, the mortgage was no more than a legitimate way for AGC to protect its loan. The loan was at ordinary commercial rates, and there was no suggestion of anything in the terms of the mortgage which of itself was harsh, oppressive, unconscionable or unjust (that is, substantively unjust, not unconscionable). Nor was it suggested that AGC in any way sought to induce Mrs West to enter into the deed or mortgage or applied any improper pressure to her (that is, procedural injustice, not unconscionability). The contract was therefore not 'unjust' within the terms of the Act.

17.4   International perspectives

17.4.1   New Zealand

[17.155] There is no substantive difference between the common law in Australia and New Zealand in relation to unconscionable conduct.[79]

17.4.2   United States

[17.160] Courts in the United States have been prepared to take the notion of an 'unconscionable' contract—that is, a contract so unfair as to offend the conscience of the court—to the extent of refusing to enforce bargains on the grounds of substantive unfairness. Relief has been denied where the sum total of contractual provisions have driven 'too hard a bargain for a court of conscience to assist'.[80] It has been suggested,

---

78   (1986) 5 NSWLR 610.
79   See *Hart v O'Connor* [1985] 1 NZLR 159 at 171; *Moffatt v Moffatt* [1984] 1 NZLR 600 at 606.
80   *Campbell Soup Co v Wentz* 172 F 2d 80 at 83–84 (3rd Cir 1948).

however, that usually the bargain is infected with something more than only substantive unfairness, such as an absence of bargaining power that does not fall to the level of incapacity, or with an abuse of bargaining process that does not rise to the level of a misrepresentation, duress, or undue influence.[81]

[17.165] Notions of unconscionability in equity gave rise to Uniform Commercial Code (UCC) 2-302(1), which provides that:

> If the court as a matter of law finds the contract or any clause of the contract to have been unconscionable at the time that it was made, the court may refuse to enforce the contract, or it may enforce the remainder of the contract without the unconscionable clause, or it may so limit the application of any unconscionable clause as to avoid any unconscionable result.

Although UCC 2-302 only applies to transactions in goods, it has been applied either by way of analogy or as expressing a more general doctrine to other kinds of contracts.[82] A section applicable to contracts in genera,l which was modelled upon it, was included in the Restatement (Second).[83]

[17.170] However, the Code provides little guidance concerning the definition of 'unconscionability'. Comment 1 to UCC 2-302 states that:

> The basic test is whether, in the light of the general background and the commercial needs of the particular trade or case, the clauses involved are so one-sided as to be unconscionable under the circumstances existing at the time of the making of the contract.

Perhaps a better definition was provided by the Federal Court of Appeals for the District of Columbia in *Williams v Walker-Thomas Furniture Co*, where it was said that 'unconscionability has generally been recognized to include an absence of meaningful choice on the part of one of the parties together with contract terms which are unreasonably favorable to the other party'.[84] An 'absence of meaningful choice' is also known as 'procedural unconscionability', while 'unreasonably favourable' terms denotes 'substantive unconscionability'.[85] It has been suggested that, provided both aspects of unconscionability are shown, the strong presence of one aspect may compensate for the lesser presence of the other.[86] Presence of one aspect only will generally be insufficient.[87]

[17.175] Procedural unconscionability has been held to include matters such as:

---

81   EA Farnsworth, *Contracts*, 3rd edn, Aspen Law and Business, New York, 1999, § 4.27. See, for example, *Woollums v Horsley* 20 SW 781 (Ky 1892) (specific performance denied in relation to contract for the sale of mineral rights for 40c per acre and actually worth $15 per acre where vendor was about 60 years old, uneducated, unable to work and knew little of the business world, while the purchaser was of large and varied experience in business including the buying of mineral rights).

82   See, for example, *Zapatha v Dairy Mart* 408 NE 2d 1370 (Mass 1980) (franchise agreement); *Lloyd v Service Corporation of Alabama* 453 So 2d 735 (A la 1984) (residential lease).

83   Restatement (Second) § 208; see also equivalent provisions in specific codes including *Uniform Consumer Credit Code* 5-108; *Uniform Land Transactions Act* 1-311; *Uniform Residential Landlord and Tenant Act* s 1.303.

84   350F 2d 445 at 449 (DC Cir 1965).

85   Leff, 'Unconscionability and the Code—the Emperor's Clause' 115 U Pa L Rev 485 at 487 (1967).

86   *Phoenix Leasing Inc v Sure Broadcasting* 89 F 3d 846 (9th Cir 1996).

87   *Wade v Austin* 524 SW 2d 79 (Tex Civ App 1975) (substantive unconscionability alone insufficient); *Communications Maintenance v Motorola* 761 F 2d 1202 (7th Cir 1985) (procedural unconscionability alone insufficient).

- sharp bargaining practices;[88]
- use of fine print;[89]
- use of complex or convoluted language; and[90]
- lack of understanding.[91]

  Substantive unconscionability has been held to include matters such as:

- a clause in a petrol station lease or franchise agreement giving the oil company or franchisor an unfettered right to terminate;[92]
- a provision that the lessee of a petrol station indemnified the oil company for any negligence of the oil company on the premises;[93] and
- a clause in a franchise agreement limiting the franchisor's liability by excluding consequential loss.[94]

Consumer protection is now provided by legislation at both federal and state levels. Such legislation addresses matters such as attempts to limit a buyer's remedies, the imposition of unfair charges, or attempts to disclaim implied warranties.[95]

It has been acknowledged that it is inappropriate to attempt to invoke notions of unconscionability in relation to dealings between large, sophisticated companies.[96]

17.4.3 Japan

[17.180] Problems that occur in the formation and performance of contracts that are dealt with as issues of 'unconscionability' in Australian common law fall under the broader concept of 'good faith' in Japanese civil law. The obligation to exercise legal rights and perform legal duties 'in accordance with the principles of good faith and fair dealing' (Civil Code article 1(2)) is a mandatory requirement of Japanese civil law, including contract. As such, the obligation of good faith is implied in all transactions. Article 1 (3) then states that 'no abuse of rights is permitted'. This 'abuse of rights' concept also has its origins in the idea of good faith. Both of these general provisions of the Civil Code have been used extensively by the courts to modify contractual relationships and to soften the impact of the strict application of doctrinal rules or the complete enforcement of standard-form or one-sided agreements.

[17.185] Japanese courts' willingness to use the Code's general provisions to modify contracts has been particularly evident since the end of the Second World War, and has some similarities to the way courts in the common law world have drawn on equity to provide remedies for complex transactions, for continuing transactions, and

---

88   EA Farnsworth, *Contracts*, 3rd edn, Aspen Law and Business, New York, 1999, § 4.28.

89   See, for example, *John Deere Leasing Co v Blubaugh* 636 F Supp 1569 (D Kan 1986) (writing in light coloured fine print on extremely light weight paper which allowed the darker print on the front page to show through to the back making it difficult to read the fine print).

90   See, for example, *Seabrook v Commuter Housing Co* 338 NYS 2d 67 (NYC Civ Ct 1972) (two clauses containing 340 words separated by 13 complex legal clauses containing approximately 2000 words).

91   See, for example, *Weaver v American Oil Co* 276 NE 2d 144 (Ind 1971) (petrol station operator with only $1^{1}/_{2}$ years of high school not expected to understand the meaning of technical terms).

92   See, for example, *Shell Oil Co v Marinello* 307 A 2d 598 (NJ 1973).

93   See, for example, *Weaver v American Oil Co* 276 NE 2d 144 (Ind 1971).

94   See, for example, *Johnson v Mobil Oil Corp* 415 F Supp 264 (ED Mich 1976).

95   See generally EA Farnsworth, *Contracts*, 3rd edn, Aspen Law and Business, New York, 1999, § 4.29.

96   See, for example, *Continental Airlines v Goodyear Tire & Rubber Co* 819 F 2d 1519 (9th Cir, 1987); *Hydraform Products Corp v American Steel & Aluminium Corp* 498 A 2d 339 (NH 1985).

in consumer protection problems. However, Japanese case law also reveals numerous situations in which courts prefer a strict interpretation of the contract.[97] One explanation for this is that the 'good faith' clause generally operates as a final argument once other defences have been tested.

[17.190] Good faith in a Japanese context can be classified into six major obligations. Uchida[98] draws these categories based on his study of 500 leading contract cases in Japan. Cast in the language of obligation, they can be listed in this way:

- the obligation to compensate the other party when contractual negotiations are wrongfully destroyed;
- the obligation to provide information and make disclosure;
- the duty to re-negotiate, including situations where there has been a change of circumstances;
- the obligation to protect the other party in a contractual relationship from loss (or expansion of loss);
- the obligation to provide an appropriate reason for mid-transaction termination of a continuing contract (or to provide compensation, when this obligation is breached); and
- the obligation to submit to court adjustment of liquidated amounts claimed.

Of course, calibrating court decisions is not an exact science—there will always be decisions that are not easily subsumed within this model. Nevertheless, Uchida's analysis is important and influential. What it shows, among other things, is that in Japan, general provisions such as the good faith obligation have generated a fairly cohesive jurisprudence that makes it possible to predict relatively easily whether or not conduct will be regarded as infringing.

[17.195] One of the better known Japanese applications of good faith is the principle of 'changed circumstances'—although this has been widely misunderstood outside Japan. The changed circumstances doctrine holds that where, after a contract has been formed, circumstances change to such an extent that performance of the contract is not impossible but would work an injustice on one party, the parties have an obligation to renegotiate in good faith, or where this fails, have the option to bring the contract to the court for either cancellation or (re)adjustment.

The doctrine has its origins in German law, and in the legal response to unforseen price fluctuations after the First World War. In Japanese law, the doctrine requires:

- that the change of circumstances be unforeseen;
- that the change be something not attributable to either party; and
- that the enforcement of the contract be a breach of the good faith principle.

In practice, the three periods in which the principle has been used in litigation in Japan have been in response to Second World War price control legislation; during the 1970s oil shock (and subsequent effect on prices); and currently, during resolution of disputes arising from the collapse of Japan's 1980s 'bubble economy'.

---

97   For examples of Japanese courts take divergent approaches to similar problems in continuing contracts see V Taylor, 'Continuing Transactions and Persistent Myths: Contracts in Contemporary Japan' (1993) 19 *Melbourne University Law Review* 352–397.

98   Takashi Uchida, 'New Developments in Contemporary Contract Law and General Clauses' [*Gendai keiyakuhô no aratana tenkai to ippanjôkô*] (1994) Nos 514, 515, 516 and 517 *NBL*.

[17.200] The effect of the doctrine is twofold. It requires the parties to renegotiate, and thus supports the continuation and validity of the contract. Where negotiation fails (or where there is a refusal to negotiate in good faith) it allows a party to either assert that the contract is terminated, or to request a readjustment of the contract. Lower-level decisions may be found that uphold the validity of both remedies. However, in the post-Second World War period, no Japanese Supreme Court decisions have upheld contract cancellation on the basis of changed circumstances. Nor are there any pre-war or post-war decisions at Supreme Court level that have upheld contractual readjustment based on this principle. The end result is that the Japanese Supreme Court, while not actually denying the validity of the doctrine of changed circum-stances, can probably be seen as reluctant to recognise its application in any but the most exceptional cases.[99]

---

99   Takashi Uchida, *Minpô II* [Civil Code Vol 2] Tokyo Daigaku Shuppankai, Tokyo, 1997, p 75.

Chapter 18
Void and illegal contracts

18.1   Introduction

[18.05] A contract may be rendered 'illegal' in two ways: it may be prohibited by statute, or it may be contrary to public policy at common law. However, not all contracts that contravene a statute or are contrary to public policy are properly described as illegal. These contracts may instead be referred to as being 'void'.

[18.10] Whether a contract contravenes a statute is a question of statutory interpretation. In relation to the concept of a contract that is contrary to public policy, Isaacs J in *Wilkinson v Osborne*[1] explained as follows:

> The 'public policy' which a Court is entitled to apply as a test of validity to a contract is in relation to some definite and governing principle which the community as a whole has already adopted either formally by law or tacitly by its general course of corporate life, and which the Courts of the country can recognize and enforce. The Court is not a legislator: it cannot initiate the principle; it can only state or formulate it if it already exists.
>
> The rule of law as to contracts against public policy is constant—namely, that every bargain contrary to such a social governing principle is regarded as prejudicial to the State ... and the State by its tribunals refuses to enforce it.[2]

[18.15] This is an area of law beset with difficulties: commentators have variously described it as 'one of the least satisfactory branches of contract law',[3] or 'complex and obscure', with cases that often seem 'hit and miss'[4] or, more generously 'often challenging and sometimes difficult'.[5] The difficulties arise from an inconsistent use of

---

1   (1915) 21 CLR 89 at 97.
2   Cited with approval in *A v Hayden* (1984) 156 CLR 532 at 558, 571.
3   JW Carter & DJ Harland, *Contract Law in Australia*, 3rd edn, Butterworths, Sydney, 1996, p 519.
4   N Seddon & MP Ellinghaus, *Cheshire and Fifoot's Law of Contract*, 7th edn, Butterworths, Sydney, 1997, p 675.
5   N Thompson, *The Rights of Parties to Illegal Transactions,* Federation Press, Sydney, 1991, p iii.

terminology and cases that are difficult to reconcile. These problems were summed up in the remark by Windeyer J that:

> It has always seemed to me likely to lead to error, in matters such as this, to adopt first one of the familiar legal adjectives—'illegal', 'void', 'unenforceable', 'ineffectual', 'nugatory'—and then having given an act a label to deduce from that its results in law. That is to invert the order of inquiry, and by so doing to beg the question, and allow linguistics to determine legal rights.[6]

The difficulties in distinguishing between different types of vitiated contract may be traced more often than not to an inconsistent and indiscriminate use of terms such as 'unenforceable', 'void' and 'illegal'.[7]

[18.20] Illegal contracts may usefully be distinguished from others on the grounds that, in the case of illegality a court will generally deny relief to one or both parties to the contract (*ex turpi causa*—no cause of action arises out of the illegality). The category of *void* contracts may then be regarded as contracts rendered void by statute or contrary to public policy, but which do not have the consequence of *ex turpi causa*.[8]

Sometimes judges describe illegal contracts as being 'illegal and void'. The term 'void' in such cases adds nothing to the term 'illegal'. Indeed, it may merely result in confusion if it leads to the conclusion that the same result follows as in, for example, a case of mistaken identity[9] or *non est factum*.[10] In such cases, the result is that the contract is regarded as being non-existent and title cannot pass under it. Money or property transferred may be recovered in restitution for total failure of consideration. By contrast, a contract that is said to be 'illegal' or 'illegal and void' cannot be enforced by one or both parties, and no restitutionary claim may be invoked to recover money or property transferred.

Somewhere in between[11] are contracts that are 'unenforceable' because, for example, they do not comply with the requirements of writing laid down by Statute of Frauds legislation.[12] The effect of such non-compliance[13] is that is that no action may be brought by either party upon the contract. However, the contract may still be specifically enforced if there is part-performance[14] and in any event the contract is effective to pass title.[15] Moreover, a contract that is unenforceable for failure to comply with statutory requirements may give rise to restitutionary remedies.[16] Denning LJ summed up unenforceable contracts in the following terms: 'They are invalid and unenforceable. The law does not punish them. It simply takes no notice of them.'[17]

---

6   *Brooks v Burns Philp Trustee Co Ltd* (1969) 121 CLR 432 at 458.
7   See also N Thompson, *The Rights of Parties to Illegal Transactions,* Federation Press, Sydney, 1991, p 12.
8   Ibid.
9   See [14.215].
10   See [14.255].
11   *Bennett v Bennett* [1952] 1 KB 249 at 260 per Denning LJ.
12   See Chapter 11.
13   See [11.05].
14   See [11.335].
15   See [11.300].
16   *Pavey & Mathews Pty Ltd v Paul* (1987) 162 CLR 221 (failure to comply with requirement of writing in *Builders Licensing Act* 1971 (NSW); see also [11.305]–[11.325].
17   *Bennett v Bennett* [1952] 1 KB 249 at 260.

18.2 Void contracts

[18.25] The category of contract that is regarded as void but to which *ex turpi causa* does not apply, would seem to embrace contracts deemed by statute to be void[18] as well as three categories of contract that are, at common law, contrary to public policy:

- contracts in restraint of trade;
- contracts containing clauses that attempt to oust the jurisdiction of the court; and
- contracts prejudicial to the status of marriage.[19]

These cases generally involve one particular provision that is contrary to public policy; the entire contract is not usually of that nature. However, if the offending provision cannot be severed from the remainder of the contract, it has the effect of voiding the whole contract.[20]

18.2.1 Contracts void by statute

[18.30] Statutes sometimes provide that particular contractual provisions are void. For example, the *Trade Practices Act* 1974 (Cth) provides that clauses purporting to exclude, restrict, or modify the liability of a corporation imposed by Division 2 of Part V of the Act (that is the implication of terms such as an implied condition of merchantability and of fitness for purpose) are void.

The operation of such legislation is a question of statutory interpretation. It is also a question of interpretation about the impact of any provision—whether it only affects a particular term, or has ramifications for the contract as a whole.

18.2.2 Terms contrary to public policy

(a) Restraint of trade

[18.35] A restraint of trade is a promise by one party, the 'covenantor', to give up a freedom that he or she would otherwise enjoy in relation to his or her trade, for the benefit of another party, the 'covenantee'.[21] The two main examples of restraints of trade have been restraints in contracts for the sale of a business and contracts of employment. In the sale of a business, the vendor may agree with the purchaser that the vendor will not set up a rival business within a particular radius of the purchased business for a period of time.[22] In contracts of employment, an employee may agree with his or her employer that should the employment end, the employee will not work for a rival employer for a certain period of time.[23] However, restraints of trade may also exist in a wide array of other types of con-

---

18 N Thompson, *The Rights of Parties to Illegal Transactions*, Federation Press, Sydney, 1991, p 6.
19 DW Greig & JLR Davis, *Law of Contract*, Law Book Co, Sydney, 1987, p 1094 added to this list an agreed damages clause that amounted to a penalty: see also [23.470].
20 See, for example, *Nordenfelt v Maxim Nordenfelt Guns and Ammunition Co Ltd* [1894] AC 535; *McFarlane v Daniell* (1938) 38 SR (NSW) 337; *Niemann v Smedley* [1973] VR 769.
21 *Amoco Aust Pty Ltd v Rocca Bros Motor Engineering Co Pty Ltd.*(1973) 133 CLR 288 at 304–305; 313–314. This includes freedom to do an activity in which the covenantor was not previously engaged.
22 See, for example, *Nordenfelt v Maxim Nordenfelt Guns and Ammunition Co Ltd* [1894] AC 535; *Papastravou v Gavan* [1968] 2 NSWR 286.
23 See, for example, *Curro v Beyond Productions Pty Ltd* (1993) 30 NSWLR 337.

tracts, including partnership agreements,[24] franchise agreements,[25] agreements to take supplies from one source, and 'salary caps' and 'players drafts' used by sporting organisations to encourage fair competition.[26]

A restraint of trade need not be contained in a contract between the covenantor and the covenantee. It has been held, for example, that a player in a sporting league may be adversely affected by, and obtain relief against, a restraint contained in a contract between the organisation running the league and the player's club.[27]

[18.40] In restraint of trade cases, the law seeks to accommodate two competing policy considerations: the policy of freedom of contract and enforcing contractual obligations, and the policy of preserving freedom of trade from unreasonable contractual restriction.[28]

[18.45] All restraints of trade are regarded as prima facie void.[29] However, this presumption may be rebutted by showing that the restraint was justified. A restraint may be justified by showing that it is:

* reasonable in the interests of the parties; and
* reasonable in the interests of the public.[30]

The onus of showing that a covenant is reasonable in the interests of the parties lies on the party seeking to rely on the restraint—the covenantee. If this onus is discharged, the burden shifts to the covenantor to show that the covenant is unreasonable from the perspective of the public interest.[31]

Interests of the parties

[18.50] Reasonableness as between the parties involves a consideration of two issues:

* whether the covenantee has a legitimate interest; and
* whether the restraint goes no further than is necessary to protect that interest.[32]

[18.55] Whether the covenantee has a legitimate interest to protect will depend upon the nature of the contract. For example, in the case of the sale of a business, the covenantee's legitimate interest will be to protect the goodwill of the business from competition by the seller.[33] In the case of a restraint on the subsequent employment of a former employee, former partner or former franchisee the covenantee's legitimate interest may be in the nature of goodwill, the prevention of solicitation of clients or

---

24 See, for example, *Bridge v Deacons* [1984] AC 705.

25 See, for example, *KA & C Smith Pty Ltd v Ward* (1999) ATPR 41-717.

26 See, for example, *Buckley v Tutty* (1971) 125 CLR 363; *Adamson v West Perth Football Club* (1979) 27 ALR 475.

27 See, for example, *Buckley v Tutty* (1971) 125 CLR 363; *Adamson v West Perth Football Club* (1979) 27 ALR 475; *Hughes v West Australian Cricket Association Inc* (1996) 69 ALR 660.

28 *Peter American Delicacy Co Ltd v Patricia's Chocolates and Candies Pty Ltd* (1947) 77 CLR 574 at 590 per Dixon J.

29 *Nordenfelt v Maxim Nordenfelt Guns and Ammunition Co Ltd* [1894] AC 535 at 565.

30 Ibid, adopted in *Buckley v Tutty* (1972) 125 CLR 353 at 396; *Amoco Aust Pty Ltd v Rocca Bros Motor Engineering Co Pty Ltd* (1973) 133 CLR 288 at 306, 315–316.

31 *Amoco Australia Pty Ltd v Rocca Bros Motor Engineering Co Pty Ltd* (1973) 133 CLR 288 at 307.

32 Ibid at 306, 316.

33 See, for example, *Bacchus Marsh Concentrated Milk Co Ltd v Joseph Nathan & Co Ltd* (1919) 26 CLR 410; *Peters American Delicacy Co Ltd v Patricia's Chocolates and Candies Pty Ltd* (1947) 77 CLR 574; *Butt v Long* (1953) 88 CLR 476 at 486.

customers,[34] or confidential information such as the secrets of the business, processes, and products.[35] A legitimate interest may also be found in ensuring the stability of a business or industry[36]—or, in the case of a sporting association employing a 'salary cap' or 'players draft', a legitimate interest in having an even competition between participating teams.[37] By contrast, it has been held that a purchaser of capital equipment has no legitimate interest in preventing competition from a later purchaser of similar equipment from the same supplier.[38]

[18.50] Whether the restraint does no more than provide adequate protection of the covenantee's legitimate interest depends upon the balancing of a number of relevant factors including:

- *The scope of the restraint, in terms of both the area and duration.* The wider the restraint in geographical terms, and longer the restraint in terms of time, the more likely the restraint will be unreasonable.[39]

- *The activities covered by the restraint.* If the restraint purports to restrict activities that are unrelated to the covenantee's legitimate interest, the restraint is more likely to be unreasonable.[40]

- *The relative bargaining power of the parties.* It will be relevant, but not conclusive, if the covenantee is in a stronger bargaining position than the covenantor.[41] The court may be prepared to show greater latitude where the parties are in a position to bargain on an equal footing,[42] although a restraint may still be unreasonable where the parties had equal bargaining power.[43]

- *The consideration paid in exchange for the restraint.* The court may be prepared to allow a greater restraint than it might otherwise have done where the covenantor has received a large consideration for the covenant.[44]

- *The context of the contract.* The setting in which the contract takes place may be an important consideration. Thus, for example, a restraint may be upheld where it is inserted into a partnership agreement between solicitors who were experienced in relation to restraints.[45]

[18.65] The courts tend to take different attitudes to the assessment of the various relevant considerations depending upon the type of contract. For example, because employees often have only their labour to trade, the courts normally adopt a strict

---

34   *Peters American Delicacy Co Ltd v Patricia's Chocolates and Candies Pty Ltd* (1947) 77 CLR 574; *KA & C Smith Pty Ltd v Ward* (1999) ATPR 41-717.
35   *Bacchus Marsh Concentrated Milk Co Ltd v Joseph Nathan & Co Ltd* (1919) 26 CLR 410 at 441; *KA & C Smith Pty Ltd v Ward* (1999) ATPR 41-717.
36   *Queensland Co-operative Milling Association v Pamag Pty Ltd* (1973) 133 CLR 260; *Amoco Australia Pty Ltd v Rocca Bros Motor Engineering Co Pty Ltd* (1973) 133 CLR 288 at 319.
37   *Buckley v Tutty* (1971) 125 CLR 363; *Buckenara v Hawthorn Football Club* [1998] VR 39.
38   *ICT Pty Ltd v Sea Containers Ltd* (1995) 39 NSWLR 640 (covenant by builder of seagoing catamaran ferries not to sell similar ferries to covenantee's competitors struck down).
39   *Butt v Long* (1953) 88 CLR 476.
40   *Nordenfelt v Maxim Nordenfelt Guns & Ammunition Co Ltd* [1894] AC 535.
41   *A Schroeder Music Publishing Co Ltd v Macauley* [1974] 1 WLR 1308.
42   *Amoco Australia Pty Ltd v Rocca Bros Motor Engineering Co Pty Ltd* (1973) 133 CLR 288 at 316.
43   *Creamoata Ltd v Rice Equalization Association Ltd* (1953) 89 CLR 286 at 318.
44   See, for example, *Nordenfelt v Maxim Nordenfelt Guns & Ammunition Co Ltd* [1894] AC 535 at 565; *Amoco Australia Pty Ltd v Rocca Bros Motor Engineering Co Pty Ltd* (1973) 133 CLR 288 at 305–306, 316.
45   *Bridge v Deacons* [1984] AC 705.

approach to judging the reasonableness of a restraint in an employment contract that restricts the activities of former employees.[46]

Example: Buckley v Tutty[47]

The defendant NSW Rugby League conducted a rugby league competition. The plaintiff was a player with the Balmain Tigers, one of the clubs in the competition. The defendant applied a retention-transfer-clearance system whereby a player placed on a club's 'retain' list could only play for that club, a player placed on a club's 'transfer' list could only play for another club if the new club paid a transfer fee to the old club, and otherwise a player could not play in Queensland, New Zealand or England (the other places where rugby league was played) without obtaining a clearance from his club. The plaintiff was placed on Balmain's retain list, but he thought he could obtain more favourable terms from a different club. He argued that the defendant's system was an unreasonable restraint of trade.

The High Court thought that it was a legitimate object of the League and its member clubs to ensure that teams in the competition were as strong and well-matched as possible, since in that way the support of the public may be attracted and maintained, and players would have the best opportunity of developing and displaying their skill. However, the system went beyond what was reasonable to protect that interest. A team could place a player on its retain list for an indefinite period—even after he had ceased to play for, or receive remuneration from, the club. Alternatively, the club could fix such a high transfer fee that it effectively stopped the player from playing for another club. The law will regard as unreasonable restraints that prevent people from earning their living in whatever lawful way they choose. That was the case here.

However, while an employer is entitled to protection against having its clients solicited or enticed away by a former employee, it cannot claim protection against competition as such. General skill and knowledge that an employee obtains in the course of employment do not qualify as 'trade secrets' capable of being protected by a reasonable restraint.[48]

[18.70] A distinction is sometimes drawn between an employment contract and a contract that provides that a party must render services exclusively to the other party. The latter is valid because the promise to render services exclusively is merely an incident of the contract and is required to enable the covenantee to obtain full benefit of the covenantor's services.[49] Such a requirement is valid if, viewed as a whole, it is directed towards absorption rather than sterilisation of the covenantor's services.

---

46   See, for example, *Forbes v NSW Trotting Club Ltd* (1979) 143 CLR 242 at 260–261; *Buckley v Tutty* (1971) 125 CLR 353 at 381; *Hughes v West Australian Cricket Association (Inc)* (1996) 69 ALR 660 at 703.
47   (1971) 125 CLR 353.
48   *Drake Personnel Ltd v Beddison* [1979] VR 13 at 20, 23–24.
49   *Esso Petroleum Co Ltd v Harper's Garage (Stourport) Ltd* [1968] AC 269 at 328–329 applied in *Buckenara v Hawthorn Football Club Ltd* [1988] VR 39; *Curro v Beyond Productions Pty Ltd* (1993) 30 NSWLR 337.

Example: Curro v Beyond Productions Pty Ltd[50]

Tracey Curro was a television presenter contracted to a documentary programme called *Beyond 2000*, broadcast on the Seven Network. The contract contained promises by Curro that during the life of the contract she would present segments and host programmes as required by the show's producers, and that she would not engage in any other presentation activity without the consent of the producers. During her contract, Curro advised the show's producers that she had been approached by the Nine Network to work as a television reporter for its *60 Minutes* current affairs programme, and that she wished to accept the offer.

The New South Wales Court of Appeal held that the *Beyond 2000* producers were entitled to an injunction restraining Curro from breaching her promise of exclusive service. The court was of the view that, as in the case of an actor, an employer in the entertainment industry who engages an employee such as Curro for television presentation work contemplates that the employee not only wants to receive the agreed remuneration but also the opportunity to keep her name and talents before the viewing public. Accordingly, even if there is no express provision, the court will imply an obligation on the employer to provide a reasonable opportunity of performing services of the kind for which the employer contracted and of appearing before the public. The absence of an express requirement for the producers to provide Curro with work did not therefore mean that they could simply pay her remuneration without giving her work and thereby 'sterilise' her talents for the life of the contract. The promise of exclusive service therefore did not amount to an unreasonable restraint of trade.[51]

However, such a tie maybe judged unreasonable where, for example, the restraint is too long or the covenantee is taking advantage of a stronger bargaining position.[52]

[18.75] By contrast, courts may be prepared to take a more robust approach to judging the reasonableness of a restraint contained in a contract for the sale of a business, since such a restraint normally allows the vendor to obtain full value for the business being purchased and enables the purchaser to obtain exactly what he or she is bargaining for.[53]

Example: Nordenfelt v Maxim Nordenfelt Guns and Ammunition Co Ltd[54]

Nordenfelt was a manufacturer of guns and ammunition. The business had clients from all around the world. Nordenfelt sold his business to a company in consideration of a payment of $1 000 000 and Nordenfelt being restrained from being involved in

---

50 (1993) 30 NSWLR 337. See also *Warner Bros Pictures Inc v Nelson* [1937] 1 KB 209; *Warner Brothers Pictures Inc v Ingolia* [1965] NSWR 988.

51 Cf *Canberra Bushrangers Baseball Team Pty Ltd v Byrne* (unreported, ACT SC, Higgins J, 21 December 1994) (restraint unreasonable where no requirement to select player during time of contract and no obligation to pay remuneration).

52 *A Schroeder Music Publishing Co. Ltd v Macaulay* [1974] 1 WLR 1308 (song writer obliged to provide all works to recording company but company not obliged to record any of his work).

53 *Esso Petroleum Co Ltd v Harper's Garage (Stourport) Ltd* [1968] AC 269 at 335–336.

54 [1894] AC 535.

the munitions industry or any other business that might be carried on by the company for a period of 25 years. There was no geographical limit to the restraint.

The House of Lords held that a degree of latitude was appropriate in the case of a restraint in the sale of a business since it enabled the purchaser to obtain the whole of the consideration it was wanting to purchase—that is, the business and its goodwill. It also allowed the vendor to obtain full value for what he was selling: in other words, without the restraint preventing him from establishing a new business in competition, the purchaser would be less inclined to pay full price for the business. While ordinarily a worldwide restraint would not be permitted, particularly for a restraint so long in duration, in the particular circumstances of this case, taking into account the worldwide nature of the business and the substantial consideration being paid to the covenantor, the restraint in relation to the munitions industry was upheld. However, that part of the restraint restricting the covenantor from competing with any business that the company might pursue at some time in the future went beyond what was reasonably necessary to protect the covenantee's interest. Accordingly, that part of the restraint was unreasonable.

[18.80] Similarly, in the case of 'solus' or exclusive dealing agreements whereby a retailer agrees to take its supplies exclusively from a particular manufacturer, the courts tend to uphold the restraint where the parties have bargained at arm's length. Such agreements are common in the petroleum industry for the supply of petrol to petrol stations. In upholding such restraints, courts have recognised that the restraint is relevant to the industry involved and facilitates the efficient distribution of the particular type of product to the public.[55] Nevertheless, factors such as the length of the restraint and an obligation to purchase minimum quantities regardless of market conditions may render an exclusive dealing arrangement unreasonable.[56]

Interests of the public

[18.85] Where a restraint goes beyond what is reasonably necessary to protect the interests of the parties, it is contrary to the public policy that underlies the whole doctrine, and for that reason is regarded as being void. Indeed, in practice, courts have to some extent treated the two branches of the *Nordenfelt* test as being merged—inasmuch as having found that a restraint was reasonable between the parties, they have concluded that it was reasonable in the interests of the public as well. However, this need not be so: the requirements of reasonableness with reference to the interests of the

---

55 See, for example, *Esso Petroleum Co Ltd v Harpur's Garage (Stauport) Ltd* [1968] AC 269; *Peters American Delicacy Co Ltd v Patricia's Chocolates and Candies Pty Ltd* (1947) 77 CLR 574; *Queensland Co-operative Milling Association Ltd v Pamag Pty Ltd* (1973) 133 CLR 260.

56 See, for example, *Queensland Cooperative Milling Association Ltd v Pamag Pty Ltd* (1973) 133 CLR 260 (requirement to purchase 'all flour wheatmeal or other commodities' required for a bakery business for a maximum period of 7 years held reasonable); cf *Esso Petroleum Co Ltd v Harper's Garage (Stourport) Ltd* [1968] AC 269 (promise to purchase 'total requirements of motor fuels' of a petrol station from petrol supplier for a period of 5 years held to be reasonable but for 21 years held to exceed what was commercially necessary for protection); *Amoco Australia Pty Ltd v Rocca Bros Motor Engineering Co Pty Ltd* (1973) 133 CLR 288 (promise to purchase minimum quantities of petrol and motor oil from petrol supplier for 15 years held to be too long and unreasonable).

parties and of reasonableness with reference to the interests of the public are still to be regarded as raising distinct questions. There may be a rare case where although a restraint satisfies the first requirement, it is nevertheless injurious to the public.[57] For example, a restraint preventing a medical practitioner practising in a country town might be reasonable as between the parties (perhaps by virtue of the consideration provided in exchange for the covenant), but be unreasonable from the public perspective, because there is a public interest in maximising the availability of medical expertise in a small and perhaps isolated community. Similarly, an indefinite ban imposed on cricket players in retaliation for breaching a ban imposed by authorities on playing in unauthorised games might be held unreasonable, at least because it is against the public interest that lies in having every opportunity to see first class cricketers in action.[58]

Time of assessment

[18.90] The validity of a restraint must be decided as at the date of the agreement imposing it—rather than, for example, the date when the covenantee seeks to enforce the covenant.[59] Accordingly, the court will take into account the probabilities of what *might* have occurred, rather than, with hindsight, what *actually* occurred.[60] Thus in the case of a restraint in an employment contract, for example, the relevant enquiry will be in relation to whether or not the restraint was reasonable as at the date when the employment contract was entered into, rather than the activities of the covenantor since leaving the covenantee's employment.[61]

Statute

[18.95] Restraints of trade may also fall within the ambit of Part IV of the *Trade Practices Act* 1974 (Cth), which generally deals with anti-competitive behaviour. An examination of those provisions is beyond the scope of this book.[62] However, s 51(2) of the Act expressly provides that Part IV does not apply to certain types of contractual provision, including:

- a provision in a contract of service or for services restricting the work in which a person may engage during or after termination of the contract;
- a provision in a contract of partnership relating to competition between the partnership and a partner before or after cessation of the partnership; and
- a provision in a contract for the sale of a business that is solely for the protection of the purchaser in respect of the goodwill of a business.[63]

Accordingly, the validity of such provisions continues to be governed by the common law.

---

57 *Amoco Australia Pty Ltd v Rocca Bros Motor Engineering Co Pty Ltd* (1973) 133 CLR 288 at 307 per Walsh J.

58 *Hughes v Western Australian Cricket Association (Inc)* (1986) 69 ALR 660 at 703 (former Australian captain banned for leading rebel team to South Africa during apartheid era); see also *Greig v Insole* [1978] 1 WLR 302 (cricketers banned from international cricket due to playing for rebel World Series Cricket).

59 *Lindner v Murdock's Garage* (1950) 83 CLR 628 at 653; *Amoco Australia Pty Ltd v Rocca Bros Motor Engineering Co Pty Ltd* (1973) 133 CLR 288 at 318.

60 Ibid.

61 *Drake Personnel Ltd v Beddison* [1979] VR 13 at 25.

62 See, for example, S Corones, *Competition Law in Australia*, LBC, Sydney, 1999.

63 Cf *Peters (WA) Ltd v Petersville Ltd* (1999) ATPR 41-714.

(b)   Attempts to oust the jurisdiction of the court

[18.100] At common law, it is contrary to public policy to attempt to deny access to the courts by one or both parties. However, this broad proposition is not to be taken as stating a universal rule.

[18.105] Thus, the parties to a contract are entitled to agree that any dispute arising between them may be settled by a particular person or body, provided that recourse to the courts remains open for determination of questions of law. Accordingly, a contract may validly provide that in the event of a dispute, questions of fact will be decided conclusively by arbitration, or by obtaining the certificate of, for example, a bank manager, engineer, or architect.[64] In such a case, going to court in lieu of referring the matter to arbitration may constitute a breach of contract, sounding in damages. Indeed, the parties may validly make a court action subject to a condition precedent such as obtaining a certificate, or making prior reference to arbitration for determination of questions of fact.[65]

[18.110] Where the rules of a voluntary association provide the decision of the committee on interpretation of the rules is 'final and conclusive', this will be contrary to public policy. However, the rules may validly make the decision of the committee final on issues of fact only.[66]

[18.115] In contrast to covenants in restraint of trade, which if unreasonable may void the whole contract, the validity of a provision that seeks to oust the jurisdiction of the court is confined to the clause itself, and has no capacity to detrimentally affect the contract as a whole. In other words, a clause seeking to oust the jurisdiction of the court may be severable, leaving the remainder of the contract binding on the parties.[67]

(c)   Clauses prejudicial to the status of marriage

[18.120] Contractual provisions that are deemed prejudicial to the status of marriage are regarded as being contrary to public policy on the grounds that 'the consortium of matrimony and all that that means should not be interfered with, hampered or embarrassed'.[68] In the past, contracts held prejudicial to the status of marriage have included contracts imposing a restraint on marriage,[69] contracts providing for future separation of married couples,[70] and marriage brokerage contracts pursuant to which money is paid in return for the organisation of a marriage.[71]

[18.125] However, this is a category of public policy of a greatly reduced relevance in modern society. Community attitudes to marriage have changed significantly from those that prevailed in, for example, the 1960s, let alone the turn of the century. This is illustrated by the adoption of a 'no fault' approach to divorce under the *Family Law Act* 1975 (Cth), different attitudes to unmarried cohabitation, and pre-nuptial agreements.

---

64   *Dobbs v National Bank Australasia Ltd* (1935) 53 CLR 643.
65   *South Australian Railways v Eagan* (1973) 130 CLR 506 at 513; *Scott v Avery* (1856) 5 HLC 811; 10 ER 1121. In relation to arbitration, see now the *Commercial Arbitration Act* in each jurisdiction.
66   *Lee v Showmen's Guild of Great Britain* [1952] 2 QB 329; *Baker v Jones* [1954] 1 WLR 1005.
67   See for example, *Lee v Showman's Guild of Great Britain* [1952] 2 QB 329.
68   *Newcastle Diocese Trustees v Ebbeck* (1960) 104 CLR 394 at 415 per Windeyer J.
69   *Lowe v Peers* (1768) 4 Burr 2225; 98 ER 160; cf *Minister of Education v Oxwell* [1966] WAR 39.
70   *Money v Money* (1966) 7 FLR 476.
71   *Hermann v Charlesworth* [1905] 2 KB 123.

In relation to the last of these, agreements regarding the division of finances following divorce were at one time regarded as contrary to public policy because they presumed that the particular marriage would not last until the death of at least one of the partners.[72] However, in December 2000 relevant amendments to the *Family Law Act* 1975 (Cth) came into effect; they provide that such a 'financial agreement' may be binding, if and only if:

* it is signed by both parties;
* the agreement states that both parties received independent legal advice;
* the agreement contains a certificate signed by the person providing the legal advice;
* the agreement has not been terminated or set aside by a court; and
* one party is given the original agreement and the other is provided with a copy.[73]

A financial agreement may be terminated either by a suitable provision in a replacement financial agreement or by a termination agreement.[74] A financial agreement may be set aside by a court where:

* the agreement resulted from fraud, including non-disclosure of a material matter;
* the agreement is 'void, voidable or unenforceable';
* performance of the agreement, or part of it, has become impracticable;
* new circumstances involving the care, welfare and development of a child of the marriage mean that the agreement will cause hardship for the child or the party caring for the child; or
* a party to the agreement engaged in unconscionable conduct when the contract was formed.[75]

[18.130] Inasmuch as public policy reflects issues of concern relevant to the contemporary community, it may be that the significance of provisions prejudicial to the status of marriage as a potential vitiating factor has today been reduced almost to the point of irrelevance.

18.3 Illegal contracts

[18.135] A contract may be rendered illegal either by statute or as a matter of public policy at common law. Where the circumstances may involve both manifestations, Kirby J in *Fitzgerald v FJ Leonhardt Pty Ltd*[76] suggested that the statutory interpretation questions and questions of public policy should be kept separate, and that logically, interpretation questions should be dealt with first. Where there is a statutory prohibition, the questions to be addressed are:

* Does the statute expressly prohibit the contract as formed or because of the way it was performed?
* If not, does the Act, by necessary inference, prohibit the contract as formed or because of the way it was performed?

---

72   See, for example, *Scott v Scott* (1904) 10 ALR 43.
73   *Family Law Act* 1975 (Cth), s 90G.
74   *Family Law Act* 1975 (Cth), s 90J.
75   *Family Law Act* 1975 (Cth), s 90K.
76   (1997) 189 CLR 215 at 245.

- If not, should the court, as a matter of public policy, allow the plaintiff to invoke its process to enforce the contract?[77]

The first two questions are questions of construction. There may also be issues that overlap the second and third questions.[78]

Where no statute is involved, the only question to be addressed is whether, as a matter of public policy, the court will lend its process to the plaintiff.

[18.140] Illegality is usually pleaded by a defendant who is seeking to avoid liability under a contract. It may also arise as a relevant issue in the course of a proceeding, in which case it must be addressed by the court even though it may not have been pleaded by either party.[79]

18.3.1   Illegality by statute

[18.145] The question of whether a contract is prohibited by statute is one to be decided on the specific statute and the facts of the particular case, with little assistance being obtained from any examination of the terms of other statutes or judicial considerations of them.[80]

[18.150] On occasions, a statute will expressly provide that a contract in breach of its terms, as formed or performed, is rendered illegal.[81] Such a case is purely a question of statutory interpretation and enforcement of the will of parliament.[82]

Example: Baird v Magripilis[83]

The defendant leased land in Babinda, Queensland, from the Crown. The plaintiffs were two Greek men who could speak little English. The defendant agreed to sub-lease the land, with an option to the plaintiffs to purchase, subject to the plaintiffs becoming naturalised or passing the dictation test by a date in June 1923. In the meantime, the plaintiffs, who had previously obtained possession, continued in possession and spent large sums of money in grubbing, clearing, and improving the land and planting sugar cane. The plaintiffs became naturalised in March 1923 but never passed a dictation test. They sought to have the agreement specifically enforced.

Looking at the substance of the agreement (including, for example, the giving of possession and immediate imposition of duties and obligations), it was a case of an agreement that was immediately effective, with a proviso that would discharge the agreement if it failed to occur by a prescribed date, rather than a condition precedent that prevented an agreement being effective until the happening of an event. Notwithstanding this, the Leases to Aliens Restriction Act 1912 provided that 'it shall not be lawful to ... enter into any agreement ... for any lease of any parcel of land ... with any alien who has not first obtained ... a certificate that he is able to read and write

---

77   See also *Yango Pastoral Co Pty Ltd v First Chicago Australia Ltd* (1978) 139 CLR 410 at 427–428.
78   *Fitzgerald v FJ Leonhardt Pty Ltd* (1997) 189 CLR 215 at 245.
79   As occurred in, for example, *Electric Acceptance Pty Ltd v Doug Thorley Caravans (Aust) Pty Ltd* [1981] VR 799.
80   *Tasker v Fullwood* [1978] 1 NSWLR 20 at 23; *Fitzgerald v F J Leonhardt Pty Ltd* (1997) 189 CLR 215 at 242 per Kirby J.
81   *Anderson Ltd v Daniel* [1924] 1 KB 138 at 149.
82   *Fitzgerald v F J Leonhardt Pty Ltd* (1997) 189 CLR 215 at 242–243.
83   (1925) 37 CLR 321.

from dictation words in such language as the Secretary of Public Lands may direct. Any such … agreement shall be null and void.' The agreement was therefore directly struck out by the express words of the statute. Since the plaintiffs had never passed a dictation test the agreement was rendered null and void.

[18.155] It will more commonly be the case, however, that the legislation will not contain such an express provision. In such a case, the duty of the court is to determine whether the legislation *impliedly* prohibited the contract as it was formed or performed. It may be the case that modern judges are more reluctant than in the past to imply illegality from a legislative provision where Parliament has refrained from expressly making the contract illegal.[84] Such a reluctance might be attributable to the modern prevalence of legislative provisions that might indirectly affect the contractual relations between parties and which might, if strictly applied, result in a harsh and unwarranted deprivation of rights.[85]

However, this is not to say that the implication of illegality by a court is no longer appropriate.[86] Apart from anything else, such a suggestion would be contrary to the long-standing doctrine that the duty of a court is to give effect to both express and implied intention of parliament as interpreted from the words used in the statute.[87]

[18.160] The effect of the legislation must be derived from its language and its objective.[88] Accordingly, there is not one single test for whether a contract as formed or performed is impliedly prohibited by a statute. A court may be reluctant to imply a prohibition of the contract as formed or performed where the legislation provides in a detailed way for sanctions and remedies of its terms. In such a case, there would need to be good reason for a court to add to the burden a civil penalty in the form of the deprivation of a contractual right that parliament has chosen to not expressly decree.[89] Such a deprivation of contractual rights might be 'enormous, supplementing in a wholly arbitrary way, the defined penalties for which the legislature has expressly provided'.[90] The form of a penalty expressly provided by the legislation may also be an indication of whether a contract as formed or performed, is also prohibited.

Example: Yango Pastoral Co Pty Ltd v First Chicago Australia Ltd[91]

The plaintiff lent the defendant a sum of money secured by a mortgage and several guarantees. When the defendant defaulted on the loan, the plaintiff sued the debtor and the guarantors. In their defence, the debtor and guarantors argued that the mort-

---

84   *Ross v Ratcliff* (1998) 91 FLR 66 at 67–68; *Fitzgerald v FJ Leonhardt Pty Ltd* (1997) 189 CLR 215 at 243.
85   *Fitzgerald v F J Leonhardt Pty Ltd* (1997) 189 CLR 215 at 243 per Kirby J, referring to Rose, 'Confining illegality' (1996) 112 *Law Quarterly Review* 545.
86   Cf DW Greig & JLR Davis, *Law of Contract*, Law Book Co, Sydney, 1987, pp 117–18.
87   *Fitzgerald v F J Leonhardt Pty Ltd* (1987) 189 CLR 215 at 243; *Re Bolton; ex parte Beane* (1987) 162 CLR 514 at 518 (duty of courts where legislation is involved to give meaning to the imputed purpose of parliament as found in the words used).
88   *St John's Shipping Corporation v Joseph Rank Ltd* [1957] 1 QB 267 at 287; *Yango Pastoral Co Pty Ltd v First Chicago Australia Ltd* (1978) 139 CLR 410 at 414; *Fitzgerald v F J Leonhardt Pty Ltd* (1997) 189 CLR 215 at 244.
89   *Yango Pastoral Co Pty Ltd v First Chicago Australia Ltd* (1978) 139 CLR 410 at 429.
90   *Fitzgerald v F J Leonhardt Pty Ltd* (1997) 189 CLR 215 at 244 per Kirby J.
91   (1978) 139 CLR 410.

gage and guarantees were illegal, based on the *Banking Act* 1959 (Cth), s 8. This section prohibited a body corporate from carrying on any banking business in Australia unless it possessed a relevant authority. The section prescribed a penalty of $10 000 for each day during which a contravention continued. At the time of the transaction, the plaintiff was carrying on the business of banking without an authority.

The High Court held that the plaintiff was able to enforce both the mortgage and the guarantees. The statutory provision did not *expressly* render it unlawful to borrow or lend money or to give or take a mortgage, supported by guarantee, to secure its repayment. Accordingly, the question was whether the section *impliedly* prohibited the making or performance of the contract. There were two relevant considerations in this case. The first was that the penalty the section imposed was a sum for each day during which the contravention continued. It was immaterial whether on any day the body corporate made one contract or one hundred: the penalty was the same. This was an indication the Parliament did not intend to prohibit each contract made in the course of the business, but only to penalise the carrying on of the business without an authority. Further, it was unlikely to have been the intention of Parliament for the section to impliedly render the contract illegal where the result would be 'grave inconvenience and injury to innocent members of the public without furthering the object of the statute'. If, in this case, if the result of prohibition on carrying on of banking business was that impliedly all contracts that were made or performed in the course of that business were prohibited, not only the loans secured by mortgage and guarantees but many other types of contract would be invalidated. This included all contracts pursuant to which the plaintiff had agreed to receive money from depositors, all contracts of employment with its employees, and all contracts with those who provided it with services. It was impossible to accept that Parliament had intended to invalidate all such contracts.

[18.165] The fact that a statute is passed for the protection of public safety may be another test for whether Parliament intended the section to render the contract illegal as formed or performed.[92]

Example: Pretorius Pty Ltd v Muir & Neil Pty Ltd[93]

The plaintiff sold to the defendants by wholesale certain therapeutic substances. These substances were admitted to be caught by the *Therapeutic Goods and Cosmetics Act* 1972, s 13, which provided that a person who sold therapeutic substances by wholesale was guilty of an offence unless the sale was authorised under the terms of a licence under the Act. This was complemented by s 49, which provided for a maximum penalty of $800 or imprisonment for a maximum of six months. The plaintiff sued for the price of the goods supplied. The defendants claimed, by way of defence, that the contract was impliedly illegal by reason of non-compliance with s 13, no relevant licence having been obtained.

---

92   *Fitzgerald v F J Leonhardt Pty Ltd* (1997) 189 CLR 215 at 245 per Kirby J; *Ambassador Refrigeration Pty Ltd v Trocadero Building and Investment Co Pty Ltd* [1968] 1 NSWR 75.
93   [1976] 1 NSWLR 213.

It was held that in order to determine whether the object of s 13 extended to forbidding contracts of sale without a licence, the Act as a whole needed to be considered. The preamble described the Act as regulating the manufacture, distribution, and advertising of certain therapeutic goods and to impose standards in relation to certain therapeutic goods. The Act gave extremely wide meanings to terms such as 'sale', 'wholesale', and 'therapeutic goods'. Each unauthorised sale rendered the seller liable to a severe penalty, and a number of means were used—including inspectors, seizure, forfeiture, and analysts, as well as licences—to impose a strict and rigid control on therapeutic goods. Accordingly, the whole Act was directed to the implementation of a policy designed to protect consumers of goods.[94] The object of the legislature expressed in the statute as a whole, and s 13 in particular, was to forbid contracts to sell therapeutic substances by wholesale, unless such sales were authorised by licence. The contract was therefore illegal and unenforceable, at least by the plaintiff.

A different result may follow where the purpose of a penalty imposed by a statute is merely to increase the revenue.[95]

18.3.2   Illegality at common law on the grounds of being contrary to public policy

(a)   The traditional approach

[18.170] Lord Mansfield, in *Holman v Johnson*, expressed the view that 'no court will lend its aid to a man who founds his cause of action upon an immoral or illegal act'.[96] Over time, the courts developed a list of specific instances of contracts that could be considered to be 'immoral or illegal'. These 'heads of public policy' were regarded as being finite: as was noted earlier, Isaacs J in *Wilkinson v Osborne* explained the concept of 'public policy' as 'some definite and governing principle' that the court could not initiate.[97] Accordingly, the courts were not at liberty to recognise new heads of public policy. Nevertheless, they were prepared to treat the existing heads as being malleable, and therefore able to include a new case that was analogous to an existing head.[98] In this way, public policy could keep apace with the times.

(b)   The modern approach

[18.175] The area of illegality must now be viewed in light of the High Court's decision in *Fitzgerald v F J Leonhardt Pty Ltd*.[99] In this case, Kirby J referred to the older cases of classification of cases in closed categories, but suggested that more recent decisions supported a principle 'of greater flexibility'.

---

94   This conclusion was not affected by s 13 being directed at sale by wholesale. It was apparent that regulation between wholesale and retail was no less effective, but easier to implement, than attempting to license retailers. The form of the regulation merely showed that those who drafted the legislation were familiar with the structure of the industry: ibid at 219.

95   *Cope v Rowlands* (1836) 2 M&W 149; 150 ER 707.

96   (1775) 1 Cowp 341 at 343; 98 ER 1120 at 1121.

97   See [18.10].

98   See, for example, *A v Hayden* (1984) 156 CLR 532.

99   (1997) 189 CLR 215.

The other members of the court also did not speak in terms of closed categories or heads of policy. McHugh and Gummow JJ merely referred to *Nelson v Nelson*,[100] where McHugh J had cited Lord Mansfield's dictum from *Holman v Johnson*. Similarly, Dawson and Toohey JJ simply referred to the principle in terms of the court not denying relief under the *ex turpi causa* principle unless the plaintiff has to rely upon an unlawful or immoral transaction to establish the cause of action.

[18.180] It would seem, therefore, that the High Court now supports a broader, more flexible concept of public policy not tied to the previously recognised separate heads of public policy. The significance of this was illustrated by Kirby J in *Fitzgerald v F J Leonhardt Pty Ltd*, where he raised the possibility of the principle extending to the deliberate drilling of precious water supplies, which would be regarded as anti-social in the Northern Territory context.[101] Such a case would not fit easily within any of the existing 'recognised' categories of public policy.

(c) Examples of contracts contrary to public policy

[18.185] If the above analysis is correct, the old categories or heads of policy may still serve a useful purpose as non-exhaustive illustrations of the type of circumstances in which a court may find that a plaintiff is basing his or her cause of action upon an 'immoral or illegal act'.

Contract to commit a crime or tort

[18.190] A contract to commit a crime or a tort is regarded as being contrary to public policy and therefore is illegal. Thus, for example, no action may be brought on a contract for the murder of a person.[102]

In this connection, it is immaterial whether the criminal offence is one created by the common law or by statute.[103] It would seem that knowledge of the particular law contravened is not necessary.[104] However, the commission of the offence must be more than incidental or subsidiary to the foundation or central purpose of the contract.[105]

[18.195] Similarly, public policy will be offended by a contract for the deliberate commission of a tort—as where a contract is designed to defraud a third party,[106] or to print material known to be defamatory.[107] Indeed, this rule may extend to contracts involving other civil wrongs.[108]

---

100 (1995) 184 CLR 538 at 604–605.
101 (1997) 189 CLR 215 at 251–252.
102 See also, for example, *Cowan v Milbourn* (1867) LR 2 Exch 230 (hire of rooms for delivery of blasphemous lectures, blasphemy being a criminal offence).
103 *Electric Acceptance Pty Ltd v Doug Thorley Caravans (Aust) Pty Ltd* [1981] VR 799 at 812.
104 *Waugh v Morris* (1873) LR 8 QB 202 at 208.
105 *Neal v Ayers* (1940) 63 CLR 524 at 532. See further [18.375]–[18.395].
106 *North v Marra Developments Limited* (1981) 148 CLR 42.
107 *Apthorp v Neville & Co* (1907) 23 TLR 575 (publication of manuscript concerning action for breach of promise of marriage in which plaintiff libelled his former fiancée and others).
108 See, for example, *Thorby v Goldberg* (1964) 112 CLR 597 (breach of fiduciary duty by company directors); *Munro v Morrison* [1980] VR 83 (agreement part of a scheme to defraud plaintiff's creditors).

Contracts to defraud the revenue

[18.200] A related concern involves a contract designed to defraud the revenue—in effect, a contract to defraud the general public. Thus, where the parties drafted a lease in two separate documents in order to defraud the revenue authorities, the documents were held to be illegal.[109]

[18.205] A different result may follow where the parties seek to minimise the stamp duty due on documents without any element of fraudulent conduct such as false statements or concealing the truth from the commissioner. In such a case, there is no plan to deceive.[110]

Contracts prejudicial to the administration of justice

[18.210] Contracts that have a tendency to affect the administration of justice are contrary to public policy.[111] This may include a contract that has the effect of concealing a crime or withholding evidence from a trial.

Example: A v Hayden[112]

The plaintiffs were Australian Secret Intelligence Service officers who were involved in a training exercise that included a mock raid on the Melbourne Sheraton Hotel. This exercise resulted in guests and staff of the hotel being disturbed, and property damaged. The Victoria Police wished to bring criminal charges against the individuals concerned. However, the plaintiffs sought to enforce an express term in their contracts of employment with the Commonwealth that their identity would be kept confidential.

The High Court held there was no basis for regarding the promise of confidentiality as objectionable in itself. It was nevertheless contrary to public policy because it prevented the investigation of a crime, and accordingly interfered with the administration of justice.

[18.215] It will be an interference with the administration of justice where a contract is made to stifle a prosecution—at least where the offence is of a public nature.[113] Where an offence is of a public nature, the public has an interest in seeing it prosecuted. Accordingly, a contract to provide compensation for any harm done to a victim by the accused will be regarded as contrary to public policy. The public interest in having the offender prosecuted outweighs the private benefit of the victim in being compensated for his or her injury.

Where, on the other hand, the offence is regarded as being of a private nature, a valid contract may be made to pay compensation in return for the victim promising to not pursue any prosecution for the offence.

---

109 *Miller v Karlinski* (1945) 62 TLR 85; *Effie Holdings Properties Pty Ltd v 3A International Pty Ltd* (1984) ANZ Conv R 503.
110 *Bouelvarde Developments Pty Ltd v Toorumba Pty Ltd* [1984] 2 Qd R 371 at 377.
111 *A v Hayden* (1984) 156 CLR 532.
112 (1984) 156 CLR 532.
113 *Clegg v Wilson* (1932) 32 SR (NSW) 109 at 116.

Example: Kerridge v Simmonds[114]

The plaintiff, a married woman, and the defendant had been cohabitating together. They had a falling out, and the defendant (in the words of Barton J) 'used an opprobrious expression to the woman whom he had brought to the condition of which the expression was a more or less gross exaggeration'. The plaintiff thereupon instituted proceedings against him for criminal defamation. The parties then executed an agreement under which the defendant agreed to pay the plaintiff a sum of money per month in return for the plaintiff agreeing to live apart from him, not to call upon or interfere or molest him in any way, to surrender certain letters and telegrams, and to withdraw the defamation proceedings. When the plaintiff tried to enforce the agreement, the defendant claimed that the agreement was illegal.

The High Court held that there was no objection to compromising a claim for private injury resulting from an act amounting to an indictable offence, provided it was not a matter of public concern. In this regard, there was no difference between common assault and defamation. In both cases, it was permissible for a complainant to withdraw a prosecution already instituted or agree not to institute a prosecution in return for payment of a sum of money or other consideration. Here it was clearly in the interest of society that the couple's dirty linen not be washed in public. The agreement was therefore not illegal.

Sometimes it can be difficult to decide whether particular proceedings in a given case can be called 'matters in which the public had an interest'.[115]

[18.220] Contracts involving maintenance or champerty are also regarded as being contrary to public policy and therefore illegal. 'Maintenance' refers to the giving of assistance or encouragement to a party to litigation by a person who has no interest in the proceedings, and who has no recognised motive for provision of support.[116] 'Champerty' refers to a particular form of maintenance in which a stranger to the proceedings agrees to maintain the action in return for a share in the proceedings or subject matter of the action.[117] In theory, champerty may embrace an agreement by a solicitor to represent a client on the basis of a 'contingency fee'—in other words, in return for a percentage of any judgment.

The original basis for the rule was the potential for maintenance of actions to give rise to an increase in litigation. Further, the champertor's financial interest provided strong temptation to suborn witnesses and pursue worthless claims.[118] However, today these concerns may be regarded as being outweighed by the problems facing an ordinary litigant in gaining access to courts. Accordingly, modern courts are likely to take a wide view of what might be acceptable, particularly where procedural safeguards are present.[119] The High Court has previously held that is proper for a solicitor to act for a

---

114 (1906) 4 CLR 253.
115 Ibid at 262 per Barton J.
116 *Clyne v NSW Bar Association* (1960) 104 CLR 186 at 203; *Magic Menu Systems Pty Ltd v AFA Facilitation Pty Ltd* (1997) 72 FCR 261 at 267 (Fed Ct FC).
117 *Re Trepca Mines Ltd (No 2)* [1962] Ch 511; *Magic Menu Systems Pty Ltd v AFA Facilitation Pty Ltd* (1997) 72 FCR 261 at 267 (Fed Ct FC).
118 *Magic Menu Systems Pty Ltd v AFA Facilitation Pty Ltd* (1997) 72 FCR 261 at 267 (Fed Ct FC).
119 Ibid.

client who has no means and to incur expenses despite there being no prospect of payment except by virtue of a judgment being obtained against the other party—subject to two requirements: the solicitor must believe that a client has a reasonable cause of action, and the solicitor must not bargain with the client for an interest in the subject matter of the litigation or for remuneration in proportion to the amount recovered by the client. Modern attitudes may have relaxed this second requirement.

Maintenance was at one time regarded as both a tort and a crime. Today, it might still be regarded as being a tort,[120] and for that reason a contract for its connection may be still regarded as contrary to public policy.[121]

Contracts tending to corrupt public officials

[18.225] A contract will be regarded as being contrary to public policy where it interferes with the impartial judgment of a public official, including but not limited to members of parliament or local councillors.[122]

Example: Wilkinson v Osborne[123]

Members of the NSW Parliament agreed with a land agent that they would use their influence to persuade the government to purchase a property belonging to the agent's client. After the conclusion of the sale, the parliamentarians sued the agent for the promised fee.

The High Court held that the contract was contrary to public policy. There was a clear conflict between the parliamentarians' contractual duty to press forward with the transaction regardless of the interests of the public, and their duty as members of the legislature to consider the matter impartially before voting on it. The contract was therefore invalidated.

[18.230] It seems to be sufficient if there is merely a potential for a conflict of interest. Actual corruption need not be shown.[124]

Contracts prejudicial to national security or foreign relations

[18.235] There is a public interest in the preservation of national security.[125] This notion may even extend to international security.[126] Contracts prejudicial to the national security are therefore regarded as being contrary to public policy.

[18.240] This concept may embrace a contract entered into with a national of a country at war with Australia,[127] or with a person voluntarily residing in such a country, or enemy occupied territory.[128] The reason for this approach is that such a

---

120 See, for example, *JC Scott Constructions v Mermaid Waters Tavern Pty Ltd* [1994] 2 Qd R 413.
121 Even where maintenance and champerty have been abolished as both criminal offences and as torts: see for example, *Maintenance and Champerty Abolition Act* 1993 (NSW).
122 *Wilkinson v Osborne* (1915) 21 CLR 89; *Horne v Barber* (1920) 27 CLR 494. *Wood v Little* (1921) 29 CLR 564.
123 (1915) 21 CLR 89.
124 *Horne v Barber* (1920) 27 CLR 494 at 499; *Wood v Little* (1921) 29 CLR 564.
125 *A v Hayden* (1984) 156 CLR 532.
126 Ibid, at 560 per Mason J.
127 *Ertel Bieber & Co v Rio Tinto Co Ltd* [1918] AC 260 at 274; *Hirsch v Zinc Corp Ltd* (1917) 24 CLR 34.
128 *Anglo-Czechoslovak & Prague Credit Bank v Janssen* [1943] VLR 185 at 200–201.

contract might hinder the prosecution of the war or increase the resources available to the enemy.[129]

[18.245] Public policy may also be contravened where a contract is entered into for the purpose of assisting a person act against the laws of a friendly state. This is because there is a public interest in maintaining relations with a friendly state.[130]

Contracts promoting sexual immorality

[18.250] There is old authority supporting the proposition that contracts involving immorality are contrary to public policy.[131] This concept requires the court to apply the moral standards of the day. Accordingly, what may in the past have been regarded as being contrary to public policy may not be so by contemporary standards. Thus, it has been held that contracts that have the purpose of the continuation of unmarried cohabitation are no longer contrary to public policy due to society's changed attitude towards de facto relationships.[132] Similarly, a more relaxed attitude has been shown towards prostitution and contracts that facilitate it.[133]

[18.255] While this may be a category of public policy of diminishing significance, a court may nevertheless deem a particular case to offend contemporary standards and consequently hold the agreement contrary to public policy.[134]

18.4 Effect of illegality

[18.260] In most respects, the same principles apply whether the illegality arises by virtue of statute or by reason of being contrary to public policy. Although there are some important differences in effect, these may be highlighted where they arise.[135]

18.4.1 Ex turpi causa: no action on contract

[18.265] It was noted earlier that the factor that distinguished illegal contracts from void contracts is that the maxim *ex turpi causa non oritur actio* ('no cause of action arises out of the base cause [the illegality]') is recognised as applying to the former but not the latter.

[18.270] The *ex turpi causa* maxim was explained by Lord Mansfield in the following terms:

> No court will lend its aid to a man who founds his cause of action upon an immoral an illegal act. If from the plaintiff's own stating or otherwise, the course of action appears to arise *ex turpi causa*, or the transgression of a positive law of this country, there the court says he has no right to be assisted. It is upon that ground the court goes; not for the sake of the defendant, but

---

129 Contracts already on foot when hostilities break out may be frustrated: see [22.115].
130 *Foster v Driscoll* [1929] 1 KB 470; *Regazzoni v KC Sethia (1944) Ltd* [1958] AC 301.
131 See, for example *Pearce v Brooks* (1886) LR 1 Exch 213 (hire of Brougham cab for the purposes of prostitution).
132 See, for example, *Andrews v Parker* [1973] Qd R 93; *Seidler v Schallofer* [1982] 2 NSWLR 80.
133 See, for example, *Barac v Farnell* (1994) 53FCR193 (receptionist in brothel entitled to enforce employment contract).
134 See, for example, *H v H* (1983) 13 Fam Law 180 (spouse-swapping agreement).
135 See also N Thompson, *The Rights of Parties to Illegal Transactions*, Federation Press, Sydney, 1991, p 11.

because they will not lend their aid to such a plaintiff. So if the plaintiff and the defendant were to change sides, and the defendant was to bring his action against the plaintiff, the latter would then have the advantage of it, for where both are equally in fault *potior est conditio defendentis*.[136]

[18.275] Thus, no action is available in the event of a breach of contract. In particular:

- no damages may be recovered;[137]
- amounts due under the contract cannot be recovered;[138]
- the contract cannot be terminated for breach.[139]
- specific performance will not be ordered;[140]
- an injunction compelling observance of a negative promise will not be ordered;[141] and
- other equitable remedies such as rectification will be refused.[142]

However, a person who has rendered services under an illegal contract may be able to recover a *quantum meruit* for those services.[143]

[18.280] While illegality may render a contract unenforceable, it has no effect on the passage of title. Accordingly, title to goods delivered or money paid may pass under a contract notwithstanding any illegality.[144] It seems that where a transaction is illegal, the rights of a person who is not a party to the illegal contract are not affected by its illegality unless he or she is a knowing participant in the illegality.[145]

[18.285] As Lord Mansfield observed in the last sentence of the passage quoted above, where both parties are equally at fault, the defendant is in the better position.[146] Where money or property has been transferred under an illegal contract, the defendant or possessor is in a better position, since no action may be brought to recover such money or property even where there has been a total failure of consideration.[147]

[18.290] Where a contract is illegal, it is possible for that illegality to taint a wider scheme or enterprise of which it forms part. In such a case, the same consequences as outlined above apply to each part of the scheme.[148] The question will be whether the

---

136 *Holman v Johnson* (1775) 1 Cowp 341 at 343; 98 ER 1120 at 1121.
137 See for example, *Adelaide Development Co Pty Ltd v Pohlner* (1933) 49 CLR 25; *Electric Acceptance Pty Ltd v Doug Thorley Caravans (Aust) Pty Ltd* [1981] VR 799; *Thomas Brown & Sons Ltd v Fazal Deen* (1962) 108 CLR 391.
138 See, for example, *Adelaide Development Company Pty Ltd v Pohlner* (1933) 49 CLR 25; *North v Marra Developments Limited* (1981) 148 CLR 42.
139 See, for example, *Gerraty v McGavin* (1914) 18 CLR 152.
140 See, for example, *Robertson v Admans* (1922) 31 CLR 250.
141 See, for example, *A v Hayden* (1984) 156 CLR 532.
142 See, for example, *DJE Constructions Pty Ltd v Maddocks* [1982] 1 NSWLR 5.
143 See, for example, *Clay v Yates* (1856) 1 H&N 73; 156 ER 1123 (printer who stopped work on book when discovered it to be defamatory held entitled to *quantum meruit* for work done). It may be that in such a case an innocent party is entitled to choose between contractual relief (as to which see [xx.x.xx]) and a *quantum meruit*: see N Thompson, *The Rights of Parties to Illegal Transactions*, Federation Press, Sydney, 1991, pp 105–106.
144 *Taylor v Chester* (1869) LR 4 QB 309 at 315; *Singh v Ali* [1960] AC 167.
145 *Cannon v Bryce* (1819) 3 B&Ald 179; 106 ER 628; *Portland Holdings v Cameo Motors* [1966] NZLR 571. See further [18.305].
146 This phrase is also sometimes stated as *in pari delicto potior est conditio possidentis*: where both parties are equally at fault, the possessor is in the better position: see, *Hatcher v White* (1953) SR (NSW) 285 at 298 per Herron J.
147 See, for example, *Berg v Sadler* [1937] 2 KB 158; *George v Greater Adelaide Land Development Co Ltd* (1929) 43 CLR 91.
148 *Electric Acceptance Pty Ltd v Doug Thorley Caravans (Aust) Pty Ltd* [1981] VR 799.

illegal dealing was an integral part of the whole arrangement entered into, which could have not been performed without that illegal dealing.[149]

Example: Electric Acceptance Pty Ltd v Doug Thorley Caravans (Aust) Pty Ltd[150]

Doug Thorley Caravans was a dealer in caravans. It entered into a trade agreement with the plaintiff, a finance company, under which the plaintiff would provide finance to purchasers of caravans on hire purchase terms. The parties also entered into an oral agreement under which the plaintiff agreed to pay secret commissions to the dealer. These payments were described as 'charges for after sales service' and the agreement was made orally in order to conceal them as contraventions of the *Hire Purchase Act* (Vic) 1959. The dealership prospered to the extent that the company's principals, the Thorley brothers, became embarrassed with riches. Accordingly, for financial reasons the defendant company was formed and the dealership sold to it. Part of the arrangement included an agreement ('the September agreement') under which the defendant company agreed to assume all obligations and liabilities of the old dealer. Subsequently, relying on the September agreement, the plaintiff sought to recover losses it incurred in respect of certain repossessed caravans.

It was held that the amounts could not be recovered under the September agreement. The oral agreement between the dealer and the plaintiff was illegal. This illegality tainted not only the larger scheme between those parties but also the September agreement between the plaintiff and the defendant, which sprang from and was the creature of the illegal scheme. Consequently, the September agreement could not be enforced against the defendant.

18.4.2   *Exceptional cases where a remedy is allowed*

[18.295] Lord Mansfield's concluding observation—that where the parties are equally to blame money paid or property transferred cannot be recovered—was subsequently interpreted as if the reverse also held true: in other words, where the parties were *not* equally to blame, recovery of money paid or property transferred *may* be allowed. There are differing views as to whether Lord Mansfield intended this consequence.[151]

[18.300] The courts developed a number of exceptions where a plaintiff would be entitled to recover money paid or property transferred under an illegal contract. It would seem from recent High Court *dicta*, however, that the exceptions operate more widely and represent circumstances in which a court may allow relief to be granted in either law or equity.[152] Such relief would include, but not be limited to, restitutionary claims.

In *Nelson v Nelson*,[153] McHugh J identified four situations in which courts will not refuse to grant relief despite the presence of illegality:

149 *DJE Constructions Pty Ltd v Maddocks* [1982] 1 NSWLR 5 affirmed (1982) 148 CLR 104.
150 [1981] VR 799.
151 DW Greig & JLR Davis, *Law of Contract*, Law Book Co, Sydney, 1987, p 1160 argue that when the phrase is taken in its context it may be seen that Lord Mansfield was merely reinforcing his message that the court will not grant its aid to either party; cf N Thompson, *The Rights of Parties to Illegal Transactions*, Federation Press, Sydney, 1991, p 39.
152 See *Nelson v Nelson* (1995) 184 CLR 538 at 604–605 per McHugh J; *Fitzgerald v F J Leonhardt Pty Ltd* (1997) 189 CLR 215 at 229–230 per McHugh and Gummow JJ, 249–250 per Kirby J.
153 (1995) 184 CLR 538 at 604–605.

(a) where the claimant was ignorant or mistaken as to the factual circumstances that rendered the contract illegal;

(b) where the statutory scheme that rendered the contract illegal was enacted for the benefit of a class of which the claimant is a member;

(c) where the illegal agreement was induced by the defendant's fraud, oppression, or undue influence; and

(d) where the illegal purpose has not been carried into effect.

These four exceptions warrant closer examination.

(a) Claimant ignorant or mistaken
Ignorance

[18.305] Generally speaking, where a contract is illegal as formed, the intent of the parties is irrelevant. The parties will be equally to blame, and the *ex turpi causa* maxim will apply to both of them.

An additional consideration arises in the case of contracts that are contrary to public policy. It is possible for a contract to be illegal despite outward appearances. For example, the parties may enter into a lease with an ulterior purpose of defrauding the revenue. Where a contract is on its face illegal as formed, the intent of the parties is once again irrelevant. Where, however, the contract is on its face *lawful*, the court must determine whether the intention to break the law was common to both parties. If it was, then the *ex turpi causa* maxim applies to both. If it was not, the parties will not be equally at fault. The party who did not intend to break the law may be granted relief in either law or equity.[154]

[18.310] Where the contract is not illegal as formed, but one party enters into the contract with an intent to perform it unlawfully, the parties will not be equally at fault. In such a case, only the guilty party will be prevented from obtaining relief by the *ex turpi causa maxim*.[155] The innocent party will be entitled to take advantage of any available remedies.[156]

Mistake

[18.315] The claimant also will not be equally at fault where he or she enters into the contract under a mistake of fact. Such a mistake may be as the result of the defendant's fraudulent misrepresentation.[157]

---

154 In this connection, a party intends to break the law where he or she knows or ought to know of the law and proceeds to break the law: *Archbolds (Freightage) Ltd v Spanglett Ltd* [1961] 1 QB 374; *Phoenix General Insurance Co of Greece SA v Halvanon Insurance Co Ltd* [1985] 2 Lloyd's Rep 599 at 609.

155 *Archbolds (Freightage) Ltd v Spanglett Ltd* [1961] 1 QB 374 at 388 per Devlin LJ. A contract does not become illegal where in the course of performance one party incidentally contravenes a statute uncontemplated as being involved when the agreement was made: ibid; *Lees v Fleming* [1980] Qd R 162 at 166.

156 *Ambassador Refrigeration Pty Ltd v Trocadero Building and Investment Co Pty Ltd* [1968] 1 NSWR 75 at 77.

157 See, for example, *Radford v Ferguson* (1946) 50 WALR 14 (plaintiff recovered money paid to builder falsely claiming to be registered under relevant legislation); *Hatcher v White* (1953) 53 SR (NSW) 285 (plaintiff builder recovered damages for fraud from defendant falsely claiming to have a permit for construction work under relevant legislation); *Cowan v Milbourn* (1867) LR 2 Exch 230 at 234, 235 (defendant landlord not liable for terminating lease when at time of contract unaware rooms to be used for delivery of blasphemous lectures).

[18.320] There is authority supporting recovery in circumstances where the mistake was common to both parties.[158]

(b)   Statutory protected class

[18.325] The parties will not be regarded as being equally at fault (*in pari delicto*) where the statute that renders the contract illegal is designed to protect a particular class of persons, of which the plaintiff is a member.[159]

Example: Kiriri Cotton Co Ltd v Dewani[160]

The plaintiff paid a sum of money to obtain the sublease of a flat in Kampala, Uganda. This payment was contrary to the provisions of a Ugandan rent restriction ordinance, which had the objective of protecting tenants from exploitation by land-lords and 'queue jumping' at a time of a shortage in housing. A sublease was exe-cuted, and the plaintiff went into possession. Subsequently, the plaintiff sought to recover the amount paid.

The Privy Council held that even though neither party knew that the payment was illegal, it was prohibited by the statute. Further, the statute provided for no express right of recovery of prohibited payments. However, the plaintiff was not equally at fault with the defendants. The ordinance provided for the imposition of a penalty on the person who asked for, solicited, or received a premium like the one paid by the plaintiff. The duty of observing the law was placed on the defendants, and was for the protection of lessees in the position of the plaintiff. The fact that there was no express right of recovery in the statute did not preclude recovery of the amount which had been paid.

It is insufficient if the statute is passed not for the protection of a particular defined group as a class but for the benefit of the general public as a whole.[161]

(c)   Fraud, oppression or undue influence
Fraud

[18.330] Where the defendant makes a fraudulent misrepresentation that induces a mistake, the parties will not be regarded as being equally at fault.[162] Similarly, an action for misleading or deceptive conduct under *Trade Practices Act* 1974 (Cth), s 52 may be pursued notwithstanding that the contract induced by the conduct is illegal.[163]

[18.335] The concept of fraud would also seem capable of extending to equitable fraud in the form of a breach of fiduciary duty. For example, where a company lent money to a director to purchase its own shares, although the loan was illegal under the rele-

---

158   See *Oom v Bruce* (1810) 12 East 225; 104 ER 87 (plaintiff able to recover insurance premium for cargo where both parties unaware that contract was illegal due to outbreak of war).
159   *Kiriri Cotton Co Ltd v Dewani* [1960] AC 192.
160   [1960] AC 192.
161   *South Australian Cold Stores Ltd v Electricity Trust of South Australia* (1965) 115 CLR 247.
162   See [13.115].
163   *Brownbill v Kenworth Truck Sales (NSW) Pty Ltd* (1982) 59 FLR 56.

vant corporations legislation, the company was able to recover the money. Due to the director's breach of fiduciary duty, the parties were not *in pari delicto*.[164]

Oppression or undue influence

[18.340] Further, the parties will not be equally at fault where the plaintiff has been subject to oppression or undue influence or duress when entering into the contract.[165] It has been seen elsewhere[166] that where a contract has been entered into under duress the court may grant equitable relief such as rescission or an order declaring that the contract is void.

[18.345] A broad approach to what constituted 'oppression' was taken in the decision in *Andrews v Parkinson*,[167] allowing a plaintiff to recover title to property he had transferred on the grounds that he was a 'weak-willed man' who had been subjected to 'the pressure of a strong-willed and … ruthless woman'.

(d)   Illegal purpose not carried into effect

[18.350] An illegal purpose may not be carried into effect for a number of reasons. Reasons that involve the plaintiff not being equally at fault with the defendant include where the contract is fully performed in a way that involved no illegality, and where the plaintiff repents before the contract is substantially performed.

[18.355] In the case of a performance that did not involve illegality, the High Court has stated that the mere existence of an unlawful intent in the transaction is irrelevant where in fact no part of that intent is manifested.[168]

[18.360] In the case of repentance, relief may be granted where the plaintiff has repented before any performance has taken place.[169] However, authority supports allowing a plaintiff to rescind the contract even where there has been partial performance, provided the illegal purpose is still wholly executory[170] and *restitutio in integrum* is still possible.[171] It is essential, therefore, that the illegal purpose has not been fully carried out —or at least substantially.[172] It has been suggested that the party seeking to obtain relief must give notice of his or her repentance to the other party either expressly or impliedly by conduct.[173]

---

164   *Re Ferguson; ex parte EN Thorne & Co Pty Ltd (in liquidation)* (1969) 14 FLR 311. See also *Weston v Beaufils (No 2)* (1994) 50 FCR 476 (plaintiff recovered property put in the name of solicitor at solicitor's advice in order to evade tax).

165   (1995) 184 CLR 538 at 605 per McHugh J. See, for example, *Williams v Bayley* (1866) LR 1 HL 200 (father coerced into agreement to stifle prosecution against son).

166   See [15.80].

167   [1973] Qd R 93 at 105.

168   *Payne v McDonald* (1908) 6 CLR 208 at 211; *Perpetual Executors and Trustees Association of Australia v Wright* (1917) 23 CLR 185 at 194, 198; *Martin v Martin* (1959) 110 CLR 297 at 305; *Gollan v Nugent* (1988) 166 CLR 18 at 48.

169   *Payne v McDonald* (1908) 6 CLR 208 at 212, 213.

170   *Clegg v Wilson* (1932) 32 SR (NSW) 109 at 125. DW Greig & JLR Davis, *Law of Contract*, Law Book Co, Sydney, 1987, p 1168 suggested that it may be better to allow plaintiffs to recover money on the basis of a total failure of consideration rather than on the basis of a repentance of the illegal purpose.

171   N Thompson, *The Rights of Parties to Illegal Transactions,* Federation Press, Sydney, 1991, p 89.

172   *Kearley v Thompson* (1890) 24 QBD 742.

173   N Thompson, *The Rights of Parties to Illegal Transactions*, Federation Press, Sydney 1991, at 79 relying on *Palyart v Leckie* (1817) 6 M&S 290; 105 ER 1251 and *Gatty v Field* (1846) 9 QB 431; 115 ER 1337 which suggests that a plaintiff is under an obligation to manifest an intention to withdraw from the contract.

[18.365] It appears that the repentance exception was developed about twenty years after the other exceptions were recognised.[174] After its recognition, the exception was found to have limitations. For example, the plaintiff's repentance must not be due to his or her illegal purpose being frustrated by others.[175] Further, there may be cases where the contract may be so grossly immoral that the court will not enter into any discussion of it, even where a party has repented—as where a person pays another to murder a third person.[176]

[18.370] Also, it would seem that the option of repentance is not available where the contract is prohibited by statute.[177] This is perhaps because in the case of a contract prohibited as formed by statute, the illegal purpose is regarded as having been effected by the mere making of the contract.[178]

18.4.3   A more flexible approach to relief

[18.375] Although these four exceptions may be regarded as being well established, recent High Court authority has signalled a more liberal approach to the granting of relief, including restitution of money paid or property transferred under an illegal contract—at least in the case of a statutory prohibition.[179] In *Fitzgerald v F J Leonhardt Pty Ltd*, McHugh and Gummow JJ stated that:

> Even if the case does not come within one of those exceptions, the court should not refuse to enforce contractual rights arising under a contract, merely because the contract is associated with or in furtherance of an illegal purpose, where the contract was not made in breach of a statutory prohibition upon its formation or upon the doing of a particular act essential to the performance of the contract or otherwise making unlawful the manner in which the contract is performed.[180]

Instead, a more flexible approach, outlined by McHugh J in *Nelson v Nelson*, was supported.[181] Under McHugh J's formula, courts should not refuse to enforce legal or equitable rights simply because they arose out of or were associated with an unlawful purpose unless one of two situations exists: either the statute discloses an intention that those rights should be unenforceable in all circumstances, or:

- the sanction of refusing to enforce those rights is not disproportionate to the seriousness of the unlawful conduct;
- the imposition of the sanctuary is necessary, having regard to the terms of the statute, to protect its objects or policies; and

---

174 N Thompson, *The Rights of Parties to Illegal Transactions*, Federation Press, Sydney, 1991, p 76.
175 *Alexander v Rayson* [1936] 1 KB 169; *Berg v Sadler & Moore* [1937] 2 KB 158.
176 *Tappenden v Randall* (1801) 2 B&P 467 at 471; 126 ER 1388 at 1390 per Heath J.
177 *George v Greater Adelaide Land Development Co* (1929) 43 CLR 91.
178 *Marks v Jolly* (1938) 38 SR (NSW) 351.
179 *Fitzgerald v F J Leonhardt Pty Ltd* (1997) 189 CLR 215 at 229–230.
180 (1997) 189 CLR 215 at 229.
181 Ibid, at 230 per McHugh and Gummow JJ, 250 per Kirby J.

- the statute does not disclose an intention that the sanction and remedies contained in the statute are to be the only legal consequences of a breach of the statute or the frustration of its policies.[182]

[18.380] McHugh J's more flexible approach to relief is better adapted and appropriate to accommodate the difficulty that arises where the illegality is a mere incidental accompaniment to performance of the contract. In *St John's Shipping Corp v Joseph Rank Ltd*, Devlin J posed the example of a taxi driver agreeing to drive at an excessive speed in order for the passenger to reach the destination on time. His Honour thought it curious if, in addition to any fine, the taxi driver could be penalised by the passenger refusing to pay the fare on the basis of the illegality.[183] If McHugh J's formula were applied, greater emphasis could be given to, for example, the disproportionality involved in such a result and the incidental nature of the illegality. The taxi driver would still be entitled to a remedy despite having incurred the penalty of a fine in performing the contract.[184]

[18.385] A question posed by McHugh J's formula is whether it also applies to contracts illegal at common law on the grounds of being contrary to public policy. The references to 'statute' in the formula might be interpreted as meaning that McHugh J only intended to state a more flexible approach for contracts prohibited by statute. Equally, it might be argued that McHugh J referred to statute because *Nelson v Nelson* itself concerned a case of illegality by statute. In *Fitzgerald v F J Leonhardt Pty Ltd*, Kirby J cited, alongside McHugh J's formula, a statement by Toohey J in *Nelson v Nelson* that:

> Although the public policy in discouraging unlawful acts and refusing them judicial approval is important it is not the only relevant policy consideration. There is also the consideration of preventing injustice and the enrichment of one party at the expense of the other.[185]

This would appear to advocate the adoption of a flexible approach both to contracts illegal by statute and to contracts contrary to public policy. Other judges have referred to an inherent flexibility associated with the application of public policy. For example, in *Hardy v Motor Insurers Bureau*,[186] Diplock LJ observed that:

---

182 (1995) 184 CLR 538 at 613. When he was a member of the New South Wales Court of Appeal, McHugh J foreshadowed his more flexible approach in *Hurst v Bestcorp* (1988) 12 NSWLR 394 at 445–446. There his Honour referred to the absence of the flexibility of equitable remedies where a plaintiff sought a legal remedy, and thought that restitutionary remedies, based on notions of unjust enrichment, may be useful in striking a balance where there would otherwise be an 'unmerited benefit'. These comments, while only *obiter*, were subsequently applied by the Full Court of the Federal Court in, for example, *Australian Breeders Co-operative Society Ltd v Jones* (1997) 150 ALR 488. See also the earlier statements in *Fire and All Risks Insurance Co Ltd v Powell* [1966] VR 513. The flexible approach is also consistent with the grant of a restitutionary remedy (ie a *quantum meruit* for services rendered) where statutory requirements of writing were not observed in a building contract: *Pavey & Matthews Pty Ltd v Paul* (1987) 162 CLR 221.

183 [1957] 1 QB 267 at 292.

184 See also *Fitzgerald v FJ Leonhardt Pty Ltd* (1997) 189 CLR 215 (remedy on contract not withheld from driller where water bores drilled without necessary licence since property owner was supposed to obtain licence and would otherwise obtain a windfall benefit of three free bores, and because denying a remedy would be disproportionate to the seriousness of the offence).

185 (1995) 184 CLR 538 at 597.

186 [1964] 2 QB 745.

All that the [*ex turpi causa* rule] means is that the courts will not enforce a right which would otherwise be enforceable if the right arises out of an act committed by the person asserting the right (or by someone who was regarded in law as his successor) *which is regarded by the court as sufficiently anti-social to justify the court's refusing to enforce that right.*[187] (emphasis added)

In other words, the court is called upon to make an assessment of whether an anti-social act is 'sufficient' to warrant application of the *ex turpi causa maxim.*[188]

[18.390] Also in support of a flexible approach to public policy, it may be argued that public policy is not necessarily served by, for example, denial of recovery of money paid or property transferred. Restitution may have a stronger deterrent effect than denial of recovery.[189]

[18.395] In light of the modern focus of restitution on the prevention of unjustly obtained benefit, it may be that flexibility is appropriate in the case of contracts illegal on the grounds of being contrary to public policy as well. Nevertheless, until directly addressed the question must be regarded as unresolved.

18.4.4   Action independent of the contract

(a)   The *Bowmakers* principle

[18.400] One means of evading the *in pari delicto* rule was for the plaintiff to base his or her claim for the return of money paid or property transferred under the contract on some ground other than the illegal contract. This principle originated in the decision of the English Court of Appeal in *Bowmakers Ltd v Barnet Instruments Ltd,*[190] where the Court held:

> In our opinion, a man's right to possess his own chattels will as a general rule be enforced against anyone who, without any claim of right, is detaining them, or has converted them to his own use, even though it may appear either from the pleadings or in the course of the trial, that the chattels in question came into the defendant's possession by reason of an illegal contract between himself and the plaintiff provided that the plaintiff does not seek, and is not forced, either to found his claim on the illegal contract or to plead its illegality in order to support his claim.[191]

The principle has been approved by the High Court[192] and the House of Lords.[193]

Example: Bowmakers Ltd v Barnet Instruments[194]

Certain machine tools were sold by Smith to the plaintiffs, who then entered into three hire purchase agreements with the defendants for the goods. After making only some of the payments under the hire purchase agreements, the defendants sold the

---

187 Ibid, at 767. See also *Fire and All Risks Insurance Co Ltd v Powell* [1966] VR 513 at 522–523.
188 See also *Andrews v Parker* [1973] Qd R 93 at 106 per Stable J.
189 JK Grodecki, '*In Pari Delicto Potior Est Conditio Defendentis*' (1955) 71 LQR 254 at 266–269.
190 [1945] KB 65.
191 Ibid, at 71.
192 *Thomas Brown & Sons Ltd v Fazal Deen* (1962) 108 CLR 391.
193 *Tinsley v Milligan* [1994] 1 AC 340.
194 [1945] 1 KB 65.

goods that were the subject of the first and third agreements, and subsequently refused to return to the plaintiffs the goods that were the subject of the second agreement. The plaintiffs sued to recover damages for conversion of the tools. It transpired that neither Smith nor the plaintiffs were in possession of a licence to dispose of the machine tools as required under certain wartime statutory orders.

The Court of Appeal held that the sale agreements and three hire purchase agreements were illegal. Nevertheless, title in goods may validly pass under an illegal contract. Accordingly, the sale from Smith to the plaintiffs validly transferred ownership of the machine tools to the plaintiffs. Moreover, the plaintiff's claim in conversion did not rely on the hire purchase agreements at all. Instead, it was just trying to enforce its right to possess its own chattels—a right that may be exercised against anyone who, without any claim of right, was detaining them or had converted them to his or her own use.

The English Court of Appeal observed, however, that the principle did not extend to cases where the goods claimed were of such a kind that it was unlawful to deal with them at all—as, for example, with obscene publications.[195]

[18.405] The application of the principle in the *Bowmakers* case itself is not without difficulty. Criticisms of the decision have centred on the prerequisites for the tortious actions for conversions and detinue—a matter not examined by the Court of Appeal itself.[196] The tortious action for conversion lies where the defendant 'converts' the plaintiff's goods to his or her own use, such as destroying the goods or selling them to a third party. The action requires the plaintiff to have an immediate right to possession of the goods.[197] By contrast, the tortious action for detinue lies where the defendant detains the plaintiff's goods despite the plaintiff's reasonable request for their return. Again, the plaintiff must show as a prerequisite an immediate right to possession of the goods.

The difficulty posed by the *Bowmakers* facts is that the hire purchase agreements constituted a bailment of the goods to the defendants. The type of bailment depends upon the particular contract. In particular, only a 'bailment at will' gives the bailor a right to immediate possession of the goods. Other types of bailment may require the satisfaction of particular preconditions such as the giving of a period of notice, or an act repugnant to the bailment such as the sale of the goods to a third party, before the bailor obtains a right to immediate possession. In any event, it would be necessary to have reference to the illegal contract before it can be determined whether there is the necessary immediate right to possession to ground an action for conversion or detinue.[198] A further difficulty is that in the case of the second hire purchase agreement there was not even a sale to a third party which, as an act repugnant to the bailment, might have conferred on the plaintiffs a right to immediate possession.

---

195 *Bowmakers Ltd v Barnet Instruments Ltd* [1945] 1 KB 65 at 72. This dictum was approved by the High Court in *Gollan v Nugent* (1988) 166 CLR 18 at 49.

196 Both the title of the plaintiffs and the defendant's act of conversion were conceded by the defendant.

197 *Penfolds Wines Pty Ltd v Elliott* (1946) 74 CLR 204 at 229.

198 See also JW Carter & DJ Harland, *Contract Law in Australia*, 3rd edn, Butterworths, Sydney, 1996, pp 582–583.

(b) Examples of independent causes of action

[18.410] Leaving aside the difficulty inherent in the *Bowmakers* case itself, the proposition that emerges from the case is that money paid or property transferred may be recovered where the plaintiff does not seek, or is not forced, to base the claim on the illegal contract. Such an independent cause of action would include the following.

Claims based on ownership

[18.415] If a plaintiff has title to goods, he or she is entitled to bring an action in tort for any interference with those goods. The available actions in such a case include trespass to goods (which the plaintiff must be in possession or have immediate right to possession),[199] conversion (for which the plaintiff must have an immediate right to possession),[200] and detinue (for which the plaintiff must have an immediate right to possession).[201] As already indicated, for a plaintiff to properly fit within this scenario, he or she should be able to identify at least an immediate right to possession without needing to rely on the illegal contract.

Collateral contract

[18.420] It seems that an action may be brought on a collateral contract notwithstanding that the main contract is illegal.[202]

Example: Strongman (1945) Ltd v Sincock[203]

An architect entered into a contract with a builder after the architect had assured him that he held all of the necessary licences. In fact the building contract was illegal because the architect did not have the necessary licences.

The court held that while the builder was unable to enforce the building contract, the architect's assurance took effect as a collateral contract. Its breach entitled the builder to damages.

However, reliance on the concept of a collateral contract in this context is an exercise in sophistry. Since the consideration for the collateral contract is the entering into of the main contract, the consideration for the collateral contract would be illegal. In turn, if the consideration is illegal, so must the collateral contract.[204]

(c) Modern attitudes to the *Bowmakers* principle

[18.425] Doubts have recently been expressed about the legitimacy of the *Bowmakers* principle. In *Nelson v Nelson*[205] McHugh J remarked:

---

199   See, for example, *Singh v Ali* [1960] AC 167.
200   Cf *Newcastle District Fishermen's Co-operative Society v Neal* (1950) 50 SR (NSW) 237 (claim dismissed because plaintiff required to rely on terms of contract to show defendant's acts were wrongful); *Thomas Brown & Sons Ltd v Fazal Deen* (1962) 108 CLR 391 (claim for conversion time-barred).
201   Cf *Thomas Brown & Sons Ltd v Fazal Deen* (1962) 108 CLR 391 (claim for detinue time-barred).
202   *Strongman (1945) Ltd v Sincock* [1955] 2 QB 525. Cf *Quin v Mutual Acceptance Co* [1968] 1 NSWR 122.
203   [1955] 2 QB 525.
204   N Thompson, *The Rights of Parties to Illegal Transactions*, Federation Press, Sydney, 1991, p 123.
205   (1995) 184 CLR 538.

A doctrine of illegality that depends upon the state of the pleadings or the need to rely on a transaction that has an unlawful purpose is neither satisfactory nor soundly based in legal policy. The results produced by such a doctrine are essentially random and produce windfall gains as well as losses, even when the parties are in pari delicto ... The *Bowmakers* rule has no regard to the legal and equitable rights of the parties, the merits of the case, the effect of the transaction in undermining the policy of the relevant legislation or the question whether the sanctions imposed by the legislation sufficiently protect the purpose of the legislation. Regard is had only to the procedural issues; and it is that issue and not the policy of the legislation or the merits of the parties which determines the outcome. Basing the grant of legal remedies on an essentially procedural criterion which has nothing to do with the equitable positions of the parties or the policy of the legislation is unsatisfactory, particularly when implementing a doctrine that is founded on public policy.[206]

The other members of the court shared McHugh J's disquiet that the *Bowmakers* principle meant that success of a claim should depend on the form of the action brought and the technicality of whether the plaintiff could be said to be 'relying' on the illegality.[207] McHugh J's solution was the more flexible approach to the granting of relief that he advocated, and which he saw as being a 'less extreme and more just process'.[208] It may be, therefore, that if a case does not fit within the four exceptions to *ex turpi causa*, application of McHugh J's flexible formula has now made resort to the *Bowmakers* principle unnecessary.

18.5 Severance

18.5.1 Where severance is available

[18.430] Where a contractual provision is regarded as being void or illegal, it may be possible to sever it to allow the remaining part of the contract to be enforced.[209] The notion of severance is readily applicable to cases involving covenants in unreasonable restraint of trade, or clauses that purport to oust the jurisdiction of the court. In England, doubt has been cast upon whether severance applies in the case of an illegal contract.[210] However, in Australia any such doubt was dispelled by the High Court in *Thomas Brown & Sons Ltd v Fazal Deen*,[211] which held that in an appropriate case, a court may sever an illegal promise.[212] It may be, however, that the court will take into account the nature of the illegality as a factor when deciding whether severance is appropriate in a particular case.[213]

---

206 Ibid, at 609.
207 Ibid, at 557–558 per Deane and Gummow JJ, 592–593 per Toohey J.
208 Ibid, at 612.
209 It has been seen elsewhere that severance may also be possible where a contractual provision is regarded as being uncertain: see, for example, *Whitlock v Brew* (1968) 118 CLR 445 at 460. See further [4.135]–[4.140].
210 *Bennett v Bennett* [1952] 2 KB 249; *Goodinson v Goodinson* [1954] 2 QB 118.
211 (1962) 108 CLR 391; *Langley v Foster* (1906) 4 CLR 167.
212 See also *Carney v Herbert* [1985] AC 301.
213 *McFarlane v Daniell* (1938) SR (NSW) 337 at 346 (difficult to imagine severance of promise to assassinate someone); *Electric Acceptance Pty Ltd v Doug Thorley Caravans (Aust) Pty Ltd* [1981] VR 799 at 818 (severance permitted where offence not of heinous character).

Example: Thomas Brown & Sons Ltd v Fazal Deen[214]

The plaintiff deposited with the defendant company a safe, nineteen bars of gold, and a quantity of gems, to be kept in safe custody for an indefinite period until such time as the plaintiff required them to be returned. At the time, wartime regulations required all persons who possessed gold to deliver it to the Commonwealth Bank. In 1959, the plaintiff demanded the return of the goods, without success. It transpired that the gold and gems had disappeared at some time while they were in the possession of the company.

The High Court held that so far as the agreement concerned the gold, it was illegal because it contravened the regulations. However, it did not follow that the bailment of the gems and of the safe was tainted by that illegality. Since the promises were divisible, the plaintiff retained his rights of action in respect of the gems and the safe.

[18.435] It may be relevant to enquire as to the seriousness of the illegality. Severance may be refused where the illegality is deemed to be calculated or oppressive.[215]

18.5.2 General guidelines to severance

[18.440] The question of severance depends upon a determination of the intention of the parties. Two other substantive rules are important:[216]

- severance must be achieved by taking out the objectionable parts, but must not require the court to rewrite the contract;[217] and
- severance may change the extent only but not the kind of the contract.[218]

18.5.3 Forms of severance

[18.445] Severance may take one of a number of forms: severance of a dealing within a larger enterprise, severance of an offending provision from the remainder of the contract, and severance of an offending part of a provision.

(a) Severance of associated dealing

[18.450] It has already been seen that illegality of one contract may taint a wider enterprise with which it is associated.[219] Where two or more contracts are so closely connected that the court regards them as being in effect a single commercial transaction, severance will not be possible, and the entire transaction will fall.[220]

Example: Amoco Australia Pty Ltd v Rocca Bros Motor Engineering Co Pty Ltd (No 2)[221]

Rocca and Amoco entered into a number of agreements that achieved three ends. First Rocca agreed to build a petrol service station on its land, with necessary

---

214 (1962) 108 CLR 391.
215 *Horwood v Millar's Timber & Trading Co Ltd* [1917] 1 KB 305.
216 See also N Thompson, *The Rights of Parties to Illegal Transactions*, Federation Press, Sydney, 1991, p 130.
217 See, for example, *Esso Petroleum Co Ltd v Harper's Garage (Stourport) Ltd* [1968] AC 269 at 295. This is known as the 'blue pencil test'.
218 *McFarlane v Daniell* (1938) 38 SR (NSW) 337 at 345.
219 *Electric Acceptance Pty Ltd v Doug Thorley Caravans (Aust) Pty Ltd* [1981] VR 799. See further [18.290].
220 *Amoco Australia Pty Ltd v Rocca Bros Motor Engineering Co Pty Ltd (No 2)* [1975] AC 561; *Electric Acceptance Pty Ltd v Doug Thorley Caravans (Aust) Pty Ltd* [1981] VR 799.
221 [1975] AC 561.

equipment being borrowed from Amoco. Secondly, Rocca leased the land to Amoco for 15 years. Thirdly, Amoco subleased the land back to Rocca for 15 years. The sub-lease contained a promise by Rocca to purchase all its petrol, motor oil lubricants and other petroleum products exclusively from Amoco. After five years, the parties extended the arrangements for a further five-year period. Two years later, however, Rocca began to negotiation with another petrol company for the supply of petrol and other products. Amoco sought to enforce the restraint.

The High Court was held that Amoco had a legitimate interest to protect in the form of a stable outlet for its products. However, 15 years exceeded what was rea-sonably necessary to protect that interest. The restraint was therefore void. On appeal to the Privy Council, it was held further that neither the restraint itself nor even the sublease that contained the restraint could be severed, because both were inextricably linked to the enterprise between the parties. In effect there was a 'single commercial transaction'. Accordingly, the whole enterprise was void, and Rocca was free to negotiate with another petrol company.

Where, on the other hand, the associated contracts are able to stand alone, the illegal-ity of one will not affect the enforceability of the other.[222]

(b) Severance of an objectionable promise

[18.455] An offending term may be severed where it does not form the whole or a sub-stantial part of the consideration promised by one of the parties.[223] In such a case, sever-ance will only be permitted where it was the intention of the parties that the contract was able to take effect notwithstanding the excision of the particular term.[224] Thus, for example, where a restraint of trade is regarded as being unreasonable, the entire restraint may be severed where it is merely an ancillary part of the contract between the parties.

[18.460] Although the covenantee in such a case will no longer be able to enforce the restraint against the covenantor, the advantage of this form of severance is that it may allow the covenantee to enforce the remaining provisions of the contract, one or more of which may have been breached by the covenantor in the particular circumstances.

(c) Severance of objectionable part of a term

[18.465] It may be possible to sever part only of a term, rather than the entire term. In such a case, the question is whether the covenant is divisible: in other words, where the covenant is 'not really a single covenant but ... in effect a combination of several distinct covenants'.[225]

[18.470] When determining whether the covenant is in effect a combination of several distinct promises, the court looks at the substance of the promise rather than the way the promise is expressed.

---

222 See, for example, *Dalgety and New Zealand Loan Limited v C Imeson Pty Limited* [1964] NSWR 638 at 646.
223 *O'Loughlin v O'Loughlin* [1958] VR 649 at 657; *Re Field* [1968] NSWLR 210 at 216.
224 *Brooks v Burns Philp Trustee Co Ltd* (1969) 121 CLR 432.
225 *Atwood v Lamont* [1920] 3KB571 at 593.

Example : Atwood v Lamont[226]

The plaintiff owned a general outfitter's business, which was conducted as a store comprising various departments. The defendant was the head of the tailoring department. The plaintiff obtained a covenant from the defendant that if the defendant left the employment, he would not engage in 'the trade or business of a tailor, dressmaker, general draper, milliner, hatter, haberdasher, gentlemen's ladies' or childrens' outfitter' within 60 kilometres of the town. The plaintiff argued that the covenant could be severed by excising the references to the various activities other than that of tailor, in order to be able to enforce the restraint against the defendant.

The English Court of Appeal held that the covenant was not divisible. Instead, in truth there was but one covenant for the protection of the plaintiff's entire business. The intention of the plaintiff must therefore have been to prevent the defendant from carrying on any and all of the listed activities. Since the covenant, in the form of which it was expressed, was adjudged too wide to be reasonable, the entire covenant was void.

[18.475] Severance may be permitted where the covenant can be divided into distinct promises.[227] For example, in the *Nordenfelt* case[228] the promise not to be involved in 'any other business' was held to be unreasonable. As a distinct promise, it could be severed from the remaining portion of the restraint on foot.

[18.480] Severance does not permit the court to selectively enforce an otherwise objectionable covenant. For example, if in the circumstances a restraint for 10 years within a radius of 100 kilometres is unreasonable, but a restraint for 1 year within a radius of 10 kilometres would have been reasonable, the court cannot merely enforce the 10 year, 100 kilometre restraint only to the extent of its validity (1 year and 10 kilometres). To do so would be to rewrite the covenant for the parties. In other words, at common law the effect of the severance rules on a covenant that is not divisible is an 'all or nothing' result.

(d)   Severance clauses

[18.485] A practice has developed among some drafters of contracts to include a 'severance clause' that purports to define a restraint according to what is valid, with any unreasonable aspect to be severed. Such a clause may be taken as reflecting the intent of the parties unless the clause is construed as merely an attempt to abdicate to the court the determination of the intended scope of the particular covenant.[229]

Example: Lloyd's Ships Holdings Pty Ltd v Davros Pty Ltd[230]

The plaintiff sold a ship building business to the defendant. To protect the goodwill of the business, the parties included a covenant that combined three alternative forms of conduct, ten alternative time periods (ranging from 1 to 10 years), and

---

226 [1920] 3 KB 571.
227 *Bacchus Marsh Concentrated Milk Co Ltd (in liq) v Joseph Nathan & Co Ltd* (1919) 26 CLR 410 at 434.
228 *Nordenfelt v Maxim Nordenfelt Guns and Ammunition Co Ltd* [1894] AC 535.
229 *Peters Ice Cream (Vic) Ltd v Todd* [1961] VR 485 at 490; *JQAT Pty Ltd v Storm* [1987] 2 Qd R 162.
230 (1987) 17 FCR 505.

three alternative areas of operation (ranging from the East Coast of Australia to Australia and other named countries). Clause 39 provided that it was to take effect 'as if it were several separate covenants' and 'if any of the said several separate covenants shall be or become invalid or unenforceable for any reason then such invalidity or unenforceability shall not affect the validity or enforceability of any of the other separate covenants.' The clause was determined to generate 120 alternative sub-clauses.

Spender J of the Federal Court of Australia held that a threshold question was whether the clause contemplated a single covenant. If it did, then it needed to provide a means by which to choose which of the combinations was to apply, or the clause would be void for uncertainty, and otherwise open to the separate policy objection that the parties had left the court to fix the extent of the restraint. The question was whether the technique of combining variables where each covenant generated was subject to severance amounted to a genuine attempt to define the covenantee's need for protection, with an agreement as to severance as a precaution against an 'all or nothing' result, or whether it was simply one where the parties have left to the court the task of making their contract for them. This was a question of degree, dependent on the parameters in each case, although the more numerous the variables and the more mechanical and indiscriminate the combinations the more likely the court is being asked to choose the extent of the restraint. Here, cl 39 appeared to be a bona fide attempt to fix the covenantee's need for protection, subject to severance as a precaution against possible invalidity of some of its covenants.[231]

(e) Severance under statute

[18.490] It has been noted that at common law, severance is an 'all or nothing' proposition: the court is not able to read down an objectionable promise, such as an unreasonable restraint of trade, and enforce it as far as is reasonable. This position has now been modified by statute in New South Wales, at least in relation to restraints of trade.

[18.495] The *Restraints of Trade Act* 1976 (NSW), s 4 provides that a 'restraint of trade is valid to the extent to which it is not against public policy, whether it is in severable terms or not.' The section therefore allows a court to read down an unreasonable restraint and enforce it so far as it is valid irrespective of whether or not the covenant is divisible in nature.[232]

This section is, however, subject to a proviso contained in ss (3). This proviso states, in effect, that the section cannot be called upon where there is a manifest failure by a person who created or joined in creating the restraint to attempt to make a reasonable restraint. In other words, the statute will not save a restraint where there has been no attempt to make a reasonable restraint in the first place. The onus in this case

---

231 Ultimately this was of little consolation for the covenantee, since it was held that while the widest geographical variable and the longest time variable were not unreasonable, even the narrowest conduct variable went beyond what was necessary to protect the covenantee's interest. The restraint was therefore invalid.

232 See, for example, *KA & C Smith Pty Ltd v Ward* (1999) ATPR 41-717.

is on the applicant to show there was a manifest failure to attempt to make a reasonable restraint.[233]

18.6 International perspectives

18.6.1 New Zealand

[18.500] The *Illegal Contracts Act* 1970 (NZ), s 6, provides that every illegal contract shall be of no effect and no person shall become entitled to any property under a disposition made by or pursuant to such a contract. However, the section proceeds to protect third parties who have acted in good faith and without notice of the circumstances affecting the original contract. Accordingly, a third party may acquire good title notwithstanding the illegal nature of the primary contract.

The statute further provides in s 7 that a court has discretion to grant relief as it thinks just to a party to an illegal contract, or to a person claiming through or under such a party.

[18.505] It has been held that the purpose of the *Illegal Contracts Act* is to provide the discretionary remedy in cases where the results of declaring a contract illegal are judged to be too harsh or unfair. This may arise whether the contract is illegal at common law or because it is prohibited by statute. Common law and prohibition by statute clearly provide the setting in which the *Illegal Contracts Act* was intended to operate in order to provide a remedy in some cases.[234] Accordingly, the same questions regarding the circumstances in which the common law renders a contract illegal on the grounds of public policy, including the finite list of recognised heads of public policy, and prohibition of a contract by statute arise equally in New Zealand.

[18.510] The judicial discretion to provide relief is subject to guidelines stated in s 7(3), namely that the court shall have regard to:

• the conduct of the parties;
• in the case of a breach of a statutory enactment, the object of the statute and the gravity of the penalty expressly provided for any breach; and
• such other matters as is proper.

There is also a general proviso that relief shall not be granted where to do so would not be in the public interest.

[18.515] Further principles have been developed by the courts in support of these guidelines.[235] These principles are as follows:

• relief should be granted if the policy of the statute would not be frustrated thereby;[236] by contrast, a court will refuse relief where the contract produces the very results the statute seeks to avoid,[237] or where the grant of relief would undermine a balance of competing public interests fixed by a statute;[238]

---

233 *Orton v Melman* [1981] 1 NSWLR 583.
234 *Harding v Coburn* [1976] 2 NZLR 577 at 582–583; *Ross v Henderson* [1977] 2 NZLR 458 at 465.
235 See JF Burrows, J Finn & S Todd, *Law of Contract in New Zealand*, Butterworths, Wellington, 1997, p 414–417.
236 *Harding v Coburn* [1976] 2 NZLR 577; *Hurrell v Townend* [1982] 1 NZLR 536.
237 *Euro-National Corporation v NZI Bank Ltd* [1992] 3 NZLR 528.
238 *Lower Hutt City Council v Martin* [1987] 1 NZLR 321.

- relief will rarely be granted where the contract is illegal because it interferes with the administration of justice;[239]
- relief should not be granted where it would increase the penalties or hardship suffered by a party to an illegal contract. The purpose of s 7 is a discretionary lifting of burdens, not a distribution of windfalls; and[240]
- an important factor will be the conduct of the parties, including whether there was a deliberate breach of statute or head of public policy by one or both parties.[241]

[18.520] Special provision is made in the statute for cases of unreasonable restraint of trade. Section 8 provides that in the case of a provision that constitutes an unreasonable restraint of trade, the court may delete the provision or modify the provision so that it would have been reasonable at the time the contract was entered into, and then allow enforcement of the modified provision. In other words, the statute is wider than common law severance, since the promise need not be divisible and the court is entitled to re-write the covenant to give effect to the restraint so far as is reasonable. Unlike the New South Wales *Restraints of Trade Act*, however, it is not necessary for the parties to have attempted to make a reasonable restraint in the first place as a prerequisite to the court's ability to enforce it so far as is reasonable.

Nevertheless, some aspects of the common law relating to enforcement of restraints of trade are preserved—such as the reluctance of courts to enforce restraint if its effect would be akin to enforcing specific performance of a contract of employment.[242]

18.6.2   United States

[18.525] As in Australia, the United States recognises that a contract may be adversely affected by a statutory prohibition, or on the grounds that it contravenes public policy. However, the American courts prefer to eschew the description 'void' because a court will not necessarily condemn the entire agreement as unenforceable and may instead hold the agreement to be enforceable by one and not the other party[243]—or may hold that part of the agreement is enforceable although another part is not. Nor is the term 'illegal' favoured if that connotes that some penalty is imposed on the parties apart from the courts refusal to enforce the contract.[244] Instead, the preferred epithet is that a contract may be rendered 'unenforceable'.[245]

[18.530] Sometimes United States courts faced with the question whether a penalty in a statute is sufficient without the necessity of also deeming the agreement to be unenforceable have framed the question in terms of whether the prohibited conduct is merely *malum prohibitum* (wrong because prohibited) or instead *malum in se* (wrong in

---

239 *Slater v Mall Finance and Investment Ltd* [1976] 2 NZLR 685; *Barsdell v Kerr* [1979] 2 NZLR 731.

240 *Broadlands Rentals Ltd v RD Bull Ltd* [1976] 2 NZLR 595 at 600.

241 *Equiticorp Industries Group (In Statutory management) v The Crown* (Judgment No 47: summary) [1996] 3 NZLR 586.

242 *Broadcasting Corporation of New Zealand v Daniels* (1988) 2 NZBLC 103,535.

243 *Short v Sun Newspapers* 300 NW 2d 781 (Minn 1980) (contract not void but voidable at the timely election of the defrauded party).

244 EA Farnsworth, *Contracts*, 3rd edn, Aspen Law and Business, New York, 1999, § 5.1.

245 *Kebzie & 103rd Currency Exchange v Hodge* 619 NE 2d 732 (Ill 1993).

itself).[246] However, the distinction may be of questionable guidance in practice. A more useful approach was suggested in the Supreme Court of Indiana decision in *Fresh Cut Inc v Fazli*,[247] which proposed a balancing process taking into account five factors:

- the nature of the subject matter of the contract;
- the strength of the public policy underlying the statute;
- the likelihood that refuses to enforce the bargain or term will further that policy;
- how serious or deserved would be the forfeiture suffered by the party attempting to enforce the bargains; and
- the parties' relative bargaining power and freedom to contract.

[18.535] It may be useful to enquire as to the history and purpose of the legislation in order to determine the intention of the legislature.[248] The disparity between a relatively small criminal penalty and the much greater consequences if enforcement is refused may suggest that rendering the contract unenforceable was not the intention of the legislature.[249] It has been suggested that the issue may also involve a comparison of the 'pros and cons of enforcement' and the 'reciprocal dangers of over-deterrence and under-deterrence'.[250]

It has been recognised by some courts that refusing to enforce the contract may not be the best means of giving effect to the object of the legislation. For example, it was argued by one court that the intent of the immigration laws, which prohibited aliens entering into employment agreements except in certain circumstances, should not also render unenforceable contracts of employment with aliens. Otherwise, employers would be able to employ aliens and justifiably refuse to pay them for their services. This would have the opposite effect to the intended purpose of the legislation of safeguarding American workers from unwanted competition.[251]

[18.540] A non-exhaustive list of public policy considerations invoked by American courts is similar to, but not identical with, those recognised in Australia. The list includes contracts involving:

- gaming and gambling;[252]
- restraint of trade;[253]
- prolongation of litigation;[254]

---

246 *Gardner v Reed* 42 So 2d 206 (Miss 1949).
247 650 NE 2d 1126 at 1130 (Ind 1995).
248 *Gates v Rivers Construction Co* 515 P 2d 1020 (Alaska 1973); *PM Palumbo Jr MD Inc v Bennett* 409 SE 2d 152 (Va 1991).
249 *De Cato Bros v Westinghouse Credit Corp* 529 A 2d 952 (NH 1987) (lender's breach of statute requiring disclosure of interest which was punishable as a misdemeanour did not entitle the borrower to the free use of the large amount of money).
250 *Northern Indiana Pub Service Co v Carbon County Coal Co* 799 F 2d 265 at 273 (7th Cir 1986).
251 *Gates v Rivers Construction Co* 515 P 2d 1020 at 1022 (Alaska 1973).
252 See *Irwin v Williar* 110 US 499 (1884) where it was pointed out that unlike England where wagers were not void a common law, a different attitude was taken in the United States. This appears to be on the basis that gaming 'perverts the activity of the mind, takes the heart ... depraves the affections ... becomes not only the resources of great private misery, but suggests constant temptations to fraud, and the perpetration of atrocious crimes': *Amory v Gilman* 2 Mass 1 (1806); EA Farnsworth, *Contracts*, 3rd edn, Aspen Law and Business, New York, 1999, § 5.2.
253 See [18.550].
254 *Plumlee v Paddock* 823 SW 2d 757 (Tex App 1992). See [18.545].

- restraints on alienating property;[255]
- interference with the administration of justice;[256]
- corruption of elected and government officials;[257]
- promises involving a contract to commit a crime, tort or fiduciary duty; and[258]
- interference with family relations.[259]

[18.545] In relation to prolongation of litigation and interference with the administration of justice American courts, unlike Australian courts, have long regarded champerty and maintenance as being rendered obsolete by modern judicial procedure and an independent judiciary.[260]

[18.550] In relation to restraint of trade, Federal antitrust laws and similar State legislation have eroded the areas of operation of the common law. Where the common law still applies, a threshold question posed by American courts is the requirement of 'ancillarity'. Shortly stated, this requirement means the restraint must be ancillary to an appropriate transaction or relationship.[261] An example of a non-ancillary restraint that serves no interest of the covenantee and will therefore be necessarily unreasonable is where one business person obtains a promise from another business person that he or she will not to compete in the same locality. Such a restraint is non-ancillary because it is not attached to any transaction.[262] Similarly, a promise not to bid at an auction has been held to be a non-ancillary restraint.[263] Apart from the requirement of ancillarity (which may be accommodated within Australian law, even if it is not made as overt as it is in America), there are the familiar concepts of the covenantee requiring a legitimate interest, the restraint going no further than is necessary to protect that interest, and the restraint not causing unreasonable hardship to the covenantor or injury to the public.[264] As in Australia, the reasonableness of the restraint is judged in terms of the type of activity, geographical area, and time.[265] American courts also recognise that where an unreasonable restraint is divisible, it may be possible to sever the offending portion of the restraint and to enforce the balance. A court may allow the contract to be enforced by a party who is excusably ignorant;[266] and the effects of illegality may also be mitigated by permitting restitution where the court decides that there has been unjust enrichment.

---

255   *Proctor v Foxmeyer Drug Co* 884 SW 2d 853 (Tex App 1994).
256   See, for example, *Griffeth v Harris* 116 NW 2d 133 (Wis 1962) (agreement by expert witness to give favourable testimony); cf *Blair Milling Co v Frutager* 15 P 286 (Kan 1923) (settlement agreement not shown to have been made in return for promise not to prosecute if the loss was paid or secured).
257   *An-Cor v Reherman* 835 P 2d 93 (Okl 1992) (a corporation agreement to pay mayor in order to secure support for its lease).
258   *Sayres v Decker Auto Co* 145 NE 744 (NE 1924) (agreement to defraud insurance company); *Dubbs v Kramer* 158 A 733 (Pa 1931) (agreement by company director to vote for a particular person as vice president amounting to breach of fiduciary duty to shareholders).
259   See [18.555].
260   *Grant v Stecker & Huff* 1 NW 2d 500 (Mich 1942).
261   *United States v Addyston Pipe & Steel Co* 85 F 271 (6 Cir 1898); Restatement (Second) § 187.
262   *Dyson Conveyor Maintenance v Young & Vann Supply Co* 529 So 2d 212 (Ala 1988).
263   *Gibbs v Smith* 115 Mass 592 (1874).
264   *Weaver v Ritchie* 478 SE 2d 363 (W Va 1996).
265   *Riggs v RR Donnelley & Sons Co* 589 F 2d 39 (1st Cir 1978).
266   *Weinsklar Realty Co v Dooley* 228 NW 515 (Wis 1930).

[18.555] In relation to interference with family relations, the primary focus is on the marriage relationship. Even here, it is recognised that society has changed and the sanctity of the marriage relationship is no longer as it once was. In a recent case the Supreme Court of California upheld a 'cohabitation contact' between married couples providing for distribution of property accumulated should they separate.[267] Such a contract was regarded by the court as being unenforceable only to the extent that they explicitly rested upon the 'immoral and illicit consideration of meretricious sexual services'.[268]

[18.560] Certain types of exemptions clauses have also been held to be unenforceable on the grounds of public policy. This has been where the exemption is regarded as affecting the public interest and the other contracting party is a member of a protected class. This may arise in the case of an employer attempting to exempt itself from liability in negligence to its employee[269] and a common carrier or public utility attempting to exempt itself from liability to a passenger or customer, although it may be possible to limit liability to a reasonable amount in return for payment of a lower rate.[270]

Some courts recognise a third category in which exemption clauses in residential leases are not enforceable,[271] while exemption clauses have also been struck down as being contrary to public policy in the case of a standardised release from liability for negligence imposed as a condition for admission to a public hospital.[272] Similar reasoning has led to exemption clauses being held unenforceable in the case of releases for inter-scholastic athletics[273] and the provision by a State University of recreational activities such as a rugby club purportedly without liability.[274] By contrast, exemption clauses have been upheld in the case of activities that are recreational in nature and known to be dangerous.[275]

18.6.3 Japan

[18.565] The legality of contract in Japan is regulated at two levels. At the more abstract level, contracts must not infringe 'public policy or good morals' (Civil Code art 90). The effect of ignoring this mandatory provision of the Civil Code is that the contract will be void. It follows that contracts that are traditionally treated as illegal in the common law, such as contracts for prostitution or contracts to murder another

---

267 *Marvin v Marvin* 557 P 106 (Cal 1976).
268 Ibid at 113.
269 *Pittsburgh CC & St Louis Railway v Kinney* 115 NE 505 (Ohio 1916).
270 *Curtiss-Wright Flying Service v Glose* 66 F 2d 2710 (3rd Cir 1933) (common carriers when dealing with passengers cannot compel them to release the carriers from liability for their own negligence); *cf Hart v Pennsylvania Rail Road* 112 US 331 (1884) (limitation of liability is just where the effect of the agreement is to cheapen the freight).
271 *Hiett v Lake Barcroft Community Association* 418 SE 2d 894 (Va 1992) ('provisions for release from liability for personal injury which may be caused by future acts of negligence are prohibited "universally"'); *McCutcheon v United Homes Corp* 486 P 2d 1093 (Wash 1971) (clause exempting land lord to anyone in common areas held invalid since it did not deal with a purely private affair).
272 *Tunkl v Regents of University of California* 383 P 2d 441 (Cal 1963).
273 *Wagenblast v Odessa School District* 758 P 2d 968 (Wash 1988).
274 *Kyriazis v University of West Virginia* 450 SE 2d 649 (W Va 1994).
275 See, for example, *Falkner v Hinckley Parachute Center* 178 Ill App 3d 597, 533 NE 2d 941 (1989) (parachute training centre); *Marshall v Blue Springs Corp* 641 Ne 2d 92 (Ind App 1994); *Huber v Hovey* 501 NW 2d 53 (Iowa 1993) (race track liability to spectator).

person are also void in Japanese law. Contracts that appear valid, but have as their purpose something that conflicts with public policy can also be avoided through the application of article 90.

[18.570] In commercial transactions, article 90 can also be used to void or partially void contracts. Examples include contracts where an undue profit has been achieved; contacts that are one-sided and take advantage of someone's ignorance, distress, or haste.[276]

[18.575] Beyond the broad application of Civil Code article 90, individual contract types are often subject to regulation under other, special laws. It follows that these contracts may be rendered illegal or wholly or partly void for failure to comply with mandatory provisions of this other legislation. Examples of key legislation include: the *Consumer Contract Law* 2000; the *Insurance Industry Law* 1995; the *Antimonopoly Law* 1947 and specific laws relating to sales—for example, the *Door to Door Sales Law*. Other examples include the *Interest Rate Restriction Law* and the *Land and House Lease Law*.

---

276   In relation to penalties, see [xx.x.xx].

Part VI

Discharge of the Contract

A validly formed contract may be discharged in several ways. In each case, the parties will be released from their future obligations under the contract—but the difference in each method of discharge lies in the residual liability of the parties to each other. First, the usual way a contract is discharged is by performance. Once both parties have performed the contract it will be discharged, and neither party will be under any obligation to the other. This is considered in Chapter 19: Discharge by performance. Secondly, the question of performance is inextricably connected with the issue of breach of contract. Generally, a party who has not performed the contract will be in breach. This may also result in a discharge of the contract, but this time for breach of the contract. Discharge of a contract for breach is referred to as termination for breach. Termination for breach will usually occur as a result of the unilateral act of one of the parties to the contract. A contract will not automatically terminate for breach. This type of discharge will also release the parties from their future obligations, but an important difference lies in the resulting liability of one party to pay compensation to the other for his or her breach. Termination for breach is considered in Chapter 20 and the issue of compensation is considered in Chapter 23: Damages. The third way a contract may be discharged is through frustration. This will occur where a supervening event has made performance of the contract in the manner contemplated impossible. In contrast to termination for breach, a frustrating event will automatically discharge the contract, but it will not result in liability to pay compensation to the other party. Both parties are released from the contract for the future, but accrued obligations are enforceable. Frustration is considered in Chapter 22. The final method of discharge discussed is by agreement of the parties. The parties may agree to discharge each other from further performance of the contract. In most cases, some form of consideration will be payable for this agreement. Discharge by agreement is discussed in Chapter 21.

Part VI examines the effect of each form of discharge on a validly formed contract and the resulting effect on the obligations of the parties.

Chapter 19

Discharge by performance

19.1   Effect of performance on a contract

[19.05] Performance of a contract according to its terms is one of the ways a party will be discharged from further performance of a contract.[1] In order to discharge a party from his or her obligations under a contract, performance must be exact, except for insignificant defects in performance.[2] What constitutes exact performance of any particular contract can only be determined after careful consideration of the contract's terms. Some contracts may require all of the particular party's obligations to be performed exactly, without defect; others may allow for discharge of the parties' obligations after only their substantial performance.[3]

[19.10] Once a contract has been performed according to its terms, it will be discharged. This means the parties are no longer obliged to perform any of the terms of the agreement and will have no liability to each other.[4] This will not be the case where one or both of the parties have failed to perform their obligations exactly. The first effect of a failure to perform is that the contract price is not payable. The obligation to pay the contract price is usually conditional upon performance of the contract by the other party exactly in accordance with its terms. The imposition of exact performance as a requirement for obtaining the contract price has been viewed as harsh and unfair,[5] giving way to the contract price being recoverable where the obligation is substantially performed. The second effect is that the party who has failed to perform his or her obligations will be liable to the other for breach of contract. This may result in the contract's being terminated for breach and damages being sought by the innocent party.[6] This chapter examines performance of the contract in two related parts:

* matters impacting upon whether the contract has been performed; and
* the effect of a failure to perform on recovery of the contract price.

[19.15] Other effects of a failure to perform—the right to terminate the contract and to seek damages—are considered separately in chapters 20 and 23.

---

1   A contract may also be discharged by termination (see Chapter 20), frustration (see Chapter 22) and agreement (see Chapter 21).

2   See *Shipton Anderson & Co v Weil Bros & Co* [1912] 1 KB 574.

3   For example, in *Luna Park (NSW) Ltd v Tramways Advertising Pty Ltd* (1938) 61 CLR 286 at 304, the Court considered that the obligation to display signs on trams for 8 hours a day was satisfied by the display of signs for substantially 8 hours a day.

4   This should be contrasted with discharge by termination where although the parties do not have to perform any future obligations under the contract, liability to pay damages for breach or pay compensation pursuant to the contract may survive.

5   *Hoenig v Isaacs* [1952] 2 All ER 176.

6   Termination for breach of contract is considered in Chapter 20. Damages for breach of contract are considered in Chapter 23.

19.2 Matters impacting on performance

[19.20] Whether a contract has been performed—and consequently, whether there is an obligation to pay the contract price—can only be determined by examining the various terms of the particular contract. Issues for consideration may fall within the following broad categories:

- Have the obligations been performed on time?
- Is the obligation to pay dependent upon the other party's obligation to perform the contract?

19.2.1 Time considerations

[19.25] Generally, a contract will provide for the obligations of the parties to be performed within certain time frames. For example, a contract for the sale of land will usually provide that the purchase monies are to be paid on a specified date in exchange for the title to the property. Similarly, in a contract for the sale of goods, delivery of the goods, and the price paid, will usually be specified to occur on a certain date. Contracts will vary in approach to the specification of time frames, but generally a contract specifies a date for performance, or is silent about the time for performance.

[19.30] Where a date for performance of the contract is stated, it will be necessary to determine whether or not the date is essential to the performance of the contract. The rules governing when time will be of the essence are considered at [20.250]–[20.260]. For the purposes of determining whether the contract has been performed, the significant issue is the effect of complying or not complying with a time provision—whether it is essential or inessential.

[19.35] Where a particular date is specified for performance of an obligation under the contract, that date may be either essential or inessential. If it is essential, a failure to perform exactly at the time specified will be a breach of the contract entitling the other party to terminate the agreement. The effect of termination is to discharge the contract for the future,[7] but the party in breach is liable to pay compensation and is not able to claim the contract price.[8] If the time provision is inessential, a failure to perform will also constitute a breach of contract. However, the difference will be that the other party will not be entitled to terminate; and although the party in breach may be liable to pay compensation, there is still a possibility that the contract price may be recoverable if the contract is substantially performed.[9]

[19.40] If the time for performance is not specified, the contract must be performed within a reasonable time.[10] What constitutes a reasonable time is a matter of fact to be determined at the time when performance is alleged to be due.[11] Failure to perform within a reasonable time will be a breach of the contract, but the other party will not

---

7   *McDonald v Dennys Lascelles Ltd* (1933) 48 CLR 457.
8   *Sumpter v Hedges* [1898] 1 QB 673.
9   See [19.140]–[19.180] in relation to the recovery of the contract price for substantial performance *Hoenig v Isaacs* [1952] 2 All ER 176.
10 *Perri v Coolangatta Investments Pty Ltd* (1982) 149 CLR 537 at 543, 554, 556, 567; *Goldcoast Oil Co Pty Ltd v Lee Properties Pty Ltd* [1985] 1 QdR 416 at 421.
11 For example, see *Perri v Coolangatta Investments Pty Ltd* (1982) 149 CLR 537 at 567.

be entitled to terminate the contract immediately. The breach will be classified and have the same effect as a breach of an inessential term. This means that although compensation may be payable, the party in breach will be entitled to recover the contract price if substantial performance of the contract has occurred.

19.2.2   Type of obligation

[19.45] An obligation to perform a contract may be broadly classified as either dependent or independent. This classification is relevant to the question of performance and a claim for the contract price because, if the obligation to pay the contract price is independent, there will be no requirement for the other party to perform his or her obligations prior to a claim for the contract price. On the other hand, if the obligation to pay the contract price is dependent, the other party will have to perform his or her' obligations before an obligation to pay the price arises.[12]

(a)   Independent obligations

[19.50] An independent obligation is where one person must perform, regardless of whether the other does so. One modern example is where a contract for the sale of goods provides for payment on a certain day, irrespective of whether the goods are delivered by that time.[13] Where the obligations are independent, either party may call upon the other to perform without having first performed his or her obligations. This may result in one party being obliged to pay the contract price without receiving goods or services in return.

(b)   Dependent obligations

[19.55] Most obligations in modern contracts for the sale of goods, land or employment are dependent. This means one party must perform his or her obligations before the other. In other words, the performance of the contract by the second party is dependent on performance by the first party. For example, a buyer is not required to pay for goods until the seller delivers the goods in accordance with the contract and they are accepted by the buyer.[14] Only once the goods are delivered and accepted is the purchaser obliged to pay the contract price. It also follows that the seller is only able to claim the contract price from the buyer once the goods are delivered and accepted by the buyer. This is because the contract price is payable for the actual goods, and not for the willingness or promise to deliver the goods. A further consequence of the obligations being dependent is that if a buyer refuses to accept the goods when delivered, the seller will only be able to claim damages, not the contract price. The reason for this is that the obligation to pay the price is dependent upon the other party's providing the goods or services as required under the contract. If the goods or

---

12   See, for example, *Automatic Fire Sprinklers v Watson* (1946) 72 CLR 435.
13   s 50(2) *Sale of Goods Act* 1896 (Qld); *Sale of Goods Act* 1954 (ACT), s 52(2); *Sale of Goods Act* 1923 (NSW), s 51(2); *Sale of Goods Act* 1972 (NT), s 51(2); *Sale of Goods Act* 1895 (SA), s 48(2); *Sale of Goods Act* (1896) (Tas), s 53(2); *Goods Act* 1958 (Vic), s 55(2); *Sale of Goods Act* 1895 (WA), s 48(2).
14   See also *Sale of Goods Act* 1896 (Qld) s 51(2); *Sale of Goods Act* 1954 (ACT), s 52(2); *Sale of Goods Act* 1923 (NSW), s 51(2); *Sale of Goods Act* 1972 (NT), s 51(2); *Sale of Goods Act* 1895 (SA), s 48(2); *Sale of Goods Act* (1896) (Tas), s 53(2); *Goods Act* 1958 (Vic), s 55(2); *Sale of Goods Act* 1895 (WA), s 48(2).

services are not provided, the obligation to pay the price does not arise.[15] Once the contract is terminated for breach, the aggrieved party is limited to a claim for damages or enforcement of the obligations that accrued prior to termination.[16]

(c) Dependent and concurrent obligations

[19.60] While the obligations under a contract for the sale of land or goods are described as dependent, it should be noted that performance of those obligations will usually take place concurrently. A purchaser of land will pay the purchase price in exchange for, and at the same time as, the vendor delivers title and possession of the property to the purchaser. Concurrent performance of a dependent obligation adds another layer of complexity when considering termination of a contract for breach, but has little impact upon a claim for recovery of the contract price. In reality, there will be little opportunity for substantial performance where the obligations are both dependent and concurrent. As the obligations are to be performed at the same time are usually obligations concerning title, delivery and payment, generally any failure to perform will not be considered to be of a minor nature.

19.3 Effect of failure to perform on recovery of the contract price

[19.65] If the contract is performed exactly according to its terms, it will be discharged. If the performance is defective in any respect, the rights of the parties need to be considered. The primary issues will be whether the contract price is recoverable despite the defective performance—and, if the contract price is not recoverable, whether any compensation is payable for the work performed. In addition, a failure to perform the contract according to its terms will be a breach of the contract. The issues related to recovery of damages for breach are considered in Chapter 23.

19.4 Overview

[19.70] Clearly, a party who performs a contract exactly according to its terms is entitled to enforce the contract by claiming the contract price, seeking damages, or pursuing an equitable remedy. In this chapter, the right of a party to claim the contract price in circumstances where the contract has not been performed exactly is considered.[17] As a general proposition, a party who has not performed a contract exactly is not entitled to payment of the contract price. This proposition is premised on the obligations under the contract being dependent.[18] In other words, if the party performing the work or providing the goods does not comply with the terms of the contract, the dependent obligation to pay the contract price will not arise. The application of this principle may vary, however, depending upon a construction of the contract entered

---

15   *Automatic Fire Sprinklers Pty Ltd v Watson* (1946) 72 CLR 435 at 464–465 per Dixon J.
16   See [20.470]–[20.530] in relation to the effect of termination on the rights of the parties.
17   Claims for damages are considered in Chapter 23 and equitable remedies are considered in Chapter 25.
18   See [19.55]. If the obligations were independent, the contract price would be recoverable despite the defective performance.

into between the parties and the type of performance rendered. Despite the fact that some contracts may appear on their face to indicate that no part of the contract price should be paid unless total performance is rendered, the courts have recognised that this causes undue hardship in most cases. There is a growing tendency by the judiciary to prefer a construction of the contract that will not lead to such a drastic result. Denning LJ gave the first indication of such an approach in *Hoenig v Issacs*:[19]

> When a contract provides for a specific sum to be paid on completion of specified work, the courts lean against a construction of the contract which would deprive the contractor of any payment at all simply because there are some defects or omissions.[20]

[19.75] This statement is consistent with the approach currently taken by the courts to the question of whether the contract price is recoverable. The court will usually give consideration to both aspects of this statement: the nature of the obligation to pay the contract price and the nature of the performance rendered by the performing party.

19.5 Construing the contract and the performance of the parties: a modern approach

[19.80] Some commentators[21] and judges have recognised the existence of two broad categories of contracts:

- entire contracts; and
- divisible contracts.

[19.85] The judgment of Denning LJ in *Hoenig v Issacs*[22] appears to create a third type of contract, which has been referred to as a 'lump sum contract' by other commentators. This type of contract may be described as containing a reference to the performance of specific work for the payment of a specific amount of money, but complete and exact performance will not be a condition precedent to payment.

[19.90] The writers of this text suggest that in reality there are only two types of contract: those that are divisible and those that are not. Contracts that are not divisible may simply be given the broad description of lump sum contracts. Any distinction between different types of lump sum contracts should be drawn on the basis of the obligations of the parties as expressed in the contracts. An approach that attempts to classify contracts as being of certain types, from which set consequences may flow, gives an unduly simplistic picture of the judicial process. In reality, the ultimate decision to allow recovery of the contract price will depend upon a detailed construction of the contract and the parties' obligations under that contract. A classification of the contract as being entire or lump sum may not account for the complexity of the actual

---

19   [1952] 2 All ER 176.
20   Ibid at 180.
21   JW Carter & DJ Harland, *Contract Law in Australia*, 3rd edn, Butterworths Sydney, pp 617; Seddon & Ellinghaus, *Cheshire & Fifoot's Law of Contract*, 7th edn, Butterworths Sydney, pp 851–852.
22   [1952] 2 All ER 176.

contract, and lead to an elementary analysis. While the obligation to pay the ultimate contract price may require entire performance, other obligations in the contract may not be entire in their nature. A more helpful analysis of the modern approach taken by the courts concentrates on:

1   Is the contract divisible?[23]

2   (a)   If it is not divisible, what is the nature of the parties' obligations under the contract?

(b)   If the contract is divisible, what is the nature of the parties' obligations in respect of each divisible part of the contract?[24]

(i)   Was the performance rendered sufficiently in accordance with the contract (was it in fact entire or substantial) so as to entitle that party to payment of the contract price either for the whole of the contract or for the relevant divisible parts?[25]

(ii)   If the contract price is not recoverable is other compensation available?

19.6   When is a contract divisible?

19.6.1   Definition

[19.95] The description 'divisible or severable contract' is most appropriately given to a contract in which the consideration and the payment for it are apportioned or are capable of apportionment according to the work to be done.[26] A contract that provides for a seller to provide 1000 carburettors to a buyer at $10 each at the following times: 350 by the 30/6/92; 350 by the 30/8/92; and the balance on or before the 30/9/92; with payment upon delivery, will be divisible. The contract itself has divided the performance of the work and the payment of the consideration expressly.

[19.100] An example of a contract where the payment was *capable* of apportionment can be found in *Steele v Tardiani*.[27] Although the contract itself did not specify that it was divisible, the High Court considered the contract to be 'infinitely' divisible.[28] This finding allowed the defendants to claim the contract price or a rateable proportion for the work performed according to its terms.[29]

[19.105] A contract which is not divisible should be classified as a lump sum contract. A lump sum contract may be defined as a contract which provides for payment of a specific sum upon the completion of specific work.

19.6.2   Relevance to recovery of the contract price

[19.110] Whether a contract is divisible or not may affect a court's ultimate decision about the payment of the contract price. A contract that is not divisible will usually

---

23   See [19.95]

24   See [19.115]–[19.185].

25   See [19.115]–[19.185].

26   *Steele v Tardiani* (1946) 72 CLR 386 at 401; *Baltic Shipping Co v Dillon* (1993) 67 ALJR 228 at 231 per Mason CJ when distinguishing an entire agreement.

27   (1946) 72 CLR 386.

28   Ibid at 401.

29   Recovery of a *quantum meruit* for work not performed in accordance with the contract in *Steele v Tardiani* (1946) 72 CLR 386 is considered at [19.265].

provide for a specific sum of money to be paid in exchange for the performance of certain work. In that case, the court would consider the whole of the performing party's obligations under the contract and whether the performance that was rendered satisfied the requirements of the contract as a whole. Where a contract is divisible, the court will consider each divisible part of the contract separately, as though they were separate agreements. Instead of considering all of the party's obligations of performance under the contract, the court will only consider the obligations relating to the particular divisible part of the contract. This will result in the party performing the contract being able to recover after each part of the contract is performed, notwithstanding that the whole contract has not been completed. For example, consider a contract that provides for a seller to provide 1000 carburettors to a buyer at $10 each at the following times: 350 by the 30/6/92; 350 by the 30/8/92; and the balance on or before the 30/9/92; payment to be made on delivery of each shipment. A seller who provided only the first two lots would be entitled to payment for those lots, as the contract is divisible into parts, and two of the parts have been performed. Payment for the final part of the contract will depend only on performance of that part. By contrast, if the contract was a lump sum contract for 1000 carburettors at $10 each, and the seller delivered 700 carburettors on the date for delivery, no part of the contract price would be recoverable.[30]

19.7 Nature of the parties' obligations under the contract

19.7.1 Dependent or independent

[19.115] After identifying whether the contract is divisible, the court will generally proceed to consider the nature of the parties' obligations under the contract, either as a whole, or considering each divisible part. The first issue of interpretation for the court will be whether the obligations of the parties are dependent or independent. Consideration has already been given to the difference between a dependent obligation and an independent obligation in a contract.[31] If the obligation to perform is independent of the obligation to pay the contract price, the issue of whether the performance is in accordance with the contract becomes redundant. An independent obligation to pay the contract price will not, by its very nature, be dependent on proper performance of the contract. This means that provided any conditions precedent—such as payment being due on a particular date—have been met, the contract price will be payable.

[19.120] If the obligations to pay the contract price and provide services or goods are dependent, the court will have to give further consideration to the parties' obligations. In particular, the court will be concerned with whether the contract price is payable only after exact performance of the obligation to provide services or goods, or whether substantial performance of the obligation will entitle that person to the contract price.

---

30   It is unlikely that this would be substantial performance of the contract. See [19.140]–[19.180] in relation to substantial performance.

31   See [19.45]–[19.60].

19.7.2 Exact performance: entire obligations

[19.125] The general rule is that the contract price or any part of it is only payable in exchange for exact performance of the whole contract—or, in the case of a divisible contract, exact performance of the particular part of the contract. Due to the often harsh and inequitable result achieved from an application of this rule, judicial opinion has swayed in favour of a less strict requirement of substantial performance.[32] Nevertheless, there may be contracts where the terms clearly indicate that 'the consideration for the payment of money or for the rendering of some other counter performance is entire and indivisible'.[33] This type of obligation may be referred to as an entire obligation (that is an obligation to perform the entire contract exactly). Essential features of such an obligation are:

1 complete performance is a condition precedent to payment of the contract price;

2 the benefit expected by the defendant is to result from the enjoyment of every part of the work jointly; and

3 the consideration is neither apportioned by the contract nor capable of apportionment.

[19.130] The mere fact the contract provides for the contract price to be payable in a lump sum or 'payable on completion'[34] is not enough for the obligation to be entire. The contract must indicate that complete performance of the obligation to provide services or goods is a *condition precedent* to payment.[35] A simple example is a contract for the making and sale of a pair of shoes. The shoemaker could not give the customer one shoe and expect the contract price. It would be clear from the contract that full and complete performance—provision of a pair of shoes—would be required prior to payment of the price.

[19.135] A further example of a contract where the contract price was only payable for exact performance (that is, entire performance of the contract) can be found in *Cutter v Powell*.[36]

Example: Cutter v Powell[37]

A seaman agreed to work on a ship making a voyage from Jamaica to Liverpool. The defendant agreed to pay him 30 guineas upon his arrival in England, provided he continued to do his duty on board for the period of the voyage. The voyage took 2 months, but Cutter died 6 weeks into the voyage. Cutter's administratrix commenced an action for the contract price or a *quantum meruit*.[38] The Court of Kings Bench held that the contract was entire and therefore, the estate was not entitled to recover either under the contract or on a *quantum meruit*. Ashhurst J said:

---

32 See *Hoenig v Isaacs* [1952] 2 All ER 176 per Denning LJ; *Steele v Tardiani* (1946) 72 CLR 386 at 401; and the commentary at [19.140]–[19.185].

33 *Baltic Shipping Co v Dillon* (1993) 67 ALJR 228 at 231. See also *Phillips v Ellinson Brothers Pty Ltd* (1941) 65 CLR 221 at 233–234 per Starke J.

34 As was the case in *Hoenig v Isaacs* [1952] 2 All ER 176 where the obligation to pay the price arose in exchange for substantial performance of the contract.

35 *Purcell v Bacon* (1914) 19 CLR 241; *Phillips v Ellinson Brothers Pty Ltd* (1941) 65 CLR 221; *Baltic Shipping Co v Dillon* (1992) 176 CLR 344.

36 (1795) 6 TR 320; 101 ER 573.

37 (1795) 6 TR 320; 101 ER 573.

38 *Quantum meruit* is discussed at [19.225]–[19.235].

as it [the contract] is entire, and as the defendant's promise depends on a condition precedent to be performed by the other party, the condition must be performed before the other party is entitled to receive anything under it.[39]

The fact that Cutter was required to proceed, continue, and do his duty for the whole of the voyage indicated that the contract—and therefore his obligation of performance—was entire, and that he was only entitled to payment if he completed the voyage. The court was also influenced by the lack of any prevailing custom in relation to the particular type of contract and the significantly high amount of money payable under the contract compared with the usual monthly wage. This in itself seemed to be an indication to the court that the parties intended an 'all or nothing' result.

19.7.3   Substantial performance

[19.140] Where the contract does not clearly and expressly provide that exact performance[40] is a condition precedent to payment of the contract price, 'the courts will lean against a construction which would deprive the party of any payment'[41] simply because of defects. If the obligation to perform is not entire in nature, the fulfilment of every part of the obligation will not necessarily be essential to payment of the contract price, even though the obligations of the parties are dependent. The very fact that exact and complete performance is not specified in the contract has allowed the courts to alleviate the strictness of the exact performance rule. It has been accepted by Australian and English courts that a promisor who substantially performs a contract (or a divisible part of the contract) will be entitled to claim the contract price (or the portion of the contract price related to the divisible part), subject to a set-off for defects in the performance.[42]

[19.145] The justification for such an approach is stated by Denning LJ in *Hoenig v Isaacs*:[43]

When a contract provides for a specific sum to be paid on completion of specified work, the courts lean against a construction of the contract which would deprive the contractor of any payment at all simply because there are some defects or omissions. The promise to complete the work is, therefore, construed as a term of the contract, but not as a condition. It is not every breach of that term which absolves the employer from his promise to pay the price, but only a breach which goes to the root of the contract, such as an abandonment of the work when it is only half done. Unless the breach goes to the root of the matter, the employer cannot resist payment of the price. He must pay it

---

39   Ibid at 576.
40   See the commentary at [19.125].
41   *Hoenig v Isaacs* [1952] 2 All ER 176 at 180.
42   *Hoenig v Isaacs* [1952] 2 All ER 176; *Bolton v Mahedeva* [1972] 1 WLR 1009; *Steele v Tardiani* (1946) 72 CLR 386; *Lemura v Coppola* [1960] QdR 308 at 314; *Phillips v Ellinson Brothers Pty Ltd* (1941) 65 CLR 221; *Williamson v Murdoch* (1912) 14 WALR 54.
43   [1952] 2 All ER 176 at 180–181.

and bring cross-claim for the defects and omissions, or alternatively, set them up in diminution of the price.

[19.150] Denning LJ suggests that the obligations of a party to perform work under the contract should be considered in the same way as a term of the contract. What type of term he had in mind is not clear. However, it should only be in cases where the breach goes to the root of the contract that the party should be prevented from recovering the contract price.[44]

[19.155] The advantages of the approach elucidated by Denning LJ are that:

- it recognises the obligation to perform as a term of the contract, which is consistent with the approach taken by the courts when considering the question of termination or damages for failure to perform; and

- it allows a court to award the contract price to a party who has substantially performed, even though there is a minor defect in performance and therefore a breach of the contract.[45]

[19.160] One difficulty with the approach is the classification of the particular term as either a condition or a warranty. Denning LJ appears to indicate that, unless the contract provides expressly for entire performance as a condition precedent, the term is not a condition. This is certainly consistent with the court's being able to grant payment of the contract price, subject to a set-off for damages. It would also mean that the other party would only be able to terminate the contract for a repudiation of the contract, rather than for a breach of the term itself, no matter how serious. This could lead to an unfair result in some situations—for example where, although the work to be performed under a building contract is finished, there has been a breach of the term to provide steel beams of a certain quality or diameter, and that has made the building unstable. This will be a breach of a term of the contract, but not a repudiation of the agreement.[46] Should the contract price be payable in this case? Why should the innocent party be forced to sue for damages, when he or she could easily retain part of the contract price to rectify the defects? Is this the type of result his Honour envisaged when he made the statement 'a breach going to the root of the matter'? An obvious solution is that the term for performance of the work should be considered intermediate.[47] Such an approach would be entirely consistent with Denning LJ's statement in *Hoenig v Isaacs*.[48] It would only be for serious breaches of the term (breaches that go to the root of the contract) that the contract could be terminated, and therefore the price would not be payable. In all other cases, the contract would remain on foot and the term would be enforceable. However, the decision of *Hongkong Fir Shipping Co Ltd v Kawasake Kissen Kaisha Ltd*,[49] which introduced the concept of intermediate terms, was decided ten years after Denning LJ made this judicial statement.

---

44   See also *Corio Guarantee Corporation Ltd v McCallum* [1956] VR 755 at 760.
45   Unless this is a case like *Luna Park (NSW) Ltd v Tramways Advertising Pty Ltd* (1938) 61 CLR 286, where substantial performance was considered to discharge the party's obligations under the contract.
46   Repudiation is discussed at [20.105].
47   See [9.175]–[9.200] for a discussion of intermediate terms.
48   [1952] 2 All ER 176.
49   [1962] 2 QB 26.

Since Denning LJ's decision in *Hoenig v Isaacs*[50] there have been very few judicial pronouncements to assist in the resolution of this uncertainty. It is suggested that courts should adopt a global approach to the problem, consistent with allowing recovery of the price for substantial performance unless the obligations of the contract are clearly entire.[51] Once it is accepted that recovery for substantial performance is available, the primary question will be whether in fact the party has substantially performed his or her obligations.

19.7.4 Requirements for substantial performance

[19.165] A party will usually be considered to have substantially performed a contract where the defects in the services or goods are of a minor nature. If the term of the contract were considered to be a warranty, then failure to perform any aspect of the term would be considered minor. However if, as suggested, the term is considered to be intermediate, or if the court takes a global approach to the issue, the focus of the court's deliberation should remain on the effect of the performance itself. What are the factors a court will consider as relevant?

[19.170] Usually, a determination of whether the performance is substantial will be a question of degree to be determined by the court after consideration of all the relevant facts.[52] The court will take into account:

- the nature of the defect; and
- the cost of rectifying the defect compared to the contract price.[53]

[19.175] Where the nature of the defect is serious and the cost of rectification is high by comparison with the contract price, a court will conclude that the party has not substantially performed his or her obligations. The contrary will be the case where the defect is minor and the cost small. The difficult question is at what point a court will no longer consider a party's performance to be substantial. In *Bolton v Mahadeva*,[54] the court considered that the drawing of a point where a party's performance would no longer be substantial is a question of degree. The facts of *Bolton v Mahadeva*[55] and *Hoenig v Issacs*[56] provide a suitable comparison.

Example: Hoenig v Issacs[57]

The plaintiff agreed to decorate and furnish the defendant's flat for the sum of £750, the terms of payment being 'net cash, as the work proceeds and balance on completion'. The defendant paid £400 as progress payments. When the work was finished, it was found that the door of a wardrobe required replacing and a book shelf that was too short would have to be remade, requiring consequential alterations to a bookcase. The defendant had occupied the flat and used the furniture but was refusing to pay the balance. The cost of the remedial work was £55.18s.2d. The Court of Appeal

50   [1952] 2 All ER 176.
51   See [19.125]–[19.135] in relation to entire obligations.
52   *Bolton v Mahadeva* [1972] 1 WLR 1009.
53   *Bolton v Mahadeva* [1972] 1 WLR 1009.
54   [1972] 1 WLR 1009.
55   Ibid.
56   [1952] 2 All ER 176.
57   Ibid.

held that as the plaintiff had substantially performed the contract, he was entitled to payment, less an amount for the rectification work.

Example: Bolton v Mahadeva[58]

The plaintiff agreed to install a water heating system for £560. The water heater had been installed but, when in operation, fumes were given out into some of the living rooms and in addition, due to insufficient radiators and insulation, the system did not work properly. The plaintiff claimed payment of the contract price.

In order to determine whether the plaintiff had substantially performed the contract, Cairns LJ considered it necessary to take into account 'both the nature of the defects and proportion between the cost of rectifying them and the contract price'. In the present case, the heating system did not heat the house adequately and gave out fumes into some rooms. The cost of rectification was £174. The Court concluded, on the above facts, that the plaintiff had failed to substantially perform the obligations under the contract. This conclusion was reached without taking into account whether the contract was an entire contract, as this was not pleaded by the defendant.

[19.180] An analysis of these two decisions provides some assistance to parties considering a claim for substantial performance.

- Where the nature of the defect is minor and the cost of rectification is 10 per cent or less of the contract price it is likely that a court would allow recovery of the contract price for substantial performance.[59]

- Where the nature of the defect is serious and the cost of rectification is 33 per cent of the contract price or more, it is likely that a court will refuse the recovery of the contract price.[60]

- Where the nature of the defect is relatively minor but costs more that 10 per cent of the contract price to remedy, recovery of the contract price for substantial performance may be allowed, subject to the cost of rectification not exceeding a reasonable amount.

- Where the nature of the defect is serious but the cost of rectifying the damage is small (less than 10 per cent) the result would be difficult to predict. If the serious nature of the defect justifies the termination of the contract by the other party it is unlikely that the contract price will be recoverable despite the small cost. However, a party who acted to terminate the contract in such a case could not be assured that a court would agree with such action. Where the defects fall into this category, the result will in all cases depend very much upon the factual matrix.

19.7.5 Substantial performance and entire obligations

[19.185] The doctrine of substantial performance has been criticised by some commentators as being uncertain in nature and scope.[61] These criticisms are made in the context of an approach that recognises contracts as being entire or divisible. As

---

58   [1972] 1 WLR 1009.
59   *Hoenig v Isaacs* [1952] 2 All ER 176.
60   *Bolton v Mahadeva* [1972] 1 WLR 1009.
61   JW Carter & DJ Harland, *Contract Law in Australia*, 3rd edn, Butterworths, Sydney 1996, p 626.

suggested above, a different approach, which focuses more on the nature of the obligations within the contract rather than the contract itself, may act to alleviate some of these uncertainties. If, as suggested, the obligations of the parties are construed in the context of the contract, the intention of the parties to allow recovery of the contract price for either exact performance or substantial performance becomes clearer. In this context it would be inconsistent to suggest that an entire obligation (as opposed to an entire contract) could be substantially performed. To suggest otherwise would render the concept of an entire obligation redundant. This would be inconsistent with current judicial opinion.[62]

19.8 Effect of different types of performance on the right to the contract price

[19.190 The different types of performance identified so far are:
- exact performance; and
- substantial performance.

[19.195] A third type of performance that occurs where the performance is neither exact nor substantial is partial performance. The difference between exact and substantial performance and their effect on a claim for recovery of the contract price has been discussed above.[63] The effect of these two types of performance on the right of a party to claim the contract price may be summarised as:

1   A party who exactly performs his or her obligations under either a lump sum contract or a divisible contract will be entitled to the contract price.

2   A party who substantially performs his or her obligations under a lump sum contract, where the obligation to provide the services or goods is not entire, will be entitled to recover the contract price less a set off for the cost of rectification. However, if the obligation to perform is entire, a party who substantially performs a lump sum contract will not be entitled to recover the contract price.[64] This will be because the condition precedent of exact and complete performance of the party's obligations will not be fulfilled.

3   A party who substantially performs a divisible part of a contract will be entitled to recover the contract price for that divisible part, less a set off for rectification of the defects. It will not be necessary to substantially perform the whole of the contract to recover any part of the price. However, if the obligation to perform that divisible part is entire, the party will only be able to recover the contract price for that divisible part if the performance is exact.

[19.200] If a party has failed to exactly perform or substantially perform the contract, his or her right to recover the contract price will be affected. A court will generally not allow a claim for recovery of the contract price (or the proportion related to a divisible part of the contract) where the claiming party has only partly performed his

---

62   See *Baltic Shipping Co v Dillon* (1993) 67 ALJR 228.
63   See [19.115]–[19.185].
64   *Cutter v Powell* (1795) 101 ER 573; *Phillips v Ellinson Brothers Pty Ltd* (1941) 65 CLR 221; *Connor v Stainton* (1924) WALR 72.

or her obligations under the contract (or a divisible part of the contract). Examples of part-performance may be where:

* the work is of no value to the defendant;
* the work is entirely different from that provided for by the contract;[65]or
* the conduct of the plaintiff constitutes a repudiation or abandonment of the contract.[66]

Example: Connor v Stainton[67]

The agreement between the parties required the plaintiff to build a fence with the posts 12 feet apart. The plaintiff instead constructed the fence with the posts at distances varying from 12 feet to 18 feet apart. The plaintiff claimed payment of the contract price on the ground that with the aid of droppers, the fence could be made as effective as that specified by the contract. The local magistrate granted the plaintiff's claim but deducted damages for the defects. The defendant appealed.

The Court held that since this procedure would cost half as much again as the contract price, it could not be said that there had been substantial performance. In the circumstances, the plaintiff was entitled to nothing. Where the work provided under a contract was of an entirely different character from that agreed, it was not open to the plaintiff to say he or she had done something different, but really as good.

[19.205] Although a party who has partly performed a contract will not be entitled to claim the contract price, he or she may, in appropriate circumstances, be able to claim either damages to compensate them for the breach of the other party or a *quantum meruit* for the value of the work performed. Each of these types of claims is considered below.[68]

19.9 Effect of termination on recovery of the contract price

[19.210] Termination of the contract will affect a party's claim for the contract price. If the party obliged to pay the price has validly terminated the contract[69] for a breach by the party performing the work, it will generally mean that the party obliged to perform the work has not substantially performed the contract. The very nature of substantial performance will mean that any defects in performance are minor and do not justify termination. If the party undertaking the work has validly terminated the contract for a breach by the party obliged to pay the price, a claim for the contract price will only succeed if there is an accrued right to claim the price prior to termination. Termination of a contract for breach, repudiation, or frustration will bring the contract to an end for the future.[70] Only obligations that have accrued, and are due, prior to

---

65   *Connor v Stainton* (1924) WALR 72; *Cooper v Australian Electric Ltd Co* (1922) 25 ALR 66.
66   For an example of abandonment see *Sumpter v Hedges* [1898] 1 QB 673.
67   (1924) 27 WALR 72.
68   See [19.215] and [19.70].
69   See Chapter 20 in relation to the requirements of a valid termination.
70   See [20.470].

termination are enforceable. Therefore, the obligation to pay the price must have arisen prior to termination because the terminating party had exactly or substantially performed his or her obligations.[71] If this is not the case, the party obliged to undertake the work may seek alternative compensation in the form of damages for breach or a *quantum meruit*.

19.10 Alternatives to claiming the contract price

[19.215] Even though the contract price may not be recoverable, a party to the contract may be able to seek alternative remedies. One approach is for the party who has undertaken work or provided goods to seek damages for the breach by the other party. Damages may be claimed only if the party seeking the damages is not himself or herself in breach.[72]

[19.220] The alternative is to make a claim in restitution for the return of a benefit provided to the other party.[73] The only type of restitutionary claim relevant to this context is a claim for *quantum meruit*[74] for the value of services provided to the other party pursuant to a contract for services.[75]

19.11 *Quantum meruit*

[19.225] *Quantum meruit* is an action for the reasonable value of services performed. A claim for *quantum meruit* may be sought where there is no contract—or no effective contract—between the parties, or the contract is at an end.[76] In such a case, the law may imply an obligation on the defendant to pay the reasonable value of the services rendered.[77] The law will only impose such an obligation if there is no subsisting contract.[78] This means that if the services were performed pursuant to a contract, a *quantum meruit* is only available if the contract has been terminated, rescinded, frustrated, or is unenforceable or void.[79]

[19.230] Unlike contractual damages, recovery of a *quantum meruit* is generally unrelated to fault, and is premised upon three elements:

1 *Benefit*: Has the plaintiff provided a benefit to the defendant?

---

71 Note if the obligation to perform is entire, the party would have to perform exactly. Substantial performance would not be sufficient.
72 The right to damages may also be subject to other limitations. See Chapter 23.
73 Restitution is considered in more detail in Chapter 24.
74 A claim for *quantum valebrant* (as much as they were worth) could be made for the recovery of the price of goods delivered. A right to recover the contract price for goods delivered also exists under the *Sale of Goods Act* in each State: *Sale of Goods Act* 1954 (ACT), s 52; *Sale of Goods Act* 1972 (NT), s 51; *Sale of Goods Act* 1923 (NSW), s 51; *Sale of Goods Act* 1896 (Qld), s 50; *Sale of Goods Act* 1895 (SA), s 48; *Sale of Goods Act* 1896 (Tas), s 53; *Goods Act* 1958 (Vic), s 55; *Sale of Goods Act* 1895 (WA), s 48.
75 In contracts for the sale of goods or land, if the other party has received a benefit, it will usually mean they have accepted the goods or land and therefore should pay the contract price.
76 See *Rover International Ltd v Cannon Film Sales Ltd* [1989] 1 WLR 912 (void contract); *Pavey & Matthews Pty Ltd v Paul* (1987) 162 CLR 221 (unenforceable contract); *Lodder v Slowery* [1904] AC 442 (terminated contract).
77 *Pavey & Matthews Pty Ltd v Paul* (1987) 162 CLR 221.
78 *Update Constructions Pty Ltd v Rozelle Child Care Centre Ltd* (1990) 20 NSWLR 251 at 275.
79 *Automatic Fire Sprinklers Pty Ltd v Watson* (1946) 72 CLR 435.

2   *Expense*: Was the benefit provided at the expense of the plaintiff?

3   *Unjustness*: Is it unjust that the defendant retains the benefit?

[19.235] Although, in theory the elements suggest a party in breach of the contract can claim a *quantum meruit* for the work performed, in practice it is more difficult for a party in breach to prove the other party has received a benefit from the defective performance of the contract. For this reason, the rights of the party not in breach are considered separately from the rights of the party in breach.

19.11.1   Recovery of a quantum meruit by party not in breach

[19.240] The party not in breach of the contract who has provided services to the other party will be entitled to elect between the recovery of damages for breach and the recovery of a *quantum meruit*.[80] It will not be possible to recover both damages and a *quantum meruit*, as this would result in double compensation (that is the party would be compensated twice for the same loss).[81] Before making a choice between the alternative remedies, the plaintiff should first establish whether there is any action on the contract. If the plaintiff has performed his or her obligations exactly or substantially, there will be a claim in contract for the price.[82] A claim for *quantum meruit* would not be available in that case, as the contract could not be terminated for breach.[83] If, however, the plaintiff has only rendered part-performance because of the other party's breach, he or she may elect to claim either damages or a *quantum meruit*, provided the contract is brought to an end by terminating for the other party's breach.

[19.245] An innocent party who elects to claim a *quantum meruit* must prove the other party has received a benefit from the work performed. Where the work is only partially performed, will the innocent party have provided a benefit? Whether a party has received a benefit from services provided will usually be based on an objective analysis. It is only where the plaintiff is in breach of a contract, and has failed to deliver what was contracted for, that the defendant is entitled to say, 'I did not want these services, therefore I have not received a benefit'. It is clear that a defendant who requests services and receives the services requested is required to pay for those services. Likewise, where the conduct of the defendant prevents the completion of requested services, a court will not allow the defendant to deny the services are a benefit.[84] This will be the case even where the services do not produce any tangible product.[85]

[19.250] An issue raised in several decisions is whether a claim for *quantum meruit* should be limited to the amount of the contract price. This is a particularly important question where the plaintiff has entered into a losing contract[86] and the value of the work actually performed exceeds the contract price. A dramatic illustration is provided

---

80   See *Automatic Fire Sprinklers Pty Ltd v Watson* (1946) 72 CLR 435 at 450; *Renard Constructions (ME) Pty Ltd v Minister for Public Works* (1992) 26 NSWLR 234 at 277; *Brenner v First Artists' Management Pty Ltd* [1993] 2 VR 221.

81   See *Baltic Shipping Co Ltd v Dillon* (1992) 176 CLR 344.

82   See [19.125]–[19.185].

83   This assumes that where the contract is substantially performed the defects in performance are minor and therefore termination of the contract is not possible.

84   The requirement of benefit in a restitutionary claim is discussed further in Chapter 24.

85   See for example *Planché v Colburn* (1831) 8 Bing 14; 131 ER 30.

86   A losing contract is a contract that results in the plaintiff's making a loss rather than a profit: *The Commonwealth v Amman Aviation Pty Ltd* (1991) 66 ALJR 123.

by *Boomer v Muir*.[87] In that case, the plaintiff was engaged in construction of a dam. When it was near completion, the defendant breached the agreement; the court held that the plaintiff was justified in terminating. The plaintiff claimed a *quantum meruit* and was awarded $250,000 even though he only entitled to a final payment of $20 000 under the contract. A similar result was reached in the case of *Lodder v Slowery*[88] by the Privy Council, which awarded the plaintiff a *quantum meruit* even though there was a losing contract and the plaintiff would have received a reduced amount in an action for damages.

In Australia, Deane J expressly stated in *Pavey & Matthews Pty Ltd v Paul*[89] that where the contract was unenforceable, the contract price would provide a ceiling for the amount of the award. However, in *Rover International Ltd v Cannon Film Sales Ltd*,[90] the English Court of Appeal rejected the submission that a *quantum meruit* should be limited to the contract price in the case of a void contract. This decision was also reached by the New South Wales Court of Appeal in *Renard Constructions (ME) Pty Ltd v Minister for Public Works*.[91] The position is therefore unclear; commentators suggest that in the case of *quantum meruit* after breach of contract, the maximum award should be limited to the contract price. This provides for consistency with the contract and avoids the reallocation of risks and obligations that had originally been agreed between the parties.[92]

19.11.2   Recovery by the party in breach

[19.255] Parties in breach of a contract will be unable to claim damages because they are unable to rely on their own breach to obtain a benefit under the contract.[93] A party in breach may also have difficulty in succeeding in a claim for *quantum meruit* because he or she will be unable to prove that a benefit was provided to the defendant. Although the notion of benefit is generally considered objectively,[94] a defendant who has not received what he or she expected under the contract may subjectively devalue the work. This means that the defendant may allege that as the work is only partly complete, it is of no benefit to him or her. For this reason services will generally only be considered to provide a benefit if:

- the services performed were requested by the defendant;
- the services were freely accepted; or
- the defendant has obtained an incontrovertible benefit from the services.

[19.260] It will be insufficient in a claim for *quantum meruit* by the party in breach to merely show the services were requested. Despite the fact that work may have been requested by the defendant, the problem will be that the work provided will usually not match the request. It will be difficult for the plaintiff to convince a court that work that does not comply with a request actually provides a benefit to the defendant.

---

87   24 P 2d 570 (1933).
88   [1904] AC 442.
89   (1987) 162 CLR 221.
90   [1989] 1 WLR 912.
91   (1992) 26 NSWLR 234 at 276–278.
92   See R Goff and G Jones, *The Law of Restitution*, 4th edn, Sweet & Maxwell, London, 1993, p 427.
93   *Suttor v Gundowda Pty Ltd* (1950) 81 CLR 418; *Alghussein Establishment v Eaton College* [1988] 1 WLR 587.
94   The concept of benefit in restitution is examined is more detail in Chapter 24.

This leaves the plaintiff having to prove that the services were freely accepted, or that there was an incontrovertible benefit. Free acceptance means that the defendant had a choice between accepting and rejecting the work, and has freely decided to accept the work, even though it does not comply with the contract. Where the work concerns improvements to land, the plaintiff will have a very difficult task in proving free acceptance. *Sumpter v Hedges*[95] provides an example of the difficulties inherent in using the principle of free acceptance in such a context. In that case, the plaintiff's claim for *quantum meruit* was refused because the court considered the defendant did not have a choice whether to accept the partly completed building or not.

Example: Sumpter v Hedges[96]

The plaintiff agreed to build two houses and a stable for the defendant, for £565. The plaintiff did part of the work amounting to £333 and received payment of part of the price. He then informed the defendant he could not go on. The trial judge found that the plaintiff abandoned the contract. The defendant finished the building using building materials the plaintiff left behind. The Court of Appeal awarded the plaintiff the value of the materials left behind, but said, in refusing the claim for *quantum meruit:*

> the circumstances must be such as to give an option to the defendant to take or not to take the benefit of the work done ... Where, as in the case of work done on land, the circumstances are such as to give the defendant no option whether he will take the benefit of the work or not then one must look to other facts than the mere taking the benefit of the work in order to ground the inference of a new contract ... The mere fact that a defendant is in possession of what he cannot help keeping, or even has done work upon it, affords no ground for such an inference. He is not bound to keep unfinished a building which in an incomplete state would be a nuisance on his land.[97]

[19.265] Where the services provided by the plaintiff do not concern the construction of improvements on land, a defendant in breach is more likely to be able to rely on either free acceptance or incontrovertible benefit. An incontrovertible benefit will arise where the defendant has converted services or goods provided by the plaintiff into money in the hands of the defendant. The defendant could not deny that money in her or his hands is a benefit.

An example of how both of these concepts may apply to assist a plaintiff is found in *Steele v Tardiani*.[98]

Example: Steele v Tardiani[99]

The defendant employed the plaintiffs to cut firewood into certain lengths and diameters. The defendant alleged that the plaintiffs were in breach of contract because the wood was not cut into the correct lengths. However, the defendant continued to take

---

95   [1898] 1 QB 673.
96   Ibid.
97   Ibid at 676.
98   (1946) 72 CLR 386.
99   Ibid.

possession of all wood cut by the plaintiff and sell it. The High Court considered that as the contract was 'infinitely divisible', the plaintiffs were entitled to be paid 8 shillings per ton for any wood split into the correct dimensions. The High Court further held that the plaintiffs were entitled to recover on a *quantum meruit* for the remaining timber they had split, and which the defendant had accepted and sold. The High Court agreed that a *quantum meruit* was available if the defendant had accepted the benefit of the work. Dixon J said:

> The defendant says that his trees were cut upon his land and the firewood left lying there was his. What was he to do? By what step could he actively 'reject' the advantage that the transmutation of his standing trees into firewood necessarily gave him, however unsuitable to his purpose might be the actual lengths and widths? Was he to allow the wood to rot on the ground? What practical choice had he except to make it clear to the plaintiff that, to obtain payment, they must split the wood to the contract width, and, when they refused or failed to do so, to employ other labour for the purpose of reducing its width or 'diameter' so far as otherwise he was unable to dispose of the firewood. Why should he be precluded from selling his wood in the shape the plaintiffs wrongfully left it? It was his wood and why should his dealing with it imply a new contract with the plaintiffs? ...
>
> If it were true that he made it clear to the plaintiffs before they departed that they must complete their contract by splitting the wood to the specified width, these considerations would indeed place him in a strong position.[100]

[19.270] Despite the fact the High Court did not consider the question of incontrovertible benefit in *Steele v Tardiani*,[101] it is possible to see the potential for this principle to also apply on the facts.

19.12 Failure to perform constitutes breach

[19.275] A breach of contract will occur where a party fails to perform a contract according to its terms. There are two types of breach: actual breach and anticipatory breach. A party who fails to perform a contract at the time nominated for performance is in actual breach of the contract. Anticipatory breach occurs if one party indicates prior to the time for performance that he or she does not intend to, or is unable to perform his or her contractual obligations.[102] The contract may be terminated immediately for anticipatory breach. There is no need to wait for the time for performance to arrive.

[19.280] Where one party is in breach, the other party to the contract will be entitled to sue for damages—and in some circumstances, terminate the contract or seek an equitable remedy, such as specific performance.[103]

---

100 Ibid at 403–404
101 (1946) 72 CLR 386.
102 For an example of anticipatory breach see *Foran v Wight* (1989) 168 CLR 385. Anticipatory breach is considered further at [20.130]–[20.135].
103 Damages are discussed in Chapter 23, termination is discussed in Chapter 20 and equitable remedies are discussed in Chapter 25.

19.13 International perspectives

19.13.1 New Zealand

[19.285] The law in New Zealand concerning discharge by performance and recovery of the contract price is in substance the same as the law in Australia, except in some minor respects. The law recognises the existence of two categories of contract – divisible and entire. A contract is entire where on a proper construction no consideration is to pass from one party unless and until the whole of the obligations of the other party have been performed.[104] If there is no intention gleaned from the contract that it is to be entire then the question will be whether the contract can be broken into a number of consideration for a number of acts and therefore be divisible.[105]

[19.290] The doctrine of substantial performance has been accepted as a method of militating against the harshness of the exact performance requirement for entire contracts. As in Australia a party who has performed their obligations except in a minor respect will be able to claim the contract price less an amount for defective performance. Whether substantial performance applies is a question of construction in each case. Where the contract is intended to be exactly performed, the doctrine will not apply.

[19.295] Some concern has been voiced in relation to the common law doctrines of entire contracts and substantial performance and their relationship to the *Contractual Remedies Act* 1979. One view is that the Act does not affect the doctrine of entire contracts at all because it is based upon a condition precedent to performance not discharged for breach. The second view is that the Act will apply where there is incomplete performance

19.13.2 United States

[19.300] The American law in relation to discharge by performance, substantial performance, and recovery for *quantum meruit* is substantially similar the Australian position. The basic concepts within the American system have English origins, like Australian law. This is reflected in the proposition that nothing less than full performance will discharge a party's obligations under a contract and the willingness to recognise both dependent and independent obligations.[106] Despite the similarity in nomenclature and origin, several notable differences exist in the application of these principles in the American context. The differences in relation to dependent obligations, substantial performance, divisible contracts, and *quantum meruit* are highlighted here.

[19.305] American contract law, like Australian, distinguishes between independent and dependent obligations; but in the case of dependent obligations, the term 'constructive conditions of exchange' is used. This principle grew out of the inadequacy of the English common law to sufficiently protect the innocent party to a bilateral contract following breach. Until the late 1700s, English law did not recognise that

---

104   For example *Staunton v Wellington Education Board* (1909) 28 NZLR 449 and Dutton v Breen (1908) 28 NZLR 717.

105   *Rosenthal & Sons Ltd v Esmail* [1965] 1 WLR 1117. The fact the contract is divided into instalments may not be enough.

106   Restatement (Second) § 235. See AE Farnsworth *Contracts*, 3rd edn, Aspen Law and Business, New York, 1999, § 8.9.

promises in a bilateral contract were dependent on each other in such a way that non-performance of the first promise relieved performance of the second.[107] American courts, in reliance upon a judgment of Lord Mansfield,[108] recognised that justice required the implication of a term in a bilateral contract to the effect that the parties intend—or would have intended, had they thought about it—that the performance of one duty is conditional on performance of the other duty. Such an implied condition or 'constructive condition of exchange' is implied in all bilateral contracts unless a contrary intention is expressed.[109]

[19.310] The doctrine of substantial performance in American law arose out of a desire by American courts to mitigate forfeiture of the contract by the party in breach. The doctrine is a natural outgrowth of the doctrine of constructive conditions. It is suggested that if a constructive condition had to be performed strictly, the development of constructive conditions as an aid to justice between the parties would be impaired. Therefore, where one party's duty to perform is a constructive condition of the other party's duty to pay, only substantial performance is required before the obligation to pay arises.[110] This principle is applied to all bilateral contracts with constructive conditions except contracts for the sale of goods.[111] However, the doctrine will not apply to a contract if strict performance has been made a condition precedent to payment.[112] Similarly, as in Australia this is a rare occurrence. If a party can satisfy the court that substantial performance has occurred, he or she will be entitled to the contract price, less any damages the other party is entitled to because of the breach. The onus of proving the amount of damage is usually placed on the defendant.

[19.315] Whether a contract has been substantially performed is a question of fact. In words reminiscent of Denning LJ,[113] Cardozo J stated 'Where the line is to be drawn between the important and the trivial cannot be settled by a formula … The question is one of degree, to be answered, if there is doubt, by the triers of facts …'.[114] No particular formula or mathematical rule related to the cost of rectification[115] is used by the courts, but it has been suggested that the following factors may be relevant:

- *How much of the benefit reasonably expected from the contract has been received?* To determine this, the court will look to the purpose of the contract. For example, where the contract is one for the construction of a building, the existence of structural defects will usually mean the contract was not substantially performed.[116]

---

107   *Kingston v Preston* (1773) 2 Doug 689; 99 ER 437.
108   Ibid.
109   Restatement (Second) § 232. See for example *Orkin Exterminating Co v Harris* 164 SE 2d 727.
110   Boon v Eyre (1777) 126 ER 160; *Brown-Marx Associates v Emigrant Savings Bank* 703 F 2d 1361 (11th Cir. 1983).
111   See UCC § 2-601, which retains the perfect tender rule subject to certain conditions. However, there is a suggestion that the Code frequently applies the doctrine of substantial performance but that the Code through its exceptions strikes a different balance from the common law: *Ramirez v Autosport* 88 NJ 277, 440 A 2d 1345 (1982).
112   EA Farnsworth, *Contracts*, 3rd edn, Aspen Law and Business, New York, 1999, § 8.3.
113   *Hoenig v Isaacs* [1952] 2 All ER 176.
114   *Jacob & Youngs v Kent* 129 NE 889 (NY 1921) at 891.
115   *Plante v Jacobs* 103 NW 2d 296 (Wis 1960). Contrast with the Australian position, [19.170].
116   *Spence v Ham* 57 NE 412 (NY 1900).

- *The extent to which the injured party can be compensated adequately by damages.* A court is more likely to find substantial performance if the breach can be paid for by damages. For example, in a building contract if the owner can easily obtain another builder to correct the defects, and can withhold a particular sum from the first builder, it is likely that substantial performance has occurred.[117] However, if the defects are serious and the amount of damages uncertain, it is unlikely that a court will find substantial performance.

- *The extent of the forfeiture that will be suffered by the party in breach.* If the performance can be returned and salvaged by the party in breach, it is less likely to be regarded as substantial. The fact that the party in breach may recover his or her performance means that the extent of the forfeiture will be reduced. This is one of the reasons that the principle of substantial performance is so important in building contracts, where the performance cannot be recouped. However, the extent of the forfeiture is reduced where progress payments are provided in the contract.

- *Whether the party in breach has deliberately breached the contract.* The failure by a party to observe standards of good faith will be one of the factors a court may take into account.[118] A lack of good faith of itself though will not be determinative.[119]

[19.320] Substantial performance is synonymous with immaterial breach. That is if the contract is substantially performed the breach will be immaterial and the injured party is unable to terminate. It is equally the case that, if performance is not substantial, a material breach will have occurred.[120]

[19.325] Another mechanism used by American courts to avoid forfeiture and allow recovery of the contract price, or a *pro rata* amount, is the concept of a divisible contract. A contract is considered to be divisible if the performances to be exchanged can be divided into corresponding pairs of part performances in such a way that a court will treat the parts of each pair as if the parties had agreed that they were equivalents. This is a flexible principle that allows a court to order payment to a party even though the contract is not expressly divisible. The Restatement (Second) sets out two criteria for a divisible contract. First, it must be possible to apportion the parties' performances into corresponding pairs of part performances. Secondly, it must be proper to regard the part of each pair as agreed equivalents. This represents a significant departure from the Australian position.[121] The American approach is not dependent upon payment or delivery of goods by instalments, and contracts where the price is payable in a lump sum may still be considered divisible.

[19.330] The first requirement of apportionment will be met if the agreement states separate prices for different parts of the work or a unit price for the work or if a price list states separate prices for items.[122] The second requirement of being an agreed equivalent is more difficult. Usually, the parties did not consider the issue of divisibility

---

117 *Alhers Building Supply v Larsen* 535 NW 2d 431 (SD 1995).

118 Restatement (Second) § 241.

119 *Vincenzi v Cerro* 442 A 2d 1352 (Conn 1982); cf JD Calamari & JM Perillo, *The Law of Contracts,* 4th edn, West Group, 1998, pp 417–418.

120 See [20.500]–[20.610] for further discussion of material breach.

121 See [19.95]–[19.105].

122 *Lowry v United Pac Ins Co* 429 P2d 577 (agreement stated prices separately for excavation and grading and for street improvement).

at the time of contract. Therefore, instead of giving effect to the assumed intention of the parties, the court will consider issues of fairness in the same way as if the court was implying a term.[123] The fundamental question is whether the part performances are of roughly equivalent value to the injured party when considered against the background of that party's expectations as to the agreement as a whole.[124] If the injured party is required to pay the contract price, the value of the part must be roughly equivalent to a proportional value of the whole. For example, if the parties enter a contract to drive logs down a river, and some actually arrive at the destination but others are swept away, the court may consider that a divisible contract. The first party would be entitled to the cost of the logs that actually arrived at the destination, according to the unit price. In respect of the logs that were swept away, the price would not be recoverable even if the logs had been driven part of the way, as the second requirement of agreed equivalents would not be met.[125] Examples of contracts that may not be divisible are:

- a construction contract with progress payments where the payments do not correspond to the value of the work performed; and[126]
- a contract where the prices are stated separately but the injured party cannot make full use of the part received without the rest.[127]

[19.335] The final point of note is that just because a contract is divisible for the purpose of payment of the price does not mean it will be divisible for all purposes. For example, it will not render the contract divisible for the purpose of deciding whether the injured party is able to recover for part performance.

[19.340] The final means employed by American courts to avoid or limit forfeiture is restitution. The elements of a claim in restitution are the same as in Australia, with the claimant being required to prove the defendant has received a benefit. Traditionally, the courts denied restitution to the party in breach of the contract not on the basis of benefit, but on policy grounds.[128] Conflicting authority recognises, however, that if restitution is not possible, the injured party may actually receive more as a result of the breach than the loss actually sustained.[129] Consequently, a party in breach should be able to recover payment for his or her performance less the amount of damages suffered by the injured party. This more liberal view has been applied to allow a defaulting builder to recover where there was no substantial performance.[130] This liberal approach has been adopted by the Restatement (Second), which allows recovery by the party in breach subject to a damages claim by the injured party.[131] The party claiming restitution will have the onus of proving the value of the benefit provided to the other party. The benefit will be measured objectively by the cost of obtaining the services from another person or the increase in value to the other party's property.

---

123 See [8.915]–[8.965] in relation to implications of terms in American law.
124 *Lowy v United Pac Ins Co* 429 P2d 577 and Farnsworth § 8.13.
125 *Gill v Johnstown Lumber Co* 25 A 120, 120 (Pa 1892).
126 *Kirkland v Archbold* 113 NE 2d 496 (Ohio App 1953).
127 For example, where a machine is provided that cannot be used without an attachment that is unavailable.
128 *Stark v Parker* 19 Mass (2 Pick) 267, 275 (1824); *Lawrence v Miller* 86 NY 131 (1881).
129 *Britton v Turner* NH 481, 487, 492 (1834).
130 *PDM Mechanical Contractors v Suffolk Constr Co* 618 NE 2d 72 (Mass App 1993).
131 Restatement (Second) § 374.

Unlike the position in Australia, a subjective analysis of the benefit will not be undertaken.[132] If the party in breach is seeking restitution, the smaller of the amounts will be recoverable.[133] For example, say A agrees to repair B's roof for $3000. A does part of the work at a cost of $2000, increasing the market price of B's house by $1200. The price to have a similar carpenter do the work already done is $1800. A's restitution interest is equal to the benefit conferred on B. This could be either the market value of the work or the increase in value of the house. If A is in breach, the restitution interest will be $1200.

19.13.3 Japan

[19.345] In Japan, discharge of the contract by performance is effected, as it is in Australia, by performing the contract according to its original terms, or according to terms subsequently changed and agreed upon by the parties.

[19.350] Unlike the common law in countries such as Australia and New Zealand, where non-contractual performance is rarely excused,[134] Japanese law follows other civil law countries in inquiring into the relative faults of both parties. Where the contract is not performed as planned, the parties and the court will inquire into the reason. This is the idea of a 'reason imputable' (or, based on the court's analysis of the facts, attributable) to the obligor (the party owing the obligation).

[19.355] The practical consequence of this stance is first that—as with the common law—when a party does not perform a contractual duty, the other party can claim compensation.[135] In cases of impossibility, the Civil Code imposes the requirement of a 'reason imputable' to the obligor as a prerequisite for compensation (art 414), but this has been interpreted to include:

- intentional non-performance;
- non-performance due to the negligence of the obligor; and
- the intentional or negligent non-performance of an assistant chosen by the obligor to perform the obligation.

[19.360] The obligor then has the burden of proof in showing that the non-performance is not attributable to his or her fault.

'Non-performance' in this context can mean either complete non-performance of the contractual obligation, or partial non-performance. The Civil Code makes no explicit mention of the consequences of partial or incomplete performance, and so the provisions relating to termination and the right to compensation are applied analogously in these situations. As a matter of practice, however, many commercial and consumer contracts in Japan are continuing contracts that are performed in instalments. This means that where there is incomplete performance—as when the quality of an instalment of service as provided is less that that agreed to or expected by the consumer—it is possible either to claim the contract price or to treat the contract as terminated, or both. However, the claim for the contract price will be assessed against the extent of real damage or loss suffered, and Japanese law recognises a concept analogous

---

132   See [19.255] in relation to the Australian position.
133   Restatement (Second) § § 370, 374.
134   See [19.275].
135   Breach of contract is regulated in articles 414–418 of the Civil Code.

to set-off, which means that benefits taken under the contract will be considered, in the calculation of loss actually suffered.

Japanese law also recognises a concept analogous to that of independent and dependent obligations. A recent Supreme Court case has made this clear.[136] The contract in question was for the purchase of an apartment bought 'off the plan'. The plan showed a swimming pool and gym, which, subsequently, were not opened. The buyer sought rescission of the sale agreement on the basis that it included an ancillary, tacit obligation to build and open the pool and gym, on which the obligations of the sales agreement depended. The Supreme Court accepted this argument. This decision is expected to have a major impact on contracts involving sale of land or goods that have a service component built into them, or which depend implicitly on the performance of service obligations.[137]

[19.365] Breach of an obligation to pay money is regulated by article 419 of the Civil Code. Where the compensation being claimed is specific performance of the contract, this will not preclude a request for damages to be paid in addition to the specific performance (Civil Code art 414(4)).

---

136 Supreme Court Decision of 12 November 1997 (HO(o)1056).
137 Note that the case could also have been, but was not, resolved on the basis of misrepresentation: see Chapter 13.

Chapter 20

Discharge by termination

20.1 Introduction

[20.05] The previous chapter dealt with the circumstances in which a contract will be discharged by the performance of the parties to a contract.[1] A contract may also be discharged unilaterally by one of the parties for the breach by the other. Discharge of the contract in this way allows the terminating party, in addition to claiming damages for breach, to be freed from his or her obligations under the contract. This chapter considers the circumstances in which a right to terminate may be exercised and the limits imposed by the law on an injured party's right of termination.[2]

---

1   See Chapter 19.
2   The right to damages is considered in Chapter 23.

[20.10] The right to terminate a contract may be conferred expressly by the contract or may be implied by the common law. The common law implies a right to terminate, unless the parties have agreed to the contrary, where one party to the contract:

- fails to perform an essential term of the contract;
- commits a serious breach of an intermediate term; or
- evinces an unwillingness or inability to continue with the contract, constituting a repudiation or anticipatory breach of the contract.

[20.15] Where the party seeking to terminate the contract proves the existence of one or more of the above situations,[3] that party may elect to terminate the contract. Termination of the contract will discharge the parties from their future obligations under the contract, but obligations that have accrued under the contract may still be enforceable after termination.[4]

[20.20] A similar result will occur where the contract provides for one party to have the right to terminate the contract in the event of default under the contract (contractual right to terminate). This type of contractual right may exist independently of the common law principles governing termination. It is considered here only briefly; the emphasis in this chapter is on the rights conferred by the common law for termination of the contract.

20.2 Termination distinguished from rescission

[20.25] The right to terminate a contract for breach should be distinguished from a right to rescind the contract *ab initio*. Termination releases the parties from future obligations to perform but accrued obligations—such as an obligation to pay a deposit—may be enforceable.[5] Rescission *ab initio* means to discharge the contract from the beginning. A court will only grant rescission if the parties can be returned substantially to their original positions. Once a contract is rescinded *ab initio*, it will be as though the contract never existed, and it will be referred to as void. Consequently, after rescission neither party is able to enforce any obligations under the rescinded contract.[6] This will apply even to obligations that were due for performance prior to rescission, such as the payment of a deposit. As part of the order for rescission the court will return all monies paid, and property passed, to the original parties.

[20.30] Both the right to rescission and the right to terminate are subject to a variety of different restrictions.[7]

---

3   The onus of proving the existence of breach or repudiation lies on the party seeking to terminate the contract: *Southern Foundries (1926) Ltd v Shirlaw* [1940] AC 701 at 729; *Hobbs v Persham Transport Co Pty Ltd* (1971) 124 CLR 220 at 230; *Minchillo v Ford Motors Co of Australia Ltd* [1995] 2 VR 594 at 616.

4   The effect of termination on the contract and on the obligations of the parties is considered at [20.470].

5   Damages may also be recoverable for the breach of contract. See Chapter 23.

6   Damages may be available in certain cases, such as negligent or fraudulent misrepresentation or misleading or deceptive conduct.

7   See [20.415]–[20.455] in relation to the restrictions on termination and [13.195]–[13.250] in relation to the restrictions on rescission.

[20.35] The right to terminate a contract will only be available for breach of contract, repudiation or frustration. Rescission of a contract is available for misrepresentation, mistake, unconscionable conduct, duress, undue influence, or misleading or deceptive conduct.[8]

20.3 Termination for breach

[20.40] A right to terminate a contract for breach will arise where there has been a breach of an essential term, serious breach of an intermediate term, or the contract expressly provides for termination in the particular situation. Breach of a term considered to be inessential, (a warranty) will only allow the injured party to sue for damages.

20.3.1 Contractual right of termination

[20.45] Whether a right to terminate given by the contract has arisen will depend upon a construction of the contract. Generally this will require an investigation into whether the events that activate the contractual right have occurred—and then, whether the party has exercised the right of termination according to the contract. The types of clauses that may give a contractual right to terminate are many and varied. In accordance with the usual approach to interpretation of contracts, the court will try to give effect to the intention of the parties in each case.[9] The contractual right to terminate will generally be construed strictly, particularly where a time limit is imposed for exercising the right.[10]

[20.50] The existence of a contractual right to terminate will generally not exclude reliance on the common law right to terminate for repudiation. For example, a contract may provide that the buyer of goods is entitled to terminate the contract if the seller for any reason does not deliver 200 cases of oranges by 20 June. In this example, the right to terminate pursuant to the contract does not arise until 20 June. Therefore, if the seller indicates prior to 20 June that only 150 cases will be delivered, the buyer cannot terminate the contract pursuant to the right in the contract. As the common law right to terminate for repudiation has not been excluded by the contract, the buyer may still be able to rely on the common law to terminate the contract.[11] The exclusion of a right to terminate for repudiation will need to be clearly excluded by the contract.[12]

[20.55] The fact that a party has exercised a contractual right to damages will not equate in all cases to a right to damages for breach of an essential term. A claim for damages will depend upon the injured party's proving that the term breached is essential, or that a repudiation has occurred. The right to damages is linked to the type of breach, rather than the right to terminate.[13]

---

8   A statutory right to rescission exists for misleading or deceptive conduct under the *Trade Practices Act* 1974 or the State *Fair Trading Acts*. This right is discussed further at [13.595].

9   *Telfair Shipping Corp v Athos Shipping Co SA (The Athos)* [1983] 1 Lloyds Rep 127; *Antaios Compania Naviera SA v Salen Rederierna AB* [1985] AC 191.

10 *Rawson v Hobbs* (1961) 107 CLR 466; *Afovos Shipping Co SA v Pagnan* [1983] 1 WLR 195; *Eriksson v Whalley* [1971] 1 NSWLR 397.

11 See for example *Rawson v Hobbs* (1961) 107 CLR 466.

12 See *Amann Aviation Pty Ltd v The Commonwealth* (1990) 92 ALR 601.

13 See *Progressive Mailing House Pty Ltd v Tabali Pty Ltd* (1985) 157 CLR 17.

20.3.2 Common law right of termination

[20.60] The common law right to terminate for breach arises where there has been a breach of an essential term, or a serious breach of an intermediate term of the contract. The different types of terms within a contract were discussed in Chapter 9 but will be briefly revised for the purpose of considering the right of termination.

(a) Breach of an essential term
Express terms

[20.65] The classification of a term as essential will be ascertained by reference to the contract as a whole and a consideration of the intention of the parties. The High Court in Associated Newspapers Ltd v Banks[14] approved the test in Tramways Advertising Pty Ltd v Luna Park (NSW) Ltd[15] pronounce by Jordan CJ:

> The test of essentiality is whether it appears from the general nature of the contract considered as a whole, or from some particular terms or terms, that the promise is of such importance to the promisee that he would not have entered into the contract unless he had been assured of a strict or a substantial performance of the promise, as the case may be, and this ought to have been apparent to the promisor.[16]

[20.70] The effect of classifying a term as essential is that all breaches of that term will allow the innocent party to terminate the contract. This consequence has given rise to reluctance on the part of the courts to construe a term as essential unless it is clear from the circumstances that such an effect was intended by the parties.[17] Where the parties described the term as a 'condition' this will not be conclusive of the fact an essential term was intended.[18] However a statement that 'time is of the essence of this agreement' will result in the court's construing the time requirements of the contract strictly.[19] Another method used to indicate the fundamental nature of a term is to provide for the right to terminate for a breach of a particular term or a right to terminate 'in the case of any breach of a term of the contract'.[20] The court will usually give effect to this type of term and allow the innocent party to terminate the contract. However, the right to damages for loss of the bargain may not follow unless the term breached is actually essential or there is a repudiation of the contract.[21]

[20.75] If the parties have not expressly stated that the term is essential the court will need to construe the contract in the light of the surrounding circumstances. If the

14   (1951) 83 CLR 322.
15   (1938) 38 SR (NSW) 632.
16   Ibid at at 641–642.
17   *Ankar Pty Ltd v National Westminster Finance (Australia) Ltd* (1987) 162 CLR 549 at 556–557.
18   *L Schuler AG v Wickman Machine Tool Sales Ltd* [1974] AC 235 at 251. Refer further to [9.145].
19   The effect of time requirements on a contract and the right of termination are considered at [20.250]–[20.260].
20   *Campbell v Payne and Fitzgerald* (1953) 53 SR (NSW) 537 at 539; *Shevill v Builders Licensing Board* (1981–82) 149 CLR 620.
21   *Shevill v Builders Licensing Board* (1981–82) 149 CLR 620; *Progressive Mailing House Pty Ltd v Tabali Pty Ltd* (1985) 157 CLR 17. See Chapter 23 in relation to the right to claim damages following breach of contract.

contract is subject to the parol evidence rule[22] the court will be unable to have regard to the prior negotiations of the parties or their subsequent conduct to ascertain their intentions. The court will be limited to the contract itself which may cause difficulties in construction and lead the court to lean in favour of a construction that encourages performance rather than one allowing termination.[23] In the absence of the parol evidence rule, however, the court may have regard to a variety of matters to ascertain the intention of the parties. These may include:

- The conduct of the parties following a breach of the term: did the parties act in a way consistent with the term's being essential?
- The motivation for entry into the contract: would the party have entered into the contract unless assured of strict performance?[24]
- Whether the term itself was set out clearly and concisely: did it state precisely the obligations of the parties?
- What the consequences of breaching the term will be. Will every breach of the term deprive the innocent party of substantially the whole benefit of the contract?[25]

[20.80] The contract will not automatically terminate for the breach. The innocent party will need to elect to terminate the contract.[26] Termination for an essential term will be available even though the loss to the innocent party may be small or the detriment to the other party large. Although if that is the case, the court may be reluctant to classify the term as essential and may consider a more suitable classification.

Implied terms

[20.85] A term implied into the contract by statute or at common law may also in some cases be an essential term of the contract. Where a term is implied by statute, the statute will regularly provide for the effect of breaching such a term. Where a term is implied into a consumer transaction, the effect of this implied term may not, as a general rule, be altered by the parties. For example s 71 of the *Trade Practices Act* 1974 provides for all contracts of sale between a corporation and a consumer to contain an implied condition that the goods are fit for the purpose. Section 68 of the *Trade Practices Act* 1974 provides that a contract may not modify, exclude or restrict a term implied by s 71. This may be contrasted with s 17 of the *Sale of Goods Act* 1867 (Qld), which also implies a condition of fitness for the purpose but allows parties to contract out of the effect of the condition.

[20.90] If the term is implied by the common law the classification of the term will depend upon the construction of the contract and the possible intention of the parties. Similar considerations relevant to express terms are also relevant to implied terms. Usually an implied term will not be an essential term of the contract, unless there is some implied agreement to that effect between the parties.[27]

---

22   See [9.25]–[9.30].
23   *Ankar Pty Ltd v National Westminster Finance (Australia) Ltd* (1987) 162 CLR 549 at 556–557.
24   *Associated Newspapers Ltd v Bancks* (1951) 83 CLR 322.
25   *Honkong Fir Shipping Co Ltd v Kawasaki Kisen Kaisha Ltd* [1962] 2 QB 26 at 29.
26   Election to terminate is discussed at [20.320]–[20.375].
27   *Shepherd v Felt and Textiles of Australia Ltd* (1931) 45 CLR 370.

(b)   Breach of an intermediate term

[20.100] As explained earlier,[28] an intermediate term is one that cannot be satisfactorily construed as a condition or a warranty. Typically an intermediate term is one which may give rise to a variety of breaches, some trivial and some serious.[29] Both express terms and implied terms may be intermediate in nature.[30] The approach to classification is the same for express and implied terms. Whether a particular breach will entitle the innocent party to terminate the contract, depends on the seriousness of the breach and the consequences both actual and foreseeable.[31] If the consequences of the breach deprive the innocent party of substantially the whole of the benefit of the contract, termination will be possible. In other cases where the consequences are less serious the innocent party will be limited to a remedy in damages. The effect of terminating for the serious breach of an intermediate term is the same as termination for an essential term.[32]

20.4   Termination for repudiation

[20.105] Repudiation occurs where one party renounces his or her liabilities under a contract—or evinces an intention no longer to be bound by the contract, or shows an intention to fulfil the contract only in a manner substantially inconsistent with his or her obligations, and not in any other way.[33] Underlying this definition of repudiation is the notion that parties should be ready, willing, and able to perform their contractual obligations at the relevant time. A party who is not ready, willing and able to perform the contract at the appointed time may be indicating an intention no longer to be bound by the contract. Repudiation may also occur prior to the time for performance, and is then referred to as 'anticipatory breach'.

[20.110] Repudiation does not automatically bring a contract to an end. As with breach of contract, the promisee must elect to terminate the contract. In the context of repudiation, termination of the contract is also necessary for acceptance of the repudiation. Acceptance of repudiation is necessary to trigger a right to damages.[34] A promisee may elect to terminate for repudiation only if the promisor's absence of readiness and willingness to perform the contract extends to all of the promisor's obligations, or it indicates the promisor will be in breach entitling the promisee to terminate. In other words, the absence of readiness and willingness to perform the contract must be a serious matter.[35]

---

28   See [9.175]–[9.200].

29   Examples of intermediate terms include a seaworthiness provision in a charterparty: *Hongkong Fir Shipping Co Ltd v Kawasaki Kisen Kaisha Ltd* [1962] 2 QB 26; or a clause requiring employees to exercise proper care in carrying out their duties.

30   For example, the implied term in employment contracts, that an employee will exercise all due care and skill, will usually be intermediate because of the range of possible breaches: *Lister v Romford Ice and Cold Storage Co Ltd* [1957] AC 555; *Bliss v South East Thames Regional Health Authority* [1987] ICR 700.

31   *Hongkong Fir Shipping Co Ltd v Kawasaki Kisen Kaisha Ltd* [1962] 2 QB 26; *Direct Acceptance Finance Ltd v Cumberland Furnishing Pty Ltd* [1965] NSWR 1504 at 1511.

32   See [20.70].

33   *Shevill v Builders Licensing Board* (1982) 149 CLR 620 at 625–626.

34   See [23.400].

35   For example *Hochster v De la Tour* (1853) 2 E&B 678; 118 ER 922 and *Federal Commerce and Navigation Co Ltd v Molena Alpha Inc* [1979] AC 757 at 779, 783, 785.

20.5   Repudiation or breach?

[20.115] The question of whether termination for repudiation is justified will focus on whether the defendant, by conduct or words, indicated an unwillingness or inability to continue further with the contract. This involves an examination of the transaction to date between the parties. Repudiation does not depend upon a conclusion that a particular term of the contract has been breached. The focus of the court's examination will be on whether a reasonable person would have concluded that the defendant had repudiated his or her obligations. This differs from the approach to a claim for termination based on the breach of a term, where the focus is on the particular term breached and the consequences of the breach. That is not to say that repudiation and breach of contract are mutually exclusive. Conduct that indicates a lack of willingness or ability to perform the contract may constitute both a repudiation and a breach of a term of the contract. For example, in *Associated Newspapers Ltd v Bancks*,[36] the failure to place the cartoonist's drawing on the front page of the comic section was a breach of an essential term of the contract. The failure to place the drawing on that page for three consecutive weeks was also considered by the court to be an indication of an unwillingness to perform the contract, and therefore a repudiation.

[20.120] Generally, where an essential term of the contract has been breached, it will be unnecessary to consider whether the promisor has repudiated the contract.[37] The promisee will be entitled to terminate the contract for the breach of the essential term. However, where the term breached is merely a warranty, the promisee will have to establish repudiation before the contract may be terminated. Repudiation may occur where there are several consecutive breaches of warranty. For example, in *Progressive Mailing House Pty Ltd v Tabali Pty Ltd*,[38] the lessee failed to pay the rent, and in addition failed to open on time, obstructed access to the premises, caused damage to the drains, and sublet the premises without consent. The individual breaches were only breaches of warranty, but taken together, the conduct evidenced a refusal to perform the contract according to its terms.

[20.125] If the repudiatory conduct of the defendant also results in a serious breach of an intermediate term, the plaintiff will need to be discriminating in his or her choice. While the difference between the two may appear to be subtle, a different range of evidence will need to be presented for each. The focus of repudiation will be on the words and conduct of the defendant and the absences of readiness and willingness, whereas the focus for breach of an intermediate term will be on the consequences of the breach. The two may merge where the absence of a willingness or readiness to perform, such as an accumulation of breaches, gives rise to the serious consequences of the breach.

20.6   Anticipatory breach

[20.130] Anticipatory breach is a form of repudiation. It occurs where a party, prior to the time for performance under the contract, evinces an intention no longer to be

---

36   (1951) 83 CLR 322.
37   See the comments in *Associated Newspapers Ltd v Bancks* (1951) 83 CLR 322 at 339–340.
38   (1985) 157 CLR 17.

bound to the contract according to its terms. A promisee may terminate for an anticipatory breach immediately, even if the time for performance has not arrived. The only proviso is that the breach must be of a sufficiently serious nature so that if it had occurred at the time for performance the promisee would have been entitled to terminate the contract. In other words, if the anticipatory breach relates to a breach of an essential term or the repudiation goes to the root of the contract,[39] the promisee may terminate prior to the time for actual performance.[40]

[20.135] The promisee may also wait until the time for performance and accept the failure to perform as an actual repudiation of the contract or a breach of an essential term. If the promisee elects to wait until the time for performance before terminating they should be aware of an important limitation. Consistently with the fact that anticipatory breach is a form of repudiation, the breach must be accepted before it may be acted upon. This means if the innocent party does not elect to terminate the contract prior to the time for performance, the contract will continue on foot, for the benefit of both parties. In that case, it is possible for the repudiating party to change his or her mind and complete the contract. For example, A agrees to sell her land to B on 1 June for $100 000. On 25 May, B states that finance is not available and he will not be able to complete on 1 June. This is an anticipatory breach entitling A to terminate the contract immediately. If A decides not to terminate on 25 May, but rather continues performing the agreement, she may terminate on 1 June for actual breach if B does not complete the contract.[41] However, if the contract remains on foot between 25 May and 1 June, B is entitled to change his mind and complete the contract on 1 June. If B decides to complete, A will not be entitled to rely on the previous anticipatory breach to terminate the contract or claim damages.[42]

20.7   Scope of repudiation

[20.140] The doctrine of repudiation applies to the majority of contractual arrangements between parties to both commercial and private transactions. A significant limitation on this proposition is that the doctrine may be excluded by the parties. This limit on the operation of the doctrine is discussed later.[43] Questions have also been raised in the past about the application of the doctrine to leases. Upon the execution of a lease, not only is a contractual arrangement formed between the parties, but in addition an interest in land is granted to the lessee. It has been suggested that the creation of this interest in land should prevent purely contractual doctrines from operating. However, Australian courts have clearly accepted that contractual principles—subject to some limitations—will have application to leases just like any other contract.[44] The complications that arise when considering the termination of a lease for repudiation do so mainly because of the parallel existence of both contractual and proprietary interests.

---

39   That is a serious breach of an intermediate term.
40   See *Foran v Wight* (1989) 168 CLR 385 at 395, 416, 441.
41   Ibid.
42   See *Foran v Wight* (1989) 165 CLR 385; *Sibbles v Highfern* (1987) 164 CLR 214; *Bowes v Chateyer* (1923) 43 CLR 159.
43   See [20.465].
44   *Shevill v Builders Licensing Board* (1981–82) 149 CLR 620; *Progressive Mailing House Pty Ltd v Tabali Pty Ltd* (1985) 157 CLR 17.

The first complication is the existence of statutory limitations on the right of a lessor to forfeit the lessee's interest in the land.[45] In most Australian jurisdictions, legislation requires the lessor to give the lessee time to rectify the breach prior to termination of the lease. The delivery of such a notice would usually be a prerequisite to exercising a right to terminate for repudiation. The second and third complications impact on the right to claim damages for the loss of the bargain following termination. Most leases will contain a clause giving the lessor the right to terminate the contract if the lessee is in default of any clause of the lease. As highlighted earlier,[46] although that type of clause may allow termination of the lease, the right to damages will depend upon the existence of the breach of an essential term or a repudiation of the contract.[47] The final problem arises from the operation of the doctrine of surrender of leases.[48] If the court considers that the lessor actually accepted a surrender of the lease rather than terminating for repudiation, no damages for the loss of future rent will be recoverable.[49]

20.8 Proof of repudiation

[20.145] Repudiation may be proved by reference to the parties' words, conduct, or position (that is, whether on the basis of the surrounding facts they are in a position to perform the contract). As discussed earlier,[50] the unwillingness or inability to perform must relate either to the whole of the party's obligations under the contract, or be sufficient to allow termination of the contract for breach of an essential term or serious breach of an intermediate term. Where the plaintiff is relying on the defendant's words or conduct as indicating a refusal to perform, there is no requirement for proof that the defendant is also unable to perform. The plaintiff may simply rely upon the defendant's stated intention not to perform, and terminate the contract. If the plaintiff is relying on the defendant's apparent inability to perform due to the circumstances, the plaintiff will be required to prove that the defendant was unable to perform at the time for performance under the contract.

20.9 Examples of repudiation

[20.150] Whether the conduct of a contracting party will amount to repudiation is a question of fact. Proof of repudiation will fall into two broad categories:

- repudiation by words or conduct; and
- repudiation through inability to perform.[51]

---

45   *Conveyancing Act* 1919 (NSW), s 129(2); *Property Law Act* 1974 (Qld), s 124; *Landlord and Tenant Act* 1936 (SA), s 11; *Conveyancing and Law of Property Act* 1884 (Tas), s 15(2); *Property Law Act* 1958 (Vic), s 146(2); *Property Law Act* 1969 (WA), s 81(2); *Forfeiture of Leases Act* 1901 (NSW), ss 1, 4; *Law of Property Act* 2000 (NT), s 137.

46   See [20.55].

47   *Shevill v Builders Licensing Board* (1981–82) 149 CLR 620; *Progressive Mailing House Pty Ltd v Tabali Pty Ltd* (1985) 157 CLR 17. See [20.105].

48   See WD Duncan *Commercial Leases*, 3rd edn, LBC Information Services, Sydney, 1998, pp 301–308, in relation to the operation of the doctrine of surrender.

49   Arrears of rent will still be recoverable.

50   See [20.105].

51   See [20.205]–[20.215].

20.9.1   *Repudiation by words or conduct*

(a)   Express refusal

[20.155] Express refusal to perform a contract is the clearest case of repudiation. Refusal to perform all of the obligations under the contract will clearly amount to repudiation.

Example: Hochster v De la Tour[52]

The defendant agreed to employ the plaintiff for a specified period as a courier. Before the employment was due to commence, the defendant told the plaintiff that his services were no longer required.

The court held that the defendant had repudiated all of his obligations under the contract. Lord Campbell said:

> The declaration in the present case, alleging a breach, states a great deal more than a passing intention on the part of the defendant which he may repent of, and could only be proved by evidence that he had utterly renounced the contract, or done some act which rendered it impossible for him to perform it.[53]

[20.160] Repudiation may also occur where the promisor refuses to perform some of his or her obligations under a contract—provided the refusal is a sufficiently serious matter. Similarly, a refusal to perform in accordance with the contract will also be a repudiation even though there is no express refusal to perform a particular term. An example is provided in *Associated Newspapers Ltd v Bancks*,[54] where the newspaper editor printed the drawing by a cartoonist but did not print it on the first page for three consecutive weeks. The court considered this to be a repudiation, irrespective of whether any term had been breached.

(b)   Implied refusal

[20.165] An express statement by words or conduct is not always necessary. Repudiation may be implied from the party's words or conduct. Brennan J in *Laurinda Pty Ltd v Capalaba Park Shopping Centre Pty Ltd*[55] stated that repudiation may be inferred where a:

> reasonable person in the shoes of the innocent party [would] clearly infer that the other party would not be bound by the contract or would fulfil it only in a manner substantially inconsistent with that party's obligations and in no other way.[56]

---

52   (1853) 2 E & B 678; 118 ER 922.
53   Ibid at 926.
54   (1951) 83 CLR 322.
55   (1989) 166 CLR 623.
56   Ibid at 648.

Example: Laurinda Pty Ltd v Capalaba Park Shopping Centre Pty Ltd[57]

The lessee executed a lease of premises and paid the stamp duty to the lessor, with authority for the lessor to complete the lease and lodge it for registration. In a nine-month period the lessee made several requests for a copy of the completed and registered lease. After nine months had elapsed and the lease was still not registered, the lessee sent a demand requesting a copy of the registered lease within 14 days. The lessor did not deliver the lease, and the lessee purported to terminate the agreement.

In deciding whether the lessor had repudiated its obligation to register the lease, the Court drew a distinction between an intention to carry out a contract only *if and when* it suited the party to do so, and an intention to carry out a contract *as and when* it suited the party. In the first case, it is easy to draw the inference that the party no longer intends to be bound by the contract because the party does not intend to carry out the contract at all if it does not suit him or her. In the second instance, it will depend on the circumstances of the case, because the party intends to perform the contract but only as and when it suits him or her. Due to the substantial delay in performance that occurred in the case, the Court held that the lessor had repudiated the contract. The clear intention only to perform the contract in a manner substantially inconsistent with its obligations was evidenced by the protracted delay in registering the lease.

[20.170] Further instances of an implied refusal to perform may be found in instalment contracts for the sale of goods. A failure to deliver or pay for one instalment may indicate that the party will be unable to deliver or pay for later instalments.[58] However, an inference of repudiation will depend in all cases upon proof of the requirement of seriousness.[59] This may involve consideration not only of whether the breach will occur again, but also the ratio that the breach bears to the whole of the contract.[60]

(c) Unjustifiable interpretation of the contract

[20.175] If a party acts on an erroneous construction and breaches one or more terms of the contract or evinces an intention not to perform except in accordance with the erroneous interpretation, the party may have repudiated his or her obligations if the requirement of seriousness is satisfied—as where the erroneous interpretation concerns the performance of significant contractual obligations. Repudiation was established in *Luna Park (NSW) Ltd v Tramways Advertising Pty Ltd*,[61] where the defendant failed to display each and every roof board on its trams for at least eight hours on each and every day. The plaintiff had advised the defendant of this failure, but the defendant continued with its inadequate performance. The defendant claimed that it was unable to control the trams, and therefore could not ensure that the signs were displayed for

---

57   Ibid.
58   *Millars' Karris and Jarrah Co v Weddel Turner & Co* (1908) 14 Com Cas 25 at 29.
59   See *Warinco AG v Samor SpA* [1979] 1 Ll Rep 450.
60   *Maple Flock Co Ltd v Universal Furniture Products (Wembley) Ltd* [1934] 1 KB 148 at 157; *Hammer v Coca-Cola* [1962] NZLR 723 at 725–726.
61   (1938) 61 CLR 286.

eight hours a day. The court concluded that the requirement to display the advertisements was a condition of the contract. Therefore, due to the breach of contract—or because the defendant was only prepared to perform on the basis of its erroneous construction (repudiating the contract, according to the terms agreed upon)—the plaintiff was entitled to terminate. The fact that the defendant could not control the trams was irrelevant.

[20.180] The position in *Luna Park* should be contrasted with *DTR Nominees Pty Ltd v Mona Homes Pty Ltd*.[62] There, the vendor agreed to sell to the purchaser nine land subdivisions, which were set out on a plan annexed to the contract. A term of the contract provided that a plan of subdivision as annexed had been lodged with the local authority. In fact a plan different from the one in the contract had been lodged. Once the plan was lodged, the vendor required settlement in accordance with the contract. The purchaser purported to terminate because the plan lodged was not the one in the contract. The vendor argued that the purchaser's termination constituted a wrongful termination of the contract. In reliance upon the wrongful termination, the vendor purported to terminate the contract and claim the deposit. The court held that lodgement of a different plan in these circumstances was not repudiation of the contract. In considering this case, the court distinguished two situations:

- where, in the face of adverse comment a party insists on an interpretation of the contract which is not tenable; and
- where the party, although asserting a wrong view of a contract is willing to perform the contract according to its tenor.

[20.185] Only the first is an example of repudiation. In the court's view, because the purchaser had not advised the vendor of the error, nor given the vendor any opportunity to rectify the position, there was no basis upon which to infer that the vendor was persisting in its interpretation in the face of a clear enunciation to the contrary. It could have been that the vendor, if apprised of the mistake, would have performed the contract according to its terms.[63]

(d)   Wrongful termination of a contract

[20.190] Generally, a wrongful termination of the contract constitutes repudiation.[64] This means that, where a party purports to terminate a contract in circumstances where he or she has no legal right to do so, the party's conduct will constitute a repudiation of the agreement. As the purported termination is wrongful, it will not be effective to terminate the contract. Consequently the innocent party will still have to elect to terminate the contract for repudiation.[65] In *Braidotti v Queensland City Properties Ltd*,[66] the vendor under an instalment contract purported to give a notice of termination before complying

---

62   (1978) 138 CLR 423.

63   This case was followed in *Trawl Industries of Australia Pty Ltd v Effem Foods Pty Ltd Trading as 'Uncle Bens of Australia'* (1992) 27 NSWLR 326. Cf *Braidotti v Queensland City Properties Ltd* (1991) 65 ALJR 387 at 392. See also: *Starlight Enterprises Ltd v Lapco Enterprises Ltd* [1979] 2 NZLR 744.

64   *Ogle v Comboyuro Investments Pty Ltd* (1976) 136 CLR 444 at 453. Note in *DTR Nominees Pty Ltd v Mona Homes Pty Ltd* (1978) 138 CLR 423 the wrongful termination by the vendor was not a repudiation entitling termination due to the abandonment of the contract by the parties.

65   *White and Carter (Councils) Ltd v McGregor* [1962] AC 413.

66   (1991) 65 ALJR 387.

with s 72 *Property Law Act* 1974 (Qld). Due to non-compliance with the section, the purported termination of the contract by the vendor was ineffective. The court considered that termination of the contract in the circumstances was a repudiation as it 'signalled an unqualified intention not to proceed with the contract'.[67]

[20.195] Where the purported wrongful termination of the contract is in reliance upon a contractual right of termination, the court may consider the bona fides of the terminating party. If the party truly believes that its termination is justified by the contract, is its conduct repudiation? In *Woodar Investment Development Ltd v Wimpey Construction UK Ltd*,[68] the House of Lords considered that a bona fide reliance upon a right to terminate a land contract was not repudiation.[69] However, the contrary view has also been expressed, as the establishment of repudiation relies upon an objective test intention and bona fides should be irrelevant.[70]

(e)   Commencement of proceedings

[20.200] The commencement of proceedings will not amount to repudiation of a contract unless those proceedings are commenced in such circumstances as to make it plain that the party commencing them thereby evinces an intention not to be bound irrespective of the outcome. As the plaintiff seeking a determination by the court will usually abide by the court's decision, such conduct will not be repudiation.[71]

20.9.2   *Repudiation based on inability to perform*

(a)   Express declaration by words or acts

[20.205] Express declaration of an inability to perform is the clearest example of repudiation based on inability to perform. For example, in *Foran v Wight*[72] the vendor informed the purchaser he would be unable to settle on the date for completion because he was unable to remove an easement from the title prior to the required date. As time was of the essence, and it was clear that the easement would not be removed within two days, the court held the vendor had repudiated his obligations.

[20.210] A party may also declare by its actions that it is unable to perform a contract—for example, if the vendor in a land transaction, after agreeing to sell the property to the purchaser, sells it to a third party. The act of selling the property to another person will be a repudiation of the first contract. The purchaser will be able to terminate the contract for repudiation, as it is clear the vendor will be unable to perform.[73]

(b)   Implied inability

[20.215] Even though the defendant has not expressly indicated an inability to perform the contract, the facts may indicate that the defendant will be unable to perform. In that

---

67   Ibid at 391. The High Court, at 392, contrasted this with *DTR Nominees Pty Ltd v Mona Homes Pty Ltd* (1978) 138 CLR 423 (see [20.180]).

68   [1980] 1 WLR 277.

69   See also *Mersey Steel and Iron Co Ltd v Naylor Benzon & Co* (1884) 9 App Cas 434.

70   *Satellite Estates Pty Ltd v Jaquet* (1967) 71 SR (NSW) 126 at 150. *Carr v JA Berriman Pty Ltd* (1953) 89 CLR 327 at 351; *Laurinda Pty Ltd v Capalaba Park Shipping Centre Pty Ltd* (1989) 166 CLR 623 at 633–634, 644, 657–658.

71   See, for example, *Lombok Pty Ltd v Supetina Pty Ltd* (1987) 71 ALR 333.

72   (1989) 168 CLR 385.

73   See also *Schmidt v Holland* [1982] 2 NZLR 406 where the purchaser entered into another contract to purchase a house. This conduct in addition to a failure to attend settlement was considered repudiation.

case, the plaintiff must prove that the defendant is wholly and finally disabled from performing the contract. It will be necessary to prove the defendant's actual position rather than what the defendant has said or done. For example, if the vendor of a property requires the consent of the Crown to the transfer of the land and this had not been given 3 days prior to completion, this is likely to indicate an inability to perform where time is of the essence of the contract. Without the consent, no transfer of the property could take place at the time nominated. If there is no possibility that the consent will be obtained within the time limits of the contract, the vendor is at that time wholly and finally disabled from performing the contract. Generally this type of repudiation is difficult to prove—which makes reliance on the conduct as anticipatory breach risky. Usually a party will wait until the time for performance and act upon the clear failure to perform, rather than attempting to prove inability in the abstract. Inability to perform may be argued where an earlier ground for termination, such as express refusal to perform, is unsuccessful. As a final resort, the terminating party may seek to rely upon factual inability to perform as justification for his or her termination.[74]

20.10 Acceptance of repudiation

[20.220] As discussed above, repudiation of a contract must be accepted by terminating the contract. Acceptance of the repudiation is a requirement both for termination and to complete the injured party's right to damages.[75] Prior to acceptance of the repudiation, it may be possible for the other (repudiating) party to retract a verbal repudiation and perform the contract. However, where the verbal repudiation has been relied upon by the innocent party in performing or failing to perform the contract, the retracting party will need to give notice to the innocent party (allowing time for performance).[76] If reasonable notice of retraction is not given, the innocent party may refuse to perform.[77]

[20.225] The consequences of accepting a repudiation are the same as electing to terminate for breach. The contract will be discharged along with the parties' obligations to perform.[78]

20.11 Termination for delay

[20.230] The circumstances in which a delay in performance gives rise to a right of termination are worthy of separate consideration. Although the general common law principles concerning breach are applicable, the overlay of equitable principles, in respect of time stipulations, acts to create issues that require separate consideration.

[20.235] A contract may be terminated for delay in performance in one of two circumstances. First, the defaulting party may not perform at the appointed time. This will involve a direct breach of a time stipulation in the contract. The second type of

---

74 A party may rely upon an alternative ground to justify the termination of a contract where the first ground is found to be untenable: *Shepherd v Felt and Textiles of Australia Ltd* (1931) 45 CLR 359; *Sunbird Plaza Pty Ltd v Maloney* (1988) 166 CLR 245. See [20.405].

75 See [23.400].

76 See *Foran v Wight* (1989) 168 CLR 385; *Cohen & Co v Ockerby & Co Ltd* (1917) 24 CLR 288 at 298.

77 *Peter Turnbull & Co Pty Ltd v Mundus Trading Co (Australasia) Pty Ltd* (1954) 90 CLR 235.

78 See [20.320]–[20.375] in relation to the election to terminate for breach.

delay may arise as a consequence of a breach of another term of the contract. For example, where a lessor provides defective goods to a lessee under a chattel lease and this means there is a delay in delivery of the goods while they are being repaired.

[20.240] The first situation involves the breach of a time provision in a contract. As with any other term of the contract, a breach of a time stipulation will only allow termination if the provision is essential. However, there may be circumstances in which the breach of an inessential time provision will also give rise to a right to terminate because of unreasonable delay. The second situation does not give rise to the direct breach of a time stipulation in the contract, but the injured party may suffer loss arising from the delay in performance. Whether the injured party may terminate the contract will depend on the nature of the other term that is breached and whether the delay in providing performance of the contract is so unreasonably long that there is an intention not to perform the contract according to its terms. Even if the breach is not serious enough for termination, the injured party will be entitled to claim damages for breach.

[20.245] It is only in the first situation described above that the rules of common law and equity concerning time provisions are relevant.

20.12 Time stipulations: general principles

[20.250] The common law and equity differ in the treatment of time provisions in contracts. At common law, a date specified in a contract will generally be considered essential unless the contrary intention is indicated in the contract. In equity, a contrary approach is taken: time is not considered to be of the essence unless it is expressly stated to be of the essence in the contract, or where 'there was something in the nature of the property or the surrounding circumstances which would render it inequitable to treat it as a non-essential term'.[79]

[20.255] The obvious conflict between the rules at common law and in equity was resolved in each State by legislation providing for the rule in equity to prevail. For example, s 62 of the *Property Law Act* 1974 (Qld) provides that:

> Stipulations in contracts, as to time or otherwise, which according to rules of equity are not deemed to be or to have become of the essence of the contract, shall be construed and have effect at law in accordance with rules of equity.[80]

[20.260] The statutory provisions override the common law rule and require a contract to be construed in accordance with the rules of equity, but only as they operated prior to the legislation. Prior to the legislation, the equitable rules operated in the context of equitable claims. This means that the rules of equity regarding time will only have application where the plaintiff is seeking specific performance, an injunction, or some other equitable remedy.[81] The statute does not prevent a claim for damages at

---

79 *Stickney v Keeble* [1915] AC 386.
80 A similar provision can also be found in s 13 *Conveyancing Act* 1919 (NSW); s 41 *Property Law Act* 1958 (Vic); s 16 *Law of Property Act* 1936 (SA); s 21 *Property Law Act* 1969 (WA); s 4 *Law of Property (Miscellaneous Provisions) Act* 1958 (ACT); s 65 *Law of Property Act* 2000 (NT).
81 *Holland v Wiltshire* (1954) 90 CLR 409 at 418–419.

common law for a failure to perform on time. Where the rule of equity applies, the failure to perform on time is a breach of a non-essential term giving rise to a right to damages unless the contract, or the circumstances, indicate time is of the essence.[82] Where no equitable remedy is being sought, the equitable presumption does not apply and the failure to comply with the time provision should be analysed in accordance with the common law rules. This means that if a date is specified it will usually be the case that the parties intended time to be of the essence expressly or by implication. In *Bunge Corp New York v Tradax Export SA Panama*,[83] neither party was claiming an equitable remedy, so the court approached the case from the perspective of the common law. The court held that, on its construction of the contract, the parties intended time to be of the essence, particularly since it was a mercantile agreement.

20.13 Breach of essential time provisions

[20.265] Time provisions in contracts are treated in the same way as any other term. Where the time provision is essential, the innocent party will be able to terminate the contract for the other party's failure to perform on time. It is therefore, necessary to consider the circumstances in which time will be considered to be of the essence of the contract. As previously discussed, whether a term of a contract will be classified as essential depends upon a construction of the contract and a consideration of the intention of the parties.[84] From this broad proposition, specific rules for determining when a time provision is essential have been developed.

[20.270] First, time will be of the essence at common law and in equity where time is expressly stated to be of the essence. This requires more than the mere provision of a date for performance, and it usually applies where the term states 'time is of the essence of this agreement'. The second circumstance where time will be considered to be of the essence at common law and in equity is where there is something in the nature of the property or the surrounding circumstances that indicates a time stipulation should be essential.[85]

Thirdly, specific dates for performance in commercial contracts will generally be treated by the common law as essential where they relate to substantive obligations under the contract.[86] These are obligations such as the time for delivery of goods, time for acceptance, and the time for shipment. However, this is not an absolute rule, and it relies to a certain extent on the court's being able to draw such an implication from the intention of the parties. Time provisions concerning procedural matters in a commercial contract will not, unless express agreement is present, be essential.

[20.275] Time provisions in land transactions are considered differently from commercial contracts. The main reason for the difference lies in the nature of a land transaction. Upon execution of a land contract, the purchaser acquires an equitable interest in

---

82   *Stickney v Keeble* [1915] AC 386.
83   [1981] 1 WLR 711. The court adopted the approach in *Holland v Wiltshire* (1954) 90 CLR 409. See also *Citicorp Australia Ltd v Hendry* (1985) 4 NSWLR 22 at 27.
84   See [20.65]–[20.80].
85   *Stickney v Keeble* [1915] AC 386; *Canning v Temby* (1905) 3 CLR 419.
86   *Bunge Corp New York v Tradax Export SA Panama* [1981] 1 WLR 711 at 720.

the land. Equitable doctrines may be used by purchasers to protect their interest in the land from forfeiture. Equity will not enforce a time stipulation unless the contract clearly indicates that time is of the essence.[87] This will occur, as for other contracts, where time is expressly stated to be of the essence, or where there is something in the nature of the property or the surrounding circumstances that indicates the time stipulation should be essential. An example of the second instance may occur with a contract for the sale of a pastoral property. The perishable nature of the stock and the variability in markets may imply that the parties intend time to be of the essence.[88] The only exception to the general proposition stated above is a provision requiring the payment of a deposit on a certain date. The requirement to pay a deposit will usually be considered an essential term even though payment at a particular time may not be expressed as essential. The classification of the term as essential is due to the nature of a deposit as a bond for performance of the agreement.[89]

[20.280] Where time is expressly stated to be of the essence, breach of the time provision will allow the innocent party to terminate the contract immediately, according to the rules of either common law or equity. However, in the case of a land transaction, the right of the vendor to terminate is subject to the right of purchasers to seek relief against forfeiture of their interest.[90]

20.14 Time as an intermediate term

[20.285] Theoretically, the principles concerning intermediate terms should be applicable to time stipulations. However, as pointed out in *Bunge Corp New York v Tradax Export SA Panama*,[91] only one type of breach of a time stipulation is possible: to be late. The subsequent High Court decision of *Ankar Pty Ltd v National Westminster Finance (Australia) Ltd*[92] seems to suggest that it might be possible for a time stipulation to be intermediate in nature, on the basis that the gravity of the breach will depend on the length of the delay. However, this overlooks the fact that a term will only be intermediate if there is a range of different types of breaches, not a range of consequences.

20.15 Termination for breach of an inessential time stipulation

[20.290] A time provision that is not essential will be inessential. As with other inessential terms, breach of an inessential time provision does not give rise to a right to terminate. However, unlike other inessential terms, the contract may be terminated for the breach of a time provision, after a notice requiring performance within a reasonable time is served and the defaulting party fails to perform. The primary purpose of the notice is to set a new date for performance by which a party in default will be consid-

---

87   See [20.250]–[20.260] in relation to when time is of the essence in equity.
88   *Carpentaria Investments Pty Ltd v Airs* [1972] Qd R 436.
89   *Brien v Dwyer* (1978) 141 CLR 378; *Millichamp v Jones* [1982] 1 WLR 1422.
90   See [20.445].
91   [1981] 1 WLR 711.
92   (1987) 162 CLR 549 at 562.

ered to have repudiated the contract through unreasonable delay. However, a notice will not be required if the conduct of the party, including the delay in performance, constitutes a repudiation of the contract.[93]

[20.295] The service of a notice in two common situations is considered here.

20.15.1 Time is inessential but a date for performance is stated in the contract

Unreasonable delay, and therefore repudiation, may be proved where the delay that extends beyond the date stated in the contract is so gross or protracted as to cause serious detriment to the other party.[94] In a commercial contract, the concept of a frustrating delay has been used: the delay must be so unreasonable as to frustrate the commercial purpose of the contract.[95] A notice to complete may be served immediately, once the date for performance has passed, giving a reasonable time for performance. The significance of the notice in this context is, first, that it fixes a day when, if the default is not remedied, the party in default will be held to have repudiated the promise. Secondly, it will show that for equity's purposes, it is fair for the innocent party to exercise that right.[96] If the contract is not completed in accordance with the notice, an unreasonable delay will be considered to have occurred.

20.15.2 No time for performance is stated in the contract

Where no date for performance is stated, it will be implied that performance of the contract should occur within a reasonable time.[97] To prove unreasonable delay in this case, there must in effect be two periods of unreasonable delay. First, there must be a failure to perform within a reasonable time. This establishes a breach of the contract. What will be a reasonable time is a question of fact and will change from case to case. A further unreasonable delay in performance is necessary to establish repudiation of the contract. A notice to complete would usually be served after a reasonable time has elapsed.[98] The purpose of the notice in this context is to set a reasonable time for performance—after which, if performance does not occur, the court will infer repudiation of the contract.[99] The notice will give a further reasonable time for performance. If the contract is not completed in accordance with the notice, the court will consider that an unreasonable delay has occurred, provided an appropriate time period has been given.[100] Although in most cases a notice to complete would be given, it is not necessary if the delay in performance by the defaulting party constitutes a repudiation.[101]

---

93 See *Laurinda Pty Ltd v Capalaba Park Shopping Centre Pty Ltd* (1989) 166 CLR 623 where although the notice was not valid the plaintiff was able to terminate the contract based upon the repudiation of the defendant.

94 *Louinder v Leis* (1982) 149 CLR 509; *Neeta (Epping) Pty Ltd v Phillips* (1974) 131 CLR 286 at 302.

95 *Hongkong Fir Shipping Co Ltd v Kawasaki Kisen Kaisha Ltd* [1962] 2 QB 26; *Universal Cargo Carriers Corp v Citati* [1957] 2 QB 402.

96 *Green v Sevin* (1879) 13 Ch D 589 at 599; *Maynard v Goode* (1926) 37 CLR 529 at 538; *Laurinda Pty Ltd v Capalaba Park Shopping Centre Pty Ltd* (1989) 166 CLR 623 at 644–645.

97 *Perri v Coolangatta Investments Pty Ltd* (1982) 149 CLR 537.

98 *Louinder v Leis* (1982) 149 CLR 509.

99 *Laurinda Pty Ltd v Capalaba Park Shopping Centre Pty Ltd* (1989) 166 CLR 623 at 645.

100 Ibid.

101 See *Laurinda Pty Ltd v Capalaba Park Shopping Centre Pty Ltd* (1989) 166 CLR 623.

20.16 Requirements of a valid notice to complete

[20.300] As discussed above, if time is not of the essence and one party fails to perform on time, the other party may terminate the contract after serving a notice, specifying a time for performance, on the first party. The notice itself does not make time of the essence of the contract where time was not stated by the contract to be essential. The real effect of the notice is to make the time fixed by the notice essential.[102]

[20.305] The notice is not required to be in any particular form, but should contain all of the following.

* *What the promisor must do to perform the contract.*[103] For example, a notice given by a seller of land to the buyer should state the amount of the balance purchase monies that should be tendered and the place for tender.

* *A reasonable time in which the contract must be completed.* What is a reasonable time will depend on the circumstances. The court will consider the nature of the transaction, the remaining actions a party is required to undertake to perform the contract, and how long the party has already been given to complete. In land transactions, a period of 24 hours will be considered too short and, as a rule of thumb, not less than 7 days should be stated. This may extend to a longer period where the transaction is complex.[104]

* *A statement of the consequences of not performing in accordance with the notice.*[105] The notice should clearly indicate to the other party, either that time is of the essence of the notice, or that, in the event of non-compliance, the notifying party will be entitled, or will regard itself as entitled, to terminate the contract. A statement such as 'our clients reserve their rights in respect of your client's default' will not be sufficient.[106]

[20.310] A notice that fails to comply with all of these requirements will be invalid. In that case, the innocent party must either serve another notice or prove repudiation by the defaulting party, to terminate the contract.

20.17 Delay constituting repudiation

[20.315] A mere delay in performance of a contract will not amount to repudiation. The delay must be unreasonably long, so that the only reasonable inference to be drawn is that the defaulting party does not intend to perform the contract substantially in accordance with its terms. In *Laurinda Pty Ltd v Capalaba Park Shopping Centre Pty Ltd*,[107] Brennan J considered that:

---

102 *Louinder v Leis* (1982) 149 CLR 509 at 532–33.
103 *Falconer v Wilson* [1973] 2 NSWLR 131.
104 *Sindel v Georgiou* (1984) 154 CLR 661; *Laurinda Pty Ltd v Capalaba Park Shopping Centre Pty Ltd* (1989) 166 CLR 623.
105 *Laurinda Pty Ltd v Capalaba Park Shopping Centre Pty Ltd* (1989) 166 CLR 623.
106 Ibid at 654.
107 Ibid.

If the inference to be drawn from the circumstances is that the defaulting party intends to perform an essential promise after some minor delay, repudiation cannot be inferred; but if the inference is that the defaulting party intends so to delay performance that the promisee will be substantially deprived of the benefit of the promise, repudiation can be inferred.[108]

20.18 Election to terminate for breach

20.18.1 Termination not automatic

[20.320] A contract will not automatically terminate due to the breach or repudiation by one of the parties.[109] The innocent party has a choice. The innocent party may either:

• accept the repudiation or breach of contract and terminate the contract; or
• affirm the contract.

[20.325] There is no requirement that the right be exercised immediately. The question may be kept open as long as the innocent party does not affirm the contract or prejudice the other party by the delay.

[20.330] The party in breach has no right to determine the contract nor any right to force the innocent party to do so. The innocent party may terminate the contract immediately for repudiation or breach of an essential term, and is not obliged to give the defaulting party the opportunity to rectify the breach unless legislation requires him or her to do so.[110] A notice giving additional time to perform the contract may also be required where a time stipulation is not considered to be essential in equity.[111]

20.18.2 Doctrine of election

[20.335] An innocent party who elects to terminate the contract will be prevented at a later date from seeking to enforce the contract, for the very reason that it no longer exists.[112] On the other hand, due to the doctrine of election, a party who elects to affirm the contract will be prevented at a later date from terminating the contract for the same breach.[113] The doctrine of election requires a party to elect between two inconsistent legal rights. A legal right is inconsistent with another right if neither can be enjoyed without the extinction of the other. This applies to a party's election between affirmation and termination of a contract. It is not possible for a party to affirm the agreement without first electing to forgo the right to terminate the contract. It necessarily follows that once an election is made to affirm, the right to terminate cannot be revived.

---

108 Ibid at 643.
109 *Kelly v Desnoe* [1985] 2 QdR 477. Compare this with the effect of frustration at [22.215]–[22.250].
110 See, for example, ss 124 and 72 *Property Law Act* 1974 (Qld); s 129 *Conveyancing Act* 1919 (NSW); s 146 *Property Law Act* 1958 (Vic); s 81 *Property Law Act* 1969 (WA); ss 137 and 69 *Law of Property Act* 2000 (NT).
111 See [20.260].
112 See *Evans v Watt* (1880) 43 LT 176.
113 See *Sargent v ASL Developments Ltd* (1974) 131 CLR 634 at 642. However, a party will not be prevented from terminating at a later date for a subsequent or continuing breach of the contract.

20.18.3　Requirements of a valid election

[20.360] Once it is recognised that the injured party is faced with a choice between inconsistent rights, it will be necessary for the court to determine whether in fact an election has occurred. The issues relevant to this determination are:

* Has the party elected by unequivocal words or conduct?
* Did the party have knowledge of the necessary facts that imply that an election was made?

[20.365] Whether the elector's words or acts are unequivocally consistent only with the exercise of one of the two rights, and inconsistent with the other, is a question of fact. In the context of termination and affirmation, the court will be concerned with whether the elector has acted in a manner consistent with the continued existence of . the contract. Actions such as tendering the purchase price for goods or land, or continuing to accept rent under a lease, will be consider as affirmations of the contract.

[20.370] The next inquiry is as to the elector's knowledge of the material circumstances which, in law, give rise to the right to elect. Great variance exists among the authorities about the nature of the knowledge required. However, it is clear that an elector must at least have knowledge of the facts that give rise to the right to terminate. This requires the elector to know that the other party has breached the contract.[114] The conflict in the authorities arises in relation to whether the elector must also have knowledge of the right of election as between two available inconsistent legal rights.

[20.375] The spectrum of authorities moves from not discussing the issue,[115] to only requiring knowledge of the facts,[116] to expressly denying the need for knowledge of legal rights,[117] to, finally, requiring actual knowledge of the right to elect.[118] It has been suggested by one member of the judiciary that the way to navigate the maze is to distinguish between contractually conferred rights and other common law rights. As parties will be deemed to know the contents of their own contract, the issue of knowledge of legal rights should not arise.[119] This may explain several of the decisions, but does not answer the question definitively. Another suggestion is that knowledge of the right to elect is not relevant where the elector's word or conduct is clear. It is only where the conduct is equivocal that the issue of conduct becomes relevant.[120] Neither of these theories adequately explains the divergent views in the cases, and the New Zealand judiciary has suggested that no plausible reconciliation is possible, relegating the issue to a question of fact in each case.[121]

114　In *Bennett v L&W Whitehead Ltd* [19412] AC 1 at 30 it was described as 'full knowledge of the material facts'.

115　*Scarf v Jardine* (1882) 7 AC 345.

116　*Matthews v Smallwood* [1910] 1 Ch 777; *Kammins Ballrooms Co Ltd v Zenith Investments (Torquay) Ltd* [1971] AC 859.

117　*O'Connor v SP Bray Ltd* (1936) 36 SR (NSW) 248 at 263–264; *Coastal Estates Pty Ltd v Melevende* [1965] VR 433.

118　*Young v Bristol Aeroplane Co Ltd* [1946] AC 163, *Dey v Victorian Railways Commissioners* (1949) 78 CLR 62.

119　*Sargent v ASL Developments Ltd* (1974) 131 CLR 634 at 644–645.

120　See *Elders Trustee & Executor Co Ltd v Commonwealth Homes & Investments Co Ltd* (1941) 65 CLR 603 at 618.

121　See [20.635] in relation to the position in the United States.

20.18.4 *Effect of specific performance on termination*

[20.380] The question of whether an election to seek specific performance precludes a later termination of the contract for breach requires consideration. Objectively it could be suggested that bringing a claim for specific performance implies an affirmation of the contract. According to the principle of election discussed above, this would mean that later termination for the same breach would be precluded.[122] Two different situations need to be considered. First, after commencing a claim for specific performance, the innocent party may discover that proceeding with the claim is useless because the other party is either unwilling or unable to perform. Can the injured party discontinue the claim for specific performance, terminate the contract and claim damages? In *Ogle v Comboyuro Investments Pty Ltd*,[123] the High Court gave consideration to the right of a party in this situation. The case involved a claim for specific performance by a vendor where the purchaser failed to complete the contract on time. The Court found that, in principle, a party who had commenced a claim for specific performance could elect to abandon the claim for specific performance, and terminate the contract, where there was a further breach of an essential term or the conduct of the other party constituted repudiation.[124] A party could take the step of abandoning the specific performance claim in that case without seeking the approval of the court. This is consistent with the general principle of election—an election to affirm does not prevent termination for a fresh or subsequent breach.

[20.385] What if the party claiming specific performance seeks to abandon the claim and terminate for the original breach? Again, that party will be able to abandon the claim for specific performance and terminate the contract. However, in this case the court may exercise its discretion to refuse a discontinuance of the claim if such a step would be inequitable to the other party.[125] This approach is based upon an analysis of specific performance as a conditional election. As stated by O'Bryan J in *McKennan v Richey*:[126]

> [a claim for specific performance is in effect saying] I don't accept your repudiation of the contract but am willing to perform my part of the contract and insist upon your performing your part—but if I cannot successfully insist on your performing your part, I will accept the repudiation and ask for damages.

[20.390] The second situation that may arise is where a claim has resulted in a decree of specific performance. It is clear that after a decree of specific performance has been obtained, a party is not entitled to elect to terminate and claim damages unless the court vacates the order for specific performance. Once an order of the court has been made, the matter is within the control of the court and not the party. In *Johnson v Agnew*,[127] Lord Wilberforce stated:

---

122 See [20.335].

123 (1976) 136 CLR 444.

124 According to *Carr v JA Berriman Pty Ltd* (1953) 89 CLR 327 a repudiation will be shown where the breach continues for such a time as to indicate an intention not to perform the contract according to its terms.

125 *Ogle v Comboyuro Investments* (1976) 136 CLR 444 at 461, *Public Trustee v Pearlberg* [1940] 1 KB 1.

126 [1950] VLR 360 at 372.

127 [1980] AC 367. Refer also to *Emeness Pty Ltd v Rigg* [1984] 1 QdR 172.

A vendor who seeks and gets specific performance is merely electing for a course which may or may not lead to implementation of the contract – what he elects for is not eternal and unconditional affirmation, but a continuance of the contract under control of the court which control involves the power in certain events to terminate it.

Once the matter has been placed in the hands of a court of equity the subsequent control of the matter will be exercised according to equitable principles. The court would not make an order dissolving the decree of specific performance and terminating the contract if to do so would be unjust, in the circumstances then existing, to the other party …

[20.400] In determining such a claim, the court will consider all of the usual issues relevant to the exercise of a discretion in equity.[128]

The final aspect of election is the fact that an election will be final. An election to affirm the contract will preclude the right to terminate for that particular breach. However, the election does not prevent the innocent party from relying on an unknown or subsequent breach or repudiation to terminate the contract at a later date. For example, a party to a contract for the sale of goods may accept one delivery of goods after the due date in the contract, where time is of the essence. This will be an election to affirm, and the right to terminate for that late delivery will be precluded. This will not prevent the buyer from exercising a right to terminate where the next delivery of the goods is also late. This will be a new breach of the contract, which is not waived by the prior affirmation. A fresh breach may also be constituted by a continuing breach of contract where it indicates an intention not to be bound by the contract.[129]

20.18.5 Justification of termination

[20.405] A party who acts to terminate a contract may be called upon to justify that termination in court. The party will not be limited, in that justification, to the reason for termination originally given, and may rely upon any justifiable reason that existed at the time of termination—even if he or she was not aware of it at that time.[130] For example, an employer may terminate the contract of its employee because the employee is failing to perform his or her duties in accordance with the contract. If, after termination, the employer becomes aware that at the time the employee was also stealing money, this would provide another justification for the termination of the employee's contract, and may be relied upon in court.[131]

[20.410] However, an alternative ground for termination may not be alleged by the innocent party where a statutory provision precludes reliance on an alternative ground,[132] or where the innocent party tries to invoke a contractual right but has not

---

128 See [25.75]–[25.120].

129 *Carr v JA Berriman Pty Ltd* (1953) 89 CLR 327; *Ogle v Comboyuro Investments* (1976) 136 CLR 444.

130 *Shepherd v Felt and Textiles of Australia Ltd* (1931) 45 CLR 359 approving *Taylor v Oakes Roncoroni & Co* (1922) 127 LT at 267; 27 Comm Cas 261 at 266; *Sunbird Plaza v Maloney* (1988) 77 ALR 205; *Pearce v Stevens* (1904) 24 NZLR 357.

131 For a further example refer to *Rawson v Hobbs* (1961) 107 CLR 466.

132 *W Devis & Sons Ltd v Atkins* [1977] AC 931; *West Midlands Co-operative Society Ltd v Tipton* [1986] AC 536.

complied with its requirements,[133] or where the innocent party is estopped from relying on an alternative ground.[134]

20.19 Restrictions on the right to terminate

[20.415] In addition to the principle of election, several other restrictions affect a party's right to terminate.

20.19.1 Further performance impossible

[20.420] The innocent party may have no alternative but to terminate if performance of the contract is dependent on the other party's co-operation. For example, in employment contracts, the employee is unable to perform unless the employer co-operates and allows the employee to continue working. An employee banned from entering the workplace may have no practical option but to accept the employer's conduct as repudiation and terminate.[135] However, if the party does not require co-operation to complete the contract, can that party elect to continue performance of the contract in order to obtain the contract price?

Example: White and Carter (Councils) Ltd v McGregor[136]

The plaintiff agreed with a representative of the defendant to display advertisements for the defendant's business for a period of three years. On the same day, the defendant wrote to the plaintiff stating that the representative was not authorised to enter the contract, and asked for it to be cancelled. The plaintiff chose to continue with performance of the contract and started advertising. The defendant did not make any payments under the contract.

The House of Lords allowed the plaintiff to recover the full price. The judgment highlights two matters for consideration:
- a plaintiff is only able to proceed with the contract if performance is not dependent on co-operation of the other party; and
- public policy may limit recovery if the plaintiff does not have a legitimate interest in performing the contract rather than claiming damages.

In relation to the first issue, Lord Reid noted the peculiarity of the contract at hand:

> Of course, if it had been necessary for the defender to do or accept anything before the contract could be completed by the pursuers, the pursuers could not and the court would not have compelled the defender to act, the contract would not have been completed and the pursuers' only remedy would have been damages. But the peculiarity in the present case, was that the

---

133 For example the contractual right of termination may require notice in writing or statement of the grounds of termination.
134 See Chapter 7 for further discussion of estoppel.
135 The court is unlikely to grant specific performance of an employment contract. See [25.65].
136 [1962] AC 413.

pursuers could completely fulfil the contract without any co-operation of the defender.[137]

Lord Reid then considered whether there should be any policy against a party's continuing to perform the contract, in order to obtain the contract price:

> It may well be that, if it can be shown that a person has no legitimate inter-est, financial or otherwise, in performing the contract rather than claiming damages, he [or she] ought not to be allowed to saddle the other party with an additional burden with no benefit to himself [or herself]. If a party has no interest to enforce a stipulation, he [or she] cannot in general enforce it: so it might be said that, if a party has no interest to insist on a particular rem-edy, he [or she] ought not to be allowed to insist on it. And, just as a party is not allowed to enforce a penalty, so he [or she] ought not to be allowed to penalise the other party by taking one course when another is equally advantageous to him [or her].[138]

[20.425] The application of this principle in Australia is uncertain. Some English deci-sions have accepted the application of the principle, but they provide little guidance on the doctrinal basis of the concept.[139] It is suggested that while a party may theoreti-cally elect to continue performance where co-operation is not required, this right should be exercised with caution. Particular regard should be given to the interest the innocent party is seeking to further.

20.19.2   Terminating party ready, willing and able

[20.430] Where the defaulting party has breached a dependent and concurrent obliga-tion,[140] the innocent party will be unable to terminate the contract unless he or she is ready, willing and able to perform his or her own obligations at the time for perform-ance. For example, a purchaser of land cannot terminate for failure of the vendor to complete if the purchaser does not have sufficient funds and also could not complete the contract.[141] A purchaser who is unable to perform his or her own obligations is unable to terminate the contract for a failure by the other party. In other words, an innocent party cannot show that he or she is ready, willing and able without tendering performance of the contract at the time specified in the contract. However, a party may be excused from tendering performance if the other party intimates, prior to the time for performance, that performance of the obligation will be futile or useless, and the innocent party acts on that intimation.[142] In that case, provided the innocent party is not wholly and finally disabled from performing the contract at the time of the inti-

---

137   Ibid at 429.
138   Ibid at 431.
139   *Gator Shipping Corp v Trans-Asiatic Oil Ltd SA* [1978] 2 Lloyd's Rep 357; *Clea Shipping Corp v Bulk Oil International Ltd (The Alaskan Trader)* [1984] 1 All ER 129.
140   See [19.60].
141   See *Foran v Wight* (1989) 168 CLR 385.
142   For an example of the operation of this principle see *Peter Turnbull and Co Pty Ltd v Mundus Trading Co (Australia) Pty Ltd* (1954) 90 CLR 235; *Mahoney v Lindsay* (1980) 55 ALJR 118; *Foran v Wight* (1989) 168 CLR 385 at 417–429.

mation (anticipatory breach), he or she will be able to terminate the contract for the repudiation of the other party at the time for performance, despite a failure to tender performance at the time stipulated in the contract.

Example: Foran v Wight[143]

The parties had entered into a contract for the sale of land. A special condition required the vendors to obtain the registration of a right of way prior to completion. The date for completion was 22 June and time was of the essence. On 20 June, the vendors told the purchasers they would not be able to complete the contract, as the right of way could not be registered by 22 June. Neither party attempted to settle on 22 June, and the purchasers purported to terminate the contract by notice on 24 June. The purchasers claimed a declaration that the contract was validly terminated and the deposit should be repaid. The vendors claimed that the purchasers could not terminate the contract as they were not ready willing and able to perform.

The majority of the High Court agreed that the vendors' statement on 20 June of an inability to perform was an anticipatory breach of contract. Although the purchasers did not terminate immediately, but waited until the time for performance, the High Court held that the purchasers were entitled to terminate and recover the deposit. Different reasons for the decision are offered by several members of the court. While each judge relies upon the previous decision of *Peter Turnbull & Co Pty Ltd v Mundus Trading Co (Australasia) Pty Ltd*,[144] each gives it a different emphasis.

Brennan J said:

> if an executory contract creates obligations which are mutually dependent and concurrent and, before the time for performance of the obligations arrives, one party, A, gives the other party, B, an intimation that it will be useless for B to tender performance and B abstains from performing his obligation in reliance on A's intimation, B is dispensed from performing his obligation and A's obligation is absolute provided that B had not repudiated the contract and he was ready and willing to perform his obligation up to the time when the intimation was given ... If at the time when the intimation was given, B was substantially incapable of future performance of his obligation or had already definitively resolved or decided not to perform it, B was not ready and willing.

Dawson J agreed with the principle stated by Brennan J.

Deane J relied upon the doctrine of estoppel to grant termination and return of the deposit. The continuing repudiation conveyed to the purchasers that performance of their concurrent obligations would be useless. The purchasers relied upon that intimation, and ceased efforts to obtain finance. This resulted in their being unable to complete at the time for performance. Unless the vendor provided sufficient notice of a change in the state of affairs, it was unnecessary for the purchasers to tender performance on the date for completion. His Honour also expressed the view that a

---

143 (1989) 168 CLR 385.
144 (1954) 90 CLR 235.

party should not have to incur the expense of performance as a precondition to termination for repudiation in all cases. To this extent, his Honour agreed with the statements by Brennan J.

[20.435] Where the obligations of the parties are not dependent and concurrent, there is no requirement to prove that at the time of termination the party was ready, willing and able to perform. Consequently, if the repudiation by one party is not accepted and the contract continues, the repudiating party may be able to exercise a right of termination provided by the contract or the common law.[145]

20.19.3   Terminating party not in default

[20.440] Clearly, a party who is in default will not be able to terminate the contract. This will usually be because the party is not ready, willing, and able to perform. There is also a strong presumption founded in policy and morality that a contracting party will not be able to take advantage of his or her own wrong to bring a contract to an end. This principle has a strong history in cases where a party wishes to avoid a contract for the failure of a special condition. A party who has acted to ensure that the special condition is not fulfilled, or that a certain event does not occur, will be unable to rescind the contract.[146] The presumption is sufficiently wide to apply also to instances of termination for breach.[147]

20.19.4   Relief in equity

[20.445] Two equitable principles may restrict a party's right to terminate. The first is equitable estoppel, considered previously.[148] The second is the principle of relief against forfeiture. Within the inherent jurisdiction of equity, the courts may relieve against the forfeiture of money or property. This jurisdiction will arise where:

- the object of the transaction and the insertion of a right to forfeit are essentially to secure the payment of money;
- the party possesses a sufficient interest under the contract; and
- intervention by equity must be appropriate, either because there has been unconscionable conduct, or because the forfeiture provision acts as a penalty.[149]

Typically, relief against the effects of termination has been given to the purchasers of interests in real property.[150] Forfeiture provisions will commonly appear in contracts for the purchase of land by instalments. The vendor will be entitled to terminate the contract, forfeiting the instalments and the property if the purchaser fails to pay any or

---

145   *Kelly v Desnoe* [1985] 2 Qd R 477 at 497.

146   *New Zealand Shipping Co v Société des Ateliers et Chantiers de France* [1919] AC 1; *Rede v Farr* (1817) 6 M&S 121 at 124–125; *Quesnel Forks Gold Mining Co Ltd v Ward* [1920] AC 222; *Cheall v Association of Professional Executive Clerical and Computer Staff* [1983] 2 AC 180.

147   *Alghussein Establishment v Eaton College* [1988] 1 WLR 587 at 594; *TCN Channel Nine Pty Ltd v Hayden Enterprises Pty Ltd* (1989) 16 NSWLR 130.

148   See Chapter 7.

149   *Shiloh Spinners Ltd v Harding* [1973] AC 691 at 722.

150   Although relief to a party in a commercial transaction is not prohibited: *BICC Plc v Burndy Corp* [1985] Ch 232.

all instalments. In deciding whether exceptional circumstances exist, the court will consider:

- whether the conduct of the vendor contributed to the purchaser's breach;
- how serious the breach was;
- whether the was breach wilful;
- the damaged actually caused to the vendor;
- the vendor's gain weighed against the purchaser's loss, and whether an award of specific performance with or without compensation would be satisfactory to the vendor.

[20.450] If the purchaser has been in possession of the property for some time, has made substantial improvements for which no compensation will be given, and the vendor will receive a windfall upon termination, the court may consider that the vendor is acting unconscionably in insisting on his or her rights.[151]

Example: Stern v McArthur[152]

The parties had entered into a contract for the sale of land by instalments over a period of 13 years. After 10 years, the seller purported to terminate the contract, relying on an express right to terminate for default in the observance of any obligation. The buyers had fallen into arrears and had become liable to pay the balance, which they failed to do as required. But the buyers had continued to pay instalments regularly for a period of eight years. During this time, they had been in possession of the land and had constructed a house. At the time of termination, all arrears in instalments had been paid or tendered and the buyers were attempting to find the balance purchase moneys. All moneys owing had been paid to the seller's bank account prior to commencement of the action for forfeiture of deposit and retention of instalments. At the time of termination, the value of the land was significantly greater than it was at the time of contract. The seller had offered to make allowances for the improvements, but none in respect of the increased value of the property.

The High Court ordered relief against forfeiture of the interest in land and specific performance of the contract of sale on behalf of the buyers. The court considered that in the circumstances, insistence on the forfeiture was unconscionable. Factors such as the increased value in the property, the conduct of the vendor in relying upon a contractual right of termination when the buyers had attempted to fulfil their obligations, and the value of the improvements on the property, were all taken into account.[153]

[20.455] Relief from the consequences of termination will not usually be granted where the failure to perform is a breach of an essential time provision. The rationale for this approach appears to lie in the recognition by equity of express provisions

---

151   *Legione v Hateley* (1982) 152 CLR 406. The granting of relief against forfeiture will usually accompany an order for specific performance by the court.

152   (1988) 165 CLR 489

153   See also *Lexane Pty Ltd v Highfern Pty Ltd* [1985] 1 Qd R 446; *Milton v Proctor* (1989) NSW Conv R 55-450; *Minister for Lands and Forests v McPherson* (1991) 22 NSWLR 687; *Sunbird Plaza Pty Ltd v Maloney* (1988) 166 CLR 245; *Berry v Hodsdon* [1989] 1 QR 361.

making time of the essence.[154] Because of this recognition, it is not considered appropriate for equity to intervene.[155] Despite some initial uncertainty on this point, courts in England and Australia have now confirmed this approach.[156] Nevertheless, the door is left open for granting relief in exceptional circumstances if such an order would not be inequitable.[157]

20.20 Procedure for termination

[20.460] The procedure for termination of a contract will depend upon the source of the right. Where the right to terminate arises under the common law, the requirements of the common law apply. Alternatively, if the right arises by virtue of the contract, the provisions of the contract may govern the method of termination. If no procedure is provided in the contract, the common law will be relevant. At common law, the innocent party must elect by unequivocal words or conduct to terminate the performance of the contract. Usually the termination must be communicated to the party in breach. For example, the service of a writ claiming termination, or the innocent party's action in selling the property after repudiation, would be effective as a termination of the contract.[158]

[20.465] If the right arises by virtue of the contract, it will usually require notice to be given to the other party—or it may go further, and require the innocent party to allow the other party time to remedy the breach or to show cause why the contract should not be terminated. Rights of termination pursuant to a contract are generally treated as being in addition to the party's rights under the common law. A common law right to terminate the contract may only be excluded or limited by clear words in the contract. The right to terminate for repudiation may only be excluded if the contract provides an exhaustive code for termination. In *Amann Aviation Pty Ltd v The Commonwealth*,[159] the High Court held that clause 24 of the contract provided an exclusive code for termination, and the Commonwealth was therefore prohibited from terminating the contract in any other way.

20.21 Consequences of termination

20.21.1 Discharge of obligations

[20.470] After termination for breach or repudiation, both parties are relieved of their obligations under the contract from that time.[160] This has previously been contrasted with rescission of the contract for misrepresentation or mistake, where the contract

---

154 See [20.250]–[20.280] for a detailed discussion on when time will be of the essence in equity.

155 See *Steedman v Drinkle* [1916] 1 AC 275

156 The initial doubts in *Legione v Hateley* (1982) 152 CLR 406 at 429 have been overcome in *Smilie Pty Ltd v Bruce* (1999) NSW Conv R 55-886; *Re Ronim Pty Ltd* [1999] 2 Qd R 172.

157 *Legione v Hateley* (1982) 152 CLR 406 at 429.

158 It should be noted that a writ which claims specific performance or termination is equivocal and not effective as a termination of the agreement: for example *Ogle v Comboyuro Investments Pty Ltd* (1976) 136 CLR 444 at 452.

159 (1990) 92 ALR 601.

160 *McDonald v Dennys Lascelles Ltd* (1933) 48 CLR 457.

itself is void.[161] Although discharge of the parties' obligations occurs at the time of termination and does not relate back to the breach or repudiation,[162] the practical effect is that all obligations, except accrued obligations, are discharged. For example, if a contract for the sale of land is discharged after the time for performance by the vendor, the obligation of the purchaser to pay the contract price will be discharged. The vendor will not be able to require payment of the balance of the contract price after termination.[163] On the other hand, the obligation of the purchaser to pay the deposit will be enforceable as an accrued right.

20.21.2   Enforcement of accrued rights

[20.475] Several types of accrued rights survive the termination of a contract. According to Dixon J in *McDonald v Dennys Lascelles Ltd*:[164]

> rights are not divested or discharged which have already been unconditionally acquired. Rights and obligations which arise from the partial execution of the contract and causes of action which have accrued from its breach alike continue unaffected.

[20.480] Two particular rights are identifiable as accrued rights. First, the right to damages for breach or repudiation survives termination. This is discussed in detail in Chapter 23. Of particular note is the fact that an accrued right to damages in favour of either party to the contract will survive termination. This means that the defaulting party may be entitled to damages for a prior breach by the innocent party.

[20.485] The second type of accrued right is the right to receive performance of a contractual obligation. Contractual obligations to pay money should be distinguished from other types of obligation. An obligation to pay money is enforceable as a debt following termination, whereas other types of obligation may only be protected by injunction. Specific performance of the obligation is not available.

[20.490] An accrued right will only be enforceable after termination if the right has been unconditionally acquired. This means performance of the obligation must not be subject to the ultimate completion of the contract. Several types of obligation to pay money, and whether they are recoverable after termination for breach, are considered here.

(a)   Recovery of contract price

[20.495] The contract price may only be recovered after termination if it has been earned prior to termination. The contract price will be earned where the obligations under the contract have been performed exactly or substantially.[165] In most cases, termination for breach will occur prior to substantial completion of the contract. For example, a builder terminates a contract for breach by the owner with one-third of the work still to be performed. The builder will only be able to seek damages, as the contract price was not payable prior to termination. Likewise, in a contract for the sale of

---

161   *Heymans v Darwins Ltd* [1942] AC 356 at 399 and See [20.25]–[20.35].
162   *Larratt v Bankers and Traders Insurances Co Ltd* (1941) 41 SR (NSW) 215 at 226.
163   Damages will be payable for the failure to perform.
164   (1933) 48 CLR 457 at 476-477.
165   See [19.140]–[19.180] for detailed discussion of when a contract is substantially performed.

land, termination prior to the passing of title to the land leaves a vendor or purchaser with a right to damages only—not a right to the contract price. The contract price will only be recoverable if title to the land has passed to the purchaser.[166]

[20.500] The same principle is applicable to a party in breach of the contract. Despite the breach, the party will be able to recover any accrued payments. For example, in a building contract where the price is payable in instalments (divisible contract), upon termination the builder is able to recover any instalments that have accrued prior to termination, but not the total price.

(b) Instalments of price

[20.505] Instalments of contract price are recoverable after termination provided they have unconditionally accrued prior to termination. The crucial point for consideration by the court is whether the consideration for the particular instalment has failed. If there is a total failure of consideration for that instalment of price, the obligation to pay the instalment will not be enforceable.

[20.510] A common example of a contract where payment of instalments of price will be enforceable after termination is a building contract. It is usual for a building contract to provide for payment of price at various stages in construction: slab stage, roof stage, and practical completion. If the contract is terminated after roof stage, the builder is entitled to payment, provided it provides proof of completion (or substantial completion) of the work related to the particular payment. Even a builder in breach of contract will be able to recover, if the work for the instalment is substantially complete.[167] However, it will be unnecessary to prove performance of the contract where the payments were not conditional on performance of the contract but were required at a specific time. For example, in *Hyundai Heavy Industries Co Ltd v Papadopoulos*,[168] a building contract provided for instalments to be paid on 1 April, 1 May, and 1 June. The contract was terminated on 3 May. In that case, the builder was entitled to payment of the first two instalments without proof of the work done.

[20.515] By contrast, in some cases, the accrual of an instalment will be dependent on performance of the whole contract. A contract for the sale of land is a typical example, where usually the instalments paid are conditional on title being provided at completion. If the contract is terminated prior to completion, the consideration for which the instalments are provided will fail.[169] The obligation to pay the instalments in this case will not be an accrued obligation. Consequently, instalments that have been paid during the course of the contract will also be recoverable after termination. The basis upon which instalments of price are recoverable is either:

- total failure of consideration; or
- relief against forfeiture.

[20.520] Instalments are recoverable on the basis of total failure of consideration if the contract has no forfeiture provision.[170] If there is a forfeiture provision, equity will

---

166 As an alternative, a party who wishes to claim the contract price may elect to continue with performance where the co-operation of the other party is not required. See [20.420].

167 See Chapter 19 for further discussion of the circumstances in which the contract price is recoverable.

168 [1980] 1 WLR 1129.

169 See *McDonald v Dennys Lascelles Ltd* (1933) 48 CLR 457.

170 Total failure of consideration is examined in detail in Chapter 24.

usually relieve against the forfeiture of instalments where it would be unconscionable for the other party to retain the payments.[171] Unconscionability will usually be found where there is a total failure of consideration.

(c)   Obligation to pay a deposit

[20.525] A deposit is a bond for performance of the contract.[172] The party giving the deposit is doing so as an indication of sincerity in performing the contract and on the basis it will be forfeited if he or she fails to perform. Forfeiture of the deposit to the other party after termination is seen as a form of compensation for the breach. The right to forfeit a deposit may be express, or the court may imply such a right[173] because of the special nature of the deposit. A distinction is drawn between the position of the party in breach who pays a deposit and the innocent party who pays a deposit. The consequent effect of this treatment is that an innocent party will not be required to pay the deposit after termination, whereas a defaulting party will be required to pay. The defaulting party will not be able to resist a claim for payment on the basis of total failure of consideration. The distinction between deposits and instalments of price in the context of termination can be best explained by example.

Example

A executes a contract to purchase land from B. A is obliged by the contract to pay a deposit of 10 per cent of the purchase price at the time of signing.

Variation 1: A signs the contract but fails to pay the deposit. This is a breach of an essential term of the contract and B is entitled to terminate. If B terminates the contract, the obligation to pay the deposit will be enforceable as an accrued right. B will be entitled to claim the deposit as a debt.[174] Because A is in breach of contract the fact that A does not have the title to the land is irrelevant and relief against forfeiture will not be given.[175]

Variation 2: A signs the contract and pays the deposit. A fails to pay the balance of the purchase moneys on the date for completion. This will be the same as variation 1. The payment of the deposit is an accrued obligation. B will be entitled to retain the deposit after termination because of A's failure to perform. The only difference is that B is not required to bring a claim in debt to retain the money.

Variation 3: A signs the contract and pays the deposit. B fails to tender the titled at completion and A terminates the contract. The payment of the deposit is an accrued obligation. This would suggest that it cannot be recovered by A. However, in this case A is the innocent party and would be entitled to recover the deposit either because of a total failure of consideration or as part of his or her damages claim.

Variation 4: A signs the contract and pays a deposit of 35 per cent. A fails to complete the contract and B terminates for breach. The difference in this example is the amount of the deposit. Although A is in breach and B will normally be entitled to

---

171   *McDonald v Dennys Lascelles Ltd* (1933) 48 CLR 457.
172   *Brien v Dwyer* (1978) 141 CLR 378.
173   *Howe v Smith* (1884) 27 Ch D 89.
174   *Pollway Ltd v Abdullah* [1974] 1 WLR 493; *Ashdown v Kirk* (1997) Q Conv R 54-487.
175   See [20.445]–[20.455].

retain the whole deposit, A may have a claim for relief against forfeiture in equity on the ground that the amount is extravagant and therefore a penalty.[176] B will be entitled to retain only 10 per cent.

20.21.3 Terms that operate after termination

[20.530] Certain contractual terms will be intended to operate after termination of the contract. Some clauses such as a confidentiality clause in an employment agreement will expressly provide for operation after the termination of the agreement. In other cases, the contract will not be express, and the court will need to assess the parties' intention. The most relevant question will usually be the nature of the clause in question. Clauses such as restraints of trade,[177] exclusionary provisions,[178] arbitration clauses, confidentiality clauses or agreed damages clauses[179] will usually be enforced by a court after termination, subject to questions of policy.[180] These types of clauses usually represent obligations of a secondary or procedural nature rather than primary obligations under the contract. Primary obligations, unless they are accrued obligations, will not be specifically enforceable after termination. Clauses that are effective after termination may generally be enforced by either party.[181]

20.22 International perspectives

20.22.1 New Zealand

[20.535] Cancellation of a contract in New Zealand is governed by the *Contractual Remedies Act* 1979. Under to this legislation, a contract may be terminated in one of two circumstances:

- where there is a repudiation of the contract; or
- where there is a serious breach.[182]

[20.540] Repudiation is constituted by a party, through words or conduct, making it clear that he or she does not intend to perform his or her obligations under a contract, or, as the case may be, to complete such performance.[183] This encapsulates the common law definition of repudiation as applied in Australia. The examples discussed previously are relevant to a finding of repudiation in New Zealand.

[20.545] The second circumstance in which a party may terminate a contract pursuant to the *Contractual Remedies Act* 1979 is for a serious breach. Section 7(4) provides that a breach is considered to be serious where:

- the stipulation breached has been agreed expressly or impliedly between the parties to be essential to the cancelling party; or

---

176 See *Coates v Sarich* [1964] WAR 2; *Smyth v Jessep* [1956] VLR 230.
177 See [18.35]–[18.95].
178 *Photo Productions Ltd v Securicor Transport Ltd* [1980] AC 827; *Port Jackson Stevedoring Pty Ltd v Salmond & Spraggon (Aust) Pty Ltd* [1981] 1 WLR 131.
179 See [23.425]–23.470].
180 For example, a restraint of trade clause may be unenforceable because of public policy. See [18.25]. The *Contracts Review Act* 1980 (NSW) may also preclude the enforcement of an unjust term.
181 *Heymans v Darwins Ltd* [1942] AC 356; cf *General Billposting Co Ltd v Atkinson* [1909] AC 118.
182 *Contractual Remedies Act* 1979, s 7.
183 *Contractual Remedies Act* 1979, s 7(2).

- the consequences of the breach are serious (that is, the contracting party has not received substantially what was bargained for).[184]

[20.550] The first circumstance appears to adopt the common law position of an essential term, but several differences are evident in the legislation. First, it is only essentiality to the cancelling party that is important, rather than the intention of either party.[185] Secondly, the section emphasises that both parties must have 'expressly or impliedly agreed' on the essentiality of the stipulation to the cancelling party. This is to be determined at the time of contract.[186] The situations in which the parties have expressly provided for essentiality in the contract raise no particular difficulties, for example, where the contract provides for 'time to be of the essence'. In contrast, whether there has been implied agreement that a term is essential to one party is more problematic. Resolution of this question will depend upon a construction of the contract taking into account the express terms and the circumstances at the time of contract. The approach taken by the New Zealand courts is reminiscent of the common law approach in *Tramways Advertising Pty Ltd v Luna Park (NSW) Ltd*.[187] Terms that satisfied the test at common law are also likely to satisfy the test of implied agreement under the Act.[188] Interestingly, most of the cases decided under the Act could also have satisfied the test of serious consequences in s 7(4)(b) of the *Contractual Remedies Act 1979*. Compliance with both tests is, however, unnecessary—each being an independent requirement.[189]

[20.555] The third circumstance in which a party may terminate a contract is where the consequences of the breach are severe. In this case, the nature of the term is irrelevant, but the breach must:

- substantially reduce the benefit of the contract to the cancelling party;
- substantially increase the burden of the cancelling party under the contract; or
- make the benefit or burden of the contract substantially different from that contracted for.

[20.560] There are no significant differences between the approach under the Act and the approach taken at common law pursuant to the principles in *Hong Kong Fir Shipping Co Ltd v Kawasaki Kisen Kaisha Ltd*.[190] The courts have refused to give further definition to the meaning of 'substantial' under the Act, preferring to treat each case as a matter of 'fact, degree and impression'.[191] This same degree of imprecision is evident in the common law approach to intermediate terms, where the requirement is that the injured party be deprived of substantially the whole benefit of the contract.[192] The

---

184   *Contractual Remedies Act* 1979, s 7(3) and (4).
185   See [20.65] in relation to the test of essentiality at common law.
186   *Wilson v Hines* (1994) 6 TCLR 163.
187   (1938) 38 SR (NSW) 632.
188   See *Marsland v J Walter Thompson New Zealand Ltd* (High Court, Wellington CP 338/86 29 November 1989): a restraint of trade clause was essential; *Wilson v Hines* (1994) 6 TCLR 163: a promise to graze and maintain cattle was essential. Refer also to the other cases in JF Burrows, J Finn, & SMD Todd, *Law of Contract in New Zealand*, Butterworths, Wellington, 1997, pp 599–601.
189   *Marsland v J Walter Thompson New Zealand Ltd* (High Court, Wellington CP 338/86, 29 November 1989).
190   [1962] 2 QB 26.
191   *MacIndoe v Mainzeal Group Ltd* [1991] 3 NZLR 273.
192   Refer for further discussion of this test to [9.190].

requirements of the Act appear to be less severe, however, in that they only require the benefit of the contract to the injured party be reduced, rather than the 'whole benefit of the contract'. But this may be a matter of semantics. The second difference between the Act and common law is the reference in the Act to the benefit *of the contract* or burden *under the contract*. This will have a greater effect on the right to cancel for misrepresentation than for breach. A misrepresentation, unlike a breach, may *relate* to the contract but may not actually impose a burden under the contract or cause loss of benefit under the contract.[193] In most cases, a breach of contract will have a direct effect on or under the contract itself. Despite these differences, the large number of cases decided under the Act would have been decided in the same way under the common law.[194]

[20.565] The common law principles governing election to terminate a contract are preserved by the *Contractual Remedies Act* 1979. Section 7 provides only that a party may exercise the right to cancel a contract. Section 7(5) recognises that a party may not terminate following affirmation, and s 8 provides that notice of cancellation of the contract must be given to the other party. The requirement for affirmation to occur by unequivocal words or acts with full knowledge of the breach is preserved. The courts will require clear evidence of affirmation before debarring a party from relief.[195] Unlike the conflicting Australian authorities, evidence that the party has knowledge of his or her legal rights will not be required.[196] New Zealand courts applying the *Contractual Remedies Act* 1979 will follow the common law position regarding actions for specific performance and affirmation. Commencement of a claim for specific performance will not be considered affirmation[197] unless accompanied by other conduct clearly indicating an affirmation of the agreement.[198]

[20.570] An election to terminate the contract must be justifiable in accordance with the Act. At common law, a party may justify his or her termination by reference to any breach that existed at the time of termination, even if the party did not know of the breach.[199] The *Contractual Remedies Act* 1979 does not expressly refer to the issue of justification. Judicial opinion suggests that the Act has discarded the common law principle, and therefore justification of termination cannot be based on a different ground.[200]

[20.575] The final important aspect of termination governed by the *Contractual Remedies Act* 1979 is the effect of cancellation on the rights of the parties. The effect of cancellation, as outlined in s 8(3) of the Act, is similar to the common law in the sense

---

193   See *Jolly v Palmer* [1985] 1 NZLR 658.
194   See *Ansell v New Zealand Insurance Finance Ltd* (High Court Wellington A 434/83, 6 June 1984; *Gallager v Young* [1981] 1 NZLR 734; *Norden v Blueport Enterprises Ltd* [1996] 3 NZLR 134. *LJ Smits Ltd v Auto-Tec International Ltd* (1992) 5 TCLR 21. For detailed discussion refer to JF Burrows, J Finn, SMD Todd, *Law of Contract in New Zealand*, Butterworths, Wellington, NZ, 1997 pp 602–606.
195   *Oldham Cullens and Co v Burbery Finance Ltd* (High Court, Christchurch, A368/83, 4 October 1985); *Wilson v Hines* (1994) 6 TCLR 163; *Westpac Merchant Finance Ltd v Winstone Industries Ltd* [1993] 2 NZLR 247.
196   See commentary at [20.375].
197   For example *Stine v Maiden* (1984) 2 NZCPR 176.
198   See *Jolly v Palmer* [1985] 1 NZLR 658
199   See [20.405]–[20.410].
200   *Mercurius Ventures Ltd v Waitakere City Council* [1996] 2 NZLR 495.

that the obligations of the parties cease as to the future, and damages may be sought by the injured party. Similarly, other rights such as arbitration clauses and restraint of trade clause have also been considered to survive cancellation.[201] Some difficulties have arisen regarding the effect of s 8 on accrued rights after cancellation. The common example in such cases involves the recovery of an unpaid deposit. In the past, some judicial and academic comment took the view that cancellation of a contract deprived an injured party of the right to sue for the deposit.[202] More recent authority has, however, held that recovery of a deposit accrued due prior to termination is available as a debt rather than a claim in contract. As such the *Contractual Remedies Act* 1979 does not affect the claim.[203] Nevertheless, recovery of a deposit may be subject to the principle of penalties and relief against forfeiture where the amount is excessive.[204]

20.22.2   United States

[20.580] American law provides a two-step response to the issue of breach or repudiation, which although more complex, is arguably less severe than the Australian approach. The basic policy underlying the American courts' approach is to keep the deal together, thereby avoiding forfeiture of the contract. This course is encouraged provided the expectations of the parties are not seriously disappointed. We have seen in relation to discharge by performance that American courts have adopted various mechanisms for avoiding forfeiture of the contract and consequent non-payment of the contract price.[205] In keeping with this philosophy, an injured party may only terminate a contract for a material breach after time has been allowed for the defaulting party to cure the breach. The contract may not be terminated for an immaterial breach unless the defaulting party has also repudiated his or her obligations.[206] A distinction is usually drawn between non-performance of the contract and repudiation. Non-performance may not lead to a breach where it is justified. On the other hand, a repudiation—whether at the time for performance or before—will always be considered a material breach.[207] Each of these concepts is considered separately here.

[20.585] Non-performance does not always lead to a breach of contract. Included in the American concept of non-performance are situations where a party may refuse to perform due to the failure of a condition, or where the contract is discharged due to impracticability of performance or frustration of purpose. Frustration is considered in Chapter 21, and conditions in Chapter 9. In those cases, non-performance is considered to be 'justified', either because the contract is frustrated or because a condition has not occurred—for example, where the obligation of a builder to begin work is

---

201   See *Broadcasting Corporation of New Zealand v Neilsen* (1988) 2 NZELC 96,404 (as clause applied upon termination, s 8 was considered to be subject to this express provision). This is consistent with the position in Australia. See [20.530].

202   *Spencer v Crowther* [1986] 1 NZLR 755 at 757; P Blanchard, *A Handbook on Agreements for Sale and Purchase of Land*, 3rd edn, Handbook Press, Auckland, 1984, p 34.

203   *Pendergrast v Chapman* [1988] 2 NZLR 177; *Bussell v Morton Read Farming Corporation Ltd* (1990) 1 NZ Conv C 190,338. This also applies to other payments: *Brown v Langwoods Photo Stores Ltd* [1991] 1 NZLR 173 at 176 (payment of franchise fees).

204   *Simanke v Liu* (1994) 2 NZ Conv C 191,888.

205   See [19.300]–[19.340].

206   Repudiation is considered separately at [20.645]–[20.675].

207   *Riess v Murchison* 329 F 2d 635 (9th Cir 1964). See also Restatement (Second) § 243.

conditioned on the owner's providing plans for the building. The builder is justified in not starting work until the plans are provided. Even if the performance by the builder was not expressly conditioned on the provision of plans, an American court would imply that performance by the builder was conditional on performance by the owner. This implied term is referred to as a 'constructive condition of exchange' and was considered in Chapter 19. The failure of either a constructive condition of exchange or of a condition may be used by a party to justify his or her non-performance of a contract. However, once performance is due, a failure to perform will be a breach of contract.

[20.590] The response of American law to a breach of contract is to offer a two-step self-help remedy of suspending performance followed by termination of the agreement if necessary.[208] The essential questions in this process are:

- When will a breach of contract be sufficiently serious to allow suspension of a contract?
- When will the breach have continued for long enough to justify termination?

[20.595] Parties who choose to suspend or terminate a contract for breach are taking a risk that the court may consider their actions precipitate. In that case, the injured party's unwarranted actions will have led to repudiation of her or his obligations under the contract.[209] A safer course would be to continue with performance and sue for damages for partial breach.[210] A party who ultimately terminates a contract will be able to seek damages for total breach.[211]

[20.600] Performance of a contract may only be suspended if the breach is material. If the breach is non-material, the injured party is entitled to seek damages for partial breach but is not able to suspend performance. For a breach to be material, it should amount to a non-occurrence of a constructive condition of exchange. In essence, a material breach is the opposite to substantial performance of the agreement. If a material breach has occurred, there will be no substantial performance.

[20.605] The materiality of the breach will be considered at the time of breach, not at the time of contract.[212] Whether a breach is material is a question of fact depending on similar factors to those that determine whether performance is substantial. The Restatement (Second)[213] lists the factors as:

(a) the extent to which the injured party will be deprived of the benefit which [she or] he reasonably expected;

(b) the extent to which the injured party can be adequately compensated for the part of that benefit of which [she or] he will be deprived;

(c) the extent to which the party failing to perform or to offer to perform will suffer forfeiture;

---

208 *Stanley Gudyka Sale Co v Lacy Forest Prods Co* 915 F 2d 273 (7th Cir 1990).

209 *Walker & Co v Harrison* 81 NW 2d 352, 355 (Mich 1957).

210 However, this will result in an election to continue and the right to terminate for breach will be lost unless there is a subsequent breach. See EA Farnsworth, *Contracts*, 3rd edn, Aspen Law and Business, New York, 1999 § 8.19 (p 595).

211 For the difference between damages for partial and total breach See [23.480]–[23.500].

212 EA Farnsworth, *Contracts*, 3rd edn, Aspen Law and Business, New York, 1999 § 8.16.

213 § 241.

(d) the likelihood that the party failing to perform or to offer to perform will cure [her or] his failure, taking account of all the circumstances including any reasonable assurances; and

(e) the extent to which the behaviour of the party failing to perform or to offer to perform comports with standards of good faith and fair dealing.[214]

[20.610] In comparison to the Australian principles regarding essentiality and serious breach of an intermediate term, these factors are imprecise, but they do provide the court with a larger degree of flexibility. The operation of these principles in any given situation will differ, but one important issue will be the extent to which the party is deprived of the benefit of the contract. For example, material breaches may occur where a vendor fails to deliver title to a purchaser; where an owner fails to pay a progress payment to a builder; where a lessee fails to maintain premises in good repair; or where a seller of goods fails to deliver the shipping documents on time. Even if the breach is material and performance has been suspended, termination of the contract does not automatically arise.

[20.615] A party may only take steps to terminate a contract after appropriate time has elapsed. The period should be sufficiently long to allow the other party an opportunity to cure the breach.[215] This would allow, for example, a vendor who delivered a defective title to remedy the defect and tender the title again. The effect of curing a breach is that the other party will be required to perform where it would otherwise be discharged. But the liability for damages is not cancelled: the defaulting party will be liable for damages for partial breach, usually amounting to the cost of the delay in performance. The Uniform Commercial Code formalises the right of a seller of goods to cure his or her default, and may be used by analogy with other contracts.[216]

[20.620] The period that an injured party must allow for the other party to cure the breach is a question of fact. The court will consider issues similar to those relevant to whether the breach was material in the first place. That is, issues such as the extent to which a further delay will deprive the injured party of the benefit that it expected from the exchange, and the degree to which the injured party can be compensated by damages for the loss. The risk of forfeiture to the defaulting party is also considered, particularly where performance of the contract has commenced. A longer time to cure the breach may be given where performance has not started.[217] The likelihood of the defaulting party's actually curing the breach is also important. Where the facts indicate an unwillingness or inability to cure, there may be a strong reason for termination in a shorter period of time.[218] The nature of the contract may also impact on the time for cure. The courts will commonly allow a much shorter period for termination in contracts for the sale of goods than in contracts for the sale of land. Even though time

---

214 The Vienna Convention and the UNIDROIT Principles add a further factor, ie foreseeability, by the party in breach, of the impact on the injured party—a factor in determining whether a breach is fundamental.

215 Restatement (Second) § 242.

216 UCC 2-508. See EA Farnsworth, *Contracts*, 3rd edn, Aspen Law and Business, New York, 1999 § 8.17 (p 588).

217 *Leazzo v Dunham* 420 NE 2d 851 (Ill App 1981).

218 *Sackett v Spindler* 56 Cal Rptr 435 (Ct App 1967). A lack of good faith or failure to observe reasonable standards of fair dealing may also shorten the waiting time.

may be considered to be of the essence in a contract for the sale of goods, time for remedying the breach will still be allowed.[219] The only exception will be where performance on time is a condition of the parties' duty to perform. The court will give strict effect to a contractual provision, but unless the party has a duty to ensure the contract is performed on time, damages will not be payable.[220] Once the appropriate period has elapsed and the defaulting party has not remedied the defect, the injured party may terminate. Damages for total breach will be recoverable to compensate for the loss of performance.

[20.625] Similarly to the Australian position, a party may choose to waive the non-occurrence of performance and continue with the contract. Waiver acts as an election to not terminate the contract. Waiver does not affect other rights under the contract; a right to damages for partial breach therefore remains. For example, an owner may agree to continue with a building contract and pay the builder, despite the fact that the builder has not substantially performed. A right to claim damages for the defects will remain.

[20.630] Election to waive a breach will also occur through the conduct of the injured party. If the injured party accepts performance of the contract or retains goods or other performance for more than a reasonable time, an election to waive will be deemed.[221] So a buyer of goods who, with knowledge of the defects, accepts the goods and keeps them for some time will lose the right to terminate. Likewise, a buyer who accepts a defective instalment will be waiving the defects in that instalment and previous instalments.[222] The acceptance of defective instalments may also indicate to the seller that the defects in subsequent instalments are also waived.[223] The principle of waiver by conduct will not apply to a contract for the construction of a building. The fact an owner moves into a building that is not substantially complete will not be a waiver of the breach.[224] The conduct must go further, and amount to an assent to be bound despite the failure to perform.

[20.635] An election to waive will not be effective unless the party knows of the relevant facts. The debate within Australia concerning the necessity for knowledge of the party's legal rights has been resolved as being irrelevant.[225] Once an election to waive the breach has occurred it is final.[226] The right to terminate will be lost unless the defaulting party commits a further breach.[227]

[20.640] One final limit on the injured party's right to terminate for non-performance is the requirement of tender. If there are concurrent conditions under an agreement—so that tender by each party is a constructive condition of the other party's duty to

---

219 *Fitz v Coutinho* 622 A 2d 1220 (NH 1993).
220 See the discussion in EA Farnsworth, *Contracts*, 3rd edn, Aspen Law and Business, New York, 1999 § 8.3 (pp 529–530).
221 *Lindsay Manufacturing Co v Universal Sur Co* 519 NW 2d 530 (Neb 1994).
222 UCC 2-612(3).
223 *Heinzman v Howard* 348 NW 2d 147 (SD 1984) (seller's acceptance of late payments waived the contract provision that time of payment was essential). See also Restatement (Second) § 247.
224 *Cawley v Weiner* 140 NE 724, 725 (NT 1923).
225 *Bertrand v Jones* 156 A 2d 161 (NJ Super 1959).
226 See Restatement (Second) § 84 and EA Farnsworth, *Contracts*, 3rd edn, Aspen Law and Business, New York, 1999 § 8.5 (p 543).
227 *K&G Construction Co v Harris* 164 A 2d 451 (Md 1960) cf *Cities Serv. Helex v United States* 543 F 2d 1306, 1313–1317 (Ct Cl 1976).

perform—a party must tender performance to put the other party in breach. This is equivalent to the requirement in Australian principles for the innocent party to be ready, willing, and able to perform.[228] If the party does not tender, the contract will merely go on until the abandonment is considered an agreement to rescind. Neither party will be able to sue for breach. The only exception to the requirement of tender is in the case of anticipatory repudiation, which the injured party may act upon prior to the time for performance.[229]

[20.645] The final aspect is the concept of repudiation. Repudiation is considered to be:

(a) a statement by the obligor to the obligee indicating that the obligor will commit a breach that would of itself give the obligee a claim for damages for total breach; or

(b) a voluntary affirmative act that renders the obligor unable or apparently unable to perform without such a breach.[230]

[20.650] Repudiation may occur by words or conduct; it usually consists of a statement that the party cannot or will not perform.[231] The statement must be understood as meaning a breach will actually occur. Expressions of doubt as to a party's willingness or ability may not constitute a repudiation.[232] The circumstances in which repudiation will arise are similar to those in Australia. One difference arises where a party relies on a mistaken understanding of his or her rights to either terminate or refuse performance. In Australia, it will not be a repudiation unless it is clear that the party would not perform, even if the true position were known.[233] In America, a statement that indicates an intention not to perform except on conditions that go beyond the contract is a repudiation, even if the party is mistaken about his or her rights.[234]

[20.655] Where the repudiation occurs in conjunction with a non-performance of the contract, the injured party is entitled to treat the breach as total, even if it would only have been partial. This would entitle the injured party to suspend performance and, depending upon the circumstances, terminate the contract within a short period.[235]

[20.660] A repudiation that occurs prior to the time for performance is an anticipatory repudiation. This type of repudiation will be treated as a prospective total breach; it immediately discharges the innocent party from further performance of the contract. Although it was initially unclear whether the innocent party could also immediately sue for damages for total breach, most states, except for Massachusetts, accept that damages are claimable immediately.[236] However, the doctrine of anticipatory repudiation does not apply if repudiation occurs after the repudiating party has received all of

---

228 See [20.430].
229 Tender is also not required for a successful claim of specific performance.
230 Restatement (Second) § 250.
231 Example : *Petrangelo v Pollard* 255 NE 2d 342 (Mass 1970).
232 *Thermo Electron Corp v Schiavone Construction Co* 958 F 2d 1158 (1st Cir 1992).
233 See [20.175]–[20.185].
234 *Chamberlin v Puckett Construction* 921 P 2d 1237 (Mont 1996); *Miller v Schwinn Inc* 113 F 2d 748 (DC Cir 1940). See also UCC 2-610.
235 See [20.620].
236 See Restatement (Second) § 253 and EA Farnsworth, *Contracts*, 3rd edn, Aspen Law and Business, New York, 1999 § 8.20 (p 602), cf *Daniels v Newton* 114 Mass 530 (1874) (no present violation of rights and therefore no present right to damages).

the agreed exchange for that duty.[237] Courts have attempted to avoid this exception by finding that some part of the agreed exchange has not been rendered.[238]

[20.665] A party faced with anticipatory repudiation in America has choices similar to a party in Australia. The party may treat the contract as terminated and sue for damages; try to save the contract by urging the other party to perform; or choose to await the time for performance. If the innocent party chooses to terminate immediately, the innocent party is discharged from further performance and does not need to tender performance.[239] However, to recover damages, the injured party will need to show that, had there been no repudiation, she or he would have been able to tender performance as required by the contract.[240] Termination will need to occur prior to any retraction of the repudiation by the defaulting party.[241] For this reason it is prudent for the injured party to give notice of its termination to the defaulting party. If notice is not given, but the injured party has relied upon the repudiation, this will be sufficient.[242] Acceptance, as it is understood in Australia, is not required.

[20.670] The second avenue open to the injured party is to urge a retraction. This is a common response by contracting parties, and it is not considered an election to waive the repudiation.[243] If the repudiating party does not retract the repudiation, the injured party may treat the contract as discharged, and terminate the contract.

[20.675] The final response is to wait and see. As with the Australian position, this is the least certain response for the injured party. Waiting until the time for performance will provide the repudiating party with an opportunity to perform the contract. However, if the repudiating party decides not to perform, the injured party will be disadvantaged by not being able to terminate immediately, and some items of loss may not be recoverable, due to the principle of avoidability.[244] This should be contrasted with the case of breach by non-performance, where the injured party may treat the breach as partial, claim damages, and await performance.

20.22.3 Japan

[20.680] The Japanese Civil Code follows German jurisprudence in classifying the reasons for non-performance into three categories: impossibility; delay; and incomplete performance. Article 415 of the Civil Code states the consequence of non-performance of contracts (other than those for payment of a sum of money):

> If an obligor fails to effect performance in accordance with the tenor and purport of the obligation, the obligee may claim damages; the same shall apply to cases where the performance becomes impossible for any cause for which the obligor is responsible.

---

237 Texas does not accept this exception: *Pitts v Wetzel* 498 SW 2d 27 (Tex Civ App 1973).
238 *Long Island RR v Northville Industrial Corp* 362 NE 2d 558 (NY 1977).
239 *Midwest Engineering & Construction Co v Electric Regulator Corp* 435 P 2d 89 (Okl 1967).
240 *Income Properties/Equity Trust v Wal-Mart Stores* 33 F 3d 987 (8th Cir 1994).
241 Retraction will prevent the other party from terminating the contract but damages for any delay or other loss suffered may be recoverable. See UCC 2-611(3).
242 *William B Tanner Co v WIOO Inc* 528 F 2d 262 (3d Cir 1975).
243 *United Cal Bank v Prudential Insurance Co* 681 P 2d 3980 (Ariz App 1983).
244 See [23.490].

[20.685] The three core categories of non-performance in Japanese law are forms of breach of contract, which generally give rise to a right to terminate the contract provided:

- the non-performance is objectively proven; and
- the innocent party can also point to fault imputable (attributable) to the other party.

The same breach may also give rise to a right to demand performance of the contract, or a right to claim damages as compensation in addition to either the demand of performance or the termination.

(a) Delay

[20.690] Delay of contractual performance is governed by Civil Code art 412, which provides that:

- Where a time is fixed for the performance of an obligation-duty, the obligor shall be responsible for any delay beyond such time.
- If an uncertain time period is agreed to for the performance of an obligation-duty, the obligor shall be responsible for the delay from the time when such obligor becomes aware of the arrival of the time for performance.
- If no time is fixed for the performance of an obligation-duty; the obligor shall be responsible for any delay from the time when performance is demanded.

[20.695] Delayed performance gives the other party the right to terminate the contract. The Civil Code provides for two kinds of termination, depending on whether time was a critical factor in the original contract or not. Where the timing in the original contract was not critical, the party seeking to terminate must first demand performance (offer the other party an opportunity to cure its defective performance). If the other party continues to fail to perform the obligation, the innocent party may then terminate the contract (Civil Code art 541).[245] However, in cases where the original time was critical, a prior demand for performance is not required. Civil Code art 542 allows immediate termination. This is similar to the position under the common law.[246] Whether or not time is critical (in the common law, whether it is of the essence) and therefore a basis for immediate termination of the contract is a question of fact. However, as a matter of business practice in Japan, delay is generally regarded as a serious issue. In sales of goods particularly, delay in delivery—depending on the circumstances and terms of the agreement—can be grounds for termination. However,

---

245 Article 541: If one of the parties does not perform his obligation, the other party may fix a reasonable period and demand its performance and may rescind the contract if no perfomance is effected within that period.

   Article 542: If, according to the nature of the contact or by a declaration of intention by the parties, the object for which the contract was made cannot be attained unless it is performed at a fixed time or within a fixed period, one of the parties has allowed the time to elapse without performance on his part, the other party may, without making a demand mentioned in the preceding article, forthwith rescind the contract.

   Article 543: If performance has become impossible in whole or in part by any cause for which the obligor is responsible, the obligee may rescind the contract.

246 See [20.265]–[20.280].

this needs to be balanced against possible defences to claims of non-performance—for example, a requirement of simultaneous performance.

(b)   Incomplete performance

[20.700] Cases of incomplete performance arise in Japanese contracts in much the same way as they do elsewhere: the performance contracted for is not completed, or has a defect (that is, the contract is breached); or the performance is effected in a way that creates some new ancillary damage.

[20.705] The Japanese Civil Code has no specific provisions governing incomplete performance of contracts. Civil Code articles 541 and 543 are applied analogously to cover this situation.

[20.710] Many Japanese commercial contracts have traditionally been continuing contracts—that is, the parties may have a long-term contract for a number of years, tacitly renewed and performed over an extended period: for example, 20–30 years. There is an ongoing debate in Japan about whether article 541 allows the termination of a continuing contract at will. The answer seems to be no. Case law seems to indicate that termination of a continuing contract—even for breach—requires, at a minimum, notice to the other party; and an opportunity to cure defective performance. Where the contract is silent about notice periods, a reasonable period of notice will be required. What is reasonable will depend on the nature and length of the contract in question. In distributorship contracts, for example, courts have imposed notice periods of between 6 months and 12 months.

[20.715] On the other hand, Japanese courts have also upheld the right of innocent parties to terminate the contract where the other party performs an act that fundamentally undermines the basis of the contractual relationship. These kinds of acts include committing an act that destroys the trust relationship between the parties—for example, sabotaging the transaction partner's business by spreading industry rumours; committing an act (for example delayed payment) that shows a lack of creditworthiness; or otherwise doing something that provides reasonable grounds for the innocent party to doubt the business integrity of his or her transaction partner.

(c)   Failure to pay an agreed sum

[20.720] Article 419 of the Civil Code governs the non-performance of money payment obligations. Unlike other forms of non-performance, where a party has failed to pay an agreed sum, the court will not inquire into any subjective issues; the obligor is treated as having a strict liability.

[20.725] The amount of damages payable will be the amount of interest due on the money, either at the rate agreed between the parties, or at the legal rate. Whether the amount of actual damages exceeds the amount of interest due, the obligor cannot be held responsible for the difference based on breach of contract. The law considers that, even though the obligor has delayed the payment, the obligee can borrow in order to cover the period of delay.

[20.730] In reality, delay in payment may have serious consequences. Courts have upheld the cancellation of a contract where there has been repeated delay in payment, as this suggests the non-performing party may be in business difficulty, and the innocent party is justified in cancelling the contract before the breaches become more serious. Conversely, a delayed payment may be the factor that pushes the innocent party into bankruptcy; where the obligor's non-performance produces such serious results, it may be possible for the innocent party to claim alternative relief based on a claim in tort.

(d)   Effect of termination

[20.735] The effect of terminating ('rescission') is debated in Japanese contract scholarship. Article 545 of the Civil Code states:

(1) If one of the parties has exercised his or her right of rescission, the other party is obligated to restore the former to his or her original position; however the rights of third persons shall not be prejudiced thereby;

(2) Interest shall be paid upon any money to be repaid in the cases referred to in the preceding paragraph from the time when such money was first received;

(3) The exercise of a right of rescission shall not preclude a demand for compensation of damages.

[20.740] These general principles apply both to termination by provision of law and to termination by the operation of the contract. Paragraph (3) applies only in cases of non-performance. Parties are free to contract out of Article 545.

[20.745] The effect of termination in Japanese law combines some aspects of both termination and rescission at common law. It is similar in requiring that innocent parties be returned to their original positions without prejudice to third parties. As in termination, however, an innocent party is entitled to compensation for non-performance.

Chapter 21

Discharge by agreement

21.1 Introduction

[21.05] Discharge of a contract as the result of performance, breach or frustration is considered in chapters 19, 20 and 22. The final circumstances in which a contract may be discharged and the parties freed from their obligations is by agreement between the parties (contractual discharge) or conduct that implies an extinguishment of the contract (non-contractual discharge). Contractual discharge may result from an express term of the contract—or the parties may just agree that they no longer wish to continue. The first situation will arise where the parties have inserted a term in the contract that allows for termination by either party, usually with a period of notice. These types of clauses typically appear in employment contracts where either party may terminate the contract by a certain period of notice to the other. Considerations relevant to the exercise of such rights are similar to those discussed in relation to contractual rights of termination for breach.[1] Valid exercise will depend, ultimately, upon a construction of the contract[2] and compliance with any restrictions imposed. Contracts of indefinite duration may also be subject to an implied right to terminate by notice—but this is subject to the usual requirements for implication of a term.[3] The second type of contractual discharge arises where the parties mutually agree, prior to the completion of the contract, to discharge their obligations. Usually such agreement will be subject to terms such as the payment of money or the relinquishment of a cause of action.

[21.10] Non-contractual discharge may occur where the parties act in a way that implies their mutual obligations are discharged and the contract abandoned.[4] The second type of contractual discharge and non-contractual discharge is the subject of this chapter.

21.2   Discharge distinguished from variation

[21.15] The complete discharge of a contract must be distinguished from the variation or partial discharge of an agreement by the parties. In contrast to the discharge of a contract, the variation of a contract will leave the original contract on foot, but modify some particulars. Whether the agreement between the parties is a discharge or variation appears to be a question of degree and intention.[5] A purported variation of the contract may alter so many particulars of a contract that a court will infer that the parties intended to abrogate the existing contract and substitute it with the 'varied' contract.[6]

[21.20] The ultimate determination of the court will not affect the enforceability of the agreement unless it is of a type required to be in writing.[7]

Example: Morris v Baron & Co[8]

Morris agreed to sell goods to Barron. He delivered only part of the goods, valued at £880.00, and six months later began proceedings to recover this sum. The company counter-claimed for £934.00 as the damages for non-delivery of the whole of the goods. Prior to trial, the parties compromised the dispute. They made an oral contract under which the action was to be withdrawn. The company was granted another three months to pay the sum due under the contract, and it was to have the option either to accept or to refuse the undelivered goods. The company was allowed £30 to meet the expenses incurred owing to the failure of Morris to make complete delivery. Ten months later, the moneys were still unpaid; Morris brought a second action to

---

1   See [20.45].
2   See *Permanent Building Society (in liq) v Wheeler* (1993) 10 WAR 109
3   Implication of a term is discussed at [8.460]–[8.820]. Where the contract is of indefinite duration for a particular project, the court will not imply a right of termination other than by mutual agreement of the parties: *Dempster v Mallina Holdings Ltd* (1994) 13 WAR 124 at 170–171.
4   See [21.75].
5   See *Tallerman & Co Pty Ltd v Nathan's Merchandise (Victoria) Pty Ltd* (1956) 98 CLR 93 at 112–112, 122–126, 135, 144. See also: *Electronic Industries Ltd v David Jones Pty Ltd* (1954) 91 CLR 288; *Civil and Civic Pty Ltd v Pioneer Concrete (NT) Pty Ltd* (1991) 103 FLR 196; *Australian Horizons (Vic) Pty Ltd v Ryan Land Co Pty Ltd* [1994] 2 VR 463.
6   *British and Beningtons Ltd v NW Cochar Tea Co* [1923] AC 48 at 62.
7   See [21.55]–[21.70].
8   [1918] AC 1.

recover the outstanding sum. The company admitted liability, but again counter-claimed for damages in respect of the undelivered goods. The action failed.

The Court gave careful consideration to the evidence, which indicated an intention by the parties to set aside and substitute the original contract for another contract. The Court noted that neither party ever referred to the original contract as governing their rights—on the contrary, they treated it as at an end, even though the original agreement was required to be in writing in accordance with the Statute of Frauds. As the compromise agreement was not itself in writing neither party was able to enforce the agreement. The parties were therefore left effectively with no contract governing their relationship.

[21.25] The distinction between discharge and variation becomes relevant when considering issues such as whether the contract is required to be in writing,[9] and at what time and place the contract was formed;[10] it is also relevant where a cause of action is compromised.

21.3 Requirements of a valid discharge by agreement

[21.30] An existing contract may be discharged by a further contract between the parties. The usual rules of contract formation will apply to the contract of discharge. Offer and acceptance will be required,[11] as will consideration and a clear intention to bring the parties' obligations to an end.[12] The provision of consideration will pose no problem where neither party has performed his or her obligations. However, where one party to the contract has performed his or her obligations, fresh consideration will be required unless the agreement is in the form of a deed.[13]

Example

A agrees to sell 100 crates of potatoes to B for $500 per crate.

Illustration 1: Prior to A's delivering any potatoes to B, A and B agree to discharge the contract. In this case, each party provides consideration to the other for the promise to discharge the contract. The consideration in each case is the relinquishment of the right to enforce the obligations under the contract.

Illustration 2: After A delivers 50 crates to B and B has paid for those crates, A and B agree to discharge the contract. This is the same as illustration 1. Each party provides consideration by agreeing to forgo her right to enforce the obligations of the other under the contract.

Illustration 3: After A has delivered all 100 crates to B and before B has paid, A and B agree to discharge the contract. In this case, no consideration is provided by B.

---

9   Considered at [21.55]–[21.70].
10   *Tallerman & Co Pty Ltd v Nathan's Merchandise (Victoria) Pty Ltd* (1956) 98 CLR 93.
11   See for example *BP Refinery (Westernport) Pty Ltd v Shire of Hastings* (1977) 52 ALJR 20.
12   *Fitzgerald v Masters* (1956) 95 CLR 420; *Tekmat Pty Ltd v Dosto Pty Ltd* (1990) 102 FLR 240.
13   *Atlantic Shipping & Trading Ltd v Louis Dreyfus & Co* [1922] AC 250 at 262–263. See [6.165].

A can provide consideration by relinquishing her rights against B. This would in effect act as a gift because B has nothing to relinquish in return.

21.4 Compromise of a cause of action

[21.35] An agreement to relinquish a cause of action against a party may act as a discharge of the original agreement. Such a contract may be called an 'accord and satisfaction' or a 'compromise'. As described by Scrutton LJ:

> Accord and satisfaction is the purchase of a release from an obligation whether arising under contract or tort by means of any valuable consideration, not being the actual performance of the obligations itself. The accord is the agreement by which the obligation is discharged. The satisfaction is the consideration which makes the agreement operative.[14]

[21.40] Within this area of law, one of the most difficult questions is *when does the discharge of the original contract occur?* The first possibility is that the original agreement is discharged immediately the compromise agreement is entered into. In that case, the agreement itself releases the cause of action and is substituted in its place. The other possibility is that the compromise is a promise to release the cause of action only once the event set out in the compromise occurs. This will usually be the payment of money or doing of an act. This is often referred to as an 'accord executory'. The original cause of action will not be discharged unless the promised conduct occurs. Deciding which interpretation applies in any given case is a matter of construction. Dixon J, in *McDermott v Black*,[15] summarises the position like this:

> one where the making of the agreement itself is what is stipulated for, and the other, where it is the doing of the things promised by the agreement. The distinction depends on what exactly is agreed to be taken in place of the existing cause of action or claim. An executory promise or series of promises given in consideration of the abandonment of the claim may be accepted in substitution of satisfaction of the existing liability. Or on the other hand, promises may be given by the party liable that he will satisfy the claim by doing an act, making over a thing or paying an ascertained sum of money and the other party may agree to accept, not the promise, but the act, thing or money in satisfaction of his claim.

[21.45] The distinction between an accord and satisfaction and an accord executory will be particularly important where a compromise agreement is breached by one of the parties. Where the compromise acts as an accord and satisfaction to discharge the original agreement immediately, the innocent party will be forced to seek damages for breach of the compromise or a claim for specific performance. The original agreement will not be revived by the breach. If, however, the compromise acts as an accord

---

14 *British Russian Gazette and Trade Outlook Ltd v Associated Newspapers Ltd* [1933] LB 616 at 643–644; see also *McDermott v Black* (1940) 63 CLR 161 at 184.
15 (1940) 63 CLR 161. See also *British Russian Gazette Ltd v Associated Newspapers Ltd* [1933] 2 KB 616 and *Auckland Bus Co Ltd v New Lynn Borough* [1965] NZLR 542.

executory, the innocent party will be entitled to revive the original cause of action or sue to specifically enforce the compromise.

Example: Fraser v Elgen Tavern Pty Ltd[16]

The plaintiff agreed to compromise a cause of action on the following terms: 'the defendants to pay and the plaintiff to accept the sum of $315 000 in full settlement of the plaintiff's claim' and 'subject to an order for the taxation and payment of the plaintiff's costs, action to be struck out.' The money was not paid, and the plaintiff gave notice that the non-payment constituted repudiation and the plaintiff considered that he was no longer bound by the compromise.

The court was required to consider whether the compromise agreement constituted an accord and satisfaction that immediately discharge the original claim or whether it was an accord executory. Murphy J considered that where a party had agreed to compromise a cause of action, the issue was that:

> If the promise is broken, the question must always be whether the giving of the promise discharged the defendant absolutely from the cause of action, so that the plaintiff could only sue thereafter on the new agreement, or whether the discharge effected by the agreement was conditional and ... has the result of 'merely suspending the original cause of action, so that if it is not performed according to its tenor the plaintiff may still maintain that original cause of action.

After considering the actual wording of the compromise, Murphy J concluded that the clear intention was that the original cause of action would only be discharged after *performance* of the promise by the defendant. This provided the plaintiff with the choice of reverting to the original contract or suing to specifically enforce the compromise.

21.5   Requirements of a valid variation

[21.50] A variation of a contract, like a discharge, is a contract between the parties. The agreement to vary a contract must contain all of the essential terms of an agreement. In particular, the parties will need to ensure there is consideration for the variation.

Example

A agrees to sell a camera to B for $1000. A and B later agree that the price should be changed to $1200. What is the consideration for this subsequent promise to pay $1200? This is a variation to the original contract and not the substitution of a new agreement. B's was already entitled to the camera for $1000. As previously discussed, A's pre-existing obligation to deliver the camera for $1000 is not good consideration for a subsequent promise to pay more money.[17] A will need to provide additional consideration or the agreement to vary the contract must be in the form of a deed.

---

16   [1982] VR 398.
17   See [6.215]–[6.305].

Where the variation to the contract involves a potential benefit and burden to both parties, consideration will be present. If, in the example above, A agreed to give B a tripod at the same time B agreed to pay $1200, there would be sufficient consideration.

21.6   Requirements of writing

[21.55] An oral agreement to discharge a contract will be enforceable. Even if the original contract was required to be in writing, it may be totally rescinded or discharged by an oral agreement.[18] The oral agreement, although not enforceable, will be effective to discharge the original contract.[19]

[21.60] In contrast, the oral variation of a contract will not be effective if the original contract is of a type required by legislation to be in writing.[20] If the variation is not in writing the original contract will remain unaffected[21] Nevertheless, where the oral agreement purports to discharge the original contract and substitute a new contract, the original contract will be discharged, but the new contract will be unenforceable.[22]

[21.65] The difference in approach to discharge and variation results from the strict interpretation give to the relevant legislation. For example, s 59 of the *Property Law Act 1974* provides that a contract for the 'disposition' of an interest in land is only enforceable if in writing.[23] If such a contract is then rescinded by the agreement of the parties, is that second agreement one for the 'disposition' of an interest in land? Arguably the agreement to rescind is not a contract *for the disposition* but merely *relates to* the disposition of an interest.[24]

[21.70] The requirement for writing does not apply to the dispensation or waiver of a mode of performance.[25] For example, an agreement to extend the time for performance under a land transaction will be considered a waiver of the mode of performance, not a variation. This waiver does not have to be in writing to be enforceable. The distinction between a variation and waiver of performance is often difficult to judge, and some

---

18   *Tallerman & Co Pty Ltd v Nathan's Merchandise (Victoria) Pty Ltd* (1956) 98 CLR 93 at 112–113, 122–124, 143–144. An agreement under seal may also be discharged by an oral agreement: *Slee v Warke* (194) 86 CLR 271 at 281, *Creamoata Ltd v Rice Equalization Association Ltd* (1953) 89 CLR 286 at 306, 326; *Buckland v Commissioner of Stamp Duties* [1954] NZLR 1194; *Booth McDonald & Co Ltd v Hall* [1931] NZLR 1086.

19   See for example *Morris v Baron & Co* (1918) AC 1.

20   *Phillips v Ellison Bros Pty Ltd* (1941) 65 CLR 221 at 244; *Tallerman & Co Pty Ltd v Nathan's Merchandise (Victoria) Pty Ltd* (1956) 98 CLR 93 at 112–113, 122–124, 143–144; *Papapetros v Carmello Mazza* (1989) 7 BCL 60; *Watson v Healy Lands Ltd* [1965] NZLR 5111 at 513. See Chapter 11 in relation to the types of contracts required to be in writing.

21   *Tallerman & Co Pty Ltd v Nathan's Merchandise (Victoria) Pty Ltd* (1956) 98 CLR 93 at 112–113; *British & Beningtons Ltd v North Western Cachar Tea Co Ltd* (1923) AC 48; cf *United Dominions Corporation (Jamiaca) Ltd v Shoucair* [1968] 3 WLR 893 at 896–897.

22   *Tallerman & Co Pty Ltd v Nathan's Merchandise (Victoria) Pty Ltd* (1956) 98 CLR 93 at 112–113, 122–123; *Morris v Baron & Co* [1918] AC 1. Specific performance may be available if part performance is present. See the discussion of part performance at [11.335]–[11.395]. In New Zealand refer to *Boviard v Brown* [1975] 2 NZLR 694.

23   See [11.105] for further discussion.

24   This rationale has been called into question in NC Seddon & MP Ellinghaus, *Cheshire and Fifoot's Law of Contract*, 7th edn, Butterworths, Sydney, 1997 at [22.7] (p769).

25   *Phillips v Ellinson Bros Pty Ltd* (1941) 65 CLR 221.

courts have made artificial distinctions to avoid injustice.[26] In any event, in the majority of cases where a party is relying upon forbearance in relation to the mode of perform- ance, the issue of estoppel will arise. A claim based on estoppel does not require written evidence to succeed, provided there is sufficient oral evidence.[27]

21.7 Abandonment

[21.75] The main type of non-contractual discharge is abandonment. The parties' con- duct may indicate that they are in fact treating the contract as discharged even though there is no express agreement. Abandonment will usually be found where an inordi- nate length of time has been allowed to pass, during which neither party has attempted to perform or called on the other to perform.[28] The court will be interested to ascer- tain the objective intention of the parties, and the mere fact that a length of time has elapsed will not be conclusive.[29]

Example: Fitzgerald v Masters[30]

Fitzgerald sold to Masters a half-interest in his farm in 1927. The balance of the price was to be paid over a period of years, during which the farm was to be worked in partnership. In 1932, Masters left the farm after more than half the price had been paid, and further payments had been offered. Before he left, Masters had the contract of sale stamped and registered but he took no further steps in relation to it until 1948. Masters commenced an action in 1953—two years after Fitzgerald's death.

The issue for the court was whether the agreement had been abandoned due to the inordinate length of time that had been allowed to elapse, during which neither party attempted to perform. The court held that the parties had not abandoned the contract. The continued existence of the plaintiff's equitable interest in the property, the fact that more than half of the price had been paid, and the registration of the contract, indicated that despite the passing of time an intention to abandon the con- tract could not be found on the facts.

21.8   International perspectives

21.8.1   New Zealand

[21.80] The law in New Zealand in relation to discharge by agreement is substantially the same as that in Australia, and does not require separate examination.

---

26   *Hartley v Hymans* [1920] 3 KB 475.
27   *Waltons Stores (Interstate) Limited v Maher* (1987) 164 CLR 387. See the detailed commentary on estop- pel in Chapter 7.
28   *Mathews v Mathews* (1941) SASR 250 at 255; cf *Fitzgerald v Masters* (1956) 95 CLR 420.
29   Contrast *Fitzgerald v Masters* (1956) 95 CLR 420 where 16 years elapsed and *DTR Nominees Pty Ltd v Mona Homes Pty Ltd* (1978) 138 CLR 42 where the conduct of parties was more important that the time elapsed. In New Zealand see *Paal Wilson & Co A/S v Partenreederei Hannah Blumenthal, The Hannah Blumenthal* [1983] 1 AC 854.
30   (1956) 95 CLR 420.

21.8.2 United States

[21.85] Similarly to Australia, American law recognises the right of the parties to mutually agree to discharge their obligations. The mutual agreement of the parties to discharge a contract is referred to as mutual rescission. Similar issues regarding the provision of consideration and the requirement of writing arise. As with the Australian position, any mutual rescission must be accompanied by consideration. Where one of the parties has fully performed his or her obligations, the other party will need to provide fresh consideration for the agreement to be binding.[31] Where no additional consideration is provided, the mutual rescission should take the form of a deed.[32] An agreement to rescind does not have to be in writing. This will be the case even if the original agreement was of a type required to be in writing.

[21.90] Distinction is also drawn between a mutual rescission and a modification of the contract. This difference is important for issues of consideration and compliance with the Statute of Frauds. The difference between the two is a question of ascertaining the intention of the parties. One judge has attempted to provide a formula:

> An alteration of details of the contract which leaves undisturbed its general purpose constitutes a modification rather then a rescission of the contract.[33]

[21.95] The treatment of an accord and satisfaction is the same as in Australia. The law recognises that an accord may take one of two forms. The accord may discharge the original contract immediately; alternatively, it will only discharge the original contract upon the happening of a future event (an executory accord).[34] The difference had some historical significance with executory accords not considered enforceable at common law.[35] The modern approach is, however, to treat an executory accord as enforceable.[36] As in Australia, the effect of an accord executory is to suspend performance of the original contract. If the accord is performed, the original contract is discharged. If the accord is breached, the original action revives and the party has the choice of suing on the original agreement or enforcing the accord.[37] If the accord discharges the original contract immediately, the original claim will not be revived by breach.[38] Even though some authorities suggest that termination of an agreement for material breach will also revive the original claim, this approach is not taken by the Restatement (Second).[39]

[21.100] The concept of abandonment is recognised in several jurisdictions, while in others the same conduct gives rise to an implied rescission. This may occur where

---

31   See the discussion in Chapter 6 concerning consideration at [6.215]–[6.305].

32   If the original agreement is in the form of a deed this may be discharged by an agreement not under seal: *Kirk v Brentwood Manor Homes* 191 Pa Super 488, 159 A 2d 48 (1960).

33   *Travellers Insurance Co v Workmen's Compensation Appeals Board* 68 Cal 2d 7, 17, 64 Cal Rptr 440, 446, 434 P 2d 992, 998 (1967).

34   Restatement (Second) § 281. See also *Alaska Creamery Products v Wells* 373 P 2d 505, 511 (Alaska 1962).

35   *Reilly v Barrett* 220 NY 170, 115 NE 453 (1917).

36   In New York, legislation has been passed to make such agreements enforceable where they are in writing signed by the party to be charged.

37   *Markowitz & Co v Toledo Metropolitan Housing Authority* 608 F 2d 699 (6th Cir 1979).

38   *Moers v Moers* 229 NY 294, 128 NE 202, 14 ALR 225 (1920), Restatement (Second) § 279(2).

39   See *Publicker Industries v Roman Ceramics Corp* 603 F 2d 1065 (3rd Cir 1979); *Christensen v Hamilton Realty* 42 Utah 70, 129 P 412 (1912). Restatement (Second) § 279(2).

there is a mutual failure to cooperate in performance of the contract,[40] or concurrent breaches by the parties[41] or repudiation by one and acquiescence by the other.

21.8.3   Japan

[21.105] Japanese law, like its common law counterparts, allows the discharge of a contract by agreement. Discharge by agreement can occur where the parties agree to discontinue a contract in light of changing conditions—or the agreement itself may provide for termination on the occurrence of events agreed at the time of making the contract.

[21.110] In the case of commercial agreements made in writing, it is common to have a clause that provides the automatic termination of the agreement, or the right of either party to avoid the contract upon the occurrence of certain events. Typical events that may be included in these clauses are:

- corporate insolvency, or the court filing of documents that signal preliminary stages of insolvency;
- corporate reorganisation pursuant to the relevant corporate law statutes;
- the criminal indictment of any of the company's directors;
- a change in the company's management (for example, merger, acquisition, the replacement or death of a company president); and
- suspension of the company's bank accounts (a measure imposed by banks when companies fail to honour their promissory notes).

---

40   *Admiral Plastics Corp v Trueblood* 436 F 2d 1335 (6th Cir 1971).
41   *Gentry v Smith* 487 F 2d 571 (5th Cir 1973).

Chapter 22

Frustration

22.1 Introduction

[22.05] In some circumstances, an event may occur after a contract has been formed that would render performance different in substance from what was originally undertaken. In such a case, the contract is said to have been discharged by frustration, and the parties are released from further obligations under the contract. The doctrine is based on the notion that 'it was not this that I promised to do'.[1]

[22.10] This common law doctrine of frustration may be contrasted with the situation where the contract includes a clause that expressly provides for the consequences of the happening of an event that might otherwise frustrate the contract by operation of law. Such a clause—sometimes described as a *force majeure* clause—might provide that both parties are discharged, that only one party is discharged, or that any obligation to perform is merely suspended rather than terminated.[2]

22.2 Test for frustration

22.2.1 General test

[22.15] In *Codelfa Construction Pty Ltd v State Rail Authority of New South Wales*,[3] the High Court endorsed the following as the general test for frustration:

> Frustration occurs whenever the law recognises that without default of either party a contractual obligation has become incapable of being performed because the circumstances in which performance is called for would render it a thing radically different from that which was undertaken by the contract.[4]

[22.20] Application of this 'change in obligation' test depends upon the individual circumstances of each case. It involves taking into account two factors:

- the terms of the particular contract in question; and
- the effect of the supervening event.

Accordingly, it is the *effect* of the supervening event rather than merely its *nature* that is important. For example, in an appropriate case, the delay in performance caused by a strike may frustrate a contract. This does not mean that a strike will necessarily result in frustration. But it does mean that it is possible for the one event to affect different contracts in different ways, frustrating some but not others.

Example: The *Evia*[5]

On the outbreak of the Iran–Iraq War on 22 September 1980, the Shatt-al-Arab Waterway was closed, trapping many vessels. Most of those vessels, including the *Evia*, were subject to charterparty.

---

1   *Davis Contractors Ltd v Fareham Urban District Council* [1956] AC 696 at 729 per Lord Radcliffe.
2   See, for example, *Ringstad v Gollin & Co Pty Ltd* (1924) 35 CLR 303. See further [22.170].
3   (1982) 149 CLR 337.
4   Ibid, at 357, 380, 408, citing Lord Radcliffe in *Davis Contractors Ltd v Fareham Urban District Council* [1956] AC 696 at 729. See also *Brisbane City Council v Group Projects Pty Ltd* (1979) 149 CLR 143 at 159–163.
5   *Kodros Shipping Corp of Monrovia v Empresa Cubana de Flets* [1983] 1 AC 736.

The House of Lords held that in the case of the *Evia* the relevant date of frustration was 4 October 1980. That date was not open to review merely because in other cases concerning vessels trapped in the waterway, arbitrators had either held that the contract had not been frustrated or had appointed another day as the relevant date of frustration. While, prima facie, similar cases should produce a similar result, in the case of frustration, questions of degree were involved. The charterparties may have been of different characteristics and of different lengths; the discharge of cargo may have been completed on different dates; and the respective masters, officers, and crew may have left their ships at different times. The various factors that may have arisen meant that it was not legitimate to adopt the one day (including the date the waterway was actually closed) as being the relevant date of frustration for all cases.

[22.25] The mere fact that the supervening event renders performance of the contract more onerous or expensive will not mean that performance has become 'radically different' from that originally undertaken. In such a case, performance is simply more burdensome.

Example: The *Eugenia*[6]

The *Eugenia* was chartered for a voyage from Genoa, Italy, to India. No time was fixed for completion of the voyage, hire being paid according to the time taken to complete the voyage. Following a breakdown in diplomatic relations, the Egyptian government closed the Suez Canal, and the *Eugenia* was trapped in the canal. The charterers argued that closure of the canal frustrated the charterparty, because completion of the voyage via the Cape of Good Hope would add 30 days to the voyage.

The English Court of Appeal held that although the closure of the canal had rendered performance of the charterparty more onerous and expensive, it had not rendered performance radically different from the original undertaking. The charterparty therefore remained on foot.

Similarly, performance may be rendered more expensive without a radical change to the parties' bargain where there has been, for example, a rise or fall in prices or through the effects of inflation.[7] However, inflation may amount to a frustrating event in an appropriate case—as where, contrary to what the parties contemplated, inflation increases 'not at a trot or a canter, but at a gallop'.[8]

[22.30] Although the 'change in obligation' approach is the prevailing test, there have in the past been different views about the theory that underlies the doctrine of frustration. For example, some cases have suggested that the courts act to give effect to an implied term that the contract should come to an end on the happening of a given event.[9] Other judges have suggested that a given event discharges the contract because

---

6   *Ocean Tramp Tankers Corp v V-O Sovfracht* [1964] 2 QB 226.

7   *British Movietonews Ltd v London and District Cinemas Ltd* [1952] AC 166 at 185; *Power Co Ltd v Gore District Council* [1997] 1 NZLR 537 at 553–554.

8   *Wates Ltd v Greater London Council* (1983) 25 BLR 1 at 35 per Stephenson LJ.

9   See, for example, *Firth v Halloran* (1926) 38 CLR 261 at 279–290; *Scanlan's New Neon Ltd v Tooheys Ltd* (1943) 67 CLR 169; *McRae v Commonwealth Disposals Commission* (1951) 84 CLR 377 at 407–409.

the imputed intention of the parties is that it is the fair and just result in all the circumstances of the case.[10] However, the fact that a decision was based on one theory does not cast doubt on the authority of other, earlier decisions, which remain valuable as illustrations of situations in which contracts will be regarded as frustrated today. Accordingly, a case may have been decided on the basis of, for example, the implied term test but will nevertheless be regarded as representing good authority for the circumstances in which the 'change in obligation' test will be satisfied.[11]

22.2.2 Common instances of frustration

[22.35] It has been pointed out that frustration depends upon the application of the 'change in obligation' test to the facts of the particular case. Accordingly, it is not possible to generate an exhaustive list of circumstances in which a contract may be recognised as having been frustrated. However, an attempt may be made to group together previous decisions that have found that the contract in question has been frustrated in order to obtain some guidance as to the type of circumstances in which the general test may be satisfied. In doing so, however, it should be recognised that any such grouping is necessarily artificial, and that there may be overlap between the various groupings.

(a) Destruction or unavailability of subject matter

[22.40] Perhaps one of the clearer instances of a contract being frustrated is where, without the fault of either party, the specific subject matter of the contract has been destroyed. For example, where a hall is hired for the purpose of holding concerts and subsequently the hall is destroyed by fire, the contract of hire will be discharged, since the hall will be regarded as having been essential to the performance of the hire contract.[12]

[22.45] A different result may follow, however, where one of the parties has either expressly or impliedly agreed to bear the risk of any destruction. For example, under a sale of land that includes a house, it is common for risk to pass to the purchaser on the execution of the contract, so that if the house were to be destroyed by fire at a time after the contract was executed but before settlement, that destruction would be at the risk of the purchaser. For this reason, the purchaser of a house normally arranges insurance cover from the time that the contract has been executed.[13]

[22.50] There may be other cases where, although the subject matter has not been destroyed, it has, nevertheless, been effectively lost to the parties. Thus, where land subject to a contract of sale is compulsorily acquired by the government,[14] or a vessel subject to a charterparty is requisitioned for government service,[15] the contract

---

10 See *Joseph Constantine Steamship Line Ltd v Imperial Smelting Corporation Ltd* [1942] AC 154 at 186 per Lord Wright. See also *Brisbane City Council v Group Projects Pty Ltd* (1979) 145 CLR 143.

11 *Codelfa Construction Pty Ltd v State Rail Authority of New South Wales* (1982) 149 CLR 337 at 357 per Mason J.

12 See *Taylor v Caldwell* (1863) 3 B&S 826; 122 ER 309.

13 *Fletcher v Manton* (1940) 64 CLR 37; cf, for example, *Property Law Act* 1974 (Qld), s 64.

14 See, for example, *Austin v Sheldon* [1974] 2 NSWLR 661.

15 See, for example, *Bank Line Ltd v Arthur Capel & Co* [1919] AC 435; *Hirji Mulji v Cheong Yue Steamship Co Ltd* [1926] AC 497.

may be regarded as being frustrated. However, temporary unavailability due to, for example, short-term requisition, may in the circumstances be insufficient to frustrate the contract.[16]

(b)   Death or incapacitation of a party

[22.55] The death or incapacitation of one of the parties may frustrate a contract of service or for services.[17] Incapacitation may be in the form of illness or for some other reason accounting for the unavailability of the party such as imprisonment,[18] internment[19] or conscription.[20]

[22.60] In the case of illness, the effect will depend upon a consideration of two factors in conjunction:

*   the nature and probable duration of the illness; and
*   the terms and nature of the contract.[21]

The effect of illness, including a long illness, must be considered in the context of modern employment contracts that normally provide for sick leave rights and benefits, and may therefore make it difficult to determine when, if at all, the contract has been frustrated.[22] Nevertheless, there may be illness of such unreasonable length that the contract may be taken as having been frustrated[23]—perhaps as at the time of the expiry of all sickness benefits under the contract.

(c)   Failure of the basis of the contract

[22.65] A contract may be frustrated where an event that the parties have agreed to be the basis of the contract does not occur.

Example: Krell v Henry[24]

The defendant hired a flat from the plaintiff for the express purpose of being able to view the Royal Coronation Procession of Edward VII. However, due to the King's illness, the procession was cancelled.

The Court held that both contracting parties had regarded the procession as being the foundation of the contract. Accordingly, its non-occurrence was sufficient to frustrate the contract.

[22.70] However, it will not always be the case that the non-occurrence of an event to which the contract is related will have this effect.

---

16   See, for example, *FA Tamplin Steamship Co Ltd v Anglo-Mexican Petroleum Products Co Ltd* [1916] 2 AC 397.
17   See, for example, *Simmons Ltd v Hay* [1965] NSWR 416.
18   See, for example, *FC Shepherd & Co v Jerrom* [1987] 1 QB 301.
19   See, for example, *Horlock v Beal* [1916] 1 AC 486.
20   See, for example, *Morgan v Manser* [1948] 1 KB 184.
21   *Carmichael v Colonial Sugar Co Ltd* (1944) 44 SR (NSW) 233 at 235–236; *Finch v Sayers* [1976] 2 NSWLR 540 at 557.
22   *Finch v Sayers* [1976] 2 NSWLR 540 at 548.
23   See JW Carter & DJ Harland, *Contract Law in Australia*, 3rd edn, Butterworths, Sydney, 1996, p 718.
24   [1903] 2 KB 740.

Example: Herne Bay Steam Boat Co v Hutton[25]

The defendant chartered a vessel from the plaintiff for the purpose of viewing the naval review associated with the coronation of Edward VII and to cruise around the assembled fleet. The review was also cancelled due to the King's illness.

The English Court of Appeal held that in this case, the contract was not frustrated by the cancellation of the naval review. The purpose or basis of the contract had not been frustrated since the defendant was still able to use the vessel is cruising around the fleet, notwithstanding that the review itself had been cancelled.

(d)   Contemplated method of performance no longer possible

[22.75] The contract may expressly provide for a particular method of performance. Where a supervening event renders that method of performance impossible, the contract may be regarded as frustrated. Accordingly, where a contract was expressed to be for the sale of onions to be shipped 'per P&O steamer sailing from Japan about 8 September and coming direct to Sydney' and due to a strike there was no such vessel steaming direct to Sydney, it was held that the contract was frustrated.[26]

[22.80] Alternatively, the parties may contemplate that a particular method of performance was to be employed, without making it the subject of an express provision in the contract. Where that jointly contemplated method becomes impossible, the contract will be discharged.

Example: Codelfa Construction Pty Ltd v State Rail Authority of NSW[27]

Codelfa entered into a contract with the State Rail Authority to perform excavation work for the construction of an underground railway. The work was required by the contract to be completed within a fixed period. The parties entered into the contract on the understanding that the work was to be carried out by three shifts for seven days a week. The work proved to be noisy; it disturbed nearby residents. As a consequence, the residents obtained an injunction restraining Codelfa from working more than two shifts a day for six days a week, not including Sundays. As an alternative to a claim that there was an implied term that the State Rail Authority would indemnify Codelfa against additional costs incurred,[28] Codelfa argued that the excavation contract had been frustrated by the grant of the injunction.

The High Court held that in the circumstances, the performance of the contract had been rendered radically different from the performance the parties had contemplated. Accordingly, the grant of the injunction had frustrated the contract.

Thus, had the contract in the *Eugenia*[29] expressly stated that the vessel was to travel via the Suez Canal, or had the vessel been chartered to carry a perishable cargo so that the parties contemplated the shortest possible carriage, the closure of the Suez Canal

---

25   [1903] 2 KB 683.
26   *Cornish & Co v Kanematsu* (1913) 13 SR (NSW) 83.
27   (1992) 149 CLR 337.
28   See [8.530].
29   [1964] 2 QB 226; see [22.25].

may have frustrated the contract because the contemplated method of performance would have been rendered impossible.

(e)   Excessive delay

[22.85] An event that causes a temporary delay in performance may frustrate the contract where the delay is such as to render performance something radically different from what was originally undertaken.[30] Some cases may require an assessment in relation to a delay in performance already incurred.[31] Other cases may involve a judgment concerning *prospective* delay. In such cases, two factors must be taken into account:

- the probabilities of the length of delay; and
- the time the contract still has left to run or during which performance might have been expected to have been completed.[32]

This is to be an informed judgment based upon all the evidence.[33] This may mean that the time at which the assessment of whether the contract is frustrated or not may vary from case to case. In some cases, the assessment of commercial probabilities soon after the delay begins. A party is not bound to wait for that delay actually to occur, but can immediately treat itself as discharged from its obligation to perform.[34] For example, in the case of delay in performance of a charterparty due to the ship being requisitioned, it may be clear at the time of the requisition that the ship will not be returned in time to allow further performance under the charter.[35]

In other cases, the parties will be expected to 'wait and see' for some undetermined time—although it has been said that 'businessmen must not be required to await events too long' because they are 'entitled to know where they stand'.[36] For example, it has been suggested that in the case of delay caused by a strike, a court is likely to say that the party should wait to see how long the strike is likely to last, and to determine the prospects for early settlement of the dispute.[37]

[22.90] If, as assessed at the relevant time, reasonable commercial probabilities point to a frustrating delay, it does not matter if in fact no such delay ever occurs.[38]

Example: Court Line v Dant & Russell[39]

A ship under charter was ordered to proceed to a port 750 miles up the Yangtze River. On its arrival in early September 1937, war broke out between China and Japan. The Chinese sank ships to form a boom to prevent the Japanese using the river, and as a result, the chartered ship was trapped in the river. The boom was breached by the Japanese on 9 December, and the ship sailed down the river on 17 December, leaving sufficient time to redeliver the ship to its owner within the period stipulated.

---

30   *Jackson v Union Marine Insurance Co Ltd* (1874) LR 10 LP 125.
31   See, for example, *Ringstad v Gollin & Co Pty Ltd* (1924) 35 CLR 303.
32   See DW Greig & JLR Davis, *Law of Contract*, Law Book Co, Sydney, 1987, pp 1310–1311.
33   *Pioneer Shipping Ltd v BTP Tioxide Ltd* [1982] AC 724 at 752.
34   *Embiricos v Sydney Reid & Co* [1914] 3 KB 45. This is sometimes referred to as 'the *Embiricos* principle.'
35   See, for example, *Bank Line Ltd v Arthur Capel and Co* [1919] AC 435.
36   *Pioneer Shipping Ltd v BTP Tioxide Ltd* [1982] AC 724 at 752.
37   See JW Carter & DJ Harland, *Contract Law in Australia*, 3rd edn, Butterworths, Sydney, 1996, p 723.
38   *Embiricos v Sydney Reid & Co* [1914] 3 KB 45.
39   (1939) 64 Ll LR 212.

It was held that the length and effect of the delay was to be assessed as at the time of the interruption, and without the benefit of the hindsight. At the time the ship was trapped by the boom, the evidence pointed to its being blocked indefinitely; it did not matter that this subsequently proved to be wrong. Accordingly, the charter was frustrated even though, as matters transpired, the contract could have been performed despite the event.

[22.95] If a reasonable person would *not* have drawn an inference of frustration, any party who treats the contract as frustrated will be regarded as having repudiated the obligation to perform.[40]

(f)   Supervening illegality

[22.100] A contract may be frustrated where at some time after formation, performance becomes illegal. Supervening illegality may arise in different ways.

Change in the law

[22.105] Where, after the contract is formed, the law changes in such a way as to prohibit further performance of the contract, the contract will be discharged.[41] However, not all government legislation will render performance of the contract radically different from what was originally undertaken. Attention must be paid to the nature and terms of the contract and the surrounding circumstances.[42]

Example: Scanlan's New Neon Ltd v Tooheys Ltd[43]

The defendant entered into a contract to lease from the plaintiff a neon advertising sign that was to be constructed and installed upon a building. Subsequently, under wartime powers, the government made orders that prohibited the illumination at any time of neon signs. The defendant claimed that the effect of the order was to frustrate the contract.

The High Court held that since the signs were visible and legible even when unilluminated, they retained substantial advertising value. Accordingly, the order prohibiting illumination did not effect a complete prohibition on the lease of the sign. The contract was therefore not frustrated.

[22.110] Where the prohibition effected by the change in law is less than complete, the question whether the contract has been rendered something radically different may depend upon, for example, the effect of any delay caused by the change of law.[44]

Contracting with the enemy

[22.115] If war were to break out between Australia and another country, any contract with a national of that other country or one voluntarily residing in that country would

---

40   See JW Carter & DJ Harland, *Contract Law in Australia*, 3rd edn, Butterworths, Sydney, 1996, p 724.
41   *Cooper & Sons v Neilson & Maxwell Ltd* [1919] VLR 66 at 76.
42   *Scanlan's New Neon Ltd v Tooheys Ltd* (1943) 67 CLR 169.
43   (1943) 67 CLR 169.
44   See, for example, *Metropolitan Water Board v Dick, Kerr & Co Ltd* [1918] AC 119.

be rendered illegal, and the contract would be frustrated.[45] Further, the contract may be frustrated where, while not with an enemy national, it may nevertheless provide assistance to the enemy or hinder the prosecution of the war.[46]

(g)   Contracts concerning land
[22.120] Differing views have been expressed concerning the extent to which the doctrine of frustration applies to contracts concerning land. This is because a contract concerning land may confer a proprietary interest that may not be affected by any discharge of the contract.[47] Notwithstanding this reservation, the weight of authority seems to be in favour of applying the doctrine of frustration to both sale contracts and leases of land.

Sale contracts
[22.125] Upon execution of the contract, a purchaser of land acquires an equitable interest in the land. Since this equitable interest is regarded as being the equivalent of the legal interest of the vendor, subject to payment of the purchase price, it has been said that anything that happens to the land between the time of the contract of sale and the time of completion is at the risk of the purchaser.[48] However, as Greig and Davis point out,[49] if there is a radical change of circumstances between the time of the execution of the contract and its settlement that prevents the vendor from transferring the legal estate to the purchaser, specific performance will no longer be available, the purchaser cannot be treated as the owner in equity nor as having been at risk, and the contract will be frustrated. An example of where the vendor will be prevented from transferring the legal estate in the land will be where, as has already been seen, the land is no longer available due to having been resumed by the government.[50] A more extreme example might be where, due to a landslide, the relevant piece of land no longer exists.[51]

[22.130] A different position applies where, for example, in a sale of land including a building, the building is destroyed prior to settlement. Such a contract is not frustrated, because the purchaser is still able to acquire the legal interest in the land, and will have been taken to have taken the risk of any damage to structures built on the land.[52]

---

45   *Hirsch v Zinc Corporation Ltd* (1917) 24 CLR 34 (contract for annual delivery of zinc to Germany commencing in 1910 frustrated on outbreak of war in 1914).

46   *Fibrosa SA v Fairbairn Lawson Combe Barbour Ltd* [1943] AC 32.

47   *Halloran v Firth* (1926) 26 SR (NSW) 183 at 187 (NSW) FC, adopted on appeal sub nom *Firth v Halloran* (1926) 38 CLR 261 at 268 per Knox CJ and Gavan Duffy J.

48   *Fletcher v Manton* (1940) 64 CLR 37 at 45 per Starke J, 48 per Dixon J.

49   DW Greig & JLR Davis, *Law of Contract*, Law Book Co, Sydney, 1987, p 1324.

50   *Austin v Sheldon* [1974] 2 NSWLR 661; *Holland v Goldtrans Pty Ltd* [1984] 1 Qd R 18.

51   See *National Carriers Ltd v Panalpina (Northern) Ltd* [1991] AC 675 at 691 per Lord Hailsham, 700–701 per Lord Simon.

52   *Fletcher v Manton* (1940) 64 CLR 37 (building demolished pursuant to government order); *British Traders' Insurance Co Ltd v Monson* (1964) 111 CLR 86 (building destroyed by fire).

Leases of land

[22.135] An agreement to lease confers an equitable interest upon the prospective lessee, while an actual grant of lease transfers a legal estate or interest to the lessee.[53] While it might be thought that similar considerations to those that may apply in the case of a sale of land should be relevant to leases and agreements to lease, the only High Court decision on point, *Firth v Halloran*,[54] has left the position in Australia in a state of confusion. While two of the judges—Knox CJ and Gavan Duffy J—were prepared to adopt the reasoning of the Court below to the effect that the doctrine of frustration did not apply to leases,[55] one judge, Isaacs J rejected 'so sweeping a rule'.[56] Of the remaining two judges, Higgins J did not believe that issue arose,[57] while Rich J merely agreed with the other judges.[58]

In England, however, the position has now been settled by a decision by a majority of the House of Lords in *National Carriers Ltd v Panalpina (Northern) Ltd*[59] as being that the doctrine of frustration could be applied to a lease but 'hardly ever'.[60] As in the case of a frustration of a contract for the sale of land, the exceptional circumstances contemplated were those where the interest granted by the lease or agreement to lease was no longer capable of being enjoyed by the lessee.[61] While destruction of leased premises will be insufficient, a 'vast convulsion' of nature [that] swallowed up the property altogether, or buried it in the depths of the sea'[62] or disappearance of the land through erosion by the action of the sea[63] may frustrate the contract.

[22.140] The effect of a supervening event on a lease must, like the effect of other instances of delay, be to render performance of the contract something radically different from the original agreement, taking into account:

- the duration of the lease and the time left to run as at the time of the supervening event;
- the nature and object of the lease; and
- the length or prospective length of any interruption to the lessee's possession.

Example: Robertson v Wilson[64]

A two-storey brick residence fell into ruin and became unfit for habitation and a danger to the public and occupiers of neighbouring homes. The local council issued an

---

53 *Progressive Mailing House Pty Ltd v Tabali Pty Ltd* (1985) 157 CLR 17; A O'Hara, 'The Frustrated Tenant—Towards a Just Solution' (1994) *Australian Property Law Journal* 1 at 4–5.
54 (1926) 38 CLR 261.
55 Ibid, at 268.
56 Ibid, at 269.
57 Ibid, at 271.
58 Ibid, at 272.
59 [1981] AC 675.
60 Ibid, at 692 per Lord Hailsham.
61 See DW Greig & JLR Davis, *Law of Contract*, Law Book Co, Sydney, 1987, p 1330.
62 *Cricklewood Property and Investment Trust Ltd v Leighton's Investment Trust Ltd* [1945] AC 221 at 229 per Viscount Simon.
63 *National Carriers Ltd v Panalpina (Northern) Ltd* [1981] AC 675 at 691 per Lord Hailsham LC, 700–701 per Lord Simon.
64 (1958) 75 WN (NSW) 503; see also *Shiell v Symons* [1951] SASR 82.

order requiring the premises to be permanently vacated unless certain repairs were carried out. The claimant acquired the building after the order had been issued, and sought to have the occupier ejected. The occupier claimed to be a weekly tenant. The claimant argued that, whatever rights the occupier may have had, they had been discharged by the order.

It was pointed out that this was not a cottage on 100 acres of farm land or a lease for 1, 3, 7 or 99 years. In this case, it had become illegal for the tenant, his family or anyone else to occupy, for an unspecified term, the whole of the thing he leased—the residence, which he leased from week to week. The council order had destroyed the basis of the tenancy by creating a situation in which everyone had to leave the premises whether they liked it or not. The tenancy was therefore held to be frustrated.

[22.145] While, in theory, application of the doctrine of frustration to commercial and building leases may be 'less difficult',[65] it may still be difficult to show that circumstances have rendered performance radically different from that undertaken.

Example: National Carriers Ltd v Panalpina (Northern) Ltd[66]

A warehouse was leased for a period of 10 years. After 5 years, the only vehicular access to the warehouse was closed by the local authority due to the dangerous condition of an abandoned building nearby. The closure rendered the warehouse useless. At the time, the interruption was likely to last for about 20 months.

The House of Lords held that the lease was of a kind that could be frustrated. However, this lease was not frustrated, because after the interruption, there was likely to be a period of about three years during which the warehouse could be used for its intended purpose.

Similarly, in another case a 99-year building lease was held to not be frustrated by building restrictions imposed during wartime.[67]

[22.150] The *National Carriers v Panalpina* approach to the frustration of leases has now received the support of some High Court judges.[68]

22.3   Limits on frustration

[22.155] In some cases the supervening event may have rendered performance radically different from what was originally undertaken, but the contract will still be on foot due to one of the limits on the doctrine of frustration.

---

65   *Cricklewood Property & Investment Trust Ltd v Leighton's Investment Trust Ltd* [1945] AC 221 at 229.
66   [1981] AC 675.
67   *Cricklewood Property & Investment Trust Ltd v Leighton's Investment Trust Ltd* [1945] AC 221.
68   See Aickin J (with whom Stephen and Wilson JJ concurred) in *Codelfa Construction Pty Ltd v State Rail Authority of New South Wales* (1982) 149 CLR 337 at 378.

22.3.1   *Express contractual provision*

[22.160] A contract will not be frustrated where there is an express contractual provision dealing with the intervening event. In such a case, the parties will be taken to have provided for the risk of the event.[69]

Example: Claude Neon Ltd v Hardie[70]

The defendant agreed to hire from the plaintiff an illuminated sign to be installed on the premises of the defendant. The agreement included a sub-clause (f) empowering the plaintiff in certain events to declare the unpaid balance of the rental to be forthwith due and payable. One of the events referred to in the clause was the interest of the lessee in the premises being 'extinguished or transferred'. About 21 months into the 60-month agreement the premises were resumed by the government. The plaintiff gave notice pursuant to sub-clause (f) declaring the balance of the rent to be due and payable. The defendant argued that the contract had been discharged by frustration.

The Full Court of the Queensland Supreme Court held that the resumption of the premises amounted to an extinguishment of the interest of the defendant within the meaning of the clause. The consequences of the resumption were therefore as provided for in that clause, the doctrine of frustration having no application.

[22.165] Whether the doctrine of frustration will apply in a given case will be a question of construction of the particular clause. It may be that even where a term in the contract applies in the circumstances of the supervening event, it is not sufficient to preclude discharge of the contract by frustration.

For example, in *Codelfa Construction Co v State Rail Authority of NSW*,[71] the construction contract contained a clause which provided that: 'the operation of all plant construction equipment shall be such that it does not cause undue noise, pollution or nuisance. This may require the use of sound insulated compressors and air tools, silencers on ventilating fans and restrictions on the working hours of plant or such other measures as approved by the Engineer.' It was held that this provision did not mean that Codelfa had undertaken to perform the contract work in any event, even though the method contemplated by the parties might prove to be impossible by reason of amounting to a nuisance and being restrained by injunction. The language of the clause was consistent with the contemplated method of work being an essential element of the contract. There was plenty of scope for an exercise of the Engineer's power provided it did not displace the continuation of the contemplated method of work, namely three shifts a day for seven days a week.

[22.170] Provisions dealing with the supervening event that have the effect of preventing the contract being discharged under the doctrine of frustration should not be confused with provisions that provide that the happening of a particular event has a specific consequence—a *force majeure* clause. *Force majeure* clauses are particularly common in long-term construction contracts such as shipbuilding agreements, public works, infrastructure projects, joint ventures, management and marketing agreements,

---

69   *Claude Neon Ltd v Hardie* [1970] Qd R 93; *Thors v Weekes* (1989) 92 ALR 131 at 142.

70   [1970] Qd R 93.

71   (1982) 149 CLR 447. The facts of this case are set out in [22.80].

long-term transport contracts, and other contracts requiring a particular performance of services or delivery of goods from a particular source of supply.[72] Such clauses typically catalogue a number of events and then provide for the consequence of the occurrence of such an event. For example, *Ringstad v Gollin & Co Pty Ltd*,[73] a contract for the sale of a quantity of carbide of calcium being shipped from a continental port in six approximately equal monthly instalments provided that 'the above sale is subject to strikes, floods, war, accidents, fire, failure of manufacturers to deliver, non-receipt, non-delivery or mistakes in cables, and/or other contingencies causing delay or non-shipment.' Accordingly, a *force majeure* clause may operate in relation to events that may not ordinarily be regarded as of a nature that would render the contemplated performance of a contract impossible. Further, a *force majeure* clause may provide that should one of the catalogued events occur, the contract will be terminated, suspended, renegotiated, or otherwise dealt with in accordance with its express terms.[74] The clause may therefore have the same effect as the common law doctrine of frustration by terminating the contract, or may provide for a different result such as suspending payment for a time, or providing one party or both parties with the option of terminating the contract.[75] It seems that, like an exemption clause, *force majeure* clauses are interpreted strictly, *contra proferentem*.[76]

[22.175] Once again, it is a question of careful construction of the clause. It is possible, having interpreted the *force majeure* clause and other terms of the contract together, for a court to find that the parties have failed to make full and complete provision for the situation created by a supervening event that otherwise makes performance impossible by rendering it radically different from what was originally undertaken. In such a case, a court may find that despite the presence of a *force majeure* clause, the doctrine of frustration is still applicable.[77]

22.3.2 Supervening event foreseeable

[22.180] When determining whether performance has been rendered radically different, reference must be made to what was originally contemplated by the parties. What was originally contemplated depends not only upon express provisions in the contract, but also upon the nature of the contract and its surrounding circumstances. This has led to the suggestion that where the supervening event was, or should have been, foreseen by the parties as a serious possibility—but for which the parties did not make

---

72 D Yates, 'Drafting *Force Majeure* and Related Clauses' (1991) 3 JCL 186 at 187.

73 (1924) 35 CLR 303.

74 Yates (1991) 3 JCL 186 at 193–194.

75 A variation of the *force majeure* clause is the 'hardship' or 'intervener' clause which may provide that in circumstances such as an increase in the burden on one of the parties caused by, for instance, the frequent rise in the price of a commodity, the parties are required to enter into renegotiations (as opposed to the parties must reach agreement) or provide for the appointment of a third party intervenor who may encourage renegotiations or in default impose a fair solution: ibid, at 187–188.

76 *Fairclough Dodd & Jones Ltd v JH Vantol Ltd* [1957] 1 WLR 136 (HL), discussed in Yates (1991) 3 JCL 186 at 196. For the *contra proferentum* rule and exemption clauses, see [9.265].

77 *Metropolitan Water Board v Dick, Kerr & Co Ltd* [1918] AC 119. Such a case may be where the *force majeure* clause is interpreted as only dealing with temporary interruptions. The doctrine of frustration would still apply where events which 'struck at the contract as a whole and render performance ... unthinkable': *Empresa Exportadora de Azucar v Industria Azucarera Nacional SA* [1983] 2 Lloyd's Rep 171 at 189.

express provision—the inference is that the parties have nevertheless assumed the risk of the event occurring. This proposition has attracted sporadic support.[78]

As Carter and Harland point out,[79] the event must be foreseen as a serious possibility, rather than merely being reasonably foreseeable. Thus, while the risk of incapacitating illness might be reasonably foreseeable in many if not most employment contracts, the risk of incapacitating illness will be foreseeable as a serious possibility in only a few cases.[80] Further, even where the event is foreseeable, it may still frustrate the contract where the effect of the interference caused by the event exceeded anything that was contemplated.[81]

Example: WJ Tatem Ltd v Gamboa[82]

During the Spanish Civil War, a vessel was chartered on behalf of the Spanish Republicans from the plaintiff for a period of 1 month for the purpose of evacuating a section of the population from northern Spain. It was contemplated by the parties that the vessel might be detained for a short time by the Spanish Nationalists. In recognition of the risk facing the vessel, the defendant agreed to pay hire at three times the market rate, and in advance. In fact the vessel was seized and detained for a period of two months. The plaintiff claimed that additional hire was payable for the second month of detention.

It was held that while both parties had contemplated the detention of the vessel, the detention that occurred far exceeded what they had contemplated. Accordingly, the contract had been frustrated by the detention, and the claimed hire was not payable.

22.3.3   Supervening event induced by one of the parties

[22.185] By definition, in order for a contract to be frustrated, the supervening event must be 'without default of either party'. The relevant question, therefore, is the meaning of 'default' for these purposes.

[22.190] It would seem that the ambit of the rule that frustration cannot be relied upon by a party if the event was brought about by that party's own default, that is, was 'self-induced', has yet to be precisely determined.[83] It would seem that some sense of blameworthiness is required.[84] This would include cases where the supervening event is brought about by the deliberate act of one of the parties.[85]

---

78   See, for example, *Krell v Henry* [1903] 2 KB 740 at 751; *Palm Co Shipping Inc v Continental Ore Corp* [1970] 2 Lloyd's Rep 21 at 31 per Mocatta J; *Fibrosa Spolka Akoyjna v Fairbairn Lawson Combe Barbour Ltd* [1943] AC 32 at 40 per Lord Symon LC; *Tamplin (FA) Steamship Co Ltd v Anglo-Mexican Petroleum Products Co Ltd* [1916] 2 AC 397 at 426 per Lord Parker; *Bank Line Ltd v Arthur Capel & Co* [1919] AC 435 at 459 per Lord Sumner; *Codelfa Construction Pty Ltd v State Rail Authority of New South Wales* (1982) 149 CLR 337 at 359 per Mason J, 381 per Aickin J.

79   JW Carter & DJ Harland, *Contract Law in Australia*, 3rd edn, Butterworths, Sydney, 1996, pp 730–731.

80   Cf *Simmons Ltd v Hay* [1965] NSWR 416.

81   *WJ Tatem Ltd v Gamboa* [1939] 1 KB 132.

82   [1939] 1 KB 132.

83   *Joseph Constantine Steamship Line Ltd v Imperial Smelting Corp Ltd* [1942] AC 154 at 166 per Viscount Simon LC.

84   J Swanton, 'The concept of self-induced frustration' (1990) 2 JCL 206 at 217–218.

85   *Cricklewood Property & Investment Trust Ltd v Leighton's Investment Trust Ltd* [1945] AC 221. *Dymocks Holdings Pty Ltd v Top Ryde Booksellers Pty Ltd* [2000] NSWSC 390 (15 May 2000).

[22.195] There is also authority to support the view that negligence on the part of one of the parties—in the sense of breach of a duty in tort—is sufficient to constitute default.[86] It may be, however, that a number of factors are relevant, including the degree of seriousness of the negligence,[87] the closeness of the cause or connection between the negligence and the frustrating event, whether the negligent conduct was directed towards performance of the contract, and the type of contract such as whether it was a commercial or personal contract.[88]

[22.200] It will be a case of self-induced frustration where a party's conduct not only causes the supervening event but also constitutes a breach of contract.[89] However, not all cases of self-induced frustration will amount to a breach of contract.[90]

[22.205] Where a party enters into a number of contracts and has a real choice whether or not to fulfil one contract out of a number, the act or election leading to the failure to perform may be classified as self-induced frustration.

Example: Maritime National Fish Ltd v Ocean Trawlers Ltd[91]

The government passed legislation that made fishing dependent upon the holding of a licence from the Minister. The charterers of a trawler called the *St Cuthbert* sought to rely on the failure of the Minister, to license the vessel's use as having frustrated the contract with the owners. However, the charterers operated four other trawlers as well as the *St Cuthbert*, and had applied for five licences. They had been granted only three, which they had elected to apply to trawlers other than the *St Cuthbert*.

The Privy Council held that while it was true that performance of the contract was dependent on a licence being granted, it was the election by the charterers not to apply one of its licences to the *St Cuthbert* that prevented performance in this case. The charterers' own default had therefore frustrated performance. The contract was therefore still on foot.[92]

[22.210] The onus of proving that a supervening event amounted to a self-induced frustration lies on the party who makes such an allegation.[93] This has been described as 'both logical and satisfactory' because the allegation of self-induced frustration is often made to support a claim for damages for breach of contract. Accordingly, the onus of proving both the existence of breach and proof of self-induced frustration should rest with the same party.[94]

---

86 *The Super Servant Two* [1990] 1 Lloyd's Rep 1.

. 87 In *Joseph Constantine Steamship Line Ltd v Imperial Smelting Corp Ltd* [1942] AC 154 at 166–167, Viscount Simon LC contrasted, without deciding, the case of a prima donna completely losing her voice from an executory contract to sing if it was proved that her condition was caused by her carelessness in changing her wet clothes after being out in the rain.

88 Swanton (1990) 2 JCL 206 at 217.

89 *The Lucille* [1984] 1 Lloyd's Rep 244 (charter of tanker trapped in Shatt-al-Arab waterway not frustrated because in the circumstances the charterer had breached its promise to send chartered vessel to only safe ports).

90 *Scanlan's New Neon Ltd v Tooheys Ltd* (1943) 67 CLR 169 at 186 per Latham CJ; *Paal Wilson & Co AS v Partenreederei Hannah Blumenthal* [1983] 1 AC 854 at 920.

91 [1935] AC 524.

92 See also *The Super Servant Two* [1990] 1 Lloyd's Rep 1.

93 *Joseph Constantine Steamship Line Ltd v Imperial Smelting Corp Ltd* [1942] AC 154 (explosion which disabled vessel under charterparty held not to be self-induced frustration because charterers could not establish that explosion was caused by owner).

94 JW Carter & DJ Harland, *Contract Law in Australia*, 3rd edn, Butterworths, Sydney, 1996, p 734.

22.4   Effect of frustration

[22.215] The effect of frustration on a contract depends upon the jurisdiction whose law governs the contract. In the majority of Australian jurisdictions, the consequences of frustration are determined by reference to the common law, while in three jurisdictions those consequences are determined by legislation.

22.4.1   Common law

[22.220] At common law, frustration automatically discharges the contract.[95] Both parties are relieved from further performance of their obligations under the contract as from the time of the frustration.

[22.225] The contract is discharged by force of law.[96] Unlike termination for breach, it is not necessary for one of the parties to elect to terminate the contract. Indeed, neither party has a choice in the matter.

[22.230] Frustration does not void the contract *ab initio*.[97] Accordingly, unconditional rights and liabilities accrued prior to the frustrating event—including accrued rights to sue for damages for prior breach of contract[98]—remain unaffected by the discharge.[99]

However, rights or liabilities accrued prior to the frustrating event will be unenforceable if there has been a total failure of consideration.[100] Thus where, for example, money has been paid prior to the supervening event, the party who paid an amount may recover it in restitution if the agreed consideration for it has totally failed. This question will therefore depend upon the true interpretation of the contract and the identification of the relevant consideration.

Example: Fibrosa Spolka Akcyjna v Fairbairn Lawson Combe Barbour Ltd[101]

A contract was entered into for the manufacture and delivery of certain machinery by an English firm for and to a Polish firm. The contract price was £4800, of which £1600 was payable on signing the contract. The Polish firm paid £1000 of that sum. The contract was frustrated when Poland was invaded by Germany at the start of the Second World War. The Polish firm subsequently sought to recover the £1000 it had paid under the contract.

The House of Lords held that the Polish firm was entitled to recover the money it had paid if the consideration for its payment had totally failed. In the circumstances, the correct reading of this contract was that the £1000 was an advance payment in return for consideration comprising not only the manufacture of the machinery, but also its delivery at Gdynia in Poland. Since the bargained-for consideration was not

---

95   *Hirji Mulji v Cheong Yue Steamship Co Ltd* [1926] AC 497 at 509; *Scanlan's New Neon Ltd v Tooheys Ltd* (1943) 67 CLR 169 at 203.
96   *Cachia v State Authorities Superannuation Board* (1993) 47 IR 254 at 274.
97   *Baltic Shipping Co v Dillan* (1993) 176 CLR 345 at 356 per Mason CJ.
98   *MacDonald v Dennys Lascelles Ltd* (1933) 48 CLR 457 at 477 per Dixon J. This case actually dealt with termination for breach but the same principle applies equally to frustration.
99   *Baltic Shipping Co v Dillan* (1993) 176 CLR 344 at 356 per Mason CJ.
100   *Fibrosa Spolka Akcyjna v Fairbairn Lawson Combe Barbour Ltd* [1943] AC 32 at 53.
101   [1943] AC 32.

provided by the English firm, the Polish firm was entitled to recover the £1000 paid as money had and received.

The *Fibrosa* decision has been approved by the High Court.[102] Therefore it is no longer the case in Australia that money paid under a frustrated contract can never be recovered, because the contract is not rendered void *ab initio*.[103]

[22.235] It is said that on frustration, 'loss lies where it falls'. Where there has only been a partial failure of the agreed consideration, there will be no right to recover any payment that has been made. For example, where the contract is for the provision of services that have been partly rendered at the time the frustrating event occurs, there will be no ground on which money that has been paid can be recovered.[104]

This will be the case even where only a small part of the consideration has passed, but a disproportionately large benefit has been conferred. Accordingly, unless there is provision in the contract for the unconditional accrual of liability for expenses incurred in performance of the contract, a party may be unable to recover in respect of any expenses—even significant expenses—incurred up to the date of frustration. Consequently, the rule that 'loss lies where it falls' may result in one party suffering hardship. As Lord Atkin in the *Fibrosa* case remarked:

> One party may have almost completed expensive work. He can get no compensation. The other party may have paid the whole price, and if he has received but a slender part of the consideration he can get no compensation. That the result of the law may cause hardship when a contract is automatically stayed during performance and any further right to performance is denied to each party is uncontrovertible.[105]

[22.240] Where, by contrast, services are rendered *after* the contract has been discharged by frustration at least with the assent of the other party, there may be a right to recover a *quantum meruit* in restitution for the work done.[106]

[22.245] Since frustration does not render the contract void *ab initio*, it is possible for some clauses—such as a clause referring any disputes to arbitration—to continue to operate, even though all performance under the contract is at an end.[107] However, for a term to operate after the contract has been frustrated, it must be clear that the parties intended this result.[108]

[22.250] While frustration automatically terminates a contract by operation of law, without either party having any input into the situation, there is no reason why the

---

102 *Baltic Shipping Co v Dillon* (1993) 176 CLR 344 at 355.
103 Cf *Re Continental C and G Rubber Co Pty Ltd* (1919) 27 CLR 194.
104 Cf *Baltic Shipping Co v Dillon* (1993) 176 CLR 344 (cruise ship passenger not entitled to a refund of the fare when the vessel sank 10 days into a 14-day cruise because there was only partial failure of consideration). Although the case concerned breach of contract, the same result would follow frustration.
105 *Fibrosa Spolka Akcyjna v Fairbairn Lawson Combe Barbour Ltd* [1943] AC 32 at 54–55.
106 *Codelfa Construction Pty Ltd v State Rail Authority of New South Wales* (1982) 149 CLR 337.
107 *Heyman v Darwins Ltd* [1942] AC 356; *Codelfa Construction Pty Ltd v State Rail Authority of New South Wales* (1982) 149 CLR 337 at 364.
108 *BP Exploration Co (Libya) Ltd v Hunt (No 2)* [1983] 2 AC 352.

parties cannot agree to treat the contract as still being on foot notwithstanding the frustrating event.[109]

22.4.2 Statute

[22.255] It has already been noted that the common law effects of the doctrine of frustration—including the 'loss lies where it falls' rule—may work hardship or injustice on a contracting party. For example, at common law, unless there is contractual provision allowing for recovery, a party who has rendered services is not entitled to recover for reasonable expenses incurred up to the time of frustration. There may also be injustice where money paid cannot be recovered on the basis of a total failure of consideration because services rendering a relatively small benefit have been performed prior to frustration. The unsatisfactory operation of the common law prompted New South Wales, Victoria, and South Australia to enact legislation aimed at overcoming these problems.[110] These statutes seek to provide for a more equitable resolution between the parties where a contract has been frustrated.[111]

(a) New South Wales

[22.260] The *Frustrated Contracts Act* 1978 (NSW) seeks to provide a scheme for the apportionment of loss resulting from frustration. Certain contracts, such as a contract for the carriage of goods by sea and charterparties (other than time or demise charterparties), and contracts of insurance, are excluded from the operation of the Act.[112]

[22.265] The Act provides that all money paid must be returned,[113] but that a part-performing party may recover compensation in respect of performance received by the other party, calculated according to a complicated formula.[114] However, the complex accounting method provided for by the Act may be disregarded in a particular case where its application 'would be excessively difficult or expensive', in which case a court may make such adjustments in money or otherwise as it considers proper.[115]

[22.270] The Act also provides that where a promise was due to be, but was not, performed before the time of frustration the promise is discharged,[116] and that where a contract is frustrated any liability for damages is assessed taking into account the fact that the contract was frustrated. This may affect, for example, any claim to damages for loss of bargain.[117]

---

109 *Heytesbury Properties Pty Ltd v Subiaco City Council* [2000] WASC 8 (28 January 2000).

110 See *Frustrated Contracts Act* 1978 (NSW); *Frustrated Contracts Act* 1959 (Vic); *Frustrated Contracts Act* 1988 (SA).

111 The provisions have effect only where a contract has first been frustrated: *Thors v Weekes* (1989) 92 ALR 131 at 142 (NSW statute did not apply where express provisions in contract governed the supervening event).

112 See s 6.

113 See s 12.

114 See s 11.

115 See s 15. For more detailed consideration of this statute see DW Greig & JLR Davis, *Law of Contract*, Law Book Co, Sydney, 1987, pp 1344–1350; JW Carter & DJ Harland, *Contract Law in Australia*, 3rd edn, Butterworths, Sydney, 1996, pp 749–753.

116 See s 7.

117 *Upper Hunter Timbers Pty Ltd v Forestry Commission of NSW* [1999] NSWCA 125 (Priestley, Shellar and Stein JJA) 21 May 1999.

(b)   Victoria

[22.275] In Victoria, the *Frustrated Contracts Act* 1959 (Vic) was modelled on the *Law Reform (Frustrated Contracts) Act* 1943 (UK). The Act applies where a 'contract has become impossible to performance or been otherwise frustrated', as well as in the case of a sale of goods contract that has been 'avoided' under *Goods Act* 1958 (Vic), s 12.[118]

[22.280] Under the Act, all sums paid before the time of discharge are recoverable by the party who made the payment, unless such money had fallen due prior to the contract being discharged.[119] Where prior to the discharge a party has incurred expenses in or for the purpose of the performance of the contract, or conferred a benefit on the other party, the court has power to order the other party to pay such sum as it considers just.[120] It seems that the onus is on the party to whom the money was paid or payable to establish that the expenses were in fact incurred in or for the purpose of performance.[121]

[22.285] Like the New South Wales legislation, the Victorian Act excludes certain contracts from its operation: contracts for the carriage of goods by sea, charterparties (other than time or demise charterparties), and contracts of insurance.[122]

(c)   South Australia

[22.290] The *Frustrated Contracts Act* 1988 (SA), s 7, provides that where a contract is frustrated, there will be an adjustment between the parties so that no party is unfairly advantaged or disadvantaged in consequence of the frustration. This object is achieved by comprehensive provisions that provide for the valuation of benefits and of performance.[123] However, the court has an overriding discretion to proceed on an equitable basis.[124]

[22.295] Once again, the Act does not apply to certain contracts: charterparties (other than time or demise charterparties), contracts for the carriage of goods by sea, insurance contracts, and constituent documents of association.[125]

22.5   International perspectives

22.5.1   New Zealand

[22.300] There is no substantive difference between the law in Australia and New Zealand in relation to the circumstances in which a contract will be frustrated and the limits on the operation of the doctrine.

---

118   See s 3(1).
119   See s 3(3). A detailed consideration of this statute may be found in, for example, DW Greig & JLR Davis, *Law of Contract*, Law Book Co, Sydney, 1987, pp 1336–1343; JW Carter & DJ Harland, *Contract Law in Australia*, 3rd edn, Butterworths, Sydney, 1996, pp 753–757.
120   See s 3(2).
121   See, for example, *Logg v Vasey Housing Auxiliary (War Widows Guild)* [1963] VR 239.
122   See s 4(3).
123   See s 3(1) and s 3(2) respectively.
124   See s 7(4). For a detailed examination of this statute see JW Carter & DJ Harland, *Contract Law in Australia*, 3rd edn, Butterworths, Sydney, 1996, pp 757–761.
125   See s 4.

[22.305] However, in relation to the effect of frustration, New Zealand enacted the *Frustrated Contracts Act* 1944. The statute has two major effects. First, s 3(2) provides that all sums paid or payable to any party in pursuance of the contract before the time when the parties were discharged is, in the case of some so paid, be recoverable from that party as money received by that party for the use of the party by whom the sums were paid, and, in the case of some so payable, cease to be so payable. The section therefore extends the decision in the *Fibrosa* case by allowing the recovery of money prepaid even where there has been no total failure of consideration. However, the section is subject to the proviso that where the payee has incurred expense in the course of performing the contract, the court may, as it considers just, allow the party to retain or recover the whole or any part of the sums paid or payable on account of those expenses. The section makes no provision for recovery of expenditure unless it was incurred before the occurrence of the frustrating event.

Secondly, s 3(3) seeks to overcome the situation where an entire contract is frustrated, leaving the party unable to claim payment for performance rendered even where that performance has been substantial. The section provides that where any party to the contract has by reason of anything done by any other party in performance of the contract, obtained a valuable benefit (other than a payment of money) before the time of discharge, he or she may recover such sum not exceeding the value of the benefit as the court considers just. In estimating the amount to be recovered, the court must consider all the circumstances of the case—particularly any expenses that the party receiving the benefit may have incurred in the performance of the contract, and whether the circumstances causing the frustration have affected the value of the benefit.

[22.310] Like the statutes in New South Wales, Victoria, and South Australia, the Act is stated as not applying to a contract for the carriage of goods by sea or a charterparty (except a time or demise charterparty), contracts of insurance and contracts for the sale of goods where the contract is frustrated by reason of the goods having perished.

22.5.2 United States

[22.315] The doctrine of frustration, as it is known in Australia, is reflected in two closely related American doctrines: the 'doctrine of impracticability' and the 'doctrine of frustration'. While these doctrines share some familiar concepts with the Australian approach, they represent a different synthesis of the field. It seems that the distinction between the two American doctrines is that generally speaking 'impracticability' of performance excuses parties who are bound to provide goods, land, services or other performance whereas 'frustration' excuses parties who are bound to pay money in return for some performance by the other party.[126]

[22.320] The modern synthesis of 'impracticability' originated with UCC 2-615, which was designed for the sale of goods—which in turn influenced the law of contract generally and has now been adapted by the Restatement (Second) §261. This synthesis has been recognised as moving the analysis away from such theories as the 'implied term' and the 'parties' contemplation' tests to a determination whether, in the

---

126 EA Farnsworth, *Contracts*, 3rd edn, Aspen Law and Business, New York, 1999, § 9.7.

light of exceptional circumstances, justice requires a departure from the general rule that a promisor bears the risk of increased difficulty of performance.[127] 'Impracticability' requires four elements to be shown:

- a supervening event must have made the agreed performance 'impracticable';
- the non-occurrence of the event must have been a basic assumption on which the contract was made;
- the impracticability must have resulted without the fault of the party seeking to be excused; and
- that party must not have assumed a greater obligation than the law imposes.[128]

[22.325] As in Australia, the first determination for the first element is what was the agreed performance.[129] If there is a choice of alternatives available, as in the *Eugenia*, it will be difficult to show performance has been rendered impracticable. Unlike Australian courts, American courts only require that performance be rendered 'impracticable' rather than 'impossible'.[130] Thus, a mere apprehension of illness unaccompanied by actual disability may excuse an obligation to render personal services,[131] and a fear of exposure to danger may excuse further performance.[132] However, there is a counter-vailing expectation that the promisor will exercise reasonable efforts in attempting to overcome impediments to performance.[133]

An increased cost of performance rendering the contract economically burdensome will generally be insufficient,[134] but a severe shortage of raw materials or supplies—due, for example, to war, embargo, local crop failure, or unforeseen closure of major sources of supply that either increase costs or prevent the supplier from obtaining supplies will do.[135]

[22.330] Instances of the event constituting the 'basic assumption' has been recognised as falling into three broad categories: the parties assuming that performance will not be affected by government intervention; the parties assuming that a person who is necessary for performance will not die or otherwise be rendered incapable; and the parties assuming that a thing that is necessary for performance will remain available and in such a condition as necessary for performance. Most cases of impracticability involve such circumstances, but there may be other cases that involve basic

---

127 *Transatlantic Fin Corp v United States* 363 F 2d 312 (DC Cir 1966); *United States v Wegematic Corp* 360 F 2d 674 (2d Cir 1966).

128 EA Farnsworth, *Contracts*, 3rd edn, Aspen Law and Business, New York, 1999, § 9.6.

129 *Florida Power & Light Co v Westinghouse Electric Corp* 826 F 2d 239 (4th Cir 1987) (first step to determine 'exact act or thing' promised and 'means whereby the parties contemplated performance').

130 The term 'impracticability' was used in the First Restatement § 454.

131 See, for example, *Wasserman Theatrical Entertainment v Harris* 77 A 2d 329 (Conn 1950) (actor's 'apprehension' that he could not perform due to a tickling in and tightening of throat sufficient grounds for cancelling show); *Lakeman v Pollard* 43 Me 463 (1857) (mill employee apprehensive of imperilling his life by working in vicinity of cholera epidemic entitled to leave his work).

132 *The Kronprinzessin Cecilie* 244 US 12 (1917) (owner of German vessel apprehending it would be seized as prize on eve of World War I excused of completing voyage between United States and England).

133 *Pennsylvania State Shopping Plazas v Olive* 120 SE 2d 372 (Va 1961) (failure by property developer to file formal application for building permit or variation of zoning).

134 *Bernina Distributions v Bernina Sewing Machine Co* 646 F 2d 434 (10th Cir 1981); *Neal-Cooper Grain Co v Texas Gulf Sulphur Co* 508 F 2d 283 (7th Cir 1974).

135 UCC 2-615 comment 4; Restatement (Second) § 261 comment d.

assumptions underlying performance.[136] Certainly the three broad categories would also seem to satisfy the Australian 'change in obligation' test.

[22.335] The third requirement reflects the Australian requirement concerning the supervening event not being self-induced. In America it would seem that negligence will suffice, although it may be that fault must be clearly established.[137] The fourth requirement means that the promisor must not have expressly or impliedly assumed the risk of the event occurring.[138] Foreseeability of the event suggests an implied assumption of risk but is not conclusive.[139]

[22.340] The doctrine of frustration has been generally accepted by United States courts,[140] and while not expressly recognised by the Uniform Commercial Code, also applies to sales of goods.[141] It was included in both the First and Second Restatements.[142] According to the Restatement (Second), 'frustration' is similar to impracticability and also has four elements:

- the supervening event must have substantially frustrated the party's principal purpose;
- a basic assumption on which the contract was made must have been that the event would not occur;
- the event came about through no fault of the party seeking to be excused; and
- that party must not have assumed a greater obligation than the law imposes.

While the elements may be similar, courts have shown a greater reluctance to uphold a claim of 'frustration' than of 'impracticability'. In this regard, the first and fourth elements in particular have proved difficult to establish.[143]

[22.345] Satisfaction of the first element involves overcoming two hurdles. First, the party's principal purpose is viewed widely. A purpose will not be frustrated where one expected advantage is no longer available but the party may gain an alternative advantage, similar to the distinction drawn in the English case *Herne Bay Steam Boat v Hutton*.[144] Secondly, frustration must be total or nearly total. Partial frustration—or an increase in the cost of performance—is insufficient.[145]

[22.350] Like impracticability, the fourth element reflects the notion that a party may expressly or impliedly assume the risk of the event. In the case of frustration, however, the courts have been prepared to readily imply an assumption of risk where, for example, the risk was foreseeable.[146] Such a high standard limits frustration to 'cases of

---

136 *Waldinger Corp v CRS Group Engineers* 775 F 2d 781 (7th Cir 1985).
137 UCC 2-613 comment 1.
138 *Rowe v Town of Peabody* 93 NE 604 (Mass 1911) (express assumption of risk); *Publicker Industries v Union Carbide Corp* 17 UCC Rep 989 (ED Pa 1975) (implied assumption of risk).
139 *United States v Winstar Corp* 518 US 839 (4th Cir 1996).
140 *Chase Precast Corp v John J Paonessa Co* 566 NE 2d 603 (Mass 1991).
141 Under UCC 1-103 unless otherwise provided the Code is supplemented by the principles of law and equity; see also *Northern Ind Public Service Co v Carbon County Coal Co* 799 F 2d 265 (7th Cir 1986).
142 Restatement § 288; Restatement (Second) § 265.
143 EA Farnsworth, *Contracts*, 3rd edn, Aspen Law and Business, New York, 1999, § 9.7.
144 See [22.70].
145 *Swift Canadian Co v Banet* 224 F 2d 36 at 38 (3d Cir 1955).
146 *Gold v Salem Lutheran Home Association* 347 P 2d 687 at 689 (Cal 1959) (death of 84-year-old reasonably foreseeable, so death did not frustrate contract with nursing home).

extreme hardship so that businessmen, who must make their arrangements in advance, can rely with certainty on their contracts.'[147]

[22.355] It would appear that impracticability and frustration have the same effects; which may be contrasted with the automatic termination and 'loss lies where it falls' rules that operate in Australia. Supervening impracticability or frustration discharges the excused party from any remaining duties of performance.[148] The other party is left in the same position as if the excused person were in breach: if the excused party's failure to perform is material the other party may suspend performance, or if the appropriate time for performance has passed the other party may elect to terminate. In any event, there is no right to claim damages for non-performance.

[22.360] On occasions, only part of the excused party's performance will have been rendered impracticable. In such a case, it may be possible to require the excused party to perform as much of his or her obligations as possible. However, in the absence of a fresh agreement, this is apt to produce difficulties about the proportion of the original compensation that is payable. In the case of a sale of goods, UCC 2-615(b) provides that where an impracticability affects only part of a seller's capacity to perform, he or she must allocate production and delivery among customers in a manner that is 'fair and reasonable' for an apportioned price.

[22.365] Where the excused party has rendered performance before the contract became impracticable or frustrated, the question will be whether the contract is divisible. The excused party will recover the appropriate apportionment with a measure of generosity generally shown to the excused party.[149] Where the contract is not divisible, the excused party will recover any benefit conferred[150] unless there is agreement to the contrary.[151]

The Restatement (Second) §272 suggests that the courts have power to order such relief as is just, including compensation for expenses in performance ('reliance interests'). However, as in Australia, American courts have generally resisted granting compensation for expenditure incurred in performance.[152]

22.5.3 Japan

[22.370] The basic category of non-performance in Japanese law that approximates to frustration in the common law is impossibility. A second category consists of claims for renegotiation based on changed circumstances, which is discussed below.

[22.375] Impossibility can be asserted under Japanese law when performance of the obligation was impossible from the outset, or has become physically impossible or impossible for 'social reasons'. Physical impossibility is analogous to its common law counterpart—for example, destruction of subject matter of the contract. 'Social

---

147 *Lloyd v Murphy* 153 P 2d 47 at 50–51 (Cal 1944).
148 *Lazzara v Wisconsin Boxing Club* 29 F 2d 483 (7th Cir 1928) (boxing club's obligation to pay boxer $10 000 for boxing ten rounds discharged when strangers wrongfully stopped bout in sixth round).
149 *Mullen v Wafer* 480 SW 2d 332 (Ark 1972).
150 *LDA Inc v Cross* 279 SE 2d 409 (W Va 1981) (contract to build modular home was not severable and builder bore entire loss when home burned during construction).
151 Cf *Parker v Arthur Murray Inc* 295 NE 2d 487 (Ill App 1973) ('no refunds will be made' held insufficient to exclude restitution).
152 *The Isle of Mull* 278 F 131 (7th Cir 1921)

impossibility' is a category open to court interpretation; it includes events such as the introduction of new regulations or legislation that would render the performance of the contact impossible.

[22.380] The consequences of impossibility are these. Contracts impossible from the outset are void. If performance has subsequently become impracticable, the court looks to the parties' relative responsibility. If the cause of the impossibility is attributable to the obligor (the party owing the obligation), then the contract may be cancelled by the obligee (the innocent party) (Civil Code art 543). If a seller can no longer deliver the contracted goods because of impracticability that is not the fault of the seller, then the risk of loss is transferred to the buyer (obligee). In all other cases, the courts will place the risk of loss on the seller (obligor) (Civil Code arts 534, 536). The court-mandated risk allocations, of course, apply only where the parties themselves has not made a specific choice about risk allocation in their contract. The contract agreement about risk allocation, impossibility, and impracticability will override the default provision of the Civil Code.

[22.385] In cases that fall short of complete impossibility of performance, many foreign commentators have focussed on the operation of the doctrine of changed circumstances in Japanese law. The statutory basis of this idea is the Civil Code requirement that all legal acts (including contracts) must be performed in good faith. The parameters of 'changed circumstances' have been set by judicial opinion and by scholarly commentary. Essentially, an innocent party can petition the court to allow them to cancel a contract where:

• circumstances has changed drastically since it made the contract;
• the innocent party did not foresee and could not have foreseen the change;
• the innocent party was not responsible for the change; and
• enforcing the contract would not violate good faith and notions of justice and fairness.

The leading case that established these requirements was *Iguchi v Ikegami*[153]—a claim by a tenant seeking to avoid eviction. The changed circumstance being asserted was the destruction of rental housing in Osaka as a result of Allied bombing during the Second World War. Note, however, that the court recognised the doctrine, but maintained that the fourth element was not fulfilled in this case and so enforced the contract and upheld the eviction.

[22.390] For those outside Japan, the best-known applications of the changed circumstances doctrine are those international contracts where the Japanese buyers have sought a renegotiation in situations where market prices have changed dramatically and have cited this doctrine in support of their arguments. In fact, the doctrine itself has seldom been used to uphold commercial contract cancellation in Japanese courts.

---

153 3 *Kaminshu* 962 Osaka High Ct 14 July 152; affirmed 8 *Saihan minshu* 448 (Supreme Court 12 Feb 1954).

Part VII
Remedies

A remedy may be defined, as in the eighth edition of *Osborn's Concise Law Dictionary*, as 'the means by which the violation of a right is prevented, redressed, or compensated'. This highlights the general essence of a remedy as the means by which a wrong (such as negligence or trespass) or a breach of contract maybe redressed or compensated. A remedy will only exist where there is a legally recognised right either at common law or in equity.

Is there a separate law of remedies?

It is suggested by some commentators that the boundaries of the law of remedies may be delineated by distinguishing between primary and secondary rights or obligations. Primary rights are rights that exist independently of other rights; secondary rights are rights that only come into existence if a primary right is breached.

In this context, the primary right is the cause of action and the secondary right is the remedy—for example, breach of contract and damages. In *Photo Productions Ltd v Securicor Transport Ltd* [1980] AC 827 Lord Diplock said:

> Every failure to perform a primary obligation is a breach of contract. The secondary obligation on the part of the contract breaker to which it gives rise by implication of the common law is to pay monetary compensation to the other party for the loss sustained by him in consequence of the breach.

The maxim *ubi ius ibi remedium*—where there is a right, there is a remedy—reflects the fact that a legal right will not exist without a remedy. In the context of contract law, this means the right to sue for breach of contract is only recognised as a legal right because of the secondary obligation by the contract-breaker to pay damages.

The categorisation of primary and secondary rights is useful to provide some delimitation for the law of remedies, but as Tilbury pointed out in 1990 in *Civil Remedies*, it does not define the final boundaries of remedies in the context of restitution. This is due to the fact that restitutionary remedies are usually imposed in response to avoiding unjust enrichment and not due to any antecedent wrong. For that reason, restitution is usually referred to as a principal and a remedial right. However, it will be possible to analysis the law of restitution as a response to an event, in the same way as a remedy is a response to a primary right. The event that requires this response may be either a wrong, a consent, or unjust enrichment.

The different types of remedies may be classified in several ways. First, remedies may be differentiated by their jurisdiction: that is, whether common law or equitable remedies. Secondly, remedies may be classified by the type of relief available. This results in the broad, three-part classification of specific relief, substitutionary relief, and declaratory relief.

It might be thought that contractual remedies would be aimed at compelling performance by promisors to prevent breach. Instead, the preoccupation of contractual remedies is with ways of redressing breach with compensation. Substitutionary relief such as damages or restitution provides compensation for the breach of a contract. Specific relief, such as specific performance or injunctions can provide enforcement of a contractual right, but only if damages is an inadequate remedy.

Part VII examines the different types of remedies available to a party in the contractual context, usually arising from a breach of contract. The substitutionary relief available in the form of damages and recovery of liquidated sums are considered first. Restitution is considered in Chapter 24, and finally, the specific relief of specific performance and injunctions is dealt with in Chapter 25. The order in which the remedies are considered does not reflect the importance of the remedies.

Chapter 23

Damages

23.1   Damages: compensation for loss suffered

[23.05] An obligation to pay damages for a failure to perform an obligation (whether by breach or repudiation) assumed under a contract arises impliedly from the entry into the contract.[1] Unlike obligations in tort, contractual obligations are assumed or agreed upon, not imposed. A party who enters a contract agrees not only to undertake the primary obligations asserted in the agreement, but also to fulfil the secondary obligations that arise upon a failure to perform a primary obligation. One of these secondary obligations is the obligation of the non-performer to make reparation in money for any loss sustained by the other party that results from the failure of the non-performer to perform the primary obligation. Unless the secondary obligation to make reparation is expressly excluded or limited, the mere entry into the contract will be sufficient to induce the other party to believe that the non-performer undertakes to pay compensation, which the non-performer knows is liable to result from the breach in the usual course of things. However, the non-performer will not be assumed to be liable for exceptional loss arising from special circumstances, peculiar to the other party, which are outside the usual course of things.[2]

---

1   *The Heron* [1996] 2 QB 695 at 727–730.
2   See *Hadley v Baxendale* (1854) 9 Exch 341; *The Heron* [1996] 2 QB 695 at 727–730.

[23.10] The primary objective of damages in contract is to compensate a party for the actual loss suffered as a result of the other party's failure to perform the contract.[3] This should be contrasted with the objective of restitution, which is to return a benefit received unjustly by the other party.[4] If no loss is suffered, only nominal damages are recoverable. Nominal damages may range from $1.00 to $100, and are awarded to a plaintiff in recognition of the breach of contract.[5] Therefore, despite a breach of contract occurring, if there is no actual loss to the plaintiff, no more than nominal damages are recoverable. Damages will not be used to punish the contract breaker.[6] An actual loss must be proven by the plaintiff.[7]

23.2   Requirements

[23.15] Will all loss suffered following a failure to perform be recoverable?[8] This question can only be answered by an examination of the limits on a claim for damages. Before a claim for damages for breach of contract will succeed, several hurdles must be overcome.

1   Is there a cause of action? A cause of action for breach of contract will arise if, after entry into a valid and binding contract, one of the parties to the contract fails to perform one or more of that party's obligations under the contract. This will be a question of fact for the court. Proof of loss or damage is not a precondition to a cause of action arising, but contractual damages will only be awarded if actual loss is proved by the plaintiff.[9] In the absence of actual loss, nominal damages may be awarded.[10]

2   Did the wrong or breach of contract cause the loss?[11]

3   Is the loss suffered by the plaintiff not too remote?[12]

4   Has the plaintiff acted reasonably to mitigate unnecessary loss?[13]

[23.20] Termination of a contract is not a precondition to recovery of damages in all cases. However, where damages are sought for anticipatory breach or repudiation, they are only available if the contract has been terminated.[14]

---

3   *Hungerfords v Walker* (1989) 63 ALJR 210 at 2215.

4   See Chapter 24.

5   *Luna Park (NSW) Ltd v Tramways Advertising Pty Ltd* (1938) 61 CLR 286.

6   *Addis v Gramophone Co Ltd* [1909] AC 488; *Butler v Fairclough* (1917) 23 CLR 78 at 89; *Whitfeld v De Lauret & Co Ltd* (1920) 29 CLR 71 at 80.

7   *Erie County Natural Gas & Fuel Co Ltd v Samuel S Carroll* [1911] AC 105; *Goldburg v Shell Oil Co of Aust* (1990) 95 ALR 711.

8   This could arise from a breach of contract or a repudiation. See Chapter 20.

9   Compare an action in tort for negligence where proof of loss or damage is necessary for the cause of action: see J Stapleton, 'The Gist of Negligence: Minimum actionable damage' (1988) 104 *LQR* 213, at 213.

10   See [23.10].

11   See [23.35]–[23.95].

12   See [23.100]–[23.165].

13   See [23.170]–[23.225].

14   See [23.400] and *Sunbird Plaza Ltd v Mahoney* (1988) 166 CLR 245.

23.3 Onus of proof

[23.25] The onus of proving the elements of the cause of action, the amount of loss suffered, causation, and remoteness lies on the plaintiff.[15] The plaintiff's case must generally be proven on the balance of probabilities,[16] but this requirement is not applied rigidly to each element in all cases. For example, in a case where the court is considering whether damages should be awarded for the loss of a chance, it will be sufficient for the plaintiff to show

> *some* loss or damage was sustained by demonstrating that the contravening conduct caused the loss of a commercial opportunity which has *some* value (not being a negligible value), the value being ascertained by reference to the degree of probabilities or possibilities.[17]

[23.30] Usually the only onus imposed on the defendant is to prove the plaintiff has failed to mitigate his or her loss.[18] If the defendant does not allege a failure to mitigate in the pleadings, it will be presumed that the plaintiff has mitigated the loss. In certain circumstances, an additional onus of proof will be placed upon the defendant where damages only for reliance loss (wasted expenditure) are claimed. If the plaintiff proves expenditure has been reasonably incurred pursuant to the contract, the onus then shifts to the defendant to establish that such expenditure would not have been recouped even if the contract had been fully performed. If the defendant discharges this onus, the plaintiff's claim will be reduced by the amount that could not be recouped. However, if the onus is not discharged, the plaintiff will be entitled to recover all of their wasted expenditure.[19]

23.4 Causation

[23.35] Not all loss arising from a breach of contract will be recoverable. Various limits have been imposed on the recovery of loss for a breach of contract. The first is that the defendant is only liable for the loss *caused* by the breach.

23.4.1 Causation at law

[23.40] The development of the concept of legal causation has been criticised by philosophers and scientists who view causation as the sum of the conditions that were jointly responsible for the event. However,

> [in] ordinary speech and practice we select one or more out of what is an infinite number of conditions to be treated as the cause. From the practical standpoint of the man in the street the cause of the setting the house on fire was the

---

15   *Goldburg v Shell Oil Co of Australia Ltd* (1990) 95 ALR 711 at 714; cf *Kargotich v Mustica* [1973] WAR 167.

16   *Sellars v Adelaide Petroleum NL* (1992–94) 179 CLR 332 at 355.

17   Ibid.

18   *TCN Channel 9 Pty Ltd v Hayden Enterprises Pty Ltd* (1989) 16 NSWLR 130 at 158; *Goldburg v Shell Oil Co of Australia Ltd* (1990) 95 ALR 711.

19   See *The Commonwealth v Amann Aviation Pty Ltd* (1991) 174 CLR 64 at 86–90.

striking of a match, while from that of the man of science it was the presence of all the conditions which enabled potential to be converted into kinetic energy.[20]

[23.45] The common law has followed the ordinary man's notion of causation instead of scientific theory.[21] The law does not accept the definition of causation as the sum of the conditions that are jointly sufficient to produce it. At law, a person may be responsible for damage when his or her wrongful conduct is one of a number of conditions sufficient to produce that damage. Although it may not be logical for one factor in a set of facts to be seen as contributing more to the loss than another, the legal position may be rationalised by reference to the object of causation. The common law is only concerned with determining whether a particular act or omission is so connected with a particular result that legal responsibility should attach to it—not that it is the only cause of the loss. However, the ultimate decision of whether a person who has caused loss should be legally responsible is a question of policy. Therefore, the common law is concerned with whether an act or omission 'contributed to the occurrence of a particular event (causation) and if so, with whether responsibility should attach to that act or omission (remoteness)'.[22] This clearly indicates that causation is a question of fact only, leaving issues of policy to the law of remoteness. This approach underlies the adoption of the 'but for' test as the primary test of causation in contract.[23]

23.4.2 The 'but for' test

[23.50] The traditional test for establishing causation in contract is the 'but for' test. That is, the loss would not have occurred *but for* the breach of the defendant. This maintains the issue of causation as a question of fact for the court. If the loss would have been suffered anyway, no more than nominal damages will be payable.[24] Pursuant to this test, it is not necessary for the defendant's conduct to be the sole contributing factor of the loss, provided it is a cause of the loss.[25] Usually the causal link between the loss suffered by the plaintiff and the breach of contract is obvious—as, for example, where the buyer of goods fails to accept and pay for the goods, and as a result, the seller is forced to sell the goods on the open market for a lesser price. In that case, it can be said that but for the breach of the buyer, the seller would have obtained the contract price and not suffered a loss.

23.4.3 The 'common sense' approach and multiple causes

[23.55] While judicial authority is in favour of maintaining the 'but for' test as the primary test for causation, it is recognised that the 'but for' test is plainly inadequate

20   *Thom (or Simpson) v Sinclair* [1917] AC 127 at 135.
21   *Leyland Shipping Co Ltd v Norwich Union Fire Insurance Society Ltd* [1918] AC 350 at 361, 362, 371; *Fitzgerald v Penn* (1954) 91 CLR 268.
22   *Alexander v Cambridge Credit Corp Ltd* (1987) 9 NSWLR 310 at 350.
23   See *Alexander v Cambridge Credit Corp Ltd* (1987) 9 NSWLR 310. The 'but for' test however, is insufficient in all cases. See [23.55].
24   See *RegGlass Pty Ltd v Rivers Locking Systems Pty Ltd* (1968) 120 CLR 516.
25   *Norton Australia Pty Ltd v Streets Ice Cream Pty Ltd* (1968) 120 CLR 635; *Barnes v Hay* (1988) 12 NSWLR 337; *Alexander v Cambridge Credit Corp Ltd* (1987) 9 NSWLR 310.

where there are two separate and independent events, each of which alone was suffi-cient to cause the damage. The judicial shift toward applying the 'but for' test in a common-sense way is typified by the New South Wales Court of Appeal decision in *Alexander v Cambridge Credit Corp Ltd*,[26] which indicated that the 'but for' test should only be used as a guide, and that the ultimate question was whether 'as a matter of common sense, the relevant act or omission was a cause' of the loss.[27] What is a common-sense approach? McHugh J in *March v E & M Stramare Pty Ltd*[28] doubted that there could be consensus about the approach, and expressed concerns about the value judgements that would underpin the application of the principal. *Alexander v Cambridge Credit Corp*[29] is itself an example of a situation where two independent events would have satisfied the 'but for' test of causation. The defendant auditors breached their contract of employment with the plaintiff by supplying audit certificates that failed to make provision for the plaintiff's poor financial position. This caused the ratio of debentures to shareholders funds, set in the plaintiff's trust deed, to be exceeded. The company continued to trade for 3 years, and during that time the gov-ernment altered monetary policies and land development policies, causing increased interest rates and increased costs of development. A receiver was not appointed for 3 years, and the plaintiff claimed the losses incurred in those years from the auditors, on the basis that if the breach of contract had not occurred, the company would have been wound up at that time, and a small amount would be owed to the creditors. The auditors' defence was that the plaintiff's plight was brought about by the government's budgetary measure of 1972–73, so any prior breaches of contract or negligence on their part were no longer causally relevant.

[23.60] The Court of Appeal in New South Wales held there was no causal connec-tion between the loss and the breach of contract. While it recognised the primary role of the 'but for' test in questions of causation, the Court also saw the need for a less-rigid approach where there was more than one possible cause of the loss. It was possi-ble for the 'but for' test to be applied in a common-sense way to determine whether the breach 'causally contributed' to the damage.[30] It was not necessary for the breach to be the only cause of the loss only that it was *a* cause.[31]

[23.65] Despite the fact that issues of causation are generally considered to revolve around questions of fact, in some circumstances, an independent act or event may as a matter of policy be treated as the sole cause of the damage. In essence, the question of whether an act or event will be sufficient to break the chain of causation is a question of legal liability or policy, not a question of fact. This is clearly indicated in *Mahony v J Kruschich (Demolitions) Pty Ltd*,[32] where the High Court said:

> a line marking the boundary of the damage for which a tortfeasor is liable in negligence may be drawn either because the relevant injury is not reasonably

---

26   (1987) 9 NSWLR 310.
27   At 358; this is also the position in tort: see *March v E & M Stramare Pty Ltd* (1991) 171 CLR 506.
28   (1991) 171 CLR 506.
29   (1987) 9 NSWLR 310.
30   Ibid at 351.
31   Ibid at 358.
32   (1985) 156 CLR 522.

foreseeable *or because the chain of causation is broken by a novus actus interveniens* ... But it must be possible to draw such a line clearly before a liability for damage that would not have occurred but for the wrongful act or omission of a tortfeasor and that is reasonably foreseeable by him is treated as the result of a second tortfeasor's negligence alone ... whether such a line can and should be drawn is very much a matter of fact and degree.[33]

[23.70] This would suggest either that the law of causation is concerned both with fact *and policy*, or that the proper place for the consideration of whether a *novus actus interveniens* has broken the chain of causation—and therefore, whether legal liability should attach—is part of the concept of remoteness, not of causation. In either case, no matter whether the effect of an intervening act is considered as part of causation or remoteness, it is logical to consider it as a separate issue, after establishing that the breach causally contributed to the loss and before examining the question of remoteness.

[23.75] Two general types of conduct may arise to reduce or limit the damages claimed by the plaintiff:

* actions of the plaintiff that contribute to the loss (contributory negligence); or
* actions of a third person that cause the loss.

(a)   Contributory negligence

[23.80] Will the court take into account the negligent acts of the plaintiff that have contributed to their loss? In tort, the contributory negligence of the plaintiff will not break the chain of causation, but will generally result in a reduction in the amount of damages payable by the defendant. This is due largely to the operation of the apportionment legislation in each State.[34]

[23.85] While there is some argument that the apportionment legislation should apply to claims for damages for breach of contract, the majority of judicial opinion is against this view.[35] This issue is particularly relevant where the plaintiff is claiming both damages for negligence and damages for breach of contract, in the alternative. If the plaintiff is awarded damages for negligence, the contributory negligence of the plaintiff will reduce the award. If, however, the plaintiff elects damages for breach of contract, the contributory negligence of the plaintiff will be largely irrelevant. As the law currently stands,[36] contributory negligence will only be relevant in a claim for damages for breach of contract, where the conduct is such as to break the chain of causation between the breach by the defendant and the loss.

---

33   Ibid at 528.

34   See *Law Reform (Miscellaneous Provisions) Act* 1965 (NSW) s 10(1); *Law Reform Act* 1995 (Qld) s 10; *Wrongs Act* 1936 (SA) s 27a(3); *Tortfeasors and Contributory Negligence Act* 1954 (Tas) s 4(1); *Wrongs Act* 1958 (Vic) s 26(1); *Law Reform (Contributory Negligence and Tortfeasors Contribution) Act* 1947 (WA) s 4(1); *Law Reform (Miscellaneous Provisions) Act* 1955 (ACT) s 15; *Law Reform (Miscellaneous Provisions) Act* 1956 (NT) s 16(1).

35   See *Astley v Austrust Ltd* (1999) 161 ALR 155 where the High Court reviewed the judicial history, concluding that a claim for contributory negligence did not reduce a claim for damages in contract.

36   See *Astley v Austrust Ltd* (1999) 161 ALR 155.

Example: Lexmead (Basingstoke) Ltd v Lewis[37]

A farmer bought a towing hitch to connect his four-wheel drive to a trailer. While using the hitch, he noticed it was broken, but continued to use it for a period of between three and six months. The trailer became loose, and careered across the road into the path of a car. The driver of the car and his son were killed. The plaintiff (another passenger in the car) brought an action for damages for personal injury, and in third party proceedings, the farmer sought damages from the seller of the hitch— claiming breach of contract for supplying goods that were not fit for the purpose, and not of merchantable quality.

It was evident from the facts that the farmer had used the coupling over a period of months in a plainly damaged state without taking steps to have it repaired, or even to ascertain whether it was safe to use. Lord Diplock in the House of Lords concluded that the loss suffered by the farmer arose from his own negligence in failing to repair the coupling, and not from the breach by the seller of any implied warranties of fitness or merchantability. It would only be where the farmer's negligence arose directly and naturally, in the ordinary course of events, from the seller's breach of warranty that the chain of causation would not have been broken. In other words, the seller would need to have warranted that the farmer did not need to take care to ensure that the coupling was safe to use.

(b) Intervening acts or events

[23.90] The act of a third party to the contract may be so substantial that it is no longer possible to conclude that the breach of contract contributed to the loss. The intervening act must 'act to supersede in potency'[38] the breach of contract so that it could no longer be considered as a cause, either in common sense or in law. However, where the defendant is under a contractual duty to guard against the very act of the intervener—or that class of act—a break in the chain of causation will not be found. For example, if a person writes a cheque in such a way as to allow another person to alter the cheque and pay the money to themselves, the person has committed a breach of duty to the bank. If a third person fraudulently cashes the cheque, the chain of causation has not been broken.[39] This is due to the fact that the customer is under a duty to protect the bank from fraud arising in this way.

[23.95] An event may also intervene to break the chain of causation between the breach of contract and the loss, provided the event was not of a kind that was reasonably to be anticipated.[40] For example, in *Monarch Steamship Co Ltd v Karlshamns Oljefabriker A/b*[41] the appellant breached its contract with the defendant to provide a seaworthy ship for the carriage of cargo from Manchuria to Sweden. The breach resulted in the vessel being delayed, so it could not reach Sweden before the outbreak of the Second World War. On the outbreak of war, the British Admiralty directed the ship to unload at Glasgow. The defendant then had to arrange for the cargo to be

---

37   [1982] AC 225.
38   *Alexander v Cambridge Credit Corp* (1987) 9 NSWLR 310 at 363.
39   See *London Joint Stock Bank v MacMillan* [1918] AC 777.
40   *The Wilhelm* (1866) 14 LT 636; *Monarch Steamship Co Ltd v Karlshamns Oljefabriker A/b* [1949] AC 196.
41   [1949] AC 196.

shipped to Sweden, and the cost was claimed from the appellant. The appellant argued that the war intervened and broke the chain of causation. The House of Lords rejected this claim, and found that at the time (1939) the appellants ought to have foreseen that war might shortly break out, and that any prolongation of the voyage might cause the loss of or diversion of the ship.

23.5 Remoteness

[23.100] Remoteness is the second control mechanism that will operate to limit a plaintiff's recovery of compensation for loss suffered. The law will place a limit on the amount and the time over which losses are recoverable.

> [T]he law cannot take account of everything that follows a wrongful act; it regards some matters as outside the scope of its selection, because it were infinite for the law to judge the cause of causes, or consequences of consequences … In the varied web of affairs, the law must abstract some consequences as relevant, not perhaps on grounds of pure logic but simply for practical reasons.[42]

[23.105] This statement reflects the fact that the principle of remoteness operates as a policy factor in the court's decision. There is a perceived injustice in imposing an intolerable burden on defendants who would otherwise be liable for all loss de facto arising from a particular breach, however improbable, and however unpredictable. In addition, if a plaintiff were entitled to all of the conceivable loss suffered from the breach, the court may not be able to calculate the actual loss for many years, clogging the court system with undecided cases. Therefore, although at first glance the principle of remoteness may seem to some plaintiffs unfair, any potential loss must be weighed against the promotion of certainty and efficiency within the court system.

23.5.1 Two Limbs of Hadley v Baxendale

[23.110] The test for deciding whether damage is too remote in contract was formulated in the case of *Hadley v Baxendale*.[43] It is clear from the judgment of Alderson B[44] that parties to a contract should only be liable for loss that could be fairly and reasonably contemplated by both parties when making the contract. The parties should first be able to contemplate that the loss would arise because the loss that actually occurred arose naturally, according to the usual course of things, as a probable result of the breach. The court will presume the parties to the contract are aware of loss that may arise in the usual course from a breach—even though the parties did not in fact consider the effect of a breach at the time of contract. The second circumstance in which the parties should be able to contemplate loss arising from a breach of contract is where the loss is reasonably supposed to have been in the contemplation of both parties at the time they made the contract as a probable result of the breach. This second limb of the principle relies on the defendant possessing knowledge of special damage

---

42   *Liesbosch Dredger v SS Edison* [1933] AC 449 at 460.
43   (1854) 9 Exch 341 at 354; 156 ER 145 at 151.
44   Ibid at 466.

that may occur as a probable result of the breach. This knowledge must be acquired from the plaintiff at or prior to contract.

[23.115] In essence, the two limbs of *Hadley v Baxendale*[45] are part of the one rule: that a party will only be liable for loss suffered that both parties would contemplate as a probable result, either because it arises in the usual course of events, or because it arises from the special facts known to both parties. To fully understand the operation of the two limbs of *Hadley v Baxendale*,[46] it is necessary to consider the operation of each in various situations.

23.5.2   Damage under the first limb of Hadley v Baxendale

[23.120] According to the first limb of the rule, damage that arises 'naturally … according to the usual course of things' as the probable result of a breach will be recoverable.[47] Since *Hadley v Baxendale*,[48] the courts have grappled with how best to explain this principle of remoteness. In *Hadley v Baxendale*[49] itself, Alderson B, in applying the principle, considered the loss under the first limb would be loss flowing 'naturally from the breach of [the] contract in the great multitude of such cases occurring under ordinary circumstances'.[50] In *Koufos v Czarnikow Ltd*,[51] Lord Reid considered this to mean that parties to a contract will have within their contemplation 'a result which will happen in the great majority of cases',[52] or a result 'not unlikely to occur'.[53] The consequence of this approach is that a result that may be foreseeable as a substantial possibility in only a minority of cases will not fairly be considered as normally within the contemplation of the two reasonable parties to a contract. All members of the court in *Koufos v Czarnikow Ltd*[54] were clearly of the view that a test of reasonable foreseeability should remain within the domain of tort law, and should not be applied to recovery of loss in contract.[55] This separate approach to remoteness in contract and tort has been followed in Australia.[56]

[23.125] To determine what loss would be within the reasonable contemplation of the parties at the time of entry into the contract, the court, in the absence of special knowledge, will look to the knowledge of a reasonable person in the position of the

---

45   Ibid at 354; at 151.
46   Ibid.
47   *Hadley v Baxendale* (1854) 156 ER 145 at 151.
48   (1854) 9 Exch 341; 156 ER 145.
49   Ibid.
50   Ibid at 151.
51   [1969] 1 AC 350 at 388, 406, 410–411, 415, 425.
52   Ibid at 384.
53   Ibid at 388. Refer also to the other formulations of 'not unlikely to result' per Lord Morris of Borth-y-gest; 'liable to result' per Lord Hodson. The court in *Monarch Steamship Co Ltd v Karlshamns Oljefabriker* [1949] AC 196 also referred to 'a serious possibility' and 'real danger' per Lord du Parq; and 'grave risk' per Lord Morton of Henryton.
54   [1969] 1 AC 350.
55   See pp 386, 406, 410–411.
56   *Burns v MAN Automotive (Aust) Pty Ltd* (1986) 161 CLR 653 at 667; *Baltic Shipping Co v Dillon* (1993) 176 CLR 334 at 368–369; *Alexander v Cambridge Credit Corporation Ltd* (1987) 9 NSWLR 310; *The Commonwealth v Amann Aviation Pty Ltd* (1991) 174 CLR 64 at 116 per Deane J 'the gradual assimilation of the tests "within the contemplation of the parties" (contract) and reasonable foreseeability (in tort)'.

parties to the contract. For example, in *Koufos v Czarnikow Ltd*,[57] the court looked to the reasonable contemplation of a reasonable shipowner at the time of making the charterparty. The question asked was whether such a shipowner would contemplate that if the sugar was delivered nine or ten days late, would a loss by reason of a fall in the market price of sugar be not unlikely to result? The House of Lords considered the result was not unlikely.

[23.130] Further guidance in relation to the operation of the principle of remoteness may be gained from the case examples.

Example: Hadley v Baxendale[58]

This is an example of a case where the first limb of the rule was not satisfied. The plaintiff owner of a flour mill contracted with the defendant (a common carrier) to have a broken crankshaft conveyed to engineers for the purpose of manufacturing a new shaft. Delivery of the shaft was delayed, and as a consequence the mill was stopped for five days longer than it should have been, and profits that would otherwise have accrued were lost.

The court held the defendant was not liable for the lost profits as he was merely a carrier who did not know that the mill would be stopped. The plaintiff might, for example, have had a spare shaft in his possession, and the plaintiff's loss of profit was therefore not something the defendant could have contemplated as occurring in the usual course of things. It was not a result that would have occurred in a 'multitude' of cases.

Example: Koufos v Czarnikow Ltd[59]

This is an example of a case where the first rule was satisfied. The defendants had agreed to carry sugar from Constanza to Basrah, but deviated during the course of the voyage, with the result that it took nine or ten days longer than it should have taken to reach Basrah. Sugar prices fell on the Basrah market, and the plaintiffs suffered loss of profit by selling at a lower price than would have been obtained had the vessel not deviated. The House of Lords held that the loss occurred in the usual course of things because the defendants knew:

1   that the plaintiffs were sugar merchants; and
2   that there was a market for sugar at Basrah.

[23.135] Accordingly, because the defendants had that knowledge, they should have contemplated that failure to deliver on time could result in a decrease in value of goods—and therefore, a loss of profit. It was not relevant that the owners did not have any knowledge of the exact contracts.

---

57   [1969] 1 AC 350.
58   (1854) 156 ER 145.
59   [1969] 1 AC 350.

Example: Victoria Laundry v Newman Industries[60]

This is an example of a case where part of the loss was recovered under the first limb, but the balance of the loss was too remote. The plaintiff had purchased from the defendant a boiler, which it proposed to use in its dyeing and dry-cleaning business. The defendant caused damage to the machinery when moving it, and the plaintiff refused to take it until it was fixed. The defendant delayed for some five months in delivery, and the court awarded the plaintiff an amount for loss of business in respect of dyeing contracts that were reasonably expected. This corresponded with the loss from the ordinary business of the plaintiff. But the plaintiff failed to recover the loss arising from the loss of its more lucrative contracts, because they were not within the contemplation of the defendant at the time of entering into the contract—nor were they something arising out of the ordinary course of things. In other words, although the loss from the contract may have been foreseeable, it was not a loss that would have occurred in the majority of cases and therefore, was not a probable result of the breach.

23.5.3   Damage under the second limb of Hadley v Baxendale[61]

[23.140] The second limb of the rule in *Hadley v Baxendale* provides for the party to a contract to be liable for loss arising as a reasonable and natural course from special facts of which the party is aware at the time of entry into the contract. This limb will only be considered by the court where the defendant is possessed of special knowledge at the time of entry into the contract. The basis of this rule is said to be that the defendant with actual knowledge of special facts is undertaking to bear a greater loss as a result of the particular facts.[62] In addition to actual knowledge of the special circumstances, it is necessary either:

- for the defendant to acquire this knowledge from the plaintiff;[63] or
- for the plaintiff to know the defendant is possessed of the knowledge at the time the contract is entered into;

so the defendant could reasonably be said to have foreseen that an enhanced loss was likely to result from a breach.

However, as with the first limb, only a loss that is likely to occur in a majority of cases will not be too remote. Where the loss arising from the special facts is likely to occur in only a minority of cases, it may not be a probable result of the breach, even though it is reasonably foreseeable.

[23.145] An example of damage that falls within the second limb can be found in *McRae v The Commonwealth*.[64] In that case, the defendants had warranted to the plaintiffs that a tanker lay on a coral reef and required salvage. The plaintiff expended moneys in trying to locate the vessel, which was not in the location given by the defendant. The court held that the expenditure for the salvage operation fell within

---

60   [1949] 2 KB 528.

61   (1854) 145 ER 145.

62   *Koufos v Czarnikow Ltd* [1969] 1 AC 350; *Robophone Finance Facilities Ltd v Blank* [1966] 1 WLR 1428 at 1448.

63   See *Panalpina International Transport Ltd v Densil Underwear Ltd* [1981] 1 Lloyds Rep 187 where the defendants were made aware of the special circumstances in the course of negotiations.

64   (1951) 84 CLR 377.

the second limb because of the defendant's actual knowledge of the need for a salvage operation.

[23.150] *McRae's case* should be contrasted with *Victoria Laundry v Newman Industries*,[65] where even though the defendant had knowledge of the business of the plaintiff and the fact that the plaintiff wished to put the boiler into immediate operation, this was not sufficient to bring the knowledge within the second limb. The defendant did not have any actual knowledge of the specific contracts the plaintiff had entered into, or that the boiler was necessary to comply with those contracts. Damages were awarded to the plaintiff, but only for the loss arising in the usual course of events.

23.5.4 Extent of the loss

[23.155] The principle of remoteness in *Hadley v Baxendale*[66] requires the parties to contemplate that the loss that occurred was a probable result of the breach—either because it would occur in the usual course of things, or because of special facts known to the parties. This raises the question of exactly what the parties must contemplate. Is it merely the type of loss—such as economic loss—or do the parties have to contemplate the actual extent of the loss? This question arose for consideration in *H Parsons (Livestock) Ltd v Uttley Ingham & Co*,[67] where pigs owned by the plaintiff had died as a result of eating contaminated nuts from a faulty hopper bought from the defendant. The loss had been caused by the negligence or breach of contract of the defendant. Although it could not be considered that the parties would have contemplated the death of the pigs as a probable result, the Court of Appeal concluded that the defendant was liable for the loss of the pigs. The majority of the court considered, as the plaintiff was suing for breach of an implied term, that the hopper as delivered and installed would be reasonably fit for its purpose. The question was whether the parties would contemplate that a breach of this implied term would lead to injury to the farm animals. The Court found that a natural consequence of feeding toxic food to an animal is damage to their health. Therefore, the parties to the contract must have appreciated that if the hopper was not suitable for the storage of pig nuts, it was a serious possibility that the pigs would become ill. Accordingly, the parties need only contemplate the type of injury that has occurred—not necessarily the full extent of the loss.

[23.160] There is also a suggestion that a different rule of remoteness should be applied where there is physical damage arising from a breach of contract. Lord Denning, in *H Parsons (Livestock) Ltd v Uttley Ingham & Co*,[68] suggested that in cases of physical damage, the test applied should be one of reasonable foreseeability, not reasonable contemplation.[69] Such an approach would reflect either a policy decision (that personal injury resulting from a breach of contract should be recoverable no matter how slight a possibility of it actually occurring), or the fact that most claims of that nature will be founded alternatively in contract and in tort (for negligence).

---

65   [1949] 2 KB 528.
66   (1854) 9 Exch 341; 156 ER 145.
67   [1978] QB 791.
68   [1978] QB 791.
69   This is also suggested in F Dawson, 'Reflections on Certain Aspects of the Law of Damages for Breach of Contract' (1995) 9 *JCL* 125 at 139.

23.5.5 Alternative claims in contract and tort

[23.165] In a majority of cases where damages for breach of contract are claimed, these may also be an alternative claim for damages for negligence arising out of the same facts. Say, for example, a person is engaged to repair a ceiling in a court. One month after the ceiling is repaired, it collapses. Several people, including the person who engaged the defendant, are injured. It may be, after considering court vacation and court sitting times, that the chances of the ceiling falling while the court was sitting is minor. But it would certainly be reasonably foreseeable that if the ceiling is not repaired properly, a natural consequence is that it may fall and injure anyone sitting in the court. The approach of any court to such a situation would be to award damages to the plaintiffs—usually for negligence in tort. The suggestion by Lord Denning in *H Parsons (Livestock) Ltd v Uttley Ingham & Co*[70] is that the plaintiff should not be disadvantaged where there are alternative claims in contract and tort.[71] This would lead to the court applying the most advantageous test of remoteness. Care should be taken when applying this principle, because of the curious nature of the facts in the case. There is no suggestion that it should be applied for recovery of economic loss.[72]

23.6 Mitigation: general principle

[23.170] The right of a plaintiff to recover all loss naturally flowing from the breach is qualified by the principle that a plaintiff is unable to claim for any damage flowing from a breach of contract that is a result of the plaintiff failing to take all reasonable steps to mitigate the loss.[73] As indicated in *Dunkirk Colliery Co v Lever*:[74]

> The person who has broken the contract is not to be exposed to additional cost by reason of the plaintiffs not doing what they ought to have done as [a] reasonable [person] and the plaintiffs not being under any obligation to do anything otherwise than in the ordinary course of business.

[23.175] The principle of mitigation acts as a negative duty upon the plaintiff. There is no positive obligation to take steps to reduce the loss suffered, provided the action or lack of action taken is reasonable in all the circumstances. There is no requirement to take unreasonable steps or risks to reduce the liability of the defendant.

[23.180] Unlike the principles of causation and remoteness, the onus of proving the plaintiff acted unreasonably is on the defendant.[75] The defendant is required to raise the issue of mitigation within their defence. If the issue is not raised, the court will assume the plaintiff has taken all reasonable steps to mitigate their loss.

---

70 [1978] QB 791.
71 This should be contrasted with the approach to contributory negligence for alternative claims in contract and tort. See [23.80]–[23.85].
72 Note the comments of Deane J in *Commonwealth v Amann Aviation Pty Ltd* (1991) 174 CLR 64 at 116.
73 *British Westinghouse Electric and Manufacturing Co Ltd v Underground Electric Railways Co of London Ltd* [1912] AC 673 at 689. The principle does not apply to a claim for debt or liquidated damages: *White and Carter (Councils) Ltd v McGregor* [1962] AC 413.
74 (1878) 9 Ch D 20 at 25.
75 *TC Industrial Plant Pty Ltd v Robert's Queensland Pty Ltd* (1963) 37 ALJR 289 at 292; *Watts v Rake* (1960) 108 CLR 158 at 159; *Fazlic v Milingimbi Community Inc* (1982) 150 CLR 345; *Metal Fabrications (Vic) Pty Ltd v Kelcey* [1986] VR 507 at 509.

23.6.1 Mitigation: a question of fact

[23.185] Whether a plaintiff has acted reasonably or unreasonably is a question of fact that will depend on the individual circumstances of the case.[76] Plaintiffs are only required to take steps that are reasonable—they do not have to resort to steps that are costly or extravagant.[77] As long as plaintiffs have acted reasonably, they should not be debarred from recovering the actual loss flowing to them simply because the defendant asserts that if the plaintiff had taken some other course, the loss might well have been lower. Accordingly, if a plaintiff is found to have acted reasonably in the circumstances, the fact that the loss is increased by its actions will not affect its right to recover the loss in full. Likewise, if the plaintiff's loss is diminished as a result of its actions, this must also be taken into account in making the award of damages.

[23.190] As the duty to mitigate is a question of fact in all the circumstances, it is useful to consider some particular situations that may arise.

(a) Should the plaintiff enter into or negotiate a further contract within the defendant?

[23.195] If the parties had the opportunity of entering into a new bargain after breach, which might have eliminated the loss suffered, the issue is whether the plaintiff has acted reasonably in refusing to enter into a new contract.[78] A difference is drawn in the cases between a commercial or mercantile contract and a contract of personal service.

Commercial contract

[23.200] The authorities indicate that in the case of a commercial contract, where the defendant makes a reasonable offer to resume the contract, it should generally be accepted by the plaintiff.[79] However, the overriding question for the Court will be whether a refusal is reasonable. Where the new offer requires the plaintiff to risk capital that must be borrowed, or to take steps that may cause their financial ruin a refusal to contract may be reasonable. Alternatively, any refusal to negotiate because of an ulterior motive may deny the plaintiff any damages where to enter into another contract with the defendant would have been reasonable.

Example: Payzu Ltd v Saunders[80]

The defendant agreed to sell 400 pieces of silk to be delivered in monthly instalments. The price was to be paid within one month of delivery. The plaintiff failed to make the first payment on time. In the bona fide belief that this reflected the plaintiff's solvency, the defendant refused to make further deliveries, but offered to deliver the goods at the contract price if the plaintiff paid in cash. The plaintiff did not accept. The market for silk had risen, so the plaintiff was unable to buy silk on the open market for the contract price. The plaintiff sued the defendant for repudiation claiming the difference between the contract price and the market value.

The Court found that the actions of the defendant amounted to repudiation, but the plaintiff had acted unreasonably and should have accepted the new offer. Both the

---

76   *Payzu Limited v Saunders* [1919] 2 KB 581 at 588, 589.
77   *Metal Fabrications Pty Ltd v Kelcey* [1986] VR 507 at 513.
78   *Shindler v Northern Raincoat Co Ltd* [1960] 1 WLR 1038.
79   *Payzu Limited v Saunders* [1919] 2 KB 581 at 589.
80   [1919] 2 KB 581.

trial judge and the Court of Appeal agreed that whether the offer of a new contract should be accepted is a question of fact in each case. There may be differences between accepting a further contract of personal service with an employer who has injured the plaintiff's reputation and accepting the offer of a new contract in a commercial situation. In a commercial situation, the offer of a new contract is generally reasonable—and, as indicated by McCardie J, an extraordinary result would arise if a plaintiff were able to reject a reasonable offer and incur substantial avoidable loss, which is then recovered from the defendant.

The plaintiff was awarded nominal damages for the loss of the credit facility.

Employment contracts

[23.205] As indicated in *Payzu Ltd v Saunders*,[81] there will generally be a difference between accepting a new contract in a commercial relationship and agreeing to another contract of employment. However, the overriding consideration for the court in each case will be whether the refusal to accept the new offer is reasonable in the circumstances. Circumstances that may make it unreasonable to accept the further offer of the defendant may be:

- the new offer of employment is at a lower status;[82]
- the new offer of employment requires the plaintiff to abandon his or her legal rights arising from the breach;[83]
- the offer of employment is made during the course of the proceedings claiming damages, where the offer is made to reduce the damages awarded.[84]

[23.210] However, where an offer of employment is made at the same salary and with the same benefits, it is unlikely to be reasonable to refuse the offer.[85]

(b)   Are reductions or increases in the amount of loss taken into account?

[23.215] The mere fact the loss of the plaintiff has increased will not bar the plaintiff from recovering the loss from the defendant. If the plaintiff has acted reasonably, the loss may be recoverable.[86] Where the plaintiff obtains extra benefits as a result of the breach of the defendant, these benefits must be accounted for in assessing the damages. For example, where an employee is unfairly dismissed, the damages payable will be reduced by the amount earned from another employer after the dismissal;[87] or the advantage of newer and more efficient machinery purchased to replace defective machinery may have to be taken into account.[88]

---

81 [1919] 2 KB 581.
82 *TCN Channel 9 v Hayden Enterprises Pty Ltd* (1989) 16 NSWLR 130.
83 *Shindler v Northern Raincoat Co Ltd* [1960] 2 All ER 239.
84 Ibid.
85 Refer for example to *Brace v Calder* [1895] 2 QB 253; *Saddington v Building Workers Industrial Union of Australia* [1993] 49 IR 323.
86 *Banco de Portugal v Waterlow & Sons Ltd* [1932] AC 452.
87 *Lavarack v Woods of Colchester Ltd* [1967] 1 QB 278.
88 *British Westinghouse Electric and Manufacturing Co Ltd v Underground Electric Railways of London Ltd* [1912] AC 673.

(c)   Should the plaintiff purchase a substitute in the market place?

[23.220] In the ordinary course it is expected that an injured party would attempt to avoid loss by making a substitute arrangement. If the buyer of goods refuses to accept them, it would be considered reasonable for the seller to go into the market place and sell the goods. Likewise, where the seller fails to deliver, the buyer would be expected to attempt to obtain a substitute. This principle also applies to contracts other than a sale of goods. For example, employees who are wrongfully terminated should take all reasonable steps to mitigate their loss by looking for other employment.

23.6.2   Anticipatory breach and mitigation

[23.225] The duty to mitigate does not arise until there is an actual breach of contract or an anticipatory breach that is accepted as a repudiation of the contract.[89] Where there is an anticipatory breach of contract, the duty to mitigate will not arise until termination has taken place; therefore, whether the plaintiff behaved reasonably in deciding to terminate or continue with performance is not a question of mitigation.[90] If the plaintiff chooses to affirm the contract, no obligation to mitigate arises.

23.7   Assessment: how are damages calculated?

[23.230] As discussed above, the general object of awarding damages in contract is to compensate a person for loss suffered as a result of a breach of contract.[91] The general measure of the loss recoverable will be in accordance with the principle in *Robinson v Harman*[92] that the plaintiff will be awarded damages to put the plaintiff in the position they would have been in had the contract been performed. In other words, the plaintiff will be awarded damages commensurate with the loss of expectation or profits from the contract. Where the contract involves the sale of goods or land, the general measure of the lost expectation will be the difference between the contract price and the market value of the goods or land on the date of breach. In other cases, where the breach of contract has prevented the opportunity to earn the expectation or profit from arising, the court will need to estimate the value of the potential expectancy.[93] In either situation, the fact that damages may be difficult to estimate is not a bar to recovery.[94]

[23.235] The general measure of damages in contract should be contrasted with the measure of damages in tort. Damages are awarded in tort to place the plaintiff in the position they would be in if the tort had not been committed.[95] Generally, in the commercial context, this will mean the plaintiff is able to recover the amount of moneys expended in reliance on the tort. For example, if a person is induced to enter

---

89   *Shindler v Northern Raincoat Co Ltd* [1960] 2 All ER 239 at 249.
90   *White and Carter (Councils) Ltd v McGregor* [1962] AC 413.
91   *Johnson v Agnew* [1980] AC 367 at 400.
92   (1848) 1 Ex 850.
93   *Tszyu v Fightvision Pty Ltd* [1999] NSWCA 323.
94   *Fink v Fink* (1946) 74 CLR 127 at 143, *McRae v Commonwealth Disposals Commission* (1951) 84 CLR 377; *Commonwealth v Amann Aviation Pty Ltd* (1991) 174 CLR 64; *Benlist Pty Limited v Olivetti Australia Pty Limited* (1990) ATPR 41-043.
95   *Gates v City Mutual Life Assurance Society Ltd* (1986) 160 CLR 1 at 11–12; *Gould v Vaggelas* (1985) 157 CLR 215 at 264–265; Refer also to [13.260]–[13.295].

into a contract by a negligent misrepresentation, the person will be able to seek damages to place them in the position as if the tort had not been committed. If the person would not have entered into the contract but for the negligent misrepresentation, the moneys expended in performing the contract or the contract price paid will be recoverable. The person will not be able to recover in tort any lost expectation, because the misrepresentation has not been fulfilled. Such damages are only recoverable in contract for a breach of warranty.[96]

23.8   Date of assessment

[23.240] In contract, damages are generally assessed at the date of the breach. However, this is not an absolute rule: the date for assessment may be altered by the court to ensure the plaintiff receives the amount of damages that most fairly compensates them for their loss.[97]

[23.245] For example, in *Johnson v Agnew*[98] the purchaser of land failed to complete a contract of sale. The vendor obtained an order for specific performance, but 7 months later, the order not having been carried out, the mortgagee enforced the security by selling the property. As the market price of the property had fallen following the default of the purchaser, the mortgagee did not realise sufficient funds to discharge the debt. The vendor sought damages from the purchaser for the balance of the moneys owing under the contract. The House of Lords considered that as the vendors acted reasonably in pursuing the remedy of specific performance, the date when that remedy was aborted should be the date on which damages are assessed. The date of that loss was the date the mortgagees contracted to sell the property. The vendor was entitled to damages being the difference between the contract price and the market value of the property at that date.[99]

[23.250] A different date for the assessment of damages is readily applied in the following cases.

*   *A situation where a debt is payable in a foreign currency:* in this case the critical date is not so much the date when the cause of action arose, but rather the dates when the debt should have been paid.[100] Where these date are not the same, the later date will be more appropriate.[101]

*   *A sale of goods for which there is no available market:* if there is a market in which the injured party can buy a substitute, the appropriate date for assessment of loss is usually the date of non-delivery of the goods. However, where there is no available market, an appropriate date will usually be a reasonable time after the date of the breach. A reasonable time will be the period after which the plaintiff

---

96   See *Marks v GIO Australia Holdings Ltd* (1998) 158 ALR 333 which provides an example of the limitations on damages in the context of a claim for misrepresentation.
97   *Johnson v Perez* (1988) 166 CLR 351 at 355–356; *Johnson v Agnew* [1980] AC 367.
98   [1980] AC 367.
99   Followed in *The Millstream Pty Ltd v Schultx* [1980] 1 NSWLR 547.
100 *Cummings v London Bullion Co Ltd* [1952] 1 KB 327 at 336.
101 *Phillips v Ward* [1956] 1 WLR 471 at 474.

might be reasonably expected to mitigate his or her loss by seeking an alternative to performance.[102]

- *Cases of anticipatory breach:* damages for anticipatory breach will usually be assessed on the date for performance of the contract.[103] The rationale of this approach is that the innocent party is to be put, financially, in the same position as—but in no better position than—they would have been in had the contract not been repudiated but had been performed.[104] Care must, however, be taken by the court if the trial takes place before the time for performance of the contract. Contingencies that may have occurred between repudiation and performance, and the fact that the defendant's liability has been accelerated, should be taken into account.[105]

[23.255] Consistently with the fact that damages are assessed once and for all, and as at a particular date, the court will usually assess the measure of damages in light of events that have occurred up to the date of breach. This includes the market value at that date, and whether the loss is capable of mitigation. Generally, events that occur after the date of the breach—such as the sale of the property or goods—are irrelevant except where they result in the plaintiff receiving a benefit that would not have occurred but for the breach of contract. A further exception to this principle also arises in the case of a breach of contract involving an income-earning asset. Loss occurring after the date of the breach—such as the loss of income from a business—will be taken into account as part of the damages recoverable by the plaintiff, provided the loss was caused by the breach and is not too remote.[106]

23.9   The 'once and for all' rule

[23.260] Damages are generally assessed 'once and for all'. That is, there is usually a lump sum payment. There is no right to return to court to recover additional payments for loss suffered at a later date. However, there are two exceptions:

- if there is more than one cause of action; or
- there is a continuing breach.

[23.265] In each of these cases, the court will award damages for the loss sustained to the date of trial, and any additional loss may be recovered in a further action—either because there is another cause of action, or because the breach has continued.[107] The distinction between a once and for all breach and a continuing breach is often difficult to determine, and will usually depend upon a construction of the document in question. For example, the obligations in a lease to insure and keep insured the premises or to keep the premises in repair will be continuing obligations. However, a covenant in a lease by the lessor to put the premises in repair will be broken once and for all when the lessee moves into the premises that have not been repaired by the landlord.

---

102 *Radford v De Froberville* [1977] 1 WLR 1262 at 1285; *Asamera Oil Corp v Sea Oil & General Corp* (1978) 89 DLR (3d) 1.
103 *Millet v Van Heck & Co* [1912] 2 KB 369; *Hoffman v Cali* [1985] 1 Qd R 253.
104 *The Mihalis Angelos* [1971] 1 QB 164.
105 *Hoffman v Cali* [1985] 1 Qd R 253.
106 *Wenham v Ella* (1972) 127 CLR 454 where the plaintiff recovered income lost after the date of the breach that was caused by the breach.
107 *Larking v Great Western (Nepean) Gravel Ltd* (1940) 64 CLR 221.

23.10 Net loss only recoverable

[23.270] To ensure that damages awarded for breach of contract place the plaintiff in the position they would be in had the contract been performed, the court will take into account any benefits or saved expenses received by the plaintiff as a result of the breach. These benefits may arise because the contract has been prematurely terminated, or due to the acts of the plaintiff in mitigation of the loss. The plaintiff should not be placed in a better position as a result of the breach. As a result, the court must take account of the following.

23.10.1   The value of any asset in the hands of the plaintiff

[23.275] If the plaintiff has purchased assets as part of the performance of the contract and those assets are retained by the plaintiff, the residual value of those assets will be taken into account in assessing the plaintiff's loss. In *The Commonwealth v Amann Aviation Pty Ltd*,[108] the value of the aircraft purchased in performance of the contract, which the plaintiff retained, was deducted from the final award.[109]

[23.280] The position is slightly more complex where the plaintiff purchases an asset for the purposes of making profit under a contract and a warranty concerning performance of the machine is breached. It will usually be necessary to account for the residual value of the machine (if any) when calculating the loss of the plaintiff. For example, a manufacturer purchases and pays $10 000 for a vacuum sealing machine from the seller and expects to make $80 000 net profit by using the machine for its full life. If the machine does not comply with a warranty given by the seller and is worthless or returned to the seller, then the manufacturer will receive $80 000.[110] If, however, the machine has some residual value, this must be taken into account in the final award.[111]

23.10.2   Expenditure necessary for performance or saved expense

[23.285] This will arise most commonly in contracts for the provision of services. Where the plaintiff is to perform services under a contract, account must be taken of any expenditure that is required for completion of the contract following the breach. For example, a builder contracts to construct a house for $100 000 and it will cost $80 000 to perform the contract. The profit is $20 000. If the contract is terminated prior to commencement of work, the builder is only entitled to $20 000 (difference between contract price and cost of performance). This is the net loss—not the contract price of $100 000.

---

108   (1991) 174 CLR 64.
109   See also *Banks v Williams* (1912) 12 SR (NSW) 382 where the value of maps retained by the plaintiff was taken into account in the award of damages.
110   *TC Industrial Plant Pty Ltd v Robert's Queensland Pty Ltd* (1963) 37 ALJR 289.
111   *Cullinane v British 'Rema' Manufacturing Co Ltd* [1954] 1 QB 292.

23.11 Heads of damage

23.11.1 Overview: loss of expectation

[23.290] The general measure of damages in contract is the amount necessary to put the plaintiff in the position they would have been in if the contract had been performed.[112] Application of this principle will provide reasonable compensation for the breach 'without imposing liability upon the other party exceeding that which he could fairly be regarded as having contemplated and been willing to accept'.[113] Depending upon the type of contract and the circumstances of the breach, there may be a variety of methods by which the court could give compensation for the breach. Generally, a breach of contract will result in an economic loss being suffered in the form of the loss of profit, the cost of rectifying defective work, wasted expenditure on the contract, or a lost opportunity to make a profit on the contract. Expectation loss is the general description of the type of loss recoverable by the plaintiff from the defendant in a claim for damages for breach of contract. Although expectation loss will generally be compensation for economic loss, it may also include compensation for physical injury, mental distress, loss of reputation, or loss of an opportunity. These types of loss may generally be referred to as heads of damage. No matter what description is given to the type of loss suffered, it is clear that:

> the expressions expectation damages, damages for loss of profits, reliance damages and damages for wasted expenditure are simply manifestations of the central principles enunciated in *Robinson v Harman* rather than discrete and truly alternative measures of damages which a party not in breach may elect to claim.[114]

[23.295] Therefore, the plaintiff need not choose between the different heads of damage. Any or all are available to a plaintiff, subject to the rule against allowing double recovery for the same loss.

Difficulties arise, however, where there is either no lost expectation or the loss of profit cannot be calculated. The fact that the plaintiff has not suffered any loss of expectation may indicate either that the plaintiff has not suffered any loss at all, or that although the plaintiff has suffered a loss, the contract was not profitable. In the first case, the plaintiff will only be entitled to nominal damages. In the second case, the court may award compensation on the basis of the wasted expenditure of the plaintiff. Although this is not consistent with the principle in *Robinson v Harman*,[115] it may be the only method available to the court to appropriately and reasonably compensate the plaintiff for the defendant's breach. Issues for the court in awarding damages on the basis of wasted expenditure alone are discussed at [23.385]–[23.395].

---

112 *Robinson v Harman* (1848) 1 Ex 850.
113 *Wenham v Ella* (1972) 127 CLR 454 at 466.
114 *Commonwealth v Amann Aviation Pty Ltd* (1991) 174 CLR 64 at 82.
115 (1848) 1 Ex 850.

23.11.2   Types of economic loss recoverable as part of expectation loss

(a)   Loss of profit or value

[23.300] The usual measure of loss for a breach of contract will be the difference between the contract price and the value of the subject matter of the contract at the date of breach. This measure of loss will apply in the case of contracts for the sale of real property and contracts for the sale of goods. For example, if the seller of apples agreed to supply 10 tonnes of apples at $1200 per tonne, but then failed to deliver them to the buyer, what would be the loss to the buyer? If the price of apples has increased and the buyer now has to pay $1500 per tonne, the seller will be liable to compensate the buyer for $300 per tonne—a total of $3000. This will represent the loss of expectation or loss of value to the buyer from the breach.

(b)   Wasted expenditure or reliance loss

[23.305] Monies expended in the performance of a contract may be recovered as part of the loss of expectation suffered as a result of the breach. The performance of a contract such as a construction contract will require the builder to expend moneys, which they usually intend to recover as part of the contract price. For example, a builder may agree to build a house for a contract price of $200 000. However, in order to construct the house the builder will have to spend $150 000 in construction and materials. This means the builder intended to make a profit of $50 000 from the contract. If the contract is breached, should the builder be able to recover the amount of any moneys expended to date in the performance of the contract in addition to the lost profit?

[23.310] Several early authorities considered that a plaintiff could not make a claim for wasted expenditure and loss of profits as this would lead to double recovery. That is, the plaintiff would be in a better position than if the contract had been performed.[116] This proposition is however, based upon a misconception of the object of damages in contract. The preferable view is that wasted expenditure and loss of profit are recoverable in the same action where the expenditure together with a profit would have been recovered upon completion of the contract. This is consistent with the principle in *Robinson v Harman*[117] that the innocent party should be placed in the same position as if the contract had been completed.

[23.315] For example, in the case of a building contract where a building contractor has finished half a building for which the contract price is $200 000, expenditure is $60 000 and the cost of completion is $90 000. Provided the builder terminates for the breach of the other party, the builder may claim two types of damage:

- expenditure actually made in performing or preparing to perform ($60 000); and
- the profit which he would have made on the whole contract ($50 000.) (This is the net profit after deduction of the expenditure necessary to complete the contract from the contract price: $200 000 minus $150 000).

[23.320] At first glance, this looks like a combination of reliance and expectation losses. But it is really a claim for what the plaintiff expected to make from the contract.[118]

---

116   *Anglia Television Ltd v Reed* [1972] 1 QB 60 at 63–64.
117   (1848) 1 Ex 850.
118   See also *The Commonwealth v Amann Aviation Pty Ltd.* (1991) 174 CLR 64 at 85.

(c)   Loss of an opportunity

[23.325] Damages for the loss of an opportunity or chance are recoverable in contract despite the fact there may be a less than a 50 per cent chance of the event occurring. It has been recognised that the loss of a chance to win a prize in a competition due to a breach of contract is subject to compensation despite the difficulty of assessment.[119] This willingness to award compensation for the loss of a chance is not limited to competitions. In *The Commonwealth v Amann Aviation Pty Ltd*,[120] the majority of the High Court concluded that a lost commercial advantage or opportunity was a compensable loss, even though there was a less than 50 per cent likelihood that the commercial advantage would have been realised. Damages for the breach were assessed by reference to the probabilities or possibilities of what would have happened.[121] The Commonwealth argued that as there was no obligation to renew the agreement, there was accordingly no obligation to pay compensation.[122] The High Court rejected this approach, stating that the rule in *Hadley v Baxendale*[123] should be applied instead. The question is what was reasonably within the contemplation of the parties as the probable result of the breach at the time of contract. It was assumed that the prospect of securing a renewal of the contract was within the contemplation of the parties. This meant that despite the fact there was no legal obligation to provide a further contract, the Commonwealth was liable for the loss of the prospect of securing a renewal.

(d)   Cost of rectification of defective work

[23.330] The general object of damages in contract is, so far as money can do it, to place the plaintiff in the same position as they would have been had the contract been performed. In the context of defective building work there can be two competing measures of damage: the cost of rectification of the defect and the loss in value of the property.

[23.335] According to McGregor,[124] in deciding between diminution in value or rectification, the appropriate test was reasonableness of the plaintiff's desire to reinstate the property. However, if the cost of remedying the defect was disproportionate to the end to be attained, the damages fall to be measured by the value of the building had it been built as required by the contract, less its value as it stands. Where the reinstatement presents no particular problem, the cost of reinstatement will be the obvious measure of damages, even where there is little or no difference in value or where the difference in value is hard to assess.

[23.340] This same approach is adopted by the High Court in *Bellgrove v Eldridge*:[125]

> the measure of the damages recoverable by the building owner for the breach
> of a building contract is ... the difference between the contract price of the

119   *Chaplin v Hicks* [1911] 2 KB 786.
120   (1991) 174 CLR 64.
121   The High Court continued this approach in *Sellars v Adelaide Petroleum NL* (1991) 179 CLR 332.
122   The Commonwealth relied on *Abrahams v Herbert Reiach Ltd* [1922] 1 KB 477 and *Lavarack v Woods of Colchester Ltd* [1967] 1 QB 278.
123   (1854) 9 Exch 341; 156 ER 145.
124   H McGregor, *McGregor on Damages*, 17th edn, Sweet & Maxwell, London, 1997, p 752; see also *Ruxley Electronics v Forsyth* [1996] AC 344.
125   (1954) 90 CLR 613.

work or building contracted for and the cost of making the work or building conform to the contract.

and continued:

the qualification, however, to which this rule is subject is that, not only must the work undertaken be necessary to produce conformity, but that also, it must be a reasonable course to adopt.[126]

[23.345] Damages are designed to compensate for an established loss—not to provide a gratuitous benefit to the aggrieved party. It follows that the reasonableness of an award of damages should be linked directly to the loss sustained. If it is unreasonable in a particular case to award the cost of reinstatement, it must be because the loss sustained does not extend to the need to reinstate. Consequently, the question of whether the work will ever be performed is relevant to the question of reasonableness, particularly where there is a significant difference between the loss in value and the rectification costs. In *Ruxley Eectronics Ltd v Forsyth*,[127] the House of Lords concluded that where a pool had been constructed at an incorrect depth, the measure of damages should not be the cost of rectification of the pool. In the circumstances it would be unreasonable, where the pool was adequately constructed, to demolish it and reconstruct it to another depth. The fact no intention to rebuild had been expressed to the court was relevant, even though usually the court will not be concerned with how an award of damages will be spent.[128]

[23.350] The House of Lords in *Ruxley* considered the historical development of this principle. The court found that four main factors were evident in the decided cases:

* the comparative cost of rectification and loss of value;
* whether the work is substantially complete or not;
* whether the owner intends to undertake the rectification work;
* whether the building is sold prior to undertaking the work.[129]

(e) Delay in the payment of money

[23.355] The general common law principle is that, in the absence of any agreement or statutory provision for the payment of interest, a court has no power to award interest as compensation for the late payment of a debt or damages.[130] However, damages may be recoverable for the cost of borrowing money to replace money paid away or withheld in consequence of the defendant's breach of contract. These losses are directly related to the wrong and are not too remote. For example, in *Hungerfords v*

---

126   Ibid at 617–618. See also *East Ham Corporation v Bernard Sunley & Sons Ltd* [1966] AC 406.
127   [1995] 3 WLR 118.
128   Contrast *DeCesare v Deluxe Motors Pty Ltd* (1996) 67 SASR 28, and *Director of War Service Homes v Harris* [1968] Qd R 275.
129   See J Swanton & B McDonald, 'Measuring contractual damages for defective building work' (1996) 70 ALJ 444.
130   *London Chatham and Dover Railway Co v South Eastern Railway Co* [1893] AC 429; *Tehno-Impex v Gebr Van Weelde Scheepvaarthantoor BV* [1981] QB 648 at 660; *Norwest Refrigeration Services Pty Ltd v Bain Dawes (WA) Pty Ltd* (1984) 157 CLR 149 at 162.

Walker,[131] accountants were employed to prepare partnership tax returns. The accountants made a mistake in the calculation of depreciation allowable as a deduction, which resulted in the plaintiff making an overpayment of tax for three successive years. The plaintiff claimed damages, including an amount for the loss of use of the money in the business. The High Court gave careful consideration to existing common law principle and its application to the facts. The Court considered that where the plaintiff's loss of the use of the money was sustained as a direct result of the breach, there was no reason why interest should not be payable as a component of the loss. This was not a case of the late payment of damages, and therefore, the general common law rule did not apply.

[23.360] The common law rule has been modified by legislation in each Australian State. Each statute empowers the Supreme Court to award interest on a judgment from the date the cause of action arose.[132]

23.11.3 Recovery of compensation for mental distress

[23.365] The general principle is that damages for injured feelings, disappointment and mental distress are not available in contract.[133] Several judicial explanations have been made for the policy foundations of this approach, and although they may in hindsight appear conceptually weak, the current approach has been defended as essentially pragmatic.[134] The first suggested rationale for rejecting compensation for this type of loss in contract is that the principles of contract provide compensation for financial loss only.[135] To allow recovery of compensation for injured feelings would lead to inflated awards of damages in commercial contracts, particularly as anxiety is an 'inevitable concomitant of expectations based on promises'.[136] Secondly, it is suggested that compensation for injured feelings is not available because of the rules of remoteness.[137] For the purpose of satisfying the rule in *Hadley v Baxendale*,[138] the disappointment or distress would have to be within the usual contemplation of the parties at the time of contract as a likely result of the breach. Unless the contract is one for the provision of enjoyment, an injury to a person's feeling as a result of a breach of contract would not usually fall within the remoteness rule.

[23.370] The strictness of this general principle has been eroded by the creation of several exceptions to the point where it must be questioned whether mental distress should continue to be treated differently from other heads of damage in contract.[139] As each of the established exceptions are re-interpreted, adapted and applied to new

---

131 (1989) 84 ALR 119 at 129.
132 Section 53A(1) *Supreme Court Act* 1933 (ACT); s 94 *Supreme Court Act* 1970 (NSW); s 30C *Supreme Court Act* 1935 (SA); s 60 *Supreme Court Act* 1986 (Vic).
133 *Addis v Gramophone Co Ltd* [1909] AC 488. This should be contrasted with the position in torts where mental distress is regularly recoverable.
134 *Baltic Shipping Co v Dillon* (1992–93) 176 CLR 344 per Deane and Dawson JJ at 380.
135 Ibid, per Mason CJ at 361–362.
136 GH Treitel, *The Law of Contract*, 8th edn, Sweet & Maxwell, London, 1991, p 878.
137 *Baltic Shipping Co v Dillon* (1992–93) 176 CLR 344 per Deane and Dawson JJ at 380–381.
138 (1854) 9 Ex 341; 156 ER 145.
139 See Mason CJ in *Baltic Shipping Co v Dillon* (1992–93) 176 CLR 344 at 365; and Wilson J in *Vorvis v Insurance Corporation of British Columbia* [1989] 1 SCR 1085 at 1121–1124.

situations the general principle of refusing recovery for disappointment or distress in contract will weaken.[140]

[23.375] Nevertheless, the Australian courts continue to favour an approach that adopts the general principle that damages are not recoverable in contract for mental distress unless one of the exceptions exist. Damages for injured feelings or mental distress are recoverable:

- where the breach of contract has caused personal injury to the plaintiff;[141]
- where the plaintiff has suffered actual physical discomfort and inconvenience and the mental suffering is directly related to that inconvenience;[142] and
- where an object of the contract is the provision of pleasure and enjoyment or freedom from mental distress.[143]

[23.380] The third exception creates some flexibility for awarding damages for disappointment. Historically, the Courts appeared to restrict their interpretation of contracts where 'the object is the provision of enjoyment' to holiday agreements. However, the House of Lords in *Ruxley Electronics Ltd v Forsyth*,[144] questioned this historical view by awarding damages for breach of a contract to construct a swimming pool—the rational being that this was a contract for the 'provision of a pleasurable amenity'.[145] To date, such an approach has not been adopted in Australia.[146] The current approach is exemplified by the High Court in *Baltic Shipping Co v Dillon*,[147] where damages for the lost enjoyment of a holiday were awarded.[148]

Example: Baltic Shipping Co v Dillon[149]

Mrs Dillon was a passenger on the cruise ship *Mikhail Lermontov*, which sank on a trip from New Zealand to Australia. Mrs Dillon had booked a 14-day cruise; the ship sank nine days after the cruise began.

The two questions before the High Court were whether Mrs Dillon was entitled to the repayment of the fare in restitution, and whether she was entitled to damages for the disappointment and distress at the loss of the holiday. In relation to the issue of disappointment and distress, the High Court unanimously favoured the retention of the general rule that damages for anxiety, disappointment, and distress are not recoverable in actions for breach of contract. However, each of the members of the High Court allowed recovery by Mrs Dillon because the object of the contract was to provide enjoyment, relaxation, or freedom from molestation. Therefore, the disappointment and distress Mrs Dillon suffered flowed directly from the breach of contract.

---

140   Refer for example to *Ruxley Electronics Ltd v Forsyth* [1995] 3 WLR 118 at 139–140.
141   *Godley v Perry, Burton & Sons* [1960] 1 WLR 9 at 13; *Mount Isa Mines Ltd v Pusey* (1970) 125 CLR 383.
142   *Hobbs v London & South Western Rly Co* (1875) LR 10 QB 111; *Bailey v Bullock* [1950] 2 All ER 1167; *Watts v Morrow* [1991] 1 WLR 1421.
143   *Heywood v Wellers* [1976] QB 446; *Jarvis v Swan Tours Ltd* [1973] QB 233; *Jackson v Horizon Holidays Ltd* [1975] 1 WLR 146.
144   [1995] 3 WLR 118 at 139–140.
145   Ibid at 139.
146   For further discussion refer to J Swanton & B McDonald, 'Measuring Contractual Damages for Defective Building Work' (1996) ALJ 444.
147   (1992–93) 176 CLR 344.
148   See also *Jarvis v Swans Tours* [1973] QB 233 and *Falko v James McEwan & Co Pty Ltd* [1977] VR 447.
149   (1992–93) 176 CLR 344.

23.11.4   Loss recoverable where no loss of profit or impossible to calculate

[23.385] A plaintiff who did not expect to make a profit on a contract may still be able to recover his or her wasted expenditure. This is merely another manifestation of the principle in *Robinson v Harman*[150] that the plaintiff is to be put in the same position as if the contract had been performed.[151] Where the evidence indicates that the plaintiff, although unlikely to make a profit, was not going to make a loss, all the plaintiff's wasted expenditure would be recoverable.[152] The amount of loss recoverable could only be reduced if it was proved that the plaintiff had entered a losing contract. The onus of proving this is on the defendant.[153] If the defendant is unable to prove it was a losing contract, all the wasted expenditure is recoverable.

[23.390] Where the defendant proves that the plaintiff entered a losing contract, it is clear that even if the contract had been performed the plaintiff would not have been able to recoup all or some of the expenditure. Consequently, if the principle in *Robinson v Harman*[154] is followed, the plaintiff should only recover the proportion of the wasted expenditure they would have recovered if the contract had been performed. For example, if a builder entered into a building contract for $200 000 but it was going to cost $220 000 for construction and materials, this would be a losing contract. If the contract was terminated for the breach of the other party after the builder had spent $60 000, the builder would only be entitled to recover $40 000 of the wasted expenditure as damages. This would put the builder in the same position as if the contract had been performed—that is, with a loss of $20 000.

[23.395] The second circumstance in which wasted expenditure may be substituted as the primary measure of loss is when it is the only available means of determining the detriment suffered as a result of the breach.[155] The mere fact that the loss of expectation may be difficult to calculate will not result in the court using this approach. Wasted expenditure as the sole loss awarded will only occur where the loss of profit is impossible to calculate.

Example: McRae v Commonwealth Disposals Commission[156]

The defendant sold to the plaintiff an oil tanker supposedly lying on Jourmaund Reef. The price was £285. The plaintiff spent 10 times that amount fitting out a salvage expedition. The plaintiff could not find the tanker, and it was subsequently found that the tanker was never at that location. The court found that the defendant had breached a warranty of the contract that the tanker was not at the promised location, and awarded damages for the breach.

---

150 (1848) 1 Ex 850.
151 *The Commonwealth v Amann Aviation Pty Ltd* (1991) 174 CLR 64.
152 Ibid. In appropriate cases include payments made and liability incurred to third parties. See *Carr v Berriman* (1959) 89 CLR 327 and pre-contractual expenditure: *Anglia Television Ltd v Reed* [1972] 1 QB 60.
153 *The Commonwealth v Amann Aviation Pty Ltd* (1991) 174 CLR 64.
154 (1848) 1 Ex 850.
155 *McRae v Commonwealth Disposals Commission* (1951) 84 CLR 377.
156 (1951) 84 CLR 377.

Damages were awarded for the plaintiff's wasted expenditure. The court considered it would be impossible to place a value on what the defendant purported to sell, thus making assessment of the expectation loss impossible. However, the court took the view that this was more than a case of mere non-delivery of goods. The substance of the action lay in recovery of expenditure wasted in reliance on the assertion that a tanker actually existed.[157] The defendant could not prove that the expenditure would have been wasted because there was no tanker.

23.12 Issues impacting on recovery of damages

23.12.1 Is termination of the contract required?

[23.400] There is no general requirement for a plaintiff to terminate a contract prior to making a claim for damages.[158] There are however, two exceptions:

- The first exception relates to the case of anticipatory breach. An anticipatory breach of contract will not be a breach until the innocent party accepts the conduct as repudiation of the contract and terminates. Consequently, until the contract is terminated, no cause of action for damages will arise.[159]
- The second exception arises in the case of a claim for loss of bargain damages. Loss of bargain damages are intended to compensate the plaintiff for the loss of the contract, and are the usual measure of damages in contracts for the sale of land.[160] As the object of such damages is to compensate for the loss of the bargain, it is only once the agreement is at an end permanently that the plaintiff can be said to have lost the benefit of the bargain.[161]

23.12.2 Should the plaintiff be ready, willing, and able to perform?

[23.405] A plaintiff seeking to claim damages for the loss of a contract terminated for the breach of the defendant will need to prove they were ready, willing, and able to perform where the obligations are dependent and concurrent.[162] This situation will arise in contracts for the sale of land and contracts for the sale of goods. A party's entitlement to damages for the other party's failure to complete, depends on two questions:

- whether the party was, at the time of the refusal to complete, substantially capable of completing the contract; and
- whether it is likely that the party actually would have completed the contract.

[23.410] The onus is on the party claiming damages to prove, on the balance of probabilities, that they could have completed the contract.[163] If the purchaser is claiming damages, this means proving the purchaser was capable of paying the purchase price. If the vendor is claiming damages, it means proving the vendor was able to hand over the title to the property or goods.

---

157 Ibid at 414 per Dixon and Fullager JJ.
158 *Luna Park (NSW) Ltd v Tramways Advertising Pty Ltd* (1938) 61 CLR 286.
159 *Ogle v Comboyuro Investments Pty Ltd* (1976) 136 CLR 444.
160 The measure of loss would usually be the difference between the contract price and the market value of the land.
161 *Progressive Mailing House Pty Ltd v Tabali Pty Ltd* (1985) 157 CLR 17 at 31; *Photo Productions Ltd v Securicor Ltd* [1980] AC 827; *Sunbird Plaza Ltd v Maloney* (1988) 166 CLR 245.
162 *Foran v Wight* (1989) 168 CLR 385. See [19.60].
163 See *Foran v Wight* (1989) 168 CLR 385 at 430; *Hensley v Reschke* (1914) 18 CLR 452 at 467.

23.12.3 Is an accrued right to damages lost after termination for breach?

[23.415] A plaintiff's right to seek damages for breach of contract that accrued prior to termination will survive.[164] This will apply even to a plaintiff where the defendant has terminated the contract for the plaintiff's breach.[165]

23.12.4 Does affirmation of a contract waive damages for breach?

[23.420] An injured party may elect, following breach, either to terminate the contract or to affirm and continue performance. An election to affirm will mean the right to terminate for that particular breach is lost. Does it act as a waiver of the breach? The better view is that an election between the inconsistent rights of termination and affirmation does not act as a waiver of the breach for other purposes.[166] This would allow a party to claim damages for breach of contract.[167] However, this does not apply to an election to affirm an anticipatory breach. An anticipatory breach is not actionable as a breach until it is accepted by the other party.[168] Therefore, any election to affirm the contract will act as a waiver of the right to terminate and the right to damages.

23.13 Liquidated damages

23.13.1 General

[23.425] As a substitute for damages at common law, parties to a contract may stipulate an amount payable in the event of breach of contract.[169] This will commonly be referred to as liquidated damages or agreed damages.[170] A liquidated damages clause is generally considered to provide a genuine pre-estimate of loss suffered in the event of breach. The advantage of an agreed damages clause is that the plaintiff does not have to prove the loss suffered, and is entitled to the sum stated in the clause. If the sum stipulated as payable on breach is a genuine pre-estimate of the loss, it will be accepted as the amount payable without proof of the actual loss.[171] However, if the amount stipulated bears little resemblance to the greatest loss that could occur, then it is likely to be a penalty. A penalty will not be enforced by the courts. A liquidated sum will be recoverable after termination of the contract for breach.[172]

[23.430] Whether a clause is a penalty involves a consideration of two broad questions:

---

164   *McDonald v Dennys Lascelles Ltd* (1933) 48 CLR 457 at 477.
165   *Ettridge v Vermin Board of the District of Murat Bay* [1928] SASR 124 at 128; *Hyundai Heavy Industries Co Ltd v Papadopoulos* [1980] 1 WLR 1129 at 1136.
166   *Mulcahy v Hoyne* (1925) 36 CLR 41 at 55, 56.
167   *Hain SS Co Ltd v Tate & Lyle Ltd* [1936] 2 All ER 597; cf *Banning v Wight* [1972] 1 WLR 972 at 990–991.
168   See [20.110].
169   If the liquidated damages clause is valid, common law damages will not be given in relation to the breach covered by the clause.
170   Liquidated damages may also be payable under a charterparty agreement if the charterer detains the vessel for longer than the time allowed under the contract. This liquidated payment is referred to as demurrage.
171   *Dunlop Pneumatic Tyre Company Limited v New Garage & Motor Company Limited* [1915] AC 79 at 86.
172   This will be subject to the right of the court to grant relief against forfeiture: *Boucat Pay Co Ltd v The Commonwealth* (1927) 40 CLR 98.

- Is the clause of a type to which the rule concerning penalties applies?
- Is the clause classified as a genuine pre-estimate of loss or a penalty?

23.13.2   Application of the doctrine of penalties

[23.435] It was generally stated that the doctrine of penalties only has application to a clause that requires the payment of money following a breach of contract. For example, a contract for the construction of a house provides that if the builder does not complete the house by the stipulated completion date, the owner is entitled to claim $200 for every additional week until completion. The doctrine of penalties will apply to such a clause in the contract.

[23.440] However, in *AMEV-UDC Finance Ltd v Austin*,[173] the High Court was required to consider whether a clause requiring the payment of liquidated damages after termination was subject to scrutiny as a penalty. The clause was contained in a hire purchase agreement and the hirer had failed to pay instalments of hire when due. The owner exercised a contractual right to determine the hiring rather than terminating for breach at common law. The owner claimed for the outstanding instalments, the whole of the amounts payable under the agreement, and the residual value of the equipment less the value of the equipment upon sale.

[23.445] According to Deane J, restricting the operation of the rule concerning penalties to a situation where moneys are payable in the event of breach is not consistent with the development of the doctrine of penalties in equity or at common law. His Honour noted that the doctrine is not applicable in all cases where the contract requires the payment of money (for example, insurance policies or wagering contracts) but that the doctrine should apply generally where there exists a contractual liability to pay or forfeit an amount or amounts.

> It is within that general area that a liability to pay or forfeit money may be discerned, as a matter of substance, as going beyond any genuine pre-estimate of damage and as representing a penal sanction or security against the occurrence or non-occurrence of an event which the obligor and obligee have seen as falling within the responsibility of the obligor.[174]

23.13.3   Distinction between agreed damages and penalties

[23.450] Once it is determined that the rules concerning penalties apply, it is necessary to construe the terms of the contract at the time the contract was made.[175] When construing the clause, the court will look to its substance—not to the classifications given by the parties. The fact the parties have described the amount payable as agreed damages will not prevent the clause from being a penalty. A penalty is generally considered to be a requirement to pay an amount out of all proportion to, or extravagant or unconscionable in comparison with, the greatest loss that could conceivably be proved to have followed

---

173   (1986) 162 CLR 170.
174   Ibid at 199–200. This view was also held by Lords Denning and Devlin in *Bridge v Campbell Discount Co Ltd* [1962] AC 600.
175   *Dunlop Pneumatic Tyre Co Limited v New Garage & Motor Company Limited* [1915] AC 79 at 87.

from the breach.[176] Several other rules and presumptions have also developed over time to assist the courts in determining whether the amount required to be paid is extravagant or unconscionable. Lord Dunedin in *Dunlop Pneumatic Tyre Co Limited v New Garage & Motor Co Limited*[177] summarised the various propositions.

1   The use of a particular expression such as penalty or liquidated damages is not conclusive of the meaning of the clause. The court must decide whether in substance the payment is a penalty.

2   The essence of a penalty is a payment of money stipulated as in terrorem of the offending party; the essence of liquidated damages is a genuine covenanted pre-estimate of damage.

3   The question whether a sum stipulated is a penalty or liquidated damages is a question of construction to be decided upon the terms and inherent circumstances of each particular contract, judged of as at the time of the making of the contract, not as at the time of the breach.

4   To assist this task of construction various test have been suggested, which if applicable to the case under consideration may prove helpful, or even conclusive. Such as:

(a)   It will be held to be a penalty if the sum stipulated for is extravagant and unconscionable in amount in comparison with the greatest loss that could conceivably be proved to have followed from the breach.[178]

(b)   It will be held to be a penalty if the breach consists only in not paying a sum of money and the sum stipulated is a sum greater than the sum which ought to have been paid.

(c)   There is a presumption that it is penalty when a single lump sum is made payable by way of compensation, on the occurrence of one or more or all of several events, some of which may occasion serious and others but trifling damage.[179]

(d)   It is no obstacle to the sum stipulated being a genuine pre-estimate of damage, that the consequences of the breach are such as to make precise pre-estimation almost an impossibility. On the contrary, that is just the situation when it is probable that pre-estimated damage was the true bargain between the parties.

Example: Dunlop Pneumatic Tyre Co Limited v New Garage & Motor Co Limited[180]

Dunlop supplied to New Garage various tyres, covers, and tubes. New Garage agreed not to alter remove or tamper with the manufacturer's marks, not to resell the goods

---

176   Adopted by the High Court in *Esanda Finance Corporation Ltd v Plessnig* (1989) 63 ALJR 238. Refer also to EV Lanyon, 'Equity and the Doctrine of Penalties' (1996) 9 JCL 234, for detailed discussion on the application of this test at common law and in equity.

177   [1915] AC 79 at 87.

178   See *Clydebank Engineering and Shipbuilding Co Ltd v Don Jose Ramos Yzquierdo y Castaneda* [1905] AC 6.

179   Considered in *Lord Elphinstone v The Monkland Iron and Coal Co* (1886) 11 App Cas 332; *Dunlop Pneumatic Tyre Co Limited v New Garage & Motor Co Limited* [1915] AC 79; *IAC (Leasing) Ltd v Humphrey* (1971) 126 CLR 131.

180   [1915] AC 79.

to private customers at less than list prices or to trade with customers at less than list prices, and not to exhibit Dunlop goods unless consent was obtained. New Garage agreed to pay Dunlop £5 for each tyre cover or tube sold or offered in breach of the agreement. New Garage breached the agreement by selling tubes and covers at less than the list price. New Garage argued that the payment of the £5 was a penalty.

The House of Lords held that the sum required to be paid by the contract was not a penalty. The fact the payment related to several types of breach did not mean it was a penalty. As the kind and magnitude of damage (eventual loss of business) that was likely to arise in relation to all breaches of the contract (as stipulated in the clause) was the same or similar, the clause was not a penalty. If the clause had specified the payment of a single sum for different breaches—some of which were trifling and some serious—the clause would in all probability have been a penalty. In addition, the fact that damage was difficult to assess also pointed toward the clause being for agreed damages particularly as the sum was not extravagant.

[23.455] Acceleration clauses commonly used in hire purchase and chattel leases have also received detailed scrutiny in the context of liquidated damages. An acceleration clause is a clause that accelerates the time for payment under the contract, usually in the event of breach.[181] The two issues that have arisen for consideration are:

- Will the doctrine of penalties apply to an agreement if the debt is expressed as presently owing and upon termination for default must be paid in full?

- What will be considered a genuine pre-estimate of loss under a hire purchase or chattel lease?

[23.460] In relation to the first issue the High Court, in *O'Dea v Allstates Leasing System Pty Ltd*,[182] considered the statements of principle from *Lamson Store Service Co Ltd v Russell Wilkens & Sons Ltd*[183] that where the agreement provided for all of the moneys to be owing at the time of entry into the agreement, but allowed it to be repaid by instalments, the acceleration clause was not a penalty. It is clear that the High Court in *O'Dea's* case was not comfortable with applying the principle to overcome the doctrine of penalties and avoided a determination by finding that after considering the agreement as a whole there was no presently existing debt. Although similar facts arose in *IAC (Leasing) Ltd v Humphrey*,[184] the High Court avoided a re-examination of *Lamson Store Service Co Ltd v Russell Wilkens & Sons Ltd*[185] by finding that the clause was not a penalty in any event. It is suggested that, having regard to the dicta of the High Court in *O'Dea v Allstates Leasing System Pty Ltd*,[186] the principle should not override the application of the doctrine of penalties.[187]

---

181 The effect of acceleration clauses has been discussed in *O'Dea v Allstates Leasing System Pty Ltd* (1982–83) 152 CLR 359; *AMEV-UDC Finance Limited v Austin* (1986) 162 CLR 170; *IAC (Leasing) Ltd v Humphrey* (1972) 126 CLR 131; *Esanda Finance Corporation Ltd v Plessnig* (1989) 63 ALJR 238.

182 (1982–83) 152 CLR 359.

183 (1906) 4 CLR 672.

184 (1971) 126 CLR 131.

185 (1906) 4 CLR 672.

186 (1982–83) 152 CLR 359.

187 Refer also to the wider approach on the basis of unconscionability discussed in EV Lanyon, 'Equity and the Doctrine of Penalties (1996) 9 JCL 234.

[23.465] The second issue that has been the subject of examination is the kind of loss recoverable as part of a liquidated damages claim. In a typical hire purchase agreement, an acceleration clause that provides for recovery of the amount of any payments of rent in arrears, together with the total of unpaid future payments appropriately rebated for acceleration of payments, and the expenses associated with termination, is likely to be a genuine pre-estimate of loss.[188] Whether other expenses are recoverable will depend on whether the total amount is out of all proportion to—or extravagant or unconscionable in comparison with—the greatest loss that could conceivably be proved to have followed from the breach. To determine if the amount is out of all proportion to the possible loss, the relevant loss will not be restricted to the loss flowing immediately from the actual breach, but will include the loss of the benefit of the contract resulting from the election to terminate for breach.[189]

23.13.4   Effect of clause being a penalty

[23.470] A clause construed as a penalty will be void and unenforceable by either party. Nevertheless, the plaintiff will be able to recover damages in the usual way by proving that loss has been suffered as a result of the breach.[190] It has been suggested that the amount of loss recoverable should be restricted to the maximum available under the liquidated damages clause. This has some analogy with restitution, where it has been argued that the amount recoverable in restitution should be limited to the contract price.[191] In the context of restitution, this argument has carried little weight where the contract is void.[192] Although this has not received any authoritative decision, the writers suggest that similar reasoning should be applied. Where the clause is considered by the court to be a penalty, and therefore void, it should not be used to indicate the maximum amount of the loss recoverable or used as the upper limit of recovery.[193] The usual rules concerning the recovery of damages in contract will apply.[194]

23.14 International perspectives

23.14.1   New Zealand

[23.475] There is no substantial difference between the law in Australia and in New Zealand with respect to the recovery of damages for breach, and separate examination is not required.

---

188   *Esanda Finance Corporation Ltd v Plessnig* (1989) 63 ALJR 238; and *IAC (Leasing) Ltd v Humphrey* (1971) 126 CLR 131.

189   *Esanda Finance Corporation Ltd v Plessnig* (1989) 63 ALJR 238 at 241, 244.

190   *W&J Investments Ltd v Bunting* [1984] 1 NSWLR 331.

191   See [19.250].

192   *Rover International Ltd v Cannon Film Sales Ltd* [1989] 1 WLR 912.

193   See *AMEV-UDC Finance Ltd v Austin* (1986) 162 CLR 170.

194   For example refer to *AMEV-UDC Finance Ltd v Austin* (1986) 162 CLR 170 where the plaintiff was refused damages for loss of bargain because there was no repudiation of the contract. Termination pursuant to a contractual right of termination in the contract did not guarantee a claim for damages. Refer on this point to *Shevill v Builders' Licensing Board* (1982) 149 CLR 620.

23.14.2   United States

[23.480] Consistently with Australian law, American law considers the object of awarding damages for breach of contract is to put the party in the position they would have been in if the contract had been performed.[195] This is referred to as the party's 'expectation interest'. Recovery of damages to compensate for the loss of that interest requires proof of loss with reasonable certainty.[196] A party who is unable to prove that any loss was suffered will be entitled to nominal damages.[197] Only the net loss proved will be recovered to ensure the plaintiff is not in a better position than if the contract was performed.[198]

[23.485] The starting point in a claim for damages is that the plaintiff is entitled to full compensation for their actual loss. A claim for damages for total breach may have four elements. First, the breach may cause the plaintiff loss in value. Secondly, the breach may cause the plaintiff other loss. Thirdly, the breach may enable the plaintiff to avoid some cost. Fourthly, it may enable the plaintiff to avoid some loss.[199] Questions of causation are considered at this stage. While obviously the breach must in fact be the cause of the loss, other causes—multiple or intervening—will not usually act to preclude the effect of the breach.[200] The acts of plaintiffs themselves may affect their claim, but are taken into account when considering mitigation. Difficult issues of causation are usually taken into account when considering issues of foreseeability or certainty of loss, which are discussed below.[201]

[23.490] Similarly to the situation in Australia, the right of a plaintiff to recover all of his or her actual loss is subject to certain restrictions:

1   *The loss that occurred must be foreseeable as a probable result of the breach.* Loss is foreseeable as a probable result if the loss flows in the ordinary course of events or is as a result of special circumstances that the party in breach had reason to know.[202] This represents an adaptation and widening of the principle in *Hadley v Baxendale*.[203] Instead of limiting the loss to what the parties would have agreed had they turned their minds to it, the loss is only limited by foreseeability. This means, in relation to the second limb, there is only a requirement that the circumstances be notified to the other party in some way.[204] What foreseeability means in the context of contractual damages is summarised in Farnsworth as:[205]

   (a) the relevant time for considering foreseeability is the time of entering the contract;

   (b) it is only necessary to foresee that loss would result, not the type or amount;

---

195   Restatement (Second) § 344, UCC § 1-106(1).
196   This is consistent with the standard of proof in Australia (on the balance of probabilities).
197   Restatement (Second) § 346.
198   Restatement (Second) § 347.
199   The third and fourth factors are only relevant to a case of total breach (that is, termination of contract). The first and second factors are relevant to both total and partial breach of contract. See [20.580]–[20.620] in relation to the difference between total and partial breach.
200   See *Krauss v Greenbarg* 137 F 2d 569 (3d Cir 1943), causes which are negligible may have no legal effect.
201   See for example *Stokes v Roberts* 711 SW 2d 757 (Ark 1986).
202   Restatement (Second) § 351.
203   (1854) 9 Exch 341; 156 ER 145.
204   Contrast with the Australian position at [23.140]–[23.150].
205   EA Farnsworth, *Contracts*, 3rd edn, Aspen Law & Business, New York, 1999, § 12.14.

(c) only foreseeability of the party in breach is relevant;

(d) foreseeability has an objective character;

(e) loss need only be foreseeable as a probable result not a necessary or certain result.

2   *Loss which the injured party could have avoided by taking reasonable steps is not recoverable.*[206] This principle is consistent with the requirement of mitigation of loss in Australian law. The onus of proving the plaintiff has not acted to avoid loss is on the defendant.[207] Whether the plaintiff has failed to act reasonably will be a question of fact in each case. Similarly to the position in Australia, the plaintiff is not expected to take unreasonable risks, incur undue burden or humiliation. Two common steps a court will expect a plaintiff to take are:

(a) Stopping performance of the contract once it is clear the other party will not perform. This action should avoid further costs of performance;

(b) Making substitute arrangements to avoid loss, such as employing a new builder or purchasing substitute goods in the market place.

3   *Damages are not recoverable beyond the amount that the evidence permits to be established with reasonable certainty.*[208] This limitation acts to preclude only those amounts of loss that are not provable with reasonable certainty. This may result in the plaintiff's recovering only nominal damages; or the plaintiff may choose to make a claim for her or his reliance interest rather than expectation interest. Recovery of damages on an alternative basis to the expectation interest is available generally where the loss in value to the injured party is not proved with sufficient certainty. The Restatement (Second) provides for different measures of loss for certain types of contracts. In particular, damages for reliance loss (or wasted expenditure), the cost of rectifying defects in work, or the rental value of a property where the breach causes a delay in the use of the property.[209] Recovery of damages on the basis of reliance loss is subject to the same limitation as in Australia. If the injured party is able to prove that all of the expenditure would not have been recovered, the amount of loss proved will be deducted from the plaintiff's claim.[210] Recovery of damages for the rectification of defective building work is subject to the requirement of reasonableness. Where the cost of rectification is all out of proportion to the loss suffered, the decrease in value of the building will be given instead.[211]

[23.495] Other principles governing an award of damages are consistent with Australia. For example, there is no bar on the recovery of reliance damages and expectation damages in the same claim, subject to the principle of double recovery for the same loss.[212] Damages for mental distress are generally not recoverable, for the same policy

206   Restatement (Second) § 350.

207   *Cates v Morgan Portable Building Corp* 780 F 2d 683 (7th Cir 1985).

208   Restatement (Second), § 352.

209   Restatement (Second) §§ 348, 349.

210   Restatement (Second) § 349. This is consistent with the position stated in *Commonwealth v Amann Aviation Pty Ltd* (1991) 174 CLR 64.

211   Restatement (Second) § 348. This is consistent with the approach adopted in Australia. See [23.330]–[23.350].

212   EA Farnsworth, *Contracts*, 3rd edn, Aspen Law & Business, New York, 1999, § 12.16.

reasons as in Australia. Generally, damages for mental distress will be given where physical injury has resulted to the plaintiff, or physical inconvenience, or the object of the contract is the provision of enjoyment.[213] Damages for breach of a concurrent obligation are only payable if the injured party was ready, willing, and able to perform on the date for performance. This is usually shown by a tender of performance.[214] Punitive damages are not recoverable for breach of contract, unless the breach is also a tort for which punitive damages are recoverable.[215]

[23.500] American courts recognise that the parties to an agreement may provide for an estimate of the loss that would be suffered following breach. Such clauses are enforceable provided the amount is reasonable in the light of the anticipated or actual loss caused by the breach and the difficulties of proof of loss. Where the amount is unreasonably large, it will be a penalty.[216] Although simpler than the test applied in Australia, it has caused difficulty in application.[217] The overriding factor is whether the amount is reasonable having regard to the actual loss. This is determined at the time of entry into the contract, not at the time of breach. However, where the difficulty of proving the loss is great, the court may be more flexible in its view of what constitutes a reasonable amount.[218]

23.14.3 Japan

[23.505] As a civil law country, Japan maintains no common law/equity distinction. The principles of contract law are unified within the Civil Code and the distinction is between the general provisions that apply universally to juristic acts (including contracts) and the Code provisions that are optional and that may have either general application or that may relate to a named contract type. The general provisions—the doctrine of good faith (art 1(2)); the prohibition on abuse of rights (art 1(3)); and the prohibition on breach of public order and good morals (art 90)—are applied by Japanese courts in their interpretation of contracts in ways that approximate to the operation of equitable principles within common law systems. However, when Japanese courts come to apply contract remedies, they select from a single, unified remedial 'package'. Accordingly, all the contractual remedies are described in this chapter. Chapter 24 contains a brief description of the key elements of unjust enrichment in Japan, a remedial route that can be pursued in situations where a contract is found to be void, for example, and so no contractual remedy is appropriate.

[23.510] At the outset it should be noted that in Japan, as elsewhere, a tort claim can often be made in the alternative to a contract claim. This will usually occur where the contract claim is difficult to prove—for example, in the complete absence of documentation.

---

213 *Jankowski v Mazzotta* 7 Mich App 483, 152 NW 2d 49 (1967); *Lamm v Shingleton* 231 NC 10, 55 SE 2d 810 (1949); Restatement (Second) § 353.
214 See [20.640].
215 Restatement (Second) § 355; for example, breach of duty by a public utility.
216 Restatement (Second) § 356.
217 *Cotheal v Talmadge* 9 NY 551 (1854), at 553 '[T]he ablest judges have declared that they felt themselves embarrassed in ascertaining the principles on which the decisions [distinguishing penalties from liquidated damages] were founded'.
218 *Williams v Dakin* 22 Wend 201 (NY 1839); *Hutchinson v Tompkins* 259 So 2d 129 (Fla 1972).

[23.515] Descriptions of civil law remedies often start with the proposition that specific performance is the basic remedy for breach of contract. This should be contrasted with the approach of the common law, which prefers the substitutionary remedy of damages as the primary remedy. In Japan, this means that civil law obligations may be enforced either through direct compulsion (*chokusetsu kyôsei*), through indirect compulsion (*kansetsu kyôsei*) or through substitutional execution (*daitai shikkô*). In theory almost all obligations may be enforced through direct compulsion (eg Civil Code art 414(1)), with the exception of those where a person is personally required to perform a specific act. Direct compulsion in practice is the strongest form of enforcement and applies to obligations to deliver, for example, debts (an obligation to deliver money) and to obligations to deliver personal or real property. In the case of default, an executor may seize the property in question.

[23.520] Substitutional execution may be ordered where, for example, someone other than the party in breach can perform the obligation owed under a contract. So when specific performance is ordered, the court orders a substitute to perform the work and collects the money to cover the cost of this from the original contracting party (art 414(2)). Indirect compulsion is employed where other forms of enforcement are not possible. A court will, for example, order the performance of an obligation within a certain period of time and where this is not done, levy a fine for non-performance.

[23.525] Certain types of contracts (particularly commercial documents) may be notarised as public documents and filed with the court in advance of performance of the obligations. The effect of doing this is that, in the event of non-performance, the document is treated as having presumptive validity, so that the party seeking to enforce it need not prove the contents of the document, all they are required to do is to apply to the court for compulsory enforcement.

[23.530] In the case of contract, a claim for damages for breach may be made in addition to and at the same time as a claim for specific performance. Damages may take the form of liquidated damages as specified in the contract, or unliquidated damages.

[23.535] The calculation of unliquidated damages is in principle very similar to the process undertaken by common law courts. Article 415 of the Civil Code states that 'If an obligor fails to effect performance in accordance with the tenor and purport of the obligation, the obligee may claim damages; the same shall apply to cases where the performance becomes impossible for any cause for which the obligor is responsible'. This is a general statement on the entitlement to damages in cases other than for the payment of money (debts).

[23.540] A claim for damages depends on the obligee's showing that the non-performance complained of occurred for a reason imputable to the other party. If this can be shown, then damages are awarded for a specific monetary value (Civil Code art 417). This is a direct counterpart of the causation principle in the common law.

[23.545] The scope of damages in Japanese law is governed by the direct importation into the Civil Code of the *Hadley v Baxendale* principle from English law: damages that would ordinarily have arisen from the non-performance of the obligation will always be awarded, while damages that have arisen through special circumstances may be recovered only if the parties have foreseen or could have foreseen these circumstances (Civil Code art 416).

[23.550] Damages may be reduced by a claim for contributory negligence (Civil Code art 418). Japanese law does not recognise punitive damages in either contract or tort. Moreover, the damages awards rendered in contract and tort have tended to be relatively conservative calculations.

[23.555] In the case of a liquidated damages clause, Japanese courts take a slightly more permissive stance that the traditional common law prohibition on penalties (Civil Code art 420). Penalty amounts are tolerated, provided that the proportion is not seen to be in breach of public policy (art 90).[219] Obviously this will be determined by the facts situation. The penalty or compensation agreed upon can be calculated in something other than money (art 421).

[23.560] In relation to debts, article 419 of the Civil Code provides that:

1. The amount of damages for non-performance of a money debt shall be determined by the statutory rate of interest; but where the agreed rate of interest exceeds the statutory rate, it shall be determined by the former.
2. With regard to the damages mentioned in the preceding paragraph, the obligee is not bound to prove actual damages nor can the obligor set up *vis major* as a defence.

[23.565] What this means is that first, the obligor remains liable for the debt regardless of the cause of the non-repayment. He or she will also be liable for interest on the debt at the statutory interest rate or at the rate agreed by the parties, whichever is higher. Conversely, the obligee is limited to recovery of this amount; even where the actual damage suffered exceeds the interest due.

---

219 Note that in loan contracts, the amount of liquidated damages is restricted to a proportion of the highest interest rate allowed under the *Interest Rate Restriction Law* (Law No 100, 15 May 1954).

Chapter 24

Restitution

24.1   Introduction

[24.05] A person may claim compensation in restitution for a benefit provided to another person where it would be unjust for the other person to retain the benefit. The emphasis in a claim for restitution is the return of a benefit; this should be distinguished from a claim for damages in contract, where the emphasis is on recovery of the loss sustained by reason of another party's default.[1] In the case of a claim for damages, the benefit received by the defaulting party is not usually relevant to calculation of the compensation payable.[2] Restitution in its modern form as based on unjust enrichment is relatively new to the Australian context. While claims in restitution have been recognised by courts since the late nineteenth century it was only in the later part of the twentieth century that Australian courts authoritatively accepted unjust enrichment as a unifying concept for restitution.[3]

[24.10] Claims for restitution are not limited to parties in a contractual relationship. A claim may be brought by any party who has provided a benefit to another party where it would now be unjust for that benefit to be retained. For this reason, restitution has the potential to cut across the boundaries of the law of contract, tort, and equity. Nevertheless, restitution is important to contracting parties as it provides a potential avenue for the recovery of money paid to another person or for services rendered. We have already discussed the benefits and limits of a *quantum meruit* claim to a party who, although in breach of contract, has provided services for the benefit of the other party to the contract.[4]

[24.15] As the law of restitution applies in so many varied situations, the discussion of restitution in this chapter is limited to the restitutionary claims most usually sought by contracting parties. The emphasis in this chapter is on claims for:

- recovery of moneys paid under a mistake;[5]

---

1   *Air Canada v Ontario (Liquor Control Board)* [1997] 2 SCR 581 at 597–598.

2   Certain exceptions to this general principle exist, such as a claim for account of profits following breach of fiduciary duty. The House of Lords appears to have widened the circumstances in which account of profits is available as the measure of loss for breach of contract. See, *Her Majesty's Attorney General v Blake* House of Lords, unreported, 27 July 2000 (available at http://www.parliament.the-stationery-office.co.uk/pa/ld199900/ldjudgmt/jd000727/blake-1.htm) where the government succeeded in a claim for profits made by a past employee through a breach of the *Official Secrets Act* 1989 (UK).

3   See [24.70]–[24.75].

4   See [19.255]–[19.270].

5   See *ANZ Banking v Westpac Banking* (1988) 164 CLR 662; *David Securities v The Commonwealth* (1992) 175 CLR 353.

- recovery of money due to a total failure of consideration;[6]
- recovery of compensation for work done in anticipation of a contract;[7]
- recovery of compensation for work done under an unenforceable, void, or partly performed contract.[8]

The recovery of compensation for work done or money paid after termination for breach is considered at [24.555]–[24.270].

[24.20] All of the above claims would previously have been classified as claims in quasi-contract and based upon an implied contract. Implied contract as a basis for restitution has, however, been abandoned in favour of unjust enrichment.[9] Each claim originally considered to be quasi-contractual is now subsumed into the law of restitution.[10]

24.2   Development of restitution in Australian law

24.2.1   Origins

[24.25] The law of restitution as based on unjust enrichment is claimed to originate with the words of Lord Mansfield in *Moses v MacFerlan*:[11]

> The gist of this kind of action is that the defendant, upon the circumstances of the case, is obliged by the ties of natural justice and equity to refund the money.

[24.30] Lord Mansfield considered the different types of claims that then abounded for moneys had and received, and sought by his statement to rationalise the typical claims: claims for moneys by mistake; monies for which the consideration had failed; and money obtained through extortion, oppression, or unfair advantage. In all of these cases, the law would impose an obligation or debt to refund the money because of the equity of the plaintiff's claim. The principles set out in *Moses v MacFerlan*[12] were followed by a number of Australian authorities early in the twentieth century,[13] prior to the decision of *Sinclair v Brougham*.[14]

---

6   *Baltic Shipping Co Ltd v Dillon* (1993) 176 CLR 344.
7   *Brewer Street Investments Ltd v Barclays Woollen Co Ltd* [1954] 1 QB 428; *Sabemo Pty Ltd v North Sydney Municipal Council* [1977] 2 NSWLR 880; *Ramsden v Dyson* (1866) LR 1 HL 129.
8   *Pavey Matthews Pty Ltd v Paul* (1987) 162 CLR 221. See [24.255]–[24.280] in relation to claims under a partly performed contract.
9   *Pavey Matthews Pty Ltd v Paul* (1987) 162 CLR 221; *David Securities Pty Ltd v Commonwealth Bank of Australia* (1992) 175 CLR 353; *Baltic Shipping Co v Dillon* (1993) 176 CLR 344.
10   See R Goff & G Jones, *The Law of Restitution*, 5th edn, Sweet & Maxwell, London, 1998, pp 3–5, where the authors indicate that quasi-contractual claims form the bulk of restitution but any claim which can be founded on unjust enrichment may be included.
11   (1760) 97 ER 676.
12   (1760) 97 ER 676.
13   *White v Copeland* (1894) 15 NSWLR 281; *Scargood Bros v The Commonwealth* (1910) 11 CLR 258; *Cambell v Kitchen & Sons Ltd* (1910) 12 CLR 515.
14   [1914] AC 398.

24.2.2 Implied contract theory

[24.35] The decision of *Sinclair v Brougham*[15] gave birth to the implied contract theory as the underlying basis for restitution of either money or services. Despite the fact that unjust enrichment was recognised in *Moses v MacFerlan*[16] as the basis of a claim for moneys had and received, for a good part of the twentieth century the authorities commonly required a plaintiff to prove an implied promise to pay. This adherence to the implied contract theory slowed the development of unjust enrichment as a concept in its own right. Although unjust enrichment is now considered the primary basis of restitution, knowledge of the implied contract theory is important to an understanding of the many authorities that relied on the theory and are now used as examples of restitutionary claims.

[24.40] With the benefit of hindsight it is clear that the court in *Sinclair v Brougham*[17] was influenced by the old forms of action—which for the recovery of money had and received were usually based in indebitatus assumpsit. This required a claim to first allege a debt or obligation and secondly a promise. The first aspect was the real basis of the cause of action and the second aspect although required for the particular writ, was merely fictitious. The requirement of assumpsit was removed by the *Common Law Procedure Act* 1852 (UK). Despite the fact that the indebitatus assumpsit count became obsolete by 1914, the court in *Sinclair v Brougham*[18] appeared to be influenced by the ghosts of the forms of action. The case involved the Birbeck Building Society, which became insolvent in 1911. The court considered the rights of depositors to recover the moneys paid to the building society. The House of Lords held that the building society had been illegally carrying on the business of banking and as such the payments by the depositors were *ultra vires*. Lord Sumner in concluding the depositors had no claim stated:

> The depositors' [claim] … that they paid their money under a mistake of fact, or for a consideration that has wholly failed, or that it has been had and received by the society to their use. My Lords, in my opinion no such actions could succeed. … All these causes of action are common species of the *genus assumpsit*. All now rest and long have rested, upon a notional or imputed promise to repay, The law cannot *de jure* impute promises to repay, whether for money had and received or otherwise, which, if made de facto, it would be inexorably avoid.[19]

[24.45] The decision in *Sinclair v Brougham* was adopted by the High Court in various cases.[20] However, the artificial nature of the implied contract theory is highlighted by the High Court's willingness to grant restitution in cases involving void or unenforceable contracts.[21] There is no difference in effect between a contract void for illegality and a contract void for mistake, except issues of policy. Eventually the flawed analysis applied in *Sinclair v Brougham*[22] was re-examined in England, and eventually in Australia.

---

15 Ibid.
16 (1760) 97 ER 676.
17 [1914] AC 398.
18 Ibid.
19 Ibid at 452.
20 *Hirsch v The Zinc Corp Ltd* (1917) 24 CLR 34; *Smith v William Charlick Ltd* (1924) 34 CLR 38.
21 *Ward v Griffiths Bros Ltd* (1928) 28 SR (NSW) 425; *Horton v Jones* (1934) 34 SR (NSW) 359.
22 [1914] AC 398.

24.2.3   Unjust enrichment as a unifying concept

[24.50] The currently accepted view in Australia is that unjust enrichment provides a unifying legal concept that explains why the law recognises, in a variety of distinct categories of case, an obligation on the part of a defendant to make fair and just restitution for a benefit derived at the expense of a plaintiff.[23]

[24.55] This view was finally reached after a series of cases in England and Australia re-examined the decision of *Moses v MacFerlan*[24] and the interpretation of that decision in *Sinclair v Brougham*.[25] The English authorities have provided valuable guidance for the Australian context, so we start with an examination of those authorities. The House of Lords was provided with the opportunity to revisit the implied contract theory in the *Fibrosa* case.[26] The parties had entered into a contract for the sale of certain machinery from an English firm to a Polish firm prior to the Second World War. The Polish firm had paid a deposit prior to the contract being frustrated by the outbreak of the war. The Polish firm was seeking to recover the deposit as monies had and received. The House of Lords ordered the repayment of the deposit to the Polish firm due to a total failure of consideration. In the course of the decision Lord Wright considered in detail the judgment in *Moses v MacFerlan*,[27] highlighting the fact that:

> Lord Mansfield does not say that the law implies a promise. The law implies a debt or obligation which is a different thing. In fact he denies that there is a contract; the obligation is as efficacious as if it were upon a contract. The obligation is a creation of the law, just as much as an obligation in tort. The obligation belongs to a third class distinct from either contract or tort, though it resembles contract rather than tort.

[24.60] Lord Wright offered several reasons why the implied contract theory should be rejected in favour of the more appropriate underlying theory of unjust enrichment. First, his Lordship noted the artificial requirement for a promise as the basis of a claim under the old forms of action for indebitatus assumpsit. This requirement was considered to have lead to the confusion apparent in *Sinclair v Brougham*[28] between a claim in contract and a claim in restitution. Secondly, the parties were no longer required to bring their claim within a particular form of writ since the *Common Law Procedure Act* 1852 (UK). Consequently the 'fantastic resemblances of contracts invented in order to meet these requirements of the law should not be allowed to affect actual rights'.[29] Thirdly, the 'ghosts of the forms of action should not be allowed to intrude in the ways of the living and impede vital functions of the law'.[30] The forms of action appeared to influence the court in *Sinclair v Brougham*,[31] where Lord Sumner stated that 'all these causes of action [for moneys had and

23   *Pavey & Matthews Pty Ltd v Paul* (1987) 162 CLR 221 at 256–257.
24   (1769) 2 Burr 1005; 97 ER 676.
25   [1914] AC 398.
26   *Fibrosa Spolka Akcynja v Fairbairn Lawson Combe Barbour* [1943] AC 32. See [22.230] for a fuller examination of this case.
27   (1769) 2 Burr 1005; 97 ER 676.
28   [1914] AC 398.
29   *United Australia Ltd v Barclays Bank Ltd* [1941] AC 1 at 29.
30   [1943] AC 32 at 64.
31   [1914] AC 398.

received] are common species of the genus assumpsit. All now rest and long have rested, upon a notional or imputed promise to repay.'[32] Lord Wright agreed that a claim for monies had and received had always rested in debt or an obligation arising by law irrespective of the procedures in use at the time. As assumpsit was merely a fictional tool used to align a claim within strict boundaries, it should not affect the true nature of a claim for monies had and received. And lastly, Lord Wright rejected any claim that the decision in *Sinclair v Brougham*[33] had closed the door to the theory of unjust enrichment in English law.

[24.65] It was not until 1991 that the House of Lords completely opened the door left ajar by Lord Wright in *Fibrosa*.[34] In *Lipkin Gorman v Karpendale*,[35] the House of Lords authoritatively abandoned the implied contract theory and recognised unjust enrichment as a basis of restitution.[36]

[24.70] Recognition of unjust enrichment in Australia followed in parallel with the English Courts. Following on from the doubts expressed in *Fibrosa*,[37] various members of the High Court expressed the view that there was no need to imply a contract in cases of monies had and received. The concept of unjust enrichment appeared more appropriate. The High Court finally settled the question in *Pavey & Matthews Pty Ltd v Paul*.[38] This case involved a claim by a builder for *quantum meruit* under an unenforceable building contract. The court unanimously rejected the implied contract theory as the basis of a claim for *quantum meruit*, concluding that the law recognised an obligation to pay independent of the contract. In the words of Deane J:

> [unjust enrichment] constitutes a unifying legal concept which explains why the law recognises, in a variety of distinct categories of case, an obligation on the party of a defendant to make fair and just restitution for a benefit derived at the expense of a plaintiff and which assists in the determination, by the ordinary processes of legal reasoning, of the question whether the law should, in justice, recognise such an obligation in a new or developing category of case.[39]

[24.75] Despite some suggestion that unjust enrichment is a vague notion that provides a court with a general discretion to grant relief where the justice of the case requires, the High Court has limited the doctrine in certain respects. First, it does not provide the court with a judicial discretion to do whatever idiosyncratic notions of what is fair and just might dictate. In reaching a decision, the court should have regard to the body of authorities where relief has previously been granted. As stated by Lord Wright in *Fibrosa*, 'what is against conscience in this context has become more or less canalised or

---

32 Ibid at 452.
33 [1914] AC 398.
34 *Fibrosa Spolka Akcynja v Fairbairn Lawson Combe Barbour* [1943] AC 32.
35 [1991] 2 AC 548.
36 This was taken up in subsequent decisions of *Westdeutsche Landesbank Girozentrale v Council of the London Borough of Islington* [1996] AC 669 and *Kleinwort Benson Ltd v Glasgow City Council* [1997] 3 WLR 923.
37 *Fibrosa Spolka Akcynja v Fairbairn Lawson Coombe Barbour* [1943] AC 32.
38 (1987) 162 CLR 221.
39 Ibid at 257.

defined'.[40] Secondly, unjust enrichment as a cause of action in itself has not been recognised in Australia. To succeed in a claim a party must allege a specific unjust ground such as mistake or total failure of consideration.[41] Unjust enrichment is merely the jurisprudential basis of the primary claim for restitution. However, as indicated by Deane J, the concept is also useful in the identification of new categories of case in which the law should imply an obligation to pay reasonable remuneration or compensation.[42] The equation of restitution with unjust enrichment provides the cohesion necessary to bring a disparate number of legal categories together under one heading.

24.3 General elements of a restitutionary claim

[24.80] Once it is accepted that unjust enrichment underlies the majority of claims for restitution, it is necessary to consider each of the individual elements prior to an examination of certain common claims. The authorities recognise three elements to a claim in restitution. First, the defendant must be enriched; secondly, the enrichment must be at the plaintiff's expense; and finally, the enrichment must be unjustified. The allegation of a specific unjust factor or reason will be necessary. It will be insufficient to plead that the defendant is 'unjustly enriched' or that it is unfair the defendant retain the benefit.

24.3.1 Enrichment of the plaintiff

[24.85] Enrichment of the plaintiff is equivalent to the receipt of a benefit by the plaintiff. Loss to the plaintiff is generally irrelevant unless there is a corresponding benefit to the defendant. The aim of a claim in restitution will be to recover the actual benefit provided to another party or to recover the value of the benefit as compensation for the fact that it cannot be returned *in specie*. Issues concerning valuation of benefit will be considered later.[43]

(a) Money as a benefit
[24.90] The types of benefit a plaintiff may seek to recover can be broadly categorised as money or goods and services. Generally, benefit should be assessed objectively as something of market value. In the case of money paid by the plaintiff to the defendant, no particular problems arise. As stated by Lord Goff in *BP Exploration Co (Lybia) Ltd v Hunt No 2*,[44] money has 'the peculiar character of a universal medium of exchange, [b]y its receipt, the recipient is inevitably benefited'.

---

40   *Fibrosa Spolka Akcynuja v Fairbairn Lawson Combe Barbour* [1943] AC 32. This approach was also confirmed by the House of Lords in *Lipkin Gorman v Karpnale Ltd* [1991] 2 AC 548 at 578.
41   *David Securities Pty Ltd v Commonwealth Bank of Australia* (1992) 175 CLR 353.
42   But it should be noted that unjust enrichment is not the only basis upon which a party may obtain restitution. See P Birks, 'Equity, conscience, and unjust enrichment' (1999) 23 MULR 1
43   See [24.155].
44   [1979] 1 WLR 783 at 799.

(b) Services as a benefit

[24.95] The identification of an objective benefit becomes more difficult when considering services. The law acts to protect individual tastes and economic priorities, allowing a defendant to subjectively devalue something that may be of objective value. Say, for example, a person cleans someone's windscreen, without their request, while their car is stopped at the lights. Although the service has some objective value, the driver (defendant) is able to say 'I did not want my windscreen cleaned, therefore I do not have to pay'. The law will, however, not allow the defendant to subjectively devalue services or the product of services in certain cases. The first circumstance is where the defendant has requested the services and the plaintiff provides the services. If, in the above example, the defendant had asked the plaintiff to clean the windscreen, the defendant would not be able to later deny the benefit. This will also be the case even where there is no discernible outcome or product from the services.

Example: Brenner v First Artists' Management Pty Ltd[45]

The second plaintiff, Fenner was engaged as manager by the second defendant, Darrell Braithwaite, in June 1987. A commission of 15 per cent was agreed between the parties, but the basis on which it was to be calculated was not determined. Subsequently, the second defendant entered into a Management Agreement with First Artists' Management (FAM), which was set up by investors to manage the artist. A Management Agreement was entered into between the second defendant and the management company. In January 1988 the first plaintiff, Brenner, joined the Management Agreement between Braithwaite and Fenner. Braithwaite then requested Fenner and Brenner to become directors of FAM for the purpose of providing managerial services, in anticipation of the finalisation of a contract. The contract between the parties was never finalised. In late 1988, Braithwaite gave notice to Fenner and Brenner of a determination of their relationship. Brenner and Fenner commenced proceedings against FAM and Braithwaite seeking remuneration. FAM was subsequently dissolved, and they pursued their remuneration claim against Braithwaite only. Byrne J found that there was no contract between the parties, and therefore refused any claim based upon the contract. Byrne J did allow the claim in restitution.

Byrne J noted that in the case before him, the plaintiff had brought its claim on the basis that there was no contract between the parties. In such a case, His Honour considered the underlying basis of the claim must have been that the defendant had actually or constructively accepted the benefit of the plaintiff's services in circumstances where it would be unjust for that party to do so without making restitution to the plaintiffs. His Honour was concerned with the difficulty that arises where services, although requested by a party, do not provide any direct or tangible outcome. His Honour said:

> It seems to me unlikely that the law would introduce into this area the difficult and somewhat arbitrary distinction which has been drawn in the law of negligence between pure economic loss and physical loss. To take an

extreme case, it may be of benefit to an artist simply that it be known that a particular person has accepted the role of his or her manager or that the manager by accepting the artist as a client is then precluded from acting for a competitor of the artist. I have referred to non-economic benefits which may be requested, conferred and accepted. I would need clear authority to deny a claimant the right to restitution for such services when all the other requirements of the cause of action are established.

His Honour went on to consider the various authorities and concluded that:

The plaintiff was required to show that the defendant accepted the benefit of their services in circumstances where he as a reasonable person should realise that the plaintiff would expect to be paid for them. His Honour emphasised the fact that it must be the defendant who accepts the services if the claim in restitution was to succeed.

[24.100] Services that are requested, but only partially performed, provide a further layer of complexity. As previously discussed, a plaintiff who provides only partial services to a defendant will have difficulty in claiming restitution if she or he is in breach of contract.[46] On the other hand, if the defendant by his or her own breach has prevented the completion of the contract, the plaintiff will usually be entitled to recover pursuant to a *quantum meruit*.[47] In the latter case, the defendant will be prevented from arguing subjective devaluation due to the implied acceptance of the work through their conduct.[48] It is also clearly the case that to allow the defendant to claim subjective devaluation would be unjust in that particular case. In the first situation, however, the defendant will be able to claim there is no subjective benefit from the partially completed work. Despite the fact that the defendant may in fact have received a benefit through saved expenses, the current authorities do not allow recovery by the plaintiff unless free acceptance of the work is proved.[49]

[24.105] The second circumstance in which the defendant is not able to use subjective devaluation is where the plaintiff's services are freely accepted by the defendant. The exact meaning of free acceptance has given rise to much academic comment, but in simple terms, free acceptance involves the acceptance of a benefit in circumstances where the defendant exercised a choice whether to accept or reject the benefit. If the defendant has had a choice whether to accept or reject, it will usually be unjust to retain the benefit without making restitution.[50]

---

46   See [19.255]–[19.270].
47   See *Brenner v First Artists' Management Pty Ltd* [1993] 2 VLR 221 at 263; *Iezzi Constructions Pty Ltd v Currumbin Development Pty Ltd* [1995] 2 Qd R 350; *Independent Grocers Co-Operative Ltd v Noble Lowndes Superannuation Consultants Ltd* (1993) 60 SASR 525.
48   K Mason and JW Carter, *Restitution Law in Australia*, Butterworths, Sydney, 1995, p 52.
49   See [19.255]–[19.270].
50   See *Brenner v First Artists' Management Pty Ltd* [1993] 2 VLR 221 at 257; *Angelopoulos v Sabatino* (1995) 65 SASR 1 at 10–11; *Steele v Tardiani* (1946) 72 CLR 386.

Example

A woman returns from holiday to find that a garage has been built beside her house by her neighbour, either thinking that the land was his or that the woman would let him have it. Assume that the garage cost $2000 to build and that the land is now worth $3000 more on the market than it was without the garage. Is the woman enriched? It would be difficult to hold that a garage was an incontrovertibly valuable benefit, since many people with means and space for a garage may prefer to have a greenhouse or leave things as they are. So the woman is not enriched. She uses the garage. That changes nothing. Privately she is delighted to have the garage and it is the case that she might very well have decided to pay for one to be built. All that she has to show is that in fact she made no choice to have it.

Assume now that the same woman comes back early and sees the work beginning. Knowing what mistake or misprediction the neighbour has made she decides to withdraw to her country cottage until the work is finished, so as to be able to take advantage of the work. She returns when the garage is finished. This time she is enriched. The reason is that she cannot conscientiously assert 'Oh but I did not choose to have this garage built'. She had her opportunity to say so earlier. It is not that her neglect of that opportunity affirmatively indicates that she attached value to the garage; it merely makes it impossible for her to get her appeal to the subjectivity of value.[51]

(c)   Incontrovertible benefit

[24.110] An incontrovertible benefit is one no reasonable person could deny.[52] It will generally take the form of a positive gain to the wealth of the defendant or a negative saving. The payment of money to the defendant will always be considered a benefit. To that extent, it is possible to say money is an incontrovertible benefit.[53] Services will generally only constitute an incontrovertible benefit if they confer a positive gain to the wealth of the defendant. This in itself raises the issue of whether the incontrovertible benefit needs to be actually realised by the defendant, or whether the defendant is liable to pay for a realisable benefit. No clear direction has been provided by the courts, but it is suggested that cases of improvements to a chattel will be treated differently from improvements to land. In *Greenwood v Bennett*,[54] the owner of a prestige automobile was ordered to provide restitution to a person who undertook repairs and improvements to the car without the knowledge of the owner. The owner had sold the car prior to the proceedings. The requirement to pay was based on the accretion to the wealth of the owner despite the fact the owner did not freely accept the work. However, in *Republic Resources Ltd v Ballem*,[55] the plaintiffs, pursuant to the terms of a

---

51   Example from P Birks, 'In defence of free acceptance', in A Burrows (ed), *Essays on the Law of Restitution*, Clarendon Press, Oxford, 1991, pp 128–131.
52   P Birks, *An Introduction to the Law of Restitution*, rev edn, Oxford University Press, Oxford, 1989, pp 116–117.
53   *BP Exploration Co (Libya) Ltd v Hunt* (No 2) (1979) 1 WLR 783.
54   [1973] 1 QB 195. Refer also to *Steele v Tardiani* (1946) 72 CLR 386.
55   [1982] 1 WLR 692.

lease, drilled the land of the defendant. After the lease had expired, the plaintiffs claimed the value of the improvements to the land. The court refused relief due to the uncertainty surrounding the valuation of the improvements and the likelihood of using the oil wells in the future. Goff and Jones[56] agree with the maintenance of this difference between land and chattels:

> It may appear odd to allow a bona fide improver of a chattel a claim for improvements and to deny the bona fide improver of land a comparable claim. But no English lawyer should be surprised that our law should treat chattels differently from land. Most chattels are not unique: they are fungible and replaceable. It may be unreasonable to require the owner of land to sell or mortgage in order to recompense the improver for unsolicited improvements.

(d) Goods as a benefit

[24.115] Restitution for goods delivered presents similar problems to services rendered. If the goods have been delivered at the request of the defendant and the defendant has accepted the goods, the defendant will be required to pay the price under the contract. This will be a claim for the contract price, not in restitution. If the defendant has not accepted the goods the defendant will not be required to pay, but the plaintiff will have a claim in damages for breach of contract. No claim in restitution can be made because the defendant has not retained the goods. The only case in which restitution will be relevant will be where the defendant has freely accepted the goods by using or consuming them.[57]

24.3.2 Enrichment at the plaintiff's expense

[24.120] In a claim for restitution based on unjust enrichment, the benefit will be provided at the expense of the plaintiff if there is a subtraction from the wealth of the plaintiff.[58] Generally, there will be no difficulty with this aspect in the context of a claim linked to a contract. The plaintiff will have provided either money or services at their expense. However, one particular issue arises in the context of moneys paid under a mistake. What if the plaintiff has recouped or can recoup the cost from a third party? As restitution is concerned with the return of benefits received by one party and not with the loss by the other, the fact payments have previously been recouped will not affect the claim. The only exception to this is where the plaintiff acts as a conduit of the payment for a third party. In that case the payment is at the expense of the third party and not the plaintiff.

---

56   R Goff & G Jones, *The Law of Restitution*, 3rd edn, Sweet & Maxwell, London 1986, pp 113–114.
57   See *Sumpter v Hedges* [1898] 1 QB 673.
58   A benefit may also be obtained at the expense of the plaintiff where a wrong is committed against the plaintiff. This will allow a claim based upon the wrong. Once the elements are proved, the plaintiff may be able to choose compensation or restitution. This type of claim is different to the type under consideration and will not be examined further.

Example: Commissioner of State Revenue v Royal Insurance Australia[59]

Royal Insurance mistakenly paid stamp duty of premiums received from the holders of certain workers' compensation insurance policies. Royal sought repayment of the moneys from the Commissioner of Stamp duties. Royal had, however, charged the stamp duty to the holders of the policies.

The Commissioner for Stamp Duties refused to refund the moneys to Royal Insurance on the basis that Royal would receive a windfall.

The court considered that although it would be difficult for Royal to seek to refund the stamp duty to all its policy-holders, this was not a bar to the relief claimed. The critical question in the case was whether the Commissioner was unjustly enriched at the expense of Royal. The fact that Royal had charged duty to its policy-holders suggested that the enrichment of the Commissioner had taken place not at the expense of Royal but at the expense of its policy holders. The Court concluded that the fact Royal had passed on the cost to its policy-holders was not sufficient to deny a remedy. It was still possible to say an unjust enrichment had occurred at the expense of the plaintiff, notwithstanding that the plaintiff may recoup the outgoing by means of transactions with the third party. The aim of restitutionary relief is not to provide compensation for loss but to restore unjust enrichments. Therefore it is irrelevant that the plaintiff may have in fact recouped the expense.[60]

24.3.3   Unjustified enrichment

[24.125] The final requirement for a claim in restitution is the existence of a factor that makes it unjust for the defendant to retain a benefit. It is not sufficient for the plaintiff to allege that the retention of the benefit is unfair or unconscientious.[61] A specific ground or unjust factor must be stated. The onus will be on the plaintiff to show that the defendant has been unjustly enriched.

[24.130] A number of unjust factors have been identified by the Australian courts:

- mistake;
- duress;
- legal compulsion;
- free acceptance;
- total failure of consideration; and
- illegality.[62]

[24.135] Other potential factors that are recognised in England but not in Australia are an *ultra vires* demand by a public authority[63] and wrongful retention of property. Whether these will become recognised within Australia is difficult to predict. The

---

59   (1994) 182 CLR 51.

60   Compare M McInnes, 'The structures and challenges of unjust enrichment', in M McInnes (ed), *Restitution: Developments in Unjust Enrichment*, LBC Information Services, Sydney, 1996 pp 32–34; M McInnes, 'Mistaken payments returned to the High Court: *Commissioner of Revenue v Royal Insurance*' (1996) 22 *Mon ULR* 209, 236–243.

61   *David Securities Pty Ltd v Commonwealth Bank of Australia* (1992) 175 CLR 353 at 378–379.

62   However, illegality may not justify the return of moneys paid under an enforceable contract. *Roxborough v Rothmans of Pall Mall Australia Ltd* (1999) 161 ALR 253.

63   *Woolich Equitable Building Society v Inland Revenue Commission* [1993] AC 70 at 171–172.

court may use the underlying concept of unjust enrichment to develop the law incrementally in these areas. Unconscionability is not recognised as an unjust factor in either England or Australia.

[24.140] The unjust factor alleged by the plaintiff must also be a cause of the defendant's receipt of the benefit.[64] The 'but for' test is usually adopted as the general test of causation in this case. Therefore, the plaintiff must be able to prove that but for the unjust factor, the benefit would not have been conferred on the defendant. Where the unjust factor is duress, it need only be one of the factors, and not the sole factor.[65]

24.4 Total failure of consideration

[24.145] Total failure of consideration will be the underlying unjust fact in the majority of claims for money had and received. The claim is premised on the fact that the plaintiff has received no consideration for his or her payment and the contract does not provide for the money to be retained by the defendant.[66] Although a softening of approach is becoming evident, the current requirement is for the failure of consideration to be total. This means a party who receives part of the consideration bargained for, in return for his or her payment, will be unable to recover the payment, as the failure will only be partial. However the strict requirement for a total failure of consideration may be overcome in some cases, where specific portions of the contract price are paid in return for discrete portions of the agreed return.[67] This approach will depend in each case upon an interpretation of the contractual terms.[68]

Consideration is used in this context to denote performance of the defendant's promise, not the promise itself. This was confirmed by the High Court in *Baltic Shipping Co v Dillon*.[69] According to the High Court, the question the plaintiff should ask is 'what did I bargain to receive for my money and have I received it?'.

Example: Rowland v Divall[70]

The plaintiff purchased a motor vehicle from the defendant and used it for several months. It subsequently appeared that the defendant had no title to the vehicle, and the plaintiff was forced to return the vehicle to the true owner.

The plaintiff succeeded in recovering the purchase price of the car based on a total failure of consideration.

The fact that the plaintiff used the vehicle for several months did not prevent the plaintiff from asserting that there was a total failure of consideration. This was because:

---

64   *David Securities v Commonwealth Bank of Australia* (1992) 175 CLR 353.
65   *Crescendo Management v Westpac Banking Corp* (1988) 19 NSWLR 40.
66   If the contract provides for the money to be retained by the defendant, the proper claim is for relief against forfeiture in equity. See [20.445]–[20.455].
67   See for example *McDonald v Dennys Lascelles Ltd* (1933) 48 CLR 457.
68   See *Roxborough v Rothmans of Pall Mall Australia Ltd* (1999) 161 ALR 253.
69   (1993) 67 ALJR 228.
70   [1923] 2 KB 500.

the buyer [did] not receive any part of that which he contracted to receive—namely, the property and right to possession—and that being so, there has been a total failure of consideration.[71]

[24.150] In *Rowland v Divall*, the bargained for consideration was property in the chattel. A similar approach is taken to contracts for the sale of land, where the purchaser will usually have bargained for the title to the property. If the purchaser does not receive the title, there is a total failure of consideration. This will not always be the case however, and each contract should be closely examined to ascertain what the party bargained for by the payment of the money.

Example: Shaw v Ball[72]

The plaintiff entered into a contract for the purchase of the defendant's business. The purchase price was £5500. The plaintiff paid the defendant £2000. The purchaser took early possession of the premises and enjoyed the goodwill for a time. During the time of possession, the plaintiff carried on the business as if it was his own. The defendant terminated the contract for the plaintiff's breach. The plaintiff claimed repayment of the £2000. The court denied restitution to the plaintiff because there was no total failure of consideration. The goodwill was part of the consideration bargained for, and the plaintiff had enjoyed it for some time.

24.5 Valuation of a benefit

[24.155] The value of a monetary benefit will obviously be equal to the money paid to the defendant. When valuing non-monetary benefits, the court will fundamentally be concerned with what is a fair and reasonable remuneration for the benefit accepted by the defendant. The court may choose to calculate the fair market value of the work done or materials supplied, or it may use the enhanced value of the property in exceptional cases. A comprehensive guide to the principles the court may adopt in determining the quantum of relief are set out by Byrne J in *Brenner v First Artists' Management Pty Ltd*.[73] It is useful to summarise these principles:

1   The fundamental yardstick is that a fair and reasonable remuneration or compensation for the benefit accepted by the other party will be awarded. Where the plaintiff performs services at the request of the defendant, the fair value of the work of the plaintiff will ordinarily be the remuneration calculated at a reasonable rate for the work actually done. The assessment will have regard to what the defendant would have had to pay had the benefit been conferred under a normal commercial arrangement. The enquiry is not primarily directed at the cost to the plaintiff of performing the work, since the law is not compensating that party for loss suffered.[74]

2   Where the parties have agreed upon a price for certain services, and those services have in fact been performed—but for some reason the agreement is no longer

---

71   Ibid at (at 507).
72   (1963) SR (NSW) 910. See also *Pitt v Curotta* (1931) 31 SR (NSW) 477.
73   [1993] 2 VR 221 at 262.
74   See *Renard Constructions (NE) Pty Ltd v Minister for Public Works* (1992) 26 NSWLR 234 at 276.

effective or on foot—the agreed price is evidence of the value that the parties themselves put on the services, and may be received as evidence of the appropriate remuneration.[75] The court may also have regard to the contract price where the services have not been totally performed by the plaintiff. In such a case, however, there may be difficulties in calculating a pro rata amount for the agreed price to the incomplete works.[76] The court is not bound to implement a pro rata method of calculation and may modify this to determine what in all the circumstances is a fair recompense.

3   In some cases, the method of assessing the benefit of the work may be by applying an hourly rate to the time involved in performing those services. If this procedure is adopted, the court may have regard to the rate of remuneration that is commonly accepted in the industry. Additional consideration should be the standing of the person performing the services, the difficulty of the task, the fact that the services required imagination and creativity that may be difficult to discern in the end product.

4   If the services are of a kind where it is difficult or impossible to assess the number of hours involved or to itemise precise services, the court may make a global assessment of the remuneration that is fair and reasonable. Regard may be had to the value of any improvements to property in the hands of the defendant.

5   Where it is customary in the industry for the services to be recompensed by commission, the court may have regard to what is a reasonable commission and apply it where appropriate.[77] This manner of valuation causes difficulties where the event giving rise to the payment of commission has not occurred. In such a case, it cannot be appropriate to treat the benefits to the employer as being the procuring of a sale that has not occurred nor is it appropriate to value the lost chance of the agent to make this sale. No authorities appear to resolve this issue.[78]

24.6   Restitution between contracting parties

[24.160] An action for restitution will operate outside of the contractual relationship of the parties; it is closely linked to considerations of justice and equity rather than compensation for loss or damage suffered. This chapter is limited to the role of restitution in the context of contractual relationships. In particular, restitution is relevant to the rights of parties to recover benefits conferred pursuant to void and unenforceable contracts and contracts that are discharged for breach. It is important to note that an action for restitution may not be brought while an enforceable contract is on foot between the parties. However, an action may be commenced after the contract is terminated or found to be void or ineffective.[79] Where a contract has been breached, the plaintiff may bring alternative claims in contract or restitution, but is only entitled to a remedy

---

75   See *Pavey & Matthews v Paul* (1987) 162 CLR 221.
76   See *Jennings Construction Ltd v O H & M Birt Pty Ltd* (Supreme Court NSW unreported, 16 December 1988, per Cole J).
77   See *Way v Latilla* [1937] 3 All ER 759 at 764.
78   See *Brenner v First Artists' Management Pty Ltd* [1993] 2 VR 221.
79   *Newitt v Leitch* (1997) 6 Tas LR 396 at 408; *Update Constructions Pty Ltd v Rozelle Child Care Centre Ltd* (1990) 20 NSWLR 251 at 275; *Pavey Matthews Pty Ltd v Paul* (1987) 162 CLR 221; *Christiani & Nielsen Pty Ltd v Foliath Portland Cement Co Ltd* (1993) 2 Tas LR 122.

pursuant to one. In *Baltic Shipping Co v Dillon*,[80] Deane and Dawson JJ concluded that a claim in restitution for return of the purchase price would not succeed if damages were awarded because:

> the promisee, having received full compensation for non-performance of the promise, is not entitled to a refund of the price upon payment of which the performance of the promise was conditioned. Were it otherwise, the promisee 'would have the equivalent' of performance of the contractual promise 'without having bourne the expense' which he or she had agreed to pay for it.[81]

A claimant will be required to make an election between damages and restitution at the time of judgment.

As a claim for restitution is available independently of the contractual relationship between the parties, does this mean that the contract will be irrelevant to the deliberations of the court? In most cases, the terms of the contract will have little impact on whether a restitutionary claim exists. However, the contract may be used as evidence of the value of goods or services provided.[82] This will apply whether the contract is terminated, unenforceable, or void. Nevertheless, some commentators have suggested that the courts should go further and use the contract price as a ceiling for the claim—but this has been rejected by the courts in some jurisdictions.[83]

[24.165] The remainder of this chapter will examine common claims in restitution related in some way to the rights of a contracting party.

24.7 Recovery of moneys paid by mistake

[24.170] The law recognises the right of a person who mistakenly pays money to another to recover the unintended payment. For example, where a cargo of goods is insured under a policy of insurance and the insurer pays out a claim in the belief that the cargo has perished, when in fact it was sold, the insurer will be able to recover the payment made because of the mistake.[84] Another common situation is where a bank pays a cheque drawn on its customer's account in favour of a third party, in circumstances where the payment has been stopped by the customer. The bank will be able to recover from the payee despite its negligence, but subject to the payee having changed their position.[85] Until recently, distinctions were drawn between the different types of mistake involved. Any payment based upon a mistake that did not relate to liability—or was not as between plaintiff and defendant, or was a mistake of law—was said to not be recoverable. Since the decision of *David Securities Pty Ltd v Commonwealth Bank of Australia*,[86] these types of limitations have been removed. Most impor-

---

80   (1993) 67 ALJR 228.
81   Ibid at 248.
82   *Pavey & Matthews Pty Ltd v Paull* (1987) 162 CLR 221; *Gino d'Alessandro Constructions Pty Ltd v Powis* [1987] 2 Qd R 40, 58–59.
83   *Renard Constructions (ME) Pty Ltd v Minister for Public Works* (1992) 26 NSWLR 234, 271, 276–278, 283; *Iezzi Constructions Pty Ltd v Watkins Pacific (Qld) Pty Ltd* [1995] 2 Qd R 350 at 355–356, 369–370.
84   *Norwich Union Fire Insurance Society Ltd v William H Price Ltd* [1934] AC 455.
85   See *Commercial Bank of Australia Ltd v Younis* [1979] 1 NSWLR 444. In relation to the defence of change of position see [24.325]–[24.335].
86   (1992) 175 CLR 353.

tantly, the High Court has recognised that no distinction should be made between mistakes of fact and mistakes of law. Instead, the court has chosen to limit recovery based upon whether the payment was made in voluntary submission to an honest claim. This change to the court's approach is due to the recognition of unjust enrichment as the basis of a claim in restitution and the basis of the claim for mistaken payments. In *Australia and New Zealand Banking Group Ltd v Westpac Banking Corp*,[87] the court clearly recognised the right to recover for a mistaken payment:

> Receipt of a payment which has been made under a fundamental mistake is one of the categories of case in which the facts give rise to a prima facie obligation to make restitution, in the sense of compensation for the benefit of unjust enrichment, to the person who has sustained the countervailing detriment.[88]

The authorities set out a variety of categories of mistake that are sufficient to support a prima facie right to recovery. Mistake in this context includes a belief as to the existence or non-existence of a state of affairs, factual or legal, which turns out to be mistaken. A person who transfers money to another may be moved to do so under the influence of a mistake. The mistake can be of several varieties, for example:

- A mistake of fact giving rise to a legal liability to make payment. For example, where the payer expends money to buy or lease land owned by the payer or expends money pursuant to a contract that is in fact void.[89]
- A mistake of fact that a legal liability will accrue in the future. For example, where a party makes a payment for the purpose of meeting an anticipated liability although they knew no actual liability had yet accrued.[90]
- The payer has deposited money thinking in error that the payer was a bank.
- Payment is made in the mistaken belief that a seller has title to the land or goods to be sold.[91]
- The payer pays in the mistaken belief that he or she was obliged to pay when in fact the payment was not legally obliged to be paid.

[24.175] Prior to the decision in *David Securities Pty Ltd v Commonwealth Bank of Australia*,[92] the payer may have been entitled to recover the payment in all but the last example. In that example, recovery would have been precluded because the mistake was one of law. Since that decision, the distinction between law and fact for the purpose of mistaken payments has become largely irrelevant. Instead, the High Court has chosen to distinguish between the types of mistaken payments on the basis that a voluntary payment is not recoverable.

---

87 (1998) 164 CLR 662.
88 Ibid at 673. See also *Hydro-electric Commission of the Township of Nipea v Ontario Hydro* (1982) 132 DLR (3d) 193 at 209 per Dickson J; *David Securities Pty Ltd v Commonwealth Bank of Australia* (1992) 175 CLR 353 at 375, 393.
89 See *Chirnside v Keating* (1889) 15 VLR 697; *Rover International Ltd v Cannon Film Sales Ltd* [1989] 1 WLR 912.
90 *Kerrison v Glyn, Mills, Currie and Co* (1911) 17 Com Cas 41.
91 *Commercial Bank of Australia Ltd v Younis* [1979] 1 NSWLR 444. See also *Bank of New South Wales v Murphett* [1983] VLR 489.
92 (1992) 175 CLR 353.

24.7.1   *Historical development: recovery for payments made under mistake of fact*

[24.180] Recovery for the types of mistakes of fact described above will prima facie be available on the basis of the unjust enrichment of the defendant. Traditionally, the law applied 'the supposed liability test' as set out in *Aiken v Short*.[93] According to Bramwell B, a person could only recover money paid under a mistake of fact. The mistake should be of a type that if the mistaken fact were true, the plaintiff would be liable to pay the money in discharge of a liability. However, if the mistaken fact were of a kind that if it had been true, it would only have been desirable that the plaintiff pay money, then the money is not recoverable. The supposed liability test was slowly eroded over time, with the courts creating exceptional categories where recovery was permitted despite the mistake not being a liability mistake. For example, recovery was permitted where the plaintiff paid money under the mistaken belief of a legal liability to a third party,[94] and where the money was paid under the mistaken belief that there was a moral as opposed to a legal obligation to pay.[95] The supposed liability test was soon replaced by the requirement for a fundamental mistake. In *Australian and New Zealand Banking Group v Westpac Corp*,[96] the High Court left open the question of whether the requirement meant any more than that the mistake had to cause the payment.[97] In England, the High Court considered that the right to the recovery of the payment made under a mistake of fact arose where the mistake caused the payment.

Example: Barclays Bank Ltd v WJ Simms & Sons[98]

A housing association drew a cheque of $24 000 on its account with Barclays in favour of a building company. The following day, the building company went into receivership, and the housing association phoned the bank and stopped the cheque. Despite noting the instruction to stop the cheque in their computer, a clerk paid the cheque in error. Barclays commenced an action against the receiver, claiming that the moneys had been paid under a mistake of fact. Croft J considered all the previous authorities including *Kelly v Solari*,[99] and established the following guidelines.

1   If a person pays money to another under a mistake of fact that causes him to make the payment, he is prima facie entitled to recover it as money paid under a mistake of fact.[100]

2   The claim may fail however if:

   (i)   the payer intends that the payer shall have the money in all events whether the fact be true or false;

---

93   (1856) 1 H & N 210; 156 ER 1180.
94   *Jones Ltd v Waring & Gillow Ltd* [1926] AC 670.
95   *Larner v London City Council* [1949] 2 KB 683. See also *Morgan v Ashcroft* [1938] 1 KB 49.
96   (1988) 164 CLR 662.
97   See however, *Bank of New South Wales v Murphett* [1983] 1 VLR 489 at 484 where Crockett J recognised that a fundamental mistake was merely one which caused the payment.
98   [1980] QB 677.
99   (1841) 9 MW 54.
100   If the money is paid under a contract then there can be no relief unless the contract is void, rescinded, terminated or frustrated.

(ii) the payment is made for a debt owed to the payee (or a principal on whose behalf he is authorised to receive the payment) by the payer or by a third party by whom he is authorised to discharge the debt;

(iii) the payee has changed his position in good faith, or is deemed in law to have done so.

His Honour rejected the previous analysis, which required the mistake to induce the payer to believe that he was liable to pay the money to the payee and that the mistake had to be as between payer and payee.[101]

24.7.2 Contemporary approach: recovery for mistakes of law and fact

[24.185] As indicated by the Restatement of the Law of Restitution:[102]

Until the 19th century no distinction was made between mistake of fact and mistake of law restitution was freely granted both in law and in equity to persons who had paid money to another because of a mistake of law.[103]

In *Bilby v Lumley*,[104] Lord Elenbrough CJ refused recovery of moneys paid under a mistake of law. It is now accepted that His Honour based his decision on an inapplicable maxim (*antia juris non excusat*), which started the whole 'fact versus law' debate. The decision became known as authority for the proposition that moneys paid under a mistake of law were not recoverable.[105] Despite the growing application of this principle, there also existed a growing mass of exemptions that tended to consume the general principle; for example:

* disbursements of public authorities with statutory authority;[106]
* payments made to an officer of the court;[107]
* certain mistakes in payments to public authorities;
* payments mistakenly made by the court;[108]
* certain payments by personal representatives and trustees.

Despite this raft of exceptions, the distinction between mistakes of fact and law is no longer relevant to the law of Canada[109] or Australia,[110] and has been doubted in the United Kingdom.[111]

---

101 These principles were approved by the High Court in *David Securities v Commonwealth Bank of Australia* (1992) 175 CLR 353 at 376.
102 American Law Institute 1937, p 179.
103 *Farmer v Rundel* (1772) 2 W Bl 824 at 825; 96 ER 485 at 486.
104 (1802) 2 East 469; 102 ER 448.
105 See *Werrin v Commonwealth* (1938) 59 CLR 150 at 158–160; *York Air-conditioning and Refrigeration (Australasia) Pty Ltd v Commonwealth* (1949) 80 CLR 111 at 30; *Yarmirr v Australian Telecommunications Corp* (1990) 96 ALR 739.
106 *Auckland Harbour Board v The King* [1924] AC 318.
107 *Re Roberts* (1976) 26 FLR 330.
108 *Re Birkbeck Permanent Benefit Building Society* (1915) 1 Chancellery 91.
109 *Air Canada v British Columbia* (1989) 59 DLR (4th) 161.
110 *David Securities Pty Ltd v Commonwealth Bank of Australia* (1992) 175 CLR 353.
111 *Woolwich Equitable Building Society v Inland Revenue Commission* [1993] AC 70 at 164.

[24.190] The current perspective is provided by the High Court in *David Securities v Commonwealth Bank of Australia*,[112] where the court decided that the distinction between mistakes of law and mistakes of fact should no longer form part of the law of Australia. Whether a recipient is unjustly enriched by a payment is not determined according to the type of mistake.

[24.195] In *David Securities*, a customer paid the mortgagee bank money, in addition to interest, pursuant to a covenant in a mortgage. The covenant was designed to gross–up the amount of withholding tax that the Australian customer deducted from interest payable to its overseas lender. Unbeknown to the customer, s 261 of the *Income Tax Assessment Act* 1936 (Cth) avoided the covenant. The customer's claim to set off the additional amounts was rejected by the Full Federal Court applying the traditional prohibition on recovery from mistake of law. On appeal, the High Court overturned this decision. The High Court indicated that where a mistake of either fact or law caused the plaintiff to make the payment, recovery in restitution for unjust enrichment would be prima facie available. The High Court considered two main issues. First, the type of mistake that will justify a prima facie right to restitution; secondly, the defence of voluntary payment. First, the Court considered that the mistake did not have to be fundamental. It was satisfactory if the mistake caused the payment. Therefore, recovery will be allowed where:

> The payer will be entitled prima facie to recover moneys paid under a mistake if it appears that the moneys were paid by the payer in the mistaken belief that he or she was under a legal obligation to pay the moneys or that the payee was legally entitled to payment of the moneys such a mistake would be causative of the payment.[113]

[24.200] Secondly, there was no need for the mistake to be one in relation to the liability of the payer to make the payment. The High court considered that the crucial factor was not the type of mistake but whether the recipient was enriched as a result of the mistake. Thirdly, in order to prove it is unjust for the money to be retained by the defendant it was only necessary to show the payment was made under a mistake. It was not necessary to show there was any compulsion, duress, or undue influence in order for the retention of the money to be unjust.[114]

[24.205] The propositions set out in *David Securities Pty Ltd v Commonwealth Bank of Australia*[115] provide only for the prima facie position of a payer under a mistake of fact or law. The payee is entitled to defend the claim first, on the basis that the payment was voluntary; secondly, on the basis that the monies were due anyway; thirdly, on the basis that the payments were made for good consideration and received in good faith; fourthly, wherever a payment would frustrate the policy of a statutory or common law rule; and lastly, where the payee has changed their position in reliance on the payment. To counter the final defence, it is important that the payer give notice to the

---

112 (1992) 175 CLR 353.
113 Ibid at 378.
114 See also *Australia New Zealand Banking Corporation Group v Westpac Banking Corporation* (1988) 164 CLR 662 at 673.
115 (1992) 175 CLR 353.

payee as soon as the mistake is discovered. This will prevent the payee from later claiming that their position was changed in reliance on, or on faith of, the payment.[116] The main exception considered by the High Court was where the payment was voluntary, and therefore the plaintiff was not labouring under any mistake at all. The High Court, with a view to maintaining certainty in transactions, considered that all of the previous cases, including *Bilbie v Lumley*,[117] could be explained on the basis of a voluntary payment. The payment was considered to be voluntary if:

> The payment is voluntary or there is an election if the plaintiff chooses to make the payment even though he or she believes the particular law or contractual provision requiring the payment is, or may be, invalid, or is not concerned to query whether payment is legally required; he or she is prepared to assume the validity of the obligation or is prepared to make the payment irrespective of the validity or invalidity of the obligation, rather than contest the claim for payment.

This would mean that where a payer has a conscious but mistaken misunderstanding of the payer's legal obligation to pay, or the payee's legal right to receive the money, the payment will be recoverable in restitution. However, where the payer intends to settle a claim honestly made by the payee, or knows the money is not due, or has no belief one way or the other on the matter, but is willing to pay because of the relationship with the payee, the decision of *David Securities* would deny payment.[118] Consequently, the majority judgment has been criticised by Brennan J[119] and Professor Birks[120] on the basis that it will refuse relief to all in a case of mistake of law unless the plaintiff has consciously considered the validity of the particular obligation and has reached a mistaken conclusion. This would result in relief being denied in relation to tax or local government payments where the taxpayer has reasonably assumed the validity of an imposition and will simply be unaware of the possibility that the payment may not be due.

24.8   Void contracts

[24.210] A void contract may arise where there is a common or mutual mistake[121] or because there is uncertainty in the terms of the agreement.[122] Once it is clear that the contract is void, a claim in restitution may be brought, even though any other claims on the contract are likely to fail. The fact the contract is void will not support a claim for restitution. The plaintiff must prove one of the accepted unjust factors.[123] Usually,

---

116 Defences are discussed further at [24.320].
117 (1802) 2 East 469; 102 ER 448.
118 See, for example, *Roxborough v Rothmans of Pall Mall Australia Ltd* (1999) 161 ALR 253 where the applicant was denied restitution of licence fees paid under a contract subsequently declared illegal after consideration of the *Business Franchise Licences (Tobacco) Act* 1987 (NSW) by the High Court. The Federal Court held that the payments had not been made under a mistaken belief but voluntarily in satisfaction of a valid contract. The fact the licence fee was later ruled invalid was irrelevant.
119 Ibid at 398.
120 P Birks, 'Modernising the Law of Restitution' (1993) 109 LQR 164 at 167.
121 See Chapter 14.
122 See Chapter 4.
123 *David Securities Pty Ltd v Commonwealth Bank of Australia* (1992) 175 CLR 353.

a plaintiff seeking to recover money paid will be able to allege a total failure of consideration. If the plaintiff is seeking payment for services rendered pursuant to the void contract, free acceptance of the services may be alleged. A contract void for illegality presents its own complex problems and is considered in another chapter.[124] Even where there is a total failure of consideration, the plaintiff still may not succeed in the recovery of money either because:

- it would be against policy for the plaintiff to recover where the contract is void for illegality;[125] or
- the plaintiff is prevented from relying on their own wrongful conduct in order to establish the claim.[126]

24.8.1   Recovery of money paid

[24.215] As indicated, money paid pursuant to a void contract may be recovered if there is a total failure of consideration.[127] For example, if a contract for the sale of land is void and the purchaser does not receive title to the land, any moneys paid may be recovered because the purchaser has not received what was bargained for: title to the land.[128] If some consideration has been received for the payments, no recovery will be allowed. In this respect, a void contract is treated no differently from an ineffective contract or a contract discharged by breach. A payment may also be recovered where it is paid under the mistaken belief that a valid contract has been formed.

Example: Rover International Ltd v Cannon Film Sales Ltd[129]

Rover entered into a joint agreement with Thorne EMI. Under this agreement, Thorne was to supply master prints of films to Rover and Rover was to arrange for the dubbing and distribution of the films to Italian cinemas. Rover made substantial advance payments in the nature of royalties to Thorne; in return, Rover acquired the right to earn a substantial share of the gross receipts from the films in Italy. Thorne was subsequently taken over by Cannon, which searched for a reason to terminate the agreement. It was discovered that Rover had not been incorporated at the date of entering the joint agreement, and that the contract was therefore void. By this time, much of the dubbing work had been done by Rover. Pending the determination of legal proceedings, the parties entered into an escrow agreement that provided that all future royalty payments were to be paid to a joint solicitor's account pending the outcome of the trial. After this time, Rover commenced distribution of a film prior to the approved date. Cannon purported to terminate the agreement for Rover's repudiation, and Rover claimed recovery of the advance royalty payments. The trial judge found that the joint venture agreement was at all times void *ab initio*.

---

124 See Chapter 18.
125 This is consistent with the approach in *Nelson v Nelson* (1995) 184 CLR 538 in relation to illegal contracts generally.
126 See, for example, *Bank of South Australia Ltd v Ferguson* (1996) SASR 77.
127 The principle of total failure of consideration will have application irrespective of the type of contract. See *Westdeutsche Landesbank Girozentrale v Council of the London Borough of Islington* [1996] AC 669 per Lord Goff.
128 See *Kleinwort Benson Ltd v Birmingham City Council* [1996] 3 WLR 1139 at 1142–1144.
129 [1989] 1 WLR 912.

The trial judge refused Rover's claim for return of the royalties on the basis that there was no failure of consideration. The English Court of Appeal overturned this decision on the basis that the judge was incorrect in law. The Court considered that if the judge had been directed to the appropriate test—that is, whether or not the party claiming total failure of consideration had in fact received any part of the benefit bargained for under the contract or purported contract, his Honour would not have reached the same conclusion. The Court of Appeal noted that this test was a settled part of English law referring to the *Fibrosa*[130] case and several others.[131] The Court considered that the position of Rover was similar to the cases cited. Although Rover had taken possession of the film, possession was merely incidental to the performance of the contract, in the sense that it enabled Rover to render services in relation to the films by dubbing them and preparing them for the market. These were associated with the delivery of the films; and delivery and possession were not what Rover bargained for. The relevant bargain was the opportunity to earn a substantial share of the gross receipts with the certainty of at least breaking even by recouping their advance. Due to the invalidity of the agreement, Rover got nothing of what it had bargained for, and there was clearly a total failure of consideration.

24.8.2   Payment for services rendered

[24.220] Compensation for services rendered pursuant to a void transaction will be possible if the other person has benefited from the services. As discussed previously services will be a benefit to the defendant if:
* the defendant requested the services; or
* the defendant freely accepted the services; or
* the defendant is incontrovertibly benefited by the services.

[24.225] It will be unnecessary for the defendant to both request and freely accept the services, although in most cases involving a contract (even a void contract) a request will usually be present.

Example: Way v Latilla[132]

The appellant and respondent entered into a contract regarding information and concessions relating to gold mines in West Africa. At the request of the respondent, the appellant obtained certain valuable information and concessions relating to the mines. The appellant argued there was a binding agreement for the services and that the respondent had agreed to give him a share in the concessions and to pay him for the information supplied. The respondent had paid nothing to the appellant. The appellant claimed damages for breach of agreement, with an alternative claim for *quantum meruit* which, he maintained, should be calculated with regard to the profit the respondent had made (approximately one million pounds).

The House of Lords found there was no concluded contract between the parties. No agreement had been reached in relation to an essential term—namely, the

---

130 *Fibrosa Spolka Akcynja v Fairbairn Lawson Combe Barbour Ltd* [1943] AC 32 at 48.
131 *Rowland v Divall* [1923] 2 KB 500; *Warman v Southern Counties Car Finance Corp Ltd* (WJ Ameris Car Sales, Third Party) [1949] 1 All ER 711.
132 [1937] 3 All ER 759.

amount of the share in the concessions that the appellant was to receive. Despite the conclusion of a void contract, the appellant was held to be entitled to remuneration upon a *quantum meruit* basis. Lord Wright said:

> the work was done by the appellant and accepted by the respondent on the basis that some remuneration was to be paid to the appellant by the respondent. There was thus an implied promise by the respondent to pay on a quantum meruit, that is, to pay what the services were worth.[133]

[24.230] *Way v Latilla*[134] provides an example of a situation here the work had been requested and accepted by the defendant.[135] The appellant's claim was assisted by the fact that the work was done in circumstances where it was obvious some remuneration was payable. However, a request is not necessary, provided the defendant freely accepts the work performed.

Example: Craven-Ellis v Canons Ltd[136]

The defendant company's articles of association required all directors to acquire a certain number of shares in the company within two months of appointment. The plaintiff was appointed the managing director of the defendant by two directors who did not hold the appropriate shareholding. This meant the contract was void; because of the director's inability to make the appointment, there was also no request for the services. Despite the lack of a request, the defendant was liable to pay the reasonable value of the services provided by the plaintiff because the defendant had freely accepted the services.

24.9   Ineffective contracts

[24.235] A contract that is unenforceable or ineffective is not a void contract. An unenforceable contract is one that has come into existence, but an action may not be commenced for enforcement or any other remedy based upon the contract. For example, in the majority of Australian States, a contract for the sale of land is unenforceable at law unless in writing and signed by the party to be charged.[137] As with a void contract, the fact the contract is unenforceable is not an unjust factor giving rise to a claim in restitution. The plaintiff will still need to rely on one of the unjust factors discussed above. Usually the plaintiff will rely on total failure of consideration or free acceptance. Since *David Securities v Commonwealth Bank*,[138] a plaintiff may also be able to rely on payment of money under a mistake of law, subject to the defence of good consideration.

---

133   Ibid at 765–766.
134   Ibid.
135   See also *Rover International Ltd v Cannon Film Sales Ltd* [1989] 1 WLR 912.
136   [1936] 2 KB 403. See also *Brenner v First Artists' Management* [1993] 2 VR 221 and [24.95].
137   See Chapter 11 for further discussion and other examples.
138   (1992) 175 CLR 353.

24.9.1   Recovery of money

[24.240] A claim for restitution of moneys paid under an ineffective contract will commonly arise in the context of a contract for the sale of land. The Statute of Frauds equivalents in each State render a contract unenforceable if the contract is not in writing and signed by the party to be charged.[139] If the contract does not proceed, the purchaser will be able to recover their deposit due to a total failure of consideration. The policy of the legislation does not prohibit such a claim.

Example: Freedom v AHR Constructions Pty Ltd[140]

The plaintiff and defendant orally agreed that the plaintiff would purchase a unit from the defendant at the price of $140 000. The price was to be defrayed in part by payment of a cash sum and in part by payments of amounts due or to be due to the plaintiff by way of commission on the sales affected by her. Although two draft contracts were prepared, neither was signed. The plaintiff paid $21 000 in cash to the defendant by March 1983 and her employer paid to the defendant $26 000 on account of commissions due to her, the total being $47 000. At the end of March, the plaintiff was dismissed, leaving her with no means of paying for the unit. She requested both orally and by letter from her solicitor that the $47 000 be refunded to her.

The court found that there was a binding oral agreement between the parties. The execution of a formal contract was not a condition precedent to the creation of contractual obligations between the parties. As the contract was not in writing and signed by the party to be charged as required by s 59 of the *Property Law Act* 1974 (Qld), the plaintiff was unable to bring a claim in contract for the return of the deposit. The plaintiff succeeded in recovering the amount by which the deposit exceeded 10 per cent of the purchase price, on the basis of a total failure of consideration.

24.9.2   Recovery for services rendered

[24.245] The principles governing restitution of services rendered pursuant to an unenforceable contract are explained in the High Court decision of *Pavey & Matthews Pty Ltd v Paul*.[141] That case involved a building contract in NSW rendered unenforceable by the operation of s 45 of the *Builders' Licensing Act* 1971 (NSW). Most of the work had been completed under the oral contract, and the trial judge awarded the plaintiff a *quantum meruit*. In the Court of Appeal, the decision was reversed on the basis that the plaintiff was in essence seeking to enforce the oral contract; in addition, the claim was against the policy of the Act. In the High Court, the claim by the builder for a *quantum meruit* succeeded.

Deane J approached the problem first by distinguishing between two distinct categories of *quantum meruit*. The first allowed recovery of a debt arising under a genuine contract, whether express or implied. The second allowed recovery of a debt owing in circumstances where the law itself imposed or imputed an obligation or promise to

---

139   See further [11.105].
140   [1987] 1 Qd R 59
141   (1987) 162 CLR 221

make payment for a benefit accepted. In the first case, the action was on the contract. In the second, the action was not based on a genuine agreement at all. Deane J pointed out that it was the absence of a genuine agreement or the fact that it was not applicable, frustrated, avoided, or unenforceable 'that provides the occasion for (and part of the circumstances giving rise to) the imposition by law of the obligation to make restitution'.[142] Approving the statement of Jordan CJ in *Horton v Jones*,[143] Deane J concluded that if the Statute of Frauds was the legislation under consideration, it would not have prevented a claim for *quantum meruit* succeeding.

However, the question was whether the legislative policy behind s 45 of the *Builders Licensing Act* 1971 (NSW) prohibited the claim. Relying on the interpretation of similar legislation in *Gino D'Alessandro Constructions Pty Ltd v Powis*,[144] Deane J concluded that the section did not affect the right to a *quantum meruit* claim.[145]

[24.250] The decision of *Pavey & Matthews Pty Ltd v Paul*[146] is significant in the context of restitution under an ineffective contract. The case clearly establishes the existence of a distinct claim in restitution for unjust enrichment outside of the contractual relationship of the parties. It follows from this that even though the parties are unable to bring a contractual claim in relation to an unenforceable contract, a claim in restitution will not be barred. The only exception may be where the policy or legislative intent prohibits the claim.

24.10 Partly performed contracts

[24.255] If a contract is discharged for breach or frustration after it has been partly performed, one or both parties may be seeking compensation for work or moneys paid under the contract. Despite the fact that recovery for restitution is not dependent on proof of fault, the rights of a party in restitution are affected in some cases by whether the contract has come to an end by reason of their fault. In the case of frustration, the contract will have come to an end without the fault of either party. In that case, the principles applicable to void contracts and unenforceable contracts will be relevant. A party will be able to recover moneys paid under the frustrated contract if there is a total failure of consideration.[147]

[24.260] The rights of a party after discharge for breach have been considered previously, in relation to both recovery of money paid and recovery for services rendered.[148] In this chapter, a summary of the issues for a party after discharge in the context of restitution is considered.

---

142 Ibid at 257.
143 (1934) 34 SR (NSW) 359 at 367–368.
144 [1987] 2 QdR 40.
145 Similar conclusions were reached in *JC Scott Constructions v Mermaid Waters Tavern Pty Ltd* [1984] 2 Qd R 413 at 424–425; *O'Connor v Leaw Pty Ltd* (1997) 42 NSWLR 285 at 291–295; *Tea Tree Gully Builders Co Pty Ltd v Martin* (1992) 59 SASR 344 at 349; *Great City Pty Ltd v Kemayan Management Services (Australia) Pty Ltd* (1999) 21 WAR 44.
146 (1987) 162 CLR 221.
147 See *Fibrosa Spolka Akcyjna v Fairbairn Lawson Combe Barbour Ltd* [1943] AC 32 at 52.
148 See [20.505]–[20.525] and [19.255]–[19.270].

24.10.1   Recovery of money paid

[24.265] Money paid under a contract discharged for breach will be recoverable if there is a total failure of consideration.[149] The two main difficulties that arise in this area relate first to whether the failure of consideration is total, and secondly to the position of the defaulting party in relation to the recovery of a deposit.

As discussed previously, it would be unjust, where the plaintiff has received none of the consideration under the contract, to allow the defendant to retain the money. If the consideration has not totally failed, it will not be unjust for the defendant to retain the money.[150] A plaintiff will face difficulties where, although the plaintiff has not received all of the consideration for the payment, some consideration—albeit of a lesser value—has been received.[151]

Example: Yeoman Credit Ltd v Apps[152]

The defendant entered into an agreement for the hire purchase of a car with the plaintiff. The agreement excluded liability for the condition of the car. When delivered, the car was unsafe and unroadworthy, but the defendant, though he complained, drove the car and paid three instalments of hire. The defendant defaulted, and the plaintiff determined the contract and sued for damages. The defendant counterclaimed for recovery of the deposit and instalments paid, on the basis of total failure of consideration.

The Court of Appeal held that the condition of the car was such that the plaintiff was in fundamental breach of the contract and so could not rely on the exclusion clause. Consequently, the defendant was entitled to reject the car and bring the contract to an end. But the Court held that the defendant could not succeed because there was no total failure of consideration. It distinguished *Rowland v Divall*[153] on the basis that the defendant had possession of the car, used the car, and effected repairs to the car.

[24.270] The second main area of dispute involves recovery of the deposit paid under the contract. The party in default of the contract will be unable to recover the deposit paid to the other party. It follows from the fact the deposit is a bond for performance that if the party paying the deposit defaults, the bond is lost. In contrast, the defaulting party will be able to recovery instalments of contract price after discharge. These differences were considered in detail previously.[154]

---

149 See the discussion at [24.145].
150 See *Rowland v Divall* [1923] 2 KB 500 concerning a total failure of consideration, and compare with *Yeoman Credit Ltd v Apps* [1962] 2 QB 508.
151 See *Dies v British & International Mining & Finance Corporation Ltd* [1939] 1 KB 724 where the payments were retained because consideration had been given.
152 [1962] 2 QB 508.
153 [1923] 2 KB 500.
154 See [20.505]–[20.525].

24.10.2 Recovery for services rendered

[24.275] The issues for a party seeking *quantum meruit* after termination for breach have already been considered in a previous chapter.[155] The issues in the context of restitution will be briefly summarised. Where payment for services rendered is sought, the plaintiff should first establish if there is any action on the contract. A claim for restitution will not be available if the contract remains enforceable. If the obligations of the plaintiff are substantially performed, a claim in contract for the price would be available.[156] An entitlement to *quantum meruit* would only be available if the contract has been terminated. Where the contract is substantially performed, termination will not be possible. The requirement to pay the contract price will have become a debt preventing an alternative claim in restitution for *quantum meruit*.

[24.280] Although a claim in restitution is not in theory dependant upon proof of fault the authorities have treated a claim for *quantum meruit* by the defaulting party differently to the party not in default. An innocent party who terminates the contract for the breach of the other party will be entitled to elect between a claim for damages and a claim for restitution.[157] The court will readily accept that the innocent party has provided a benefit, even if the work is only partly completed.[158] The party in default, however, will need to go further in proving a benefit was provided to the other party to the contract where the services were only partly performed. The defaulting party will need to provide evidence that the services were freely accepted, or that the other party received an incontrovertible benefit.[159]

24.11 Anticipated contracts

[24.285] If a party pays money or performs services in anticipation of the formation of a contract, the question is whether the money or the value of the services is recoverable. The plaintiff will be unable to claim damages, as no contract was ever entered into. Subject to claims for unfair conduct such as estoppel, misrepresentation, or misleading conduct, the party's only possible claim will lie in restitution.[160]

[24.290] A claim for moneys prior to formation of a contract will be recoverable on similar bases to moneys paid pursuant to the contract. A claim for moneys had and received will succeed if there is a total failure of consideration or the money was paid under a mistake.[161] Recovery of compensation for services, however, is complicated by the different approaches in the authorities. In particular, the question of which party has assumed the risk of the contract not materialising appears relevant. Situations where services provided in anticipation of a contract are of no benefit to the other

---

155 See Chapter 19.
156 See [19.195] for discussion of a party's right to the contract price.
157 See *Automatic Fire Sprinklers Pty Ltd v Watson* (1946) 72 CLR 435 at 450 noted at [17.2.4] and *Renard Constructions (ME) Pty Ltd v Minister for Public Works* (1992) 26 NSWLR 234 at 277; *Brenner v First Artists' Management Pty Ltd* [1993] 2 VR 221.
158 See [19.240]–[19.250].
159 See [19.255]–[19.270].
160 See Chapter 7 in relation to estoppel, Chapter 13 in relation to misrepresentation, and Chapter 13 in relation to misleading conduct.
161 See [24.145]–[24.170].

party do not sit comfortably with the concept of unjust enrichment. No clear indication is given by the authorities of the unjust factor that will be relevant to recovery in this type of situation. In *Angelopoulos v Sabatino*,[162] the court suggests free acceptance as the basis of relief; but this has been doubted by commentators who suggest failure of an anticipated event[163] or unconscionability[164] as being more appropriate. The authorities also consider issues of risk assumption, why the negotiations failed, and the extent of the work that is normally considered to fall outside that expected.[165] The cases fall into two broad classes: those where an objective benefit is conferred, and those where no benefit or end product is conferred.

[24.295] A common example of an end product being produced from the plaintiff's work is where a lessee is allowed into possession of premises prior to the commencement of the lease. This will usually be with the consent of the landlord, who may be considered to have freely accepted the work. If negotiations collapse, the lessee will usually be entitled to claim the value of the work performed.

Example: Angelopoulos v Sabatino[166]

The parties had entered into preliminary negotiations for the lease of a hotel after the tenant operating the business became insolvent. The owner, Mr Angelopoulos, was anxious to return the hotel to an operational state; he requested the plaintiff, Sabatino, to organise and oversee the necessary restoration work on the hotel. The plaintiff hired contractors and casual workers to carry out the restoration work, and purchased and installed plant and equipment to a value of $57 000. Negotiations broke down, and the owner then leased the property to a third party and sold a lot of the plant and equipment, including that purchased by the plaintiff.

The court found that an obligation to pay for the services and plant and equipment arose from the free acceptance of the work and other items by the defendant. The court considered it was unnecessary for the plaintiff to prove that the defendant had requested the work because, in the circumstances, it was shown that the defendant actually encouraged and acquiesced in the work being carried out. Eight factors were relevant to the court's decision.

1   This was not a case where the plaintiff intended to provide his services gratuitously.

2   The plaintiff did not provide services or plant and equipment solely at his own initiative.

3   The plaintiff did not provide his services on the basis that there would be no payment unless a certain event came to pass.

162 (1995) 65 SASR 1.

163 K Liew, 'Restitution and contract risk: commentary' in M McInnes (ed), *Restitution: Developments in Unjust Enrichment*, LBC Information Services, Sydney, 1996, Ch 10.

164 SA Christensen, 'Recovery for Work Performed in Anticipation of Contract' (1993) 11 ABR 144, pp 156–160; G Jones, 'Claims Arising out of Anticipated Contracts which do not Materialise'(1980) 18 *University of Western Ontario LR* 447; J Carter, 'Contract, Restitution and Promissory Estoppel' (1989) 12 *UNSW Law Journal* 30.

165 Work which is normally considered to be part of the tender work would not be recoverable. See *Brenner v First Artists' Management* [1993] 2 VR 221; Byrne, 'Restitution for work done in anticipation of contract' (1997) 13 BCL 4.

166 (1995) 65 SASR 1.

4   This was not a case in which the services were provided on a basis from which the plaintiffs chose to depart; that is, the plaintiff did not unilaterally or unreasonably terminate negotiations.

5   The defendant benefited from what the plaintiff did.

6   The benefit was at the expense of the plaintiff.

7   The defendant approved or agreed to the plaintiff carrying out the work that he did, and by his later sale and lease of the premises, he accepted the benefit.

8   The defendant must have known that the plaintiff expected to be remunerated for his services.

[24.300] Reference should also be made to the case of *A-G Hong Kong v Humprheys Estate Ltd*,[167] where prior to and in anticipation of a contract the plaintiff improved property of the defendant. After negotiations broke down, the plaintiff attempted to recover the value of the improvements from the defendant. The court based its refusal to award payment on the fact that the defendant did not create or encourage a belief in the plaintiff that the contract would be concluded—or alternatively, that the defendant would not withdraw from the negotiations.

[24.305] Both *Angelopoulos v Sabatino*[168] and the *Humprey* case[169] can be explained by reference to the principles governing estoppel. Both estoppel and the restitutionary remedy given in *Angelopoulos v Sabatino*[170] operate where there is no existing contractual relationship between the parties with the mutual purpose of the remedies being to relieve against the conduct of the defendant that has encouraged or induced the plaintiff into an assumption that a contract will be entered into. The plaintiff then relies upon the assumption to their detriment. It is arguable that estoppel provides a preferable juristic basis for relief.

[24.310] In cases where the collapse of the contract renders the work of no benefit to the defendant, it is more difficult to given a restitutionary analysis of the cases.

In *Brewer Street Investments Ltd v Barclays Woollen Co Ltd*,[171] the plaintiff and defendant were negotiating the terms of a lease. The parties agreed on the material terms subject to a formal lease being entered into. The defendant was anxious to enter the premises, and the plaintiff agreed to make certain alterations that the defendant required. The defendant accepted responsibility for the cost. The negotiations fell through, and the plaintiff claimed reimbursement of the value of the work done to the property.

Denning LJ approached the question as one of risk. On whom is the loss to fall? He referred to the judgment of Morris LJ in *Jennings and Chapman Ltd v Woodman, Mathews and Co*[172] who stated the question as: *What was the reason for the negotiations breaking down?* If it was the landlord's fault—as, for instance, if it refused to go on with the lease for no reason at all, or because it demanded a higher rent than what had been agreed—then it should not be allowed to recover any part of the cost of the altera-

---

167   [1987] 1 AC 114.
168   (1995) 65 SASR 1.
169   [1987] 1 AC 114.
170   (1995) 65 SASR 1.
171   [1954] 1 QB 428.
172   [1952] 2 TLR 409.

tions. Even if the landlord derived no benefit from the work, it should not be allowed to recover the costs from the prospective tenants—seeing it was by its own fault that the prospective tenants were deprived of it. On the other hand, if it was the prospective tenants' fault that the negotiations broke down—for example if they sought lower rent than what had been agreed upon—then they ought to pay the cost of the alterations up to the time they were stopped. After all, the prospective tenants did promise to pay for the work, and they should not be able to get out of their promise by their own fault even though the alterations were not completed. In the particular case before the court, the negotiations did not fall down due to the fault of either party. In this case therefore, the tenant should pay the cost for the work done at their request, which was prima facie for their benefit. If some of the work was actually of benefit to the landlord, a credit should be given.

[24.315] The question of whether the negotiations had broken down due to the fault of one of the parties was the central issue for the court in *Brewer Street Investments Ltd*.[173] It was unclear from the case, however, what position the tenant would be in if it had not undertaken to pay for the work in circumstances where negotiations breakdown without the fault of either party. It may be difficult in those circumstances to argue that the tenant had obtained a benefit unless it was accepted that fulfilment of the request was the benefit. Although Denning LJ said the action should be founded in restitution, it appears that the other members of the court—Somerville and Rommer LJJ—based their decisions on the fact the defendant was assuming a risk the contract would not go ahead, rather than whether any benefit accrued to the defendant. The defendant requested the work, but there was no tangible benefit to it. However, it may be argued that the landlord did receive some benefit from the improvement of the premises. The same could not be said however, where the defendant does not have any tangible or physical benefit in its hands as a result of the services of the plaintiff.

Example: Sabemo Pty Ltd v North Sydney Municipal Council[174]

The plaintiff (Sabemo) was the successful tenderer for the development of a civic centre. Sabemo carried out considerable work in developing three alternative schemes. The last of these satisfied the Minister's planning requirements for the site. Most of the work done in developing the schemes was done at the request of the defendant. The defendant decided to abandon the proposed scheme prior to a concluded agreement ever being reached. The decision not to proceed was purely on the part of the council and had nothing to do with the quality of Sabemo's work.

In the view of Sheppard J, the case revolved around the question: *On whom in all the circumstances of the case should the risk fall?* Should the loss lie where it falls, or were there circumstances in which one of the parties should pay for the expenditure of the other? In the light of certain decisions,[175] Sheppard J considered the plaintiff was entitled to recover based on the following principle:

---

173   [1954] 1 QB 428.
174   [1977] 2 NSWLR 880.
175   *William Lacey (Hounslow) Ltd v Davis* [1957] 1 WLR 932; *Jennings and Chapman Ltd v Woodman, Mathews and Co* [1952] 2 TLR 409 and *Brewer Street Investments Ltd v Barclays Woollen Co Ltd* [1954] 1 QB 428.

> Where two parties proceed upon the joint assumption that a contract will be entered into between them and one does work beneficial for the project and thus in the interests of the two parties, which work he would not be expected in other circumstances to do gratuitously, he will be entitled to compensation or restitution if the other party unilaterally decides to abandon the project, not for any reason associated with bona fide disagreement concerning the terms of the contract to be entered into but for reasons which however valid pertain only to his own position and do not relate to that of the other party.[176]

It was critical to the case that the project was unilaterally abandoned by the council, as this established a degree of fault on its part. Questions of benefit were not relevant to the court. The ability of the plaintiff to establish a benefit in the case was complicated by the fact that the work did not produce any end product, and was not necessary for the saving of any expense. To show benefit in this case it would need to be accepted that a benefit to the defendant was established where there was a depletion in the plaintiff's assets or income forgone, sustained at the request of the defendant.[177] A restitutionary analysis of *Sabemo* and similar cases may be open to the criticism that it creates a fiction not unlike the implied contracts theory. It was true that the work performed by Sabemo was beneficial to the project; but as the project did not go ahead, there was no benefit to the council in the work. The real basis of the case rested on the conduct of the defendant.

24.12 Defences

[24.320] There are several accepted defences to a claim for restitution based on unjust enrichment. Goff and Jones[178] identify six factors that may prevent a claim or be referred to as defences.

- Services, goods or money that are part of a valid gift or benefit conferred in the course of an obligation owed at law, in equity, or under statute are not recoverable—for example, where a contract provides for the payment of a deposit that is to be forfeited in the event of breach. If the plaintiff is in breach of contract, the deposit will not be recovered in restitution.
- The plaintiff has submitted to the honest claim of the defendant. This applies in the context of moneys paid under a mistake of law.[179]
- The benefit was conferred voluntarily while the plaintiff was acting in his or her own self-interest.
- The plaintiff acted officiously in conferring the benefit.
- The defendant cannot be restored to their original position (that is, the plaintiff has changed his or her position).
- Public policy, such as issues of illegality, precludes restitution.

---

176 Ibid at 902–903.
177 See JW Carter, 'Services Rendered Under Ineffective Contracts' [1990] LMCLQ 495 at 504.
178 R Goff & G Jones *The Law of Restitution*, 5th edn, Sweet & Maxwell, London, 1998, pp 46–47.
179 See [24.185]–[24.205].

[24.325] The defence of most interest to the claims discussed in this chapter is the defence of change of position. This is a concept separate from equitable estoppel, although some of the nomenclature is similar. Change of position has been recognised as a defence to a claim for restitution particularly in the case of mistaken payments. Defendants are required to prove that they acted to their detriment on the faith of the receipt of the benefit, such that it would now be inequitable for the money to be returned.

[24.330] The defence has been accepted as applying to a situation where the defendant receives money that is paid by the plaintiff under a mistake, and then expends the money before learning of the mistake.[180] This was confirmed by the High Court in *David Securities Pty Ltd v The Commonwealth Bank of Australia*.[181] The High Court acknowledged the application of the defence to cases of mistaken payments, stating that the defendant must be able to prove not only that it acted to its detriment on the faith of the payment, but also that it committed to some expenditure or financial commitment that was attributable to the mistaken payment.[182]

[24.335] In England, the House of Lords in *Lipkin Gorman v Karpnale Ltd*[183] allowed a claim for change of position. There, a solicitor called Case (a partner in the plaintiff's firm) misappropriated the sum of £323 222 from the firm's client account. Case paid back into the account various amounts totally £100 331 leaving a shortfall of £222 909. Case used the money to gamble at the defendant's club. The defendant had no knowledge that the money was stolen. The total amount spent by Case at the club was £561 014, which comprised the misappropriated moneys, some of Case's own money, and some of Case's winnings. Case's total winnings amounted to £378 294; the net sum won by the club from Case's losing bets over the relevant period was £174 745. On the basis that £20 000 of the club's earnings had been derived from stakes of Case's own money, the parties agreed that at least £154 695 of the club's gain had been derived from the money misappropriated from the client's account.

The House of Lords held that the plaintiff had a prima facie right to recover the sum of money in restitution on the basis of a total failure of consideration. The club argued, however, that it had changed its position by paying out on the winning bets. Lord Goff discussed generally the defence of change of position, and accepted its application to a case for moneys had and received. His Lordship gave careful consideration to the differences between the defence of change of position and estoppel. One important difference is the inability of estoppel to operate *pro tanto*. For example, where defendants have innocently changed their position by disposing of part of the money, a defence of estoppel would provide them a defence to the whole of the claim. The defence of change of position would only operate in respect of that part of the money expended. Lord Goff went on to make some suggestions about the width of the defence of change of position:

- it would not be open to any one acting in bad faith, or to a wrong-doer;

---

180 *ANZ Banking Group Ltd v Westpac Banking Corporation* (1988) 164 CLR 662.
181 (1992) 175 CLR 353.
182 Approved in *State Bank of NSW v Swiss Bank Corporation Ltd* (1995) 39 NSWLR 350.
183 [1991] 2 AC 548.

- merely disposing of the money in good faith is not of itself sufficient to render it inequitable that it be repaid 'because the expenditure might in any event have been incurred by him [or her] in the ordinary course of things';[184]
- although there are resemblances between bona fide purchase and change of position, the two cannot properly be equated, because in the former there is no inquiry into the adequacy of the consideration, while in the latter the defence only operates *pro tanto* to the extent of the change.

In applying this principle to the facts of the case, Goff LJ gave careful consideration to what would be just in the circumstances. Even though the casino would have incurred a risk by taking the bets, if the bet did not win, the casino would have paid out nothing to the gambler, and therefore it would not be inequitable to require the casino to repay the bet. The defendant was ordered to repay the moneys received from Case after taking into account the amount paid by the defendant in winnings to Case.

24.13 International perspectives

24.13.1 New Zealand

[24.340] The law in New Zealand concerning recovery of money and compensation for services in restitution is in substance the same as the law in Australia, and does not require separate examination.[185]

24.13.2 United States

[24.345] As in Australia, the law of restitution in the United States is largely based upon the notion of unjust enrichment. This is recognised in the Restatement of Restitution, which states that 'one person is accountable to another on the ground that otherwise he would unjustly benefit or the other would unjustly suffer loss'.[186] The principle of unjust enrichment is considered to underpin many of the claims that are classified as restitution but it is not the only bases for recovery.[187] Substantially the same principles apply to a claim for restitution in the context of a contractual relationship as in Australia. A claim is only available if the contract is terminated for total breach;[188] also, damages and restitution will not be given together.[189] A restitutionary remedy is available as an alternative to the remedy of damages, and the value of the benefit received is calculated in the same manner. Generally, the same principles apply to a claim for *quantum meruit* or return of moneys paid as in Australia, and further examination of the area is beyond the scope of this text.

---

184 *Lipkin Gorman v Karapnale Ltd* [1991] 2 AC 548 at 580.
185 See, for example, *National Bank of NZ Ltd v Waitaki International Processing (NI) Ltd* [1997] 1 NZLR 724.
186 Restatement of Restitution (2d) Ch 1.
187 Restatement of Restitution (1937) p 11.
188 See *United States for Use of Building Rentals Corp v Western Cas & Sur Co* 498 F 2d 335 (9th Cir. 1974). See [20.595]–[20.605] in relation to the circumstances in which termination for total breach will be available.
189 *Downs v Jersey Central Power & Light Co* 117 NJ Eq 138, 174 A 887 (1934).

24.13.3 Japan

[24.350] The principles of unjust enrichment in Japanese civil law are set out in the Civil Code, operating as a parallel system alongside the rules of contract, tort, and real property. Article 703 provides that: 'A person who without any legal ground derives a benefit from the property or services of another and thereby causes loss to the latter, is bound to return such benefit to the extent that it still exists.' Article 704 provides that: 'A person enriched in bad faith must return the benefit received by him with interest, and if there has been any damage, he is bound also to make compensation for it.' In general terms, the elements of unjust enrichment are similar to their common law counterparts—a benefit taken without a legal basis, either intentionally or unintentionally, and a corresponding harm to the other party, which must be compensated.

[24.355] Where the thing possessed has been lost or damaged or is unable to be returned because of the fault of the person in possession, article 91 of the Civil Code provides that a person possessing in bad faith is liable to compensate the person entitled to restoration of the rights for the full amount of the damage. A person holding the thing in good faith is liable to the extent of the enrichment he or she enjoys as a result of the loss of damage. Someone in possession but with no intention of taking ownership is bound to compensate for the full amount of the damage, regardless of whether or not they were acting in good faith.

The typical situations in which the unjust enrichment principles work is where a contract was formed but was subsequently found to be void. Monies paid under the contract, or property transferred under the contract, may be ordered to be returned in order to avoid unjust enrichment on either side—an application analogous to restitution principles in the common law.

[24.360] One explicit restriction on the operation of these principles is set out in article 708, which denies restitution in the case of a contract void for reasons of public policy or good morals (article 90), except where the immorality existed only on the side of the defendant. This is an application of an idea analogous to the 'clean hands' maxim of equity in common law systems—claimants may not themselves be in breach of the law.[190]

---

190 For a fuller exposition of the operation of unjust enrichment across the spectrum of contract and property in Japan see: Takashi Uchida, *Minpô II* [Civil Code Vol 2], Tokyo Daigaku Shuppankai, Tokyo, 1997, 519–572.

Chapter 25

Equitable remedies

25.1   Introduction

[25.05] The remedy of damages at common law has already been considered.[1] It is now appropriate to consider how an innocent party to a breach of contract may enforce the contract by means of an equitable remedy.

[25.10] There are several important features of equitable remedies that distinguish them from common law remedies. First, equitable remedies are usually only given where common law damages are an inadequate remedy. The remedy of damages can only compensate injured parties financially for the default of another party. In the case of certain contracts—particularly those conveying land, or for the purchase of a custom-built chattel—this remedy will usually be insufficient for the disappointed party. For example, breach of a contract by a vendor to sell a common make of motor vehicle would only sound in common law damages. However, a breach of a contract to sell a taxi cab together with its licence and registration has attracted specify performance of the obligation, because at the time, the registration and licence of a taxi cab were difficult to obtain.[2] An award of damages would not have greatly assisted the plaintiff.

[25.15] Secondly, unlike legal remedies, equitable remedies are discretionary. At common law, if there has been a breach of contract by a defendant, and the plaintiff can prove loss, damages will be awarded. The conduct of the plaintiff who has suffered loss is generally not relevant; only the fact of a breach by the defendant and the loss suffered are relevant. In equity, the conduct of both the plaintiff and the defendant will relevant when the Court considers whether or not to grant a remedy. A plaintiff seeking any equitable remedy—particularly specific performance, injunction, or equitable damages—may be refused relief where the plaintiff is in breach of his or her own obligations, where the plaintiff has failed to take the action within a reasonable time,[3] or where the claim would produce unfair or harsh results to a defendant.[4] Where these equitable defences can be proved, a plaintiff would be left to his or her remedy at common law.

[25.20] Thirdly, equity acts in *personam*. This means that a defendant would be ordered personally to perform a contract (specific performance) or conversely, abstain from breaching it (injunction). The failure to comply with an order of a court of equity may lead to committal or attachment for contempt of court, depending upon the circumstances.

[25.25] This chapter will deal with the more significant equitable remedies relating to contracts. These are specific performance, injunctions, and equitable damages. In respect of the latter, equity has the power to award damages in its auxiliary jurisdiction in much the same way as damages are awarded in common law to compensate a plaintiff for loss. These damages may be awarded concurrently with a decree for specific performance or

---

1   See Chapter 23.
2   *Dougan v Ley* (1946) 71 CLR 147.
3   See the defence of Laches [25.5.5].
4   The defence of hardship.

an order for an injunction.[5] The power to grant damages was conferred initially by *Lord Cairns' Act* 1858[6] and has been re-enacted in all Australian states.[7]

25.2 Specific performance

[25.30] A decree of specific performance may be ordered to force a party to an executory (unperformed) contract to perform that contract, or may be ordered against a party to enforce the fulfilment of any one or more obligations remaining unperformed under a contract. In the words of Lord Selborne in *Wolverhampton & Wallsall Railway Co v London & Northwestern Railway Co*, a decree of specific performance:[8]

> presupposes an executory as distinct from an executed agreement, something remaining to be done, such as the execution of a deed or a conveyance, in order to put the parties in a position relative to each other which by the preliminary agreement they were intended to be placed.[9]

[25.35] Where a contract has been executed, and is not an agreement preliminary to a further transaction which, when carried out, may define the relative positions of the parties, specific performance will be inappropriate.[10] The best and most common example of an executory contract is the contract for the sale of land. Here, a vendor agrees in writing to sign the appropriate transfer to vest the title of the land in the purchaser. The contract is not completed until that occurs. If a vendor fails to sign the transfer, a purchaser may seek a decree of specific performance ordering that it be done.

[25.40] While generally it cannot be said absolutely that there are any contracts to which the remedy of specific performance would not be available,[11] relief by way of this order is more readily given in some contracts than in others. Before looking at these types of contracts, it is as well to recognise categories of contract where specific performance is not usually available. Two of these are especially worthy of note, because they are commonplace. Firstly, a contract to lend money may only be specifically enforced in exceptional circumstances.[12] This is because, generally, in such cases, damages would be an adequate remedy.[13] Financial compensation is normally an adequate remedy for breach of a contract to lend money, except where the consequences of such a breach may not give rise to adequate recovery.[14]

[25.45] Another common category of contract held not to be amenable to specific performance is a licence to use land for a limited period. The general rule is that a

---

5   *Fullers' Theatres Ltd v Musgrove* (1923) 31 CLR 524 at 547.
6   21 & 22 Vict c 27 s 2 (Imp).
7   *Supreme Court Act* 1970, s 68 (NSW); *Supreme Court Act* 1958 (Vic), s 62; *Equity Act* 1867 (Qld), 62, *Barbagallo v Catelan Pty Ltd* [1986] 1 Qd R 245 at 250-251; *Supreme Court Act* 1935 (SA), s 30; *Supreme Court Act* 1935 (WA), s 25; *Supreme Court Civil Procedure Act* 1932 (Tas), s 11.
8   (1873) LR 16 Eq 433.
9   Ibid at 439.
10 *JC Williamson v Lukey & Mulholland* (1931) 45 CLR 282 at 297.
11 *Coulls v Bagott's Executor and Trustee Co Ltd* (1967) 119 CLR 460 at 503.
12 *Wight v Haberdan Pty Ltd* [1984] 2 NSWLR 280 at 289.
13 *South African Territories Ltd v Wallington* [1898] AC 309; *Loan Investment Corp of Australasia Ltd v Bonner* [1970] NZLR 724.
14 *Wight v Haberdan Pty Ltd* [1984] 2 NSWLR 280 at 290.

grant of a licence does not create an interest in land.[15] Thus, if a licence is revoked in breach of contract, the remedy is damages, and nothing else.[16] However, this rule itself is not invariable; in the United Kingdom, specific performance of a contractual licence for a limited period has been granted, notwithstanding the licence did not create an interest in land in the true sense.[17]

25.3 Contracts commonly amenable to specific performance

[25.50] By far the most common form of contract that is specifically enforceable is a contract for the sale of an interest in land. Such a contract is uniquely suited to that treatment because of the two-stage process of the land transaction. First, there is a contract to convey title by the vendor; following that, an assurance or transfer of the land to the purchaser's name is executed. The remedy is also available to a vendor against a purchaser who fails to complete.[18] A court of equity recognises that damages is not an adequate remedy for failure to complete a contract for the sale of land, because theoretically, every block of land is unique.[19]

[25.55] Secondly, some contracts for the sale of personalty may be specifically enforced where the item of personality is unique—that is, not readily available on the open market or only obtainable if the plaintiff is put to considerable inconvenience and difficulty. However, by way of example, a contract for the sale of shares may not be specifically enforceable if those shares are readily obtainable on the open market,[20] because damages will be adequate to replace them. Thus, if the shares become more valuable than their market price agreed to be paid, the damages can be used to pay a higher price and thus obtain the shares.[21]

[25.60] It has long been held that a contract for the sale of specific goods—that is, either custom built goods or articles that are one or few of a kind—may be specifically enforced. This rule has been given statutory endorsement in all sale of goods legislation except that in New South Wales.[22] In considering the application of this principle, a court will take into account the nature of the transaction in which the sale is embodied, the nature of the goods involved in that transaction, and the general question of the inadequacy of damages should specific performance be refused.[23]

---

15 *Cowell v Rosehill Racecourse Co Ltd* (1937) 56 CLR 605.
16 *Booker v Palmer* [1942] 2 All ER 674 at 677.
17 *Verrall v Great Yarmouth Borough Council* [1981] QB 202.
18 *Turner v Bladin* (1951) 82 CLR 463 at 473.
19 *Adderley v Dixon* (1824) 1 Sim & St 607 at 610; 57 ER 239 at 240.
20 *Re Shwabacher* (1907) 98 LT 127 at 128.
21 *Rudder v George Hudson Holdings Ltd* [1972] 1 NSWLR 529 at 535.
22 *Goods Act* 1958 (Vic), s 58; *Sale of Goods Act* 1894 (Qld), s 53; *Sale of Goods Act* 1895 (SA), s 51; *Sale of Goods Act* 1895 (WA), s 51; *Sale of Goods Act* 1954 (ACT), s 55; *Sale of Goods Act* (NT), s 53; s 56 of the *Sale of Goods Act* 1923 (NSW) provides that nothing in the Act shall affect any remedy in equity of the buyer or the seller in respect of any breach of a contract of sale or any breach of warranty. In a negative sense, it would appear that this section permits specific performance of a sale of goods contract in New South Wales where the remedy of common law would be inadequate; *Aristoc Industries Pty Ltd v RA Wenham (Builders) Pty Ltd* [1965] NSWR 581 at 588.
23 *Timmerman v Nervina Industries (International) Pty Ltd* [1983] 1 Qd R 1.

25.4 Common obligations not amenable to specific performance

[25.65] There are two common forms of contract in which an award for specific performance will not be made. These can generally be described as contracts in which performance would require constant supervision (such as contracts which involve the undertaking of personal services), and contracts in which the obligations are imprecisely stated. In respect of the former, because it is not possible for a court to constantly supervise an individual, an order for specific performance will not be made, as it could be easily ignored.[24] Some contracts provide for the sale of an asset combined with the provision of personal services.[25] In such cases, the court will weigh up the extent to which the overall obligations in the contract are to provide the services, then make a decision accordingly, on the specific enforceability of the bargain—with the overriding test being whether or not there are practical difficulties in supervising the performance of those obligations.[26] Secondly, the court may be reluctant to order the performance of a contract that requires continuous supervision.

Example: JC Williamson Ltd v Lukey & Mulholland[27]

The lessees of a theatre made an oral agreement with confectioners to give the confectioners an exclusive right to sell ice cream, confectionery, and soft drinks in the theatre during the continuance of a lease of a shop that the confectioners had taken from the owner of the theatre for 5 years. The confectioners exercised their rights for some time, but the lessee later repudiated the agreement and revoked the licence. The confectioners took proceedings for an injunction and equitable damages in addition, or in lieu thereof. They failed on both counts. The court also held that specific performance was not available, amongst other reasons, because the agreement required the continued supervision of the court to ensure the fulfilment of the contract. As the right of the confectioners and their servants to enter the theatre depended upon such issues as the character of the goods supplied and the dress and behaviour of their servants, this was not possible.

[25.70] To answer the question whether a contract is amenable to the supervision of the court, one has to ask whether, if a decree were to be granted, the plaintiff would be entitled to have the defendant committed for contempt if the plaintiff can prove a breach of the terms of the order.[28] If the obligations to be performed are imprecise, proof of breach will be difficult, so a decree will not be made.[29]

---

24 *Giles (CH) & Co Ltd v Morris* [1972] 1 WLR 307.
25 *Maiden v Maiden* (1909) 7 CLR 727 (the sale of a farm and its subsequent management).
26 *Thomas Borthwick & Sons (Australasia) Ltd v South Otago Freezing Co Ltd* [1978] 1 NZLR 538 at 551.
27 (1931) 45 CLR 282.
28 *Pakenham Upper Fruit Co Ltd v Crosby* (1924) 35 CLR 386 at 396–397.
29 *Richardson v Linehan* (1930) 30 SR (NSW) 457.

25.5 Defences to specific performance

[25.75] As specific performance is a discretionary remedy, although a breach of a contract by a defendant may be proved, an order will not be made as a matter of course without consideration of the conduct of the plaintiff and the circumstances of the defendant, so far as they may be relevant. There are a number of accepted categories of case where an order will not be made; these are categorised below.

25.5.1 Where the contract was entered as a result of mistake or misrepresentation

[25.80] Where a party to a contract against whom specific performance is being sought may have entered the contract as a result of a misrepresentation by the plaintiff, or as a result of a mistake by the plaintiff, the decree will not be made. For this rule to apply, in the case of a mistake, the defendant's mistaken belief would have to be induced wholly or substantially by the plaintiff.[30] Conversely, where the mistake is entirely that of the defendant and not contributed to by the plaintiff, specific performance may be granted where it would be a hardship upon the plaintiff not to do so.[31] Much depends upon the circumstances of the particular case, but generally, a decree will be made where there has been a unilateral mistake on the part of the defendant not contributed to by the plaintiff—given the nature of allegations of unilateral mistake on the part of those resisting performance of a contract and the difficulties of proof in genuine cases.[32]

25.5.2 Where enforcement would create undue hardship upon the defendant

[25.85] This defence is only raised in exceptional cases. It arises where the order of the court might place the defendant in such a position that the defendant would be, for example, exposed to the risk of prosecution.[33] The defence may also be successful where the defendant may have entered into the contract as a result of undue influence due to the defendant's infirm condition[34]—or, in rare cases, where the contract is excessively one-sided, to the point that to seek to enforce it would be totally unfair.[35] While the court will only usually consider the defendant's position prior to contract,[36] in exceptional circumstances the court will take into account the defendant's position after contract.[37]

[25.90] However, true cases of hardship must be distinguished from a case where the terms of the contract may be unbusinesslike or create a risk for one of the parties that the defendant may later have regretted,[38] or where, for example, there has been a

---

30 *Neild v Davidson* (1890) 11 LR (NSW) Eq 209.
31 *Tamplin v James* (1880) 15 Ch D 215 at 221; *Borg v Howlett* (unreported, SC NSW, Young J, 24 May 1996).
32 *Slee v Warke* (1949) 86 CLR 271 at 278; *Fragomeni v Fogliani* (1968) 42 ALJR 263.
33 *Pottinger v George* (1967) 116 CLR 328 at 337 (breach of local government regulations).
34 *Blomley v Ryan* (1956) 99 CLR 362 at 405.
35 *Dowsett v Reid* (1912) 15 CLR 695.
36 *Ready Constructions Pty Ltd v Jenno* [1984] 2 Qd R 7 (financial difficulties not hardship).
37 *Patel v Ali* [1984] Ch 283 at 286–287 (medical condition arising post contract).
38 *Axelsen v O'Brien* (1949) 80 CLR 219 at 226.

considerable drop in the price of land the subject of the contract and the purchaser does not wish to proceed upon that basis alone.[39]

[25.95] As a general rule, the hardship of third persons entirely unconnected with the property is immaterial. For example, in *Gall v Mitchell*,[40] specific performance was ordered against a father who contracted to sell his own land and land of his children, notwithstanding the decree caused hardship for his children on the grounds that their land remaining could not be worked as profitably as it had been, unless it was worked in conjunction with the land that the father sold.[41]

25.5.3   Where the plaintiff is in breach of contract or not ready, willing and able to perform his or her obligations under the contract

[25.100] This principle is an example of the maxim that a person seeking equity must come to court 'with clean hands'. If a party is in breach of his or her obligations imposed by the contract, the plaintiff will have no merit and, in the discretion of the court, a decree will not usually be made.[42] A plaintiff seeking specific performance of a contract of sale must, as part of the pleading, state that he or she is ready, willing, and able to perform the contract or any outstanding obligations due under the contract to that point which have to be performed.[43] However, in rare cases, a plaintiff in breach of an inessential term of a contract may be granted specific performance where those breaches would not permit a defendant to terminate the contract.[44]

[25.105] In such a case, if specific performance were ordered, any loss suffered by the defendant could be the subject of an order for the payment of equitable damages with the decree of specific performance.[45] Exceptionally, a plaintiff who is in breach of an essential term of a contract may be awarded specific performance against a defendant where it can be shown that the conduct of the defendant was unconscionable or in some other way contributed to the plaintiff's breach.[46] Before specific performance may be given in that circumstance, in relation to a contract for the sale of land, the Court would have to be satisfied that circumstances existed—such as the unconscionable conduct of the vendor—to permit relief against forfeiture of the purchaser's estate based upon that breach of an essential term. In the absence of such a finding, it is doubtful whether a specific performance could be ordered.[47]

25.5.4   Performance of the contract is not possible or would be futile

[25.110] As a general rule, equity will not specifically enforce that which cannot be done.[48] In a suit for specific performance for the sale of land, an order cannot be made if

---

39   *Fitzgerald v Masters* (1956) 95 CLR 420 at 433.
40   (1924) 35 CLR 222.
41   Ibid at 230–231.
42   *Australian Hardwoods Pty Ltd v Commissioner for Railways* [1961] 1 WLR 425 at 432–433.
43   *Fullers' Theatres Ltd v Musgrove* (1923) 31 CLR 524 at 550.
44   *Mehmet v Benson* (1965) 113 CLR 295 at 307–308 (plaintiff not in a position to perform contract within the stipulated time; however, time not the essence of the contract at that point).
45   Ibid at 315.
46   *Legione v Hateley* (1983) 152 CLR 406 at 449.
47   *Stern v McArthur* (1988) 165 CLR 489.
48   *Ferguson v Wilson* (1866) LR 2 Ch App 77.

the defendant has disposed of the land to a third party.[49] The plaintiff seeking such an order must be left to an action for damages at common law.[50] A defendant may still be ordered to perform an obligation notwithstanding a condition precedent to performance of that obligation may be the obtaining of the consent of a third party, whose consent the defendant has no power to require. In *Brown v Heffer*,[51] a contract for the sale of land was conditional upon ministerial approval which, if refused, would bring the contract to an end. However, before the approval was obtained, a conditional order was made.[52] Likewise, and somewhat differently from the defence of impossibility, if the performance of a contract would in all practical terms be futile, specific performance will not be ordered by a court. For example, specific performance has been refused where an agreement for leases is for an expired term or short term. However, an order for specific performance may be made to permit an action to be bought at law upon a covenant in a lease notwithstanding the term may have expired.[53]

25.5.5 *Where the plaintiff is guilty of laches*

[25.115] A plaintiff may be refused an order for specific performance if the plaintiff is guilty of unreasonable delay in pursuing the action, and this delay unfairly prejudices the defendant's position. For example, in *Lamshed v Lamshed*,[54] a plaintiff commenced an action for specific performance of a contract for the sale of land in 1956, but did not prosecute it further until 1962, during which time the defendant had contracted to sell it to a third party. The plaintiff was held to be disentitled to an order on the basis that the plaintiff's delay unfairly placed the appellant in a position of uncertainty over a substantial period of time, and if the case was prosecuted further, this would unfairly prejudice the rights of third parties who had acquired an interest in the land.[55] Generally, a plaintiff seeking specific performance should prosecute his or her claim with diligence and should at all times be ready, willing, and able to complete the contract.[56]

25.5.6 *That the contract is unenforceable because of informality*

[25.120] Contracts for the sale or disposition of any interest in land are required by legislation to be in writing, signed by the party to be charged with their performance.[57] A contract that does not comply with the requirements of these respective statutes would be unenforceable but not void; although not amenable to a decree of specific performance, the contract could pass title to the property.

Nevertheless, the contract may still be specifically enforceable through the application of the doctrine of part-performance. This doctrine relies not upon the oral

---

49 The fact the improvements no longer exist is not a bar: *Black Creek Deer Farm Pty Ltd v Australia & New Zealand Banking Group Ltd* [1996] V Conv R 54-549.
50 *Duncombe v New York Properties Pty Ltd* [1986] 1 Qd R 16.
51 (1967) 116 CLR 344.
52 See also *Kennedy v Vercoe* (1960) 106 CLR 521.
53 *Mundy v Joliffe* (1839) 9 LJ Ch 95; *Chan v Cresdon Pty Ltd* (1989) 168 CLR 242 at 254–255.
54 (1963) 109 CLR 440.
55 Ibid at 455.
56 *Mehmet v Benson* (1965) 113 CLR 295.
57 *Conveyancing Act* 1919 (NSW), s 54A; *Instruments Act* 1958 (Vic), ss 126, 127; *Property Law Act* 1974 (Qld), s 59; *Land of Property Act* 1936 (SA), s 26; *Land Reform (Statute of Frauds) Act* 1962 (WA), s 2; *Conveyancing and Law of Property Act* 1884 (Tas), s 36; *Law of Property Act* 2000 (NT), s 62.

contract or partly oral and partly written contract, but upon acts performed by the plaintiff on the faith of the existence of an enforceable contract, such that, to plead the informality, would amount to equitable fraud on the part of the defendant.[58] The plaintiff must have performed acts that are referable to obligations under the oral contract. This will give rise to the equity required to support a claim for specific performance, on the basis that it would be unconscientious for the defendant to plead the lack of statutory formalities.[59] Where material elements of a contract are not in writing, a court will not permit the plaintiff to give oral evidence of those terms, but will allow a plaintiff to give oral evidence of acts performed, which are unequivocally referable to the alleged contract. To successfully propound part-performance of a contract for the sale of land, it is not sufficient merely to prove that purchase money was paid.[60] More substantial acts performed by the plaintiff in reliance upon the fact that the plaintiff considered the contract enforceable are necessary. For example, the taking of possession of land and making improvements or alterations to it, and the paying of rates and taxes upon it, can be sufficient acts of part-performance.[61] It is fair to say that there has been much criticism of this law, both in the United Kingdom and in Australia, on the ground that the application of the doctrine of part-performance makes a mockery of the requirements of the legislation.[62] While the equivalent provisions have been repealed in the United Kingdom, they still remain in effect in Australia, and the doctrine is still relevant to the specific enforcement of informal agreements for the sale or disposition of interests in land.

25.6 Injunctions

[25.120] An injunction is an order of a court exercising inherent equitable jurisdiction, or a jurisdiction conferred by statute that equates to the same thing—most commonly compelling a party to refrain from doing an act (a negative or prohibitory injunction) or, more rarely, to perform some positive act (a mandatory injunction). Originally, injunctions were available only in the exclusive jurisdiction of a court of equity as a means of enforcing equitable obligations and protecting equitable rights. However, they later came to be used in what was known as the auxiliary jurisdiction of equity, when injunctions were used to protect and enforce legal rights in cases where damages at common law were inadequate. An injunction in that jurisdiction may be granted to restrain a breach of contract—or, as is often the case, a threatened breach of contract. There are many other circumstances in which injunctions may be awarded by the courts, but the concentration in this part is on injunctions restraining breaches of contract.

25.7 Procedural considerations

[25.125] A claim for an injunction by a plaintiff is a two-step procedure. In the first instance, a plaintiff will seek an interlocutory injunction which, if granted, serves as an interim measure to freeze the position of the parties pending a final outcome. Often,

---

58   *Maddison v Alderson* (1883) 8 App Cas 467 at 475–476.
59   *McBride v Sandland* (1918) 25 CLR 69 at 77.
60   *Steadman v Steadman* [1976] AC 536 at 541, 570–571.
61   *Regent v Millett* (1976) 50 ALJR 799.
62   *Wakeham v Mackenzie* [1968] 2 All ER 783 at 788.

an interlocutory injunction must be sought quickly before all the evidence in the case is available; it is granted on the basis that further evidence will be led, and argument advanced, before a final injunction may or may not be awarded. The whole point of the interim injunction is to preserve the status quo until the time when this can occur.

[25.130] The courts have, over a long period, laid down rules for the granting of interim relief by way of an interlocutory injunction. Before such relief will be ordered, a court must consider whether the plaintiff has made out a prima facie case in the sense that upon the evidence before the court, there is a probability that at the trial of the action, the plaintiff will be entitled to a final injunction. Secondly, the court will consider the inconvenience or damage the plaintiff might be likely to suffer if an injunction were refused at that point, weighed against the injury the defendant would suffer if an injunction were granted. This is called the balance of convenience.[63] There has been much disputation as to what constitutes a prima facie case, and over time, this has been reduced to the principle that a plaintiff must show there is a serious question to be argued.[64] If the claim for an interlocutory injunction meets these criteria, the plaintiff will normally have to give the defendant an undertaking as to damages to protect the defendant's position, should a final injunction not be awarded and the defendant suffer loss as a result.[65] Despite a great deal of court time being consumed in seeking to identify nuances between the concept of probability of success in an action and a seriously arguable case, generally it can now be said that an interlocutory injunction will be granted if:

- the plaintiff can show that damages at common law would not be an adequate final remedy; and
- the court is satisfied that there is a serious question to be tried; and
- such interim relief is justified on the balance of convenience.

This test applies to the award of all interlocutory injunctions.

25.8 Contract enforcement and prohibitory orders

[25.135] It may be assumed that the greater part of injunctive relief given is negative in nature: that is, there is an order restraining the defendant from doing some particular act. This is in direct contrast to an order for specific performance, where the defendant is positively ordered to perform the contract according to its terms. The view has been judicially expressed that there is no real conceptual difficulty in applying prohibitory orders to aid the enforcement of a contract. In *Whitwood Chemical Co v Hardman*,[66] Lindley LJ (as he then was) made the point that every contract involves an obligation, implied if not expressed, that neither party shall do anything to destroy the efficiency of the bargain that has been made.[67] On this basis, a party to a contract could be restrained from acting in a manner inimical to the integrity of the bargain. Whether or not a defendant who is in breach of contract, or threatening seriously to breach a contract, is forced by the court to positively perform the conditions of the contract by

---

63   *Beecham Group Ltd v Bristol Laboratories Pty Ltd* (1968) 118 CLR 618 at 622.
64   *American Cyanamid Co v Ethicon Ltd* [1975] AC 396.
65   *Ansett Transport Industries (Operations) Pty Ltd v Halton* (1979) 146 CLR 249 at 306.
66   [1891] 2 Ch 416.
67   Ibid at 426.

means of an order for specific performance or prevent it from breaching the conditions of the contract by means of an injunction, may ultimately reside in the discretion of the court.[68] There is undoubtedly a contradiction in granting a prohibitory injunction to restrain a breach of a negative stipulation in a contract. However, courts have been alive to the existence of this analogy and have, for the purposes of exercising discretion, whittled down the distinction between what might be an express negative stipulation and an implied negative stipulation—and doing this by looking at the substance of the agreement rather than the form in which it is expressed.[69] Generally, no injunction will be granted to restrain a breach of a negative stipulation that is interpreted by the court as being positive in substance. In *Dalgety Wine Estates Pty Ltd v Rizzon*,[70] Mason J (as he then was) observed:

> that the attitudes of the courts to the enforcement of negative stipulations have varied according to the nature of the stipulation, the nature of the contract in which it is found, the effect which the enforceable will have on the relationship of the parties under the contract and the character of the order required to enforce the stipulation.[71]

[25.140] As an overriding consideration, an injunction will not be granted in these circumstances where it is clear that damages would be an adequate remedy.[72]

25.9 Limitations on the grant of an injunction

[25.145] There are standard cases where an injunction to enforce a contract is not usually granted. First, express or implied negative stipulations contained in contracts for the sale of chattels will not be enforced by injunction unless they are for some reason unique, or damages for breach of the contract will not otherwise be an adequate remedy.[73] Secondly, injunctions will not usually be granted in circumstances compelling a defendant to perform the defendant's side of the bargain when the continuance of the obligation to do so depends upon the future conduct of the plaintiff. This would have the effect of binding one party to perform in specie, leaving that party to a remedy in damages only, if the other party failed to fulfil his or her contractual conditions. However, this rule might not be invariable when there are clear, negative duties imposed by the contract. Here, an injunction may be granted when the remedy at law is inadequate to protect the right.[74] This is because as a matter of practice, equity when ordering specific relief against one party, expects that party to perform the whole of his or her obligations as they stand, and orders are drawn accordingly.[75]

[25.150] Thirdly, contracts of personal service in which there are negatively phrased covenants—for example, not to give notice or not to terminate a contract of employ-

---

68   *Doherty v Allman* (1878) 3 App Cas 709 at 728.
69   *Wolverhampton & Walsall Railway Co v London & Northwest Railway Co* (1873) LR 16 Eq 433 at 440.
70   (1979) 141 CLR 552.
71   Ibid at 573–574.
72   *Aristoc Industries Pty Ltd v RA Wendam (Builders) Pty Ltd* [1965] NSWR 581 at 587–589.
73   *Wood v Corrigan* (1928) 28 SR (NSW) 492; *Sky Petroleum v VIP Petroleum* [1974] 1 All ER 954.
74   *JC Williamson Ltd v Lukey & Mulholland* (1931) 45 CLR 282 at 299–300.
75   *Ryan v Mutual Tontine Westminster Chambers Association* [1893] 1 Ch 116 at 123.

ment—will normally not be enforceable by injunction. This is because the effect of granting an injunction (or specific performance) would be to force the parties to maintain a relationship with each other that may be unsatisfactory.[76] Two factors are of significance in the exercise of the court's discretion in these cases: the length of time the contract has yet to run, and the nature of the relationship between the parties. Naturally, the longer the time and the closer the relationship, the less likely that an injunction will be granted.

Example: Lumley v Wagner[77]

The defendant, a well-known opera singer, agreed to sing at the plaintiff's theatre, Covent Garden, for three months. She also agreed not to perform at any other theatre in England without the plaintiff's consent. When she threatened to breach her contract, having been offered a larger fee to sing elsewhere, an injunction was granted to restrain her from doing so. This effectively was an injunction to restrain breach of a negative covenant. In granting the injunction, Lord St Leonards LC conceded that he could not order the defendant to sing at Covent Garden but that, in the circumstances, it was appropriate to restrain her from singing elsewhere. Notably, the agreement was only for a period of three months, and would not have forced the parties to maintain a relationship that had fractured.

[25.155] On the other hand if, at the time of the breach, the length of time an agreement has to run is much longer, an injunction may not be granted. In *Page One Records Pty Ltd v Britton*,[78] a group of pop musicians agreed to appoint a manager for 5 years; the contract stipulated they would not employ anyone else as their manager during that period. Concurrently, they entered into a publishing agreement with another party not to publish their music through any other source. One year into the agreement, they threatened both to employ a rival manager and to commit breaches of both agreements. Injunctions were sought to restrain these apprehended breaches. They were refused. Clearly, granting an injunction would have forced the maintenance of the business relationship, which had become unworkable in the circumstances; damages were obviously an adequate remedy for breach of the agreement. The situation may well have been different if the nature of the agreement had been more commercial, rather than requiring the performance of personal management services.[79]

25.10 Damages in equity

[25.160] Damages are traditionally a remedy sought at common law for breach of a legal right or duty. Whilst equity had no power to award damages, as such, for breach of an equitable duty, it did have inherent power to award compensation for loss or damage suffered as a result of a breach of a purely equitable obligation—for example,

---

76   *Davis v Foreman* [1894] 3 Ch 654; *Heine Bros (Aust) Pty Ltd v Forrest* [1963] VR 383.
77   (1852) 1 De G M & G 604; 42 ER 687.
78   [1968] 1 WLR 157.
79   *Thomas Borthwick & Sons (Australasia) Ltd v South Otago Freezing Co Ltd* [1978] 1 NZLR 538 at 549–
       550; *Sanderson Motors (Sales) Pty Ltd v Yorkstar Motors Pty Ltd* [1983] 1 NSWLR 513.

misappropriation of trust property by a trustee.[80] However, in the concurrent and auxiliary jurisdiction of equity, where equitable remedies such as specific performance and
injunction were awarded in support of legal rights, damages in the form of compensation were sought in addition to or in substitution for equitable relief when that was
denied.[81] By the mid-nineteenth century, some doubt had arisen[82] about the ability of
the Court of Chancery to award damages. This led to the enactment of *Lord Cairns'
Act*[83] in 1858. Section 2 of that Act provided (in paraphrase) that in all cases where a
Court of Chancery has jurisdiction to grant an injunction for breach of any covenant,
contract or agreement, or for specific performance of any covenant, contract, or agreement, the court shall, if it thinks fit, award damages to the party injured either in addition to or in substitution for such injunction or specific performance.

[25.165] In each Australian State other than Queensland, there is legislative provision
to the same effect.[84] While the legislation allows an award of damages in lieu of either
specific performance or an injunction, in relation to breaches of contract, it is most
commonly applied to award financial compensation in substitution for or in lieu of a
decree of specific performance. This part of the chapter is confined to those issues.

25.11 Nature of claim

[25.170] Since the fusion of law and equity through the successive re-enactment of the
English *Judicature Act* 1873 in each State,[85] it has been possible to obtain both common
law and equitable relief in the one court. This effectively means that a plaintiff seeking
to specifically enforce a contract may claim, in the one writ or application (as the case
may be), an order for specific performance of the contract, an order for damages in
lieu of or in addition to specific performance, and alternatively to both of these, damages at common law.[86] The plaintiff would seek damages at common law where the
action for specific performance may have been abandoned or due to the failure of the
defendant to obey the order.[87] At that point, the defendant's failure to perform can be
treated by the plaintiff as a repudiation of the defendant's obligations under a contract,
thus permitting the plaintiff the right to terminate the contract based upon that repudiation.[88] In these cases, no question of equitable damages arises.

---

80   *Re Dawson (dec'd)* [1966] 2 NSWR 211.
81   *Phelps v Prothero* (1855) 7 De G M & G 722 at 734; ER 280 at 285; *King v Poggioli* (1923) 32 CLR 222
     at 246–247; *Fullers' Theatres Ltd v Musgrove* (1923) 31 CLR 524 at 547.
82   See, for example, *Todd v Gee* (1810) 17 Ves 273 at 277–278; 34 ER 106 at 107.
83   21 & 22 Vict c 27.
84   *Supreme Court Act* 1970 (NSW), s 68; *Supreme Court Act* 1958 (Vic), s 62(3); *Equity Act* 1867 (Qld), s 62
     (repealed by *Statute Law Revision Act* 1908 (Qld) but with its substantive effect retained by a saving pro-
     vision), *Conroy v Lowndes* [1958] Qd R 375 at 383; *Supreme Court Act* 1935 (SA), s 30; *Supreme Court Act*
     1935 (WA), s 25(10); *Supreme Court Civil Procedure Act* 1932 (Tas), s 11(13).
85   *Supreme Court Act* 1970 (NSW), ss 57–64; *Supreme Court Act* 1958 (Vic), s 62; *Supreme Court Act* 1995
     (Qld), s 44; *Supreme Court Act* 1935 (SA), ss 17–28; *Supreme Court Act* 1935 (WA), ss 24, 25; *Supreme
     Court Civil Procedure Act* 1932 (Tas), ss 10, 11.
86   *Public Trustee v Pearlberg* [1940] 2 KB 1 at 11–12; *Bosaid v Andry* [1963] VR 465 at 486–487.
87   *Ogle v Comboyuro Investments Pty Ltd* (1976) 136 CLR 444 at 453.
88   *McDonald v Dennys Lascelles Ltd* (1933) 48 CLR 457 at 476–477; *Johnson v Agnew* [1980] AC 367. See
     Chapter 20 [20.105] in relation to termination for repudiation.

[25.175] However, when specific performance is refused and the plaintiff still suffers loss, the question of compensation through equitable damages arises at that point.

25.12 When equitable damages may be awarded

[25.180] It is clear that equitable damages will only be awarded where a plaintiff demonstrates a right to specific performance at the hearing.[89] The circumstances in which a plaintiff may have a right to specific performance, but it is not awarded, are where the defendant raises a successful equitable defence such as, for example, hardship or laches. For example, in *Edward Street Properties Pty Ltd v Collins*,[90] a court refused specific performance to a plaintiff on the ground of laches, but recognised that the defendant had still committed a breach of contract in failing to complete, and that the plaintiff had suffered loss and damage. The court accordingly awarded equitable damages to the plaintiff.

[25.185] However, where the plaintiff is not entitled to specific performance because the plaintiff is in breach of his own obligations, equitable damages will not be awarded. In *King v Poggioli*,[91] a plaintiff purchaser under a contract for the sale of land was denied specific performance because of his failure to show that he was ready, willing and able to perform the contract; he was also denied equitable damages for that reason.[92] The same principle would apply where a plaintiff was denied specific performance based upon his or her unconscionable conduct.[93]

[25.190] This accords with an application of the general principles of equity and, in particular, the principle that for any equitable relief to be granted, is a matter for the discretion of the court, and the plaintiff must come to equity with clean hands.[94]

[25.195] Equitable damages might also be awarded where a contract for the sale of land does not meet the requirements of writing but can be enforced in equity through part performance. In such a case, equitable damages may be awarded in lieu of or in substitution for specific performance.[95]

25.13 Measure of equitable damages

[25.200] Where equitable damages are awarded in lieu of specific performance, effectively the contract is brought to an end and the plaintiff would be seeking to recover the same damages recoverable for loss of bargain as if the plaintiff had rescinded the contract based upon the defendant's breach. The measure of damages is, therefore, the difference between the contract price and market value of the property at the date of breach.[96] The date of breach will effectively be the date of the judgment of the court.[97]

---

89 *Bosaid v Andry* [1963] VR 465 at 484.
90 [1977] Qd R 399.
91 (1923) 32 CLR 222.
92 *Boyns v Lackey* (1958) 58 SR (NSW) 395.
93 *Dowsett v Reid* (1912) 15 CLR 695; *Summers v Cocks* (1927) 40 CLR 321.
94 See also *McKenna v Richey* [1950] VLR 360 at 375.
95 *Dillon v Nash* [1950] VLR 293 at 300–301.
96 *Bosaid v Andry* [1963] VR 465 at 484; *Souster v Epson Plumbing Contractors Ltd* [1974] 2 NZLR 515 at 520.
97 *Wroth v Tyler* [1974] Ch 30 at 57–58.

[25.205] Because the question of damages in equity is discretionary, the court may take into account conduct that may disentitle the plaintiff to specific performance. For example, if the plaintiff were guilty of laches (delay) so as to disentitle the plaintiff to specific performance of a contract for the sale of land, equitable damages may be reduced as the plaintiff should not profit out of the delay and gain the effects of inflation on the value of the land to the date of judgment.[98] If, as stated, the date of judgment can be equated to the date of acceptance by the plaintiff of a repudiation of a contract by the defendant as being the date of breach, for the purposes of determining damages, it is now clear that there is little difference in that respect between the quantum of damages in equity and that at common law.[99]

25.14 International perspectives

25.14.1 New Zealand

[25.210] There is no substantive difference between the law in Australia and in New Zealand with respect to equitable remedies, so New Zealand law does not require separate examination here.

25.14.2 United States

[25.215] The American law in relation to enforcement of a contract by specific performance and injunction is substantively the same as in Australia. Specific performance and injunction are recognised as alternative remedies to damages for breach of contract. An award of specific performance or injunction is subject to all of the usual equitable limitations, such as adequacy of damages, discretion of the court, clean hands, and laches. The contrasting features of American law lie not in the statements of principle, but in the interpretation of these principles. The primary area of difference is in the circumstances in which an American court will consider damages an inadequate remedy.

[25.220] Whether damages are an adequate remedy is directly relevant to the granting of an equitable remedy. In contrast to English and Australian courts, American courts have taken a liberal view of this requirement by tending to enlarge the class of cases in which damages will be considered inadequate. The underlying objective of the court will be to choose the form of relief that will adequately protect the legally recognised interest of the injured party, which is usually the expectation interest of the party. Factors a court may consider are:

- the difficulty of proving damages with reasonable certainty;[100]
- the difficulty of procuring a reasonable substitute;
- the likelihood that an award of damages could not be collected.[101]

---

98   *Hickey v Bruhns* [1977] 2 NZLR 71 at 79.
99   *Johnson v Agnew* [1980] AC 367 at 400.
100 For example, where damages may only be nominal or the contract involves matters of taste or sentiment.
101 Usually where the defendant is insolvent. Refer generally to Restatement (Second) § 360.

[25.225] This may lead to a wider range of contracts being capable of specific perform-ance than under the Australian law.[102] The fact that damages are an adequate remedy for failure to complete one part of the contract will not preclude specific performance of the contract as a whole.[103] Nor does the existence of a liquidated damages clause necessarily preclude specific performance.[104]

[25.230] In all other respects, the same considerations are relevant to the court's exer-cise of their discretion to award specific performance or an injunction, as in the Aus-tralian system.[105]

25.14.3 Japan

[25.235] As a civil law country, Japan has no equitable jurisdiction as such. It follows that there are no equitable remedies in the common law sense. The legal principles that operate as functional equivalents of equitable principles in the common law are described in chapters 7, 17, and 23.

---

102 For example, contracts for the sale of artwork, heirlooms, shares (where a loss in control of a corpora-tion is involved), covenant for an indemnity, even a contract for goods where they are not easily obtain-able in the market place.

103 *Taylor v Highland Park Corp* 42 SE 2d 335 (SC 1947) (contract for the sale of personalty and land). See Restatement (Second) § 359.

104 The existence of such a clause may not necessarily afford an adequate remedy. See Restatement (Sec-ond) § 361.

105 See the Restatement (Second) § 362–369.

Part VIII

International Contracts

Globalisation is an indisputable aspect of modern society. Australia, like most other countries, depends upon trade with other nations. As international trade makes up a considerable part of this country's economy, it is important to understand the international contracts facilitating that trade, and appreciate the special issues they entail. This Part considers the wider implications of contract law in the context of globalisation and regionalisation. It considers the way international approaches are harmonising and unifying substantive contract law, and the way standard-form and generally accepted international commercial contracts have been accepted in commerce. It also discusses choice of law and choice of forum—the two major issues for private international law.

Chapter 26

International contracts

26.1   Introduction

[26.05] This chapter examines international contracts, using a variety of frameworks. It begins with an examination of the globalisation and regionalisation of contract law, the aim of which is to situate Australian contract law within broader global and regional legal frameworks. The macroscopic approach to international contracts is then considered, concentrating on the harmonisation and unification of substantive contract law. The chapter looks at what has been accomplished through international treaties and statements of principle made by the peak bodies with an interest in commercial and contract law. Attention then shifts to the microscopic approach to international contracts, with a focus on standard-form contracts and generally accepted international commercial contracts. The chapter concludes with an examination of private international law as it relates to choice of law and choice of forum in international contracting.

26.2   The globalisation and regionalisation of contract law

[26.10] This section examines two distinct but related phenomena: the globalisation of contract law and the regionalisation of contract law.

One of the modern buzzwords, particularly in the international business market place, is 'globalisation'. Globalisation has been defined in these terms by one commentator, McGrew:

> Globalisation refers to the multiplicity of linkages and interconnections between the states and the societies which make up the present world system. It describes the process by which events, decisions and activities in one part of the world come to have significant consequences for individuals and communities in quite distant parts of the globe. Globalisation has two distinct phenomena: scope (or stretching) and intensity (or deepening). On the one hand, it defines a set of processes which embrace most of the globe or which operate worldwide; the concept therefore has a spatial connotation ... On the other hand, it also implies an intensification of the levels of interaction, interconnectedness or interdependence between the states and societies which constitute

the world community. Accordingly, alongside the stretching goes a deepening of global processes.[1]

Goldring has referred to globalisation in these terms:

'Globalisation' is said to mean the end of national politics, which will be replaced by exchange in a totally free global market for goods, services and ideas.[2]

[26.15] These commentators have viewed globalisation as an extra-legal phenomenon in its nature, scope, operation, and effect.[3] Yet globalisation does resonate within parts of contract law, and the task at present is to identify briefly the key points of connection between globalisation and contract law. Scholars have already identified some points of connection between the body of commercial law and globalisation.[4] As commercial law is underpinned by so much contract law[5], it follows that it is proper to ask the question: what is the confluence of contract law and globalisation? Four distincte phenomena are relevant here: the advent of international standard business contracts; harmonisation; standardisation; and unification.

[26.20] The advent of international standard business contracts demonstrates just how much contract law is becoming globalised. An international standard business contract is a contract drawn up by or sponsored by an international business organisation (for example, the International Chamber of Commerce). The members of that organisation—and even non-members—use these contracts to document and record cross-border transactions. One explanation for this phenomenon is the supremacy of *transactional law*. Some commentators consider that international business law has reached the point where it accentuates the primacy of contracts above other types of legal instruments.[6] This could be explained, in part, by the importance of the

---

1   See A McGrew, 'Conceptualising Global Politics', in A McGrew & P Lewis (eds), *Global Politics: Globalisation and the Nation State*, Polity Press, Cambridge Press, Mass, 1992 (cited by J Dunning, 'The Role of FDI in a Globalising Economy', Chapter 3 in C Green & T Brewer (eds), *Investment in Asia and the Pacific Rim*, Oceana Publications, New York, 1995, p 44).

2   See J Goldring, 'Globalisation, National Sovereignty and the Harmonisation of Laws' [1998] 3 *Uniform Law Review (NS)* Nos 2/3, 435 at 437.

3   See F Lechner & J Boli (eds), *The Globalisation Reader*, Blackwell Publishers, Oxford, 2000 for a well-assembled collection of contemporary resources on globalisation.

4   For a study addressing the connections between commercial law and globalisation see S Fisher, 'Commercial Law in a Global Context: Current Influences and the Future for Australia', Chapter 10 in A Mugasha (ed), *Commercial Law: Issues for the 21st Century*, Prospect Media Pty Ltd, Sydney, 2001, especially pp 115-117; U Geiger, 'The Case for the Harmonisation of the Securities Disclosure Rules in the Global Market' [1997] 2 & 3 *Columbia Business Law Review* 241 at 298. See also H Sigman, 'The Case for Worldwide Reform of the Law Governing Secured Transactions in Movable Property', Chapter 11 in J Ziegel (ed), *New Developments in International Commercial and Consumer Law*, Hart Publishing, Oxford, 1998, pp 239-244 and R Goode, 'Reflections on the Harmonisation of Commercial Law' in R Cranston & R Goode (eds), *Commercial and Consumer Law: National and International Dimensions*, Clarendon Press, New York, 1993, p 1.

5   For example, the standard works on commercial law contain a significant leavening of contract law. See R Goode, *Commercial Law*, 2nd edn, Penguin Books, London, 1995; and I Turley, *Principles of Commercial Law*, Cavendish Publishing (Australia) Pty Ltd, Sydney, 1995; and S Fisher, *Commercial and Personal Property Law*, Butterworths, Sydney, 1997.

6   See C Schmitthoff, *Commercial Law in a Changing Economic Climate*, 2nd edn, Sweet & Maxwell, London, 1981, pp 21–22 (speaking particularly of the law of international trade). For a recent review of international contracts concentrating on commercial contracts, see M Koppenol-Laforce et al, *International Contracts: Aspects of Jurisdiction, Arbitration and Private International Law*, Sweet & Maxwell, London, 1996.

contract to international trade—a point that is so obvious it hardly needs restating here. This development is not without its critics, who point to the efforts made by international traders to select the body of law most likely to contribute to the successful consummation of their transaction, even though this reduces the impact of national laws.[7] But one interesting development in some branches of Australian law that contain international elements is that standard-form contracts have become accepted vehicles with which to conduct business.[8]

[26.25] In the field of trade finance, for example, one of the most common methods used by exporters to secure payment from the importer (when the exporter does not wish to extend credit or open account terms) is the letter of credit. The letter of credit originated with the mediaeval letter of payment that was in use in northern Italy in the fourteenth century.[9] From this beginning, the documentary letter of credit has become one of the critical commercial and legal elements of international trade—so much so that English judges have described it as the 'lifeblood of international commerce'.[10] The predominant legal instrument governing the use of the documentary letter of credit is the ICC's *Uniform Customs and Practice for Documentary Credits*.[11] Banks in more than 140 countries have signified their acceptance to the UCP.[12] This is remarkable, considering that the ICC is a non-governmental body, and that its work is adopted by interested parties on a voluntary basis without legislative backing.[13] Another ICC publication that is influential in international trade in goods is *Incoterms 2000*.[14] *Incoterms 2000* is incorporated into individual cross-border sale of goods contracts. A third example is the documentation sponsored by the International Swap Dealers' Association (ISDA), which is widely used in international currency and interest rate swap transactions.

[26.30] What these standardised contracts signify is the emergence of standardised trade terms on the basis of the activities of merchants rather than by imposed law. Collins has described this quite neatly as the case where 'international business transactions ... [forge] their own miniature legal orders'.[15] This in fact may provide a speedier method to the unification of international business laws than positive enacted law. According to the Australian Law Reform Commission, this type of legal activity may provide a

---

7   See J Goldring, 'Globalisation, National Sovereignty and the Harmonisation of Laws' [1998] 3 *Uniform Law Review (NS)* Nos 2/3, 435 at 445.

8   There are some Queensland examples, too: the REIQ Conveyancing Contracts and the REIQ Contract for Sale of a Business.

9   C Hugo, *The Law Relating to Documentary Credits from a South African Perspective with Special Reference to the Legal Position of the Issuing and Confirming Banks*, LLD Thesis, University of Stellenbosch, August 1997, paragraph [2 4 2].

10 *RD Harbottle (Mercantile) Ltd v National Westminster Bank Ltd* [1978] 1 QB 146 at 155; *Intraco Ltd v Notis Shipping Corporation (The 'Bhoja Trader')* [1981] 2 Lloyds Rep 256 at 257.

11 UCP 500, ICC, ICC Publishing SA, Paris, 1993. The UCP is cited by reference to the publication number assigned to it by the ICC, and in the case of the 1993 revision, this is UCP 500. The 1983 revision was called the UCP 400.

12 C Hugo, *The Law Relating to Documentary Credits from a South African Perspective with Special Reference to the Legal Position of the Issuing and Confirming Banks*, LLD Thesis, University of Stellenbosch, August 1997, paragraph 3 1 (citing data as at 5 April 1990 provided by the ICC).

13 It is rarer still to find domestic legislation governing letters of credit. The best-known example is Article 5 of the *Uniform Commercial Code* (USA).

14 See [26.285]–[26.300].

15 H Collins, *The Law of Contract*, 3rd edn, Butterworths, London, 1997, p 44.

more flexible and rapid method of cementing internationally accepted business practices, and is likely to be developed with more expertise than any formal international legal initiative.[16] At bottom, this is a form of self-help of the law reform variety. These types of standardised contracts depend on the operation of a legal principle of party autonomy, so this norm has a distributive operation when invoked to support the notion of the supremacy of transactional law. The widespread use of these international standard-form contracts shows that contract law is becoming globalised in very distinct sectors or market niches. This phenomenon may also be explained on the basis that there is a breakdown in legal insularity if international merchants and traders select and voluntarily adopt their own standard-form contracts.[17]

[26.35] It is appropriate to consider why the legal system should be supportive of standard-form contracts when they can also produce injustice, particularly in the consumer arena. There are several quite strong reasons why legal systems generally, and Australia's in particular, support standard-form contracts.

The first reason is that standard-form contracts facilitate contracting because they eliminate the need for the contracting parties to renegotiate the complete range of terms every time they deal with each other. Secondly—and this is a corollary of the first point—standard-form contracts reduce transaction costs. Transaction costs are incurred primarily when the standard-form contract is first prepared, and they are amortised over the subsequent uses of the contract. Thirdly, standard-form contracts become known to users and lawyers as authoritative compilations of terms that are used in a particular industry or business sector, and this familiarity leads to the promotion of trust and confidence in the standard-form contract. When peak bodies for particular industries or professions sponsor standard-form contracts, participants in those industries or professions may feel secure that the specific nuances that reflect the basis upon which their business or profession is conducted, are incorporated into the standard-form contract sponsored by the relevant peak body. Fourthly, standard-form contracts lead to greater certainty in terms of the contents of a contract—reducing, but not eliminating, the need to have recourse to implied terms to give effect to the intentions of the parties.

26.2.1   Convergences in contract law

[26.40] Standard-form contracts are adopted by international traders, as we have seen; but the remaining three processes to be discussed—harmonisation, standardisation, and unification of contract law—differ markedly from the phenomenon of international standard-form contracts because they represent positivist legal interventions in contract law by law-making agencies.

26.2.2   Harmonisation

[26.45] Where laws are harmonised between two or more jurisdictions, the underlying process is that the laws are not made identical in each of the jurisdictions, but are brought generally into line, so that there is equivalence in the content of the laws as

---

16   Australian Law Reform Commission, *Legal Risk in International Transactions,* ALRC Report No 80, Canberra, 1996, paragraph 2.33.

17   This decline in insularity is considered in H Collins, *The Law of Contract*, 3rd edn, Butterworths, London 1997, p 41.

between the different jurisdictions.[18] The general corpus of contract law has not been harmonised between any two major economic powers, but there are isolated examples of harmonisation of contract law in discrete areas.

[26.50] One illustration of this is the *Contract (Applicable Law) Act* 1990 (UK), which incorporates into domestic English law the Rome Convention 1980 on the Law Applicable to Contractual Obligations. A harmonisation initiative of a different order is that in the European Union; there has been some political intervention in the arena of the harmonisation of private laws. One example of this is the Resolution of the European Parliament on the Harmonisation of Certain Sectors of Private Law of the Member States.[19] Harmonisation of laws is needed in federated legal systems such as Australia's.[20]

26.2.3   Standardisation

[26.55] The standardisation of laws is a process by which laws in different jurisdictions conform to a particular standard enunciated by a body having competence or authority, and received or adopted by anther body having legislative competence to translate that standard into applicable positive law.

The paradigm of standardisation of laws is the European Union, where instruments promulgated by the various organs of the European Union identify standards of behaviour that are to be observed by everyone to whom the standards are expressed to be applicable. Law-making agencies of Member States of the European Union then translate those standards into national, positive law.[21] The intervention of the European Union within contract law has been piecemeal and isolated, but nonetheless quite important. One illustration of this is the Directive on Unfair Contract Terms, which has influenced contracting between business operators and consumers. In the United Kingdom, the resulting legislation is the *Unfair Contract Terms Act* 1977 (UK).[22] The European Union's initiative in one area of the law—product liability—has been influential in reshaping and reforming Australia's product liability law under Part VA of the *Trade Practices Act* 1974 (Cth).[23]

26.2.4   Unification

[26.60] The third process that can be used to accomplish the globalisation of contract law is unification. In general, unification refers to the effort made by

---

18   Harmonisation is more complex than has been portrayed here. One commentator has divided harmonisation into two types, harmonisation by commonality and harmonisation by reciprocity: see U Geiger, 'The Case for the Harmonisation of the Securities Disclosure Rules in the Global Market' [1997] 2 & 3 *Columbia Business Law Review* 241 at 298. The former embraces the modification or replacement of domestic rules with substantially similar rules as those of other jurisdictions, while the latter involves the deference by the host jurisdiction to the laws or standards of other jurisdictions.

19   OJ C 205/518, 6 May 1994.

20   See J Ziegel, 'Harmonization of Private Laws in Federal Systems of Government: Canada, the USA, and Australia', Chapter 5 in R Cranston (ed), *Making Commercial Law: Essays in Honour of Roy Goode*, Clarendon Press, Oxford, 1997, pp 131–166.

21   See, S Bronitt, F Burns & D Kinley, *Principles of European Community Law: Commentary and Materials*, Law Book Company, Sydney, 1995.

22   See M Furmston, *Sale and Supply of Goods*, 2nd edn, Cavendish Publishing Limited, London, 1995, pp 142–155 and M Vranken, *Fundamentals of European Civil Law*, The Federation Press, Sydney, 1997, Section 5.5. This has inspired provisions such as ss 68 and 68A of the *Trade Practices Act*, discussed at [9.3.3] above.

23   On product liability law, see J Goldring & Ors, *Consumer Protection Law in Australia*, 5th edn, The Federation Press, Sydney, 1998; S Corones & P Clarke, *Consumer Protection and Product Liability Law: Cases and Materials*, LBC Information Services, Sydney, 1999.

international organisations to make the municipal laws of the countries of a region as uniform as possible[24].

One of the best-know examples of unified laws is the *United Nations Convention on Contracts for the International Sale of Goods* signed in Vienna in April 1980.[25] Australia was a participant in the negotiation of this Convention, and it has been incorporated into domestic law via the generically entitled *Sale of Goods (Vienna Convention) Act*, which was enacted in 1986 in New South Wales, Victoria, Queensland, Western Australia, South Australia, and Tasmania and in 1987 in the Northern Territory and the Australian Capital Territory.[26] With unification of laws, the law is made identical in each of the adopting or implementing jurisdictions. This reduces the prospect of divergent results being caused by differences in substantive law (which are eliminated with unification). And even if the application of private international law is taken into account, the unified national laws are not bypassed as a result.[27]

26.2.5   Regionalisation

[26.70] The examination of the globalisation of contract law above did not deal directly with the regionalisation of contract law. It was touched on implicitly, however, in the mention of the specific European interventions in contract law.

Regionalisation refers to the formation and interplay of multiple linkages and connections between the states and societies of particular regions in the world, rather than the world as a whole. Regionalisation might be evident in the existence and operation of many of the peak international bodies such as the Association of South East Asian Nations (ASEAN), the European Union (EU), and the North American Free Trade Agreement (NAFTA).

26.2.6   Institutions and principles

[26.75] Besides the four phenomena just examined, some institutions and principles need to be identified so far as the globalisation and regionalisation of contract law is concerned.

[26.80] The institutions that are important in this respect, and whose mandates have some demonstrable point of connection with contract law, are the United Nations Commission on International Trade Law (UNCITRAL), the International Institute for the Unification of Private Law (UNIDROIT), the Hague Conference on Private International Law, and the International Chamber of Commerce (ICC). Each of these institutions has sponsored treaties or other instruments (such as Model Laws, standard terms and conditions, explanatory guides, and compilations of industry practices) that are binding to different degrees, and have reached into the body of contract law in discrete areas.[28] What is interesting to note here about the institutions that have been

---

24   See J Fox, *Dictionary of International and Comparative Law,* Oceana Publications Inc, New York, 1997, p 325.

25   Vienna, 11 April 1980; Aust TS 1988 No 32; 19 ILM 671 (1980).

26   See [26.100] below. As it turns out, this is another illustration of intervention into a specific branch of contract law (international contracts for the sale of goods) rather than in contract law as a whole.

27   Some unification Conventions (such as, but not limited to the Vienna Sales Convention) also provide common private international law rules so eliminating divergences in the substantive conflict of laws rules (for example, Article 1(b) of the Vienna Sales Convention). See further [26.345] below.

28   Australian Law Reform Commission, *Legal Risk in International Transactions*, ALRC Report No 80, Canberra, 1996, p 71.

selected is that not all of them are supranational intergovernmental, since the ICC is a private body with an international mandate.

[26.85] The principles that inform the globalisation and regionalisation of contract law are derived, in part, from generally accepted principles of contract law that have circulated across borders and taken root into domestic legal orders. Two are examined later in this chapter: the UNIDROIT Principles of International Commercial Contracts and the European Contract Code. Amissah has identified some of the underlying principles in these terms:

> In sum, a transnational/non-national regulatory order governing the contractual rights and obligations of private individuals is made possible by: (a) States' acceptance of freedom of contract (public policy excepted); (b) Sanctity of contract embodied in the principle *pacta sunt servanda* (c) Written contractual selection of dispute resolution by international commercial arbitration, whether *ad hoc* or institutional, usually under internationally accepted arbitration rules; (d) Guaranteed enforcement, arbitration where necessary borrowing the State apparatus for law enforcement through the NY Convention on International Commercial Arbitration, which has secured for international commercial arbitration a recognition and enforcement regime unparalleled by municipal courts in well over a hundred contracting States; (e) Transnational effect or non-nationality being achievable through international commercial arbitration accepting the parties' ability to select the basis upon which the dispute would be resolved outside municipal law, such as through the selection of general principles of law or *lex mercatoria*, or calling upon the arbitrators to act as *amiable compositeur* or *ex aequo et bono*.[29]

[26.90] To sum up: globalisation and regionalisation of contract law have been influenced by a variety of forces, including the quest for party autonomy in international contracting; the desire to even out differences in substantive contract law; the desire to remove legal insularity; and the wish of international business traders to establish and maintain their own private legal domains. The application and impact of these forces has resulted in harmonised contract law in discrete sectors of international contract law; some harmonised contract law in the sphere of private international law; and the growth in number, and widespread adoption and use, of international standardised business contracts.

26.3   The macro approach to international contracts: the harmonisation and unification of substantive contract law

[26.95] Having explained the processes underlying the globalisation and regionalisation of substantive contract law, this section moves to an examination of some important legal regimes where harmonisation or unification of substantive contract law has taken

---

29   See R Amissah, 'Revisiting the Autonomous Contract: Transnational Contracting, Trends and Supporting Structures' available at: <http://www.jus.uio.no/lm/autonomous.contract.2000.amissah/doc.html> (accessed 6 January 2001). For a study of related principles, again in the commercial law arena, see S Fisher, 'Commercial Law in a Global Context: Current Influences and the Future for Australia', Chapter 10 in A Mugasha (ed), *Commercial Law: Issues for the 21st Century*, Prospect Media Pty Ltd, Sydney, 2001, pp 129–137.

place. Hopes that the globalisation and regionalisation of international trade law—which, as stated before, rests on a foundation of contract law—might assist in the quest for world peace have not been realised in practice.[30]

26.3.1   The United Nations Convention on Contracts for the International Sale of Goods 1980

(a)   Background to the Convention

[26.100] The United Nations Convention on Contracts for the International Sale of Goods[31] (known as the Vienna Sales Convention or the CISG) is an international treaty that has unified an important body of contract law on a cross-border basis, namely the contract for the international sale of goods. It represents the culmination of literally decades of efforts by some international agencies and by leading scholars to unify the law governing the international sale of goods.[32]

The Vienna Sales Convention has led to a bifurcation of international sale of goods law.[33] It has enjoyed widespread acceptance by leading international trading nations, including many of Australia's major trading partners, as well as developing nations.[34] This section explores the foundation principles and rules of the Convention that concentrate on the formation of contracts for the international sale of goods.

(b)   Application of the Convention

[26.105] The Convention itself came into force internationally on 1 January 1988. It applies to international sale contracts entered into by Australian exporters and importers after 1 April 1989. Many Australian lawyers are unaware of the Convention, so

---

30   F Fabricus, 'The Universal and Regional Harmonisation of International Trade Law As a Means of Maintaining World Peace', Chapter 18 in C Schmitthoff & K Simmonds (eds), *International Economic and Trade Law: Universal and Regional Integration*, AW Sithoff, Leyden, 1976, pp 201–225.

31   Vienna, 11 April 1980; Aust TS 1988 No 32; 19 ILM 671 (1980).

32   The history of previous attempts to unify international sale of goods law before the advent of the Vienna Sales Convention is traced by J Honnold, *Uniform Law for International Sales under the 1980 United Nations Convention*, 3rd edn, Kluwer Law International, The Hague, 1999.

33   See M Bridge, 'The Bifocal World of International Sales: Theatre and Non-Vienna', Chapter 11 in R Cranston (ed), *Making Commercial Law: Essays in Honour of Roy Goode*, Clarendon Press, Oxford, 1997, pp 277–296.

34   For a list of the States that are party to the Vienna Sales Convention, see S Fisher & D Fisher, *Export Best Practice: Commercial and Legal Aspects*, The Federation Press, Sydney, July 1998, paragraph [5.3.2]. This can be updated by accessing the UN International Trade Centre's Juris International website: <http://www.jurisint.org/pub/01/en/113.htm> (accessed 17 January 2001).

For analyses of the Vienna Sales Convention, see J Honnold, *Uniform Law for International Sales under the 1980 United Nations Convention* (Professor Honnold was one of the principal architects of the Vienna Sales Convention); P Gillies, 'The UN Convention on Contracts for the International Sale of Goods', Chapter 1 in G Moens & P Gillies (eds), *International Trade and Business: Law, Policy and Ethics*, Cavendish Publishing (Australia) Pty Ltd, Sydney, 1998, pp 1–77; S Fisher & D Fisher, *Export Best Practice: Commercial and Legal Aspects*, Chapter 5; MR Islam, *International Trade Law*, LBC Information Services, Sydney, 1999, pp 307–320; P Schlechtriem, *Uniform Sales Law: the UN Convention on Contracts for International Sale of Goods*, Manzsche Verlags-Und-Universitäsbuchhandlung, Vienna, 1986; P Schlechtriem, *Commentary on the UN Convention on Contracts for International Sale of Goods*, 2nd edn, trans G Thomas, Clarendon Press, Oxford, 1998; J Lookofsky, *Understanding the CISG in the USA: A Compact Guide to the 1980 United Nations Convention on Contracts in International Sale of Goods*, Kluwer Law International, Boston, 1995; S Fisher, 'International and Domestic Sale of Goods Remedies' (1994) 8 Comm LQ (No. 2) 19; G Corney, 'Obligations and Remedies Under the 1980 Vienna Sales Convention' (1993) 23 QLSJ 37; J. Roberts, 'International Sale of Goods', Chapter 2 in K Wilde (ed), *International Transactions: Trade and Investment, Law and Finance*, Law Book Company Ltd, Sydney, 1993, pp 31–73.

they do not realise that its terms may govern an export sales contract that has been concluded with an overseas buyer or seller.

[26.110] The important point to keep in mind is that the Convention applies automatically to certain international sale of goods contracts, whether the parties realise this or not. It is not a convention that requires or allows the parties to *opt in*; rather, it is an international convention that the parties can opt out of if they wish (subject to some exceptions that do not need to be detailed in this book). The rules detailed below function as a set of default rules; if the parties do not expressly or impliedly provide contrary rules in their sale contract, then these rules will comprise the content of the contract they have formed. It is possible for the seller and the buyer under an international sale of goods contract governed by the Convention to include only part of the Convention regime within the ambit of a given sale contract. The content of the contract is then split between the actual contract formed and the provisions of the Convention that have not been excluded by the other, more specific terms of the contract. If this occurs—and a dispute arises between the seller and the buyer—then it can be difficult to determine exactly what is the content of the contract before deciding (or advising) on the rights and duties of the parties. It is preferable for sellers and buyers to negotiate the terms (or contents) of their sale contract in advance, so these difficult issues of construction are avoided, or at least minimised.

[26.115] The Convention applies to contracts of sale of goods between parties whose places of business are in different states:
- when the states are Contracting States; or
- when the rules of private international law lead to the application of the law of a Contracting State.[35]

The fact that the parties have their places of business in different states is to be disregarded whenever this fact does not appear either from the contract, or from any dealings between the parties, or from information disclosed by the parties, at any time before or at the conclusion of the contract.[36] If a party has more than one place of business, the place of business is the one with the closest relationship to the contract and its performance, having regard to the circumstances known to, or contemplated by, the parties at any time before (or at) the conclusion of the contract.[37] Where a party does not have a place of business, reference is to be made to the habitual residence of that party.[38]

Neither the nationality of the parties, nor the civil or commercial character of the parties or the contract, is to be taken into consideration in determining the application of the Convention.[39]

(c) International sales excluded by the Convention

[26.120] The Convention provides in Article 2 that it does not apply to sales:

---

35 Art 1(1). On private international law, see [26.345].
36 Art 1(2).
37 Art 10(a)
38 Art 10(b).
39 Art 1(3).

(1) of goods bought for personal, family or household use, unless the seller (at any time before or at the conclusion of the contract), neither knew nor ought to have known that the goods were bought for any such use;

(2) by auction;

(3) on execution or otherwise by authority of law;

(4) of stocks, shares, investment securities, negotiable instruments or money;

(5) of ships, vessels, hovercraft or aircraft;

(6) of electricity.

Contracts for the supply of goods to be manufactured or produced are to be considered sales, unless the party who orders the goods undertakes to supply a substantial part of the materials necessary for their manufacture or production.[40] The Convention does not apply to contracts in which the supply of labour or other services is the preponderant part of the obligations of the party who furnishes the goods.[41]

(d) Matters excluded from the Convention

[26.125] The Convention governs only the formation of the contract of sale and the rights and obligations of the seller and the buyer arising from such a contract. In particular, except as otherwise expressly provided in the Convention, the Convention is not concerned with:

- the validity of the contract or of any of its provisions or of any usage; or[42]
- the effect which the contract may have on the property in the goods sold.[43]

[26.130] The Convention does not apply to the liability of the seller for death or personal injury caused to any person by the goods.[44] This has the effect of preserving domestic law regimes governing product liability (for example, Part VA of the *Trade Practices Act* 1974). See also Article 2(a), which excludes sales of goods bought for personal, family or household use from the Convention, unless the seller was not actually or constructively aware that the goods were bought for such a purpose. Article 2(a) reinforces the operation of Article 5.

(e) Autonomy of the parties

[26.135] The Convention provides that the parties may exclude its application, or derogate from or vary the effect of any of its provisions.[45] Any derogation from, or variation of, the effects of any of the provisions of the Convention applies subject to the proviso that if a party has its place of business in a Contracting State that has made a declaration that contracts of sale by any party who has its place of business in that Contracting State are to be concluded in or evidenced by writing, then the contract of sale—or its modification or termination by agreement, or any offer, acceptance, or other indication of intention—must be in writing.[46]

---

40 Art 3(1).
41 Art 3(2).
42 Art 4(a).
43 Art 4(b).
44 Art 5.
45 Art 6.
46 Arts 6 and 12.

Underlying Article 6 is the idea that the dominant theme of the Convention is the primacy of the contract. The parties have virtually complete autonomy to determine the content of their contract. An example emerges from *Filanto SpA v Chilewich International Corporation*,[47] where the United States District Court allowed the parties to a contract covered by the Convention to include an arbitration clause (arbitration is not a topic covered by the Convention).

(f)   Formalities of an international sale contract

[26.140] The Convention contains provisions that govern the formalities associated with the formation of an international sale contract and the modification or termination of such a contract.[48] At the point of formation, a contract of sale need not be concluded in, or evidenced by, writing, and is not subject to any other requirement as to form.[49] A contract of sale may be proved by any means, including witnesses.[50] Where any party has its place of business in a Contracting State that has made a declaration under the Convention relating to the conclusion of contracts of sale in writing or for those contracts to be evidenced by writing,[51] any contract of sale—or its modification or termination by agreement, or any offer, acceptance, or other indication of intention—must be made in writing.[52] For the purposes of the Convention, 'writing' includes telegram and telex, and presumably now would include electronic means of communication such as e-mail.[53]

[26.145] A sale contract governed by the Convention may be modified or terminated by the mere agreement of the parties.[54] This is an advance on the common law position in Australia and other common law countries, where consideration is needed to modify a contract (unless the doctrine of estoppel can be invoked).[55] The offeree of an offer to vary a contract may indicate assent by conduct.[56] A contract in writing that contains a provision requiring any modification or termination by agreement to be in writing may not be otherwise modified or terminated by agreement.[57] A party may be precluded, by its conduct, from asserting such a formal requirement, to the extent that the other party has relied on the conduct of the first party.[58] This mimics the doctrine of estoppel.[59]

(g)   Offers

[26.150] Under the Convention, a proposal to conclude a contract must:
*   be addressed to one or more specific persons;

---

47   789 F Supp 1229 SDNY (1992).
48   Arts 11 and 12.
49   Art 28.
50   Art 11.
51   Art 96.
52   Art 12.
53   Art 13.
54   Art 29(1).
55   See Chapter 6.
56   Art 18(3).
57   Art 29(2).
58   Art 29(2).
59   See Chapter 7.

- be sufficiently definite—a proposal is sufficiently definite if it indicates the goods, and expressly or implicitly fixes, or makes provision for determining, the quantity and the price of the goods; and
- indicate the intention of the offerer to be bound in case of acceptance.[60]

A proposal that is not addressed to one or more specific persons is to be considered merely as an invitation to make offers, unless the contrary is clearly indicated by the person making the proposal.[61]

[26.155] Under the Convention, an offer:

1   becomes effective when it reaches the offeree;[62]

2   may be withdrawn (even if expressed to be irrevocable), if the withdrawal reaches the offeree before or at the same time as the offer;[63]

3   may be revoked before a contract is concluded, if the revocation reaches the offeree before the offeree has dispatched an acceptance;[64]

4   cannot be revoked:

    (a) if it indicates, whether by stating a fixed time for acceptance or otherwise, that it is irrevocable;[65] or

    (b) if it was reasonable for the offeree to rely on the offer as being irrevocable and the offeree has acted in reliance on the offer;[66]

4   is terminated (even if it is irrevocable) when a rejection reaches the offeror.[67]

(h)   Acceptances

[26.160] Under the Convention, an acceptance of the offer of an offeror is constituted by:

1   a statement made by, or other conduct of the offeree, indicating assent to an offer;[68]

2   if, by virtue of the offer, or as a result of practices that the parties have established between themselves, or of usage, the offeree may indicate assent by performing an act, such as one relating to the dispatch of the goods or payment of the price, without notice to the offeror;[69]

3   a reply to an offer that purports to be an acceptance but contains additions, limitations, or other modifications, or different terms that do not materially alter the terms of the offer,[70] will be effective unless the offeror, without undue delay, objects orally to the discrepancy or despatches a notice to that effect. If the offerer does not so object, the terms of the contract are the terms of the offer with the modifications contained in the acceptance.[71]

---

60   Art 14(1).
61   Art 14(2).
62   Art 15(1).
63   Art 15(2).
64   Art 16(1).
65   Art 16(2)(a).
66   Art 16(2)(b).
67   Art 17.
68   Art 18(1).
69   Art 18(3).
70   Art 19.
71   Art 19(2).

[26.165] An acceptance of an offer:

1   becomes effective at the moment the indication of assent reaches the offeror;[72]
2   is not effective if the indication of assent does not reach the offeror within the time fixed—or, where no time is fixed, within a reasonable time. Due account must be taken of the circumstances of the transaction, including the rapidity of the means of communication employed by the offeror.[73]

[26.170] The machinery for offer and acceptance under the Convention is broadly similar to the Australian law on these topics,[74] but there are some differences. An example is the rule in Article 19 that an acceptance containing additions, limitations, or other modifications or different terms that do not materially alter the terms of the offer, is not a counter-offer. This is at variance with Australian law, which characterises it as a counter-offer and therefore a rejection of the original offer.

26.3.2   Fundamental breach

[26.175] A breach of contract committed by one of the parties is fundamental if it results in such detriment to the other party as substantially to deprive that other party of what he or she or it is entitled to expect under the contract. This will be the case unless the party in breach did not foresee—and a reasonable person of the same kind in the same circumstances would not have foreseen—such a result.[75] This should be contrasted with the test for breach of contract under Australian law.[76]

26.3.3   Interpreting the Convention

[26.180] A few comparisons were made above between the Convention and Australian law. This raises the issue whether it is proper, under the Convention itself, to interpret it in light of common law principles of contract law and general law.

[26.185] The Convention contains a rule that is designed to shift attention away from the common law and civil law sources that inspired it. So it enjoins that '[i]n the interpretation of this Convention, regard is to be had to its international character and to the need to promote uniformity in its application and the observance of good faith in international trade'[77] While the Convention is meant to be self-contained law,[78] it is not isolationist in scope or effect, since there is a clear signal in Article 7(1) that users of the Convention are not to be insular in interpreting it. Article 7 has been criticised as vague and abstract and not offering a clear hierarchy of standards with which to apply it.[79]

---

72   Art 18(2).
73   Art 18(2).
74   See Chapter 3.
75   Art 25.
76   See Chapter 20.
77   Art 7(1).
78   See P Gillies 'The UN Convention on Contracts for the International Sale of Goods', Chapter 1 in G Moens & P Gillies (eds), *International Trade and Business: Law, Policy and Ethics*, Cavendish Publishing (Australia) Pty Ltd, Sydney, 1998, p 11.
79   MR Islam, *International Trade Law*, LBC Information Services, Sydney, 1999, p 316.

26.3.4   The UNIDROIT Principles of International Commercial Contracts 1994

(a)   Context, uses and approaches to the UNIDROIT Principles

[26.190] The Vienna Sales Convention is an example of an international treaty reaching into both contract law and international commercial law. Treaties represent only one of the many forms of instrument that have been used in the international arena to promote harmonisation and standardisation of laws. Another is the restatement of the principles. Perhaps the best-known example of this is the UNIDROIT *Principles of International Commercial Contracts.*[80]

[26.195] The UNIDROIT *Principles of International Commercial Contracts* have been hailed as a restatement of the principles of international trade law relevant to international commercial contracts.[81] Further, they may be incorporated into contracts as if they were the governing law—or indeed the terms of the contract—subject to any exclusion or modification agreed to by the parties.[82] The view has even been expressed that the UNIDROIT *Principles* can be used to augment any gaps found in international legal instruments such as the Vienna Sales Convention.[83] It has been suggested that they provide a model for the unification of contractual practices in the Americas.[84] They have also appealed to Quebec lawyers.[85]

The UNIDROIT *Principles* promise to provide comparative business lawyers with a rich vein to tap into to stimulate the study of commercial law. They show the cross-pollination of legal cultures, particularly across the common law/civil law divide. It is important that readers of the *Principles* do not bring too much of their own intellectual and cultural baggage to the document, for that would rob it of its role as the

---

80   Available from UNIDROIT, in both paper form: UNIDROIT, *Principles of International Commercial Contracts*, UNIDROIT, Rome, 1994; and from the UNIDROIT Internet website: <http://www.unidroit.org/english/principles/pr-main.htm> (accessed 19 January 2001). Work on a second edition is being undertaken by a UNIDROIT Working Party; Australia's representative on that body is Justice Paul Finn of the Federal Court of Australia. For a review of the *UNIDROIT Principles of International Commercial Contracts*, see J Wagner & G Moens, 'The UNIDROIT Principles of International Commercial Contracts', Chapter 2 in G Moens & P Gillies (eds), *International Trade and Business: Law, Policy and Ethics*, Cavendish Publishing (Australia) Pty Ltd, Sydney 1998, pp 79–119; and M Bonell (ed), *A New Approach to International Commercial Contracts—The UNIDROIT Principles of International Commercial Contracts*, XVth International Congress of Comparative Law, The Hague, Kluwer Law International, London, 1999.

81   J Wagner & G Moens, 'The UNIDROIT Principles of International Commercial Contracts', Chapter 2 in G Moens & P Gillies (eds), *International Trade and Business: Law, Policy and Ethics*, Cavendish Publishing (Australia) Pty Ltd, Sydney 1998, p 80. See M Bonell, 'The UNIDROIT Principles of International Commercial Contracts: Nature, Purposes and First Experiences in Practice,' available online at <http://www.unidroit.org/english/principles/pr-exper.htm> (accessed 19 January 2001).

82   J Wagner & G Moens, 'The UNIDROIT Principles of International Commercial Contracts', Chapter 2 in G Moens & P Gillies (eds), *International Trade and Business: Law, Policy and Ethics*, Cavendish Publishing (Australia) Pty Ltd, Sydney 1998, p 81.

83   See A Garro, 'The Gap-filling Role of the UNIDROIT Principles in International Sales Law: Some Comments on the Interplay Between the Principles and the CISG' (1995) 69 *Tulane Law Review* 1149.

84   See B Kozolchyk, 'The UNIDROIT Principles as a Model for the Unification of the Best Contractual Practices in the Americas' (1998) 46 *American Journal of Comparative Law* 151.

85   See Paul-A Crépeau (with E Charpentier), *The UNIDROIT Principles and the Civil Code of Quebec: Shared Values?* Carswell, Scarborough, Ont., 1998.

conscience of the modern law of international commercial contracts.[86] There is a suggestion that the UNIDROIT *Principles* might eventually attain the status of customary law. This would make recourse to these Principles more palatable in terms of the hierarchy of legal norms rather than their current status as unenacted principles.[87]

[26.200] The reference by academic commentators to the UNIDROIT *Principles of International Commercial Contracts* is understandable enough, but what is their penetration or acceptance within the fabric of domestic Australian law? The evidence so far is weak in arguing for a widespread acceptance of the UNIDROIT *Principles* to supplement domestic Australian law, and in particular the law of voluntary obligations (or contract law). The one ray of light comes in the form of Justice Finn's judgment in *Hughes Aircraft Systems International v Airservices Australia*.[88] Finn J spoke positively of the duty of 'fair dealing' as a major (if not openly articulated) organising idea in Australian contract law, and cited Article 1.7 of the *Principles of International Commercial Contracts* in support of this.[89] Of course, one isolated citation does not mean that there has been widespread acceptance of the UNIDROIT *Principles* as being normative in domestic Australian law. Yet it is interesting that in the *Hughes Aircraft Systems* case, Finn J was prepared to have recourse to them in order to make the claim that the concepts of 'fair dealing and its cousin, good faith' were pervasive norms in international contract law, and so should be afforded some acceptance within Australian contract law.

[26.205] The UNIDROIT Principles have been said to incorporate two fundamental themes: contractual freedom and contractual justice.[90] The interplay of these two fundamental themes provides much of the academic interest in the UNIDROIT Principles as an instrument concerning contract law.

(b)   Contents, themes and values of the UNIDROIT Principles of International Commercial Contracts

[26.210] The Preamble to the UNIDROIT *Principles of International Commercial Contracts* (the 'UNIDROIT Principles') captures something of their intended purpose and use:

Preamble

- These Principles set forth general rules for international commercial contracts.
- They shall be applied when the parties have agreed that their contract be governed by them.
- They may be applied when the parties have agreed that their contract be governed by 'general principles of law', the 'lex mercatoria' or the like.

---

86   See N Kasirer, "'Values', Law Reform and the Law's Conscience', Introductory Essay in Paul-A Crépeau (with E Charpentier), *The UNIDROIT Principles and the Civil Code of Quebec: Shared Values?* Carswell, Scarsborough, Ont., 1998, p xix at p xxiii.

87   Ibid (citing G Rouette, 'Les codifications du droit des contrats' (1996) 24 *Droits* 113 at 122–123).

88   (1997) 76 FCR 151; [1997] 558 FCA (30 June 1998) at 43.

89   *UNIDROIT Principles*, Article 1.7.1 says that each party (to an international commercial contract) 'must act in accordance with good faith and fair dealing in international trade'. By Article 1.7.2, this duty cannot be excluded or limited.

90   Paul-A Crépeau (with E Charpentier), *The UNIDROIT Principles and the Civil Code of Quebec: Shared Values?* Carswell, Scarsborough, Ont., 1998, p 5.

- They may provide a solution to an issue raised when it proves impossible to establish the relevant rule of the applicable law.
- They may be used to interpret or supplement international uniform law instruments.
- They may serve as a model for national and international legislators.

The Preamble to the UNIDROIT Principles provides some guidance about the way these Principles may in fact become part of any particular contract: by express adoption (see Preamble No 2), or by indirect adoption via selection of the legal standards of 'general principles of law', the *lex mercatoria* or the like. According to the Preamble, that would be sufficient to uplift the UNIDROIT Principles so they form the contents of any given contract (see Preamble No 3). Essentially, this depends on the cooperation of domestic contract law in order to accomplish such an object. Since Australian contract law incorporates and responds to a notion of contractual freedom (subject to some legislative override from common law public policy exceptions), it can be expected that, all other things being equal, Australian contracts whose contents are referable to the UNIDROIT Principles should be enforced under Australian law.

[26.215] The UNIDROIT Principles are expressed to apply only to international commercial contracts. Comment No 2 of the Preamble explains the nature and meaning of *commercial contracts* as follows:

> The restriction to 'commercial' contracts is in no way intended to take over the distinction traditionally made in some legal systems between 'civil' and 'commercial' parties and/or transactions, i.e. to make the application of the Principles dependent on whether the parties have the formal status of 'merchants' (*commerçants*, *Kaufleute*) and/or the transaction is commercial in nature. The idea is rather that of excluding from the scope of the Principles so-called 'consumer transactions' which are within the various legal systems being increasingly subjected to special rules, mostly of a mandatory character, aimed at protecting the consumer, i.e. a party who enters into the contract otherwise than in the course of its trade or profession.

[26.220] It is open also for the UNIDROIT Principles to cross-pollinate with the regime governing contracts for the international sale of goods under the Vienna Sales Convention.[91] This could happen if the parties to an international sales contract that is governed by the Vienna Sales Convention expressly uplift the UNIDROIT Principles into their contract. The result would be that the basic superstructure of such a contract would comprise distinct sale of goods elements (the nature, type and description of goods to be sold, coupled with provisions concerning the price of the goods, the standards of performance of the goods to be bought and sold, and performance of the contract of sale), overlaid by the UNIDROIT Principles. This is capped off with a residue or layer of contractual terms, comprising whatever elements of the Vienna Sales Convention had not been displaced by the adoption of the UNIDROIT Principles. The basis for this result stems from the operation of Article 6 of the Vienna Sales

---

91   See [26.95]–[26.185].

Convention, which reads in part '[t]he parties may exclude the application of this Convention or … derogate from or vary the effect of any of its provisions.'

[26.225] To return for the moment to the contents of the UNIDROIT Principles, the skeletal outline below captures something of the breadth, depth and comprehensiveness of these Principles as they reach into the corpus of contract law:

Chapter 1—General Provisions
Chapter 2—Formation
Chapter 3—Validity
Chapter 4—Interpretation
Chapter 5—Content
Chapter 6—Performance
    Section 1—Performance in general
    Section 2—Hardship
Chapter 7—Non-performance
    Section 1—Non-performance in general
    Section 2—Right to performance
    Section 3—Termination
    Section 4—Damages

[26.230] As this chapter cannot do justice to the detail or the rich jurisprudence that sits beneath the provisions of the UNIDROIT Principles,[92] it concentrates instead on a selection of matters that reflect the themes of contractual freedom and contractual justice.

[26.235] Article 1.1 sets the tone for the content and operation of the UNIDROIT Principles in these terms: 'The parties are free to enter into a contract and to determine its content'. The UNIDROIT Comment to this Article records:

> The principle of freedom of contract is of paramount importance in the context of international trade. The right of business people to decide freely to whom they will offer their goods or services and by whom they wish to be supplied, as well as the possibility for them freely to agree on the terms of individual transactions, are the cornerstones of an open, market-oriented and competitive international economic order.[93]

[26.240] Article 1.1 captures two important elements that are central to a general concept of freedom of contract. The first is that freedom of contract is a norm that sits beneath the very act of contracting; that is, contracting parties are free (or at liberty) to contract (this could be easily described as *freedom to contract*). As much as anything else, this notion of freedom of contract could be situated within human rights or a law of persons (to the extent that artificial juristic entities are concerned, this depends on corporate law). The second element embedded within Article 1.1 is the freedom to determine the content of a contract; that is, the liberty to decide what will be the subject matter of the contract and what will be the terms of the contract. The second freedom is not anterior to contract in the same sense that freedom to contract is; rather

---

92   For fuller treatments, see above, notes 34–43 and the sources cited by these commentators.
93   Comment 1 to Article 1.1.

it derives from contracting as a juridical act. Both of these freedoms work together to provide an expansive view of freedom of contract.

[26.245] Australian contract lawyers and most contract law scholars are unlikely to object to the sentiment expressed either in Article 1.1 of the UNIDROIT Principles or the associated Comment. Yet in some legal systems—in the interests of their own perceptions or understandings of public policy—freedom of contract is restricted beyond what would be allowed under a Western concept of contract law. One example comes from Islamic law, which prohibits charging interest on loans of money (the so-called *riba*).[94] Another example comes from China where, under Article 57 of the *Contract Law*, a contract that impairs the social and public interest is deemed to be void.[95] Thus the UNIDROIT Principles may not, on account of their generality and their cultural and liberal democratic specificity, necessarily inform or influence the contract law of non-Western States.[96]

[26.250] Another manifestation of freedom of contract involves the micro-climate of contracting. That concerns the role of usages and practices that spring up between contracting parties to deal with each other on a repeated or regular basis. Article 1.8(1) of the UNIDROIT Principles states: 'The parties are bound by any usage to which they have agreed and by any practices which they have established between themselves.' Article 1.8(2) adds 'The parties are bound by a usage that is widely known to and regularly observed in international trade by parties in the particular trade concerned except where the application of such a usage would be unreasonable.'[97] Article 1.8 is consistent with freedom to determine the content of a contract, which is in some respects also a corollary of the freedom to contract.

[26.255] Alongside contractual freedom sits contractual justice. Contractual justice is not an accepted term of art under Australian contract law, although it has been used in connection with the civil law systems.[98] The civil law commentator Crépeau has described contractual justice in terms of concepts such as:

> the renaissance of contractual morality, the search for equilibrium, the refusal of exploitation of one's neighbours, the heightened awareness of inequitable situations, the prevention of abuse or the fostering of reasonable behaviour all serve to elucidate the concept of contractual justice … Contractual fairness depends on the view that each individual takes of what is just or unjust in social relations, which in turn depends on prevailing community values.[99]

---

94   For details, see N Coulson, *Commercial Law in the Gulf States: the Islamic Legal Tradition*, Graham & Trotman, London, 1984, Chapter 7 (dealing with freedom of contract).

95   See Kui Hua Wang, *Chinese Commercial Law*, OUP, Melbourne, 2000, p 67. Presumably, the socialist orientation of the Chinese economy and political system imbues the concept of 'social and public interest' with different meaning from its meaning in Western usage and currency.

96   Article 1.4 is an explicit concession to normative rules that have a mandatory, non-derogable, nature: 'Nothing in these Principles shall restrict the application of mandatory rules, whether of national, international or supranational origin, which are applicable in accordance with the relevant rules of private international law.'

97   On the role of practice or usage (or custom or usage), see Chapter 8.

98   See Paul-A Crépeau (with E Charpentier), *The UNIDROIT Principles and the Civil Code of Quebec: Shared Values?* Carswell, Scarsborough, Ont., 1998, pp 39, 41, 43.

99   Ibid p 39.

The essence or the spirit of contractual justice aims to establish a just equilibrium between obligations of contracting parties.[100] If the UNIDROIT Principles are analysed according to the standard of contractual justice, contractual justice resonates in four key values of the UNIDROIT Principles, namely public order (Article 3.1), good faith (Article 1.7(1)), the search for a just equilibrium (Article 3.10(1)),[101] and the promotion of reasonableness as corresponding to the normal and foreseeable expectation of parties (which appears 53 times in various forms within the UNIDROIT Principles—early examples being in Articles 4.1 and 4.2).[102]

26.3.5   The Principles of European Contract Law 1998

[26.260] The Principles of European Contract Law 1998 are sponsored by the Commission on European Contract Law, based in Copenhagen, Denmark.[103] They are a response to a need for a European Union-wide infrastructure of contract law to consolidate the rapidly expanding volume of European Union law regulating specific types of contract.[104] In general, the Principles of European Contract Law 1998 are similar to the UNIDROIT Principles, as shown by the skeletal outline, set out below.

Chapter 1—general provisions
    Section 1—scope of the Principles
    Section 2—general obligations
    Section 3—terminology and other provisions
Chapter 2—formation
    Section 1—general provisions
    Section 2—offer and acceptance
    Section 3—liability for negotiations
Chapter 3—authority of agents
    Section 1—general provisions
    Section 2—direct representation
    Section 3—in direct representation
Chapter 4—validity
Chapter 5—interpretation
Chapter 6—contents and effects
Chapter 7—performance
Chapter 8—non-performance and remedies in general
Chapter 9—particular remedies for non-performance
    Section 1—right to performance
    Section 2—right to withhold performance

---

100 Ibid, p 41.

101 *Lésion* [lesion] in the civil law system, that is, the presence of a gross disparity or an unfair advantage between the contracting parties. For a wider critical and historical study, see R Zimmermann, *The Law of Obligations: Roman Foundations of the Civilian Tradition*, Juta & Co Ltd, Cape Town, 1990, Chapter 22.

102 These four values are examined at length in Paul-A Crépeau (with E Charpentier), *The UNIDROIT Principles and the Civil Code of Quebec: Shared Values?* Carswell, Scarsborough, Ont., 1998, pp 39–137.

103 These can be accessed online at Lex Mercatoria: <http://www.jus.uio.no/lm/eu.contract.principles.1998/index.html> (accessed 19 January 2001).

104 See preceding note.

Section 3—termination of the contract

Section 4—price reduction

Section 5—damages and interest.[105]

[26.265] The Principles of European Contract Law 1998 (called here the European Principles) differ from the UNIDROIT Principles in that they include a section on agency and they cover all contracts, not just commercial contracts.[106] The European Principles have a European focus, while the UNIDROIT Principles have a broader international, non-regional focus. Each instrument is also sponsored by a different agency.[107] The same themes of freedom of contract and contractual justice identified in relation to the UNIDROIT Principles pervade the Principles of European Contract Law 1998.

[26.270] One of the architects of the UNIDROIT Principles, Professor Lando of Denmark, has reduced the UNIDROIT Principles to eight principles, which deserve repetition here:

I.   You shall keep your contract.

II.   You shall keep your promise.

III.   Certain stipulations in favour of the third party are enforceable.

IV.   You shall render the performance you promised.

V.   The other party's fundamental non-performance gives the innocent party access to remedies, ranging from the right to claim damages, to withholding his or her own performance, to reduce his or her performance or to terminate the contract.

VI.   Events such as *vis major* and force majeure[108] may relieve parties from performance that has become impossible in law or in fact.

VII.   You shall act in accordance with good faith and fair dealing.

VIII. Unfair terms which have not been individually negotiated need regulation, particularly in the consumer sphere.[109]

[26.275] In a programmatic sense, the ultimate project of each of these two contract law restatements is to influence national, regional, or international legislators, with the Principles of European Contract Law 1998 being intended to result in a European

---

105 For a detailed analysis and treatment of the Principles of European Contract Law 1998, see O Lando & H Beale (eds), *Principles of European Contract Law: Parts I and II* (prepared by The Commission on European Contract Law), 2nd edn, Kluwer Law International: The Hague, London, Boston, 1999.

106 On agency under Australian law, see S Fisher, *Agency Law*, Butterworths, Sydney, 2000.

107 The history behind the formation and the operation of the sponsoring agencies to the Principles of European Contract Law 1998 and the UNIDROIT Principles is traced by F Blase in 'Leaving the Shadow for the Test of Practice: on the Future of the Principles of European Contract Law', (1999) 3(1) *Vindobona Journal of International Commercial Law and Arbitration*; available online at Lex Mercatoria: <http://www.jus.uio.no/lm/leaving.the.shadow.for.the.test.of.practice.future.of.pecl.1999.friedrich.blase/doc.html> (accessed 19 January 2001). For a comparison of the two instruments, see M Bonell, 'The UNIDROIT Principles of International Commercial Contracts and the Principles of European Contract Law: A Comparison', Chapter 3 in R Cranston (ed), *Making Commercial Law: Essays in Honour of Roy Goode*, Clarendon Press, Oxford, 1997, pp 91–101.

108 *Vis major* and force majeure approximate to frustration in the common law. See Chapter 22.

109 O Lando, 'Eight Principles of European Contract Law', Chapter 4 in R Cranston (ed), *Making Commercial Law: Essays in Honour of Roy Goode*, Clarendon Press, Oxford, 1997, pp 103–129.

Contract Code promulgated by the European Parliament. The work of the sponsoring agency of the European Principles (the Commission on European Contract Law) has been endorsed by a Resolution of the European Parliament,[110] and considered opinion holds that they could eventually ripen into a European Contract Code.[111]

26.4   The micro approach to international contracts: standard form and generally accepted international commercial contracts

[26.280] The following exploration of the microscopic approach to international contracts will examine one example of a standard-form contract commonly used in the international arena (*Incoterms 2000*) and two examples of standardised international trade terms in cross-border sale of goods contracts (FOB and CIF).

26.4.1   *International Commercial Terms (Incoterms) 2000*

[26.285] The word 'Incoterms' is a contraction of *international commercial terms*. Incoterms is a private compilation of international commercial terms used in international sale of goods contracts. Their status is similar to the Principles of European Contract Law 1998—that is, they are created and promoted by a non-government organisation. Incoterms is created and sponsored by the International Chamber of Commerce (ICC), the world business organisation headquartered in Paris, France. The current version of Incoterms is *Incoterms 2000*,[112] which came into force on 1 January 2000, replacing *Incoterms 1990*.[113]

[26.290] Incoterms consist of 13 standardised trade terms, such as EXW (ex works), FOB (free on board), and CIF (cost insurance freight). The United Nations Commission on International Trade Law (UNCITRAL) endorsed and commended Incoterms 1990 as providing a modern set of rules for the interpretation of the most commonly used terms in international trade in goods.[114] For an instrument having the status of voluntary law,[115] this is as close as is possible to having an official endorsement short of being enacted as positive law.

---

110   Resolution of 6 May 1994 (Dok. A3—0329/94), Official Journal of the European Communities C 205/518.

111   See F Blase, 'Leaving the Shadow for the Test of Practice: on the Future of the Principles of European Contract Law', (1999) 3(1) *Vindobona Journal of International Commercial Law and Arbitration*; available online at Lex Mercatoria: <http://www.jus.uio.no/lm/leaving.the.shadow.for.the.test.of.practice.future. of.pecl.1999.friedrich.blase/doc.html> (accessed 19 January 2001) section 4.

112   Publication 560, ICC Publishing SA, Paris, 2000.

113   For commentary on Incoterms 1990, see P Gillies, 'International Commercial Trade Terms—Incoterms 1990', Chapter 3 in G Moens & P Gillies (eds), *International Trade and Business: Law, Policy and Ethics*, Cavendish Publishing (Australia) Pty Ltd, Sydney, 1998, pp 121–173.

114   *Report of the United Nations Commission on International Trade Law on the work of its twenty-fifth session*, 4–22 May 1992, Official Records of the General Assembly, Forty-seventh Session, Supplement No 17 (UN Doc A/47/17), paragraph 161. There is a similar endorsement from UNCITRAL in relation to *Incoterms 2000*: see <http://www.iccwbo.org/home/news_archives/2000/un_incoterms.asp> for details (accessed 19 January 2001).

115   Schmitthoff, *Commercial Law in a Changing Economic Climate*, p 21 calls it 'optional law'.

INTERNATIONAL CONTRACTS   **807**

Incoterms 2000 sets out the precise rights, duties and responsibilities of the international sale and buyer of goods in 13 standardised trade terms:

- EXW—ex works (… named place)
- FCA—free carrier (… named place)
- FAS—free alongside ship (… named port of shipment)
- FOB—free on board (… named port of shipment)
- CFR—cost and freight (… named port of destination)
- CIF—cost, insurance and freight (… named port of destination)
- CPT—carriage paid to (… named place of destination)
- CIP—carriage and insurance paid to (… named place of destination)
- DAF—delivered at frontier (… named place)
- DES—delivered ex ship (… named port of destination)
- DEQ—delivered ex quay (… named port of destination)
- DDU—delivered duty unpaid (… named place of destination)
- DDP—delivered duty paid (… named place of destination).[116]

[26.295] *Incoterms 2000* can apply to the sale of goods that are transported by land, sea and air as well as combinations of these modes of transport (multi-modal transport). They may be incorporated into an international sale of goods contract by use of the phrase '*Incoterms 2000*' in conjunction with the particular trade term selected (such as CIF, FOB, EXW and so on). An example is '*CIF (Calais) (Incoterms 2000)*'—meaning that the goods are being shipped to Calais in France, and the contents of the sale of goods contract comprise the CIF term of *Incoterms 2000*. This is an example of the incorporation of terms into a contract by reference to an external standard.[117]

[26.300] If international sellers and buyers of goods are using *Incoterms 2000*, and the Vienna Sales Convention also applies to that contract,[118] then that particular contract consists of two layers. The first layer is whichever term within *Incoterms 2000* has been incorporated into the particular sale contract between those sellers and buyers; the second layer consists of whatever provisions of the Vienna Sales Convention are not incompatible with the first layer. Exactly how those two layers mesh together depends upon the extent to which *Incoterms 2000* adds to, subtracts from, or modifies the provisions of the Vienna Sales Convention. In the end, this exercise is a question of construction for the court or tribunal determining any disputes arising out of such a 'blended' contract.

26.4.2   FOB (Free on Board) contracts[119]

[26.305] FOB and CIF contracts of sale of goods are two of the most common forms of international contracts for the sale of goods. In the interests of brevity, the following

---

116   See the ICC's website, Incoterms webpage: <http://www.iccwbo.org/home/incoterms/the_thirteen_incoterms.asp> (accessed 6 January 2001). The detailed text of *Incoterms 2000* is not available online, and must be purchased in either CD-ROM format or as a paper-based product from the ICC in Paris or from their national offices. For commentary on *Incoterms 2000*, see J Ramberg, *ICC Guide to Incoterms 2000*, ICC Publication No 620, ICC Publishing SA, Paris, 2000; J Ramberg, P Rapatout, F Reynolds & C Debattista, *Incoterms 2000: A Forum of Experts*, ICC Publication No 617, ICC Publishing SA, Paris, 2000; and J Mo, *International Commercial Law*, 2nd edn, Butterworths, Sydney, 2000, paras [1.12]–[1.30].

117   See [8.2.5].

118   See [26.105]–[26.115].

119   See Fisher & Fisher, *Export Best Practice: Commercial and Legal Aspects*, paragraph [5.4.2].

treatment of export contracts will be confined to these two main kinds, rather than attempting to survey them all (a task undertaken by other commentators in authoritative works).[120]

[26.310] Use of the terms 'FOB' and 'CIF' implicitly demarcates the division of responsibility between the seller and buyer concerning their mutual rights and duties and, in particular, the performance of the sale contract.[121] In keeping with this idea of the division of responsibility between sellers and buyers of goods, commercial practice has divided international sale of goods contract into two categories: *shipment contracts* and *arrival contracts*. A shipment contract means that the seller's duties are limited in time up to the point of delivery to the carrier. An arrival contract means that the seller's duties extend to the point of time when the goods arrive in the country of destination. The FOB contract is a shipment contract. The CIF contract is an arrival contract.

[26.315] There are generally accepted incidents (or components) of the FOB and CIF contracts. They are covered in this section and the next.

The FOB contract has these incidents:

1   A sale of goods on FOB terms imposes a duty on the seller to put the goods on board the ship and to procure a bill of lading in terms usual in the trade. The essence of any FOB contract is that the seller, by itself or with another party, must place the goods, whether specific or unascertained, 'on board' the ship; and when those goods are placed on board they are appropriated to the contract and are then at the risk of the buyer, who has at that point in insurable interest in the goods.[122]

2   The seller must bear the expense of putting the goods on board the ship.[123]

3   Correlatively, the buyer must, under the classic form of FOB contract, nominate the ship on board which the goods must be loaded.[124]

4   The buyer must also bear all expenses associated with the provisions of the vessel upon which the goods will be transported, including port charges, stowage charges, freight duties, consular fees, and arrival charges.[125]

---

120   See CM Schmitthoff, *Schmitthoff's Export Trade: the Law and Practice of International Trade*, 9th edn, Stevens & Sons, London, 1990, pp 16–33; R Burnett, *The Law of International Business Transactions* 2nd edn, The Federation Press, Sydney, 1999; and J Mo, *International Commercial Law* 2nd edn, Butterworths, Sydney, 2000, paragraph [1.20].

121   For an example of FOB, see *Pagnan SpA v Tradax Ocean Transportation SA* [1987] 3 All ER 565, [1987] 2 Lloyd's Rep 342 (CA). For CIF, see *Bowden Bros and Co Ltd v Little* (1907) 4 CLR 1364 at 1376 per Griffith CJ, at 1390–1391 per Isaacs J; *Plaimar Ltd v Waters Trading Co Ltd* (1945) 72 CLR 304 at 311 per Rich, Dixon and McTiernan JJ.

122   *Martin v Hogan* (1917) 24 CLR 234 at 257, 259; 18 SR (NSW) 153; 35 WN (NSW)78 per Isaacs and Rich JJ (a pre-NSW *Sale of Goods Act* 1923 case). See also *Pyrene Co Ltd v Scindia Navigation Co Ltd* [1954] 2 QB 402 at 424; [1954] 2 All ER 158 at 167; [1954] 2 Wlr 1005; [1954] 1 Lloyd's Rep 321 at 332 per Devlin J; *Wimble, Sons & Co v Rosenberg & Sons* [1913] 3 KB 743; *The El Amria and The El Minia* [1982] 2 Lloyd's Rep 28 at 32 per Donaldson LJ.

123   See *J Raymond Wilson & Co Ltd v Norman Scratchard Ltd* (1944) 77 Ll L Rep 373 at 374 per Lord Caldecote CJ, KB; *Tradax Export SA v Ambrosio* [1986] 1 Lloyd's Rep 112; *Pagnan SpA v Tradax SA* [1987] 3 All ER 565; [1987] 2 Lloyd's Rep 342; *Ninth Street East Ltd v Harrison* 259 A 2d 772 (1968) at 773–774 per Levine J.

124   See *Pyrene Co Ltd v Scindia Navigation Co Ltd* [1954] 1 Lloyd's Rep 321 at 332 per Devlin J; *J & J Cunningham Ltd v Robert A Munro & Co Ltd* (1922) 28 Com Cas 42 at 45 per Lord Hewart LCJ.

125   See *Cargill UK Ltd v Continental UK Ltd* [1989] 2 Lloyd's Rep 290; *Gill & Duffus SA v Société pour l'Exportation des Sucres SA* [1986] 1 Lloyd's Rep 322; *Richco International Ltd v Bunge & Co Ltd* [1991] 2 Lloyd's Rep 93; *The New Prosper* [1991] 2 Lloyd's Rep 93; *President of India v Metcalfe Shipping Co Ltd* [1969] 1 All ER 861 (affirmed *President of India v Metcalfe Shipping Co Ltd* [1970] 1 QB 289, CA); *Pagnan SPA v Tradax Ocean Transportation SA* [1987] 3 All ER 565; [1987] 2 Lloyd's Rep 342.

[26.320] There are two judicially recognised variants of the classic FOB contract. The first variant differs from the classic FOB contract in that the seller arranges for the ship to come onto the berth, with the remaining legal incidents being the same as for the classic version. The second variant of FOB contract is where the seller puts the goods on board, takes a mate's receipt and gives this to the buyer or the buyer's agent, who then takes a bill of lading from the carrier.[126] The buyer's agent may be a forwarding agent.[127]

The difference between the first two kinds of FOB contract and the third one is that under the first two, the seller is a party to the contract of carriage and if the bill of lading is made out to the seller's order, the buyer may only obtain rights under the contract of carriage if and when the bill of lading is endorsed in the buyer's name.[128]

26.4.3 CIF (Cost Insurance Freight) contracts[129]

[26.325] In a series of leading cases dealing with the classic CIF contract, the seller's duties have crystallised into a well-settled list.

The CIF seller must:

1   make out an invoice of the goods sold;
2   ship at the port of shipment goods of the description contained in the contract;
3   procure on shipment a contract of affreightment by sea under which the goods will be delivered at the destination contemplated by the contract;
4   arrange for marine insurance, upon the terms current in the trade, which will be available for the benefit of the buyer; and
5   with all reasonable dispatch, send forward and tender to the buyer shipping documents comprising the invoice, bill of lading and policy of assurance.[130]

[26.330] In the leading CIF case of *Ross T Smyth & Co Ltd v TD Bailey, Son & Co*,[131] Lord Wright had this to say about the function and ubiquity of the CIF sale contract:

I.   The CIF contract is a type of contract which is more widely and more frequently in use than any other contract used for purposes of sea-borne commerce.

II. The CIF contract facilitates dealings in the goods by effecting dealings in the bill of lading.

---

126 See *Pyrene Co Ltd v Scindia Navigation Co Ltd* [1954] 2 QB 402 at 424; [1954] 2 All Er 158 at 167; [1954] 2 WLR 1005; [1954] 1 Lloyd's Rep 321 per Devlin J; *Wimble, Sons & Co v Rosenberg & Sons* [1913] 3 KB 743; *The El Amria and the El Minia* [1982] 2 Lloyd's Rep 28 at 32 per Donaldson LJ.

127 See *Pyrene Co Ltd v Scindia Navigation Co Ltd* [1954] 2 QB 402 at 424; [1954] 2 All ER 158 at 167; [1954] 2 WLR 1005; [1954] 1 Lloyd's Rep 321 at 332 per Devlin J.

128 *Pyrene Co Ltd v Scindia Navigation Co Ltd* [1954] 2 QB 402 at 424; [1954] 2 All ER 158 at 167; [1954] 2 WLR 1005; [1954] 1 Lloyd's Rep 321 per Devlin J; *The El Amria and the El Minia* [1982] 2 Lloyd's Rep 28 at 32 per Donaldson LJ.

129 Fisher & Fisher, *Export Best Practice: Commercial and Legal Aspects*, paragraph [5.4.3].

130 The authorities supporting this catalogue include: *Plaimar Ltd v Waters Trading Co Ltd* (1945) 72 CLR 304 at 311; [1945] ALR 469 per Rich, Dixon and McTiernan JJ; *Johnson v Taylor Bros & Co Ltd* [1920] AC 144 at 155 per Lord Atkinson; *Ireland v Livingston* (1872) LR 5 HL 395 at 406; 27 LT 79; [1861–73] All ER Rep 585 per Blackburn J; *Biddell Bros v E Clemens Horst Co* [1911] 1 KB 214 at 220 per Hamilton J (affirmed *E Clemens Horst Co v Biddell Bros* [1912] AC 18; [1911–13] All ER Rep 93); *C Sharpe & Co Ltd v Nosawa & Co* [1917] 2 KB 814 at 818 per Atkin J; *Ross T Smyth & Co Ltd v TD Bailey, Son & Co* [1940] 3 All ER 60 at 68; (1940) 164 LT 102 per Lord Wright; *The Gabbiano* [1940] P 166; *Comptoir d'Achat et de Vente du Boerenbond Belge SA v Luis de Ridder Lda (The Julia)* [1949] AC 293 at 309; [1949] 1 All ER 269 per Lord Porter.

131 [1940] 3 All ER 60 at 67–68; (1940) 164 LT 102.

The bill of lading may be pledged as security for financial accommodation as 'by mercantile law, the bills of lading are the symbol of the
goods'.[132]

[26.335] Even after the goods have been shipped and are in the possession of the carrier, and the shipping documents have been delivered to the buyer, the buyer can
effect a sale of goods afloat by dealing in the shipping documents (in particular the bill
of lading) even though the buyer does not have physical possession of the goods.[133]

[26.340] The CIF contract actually accomplishes more than simply the sale of goods
between seller and buyer. Because it includes insurance and freight components, it
deals with risk management (insurance) as well as with transport (freight) (the *cost* in
the Cost Insurance Freight contract means the price of the goods). Since international
trade in goods involves some element of risk, the CIF contract seeks to deal with all
major components of the cross-border sale of goods, with the exception of payment.
Payment for international sale of goods contracts usually takes place by means of the
letter of credit.[134]

26.5   Private international law

[26.345] Private international law has been described as the body of principles dealing
with conflicts between the domestic laws of two or more states; it is concerned with
private matters arising in an international context. Private international law is also
known as 'conflict of laws'.[135] The basic contours of private international law have
been described in these terms:

Conflict of laws is concerned with resolving the issues which arise because a
matter has a connection or claimed connection with the legal system of more
than one law area or country. In such a case the court in which the proceedings have been brought (the 'forum') must decide whether it should extend its
jurisdiction, law or institutions to the matter before it, or recognise and/or
apply the jurisdiction, law or institutions of another law area.

I.   Issues of conflict of laws may arise because:

---

132   On pledges of goods as a form of security, see S Fisher, *Commercial and Personal Property Law,* Butterworths, Sydney, 1997, Chapter 6.

133   See *JH Vantol Ltd v Fairclough Dodd & Jones Ltd v JH Vantol Ltd* [1956] 3 All ER 921, HL); *Tradax Export
SA v Andre & Cie SA* [1976] 1 Lloyd's Rep 416, CA.

134   See the text accompanying notes 9–12 above for discussion of the role of letters of credit in interna-
tional trade. See also G Moens & T Tzovaras, 'Financing Exports: Letters of Credit', Chapter 6 in G
Moens & P Gillies (eds), *International Trade and Business: Law, Policy and Ethics,* Cavendish Publishing
(Australia) Pty Ltd, Sydney, 1998, pp 387–442 and MR Islam, *International Trade Law,* LBC Information
Services, Sydney, 1999, Chapter 7, for discussion and analysis of letters of credit and of the UCP 500
issued and promoted by the ICC.

135   See *Butterworths Concise Australian Legal Dictionary,* Butterworths, Sydney, 1997, p 316. In M Koppenol-
Laforce et al, *International Contracts: Aspects of Jurisdiction, Arbitration and Private International Law,* Sweet &
Maxwell, London, 1996, p 113 private international law is described as the part of domestic law which
provides rules on how to deal with cases containing a foreign element.

II.   the forum in which the proceedings are brought is asked to hear a matter which has arisen in whole or in part outside its territory, or which involves persons who normally reside outside its territory;

III.   the forum is asked by one of the parties to the proceedings to apply the law of another law area or country; or

the forum is asked to recognise and/or give effect to, a decree or order pronounced by a court or tribunal sitting outside the forum, or acting in accordance with the law of another law area or country.[136]

[26.350] In this section dealing with private international law, only two of the many rich and varied facets of private international law will be considered: choice of law and choice of forum, as they have a bearing on international contracts. These matters are of vital importance to international contracts, for as Schmitthoff says, '[t]he central problem in an international contract is the ascertainment of the law applicable to the contract'.[137]

[26.355] The reason why private international law connects with international contracts is because if each of two (or more) contracting parties resides in or is domiciled in a different country, then if a dispute arises, it is necessary for a court or tribunal to determine what system of law governs the particular contract between those parties. Moreover, it is not possible even to characterise a relationship as a contract unless one does so by reference to the legal rules and principles that apply to or within a particular legal system. The choice of law and choice of forum enquiries in private international law are designed to provide a body of rules and principles that are referable to a given jurisdiction, to assist courts and tribunals to determine what body of contract law applies to a given dispute.

26.5.1   Choice of law

[26.360] In an international contract setting, the phrase 'choice of law' denotes the task of identifying the law that will govern an issue between the contracting parties.[138] The particular choice of law technique that predominates in determining what body of law should apply to a given international contract is the so-called 'proper law of contract'. In *Akai Pty Limited v The People's Insurance Company Limited*,[139] the High Court reviewed much of the earlier case law on the notion of the proper law of contract.[140] In *Amin Rasheed Shipping Corp v Kuwait Insurance Co*,[141] Lord Diplock described the proper law of

---

136   See *Halsbury's Laws of Australia* CONFLICT OF LAWS paragraph [85-1] (footnotes omitted), and R Mortensen, *Private International Law*, Butterworths, Sydney, 2000, p 1. For other works on private international law, see P North, *Essays in Private International Law* Clarendon Press, Oxford, 1993; P Nygh, *Conflict of Laws in Australia*, 6th edn, Butterworths, Sydney, 1994; M Davies, S Ricketson & G Lindell, *Conflict of Laws: Commentary and Materials*, Butterworths, Sydney, 1997; E Sykes & M Pryles, *Australian Private International Law*, 3rd edn, Law Book Company Ltd, Sydney, 1991.

137   See C Schmitthoff, 'The Limits of Party Autonomy', in C Cheng (ed), *Clive M Schmitthoff's Select Essays on International Trade Law*, Graham & Trotman, London, 1988, p 584.

138   See G Fisher, 'International Joint Venture Contracts: Choice of Law', Chapter 11 in W Duncan (ed), *Joint Venture Law in Australia*, The Federation Press, Sydney, 1994, paragraph [11.1.3].

139   (1996) 188 CLR 418.

140   Ibid at 440–442 per Toohey, Gaudron and Gummow JJ.

141   [1984] AC 50 at 65.

a contract as the system of domestic law that defines the obligations (that is, the complex of rights-and-duties) assumed by the parties to the contract. Another way of describing the proper law of the contract comes from Lord Simonds in the decision of the Privy Council in *Bonython v The Commonwealth*:[142] '(1) the system of law by reference to which the contract was made *or* (2) that with which the transaction has its closest and most real connection'.[143] This description was approved by a majority of the High Court in *Akai*.[144] The *Bonython* test is discussed next.

[26.365] The first limb of the *Bonython* proper law test is known as the *subjective proper law*. It denotes the selection by the parties of the law to govern the contract they have made. In turn, this is justified by the liberty, accorded by the common law to the parties to contract, to choose the proper law applicable to the contract[145] (that is, party autonomy). The generally accepted limits to the principle of party autonomy embedded within the first limb of the *Bonython* proper law test are bad faith, an unconnected law, overriding legislation, and public policy.[146]

[26.370] The second limb of the *Bonython* test is known as the *objective proper law*. It engages a search by the court or tribunal for the legal system of a given jurisdiction in which the contract has its 'natural seat or centre of gravity'. In *Akai*,[147] Toohey, Gaudron and Gummow JJ went on to say that, in conducting that search, it is proper have regard to a number of factors including the places of residence or business of the parties, the place of contracting, the place of performance, and the nature and subject matter of the contract (citing by comparison *In Re United Railways of the Havana and Regla Warehouses Ltd*).[148]

[26.375] Since the *Bonython* test of the proper law of contract contains two limbs, the next question to consider is which of the two prevails and why. In *Akai*, a majority of the High Court said:

> There is, in truth, only one question here, and that is whether, upon the proper construction of the contract (which may include an expression of choice in direct language), the court properly may conclude the parties exercised liberty given by the common law to choose the governing law for their contract. If the answer to this is in the negative, the law itself will select a proper law.[149]

In other words, when applying the *Bonython* test of the proper law of contract, courts in Australia are directed to apply the first limb first and the second limb second.

[26.380] Chapter 3 explored[150] the case of what contract formation rules apply when people engage in online commerce using a facility such as the Internet. What private

---

142 (1950) 81 CLR 486; [1951] AC 201.
143 (1950) 81 CLR 486 at 498; [1951] AC 201 at 219; number breaks and emphasis supplied.
144 (1996) 188 CLR 418 at 440–441 per Toohey, Gaudron and Gummow JJ.
145 *Cie Tunisiènne v Cie d'Armement* [1971] AC 572 at 603 per Lord Diplock.
146 R Mortensen, *Private International Law*, Butterworths, Sydney, 2000, paras [13.2.3]–[13.2.9]. *Akai Pty Limited v The People's Insurance Company Limited* (1996) 188 CLR 418 is an example of the last two factors in operation (overriding legislation and public policy).
147 (1996) 188 CLR 418 at 437.
148 [1960] Ch 52 at 91.
149 (1996) 188 CLR 418 at 442.
150 See [3.665].

international law rules govern this issue was left open. Despite some of the mystique associated with online contracting laws in the legal and commercial marketplaces, the nexus between electronic commerce and private international law does not raise significant issues of policy. Instead, the nexus between these two domains rests on the application of settled principles of private international law in the online contracting environment.[151] Neither the UNCITRAL Model Law on Electronic Commerce (1996) (endorsed by UN General Assembly, on 16 December 1996)[152] nor the Australian implementing legislation, the *Electronic Transactions Act* 1999 (Cth), provides any specialised private international law rules to govern online contracting. To the knowledge of the authors, none of the agencies concerned with the reform of private international rules (including The Hague Conference on Private International Law and UNIDROIT) currently has a program of works or research that embraces the nexus between online contracting and private international law.

[26.385] Referring back to the example raised in [3.665], the settled principles of private international law would require consideration of two issues: whether a particular court has jurisdiction to hear the matter; and, once jurisdiction is established, the proper law to be applied to resolve the contractual issue in dispute. It is beyond the scope of this work to examine these principles in detail.[153] However, a brief consideration of the kind of matters that are likely to be relevant, should such a matter be litigated in Australia, may be helpful. The following exercise assumes that the purchaser of the CD in the example in [3.665] was a resident of Queensland.

[26.390] Whether a court has jurisdiction to hear and determine a matter is resolved by reference to both the common law and relevant statutes. A court will be regarded as having jurisdiction if there are grounds upon which service on a person who is outside the jurisdiction can be effected. To have valid service outside the jurisdiction, there must be some connection between the cause of action and the jurisdiction. Where the action concerns a contract (such as the purchase of a CD by email), that connection will be demonstrated if the contract is made within the jurisdiction, is governed by the law of the jurisdiction, or is broken in that jurisdiction.[154]

[26.395] Assuming that the jurisdiction (in this example, of a Queensland court) is established, the next issue is to determine the 'proper law' to govern the dispute. In other words, it must be decided whether Queensland, English (that of the place where the seller operates the CD business), or some other law should be applied to determine the matter. In *Akai Pty Limited v The People's Insurance Company Limited*,

---

151 Drew & Napier, *Your Guide to E-commerce Law in Singapore*, Drew & Napier, Singapore, 2000, paragraph 1.7.2 supports this conclusion.

152 UN General Assembly Resolution 51/162.

153 For a comprehensive review of the law in this area, reference should be made to the relevant texts in this area, including: PE Nygh, *Conflict of Law in Australia*, 6th edn, Butterworths, North Ryde, 1995; AV Dicey and JHC Morris, *Dicey and Morris on the Conflict of Laws*, 12th edn, Sweet and Maxwell, London 1993; and EI Sykes & MC Pryles, *Australian Private International Law*, 3rd edn, Law Book Co, Sydney 1991.

154 PE Nygh, *Conflict of Laws in Australia*, 6th edn, Butterworths, North Ryde, 1995, p 51. See also *Uniform Civil Procedure Rules* (Qld) r 124(1)(g) and (h); (NSW) *Supreme Court Rules 1970*, Order 10; (Vic) *General Rules of Procedure in Civil Proceedings 1996*, Order 7; (SA) *Supreme Court Rules 1987*, Order 18; (Tas) *Rules of the Supreme Court 1965*, Order 11; (WA) *Rules of the Supreme Court 1971*, Order 10; (ACT) *Supreme Court Rules*, Order 12 Rule 2, (NT) *Supreme Court Rules*, Part 7.

Toohey, Gaudron and Gummow JJ said the following concerning the 'proper law' of the contract:

> In *Amin Rasheed Corporation v Kuwait Insurance* [1984] AC 50 at 61, Lord Diplock referred to what he described as the 'pithy definition' of the 'proper law' of the contract by Lord Simonds in *Bonython v The Commonwealth* (1950) 81 CLR 486 at 498; [1951] AC 201 at 219, namely, 'the system of law by reference to which the contract was made or that with which the transaction has its closest and most real connection'.[155]

[26.400] However, this example raises a complicating factor, in that the real issue in dispute is whether, in fact, there is a contract at all. While the Australian law on this point is not entirely settled, it appears that the law of the place where the matter is tried (the *lex fori*) will govern the issue.[156] Therefore, if the purchaser brought the action in a Queensland court, the law of Queensland would govern the issue of contract formation.

26.5.2   Choice of forum

[26.405] Private international law also determines the extent to which parties to contract may select the forum in which any disputes that arise out of their contract are to be settled. The fundamental premise in this area is that the parties have relative freedom to select any system of law they wish for this purpose.[157] The choice of forum issue is also known as the curial law applicable to the contract, if it takes the form of a clause in a contract which states that the parties select the court or tribunals of a given country before which disputes are to be settled. In principle, there is no reason why the parties to an international contract cannot select, as the proper law of their contract, the law in country A as well as providing that disputes are to be resolved according to the law of country B.[158] Freedom to nominate the choice of forum does have its limits, including overriding legislation and public policy.

[26.410] Not only is it possible for the parties to an international contract to select one or other of the countries as the curial law of their contract; so, too, the parties can select a range of dispute resolution processes that can be used to resolve any disputes that emerge out of their relationship.[159]

---

155 (1998) 188 CLR 418 at 440–441. See also *Merwin Pastoral Co Pty Ltd v Moolpa Pastoral Co Pty Ltd & McKindlay* (1933) 48 CLR 565 at 573. As to the effect of the proper law of the contract, the Supreme Court of Queensland said in *Transfield Pty Ltd v Fondside Australia Pty Ltd (Receivers and Managers Appointed) (In Liquidation)* [2000] QSC 480 (21 December 2000) at [19] that 'The proper law of a contract determines what law is applied in relation to the meaning, validity and effect of the contractual obligations: *Amin Rasheed Shipping Corporation v Kuwait Insurance Co* [1984] AC 50'.

156 *Oceanic Sun Line Special Shipping Company Inc v Fay* (1987) 165 CLR 197.

157 *Akai* at 436 per Toohey, Gaudron and Gummow JJ; *Cie Tunisienne v Cie d'Armement* [1971] AC 572 at 603 per Lord Diplock.

158 *Akai* at 436 per Toohey, Gaudron and Gummow JJ; *Cie Tunisienne v Cie d'Armement* [1971] AC 572 at 604 per Lord Diplock. See Fisher & Fisher, *Export Best Practice: Commercial and Legal Aspects*, paragraph [2.10.1.3] for a discussion of this issue.

159 For a general treatment of dispute resolution, see G Clarke, 'Dispute Resolution', Chapter 6 in S Fisher (ed), *The Law of Commercial and Professional Relationships*, FT Law & Law, Melbourne, 1996, pp 147–161. See also L Boulle, *Mediation: Principles, Process, Practice*, Butterworths, Sydney, 1996.

[26.415] In international contracts, it is quite common for the parties to provide for arbitration as the preferred dispute resolution process.[160] Various institutions have long-standing arbitral competencies—they include the Australian Commercial Disputes Centre, the ICC International Court of Arbitration, the Hong Kong International Arbitration Centre, the Singapore International Arbitration Centre, the Chartered Institute of Arbitrators, the London Court of International Arbitration, and the American Arbitration Association. The UNCITRAL Model Law on International Commercial Arbitration,[161] adopted on 21 June 1985, has been given the force of law for Australia, under section 16 of the *International Arbitration Act* 1974 (Cth).[162] Schedule 2 of that Act now sets out the text of the UNCITRAL Model Law on International Commercial Arbitration.

---

160 See S Ratnapala & L Haller, 'International Commercial Arbitration', Chapter 11 in G Moens & P Gillies (eds), *International Trade and Business: Law, Policy and Ethics*, Cavendish Publishing (Australia) Pty Ltd, Sydney, 1998, pp 729–768; Koppenol-Laforce et al, *International Contracts: Aspects of Jurisdiction, Arbitration and Private International Law*, Chapter 3; M. Jacobs, *International Commercial Arbitration in Australia: Law in Practice*, Law Book Company Ltd, Sydney, 1992. A useful and comprehensively linked website is the one at University of Chicago Law School, Law Library <http://www.lib.uchicago.edu/~llou/intlarb.html> (accessed 19 January 2001).

161 24 ILM 1302 (1985).

162 Even though the enactment of the *International Arbitration Act* 1974 (Cth) predates the promulgation of the UNCITRAL Model Law, it was amended by the *International Arbitration Amendment Act* 1989 (Cth), inserting a new Part III, to give the Model Law the force of law in Australia. See *Halsbury's Laws of Australia* ARBITRATION paragraph [25-555] and *Halsbury's Laws of Australia* TRADE AND COMMERCE [420-2500]–[420-2515].

Part IX

Themes, Critical Perspectives, and Ideologies

A true appreciation of contract law does not end with an understanding of the various doctrines, rules and principles considered in the preceding chapters. Contract law is not two-dimensional; to grasp the full picture requires a much broader understanding. This Part contemplates the contextual settings of this area of law—the underlying assumptions that provide its systemic organisation—and explain why contract law is what it is. It also embraces as the various themes that run through the body of law and the broad ideologies—the system of ideas—that may be reflected in that law.

Chapter 27

Themes, critical perspectives, and ideologies

27.1   Theories explaining contract law

[27.05] Every body of substantive and procedural law can (or should) be explained in terms of its theoretical underpinnings. Contract law is no exception. For many contract law students, the emphasis is on understanding contract law and developing a working knowledge of its main doctrines, principles and rules as well as of its contours and controversies. Yet this otherwise worthwhile endeavour is futile in the absence of some connection with the principal theories that have been developed to explain contract law. As Gordley observes, 'a legal system can have rules to govern contracts and still not have a theory of contract or even a set of doctrines that systematically organize these rules'.[1] And Barnett claims ' [a] theory is a problem-solving device. We assess the merits of particular theory by its ability to solve problems that give rise to the need for a theory'.[2] So this section provides an overview of the main theories that have been used to explain contract law. The account that follows is necessarily selective and brief, and takes the form of an overview. Some jurists despair of ever finding a theory of contract law.[3]

27.1.1   Social contract theory

[27.10] Not every theory using the word 'contract' is in fact a theory about contract law. An illustration of this is the political theory known as *social contract theory*. Pared to its essence, social contract theory holds that there is some kind of compact or contract between the governors and the governed in any civil society. This can be traced back to political theorists as such as Rousseau, who published the famous work *Du contrat social* in 1762, and before him, to Hobbes and Locke. Lessnoff writes that social contract is a branch of political philosophy; it may be defined as a theory that grounds the legitimacy of political authority, and the rights and duties of rulers and subjects, all premised on a contract or contracts relating to such matters.[4]

The contractarian origins of social contract theory are grounded in the idea that those who are governed, consent to be governed. This is put in opposition to the notion of the 'divine right' of kings or queens to rule their subjects, where the subjects do not consent to be governed. This consent is implied or derived from a more fundamental concept. That is, by living in society, people place themselves under an obligation to obey laws and political rulers.[5] What social contract theory really does is to harness the idea of contract or agreement and to deploy it as an explanatory justification about a particular form of political dispensation.

27.1.2   Barnett's explanation of contractual obligations

[27.15] Barnett has identified five theories to explain contractual obligations.[6] These are summarised below.

1   *Will theories* of contract law take as their prime focus a concern of protecting the promise-maker, that is the promisor. This is described as a *party-based* theory.

---

1   J Gordley, 'Natural Law Origins of the Common Law of Contract', in J Barton (ed), *Towards a General Law of Contract,* Comparative Studies in Continental and Anglo-American Legal History, Vol 8, Duncker & Humblot, Berlin, p 367.

2   R Barnett, ' A Consent Theory of Contract' 86 *Columbia Law Review* 269, 269 (1986).

3   J Gordley, *The Philosophical Origins of Modern Contract Doctrine*, Clarendon Press, Oxford, 1991, p 230.

4   See M Lessnoff, 'Introduction: Social Contract' in M Lessnoff (ed), *Social Contract Theory*, New York University Press, New York, 1990, pp 2–3. See also M Tebbit, *Philosophy of Law: an Introduction*, Routledge, London, 1999, p 80, tracing contractarian theory back to Plato. J Rawls, *A Theory of Justice*, Belknap Press, Harvard, Cambridge, Mass., 1971, pp 11–17 firmly embedded into social contract theory the fact that the objects of the social contract are the principles of justice that make for the basic structure of society.

5   M Tebbit, *Philosophy of Law: an Introduction*, Routledge, London, 1999, p 79. On the duty to obey the law, see J Raz, *The Authority of Law: Essays on Law and Morality*, Clarendon Press, Oxford, 1979, Chapters 12–15; MBE Smith, 'The Duty to Obey the Law', in D Patterson (ed), *A Companion to Philosophy of Law and Legal Theory*, Blackwell Publishers, Oxford, 1999, pp 465–474.

6   R Barnett, ' A Consent Theory of Contract' 86 *Columbia Law Review* 269, 271–291 (1986).

2   *Reliance theories* of contract law explain contractual obligations as an effort to protect a promisee's reliance on the promises of others. Reliance theories are based
on the intuition that a promise-maker should be liable if it is foreseeable or justifiable that others may rely on the promise made. Reliance theories are also
described as party-based theories.

3   *Efficiency theories* of contract law, derived from the law and economics movement,
explain contract law in particular (and legal rules and practices in general) to determine whether or not some concept of social wealth or welfare is maximised. The
yardstick of efficiency is used to measure whether the aggregate benefits of a given
situation outweigh the aggregate costs of the same situation. In other words, this is a
type of cost–benefit analysis. Efficiency theories of contract law are what Barnett
describes as *standards-based* theories. That is, they examine the substance of a contractual transaction to determine whether it conforms to or departs from a standard
of evaluation that the particular theory specifies as primary or determinative.

4   *Substantive fairness* theories evaluate the substance of the transaction to determine
whether or not it is fair, or otherwise complies with some yardstick of conduct.
These theories have a long pedigree, going back at least to the 'just price' Christian theorists of the Middle Ages—and perhaps even back to Aristotle.[7] Substantive fairness theories are also standards-based. They have a particular resonance
with the equitable concept of unconscionable conduct.[8]

5   *Process-based* theories of contract explain the manner by which the parties reached
their agreement, rather than accentuating the contracting parties themselves or the
substance of their agreement. The bargain theory of consideration is the best-
known example of this type of theory.

27.1.3   'Agreement' in contract law

[27.20] Contract law implies agreement. What is the *essence* of agreement? According
to Rinkes and Samuel, the history of English contract law reveals that behind the often
recited rhetoric that agreement is the essence of contract, is the idea that English contract law is basically concerned with promisory liability. That is, promise-makers
should be liable to promise-takers for breaching promises on an objective frame of
reference, rather than for non-performance of an agreement—itself a subjective frame
of reference. In *Ashington Piggeries Ltd v Christopher Hill Ltd*,[9] Lord Diplock described a
contract as 'a promise or set of promises which the law will enforce'.[10] This suggests
that the legal act of a promise may count for more than simply the phenomenon of
agreement standing alone (although these two phenomena of promising and

---

7   See his *Nichomachean Ethics* 125. This connects also with the idea of an equal exchange of value in contract between contracting parties, as to which see J Gordley, 'Equality in Exchange' 69 *California Law
Review* 1587 (1981).
8   See Chapter 17 above.
9   [1972] AC 441.
10   Ibid at 501. See J Rinkes & G Samuel, *Contractual and Non-contractual Obligations in English Law*, Ars
Aequi Libri, Nijmegen, 1992, pp 103–105 (cited in S Wheeler & J Shaw, *Contract Law: Cases, Materials
and Commentary*, OUP, Oxford, 1994, p 25). See also G Samuel & J Rinkes, *Law of Obligations and Legal
Remedies*, Cavendish Publishing Ltd, London, 1996, § 5(c); and Chapter 10 where this idea is developed
more fully.

agreement should not be divorced too far from each other, since the subject of a promise can be some agreement).

27.1.4   *Autonomy-based theories of contract law*

[27.25] With an understanding of what underpins the legal acts of promising and agreement, one can move to a deeper analysis of the role of agreement in contract law. Agreement in contract law implies, among other things, that people making an agreement have some degree of *autonomy* to participate in the contract-making process and to reach a concluded contract. Benson has identified three autonomy-based theories of contract law. What these reduce to, initially, is the concept that contract law is a legal institution that recognises and respects the power of private individuals to effect changes in their legal relations *inter se*, within certain limits. These theories resist the reduction of obligations, whether promissory or contractual, to tort and unjust enrichment.[11]

[27.30] The first autonomy-based theory of contract law that Benson discusses is that by the theorist Raz. Raz distinguishes between intention and obligations as dimensions to promising, and asserts that it is the obligation concept that embraces the common law concept of promising.[12] From this baseline, Raz holds that the purpose of contract law is to protect the practice of undertaking voluntary obligations (including promises) and the individuals who rely on this practice. The goal of contract law, says Raz, is not to enforce promises as much as to prevent harm to others by requiring that contracts be performed.[13]

[27.35] The second autonomy-based theory of contractual obligation that Benson identifies and discusses is that by Fried.[14] Fried argues that for promises to be binding, there must be an underlying general convention of promising that provides individuals with a way to commit themselves to future performances, if they wish. Fried argues that it is in fact rational for legal actors to behave in this way. The step that follows this first one is that by invoking the convention of promising, the promisor invites the promisee to trust the promisor on moral grounds. For Fried, it is the idea of the promisee's trusting the promisor to perform his or her promise that provides the basis of the obligation to keep promises.[15]

---

11   P Benson, 'Contract' in D Patterson (ed), *A Companion to Philosophy of Law and Legal Theory*, Blackwell Publishers, Oxford, 1999, p 33.

12   The concept of promise looms large in contract law: see R Crasswell, 'Contract Law, Default Rules and the Philosophy of Promising' 88 *Michigan Law Review* 489 (1989); PS Atiyah, *Promises, Morals and Law*, Clarendon Press, Oxford, 1981; and C Fried, *Contract as Promise: a Theory of Contractual Obligation*, Harvard University Press, Cambridge, Mass, 1981.

13   P Benson, 'Contract' in D Patterson (ed), *A Companion to Philosophy of Law and Legal Theory*, Blackwell Publishers, Oxford, 1999, pp 33–35. There is an apparent (but not sustained or extended) point of contact here with the natural law origins of the common law of contract in that some of the leading commentators of the late scholastic era, Grotius and Pudendorf, argued that for promises to be promises, they must be made voluntarily and that they must emanate from the *will* of the promisor: see J Gordley, 'Natural Law Origins of the Common Law of Contract' in J Barton (ed), *Towards a General Law of Contract,* Comparative Studies in Continental and Anglo-American Legal History, Vol 8, Duncker & Humblot, Berlin, p 384.

14   Benson cites the well-known work of C Fried, *Contract as Promise: a Theory of Contractual Obligation*, Harvard University Press, Cambridge, Mass, 1981.

15   P Benson, 'Contract' in D Patterson (ed), *A Companion to Philosophy of Law and Legal Theory*, Blackwell Publishers, Oxford, 1999, pp 37–40. Trust is obviously not confined to contract law alone, it is a virtue that is integral to many commercial and professional relationships. See S Longstaff, 'The Role of Ethics in Commercial and Professional Relationships' in S Fisher (ed), *The Law of Commercial and Professional Relationships*, FT Law and Tax, Melbourne, 1996, paragraph [4.5.7].

[27.40] The third autonomy-based theory that Benson identifies and discusses is the one by Barnett.[16] Barnett argues that the essential basis for the legal obligation to perform a contract is that a contracting party has manifested an intent to alienate his or her rights to another, via the very act of contracting. Corresponding with this act of alienation of rights on the part of a contracting party is the act of acceptance of the act of alienation by the other contracting party. This provides the basis for Barnett's assertion that essentially, contract is inter-relational rather than uni-dimensional (in the sense of the making of the promise by a one person to another as the basis for a contract).[17]

27.1.5 Teleological theories of contract law

[27.45] In contrast with autonomy-based theories of contract stand the so-called *teleological* theories of contract. Teleology, in its philosophical sense, refers to the explanation of phenomena by the purpose they serve rather than by postulated causes.[18] Teleological thinking has crept into various branches of the law—not the least of which is statutory interpretation. Section 15AA of the *Acts Interpretation Act* 1901 (Cth) states that in connection with the interpretation of a provision of a Commonwealth Act, 'a construction that would promote the purpose or object underlying the Act (whether that purpose or object is expressly stated in the Act or not) shall be preferred to a construction that would not promote that purpose or object.'[19] Benson, again, provides a concise and insightful account of the three leading contemporary teleological theories of contract law (only two of which are examined here).

[27.50] Benson begins with the legal philosopher Gordley. Gordley argues that the virtues of liberality or commutative (or corrective) justice, derived from Aristotelean thought, constitute the two main ends of contracting. This means that a party's contractual obligations should depend on which virtues he or she has exercised.[20] In terms of contractual liability, this means that a commitment only counts as a promise, and is therefore enforceable by the promisee, if this will instantiate liberality or commutative justice.[21]

[27.55] The second teleological theory Benson discusses is that of Kronman.[22] Kronman argues that contracts cannot be explained unless they reflect distributional concerns: they must achieve a fair division of wealth and power among contracting citizens. There are three basic steps involved in this thesis. First, contracts embody voluntary exchanges, and this involves advantage-taking of some kind. Secondly, Kronman requires that advantage-taking by one person at another's expense should be

---

16 R Barnett, 'A Consent Theory of Contract' 86 *Columbia Law Review* 269 (1986).

17 P Benson, 'Contract' in D Patterson (ed), *A Companion to Philosophy of Law and Legal Theory*, Blackwell Publishers, Oxford, 1999, pp 40–43. Collins also refers to trust as a causative phenomenon in contract law: H Collins, *Regulating Contracts*, Oxford University Press, Oxford 1999, p 3.

18 B Moore (ed), *The Australian Pocket Oxford Dictionary*, 3rd edn, Oxford University Press, 1993, p 1092. SE Stumpf, *Philosophy: History & Problems*, 5th edn, McGraw-Hill Inc, New York, 1994, p 939 says '*Teleos* is the Greek work for "purpose"; hence teleology is the study of purpose in human nature and in the events of history. In ethical theory (teleological ethics), an action is considered good if it helps to fulfil the purposes of human nature'. See too M Hunnex, *Chronological and Thematic Charts of Philosophies and Philosophers*, Zondervan Publishing House, Grand Rapids, Mich, 1986, pp 8, 15, 17, 39, 41 and 45.

19 See also J Evans, *Statutory Interpretation: Problems of Communication,* OUP, 1988, pp 13, 49–71.

20 P Benson, 'Contract' in D Patterson (ed), *A Companion to Philosophy of Law and Legal Theory*, Blackwell Publishers, Oxford, 1999, pp 43–45.

21 Ibid, p 44.

22 A Kronman, 'Contract Law and Distributive Justice' 89 *Yale Law Journal* 472 (1980).

allowed, unless it violates the rights of the person of whom advantage is taken or those of a third party. The third part of Kronman's teleological theory of contract is that one differentiates permissible advantage-taking from impermissible advantage-taking if, but only if, the person taken advantage of will be better off in the long run with this type of advantage-taking.[23]

[27.60] Both of these teleological theories accentuate the end or goal of contracting rather than its causative events. These teleological theories underscore a type of pragmatism about contract law: what it hopes to achieve. While contracting theories can be presented in terms of opposing competing theories, and are prosecuted by theoreticians sometimes on an 'all-or-nothing' basis, this is not to say that the autonomy-based theories summarised above have no point of connection at all with the teleological accounts. For example, the teleological accounts do not deny the importance of value of human autonomy to the process of contracting, but those accounts do not rest the ultimate ground of contract on the human will. That said, however, the autonomy-based theories of contract are concerned with the root cause of contract—that is, the human will expressed via the act of contracting. These theories do not depend for their efficacy upon the purpose or end of contracting, which is a subsidiary matter for those theories. Both the autonomy-based theories and the teleological-based theories provide valuable insights into the nature of contract law. It would be a mistake for the student of contract law to adopt one and reject the other out of hand without critical examination of the merits and demerits of each cluster of theories.

27.1.6   Feminism

[27.65] Another theory that informs contract law is feminism (or as some theorists would put it, feminisms or feminist theories).[24] As a branch of jurisprudence, feminism embraces all schools of thought that reject a patriarchal view of the world in favour of one that seeks justice and equality for women. As Smith has put it, 'all feminist theories are intended to liberate women from sexist domination in one form or another'.[25] The intersection of feminism and contract law is among the least-developed forms of feminist legal scholarship to date, with most feminist jurists concentrating their efforts on criminal law, family law, employment law, labour relations, and corporate law,[26] to name the leading fields of feminist law.

[27.70] Feminist thought in general can be grouped under three brands. The first brand is *liberal feminism*, which has concentrated on the need for gender equality in

---

23   P Benson, 'Contract' in D Patterson (ed), *A Companion to Philosophy of Law and Legal Theory*, Blackwell Publishers, Oxford, 1999, pp 45–46.

24   This is related to, and a sub-set of, the claim theory that law is *sexed*: see F Olsen, 'The Sex of Law', in D Kairys (ed), *The Politics of Law: a Progressive Critique*, 3rd edn, Basic Books, New York, 1998, pp 691–707.

25   P Smith, 'Feminist Jurisprudence', in D Patterson (ed), *A Companion to Philosophy of Law and Legal Theory*, Blackwell Publishers, Oxford, 1999, pp 302–310, 307.

26   For recent Australian feminist contributions to corporate law, see S Berns & P Baron, *Company Law and Governance: An Australian Perspective*, OUP, Sydney, 1998, Chapter 15; and S Corcoran, 'Does a Corporation Have a Sex? Corporations as Legal Persons' in N Naffine & R Owens (eds), *Sexing the Subject of Law*, LBC Information Services, Sydney, 1997, pp 215–232. Interestingly, one area where feminist concerns about the incidence of sexually transmitted debt have been heeded is in the introduction of one director, one shareholder proprietary companies under the *Corporations Law*, ss 112–114, which removes the need in small business and family corporate structures to have two member, two director companies comprising male and female 'partners' (using the term 'partners' in a relational, not strictly legal sense).

society at large, and within social and business structures in particular. The second brand is *socialist feminism*, where the perspective is outside the capitalist system. Socialist feminism argues for the reconstruction of economic and social structures on socialist lines; it rejects capitalist thought and systems as normative. The third brand of feminism is the *radical feminist* position. Radical feminism argues that modern society, and modern business, is shaped fundamentally by male values. Radical feminists contend that the interests of women and men are fundamentally divergent and irreconcilable, and that patriarchy is the prime cause of social division and oppression. The goal of the radical feminist project is to break down patriarchal social structures and to secure a position of female separatism.[27] There have also been feminist critiques of the social contract where the argument is that the so-called 'sexual contract' is the hidden half of the social contract under which the sexual contract preserves the dominance of men over women and creates a patriarchal social order.[28]

[27.75] In terms of the way feminism and contract law intersect, the feminist project within contract law may be described as the use of feminist strategies as a means of contesting and restructuring conventional and stalemated understandings of contract law principles, rules and doctrines, so that there is a disruption of 'cultural dichotomies—especially, and controversially, the dichotomy of male/female'.[29] In terms of contemporary contract law, some concerns of feminism are being manifested in the current reference of the New South Wales Law Reform Commission into the law concerning third party guarantees, which connects with feminist concerns about Sexually Transmitted Debt.[30] Sexually Transmitted Debt involves the use of contracts to shift debt loads and risks between spouses by the use of guarantees and indemnities.[31] Since women have attained formal (but perhaps not substantive) equality with men (also reinforced by anti-discrimination legislation), the main preoccupation of modern feminism is on social justice for women and how they can share power with men in a patriarchally ordered society.

27.1.7   Sociology and contract law

[27.80] Sociology is the study of society. Its central project concerns the observation and description of social phenomena and the articulation and application to these phenomena of a coherent conceptual scheme.[32] The contribution of sociology to contract law is that it explores the nature of contracting as a social phenomenon and offers insights into contract law as a social institution. In keeping with academic disciplines, it may be noted that as a social science, sociology has its own tensions and divisions

---

27   See D Strinati, *An Introduction to Theories of Popular Culture*, Routledge, London, 1995, p 178.

28   C Pateman, 'Contracting In', in C Pateman (ed), *The Sexual Contract*, Polity Press, Cambridge, 1988, pp 1–7 (as cited in S Wheeler & J Shaw, *Contract Law: Cases, Materials and Commentary*, Clarendon Press, Oxford, 1994, pp 125–28).

29   See M Frug, 'Rescuing Impossibility Doctrine: A Postmodernist Feminist Analysis of Contract Law' 140 *University of Pennsylvania Law Review* 1029, 1029 and 1033 (1992). For insights into gender and the law going beyond contract law, see R Graycar & J Morgan (eds), *The Hidden Gender of Law*, The Federation Press, Sydney, 1990 and F Olsen (ed), *Feminist Legal Theory*, Vols I and II, Dartmouth, Aldershot, 1995.

30   New South Wales Law Reform Commission, *Guaranteeing Someone Else's Debts: Summary of Issues Paper 17*, New South Wales Law Reform Commission, April 2000.

31   See B Fehlberg, *Sexually Transmitted Debt : Surety Experience and English Law*, Clarendon Press, Oxford, 1997.

32   A Bullock, O Stallybrass & S Trombley (eds), *The Fontana Dictionary of Modern Thought*, 2nd edn, Fontana Press, 1998, p 793.

and schools of thought,[33] so that there is perhaps no uniform sociological construct that should be regarded as authoritative. This allows us to be selective, rather than eclectic, in terms of how sociology informs contract law.

[27.85] Consider the approach of Durkheim (1858–1917), a leading figure in sociology, to contract law. Hunt argues that Durkheim used a diametrically opposed analytical tool to examine and explain contract as a social institution. According to Hunt's interpretation of Durkheim, Durkheim held contract to be a pre-eminently individualistic act as the expression of individual free will. This is then put into opposition with the notion that contracts are inherently social in character. Durkheim argued that contract is a trilateral relationship of society–party–party, rather than the traditional bilateral relationship of party–party. The trilateral model holds that society lays down in advance the permitted framework of contractual activity, so that it is really society that provides the foundations for contracting as a social activity.[34]

[27.90] The social theorist Selznick argues that contract as a relationship exhibits four core aspects. The first is that contract is voluntary, not involuntary. Secondly, contract implies a limited commitment that is impermanent in terms of the undertakings it embodies. Thirdly, contract consists of mutuality and exchanges, which connect with a largely self-enforcing system founded on self-interest and reciprocity. Fourthly, contract is a narrow bounded relationship that affects only the parties to it rather than any broader social group.[35] Collins criticises Selznick for this view of contract law on the basis that it is too narrow, and too closely tied to the legal conception of contract—and that it does not encompass the idea that contracts establish a discrete communication system between the parties to it.[36] Instead, Collins constructs an alternative framework of contractual relations centring on four dimensions. First, Collins argues that contracts circumscribe the valuation of conduct by reference to the terms recorded for the terms of that transaction. Secondly, contracts establish social relations with a currency of exchange that is quantifiable and measurable. Thirdly, contractualisation consists in the atomisation of social relations so that the effects of a transaction upon other people are regarded as irrelevant or externalities. Fourthly, contracts allow parties to construct their own type of power relation under which some person in an ascendant position creates a system of rules and governance for the particular relationship.[37]

---

33   The principal branches of sociology are described in A Bullock, O Stallybrass & S Trombley (eds), *The Fontana Dictionary of Modern Thought*, 2nd edn, Fontana Press, 1998, pp 793–795.

34   A Hunt, *The Sociological Movement in Law*, Macmillan, London, 1978, pp 85–88 (as cited in S Wheeler & J Shaw, *Contract Law: Cases, Materials and Commentary*, Clarendon Press, Oxford, 1994, pp 46–49). The same trilateral model also holds good for property law (substituting 'state' for 'society'), as to which see B Welling, *Property in Things in the Common Law System*, Scribblers Publishing, Gold Coast, 1996, pp 5–7.

35   P Selznick, *Law, Society and Industrial Justice*, Russell Sage Foundation, New York, 1969, pp 52–62, cited by H Collins, *Regulating Contracts*, OUP, Oxford, 1999, p 14.

36   H Collins, *Regulating Contracts*, OUP, Oxford, 1999, pp 14–15.

37   Ibid, pp 21–25.

27.1.8 Critical legal studies and contract law

[27.95] Critical legal studies (CLS)[38] is a branch of legal knowledge that is difficult to define precisely. CLS traces its origins to the Conference on Critical Legal Studies at the University of Wisconsin in 1977.[39] The CLS movement is commonly portrayed as the successor to the movement of legal realism,[40] and has taken up and expanded the themes of the legal realists.[41] There are three main schools of CLS thought: The Frankfurt School of Marxist Criticism; 'Orthodox' or 'Scientific' Marxism; and the Law and Social Science Perspective.[42]

[27.100] CLS adherents reject the idea that law is a value-neutral tool of social ordering, and argue instead that law is an ideological power that reinforces a dominant hierarchy of values and interests within society—usually based on race, gender, and class. CLS combines legal realism, critical Marxism, and structuralist and post-structuralist literary theory into an enterprise whose basic tenets speak to the domain of social and political theory rather than analytical jurisprudence[43] (or, for that matter, private law). CLS is implacably opposed to liberalism[44] as a social and philosophical movement. Since liberalism is one of the root platforms of societies modelled on Western democratic societies, the commitment of CLS to Western-style democratic institutions may be questioned, despite rhetoric from CLS proponents that it is democratic.[45]

[27.105] The CLS project in its application to contract law theory challenges the very notion of a theory of contract in the first place.[46] It seems to be unified by its opposition to classical and neo-classical contract law rather than by its articulation of a theory

---

38　On CLS generally, see G Binder, 'Critical Legal Studies' in D Patterson (ed), *A Companion to Philosophy of Law and Legal Theory*, Blackwell Publishers, Oxford, 1999, pp 280–290; J Stuart Russell, 'The Critical Legal Studies Challenge to Contemporary Mainstream Legal Philosophy' 18 *Ottawa Law Review* 1 (1986); and R Unger, *The Critical Legal Studies Movement*, Harvard University Press, Cambridge, Mass, 1986. A collection of some leading journal articles on CLS is found in J Boyle (ed), *Critical Legal Studies*, Dartmouth Publishing, Aldershot, 1992. CLS writers are occasionally called 'crits' or 'critters', sometimes pejoratively, sometimes not. A writer on both feminism and CLS can be called a 'femcrit': see J Boyle (ed), *Critical Legal Studies*, Dartmouth Publishing, Aldershot, 1992, p v.

39　J Stuart Russell, 'The Critical Legal Studies Challenge to Contemporary Mainstream Legal Philosophy' 18 *Ottawa Law Review* 1, 3 (1986).

40　On legal realism, see WW Fisher III, MJ Horwitz & TA Reed, *American Legal Realism*, Oxford University Press, New York, 1993, and B Leiter, 'Legal Realism' in D Patterson (ed), *A Companion to Philosophy of Law and Legal Theory*, Blackwell Publishers, Oxford, 1999, pp 261–279.

41　R Hillman, *The Richness of Contract Law: An Analysis and Critique of Contemporary Theories of Contract Law*, Kluwer Academic Publishers, Dordrecht, 1997, p 191.

42　J Stuart Russell, 'The Critical Legal Studies Challenge to Contemporary Mainstream Legal Philosophy' 18 *Ottawa Law Review* 1, 4–5 (1986). Hillman says that CLS writers often disagree among themselves and 'it is as difficult to synthesise the CLS view as it is to capture one for any other school of thought': R Hillman, *The Richness of Contract Law: An Analysis and Critique of Contemporary Theories of Contract Law*, Kluwer Academic Publishers, Dordrecht, 1997, p 191 (n 67).

43　G Binder, 'Critical Legal Studies' in D Patterson (ed), *A Companion to Philosophy of Law and Legal Theory*, Blackwell Publishers, Oxford, 1999, pp 280–281.

44　By this we mean 'small-l' liberalism, not conservatism, as a social and political movement. Liberalism is the social and political movement that springs from a vision of individuals, not classes, and of the liberty of individuals as the primary social good. This plays into the defence of rights such as free political institutions, religious practice, intellectual and artistic expression: see A Bullock, O Stallybrass & S Trombley (eds), *The Fontana Dictionary of Modern Thought*, 2nd edn, Fontana Press, 1998, p 475.

45　See D Kennedy & K Klare, 'A Bibliography of Critical Legal Studies' 94 Yale LJ 461 (1984).

46　For an account that is not quite so dismissive of a theory of contract law (and which did not set out to create one either), see P Drahos & S Parker, 'Critical Contract Law in Australia' (1990) 3 JCL 30.

that explains contract law as a legal institution.[47] One CLS proponent says that the 'ideological imagery of contract law served to legitimate an oppressive socio-economic reality by denying its oppressive character and representing it in imaginary terms'.[48] CLS contract law asserts that contract law is indeterminate because the formal rules of contract law rarely dictate a particular result in a landmark case.[49] The result of this indeterminacy thesis is that contract law and doctrine cannot really sustain its claim to generating certainty and predictability in contract law.

The CLS project generally offers sustained, polemical (including the use of a technique called 'trashing')[50] and, at times, justified criticisms of legal institutions but it offers very little of a programmatic nature that can be used to redress the defects identified. It offers little that is new in its insistence that ideology permeates legal institutions, since this had been known for a long time before CLS emerged as a recent ideology. CLS faces the prospect that it is possible to deconstruct it using its own tools and methodologies—which will leave little of value to future scholars.

27.1.9 *Economic analysis of contract law*

[27.110] Economics is the branch of the social sciences that is concerned with the production, distribution and consumption of wealth in human society.[51] The connection between law and economics is seen in public law (international economic law) and private law, and an entire discipline, the law-and-economics movement, has been constructed to state and explore the interface between law and economics.

[27.115] The law-and-economics movement has had a significant effect on restrictive trade practices[52] (in United States terminology, anti-trust law) and has been influential in theorising about some aspects of contract law.[53] Basically, there are two pathways: the first is the economic function of contract law, and the second is the contract law and economics overlap. The former is considered in this section.

[27.120] The economic role of contract law is to deter people from behaving opportunistically towards their contracting parties, in order to encourage the optimal timing of economic activity and obviate costly self-protective measures.[54] Further, contracts

---

47   S Wheeler & J Shaw, *Contract Law: Cases, Materials and Commentary*, Clarendon Press, Oxford, 1994, p 113. See further T Wilhelmsson (ed), *Perspectives of Critical Contract Law*, Dartmouth, Aldershot, 1993.

48   See P Gabel & J Feinman, 'Contract Law as Ideology' in D Kairys (ed), *The Politics of Law—a Progressive Critique*, 2nd edn, Basic Books, New York, 1998, p 179, cited in J Stuart Russell, 'The Critical Legal Studies Challenge to Contemporary Mainstream Legal Philosophy' 18 *Ottawa Law Review* 1, 14 (1986).

49   See R Hillman, *The Richness of Contract Law: An Analysis and Critique of Contemporary Theories of Contract Law*, Kluwer Academic Publishers, Dordrecht, 1997, p 191. On indeterminacy generally, see L Solum, 'Indeterminacy', Chapter 34 in D Patterson (ed), *A Companion to Philosophy of Law and Legal Theory*, Blackwell Publishers, Oxford, 1996, pp 488–502.

50   See M Kelman, 'Trashing' 36 *Stanford L Rev* 293 (1984) and J Stuart Russell, 'The Critical Legal Studies Challenge to Contemporary Mainstream Legal Philosophy' 18 *Ottawa Law Review* 1, 14–16 (1986).

51   G Bannock, R Baxter & E Davis, *Dictionary of Economics*, 6th edn, Penguin Books, London, 1998, p 122 and P Samuelson & W Nordhaus, *Economics*, 13th edn, McGraw-Hill, New York, p 5.

52   See S Corones, *Competition Law in Australia*, 2nd edn, LBC Information Services, 1999, Chapter 1, R Posner, *Economic Analysis of Law*, 5th edn, Aspen Law & Business, 1998, Chapter 10 and W Hirsch, *Law and Economics: An Introductory Analysis*, 3rd edn, Academic Press, San Diego, 1999, Chapter 10.

53   See R Posner, *Economic Analysis of Law*, 5th edn, Aspen Law & Business, 1998, Chapter 4 and W Hirsch, *Law and Economics: An Introductory Analysis*, 3rd edn, Academic Press, San Diego, 1999, Chapter 5.

54   R Posner, *Economic Analysis of Law*, 5th edn, Aspen Law & Business, 1998, p 103.

are social institutions that facilitate efficient exchange by providing a mechanism for enforcing those agreements where aggregate value between contracting parties is presumed to have increased.[55] As a discipline, economics reaches into the legal domain of contract to reduce transaction costs of contracting parties.[56]

[27.125] Some of the critical points of connection between contract law and economics lie in the following propositions.

1 A contract involves an exchange of some form of value for another form of value, and the law-and-economics approach to contract law seeks to discover and reduce the transaction costs in such exchange transactions.

2 The bargaining power of parties to contracts is rarely equal, so the spread of transaction costs between parties can be tightly constrained (in the case of a one-off purchase of consumer goods by a consumer) or widely distributed (in the case of the sale by a retailer of those same consumer goods using the same version of a standard-form contract in repeated sales to consumers).

3 Transaction costs can be reduced by the use of add-on clauses, waiver-of-defence clauses, due-on-sale clauses, liquidated damages clauses, and termination-at-will clauses.

4 Economies of scale ensue from the repeated use of standard-form contracts while 'contracts of adhesion' are those contracts entered into between a stronger party and a weaker party on a 'take-it-or-leave-it' basis.[57]

5 Any party to a contract has a choice of performing it or paying damages.[58]

6 The basic measure of damages for breach of contract is the rule of financial equivalent performance, under which the contract-breaker must pay the party not in breach the financial equivalent of the breach.[59]

7 The doctrine of mitigation of damages seeks to prevent resource misallocation— particularly in the case of an executory or partly performed contract, so that the party not in breach is not required to perform his or her side of the contract in order to obtain damages, but is instead able to enter into a substitute (or 'cover') transaction to gain what the defaulting party has not performed.[60] This is also called the avoidable-consequences rule.[61]

[27.130] In the end, the value of the law-and-economics movement is that it cross-pollinates law with economic considerations of efficiency in resource allocation. The effect of the law-and-economics movement on contract law is that it also focuses on the economic functions of contract law. These are summarised by Posner as (1) to prevent

---

55   W Hirsch, *Law and Economics: An Introductory Analysis*, 3rd edn, Academic Press, San Diego, 1999, p 106.

56   Ibid, p 17.

57   Ibid; points 1–4 are adapted from pp 120–135.

58   OW Holmes Jr, 'The Path of the Law' 10 *Harv L Rev* 457, 462 (1897): 'The duty to keep a contract at common law means a prediction that you must pay damages if you do not keep it—and nothing else', cited by R Posner, *Economic Analysis of Law*, 5th edn, Aspen Law & Business, 1998, p 131 (n 1). See also OW Holmes Jr, *The Common Law*, Little, Brown and Co, Boston, 1881, pp 234–237.

59   W Hirsch, *Law and Economics: An Introductory Analysis*, 3rd edn, Academic Press, San Diego, 1999, pp 116–117.

60   R Posner, *Economic Analysis of Law*, 5th edn, Aspen Law & Business, 1998, p 131.

61   W Hirsch, *Law and Economics: An Introductory Analysis*, 3rd edn, Academic Press, San Diego, 1999, p 117.

opportunism, (2) to interpolate efficient terms, (3) to prevent avoidable mistakes in the contracting process, (4) to allocate risk to the superior risk bearer, and (5) to reduce the costs of resolving contract disputes.[62]

27.2 Themes in contract law

[27.135] Having scanned the main theories that have been developed or used to explain contract law as a coherent and distinctive body of legal knowledge, consideration is now be given to the *themes* of contract law. The first point to reflect upon is the way the themes of contract law differ from the theories just considered. The themes of contract law are the internal working principles of contract law that determine, directly or indirectly, the make-up of contract law and its principles, doctrines, and rules. Contract law has a variety of themes. In the interests of brevity, four are selected for discussion: (1) autonomy; (2) altruism; (3) consumer welfarism; (4) fairness.

27.2.1 Autonomy

[27.140] *Autonomy* refers to the capacity of people to make their own laws. Within contract law, autonomy is harnessed to support the idea that there is a notion of freedom of contract. An important norm that underpins many (if not all) contracts is the *party autonomy principle* (sometimes called freedom of contract, although it is not quite the same).[63] This means parties have freedom to select how and in what form they will conclude a given contract—subject usually only to restraints such as compliance with public laws and public policy.

[27.145] This type of norm is present in only a diluted form in domestic Australian consumer protection laws (such as the *Trade Practices Act* 1974 (Cth) and the uniform *Consumer Credit Code*) but it is alive and well in international transactions outside the retail sector. For example, under the *United Nations Convention on Contracts for the International Sale of Goods*, the parties to an international sale of goods contract have the power to exclude the application of the Convention, or to derogate from or vary the effect of any of its provisions.[64]

[27.150] Another example of the autonomy principle at work appears in the draft *Convention on International Interests in Mobile Equipment* being prepared by UNIDROIT.[65] Article 6 of this instrument allows the parties to derogate from or vary any of the effects

---

62 R Posner, *Economic Analysis of Law*, 5th edn, Aspen Law & Business, 1998, p 108.

63 The relationship between the two might be explained by saying that the concept of freedom of contract precedes the concept of party autonomy. See also S Wiliston, 'Freedom of Contract' 6 *Cornell LQ* 365 (1921) and R Pound, 'Liberty of Contract' 18 *Yale LJ* 454.

64 *United Nations Convention on Contracts for the International Sale of Goods*, Article 6 (subject to a Statute of Frauds type of writing requirement under Article 12 which cannot be varied or derogated from). This Convention is an 'opt-out', not an 'opt-in' style of Convention, meaning it applies unless the parties have excluded its application in whole or in part in a given international sales contract. Of course, the Convention will not apply if the connecting factors of the Convention are not satisfied in acutality or if the transaction cannot be characterised as a sale of goods contract.

65 It is of interest to note that UNIDROIT has prepared, under the chairmanship of Professor Roy Goode and a UNIDROIT Study Group, a preliminary draft Convention on the International Interest in Mobile Equipment. For a review of this work to date, see (1998) 3 *Uniform Law Review* (NS) 52. This work is designed to lead to an international convention governing the creation of international security and related interests in equipment of a kind which crosses States (ie, aircraft, registered ships, oil rigs, containers, satellites and other tangible uniquely identifiable property).

of Chapter III of the Convention (with stated exceptions to this facility that do not need to be stated here). These provisions are imbued with a strong party autonomy principle that can be taken one step further back to one of the key drivers of a civilised system of a law of voluntary obligations, namely *pacta sunt servanda* (contracts should be faithfully performed). Contracts can be performed if they are entered into by parties having autonomy to select the range of provisions they consider will give effect to their bargain. The principle of party autonomy is not uniquely of international origin; traces of it can be seen in the development of contract law in England and its growth in Australia.[66] Yet what is interesting is to see the principle of party autonomy circulating internationally and being re-absorbed into domestic Australian law via the localisation of international commercial treaties. Article 1.1 of the influential UNIDROIT *Principles of International Commercial Contracts* provides 'The parties are free to enter into a contract and to determine its content'. This provision clearly reflects the party autonomy principle.[67]

This movement shows the vitality of the party autonomy principle and its widespread acceptance internationally. Its presence in the UNIDROIT *Principles* also shows how business norms can migrate across legal cultures and barriers and how they can operate as international best practice statements. The party autonomy principle flows into a related, if not indistinguishable, principle of *freedom of commerce*.[68] From a feminist viewpoint,[69] some feminists might argue that the notion of autonomy is absent for women as contractual actors who may not be in a position to act autonomously due to patriarchal dominance in the contracting arena.

27.2.2 Altruism

[27.155] Altruism is basically selflessness. The question for contract law is the extent to which—if at all—altruism has any significant reach or resonance within the law of contract. Or, in a recast form, whether contract law requires contracting parties to behave selflessly, or whether they may behave selfishly—that is, to regard only their own interests. If either the former or the latter represents the current state of the law of contract, then a subsidiary question emerges: is there some kind of balance between selflessness and selfishness that contract law attempts to accommodate? In *Walford v Miles*,[70] Lord Ackner said '[the] duty to carry on negotiations in good faith is inherently repugnant to the adversarial position of the parties when involved in the negotiations. Each party to the negotiations is entitled to pursue his (or her) own interests, so long as he (or she) avoids making misrepresentations'.[71] Ignoring for the moment the

---

66 For a brief review, see D Greig & J Davis, *The Law of Contract*, Law Book Company Ltd, Sydney, 1987, pp 22–23, 30–32. For a wider study of the history of contract law, see SJ Stoljar, *A History of Contract at Common Law*, ANU Press, Canberra, 1975.

67 What is interesting is its placement within the *UNIDROIT Principles* as the first article, surely not unintended or accidental.

68 The notion of freedom of commerce received explicit recognition by the Supreme Court of Canada in *Christie v York Corporation* [1940] SCR 139 at 142. Within Australian constitutional law, it is reflected within the text and jurisprudence of s 92 of the Commonwealth Constitution, which reads: ' On the imposition of uniform duties of customs, trade, commerce, and intercourse among the States, whether by means of internal carriage or ocean navigation, shall be absolutely free' (first paragraph). See *Cole v Whitfield* (1988) 165 CLR 360.

69 See 27.1.6 above.

70 [1992] 2 WLR 174.

71 Ibid at 181.

'good faith' context in which these remarks were made, his Lordship's remarks clearly signal a position closer to the 'selfish' rather than the 'selfless' end of the spectrum of interests that contracting parties can pursue. If one considers the nature of contract as involving a promise, and in particular when a promise maker exercises an act of liberality by making a promise for the benefit of another person, then his Lordship's remarks appear to miss the whole point of contracting in the first place.

The teleological theories of contract are much more amenable to embodying a virtue of altruism than the autonomy-based theories of contract, because the teleological theories of contract consider the purpose of contract, while the autonomy-based theories accentuate the human will as the prime cause of contracting. A connection could also be made between altruism and egalitarianism in contract law—a connection made by Kennedy in a different context.[72] A notion of egalitarianism in contract law might be present in some weak form in the idea that some contract scholars hold, that there should be equality (or perhaps relative equality) in contracting.[73] As far as Anglo-Australian contract law is concerned, there is little evidence to suggest that altruism is a prime mover of either the process of contracting or, for that matter, the substantive outcomes of contracting. Altruism is aspirational, not normative. Contract law does not strike a balance, explicitly at least, between selflessness and selfishness. Instead, contract law favours selfishness over selflessness.

[27.160] If altruism is considered from the viewpoint of economics, it could be said that the economically rational person seeks to maximise his or her own self-interest, not to enhance the well-being of others.[74] On this view, economics is selfish in the sense used in this chapter, and is not concerned with altruism. This is not to say that of and by itself economics imposes unjustified social costs, but that one of the guiding impulses of economics—like contract law—is to benefit self over others. Economics, in the classic Western model, is the antithesis of communitarianism or forms of collective ownership of economic assets such as socialism.

27.2.3   Consumer welfarism

[27.165] According to some Australian commentators 'consumer welfare' or 'consumerism' is:

> the movement of which the aim is to give consumers some equality of power, some redress against those forces which ply them with goods and services which they have been convinced to buy on the basis of a choice which may be informed but informed on an artificial basis. The objectives of the movement are probably best achieved by wide education of consumers in the community and, though law has a slight educative role, consumer education is not a prime function of laws which protect the consumer.[75]

---

72   See D Kennedy, 'Distributive and Paternalistic Motives in Contract and Tort Law, with Special Reference to Compulsory Terms and Unequal Bargaining Power' 41 *Maryland Law Review* 563, 584–586 (1982).

73   See J Gordley, 'Equality in Exchange' 69 *California Law Review* 1587 (1981).

74   W Hirsch, *Law and Economics: An Introductory Analysis*, 3rd edn, Academic Press, San Diego, 1999, p 12.

75   J Goldring, L Maher, J McKeough & G Pearson, *Consumer Protection Law*, 5th edn, The Federation Press, Sydney, 1998, p 2.

[27.170] A consumer is any person who buys goods or services for personal consumption, usually from a business operator (whether a corporation or another type of business entity such as a partnership (or firm) or a sole trader).[76] In the modern terminology of business law and commerce, this is what would be called a 'business-to-consumer' ('B2C') transaction. The Canadian commentator Ziegel has collated the following principles that inform consumerism as a movement, and provide the rationale for consumer protection laws:

1   The right to safety.
2   The right to honesty.
3   The right to fair agreements.
4   The right to know.
5   The right to choose.
6   The rights to privacy, to correct abuses, and to security of employment and peace of mind.
7   The right to be heard.[77]

[27.175] The principal bodies of law in Australia that protect consumers are the *Trade Practices Act* 1974 (Cth) (see in particular Parts IVA, IVB, V, VA)[78] and the largely equivalent pieces of legislation under State and Territorial law, namely the *Fair Trading Acts*.[79]

[27.180] Besides legislative intervention implementing ideals of consumerism and, in particular, translating consumer protection into positive law, judicial approaches to consumer welfare must be considered. Some judgments of the High Court of Australia have identified consumer welfare as an element of adjudication, and it has proved to be normative in the judicial elaboration of section 52 of the *Trade Practices Act* 1974 (Cth).[80] The *Trade Practices Act* has proved a fertile source of jurisdiction for the High Court. Juxtaposed against consumer welfare is the ideology of individual freedom, particularly in transactions between business people and consumers. This is seen in *Darlington Futures Ltd v Delco Australia Pty Ltd*[81] where the Court upheld the efficacy of a limitation of exemption clause in a contract between a futures trader and a commercial customer.[82]

[27.185] The principles of consumerism have an impact on a range of areas in business and commerce, including sale of goods,[83] supply of services,[84] consumer finance (or

---

76   For the purposes of the *Trade Practices Act* 1974 (Cth), there is a specific definition of 'consumer' in section 4B.
77   J Ziegel, 'The Future of Canadian Consumerism' (1973) 52 *Can Bar Rev* 191 (cited by Goldring & Ors, *Consumer Protection Law*, 5th edn, The Federation Press, Sydney, 1998, pp 2–3).
78   On Part VA of the *Trade Practices Act* 1974, see J Kellam, *A Practical Guide to Australian Product Liability*, CCH Australia Ltd, Sydney, 1992.
79   See *Fair Trading Act* 1987 (NSW); *Fair Trading Act* 1999 (Vic); *Fair Trading Act* 1989 (Qld); *Fair Trading Act* 1987 (SA); *Fair Trading Act* 1987 (WA); *Consumer Affairs and Fair Trading Act* 1990 (NT); *Fair Trading Act* 1990 (Tas). For a practical account of these bodies of law and of commentary associated with them, see 11 *SALE OF GOODS AND PRODUCT LIABILITY, Australian Encyclopaedia of Forms and Precedents*, 3rd edn, Butterworths, Sydney, 2000, paras [1860]–[2040], [2050]–[2090].
80   See *Concrete Constructions (NSW) Pty Ltd v Nelson* (1990) 169 CLR 594 and *Qantas Airways Limited v Aravco Limited* (1996) 185 CLR 43 and Chapter 13 above.
81   (1986) 161 CLR 500.
82   See Chapter 9 on exclusion clauses.
83   On sale of goods contracts, see A Tyree, *Sale of Goods*, Butterworths, Sydney, 1998; KCT Sutton, *Sales and Consumer Law*, 4th edn, LBC Information Services, 1995; and S Fisher, *Commercial and Personal Property Law*, Butterworths, Sydney, 1997, Chapter 12.
84   See s 74 of the *Trade Practices Act* 1974 (Cth).

retail finance),[85] banking law and product liability regimes.[86] While this catalogue is illustrative and not exhaustive, it does demonstrate the reach of the fields of activity that are impacted by consumerism.

27.2.4   *Fairness*

[27.190] The idea that any legal system not only should, but *must* embody a virtue of fairness is hardly controversial in twenty-first century Australia. While Australian law should be fair, this does not mean that fairness is a legal virtue. Certainly, fairness is integral to justice. Fairness is connected to equity (and a related sense in which this claim can be made is that the body of jurisprudence known as 'equity' is also under-pinned or informed by the virtue of equity). It is not necessary here to chart the metes and bounds of 'justice as fairness' in the sense that Rawls develops this concept of jus-tice.[87] But it is important to consider whether Australian contract law requires or rec-ognises fairness. If this can be answered affirmatively, then the question becomes: is fairness a norm of contract law or simply a virtue within contract law? The working definition of fairness in the present context is this: fairness is the virtue that dictates that there ought to be equity in the process of contracting and in contracts themselves.

[27.195] 'Fairness' within contract law has several dimensions that need to be articu-lated explicitly. One may speak of the *process* of contracting being fair to the contract-ing parties. One may also say that the *outcomes* of contract must be fair. In a third sense, the effect of fairness is that it *informs* specific contract rules.

[27.200] The first enquiry is whether contract law requires fairness in the contracting process—that is, the negotiation of contracts. Arguably it does, but the law accom-plishes this objective by an aggregation of specific contractual rules rather than by a specific doctrine to that effect. The law governing misrepresentation and its effect in the negotiation of contracts could be rationalised as requiring fairness. Thus in *Curwen v Yan Yean Land Co Ltd*,[88] Higinbotham CJ said 'A true representation, coupled with concealment, thus became a positive misrepresentation calculated to deceive and which did in fact deceive the plaintiff to his detriment.'[89] Underlying a statement of law to this effect is the idea that concealment of material facts can operate unfairly between contracting parties, so this unfairness in the contracting process needs to be corrected by judicial decree. So in terms of the specific chapters of this book that deal with misrepresentation, fraud, duress, and other vitiating factors affecting the contract-ing process,[90] the result is that these specific branches of contract law contain a virtu-ous underpinning that requires the contracting parties to negotiate fairly. Recently, Phang has made the same point in the context of security of contract. His thesis is that fairness ought to be the main focus of modern contract law.[91]

[27.205] The second enquiry is whether the *outcomes* of contracts must be fair. In other words, does contract law require fair terms—that is, must the *content* or *substance* of contracts be equitable or even-handed or balanced between the contracting parties? As

---

85   See D McGill & L Willmott, *Annotated Consumer Credit Code*, LBC Information Services, Sydney, 1999.
86   See Part VA of the *Trade Practices Act* 1974 (Cth).
87   See J Rawls, *A Theory of Justice*, Belknap Press, Harvard, Cambridge, Mass, 1971, §§ 18 and 52 and also M Tebbit, *Philosophy of Law: an Introduction*, Routledge, London, 1999, pp 85–86.
88   (1891) 17 VLR 745.
89   Ibid at p 751.
90   See chapters 13–16 above.
91   See A Phang, 'Security of Contract and the Pursuit of Fairness' (2000) 16 JCL 158.

the law currently stands, Australian law (and the common law generally) does not support the proposition that the substance of a contract must be fair; and if it is not, then there are grounds for judicial intervention or re-adjustment of the terms of the bargain enshrined in the contract.[92] In the case of standard-form contracts (particularly those in use within industry and professional associations), it has been argued that some courts interpret these forms of contract against a developing doctrine that fairness can temper the operation of substantive provisions of the standard-form contract such as exclusion clauses.[93] The evidence for substantive fairness in contracts is lacking. This is not to say that contract should be fair, just that the legal system does not hold, for now, that they must be.

[27.210] The third enquiry is whether fairness is also a virtue that informs some specific rules of contract law. For example, in *Wieder v Skala & Lubin*[94] the New York Court of Appeals said 'The idea is simply that when A and B agree that B will do something it is understood that A will not prevent B from doing it. The concept is rooted in notions of common sense and fairness (see Farnsworth, *The Law of the Contract*, § 7.16, at 307).'[95] The platform of fairness (and common sense) that props up this rule is articulated clearly, but this does not mean that fairness is normative in the sense of constituting a rule or principle that can be used to adjudicate contractual disputes. Fairness is used as an ethical prop that explains or justifies contractual rules but it is not, of and by itself, a norm that has a hard legal edge.

27.3 Conclusions: the ideologies of contract law

[27.215] To conclude this chapter, it would be instructive to identify some of the ideologies of contract law, and assess (briefly) their impact on this work and on the project of understanding contract law. This requires firstly a definition of 'ideology'.

[27.220] While the term 'ideology' carries several meanings (sometimes pejoratively, particularly when used to denounce right-of-centre political theories and 'isms'), the one relevant to this analysis is 'a system of ideas or way of thinking pertaining to a class or an individual, especially as the basis of some economic or political theory or system, regarded as justifying actions and especially to be maintained irrespective of events'.[96] Law is considered by some commentators to be inherently ideological. For example, Hunt says that law is ideological in a double sense. Thus, law is 'ideologically constructed and is itself a significant (and possibly

---

92 See *Blomley v Ryan* (1956) 99 CLR 362 at 374, and at 405. For a fuller treatment, see M Chen-Wishart, *Unconscionable Bargains*, Butterworths, Wellington, 1989, Part V.

93 See A Boggiano, *International Standard Contracts: the Price of Fairness*, Graham & Trotman/Martinus Nihoff, London/Dordrecht, 1991. His discussion of *George Mitchell (Chesterhall) Ltd v Finney Lock Seeds Ltd* [1983] 2 AC 803 (at pp 144–148) ignores the fact that the basis for the operation of a fairness doctrine was legislatively mandated by the *Unfair Contracts Terms Act* 1977 (UK), Schedule 1, paragraph 11, so it is overstating the conclusion drawn from that case to say it is warrant for judicial intervention of substantive provisions of contracts on the basis of substantive fairness. H Collins, *Regulating Contracts*, OUP, Oxford, 1999, Chapter 11 provides a broader study of unfair contracts that argues that the regulation of substantive fairness should comprise an important ingredient of the legal system.

94 80 NY 2d 628.

95 Ibid at 637.

96 L. Brown (ed), *The New Shorter Oxford English Dictionary on Historical Principles*, Clarendon Press, Oxford, Vol 1, 1993, p 1035.

major) bearer of ideology.'[97] The real issue is not whether law is ideological, but rather which ideology lawyers (whether judges, academics and practitioners) select to explain and inform their work. Just as much as law is ideologically constructed, so too are individual branches of the law, such as contract law.

[27.225] Leading contract commentators Adams and Brownsword have reduced the ideologies of contract to two extremes: Market-Individualism and Consumer-Welfarism.[98] Market-Individualism signifies the pre-eminence of the market for competitive exchange in which individual legal actors are voluntary participants and where courts play a non-interventionist role.[99] Consumer-Welfarism signifies a policy of consumer protectionism under which all consumer contracts are closely regulated and commercial contracts attract more regulation than Market-Individualism would allow.[100] Consumer-Welfarism contemplates that legislatures will set standards for the contents of contracts and courts will enforce those standards, faithfully implementing Parliament's policies as expressed in those legally binding standards. Although these ideologies were identified in the context of English law, they hold good for Australia. Both of these ideologies continue to imprint modern Australian contract law.

[27.230] How do these ideologies imprint this work? Market-Individualism is played out in those sections of the work that stress the self-selecting nature of contract law as legal actors map out and create their own private legal domains. The rules about content-setting in contracts (express and implied terms) and giving people autonomy to select the terms on which they will contract with each other, reinforce the ideology of Market-Individualism. As far as Consumer-Welfarism is concerned, it finds expression in legislative provisions in Federal, State and Territorial law that restrain freedom of contract and sanctity of contract in the interests of protecting consumers.

[27.235] Both ideologies continue to exert a powerful influence on the content and trajectory of contract law, and they provide some of the tensions that underpin both the theory and practice of contract law. One thing is clear: the halcyon days of *laissez-faire* contract law have been jettisoned in favour of a contract law that is far more protective of the interests of contracting parties—particularly those who are consumers. Even in the case of commercial contracts, the law is more cautiously interventionist than was historically the case. The future of contract law, as depicted in this work, is a mixture of self-selection and state legislative and judicial regulation, so that contract law, as an integral component of private law, is now irreversibly transformed.

---

97   A Hunt, 'Marxist Theory of Law', Chapter 23 in D Patterson (ed), *A Companion to Philosophy of Law and Legal Theory*, Blackwell Publishers, Oxford, 1999, p 361.

98   J Adams & R Brownsword, 'The Ideologies of Contract' (1987) 7 *Legal Studies* 205. Each of these ideologies finds expression in a number of subsidiary principles.

99   Ibid, pp 206–208.

100 J Adams & R Brownsword, 'The Ideologies of Contract' (1987) 7 *Legal Studies* 205, 210–213.

Index